The Reconstruction Amendments

The Reconstruction Amendments

THE ESSENTIAL DOCUMENTS / VOLUME 1

Edited by Kurt T. Lash

THE UNIVERSITY OF CHICAGO PRESS   CHICAGO AND LONDON

The University of Chicago Press, Chicago 60637
The University of Chicago Press, Ltd., London
© 2021 by The University of Chicago
All rights reserved. No part of this book may be used or reproduced in any manner whatsoever
without written permission, except in the case of brief quotations in critical articles and reviews.
For more information, contact the University of Chicago Press, 1427 E. 60th St., Chicago, IL 60637.
Published 2021
Printed in the United States of America

30 29 28 27 26 25 24 23 22 21   1 2 3 4 5

ISBN-13: 978-0-226-68878-7 (cloth)
ISBN-13: 978-0-226-68881-7 (e-book)
DOI: https://doi.org/10.7208/chicago/9780226688817.001.0001

Library of Congress Cataloging-in-Publication Data

Names: Lash, Kurt T., editor.
Title: The Reconstruction amendments : the essential documents / edited by Kurt T. Lash.
Description: Chicago ; London : The University of Chicago Press, 2021 | Includes bibliographical references
and index. | Contents: Volume 1. Part 1. The antebellum Constitution; Part 2. The Thirteenth Amendment —
Volume 2. Part 1. The Fourteenth Amendment; Part 2. The Fifteenth Amendment.
Identifiers: LCCN 2020013708 | ISBN 9780226688787 (v. 1 ; cloth) | ISBN 9780226688954 (v. 2 ; cloth) |
ISBN 9780226688817 (v. 1 ; ebook) | ISBN 9780226689005 (v. 2 ; ebook)
Subjects: LCSH: United States. Constitution. 13th–15th Amendments—History—Sources. | Constitutional amendments—
United States—History—19th century—Sources. | Constitutional history—United States—19th century—Sources.
Classification: LCC KF4757 .R43 2021 | DDC 342.7303/909034—dc23
LC record available at https://lccn.loc.gov/2020013708

♾ This paper meets the requirements of ANSI/NISO Z39.48-1992 (Permanence of Paper).

Contents

Introduction to the Collection

This two-volume collection presents major speeches, debates, and public discussions relating to the adoption of the Thirteenth, Fourteenth, and Fifteenth Amendments to the American Constitution. Known as the Reconstruction Amendments, these three amendments were framed and adopted over a roughly five-year period immediately following the American Civil War. The Thirteenth Amendment abolished slavery, the Fourteenth Amendment protected fundamental national liberties against state abridgment and established conditions for the readmission of the rebel states, and the Fifteenth Amendment declared that the right to vote could not be denied on the basis of race. Together, these three amendments reshaped the nature of American constitutional liberty.

At the time of this writing, no similar collection exists. Although historians have produced multiple collections of primary historical documents relating to the adoption of the original Constitution, only partial collections exist relating to the Fourteenth Amendment and none at all relating to the Thirteenth and Fifteenth Amendments. The only serious prior attempt, now long out of print, at gathering materials relating to the Fourteenth Amendment includes only congressional debates and omits any document relating to the amendment's ratification. Given the importance of all three amendments to the structure of modern American liberty, it seemed appropriate to undertake an effort to fill this gap in historical constitutional scholarship.

The greatest difficulty in creating such a collection lies in making it long enough to be *useful* for a broad range of writers and researchers but short enough to be *usable* by that same group. The subject of Reconstruction and its reshaping of the American Constitution is one that potentially includes thousands of documents relating to law, politics, culture, and religion. Furthermore, the time period involved can be reasonably viewed as extending from the 1780s to the 1880s — a full century. It seems almost inevitable that a collection covering the topic of constitutional reconstruction must be either impossibly long or unhelpfully "thin." It is hoped that this collection avoids both extremes. Even if successful, however, that success comes at the cost

of excluding a number of important documents and including what, to some scholars, may appear to be an unnecessarily deep collection of other materials.

Two basic principles guided the selection of documents for this collection. First, this was to be a collection of documents involving a public discussion of legal issues: *legal* issues because the collection is meant to assist lawyers, judges, and legal scholars in understanding a moment of legal change, and *public* discussion because the collection is meant to provide insight into what most people thought they were doing when they adopted these amendments. Unlike the secret debates of the original Constitutional Convention, the public could follow — and comment on — the framing debates of the Reconstruction Amendments as they occurred. Major newspapers published these debates daily and commented on the same, and regional papers throughout the country reprinted or reported much of this content. Political parties distributed congressional speeches as campaign documents, and party-aligned newspapers kept their constituents informed regarding the progress of the debates and the odds of constitutional ratification. In short, the public was able to follow and comment on constitutional reconstruction at every step in the process, from its early framing to ultimate ratification. In order to capture this public aspect of the debates, I have inserted newspaper and public commentary on the congressional debates as they occurred at the time.

With the exception of the first part of volume 1, all documents are presented in chronological order. Thus, rather than present in one section all the discussions relating to the Due Process Clause of the Fourteenth Amendment, for example, I have chosen to present the debates as they occurred. This approach is essential in order to track the origin and development of ideas in the two houses of Congress. The Senate and the House of Representatives did not discuss the same proposals at the same time; one house might discuss an early version of the Fourteenth Amendment while the other house debated a version of the 1866 Civil Rights Act. Advocates and opponents of proposals developed their arguments over time, modifying them in response to persuasive counterarguments or major events. Arranging the historical documents by constitutional text would have obscured the important and often revealing modification or abandonment of early arguments in favor of more broadly persuasive rationales. A chronological presentation also allows the reader to view the "real-time" commentary by outside groups who were deeply concerned about the shape and success of the proposed amendments. Abolitionist groups, women's rights organizations and commentators, freedmen associations, and loyal Southerners all closely followed—and sought to influence—the direction of constitutional change. In order to capture this aspect of the event, I have added commentary from advocacy journals such as the *National Anti-Slavery Standard*, the *Liberator*, and the *Revolution*.

The players in this grand constitutional drama brought to the debates conceptions of the antebellum Constitution forged from decades of political disputes and constitutional crises. Despite their differences, they shared a common constitutional heritage and often used the same legal and constitutional treatises. Citations and extended quotations from antebellum works such as the *Federalist Papers*, the published writings of James Madison, Joseph Story's *Commentaries on the Constitution*, and Chancellor Kent's *Commentaries on American Law* are ubiquitous throughout the Reconstruction debates. Participants held a general knowledge of the writings and theories of John C. Calhoun, and most knew where and how Calhoun's ideas differed from those of James Madison and Chief Justice John Marshall. In the Reconstruction debates, the ideas of Madison and the decisions of Chief Justice Marshall were presumed authoritative, and all sides developed their own interpretations of cases like *McCulloch v. Maryland* and *Prigg v. Pennsylvania* and of canonical works like the *Federalist Papers*.

It is because so much of Reconstruction thought involved a reliance upon, or a rethinking of, antebellum constitutionalism that the collection begins with a section on the antebellum Constitution. The debates over issues like secession, abolition, the exclusion from Congress of the former rebel states, the decision to proceed by way of constitutional amendment rather than purely legislation, and the ultimate form of the Fifteenth Amendment all involved competing conceptions of federalism and liberty—conceptions that emerged in the years between America's founding and the Civil War. Volume 1 therefore presents those aspects

of antebellum constitutionalism that came to play important roles in the later Reconstruction amendment debates regarding federalism and liberty, slavery and abolitionism, and the constitutional crises of secession and the Civil War. Rather than reflect a single vision of the antebellum Constitution, these opening materials are meant to inform the reader about the key constitutional ideas and disputes that emerged during this period. A proper understanding of these initial ideas and debates is essential to understanding the later debates of constitutional reconstruction. This is especially true regarding disputes over American federalism. Unless one is familiar with the federalism of James Madison and understands how it differed from the federalism of John C. Calhoun, one cannot understand why abolitionists embraced the former even as they rejected the latter. A grounding in these antebellum ideas also helps shed light on why so many major figures in Reconstruction, including Frederick Douglass, continued to embrace constitutional federalism as a key component of American liberty.

My decision to limit the collection to a manageable two-volume publication was driven by a desire to place the collection within reach of as many readers as reasonably possible. Doing so, however, required the exclusion of innumerable important and illuminating works. For example, literary works such as Frederick Douglass's magnificent *Narrative of the Life of Frederick Douglass, an American Slave*, and Harriet Beecher Stowe's *Uncle Tom's Cabin* played key roles in driving the public debate over slavery and abolition. Hinton Helper's *Impending Crisis of the South* is important not only for its economic analysis of slavery but also because Southern efforts to suppress the book gave rise to a new appreciation in the North of the national right to free speech. There are countless additional literary works that played important roles in driving public discussions of constitutional freedom in the years leading up to the Civil War. Nevertheless, they are excluded from this collection for two reasons: sufficiently representative excerpts would be too long for a limited collection, and the works themselves involve constitutional issues only by implication.

That last point illustrates the bias of this collection: it tilts toward works representing the public discussion of constitutional theory and law. Amending the Constitution is a profoundly public act; it results in rules of law representative of the people themselves. These rules bind public officials precisely because they embody the considered judgment of the sovereign people. It is for this reason that lawyers and judges since the opening days of the Republic have sought to determine and enforce that understanding of the text shared by the people who engaged in the extraordinary effort to amend their Constitution. Recovering public understanding necessarily focuses on those ideas that were placed in the crucible of public debate and earned the right to be enshrined as the people's fundamental law.

The job of collecting these public discussions and debates has been greatly assisted by the rise of digital technologies that have brought thousands of historical documents within reach of anyone with access to the internet. The Library of Congress's digitized *Congressional Globe* allows researchers to access written records of the debates in the Thirty-Eighth, Thirty-Ninth, and Fortieth Congresses. The Hathi Trust has digitized the Senate and House journals of several states. Digitized historical newspapers and pamphlets are available from a variety of sources, including the Library of Congress database Chronicling America: Historical American Newspapers, Readex's Archive of Americana collection, and the websites of individual newspapers, such as the *New York Times* Times Machine. Digitized newspapers are an especially valuable resource for researching state ratification debates. While state legislative journals, for example, reproduced spare accounts of votes and proceedings but rarely more, local newspapers often included detailed accounts of the debates in the state legislatures. Since few states had professional reporters, these local newspapers are the best and often sole sources of information regarding these important discussions. Digital archives of historical newspapers also provide access to those voices *not* included in legislative debates. In publications like the *Revolution,* the *Liberator,* and the *National Anti-Slavery Standard,* one hears the voices of women and blacks, including former slaves. These Americans played an important role in driving the country toward constitutional reform—even as they remained excluded from the political franchise.

Finally, a word about this book's title, *The Reconstruction Amendments: Essential Documents.* In some cases, "essential" refers to the importance of the included documents themselves, such as the documents presenting the drafting debates in the Thirty-Ninth Congress. No responsible academic investigation of the historical understanding of the Fourteenth Amendment can avoid grappling with these debates, as they reveal the issues underlying the amendment and, given their widespread contemporary publication and dissemination, provide significant evidence of the likely public understanding of the proposed text. But in other cases, "essential" refers not to a particular document or newspaper article itself but to the essential importance of the issue discussed within that document. For example, for each amendment, I have included newspapers' editorial coverage of the framing and ratification efforts. The inclusion of these articles is meant to illustrate how closely the public was able to track the progress of constitutional framing, assess the likelihood of ratification, and consider the substantive implications of failure or success.

PART 1

The Antebellum Constitution

Introduction to Part 1

Part 1 of this volume contains those antebellum historical documents that, either in and of themselves or because of the issues they discussed, played a critical role in the later debates over the Thirteenth, Fourteenth, and Fifteenth Amendments. Participants in the Reconstruction debates came of age in the midst of an increasingly strident national discussion regarding the nature of American government and the scope of human freedom. Ideas developed in the crucible of antebellum political and legal arguments became the building blocks of constitutional reconstruction.

The nature of the original Constitution, the proper division of national and state power, the meaning of American citizenship and human freedom, and the significance of race—all were subjects of nationwide debate long before the Civil War. In the decades following the nation's founding, driven by the increasingly divisive subject of chattel slavery, competing theories of federalism and the nature of the federal Constitution emerged and clashed as the country debated whether it could remain half slave and half free. The positions staked out in these antebellum disputes informed later debates over the legality of secession, the powers of the Reconstruction Congress, and the rights of persons and citizens in post–Civil War America.

As antebellum America struggled to determine whether the Constitution was an indestructible agreement among a unitary national people or a dissolvable compact between the states, conceptions of national liberty emerged as counterpoints to state-centered theories of legal privileges and immunities. Americans north and south increasingly invoked the revered Declaration of Independence and the sonorous language of the Bill of Rights as foundational statements of national liberty—statements that would lead the residents of free states and slave states to very different conclusions about the duties of the national government and the rights of people in the several states. These conclusions were rarely stable of course, as shifting political fortunes led both sides in the debate over slavery to embrace or abandon constitutional nationalism as the case required. As a result, participants in the Reconstruction debates brought with them a complicated and sometimes conflicting set of ideas regarding federalism and national freedom, ideas that resisted characterization as "North versus South" or "free versus slave."

Although the documents in part 1 of this volume are divided by subject as relating to federalism and liberty, slavery, or secession, these cannot be viewed as distinct legal and political topics. Discussions about national rights often involved deliberations about the meaning of canonical documents such as the Declaration of Independence and the scope of constitutional federalism. These discussions, in turn, were often deeply affected by one's position on the institution of chattel slavery. Similarly, one's position on the legality of secession heavily depended on an individual's theory of constitutional federalism. Finally, an individual's theory of constitutional federalism influenced that person's position on the necessity and scope of post–Civil War amendments. In sum, understanding the constitutional theories of Reconstruction requires a basic grasp of the crisscrossing antebellum theories of the American founding, constitutional federalism, and individual freedom.

Though the subjects in volume 1 involve intertwining and often chronologically overlapping discussions, the manner in which the volume presents them reflects a rough movement through time and degree of generality. The general subjects of America's founding, federalism, and the structure of antebellum liberty come first, followed by the more particular subjects of slavery, secession, and Civil War.

A. FOUNDATIONAL DOCUMENTS

1

The Declaration of Independence

July 4, 1776*

In Congress, July 4, 1776

THE UNANIMOUS DECLARATION OF THE

THIRTEEN UNITED STATES OF AMERICA

When in the course of human events, it becomes necessary for one people to dissolve the political bands which have connected them with another, and to assume among the powers of the earth, the separate and equal station to which the Laws of Nature and of Nature's God entitle them, a decent respect to the opinions of mankind requires that they should declare the causes which impel them to the separation.—We hold these truths to be self-evident, that all men are created equal, that they are endowed by their Creator with certain unalienable Rights, that among these are Life, Liberty and the pursuit of Happiness.—That to secure these rights, Governments are instituted among Men, deriving their just powers from the consent of the governed,—That whenever any Form of Government becomes destructive of these ends, it is the Right of the People to alter or to abolish it, and to institute new Government, laying its foundation on such principles and organizing its powers in such form, as to them shall seem most likely to effect their Safety and Happiness. Prudence, indeed, will dictate that Governments long established should not be changed for light and transient causes; and accordingly all experience hath shown, that mankind are more disposed to suffer, while evils are sufferable, than to right themselves by abolishing the forms to which they are accustomed. But when a long train of abuses and usurpations, pursuing invariably the same Object evinces a design to reduce them under absolute Despotism, it is their right, it is their duty, to throw off such Government, and to provide new Guards for their fu-

* Charles C. Tansill, ed., *Documents Illustrative of the Formation of the Union of the American States* (Washington, DC: Government Printing Office, 1927), 22.

ture security.—Such has been the patient sufferance of these Colonies; and such is now the necessity which constrains them to alter their former Systems of Government. The history of the present King of Great Britain is a history of repeated injuries and usurpations, all having in direct object the establishment of an absolute Tyranny over these States. To prove this, let Facts be submitted to a candid world.—He has refused his Assent to Laws, the most wholesome and necessary for the public good.—He has forbidden his Governors to pass Laws of immediate and pressing importance, unless suspended in their operation till his Assent should be obtained; and when so suspended, he has utterly neglected to attend to them.—He has refused to pass other Laws for the accommodation of large districts of people, unless those people would relinquish the right of Representation in the Legislature, a right inestimable to them and formidable to tyrants only.—He has called together legislative bodies at places unusual, uncomfortable, and distant from the depository of their public Records, for the sole purpose of fatiguing them into compliance with his measures.—He has dissolved Representative Houses repeatedly, for opposing with manly firmness his invasions on the rights of the people.— He has refused for a long time, after such dissolutions, to cause others to be elected; whereby the Legislative powers, incapable of Annihilation, have returned to the People at large for their exercise; the State remaining in the mean time exposed to all the dangers of invasion from without, and convulsions within.—He has endeavoured to prevent the population of these States; for that purpose obstructing the Laws for Naturalization of Foreigners; refusing to pass others to encourage their migration hither, and raising the conditions of new Appropriations of Lands.—He has obstructed the Administration of Justice, by refusing his Assent to Laws for establishing Judiciary powers.—He has made Judges dependent on his Will alone, for the tenure of their offices, and the amount and payment of their salaries.— He has erected a multitude of New Offices, and sent hither swarms of Officers to harass our people, and eat out their substance.—He has kept among us, in times of peace, Standing Armies, without the Consent of our

5

legislatures.—He has affected to render the Military independent of and superior to the Civil power.—He has combined with others to subject us to a jurisdiction foreign to our constitution, and unacknowledged by our laws; giving his Assent to their Acts of pretended Legislation:—For quartering large bodies of armed troops among us:—For protecting them, by a mock Trial, from punishment for any Murders which they should commit on the Inhabitants of these States:—For cutting off our Trade with all parts of the world:—For imposing Taxes on us without our Consent:—For depriving us in many cases, of the benefits of Trial by Jury:—For transporting us beyond Seas to be tried for pretended offences:—For abolishing the free System of English Laws in a neighbouring Province, establishing therein an Arbitrary government, and enlarging its Boundaries so as to render it at once an example and fit instrument for introducing the same absolute rule into these Colonies:—For taking away our Charters, abolishing our most valuable Laws, and altering fundamentally the Forms of our Governments:—For suspending our own Legislatures, and declaring themselves invested with power to legislate for us in all cases whatsoever.—He has abdicated Government here, by declaring us out of his Protection and waging War against us.—He has plundered our seas, ravaged our Coasts, burnt our towns, and destroyed the lives of our people.—He is at this time transporting large Armies of foreign Mercenaries to compleat the works of death, desolation and tyranny, already begun with circumstances of Cruelty & perfidy scarcely paralleled in the most barbarous ages, and totally unworthy the Head of a civilized nation.—He has constrained our fellow Citizens taken Captive on the high Seas to bear Arms against their Country, to become the executioners of their friends and Brethren, or to fall themselves by their Hands.—He has excited domestic insurrections amongst us, and has endeavoured to bring on the inhabitants of our frontiers, the merciless Indian Savages, whose known rule of warfare, is an undistinguished destruction of all ages, sexes and conditions. In every stage of these Oppressions We have Petitioned for Redress in the most humble terms: Our repeated Petitions have been answered only by repeated injury. A Prince, whose character is thus marked by every act which may define a Tyrant, is unfit to be the ruler of a free people. Nor have We been wanting in attentions to our British brethren. We have warned them from time to time of attempts by their legislature to extend an unwarrantable jurisdiction over us. We have reminded them of the circumstances of our emigration and settlement here. We have appealed to their native justice and magnanimity, and we have conjured them by the ties of our common kindred to disavow these usurpations, which, would inevitably interrupt our connections and correspondence. They too have been deaf to the voice of justice and of consanguinity. We must, therefore, acquiesce in the necessity, which denounces our Separation, and hold them, as we hold the rest of mankind, Enemies in War, in Peace Friends.—

WE, THEREFORE, THE REPRESENTATIVES OF THE UNITED STATES OF AMERICA, in General Congress, Assembled, appealing to the Supreme Judge of the world for the rectitude of our intentions, do, in the Name, and by Authority of the good People of these Colonies, solemnly publish and declare, That these United Colonies are, and of Right ought to be FREE AND INDEPENDENT STATES; that they are Absolved from all Allegiance to the British Crown, and that all political connection between them and the State of Great Britain, is and ought to be totally dissolved; and that as Free and Independent States, they have full Power to levy War, conclude Peace, contract Alliances, establish Commerce, and to do all other Acts and Things which Independent States may of right do.—And for the support of this Declaration, with a firm reliance on the protection of Divine Providence, we mutually pledge to each other our Lives, our Fortunes and our sacred Honor.

2

The Northwest Ordinance
July 13, 1787*

Ordinance of 1787, July 13, 1787
AN ORDINANCE FOR THE GOVERNMENT OF THE TERRITORY OF THE UNITED STATES NORTHWEST OF THE RIVER OHIO

Section 1. *Be it ordained by the United States in Congress assembled,* That the said Territory, for the purpose of temporary government, be one district, subject, however, to be divided into two districts, as future circumstances may, in the opinion of Congress, make it expedient.

*Tansill, *Documents*, 47–54.

Sec. 2. *Be it ordained by the authority aforesaid,* That the estates both of resident and non-resident proprietors in the said territory, dying intestate, shall descend to, and be distributed among, their children and the descendants of a deceased child in equal parts, the descendants of a deceased child or grandchild to take the share of their deceased parent in equal parts among them; and where there shall be no children or descendants, then in equal parts to the next of kin, in equal degree; and among collaterals, the children of a deceased brother or sister of the intestate shall have, in equal parts among them, their deceased parent's share; and there shall, in no case, be a distinction between kindred of the whole and half blood; saving in all cases to the widow of the intestate, her third part of the real estate for life, and one-third part of the personal estate; and this law relative to descents and dower, shall remain in full force until altered by the legislature of the district. And until the governor and judges shall adopt laws as hereinafter mentioned, estates in the said territory may be devised or bequeathed by wills in writing, signed and sealed by him or her in whom the estate may be, (being of full age,) and attested by three witnesses; and real estates may be conveyed by lease and release, or bargain and sale, signed, sealed, and delivered by the person, being of full age, in whom the estate may be, and attested by two witnesses, provided such wills be duly proved, and such conveyances be acknowledged, or the execution thereof duly proved, and be recorded within one year after proper magistrates, courts, and registers, shall be appointed for that purpose; and personal property may be transferred by delivery, saving, however, to the French and Canadian inhabitants, and other settlers of the Kaskaskies, Saint Vincents, and the neighboring villages, who have heretofore professed themselves citizens of Virginia, their laws and customs now in force among them, relative to the descent and conveyance of property.

Sec. 3. *Be it ordained by the authority aforesaid,* That there shall be appointed, from time to time, by Congress, a governor, whose commission shall continue in force for the term of three years, unless sooner revoked by Congress; he shall reside in the district, and have a freehold estate therein, in one thousand acres of land, while in the exercise of his office.

Sec. 4. There shall be appointed from time to time, by Congress, a secretary, whose commission shall continue in force for four years, unless sooner revoked; he shall reside in the district, and have a freehold estate therein, in five hundred acres of land, while in the exercise of his office. It shall be his duty to keep and preserve the acts and laws passed by the legislature, and the public records of the district, and the proceedings of the governor in his executive department, and transmit authentic copies of such acts and proceedings every six months to the Secretary of Congress. There shall also be appointed a court, to consist of three judges, any two of whom to form a court, who shall have a common-law jurisdiction and reside in the district, and have each therein a freehold estate, in five hundred acres of land, while in the exercise of their offices; and their commissions shall continue in force during good behavior.

Sec. 5. The governor and judges, or a majority of them, shall adopt and publish in the district such laws of the original States, criminal and civil, as may be necessary, and best suited to the circumstances of the district, and report them to Congress from time to time, which laws shall be in force in the district until the organization of the general assembly therein, unless disapproved of by Congress; but afterwards the legislature shall have authority to alter them as they shall think fit.

Sec. 6. The governor, for the time being, shall be commander-in-chief of the militia, appoint and commission all officers in the same below the rank of general officers; all general officers shall be appointed and commissioned by Congress.

Sec. 7. Previous to the organization of the general assembly the governor shall appoint such magistrates, and other civil officers, in each county or township, as he shall find necessary for the preservation of the peace and good order in the same. After the general assembly shall be organized the powers and duties of magistrates and other civil officers shall be regulated and defined by the said assembly; but all magistrates and other civil officers, not herein otherwise directed, shall, during the continuance of this temporary government, be appointed by the governor.

Sec. 8. For the prevention of crimes, and injuries, the laws to be adopted or made shall have force in all parts of the district, and for the execution of process, criminal and civil, the governor shall make proper divisions thereof; and he shall proceed, from time to time, as circumstances may require, to lay out the parts of the district in which the Indian titles shall have been extinguished, into counties and townships, subject, however, to such alterations as may thereafter be made by the legislature.

Sec. 9. So soon as there shall be five thousand free

male inhabitants, of full age, in the district, upon giving proof thereof to the governor, they shall receive authority, with time and place, to elect representatives from their counties or townships, to represent them in the general assembly: *Provided*, That for every five hundred free male inhabitants there shall be one representative, and so on, progressively, with the number of free male inhabitants, shall the right of representation increase, until the number of representatives shall amount to twenty-five; after which the number and proportion of representatives shall be regulated by the legislature: *Provided*, That no person be eligible or qualified to act as a representative, unless he shall have been a citizen of one of the United States three years, and be a resident in the district, or unless he shall have resided in the district three years; and, in either case, shall likewise hold in his own right, in fee-simple, two hundred acres of land within the same: *Provided also*, That a free-hold in fifty acres of land in the district, having been a citizen of one of the States, and being resident in the district, or the like freehold and two years' residence in the district, shall be necessary to qualify a man as an elector of a representative.

Sec. 10. The representatives thus elected shall serve for the term of two years; and in case of the death of a representative, or removal from office, the governor shall issue a writ to the county or township, for which he was a member, to elect another in his stead, to serve for the residue of the term.

Sec. 11. The general assembly, or legislature, shall consist of the governor, legislative council, and a house of representatives. The legislative council shall consist of five members, to continue in office five years, unless sooner removed by Congress; any three of whom to be a quorum; and the members of the council shall be nominated and appointed in the following manner, to wit: As soon as representatives shall be elected the governor shall appoint a time and place for them to meet together, and when met they shall nominate ten persons, resident in the district, and each possessed of a freehold in five hundred acres of land, and return their names to Congress, five of whom Congress shall appoint and commission to serve as aforesaid; and whenever a vacancy shall happen in the Council, by death or removal from office, the house of representatives shall nominate two persons, qualified as aforesaid, for each vacancy, and return their names to Congress, one of whom Congress shall appoint and commission for the residue of the term; and every five years, four months at least be-

fore the expiration of the time of service of the members of the council, the said house shall nominate ten persons, qualified as aforesaid, and return their names to Congress, five of whom Congress shall appoint and commission to serve as members of the council five years, unless sooner removed. And the governor, legislative council, and house of representatives shall have authority to make laws in all cases for the good government of the district, not repugnant to the principles and articles in this ordinance established and declared. And all bills, having passed by a majority in the house, and by a majority in the council, shall be referred to the governor for his assent; but no bill, or legislative act whatever, shall be of any force without his assent. The governor shall have power to convene, prorogue, and dissolve the general assembly when, in his opinion, it shall be expedient.

Sec. 12. The governor, judges, legislative council, secretary, and such other officers as Congress shall appoint in the district, shall take an oath or affirmation of fidelity, and of office; the governor before the President of Congress, and all other officers before the governor. As soon as a legislature shall be formed in the district, the council and house assembled, in one room, shall have authority, by joint ballot, to elect a delegate to Congress, who shall have a seat in Congress, with a right of debating, but not of voting, during this temporary government.

Sec. 13. And for extending the fundamental principles of civil and religious liberty, which form the basis whereon these republics, their laws and constitutions, are erected; to fix and establish those principles as the basis of all laws, constitutions, and governments, which forever hereafter shall be formed in the said territory; to provide, also, for the establishment of States, and permanent government therein, and for their admission to a share in the Federal councils on an equal footing with the original States, at as early periods as may be consistent with the general interest:

Sec. 14. It is hereby ordained and declared, by the authority aforesaid, that the following articles shall be considered as articles of compact, between the original States and the people and States in the said territory, and forever remain unalterable, unless by common consent, to wit:

ARTICLE I

No person, demeaning himself in a peaceable and orderly manner, shall ever be molested on account of his mode of worship, or religious sentiments, in the said territory.

ARTICLE II

The inhabitants of the said territory shall always be entitled to the benefits of the writs of *habeas corpus*, and of the trial by jury; of a proportionate representation of the people in the legislature, and of judicial proceedings according to the course of the common law. All persons shall be bailable, unless for capital offences, where the proof shall be evident, or the presumption great. All fines shall be moderate; and no cruel or unusual punishment shall be inflicted. No man shall be deprived of his liberty or property, but by the judgment of his peers, or the law of the land, and should the public exigencies make it necessary, for the common preservation, to take any person's property, or to demand his particular services, full compensation shall be made for the same. And, in the just preservation of rights and property, it is understood and declared, that no law ought ever to be made or have force in the said territory, that shall, in any manner whatever, interfere with or affect private contracts, or engagements, *bona fide*, and without fraud previously formed.

ARTICLE III

Religion, morality, and knowledge being necessary to good government and the happiness of mankind, schools and the means of education shall forever be encouraged. The utmost good faith shall always be observed towards the Indians; their lands and property shall never be taken from them without their consent; and in their property, rights, and liberty they never shall be invaded or disturbed unless in just and lawful wars authorized by Congress; but laws founded in justice and humanity shall, from time to time, be made, for preventing wrongs being done to them, and for preserving peace and friendship with them.

ARTICLE IV

The said territory, and the States which may be formed therein, shall forever remain a part of this confederacy of the United States of America, subject to the Articles of Confederation, and to such alterations therein as shall be constitutionally made; and to all the acts and ordinances of the United States in Congress assembled, conformable thereto. The inhabitants and settlers in the said territory shall be subject to pay a part of the Federal debts, contracted, or to be contracted, and a pro-

portional part of the expenses of government to be apportioned on them by Congress, according to the same common rule and measure by which apportionments thereof shall be made on the other States; and the taxes for paying their proportion shall be laid and levied by the authority and direction of the legislatures of the district, or districts, or new States, as in the original States, within the time agreed upon by the United States in Congress assembled. The legislatures of those districts, or new States, shall never interfere with the primary disposal of the soil by the United States in Congress assembled, nor with any regulations Congress may find necessary for securing the title in such soil to the *bona fide* purchasers. No tax shall be imposed on lands the property of the United States; and in no case shall nonresident proprietors be taxed higher than residents. The navigable waters leading into the Mississippi and Saint Lawrence, and the carrying places between the same, shall be common highways, and forever free, as well to the inhabitants of the said territory as to the citizens of the United States, and those of any other States that may be admitted into the confederacy, without any tax, impost, or duty therefor.

ARTICLE V

There shall be formed in the said territory not less than three nor more than five States; and the boundaries of the States, as soon as Virginia shall alter her act of cession, and consent to the same, shall become fixed and established as follows, to wit: The western State, in the said territory, shall be bounded by the Mississippi, the Ohio, and the Wabash Rivers; a direct line drawn from the Wabash and Post Vincents, due north, to the territorial line between the United States and Canada; and by the said territorial line to the Lake of the Woods and Mississippi. The middle State shall be bounded by the said direct line, the Wabash from Post Vincents to the Ohio, by the Ohio, by a direct line drawn due north from the mouth of the Great Miami to the said territorial line, and by the said territorial line. The eastern State shall be bounded by the last-mentioned direct line, the Ohio, Pennsylvania, and the said territorial line: *Provided, however*, And it is further understood and declared, that the boundaries of these three States shall be subject so far to be altered, that, if Congress shall hereafter find it expedient, they shall have authority to form one or two States in that part of the said territory which lies north of an east and west line drawn through the southerly bend or extreme of Lake Michigan. And whenever any of the said States shall have sixty thousand free inhabitants therein, such State shall be admitted by its delegates, into the Congress of the United States, on an equal footing with the original States, in all respects whatever; and shall be at liberty to form a permanent constitution and State government: *Provided,* The constitution and government, so to be formed, shall be republican, and in conformity to the principles contained in these articles, and, so far as it can be consistent with the general interest of the confederacy, such admission shall be allowed at an earlier period, and when there may be a less number of free inhabitants in the State than sixty thousand.

ARTICLE VI

There shall be neither slavery nor involuntary servitude in the said territory, otherwise than in the punishment of crimes, whereof the party shall have been duly convicted: *Provided always,* That any person escaping into the same, from whom labor or service is lawfully claimed in any one of the original States, such fugitive may be lawfully reclaimed, and conveyed to the person claiming his or her labor or service as aforesaid.

Be it ordained by the authority aforesaid, That the resolutions of the 23d of April, 1784, relative to the subject of this ordinance be, and the same are hereby repealed and declared null and void.

Done by the United States, in Congress assembled, the 13th day of July, in the year of our Lord 1787, and of their sovereignty and independence the twelfth.

3

The Constitution of the United States and the First Twelve Amendments

1787–1804*

We the People of the United States, in Order to form a more perfect Union, establish Justice, insure domestic Tranquility, provide for the common defence, promote the general Welfare, and secure the Blessings of Liberty to ourselves and our Posterity, do ordain and establish this Constitution for the United States of America.

*Tansill, *Documents,* 989–1002, 1066–69.

ARTICLE I.

Section 1. All legislative Powers herein granted shall be vested in a Congress of the United States, which shall consist of a Senate and House of Representatives.

Section 2. The House of Representatives shall be composed of Members chosen every second Year by the People of the several States, and the Electors in each State shall have the Qualifications requisite for Electors of the most numerous Branch of the State Legislature.

No person shall be a Representative who shall not have attained to the Age of twenty five Years, and been seven Years a Citizen of the United States, and who shall not, when elected, be an Inhabitant of that State in which he shall be chosen.

Representatives and direct Taxes shall be apportioned among the several States which may be included within this Union, according to their respective Numbers, which shall be determined by adding to the whole Number of free Persons, including those bound to Service for a Term of Years, and excluding Indians not taxed, three fifths of all other Persons. The actual Enumeration shall be made within three Years after the first Meeting of the Congress of the United States, and within every subsequent Term of ten Years, in such Manner as they shall by Law direct. The Number of Representatives shall not exceed one for every thirty Thousand, but each State shall have at Least one Representative; and until such enumeration shall be made, the State of New Hampshire shall be entitled to chuse three, Massachusetts eight, Rhode-Island and Providence Plantations one, Connecticut five, New-York six, New Jersey four, Pennsylvania eight, Delaware one, Maryland six, Virginia ten, North Carolina five, South Carolina five, and Georgia three.

When vacancies happen in the Representation from any State, the Executive Authority thereof shall issue Writs of Election to fill such Vacancies.

The House of Representatives shall chuse their Speaker and other Officers; and shall have the sole Power of Impeachment.

Section 3. The Senate of the United States shall be composed of two Senators from each State, chosen by the Legislature thereof, for six Years; and each Senator shall have one Vote.

Immediately after they shall be assembled in Consequence of the first Election, they shall be divided as equally as may be into three Classes. The Seats of the Senators of the first Class shall be vacated at the Expiration of the second Year, of the second Class at the Expiration of the fourth Year, and of the third Class at the Expiration of the sixth Year, so that one third may be chosen every second Year; and if Vacancies happen by Resignation, or otherwise, during the Recess of the Legislature of any State, the Executive thereof may make temporary Appointments until the next Meeting of the Legislature, which shall then fill such Vacancies.

No Person shall be a Senator who shall not have attained to the Age of thirty Years, and been nine Years a Citizen of the United States, and who shall not, when elected, be an Inhabitant of that State for which he shall be chosen.

The Vice President of the United States shall be President of the Senate, but shall have no Vote, unless they be equally divided.

The Senate shall chuse their other Officers, and also a President pro tempore, in the Absence of the Vice President, or when he shall exercise the Office of President of the United States.

The Senate shall have the sole Power to try all Impeachments. When sitting for that Purpose, they shall be on Oath or Affirmation. When the President of the United States is tried, the Chief Justice shall preside: And no Person shall be convicted without the Concurrence of two thirds of the Members present.

Judgment in Cases of Impeachment shall not extend further than to removal from Office, and disqualification to hold and enjoy any Office of honor, Trust or Profit under the United States: but the Party convicted shall nevertheless be liable and subject to Indictment, Trial, Judgment and Punishment, according to Law.

Section 4. The Times, Places and Manner of holding Elections for Senators and Representatives, shall be prescribed in each State by the Legislature thereof; but the Congress may at any time by Law make or alter such Regulations, except as to the Places of chusing Senators.

The Congress shall assemble at least once in every Year, and such Meeting shall be on the first Monday in December, unless they shall by Law appoint a different Day.

Section 5. Each House shall be the Judge of the Elections, Returns and Qualifications of its own Members, and a Majority of each shall constitute a Quorum to do Business; but a smaller Number may adjourn from day to day, and may be authorized to compel the Attendance of absent Members, in such Manner, and under such Penalties as each House may provide.

Each House may determine the Rules of its Proceedings, punish its Members for disorderly Behaviour, and, with the Concurrence of two thirds, expel a Member.

Each House shall keep a Journal of its Proceedings, and from time to time publish the same, excepting such Parts as may in their Judgment require Secrecy; and the Yeas and Nays of the Members of either House on any question shall, at the Desire of one fifth of those Present, be entered on the Journal.

Neither House, during the Session of Congress, shall, without the Consent of the other, adjourn for more than three days, nor to any other Place than that in which the two Houses shall be sitting.

Section 6. The Senators and Representatives shall receive a Compensation for their Services, to be ascertained by Law, and paid out of the Treasury of the United States. They shall in all Cases, except Treason, Felony and Breach of the Peace, be privileged from Arrest during their Attendance at the Session of their respective Houses, and in going to and returning from the same; and for any Speech or Debate in either House, they shall not be questioned in any other Place.

No Senator or Representative shall, during the Time for which he was elected, be appointed to any civil Office under the Authority of the United States, which shall have been created, or the Emoluments whereof shall have been encreased during such time; and no Person holding any Office under the United States, shall be a Member of either House during his Continuance in Office.

Section 7. All Bills for raising Revenue shall originate in the House of Representatives; but the Senate may propose or concur with Amendments as on other Bills.

Every Bill which shall have passed the House of Representatives and the Senate, shall, before it become a Law, be presented to the President of the United States; If he approve he shall sign it, but if not he shall return it, with his Objections to that House in which it shall have originated, who shall enter the Objections at large on their Journal, and proceed to reconsider it. If after such Reconsideration two thirds of that House shall agree to pass the Bill, it shall be sent, together with the Objections, to the other House, by which it shall likewise be reconsidered, and if approved by two thirds of that House, it shall become a Law. But in all such Cases the Votes of both Houses shall be determined by yeas and Nays, and the Names of the Persons voting for and against the Bill shall be entered on the Journal of each

House respectively. If any Bill shall not be returned by the President within ten days (Sundays excepted) after it shall have been presented to him, the Same shall be a Law, in like Manner as if he had signed it, unless the Congress by their Adjournment prevent its Return in which Case it shall not be a Law.

Every Order, Resolution, or Vote to which the Concurrence of the Senate and House of Representatives may be necessary (except on a question of Adjournment) shall be presented to the President of the United States; and before the Same shall take Effect, shall be approved by him, or being disapproved by him, shall be repassed by two thirds of the Senate and House of Representatives, according to the Rules and Limitations prescribed in the Case of a Bill.

Section 8. The Congress shall have Power To lay and collect Taxes, Duties, Imposts and Excises, to pay the Debts and provide for the common Defence and general Welfare of the United States; but all Duties, Imposts and Excises shall be uniform throughout the United States;

To borrow Money on the credit of the United States;

To regulate Commerce with foreign Nations, and among the several States, and with the Indian Tribes;

To establish an uniform Rule of Naturalization, and uniform Laws on the subject of Bankruptcies throughout the United States;

To coin Money, regulate the Value thereof, and of foreign Coin, and fix the Standard of Weights and Measures;

To provide for the Punishment of counterfeiting the Securities and current Coin of the United States;

To establish Post Offices and post Roads;

To promote the progress of Science and useful Arts, by securing for limited Times to Authors and Inventors the exclusive Right to their respective Writings and Discoveries;

To constitute Tribunals inferior to the supreme Court;

To define and punish Piracies and Felonies committed on the high Seas, and Offences against the Law of Nations;

To declare War, grant Letters of Marque and Reprisal, and make Rules concerning Captures on Land and Water;

To raise and support Armies, but no Appropriation of Money to that Use shall be for a longer Term than two Years;

To provide and maintain a Navy;

To make Rules for the Government and Regulation of the land and naval Forces;

To provide for calling forth the Militia to execute the Laws of the Union, suppress Insurrections and repel Invasions;

To provide for organizing, arming, and disciplining, the Militia, and for governing such Part of them as may be employed in the Service of the United States, reserving to the States respectively, the Appointment of the Officers, and the Authority of training the Militia according to the discipline prescribed by Congress;

To exercise exclusive Legislation in all Cases whatsoever, over such District (not exceeding ten Miles square) as may, by Cession of particular States, and the Acceptance of Congress, become the Seat of the Government of the United States, and to exercise like Authority over all Places purchased by the Consent of the Legislature of the State in which the Same shall be, for the Erection of Forts, Magazines, Arsenals, dock-Yards, and other needful Buildings;—And

To make all Laws which shall be necessary and proper for carrying into Execution the foregoing Powers, and all other Powers vested by this Constitution in the Government of the United States, or in any Department or Officer thereof.

Section 9. The Migration or Importation of such Persons as any of the States now existing shall think proper to admit, shall not be prohibited by the Congress prior to the Year one thousand eight hundred and eight, but a Tax or duty may be imposed on such Importation, not exceeding ten dollars for each Person.

The Privilege of the Writ of Habeas Corpus shall not be suspended, unless when in Cases of Rebellion or Invasion the public Safety may require it.

No Bill of Attainder or ex post facto Law shall be passed.

No Capitation, or other direct, Tax shall be laid, unless in Proportion to the Census or Enumeration herein before directed to be taken.

No Tax or Duty shall be laid on Articles exported from any State.

No Preference shall be given by any Regulation of Commerce or Revenue to the Ports of one State over those of another: nor shall Vessels bound to, or from, one State, be obliged to enter, clear, or pay Duties in another.

No Money shall be drawn from the Treasury, but in Consequence of Appropriations made by Law; and a regular Statement and Account of the Receipts and Expenditures of all public Money shall be published from time to time.

No Title of Nobility shall be granted by the United States: And no Person holding any Office of Profit or Trust under them, shall, without the Consent of the Congress, accept of any present, Emolument, Office, or Title, of any kind whatever, from any King, Prince, or foreign State.

Section 10. No State shall enter into any Treaty, Alliance, or Confederation; grant Letters of Marque and Reprisal; coin Money; emit Bills of Credit; make any Thing but gold and silver Coin a Tender in Payment of Debts; pass any Bill of Attainder, ex post facto Law, or Law impairing the Obligation of Contracts, or grant any Title of Nobility.

No State shall, without the Consent of the Congress, lay any Imposts or Duties on Imports or Exports, except what may be absolutely necessary for executing it's inspection Laws: and the net Produce of all Duties and Imposts, laid by any State on Imports or Exports, shall be for the Use of the Treasury of the United States; and all such Laws shall be subject to the Revision and Controul of the Congress.

No State shall, without the Consent of Congress, lay any Duty of Tonnage, keep Troops, or Ships of War in time of Peace, enter into any Agreement or Compact with another State, or with a foreign Power, or engage in War, unless actually invaded, or in such imminent Danger as will not admit of delay.

ARTICLE II.

Section 1. The executive Power shall be vested in a President of the United States of America. He shall hold his Office during the Term of four Years, and, together with the Vice President, chosen for the same Term, be elected as follows:

Each State shall appoint, in such Manner as the Legislature thereof may direct, a Number of Electors, equal to the whole Number of Senators and Representatives to which the State may be entitled in the Congress: but no Senator or Representative, or Person holding an Office of Trust or Profit under the United States, shall be appointed an Elector.

The Electors shall meet in their respective States, and vote by Ballot for two Persons, of whom one at least shall not be an Inhabitant of the same State with themselves. And they shall make a List of all the Persons voted for, and of the Number of Votes for each; which List they shall sign and certify, and transmit sealed to the Seat of the Government of the United States, directed to the President of the Senate. The President of the Senate shall, in the Presence of the Senate and House of Representatives, open all the Certificates, and the Votes shall then be counted. The Person having the greatest Number of Votes shall be the President, if such Number be a Majority of the whole Number of Electors appointed; and if there be more than one who have such Majority, and have an equal Number of Votes, then the House of Representatives shall immediately chuse by Ballot one of them for President; and if no Person have a Majority, then from the five highest on the List the said House shall in like Manner chuse the President. But in chusing the President, the Votes shall be taken by States, the Representation from each State having one Vote; A quorum for this Purpose shall consist of a Member or Members from two thirds of the States, and a Majority of all the States shall be necessary to a Choice. In every Case, after the Choice of the President, the Person having the greatest Number of Votes of the Electors shall be the Vice President. But if there should remain two or more who have equal Votes, the Senate shall chuse from them by Ballot the Vice President.

The Congress may determine the Time of chusing the Electors, and the Day on which they shall give their Votes; which Day shall be the same throughout the United States.

No Person except a natural born Citizen, or a Citizen of the United States, at the time of the Adoption of this Constitution, shall be eligible to the Office of President; neither shall any Person be eligible to that Office who shall not have attained to the Age of thirty five Years, and been fourteen Years a Resident within the United States.

In Case of the Removal of the President from Office, or of his Death, Resignation, or Inability to discharge the Powers and Duties of the said Office, the Same shall devolve on the Vice President, and the Congress may by Law provide for the Case of Removal, Death, Resignation or Inability, both of the President and Vice President, declaring what Officer shall then act as President, and such Officer shall act accordingly, until the Disability be removed, or a President shall be elected.

The President shall, at stated Times, receive for his Services, a Compensation, which shall neither be encreased nor diminished during the Period for which he shall have been elected, and he shall not receive within that Period any other Emolument from the United States, or any of them.

Before he enter on the Execution of his Office, he shall take the following Oath or Affirmation:—"I do solemnly swear (or affirm) that I will faithfully execute the Office of President of the United States, and will to the best of my Ability, preserve, protect and defend the Constitution of the United States."

Section 2. The President shall be Commander in Chief of the Army and Navy of the United States, and of the Militia of the several States, when called into the actual Service of the United States; he may require the Opinion, in writing, of the principal Officer in each of the executive Departments, upon any Subject relating to the Duties of their respective Offices, and he shall have Power to grant Reprieves and Pardons for Offences against the United States, except in Cases of Impeachment.

He shall have Power, by and with the Advice and Consent of the Senate, to make Treaties, provided two thirds of the Senators present concur; and he shall nominate, and by and with the Advice and Consent of the Senate, shall appoint Ambassadors, other public Ministers and Consuls, Judges of the supreme Court, and all other Officers of the United States, whose Appointments are not herein otherwise provided for, and which shall be established by Law: but the Congress may by Law vest the Appointment of such inferior Officers, as they think proper, in the President alone, in the Courts of Law, or in the Heads of Departments.

The President shall have Power to fill up all Vacancies that may happen during the Recess of the Senate, by granting Commissions which shall expire at the End of their next Session.

Section 3. He shall from time to time give to the Congress Information of the State of the Union, and recommend to their Consideration such Measures as he shall judge necessary and expedient; he may, on extraordinary Occasions, convene both Houses, or either of them, and in Case of Disagreement between them, with Respect to the Time of Adjournment, he may adjourn them to such Time as he shall think proper; he shall receive Ambassadors and other public Ministers; he shall take Care that the Laws be faithfully executed, and shall Commission all the Officers of the United States.

Section 4. The President, Vice President and all civil Officers of the United States, shall be removed from Office on Impeachment for, and Conviction of, Treason, Bribery, or other high Crimes and Misdemeanors.

ARTICLE III.

Section 1. The judicial Power of the United States, shall be vested in one supreme Court, and in such inferior Courts as the Congress may from time to time ordain and establish. The Judges, both of the supreme and inferior Courts, shall hold their Offices during good Behaviour, and shall, at stated Times, receive for their Services, a Compensation, which shall not be diminished during their Continuance in Office.

Section 2. The judicial Power shall extend to all Cases, in Law and Equity, arising under this Constitution, the Laws of the United States, and Treaties made, or which shall be made, under their Authority;—to all Cases affecting Ambassadors, other public Ministers and Consuls;—to all Cases of admiralty and maritime Jurisdiction;—to Controversies to which the United States shall be a Party;—to Controversies between two or more States;—between a State and Citizens of another State;—between Citizens of different States,—between Citizens of the same State claiming Lands under Grants of different States, and between a State, or the Citizens thereof, and foreign States, Citizens or Subjects.

In all Cases affecting Ambassadors, other public Ministers and Consuls, and those in which a State shall be Party, the supreme Court shall have original Jurisdiction. In all the other Cases before mentioned, the supreme Court shall have appellate Jurisdiction, both as to Law and Fact, with such Exceptions, and under such Regulations as the Congress shall make.

The Trial of all Crimes, except in Cases of Impeachment, shall be by Jury; and such Trial shall be held in the State where the said Crimes shall have been committed; but when not committed within any State, the Trial shall be at such Place or Places as the Congress may by Law have directed.

Section 3. Treason against the United States, shall consist only in levying War against them, or in adhering to their Enemies, giving them Aid and Comfort. No Person shall be convicted of Treason unless on the Testimony of two Witnesses to the same overt Act, or on Confession in open Court.

The Congress shall have Power to declare the Punishment of Treason, but no Attainder of Treason shall work Corruption of Blood, or Forfeiture except during the Life of the Person attainted.

ARTICLE IV.

Section 1. Full Faith and Credit shall be given in each State to the public Acts, Records, and judicial Proceedings of every other State. And the Congress may by general Laws prescribe the Manner in which such Acts, Records and Proceedings shall be proved, and the Effect thereof.

Section 2. The Citizens of each State shall be entitled to all Privileges and Immunities of Citizens in the several States.

A Person charged in any State with Treason, Felony, or other Crime, who shall flee from Justice, and be found in another State, shall on Demand of the executive Authority of the State from which he fled, be delivered up, to be removed to the State having Jurisdiction of the Crime.

No Person held to Service or Labour in one State, under the Laws thereof, escaping into another, shall, in Consequence of any Law or Regulation therein, be discharged from such Service or Labour, but shall be delivered up on Claim of the Party to whom such Service or Labour may be due.

Section 3. New States may be admitted by the Congress into this Union; but no new State shall be formed or erected within the Jurisdiction of any other State; nor any State be formed by the Junction of two or more States, or Parts of States, without the Consent of the Legislatures of the States concerned as well as of the Congress.

The Congress shall have Power to dispose of and make all needful Rules and Regulations respecting the Territory or other Property belonging to the United States; and nothing in this Constitution shall be so construed as to Prejudice any Claims of the United States, or of any particular State.

Section 4. The United States shall guarantee to every State in this Union a Republican Form of Government, and shall protect each of them against Invasion; and on Application of the Legislature, or of the Executive (when the Legislature cannot be convened) against domestic Violence.

ARTICLE V.

The Congress, whenever two thirds of both Houses shall deem it necessary, shall propose Amendments to this Constitution, or, on the Application of the Legislatures of two thirds of the several States, shall call a Convention for proposing Amendments, which, in either Case, shall be valid to all Intents and Purposes, as Part of this Constitution, when ratified by the Legislatures of three fourths of the several States, or by Conventions in three fourths thereof, as the one or the other Mode of Ratification may be proposed by the Congress; Provided that no Amendment which may be made prior to the Year One thousand eight hundred and eight shall in any Manner affect the first and fourth Clauses in the Ninth Section of the first Article; and that no State, without its Consent, shall be deprived of it's equal Suffrage in the Senate.

ARTICLE VI.

All Debts contracted and Engagements entered into, before the Adoption of this Constitution, shall be as valid against the United States under this Constitution, as under the Confederation.

This Constitution, and the Laws of the United States which shall be made in Pursuance thereof; and all Treaties made, or which shall be made, under the Authority of the United States, shall be the supreme Law of the Land; and the Judges in every State shall be bound thereby, any Thing in the Constitution or Laws of any State to the Contrary notwithstanding.

The Senators and Representatives before mentioned, and the Members of the several State Legislatures, and all executive and judicial Officers, both of the United States and of the several States, shall be bound by Oath or Affirmation, to support this Constitution; but no religious Test shall ever be required as a Qualification to any Office or public Trust under the United States.

ARTICLE VII.

The Ratification of the Conventions of nine States, shall be sufficient for the Establishment of this Constitution between the States so ratifying the Same.

AMENDMENTS TO THE CONSTITUTION

Article I

Congress shall make no law respecting an establishment of religion, or prohibiting the free exercise thereof; or abridging the freedom of speech, or of the press; or the right of the people peaceably to assemble, and to petition the Government for a redress of grievances.

Article II

A well regulated Militia, being necessary to the security of a free State, the right of the people to keep and bear Arms, shall not be infringed.

Article III

No Soldier shall, in time of peace be quartered in any house, without the consent of the Owner, nor in time of war, but in a manner to be prescribed by law.

Article IV

The right of the people to be secure in their persons, houses, papers, and effects, against unreasonable searches and seizures, shall not be violated, and no Warrants shall issue, but upon probable cause, supported by Oath or affirmation, and particularly describing the place to be searched, and the persons or things to be seized.

Article V

No person shall be held to answer for a capital, or otherwise infamous crime, unless on a presentment or indictment of a Grand Jury, except in cases arising in the land or naval forces, or in the Militia, when in actual service in time of War or public danger; nor shall any person be subject for the same offence to be twice put in jeopardy of life or limb; nor shall be compelled in any criminal case to be a witness against himself, nor be deprived of life, liberty, or property, without due process of law; nor shall private property be taken for public use, without just compensation.

Article VI

In all criminal prosecutions, the accused shall enjoy the right to a speedy and public trial, by an impartial jury of the State and district wherein the crime shall have been committed, which district shall have been previously ascertained by law, and to be informed of the nature and cause of the accusation; to be confronted with the witnesses against him; to have compulsory process for obtaining witnesses in his favor, and to have the Assistance of Counsel for his defence.

Article VII

In Suits at common law, where the value in controversy shall exceed twenty dollars, the right of trial by jury shall be preserved, and no fact tried by a jury, shall be otherwise re-examined in any Court of the United States, than according to the rules of the common law.

Article VIII

Excessive bail shall not be required, nor excessive fines imposed, nor cruel and unusual punishments inflicted.

Article IX

The enumeration in the Constitution, of certain rights, shall not be construed to deny or disparage others retained by the people.

Article X

The powers not delegated to the United States by the Constitution, nor prohibited by it to the States, are reserved to the States respectively, or to the people.

Article XI

The Judicial power of the United States shall not be construed to extend to any suit in law or equity, commenced or prosecuted against one of the United States by Citizens of another State, or by Citizens or Subjects of any Foreign State.

Article XII

The Electors shall meet in their respective states, and vote by ballot for President and Vice-President, one of whom, at least, shall not be an inhabitant of the same state with themselves; they shall name in their ballots the person voted for as President, and in distinct ballots the person voted for as Vice-President, and they shall make distinct lists of all persons voted for as President, and of all persons voted for as Vice-President, and of the number of votes for each, which lists they shall sign and certify, and transmit sealed to the seat of the government of the United States, directed to the President of the Senate;—The President of the Senate shall, in the presence of the Senate and House of Representatives, open all the certificates and the votes shall then be counted;—The person having the greatest number of votes for President, shall be the President, if such number be a majority of the whole number of Electors appointed; and if no person have such majority, then from the persons having the highest numbers not exceeding three on the list of those voted for as President, the House of Representatives shall choose immediately, by ballot, the President. But in choosing the President, the votes shall be taken by states, the representation from each state having one vote; a quorum for this purpose shall consist of a member or members from two-thirds of the states, and a majority of all the states shall be necessary to a choice. And if the House of Representatives shall not choose a President whenever the right of choice shall devolve upon them, before the fourth day of March next following, then the Vice-President shall act as President, as in the case of the death or other constitutional disability of the President. The person having the greatest number of votes as Vice-President, shall be the Vice-President, if such number be a majority of the whole number of Electors appointed, and if no person have a majority, then from the two highest numbers on the list, the Senate shall choose the Vice-President; a quorum for the purpose shall consist of two-thirds of the whole number of Senators, and a majority of the whole number shall be necessary to a choice. But no person constitutionally ineligible to the office of President shall be eligible to that of Vice-President of the United States.

B. FEDERALISM AND THE STRUCTURE OF ANTEBELLUM CONSTITUTIONAL LIBERTY

Introduction to Part 1B

The adoption of the American Constitution triggered a decades-long debate regarding the postratification status of "the several states" and the nature of American liberty. The Constitution's federalist structure was something new under the sun, and articulating the nature of federal and state sovereignty under such a document was both supremely critical and excruciatingly difficult.

Most antebellum legal and political theorists accepted the ratification-era writings of "Publius" in the *Federalist Papers* as canonical interpretations of the original Constitution—bestowing them with an authoritative status that would remain generally unchallenged even after the Civil War. These essays presented the American Constitution as creating a system of dual and competing sovereign governments. As Alexander Hamilton explained in *Federalist* No. 32, "as the plan of the convention aims only at a partial union or con-

solidation, the state governments would clearly retain all the rights of sovereignty which they before had, and which were not, by that act, *exclusively* delegated to the United States" (doc. 1). James Madison similarly assured his readers that the proposed Constitution was "neither a national nor a federal Constitution, but a composition of both" (doc. 3), in which the powers of the federal government would be "few and defined" and those reserved to the states "numerous and indefinite" (doc. 6). Finally, should the federal government transgress the boundaries of its enumerated powers, the states would be the first to "sound the alarm" and alert the people to the violation (doc. 5).

Although generally accepted as authoritative descriptions of the original Constitution, the *Federalist Papers* left a great deal ambiguous or unresolved regarding the precise nature of federal power and the right of state governments to resist potentially unconstitutional actions of the national government. In response to the 1798 Alien and Sedition Acts (doc. 8), James Madison and Thomas Jefferson authored the 1798 Virginia and Kentucky Resolutions, which denounced the acts as violations of the First Amendment and the reserved rights of the states. The resolutions articulated a powerful vision of states as cosigners of a constitutional compact who retained the right "to interpose" in cases involving "a deliberate, palpable and dangerous exercise" of powers "not granted by the said compact" (doc. 10). In 1799, Kentucky issued an even stronger version of its original resolution, declaring that "a nullification, by those sovereignties, of all unauthorized acts . . . is the rightful remedy" (doc. 11). In 1800, James Madison authored an extended report on the Virginia Resolutions and articulated what became the most influential theory of the federalist Constitution written between the nation's founding and the Civil War (doc. 12). According to Madison's Report of 1800, not only was the Constitution a compact between the independent states and the new federal government, but the states, as parties to that original compact, retained the right to judge for themselves whether the national government had violated the original agreement:

> It appears to your committee to be a plain principle, founded in common sense, illustrated by common practice, and essential to the nature of compacts; that where resort can be had to no tribunal superior to the authority of the parties, the parties themselves must be the rightful judges in the last resort, whether the bargain made, has been pursued or violated. (doc. 12)

Although Madison wrote of the rights of states to "interpose" in cases of unconstitutional national actions, the nature of such interposition remained undefined. In the case of the Virginia and Kentucky Resolutions, interposition involved nothing more than "sounding the alarm" to sister states and advocating a coordinated political response. Later decades would witness far more aggressive interpretations of the rights of interposition (see below).

The very first constitutional treatise, St. George Tucker's *A View of the Constitution* (doc. 13), borrowed copiously from Madison's Report of 1800 and set out a detailed vision of what became known as the "compact theory" of the Constitution. Since the preexisting sovereign states would have delegated to the new federal government no more power than was absolutely neces-

sary to remedy the problems with the Articles of Confederation, Tucker maintained that federal power ought to be "strictly" construed. The Federalist Party members who met at the Hartford Convention also relied on Madison's Report of 1800 as they considered whether secession was a viable response to the policies of President Madison's administration (doc. 15). During the Nullification Crisis, John C. Calhoun cited Madison's report in his support of South Carolina's refusal to submit to the federal "Tariff of Abominations" (docs. 20 and 22), although Madison himself denied that his theory of federalism justified state nullification (docs. 21 and 24). Ultimately, Calhoun himself would reject Madison's dual federalism approach and embrace an ultra–states' rights theory justifying unilateral secession (doc. 30). In moving away from Madison, Calhoun and other states' rights theorists and politicians ultimately embraced the more radical theory of the two Kentucky resolutions issued during the Alien and Sedition Acts crisis (docs. 9 and 11). Declaring that states had the right to unilaterally nullify allegedly unconstitutional acts by the national government, this more radical theory of nullification morphed into theories of unilateral secession (doc. 30). Interestingly, prior to secession, the most dramatic examples of state nullification involved Northern free states' use of the Virginia and Kentucky resolutions in defending their rights to ignore the decisions of the United States Supreme Court and reject the constitutionality of the federal fugitive slave law (see section C, docs. 36 and 38).

Although Madisonian federalism and its Jeffersonian variants dominated antebellum political theory and debate, more nationalist theories of the Constitution emerged soon after America's founding and played an increasingly important role as the country hurtled toward Civil War. From the earliest years of the Constitution, influential voices insisted that the document was not a compact between the states but an agreement among and between the undifferentiated people of the United States. Chief Justice John Marshall embraced this nationalist interpretation of our constitutional origin in *McCulloch v. Maryland* (doc. 16), prompting Madison's criticism of the opinion in what historians refer to as his *Detached Memoranda* (doc. 17). In fact, in his later years, Madison found himself pushing back against both secessionist and ultranationalist readings of the Constitution (see docs. 17, 21, and 24). Meanwhile, politicians gave the nationalist view of the Constitution rhetorical force in speeches like Daniel Webster's "The

Constitution Is Not a Compact" (doc. 23), and legal theorists like John Marshall's protégé Joseph Story gave the theory intellectual heft in his 1833 *Commentaries on the Constitution* (doc. 26). Story's influential *Commentaries* expressly and repeatedly challenged Tucker's compact theory of the Constitution and presented an alternative view of the nation's founding, in which a unitary national people preexisted the peoples of the several states. Abraham Lincoln embraced the nationalist theories of Webster and Story and used them to oppose the secessionist theories of John C. Calhoun and the Southern slave states (see section D, doc. 8).

The development of nationalist theories of federal authority coincided with emerging theories of national rights. The Bill of Rights, originally demanded by the states' ratifying conventions as a guard against national tyranny (docs. 7 and 25), over time became associated with theories of national rights—rights that both state and federal governments ought to respect. In the years prior to the Civil War, a number of judges, abolitionists, and politicians read the Bill of Rights as binding both state and federal officials (see doc. 31 and section C, docs. 26 and 29, respectively). In John Bingham's speech opposing the admission of Oregon, for example, the Ohio representative and future author of Section One of the Fourteenth Amendment declared that states were duty-bound to enforce the protections of the Fifth Amendment's Due Process Clause (doc. 33). Bingham's reasoning in this important speech contains the seeds of his theory of American freedom, which later matured during the Thirty-Ninth Congress.

Even more influential than the Bill of Rights as a statement of the *national* rights of freedom were the inspiring words of the Declaration of Independence. The Declaration's assertion of the natural-born equality of all people and the inalienable rights of life, liberty, and the pursuit of happiness provided rich soil for the growth of antebellum national rights movements. The very words and structure of the Declaration inspired the Women's Rights Convention at Seneca Falls to declare, "We hold these truths to be self-evident: that all men and women are created equal" (doc. 28). Again and again, opponents of slavery returned to the Declaration and to what they saw as its irrefutable assertion that "*all* men are created equal" (emphasis added; see section C, docs. 12, 23, 26, 28, and 29). The Declaration became the rock upon which the abolitionist movement built its house, representing as it did the nation's original commitment to the equality and freedom of *every person*,

regardless of citizenship or the laws of any individual state. Abraham Lincoln channeled this national rights reading of the Declaration in his speech at Gettysburg, explaining that "our fathers brought forth on this continent a new nation, conceived in liberty and dedicated to the proposition that all men are created equal" (section D, doc. 15).

The proponents of slavery, of course, also held a nationalist understanding of American freedom. This faction increasingly demanded that their "property rights" be respected throughout the United States and not just in the Southern slaveholding states (see section C, docs. 12, 19, 21, 25, 31, and 34). When Northern states and the Republican Party refused, the slaveholding states relied on *their* reading of the Declaration of Independence and the right of "free and independent states" to "alter or to abolish" their form of government whenever they saw fit (see section D, docs. 5 and 6). The original Constitution's federalist balance of state and national power could not be maintained in a house divided by slavery.

1

The Federalist, No. 32 (Hamilton)
January 3, 1788*

ALTHOUGH I am of opinion that there would be no real danger of the consequences which seem to be apprehended to the State governments from a power in the Union to control them in the levies of money, because I am persuaded that the sense of the people, the extreme hazard of provoking the resentments of the State governments, and a conviction of the utility and necessity of local administrations for local purposes, would be a complete barrier against the oppressive use of such a power; yet I am willing here to allow, in its full extent, the justness of the reasoning which requires that the individual States should possess an independent and uncontrollable authority to raise their own revenues for the supply of their own wants. And making this concession, I affirm that (with the sole exception of duties on imports and exports) they would, under the plan of the

* Clinton Rossiter, ed., *The Federalist Papers*, McLean edition (New York: Mentor, 1961), 197–201.

convention, retain that authority in the most absolute and unqualified sense; and that an attempt on the part of the national government to abridge them in the exercise of it, would be a violent assumption of power, unwarranted by any article or clause of its Constitution.

An entire consolidation of the States into one complete national sovereignty would imply an entire subordination of the parts; and whatever powers might remain in them, would be altogether dependent on the general will. But as the plan of the convention aims only at a partial union or consolidation, the State governments would clearly retain all the rights of sovereignty which they before had, and which were not, by that act, *exclusively* delegated to the United States. . . .

The necessity of a concurrent jurisdiction in certain cases results from the division of the sovereign power; and the rule that all authorities, of which the States are not explicitly divested in favor of the Union, remain with them in full vigor, is not a theoretical consequence of that division, but is clearly admitted by the whole tenor of the instrument which contains the articles of the proposed Constitution. We there find that, notwithstanding the affirmative grants of general authorities, there has been the most pointed care in those cases where it was deemed improper that the like authorities should reside in the States, to insert negative clauses prohibiting the exercise of them by the States. The tenth section of the first article consists altogether of such provisions. This circumstance is a clear indication of the sense of the convention, and furnishes a rule of interpretation out of the body of the act, which justifies the position I have advanced and refutes every hypothesis to the contrary.

PUBLIUS.

2

The Federalist, No. 33 (Hamilton)

January 3, 1788*

THE residue of the argument against the provisions of the Constitution in respect to taxation is ingrafted upon the following clause. The last clause of the eighth section of the first article of the plan under consideration authorizes the national legislature "to make all laws

*Rossiter, *Federalist,* 201–5.

which shall be *necessary* and *proper* for carrying into execution *the powers* by that Constitution vested in the government of the United States, or in any department or officer thereof"; and the second clause of the sixth article declares, "that the Constitution and the laws of the United States made *in pursuance thereof,* and the treaties made by their authority shall be the *supreme law* of the land, anything in the constitution or laws of any State to the contrary notwithstanding."

These two clauses have been the source of much virulent invective and petulant declamation against the proposed Constitution. They have been held up to the people in all the exaggerated colors of misrepresentation as the pernicious engines by which their local governments were to be destroyed and their liberties exterminated; as the hideous monster whose devouring jaws would spare neither sex nor age, nor high nor low, nor sacred nor profane; and yet, strange as it may appear, after all this clamor, to those who may not have happened to contemplate them in the same light, it may be affirmed with perfect confidence that the constitutional operation of the intended government would be precisely the same, if these clauses were entirely obliterated, as if they were repeated in every article. They are only declaratory of a truth which would have resulted by necessary and unavoidable implication from the very act of constituting a federal government, and vesting it with certain specified powers. This is so clear a proposition, that moderation itself can scarcely listen to the railings which have been so copiously vented against this part of the plan, without emotions that disturb its equanimity.

What is a power, but the ability or faculty of doing a thing? What is the ability to do a thing, but the power of employing the *means* necessary to its execution? What is a LEGISLATIVE power, but a power of making LAWS? What are the *means* to execute a LEGISLATIVE power but LAWS? What is the power of laying and collecting taxes, but a *legislative power,* or a power of *making laws,* to lay and collect taxes? What are the proper means of executing such a power, but *necessary* and *proper* laws?

This simple train of inquiry furnishes us at once with a test by which to judge of the true nature of the clause complained of. It conducts us to this palpable truth, that a power to lay and collect taxes must be a power to pass all laws *necessary* and *proper* for the execution of that power; and what does the unfortunate and calumniated provision in question do more than declare the same truth, to wit, that the national legislature, to whom the power of laying and collecting taxes had been previously given, might, in the execution of that power, pass all laws *necessary* and *proper* to carry it into effect? I have applied these observations thus particularly to the power of taxation, because it is the immediate subject under consideration, and because it is the most important of the authorities proposed to be conferred upon the Union. But the same process will lead to the same result, in relation to all other powers declared in the Constitution. And it is *expressly* to execute these powers that the sweeping clause, as it has been affectedly called, authorizes the national legislature to pass all *necessary* and *proper* laws. If there be anything exceptionable, it must be sought for in the specific powers upon which this general declaration is predicated. The declaration itself, though it may be chargeable with tautology or redundancy, is at least perfectly harmless.

But SUSPICION may ask, Why then was it introduced? The answer is, that it could only have been done for greater caution, and to guard against all caviling refinements in those who might hereafter feel a disposition to curtail and evade the legitimate authorities of the Union. The Convention probably foresaw, what it has been a principal aim of these papers to inculcate, that the danger which most threatens our political welfare is that the State governments will finally sap the foundations of the Union; and might therefore think it necessary, in so cardinal a point, to leave nothing to construction. Whatever may have been the inducement to it, the wisdom of the precaution is evident from the cry which has been raised against it; as that very cry betrays a disposition to question the great and essential truth which it is manifestly the object of that provision to declare.

But it may be again asked, Who is to judge of the *necessity* and *propriety* of the laws to be passed for executing the powers of the Union? I answer, first, that this question arises as well and as fully upon the simple grant of those powers as upon the declaratory clause; and I answer, in the second place, that the national government, like every other, must judge, in the first instance, of the proper exercise of its powers, and its constituents in the last. If the federal government should overpass the just bounds of its authority and make a tyrannical use of its powers, the people, whose creature it is, must appeal to the standard they have formed, and take such measures to redress the injury done to the Constitution as the exigency may suggest and prudence justify. The propriety of a law, in a constitutional light,

must always be determined by the nature of the powers upon which it is founded. Suppose, by some forced constructions of its authority (which, indeed, cannot easily be imagined), the federal legislature should attempt to vary the law of descent in any State, would it not be evident that, in making such an attempt, it had exceeded its jurisdiction, and infringed upon that of the State? Suppose, again, that upon the pretense of an interference with its revenues, it should undertake to abrogate a land tax imposed by the authority of a State; would it not be equally evident that this was an invasion of that concurrent jurisdiction in respect to this species of tax, which its Constitution plainly supposes to exist in the State governments? If there ever should be a doubt on this head, the credit of it will be entirely due to those reasoners who, in the imprudent zeal of their animosity to the plan of the convention, have labored to envelop it in a cloud calculated to obscure the plainest and simplest truths.

But it is said that the laws of the Union are to be the *supreme law* of the land. But what inference can be drawn from this, or what would they amount to, if they were not to be supreme? It is evident they would amount to nothing. A LAW, by the very meaning of the term, includes supremacy. It is a rule which those to whom it is prescribed are bound to observe. This results from every political association. If individuals enter into a state of society, the laws of that society must be the supreme regulator of their conduct. If a number of political societies enter into a larger political society, the laws which the latter may enact, pursuant to the powers intrusted to it by its constitution, must necessarily be supreme over those societies, and the individuals of whom they are composed. It would otherwise be a mere treaty, dependent on the good faith of the parties, and not a government, which is only another word for POLITICAL POWER AND SUPREMACY. But it will not follow from this doctrine that acts of the large society which are *not pursuant* to its constitutional powers, but which are invasions of the residuary authorities of the smaller societies, will become the supreme law of the land. These will be merely acts of usurpation, and will deserve to be treated as such. Hence we perceive that the clause which declares the supremacy of the laws of the Union, like the one we have just before considered, only declares a truth, which flows immediately and necessarily from the institution of a federal government. It will not, I presume, have escaped observation, that it *expressly* confines this supremacy to laws made *pursuant to the*

Constitution; which I mention merely as an instance of caution in the convention; since that limitation would have been to be understood, though it had not been expressed.

Though a law, therefore, laying a tax for the use of the United States would be supreme in its nature, and could not legally be opposed or controlled, yet a law for abrogating or preventing the collection of a tax laid by the authority of the State, (unless upon imports and exports), would not be the supreme law of the land, but a usurpation of power not granted by the Constitution. As far as an improper accumulation of taxes on the same object might tend to render the collection difficult or precarious, this would be a mutual inconvenience, not arising from a superiority or defect of power on either side, but from an injudicious exercise of power by one or the other, in a manner equally disadvantageous to both. It is to be hoped and presumed, however, that mutual interest would dictate a concert in this respect which would avoid any material inconvenience. The inference from the whole is, that the individual States would, under the proposed Constitution, retain an independent and uncontrollable authority to raise revenue to any extent of which they may stand in need, by every kind of taxation, except duties on imports and exports. It will be shown in the next paper that this *concurrent jurisdiction* in the article of taxation was the only admissible substitute for an entire subordination, in respect to this branch of power, of the State authority to that of the Union.

PUBLIUS.

3

The Federalist, No. 39 (Madison)

January [15–18], 1788*

THE last paper having concluded the observations which were meant to introduce a candid survey of the plan of government reported by the convention, we now proceed to the execution of that part of our undertaking.

The first question that offers itself is, whether the general form and aspect of the government be strictly

* Rossiter, *Federalist*, 240–46.

republican. It is evident that no other form would be reconcilable with the genius of the people of America; with the fundamental principles of the Revolution; or with that honorable determination which animates every votary of freedom, to rest all our political experiments on the capacity of mankind for self-government. If the plan of the convention, therefore, be found to depart from the republican character, its advocates must abandon it as no longer defensible.

What, then, are the distinctive characters of the republican form? Were an answer to this question to be sought, not by recurring to principles, but in the application of the term by political writers, to the constitution of different States, no satisfactory one would ever be found. Holland, in which no particle of the supreme authority is derived from the people, has passed almost universally under the denomination of a republic. The same title has been bestowed on Venice, where absolute power over the great body of the people is exercised, in the most absolute manner, by a small body of hereditary nobles. Poland, which is a mixture of aristocracy and of monarchy in their worst forms, has been dignified with the same appellation. The government of England, which has one republican branch only, combined with an hereditary aristocracy and monarchy, has, with equal impropriety, been frequently placed on the list of republics. These examples, which are nearly as dissimilar to each other as to a genuine republic, show the extreme inaccuracy with which the term has been used in political disquisitions.

If we resort for a criterion to the different principles on which different forms of government are established, we may define a republic to be, or at least may bestow that name on, a government which derives all its powers directly or indirectly from the great body of the people, and is administered by persons holding their offices during pleasure, for a limited period, or during good behavior. It is *essential* to such a government that it be derived from the great body of the society, not from an inconsiderable proportion, or a favored class of it; otherwise a handful of tyrannical nobles, exercising their oppressions by a delegation of their powers, might aspire to the rank of republicans, and claim for their government the honorable title of republic. It is *sufficient* for such a government that the persons administering it be appointed, either directly or indirectly, by the people; and that they hold their appointments by either of the tenures just specified; otherwise every government in the United States, as well as every other popular government that has been or can be well or-ganized or well executed, would be degraded from the republican character. According to the constitution of every State in the Union, some or other of the officers of government are appointed indirectly only by the people. According to most of them, the chief magis-trate himself is so appointed. And according to one, this mode of appointment is extended to one of the co-ordinate branches of the legislature. According to all the constitutions, also, the tenure of the highest offices is extended to a definite period, and in many instances, both within the legislative and executive departments, to a period of years. According to the provisions of most of the constitutions, again, as well as according to the most respectable and received opinions on the subject, the members of the judiciary department are to retain their offices by the firm tenure of good behavior.

On comparing the Constitution planned by the con-vention with the standard here fixed, we perceive at once that it is, in the most rigid sense, conformable to it. The House of Representatives, like that of one branch at least of all the State legislatures, is elected immedi-ately by the great body of the people. The Senate, like the present Congress, and the Senate of Maryland, de-rives its appointment indirectly from the people. The President is indirectly derived from the choice of the people, according to the example in most of the States. Even the judges, with all other officers of the Union, will, as in the several States, be the choice, though a remote choice, of the people themselves, the duration of the appointments is equally conformable to the re-publican standard, and to the model of State constitu-tions. The House of Representatives is periodically elec-tive, as in all the States; and for the period of two years, as in the State of South Carolina. The Senate is elec-tive, for the period of six years; which is but one year more than the period of the Senate of Maryland, and but two more than that of the Senates of New York and Virginia. The President is to continue in office for the period of four years; as in New York and Delaware, the chief magistrate is elected for three years, and in South Carolina for two years. In the other States the election is annual. In several of the States, however, no consti-tutional provision is made for the impeachment of the chief magistrate. And in Delaware and Virginia he is not impeachable till out of office. The President of the United States is impeachable at any time during his continuance in office. The tenure by which the judges are to hold their places, is, as it unquestionably ought to

be, that of good behavior. The tenure of the ministerial offices generally, will be a subject of legal regulation, conformably to the reason of the case and the example of the State constitutions.

Could any further proof be required of the republi-can complexion of this system, the most decisive one might be found in its absolute prohibition of titles of nobility, both under the federal and the State govern-ments; and in its express guaranty of the republican form to each of the latter.

"But it was not sufficient," say the adversaries of the proposed Constitution, "for the convention to adhere to the republican form. They ought, with equal care, to have preserved the *federal* form, which regards the Union as a *Confederacy* of sovereign states; instead of which, they have framed a *national* government, which regards the Union as a *consolidation* of the States." And it is asked by what authority this bold and radical inno-vation was undertaken? The handle which has been made of this objection requires that it should be exam-ined with some precision.

Without inquiring into the accuracy of the distinc-tion on which the objection is founded, it will be neces-sary to a just estimate of its force, first, to ascertain the real character of the government in question; secondly, to inquire how far the convention were authorized to propose such a government; and thirdly, how far the duty they owed to their country could supply any defect of regular authority.

First. In order to ascertain the real character of the government, it may be considered in relation to the foundation on which it is to be established; to the sources from which its ordinary powers are to be drawn; to the operation of those powers; to the extent of them; and to the authority by which future changes in the gov-ernment are to be introduced.

On examining the first relation, it appears, on one hand, that the Constitution is to be founded on the as-sent and ratification of the people of America, given by deputies elected for the special purpose; but, on the other, that this assent and ratification is to be given by the people, not as individuals composing one entire na-tion, but as composing the distinct and independent States to which they respectively belong. It is to be the assent and ratification of the several States, derived from the supreme authority in each State, the authority of the people themselves. The act, therefore, establishing the Constitution, will not be a *national*, but a *federal* act.

That it will be a federal and not a national act, as

these terms are understood by the objectors; the act of the people, as forming so many independent States, not as forming one aggregate nation, is obvious from this single consideration, that it is to result neither from the decision of a *majority* of the people of the Union, nor from that of a *majority* of the States. It must result from the *unanimous* assent of the several States that are parties to it, differing no otherwise from their ordinary assent than in its being expressed, not by the legislative authority, but by that of the people themselves. Were the people regarded in this transaction as forming one nation, the will of the majority of the whole people of the United States would bind the minority, in the same manner as the majority in each State must bind the minority; and the will of the majority must be determined either by a comparison of the individual votes, or by considering the will of the majority of the States as evidence of the will of a majority of the people of the United States. Neither of these rules have been adopted. Each State, in ratifying the Constitution, is considered as a sovereign body, independent of all others, and only to be bound by its own voluntary act. In this relation, then, the new Constitution will, if established, be a *federal*, and not a *national* constitution.

The next relation is, to the sources from which the ordinary powers of government are to be derived. The House of Representatives will derive its powers from the people of America; and the people will be represented in the same proportion, and on the same principle, as they are in the legislature of a particular State. So far the government is *national*, not *federal*. The Senate, on the other hand, will derive its powers from the States, as political and coequal societies; and these will be represented on the principle of equality in the Senate, as they now are in the existing Congress. So far the government is *federal*, not *national*. The executive power will be derived from a very compound source. The immediate election of the President is to be made by the States in their political characters. The votes allotted to them are in a compound ratio, which considers them partly as distinct and coequal societies, partly as unequal members of the same society. The eventual election, again, is to be made by that branch of the legislature which consists of the national representatives; but in this particular act they are to be thrown into the form of individual delegations, from so many distinct and coequal bodies politic. From this aspect of the government it appears to be of a mixed character, presenting at least as many *federal* as *national* features.

The difference between a federal and national government, as it relates to the *operation of the government*, is supposed to consist in this, that in the former the powers operate on the political bodies composing the Confederacy, in their political capacities; in the latter, on the individual citizens composing the nation, in their individual capacities. On trying the Constitution by this criterion, it falls under the *national*, not the *federal* character; though perhaps not so completely as has been understood. In several cases, and particularly in the trial of controversies to which States may be parties, they must be viewed and proceeded against in their collective and political capacities only. So far the national countenance of the government on this side seems to be disfigured by a few federal features. But this blemish is perhaps unavoidable in any plan; and the operation of the government on the people, in their individual capacities, in its ordinary and most essential proceedings, may, on the whole, designate it, in this relation, a *national* government.

But if the government be national with regard to the *operation* of its powers, it changes its aspect again when we contemplate it in relation to the *extent* of its powers. The idea of a national government involves in it, not only an authority over the individual citizens, but an indefinite supremacy over all persons and things, so far as they are objects of lawful government. Among a people consolidated into one nation, this supremacy is completely vested in the national legislature. Among communities united for particular purposes, it is vested partly in the general and partly in the municipal legislatures. In the former case, all local authorities are subordinate to the supreme; and may be controlled, directed, or abolished by it at pleasure. In the latter, the local or municipal authorities form distinct and independent portions of the supremacy, no more subject, within their respective spheres, to the general authority, than the general authority is subject to them, within its own sphere. In this relation, then, the proposed government cannot be deemed a *national* one; since its jurisdiction extends to certain enumerated objects only, and leaves to the several States a residuary and inviolable sovereignty over all other objects. It is true that in controversies relating to the boundary between the two jurisdictions, the tribunal which is ultimately to decide, is to be established under the general government. But this does not change the principle of the case. The decision is to be impartially made, according to the rules of the Constitution; and all the usual and most effectual precautions are taken to secure this impartiality. Some such tribunal is clearly essential to prevent an appeal to the sword and a dissolution of the compact; and that it ought to be established under the general rather than under the local governments, or, to speak more properly, that it could be safely established under the first alone, is a position not likely to be combated.

If we try the Constitution by its last relation to the authority by which amendments are to be made, we find it neither wholly *national* nor wholly *federal*. Were it wholly national, the supreme and ultimate authority would reside in the *majority* of the people of the Union; and this authority would be competent at all times, like that of a majority of every national society, to alter or abolish its established government. Were it wholly federal, on the other hand, the concurrence of each State in the Union would be essential to every alteration that would be binding on all. The mode provided by the plan of the convention is not founded on either of these principles. In requiring more than a majority, and principles. In requiring more than a majority, and particularly in computing the proportion by *States*, not by *citizens*, it departs from the *national* and advances towards the *federal* character; in rendering the concurrence of less than the whole number of States sufficient, it loses again the *federal* and partakes of the *national* character.

The proposed Constitution, therefore, is, in strictness, neither a national nor a federal Constitution, but a composition of both. In its foundation it is federal, not national; in the sources from which the ordinary powers of the government are drawn, it is partly federal and partly national; in the operation of these powers, it is national, not federal; in the extent of them, again, it is federal, not national; and, finally, in the authoritative mode of introducing amendments, it is neither wholly federal nor wholly national.

PUBLIUS.

4

The Federalist, No. 43 (Madison)

January 23, 1788*

In a confederacy founded on republican principles, and composed of republican members, the superintending

* Rossiter, *Federalist*, 274–78.

government ought clearly to possess authority to defend the system against aristocratic or monarchical innovations. The more intimate the nature of such a Union may be, the greater interest have the members in the political institutions of each other; and the greater right to insist that the forms of government under which the compact was entered into, should be *substantially* maintained. But a right implies a remedy; and where else could the remedy be deposited, than where it is deposited by the Constitution? Governments of dissimilar principles and forms have been found less adapted to a federal coalition of any sort, than those of a kindred nature. "As the confederate republic of Germany," says Montesquieu, "consists of free cities and petty states subject to different Princes, experience shews us that it is more imperfect than that of Holland and Switzerland." "Greece was undone" he adds, "as soon as the King of Macedon obtained a seat among the Amphictyons." In the latter case, no doubt, the disproportionate force, as well as the monarchical form of the new confederate, had its share of influence on the events. It may possibly be asked what need there could be of such a precaution, and whether it may not become a pretext for alterations in the state governments, without the concurrence of the states themselves. These questions admit of ready answers. If the interposition of the general government should not be needed, the provision for such an event will be a harmless superfluity only in the Constitution. But who can say what experiments may be produced by the caprice of particular states, by the ambition of enterprising leaders, or by the intrigues and influence of foreign powers? To the second question it may be answered, that if the general government should interpose by virtue of this constitutional authority, it will be of course bound to pursue the authority. But the authority extends no farther than to a guaranty of a republican form of government, which supposes a pre-existing government of the form which is to be guaranteed. As long therefore as the existing republican forms are continued by the States, they are guaranteed by the Federal Constitution. Whenever the states may choose to substitute other republican forms, they have a right to do so, and to claim the federal guaranty for the latter. The only restriction imposed on them is, that they shall not exchange republican for anti-republican Constitutions; a restriction which it is presumed will hardly be considered as a grievance.

A protection against invasion is due from every society to the parts composing it. The latitude of the expression here used, seems to secure each state not only against foreign hostility, but against ambitious or vindictive enterprises of its more powerful neighbors. The history both of ancient and modern confederacies, proves that the weaker members of the Union ought not to be insensible to the policy of this article.

Protection against domestic violence is added with equal propriety. It has been remarked that even among the Swiss Cantons, which properly speaking are not under one government, provision is made for this object; and the history of that league informs us, that mutual aid is frequently claimed and afforded; and as well by the most democratic, as the other Cantons. A recent and well known event among ourselves, has warned us to be prepared for emergencies of a like nature.

At first view it might seem not to square with the republican theory, to suppose either that a majority have not the right, or that a minority will have the force to subvert a government; and consequently that the federal interposition can never be required but when it would be improper. But theoretic reasoning in this, as in most other cases, must be qualified by the lessons of practice. Why may not illicit combinations for purposes of violence be formed as well by a majority of a State, especially a small State, as by a majority of a county or a district of the same State; and if the authority of the State ought in the latter case to protect the local magistracy, ought not the federal authority in the former to support the State authority? Besides, there are certain parts of the State Constitutions which are so interwoven with the federal Constitution, that a violent blow cannot be given to the one without communicating the wound to the other. Insurrections in a State will rarely induce a federal interposition, unless the number concerned in them, bear some proportion to the friends of government. It will be much better that the violence in such cases should be repressed by the Superintending power, than that the majority should be left to maintain their cause by a bloody and obstinate contest. The existence of a right to interpose will generally prevent the necessity of exerting it.

Is it true that force and right are necessarily on the same side in republican governments? May not the minor party possess such a superiority of pecuniary resources, of military talents and experience, or of secret succors from foreign powers, as will render it superior also in an appeal to the sword? May not a more compact and advantageous position turn the scale on the same side against a superior number so situated as to be less capable of a prompt and collected exertion of its strength? Nothing can be more chimerical than to imagine that in a trial of actual force, victory may be calculated by the rules which prevail in a census of the inhabitants, or which determine the event of an election! May it not happen in fine that the minority of *citizens* may become a majority of *persons*, by the accession of alien residents, of a casual concourse of adventurers, or of those whom the Constitution of the State has not admitted to the rights of suffrage? I take no notice of an unhappy species of population abounding in some of the States, who during the calm of regular government are sunk below the level of men; but who in the tempestuous scenes of civil violence may emerge into the human character, and give a superiority of strength to any party with which they may associate themselves.

In cases where it may be doubtful on which side justice lies, what better umpires could be desired by two violent factions, flying to arms and tearing a State to pieces, than the representatives of confederate States not heated by the local flame? To the impartiality of judges they would unite the affection of friends. Happy would it be if such a remedy for its infirmities, could be enjoyed by all free governments; if a project equally effectual could be established for the universal peace of mankind.

Should it be asked what is to be the redress for an insurrection pervading all the States, and comprising a superiority of the entire force, though not a constitutional right; the answer must be, that such a case, as it would be without the compass of human remedies, so it is fortunately not within the compass of human probability; and that it is a sufficient recommendation of the federal Constitution, that it diminishes the risk of a calamity, for which no possible constitution can provide a cure.

Among the advantages of a confederate republic enumerated by Montesquieu, an important one is, "that should a popular insurrection happen in one of the States, the others are able to quell it. Should abuses creep into one part, they are reformed by those that remain sound."

5

The Federalist, No. 44 (Madison)

January 25, 1788*

If it be asked what is to be the consequence, in case the Congress shall misconstrue this part of the Constitution, and exercise powers not warranted by its true meaning, I answer, the same as if they should misconstrue or enlarge any other power vested in them; as if the general power had been reduced to particulars, and any one of these were to be violated; the same, in short, as if the State legislatures should violate the irrespective constitutional authorities. In the first instance, the success of the usurpation will depend on the executive and judiciary departments, which are to expound and give effect to the legislative acts; and in the last resort a remedy must be obtained from the people who can, by the election of more faithful representatives, annul the acts of the usurpers. The truth is, that this ultimate redress may be more confided in against unconstitutional acts of the federal than of the State legislatures, for this plain reason, that as every such act of the former will be an invasion of the rights of the latter, these will be ever ready to mark the innovation, to sound the alarm to the people, and to exert their local influence in effecting a change of federal representatives.

6

The Federalist, No. 45 (Madison)

January [25–29], 1788†

The powers delegated by the proposed Constitution to the federal government are few and defined. Those which are to remain in the State governments are numerous and indefinite. The former will be exercised principally on external objects, as war, peace, negotiation, and foreign commerce; with which last the power of taxation will, for the most part, be connected. The powers reserved to the several States will extend to all

the objects which, in the ordinary course of affairs, concern the lives, liberties, and properties of the people, and the internal order, improvement, and prosperity of the State.

The operations of the federal government will be most extensive and important in times of war and danger; those of the State governments, in times of peace and security. As the former periods will probably bear a small proportion to the latter, the State governments will here enjoy another advantage over the federal government. The more adequate, indeed, the federal powers may be rendered to the national defense, the less frequent will be those scenes of danger which might favor their ascendancy over the governments of the particular States.

If the new Constitution be examined with accuracy and candor, it will be found that the change which it proposes consists much less in the addition of NEW POWERS to the Union, than in the invigoration of its ORIGINAL POWERS. The regulation of commerce, it is true, is a new power; but that seems to be an addition which few oppose, and from which no apprehensions are entertained. The powers relating to war and peace, armies and fleets, treaties and finance, with the other more considerable powers, are all vested in the existing Congress by the articles of Confederation. The proposed change does not enlarge these powers; it only substitutes a more effectual mode of administering them.

7

James Madison, Speech Introducing Proposed Amendments

June 8, 1789‡

MR. MADISON.

. . .

When I first hinted to the house my intention of calling their deliberations to this object, I mentioned the pressure of other important subjects, and submitted the propriety of postponing this till the more urgent business was dispatched; but finding that business not dispatched, when the order of the day for considering

* Rossiter, *Federalist*, 285–86.
† Rossiter, *Federalist*, 292–93.

‡ James Madison, *James Madison: Writings*, ed. Jack N. Rakove (New York: Library of America, 1999), 437–52.

amendments arrived, I thought it a good reason for a farther delay, I moved the postponement accordingly. I am sorry the same reason still exists in some degree; but operates with less force when it is considered, that it is not now proposed to enter into a full and minute discussion of every part of the subject, but merely to bring it before the house, that our constituents may see we pay a proper attention to a subject they have much at heart; and if it does not give that full gratification which is to be wished, they will discover that it proceeds from the urgency of business of a very important nature. But if we continue to postpone from time to time, and refuse to let the subject come into view, it may occasion suspicions, which, though not well founded, may tend to inflame or prejudice the public mind, against our decisions: they may think we are not sincere in our desire to incorporate such amendments in the constitution as will secure those rights, which they consider as not sufficiently guarded. The applications for amendments come from a very respectable number of our constituents, and it is certainly proper for congress to consider the subject, in order to quiet that anxiety which prevails in the public mind: Indeed I think it would have been of advantage to the government, if it had been practicable to have made some propositions for amendments the first business we entered upon; it would stifle the voice of complaint, and make friends of many who doubted its merits. Our future measures would then have been more universally agreeable and better supported; but the justifiable anxiety to put the government in operation prevented that; it therefore remains for us to take it up as soon as possible. I wish then to commence the consideration at the present moment; I hold it to be my duty to unfold my ideas, and explain myself to the house in some form or other without delay. I only wish to introduce the great work, and as I said before I do not expect it will be decided immediately; but if some step is taken in the business it will give reason to believe that we may come at a final result. This will inspire a reasonable hope in the advocates for amendments, that full justice will be done to the important subject; and I have reason to believe their expectation will not be defeated. I hope the house will not decline my motion for going into a committee.

...

MR. MADISON. I am sorry to be accessary to the loss of a single moment of time by the house. If I had been indulged in my motion, and we had gone into a committee of the whole, I think we might have rose, and re-

sumed the consideration of other business before this time; that is, so far as it depended on what I proposed to bring forward. As that mode seems not to give satisfaction, I will withdraw the motion, and move you, sir, that a select committee be appointed to consider and report such amendments as are proper for Congress to propose to the legislatures of the several States, conformably to the 5th article of the constitution. I will state my reasons why I think it proper to propose amendments; and state the amendments themselves, so far as I think they ought to be proposed. If I thought I could fulfil the duty which I owe to myself and my constituents, to let the subject pass over in silence, I most certainly should not trespass upon the indulgence of this house. But I cannot do this; and am therefore compelled to beg a patient hearing to what I have to lay before you. And I do most sincerely believe that if congress will devote but one day to this subject, so far as to satisfy the public that we do not disregard their wishes, it will have a salutary influence on the public councils, and prepare the way for a favorable reception of our future measures. It appears to me that this house is bound by every motive of prudence, not to let the first session pass over without proposing to the state legislatures some things to be incorporated into the constitution, as will render it as acceptable to the whole people of the United States, as it has been found acceptable to a majority of them. I wish, among other reasons why something should be done, that those who have been friendly to the adoption of this constitution, may have the opportunity of proving to those who were opposed to it, that they were as sincerely devoted to liberty and a republican government, as those who charged them with wishing the adoption of this constitution in order to lay the foundation of an aristocracy or despotism. It will be a desirable thing to extinguish from the bosom of every member of the community any apprehensions, that there are those among his countrymen who wish to deprive them of the liberty for which they valiantly fought and honorably bled. And if there are amendments desired, of such a nature as will not injure the constitution, and they can be ingrafted so as to give satisfaction to the doubting part of our fellow citizens; the friends of the federal government will evince that spirit of deference and concession for which they have hitherto been distinguished.

It cannot be a secret to the gentlemen in this house, that, notwithstanding the ratification of this system of government by eleven of the thirteen United States, in some cases unanimously, in others by large majorities; yet still there is a great number of our constituents who are dissatisfied with it; among whom are many respectable for their talents, their patriotism, and respectable for the jealousy they have for their liberty, which, though mistaken in its object, is laudable in its motive. There is a great body of the people falling under this description, who at present feel much inclined to join their support to the cause of federalism, if they were satisfied in this one point: We ought not to disregard their inclination, but, on principles of amity and moderation, conform to their wishes, and expressly declare the great rights of mankind secured under this constitution. The acquiescence which our fellow citizens shew under the government, calls upon us for a like return of moderation. But perhaps there is a stronger motive than this for our going into a consideration of the subject; it is to provide those securities for liberty which are required by a part of the community. I allude in a particular manner to those two states who have not thought fit to throw themselves into the bosom of the confederacy: it is a desirable thing, on our part as well as theirs, that a re-union should take place as soon as possible. I have no doubt, if we proceed to take those steps which would be prudent and requisite at this juncture, that in a short time we should see that disposition prevailing in those states that are not come in, that we have seen prevailing in those states which are.

But I will candidly acknowledge, that, over and above all these considerations, I do conceive that the constitution may be amended; that is to say, if all power is subject to abuse, that then it is possible the abuse of the powers of the general government may be guarded against in a more secure manner than is now done, while no one advantage, arising from the exercise of that power, shall be damaged or endangered by it. We have in this way something to gain, and, if we proceed with caution, nothing to lose; and in this case it is necessary to proceed with caution; for while we feel all these inducements to go into a revisal of the constitution, we must feel for the constitution itself, and make that revisal a moderate one. I should be unwilling to see a door opened for a re-consideration of the whole structure of the government, for a re-consideration of the principles and the substance of the powers given; because I doubt, if such a door was opened, if we should be very likely to stop at that point which would be safe to the government itself: But I do wish to see a door opened to consider, so far as to incorporate those provisions for the security of rights, against which I believe no serious ob-

jection has been made by any class of our constituents, such as would be likely to meet with the concurrence of two-thirds of both houses, and the approbation of three-fourths of the state legislatures. I will not propose a single alteration which I do not wish to see take place, as intrinsically proper in itself, or proper because it is wished for by a respectable number of my fellow citizens; and therefore I shall not propose a single alteration but is likely to meet the concurrence required by the constitution.

There have been objections of various kinds made against the constitution: Some were levelled against its structure, because the president was without a council; because the senate, which is a legislative body, had judicial powers in trials on impeachments; and because the powers of that body were compounded in other respects, in a manner that did not correspond with a particular theory; because it grants more power than is supposed to be necessary for every good purpose; and controls the ordinary powers of the state governments. I know some respectable characters who opposed this government on these grounds; but I believe that the great mass of the people who opposed it, disliked it because it did not contain effectual provision against encroachments on particular rights, and those safeguards which they have been long accustomed to have interposed between them and the magistrate who exercised the sovereign power: nor ought we to consider them safe, while a great number of our fellow citizens think these securities necessary.

It has been a fortunate thing that the objection to the government has been made on the ground I stated; because it will be practicable on that ground to obviate the objection, so far as to satisfy the public mind that their liberties will be perpetual, and this without endangering any part of the constitution, which is considered as essential to the existence of the government by those who promoted its adoption.

The amendments which have occurred to me, proper to be recommended by congress to the state legislatures, are these:

First. That there be prefixed to the constitution a declaration—That all power is originally vested in, and consequently derived from the people.

That government is instituted, and ought to be exercised for the benefit of the people; which consists in the enjoyment of life and liberty, with the right of acquiring and using property, and generally of pursuing and obtaining happiness and safety.

That the people have an indubitable, unalienable, and indefeasible right to reform or change their government, whenever it be found adverse or inadequate to the purposes of its institution.

Secondly. That in article 1st, section 2, clause 3, these words be struck out, to wit: "The number of Representatives shall not exceed one for every thirty thousand, but each State shall have at least one Representative, and until such enumeration shall be made;" and that in place thereof be inserted these words, to wit: "After the first actual enumeration, there shall be one Representative for every thirty thousand, until the number amounts to ——, after which the proportion shall be so regulated by Congress, that the number shall never be less than ——, nor more than ——, but each State shall, after the first enumeration, have at least two Representatives; and prior thereto."

Thirdly. That in article 1st, section 6, clause 1, there be added to the end of the first sentence, these words, to wit: "But no law varying the compensation last ascertained shall operate before the next ensuing election of Representatives."

Fourthly. That in article 1st, section 9, between clauses 3 and 4, be inserted these clauses, to wit, The civil rights of none shall be abridged on account of religious belief or worship, nor shall any national religion be established, nor shall the full and equal rights of conscience be in any manner, or on any pretext infringed.

The people shall not be deprived or abridged of their right to speak, to write, or to publish their sentiments; and the freedom of the press, as one of the great bulwarks of liberty, shall be inviolable.

The people shall not be restrained from peaceably assembling and consulting for their common good; nor from applying to the legislature by petitions, or remonstrances for redress of their grievances.

The right of the people to keep and bear arms shall not be infringed; a well armed, and well regulated militia being the best security of a free country: but no person religiously scrupulous of bearing arms, shall be compelled to render military service in person.

No soldier shall in time of peace be quartered in any house without the consent of the owner; nor at any time, but in a manner warranted by law.

No person shall be subject, except in cases of impeachment, to more than one punishment, or one trial for the same offence; nor shall be compelled to be a witness against himself; nor be deprived of life, liberty, or property without due process of law; nor be obliged to relinquish his property, where it may be necessary for public use, without a just compensation.

Excessive bail shall not be required, nor excessive fines imposed, nor cruel and unusual punishments inflicted.

The rights of the people to be secured in their persons, their houses, their papers, and their other property from all unreasonable searches and seizures, shall not be violated by warrants issued without probable cause, supported by oath or affirmation, or not particularly describing the places to be searched, or the persons or things to be seized.

In all criminal prosecutions, the accused shall enjoy the right to a speedy and public trial, to be informed of the cause and nature of the accusation, to be confronted with his accusers, and the witnesses against him; to have a compulsory process for obtaining witnesses in his favor; and to have the assistance of counsel for his defence.

The exceptions here or elsewhere in the constitution, made in favor of particular rights, shall not be so construed as to diminish the just importance of other rights retained by the people; or as to enlarge the powers delegated by the constitution; but either as actual limitations of such powers, or as inserted merely for greater caution.

Fifthly. That in article 1st, section 10, between clauses 1 and 2, be inserted this clause, to wit:

No state shall violate the equal rights of conscience, or the freedom of the press, or the trial by jury in criminal cases.

Sixthly. That article 3d, section 2, be annexed to the end of clause 2d, these words to wit: but no appeal to such court shall be allowed where the value in controversy shall not amount to —— dollars: nor shall any fact triable by jury, according to the course of common law, be otherwise re-examinable than may consist with the principles of common law.

Seventhly. That in article 3d, section 2, the third clause be struck out, and in its place be inserted the clauses following, to wit:

The trial of all crimes (except in cases of impeachments, and cases arising in the land or naval forces, or the militia when on actual service in time of war or public danger) shall be by an impartial jury of freeholders of the vicinage, with the requisite of unanimity for conviction, of the right of challenge, and other accustomed requisites; and in all crimes punishable with loss of life or member, presentment or indictment by a grand jury, shall be an essential preliminary, provided that in cases of crimes committed within any county which may be in possession of an enemy, or in which a general insurrection may prevail, the trial may by law be authorised in some other county of the same state, as near as may be to the seat of the offence.

In cases of crimes committed not within any county, the trial may by law be in such county as the laws shall have prescribed. In suits at common law, between man and man, the trial by jury, as one of the best securities to the rights of the people, ought to remain inviolate.

Eighthly. That immediately after article 6th, be inserted, as article 7th, the clauses following, to wit:

The powers delegated by this constitution, are appropriated to the departments to which they are respectively distributed: so that the legislative department shall never exercise the powers vested in the executive or judicial; nor the executive exercise the powers vested in the legislative or judicial; nor the judicial exercise the powers vested in the legislative or executive departments.

The powers not delegated by this constitution, nor prohibited by it to the states, are reserved to the States respectively.

Ninthly. That article 7th, be numbered as article 8th.

The first of these amendments, relates to what may be called a bill of rights; I will own that I never considered this provision so essential to the federal constitution, as to make it improper to ratify it, until such an amendment was added; at the same time, I always conceived, that in a certain form and to a certain extent, such a provision was neither improper nor altogether useless. I am aware, that a great number of the most respectable friends to the government and champions for republican liberty, have thought such a provision, not only unnecessary, but even improper, nay, I believe some have gone so far as to think it even dangerous. Some policy has been made use of perhaps by gentlemen on both sides of the question: I acknowledge the ingenuity of those arguments which were drawn against the constitution, by a comparison with the policy of Great-Britain, in establishing a declaration of rights; but there is too great a difference in the case to warrant the comparison: therefore the arguments drawn from that source, were in a great measure inapplicable. In the declaration of rights which that country has established, the truth is, they have gone no farther, than to raise a barrier against the power of the crown; the power of the legislature is left altogether indefinite. Altho' I know whenever

the great rights, the trial by jury, freedom of the press, or liberty of conscience, came in question in that body, the invasion of them is resisted by able advocates, yet their Magna Charta does not contain any one provision for the security of those rights, respecting which, the people of America are most alarmed. The freedom of the press and rights of conscience, those choicest privileges of the people, are unguarded in the British constitution.

But altho' the case may be widely different, and it may not be thought necessary to provide limits for the legislative power in that country, yet a different opinion prevails in the United States. The people of many states, have thought it necessary to raise barriers against power in all forms and departments of government, and I am inclined to believe, if once bills of rights are established in all the states as well as the federal constitution, we shall find that altho' some of them are rather unimportant, yet, upon the whole, they will have a salutary tendency.

It may be said, in some instances they do no more than state the perfect equality of mankind; this to be sure is an absolute truth, yet it is not absolutely necessary to be inserted at the head of a constitution.

In some instances they assert those rights which are exercised by the people in forming and establishing a plan of government. In other instances, they specify those rights which are retained when particular powers are given up to be exercised by the legislature. In other instances, they specify positive rights, which may seem to result from the nature of the compact. Trial by jury cannot be considered as a natural right, but a right resulting from the social compact which regulates the action of the community, but is as essential to secure the liberty of the people as any one of the pre-existent rights of nature. In other instances they lay down dogmatic maxims with respect to the construction of the government; declaring, that the legislative, executive, and judicial branches shall be kept separate and distinct: Perhaps the best way of securing this in practice is to provide such checks, as will prevent the encroachment of the one upon the other.

But whatever may be the form which the several states have adopted in making declarations in favor of particular rights, the great object in view is to limit and qualify the powers of government, by excepting out of the grant of power those cases in which the government ought not to act, or to act only in a particular mode. They point these exceptions sometimes against the abuse of the executive power, sometimes against the legislative, and, in some cases, against the community itself; or, in other words, against the majority in favor of the minority.

In our government it is, perhaps, less necessary to guard against the abuse in the executive department than any other; because it is not the stronger branch of the system, but the weaker: It therefore must be levelled against the legislative, for it is the most powerful, and most likely to be abused, because it is under the least controul; hence, so far as a declaration of rights can tend to prevent the exercise of undue power, it cannot be doubted but such declaration is proper. But I confess that I do conceive, that in a government modified like this of the United States, the great danger lies rather in the abuse of the community than in the legislative body. The prescriptions in favor of liberty, ought to be levelled against that quarter where the greatest danger lies, namely, that which possesses the highest prerogative of power: But this is not found in either the executive or legislative departments of government, but in the body of the people, operating by the majority against the minority.

It may be thought all paper barriers against the power of the community, are too weak to be worthy of attention. I am sensible they are not so strong as to satisfy gentlemen of every description who have seen and examined thoroughly the texture of such a defence; yet, as they have a tendency to impress some degree of respect for them, to establish the public opinion in their favor, and rouse the attention of the whole community, it may be one mean to control the majority from those acts to which they might be otherwise inclined.

It has been said by way of objection to a bill of rights, by many respectable gentlemen out of doors, and I find opposition on the same principles likely to be made by gentlemen on this floor, that they are unnecessary articles of a republican government, upon the presumption that the people have those rights in their own hands, and that is the proper place for them to rest. It would be a sufficient answer to say that this objection lies against such provisions under the state governments as well as under the general government; and there are, I believe, but few gentlemen who are inclined to push their theory so far as to say that a declaration of rights in those cases is either ineffectual or improper. It has been said that in the federal government they are unnecessary, because the powers are enumerated, and it follows that all that are not granted by the constitution are retained: that the constitution is a bill of powers, the great residuum being the rights of the people; and therefore a bill of rights cannot be so necessary as if the residuum was thrown into the hands of the government. I admit that these arguments are not entirely without foundation; but they are not conclusive to the extent which has been supposed. It is true the powers of the general government are circumscribed; they are directed to particular objects; but even if government keeps within those limits, it has certain discretionary powers with respect to the means, which may admit of abuse to a certain extent, in the same manner as the powers of the state governments under their constitutions may to an indefinite extent; because in the constitution of the United States there is a clause granting to Congress the power to make all laws which shall be necessary and proper for carrying into execution all the powers vested in the government of the United States, or in any department or officer thereof; this enables them to fulfil every purpose for which the government was established. Now, may not laws be considered necessary and proper by Congress, for it is them who are to judge of the necessity and propriety to accomplish those special purposes which they may have in contemplation, which laws in themselves are neither necessary or proper; as well as improper laws could be enacted by the state legislatures, for fulfilling the more extended objects of those governments. I will state an instance which I think in point, and proves that this might be the case. The general government has a right to pass all laws which shall be necessary to collect its revenue; the means for enforcing the collection are within the direction of the legislature: may not general warrants be considered necessary for this purpose, as well as for some purposes which it was supposed at the framing of their constitutions the state governments had in view. If there was reason for restraining the state governments from exercising this power, there is like reason for restraining the federal government.

It may be said, because it has been said, that a bill of rights is not necessary, because the establishment of this government has not repealed those declarations of rights which are added to the several state constitutions: that those rights of the people, which had been established by the most solemn act, could not be annihilated by a subsequent act of that people, who meant, and declared at the head of the instrument, that they ordained and established a new system, for the express purpose of securing to themselves and posterity the liberties they had gained by an arduous conflict.

I admit the force of this observation, but I do not look upon it to be conclusive. In the first place, it is too uncertain ground to leave this provision upon, if a provision is at all necessary to secure rights so important as many of those I have mentioned are conceived to be, by the public in general, as well as those in particular who opposed the adoption of this constitution. Beside some states have no bills of rights, there are others provided with very defective ones, and there are others whose bills of rights are not only defective, but absolutely improper; instead of securing some in the full extent which republican principles would require, they limit them too much to agree with the common ideas of liberty.

It has been objected also against a bill of rights, that, by enumerating particular exceptions to the grant of power, it would disparage those rights which were not placed in that enumeration, and it might follow by implication, that those rights which were not singled out, were intended to be assigned into the hands of the general government, and were consequently insecure. This is one of the most plausible arguments I have ever heard urged against the admission of a bill of rights into this system; but, I conceive, that may be guarded against. I have attempted it, as gentlemen may see by turning to the last clause of the 4th resolution.

It has been said, that it is unnecessary to load the constitution with this provision, because it was not found effectual in the constitution of the particular states. It is true, there are a few particular states in which some of the most valuable articles have not, at one time or other, been violated; but does it not follow but they may have, to a certain degree, a salutary effect against the abuse of power. If they are incorporated into the constitution, independent tribunals of justice will consider themselves in a peculiar manner the guardians of those rights; they will be an impenetrable bulwark against every assumption of power in the legislative or executive; they will be naturally led to resist every encroachment upon rights expressly stipulated for in the constitution by the declaration of rights. Beside this security, there is a great probability that such a declaration in the federal system would be inforced; because the state legislatures will jealously and closely watch the operations of this government, and be able to resist with more effect every assumption of power than any other power on earth can do; and the greatest opponents to a federal government admit the state legislatures to be sure guardians of the people's liberty. I conclude from this view of the subject, that it will be proper in itself, and highly politic, for the tranquility of the public mind, and the stability of the government, that we should offer something, in the form I have proposed, to be incorporated in the system of government, as a declaration of the rights of the people.

. . .

I wish also, in revising the constitution, we may throw into that section, which interdicts the abuse of certain powers in the state legislatures, some other provisions of equal if not greater importance than those already made. The words, "No state shall pass any bill of attainder, ex post facto law, &c." were wise and proper restrictions in the constitution. I think there is more danger of those powers being abused by the state governments than by the government of the United States. The same may be said of other powers which they possess, if not controuled by the general principle, that laws are unconstitutional which infringe the rights of the community. I should therefore wish to extend this interdiction, and add, as I have stated in the 5th resolution, that no state shall violate the equal right of conscience, freedom of the press, or trial by jury in criminal cases; because it is proper that every government should be disarmed of powers which trench upon those particular rights. I know in some of the state constitutions the power of the government is controuled by such a declaration, but others are not. I cannot see any reason against obtaining even a double security on those points; and nothing can give a more sincere proof of the attachment of those who opposed this constitution to these great and important rights, than to see them join in obtaining the security I have now proposed; because it must be admitted, on all hands, that the state governments are as liable to attack these invaluable privileges as the general government is, and therefore ought to be as cautiously guarded against.

I think it will be proper, with respect to the judiciary powers, to satisfy the public mind on those points which I have mentioned. Great inconvenience has been apprehended to suitors from the distance they would be dragged to obtain justice in the supreme court of the United States, upon an appeal on an action for a small debt. To remedy this, declare, that no appeal shall be made unless the matter in controversy amounts to a particular sum: This, with the regulations respecting jury trials in criminal cases, and suits at common law, it is to be hoped will quiet and reconcile the minds of the people to that part of the constitution.

I find, from looking into the amendments proposed by the state conventions, that several are particularly anxious that it should be declared in the constitution, that the powers not therein delegated, should be reserved to the several states. Perhaps words which may define this more precisely, than the whole of the instrument now does, may be considered as superfluous. I admit they may be deemed unnecessary; but there can be no harm in making such a declaration, if gentlemen will allow that the fact is as stated. I am sure I understand it so, and do therefore propose it.

These are the points on which I wish to see a revision of the constitution take place. How far they will accord with the sense of this body, I cannot take upon me absolutely to determine; but I believe every gentleman will readily admit that nothing is in contemplation, so far as I have mentioned, that can endanger the beauty of the government in any one important feature, even in the eyes of its most sanguine admirers. I have proposed nothing that does not appear to me as proper in itself, or eligible as patronised by a respectable number of our fellow citizens; and if we can make the constitution better in the opinion of those who are opposed to it, without weakening its frame, or abridging its usefulness, in the judgment of those who are attached to it, we act the part of wise and liberal men to make such alterations as shall produce that effect.

Having done what I conceived was my duty, in bringing before this house the subject of amendments, and also stated such as I wish for and approve, and offered the reasons which occurred to me in their support; I shall content myself for the present with moving, that a committee be appointed to consider of and report such amendments as ought to be proposed by congress to the legislatures of the states, to become, if ratified by three-fourths thereof, part of the constitution of the United States. By agreeing to this motion, the subject may be going on in the committee, while other important business is proceeding to a conclusion in the house. I should advocate greater dispatch in the business of amendments, if I was not convinced of the absolute necessity there is of pursuing the organization of the government; because I think we should obtain the confidence of our fellow citizens, in proportion as we fortify the rights of the people against the encroachments of the government.

8

The Alien and Sedition Acts

1 Stat. 577, 596, July 6 and July 14, 1798[*]

AN ACT RESPECTING ALIEN ENEMIES

Section 1. Be it enacted by the Senate and House of Representatives of the United States of America in Congress assembled, That whenever there shall be a declared war between the United States and any foreign nation or government, or any invasion or predatory incursion shall be perpetrated, attempted, or threatened against the territory of the United States, by any foreign nation or government, and the President of the United States shall make public proclamation of the event, all natives, citizens, denizens, or subjects of the hostile nation or government, being males of the age of fourteen years and upwards, who shall be within the United States, and not actually naturalized, shall be liable to be apprehended, restrained, secured and removed, as alien enemies. And the President of the United States shall be, and he is hereby authorized, in any event, as aforesaid, by his proclamation thereof, or other public act, to direct the conduct to be observed, on the part of the United States, towards the aliens who shall become liable, as aforesaid; the manner and degree of the restraint to which they shall be subject, and in what cases, and upon what security their residence shall be permitted, and to provide for the removal of those, who, not being permitted to reside within the United States, shall refuse or neglect to depart therefrom; and to establish any other regulations which shall be found necessary in the premises and for the public safety: Provided, that aliens resident within the United States, who shall become liable as enemies, in the manner aforesaid, and who shall not be chargeable with actual hostility, or other crime against the public safety, shall be allowed, for the recovery, disposal, and removal of their goods and effects, and for their departure, the full time which is, or shall be stipulated by any treaty, where any shall have been between the United States, and the hostile nation or government, of which they shall be natives, citizens, denizens or subjects: and where no such treaty

[*] Richard Peters, ed., *United States Statutes at Large* (Boston: Little, Brown, 1845), 1:577, 596.

shall have existed, the President of the United States may ascertain and declare such reasonable time as may be consistent with the public safety, and according to the dictates of humanity and national hospitality.

Sec. 2. And be it further enacted, That after any proclamation shall be made as aforesaid, it shall be the duty of the several courts of the United States, and of each state, having criminal jurisdiction, and of the several judges and justices of the courts of the United States, and they shall be, and are hereby respectively, authorized upon complaint, against any alien or alien enemies, as aforesaid, who shall be resident and at large within such jurisdiction or district, to the danger of the public peace or safety, and contrary to the tenor or intent of such proclamation, or other regulations which the President of the United States shall and may establish in the premises, to cause such alien or aliens to be duly apprehended and convened before such court, judge or justice; and after a full examination and hearing on such complaint and sufficient cause therefor appearing, shall and may order such alien or aliens to be removed out of the territory of the United States, or to give sureties of their good behaviour, or to be otherwise restrained, conformably to the proclamation or regulations which shall and may be established as aforesaid, and may imprison, or otherwise secure such alien or aliens, until the order which shall and may be made, as aforesaid, shall be performed.

Sec. 3. And be it further enacted, That it shall be the duty of the marshal of the district in which any alien enemy shall be apprehended, who by the President of the United States, or by order of any court, judge or justice, as aforesaid, shall be required to depart, and to be removed, as aforesaid, to provide therefor, and to execute such order, by himself or his deputy, or other discreet person or persons to be employed by him, by causing a removal of such alien out of the territory of the United States; and for such removal the marshal shall have the warrant of the President of the United States, or of the court, judge or justice ordering the same, as the case may be.

APPROVED, July 6, 1798.

AN ACT IN ADDITION TO THE ACT, ENTITLED "AN ACT FOR THE PUNISHMENT OF CERTAIN CRIMES AGAINST THE UNITED STATES"

Section 1. Be it enacted by the Senate and House of Representatives of the United States of America, in Congress assembled, That if any persons shall unlaw-

fully combine or conspire together, with intent to oppose any measure or measures of the government of the United States, which are or shall be directed by proper authority, or to impede the operation of any law of the United States, or to intimidate or prevent any person holding a place or office in or under the government of the United States, from undertaking, performing or executing his trust or duty, and if any person or persons, with intent as aforesaid, shall counsel, advise or attempt to procure any insurrection, riot, unlawful assembly, or combination, whether such conspiracy, threatening, counsel, advice, or attempt shall have the proposed effect or not, he or they shall be deemed guilty of a high misdemeanor, and on conviction, before any court of the United States having jurisdiction thereof, shall be punished by a fine not exceeding five thousand dollars, and by imprisonment during a term not less than six months nor exceeding five years; and further, at the discretion of the court may be holden to find sureties for his good behaviour in such sum, and for such time, as the said court may direct.

Sec. 2. And be it farther enacted, That if any person shall write, print, utter or publish, or shall cause or procure to be written, printed, uttered or published, or shall knowingly and willingly assist or aid in writing, printing, uttering or publishing any false, scandalous and malicious writing or writings against the government of the United States, or either house of the Congress of the United States, or the President of the United States, with intent to defame the said government, or either house of the said Congress, or the said President, or to bring them, or either of them, into contempt or disrepute; or to excite against them, or either or any of them, the hatred of the good people of the United States, or to stir up sedition within the United States, or to excite any unlawful combinations therein, for opposing or resisting any law of the United States, or any act of the President of the United States, done in pursuance of any such law, or of the powers in him vested by the constitution of the United States, or to resist, oppose, or defeat any such law or act, or to aid, encourage or abet any hostile designs of any foreign nation against the United States, their people or government, then such person, being thereof convicted before any court of the United States having jurisdiction thereof, shall be punished by a fine not exceeding two thousand dollars, and by imprisonment not exceeding two years.

Sec. 3. And be it further enacted and declared, That if any person shall be prosecuted under this act, for the writing or publishing any libel aforesaid, it shall be lawful for the defendant, upon the trial of the cause, to give in evidence in his defence, the truth of the matter contained in publication charged as a libel. And the jury who shall try the cause, shall have a right to determine the law and the fact, under the direction of the court, as in other cases.

Sec. 4. And be it further enacted, That this act shall continue and be in force until the third day of March, one thousand eight hundred and one, and no longer: Provided, that the expiration of the act shall not prevent or defeat a prosecution and punishment of any offence against the law, during the time it shall be in force.

APPROVED, July 14, 1798.

9

The Kentucky Resolutions of 1798

November 10, 1798*

In the House of Representatives, November 10th, 1798.

I. *Resolved*, that the several States composing the United States of America are not united on the principle of unlimited submission to their General Government; but that by compact, under the style and title of a Constitution for the United States and of amendments thereto, they constituted a general government for special purposes, delegated to that government certain definitive powers, reserving each State to itself, the residuary mass of right to their own self-government; and that whensoever the general government assumes undelegated powers, its acts are unauthoritative, void, and of no force: That to this compact each State acceded as a State and is an integral party; that the government created by this compact, was not made the exclusive or final *judge* of the extent of the powers delegated to itself; since that would have made its discretion, and not the Constitution, the measure of its powers; but that, as in all other cases of compact among parties having no common judge, each party has an equal right to judge for itself, as well of infractions as of the mode and measure of redress.

...

III. *Resolved*, That it is true, as a general principle, and is also expressly declared by one of the amendments to the Constitution, that "the powers not delegated to the United States by the Constitution, nor prohibited by it to the states, are reserved to the states respectively, or to the people;" and that, no power over the freedom of religion, freedom of speech, or freedom of the press, being delegated to the United States by the Constitution, nor prohibited by it to the States, all lawful powers respecting the same did of right remain, and were reserved to the states, or the people: That thus was manifested their determination to retain to themselves the right of judging how far the licentiousness of speech, and of the press, may be abridged without lessening their useful freedom, and how far those abuses which cannot be separated from their use, should be tolerated rather than the use be destroyed; and thus also they guarded against all abridgment, by the United States, of the freedom of religious principles and exercises, and retained to themselves the right of protecting the same, as this State, by a law passed on the general demand of its citizens, had already protected them from all human restraint or interference: And that in addition to this general principle and express declaration, another and more special provision has been made by one of the amendments to the Constitution, which expressly declares, that "Congress shall make no law respecting an establishment of religion, or prohibiting the free exercise thereof, or abridging the freedom of speech, or of the press," thereby guarding in the same sentence, and under the same words, the freedom of religion, of speech, and of the press, insomuch, that whatever violates either, throws down the sanctuary which covers the others, and that libels, falsehoods, and defamation, equally with heresy and false religion, are withheld from the cognizance of Federal tribunals. That therefore the act of the Congress of the United States passed on the 14th day of July 1798, entitled "An act in addition to the act for the punishment of certain crimes against the United States," which does abridge the freedom of the press, is not law, but is altogether void and of no effect.

* *The Papers of Thomas Jefferson, Volume 30: 1 January 1798 to 31 January 1799* (Princeton, NJ: Princeton University Press, 2003), 550.

10

The Virginia Resolutions

December 24, 1798[*]

RESOLVED, That the General Assembly of Virginia, doth unequivocally express a firm resolution to maintain and defend the Constitution of the United States, and the Constitution of this State, against every aggression either foreign or domestic, and that they will support the government of the United States in all measures warranted by the former.

That this assembly most solemnly declares a warm attachment to the Union of the States, to maintain which it pledges all its powers; and that for this end, it is their duty to watch over and oppose every infraction of those principles which constitute the only basis of that Union, because a faithful observance of them, can alone secure its existence and the public happiness.

That this Assembly doth explicitly and peremptorily declare, that it views the powers of the federal government, as resulting from the compact, to which the states are parties; as limited by the plain sense and intention of the instrument constituting the compact; as no further valid that they are authorized by the grants enumerated in that compact; and that in case of a deliberate, palpable, and dangerous exercise of other powers, not granted by the said compact, the states who are parties thereto, have the right, and are in duty bound, to interpose for arresting the progress of the evil, and for maintaining within their respective limits, the authorities, rights and liberties appertaining to them.

That the General Assembly doth also express its deep regret, that a spirit has in sundry instances, been manifested by the federal government, to enlarge its powers by forced constructions of the constitutional charter which defines them; and that implications have appeared of a design to expound certain general phrases (which having been copied from the very limited grant of power, in the former articles of confederation were the less liable to be misconstrued) so as to destroy the meaning and effect, of the particular enumeration which necessarily explains and limits the general phrases; and so as to consolidate the states by degrees,

into one sovereignty, the obvious tendency and inevitable consequence of which would be, to transform the present republican system of the United States, into an absolute, or at best a mixed monarchy.

That the General Assembly doth particularly protest against the palpable and alarming infractions of the Constitution, in the two late cases of the "Alien and Sedition Acts" passed at the last session of Congress; the first of which exercises a power no where delegated to the federal government, and which by uniting legislative and judicial powers to those of executive, subverts the general principles of free government; as well as the particular organization, and positive provisions of the federal constitution; and the other of which acts, exercises in like manner, a power not delegated by the constitution, but on the contrary, expressly and positively forbidden by one of the amendments thereto; a power, which more than any other, ought to produce universal alarm, because it is levelled against that right of freely examining public characters and measures, and of free communication among the people thereon, which has ever been justly deemed, the only effectual guardian of every other right.

That this state having by its Convention, which ratified the federal Constitution, expressly declared, that among other essential rights, "the Liberty of Conscience and of the Press cannot be cancelled, abridged, restrained, or modified by any authority of the United States," and from its extreme anxiety to guard these rights from every possible attack of sophistry or ambition, having with other states, recommended an amendment for that purpose, which amendment was, in due time, annexed to the Constitution; it would mark a reproachable inconsistency, and criminal degeneracy, if an indifference were now shewn, to the most palpable violation of one of the Rights, thus declared and secured; and to the establishment of a precedent which may be fatal to the other.

That the good people of this commonwealth, having ever felt, and continuing to feel, the most sincere affection for their brethren of the other states; the truest anxiety for establishing and perpetuating the union of all; and the most scrupulous fidelity to that constitution, which is the pledge of mutual friendship, and the instrument of mutual happiness; the General Assembly doth solemnly appeal to the like dispositions of the other states, in confidence that they will concur with this commonwealth in declaring, as it does hereby declare, that the acts aforesaid, are unconstitutional; and

[*] Madison, *Writings*, 589–91.

that the necessary and proper measures will be taken by each, for co-operating with this state, in maintaining the Authorities, Rights, and Liberties, reserved to the States respectively, or to the people.

That the Governor be desired, to transmit a copy of the foregoing Resolutions to the executive authority of each of the other states, with a request that the same may be communicated to the Legislature thereof; and that a copy be furnished to each of the Senators and Representatives representing this state in the Congress of the United States.

Agreed to by the Senate, December 24, 1798.

11

The Kentucky Resolutions of 1799

November 22, 1799*

THE representatives of the good people of this commonwealth in General Assembly convened, having maturely considered the answers of sundry states in the Union, to their resolutions, passed at the last session, respecting certain unconstitutional laws of Congress, commonly called the Alien and Sedition laws, would be faithless, indeed, to themselves, and to those they represent, were they silently to acquiesce in principles and doctrines attempted to be maintained in all those answers, that of Virginia only excepted. To again enter the field of argument, and attempt more fully or forcibly to expose the unconstitutionality of those obnoxious laws, would, it is apprehended, be as unnecessary as unavailing. We cannot, however, but lament that, in the discussion of those interesting subjects by sundry of the legislatures of our sister states, unfounded suggestions and uncandid insinuations, derogatory of the true character and principles of the good people of this commonwealth, have been substituted in place of fair reasoning and sound argument. Our opinions of those alarming measures of the general government, together with our reasons for those opinions, were detailed with decency and with temper, and submitted to the discussion and judgment of our fellow citizens throughout the Union.

Whether the like decency and temper have been observed in the answers of most of those states who have denied, or attempted to obviate, the great truths contained in those resolutions, we have now only to submit to a candid world. Faithful to the true principles of the federal Union, unconscious of any designs to disturb the harmony of that Union, and anxious only to escape the fangs of despotism, the good people of this commonwealth are regardless of censure or calumniation. Lest, however, the silence of this commonwealth should be construed into an acquiescence in the doctrines and principles advanced, and attempted to be maintained, by the said answers; or least those of our fellow citizens throughout the Union, who so widely differ from us on those important subjects, should be deluded by the expectation that we shall be deterred from what we conceive our duty, or shrink from the principles contained in those resolutions, —therefore.

Resolved, That this commonwealth considers the federal Union, upon the terms and for the purposes specified in the late compact, conducive to the liberty and happiness of the several states: That it does now unequivocally declare its attachment to the Union, and to that compact, agreeable to its obvious and real intention, and will be among the last to seek its dissolution: That, if those who administer the general government be permitted to transgress the limits fixed by that compact, by a total disregard to the special delegations of power therein contained, annihilation of the state governments, and the creation, upon their ruins, of a general consolidated government, will be the inevitable consequence: That the principle and construction contended for by sundry of the state legislatures, that the general government is the exclusive judge of the extent of the powers delegated to it, stop not short of *despotism*—since the discretion of those who administer the government, and not the *Constitution*, would be the measure of their powers: That the several states who formed that instrument, being sovereign and independent, have the unquestionable right to judge of its infraction; and, *That a nullification, by those sovereignties, of all unauthorized acts done under color of that instrument, is the rightful remedy*: That this commonwealth does, upon the most deliberate reconsideration, declare, that the said Alien and Sedition laws are, in their opinion, palpable violations of the said Constitution; and however cheerfully it may be disposed to surrender its opinion to a majority of its sister states, in matters of ordinary or doubtful policy, yet, in momentous regula-

*Jonathan Elliot, ed., *The Debates in the Several State Conventions on the Adoption of the Federal Constitution* (Washington, DC, 1836), 4:544–45. Subsequently cited as *Elliot's Debates*.

tions like the present, which so vitally wound the best rights of the citizen, it would consider a silent acquiescence as highly criminal: That, although this commonwealth, as a party to the federal compact, will bow to the laws of the Union, yet it does, at the same time, declare, that it will not now, or ever hereafter, cease to oppose, in a constitutional manner, every attempt, at what quarter soever offered, to violate that compact: And finally, in order that no pretext or arguments may be drawn from a supposed acquiescence, on the part of this commonwealth, in the constitutionality of those laws, and be thereby used as precedents for similar future violations of federal compact; this commonwealth does now enter against them, its solemn PROTEST.

...

In Senate, Nov. 22, 1799.—Read and concurred in.

12

James Madison, Report on the Virginia Resolutions

January 7, 1800*

Report of the committee to whom were referred the communications of various states relative to the resolutions of the General Assembly of this state, concerning the Alien and Sedition-Laws.

Whatever room might be found in the proceedings of some of the states, who have disapproved of the resolutions of the General Assembly of this commonwealth, passed on the 21st day of December, 1798, for painful remarks on the spirit and manner of those proceedings, it appears to the committee, most consistent with the duty, as well as dignity of the General Assembly, to hasten an oblivion of every circumstance, which might be construed into a diminution of mutual respect, confidence and affection, among the members of the union.

The committee have deemed it a more useful task, to revise with a critical eye, the resolutions which have met with this disapprobation; to examine fully the several objections and arguments which have appeared against them; and to enquire, whether there be any errors of fact, of principle, or of reasoning, which the candour of

*Madison, *Writings*, 608–62.

the General Assembly ought to acknowledge and correct.

The first of the resolutions is in the words following:

Resolved, that the General Assembly of Virginia, doth unequivocally express a firm resolution to maintain and defend the Constitution of the United States, and the Constitution of this state, against every aggression either foreign or domestic, and that they will support the government of the United States in all measures warranted by the former.

No unfavorable comment can have been made on the sentiments here expressed. To maintain and defend the Constitution of the United States, and of their own state, against every aggression both foreign and domestic, and to support the government of the United States in all measures warranted by their constitution, are duties, which the General Assembly ought always to feel, and to which on such an occasion, it was evidently proper to express their sincere and firm adherence.

In their next resolution—*The General Assembly most solemnly declares a warm attachment to the union of the states, to maintain which, it pledges all its powers; and that for this end, it is their duty to watch over and oppose every infraction of those principles, which constitute the only basis of that union, because a faithful observance of them, can alone secure its existence and the public happiness.*

The observation just made is equally applicable to this solemn declaration, of warm attachment to the union, and this solemn pledge to maintain it: nor can any question arise among enlightened friends of the union, as to the duty of watching over and opposing every infraction of those principles which constitute its basis, and a faithful observance of which, can alone secure its existence, and the public happiness thereon depending.

The third resolution is in the words following:

That this Assembly doth explicitly and peremptorily declare, that it views the powers of the Federal Government, as resulting from the compact, to which the states are parties, as limited by the plain sense and intention of the instrument constituting that compact; as no farther valid than they are authorized by the grants enumerated in that compact; and that in case of a deliberate, palpable and dangerous exercise of other powers, not granted by the said compact, the states who are parties thereto, have the right, and are in duty bound, to interpose, for arresting the progress of the evil, and for maintaining within their respective limits, the authorities, rights and liberties appertaining to them.

On this resolution, the committee have bestowed all the attention which its importance merits: They have scanned it not merely with a strict, but with a severe eye; and they feel confidence in pronouncing, that in its just and fair construction, it is unexceptionably true in its several positions, as well as constitutional and conclusive in its inferences.

The resolution declares, *first,* that "it views the powers of the Federal Government, as resulting from the compact to which the states are parties," in other words, that the federal powers are derived from the Constitution, and that the Constitution is a compact to which the states are parties.

Clear as the position must seem, that the federal powers are derived from the Constitution, and from that alone, the committee are not unapprised of a late doctrine which opens another source of federal powers, not less extensive and important, than it is new and unexpected. The examination of this doctrine will be most conveniently connected with a review of a succeeding resolution. The committee satisfy themselves here with briefly remarking, that in all the co-temporary discussions and comments, which the Constitution underwent, it was constantly justified and recommended on the ground, that the powers not given to the government, were withheld from it; and that if any doubt could have existed on this subject, under the original text of the Constitution, it is removed as far as words could remove it, by the 12th amendment, now a part of the Constitution, which expressly declares, "that the powers not delegated to the United States, by the Constitution, nor prohibited by it to the states, are reserved to the states respectively, or to the people."

The other position involved in this branch of the resolution, namely, "that the states are parties to the Constitution or compact," is in the judgment of the committee, equally free from objection. It is indeed true that the term "States," is sometimes used in a vague sense, and sometimes in different senses, according to the subject to which it is applied. Thus it sometimes means the separate sections of territory occupied by the political societies within each; sometimes the particular governments, established by those societies; sometimes those societies as organized into those particular governments; and lastly, it means the people composing those political societies, in their highest sovereign capacity.

Although it might be wished that the perfection of language admitted less diversity in the signification of the same words, yet little inconveniency is produced by it, where the true sense can be collected with certainty from the different applications. In the present instance whatever different constructions of the term "States," in the resolution may have been entertained, all will at least concur in that last mentioned; because in that sense, the Constitution was submitted to the "States": In that sense the "States" ratified it; and in that sense of the term "States," they are consequently parties to the compact from which the powers of the Federal Government result.

The next position is, that the General Assembly views the powers of the Federal Government, "as limited by the plain sense and intention of the instrument constituting that compact," and "as no farther valid than they are authorized by the grants therein enumerated." It does not seem possible that any just objection can lie against either of these clauses. The first amounts merely to a declaration that the compact ought to have the interpretation, plainly intended by the parties to it; the other, to a declaration, that it ought to have the execution and effect intended by them. If the powers granted, be valid, it is solely because they are granted; and if the granted powers are valid, because granted, all other powers not granted, must not be valid.

The resolution having taken this view of the federal compact, proceeds to infer, "that in case of a deliberate, palpable, and dangerous exercise of other powers not granted by the said compact, the states who are parties thereto, have the right, and are in duty bound to interpose for arresting the progress of the evil, and for maintaining within their respective limits, the authorities, rights and liberties appertaining to them."

It appears to your committee to be a plain principle, founded in common sense, illustrated by common practice, and essential to the nature of compacts; that where resort can be had to no tribunal superior to the authority of the parties, the parties themselves must be the rightful judges in the last resort, whether the bargain made, has been pursued or violated. The constitution of the United States was formed by the sanction of the states, given by each in its sovereign capacity. It adds to the stability and dignity, as well as to the authority of the constitution, that it rests on this legitimate and solid foundation. The states then being the parties to the constitutional compact, and in their sovereign capacity, it follows of necessity, that there can be no tribunal above their authority, to decide in the last resort, whether the compact made by them be violated; and consequently that as the parties to it, they must themselves decide in the last resort, such questions as may be of sufficient magnitude to require their interposition.

It does not follow, however, that because the states as sovereign parties to their constitutional compact, must ultimately decide whether it has been violated, that such a decision ought to be interposed either in a hasty manner, or on doubtful and inferior occasions. Even in the case of ordinary conventions between different nations, where, by the strict rule of interpretation, a breach of a part may be deemed a breach of the whole; every part being deemed a condition of every other part, and of the whole, it is always laid down that the breach must be both willful and material to justify an application of the rule. But in the case of an intimate and constitutional union, like that of the United States, it is evident that the interposition of the parties, in their sovereign capacity, can be called for by occasions only, deeply and essentially affecting the vital principles of their political system.

The resolution has accordingly guarded against any misapprehension of its object, by expressly requiring for such an interposition "the case of a *deliberate, palpable* and *dangerous* breach of the constitution, by the exercise of *powers not granted* by it." It must be a case, not of a light and transient nature, but of a nature *dangerous* to the great purposes for which the constitution was established. It must be a case moreover not obscure or doubtful in its construction, but plain and *palpable.* Lastly, it must be a case not resulting from a partial consideration, or hasty determination; but a case stampt with a final consideration and *deliberate* adherence. It is not necessary because the resolution does not require, that the question should be discussed, how far the exercise of any particular power, ungranted by the constitution, would justify the interposition of the parties to it. As cases might easily be stated, which none would contend, ought to fall within that description: Cases, on the other hand, might, with equal ease, be stated, so flagrant and so fatal as to unite every opinion in placing them within the description.

But the resolution has done more than guard against misconstruction, by expressly referring to cases of a *deliberate, palpable* and *dangerous* nature. It specifies the object of the interposition which it contemplates, to be solely that of arresting the progress of the *evil* of usurpation, and of maintaining the authorities, rights and liberties appertaining to the states, as parties to the constitution.

From this view of the resolution, it would seem inconceivable that it can incur any just disapprobation from those, who laying aside all momentary impressions, and recollecting the genuine source and object of the federal constitution, shall candidly and accurately interpret the meaning of the General Assembly. If the deliberate exercise, of dangerous powers, palpably withheld by the constitution, could not justify the parties to it, in interposing even so far as to arrest the progress of the evil, and thereby to preserve the constitution itself as well as to provide for the safety of the parties to it; there would be an end to all relief from usurped power, and a direct subversion of the rights specified or recognized under all the state constitutions, as well as a plain denial of the fundamental principle on which our independence itself was declared.

But it is objected that the judicial authority is to be regarded as the sole expositor of the constitution, in the last resort; and it may be asked for what reason, the declaration by the General Assembly, supposing it to be theoretically true, could be required at the present day and in so solemn a manner.

On this objection it might be observed *first*, that there may be instances of usurped power, which the forms of the constitution would never draw within the controul of the judicial department: secondly, that if the decision of the judiciary be raised above the authority of the sovereign parties to the constitution, the decisions of the other departments, not carried by the forms of the constitution before the judiciary, must be equally authoritative and final with the decisions of that department. But the proper answer to the objection is, that the resolution of the General Assembly relates to those great and extraordinary cases, in which all the forms of the constitution may prove ineffectual against infractions dangerous to the essential rights of the parties to it. The resolution supposes that dangerous powers not delegated, may not only be usurped and executed by the other departments, but that the Judicial Department also may exercise or sanction dangerous powers beyond the grant of the constitution; and consequently that the ultimate right of the parties to the constitution, to judge whether the compact has been dangerously violated, must extend to violations by one delegated authority, as well as by another; by the judiciary, as well as by the executive, or the legislature.

However true therefore it may be that the Judicial Department, is, in all questions submitted to it by the forms of the constitution, to decide in the last resort, this resort must necessarily be deemed the last in relation to the authorities of the other departments of the government; not in relation to the rights of the parties to the constitutional compact, from which the judicial as well as the other departments hold their delegated trusts. On any other hypothesis, the delegation of judicial power, would annul the authority delegating it; and the concurrence of this department with the others in usurped powers, might subvert forever, and beyond the possible reach of any rightful remedy, the very constitution, which all were instituted to preserve.

The truth declared in the resolution being established, the expediency of making the declaration at the present day, may safely be left to the temperate consideration and candid judgment of the American public. It will be remembered that a frequent recurrence to fundamental principles is solemnly enjoined by most of the state constitutions, and particularly by our own, as a necessary safeguard against the danger of degeneracy to which republics are liable, as well as other governments, though in a less degree than others. And a fair comparison of the political doctrines not unfrequent at the present day, with those which characterized the epoch of our revolution, and which form the basis of our republican constitutions, will best determine whether the declaratory recurrence here made to those principles ought to be viewed as unseasonable and improper, or as a vigilant discharge of an important duty. The authority of constitutions over governments, and of the sovereignty of the people over constitutions, are truths which are at all times necessary to be kept in mind; and at no time perhaps more necessary than at the present.

The fourth resolution stands as follows:—

That the General Assembly doth also express its deep regret, that a spirit has in sundry instances, been manifested by the Federal Government, to enlarge its powers by forced constructions of the Constitutional charter which defines them; and that indications have appeared of a design to expound certain general phrases, (which, having been copied from the very limited grant of powers in the former articles of confederation were the less liable to be misconstrued) so as to destroy the meaning and effect, of the particular enumeration which necessarily explains, and limits the general phrases; and so as to consolidate the states by degrees, into one sovereignty, the obvious tendency and inevitable result of which would be, to transform the present Republican system of the United States, into an absolute, or at best a mixed monarchy.

The *first* question here to be considered is, whether a spirit has in sundry instances been manifested by the Federal Government to enlarge its powers by forced constructions of the Constitutional charter.

The General Assembly having declared their opinion merely by regretting in general terms that forced constructions for enlarging the federal powers have taken place, it does not appear to the committee necessary to go into a specification of every instance to which the resolution may allude. The alien and Sedition acts being particularly named in a succeeding resolution are of course to be understood as included in the allusion. Omitting others which have less occupied public attention, or been less extensively regarded as unconstitutional, the resolution may be presumed to refer particularly to the bank law, which from the circumstances of its passage as well as the latitude of construction on which it is founded, strikes the attention with singular force; and the carriage tax, distinguished also by circumstances in its history having a similar tendency. Those instances alone, if resulting from forced construction and calculated to enlarge the powers of the Federal government, as the committee cannot but conceive to be the case, sufficiently warrant this part of the resolution. The committee have not thought it incumbent on them to extend their attention to laws which have been objected to, rather as varying the Constitutional distribution of powers in the Federal government, than as an absolute enlargement of them; because instances of this sort however important in their principles and tendencies, do not appear to fall strictly within the text under review.

The other questions presenting themselves, are— 1. Whether indications have appeared of a design to expound certain general phrases copied from the "articles of confederation," so as to destroy the effect of the particular enumeration explaining and limiting their meaning. 2. Whether this exposition would by degrees consolidate the states into one sovereignty. 3. Whether the tendency and result of this consolidation would be to transform the Republican system of the United States into a monarchy.

1. The general phrases here meant must be those "of providing for the common defence and general welfare."

In the "articles of confederation" the phrases are

used as follows, in article VIII. "All charges of war, and all other expences that shall be incurred *for the common defence and general welfare*, and allowed by the United States in Congress assembled, shall be defrayed out of a common treasury, which shall be supplied by the several states, in proportion to the value of all land within each state, granted to or surveyed for any person, as such land and the buildings and improvements thereon shall be estimated, according to such mode as the United States in Congress assembled, shall from time to time direct and appoint."

In the existing constitution, they make the following part of section 8. "The Congress shall have power, to lay and collect taxes, duties, imposts and excises to pay the debts, and provide for the common defence and general welfare of the United States."

This similarity in the use of these phrases in the two great federal charters, might well be considered, as rendering their meaning less liable to be misconstrued in the latter; because it will scarcely be said that in the former they were ever understood to be either a general grant of power, or to authorize the requisition or application of money by the old Congress to the common defence and general welfare, except in the cases afterwards enumerated which explained and limited their meaning; and if such was the limited meaning attached to these phrases in the very instrument revised and remodelled by the present constitution, it can never be supposed that when copied into this constitution, a different meaning ought to be attached to them.

That notwithstanding this remarkable security against misconstruction, a design has been indicated to expound these phrases in the Constitution so as to destroy the effect of the particular enumeration of powers by which it explains and limits them, must have fallen under the observation of those who have attended to the course of public transactions. Not to multiply proofs on this subject, it will suffice to refer to the debates of the Federal Legislature in which arguments have on different occasions been drawn, with apparent effect from these phrases in their indefinite meaning.

To these indications might be added without looking farther, the official report on manufactures by the late Secretary of the Treasury, made on the 5th of December, 1791; and the report of a committee of Congress in January 1797, on the promotion of agriculture. In the first of these it is expressly contended to belong "to the discretion of the National legislature to pronounce upon the objects which concern the *general welfare*, and

for which under that description, an appropriation of money is requisite and proper. And there seems to be no room for a doubt that whatever concerns the general interests of learning, of agriculture, of manufactures, and of commerce, are within the sphere of the national councils, *as far as regards an application of money*." The latter report assumes the same latitude of power in the national councils and applies it to the encouragement of agriculture, by means of a society to be established at the seat of government. Although neither of these reports may have received the sanction of a law carrying it into effect; yet, on the other hand, the extraordinary doctrine contained in both, has passed without the slightest positive mark of disapprobation from the authority to which it was addressed.

Now whether the phrases in question be construed to authorise every measure relating to the common defence and general welfare, as contended by some; or every measure only in which there might be an application of money, as suggested by the caution of others, the effect must substantially be the same, in destroying the import and force of the particular enumeration of powers, which follow these general phrases in the Constitution. For it is evident that there is not a single power whatever, which may not have some reference to the common defence, or the general welfare; nor a power of any magnitude which in its exercise does not involve or admit an application of money. The government therefore which possesses power in either one or other of these extents, is a government without the limitations formed by a particular enumeration of powers; and consequently the meaning and effect of this particular enumeration, is destroyed by the exposition given to these general phrases.

This conclusion will not be affected by an attempt to qualify the power over the "general welfare," by referring it to cases where the *general welfare* is beyond the reach of *separate* provisions by the *individual states*; and leaving to these their jurisdictions in cases, to which their separate provisions may be competent. For as the authority of the individual states must in all cases be incompetent to general regulations operating through the whole, the authority of the United States would be extended to every object relating to the general welfare, which might by any possibility be provided for by the general authority. This qualifying construction therefore would have little, if any tendency, to circumscribe the power claimed under the latitude of the terms "general welfare."

The true and fair construction of this expression, both in the original and existing federal compacts appears to the committee too obvious to be mistaken. In both, the Congress is authorized to provide money for the common defence and *general welfare*. In both, is subjoined to this authority, an enumeration of the cases, to which their powers shall extend. Money cannot be applied to the *general welfare*, otherwise than by an application of it to some *particular* measure conducive to the general welfare. Whenever therefore, money has been raised by the general authority, and is to be applied to a particular measure, a question arises, whether the particular measure be within the enumerated authorities vested in Congress. If it be, the money requisite for it may be applied to it; if it be not, no such application can be made. This fair and obvious interpretation coincides with, and is enforced by, the clause in the Constitution which declares that "no money shall be drawn from the treasury, but in consequence of appropriations by law." An appropriation of money to the general welfare, would be deemed rather a mockery than an observance of this constitutional injunction.

2. Whether the exposition of the general phrases here combated, would not, by degrees consolidate the states into one sovereignty, is a question concerning which, the committee can perceive little room for difference of opinion. To consolidate the States into one sovereignty, nothing more can be wanted, than to supercede their respective sovereignties in the cases reserved to them, by extending the sovereignty of the United States to all cases of the "general welfare," that is to say, to *all cases whatever*.

3. That the obvious tendency and inevitable result of a consolidation of the states into one sovereignty, would be, to transform the republican system of the United States into a monarchy, is a point which seems to have been sufficiently decided by the general sentiment of America. In almost every instance of discussion, relating to the consolidation in question, its certain tendency to pave the way to monarchy, seems not to have been contested. The prospect of such a consolidation has formed the only topic of controversy. It would be unnecessary therefore, for the committee to dwell long on the reasons which support the position of the General Assembly. It may not be improper however to remark two consequences evidently flowing from an extension of the federal powers to every subject falling within the idea of the "general welfare."

One consequence must be, to enlarge the sphere of discretion allotted to the executive magistrate. Even within the legislative limits properly defined by the constitution, the difficulty of accommodating legal regulations to a country so great in extent, and so various in its circumstances, has been much felt; and has led to occasional investments of power in the executive, which involve perhaps as large a portion of discretion, as can be deemed consistent with the nature of the executive trust. In proportion as the objects of legislative care might be multiplied, would the time allowed for each be diminished, and the difficulty of providing uniform and particular regulations for all, be increased. From these sources would necessarily ensue, a greater latitude to the agency of that department which is always in existence, and which could best mould regulations of a general nature, so as to suit them to the diversity of particular situations. And it is in this latitude, as a supplement to the deficiency of the laws, that the degree of executive prerogative materially consists.

The other consequence would be, that of an excessive augmentation of the offices, honors, and emoluments depending on the executive will. Add to the present legitimate stock, all those of every description which a consolidation of the states would take from them, and turn over to the federal government, and the patronage of the executive would necessarily be as much swelled in this case, as its prerogative would be in the other.

This disproportionate increase of prerogative and patronage must, evidently, either enable the chief magistrate of the union, by quiet means, to secure his re-election from time to time, and finally, to regulate the succession as he might please; or, by giving so transcendent an importance to the office, would render the elections to it so violent and corrupt, that the public voice itself might call for an hereditary, in place of an elective succession. Which ever of these events might follow, the transformation of the Republican system of the United States into a monarchy, anticipated by the General Assembly from a consolidation of the states into one sovereignty, would be equally accomplished; and whether it would be into a mixt or an absolute monarchy, might depend on too many contingencies to admit of any certain foresight.

The resolution next in order, is contained in the following terms:

That the General Assembly doth particularly protest against the palpable, and alarming infractions of the constitution, in the two late cases of the "Alien and Sedition acts," passed at the last session of Congress; the first of which, exercises a power no where delegated to the federal government; and which by uniting legislative and judicial powers to those of executive, subverts the general principles of a free government, as well as the particular organization, and positive provisions of the federal constitution; and the other of which acts, exercises in like manner, a power not delegated by the constitution, but on the contrary, expressly and positively forbidden by one of the amendments thereto; a power, which more than any other, ought to produce universal alarm; because it is levelled against that right of freely examining public characters and measures, and of free communication among the people thereon, which has ever been justly deemed the only effectual guardian of every other right.

The subject of this resolution having, it is presumed, more particularly led the General Assembly into the proceedings which they communicated to the other states, and being in itself of peculiar importance; it deserves the most critical and faithful investigation; for the length of which no other apology will be necessary.

The subject divides itself into *first*, "The Alien Act," *secondly*, "The Sedition Act."

...

The *second* object against which the resolution protests is the sedition act.

Of this act it is affirmed 1. That it exercises in like manner a power not delegated by the constitution. 2d. That the power, on the contrary, is expressly and positively forbidden by one of the amendments to the constitution. 3d. That this is a power, which more than any other ought to produce universal alarm; because it is levelled against that right of freely examining public characters and measures, and of free communication thereon; which has ever been justly deemed the only effectual guardian of every other right.

I. That it exercises a power not delegated by the constitution.

Here, again it will be proper to recollect, that the Federal Government being composed of powers specifically granted, with a reservation of all others to the states or to the people, the positive authority under which the sedition act could be passed must be produced by those who assert its constitutionality. In what part of the constitution then is this authority to be found?

Several attempts have been made to answer this question, which will be examined in their order. The committee will begin with one, which has filled them with equal astonishment and apprehension; and which, they cannot but persuade themselves, must have the same effect on all, who will consider it with coolness and impartiality, and with a reverence for our constitution, in the true character in which it issued from the sovereign authority of the people. The committee refer to the doctrine lately advanced as a sanction to the sedition act: "that the common or unwritten law," a law of vast extent and complexity, and embracing almost every possible subject of legislation, both civil and criminal, "makes a part of the law of these states; in their united and national capacity."

The novelty, and in the judgment of the committee, the extravagance of this pretension, would have consigned it to the silence, in which they have passed by other arguments, which an extraordinary zeal for the act has drawn into the discussion. But the auspices, under which this innovation presents itself, have constrained the committee to bestow on it an attention, which other considerations might have forbidden.

In executing the task, it may be of use, to look back to the colonial state of this country, prior to the revolution; to trace the effect of the revolution which converted the colonies into independent states; to enquire into the import of the articles of confederation, the first instrument by which the union of the states was regularly established; and finally to consult the Constitution of 1788, which is the oracle that must decide the important question.

In the state prior to the revolution, it is certain that the common law under different limitations, made a part of the colonial codes. But whether it be understood that the original colonists brought the law with them, or made it their law by adoption; it is equally certain that it was the separate law of each colony within its respective limits, and was unknown to them, as a law pervading and operating through the whole, as one society.

It could not possibly be otherwise. The common law was not the same in any two of the colonies; in some, the modifications were materially and extensively different. There was no common legislature, by which a common will, could be expressed in the form of a law; nor any common magistracy, by which such a law could be carried into practice. The will of each colony alone and separately, had its organs for these purposes.

This stage of our political history, furnishes no foothold for the patrons of this new doctrine.

Did then, the principle or operation of the great event which made the colonies, independent states, imply or introduce the common law, as a law of the union?

The fundamental principle of the revolution was,

that the colonies were co-ordinate members with each other, and with Great-Britain; of an Empire, united by a common Executive Sovereign, but not united by any common Legislative Sovereign. The Legislative power was maintained to be as complete in each American Parliament, as in the British Parliament. And the royal prerogative was in force in each colony, by virtue of its acknowledging the King for its Executive Magistrate, as it was in Great-Britain, by virtue of a like acknowledgment there. A denial of these principles by Great-Britain, and the assertion of them by America, produced the revolution.

There was a time indeed, when an exception to the Legislative separation of the several component and co-equal parts of the Empire, obtained a degree of acquiescence. The British Parliament was allowed to regulate the trade with foreign nations, and between the different parts of the Empire. This was however mere practice without right, and contrary to the true theory of the constitution. The conveniency of some regulations in both those cases, was apparent; and as there was no Legislature with power over the whole, nor any constitutional pre-eminence among the Legislatures of the several parts; it was natural for the Legislature of that particular part which was the eldest and the largest, to assume this function, and for the others to acquiesce in it. This tacit arrangement was the less criticised, as the regulations established by the British Parliament, operated in favor of that part of the Empire, which seemed to bear the principal share of the public burdens, and were regarded as an indemnification of its advances for the other parts. As long as this regulating power was confined to the two objects of conveniency and equity, it was not complained of, nor much enquired into. But no sooner was it perverted to the selfish views of the party assuming it, than the injured parties began to feel and to reflect; and the moment the claim to a direct and indefinite power was ingrafted on the precedent of the regulating power, the whole charm was dissolved, and every eye opened to the usurpation. The assertion by G.B. of a power to make laws for the other members of the Empire *in all cases whatsoever*, ended in the discovery, that she had a right to make laws for them, *in no cases whatsoever*.

Such being the ground of our revolution, no support nor colour can be drawn from it, for the doctrine that the common law is binding on these states as one society. The doctrine on the contrary, is evidently repugnant to the fundamental principle of the revolution.

The articles of confederation, are the next source of information on this subject.

In the interval between the commencement of the revolution, and the final ratification of these articles, the nature and extent of the union was determined by the circumstances of the crisis, rather than by any accurate delineation of the general authority. It will not be alleged that the "common law," could have had any legitimate birth as a law of the United States, during that state of things. If it came as such, into existence at all, the charter of confederation must have been its parent.

Here again, however, its pretensions are absolutely destitute of foundation. This instrument does not contain a sentence or syllable, that can be tortured into a countenance of the idea, that the parties to it were with respect to the objects of the common law, to form one community. No such law is named or implied, or alluded to, as being in force, or as brought into force by that compact. No provision is made by which such a law could be carried into operation; whilst on the other hand, every such inference or pretext is absolutely precluded, by article 2d, which declares, "that each state retains its sovereignty, freedom and independence, and every power, jurisdiction and right, which is not by this confederation expressly delegated to the United States, in Congress assembled."

Thus far it appears, that not a vestige of this extraordinary doctrine can be found, in the origin or progress of American institutions. The evidence against it, has, on the contrary, grown stronger at every step; till it has amounted to a formal and positive exclusion, by written articles of compact among the parties concerned.

Is this exclusion revoked, and the common law introduced as a national law, by the present constitution of the United States? This is the final question to be examined.

It is readily admitted, that particular parts of the common law, may have a sanction from the constitution, so far as they are necessarily comprehended in the technical phrases which express the powers delegated to the government; and so far also, as such other parts may be adopted as necessary and proper, for carrying into execution the powers expressly delegated. But the question does not relate to either of these portions of the common law. It relates to the common law, beyond these limitations.

The only part of the constitution which seems to have been relied on in this case, is the 2d sect. of art. III. "The judicial power shall extend to all cases, *in law*

47

and equity, arising *under this constitution*, the laws of the United States, and treaties made or which shall be made under their authority."

It has been asked what cases distinct from those arising under the laws and treaties of the United States, can arise under the constitution, other than those arising under the common law; and it is inferred, that the common law is accordingly adopted or recognized by the constitution.

Never perhaps was so broad a construction applied to a text so clearly unsusceptible of it. If any colour for the inference could be found, it must be in the impossibility of finding any other cases in law and equity, within the provisions of the constitution, to satisfy the expression; and rather than resort to a construction affecting so essentially the whole character of the government, it would perhaps be more rational to consider the expression as a mere pleonasm or inadvertence. But it is not necessary to decide on such a dilemma. The expression is fully satisfied, and its accuracy justified, by two descriptions of cases, to which the judicial authority is extended, and neither of which implies that the common law is the law of the United States. One of these descriptions comprehends the cases growing out of the restrictions on the legislative power of the states. For example, it is provided that "no state shall emit bills of credit," or "make any thing but gold and silver coin a tender in payment of debts." Should this prohibition be violated, and a suit *between citizens of the same state* be the consequence, this would be a case arising under the constitution before the judicial power of the United States. A second description comprehends suits between citizens and foreigners, or citizens of different states, to be decided according to the state or foreign laws; but submitted by the constitution to the judicial power of the United States; the judicial power being, in several instances, extended beyond the legislative power of the United States.

To this explanation of the text, the following observations may be added.

The expression, cases in law and equity, is manifestly confined to cases of a civil nature; and would exclude cases of criminal jurisdiction. Criminal cases in law and equity, would be a language unknown to the law.

The succeeding paragraph of the same section, is in harmony with this construction. It is in these words— "In all cases affecting ambassadors, other public ministers and consuls, and those in which a state shall be a party, the Supreme Court shall have original jurisdic-tion. *In all* the other cases (including cases in law and equity arising under the constitution) the Supreme Court shall have *appellate* jurisdiction both as to law and *fact*; with such exceptions, and under such regulations as Congress shall make."

This paragraph, by expressly giving an *appellate* jurisdiction, in cases of law and equity arising under the constitution, to *fact*, as well as to law, clearly excludes criminal cases, where the trial by jury is secured; because the fact, in such cases, is not a subject of appeal. And although the appeal is liable to such *exceptions* and regulations as Congress may adopt; yet it is not to be supposed that an exception of all criminal cases could be contemplated; as well because a discretion in Congress to make or omit the exception would be improper; as because it would have been unnecessary. The exception could as easily have been made by the constitution itself, as referred to the Congress.

Once more, the amendment last added to the constitution, deserves attention, as throwing light on this subject. "The judicial power of the United States shall not be construed to extend to any suit in *law* or *equity*, commenced or prosecuted against one of the United States, by citizens of another state, or by citizens or subjects of any foreign power." As it will not be pretended that any criminal proceeding could take place against a state; the terms *law* or *equity*, must be understood as appropriate to *civil* in exclusion of *criminal* cases.

From these considerations, it is evident, that this part of the constitution, even if it could be applied at all, to the purpose for which it has been cited, would not include any cases whatever of a criminal nature; and consequently, would not authorise the inference from it, that the judicial authority extends to offences against the common law, as offences arising under the constitution.

It is further to be considered, that even if this part of the constitution could be strained into an application to every common law case, criminal as well as civil, it could have no effect in justifying the sedition act; which is an exercise of legislative, and not of judicial power: and it is the judicial power only of which the extent is defined in this part of the constitution.

There are two passages in the constitution, in which a description of the law of the United States, is found— The first is contained in article III. sect. 2, in the words following: "This constitution, the laws of the United States, and treaties made, or which shall be made under their authority." The second is contained in the 2d paragraph of art. VI. as follows: "This constitution and the laws of the United States which shall be made in pursuance thereof, and all treaties made, or which shall be made under the authority of the United States, shall be the supreme law of the land." The first of these descriptions was meant as a guide to the judges of the United States; the second as a guide to the judges in the several states. Both of them consist of an enumeration, which was evidently meant to be precise and complete. If the common law had been understood to be a law of the United States, it is not possible to assign a satisfactory reason why it was not expressed in the enumeration.

In aid of these objections, the difficulties and confusion inseparable from a constructive introduction of the common law, would afford powerful reasons against it.

Is it to be the common law with, or without the British statutes?

If without the statutory amendments, the vices of the code would be insupportable.

If with these amendments, what period is to be fixed for limiting the British authority over our laws?

Is it to be the date of the eldest or the youngest of the colonies?

Or are the dates to be thrown together, and a medium deduced?

Or is our independence to be taken for the date?

Is, again, regard to be had to the various changes in the common law made by the local codes of America?

Is regard to be had to such changes, subsequent, as well as prior, to the establishment of the constitution?

Is regard to be had to future, as well as past changes?

Is the law to be different in every state, as differently modified by its code; or are the modifications of any particular state, to be applied to all?

And on the latter supposition, which among the state codes would form the standard?

Questions of this sort might be multiplied with as much ease, as there would be difficulty in answering them.

The consequences flowing from the proposed construction, furnish other objections equally conclusive; unless the text were peremptory in its meaning, and consistent with other parts of the instrument.

These consequences may be in relation; to the legislative authority of the United States; to the executive authority; to the judicial authority, and to the governments of the several states.

If it be understood that the common law is established by the constitution, it follows that no part of the law can be altered by the legislature; such of the statutes already passed as may be repugnant thereto, would be nullified, particularly the "sedition act" itself which boasts of being a melioration of the common law; and the whole code with all its incongruities, barbarisms, and bloody maxims would be inviolably saddled on the good people of the United States.

Should this consequence be rejected, and the common law be held, like other laws, liable to revision and alteration, by the authority of Congress; it then follows, that the authority of Congress is co-extensive with the objects of common law; that is to say, with every object of legislation: For to every such object, does some branch or other of the common law extend. The authority of Congress would therefore be no longer under the limitations, marked out in the constitution. They would be authorized to legislate in all cases whatsoever.

In the next place, as the President possesses the executive powers of the constitution, and is to see that the laws be faithfully executed, his authority also must be co-extensive with every branch of the common law. The additions which this would make to his power, though not readily to be estimated, claim the most serious attention.

This is not all; it will merit the most profound consideration, how far an indefinite admission of the common law, with a latitude in construing it, equal to the construction by which it is deduced from the constitution, might draw after it the various prerogatives making part of the unwritten law of England. The English constitution itself is nothing more than a composition of unwritten laws and maxims.

In the third place, whether the common law be admitted as of legal or of constitutional obligation, it would confer on the judicial department a discretion little short of a legislative power.

On the supposition of its having a constitutional obligation, this power in the judges would be permanent and irremediable by the legislature. On the other supposition, the power would not expire, until the legislature should have introduced a full system of statutory provisions. Let it be observed too, that besides all the uncertainties above enumerated, and which present an immense field for judicial discretion, it would remain with the same department to decide what parts of the common law would, and what would not, be properly applicable to the circumstances of the United States.

A discretion of this sort, has always been lamented as incongruous and dangerous, even in the colonial and state courts; although so much narrowed by positive provisions in the local codes on all the principal subjects embraced by the common law. Under the United States, where so few laws exist on those subjects, and where so great a lapse of time must happen before the vast chasm could be supplied, it is manifest that the power of the judges over the law would, in fact, erect them into legislators; and that for a long time, it would be impossible for the citizens to conjecture, either what was, or would be law.

In the last place, the consequence of admitting the common law as the law of the United States, on the authority of the individual states, is as obvious as it would be fatal. As this law relates to every subject of legislation, and would be paramount to the constitutions and laws of the states; the admission of it would overwhelm the residuary sovereignty of the states, and by one constructive operation new model the whole political fabric of the country.

From the review thus taken of the situation of the American colonies prior to their independence; of the effect of this event on their situation; of the nature and import of the articles of confederation; of the true meaning of the passage in the existing constitution from which the common law has been deduced; of the difficulties and uncertainties incident to the doctrine; and of its vast consequences in extending the powers of the federal government, and in superseding the authorities of the state governments; the committee feel the utmost confidence in concluding that the common law never was, nor by any fair construction, ever can be, deemed a law for the American people as one community; and they indulge the strongest expectation that the same conclusion will finally be drawn, by all candid and accurate enquirers into the subject. It is indeed distressing to reflect, that it ever should have been made a question, whether the constitution, on the whole face of which is seen so much labour to enumerate and define the several objects of federal power, could intend to introduce in the lump, in an indirect manner, and by a forced construction of a few phrases, the vast and multifarious jurisdiction involved in the common law; a law filling so many ample volumes; a law overspreading the entire field of legislation; and a law that would sap the foundation of the constitution as a system of limited and specified powers. A severer reproach could not in the opinion of the committee be thrown on the constitution, on those who framed, or on those who established it, than such a supposition would throw on them.

The argument then drawn from the common law, on the ground of its being adopted or recognized by the constitution, being inapplicable to the Sedition act, the committee will proceed to examine the other arguments which have been founded on the constitution.

They will waste but little time on the attempt to cover the act by the preamble to the constitution; it being contrary to every acknowledged rule of construction, to set up this part of an instrument, in opposition to the plain meaning, expressed in the body of the instrument. A preamble usually contains the general motives or reasons, for the particular regulations or measures which follow it; and is always understood to be explained and limited by them. In the present instance, a contrary interpretation would have the inadmissible effect, of rendering nugatory or improper, every part of the constitution which succeeds the preamble.

The paragraph in art. I, sect. 8, which contains the power to lay and collect taxes, duties, imposts, and excises, to pay the debts, and provide for the common defence and general welfare, having been already examined, will also require no particular attention in this place. It will have been seen that in its fair and consistent meaning, it cannot enlarge the enumerated powers vested in Congress.

The part of the constitution which seems most to be recurred to, in defence of the "Sedition Act," is the last clause of the above section, empowering Congress "to make all laws which shall be necessary and proper for carrying into execution the foregoing powers, and all other powers vested by this constitution in the government of the United States, or in any department or officer thereof."

The plain import of this clause is, that Congress shall have all the incidental or instrumental powers, necessary and proper for carrying into execution all the express powers; whether they be vested in the government of the United States, more collectively, or in the several departments, or officers thereof. It is not a grant of new powers to Congress, but merely a declaration, for the removal of all uncertainty, that the means of carrying into execution, those otherwise granted, are included in the grant.

Whenever, therefore a question arises concerning the constitutionality of a particular power; the first question is, whether the power be expressed in the constitution. If it be, the question is decided. If it be not expressed; the next enquiry must be, whether it is properly an incident to an express power, and necessary to its execution. If it be, it may be exercised by Congress. If it be not; Congress cannot exercise it.

Let the question be asked, then, whether the power over the press exercised in the "sedition act," be found among the powers expressly vested in the Congress? This is not pretended.

Is there any express power, for executing which, it is a necessary and proper power?

The power which has been selected, as least remote, in answer to this question, is that of "suppressing insurrections"; which is said to imply a power to *prevent* insurrections, by punishing whatever may *lead* or *tend* to them. But it surely cannot, with the least plausibility, be said, that a regulation of the press, and a punishment of libels, are exercises of a power to suppress insurrections. The most that could be said, would be, that the punishment of libels, if it had the tendency ascribed to it, might prevent the occasion, of passing or executing laws, necessary and proper for the suppression of insurrections.

Has the federal government no power, then, to prevent as well as to punish resistance to the laws?

They have the power which the constitution deemed most proper in their hands for the purpose. The Congress has power, before it happens, to pass laws for punishing it; and the Executive and Judiciary have power to enforce those laws when it does happen.

It must be recollected by many, and could be shewn to the satisfaction of all, that the construction here put on the terms 'necessary and proper' is precisely the construction which prevailed during the discussions and ratifications of the constitution. It may be added, and cannot too often be repeated, that it is a construction absolutely necessary to maintain their consistency with the peculiar character of the government, as possessed of particular and defined powers only; not of the general and indefinite powers vested in ordinary governments. For if the power to *suppress insurrections*, includes a power to *punish libels*; or if the power to *punish*, includes a power to *prevent*, by all the means that may have that *tendency*; such is the relation and influence among the most remote subjects of legislation, that a power over a very few, would carry with it a power over all. And it must be wholly immaterial, whether unlimited powers be exercised under the name of unlimited powers, or be exercised under the name of unlimited means of carrying into execution, limited powers.

This branch of the subject will be closed with a reflection which must have weight with all; but more especially with those who place peculiar reliance on the Judicial exposition of the constitution, as the bulwark provided against undue extensions of the Legislative power. If it be understood that the powers implied in the specified powers, have an immediate and appropriate relation to them, as means, necessary and proper for carrying them into execution, questions on the constitutionality of laws passed for this purpose, will be of a nature sufficiently precise and determinate for Judicial cognizance and controul. If, on the other hand, Congress are not limited in the choice of means by any such appropriate relation of them to the specified powers; but may employ all such means as they may deem fitted to *prevent* as well as to *punish*, crimes subjected to their authority; such as may have a *tendency* only to *promote* an object for which they are authorized to provide; every one must perceive that questions relating to means of this sort, must be questions of mere policy and expediency; on which legislative discretion alone can decide, and from which the judicial interposition and controul are completely excluded.

II. The next point which the resolution requires to be proved, is, that the power over the press exercised by the sedition act, is positively forbidden by one of the amendments to the constitution.

The amendment stands in these words—"Congress shall make no law respecting an establishment of religion, or prohibiting the free exercise thereof, *or abridging the freedom of speech or of the press*; or the right of the people peaceably to assemble, and to petition the government for a redress of grievances."

In the attempts to vindicate the "Sedition act," it has been contended, 1. That the "freedom of the press" is to be determined by the meaning of these terms in the common law. 2. That the article supposes the power over the press to be in Congress, and prohibits them only from *abridging* the freedom allowed to it by the common law.

Although it will be shewn, in examining the second of these positions, that the amendment is a denial to Congress of all power over the press; it may not be useless to make the following observations on the first of them.

It is deemed to be a sound opinion, that the sedition act, in its definition of some of the crimes created, is an abridgment of the freedom of publication, recognized by principles of the common law in England.

The freedom of the press under the common law, is, in the defences of the sedition act, made to consist in an exemption from all *previous* restraint on printed publications, by persons authorized to inspect and prohibit them. It appears to the committee, that this idea of the freedom of the press, can never be admitted to be the American idea of it: since a law inflicting penalties on printed publications, would have a similar effect with a law authorizing a previous restraint on them. It would seem a mockery to say, that no law should be passed, preventing publications from being made, but that laws might be passed for punishing them in case they should be made.

The essential difference between the British government, and the American constitutions, will place this subject in the clearest light.

In the British government, the danger of encroachments on the rights of the people, is understood to be confined to the executive magistrate. The representatives of the people in the legislature, are not only exempt themselves, from distrust, but are considered as sufficient guardians of the rights of their constituents against the danger from the executive. Hence it is a principle, that the parliament is unlimited in its power; or in their own language, is omnipotent. Hence too, all the ramparts for protecting the rights of the people, such as their magna charta, their bill of rights, &c. are not reared against the parliament, but against the royal prerogative. They are merely legislative precautions, against executive usurpations. Under such a government as this, an exemption of the press from previous restraint by licensers appointed by the king, is all the freedom that can be secured to it.

In the United States, the case is altogether different. The people, not the government, possess the absolute sovereignty. The legislature, no less than the executive, is under limitations of power. Encroachments are regarded as possible from the one, as well as from the other. Hence in the United States, the great and essential rights of the people are secured against legislative, as well as against executive ambition. They are secured, not by laws paramount to prerogative; but by constitutions paramount to laws. This security of the freedom of the press, requires that it should be exempt, not only from previous restraint by the executive, as in Great Britain; but from legislative restraint also; and this exemption, to be effectual, must be an exemption, not only from the previous inspection of licensers, but from the subsequent penalty of laws.

The state of the press, therefore, under the common law, can not in this point of view, be the standard of its freedom, in the United States.

But there is another view, under which it may be necessary to consider this subject. It may be alleged, that although the security for the freedom of the press, be different in Great Britain and in this country; being a legal security only in the former, and a constitutional security in the latter; and although there may be a further difference, in an extension of the freedom of the press, here, beyond an exemption from previous restraint, to an exemption from subsequent penalties also; yet that the actual legal freedom of the press, under the common law, must determine the degree of freedom, which is meant by the terms and which is constitutionally secured against both previous and subsequent restraints.

The committee are not unaware of the difficulty of all general questions which, may turn on the proper boundary between the liberty and licentiousness of the press. They will leave it therefore for consideration only, how far the difference between the nature of the British government, and the nature of the American governments, and the practice under the latter, may shew the degree of rigor in the former, to be inapplicable to, and not obligatory in, the latter.

The nature of governments elective, limited and responsible, in all their branches, may well be supposed to require a greater freedom of animadversion, than might be tolerated by the genius of such a government as that of Great Britain. In the latter, it is a maxim, that the king, an hereditary, not a responsible magistrate, can do no wrong; and that the legislature, which in two thirds of its composition, is also hereditary, not responsible, can do what it pleases. In the United States, the executive magistrates are not held to be infallible, nor the legislatures to be omnipotent; and both being elective, are both responsible. Is it not natural and necessary, under such different circumstances, that a different degree of freedom, in the use of the press, should be contemplated?

Is not such an inference favored by what is observable in Great Britain itself? Notwithstanding the general doctrine of the common law, on the subject of the press, and the occasional punishment of those, who use it with a freedom offensive to the government; it is well known, that with respect to the responsible members of the government, where the reasons operating here, become applicable there; the freedom exercised by the press, and protected by the public opinion, far exceeds the limits prescribed by the ordinary rules of law. The ministry, who are responsible to impeachment, are at all times, animadverted on, by the press, with peculiar freedom; and during the elections for the House of Commons, the other responsible part of the government, the press is employed with as little reserve towards the candidates.

The practice in America must be entitled to much more respect. In every state, probably, in the union, the press has exerted a freedom in canvassing the merits and measures of public men, of every description, which has not been confined to the strict limits of the common law. On this footing, the freedom of the press has stood; on this footing it yet stands. And it will not be a breach, either of truth or of candour, to say, that no persons or presses are in the habit of more unrestrained animadversions on the proceedings and functionaries of the state governments, than the persons and presses most zealous, in vindicating the act of Congress for punishing similar animadversions on the government of the United States.

The last remark will not be understood, as claiming for the state governments, an immunity greater than they have heretofore enjoyed. Some degree of abuse is inseparable from the proper use of every thing; and in no instance is this more true, than in that of the press. It has accordingly been decided by the practice of the states, that it is better to leave a few of its noxious branches, to their luxuriant growth, than by pruning them away, to injure the vigor of those yielding the proper fruits. And can the wisdom of this policy be doubted by any who reflect, that to the press alone, chequered as it is with abuses, the world is indebted for all the triumphs which have been gained by reason and humanity, over error and oppression; who reflect that to the same beneficent source, the United States owe much of the lights which conducted them to the rank of a free and independent nation; and which have improved their political system, into a shape so auspicious to their happiness. Had "Sedition acts," forbidding every publication that might bring the constituted agents into contempt or disrepute, or that might excite the hatred of the people against the authors of unjust or pernicious measures, been uniformly enforced against the press; might not the United States have been languishing at this day, under the infirmities of a sickly confederation? Might they not possibly be miserable colonies, groaning under a foreign yoke?

To these observations one fact will be added, which demonstrates that the common law cannot be admitted as the *universal* expositor of American terms, which may be the same with those contained in that law. The

freedom of conscience, and of religion, are found in the same instruments, which assert the freedom of the press. It will never be admitted, that the meaning of the former, in the common law of England, is to limit their meaning in the United States.

Whatever weight may be allowed to these considerations, the committee do not, however, by any means, intend to rest the question on them. They contend that the article of amendment, instead of supposing in Congress, a power that might be exercised over the press, provided its freedom be not abridged, was meant as a positive denial to Congress, of any power whatever on the subject.

To demonstrate that this was the true object of the article, it will be sufficient to recall the circumstances which led to it, and to refer to the explanation accompanying the article.

When the constitution was under the discussions which preceded its ratification, it is well known, that great apprehensions were expressed by many, lest the omission of some positive exception from the powers delegated, of certain rights, and of the freedom of the press particularly, might expose them to the danger of being drawn by construction within some of the powers vested in Congress; more especially of the power to make all laws necessary and proper, for carrying their other powers into execution. In reply to this objection, it was invariably urged to be a fundamental and characteristic principle of the constitution; that all powers not given by it, were reserved; that no powers were given beyond those enumerated in the constitution, and such as were fairly incident to them; that the power over the rights in question, and particularly over the press, was neither among the enumerated powers, nor incident to any of them; and consequently that an exercise of any such power, would be a manifest usurpation. It is painful to remark, how much the arguments now employed in behalf of the sedition act, are at variance with the reasoning which then justified the constitution, and invited its ratification.

From this posture of the subject, resulted the interesting question in so many of the conventions, whether the doubts and dangers ascribed to the constitution, should be removed by any amendments previous to the ratification, or be postponed, in confidence that as far as they might be proper, they would be introduced in the form provided by the constitution. The latter course was adopted; and in most of the states, the ratifications were followed by propositions and instructions for rendering the constitution more explicit, and more safe to the rights, not meant to be delegated by it. Among those rights, the freedom of the press, in most instances, is particularly and emphatically mentioned. The firm and very pointed manner, in which it is asserted in the proceedings of the convention of this state will be hereafter seen.

In pursuance of the wishes thus expressed, the first Congress that assembled under the constitution, proposed certain amendments which have since, by the necessary ratifications, been made a part of it; among which amendments is the article containing, among other prohibitions on the Congress, an express declaration that they should make no law abridging the freedom of the press.

Without tracing farther the evidence on this subject, it would seem scarcely possible to doubt, that no power whatever over the press, was supposed to be delegated by the constitution, as it originally stood; and that the amendment was intended as a positive and absolute reservation of it.

But the evidence is still stronger. The proposition of amendments made by Congress, is introduced in the following terms: *"The Conventions of a number of the states having at the time of their adopting the Constitution, expressed a desire, in order to prevent misconstructions or abuse of its powers, that further declaratory and restrictive clauses should be added; and as extending the ground of public confidence in the government, will best ensure the beneficent ends of its institution."*

Here is the most satisfactory and authentic proof, that the several amendments proposed, were to be considered as either declaratory or restrictive; and whether the one or the other, as corresponding with the desire expressed by a number of the states, and as extending the ground of public confidence in the government.

Under any other construction of the amendment relating to the press, than that it declared the press to be wholly exempt from the power of Congress, the amendment could neither be said to correspond with the desire expressed by a number of the states, nor be calculated to extend the ground of public confidence in the government.

Nay more; the construction employed to justify the "sedition act," would exhibit a phenomenon, without a parallel in the political world. It would exhibit a number of respectable states, as denying first that any power over the press was delegated by the constitution; as proposing next, that an amendment to it, should explicitly declare that no such power was delegated; and finally, as concurring in an amendment actually recognizing or delegating such a power.

Is then the federal government, it will be asked, destitute of every authority for restraining the licentiousness of the press, and for shielding itself against the libelous attacks which may be made on those who administer it?

The constitution alone can answer this question. If no such power be expressly delegated, and it be not both necessary and proper to carry into execution an express power; above all, if it be expressly forbidden by a declaratory amendment to the constitution, the answer must be, that the federal government is destitute of all such authority.

And might it not be asked in turn, whether it is not more probable, under all the circumstances which have been reviewed, that the authority should be withheld by the constitution, than that it should be left to a vague and violent construction: whilst so much pains were bestowed in enumerating other powers, and so many less important powers are included in the enumeration.

Might it not be likewise asked, whether the anxious circumspection which dictated so many *peculiar* limitations on the general authority, would be unlikely to exempt the press altogether from that authority? The peculiar magnitude of some of the powers necessarily committed to the federal government; the peculiar duration required for the functions of some of its departments; the peculiar distance of the seat of its proceedings from the great body of its constituents; and the peculiar difficulty of circulating an adequate knowledge of them through any other channel; will not these considerations, some or other of which produced other exceptions from the powers of ordinary governments, all together, account for the policy of binding the hand of the federal government, from touching the channel which alone can give efficacy to its responsibility to its constituents; and of leaving those who administer it, to a remedy for injured reputations, under the same laws, and in the same tribunals, which protect their lives, their liberties, and their properties.

But the question does not turn either on the wisdom of the constitution, or on the policy which gave rise to its particular organization. It turns on the actual meaning of the instrument; by which it has appeared, that a power over the press is clearly excluded, from the number of powers delegated to the federal government.

III. And in the opinion of the committee well may it be said, as the resolution concludes with saying, that the unconstitutional power exercised over the press by the "sedition act," ought "more than any other, to produce universal alarm; because it is leveled against that right of freely examining public characters and measures, and of free communication among the people thereon, which has ever been justly deemed the only effectual guardian of every other right."

Without scrutinizing minutely into all the provisions of the "sedition act," it will be sufficient to cite so much of section 2. as follows: "And be it further enacted, that if any person shall write, print, utter or publish, or shall cause or procure to be written, printed, uttered or published, or shall knowingly and willingly assist or aid in writing, printing, uttering or publishing any false, scandalous, and malicious writing or writings against the government of the United States, or either house of the Congress of the United States, or the President of the United States, *with an intent to defame the said government, or either house of the said Congress, or the President, or to bring them, or either of them, into contempt or disrepute; or to excite against them, or either, or any of them, the hatred of the good people of the United States, &c. then such person being thereof convicted before any court of the United States, having jurisdiction thereof, shall be punished by a fine not exceeding two thousand dollars, and by imprisonment not exceeding two years."*

On this part of the act the following observations present themselves.

1. The constitution supposes that the President, the Congress, and each of its houses, may not discharge their trusts, either from defect of judgment, or other causes. Hence, they are all made responsible to their constituents, at the returning periods of election; and the President, who is singly entrusted with very great powers, is, as a further guard, subjected to an intermediate impeachment.

2. Should it happen, as the constitution supposes it may happen, that either of these branches of the government, may not have duly discharged its trust; it is natural and proper, that according to the cause and degree of their faults, they should be brought into contempt or disrepute, and incur the hatred of the people.

3. Whether it has, in any case, happened that the proceedings of either, or all of those branches, evinces such a violation of duty as to justify a contempt, a disrepute or hatred among the people, can only be determined by a free examination thereof, and a free communication among the people thereon.

4. Whenever it may have actually happened, that pro-

ceedings of this sort are chargeable on all or either of the branches of the government, it is the duty as well as right of intelligent and faithful citizens, to discuss and promulge them freely, as well to controul them by the censorship of the public opinion, as to promote a remedy according to the rules of the constitution. And it cannot be avoided, that those who are to apply the remedy must feel, in some degree, a contempt or hatred against the transgressing party.

5. As the act was passed on July 14, 1798, and is to be in force until March 3, 1801, it was of course, that during its continuance, two elections of the entire House of Representatives, an election of a part of the Senate, and an election of a President, were to take place.

6. That consequently, during all these elections, intended by the constitution to preserve the purity, or to purge the faults of the administration, the great remedial rights of the people were to be exercised, and the responsibility of their public agents to be skreened, under the penalties of this act.

May it not be asked of every intelligent friend to the liberties of his country whether, the power exercised in such an act as this, ought not to produce great and universal alarm? Whether a rigid execution of such an act, in time past, would not have repressed that information and communication among the people, which is indispensable to the just exercise of their electoral rights? And whether such an act, if made perpetual, and enforced with rigor, would not, in time to come, either destroy our free system of government, or prepare a convulsion that might prove equally fatal to it.

In answer to such questions, it has been pleaded that the writings and publications forbidden by the act, are those only which are false and malicious, and intended to defame; and merit is claimed for the privilege allowed to authors to justify, by proving the truth of their publications, and for the limitations to which the sentence of fine and imprisonment is subjected.

To those who concurred in the act, under the extraordinary belief, that the option lay between the passing of such an act, and leaving in force the common law of libels, which punishes truth equally with falsehood, and submits the fine and imprisonment to the indefinite discretion of the court, the merit of good intentions ought surely not to be refused. A like merit may perhaps be due for the discontinuance of the *corporal punishment* which the common law also leaves to the discretion of the court. This merit of *intention*, however, would have been greater, if the several mitigations had not been limited to so short a period; and the apparent inconsistency would have been avoided, between justifying the act at one time, by contrasting it with the rigors of the common law, otherwise in force; and at another time by appealing to the nature of the crisis, as requiring the temporary rigor exerted by the act.

But whatever may have been the meritorious intentions of all or any who contributed to the sedition act; a very few reflections will prove, that its baneful tendency is little diminished by the privilege of giving in evidence the truth of the matter contained in political writings.

In the first place, where simple and naked facts alone are in question, there is sufficient difficulty in some cases, and sufficient trouble and vexation in all, of meeting a prosecution from the government, with the full and formal proof, necessary in a court of law.

But in the next place, it must be obvious to the plainest minds, that opinions, and inferences, and conjectural observations, are not only in many cases inseparable from the facts, but may often be more the objects of the prosecution than the facts themselves; or may even be altogether abstracted from particular facts; and that opinions and inferences, and conjectural observations, cannot be subjects of that kind of proof which appertains to facts, before a court of law.

Again, it is no less obvious, that the *intent* to defame or bring into contempt or disrepute, or hatred, which is made a condition of the offence created by the act; cannot prevent its pernicious influence, on the freedom of the press. For omitting the enquiry, how far the malice of the intent is an inference of the law from the mere publication; it is manifestly impossible to punish the intent to bring those who administer the government into disrepute or contempt, without striking at the right of freely discussing public characters and measures: because those who engage in such discussions, must expect and *intend* to excite these unfavorable sentiments, so far as they may be thought to be deserved. To prohibit therefore the intent to excite those unfavorable sentiments against those who administer the government, is equivalent to a prohibition of the actual excitement of them; and to prohibit the actual excitement of them, is equivalent to a prohibition of discussions having that tendency and effect; which, again, is equivalent to a protection of those who administer the government, if they should at any time deserve the contempt or hatred of the people, against being exposed to it, by free animadversions on their characters and conduct. Nor can

there be a doubt, if those in public trust be shielded by penal laws from such strictures of the press, as may expose them to contempt or disrepute, or hatred, where they may deserve it, that in exact proportion as they may deserve to be exposed, will be the certainty and criminality of the intent to expose them, and the vigilance of prosecuting and punishing it; nor a doubt, that a government thus intrenched in penal statutes, against the just and natural effects of a culpable administration, will easily evade the responsibility, which is essential to a faithful discharge of its duty.

Let it be recollected, lastly, that the right of electing the members of the government, constitutes more particularly the essence of a free and responsible government. The value and efficacy of this right, depends on the knowledge of the comparative merits and demerits of the candidates for public trust; and on the equal freedom, consequently, of examining and discussing these merits and demerits of the candidates respectively. It has been seen that a number of important elections will take place whilst the act is in force; although it should not be continued beyond the term to which it is limited. Should there happen, then, as is extremely probable in relation to some or other of the branches of the government, to be competitions between those who are, and those who are not, members of the government; what will be the situations of the competitors? Not equal; because the characters of the former will be covered by the "sedition act" from animadversions exposing them to disrepute among the people; whilst the latter may be exposed to the contempt and hatred of the people, without a violation of the act. What will be the situation of the people? Not free; because they will be compelled to make their election between competitors, whose pretensions they are not permitted by the act, equally to examine, to discuss, and to ascertain. And from both these situations, will not those in power derive an undue advantage for continuing themselves in it; which by impairing the right of election, endangers the blessings of the government founded on it.

It is with justice, therefore, that the General Assembly hath affirmed in the resolution, as well that the right of freely examining public characters and measures, and of free communication thereon, is the only effectual guardian of every other right; as that this particular right is leveled at, by the power exercised in the "sedition act."

The resolution next in order is as follows:

That this state having by its Convention, which ratified

the Federal Constitution expressly declared, that among other essential rights, "the liberty of conscience and of the press cannot be cancelled, abridged, restrained or modified by any authority of the United States," and from its extreme anxiety to guard these rights from every possible attack of sophistry and ambition, having with other states, recommended an amendment for that purpose, which amendment was, in due time, annexed to the constitution; it would mark a reproachful inconsistency, and criminal degeneracy, if an indifference were not shewn, to the most palpable violation of one of the rights, thus declared and secured; and to the establishment of a precedent, which may be fatal to the other.

To place this resolution in its just light, it will be necessary to recur to the act of ratification by Virginia which stands in the ensuing form.

We, the Delegates of the people of Virginia, duly elected in pursuance of a recommendation from the General Assembly, and now met in Convention, having fully and freely investigated and discussed the proceedings of the federal convention, and being prepared as well as the most mature deliberation hath enabled us, to decide thereon; Do, in the name and in behalf of the people of Virginia, declare and make known, that the powers granted under the constitution, being derived from the people of the United States, may be resumed by them, whensoever the same shall be perverted to their injury or oppression; and that every power not granted thereby, remains with them, and at their will. That therefore, no right of any denomination can be cancelled, abridged, restrained or modified, by the Congress, by the Senate or House of Representatives acting in any capacity, by the President, or any department or officer of the United States, except in those instances in which power is given by the constitution for those purposes; and, that among other essential rights, the liberty of conscience and of the press, cannot be cancelled, abridged, restrained or modified by any authority of the United States.

Here is an express and solemn declaration by the convention of the state, that they ratified the constitution in the sense, that no right of any denomination can be cancelled, abridged, restrained or modified by the government of the United States or any part of it; except in those instances in which power is given by the constitution; and in the sense particularly, "that among other essential rights, the liberty of conscience and freedom of the press cannot be cancelled, abridged, restrained or modified, by any authority of the United States."

Words could not well express, in a fuller or more forcible manner, the understanding of the convention, that the liberty of conscience and the freedom of the press, were *equally* and *completely* exempted from all authority whatever of the United States.

Under an anxiety to guard more effectually these rights against every possible danger, the convention, after ratifying the constitution, proceeded to prefix to certain amendments proposed by them, a declaration of rights, in which are two articles providing, the one for the liberty of conscience, the other for the freedom of speech and of the press.

Similar recommendations having proceeded from a number of other states; and Congress, as has been seen, having in consequence thereof, and with a view to extend the ground of public confidence, proposed among other declaratory and restrictive clauses, a clause expressly securing the liberty of conscience and of the press; and Virginia having concurred in the ratifications which made them a part of the constitution; it will remain with a candid public to decide, whether it would not mark an inconsistency and degeneracy, if an indifference were now shewn to a palpable violation of one of those rights, the freedom of the press; and to a precedent therein, which may be fatal to the other, the free exercise of religion.

That the precedent established by the violation of the former of these rights, may, as is affirmed by the resolution, be fatal to the latter, appears to be demonstrable, by a comparison of the grounds on which they respectively rest; and from the scope of reasoning, by which the power over the former has been vindicated.

First. Both of these rights, the liberty of conscience and of the press, rest equally on the original ground of not being delegated by the constitution, and consequently withheld from the government. Any construction therefore, that would attack this original security for the one must have the like effect on the other.

Secondly. They are both equally secured by the supplement to the constitution; being both included in the same amendment, made at the same time, and by the same authority. Any construction or argument then which would turn the amendment into a grant or acknowledgment of power with respect to the press, might be equally applied to the freedom of religion.

Thirdly. If it be admitted that the extent of the freedom of the press secured by the amendment, is to be measured by the common law on this subject; the same authority may be resorted to, for the standard which is to fix the extent of the "free exercise of religion." It cannot be necessary to say what this standard would be; whether the common law be taken solely as the unwritten, or as varied by the written, law of England.

Fourthly. If the words and phrases in the amendment, are to be considered as chosen with a studied discrimination, which yields an argument for a power over the press, under the limitation that its freedom be not abridged; the same argument results from the same consideration, for a power over the exercise of religion, under the limitation that its freedom be not prohibited.

For if Congress may regulate the freedom of the press, provided they do not abridge it: because it is said only, "they shall not abridge it"; and is not said, "they shall make no law respecting it": the analogy of reasoning is conclusive, that Congress may *regulate* and even *abridge* the free exercise of religion; provided they do not *prohibit* it; because it is said only "they shall not prohibit it"; and is *not* said "they shall make no law *respecting* or no law *abridging* it."

The General Assembly were governed by the clearest reason, then, in considering the "Sedition act," which legislates on the freedom of the press, as establishing a precedent that may be fatal to the liberty of conscience and it will be the duty of all, in proportion as they value the security of the latter, to take the alarm at every encroachment on the former.

The two concluding resolutions only remain to be examined. They are in the words following.

"That the good people of this commonwealth, having ever felt, and continuing to feel the most sincere affection for their brethren of the other states; the truest anxiety for establishing and perpetuating the union of all; and the most scrupulous fidelity to that constitution, which is the pledge of mutual friendship, and the instrument of mutual happiness; the General Assembly doth solemnly appeal to the like dispositions in the other states, in confidence that they will concur with this commonwealth in declaring, as it does hereby declare, that the acts aforesaid, are unconstitutional; and, that the necessary and proper measures will be taken by each, for co-operating with this state, in maintaining unimpaired, the authorities, rights, and liberties, reserved to the states respectively, or to the People."

"That the Governor be desired, to transmit a copy of the foregoing resolutions to the executive authority of each of the other states, with a request that the same may be communicated to the Legislature thereof; and that a copy be furnished to each of the Senators and Representatives representing this state in the Congress of the United States."

The fairness and regularity of the course of proceeding, here pursued, have not protected it, against objections even from sources too respectable to be disregarded.

It has been said that it belongs to the judiciary of the United States, and not to the state legislatures, to declare the meaning of the Federal Constitution.

But a declaration that proceedings of the Federal Government are not warranted by the constitution, is a novelty neither among the citizens nor among the legislatures of the states; nor are the citizens or the legislature of Virginia, singular in the example of it.

Nor can the declarations of either, whether affirming or denying the constitutionality of measures of the Federal Government; or whether made before or after judicial decisions thereon, be deemed, in any point of view, an assumption of the office of the judge. The declarations in such cases, are expressions of opinion, unaccompanied with any other effect, than what they may produce on opinion, by exciting reflection. The expositions of the judiciary, on the other hand, are carried into immediate effect by force. The former may lead to a change in the legislative expression of the general will; possibly to a change in the opinion of the judiciary: the latter enforces the general will, whilst that will and that opinion continue unchanged.

And if there be no impropriety in declaring the unconstitutionality of proceedings in the Federal Government; where can be the impropriety of communicating the declaration to other states, and inviting their concurrence in a like declaration? What is allowable for one, must be allowable for all; and a free communication among the states, where the constitution imposes no restraint, is as allowable among the state governments, as among other public bodies, or private citizens. This consideration derives a weight, that cannot be denied to it, from the relation of the state legislatures, to the federal legislature, as the immediate constituents of one of its branches.

The legislatures of the states have a right also, to originate amendments to the constitution, by a concurrence of two thirds of the whole number, in applications to Congress for the purpose. When new states are to be formed by a junction of two or more states, or parts of states, the legislatures of the states concerned, are, as well as Congress, to concur in the measure. The states have a right also, to enter into agreements, or compacts, with the consent of Congress. In all such cases, a communication among them, results from the object which is common to them.

It is lastly to be seen, whether the confidence expressed by the resolution, that the *necessary and proper measures*, would be taken by the other states, for co-operating with Virginia, in maintaining the rights reserved to the states, or to the people, be in any degree liable to the objections which have been raised against it.

If it be liable to objection, it must be, because either the object, or the means, are objectionable.

The object being to maintain what the constitution has ordained, is in itself a laudable object.

The means are expressed in the terms "the necessary and proper measures." A proper object was to be pursued, by means both necessary and proper.

To find an objection then, it must be shewn, that some meaning was annexed to these general terms, which was not proper; and for this purpose, either that the means used by the General Assembly, were an example of improper means, or that there were no proper means to which the terms could refer.

In the example given by the state, of declaring the alien and sedition acts to be unconstitutional, and of communicating the declaration to the other states, no trace of improper means has appeared. And if the other states had concurred in making a like declaration, supported too by the numerous applications flowing immediately from the people, it can scarcely be doubted, that these simple means would have been as sufficient, as they are unexceptionable.

It is no less certain, that other means might have been employed, which are strictly within the limits of the constitution. The legislatures of the states might have made a direct representation to Congress, with a view to obtain a rescinding of the two offensive acts; or they might have represented to their respective senators in Congress, their wish, that two thirds thereof would propose an explanatory amendment to the constitution; or two thirds of themselves, if such had been their option, might, by an application to Congress, have obtained a convention for the same object.

These several means, though not equally eligible in themselves, nor probably, to the states, were all constitutionally open for consideration. And if the General Assembly, after declaring the two acts to be unconstitutional, the first and most obvious proceeding on the subject, did not undertake to point out to the other states, a choice among the farther measures that might become necessary and proper, the reserve will not be misconstrued by liberal minds, into any culpable imputation.

These observations appear to form a satisfactory reply, to every objection which is not founded on a misconception of the terms, employed in the resolutions. There is one other however, which may be of too much importance not to be added. It cannot be forgotten, that among the arguments addressed to those, who apprehended danger to liberty, from the establishment of the general government over so great a country; the appeal was emphatically made to the intermediate existence of the state governments, between the people and that government, to the vigilance with which they would descry the first symptoms of usurpation, and to the promptitude with which they would sound the alarm to the public. This argument was probably not without its effect; and if it was a proper one, then, to recommend the establishment of the constitution; it must be a proper one now, to assist in its interpretation.

The only part of the two concluding resolutions, that remains to be noticed, is the repetition in the first, of that warm affection to the union and its members, and of that scrupulous fidelity to the constitution which have been invariably felt by the people of this state. As the proceedings were introduced with these sentiments, they could not be more properly closed, than in the same manner. Should there be any so far misled, as to call in question the sincerity of these professions, whatever regret may be excited by the error, the General Assembly cannot descend into a discussion of it. Those who have listened to the suggestion, can only be left to their own recollection, of the part which this state has borne in the establishment of our national independence; in the establishment of our national constitution; and in maintaining under it, the authority and laws of the union, without a single exception of internal resistance or commotion. By recurring to these facts, they will be able to convince themselves, that the representatives of the people of Virginia must be above the necessity of opposing any other shield to attacks on their national patriotism, than their own consciousness and the justice of an enlightened public; who will perceive in the resolutions themselves, the strongest evidence of attachment both to the constitution and to the union, since it is only by maintaining the different governments and departments within their respective limits, that the blessings of either can be perpetuated. The extensive view of the subject thus taken by the committee, has led them to report to the house, as the result of the whole, the following resolution.

Resolved, That the General Assembly, having carefully and respectfully attended to the proceedings of a number of the states, in answer to their resolutions of December 21, 1798, and having accurately and fully re-examined and re-considered the latter, find it to be their indispensable duty to adhere to the same, as founded in truth, as consonant with the constitution, and as conducive to its preservation; and more especially to be their duty, to renew, as they do hereby renew, their protest against "the alien and sedition acts," as palpable and alarming infractions of the constitution.

13

St. George Tucker,
A View of the Constitution
1803[*]

Having in the preceding pages taken a slight view of the several forms of government, and afterwards examined with somewhat closer attention the constitution of the commonwealth of Virginia, as a sovereign, and independent state, it now becomes necessary for the American student to inquire into the connection established between the several states in the union by the constitution of the United States. To assist him in this inquiry, I shall now proceed to consider: First, the nature of that instrument, with the manner in which it hath been adopted; and, Secondly, its structure, and organization; with the powers, jurisdiction, and rights of the government thereby established, either independent of, or connected with, those of the state governments; together with the mutual relation which subsists between the federal, and state governments, in virtue of that instrument.

I. I am to consider the nature of that instrument by

which the federal government of the United States, has been established, with the manner of its adoption.

The constitution of the United States of America, then, is an original, written, federal, and social compact, freely, voluntarily, and solemnly entered into by the several states of North-America, and ratified by the people thereof, respectively; whereby the several states, and the people thereof, respectively, have bound themselves to each other, and to the federal government of the United States; and by which the federal government is bound to the several states, and to every citizen of the United States.

1. It is a compact; by which it is distinguished from a charter, or grant; which is either the act of a superior to an inferior; or is founded upon some consideration moving from one of the parties, to the other, and operates as an exchange, or sale: but here the contracting parties, whether considered as states, in their politic capacity and character; or as individuals, are all equal; nor is there any thing granted from one to another: but each stipulates to part with, and to receive the same thing, precisely, without any distinction or difference in favor of any of the parties. The considerations upon which this compact was founded, and the motives which led to it, as declared in the instrument itself, were, to form a more perfect union than theretofore existed between the confederated states; to establish justice, and ensure domestic tranquility, between them; to provide for their common defense, against foreign force, or such powerful domestic insurrections as might require aid to suppress them; to promote their general welfare; and to secure the blessings of liberty to the people of the United States, and their posterity.[1]

2. It is a federal compact; several sovereign and independent states may unite themselves together by a perpetual confederacy, without each ceasing to be a perfect state. They will together form a federal republic: the deliberations in common will offer no violence to each member, though they may in certain respects put some constraint on the exercise of it, in virtue of voluntary engagements.[2] The extent, modifications, and objects of the federal authority are mere matters of discretion; so long as the separate organization of the members remains, and from the nature of the compact must continue to exist, both for local and domestic, and for federal purposes; the union is in fact, as well as in theory,

[*] St. George Tucker, *Blackstone's Commentaries with Notes of Reference, to the Constitution and Laws of the Federal Government of the United States and of the Commonwealth of Virginia* (Clark, NJ: Lawbook Exchange, 1996), 140–73, 296–316. First published 1803. [Footnote numbers have been changed for this collection. —Ed.]

1. Preamble to the C.U.S.
2. Vattel, B. 1. c. 1. §. 10.

an association of states, or, a confederacy.[3] The state governments not only retain every power, jurisdiction, and right not delegated to the United States, by the constitution, nor prohibited by it to the states,[4] but they are constituent and necessary parts of the federal government; and without their agency in their politic character, there could be neither a senate, nor president of the United States; the choice of the latter depending mediately, and of the former, immediately, upon the legislatures of the several states in the union.[5]

This idea of a confederate, or federal, republic, was probably borrowed from Montesquieu, who treats of it as an expedient for extending the sphere of popular government, and reconciling internal freedom with external security,[6] as hath been mentioned elsewhere.[7] The experience of the practicability and benefit of such a system, was recent in the memory of every American, from the success of the revolutionary war, concluded but a few years before; during the continuance of which the states entered into a perpetual alliance and confederacy with each other. Large concessions of the rights of sovereignty were thereby made to congress; but the system was defective in not providing adequate means, for a certain, and regular revenue; congress being altogether dependent upon the legislatures of the several states for supplies, although the latter, by the terms of compact, were bound to furnish, whatever the former should deem it necessary to require. At the close of the war, it was found that congress had contracted debts, without a revenue to discharge them; that they had entered into treaties, which they had not power to fulfil; that the several states possessed sources of an extensive commerce, for which they could not find any vent. These evils were ascribed to the defects of the existing confederation; and it was said that the principles of the proposed constitution were to be considered less as absolutely new, than as the expansion of the principles contained in the articles of confederation: that in the latter those principles were so feeble and confined, as to justify all the charges of inefficiency which had been urged against it; that in the new government, as in the old, the general powers are limited, and that the states, in all unenumerated cases, are left in the enjoy-

ment of their sovereign and independent jurisdictions.[8] This construction has since been fully confirmed by the twelfth article of amendments, which declares, "that the powers not delegated to the United States by the constitution, nor prohibited by it to the states, are reserved to the states respectively, or to the people." This article was added "to prevent misconstruction or abuse" of the powers granted by the constitution,[9] rather than supposed necessary to explain and secure the rights of the states, or of the people. The powers delegated to the federal government being all positive, and enumerated, according to the ordinary rules of construction, whatever is not enumerated is retained; for, *expressum facit tacere tacitum* is a maxim in all cases of construction: it is likewise a maxim of political law, that sovereign states cannot be deprived of any of their rights by implication; nor in any manner whatever by their own voluntary consent, or by submission to a conqueror.

Some of the principal points mutually insisted on, and conceded, by the several states, as such, to each other, were, that representatives and direct taxes should be apportioned among the states, according to a decennial census; that each state should have an equal number of senators; and that the number of electors of the president of the United States, should in each state be equal to the whole number of senators and representatives to which such state may be entitled in the congress; that no capitation or other direct tax shall be laid, unless in proportion to the census; that full faith and credit shall be given in each state to the public acts, records, and proceedings of every other state; that the citizens of each state shall be entitled to all the privileges and immunities of citizens in the several states; that persons charged with treason, felony, or other crime, in one state, and fleeing from justice to another state, shall be delivered up, on demand of the executive authority of the state from which he fled; that no new state shall be formed or erected within the jurisdiction of any other state; nor any state be formed by the junction of two or more states, or parts of states, without the consent of the legislatures of the states concerned; that the United States shall guarantee to every state in the union a republican form of government, and shall protect each of them against invasion; and, on application of the legislature, or of the executive (when the legislature cannot be convened) against domestic violence;

3. Federalist, vol. 1. p. 51. 52.
4. Amendments to C.U.S. art. 12.
5. C.U.S. art. 1. 2.
6. Spirit of Laws, vol. 1. B. 9. c. 1.
7. See Note B. Title Federal Government.

8. 2 Federalist, p. 32. 33.
9. Preamble to the amendments.

that amendments to the constitution, when proposed by congress, shall not be valid unless ratified by the legislatures of three fourths of the several states; and that congress shall, on the application of two thirds of the legislatures of the several states, call a convention for proposing amendments, which when ratified by the conventions in three fourths of the states shall be valid to all intents and purposes, as a part of the constitution; that the ratification of the conventions of nine states, should be sufficient for the establishment of the constitution, between the states so ratifying; and lastly, by the amendment before mentioned, it is declared, that the powers not delegated to the United States by the constitution, nor prohibited by it to the states, are reserved to the states respectively, or to the people. Thus far every feature of the constitution appears to be strictly federal.

3. It is also, to a certain extent, a social compact; the end of civil society is the procuring for the citizens whatever their necessities require, the conveniences and accommodations of life, and, in general, whatever constitutes happiness: with the peaceful possession of property, a method of obtaining justice with security; and in short, a mutual defense against all violence from without. In the act of association, in virtue of which a multitude of men form together a state or nation, each individual is supposed to have entered into engagements with all, to procure the common welfare: and all are supposed to have entered into engagements with each other, to facilitate the means of supplying the necessities of each individual, and to protect and defend him.[10] And this is, what is ordinarily meant by the original contract of society. But a contract of this nature actually existed in a visible form, between the citizens of each state, respectively, in their several constitutions; it might therefore be deemed somewhat extraordinary, that in the establishment of a federal republic, it should have been thought necessary to extend its operation to the persons of individuals, as well as to the states, composing the confederacy. It was apprehended by many, that this innovation would be construed to change the nature of the union, from a confederacy, to a consolidation of the states; that as the tenor of the instrument imported it to be the act of the people, the construction might be made accordingly: an interpretation that would tend to the annihilation of the states, and their authority. That this was the more to be apprehended,

10. Vattel, B.1. c. 2. § 15. 16.

since all questions between the states, and the United States, would undergo the final decision of the latter.

That the student may more clearly apprehend the nature of these objections, it may be proper to illustrate the distinction between federal compacts and obligations, and such as are social by one or two examples. A federal compact, alliance, or treaty, is an act of the state, or body politic, and not of an individual; on the contrary, the social contract is understood to mean the act of individuals, about to create, and establish, a state, or body politic, among themselves.... Again; if one nation binds itself by treaty to pay a certain tribute to another; or if all the members of the same confederacy oblige themselves to furnish their quotas of a common expense, when required; in either of the cases, the state, or body politic, only, and not the individual is answerable for this tribute, or quota; for although every citizen in the state is bound by the contract of the body politic, who may compel him to contribute his part, yet that part can neither be ascertained nor levied, by any other authority than that of the state, of which he is a citizen. This is, therefore, a federal obligation; which cannot reach the individual, without the agency of the state who made it. But where by any compact, express, or implied, a number of persons are bound to contribute their proportions of the common expense; or to submit to all laws made by the common consent; and where, in default of compliance with these engagements the society is authorized to levy the contribution, or, to punish the person of the delinquent; this seems to be understood to be more in the nature of a social than a federal obligation.... Upon these grounds, and others of a similar nature, a considerable alarm was excited in the minds of many, who considered the constitution as in some danger of establishing a national, or consolidated government, upon the ruins of the old federal republic.

To these objections the friends and supporters of the constitution replied, "that although the constitution would be founded on the assent and ratification of the people of America, yet that assent and ratification was to be given by the people, not as individuals composing one entire nation; but as composing the distinct and independent states, to which they respectively belong. It is to be the assent and ratification of the several states, derived from the supreme authority in each state, the authority of the people themselves. The act, therefore establishing the constitution, will not," said they, "be a national but a federal act.

"That it will be a federal and not a national act, as these terms are understood by the objectors, the act of the people, as forming so many independent states, not as forming one aggregate nation, is obvious from this single consideration, that it is the result neither from the decision of a majority of the people of the union, nor from a majority of the states. It must result from the unanimous assent of the several states that are parties to it, differing no otherwise from their ordinary assent, than in its being expressed, not by the legislative authority, but by that of the people themselves. Were the people regarded in this transaction as forming one nation, the will of the majority of the whole people of the United States would bind the minority; in the same manner as the majority in each state must bind the minority; and the will of the majority must be determined either by a comparison of the individual votes; or by considering the will of the majority of the states, as evidence of the will of the majority of the people of the United States. Neither of these rules have been adopted. Each state in ratifying the constitution, is considered as a sovereign body, independent of all others, and only to be bound by its own voluntary act. In this relation then the new constitution will be a federal, and not a national, constitution.

"With regard to the sources from which the ordinary powers of government are to be derived. The house of representatives will derive its powers from the people of America, and the people will be represented in the same proportion, and on the same principle, as they are in the legislature of a particular state. So far the government is national, not federal. The senate, on the other hand, will derive its powers from the states, as political and co-equal societies; and these will be represented on the principle of equality in the senate, as under the confederation. So far the government is federal, not national. The executive power will be derived from a very compound source. The immediate election of the president is to be made by the states, in their political character. The votes allotted to them are in a compound ratio, which considers them partly as distinct and co-equal societies; partly as unequal members of the same societies. The eventual election again is to be made, by that branch of the legislature which consists of the national representatives: but in this particular act they are to be thrown into the form of individual delegations, from so many distinct and co-equal bodies politic. From this aspect of the government it appears to be of a mixed char-

acter, presenting at least as many federal, as national features.[11]

"The difference between a federal and national government, as it relates to the operation of the government, is, by the adversaries of the plan of the convention, supposed to consist in this, that in the former the powers operate on the political bodies composing the confederacy in their political capacities; in the latter, on the individual citizens composing the nation in their individual capacities. On trying the constitution by this criterion, it falls under the national, not the federal character, though perhaps not so completely as has been understood. In several cases, and particularly in the trial of controversies to which states may be parties, they must be viewed and proceeded against in their collective and political capacities only."[12] "In some instances the powers of the federal government, established by the confederation, act immediately on individuals: in cases of capture, of piracy, of the post office, of coins, weights, and measures, of trade with the Indians, of claims under grants of land by different states, and, above all, in the cases of trials by courts martial in the army and navy, by which death may be inflicted without the intervention of a jury, or even of a civil magistrate; in all these cases the powers of the confederation operate immediately on the persons and interests of individual citizens. The confederation itself authorizes a direct tax to a certain extent on the post-office; and the power of coinage has been so construed by congress, as to levy a tribute immediately from that source also.[13] The operation of the new government on the people in their individual capacities, in its ordinary and most essential proceedings, will, on the whole, in the sense of its opponents, designate it, in this relation, a national government.

"But if the government be national with regard to the operation of its powers, it changes its aspect again when we contemplate it in relation to the extent of its powers. The idea of a national government involves in it, not only an authority over the individual citizens, but an indefinite supremacy over all persons and things, so far as they are objects of lawful government. Among a people consolidated into one nation, this supremacy is completely vested in the national legislature. Among

11. Federalist, vol. II. p. 23. 24. 25.
12. Ibidem p. 25.
13. Federalist, vol. II. p. 31. 32.

communities united for particular purposes, it is vested partly in the general, and partly in the municipal legislatures. In the former case, all local authorities are subordinate to the supreme; and may be controlled, directed, or abolished by it at pleasure. In the latter, the local or municipal authorities form distinct and independent portions of the supremacy, no more subject within their respective spheres to the general authority, than the general authority is subject to them within its own sphere. In this relation then the government cannot be deemed a national one, since its jurisdiction extends to certain enumerated objects, only, and leaves to the several states a residuary and inviolable sovereignty over all other objects. It is true that in controversies relating to the boundary between the two jurisdictions, the tribunal which is ultimately to decide, is to be established under the general government. But this does not change the principle of the case. The decision is to be impartially made according to the rules of the constitution; and all the usual and most effectual precautions are taken to secure the impartiality.

"If we try the constitution by its last relation, to the authority by which amendments are to be made, we find it neither wholly national, nor wholly federal. Were it wholly national, the supreme and ultimate authority would reside in a majority of the people of the union; and this authority would be competent at all times, like that of a majority of every national society, to alter or abolish its established government. Were it wholly federal on the other hand, the concurrence of each state in the union would be essential to every alteration that would be binding on all. The mode provided by the plan of the convention is not founded on either of these principles. In requiring more than a majority, and particularly in computing the proportion by states, not by citizens, it departs from the national, and advances towards the federal character; in rendering the concurrence of less than the whole number of states sufficient, it loses again the federal, and partakes of the national character.

"The proposed constitution, therefore, even when tested by the rules laid down by its antagonists, is in strictness neither a national nor a federal constitution, but a composition of both. In its foundation it is federal, not national; in the sources from which the ordinary powers of the government are drawn, it is partly federal, and partly national; in the operation of those powers, it is national, not federal; in the extent of them, it is federal, not national; and finally, in the authoritative mode

of introducing amendments, it is neither wholly federal, nor wholly national."[14]

4. It is an original compact; whatever political relation existed between the American colonies, antecedent to the revolution, as constituent parts of the British empire, or as dependencies upon it, that relation was completely dissolved and annihilated from that period. … From the moment of the revolution they became severally independent and sovereign states, possessing all the rights, jurisdictions, and authority, that other sovereign states, however constituted, or by whatever title denominated, possess; and bound by no ties but of their own creation, except such as all other civilized nations are equally bound by, and which together constitute the customary law of nations. A common council of the colonies, under the name of a general congress, had been established by the legislature, or rather conventional authority in the several colonies. The revolutionary war had been begun, and conducted under its auspices; but the first act of union which took place among the states after they became independent, was the confederation between them, which was not ratified until March 1781, near five years from the commencement of their independence. The powers thereby granted to congress, though very extensive in point of moral obligation upon the several states, were perfectly deficient in the means provided for the practical use of them, as has been already observed. The agency and cooperation of the states, which was requisite to give effect to the measures of congress, not infrequently occasioned their total defeat. It became an unanimous opinion that some amendment to the existing confederation was absolutely necessary, and after a variety of unsuccessful attempts for that purpose, a general convention was appointed by the legislatures of twelve states, who met, consulted together, prepared, and reported a plan, which contained such an enlargement of the principles of the confederation, as gave the new system the aspect of an entire transformation of the old.[15] The mild tone of requisition was exchanged for the active operations of power, and the features of a federal council for those of a national sovereignty. These concessions it was seen were, in many instances, beyond the power of the state legislatures, (limited by their respective constitutions) to make, without the express assent of the people. A convention was therefore summoned, in every state

14. Federalist, vol. II. p. 26. 27.
15. Federalist, vol. II. p. 33.

by the authority of their respective legislatures, to consider of the propriety of adopting the proposed plan; and their assent made it binding in each state; and the assent of nine states rendered it obligatory upon all the states adopting it. Here then are all the features of an original compact, not only between the body politic of each state, but also between the people of those states in their highest sovereign capacity.

Whether this original compact be considered as merely federal, or social, and national, it is that instrument by which power is created on the one hand, and obedience exacted on the other. As federal it is to be construed strictly, in all cases where the antecedent rights of a state may be drawn in question;[16] as a social compact it ought likewise to receive the same strict construction, wherever the right of personal liberty, of personal security, or of private property may become the subject of dispute; because every person whose liberty, or property was thereby rendered subject to the new government, was antecedently a member of a civil society to whose regulations he had submitted himself, and under whose authority and protection he still remains, in all cases not expressly submitted to the new government.[17] The few particular cases in which he submits himself to the new authority, therefore, ought not to be extended beyond the terms of the compact, as it might endanger his obedience to that state to whose laws he still continues to owe obedience; or may subject him to a double loss, or inconvenience for the same cause.

And here it ought to be remembered that no case of municipal law can arise under the constitution of the United States, except such as are expressly comprehended in that instrument. For the municipal law of one state or nation has no force or obligation in any other nation; and when several states, or nations unite themselves together by a federal compact, each retains its own municipal laws, without admitting or adopting those of any other member of the union, unless there be an article expressly to that effect. The municipal laws of the several American states differ essentially from each other; and as neither is entitled to a preference over the other, on the score of intrinsic superiority, or obligation, and as there is no article in the compact which bestows any such preference upon any, it follows, that the municipal laws of no one state can be resorted to as a general rule for the rest. And as the states, and their respective legislatures are absolutely independent of each other, so neither can any common rule be extracted from their several municipal codes. For, although concurrent laws, or rules may perhaps be met within their codes, yet it is in the power of their legislatures, respectively to destroy that concurrence at any time, by enacting an entire new law on the subject; so that it may happen that that which is a concurrent law in all the states today may cease to be law in one, or more of them tomorrow. Consequently neither the particular municipal law of any one, or more, of the states, nor the concurrent municipal laws of the whole of them, can be considered as the common rule, or measure of justice in the courts of the federal republic; neither hath the federal government any power to establish such a common rule, generally; no such power being granted by the constitution. And the principle is certainly much stronger, that neither the common nor statute law of any other nation, ought to be a standard for the proceedings of this, unless previously made its own by legislative adoption[18]: which, not being permitted by the original compact, by which the government is created, any attempt to introduce it, in that or any other mode, would be a manifest breach of the terms of that compact.

Another light in which this subject may be viewed is this. Since each state in becoming a member of a federal republic retains an uncontrolled jurisdiction over all cases of municipal law, every grant of jurisdiction to the confederacy, in any such case, is to be considered as special, inasmuch as it derogates from the antecedent rights and jurisdiction of the state making the concession, and therefore ought to be construed strictly, upon the grounds already mentioned. Now, the cases falling under the head of municipal law, to which the authority of the federal government extends, are few, definite, and enumerated, and are all carved out of the sovereign authority, and former exclusive, and uncontrollable jurisdiction of the states respectively: they ought therefore to receive the strictest construction. Otherwise the gradual and sometimes imperceptible usurpations of power, will end in the total disregard of all its intended limitations.

If it be asked, what would be the consequence in case the federal government should exercise powers not warranted by the constitution, the answer seems

16. Vattel, B. 2. c. 17. §. 305, 308. Amendments to the C.U.S. art. 12.

17. Vattel, ibid. Amendments, C.U.S. art. 11. 12.

18. Federalist, p. 50.

to be, that where the act of usurpation may immediately affect an individual, the remedy is to be sought by recourse to that judiciary, to which the cognizance of the case properly belongs. Where it may affect a state, the state legislature, whose rights, will be invaded by every such act, will be ready to mark the innovation and sound the alarm to the people[19]: and thereby either effect a change in the federal representation, or procure in the mode prescribed by the constitution, further "declaratory and restrictive clauses," by way of amendment thereto. An instance of which may be cited in the conduct of the Massachusetts legislature: who, as soon as that state was sued in the federal court, by an individual, immediately proposed, and procured an amendment to the constitution, declaring that the judicial power of the United States shall not be construed to extend to any suit brought by an individual against a state.

5. It is a written contract; considered as a federal compact, or alliance between the states, there is nothing new or singular in this circumstance, as all national compacts since the invention of letters have probably been reduced to that form: but considered in the light of an original, social, compact, it may be worthy of remark, that a very great lawyer, who wrote but a few years before the American revolution, seems to doubt whether the original contract of society had in any one instance been formally expressed at the first institution of a state.[20] The American revolution seems to have given birth to this new political phenomenon: in every state a written constitution was framed, and adopted by the people, both in their individual and sovereign capacity, and character. By this means, the just distinction between the sovereignty, and the government, was rendered familiar to every intelligent mind; the former was found to reside in the people, and to be unalienable from them; the latter in their servants and agents: by this means, also, government was reduced to its elements; its object was defined, its principles ascertained; its powers limited, and fixed; its structure organized; and the functions of every part of the machine so clearly designated, as to prevent any interference, so long as the limits of each were observed. The same reasons operated in behalf of similar restrictions in the federal constitution. Whether considered as the act of the body politic of the several states, or, of the people of the states, respectively, or, of the

people of the United States, collectively. Accordingly we find the structure of the government, its several powers and jurisdictions, and the concessions of the several states, generally, pretty accurately defined, and limited. But to guard against encroachments on the powers of the several states, in their politic character, and of the people, both in their individual and sovereign capacity, an amendatory article was added, immediately after the government was organized, declaring; that the powers not delegated to the United States, by the constitution, nor prohibited by it to the states, are reserved to the states, respectively, or to the people.[21] And, still further, to guard the people against constructive usurpations and encroachments on their rights, another article declares; that the enumeration of certain rights in the constitution, shall not be construed to deny, or disparage, others retained by the people.[22] The sum of all which appears to be, that the powers delegated to the federal government, are, in all cases, to receive the most strict construction that the instrument will bear, where the rights of a state or of the people, either collectively, or individually, may be drawn in question.

The advantages of a written constitution, considered as the original contract of society must immediately strike every reflecting mind; power, when undefined, soon becomes unlimited; and the disquisition of social rights where there is no text to resort to, for their explanation, is a task, equally above ordinary capacities, and incompatible with the ordinary pursuits, of the body of the people. But, as it is necessary to the preservation of a free government, established upon the principles of a representative democracy, that every man should know his own rights, it is also indispensably necessary that he should be able, on all occasions, to refer to them. In those countries where the people have been deprived of the sovereignty, and have no share, even in the government, it may perhaps be happy for them, so long as they remain in a state of subjection, to be ignorant of their just rights. But where the sovereignty is, confessedly, vested in the people, government becomes a subordinate power, and is the mere creature of the people's will: it ought therefore to be so constructed, that its operations may be the subject of constant observation, and scrutiny. There should be no hidden machinery, nor secret spring about it.

---

19. Federalist vol. 2. 74.
20. 1. Blacks. Com. 47.

21. Amendments to C.U.S. art. 12.
22. Ibidem. art. 11.

The boasted constitution of England, has nothing of this visible form about it; being purely constructive, and established upon precedents or compulsory concessions betwixt parties at variance. The several powers of government, as has been elsewhere observed, are limited, though in an uncertain way, with respect to each other; but the three together are without any check in the constitution, although neither can be properly called the representative of the people. And from hence, the union of these powers in the parliament hath given occasion to some writers of that nation to stile it omnipotent: by which figure it is probable they mean no more, than to inform us that the sovereignty of the nation resides in that body; having by gradual and immemorial usurpations been completely wrested from the people.

6. It is a compact freely, voluntarily, and solemnly entered into by the several states, and ratified by the people thereof, respectively: freely, there being neither external, nor internal force, or violence to influence, or promote the measure; the United States being at peace with all the world, and in perfect tranquility in each state: voluntarily, because the measure had its commencement in the spontaneous acts of the state-legislatures, prompted by a due sense of the necessity of some change in the existing confederation: and, solemnly, as having been discussed, not only by the general convention who proposed, and framed it; but afterwards in the legislatures of the several states, and finally, in the conventions of all the states, by whom it was adopted and ratified.

The progress of this second revolution in our political system was extremely rapid. Its origin may be deduced from three distinct sources: The discontents of the army, and other public creditors; . . . the decay of commerce, which had been diverted from its former channels; and the backwardness, or total neglect of the state-legislatures in complying with the requisitions, or recommendations of congress.

The discontents of the army had at several periods, during the war, risen to an alarming height, and threatened, if not a total revolt, at least a general disbandment. They were checked, or palliated by various temporary expedients and resolves of congress; but, not long before the cessation of hostilities, some late applications to congress, respecting the arrears of their pay and depreciation, not having produced the desired effect; an anonymous address to the army, couched in the most nervous language of complaint, made its appearance

in camp;[23] it contained a most spirited recapitulation of their services, grievances, and disappointments, and concluded with advising, "an appeal from the justice to the fears of government." The effects, naturally to have been apprehended from so animated a performance, addressed to men who felt their own injuries in every word, were averted by the prudence of the commander in chief;[24] and congress, as far as in them lay, endeavoured to do ample justice to the army; which was soon after entirely disbanded: but, as congress had not the command of any revenue, requisitions to the states were the only mode, by which funds for the discharge of so honorable a debt, could be procured. The states, already exhausted by a long and burthensome war, were either in no condition to comply with the recommendations of congress, or were so tardy and parsimonious in furnishing the supplies required, that the clamors against the government became every day louder and louder. Every creditor of government, of which there were thousands, besides the army now dispersed among the citizens, became an advocate for the change of such an inefficient government, from which they saw it was in vain to hope for satisfaction of their various demands.

But it is not probable that the discontents or clamors of the creditors of government, alone, would have been sufficient to effectuate a fundamental change in the government, had not other causes conspired to render its inefficiency the subject of observation and complaint, among another very numerous class of citizens . . . these were the commercial part of the people, inhabiting almost exclusively all the sea-ports, and other towns on the continent, and dispersed at small intervals through the whole country. The New-England states, in a great measure, dependent upon commerce, had before the war enjoyed a free trade with the West-India Islands, subject to the crown of Great-Britain; they had likewise maintained a very beneficial intercourse with the French Islands, from whence they drew supplies of molasses for their distilleries. The whale and cod-fisheries might be said to have been almost monopolized by them, on the American coast; at least the ad-

23. See the Remembrancer vol. 18. p. 72. Carey's Museum vol. 1. 302.

24. Ibidem, p. 120. Had General Washington no other claim to the gratitude of his country, his conduct on that occasion, alone, would have entailed an unextinguishable debt of gratitude upon it, to all posterity.

vantages they enjoyed for carrying on these branches of trade, bade fair to exclude every other nation from a competition with them on their native coasts. New-York and Pennsylvania had likewise the benefit of an advantageous fur-trade, through the channels lately occupied by the British posts, on the frontiers of the United States, which by the treaty of peace were to have been evacuated with all convenient speed. The possession of these being still retained, and the utmost vigilance exerted by the British government to prevent any communication with the Indian country; that very lucrative branch of the trade of the United States had been wholly diverted into the channel of Canada.... The ports of the English West-India Islands, which, it was expected would have been open to our vessels, as before the revolution, were, immediately after the conclusion of the peace, strictly prohibited to the American traders: ... those of the French islands were under such restrictions as greatly impaired the former advantageous intercourse with them: ... The protection formerly enjoyed under the British flag from the depredations of the corsairs of the Barbarian states, being now withdrawn, the commerce with the Mediterranean and the ports bordering thereupon, whither a great part of the produce of the fisheries, as well as the surplus of grain, was exported, was entirely cut off, from the danger of annoyance from those piratical states.... Great-Britain had, formerly, not only afforded a market for the whale oil, but had given a liberal bounty on it, both of which she now ceased to do, and no other country could be found to supply either of these advantages. Thus the sources of commerce in those states, were either dried up, or obstructed on every side, and the discontents prevailing among the newly liberated states, were little short of those of the Israelites in the wilderness.... Commotions in the northern states, seemed to threaten a repetition of the horrors of a civil war; these were ascribed to the inadequacy of the general government to secure or promote the interest and prosperity of the federal union: but whether their origin was not also to be ascribed to the administration of the state governments, is at least highly questionable.

The little regard which was paid to the requisitions of congress for money from the states, to discharge the interest of the national debt, and in particular that part due to foreigners, or foreign states, and to defray the ordinary expenses of the federal government, gave rise to a proposition,[25] that congress should be authorized, for the period of twenty-five years, to impose a duty of five percent on all goods imported into the United States. Most of the states had consented to the measure,[26] but the number required by the confederation could not be prevailed on to adopt it: New-York and Rhode-Island were particularly opposed to it. Thus a project which might perhaps have answered every beneficial purpose, proposed afterwards by the new constitution, was disconcerted, from the jealousy of granting a limited power for a limited time, by the same people, who, within three years after, surrendered a much larger portion of the rights of sovereignty without reserve.

In addition to this measure, congress in their act of April 18th, 1783, had proposed, that the eighth article of the confederation, which made the value of lands the ratio of contribution from the several states, should be revoked, and instead thereof the ratio should be fixed among the states, in proportion to the whole number of white inhabitants and three-fifths of all other persons, according to a triennial census. This proposition was agreed to in Virginia,[27] but like the former, was not acceded to by a sufficient number of the states to form an article of the confederation.... Yet this ratio is precisely the same, which has been since fixed by the new constitution as the rate by which direct taxes shall be imposed on the several states.

The total derangement of commerce, as well as of the finances of the United States, had proceeded to such lengths before the conclusion of the year 1785, that early in the succeeding year commissioners were appointed by the state of Virginia, to meet such commissioners as might be appointed by other states, for the purpose of "considering how far an uniform system in the commercial regulations may be necessary to their common interests, and their permanent harmony; and to report to the several states such an act, relative to that object, as when unanimously ratified by them, would enable congress effectually to provide for the same." The commissioners assembled at Annapolis accordingly, in September 1786, but were met only by commissioners from four of the other twelve states.... They considered the number of states represented to be too few to proceed to business ... but before they separated, wrote a letter to their constituents, recommending the appointment of deputies to meet in Philadelphia the succeeding May,

25. See Resolves of Congress, April 18th, 1783.

26. Oct. 1783, c. 31. Revised Code, p. 219. May 1784. c. 21.
27. Acts of 1784, c. 31.

for the purpose of extending the revision of the federal system to all its defects. . . .

In pursuance whereof the legislature of Virginia passed an act, appointing seven commissioners to meet such deputies as may be appointed by other states, to assemble, as recommended, and join in "devising and discussing, all such alterations, and further provisions as may be necessary to render the federal constitution adequate to the exigencies of the union; and in reporting such an act for that purpose to the United States in congress, as when agreed to by them, and duly confirmed by the several states, would effectually provide for the same."[28] Similar measures were adopted by all the states in the union, except Rhode Island: deputies assembled from all the other states; but instead of amendments to the confederation, they produced a plan for an entire change of the form of the federal government, and not without some innovation of its principles. The moment of its appearance all the enemies of the former government lifted up their voices in its favor. Party zeal never ran higher without an actual breach of the peace. Had the opposers of the proposed constitution been as violent as its advocates, it is not impossible that matters would have proceeded to some pernicious lengths: but the former were convinced that some change was necessary, which moderated their opposition; whilst the latter were animated in the pursuit of their favorite plan, from an apprehension that no other change was practicable. In several of the states, the question was decided in favor of the constitution by a very small majority of the conventions assembled to consider of its adoption. In North Carolina it was once rejected, and in Rhode Island twice: nor was it adopted by either, until the new government was organized by the ratifying states. Considerable amendments were proposed by several states; by the states of Massachusetts, South Carolina, Virginia, and New York, particularly. It was finally adopted by all the States, after having been the subject of consideration and discussion for a period little short of two years.[*]

I have said that the constitution was ratified by the conventions of the several states, assembled for the purpose of considering the propriety of adopting it. As the tenor of the instrument imports that it is the act of the people, and as every individual may, to a certain degree, be considered as a party to it, it will be necessary to add a few words on the subject of representation, and of the power which a majority have to bind the minority.

The right of suffrage is one of the most important rights of a free citizen; and in small states where the citizens can easily be collected together, this right ought never to be dispensed with on any great political question. But in large communities, such a measure, however desirable, is utterly impracticable, for reasons too obvious to be dwelt upon: hence the necessity that the people should appoint a smaller and more convenient number to represent the aggregate mass of the citizens. This is done not only for the purposes of ordinary legislation, but in large states, and on questions which require discussion and deliberation, is the most eligible mode of proceeding, even where the vote of every individual of the nation should be desired. Therefore, when the convention at Philadelphia had made their report, the ordinary legislatures, with great propriety, recommended the appointment of state-conventions, for the sole and especial purpose of considering the propriety of adopting the constitution, thus proposed by the convention of the states. The deputies in most of the counties were chosen according to the prevailing sentiments of the people in favor of the constitution, the opinions of the candidates being generally previously known. It is much to be wished that this had been universally the case, since the will of the people would in that case have been unequivocally expressed.

The right of the majority to bind the minority, results from a due regard to the peace of society; and the little chance of unanimity in large societies or assemblies, which, if obtainable, would certainly be very desirable; but inasmuch as that is not to be expected, whilst the passions, interests, and powers of reason remain upon their present footing among mankind, in all matters relating to the society in general, some mode must be adopted to supply the want of unanimity. The most reasonable and convenient seems to be, that the will of the majority should supply this defect; for if the will of the majority is not permitted to prevail in questions where the whole society is interested, that of the minority necessarily must. The society therefore, in such a case, would be under the influence of a minority of its members, which, generally speaking, can on no principle be justified.

It is true there are cases, even under our own constitution, where the vote of a bare majority is not permitted to take effect; but this is only in points which

28. Acts of 1786, c. 8.
* [Here Tucker adds a lengthy footnote quoting Virginia's notice of ratification and recommended amendments. —Ed.]

have, or may be presumed to have, received the sanction of a former majority, as where an alteration in the constitution is proposed. In order, therefore, to give the greater stability to such points, they are not permitted to be altered by a bare majority: in cases also which are to be decided by a few, but which may, nevertheless, affect a variety of interests, it was conceived to be safest to require the assent of more than a bare majority; as, in concluding treaties with foreign nations, where the interests of a few states may be vitally affected, while that of a majority may be wholly unconcerned. Or, lastly, where the constitution has reposed a corresponding trust in different bodies who may happen to disagree in opinion; as, where the president of the United States shall return a bill to congress with his reasons for refusing his assent to it; in all these cases more than a bare majority are required to concur in favor of any measure, before it can be carried into complete effect.

7th. It is a compact by which the several states and the people thereof, respectively, have bound themselves to each other, and to the federal government.

Having shewn that the constitution had its commencement with the body politic of the several states; and, that its final adoption and ratification was by the several legislatures referred to, and completed by conventions, especially called and appointed for that purpose, in each state; the acceptance of the constitution was not only an act of the body politic of each state, but of the people thereof respectively, in their sovereign character and capacity: the body politic was competent to bind itself so far as the constitution of the state permitted; but not having power to bind the people, in cases beyond their constitutional authority, the assent of the people was indispensably necessary to the validity of the compact, by which the rights of the people might be diminished, or submitted to a new jurisdiction, or in any manner affected. From hence, not only the body politic of the several states, but every citizen thereof, may be considered parties to the compact, and to have bound themselves reciprocally to each other, for the due observance of it; and, also to have bound themselves to the federal government, whose authority has been thereby created, and established.

8. Lastly. It is a compact by which the federal government is bound to the several states, and to every citizen of the United States.

Although the federal government can, in no possible view, be considered as a party to a compact made anterior to its existence, and by which it was, in fact,

created; yet as the creature of that compact, it must be bound by it, to its creators, the several states in the union, and the citizens thereof. Having no existence but under the constitution, nor any rights, but such as that instrument confers; and those very rights being in fact duties; it can possess no legitimate power, but such as is absolutely necessary for the performance of a duty, prescribed and enjoined by the constitution. Its duties, then, become the exact measure of its powers; and wherever it exerts a power for any other purpose, than the performance of a duty prescribed by the constitution, it transgresses its proper limits, and violates the public trust. Its duties, being moreover imposed for the general benefit and security of the several states, in their politic character; and of the people, both in their sovereign, and individual capacity, if these objects be not obtained, the government will not answer the end of its creation: it is therefore bound to the several states, respectively, and to every citizen thereof, for the due execution of those duties. And the observance of this obligation is enforced, by the solemn sanction of an oath, from all who administer the government.[29]

The constitution of the United States, then being that instrument by which the federal government hath been created; its powers defined, and limited; and the duties, and functions of its several departments prescribed; the government, thus established, may be pronounced to be a confederate republic, composed of several independent, and sovereign democratic states, united for their common defense, and security against foreign nations, and for the purposes of harmony, and mutual intercourse between each other; each state *retaining an entire liberty* of exercising, as it thinks proper, all those parts of its sovereignty, which are not mentioned in the constitution, or act of union, as parts that ought to be exercised in common. It is the supreme law of the land,[30] and as such binding upon the federal government; the several states; and finally upon all the citizens of the United States. . . . It can not be controlled, or altered without the express consent of the body politic of three fourths of the states in the union, or, of the people, of an equal number of the states. To prevent the necessity of an immediate appeal to the latter, a method is pointed out, by which amendments may be proposed and ratified by the concurrent act of two thirds of both houses of congress, and three fourths of the state legislatures;

29. C.U.S. Art. 2. §. 1. and Art. 6.
30. C.U.S. Art. 6.

but if congress should neglect to propose amendments in this way, when they may be deemed necessary, the concurrent sense of two thirds of the state legislatures may enforce congress to call a convention, the amendments proposed by which, when ratified by the conventions of three fourths of the states, become valid, as a part of the constitution. In either mode, the assent of the body politic of the states, is necessary, either to complete, or to originate the measure.[31]

Here let us pause a moment, and reflect on the peculiar happiness of the people of the United States, thus to possess the power of correcting whatever errors may have crept into the constitution, or may hereafter be discovered therein, without the danger of those tremendous scenes which have convulsed every nation of the earth, in their attempts to ameliorate their condition; a power which they have already more than once successfully exercised. "Americans," says a writer whom I have before quoted, "ought to look upon themselves, at present, as almost the sole guardians and trustees of republican freedom: for other nations are not, as we are, at leisure to show it in its true and most enticing form. Whilst we contemplate with a laudable delight, the rapid growth of our prosperity, let us ascribe it to its true cause, the wholesome operation of our new political philosophy. Whatever blessings we enjoy, over and above what are to be found under the British government, whatever evils we avoid, to which the people of that government are exposed; for all these advantages are we indebted to the separation that has taken place, and the new order of things that has obtained among us. Let us be thankful to the parent of the universe, that he has given us, the first enjoyment of that freedom, which is intended in due time for the whole race of man. Let us diligently study the nature of our situation, that we may better know how to preserve and improve its advantages. But above all, let us study the genuine principles of democracy, and steadily practice them, that we may refute the calumnies of those who would bring them into disgrace.

"Let us publish to the world, and let our conduct verify our assertions, that by democracy we mean not a state of licentiousness, nor a subversion of order, nor a defiance of legal authority. Let us convince mankind, that we understand by it, a well ordered government, endued with energy to fulfill all its intentions, to act with effect upon all delinquents, and to bring to punishment all offenders against the laws: but, at the same time, not a government of usurpation; not a government of prescription; but a government of compact, upon the ground of equal right, and equal obligation; in which the rights of each individual spring out of the engagement he has entered into, to perform the duties required of him by the community, whereby the same rights in others, are to be maintained inviolate."

That mankind have a right to bind themselves by their own voluntary acts, can scarcely be questioned: but how far have they a right to enter into engagements to bind their posterity likewise? Are the acts of the dead binding upon their living posterity, to all generations; or has posterity the same natural rights which their ancestors have enjoyed before them? And if they have, what right have any generation of men to establish any particular form of government for succeeding generations?

The answer is not difficult: "Government," said the congress of the American States, in behalf of their constituents, "derives its just authority from the consent of the governed." This fundamental principle then may serve as a guide to direct our judgment with respect to the question. To which we may add, in the words of the author of Common Sense, a law is not binding upon posterity, merely, because it was made by their ancestors; but, because posterity have not repealed it. It is the acquiescence of posterity under the law, which continues its obligation upon them, and not any right which their ancestors had to bind them.

Until, therefore, the people of the United States, whether the present, or any future generation, shall think it necessary to alter, or revoke the present constitution of the United States, it must be received, respected, and obeyed among us, as the great and unequivocal declaration of the will of the people, and the supreme law of the land.

. . .

Thus far the restrictions contained in the constitution extend: "The conventions of a number of the states having, at the time of adopting the constitution, expressed a desire, in order to prevent misconstruction, or abuse of its powers, that further declaratory and restrictive clauses should be added; and as extending the ground of public confidence in the government, will best ensure the beneficent ends of its institution."[32] The follow-

---

31. Ibidem, Art. 5.

32. Preamble to the amendments proposed by the 1 Cong. 1 Sess.

ing articles were proposed by congress, as amendments to the constitution, which having been duly ratified by the several states, now form a part thereof.

7. Congress shall make no law respecting an establishment of religion, or prohibiting the free exercise thereof, or abridging the freedom of speech, or of the press, or the right of the people peaceably to assemble, and to petition the government for a redress of grievances.... Amendments to C.U.S. Art. 3.

On the first of these subjects, our state bill of rights contains, what, if prejudice were not incapable of perceiving truth, might be deemed an axiom, concerning the human mind. That "religion, or the duty we owe to our Creator, and the manner of discharging it, can be dictated only by reason and conviction, not by force or violence." In vain, therefore, may the civil magistrate interpose the authority of human laws, to prescribe that belief, or produce that conviction, which human reason rejects: in vain may the secular arm be extended, the rack stretched, and the flames kindled, to realize the tortures denounced against unbelievers by all the various sects of the various denominations of fanatics and enthusiasts throughout the globe. The martyr at the stake, glories in his tortures, and proves that human laws may punish, but cannot convince. The pretext of religion, and the pretenses of sanctity and humility, have been employed throughout the world, as the most direct means of gaining influence and power. Hence the numberless martyrdoms and massacres which have drenched the whole earth, with blood, from the first moment that civil and religious institutions were blended together. To separate them by mounds which can never be overleaped, is the only means by which our duty to God, the peace of mankind, and the genuine fruits of charity and fraternal love, can be preserved or properly discharged. This prohibition, therefore, may be regarded as the most powerful cement of the federal government, or rather, the violation of it will prove the most powerful engine of separation. Those who prize the union of the states will never think of touching this article with unhallowed hands. The ministry of the unsanctified sons of Aaron scarcely produced a flame more sudden, more violent, or more destructive, than such an attempt would inevitably excite.... I forbear to say more, in this place, upon this subject, having treated of it somewhat at large in a succeeding note.

The second part of this clause provides, against any law, abridging the freedom of speech, or of the press.

It being one of the great fundamental principles of the American governments, that the people are the sovereign, and those who administer the government their agents, and servants, not their kings and masters, it would have been a political solecism to have permitted the smallest restraint upon the right of the people to inquire into, censure, approve, punish or reward their agents according to their merit, or demerit. The constitution, therefore, secures to them the unlimited right to do this, either by speaking, writing, printing, or by any other mode of publishing, which they may think proper. This being the only mode by which the responsibility of the agents of the public can be secured, and practically enforced, the smallest infringement of the rights guaranteed by this article, must threaten the total subversion of the government. For a representative democracy ceases to exist the moment that the public functionaries are by any means absolved from their responsibility to their constituents; and this happens whenever the constituent can be restrained in any manner from speaking, writing, or publishing his opinions upon any public measure, or upon the conduct of those who may advise or execute it.

Our state bill of rights declares, that the freedom of the press is one of the great bulwarks of liberty, and can never be restrained but by despotic governments. The constitutions of most of the other states in the union contain articles to the same effect. When the constitution of the United States was adopted by the convention of Virginia, they inserted the following declaration in the instrument of ratification: "that among other essential rights, the liberty of conscience, and of the press, cannot be cancelled, abridged, restrained, or modified by any authority of the United States."

An ingenious foreigner seems to have been a good deal puzzled to discover the law which establishes the freedom of the press in England: after many vain researches, he concludes, (very rightly, as it relates to that government,) that the liberty of the press there, is grounded on its not being prohibited.[33] But with us, there is a visible solid foundation to be met with in the constitutional declarations which we have noticed. The English doctrine, therefore, that the liberty of the press consists only in this, that there shall be no previous restraint laid upon the publication of anything which any person may think proper, as was formerly the case in that country, is not applicable to the nature of our government, and still less to the express tenor of the con-

33. De Lolme on the English constitution. 317 Phila. printed.

stitution. That this necessary and invaluable liberty has been sometimes abused, and "carried to excess; that it has sometimes degenerated into licentiousness, is seen and lamented; but the remedy has not been discovered. Perhaps it is an evil inseparable from the good to which it is allied: perhaps it is a shoot which cannot be stripped from the stalk, without wounding vitally the plant from which it is torn. However desirable those measures might be which correct without enslaving the press, they have never yet been devised in America."

It may be asked, is there no protection for any man in America from the wanton, malicious, and unfounded attacks of envenomed calumny? Is there no security for his good name? Is there no value put upon reputation? No reparation for an injury done to it?

To this we may answer with confidence, that the judicial courts of the respective states are open to all persons alike, for the redress of injuries of this nature; there, no distinction is made between one individual and another; the farmer, and the man in authority, stand upon the same ground: both are equally entitled to redress for any false aspersion on their respective characters, nor is there any thing in our laws or constitution which abridges this right. But the genius of our government will not permit the federal legislature to interfere with the subject; and the federal courts are, I presume, equally restrained by the principles of the constitution, and the amendments which have since been adopted.

Such, I contend, is the true interpretation of the constitution of the United States: it has received a very different interpretation both in congress and in the federal courts. This will form a subject for a discussion on the freedom of the press, which the student will find more at large in another place.

The same article secures to the people the right of assembling peaceably; and of petitioning the government for the redress of grievances. The convention of Virginia proposed an article expressed in terms more consonant with the nature of our representative democracy, declaring, that the people have a right, peaceably to assemble together to consult for their common good, or to instruct their representatives: that every freeman has a right to petition, or apply to the legislature, for the redress of grievances. This is the language of a free people asserting their rights: the other savors of that style of condescension, in which favors are supposed to be granted. In England, no petition to the king, or either house of parliament for any alteration in church or state, shall be signed by above twenty persons, unless the matter thereof be approved by three justices of the peace, or a major part of the grand-jury in the county; nor be presented by more than ten persons. In America, there is no such restraint.

8. A well regulated militia being necessary to the security of a free state, the right of the people to keep, and bear arms, shall not be infringed. Amendments to C.U.S. Art. 4.

This may be considered as the true palladium of liberty.... The right of self defense is the first law of nature: in most governments it has been the study of rulers to confine this right within the narrowest limits possible. Wherever standing armies are kept up, and the right of the people to keep and bear arms is, under any color or pretext whatsoever, prohibited, liberty, if not already annihilated, is on the brink of destruction. In England, the people have been disarmed, generally, under the specious pretext of preserving the game: a never failing lure to bring over the landed aristocracy to support any measure, under that mask, though calculated for very different purposes. True it is, their bill of rights seems at first view to counteract this policy: but the right of bearing arms is confined to protestants, and the words suitable to their condition and degree, have been interpreted to authorize the prohibition of keeping a gun or other engine for the destruction of game, to any farmer, or inferior tradesman, or other person not qualified to kill game. So that not one man in five hundred can keep a gun in his house without being subject to a penalty.

9. No soldier shall in time of peace be quartered in any house without the consent of the owner; nor in time of war, but in a manner to be prescribed by law. Amendments to C.U.S. Art. 5.

Our state bill of rights, conforming to the experience of all nations, declares, that standing armies in time of peace, should be avoided as dangerous to liberty; this article of the constitution, seems by a kind of side wind, to countenance, or at least, not to prohibit them. The billeting of soldiers upon the citizens of a state, has been generally found burthensome to the people, and so far as this article may prevent that evil it may be deemed valuable; but it certainly adds nothing to the national security.

10. The right of the people to be secure in their persons, houses, papers, and effects, against unreasonable searches and seizures, shall not be violated; and no warrant shall issue, but upon probable cause supported by oath, or affirmation, and particularly describing the place to be searched, and the person or things

to be seized. Amendments to C.U.S. Art. 6, and herewith agrees the tenth article of our state bill of rights.

The case of general warrants, under which term all warrants not comprehended within the description of the preceding article may be included, was warmly contested in England about thirty or thirty-five years ago, and after much alteration they were finally pronounced to be illegal by the common law.[34] The constitutional sanction here given to the same doctrine, and the test which it affords for trying the legality of any warrant by which a man may be deprived of his liberty, or disturbed in the enjoyment of his property, cannot be too highly valued by a free people.

But, notwithstanding this constitutional sanction, and the security which it promises to all persons, an act passed during the second session of the fifth congress, entitled an act concerning aliens, which was supposed to violate this article of the constitution, in the most flagrant and unjustifiable degree: by authorizing the president of the United States to order all such aliens as he should judge dangerous to the peace and safety of the United States, or have reasonable grounds to suspect of any treasonable or secret machinations against the government thereof, to depart out of the territory of the United States within a limited time; and in case of disobedience, every alien so ordered was liable on conviction to be imprisoned for any term not exceeding three years. And any alien so ordered to depart, and remaining in the United States without a license from the president might be arrested, and sent out of them, by his order: and, in case of his voluntary return, might be imprisoned so long, as in the opinion of the president, the public safety might require. Alien friends, only, were the objects of this act, another act being passed at the same session, respecting alien enemies. . . . The general assembly of Virginia at their session in 1798, "protested against the palpable, and alarming infractions of the constitution in this act; which exercises a power no where delegated to the federal government; and which, by uniting legislative and judicial powers to those of executive, subverts the general principles of a free government, as well as the particular organization, and positive provisions of the federal constitution." Kentucky had before adopted a similar conduct.

Among the arguments used by the general assembly of Virginia in their strictures upon this act, the follow-

ing seem to be more peculiarly apposite to the subject of this article.

In the administration of preventive justice, the following principles have been held sacred; that some probable ground of suspicion be exhibited before some judicial authority; that it be supported by oath or affirmation; that the party may avoid being thrown into confinement, by finding pledges or securities for his legal conduct, sufficient in the judgment of some judicial authority; that he may have the benefit of a writ of habeas corpus, and thus obtain his release, if wrongfully confined; and that he may at any time be discharged from his recognizance, or his confinement, and restored to his former liberty and rights, on the order of the proper judicial authority; if it shall see sufficient cause.[35]

Let the student diligently compare these principles of the only preventive justice known to American jurisprudence, and he will probably find that they are all violated by the alien act. The ground of suspicion is to be judged of, not by any judicial authority, but by the executive magistrate, alone; no oath, or affirmation is required; if the suspicion be held reasonable by the president, (whatever be the grounds of it) he may order the suspected alien to depart, without the opportunity of avoiding the sentence by finding pledges for his future good conduct, as the president may limit the time of departure as he pleases, the benefit of the writ of habeas corpus may be suspended with respect to the party, although the constitution ordains, that it shall not be suspended, unless when the public safety may require it, in case of rebellion, or invasion, neither of which existed at the passage of that act: and the party being, under the sentence of the president, either removed from the United States, or punished by imprisonment, or disqualification ever to become a citizen on conviction of his not obeying the order of removal, or on returning without the leave of the president, he can not be discharged from the proceedings against him, and restored to the benefits of his former situation, although the highest judicial authority should see the most sufficient cause for it.[36]

Among the reasons alleged by a committee of congress, in support of the constitutionality of the alien law, one was; "that the constitution was made for citizens, not for aliens, who of consequence have no rights under

34. See 3 Burrows Rep. 1743. 1 Blacks. Reports, 555. 4 Blacks Com. 291.

35. Report of the committee of the general assembly of Virginia, on the alien and sedition laws, January 20, 1800.

36. Report of the committee of the general assembly of Virginia, &c.

it, but remain in the country, and enjoy the benefit of the laws, not as matter of right, but merely as matter of favor and permission; which may be withdrawn whenever the government may judge their further continuance dangerous."[37]

To this it was answered; that, "although aliens are not parties to the constitution, it does not follow that the constitution has vested in Congress an absolute right over them; or that whilst they actually conform to it, they have no right to its protection. That if they had no rights under it, they might not only be banished, but even capitally punished, without a jury, or other incidents to a fair trial."[38] A doctrine so far from being sound, that a jury, one half of which shall be aliens, is allowed, it is believed, by the laws of every state, except in cases of treason. To which we may add that the word "persons" in this, and the subsequent articles of the amendments to the constitution, most clearly designate, that aliens, as persons, must be entitled to the benefits therein secured to all persons alike. . . . As we shall have occasion to mention the subject of this interesting controversy, again, in another place, I shall only add here, that the act was permitted to expire at the end of two years, without any attempt, I believe, to continue it.

11. No person shall be held to answer for a capital, or otherwise infamous crime, unless on a presentment, or indictment of a grand jury, except in cases arising in the land or naval forces, or in the militia in the time of war, or public danger; nor shall any person be subject for the same offense to be twice put in jeopardy of life or limb; nor be compelled in any criminal case, to be witness against himself, nor be deprived of life, liberty, or property, without due process of law; nor shall private property be taken for public use without just compensation. Amendments to C.U.S. Art. 7, and,

12. In all criminal prosecutions, the accused shall enjoy the right to a speedy and public trial, by an impartial jury of the state, and district, wherein the crime shall have been committed, which district shall have been previously ascertained by law, and to be informed of the nature and cause of the accusation; to be confronted with witnesses against him; to have compulsory process for obtaining witnesses in his favor, and to have the assistance of counsel for his defense. Amendments to C.U.S. Art. 8.

13. Excessive bail shall not be required, nor excessive fines imposed, nor cruel, and unusual punishments inflicted. Amendments to C.U.S. Art. 10.

The subjects of these three articles are so immediately connected with each other, that I have chosen not to separate them. The first may be considered as a liberal exposition, and confirmation of the principles of that important chapter of Magna Carta, which declares, *"Nullus liber Homo aliquo modo destruatur nisi per legale judicium parium suorum,"* which words, *aliquo modo destruatur*, according to Sir Edward Coke, include a prohibition not only of killing and maiming, but also of torturing, and of every oppression by color of legal authority: and the words liber Homo, extend to every one of the king's subjects, "be he ecclesiastical or temporal, free or bond, man or woman, old or young, or be he outlawed, excommunicated, or any other, without exception"[39] . . . for even a villein, as he tells us elsewhere, is comprehended under the term liber Homo, except against his lord.[40]

The common law maxim, that no man is to be brought in jeopardy of his life more than once for the same offense, is here rendered a fundamental law of the government of the United States; as, is also, that other inestimable maxim of the common law, that no man shall be compelled in any criminal case to give evidence against himself; that he shall, moreover, be informed of the nature and cause of his accusation: that he shall be confronted with the witnesses against him; that he shall have compulsory process for obtaining witnesses in his favor; . . . a benefit long denied by the courts in England: and that he shall have the assistance of counsel for his defense; . . . not as a matter of grace, but of right; . . . not for his partial defense, upon a point of law, but for his full defense, both on the law, and the evidence: and, that he shall, in no case, be deprived of life, liberty, or property, without due process of law. To all which, is added, the inestimable right of a trial by jury, of the state and district in which the crime shall have been committed. The importance of all which articles will more evidently appear, in the course of our examination of the various subjects to which they relate, in the first and fourth book of the Commentaries on the Laws of England. That part of the seventh article which declares that private property shall not be taken for public use, without just compensation, was probably intended to restrain the

37. Report of the committee of congress, on the petitions for the repeal of the alien and sedition laws; February 25, 1799.
38. Report of the Virginia assembly . . . ut supra.

39. 2 Inst. 55.
40. Ibid. c. 45.

arbitrary and oppressive mode of obtaining supplies for the army, and other public uses, by impressment, as was too frequently practiced during the revolutionary war, without any compensation whatever. A law of the state of Virginia describes by whom, and in what cases, impresses may be made; and authorizes the commitment of the offender in case of any illegal impressment.[41]

We have already noticed the act concerning aliens,[42] as violating the sixth article of the amendments to the constitution. It was said, moreover, to violate the seventh and eighth. To this the congress answered, "that the provisions in the constitution relative to presentment and trial of offenses by juries, do not apply to the revocation of an asylum given to aliens. Those provisions solely respect crimes, and the alien may be removed without having committed any offense, merely from motives of policy, or security. The citizen, being a member of society, has a right to remain in the country, of which he cannot be disfranchised, except for offenses first ascertained, on presentment and trial by jury. . . . That the removal of aliens, though it may be inconvenient to them, cannot be considered as a punishment inflicted for an offense, but merely the removal, from motives of general safety, of an indulgence, which there is danger of their abusing, and which we are in no manner bound to grant or continue."[43]

To these arguments the general assembly of Virginia replied; that it can never be admitted that the removal of aliens authorized by the act, is to be considered, not as a punishment for an offense, but as a measure of precaution and prevention. If the banishment of an alien from a country into which he has been invited, as the asylum most auspicious to his happiness; a country where he may have formed the most tender connections, where he may have vested his entire property, and acquired property of the real and permanent, as well as the moveable and temporary kind; where he enjoys under the laws, a greater share of the blessings of personal security, and personal liberty, than he can elsewhere hope for, and where he may have nearly completed his probationary title to citizenship; if, moreover, in the execution of the sentence against him, he is to be exposed, not only to the ordinary dangers of sea, but to the peculiar casualties incident to a crisis of war, and of unusual licentiousness on that element, and pos-

sibly to vindictive purposes which his emigration itself may have provoked; if a banishment of this sort be not a punishment, and among the severest of punishments, it will be difficult to imagine a doom, to which the name can be applied. And, if it be a punishment, it will remain to be shown, whether, according to the express provisions of these articles, it can be constitutionally inflicted, on mere suspicion, by the single will of the executive magistrate, on persons convicted of no personal offense against the laws of the land, nor involved in any offense against the law of nations, charged on the foreign state of which they were members.[44]

14. In suits at common law, where the value in controversy shall exceed twenty dollars, the right of trial by jury shall be preserved, and no fact tried by a jury shall be otherwise reexamined in any court of the United States than according to the rules of the common law. C.U.S. Art. 9, Amendments.

This article provides for the trial by jury in civil cases, as well as criminal, and supplies some omission in the constitution.

15. The enumeration in the constitution, of certain rights, shall not be construed to deny, or disparage others retained by the people. Amendments to C.U.S. Art. 11, and,

16. The powers not delegated to the United States by the constitution, nor prohibited by it to the states, are reserved to the states respectively, or to the people. C.U.S. Art. 12, Amendments.

All the powers of the federal government being either expressly enumerated, or necessary and proper to the execution of some enumerated power; and it being one of the rules of construction which sound reason has adopted; that, as exception strengthens the force of a law in cases not excepted, so enumeration weakens it, in cases not enumerated; it follows, as a regular consequence, that every power which concerns the right of the citizen, must be construed strictly, where it may operate to infringe or impair his liberty; and liberally, and for his benefit, where it may operate to his security and happiness, the avowed object of the constitution: and, in like manner, every power which has been carved out of the states, who, at the time of entering into the confederacy, were in full possession of all the rights of sovereignty, is in like manner to be construed strictly, wherever a different construction might

41. L. V. Edi. 1794, c. 121.
42. L.U.S. 5 Cong. c. 75.
43. Report of the committee of congress, February 25, 1799.

44. Report of the committee of the general assembly of Virginia, on the alien and sedition laws . . . January 20, 1800.

derogate from the rights and powers, which by the latter of these articles, are expressly acknowledged to be reserved to them respectively.

The want of a bill of rights was among the objections most strongly urged against the constitution in its original form. The author of the Federalist undertakes to show, that a bill of rights was not only unnecessary, but would be dangerous.[45] A bill of rights may be considered, not only as intended to give law, and assign limits to a government about to be established, but as giving information to the people. By reducing speculative truths to fundamental laws, every man of the meanest capacity and understanding may learn his own rights, and know when they are violated; a circumstance, of itself, sufficient, I conceive, to counterbalance every argument against one.

To comprehend the full scope and effect of the twelfth article, by which certain rights are said to be reserved to the states respectively, or to the people, it is to be recollected, that there are powers, exercised by most other governments, which in the United States are withheld by the people, both from the federal government and from the state governments: for instance, a tax on exports can be laid by no constitutional authority whatever, whether of the United States, or of any state; no bill of attainder, or ex post facto law can be passed by either; no title of nobility can be granted by either. Many other powers of government are neither delegated to the federal government, nor prohibited to the states, either by the federal or state constitutions. These belong to that indefinite class of powers which are supposed necessarily to devolve upon every government, in consequence of the very act of its establishment, where no restrictions are imposed on the exercise of them; such as the power of regulating the course in which property may be transmitted by deed, will, or inheritance; the manner in which debts may be recovered, or injuries redressed; the right of defining and punishing offenses against the society, other than such as fall under the express jurisdiction of the federal government; all which, and all others of a similar nature are reserved to, and may be exercised by the state governments. From those powers, which are in express terms granted to the United States, and though not prohibited to the states respectively, are not susceptible of a concurrent exercise of authority by them, the states, notwithstanding this article, will continue to be excluded; such is the power to regulate commerce, and to define and punish piracies and felonies committed upon the high seas; from which the states, respectively, are by necessary and unavoidable construction excluded from any share or participation. On the other hand, such of the powers granted by the constitution to the federal government, as will admit of a concurrent exercise of authority, both in the federal and the state governments; such for example, as the right of imposing taxes, duties, and excises (except duties upon imports or exports, or upon tonnage, which the states cannot do without consent of congress) may be exercised by the states respectively, concurrently with the federal government. And here it may not be improper to take a short review of the powers which are expressly prohibited to the individual states by the constitution; or can be exercised by them only with the consent of congress; they have been enumerated elsewhere, but seem to require a more particular notice in this place.

1. First, then; no state shall enter into any treaty, alliance, or confederation. C.U.S. Art. 1. §. 10.

A similar provision was contained in the articles of confederation, the terms of which are in reality more strong and definite than those of the constitution. The federal government being the organ through which the individual states communicate with foreign nations, and the interest of the whole confederacy being paramount to that of any member thereof; the power of making treaties and alliances with foreign nations, is with propriety vested exclusively in the federal government. Moreover, as congress is vested with the power of admitting new states into the union, it was necessary to prohibit any alliance or confederacy with such state, antecedent to its admission into the union; for such an alliance might contravene the principles of the constitution, and prevent or retard the proposed admission. And lastly, to preserve the union entire, and unbroken, no partial confederacy between any two or more states, can be entered into: for that would in fact dissolve the government of the United States, as now established.

2. Secondly; no state shall, without the consent of congress, enter into any agreement or compact with another state, or with any foreign power. C.U.S. Art. 1. §. 10.

Here we find a distinction between treaties, alliances, and confederations; and agreements or compacts. The former relate ordinarily to subjects of great national magnitude and importance, and are often perpetual, or made for a considerable period of time;[46] the power of

45. Vol. II. 349.

46. See Vattel, 296, 297.

making these is altogether prohibited to the individual states: but agreements, or compacts, concerning transitory or local affairs, or such as cannot possibly affect any other interest but that of the parties, may still be entered into by the respective states, with the consent of congress. The compact between this state and Maryland, entered into in the year 1786, may serve as an example of this last class of public agreements.[47]

3. No state shall grant letters of marque or reprisal.[48]

As these measures ordinarily precede a declaration of war, the reasons for the total prohibition of the exercise of this power, by the states respectively, have been already mentioned: for otherwise the petulance and precipitation of any one state, whose citizens may have been injured by the subjects of a foreign nation, might plunge the union into a war.

4. No state shall, without consent of congress, keep troops, or ships of war, in time of peace; or engage in war, unless actually invaded, or in such imminent danger as will not admit of delay.[49]

The prohibitions contained in this clause are not absolute, but are subject to the consent of congress, or imperious circumstances. The setting on foot an army or navy, in the time of profound peace, is often a just cause of jealousy between neighboring, and even remote nations. But there is not infrequently a period between the commencement of a quarrel between two nations, and a declaration of war, or commencement of actual hostility, when prudence makes it necessary to prepare for the issue of the dispute. During such a period, it might be necessary to call for the exertions of the several states, in aid of the federal strength. At this epoch, it might be the summit of indiscretion to check the ardor of the respective states, if disposed to raise an army or navy from its own resources. Congress therefore may permit it; and if the danger of an attack upon any particular state be so imminent, as not to admit of delay, or if it be actually invaded, it may adopt measures for its own defense, without waiting for the consent of congress. And when a war is actually begun, under the authority of the federal union, any state may, according to its resources and discretion, keep any number of troops or ships: for the prohibition ceases as soon as war begins.

5. No state shall coin money: emit bills of credit, make any thing but gold and silver coin a tender in payment of debts: or pass any law impairing the obligation of contracts.[50]

The right of coining, and regulating the value of coin, being vested in the federal government, a participation in those rights could not be permitted to the respective states with any propriety. For the government must be responsible for the purity and weight of all coin issued under its authority: this could not be if the states were permitted to coin money according to the standard prescribed by the United States, as the officers of the mint would be under the directions of the state government. And if the several states were to issue coin of different standards, or denominations, the inconveniences to commerce would be infinite. They are therefore prohibited altogether from coining money. . . . The evils of paper money, the injury produced by it to public credit; the utter destruction of the fortunes of numberless individuals, by a rapid and unparalleled depreciation during the revolutionary war; the grievous hardships introduced, at the same period, by the tender laws, (an unhappy, but perhaps unavoidable expedient, to which both the federal, and state governments were constrained to have recourse, at the same time) by which a creditor was in some instances obliged to accept paper in a most depreciated state, for a just debt of an hundred times its real value, or incur the general odium of his fellow-citizens, probably gave rise to the prohibition against any state's emitting paper money, or making any thing but gold or silver a tender in payment of debts, or passing any law impairing the obligation of contracts. . . . But why was not the prohibition extended to the federal, as well as to the state governments? The federal government, during the revolutionary war, was not more exempt from just cause of censure upon these grounds, than the states respectively. Many of the laws passed by the states to support the credit of the continental money, by making it a tender in payment of debts, were passed on the recommendation of congress. The forty for one scheme originated there; why not prohibit some future congress from renewing the same breach of faith?

6. No state shall pass any bill of attainder, or ex post facto law; or grant any title of nobility. . . . Ibid.

These prohibitions being extended equally to the federal government, as to the states, have been already sufficiently noticed.

47. L. V. Edi. 1794, c. 18.
48. C.U.S. Art. 1. §. 10.
49. C.U.S. Art. 1. Sec. 10.

50. Ibidem.

7. No state shall, without the consent of congress, lay any imposts or duties on imports or exports, except what may be absolutely necessary for executing its inspection laws; and the net produce of all duties and imposts, laid by any state on imports, or exports, shall be for the use of the treasury of the United States: and all such laws shall be subject to the revision and control of congress. Nor shall any state, without the consent of congress lay any duty of tonnage.

On the subject of these prohibitions, respectively, sufficient hath already been said, under the article which authorizes congress to regulate commerce.

Having thus taken a survey of the powers delegated to the congress of the United States, and of those prohibited thereto, by the constitution; as also, of those, which are either altogether prohibited to the states, individually, or can be exercised by them only, with the consent, and under the control of congress; and in the course of that survey, having pointed out according to the best of my abilities, those powers which are exclusively vested in the federal government; secondly, those powers, in which the federal, and state governments, may be presumed to possess concurrent jurisdiction, and authority: thirdly, those powers which are equally prohibited to the states, respectively, or can be exercised by them only, with the approbation and consent of the federal government; it follows that all other powers of government compatible with the nature and principle of democratic governments, and not prohibited by the bill of rights, or constitution of the respective states, remain with them, and may be exercised by them, respectively, in such manner as their several constitutions, and laws, may permit, or direct. And this right, is expressly recognized, as before-mentioned, by the twelfth article of the amendments to the federal constitution; declaring, that the powers not delegated to the United States by the constitution, not prohibited by it to the states, are reserved to the states respectively, or to the people. This numerous class of powers relates altogether to the civil institutions, or laws of the states; and the subject of them forms their several municipal codes, according to the constitutions and laws of each state, respectively.

Here let us again pause, and reflect, how admirably this division, and distribution of legislative power is adapted to preserve the liberty, and to promote the happiness of the people of the United States; by assigning to the federal government, objects which relate only to the common interests of the states, as composing one general confederacy, or nation; and reserving to each member of that confederacy, a power over whatever may affect, or promote its domestic peace, happiness, or prosperity: at the same time limiting, and restraining both, from the exercises, or assumption of powers, which experience has demonstrated, either in this, or in other countries, to be too dangerous to be entrusted with any man or body of men whatsoever.... Restraints upon the power of the legislature, says De Lolme,[51] are more necessary than upon the executive; the former does in a moment, what the latter accomplishes only by successive steps. In England, all legislative power, without limitation, and without control, is concentrated in the two houses of parliament, with the king at their head; and their united power according to the maxims of that government, is omnipotent. In the United States, the great and essential rights of the people are secured against legislative as well as executive ambition.... They are secured, not by laws, only, which the legislature who makes them may repeal, and annul at its pleasure; but by constitutions, paramount to all laws: defining and limiting the powers of the legislature itself, and opposing barriers against encroachments, which it can not pass, without warning the people of their danger. Secondly, by that division, and distribution of power between the federal, and the state governments, by which each is in some degree made a check upon the excesses of the other. For although the states possess no constitutional negative upon the proceedings of the congress of the United States, yet it seems to be a just inference and conclusion, that as the powers of the federal government result from the compact to which the states are parties; and are limited by the plain sense of the instrument constituting that compact; they are no further valid, than as they are authorized by the grants enumerated therein: and, that in case of a deliberate, palpable, and dangerous exercise of other powers, not granted by that compact, the states, who are parties thereto, have the right, and are in duty bound, to interpose, for arresting the progress of the evil, and for maintaining within their respective limits, the authorities, rights, and liberties appertaining to them.[52] Thirdly, by the constitution of the legislative department itself, and the separation and division of powers, between the different branches,

51. On the British constitution, p. 164.
52. Resolutions of the general assembly of Virginia, December 21, 1798. Also the resolution of the general convention of Virginia, ratifying the constitution of the U. States ... for which see ante.

both of the congress, and of the state legislatures: in all which, an immediate dependence, either from the people, or the states, is happily, in a very great degree preserved. Fourthly, by the qualified negative which the constitution of the United States, gives to the president, upon all the proceedings of congress, except a question of adjournment. Fifthly, and lastly; by the separation of the judiciary from the legislative department; and the independence of the former, of the control, or influence of the latter, in any case where any individual may be aggrieved or oppressed, under color of an unconstitutional act of the legislature, or executive. In England, on the contrary, the greatest political object may be attained, by laws, apparently of little importance, or amounting only to a slight domestic regulation: the game-laws, as was before observed, have been converted into the means of disarming the body of the people: the statute *de donis conditionalibus* has been the rock, on which the existence and influence of a most powerful aristocracy, has been founded, and erected: the acts directing the mode of petitioning parliament, &c. and those for prohibiting riots: and for suppressing assemblies of free-masons, &c. are so many ways for preventing public meetings of the people to deliberate upon their public, or national concerns. The congress of the United States possesses no power to regulate, or interfere with the domestic concerns, or police of any state: it belongs not to them to establish any rules respecting the rights of property; nor will the constitution permit any prohibition of arms to the people; or of peaceable assemblies by them, for any purposes whatsoever, and in any number, whenever they may see occasion.

French People desiring to remove all Source of misunderstanding relative to objects of discussion mentioned in the Second and fifth articles of the Convention of the 8th Vendémiaire an 9 (30 September 1800) relative to the rights claimed by the United States in virtue of the Treaty concluded at Madrid the 27 of October 1795, between His Catholic Majesty & the Said United States, & willing to Strengthen the union and friendship which at the time of the Said Convention was happily reestablished between the two nations have respectively named their Plenipotentiaries to wit The President of the United States, by and with the advice and consent of the Senate of the Said States; Robert R. Livingston Minister Plenipotentiary of the United States and James Monroe Minister Plenipotentiary and Envoy extraordinary of the Said States near the Government of the French Republic; And the First Consul in the name of the French people, Citizen Francis Barbé Marbois Minister of the public treasury who after having respectively exchanged their full powers have agreed to the following Articles.

. . .

ARTICLE III

The inhabitants of the ceded territory shall be incorporated in the Union of the United States and admitted as soon as possible according to the principles of the federal Constitution to the enjoyment of all these rights, advantages and immunities of citizens of the United States, and in the mean time they shall be maintained and protected in the free enjoyment of their liberty, property and the Religion which they profess.

14

Louisiana Purchase Treaty

April 30, 1803*

TREATY BETWEEN THE UNITED STATES OF AMERICA AND THE FRENCH REPUBLIC

The President of the United States of America and the First Consul of the French Republic in the name of the

---

* Hunter Miller, ed., *Treaties and Other International Acts of the United States of America* (Washington, DC: Government Printing Office, 1931), 2:498–505.

15

Report and Resolutions of the Hartford Convention

January 4, 1815[*]

The Delegates from the Legislatures of the States of Massachusetts, Connecticut, and Rhode-Island, and from the Counties of Grafton and Cheshire in the State of New-Hampshire and the county of Windham in the State of Vermont, assembled in Convention, beg leave to report the following result of their conference.

The Convention is deeply impressed with a sense of the arduous nature of the commission which they were appointed to execute, of devising the means of defence against dangers, and of relief from oppressions proceeding from the act of their own Government, without violating constitutional principles, or disappointing the hopes of a suffering and injured people. To prescribe patience and firmness to those who are already exhausted by distress, is sometimes to drive them to despair, and the progress towards reform by the regular road, is irksome to those whose imaginations discern, and whose feelings prompt, to a shorter course.—But when abuses, reduced to system and accumulated through a course of years, have pervaded every department of Government, and spread corruption through every region of the State; when these are clothed with the forms of law, and enforced by an Executive whose will is their source, no summary means of relief can be applied without recourse to direct and open resistance. This experiment, even when justifiable, cannot fail to be painful to the good citizen; and the success of the effort will be no security against the danger of the example. Precedents of resistance to the worst administration, are eagerly seized by those who are naturally hostile to the best. Necessity alone can sanction a resort to this measure; and it should never be extended in duration or degree beyond the exigency, until the people, not

[*] *Proceedings of a Convention of Delegates from the States of Massachusetts, Connecticut, and Rhode Island, the Counties of Cheshire and Grafton in the State of New Hampshire and the County of Windham, in the State of Vermont, Convened at Hartford in the State of Connecticut, December 15, 1814* (Boston: Wells and Lilly, 1815), 3–22.

merely in the fervour of sudden excitement, but after full deliberation, are determined to change the Constitution.

It is a truth, not to be concealed, that a sentiment prevails to no inconsiderable extent, that Administration have given such constructions to that instrument, and practised so many abuses under colour of its authority, that the time for a change is at hand. Those who so believe, regard the evils which surround them as intrinsic and incurable defects in the Constitution. They yield to a persuasion, that no change, at any time, or on any occasion, can aggravate the misery of their country. This opinion may ultimately prove to be correct. But as the evidence on which it rests is not yet conclusive, and as measures adopted upon the assumption of its certainty might be irrevocable, some general considerations are submitted, in the hope of reconciling all to a course of moderation and firmness, which may save them from the regret incident to sudden decisions, probably avert the evil, or at least insure consolation and success in the last resort.

The Constitution of the United States, under the auspices of a wise and virtuous Administration, proved itself competent to all the objects of national prosperity; comprehended in the views of its framers. No parallel can be found in history, of a transition so rapid as that of the United States from the lowest depression to the highest felicity—from the condition of weak and disjointed republicks, to that of a great, united, and prosperous nation.

Although this high state of publick happiness has undergone a miserable and afflicting reverse, through the prevalence of a weak and profligate policy, yet the evils and afflictions which have thus been induced upon the country, are not peculiar to any form of Government. The lust and caprice of power, the corruption of patronage, the oppression of the weaker interests of the community by the stronger, heavy taxes, wasteful expenditures, and unjust and ruinous wars, are the natural offspring of bad Administrations, in all ages and countries. It was indeed to be hoped, that the rulers of these States would not make such disastrous haste to involve their infancy in the embarrassments of old and rotten institutions. Yet all this have they done; and their conduct calls loudly for their dismission and disgrace. But to attempt upon every abuse of power to change the Constitution, would be to perpetuate the evils of revolution.

Again, the experiment of the powers of the Constitution, to regain its vigour, and of the people to recover from their delusions, has been hitherto made under the greatest possible disadvantages arising from the state of the world. The fierce passions which have convulsed the nations of Europe, have passed the Ocean, and finding their way to the bosoms of our citizens, have afforded to Administration the means of perverting publick opinion, in respect to our foreign relations, so as to acquire its aid in the indulgence of their animosities, and increase of their adherents. Further, a reformation of publick opinion, resulting from dear bought experience, in the Southern Atlantick States, at least, is not to be despaired of. They will have felt, that the Eastern States cannot be made exclusively the victims of a capricious and impassioned policy.—They will have seen that the great and essential interests of the people, are common to the South and to the East. They will realize the fatal errours of a system, which seeks revenge for commercial injuries in the sacrifice of commerce, and aggravates by needless wars, to an immeasurable extent, the injuries it professes to redress. They may discard the influence of visionary theorists, and recognize the benefits of a practical policy. Indications of this desirable revolution of opinion, among our brethren in those States, are already manifested.—While a hope remains of its ultimate completion, its progress should not be retarded or stopped, by exciting fears which must check these favourable tendencies, and frustrate the efforts of the wisest and best men in those States, to accelerate this propitious change.

Finally, if the Union be destined to dissolution, by reason of the multiplied abuses of bad administrations, it should, if possible, be the work of peaceable times, and deliberate consent.—Some new form of confederacy should be substituted among those States, which shall intend to maintain a federal relation to each other.—Events may prove that the causes of our calamities are deep and permanent. They may be found to proceed, not merely from the blindness of prejudice, pride of opinion, violence of party spirit, or the confusion of the times; but they may be traced to implacable combinations of individuals, or of States, to monopolize power and office, and to trample without remorse upon the rights and interests of commercial sections of the Union. Whenever it shall appear that these causes are radical and permanent, a separation by equitable arrangement, will be preferable to an alliance by constraint, among nominal friends, but real enemies, in-flamed by mutual hatred and jealousies, and inviting by intestine divisions, contempt, and aggression from abroad. But a severance of the Union by one or more States, against the will of the rest, and especially in a time of war, can be justified only by absolute necessity. These are among the principal objections against precipitate measures tending to disunite the States, and when examined in connexion with the farewell address of the Father of his country, they must, it is believed, be deemed conclusive.

Under these impressions, the Convention have proceeded to confer and deliberate upon the alarming state of publick affairs, especially as affecting the interests of the people who have appointed them for this purpose, and they are naturally led to a consideration, in the first place, of the dangers and grievances which menace an immediate or speedy pressure, with a view of suggesting means of present relief; in the next place, of such as are of a more remote and general description, in the hope of attaining future security.

Among the subjects of complaint and apprehension, which might be comprised under the former of these propositions, the attention of the Convention has been occupied with the claims and pretensions advanced, and the authority exercised over the militia, by the executive and legislative departments of the National Government. Also, upon the destitution of the means of defence in which the Eastern States are left; while at the same time they are doomed to heavy requisitions of men and money for national objects.

The authority of the National Government over the militia is derived from those clauses in the Constitution which give power to Congress "to provide for calling forth the militia, to execute the laws of the Union, suppress insurrections and repel invasions"—Also, "to provide for organizing, arming and disciplining the militia, and for governing such parts of them as may be employed in the service of the United States, reserving to the States respectively the appointment of the officers, and the authority of training the militia according to the discipline prescribed by Congress." Again, "The President shall be Commander in Chief of the army and navy of the United States, and of the militia of the several States, when called into the actual service of the United States." In these specified cases only, has the National Government any power over the militia; and it follows conclusively, that for all general and ordinary purposes, this power belongs to the States respectively, and to them alone. It is not only with regret, but with astonishment, the Convention perceive that under colour of an authority conferred with such plain and precise limitations, a power is arrogated by the executive government, and in some instances sanctioned by the two Houses of Congress, of control over the militia, which if conceded, will render nugatory the rightful authority of the individual States over that class of men, and by placing at the disposal of the National Government the lives and services of the great body of the people, enable it at pleasure to destroy their liberties, and erect a military despotism on the ruins.

...

That acts of Congress in violation of the Constitution are absolutely void, is an undeniable position. It does not, however, consist with the respect and forbearance due from a confederate State towards the General Government, to fly to open resistance upon every infraction of the Constitution. The mode and the energy of the opposition should always conform to the nature of the violation, the intention of its authors, the extent of the injury inflicted, the determination manifested to persist in it, and the danger of delay. But in cases of deliberate, dangerous, and palpable infractions of the Constitution, affecting the sovereignty of a State, and liberties of the people; it is not only the right but the duty of such a State to interpose its authority for their protection, in the manner best calculated to secure that end. When emergencies occur which are either beyond the reach of the judicial tribunals, or too pressing to admit of the delay incident to their forms, States, which have no common umpire, must be their own judges, and execute their own decisions. It will thus be proper for the several States to await the ultimate disposal of the obnoxious measures, recommended by the Secretary of War, or pending before Congress, and so to use their power according to the character these measures shall finally assume, as effectually to protect their own sovereignty, and the rights and liberties of their citizens.

...

This Convention will not trust themselves to express their conviction of the catastrophe to which such a state of things inevitably tends. Conscious of their high responsibility to God and their country, solicitous for the continuance of the Union, as well as the sovereignty of the States, unwilling to furnish obstacles to peace—resolute never to submit to a foreign enemy, and confiding in the Divine care and protection, they will, until the last hope shall be extinguished, endeavour to avert such consequences.

...

THEREFORE RESOLVED—

That it be and hereby is recommended to the Legislatures of the several States represented in this Convention, to adopt all such measures as may be necessary effectually to protect the citizens of said States from the operation and effects of all acts which have been or may be passed by the Congress of the United States, which shall contain provisions, subjecting the militia or other citizens to forcible drafts, conscriptions, or impressments, not authorized by the Constitution of the United States.

Resolved, That it be and hereby is recommended to the said Legislatures, to authorize an immediate and earnest application to be made to the Government of the United States, requesting their consent to some arrangement, whereby the said States may, separately or in concert, be empowered to assume upon themselves the defence of their territory against the enemy; and a reasonable portion of the taxes, collected within said States, may be paid into the respective treasuries thereof, and appropriated to the payment of the balance due said States, and to the future defence of the same. The amount so paid into the said treasuries to be credited, and the disbursements made as aforesaid to be charged to the United States.

Resolved, That it be, and it hereby is, recommended to the Legislatures of the aforesaid States, to pass laws (where it has not already been done) authorizing the Governours or Commanders in Chief of their militia to make detachments from the same, or to form voluntary corps, as shall be most convenient and conformable to their Constitutions, and to cause the same to be well armed, equipped and disciplined, and held in readiness for service; and upon the request of the Governour of either of the other States, to employ the whole of such detachment or corps, as well as the regular forces of the State, or such part thereof as may be required and can be spared consistently with the safety of the State, in assisting the State, making such request to repel any invasion thereof which shall be made or attempted by the publick enemy.

Resolved, That the following amendments of the Constitution of the United States, be recommended to the States represented as aforesaid, to be proposed by them for adoption by the State Legislatures, and, in such cases as may be deemed expedient, by a Convention chosen by the people of each State.

And it is further recommended, that the said States shall persevere in their efforts to obtain such amendments, until the same shall be effected.

First. Representatives and direct taxes shall be apportioned among the several States which may be included within this union, according to their respective numbers of free persons, including those bound to serve for a term of years, and excluding Indians not taxed, and all other persons.

Second. No new State shall be admitted into the union by Congress in virtue of the power granted by the Constitution, without the concurrence of two thirds of both Houses.

Third. Congress shall not have power to lay any embargo on the ships or vessels of the citizens of the United States, in the ports or harbours thereof, for more than sixty days.

Fourth. Congress shall not have power, without the concurrence of two thirds of both Houses, to interdict the commercial intercourse between the United States and any foreign nation or the dependencies thereof.

Fifth. Congress shall not make or declare war, or authorize acts of hostility against any foreign nation, without the concurrence of two thirds of both Houses, except such acts of hostility be in defence of the territories of the United States when actually invaded.

Sixth. No person who shall hereafter be naturalized, shall be eligible as a member of the Senate or House of Representatives of the United States, nor capable of holding any civil office under the authority of the United States.

Seventh. The same person shall not be elected President of the United States a second time; nor shall the President be elected from the same State two terms in succession.

Resolved, That if the application of these States to the government of the United States, recommended in a foregoing Resolution, should be unsuccessful, and peace should not be concluded, and the defence of these States should be neglected, as it has been since the commencement of the war, it will in the opinion of this Convention be expedient for the Legislatures of the several States to appoint Delegates to another Convention, to meet at Boston, in the State of Massachusetts, on the third Thursday of June next, with such powers and instructions as the exigency of a crisis so momentous may require.

Resolved, That the Hon. George Cabot, the Hon. Chauncey Goodrich, and the Hon. Daniel Lyman, or any two of them, be authorized to call another meeting of this Convention, to be holden in Boston, at any time before new Delegates shall be chosen, as recommended in the above Resolutions, if in their judgment the situation of the Country shall urgently require it.

Hartford, January 4th, 1815.

16

McCulloch v. Maryland

17 U.S. 316 (1819)

MARSHALL, Chief Justice, delivered the opinion of the Court.

In the case now to be determined, the defendant, a sovereign State, denies the obligation of a law enacted by the legislature of the Union, and the plaintiff, on his part, contests the validity of an act which has been passed by the legislature of that State. The Constitution of our country, in its most interesting and vital parts, is to be considered; the conflicting powers of the Government of the Union and of its members, as marked in that Constitution, are to be discussed, and an opinion given, which may essentially influence the great operations of the Government. No tribunal can approach such a question without a deep sense of its importance, and of the awful responsibility involved in its decision. But it must be decided peacefully, or remain a source of hostile legislation, perhaps, of hostility of a still more serious nature; and if it is to be so decided, by this tribunal alone can the decision be made. On the Supreme Court of the United States has the Constitution of our country devolved this important duty.

The first question made in the cause is—has Congress power to incorporate a bank?

It has been truly said that this can scarcely be considered as an open question entirely unprejudiced by the former proceedings of the Nation respecting it. The principle now contested was introduced at a very early period of our history, has been recognised by many successive legislatures, and has been acted upon by the Judicial Department, in cases of peculiar delicacy, as a law of undoubted obligation.

It will not be denied that a bold and daring usurpation might be resisted after an acquiescence still longer and more complete than this. But it is conceived that a doubtful question, one on which human reason may pause and the human judgment be suspended, in the decision of which the great principles of liberty are not concerned, but the respective powers of those who are equally the representatives of the people, are to be adjusted, if not put at rest by the practice of the Government, ought to receive a considerable impression from that practice. An exposition of the Constitution, deliberately established by legislative acts, on the faith of which an immense property has been advanced, ought not to be lightly disregarded.

The power now contested was exercised by the first Congress elected under the present Constitution. The bill for incorporating the Bank of the United States did not steal upon an unsuspecting legislature and pass unobserved. Its principle was completely understood, and was opposed with equal zeal and ability. After being resisted first in the fair and open field of debate, and afterwards in the executive cabinet, with as much persevering talent as any measure has ever experienced, and being supported by arguments which convinced minds as pure and as intelligent as this country can boast, it became a law. The original act was permitted to expire, but a short experience of the embarrassments to which the refusal to revive it exposed the Government convinced those who were most prejudiced against the measure of its necessity, and induced the passage of the present law. It would require no ordinary share of intrepidity to assert that a measure adopted under these circumstances was a bold and plain usurpation to which the Constitution gave no countenance. These observations belong to the cause; but they are not made under the impression that, were the question entirely new, the law would be found irreconcilable with the Constitution.

In discussing this question, the counsel for the State of Maryland have deemed it of some importance, in the construction of the Constitution, to consider that instrument not as emanating from the people, but as the act of sovereign and independent States. The powers of the General Government, it has been said, are delegated by the States, who alone are truly sovereign, and must be exercised in subordination to the States, who alone possess supreme dominion.

It would be difficult to sustain this proposition. The convention which framed the Constitution was indeed elected by the State legislatures. But the instrument, when it came from their hands, was a mere proposal,

without obligation or pretensions to it. It was reported to the then existing Congress of the United States with a request that it might be submitted to a convention of delegates, chosen in each State by the people thereof, under the recommendation of its legislature, for their assent and ratification.

This mode of proceeding was adopted, and by the convention, by Congress, and by the State legislatures, the instrument was submitted to the people. They acted upon it in the only manner in which they can act safely, effectively and wisely, on such a subject by assembling in convention. It is true, they assembled in their several States—and where else should they have assembled? No political dreamer was ever wild enough to think of breaking down the lines which separate the States, and of compounding the American people into one common mass. Of consequence, when they act, they act in their States. But the measures they adopt do not, on that account, cease to be the measures of the people themselves, or become the measures of the State governments.

From these conventions the Constitution derives its whole authority. The government proceeds directly from the people; is "ordained and established" in the name of the people, and is declared to be ordained, in order to form a more perfect union, establish justice, insure domestic tranquility, and secure the blessings of liberty to themselves and to their posterity.

The assent of the States in their sovereign capacity is implied in calling a convention, and thus submitting that instrument to the people. But the people were at perfect liberty to accept or reject it, and their act was final. It required not the affirmance, and could not be negatived, by the State Governments. The Constitution, when thus adopted, was of complete obligation, and bound the State sovereignties.

It has been said that the people had already surrendered all their powers to the State sovereignties, and had nothing more to give. But surely the question whether they may resume and modify the powers granted to Government does not remain to be settled in this country. Much more might the legitimacy of the General Government be doubted had it been created by the States. The powers delegated to the State sovereignties were to be exercised by themselves, not by a distinct and independent sovereignty created by themselves. To the formation of a league such as was the Confederation, the State sovereignties were certainly competent. But when, "in order to form a more perfect union," it was deemed necessary to change this alliance into an effective Government, possessing great and sovereign powers and acting directly on the people, the necessity of referring it to the people, and of deriving its powers directly from them, was felt and acknowledged by all. The Government of the Union then (whatever may be the influence of this fact on the case) is, emphatically and truly, a Government of the people. In form and in substance, it emanates from them. Its powers are granted by them, and are to be exercised directly on them, and for their benefit.

This Government is acknowledged by all to be one of enumerated powers. The principle that it can exercise only the powers granted to it would seem too apparent to have required to be enforced by all those arguments which its enlightened friends, while it was depending before the people, found it necessary to urge; that principle is now universally admitted. But the question respecting the extent of the powers actually granted is perpetually arising, and will probably continue to arise so long as our system shall exist. In discussing these questions, the conflicting powers of the General and State Governments must be brought into view, and the supremacy of their respective laws, when they are in opposition, must be settled.

If any one proposition could command the universal assent of mankind, we might expect it would be this—that the Government of the Union, though limited in its powers, is supreme within its sphere of action. This would seem to result necessarily from its nature. It is the Government of all; its powers are delegated by all; it represents all, and acts for all. Though any one State may be willing to control its operations, no State is willing to allow others to control them. The nation, on those subjects on which it can act, must necessarily bind its component parts. But this question is not left to mere reason; the people have, in express terms, decided it by saying, "this Constitution, and the laws of the United States, which shall be made in pursuance thereof," "shall be the supreme law of the land," and by requiring that the members of the State legislatures and the officers of the executive and judicial departments of the States shall take the oath of fidelity to it. The Government of the United States, then, though limited in its powers, is supreme, and its laws, when made in pursuance of the Constitution, form the supreme law of the land, "anything in the Constitution or laws of any State to the contrary notwithstanding."

Among the enumerated powers, we do not find that of establishing a bank or creating a corporation. But there is no phrase in the instrument which, like the Articles of Confederation, excludes incidental or implied powers and which requires that everything granted shall be expressly and minutely described. Even the 10th Amendment, which was framed for the purpose of quieting the excessive jealousies which had been excited, omits the word "expressly," and declares only that the powers "not delegated to the United States, nor prohibited to the States, are reserved to the States or to the people," thus leaving the question whether the particular power which may become the subject of contest has been delegated to the one Government, or prohibited to the other, to depend on a fair construction of the whole instrument. The men who drew and adopted this amendment had experienced the embarrassments resulting from the insertion of this word in the Articles of Confederation, and probably omitted it to avoid those embarrassments. A Constitution, to contain an accurate detail of all the subdivisions of which its great powers will admit, and of all the means by which they may be carried into execution, would partake of the prolixity of a legal code, and could scarcely be embraced by the human mind. It would probably never be understood by the public. Its nature, therefore, requires that only its great outlines should be marked, its important objects designated, and the minor ingredients which compose those objects be deduced from the nature of the objects themselves. That this idea was entertained by the framers of the American Constitution is not only to be inferred from the nature of the instrument, but from the language. Why else were some of the limitations found in the 9th section of the 1st article introduced? It is also in some degree warranted by their having omitted to use any restrictive term which might prevent its receiving a fair and just interpretation. In considering this question, then, we must never forget that it is a Constitution we are expounding.

Although, among the enumerated powers of Government, we do not find the word "bank" or "incorporation," we find the great powers, to lay and collect taxes; to borrow money; to regulate commerce; to declare and conduct a war; and to raise and support armies and navies. The sword and the purse, all the external relations, and no inconsiderable portion of the industry of the nation are intrusted to its Government. It can never be pretended that these vast powers draw after them others of inferior importance merely because they are inferior. Such an idea can never be advanced. But it may

with great reason be contended that a Government intrusted with such ample powers, on the due execution
of which the happiness and prosperity of the Nation
so vitally depends, must also be intrusted with ample
means for their execution. The power being given, it is
the interest of the Nation to facilitate its execution. It
can never be their interest, and cannot be presumed
to have been their intention, to clog and embarrass its
execution by withholding the most appropriate means.
Throughout this vast republic, from the St. Croix to the
Gulf of Mexico, from the Atlantic to the Pacific, revenue is to be collected and expended, armies are to be
marched and supported. The exigencies of the Nation
may require that the treasure raised in the north should
be transported to the south, that raised in the east, conveyed to the west, or that this order should be reversed.
Is that construction of the Constitution to be preferred
which would render these operations difficult, hazard-
ous and expensive? Can we adopt that construction
(unless the words imperiously require it) which would
impute to the framers of that instrument, when granting these powers for the public good, the intention of
impeding their exercise, by withholding a choice of
means? If, indeed, such be the mandate of the Constitution, we have only to obey; but that instrument does not
profess to enumerate the means by which the powers it
confers may be executed; nor does it prohibit the creation of a corporation, if the existence of such a being
be essential, to the beneficial exercise of those powers.
It is, then, the subject of fair inquiry how far such means
may be employed.

It is not denied that the powers given to the Government imply the ordinary means of execution. That, for
example, of raising revenue and applying it to national
purposes is admitted to imply the power of conveying
money from place to place as the exigencies of the Nation may require, and of employing the usual means of
conveyance. But it is denied that the Government has its
choice of means, or that it may employ the most convenient means if, to employ them, it be necessary to erect
a corporation. On what foundation does this argument
rest? On this alone: the power of creating a corporation
is one appertaining to sovereignty, and is not expressly
conferred on Congress. This is true. But all legislative
powers appertain to sovereignty. The original power of
giving the law on any subject whatever is a sovereign
power, and if the Government of the Union is restrained
from creating a corporation as a means for performing
its functions, on the single reason that the creation of a

corporation is an act of sovereignty, if the sufficiency of
this reason be acknowledged, there would be some difficulty in sustaining the authority of Congress to pass
other laws for the accomplishment of the same objects. The Government which has a right to do an act
and has imposed on it the duty of performing that act
must, according to the dictates of reason, be allowed to
select the means, and those who contend that it may not
select any appropriate means that one particular mode
of effecting the object is excepted take upon themselves
the burden of establishing that exception.

The creation of a corporation, it is said, appertains
to sovereignty. This is admitted. But to what portion of
sovereignty does it appertain? Does it belong to one
more than to another? In America, the powers of sovereignty are divided between the Government of the
Union and those of the States. They are each sovereign
with respect to the objects committed to it, and neither
sovereign with respect to the objects committed to the
other. We cannot comprehend that train of reasoning,
which would maintain that the extent of power granted
by the people is to be ascertained not by the nature and
terms of the grant, but by its date. Some State Constitutions were formed before, some since, that of the United
States. We cannot believe that their relation to each
other is in any degree dependent upon this circumstance. Their respective powers must, we think, be precisely the same as if they had been formed at the same
time. Had they been formed at the same time, and had
the people conferred on the General Government the
power contained in the Constitution, and on the States
the whole residuum of power, would it have been asserted that the Government of the Union was not sovereign, with respect to those objects which were intrusted
to it, in relation to which its laws were declared to be
supreme? If this could not have been asserted, we cannot well comprehend the process of reasoning which
maintains that a power appertaining to sovereignty cannot be connected with that vast portion of it which is
granted to the General Government, so far as it is calculated to subserve the legitimate objects of that Government. The power of creating a corporation, though
appertaining to sovereignty, is not, like the power of
making war or levying taxes or of regulating commerce,
a great substantive and independent power which cannot be implied as incidental to other powers or used as
a means of executing them. It is never the end for which
other powers are exercised, but a means by which other
objects are accomplished. No contributions are made

to charity for the sake of an incorporation, but a corporation is created to administer the charity; no seminary of learning is instituted in order to be incorporated, but the corporate character is conferred to subserve the purposes of education. No city was ever built with the sole object of being incorporated, but is incorporated as affording the best means of being well governed. The power of creating a corporation is never used for its own sake, but for the purpose of effecting something else. No sufficient reason is therefore perceived why it may not pass as incidental to those powers which are expressly given if it be a direct mode of executing them.

But the Constitution of the United States has not left the right of Congress to employ the necessary means for the execution of the powers conferred on the Government to general reasoning. To its enumeration of powers is added that of making all laws which shall be necessary and proper for carrying into execution the foregoing powers, and all other powers vested by this Constitution in the Government of the United States or in any department thereof.

The counsel for the State of Maryland have urged various arguments to prove that this clause, though in terms a grant of power, is not so in effect, but is really restrictive of the general right which might otherwise be implied of selecting means for executing the enumerated powers. In support of this proposition, they have found it necessary to contend that this clause was inserted for the purpose of conferring on Congress the power of making laws. That, without it, doubts might be entertained whether Congress could exercise its powers in the form of legislation.

But could this be the object for which it was inserted? A Government is created by the people having legislative, executive and judicial powers. Its legislative powers are vested in a Congress, which is to consist of a senate and house of representatives. Each house may determine the rule of its proceedings, and it is declared that every bill which shall have passed both houses shall, before it becomes a law, be presented to the President of the United States. The 7th section describes the course of proceedings by which a bill shall become a law, and then the 8th section enumerates the powers of Congress. Could it be necessary to say that a legislature should exercise legislative powers, in the shape of legislation? After allowing each house to prescribe its own course of proceeding, after describing the manner in which a bill should become a law, would it have entered into the mind of a single member of the convention that

an express power to make laws was necessary to enable the legislature to make them? That a legislature, endowed with legislative powers, can legislate is a proposition too self-evident to have been questioned.

But the argument on which most reliance is placed is drawn from that peculiar language of this clause. Congress is not empowered by it to make all laws which may have relation to the powers conferred on the Government, but such only as may be "necessary and proper" for carrying them into execution. The word "necessary" is considered as controlling the whole sentence, and as limiting the right to pass laws for the execution of the granted powers to such as are indispensable, and without which the power would be nugatory. That it excludes the choice of means, and leaves to Congress in each case that only which is most direct and simple.

Is it true that this is the sense in which the word "necessary" is always used? Does it always import an absolute physical necessity so strong that one thing to which another may be termed necessary cannot exist without that other? We think it does not. If reference be had to its use in the common affairs of the world or in approved authors, we find that it frequently imports no more than that one thing is convenient, or useful, or essential to another. To employ the means necessary to an end is generally understood as employing any means calculated to produce the end, and not as being confined to those single means without which the end would be entirely unattainable. Such is the character of human language that no word conveys to the mind in all situations one single definite idea, and nothing is more common than to use words in a figurative sense. Almost all compositions contain words which, taken in their rigorous sense, would convey a meaning different from that which is obviously intended. It is essential to just construction that many words which import something excessive should be understood in a more mitigated sense—in that sense which common usage justifies. The word "necessary" is of this description. It has not a fixed character peculiar to itself. It admits of all degrees of comparison, and is often connected with other words which increase or diminish the impression the mind receives of the urgency it imports. A thing may be necessary, very necessary, absolutely or indispensably necessary. To no mind would the same idea be conveyed by these several phrases. The comment on the word is well illustrated by the passage cited at the bar from the 10th section of the 1st article of the Constitution. It is, we think, impossible to compare the sentence which prohibits a State from laying "imposts, or duties on imports or exports, except what may be absolutely necessary for executing its inspection laws," with that which authorizes Congress "to make all laws which shall be necessary and proper for carrying into execution" the powers of the General Government without feeling a conviction that the convention understood itself to change materially the meaning of the word "necessary," by prefixing the word "absolutely." This word, then, like others, is used in various senses, and, in its construction, the subject, the context, the intention of the person using them are all to be taken into view.

Let this be done in the case under consideration. The subject is the execution of those great powers on which the welfare of a Nation essentially depends. It must have been the intention of those who gave these powers to insure, so far as human prudence could insure, their beneficial execution. This could not be done by confiding the choice of means to such narrow limits as not to leave it in the power of Congress to adopt any which might be appropriate, and which were conducive to the end. This provision is made in a Constitution intended to endure for ages to come, and consequently to be adapted to the various crises of human affairs. To have prescribed the means by which Government should, in all future time, execute its powers would have been to change entirely the character of the instrument and give it the properties of a legal code. It would have been an unwise attempt to provide by immutable rules for exigencies which, if foreseen at all, must have been seen dimly, and which can be best provided for as they occur. To have declared that the best means shall not be used, but those alone without which the power given would be nugatory, would have been to deprive the legislature of the capacity to avail itself of experience, to exercise its reason, and to accommodate its legislation to circumstances.

If we apply this principle of construction to any of the powers of the Government, we shall find it so pernicious in its operation that we shall be compelled to discard it. The powers vested in Congress may certainly be carried into execution, without prescribing an oath of office. The power to exact this security for the faithful performance of duty is not given, nor is it indispensably necessary. The different departments may be established; taxes may be imposed and collected; armies and navies may be raised and maintained; and money may be borrowed, without requiring an oath of office. It might be argued with as much plausibility as other inci-

dental powers have been assailed that the convention was not unmindful of this subject. The oath which might be exacted—that of fidelity to the Constitution—is prescribed, and no other can be required. Yet he would be charged with insanity who should contend that the legislature might not superadd to the oath directed by the Constitution such other oath of office as its wisdom might suggest.

So, with respect to the whole penal code of the United States, whence arises the power to punish in cases not prescribed by the Constitution? All admit that the Government may legitimately punish any violation of its laws, and yet this is not among the enumerated powers of Congress. The right to enforce the observance of law by punishing its infraction might be denied with the more plausibility because it is expressly given in some cases.

Congress is empowered "to provide for the punishment of counterfeiting the securities and current coin of the United States," and "to define and punish piracies and felonies committed on the high seas, and offences against the law of nations." The several powers of Congress may exist in a very imperfect State, to be sure, but they may exist and be carried into execution, although no punishment should be inflicted, in cases where the right to punish is not expressly given.

Take, for example, the power "to establish post-offices and post-roads." This power is executed by the single act of making the establishment. But from this has been inferred the power and duty of carrying the mail along the post road from one post office to another. And from this implied power has again been inferred the right to punish those who steal letters from the post office, or rob the mail. It may be said with some plausibility that the right to carry the mail, and to punish those who rob it, is not indispensably necessary to the establishment of a post office and post road. This right is indeed essential to the beneficial exercise of the power, but not indispensably necessary to its existence. So, of the punishment of the crimes of stealing or falsifying a record or process of a Court of the United States, or of perjury in such Court. To punish these offences is certainly conducive to the due administration of justice. But Courts may exist, and may decide the causes brought before them, though such crimes escape punishment.

The baneful influence of this narrow construction on all the operations of the Government, and the absolute impracticability of maintaining it without rendering the Government incompetent to its great objects, might be illustrated by numerous examples drawn from the Constitution and from our laws. The good sense of the public has pronounced without hesitation that the power of punishment appertains to sovereignty, and may be exercised, whenever the sovereign has a right to act, as incidental to his Constitutional powers. It is a means for carrying into execution all sovereign powers, and may be used although not indispensably necessary. It is a right incidental to the power, and conducive to its beneficial exercise.

If this limited construction of the word "necessary" must be abandoned in order to punish, whence is derived the rule which would reinstate it when the Government would carry its powers into execution by means not vindictive in their nature? If the word "necessary" means "needful," "requisite," "essential," "conducive to," in order to let in the power of punishment for the infraction of law, why is it not equally comprehensive when required to authorize the use of means which facilitate the execution of the powers of Government, without the infliction of punishment?

In ascertaining the sense in which the word "necessary" is used in this clause of the Constitution, we may derive some aid from that with which it is associated. Congress shall have power "to make all laws which shall be necessary and proper to carry into execution" the powers of the Government. If the word "necessary" was used in that strict and rigorous sense for which the counsel for the State of Maryland contend, it would be an extraordinary departure from the usual course of the human mind, as exhibited in composition, to add a word the only possible effect of which is to qualify that strict and rigorous meaning, to present to the mind the idea of some choice of means of legislation not strained and compressed within the narrow limits for which gentlemen contend.

But the argument which most conclusively demonstrates the error of the construction contended for by the counsel for the State of Maryland is founded on the intention of the convention as manifested in the whole clause. To waste time and argument in proving that, without it, Congress might carry its powers into execution would be not much less idle than to hold a lighted taper to the sun. As little can it be required to prove that, in the absence of this clause, Congress would have some choice of means. That it might employ those which, in its judgment, would most advantageously effect the object to be accomplished. That any means adapted to the end, any means which tended directly to the execution

of the Constitutional powers of the Government, were in themselves Constitutional. This clause, as construed by the State of Maryland, would abridge, and almost annihilate, this useful and necessary right of the legislature to select its means. That this could not be intended is, we should think, had it not been already controverted, too apparent for controversy.

We think so for the following reasons:

1st. The clause is placed among the powers of Congress, not among the limitations on those powers.

2d. Its terms purport to enlarge, not to diminish, the powers vested in the Government. It purports to be an additional power, not a restriction on those already granted. No reason has been or can be assigned for thus concealing an intention to narrow the discretion of the National Legislature under words which purport to enlarge it. The framers of the Constitution wished its adoption, and well knew that it would be endangered by its strength, not by its weakness. Had they been capable of using language which would convey to the eye one idea and, after deep reflection, impress on the mind another, they would rather have disguised the grant of power than its limitation. If, then, their intention had been, by this clause, to restrain the free use of means which might otherwise have been implied, that intention would have been inserted in another place, and would have been expressed in terms resembling these. "In carrying into execution the foregoing powers, and all others," &c., "no laws shall be passed but such as are necessary and proper." Had the intention been to make this clause restrictive, it would unquestionably have been so in form, as well as in effect.

The result of the most careful and attentive consideration bestowed upon this clause is that, if it does not enlarge, it cannot be construed to restrain, the powers of Congress, or to impair the right of the legislature to exercise its best judgment in the selection of measures to carry into execution the Constitutional powers of the Government. If no other motive for its insertion can be suggested, a sufficient one is found in the desire to remove all doubts respecting the right to legislate on that vast mass of incidental powers which must be involved in the Constitution if that instrument be not a splendid bauble.

We admit, as all must admit, that the powers of the Government are limited, and that its limits are not to be transcended. But we think the sound construction of the Constitution must allow to the national legislature that discretion with respect to the means by which the powers it confers are to be carried into execution which will enable that body to perform the high duties assigned to it in the manner most beneficial to the people. Let the end be legitimate, let it be within the scope of the Constitution, and all means which are appropriate, which are plainly adapted to that end, which are not prohibited, but consist with the letter and spirit of the Constitution, are Constitutional.

That a corporation must be considered as a means not less usual, not of higher dignity, not more requiring a particular specification than other means has been sufficiently proved. If we look to the origin of corporations, to the manner in which they have been framed in that Government from which we have derived most of our legal principles and ideas, or to the uses to which they have been applied, we find no reason to suppose that a Constitution, omitting, and wisely omitting, to enumerate all the means for carrying into execution the great powers vested in Government, ought to have specified this. Had it been intended to grant this power as one which should be distinct and independent, to be exercised in any case whatever, it would have found a place among the enumerated powers of the Government. But being considered merely as a means, to be employed only for the purpose of carrying into execution the given powers, there could be no motive for particularly mentioning it.

The propriety of this remark would seem to be generally acknowledged by the universal acquiescence in the construction which has been uniformly put on the 3d section of the 4th article of the Constitution. The power to "make all needful rules and regulations respecting the territory or other property belonging to the United States" is not more comprehensive than the power "to make all laws which shall be necessary and proper for carrying into execution" the powers of the Government. Yet all admit the constitutionality of a Territorial Government, which is a corporate body.

If a corporation may be employed, indiscriminately with other means, to carry into execution the powers of the Government, no particular reason can be assigned for excluding the use of a bank, if required for its fiscal operations. To use one must be within the discretion of Congress if it be an appropriate mode of executing the powers of Government. That it is a convenient, a useful, and essential instrument in the prosecution of its fiscal operations is not now a subject of controversy. All those who have been concerned in the administration of our finances have concurred in representing its importance

and necessity, and so strongly have they been felt that Statesmen of the first class, whose previous opinions against it had been confirmed by every circumstance which can fix the human judgment, have yielded those opinions to the exigencies of the nation. Under the Confederation, Congress, justifying the measure by its necessity, transcended, perhaps, its powers to obtain the advantage of a bank; and our own legislation attests the universal conviction of the utility of this measure. The time has passed away when it can be necessary to enter into any discussion in order to prove the importance of this instrument as a means to effect the legitimate objects of the Government.

But were its necessity less apparent, none can deny its being an appropriate measure; and if it is, the decree of its necessity, as has been very justly observed, is to be discussed in another place. Should Congress, in the execution of its powers, adopt measures which are prohibited by the Constitution, or should Congress, under the pretext of executing its powers, pass laws for the accomplishment of objects not intrusted to the Government, it would become the painful duty of this tribunal, should a case requiring such a decision come before it, to say that such an act was not the law of the land. But where the law is not prohibited, and is really calculated to effect any of the objects intrusted to the Government, to undertake here to inquire into the decree of its necessity would be to pass the line which circumscribes the judicial department and to tread on legislative ground. This Court disclaims all pretensions to such a power.

After this declaration, it can scarcely be necessary to say that the existence of State banks can have no possible influence on the question. No trace is to be found in the Constitution of an intention to create a dependence of the Government of the Union on those of the States, for the execution of the great powers assigned to it. Its means are adequate to its ends, and on those means alone was it expected to rely for the accomplishment of its ends. To impose on it the necessity of resorting to means which it cannot control, which another Government may furnish or withhold, would render its course precarious, the result of its measures uncertain, and create a dependence on other Governments which might disappoint its most important designs, and is incompatible with the language of the Constitution. But were it otherwise, the choice of means implies a right to choose a national bank in preference to State banks, and Congress alone can make the election.

After the most deliberate consideration, it is the

unanimous and decided opinion of this Court that the act to incorporate the Bank of the United States is a law made in pursuance of the Constitution, and is a part of the supreme law of the land.

17

James Madison, *Detached Memoranda*

1819*

Force of precedents in case of the Bank—& in expounding the Constn. equal division of Senate, when the Bill negatived by V. P. not occasioned by unconstitutionality *but inexpediency of the Bill.* reasoning of Sup. Ct [in *McCulloch v. Maryland*—Ed.]—founded on erroneous views &—1. as to the ratification of Const: by people if meant people collectively & not by States. 2. imputing concurrence of those formerly opposed to change of opinion, instead of precedents superseding opinion. 3. endeavoring to retain right of Court to pronounce on the consty of law after making Legisl omnipotent as to the expediency of means. 4. expounding power of Congs—as if no other Sovereignty existed *in the States* supplemental to the enumerated powers *of Congs*—5. making the Judy. exclusive expositor of the Constitutionality of laws: the co-ordinate authorities Legisl—& Execut—being equally expositors within the scope of their functions.

18

Corfield v. Coryell

6 Fed. Cas. 546 (C.C.E.D.Pa. 1823)

WASHINGTON, Circuit Justice. The points reserved present for the consideration of the court, many interesting and difficult questions, which will be examined in the shape of objections made by the plaintiff's counsel to the seizure of the Hiram, and the proceedings of the magistrates of Cumberland county, upon whose

*Madison, *Writings*, 756.

sentence the defendant rests his justification of the alleged trespass. These objections are,—

First. That the act of the legislature of New Jersey of the 9th of June 1820, under which this vessel, found engaged in taking oysters in Maurice river cove by means of dredges, was seized, condemned, and sold, is repugnant to the constitution of the United States in the following particulars: 1. To the eighth section of the first article, which grants to congress the power to regulate commerce with foreign nations, and among the several states, and with the Indian tribes. 2. To the second section of the fourth article, which declares, that the citizens of each state shall be entitled to all privileges and immunities of citizens in the several states. 3. To the second section of the third article, which declares, that the judicial power of the United States should extend to all cases of admiralty and maritime jurisdiction.

In case the act should be considered as not being exposed to these constitutional objections, it is then insisted,

Secondly. That the locus in quo was not within the territorial limits of New Jersey. But if it was, then

Thirdly. It was not within the jurisdiction of the magistrates of Cumberland county.

Fourthly. We have to consider the objection made by the defendant's counsel to the form of this action.

The first section of the act of New Jersey declares, that, from and after the 1st of May, till the 1st of September in every year, no person shall rake on any oyster bed in this state, or gather any oysters on any banks or beds within the same, under a penalty of $10. Second section: No person residing in, or out of this state, shall, at any time, dredge for oysters in any of the rivers, bays, or waters of the state, under the penalty of $50. The third section prescribes the manner of proceeding, in cases of violations of the preceding sections. The two next sections have nothing to do with the present case. The sixth section enacts, that it shall not be lawful for any person, who is not, at the time, an actual inhabitant and resident of this state, to gather oysters in any of the rivers, bays, or waters in this state, on board of any vessel, not wholly owned by some person, inhabitant of, or actually residing in this state; and every person so offending, shall forfeit $10, and shall also forfeit the vessel employed in the commission on such offence, with all the oysters, rakes, &c. belonging to the same. The seventh section provides, that it shall be lawful for any person to seize and secure such vessel, and to give information to two justices of the county where such seizure shall be made, who are required to meet for the trial of the said case, and to determine the same; and in case of condemnation, to order the said vessel, &c. to be sold.

The first question then is, whether this act, or either section of it, is repugnant to the power granted to congress to regulate commerce? Commerce with foreign nations, and among the several states, can mean nothing more than intercourse with those nations, and among those states, for purposes of trade, be the object of the trade what it may; and this intercourse must include all the means by which it can be carried on, whether by the free navigation of the waters of the several states, or by a passage over land through the states, where such passage becomes necessary to the commercial intercourse between the states. It is this intercourse which congress is invested with the power of regulating, and with which no state has a right to interfere. But this power, which comprehends the use of, and passage over the navigable waters of the several states, does by no means impair the right of the state government to legislate upon all subjects of internal police within their territorial limits, which is not forbidden by the constitution of the United States, even although such legislation may indirectly and remotely affect commerce, provided it do not interfere with the regulations of congress upon the same subject. Such are inspection, quarantine, and health laws; laws regulating the internal commerce of the state; laws establishing and regulating turnpike roads, ferries, canals, and the like.

In the case of Gibbons v. Ogden, 9 Wheat. [22 U. S.] 1, which we consider as full authority for the principles above stated, it is said, 'that no direct power over these objects is granted to congress, and consequently they remain subject to state legislation. If the legislative power of the Union can reach them, it must be for national purposes; it must be when the power is expressly given for a specified purpose, or is clearly incident to some power which is expressly given.' But if the power which congress possesses to regulate commerce does not interfere with that of the state to regulate its internal trade, although the latter may remotely affect external commerce, except where the laws of the state may conflict with those of the general government; much less can that power impair the right of the state governments to legislate, in such manner as in their wisdom may seem best, over the public property of the state, and to regulate the use of the same, where such regulations do not interfere with the free navigation of the waters of the state, for purposes of commercial intercourse,

nor with the trade within the state, which the laws of the United States permit to be carried on. The grant to congress to regulate commerce on the navigable waters belonging to the several states, renders those waters the public property of the United States, for all the purposes of navigation and commercial intercourse; subject only to congressional regulation. But this grant contains no cession, either express or implied, of territory, or of public or private property. The jus privatum which a state has in the soil covered by its waters, is totally distinct from the jus publicum with which it is clothed. The former, such as fisheries of all descriptions, remains common to all the citizens of the state to which it belongs, to be used by them according to their necessities, or according to the laws which regulate their use. 'Over these,' says Vattel (book 1, c. 20, §§ 235, 246), 'sovereignty gives a right to the nation to make laws regulating the manner in which the common goods are to be used.' 'He may make such regulations respecting hunting and fishing, as to seasons, as he may think proper, prohibiting the use of certain nets and other destructive methods.' Vattel, bk. 1, c. 20, § 248. The jus publicum consists in the right of all persons to use the navigable waters of the state for commerce, trade, and intercourse; subject, by the constitution of the United States, to the exclusive regulation of congress. If then the fisheries and oyster beds within the territorial limits of a state are the common property of the citizens of that state, and were not ceded to the United States by the power granted to congress to regulate commerce, it is difficult to perceive how a law of the state regulating the use of this common property, under such penalties and forfeitures as the state legislature may think proper to prescribe, can be said to interfere with the power so granted. The act under consideration forbids the taking of oysters by any persons, whether citizens or not, at unseasonable times, and with destructive instruments; and for breaches of the law, prescribes penalties in some cases, and forfeitures in others. But the free use of the waters of the state for purposes of navigation and commercial intercourse, is interdicted to no person; nor is the slightest restraint imposed upon any to buy and sell, or in any manner to trade within the limits of the state.

It was insisted by the plaintiff's counsel, that, as oysters constituted an article of trade, a law which abridges the right of the citizens of other states to take them, except in particular vessels, amounts to a regulation of the external commerce of the state. But it is a manifest mistake to denominate that a commercial regulation which merely regulates the common property of the citizens of the state, by forbidding it to be taken at improper seasons, or with destructive instruments. The law does not inhibit the buying and selling of oysters after they are lawfully gathered, and have become articles of trade; but it forbids the removal of them from the beds in which they grow, (in which situation they cannot be considered articles of trade,) unless under the regulations which the law prescribes. What are the state inspection laws, but internal restraints upon the buying and selling of certain articles of trade? And yet, the chief justice, speaking of those laws [Gibbons v. Ogden] 9 Wheat. [22 U.S.] 203, observes, that 'their object is to improve the quality of articles produced by the labour of a country; to fit them for exportation, or, it may be, for domestic use. They act upon the subject before it becomes an article of foreign commerce, or of commerce among the states, and prepare it for that purpose.' Is this not precisely the nature of those laws which prescribe the seasons when, and the manner in which, the taking of oysters is permitted? Paving stones, sand, and many other things, are as clearly articles of trade as oysters; but can it be contended, that the laws of a state, which treat as tort feasors those who shall take them away without the permission of the owner of them, are commercial regulations? We deem it superfluous to pursue this subject further, and close it by stating our opinion to be, that no part of the act under consideration amounts to a regulation of commerce, within the meaning of the eighth section of the first article of the constitution.

2. The next question is, whether this act infringes that section of the constitution which declares that 'the citizens of each state shall be entitled to all the privileges and immunities of citizens in the several states?' The inquiry is, what are the privileges and immunities of citizens in the several states? We feel no hesitation in confining these expressions to those privileges and immunities which are, in their nature, fundamental; which belong, of right, to the citizens of all free governments; and which have, at all times, been enjoyed by the citizens of the several states which compose this Union, from the time of their becoming free, independent, and sovereign. What these fundamental principles are, it would perhaps be more tedious than difficult to enumerate. They may, however, be all comprehended under the following general heads: Protection by the government; the enjoyment of life and liberty, with the right to acquire and possess property of every kind, and to

pursue and obtain happiness and safety; subject nevertheless to such restraints as the government may justly prescribe for the general good of the whole. The right of a citizen of one state to pass through, or to reside in any other state, for purposes of trade, agriculture, professional pursuits, or otherwise; to claim the benefit of the writ of habeas corpus; to institute and maintain actions of any kind in the courts of the state; to take, hold and dispose of property, either real or personal; and an exemption from higher taxes or impositions than are paid by the other citizens of the state; may be mentioned as some of the particular privileges and immunities of citizens, which are clearly embraced by the general description of privileges deemed to be fundamental: to which may be added, the elective franchise, as regulated and established by the laws or constitution of the state in which it is to be exercised. These, and many others which might be mentioned, are, strictly speaking, privileges and immunities, and the enjoyment of them by the citizens of each state, in every other state, was manifestly calculated (to use the expressions of the preamble of the corresponding provision in the old articles of confederation) 'the better to secure and perpetuate mutual friendship and intercourse among the people of the different states of the Union.'

But we cannot accede to the proposition which was insisted on by the counsel, that, under this provision of the constitution, the citizens of the several states are permitted to participate in all the rights which belong exclusively to the citizens of any other particular state, merely upon the ground that they are enjoyed by those citizens; much less, that in regulating the use of the common property of the citizens of such state, the legislature is bound to extend to the citizens of all the other states the same advantages as are secured to their own citizens. A several fishery, either as the right to it respects running fish, or such as are stationary, such as oysters, clams, and the like, is as much the property of the individual to whom it belongs, as dry land, or land covered by water; and is equally protected by the laws of the state against the aggressions of others, whether citizens or strangers.

...

Let judgment be entered for the defendant.

19

James Kent, *Commentaries; Of the Absolute Rights of Persons*

1827[*]

OF THE ABSOLUTE RIGHTS OF PERSONS.

The rights of persons in private life are either absolute, being such as belong to individuals in a single unconnected state; or relative, being those which arise from the civil and domestic relations.

The absolute rights of individuals may be resolved into the right of personal security, the right of personal liberty, and the right to acquire and enjoy property. These rights have been justly considered, and frequently declared, by the people of this country, to be natural, inherent, and unalienable. The history of our colonial governments bears constant marks of the vigilance of a free and intelligent people, who understood the best securities for political happiness, and the true foundation of the social ties. The inhabitants of Massachusetts, in the very infancy of their establishments, declared by law that the free enjoyment of the liberties which humanity, civility and Christianity called for, was due to every man in his place and proportion, and ever had been, and ever would be, the tranquility and stability of the commonwealth. They insisted that they brought with them into this country the privileges of English freemen; and they defined and declared those privileges, with a caution, sagacity and precision, that has not been surpassed by their descendants. Those rights were afterwards, in the year 1692, on the receipt of their new charter, re-asserted and declared. It was their fundamental doctrine, that no tax, aid or imposition whatever could rightfully be assessed or levied upon them, without the act and consent of their own legislature; and that justice ought to be equally, impartially, freely and promptly administered. The right of trial by jury, and the necessity of due proof preceding conviction, were claimed as undeniable rights; and it was further expressly ordained, that no person should suffer without express law, either in life, limb, liberty,

good name, or estate; nor without being first brought to answer by due course and process of law.

The first act of the General Assembly of the colony of Connecticut, in 1639, contained a declaration of rights in nearly the same language; and among the early resolutions of the General Assembly of the colony of New-York, we meet with similar proofs of an enlightened sense of the provisions requisite for civil security. It was declared by them, that the imprisonment of subjects without due commitment for legal cause, and proscribing and forcing them into banishment, and forcibly seizing their property, were illegal and arbitrary acts. It was held to be the unquestionable right of every freeman, to have a perfect and entire property in his goods and estate; and that no money could be imposed or levied, without the consent of the General Assembly. The erection of any court of judicature without the like consent, and exactions upon the administration of justice, were declared to be grievances. Testimonies of the same honourable character are doubtless to be met with in the records of other colonial legislatures. But we need not pursue our researches on this point, for the best evidence that can be produced of the deep and universal sense of the value of our natural rights, and of the energy of the principles of the common law, are the memorials of the spirit which pervaded and animated every part of our country, after the peace of 1763, when the same parent power which had nourished and protected us, attempted to abridge our immunities, and retard the progress of our rising greatness.

The House of Burgesses in Virginia, took an early and distinguished part, upon the first promulgation of the stamp act, in the assertion of their public rights as free-born English subjects. The claim to common law rights, soon became a topic of universal concern and national vindication. In October, 1765, a convention of delegates from nine colonies, assembled at New-York, and made and published a declaration of rights, in which they insisted that the people of the colonies were entitled to all the inherent rights and liberties of English subjects, of which the most essential were, the exclusive power to tax themselves, and the privilege of trial by jury. The sense of America was, however, more fully ascertained, and more explicitly and solemnly promulgated, in the memorable declaration of rights of the first continental congress, in October, 1774. That declaration contained the assertion of several great and fundamental principles of American liberty, and it constituted the basis

---

[*] James Kent, *Commentaries on American Law*, 1st ed. (New York: O. Halsted, 1827), 2:1–34.

of those subsequent bills of rights, which, under various modifications, pervaded all our constitutional charters. It was declared, "that the inhabitants of the English colonies in North America, by the immutable laws of nature, the principles of the English constitution, and their several charters or compacts, were entitled to life, liberty, and property; and that they had never ceded to any sovereign power whatever right to dispose of either, without their consent; that their ancestors, who first settled the colonies, were, at the time of their emigration from the mother country, entitled to all the rights, liberties, and immunities of free and natural born subjects; and by such emigration, they by no means forfeited, surrendered, or lost any of those rights;—that the foundation of English liberty, and of all free government, was a right in the people to participate in the legislative power, and that they were entitled to a free and exclusive power of legislation, in all matters of taxation and internal policy, in their several provincial legislatures, where their right of representation could alone be preserved;—that the respective colonies were entitled to the common law of England, and more especially to the great and inestimable privilege of being tried by their peers of the vicinage, according to the course of that law; that they were entitled to the benefit of such of the English statutes as existed at the time of their colonization, and which they had by experience found to be applicable to their several local and other circumstances;—that they were likewise entitled to all the immunities and privileges granted and confirmed to them by royal charters, or secured by their several codes of provincial laws." Upon the formation of the several state constitutions, after the colonies had become independent states, it was, in most instances, thought proper to collect, digest, and declare, in a precise and definite manner, and in the shape of abstract propositions and elementary maxims, the most essential articles appertaining to civil liberty and the natural rights of mankind.

The precedent for these declaratory bills of rights was to be found, not only in the colonial annals to which I have alluded, but in the practice of the English nation, who had frequently been obliged to recover by intrepid councils, or by force of arms, and then to proclaim by the most solemn and positive enactments, their indefeasible rights, as a barrier against the tyranny of the executive power. The establishment of magna carta, and its generous provisions for all classes of freemen against the complicated oppressions of the feudal system; the petition of right, early in the reign of Charles I., assert-ing by statute the rights of the nation as contained in their ancient laws, and especially in "the great charter of the liberties of England;" and the bill of rights at the revolution, in 1688, are illustrious examples of the intelligence and spirit of the English nation, and they form distinguished eras in their constitutional history.

But the necessity in our representative republics of these declaratory codes, has been frequently questioned, inasmuch as the government, in all its parts, is the creature of the people, and every department of it is filled by their agents, duly chosen or appointed, according to their will, and made responsible for maladministration. It may be observed, on the one hand, that no gross violation of those absolute private rights, which are clearly understood and settled by the common reason of mankind, is to be apprehended in the ordinary course of public affairs; and as to extraordinary instances of faction and turbulence, and the corruption and violence which they necessarily engender, no parchment checks can be relied on as affording, under such circumstances, any effectual protection to public liberty. When the spirit of liberty has fled, and truth and justice are disregarded, private rights can easily be sacrificed under the forms of law. On the other hand, there is weight due to the consideration, that a bill of rights is of real efficacy in controlling the excesses of party spirit. It serves to guide and enlighten public opinion, and to render it more quick to detect, and more resolute to resist, attempts to disturb private right. It requires more than ordinary hardness and audacity of character, to trample down principles, which our ancestors cultivated with reverence, which we imbibed in our early education, which recommend themselves to the judgment of the world by their truth and simplicity, and which are constantly placed before the eyes of the people, accompanied with the imposing force and solemnity of a constitutional sanction. Bills of rights are part of the muniments of freemen, showing their title to protection, and they become of increased value when placed under the protection of an independent judiciary, instituted as the appropriate guardian of private right. Care, however, is to be taken in the digest of these declaratory provisions, to confine the manual to a few plain and unexceptionable principles. We weaken greatly the force of them, if we incumber the constitution, and perhaps embarrass the future operations and more enlarged experience of the legislature, with a catalogue of ethical and political aphorisms, which, in some instances, may reasonably be questioned, and in others, justly condemned.

In the revision of the constitution of New-York, in 1821; the declaration of rights was considerably enlarged, and yet the most comprehensive, and the most valuable and effectual of its provisions, were to be found in the original constitution of 1777, as it was digested by some master statesmen, in the midst of the tempest of war and invasion. It was declared, that no authority should be exercised over the people or members of this state, on any pretence whatever, but such as should be derived from, and granted by them; and that trial by jury, as formerly used, should remain inviolate for ever; and that no bills of attainder should be passed, and no new courts instituted, but such as should proceed according to the course of the common law; and that no member of the state should be disfranchised, or deprived of any of his rights or privileges under the constitution, unless by the law of the land, or the judgment of his peers. Several of the early state constitutions had no formal bill of rights inserted in them; and experience teaches us, that the most solid basis of public safety, and the most certain assurance of the uninterrupted enjoyment of our personal rights and liberties, consists, not so much in bills of rights, as in the skillful organization of the government, and its aptitude, by means of its structure and genius, and the spirit of the people which pervades it, to produce wise laws, and a just, firm, and intelligent administration of justice.

I shall devote the remainder of the present lecture to examine more particularly the right of personal security and personal liberty, and postpone the consideration of the right of private property, until we arrive at another branch of our inquiries.

(1.) The right of personal security is guarded by provisions which have been transcribed into the constitutions in this country from Magna Charta, and other fundamental acts of the English Parliament, and it is enforced by additional and more precise injunctions. The substance of the provisions is, that no person, except on impeachment, and in cases arising in the military and naval service, shall be held to answer for a capital, or otherwise infamous crime, or for any offence above the common law degree of petit larceny, unless he shall have been previously charged on the presentment or indictment of a grand jury; that no person shall be subject, for the same offence, to be twice put in jeopardy of life or limb; nor shall he be compelled in any criminal case, to be a witness against himself and in all criminal prosecutions, the accused is entitled to speedy and public trial by an impartial jury; and upon the trial he is entitled to be confronted with the witnesses against him; to have compulsory process for obtaining witnesses in his favour, and to have the assistance of counsel for his defence. And as a further guard against abuse and oppression in criminal proceedings, it is declared, that excessive bail cannot be required, nor excessive fines imposed, or cruel and unusual punishments inflicted; nor can any bill of attainder, or ex post facto law, be passed. The constitution of the United States, and the constitutions of almost every state in the Union, contain the same declarations in substance, and nearly in the same language. And where express constitutional provisions on this subject appear to be wanting, the same principles are probably asserted by declaratory legislative acts; and they must be regarded as fundamental doctrines in every state, for all the colonies were parties to the national declaration of rights in 1774, in which the trial by jury, and the other rights and liberties of English subjects were peremptorily claimed as their undoubted inheritance and birthright. It may be received as a self-evident proposition, universally understood and acknowledged throughout this country, that no person can be taken, or imprisoned, or disseised of his freehold, or liberties, or estate, or exiled, or condemned, or deprived of life, liberty, or property, unless by the law of the land, or the judgment of his peers. The words, by the law of the land, as used in Magna Charta, in reference to this subject, are understood to mean due process of law, that is, by indictment or presentment of good and lawful men; and this, says Lord Coke, is the true sense and exposition of those words.

20

John C. Calhoun, South Carolina Exposition

December 1828[*]

The committee [of the South Carolina Legislature] have bestowed on the subjects referred to them the deliberate attention which their importance demands; and the result, on full investigation, is a unanimous opinion that the act of Congress of the last session, with the whole

[*] H. Lee Cheek Jr., ed., *John C. Calhoun: Selected Writings and Speeches* (Washington, DC: Regnery, 2003), 268–306.

system of legislation imposing duties on imports, not for revenue, but the protection of one branch of industry at the expense of others, is unconstitutional, unequal, and oppressive, and calculated to corrupt the public virtue and destroy the liberty of the country; which propositions they propose to consider in the order stated, and then to conclude their report with the consideration of the important question of the remedy.

The committee do not propose to enter into an elaborate or refined argument on the question of the constitutionality of the Tariff system. The General Government is one of specific powers, and it can rightfully exercise only the powers expressly granted, and those that may be necessary and proper to carry them into effect, all others being reserved expressly to the States or the people. It results, necessarily, that those who claim to exercise power under the Constitution, are bound to show that it is expressly granted, or that it is necessary and proper as a means of the granted powers. The advocates of the Tariff have offered no such proof. It is true that the third section of the first article of the Constitution authorizes Congress to lay and collect an impost duty, but it is granted as a tax power for the sole purpose of revenue, a power in its nature essentially different from that of imposing protective or prohibitory duties. Their objects are incompatible. The prohibitory system must end in destroying the revenue from imports. It has been said that the system is a violation of the spirit, and not the letter of the Constitution. The distinction is not material. The Constitution may be as grossly violated by acting against its meaning as against its letter.

. . .

The committee has demonstrated that the present disordered state of our political system originated in the diversity of interests which exists in the country; a diversity recognized by the Constitution itself, and to which it owes one of its most distinguished and peculiar features, the division of the delegated powers between the State and General Governments. Our short experience, before the formation of the present Government, had conclusively shown that, while there were powers which in their nature were local and peculiar, and which could not be exercised by all, without oppression to some of the parts, so, also, there were those which, in their operation, necessarily affected the whole, and could not, therefore, be exercised by any of the parts, without affecting injuriously the others. On this different character, by which powers are distinguished in their geographical operation, our political system was

constructed. Viewed in relation to them, to a certain extent we have a community of interests, which can only be justly and fairly supervised by concentrating the will and authority of the several States in the General Government; while, at the same time, the States have distinct and separate interests, over which no supervision can be exercised by the general power without injustice and oppression. Hence the division in the exercise of sovereign powers. In drawing the line between the powers of the two—the General and State Governments—the great difficulty consisted in determining correctly to which of the two the various political powers ought to belong. This difficult task was, however, performed with so much success that, to this day, there is an almost entire acquiescence in the correctness with which the line was drawn. It would be extraordinary if a system, thus resting with such profound wisdom on the diversity of geographical interests among the States, should make no provision against the dangers to which its very basis might be exposed. The framers of our Constitution have not exposed themselves to the imputation of such weakness. When their work is fairly examined, it will be found that they have provided, with admirable skill, the most effective remedy; and that, if it has not prevented the danger with which the system is now threatened, the fault is not theirs, but ours, in neglecting to make its proper application. In the primary division of the sovereign powers, and in their exact and just classification, as stated, are to be found the first provisions or checks against the abuse of authority on the part of the absolute majority. The powers of the General Government are particularly enumerated and specifically delegated; and all powers not expressly delegated, or which are not necessary and proper to carry into effect those that are so granted, are reserved expressly to the States or the people. The Government is thus positively restricted to the exercise of those general powers that were supposed to act uniformly on all the parts, leaving, the residue to the people of the States, by whom alone, from the very nature of these powers, they can be justly and fairly exercised, as has been stated.

Our system, then, consists of two distinct and independent Governments. The general powers, expressly delegated to the General Government, are subject to its sole and separate control; and the States cannot, without violating the constitutional compact, interpose their authority to check, or in any manner to counteract its movements, so long as they are confined to the proper sphere. So, also, the peculiar and local powers reserved to the States are subject to their exclusive control; nor can the General Government interfere, in any manner, with them, without violating the Constitution.

In order to have a full and clear conception of our institutions, it will be proper to remark that there is, in our system, a striking distinction between Government and Sovereignty. The separate governments of the several States are vested in their Legislative, Executive, and judicial Departments; while the sovereignty resides in the people of the States respectively. The powers of the General Government are also vested in its Legislative, Executive, and judicial Departments, while the sovereignty resides in the people of the several States who created it. But, by an express provision of the Constitution, it may be amended or changed by three fourths of the States; and thus each State, by assenting to the Constitution with this provision, has modified its original right as a sovereign, of making its individual consent necessary to any change in its political condition; and, by becoming a member of the Union, has placed this important power in the hands of three fourths of the States, in whom the highest power known to the Constitution actually resides. Not the least portion of this high sovereign authority resides in Congress, or any of the departments of the General Government. They are but the creatures of the Constitution, and are appointed but to execute its provisions; and, therefore, any attempt by all, or any of these departments, to exercise any power which, in its consequences, may alter the nature of the instrument, or change the condition of the parties to it, would be an act of usurpation.

. . .

It is manifest that, so long as this beautiful theory is adhered to in practice, the system, like the atmosphere, will press equally on all the parts. But reason and experience teach us that theory of itself, however excellent, is nugatory, unless there be means of efficiently enforcing it in practice;—which brings under consideration the highly important question, What means are provided for the system for enforcing this fundamental provision?

If we look at the history and practical operation of the system, we shall find, on the side of the States, no means resorted to in order to protect their reserved rights against the encroachments of the General Government; while the latter has, from the beginning, adopted the most efficient to prevent the States from encroaching on those delegated to them. The 25th section of the Judiciary Act, passed in 1789,—immediately after

the Constitution went into operation,—provides for an appeal from the State courts to the Supreme Court of the United States in all cases, in the decision of which, the construction of the Constitution,—the laws of Congress, or treaties of the United States may be involved; thus giving to that high tribunal the right of final interpretation, and the power, in reality, of nullifying the acts of the State Legislatures whenever, in their opinion, they may conflict with the powers delegated to the General Government. A more ample and complete protection against the encroachments of the governments of the several States cannot be imagined; and to this extent the power may be considered as indispensable and constitutional. But, by a strange misconception of the nature of our system,—and, in fact, of the nature of government,—it has been regarded as the ultimate power, not only of protecting the General Government against the encroachments of the governments of the States, but also of the encroachments of the former on the latter;—and as being, in fact, the only means provided by the Constitution of confining all the powers of the system to their proper constitutional spheres; and, consequently, of determining the limits assigned to each. Such a construction of its powers would, in fact, raise one of the departments of the General Government above the parties who created the constitutional compact, and virtually invest it with the authority to alter, at its pleasure, the relative powers of the General and State Governments, on the distribution of which, as established by the Constitution, our whole system rests;—and by which, by an express provision of that instrument, can only be altered by three fourths of the States, as has already been shown. It would go further. Fairly considered, it would in effect, divest the people of the States of the sovereign authority, and clothe that department with the robe of supreme power. A position more false and fatal cannot be conceived.

Fortunately, it has been so ably refuted by Mr. Madison, in his Report to the Virginia Legislature in 1800, on the Alien and Sedition Acts, as to supersede the necessity of further comments on the part of the committee. Speaking of the right of the State to interpret the Constitution for itself, in the last resort, he remarks:—"It has been objected that the judicial authority is to be regarded as the sole expositor of the Constitution. On this objection, it might be observed,—*first*—that there may be instances of usurped power" (the case of the Tariff is a striking illustration of the truth), "which the forms of the Constitution could never draw within the control of the Judicial Department;—*secondly*,—that if the decision of the Judiciary be raised above the authority of the sovereign parties to the Constitution, the decision of the other departments, not carried by the forms of the Constitution before the Judiciary, must be equally authoritative and final with the decision of that department. But the proper answer to the objection is, that the resolution of the General Assembly relates to those great and extraordinary cases, in which all the forms of the Constitution may prove ineffectual against infractions dangerous to the essential rights of the parties to it. The resolution supposes that dangerous powers, not delegated, may not only be usurped and executed by the other departments, but that the judicial department also may exercise or sanction dangerous powers beyond the grant of the Constitution; and, consequently, that the ultimate right of the parties to the Constitution, to judge whether the compact has been dangerously violated, must extend to violations by one delegated authority, as well as by another; by the judiciary, as well as by the executive, or the legislature. However true, therefore, it may be, that the judicial department, is, in all questions submitted to it by the forms of the Constitution, to decide in the last resort, this resort must necessarily be deemed the last in relation to the authorities of the other departments of the government; not in relation to the rights of the parties to the constitutional compact, from which the judicial as well as the other departments hold their delegated trusts. On any other hypothesis, the delegation of judicial power would annul the authority delegating it; and the concurrence of this department with the others in usurped powers, might subvert for ever, and beyond the possible reach of any rightful remedy, the very Constitution which all were instituted to preserve."

As a substitute for the rightful remedy, in the last resort, against the encroachments of the General Government on the reserved powers, resort has been to a rigid construction of the Constitution. A system like ours, of divided powers, must necessarily give great importance to a proper system of construction; but it is perfectly clear that no rule of construction, however perfect, can, in fact, prescribe bounds to the operation of power. All such rules constitute, in fact, but an appeal from the minority to the justice and reason of the majority; and if such appeals were sufficient of themselves to restrain the avarice or ambition of those vested with power, then may a system of technical construction be sufficient to protect against the encroachment of power; but, on

such supposition, reason and justice might alone be relied on, without the aid of any constitutional or artificial restraint whatever. Universal experience, in all ages and countries, however, teaches that power can only be restrained by power, and not by reason and justice; and that all restrictions on authority, unsustained by an equal antagonist power, must ever prove wholly inefficient in practice. Such, also, has been the decisive proof of our own short experience. From the beginning, a great and powerful minority gave every force of which it was susceptible to construction, as a means of restraining the majority of Congress to the exercise of its proper powers; and though that original minority, through the force of circumstance, has had the advantage of becoming a majority, and to possess, in consequence, the administration of the General Government during the greater portion of its existence, yet we this day witness, under these most favorable circumstances, such an extension of its power as to leave the States scarcely a right worth possessing....

If it be conceded, as it must be by every one who is the least conversant with our institutions, that the sovereign powers delegated are divided between the General and State Governments, and that the latter hold their portion by the same tenure as the former, it would seem impossible to deny to the States the right of deciding on the infractions of their powers, and the proper remedy to be applied for their correction. The right of judging, in such cases, is an essential attribute of sovereignty,—of which the States cannot be divested without losing their sovereignty itself,—and being reduced to a subordinate corporate condition. In fact, to divide power, and to give to one of the parties the exclusive right of judging of the portion allotted to each, is, in reality, not to divide it at all; and to reserve such exclusive right to the General Government (it matters not by what department to be exercised,) is to convert it, in fact, into a great consolidated government, with unlimited powers, and to divest the States, in reality, of all their rights, It is impossible to understand the force of terms, and to deny so plain a conclusion. The opposite opinion can be embraced only on hasty and imperfect views of the relation existing between the States and the General Government. But the existence of the right of judging of their powers, so clearly established from the sovereignty of States, as clearly implies a veto or control, within its limits, on the action of the General Government, on contested points of authority; and this very control is the remedy which the Constitution has provided to prevent the encroachments of the General Government on the reserved rights of the States; and by which the distribution of power, between the General and State Governments, may be preserved for ever inviolable, on the basis established by the Constitution. It is thus effectual protection is afforded to the minority, against the oppression of the majority. Nor does this important conclusion stand on the deduction of reason alone. It is sustained by the highest contemporary authority. Mr. Hamilton, in the number of the Federalist already cited remarks that,— "in a single republic, all the power surrendered by the people is submitted to the administration of a single government; and usurpations are guarded against, by a division of the government into distinct and separate departments. In the compound republic of America, the power surrendered by the people is first divided between two distinct governments, and then the portion allotted to each subdivided among distinct and separate departments. Hence a double security arises as to the rights of the people. The different governments will control each other; at the same time that each will be controlled by itself." He thus clearly affirms the control of the States over the General Government, which he traces to the division in the exercise of the sovereign powers under our political system; and by comparing this control to the veto, which the departments in most of our constitutions respectively exercise of the acts of each other, clearly indicates it is his opinion, that the control between the General and State Governments is of the same character.

Mr. Madison is still more explicit. In his report, already alluded to, in speaking on this subject, he remarks;— "The resolutions, having taken this view of the Federal compact, proceed to infer that, in cases of a deliberate, palpable, and dangerous exercise of other powers, not granted by the said compact, the States, who are parties thereto, have the right, and are duty bound to interpose to arrest the evil, and for maintaining, within their respective limits, the authorities, rights, and liberties appertaining to them. It appears to your committee to be a plain principle, founded in common sense, illustrated by common practice, and essential to the nature of compacts, that where resort can be had to no tribunal superior to the rights of the parties, the parties themselves must be the rightful judges, in the last resort, whether the bargain has been pursued or violated. The Constitution of the United States was formed by the sanction of the States, given by each in its sovereign capacity. It adds to the stability and dignity, as well as

to the authority of the Constitution, that it rests on this solid foundation. The States, then, being parties to the constitutional compact, and in their sovereign capacity, it flows of necessity that there can be no tribunal above their authority to decide, in the last resort, whether the compact made by them be violated; and, consequently, as parties to it, they must themselves decide, in the last resort, such questions as may be of sufficient magnitude to require their interposition." To these the no less explicit opinions of Mr. Jefferson may be added; who, in the Kentucky resolutions on the same subject, which have always been attributed to him, states that— "The Government, created by this compact, was not made the exclusive or final judge of the extent of the powers delegated to itself; since that would have made its discretion, and not the Constitution, the measure of its powers;— but, as in all other cases of compact between parties having no common judge, each party has an equal right to judge for itself, as well of infractions as of the mode and measure of redress."

...

The committee have thus arrived, by what they deem conclusive reasoning, and the highest authority, at the constitutional and appropriate remedy against the unconstitutional oppression under which this, in common with the other staple States, labors,— and the menacing danger which now hangs over the liberty and happiness of our country;— and this brings them to the inquiry,— How is the remedy to be applied by the States? ... Whatever doubts may be raised to this question,— whether the respective Legislatures fully represent the sovereignty of the States for this high purpose, there can be none as to the fact that a Convention fully represents them for all purposes whatever. Its authority, therefore, must remove every objection as to form, and leave the question on the single point of the right of the States to interpose at all. When convened, it will belong to the Convention itself to determine, authoritatively, whether the acts of which we complain be unconstitutional; and, if so, whether they constitute a violation so deliberate, palpable, and dangerous, as to justify the interposition of the State to protect its rights. If this question be decided in the affirmative, the Convention will then determine in what manner they ought to be declared null and void within the limits of the State.

...

And, finally, may this power be abused by a State, so as to interfere improperly with the powers delegated to the General Government? There is provided a power, even over the Constitution itself, vested in three fourths of the States, which Congress has the authority to invoke, and may terminate all controversies in reference to the subject, by granting or withholding the right in contest. Its authority is acknowledged by all; and to deny or resist it, would be, on the part of the State, a violation of the constitutional compact, and a dissolution of the political association, as far as it is concerned. This is the ultimate and highest power, and the basis on which the whole system rests.

…

With these views the committee are solemnly of the impression, if the present usurpations and the professed doctrines of the existing system be persevered in, after due forbearance on the part of the State, that it will be her sacred duty to interpose;—a duty to herself—to the Union, to the present, and to future generations, and to the cause of liberty over the world, to arrest the progress of a usurpation which, if not arrested, must, in its consequences, corrupt the public morals and destroy the liberty of the country.

21

James Madison to Edward Everett

August 28, 1830*

I have duly recd. your letter in wch. you refer to the "nullifying doctrine" advocated, as a Constitutional right, by some of our distinguished fellow citizens; and to the proceedings of the Virga. Legislature in 98 & 99, as appealed to in behalf of that doctrine; and you express a wish for my ideas on those subjects.

I am aware of the delicacy of the task in some respects, and the difficulty in every respect of doing full justice to it. But having in more than one instance complied with a like request from other friendly quarters, I do not decline a sketch of the views which I have been led to take of the doctrine in question, as well as some

others connected with them; and of the grounds from which it appears, that the proceedings of Virginia have been misconceived by those who have appealed to them. In order to understand the true character of the Constitution of the U. S. the error, not uncommon, must be avoided, of viewing it through the medium, either of a consolidated Government, or of a confederated Govt. whilst it is neither the one nor the other; but a mixture of both. And having in no model, the similitudes and analogies applicable to other systems of Govt. it must more than any other, be its own interpreter, according to its text and *the facts of the case.*

From these it will be seen, that the characteristic peculiarities of the Constitution are 1. The mode of its formation, 2. The division of the supreme powers of Government between the States in their united capacity, and the States in their individual capacities.

1. It was formed not by the Governments of the component States, as the Federal Govt. for which it was substituted was formed; nor was it formed by a majority of the people of the U.S. as a single community, in the manner of a consolidated Government.

It was formed by the States—that is by the people in each of the States, acting in their highest sovereign capacity; and formed, consequently by the same authority which formed the State Constitutions.

Being thus derived from the same source as the Constitutions of the States, it has within each State, the same authority as the Constitution of the State; and is as much a Constitution, in the strict sense of the term, within its prescribed sphere, as the Constitutions of the States are within their respective spheres; but with this obvious & essential difference, that being a compact among the States in their highest sovereign capacity, and constituting the people thereof one people for certain purposes, it cannot be altered or annulled at the will of the States individually, as the Constitution of a State may be at its individual will.

2. And that it divides the supreme powers of Govt. between the Govt. of the United States, & the Govts. of the individual States, is stamped on the face of the instrument; the powers of war and of taxation, of commerce and of treaties, and other enumerated powers vested in the Govt. of the U.S. being of as high and sovereign a character as any of powers reserved to the State Govts.

Nor is the Govt. of the U.S. created by the Constitution, less a Govt. in the strict sense of the term, within the sphere of its powers, than the Govts. created by the constitutions of the States are within their several spheres.

*Madison, *Writings*, 842. [Madison agreed to publish this letter as a response to Calhoun and others who cited the Virginia resolutions and Madison's Report of 1800 in support of the doctrine of nullification. See Ralph Ketcham, *James Madison* (Newton, CT: American Political Biography, 2003), 641–42. —Ed.]

It is like them organized into Legislative, Executive and Judiciary Departments. It operates like them, directly on persons & things. And, like them, it has at command a physical force for executing the powers committed to it. The concurrent operation in certain cases is one of the features marking the peculiarity of the system.

Between these different constitutional Govts.—the one operating in all the States, the others operating separately in each, with the aggregate powers of Govt. divided between them, it could not escape attention that controversies would arise concerning the boundaries of jurisdiction; and that some provision ought to be made for such occurrences. A political system that does not provide for a peaceable & authoritative termination of occurring controversies, would not be more than the shadow of a Govt.; the object & end of a real Govt. being the substitution of law & order for uncertainty confusion, and violence.

That to have left a final decision, in such cases, to each of the States, then 13 & already 24, could not fail to make the Constn. and laws of the U.S. different in different States was obvious; and not less obvious, that this diversity of independent decisions, must altogether distract the Govt. of the Union & speedily put an end to the Union itself. A uniform authority of the laws, is in itself a vital principle. Some of the most important laws could not be partially executed. They must be executed in all the States or they could be duly executed in none. An impost or an excise, for example, if not in force in some States, would be defeated in others. It is well known that this was among the lessons of experience wch. had a primary influence in bringing about the existing Constitution. A loss of its general authy. would moreover revive the exasperating questions between the States holding ports for foreign commerce and the adjoining States without them, to which are now added all the inland States necessarily carrying on their foreign commerce through other States.

. . .

The reply to all such suggestions seems to be unavoidable and irresistible, that the Constitution is a compact; that its text is to be expounded according to the provisions for expounding it, making a part of the compact; and that none of the parties can rightfully renounce the expounding provision more than any other part. When such a right accrues, as may accrue, it must grow out of abuses of the compact releasing the sufferers from their fealty to it.

In favor of the nullifying claim for the States individually, it appears, as you observe, that the proceedings of the Legislature of Virga. in 98 & 99 agst. the Alien and Sedition Acts are much dwelt upon.

It may often happen, as experience proves, that erroneous constructions, not anticipated, may not be sufficiently guarded against in the language used; and it is due to the distinguished individuals who have misconceived the intention of those proceedings to suppose that the meaning of the Legislature, though well comprehended at the time, may not now be obvious to those unacquainted with the contemporary indications and impressions.

But it is believed that by keeping in view the distinction between the Govt. of the States & the States in the sense in which they were parties to the Constn.; between the rights of the parties, in their concurrent and in their individual capacities; between the several modes and objects of interposition agst. the abuses of power, and especially between interpositions within the purview of the Constn. & interpositions appealing from the Constn. to the rights of nature paramount to all Constitutions; with these distinctions kept in view, and an attention, always of explanatory use, to the views & arguments which were combated, a confidence is felt, that the Resolutions of Virginia, as vindicated in the Report on them, will be found entitled to an exposition, showing a consistency in their parts and an inconsistency of the whole with the doctrine under consideration.

That the Legislature cd. not have intended to sanction such a doctrine is to be inferred from the debates in the House of Delegates, and from the address of the two Houses to their constituents on the subject of the resolutions. The tenor of the debates wch. were ably conducted and are understood to have been revised for the press by most, if not all, of the speakers, discloses no reference whatever to a constitutional right in an individual State to arrest by force the operation of a law of the United States. Concert among the States for redress against the alien & sedition laws, as acts of usurped power, was a leading sentiment, and the attainment of a concert, the immediate object of the course adopted by the Legislature, which was that of inviting the other States "to *concur* in declaring the acts to be unconstitutional, and to *co-operate* by the necessary & proper measures in maintaining unimpaired the authorities rights & liberties reserved to the States respectively & to the people." That by the necessary and proper measures to be *concurrently* and co-operatively taken, were meant measures known to the Constitution, particularly the ordinary controul of the people and Legislatures of the States over the Govt. of the U.S. cannot be doubted; and the interposition of this controul as the event showed was equal to the occasion.

It is worthy of remark, and explanatory of the intentions of the Legislature, that the words "not law, but utterly null, void, and of no force or effect," which had followed, in one of the Resolutions, the word "unconstitutional," were struck out by common consent. Tho the words were in fact but synonymous with "unconstitutional," yet to guard against a misunderstanding of this phrase as more than declaratory of opinion, the word unconstitutional alone was retained, as not liable to that danger.

The published address of the Legislature to the people their constituents affords another conclusive evidence of its views. The address warns them against the encroaching spirit of the Genl. Govt., argues the unconstitutionality of the alien & sedition acts, points to other instances in which the constl. limits had been overleaped; dwells on the dangerous mode of deriving power by implications; and in general presses the necessity of watching over the consolidating tendency of the Fedl. policy. But nothing is sd. that can be understood to look to means of maintaining the rights of the States beyond the regular ones within the forms of the Constn.

If any farther lights on the subject cd. be needed, a very strong one is reflected in the answers to the Resolutions by the States which protested agst. them. The main objection of these, beyond a few general complaints agst. the inflammatory tendency of the resolutions was directed agst. the assumed authy. of a State Legisle. to declare a law of the U.S. unconstitutional, which they pronounced an unwarrantable interference with the exclusive jurisdiction of the Supreme Ct. of the U.S. Had the resolns. been regarded as avowing & maintaining a right, in an indivl. State, to arrest by force the execution of a law of the U.S. it must be presumed that it wd. have been a conspicuous object of their denunciation.

22

South Carolina, Ordinance of Nullification

November 24, 1832[*]

AN ORDINANCE
To Nullify Certain Acts of the Congress of the United States, Purporting to be Laws, Laying Duties and Imposts on the Importation of Foreign Commodities.

Whereas, the Congress of the United States, by various acts, purporting to be acts laying duties and imposts on foreign imports, but in reality intended for the protection of domestic manufactures, and the giving of bounties to classes and individuals engaged in particular employments, at the expense and to the injury and oppression of other classes and individuals, and by wholly exempting from taxation certain foreign commodities, such as are not produced or manufactured in the United States, to afford a pretext for imposing higher and excessive duties on articles similar to those intended to be protected, hath exceeded its just powers under the Constitution, which confers on it no authority to afford such protection, and hath violated the true meaning and intent of the Constitution, which provides for equality in imposing the burdens of taxation upon the several States and portions of the Confederacy. And whereas, the said Congress, exceeding its just power to impose taxes and collect revenue for the purpose of effecting and accomplishing the specific objects and purposes which the Constitution of the United States authorizes it to effect and accomplish, hath raised and collected unnecessary revenue, for objects unauthorized by the Constitution. —

We, therefore, the People of the State of South Carolina, in Convention assembled, do Declare and Ordain, and it is hereby Declared and Ordained, That the several acts and parts of acts of the Congress of the United States, purporting to be laws for the imposing of duties and imposts on the importation of foreign commodities, and now having actual operation and effect within

[*]Alexander Hamilton, James Madison, and John Jay, *The Federalist: A Commentary on the Constitution of the United States*, ed. Paul Leicester Ford (New York: Henry Holt, 1898).

the United States, and more especially an act entitled "an act in alteration of the several acts imposing duties on imports," approved on the nineteenth day of May, one thousand eight hundred and twenty-eight, and also, an act entitled "an act to alter and amend the several acts imposing duties on imports," approved on the fourteenth day of July, one thousand eight hundred and thirty-two, are unauthorized by the Constitution of the United States, and violate the true meaning and intent thereof, and are null, void and no law, nor binding upon this State, its officers, or citizens; and all promises, contracts and obligations, made or entered into, or to be made or entered into, with purpose to secure the duties imposed by said acts, and all judicial proceedings which shall be hereafter had in affirmance thereof, are, and shall be held, utterly null and void.

And it is further Ordained, That it shall not be lawful for any of the constituted authorities, whether of this State, or of the United States, to enforce the payment of duties imposed by the said acts, within the limits of this State; but it shall be the duty of the Legislature to adopt such measures and pass such acts as may be necessary to give full effect to this Ordinance, and to prevent the enforcement and arrest the operation of the said acts and parts of acts of Congress of the United States within the limits of this State, from and after the first day of February next; and the duty of all other constituted authorities, and of all persons residing or being within the limits of this State, and they are hereby required and enjoined, to obey and give effect to this Ordinance, and such acts and measures of the Legislature as may be passed or adopted in obedience thereto.

And it is further Ordained, That in no case of law or equity, decided in the Courts of this State, wherein shall be drawn in question the authority of this Ordinance, or the validity of such act or acts of the Legislature as may be passed for the purpose of giving effect thereto, or the validity of the aforesaid acts of Congress, imposing duties, shall any appeal be taken or allowed to the Supreme Court of the United States; nor shall any copy of the record be permitted or allowed for that purpose; and if any such appeal shall be attempted to be taken, the Courts of this State shall proceed to execute and enforce their judgment, according to the laws and usages of the State, without reference to such attempted appeal, and the person or persons attempting to take such appeal may be dealt with as for a contempt of the Court.

And it is further Ordained, That all persons now holding any office of honor, profit or trust, civil or military, under this State, (members of the Legislature excepted) shall, within such time, and in such manner as the Legislature shall prescribe, take an oath, well and truly to obey, execute and enforce this Ordinance, and such act or acts of the Legislature as may be passed in pursuance thereof, according to the true intent and meaning of the same; and on the neglect or omission of any person or persons so to do, his or their office or offices shall be forthwith vacated, and shall be filled up as if such person or persons were dead or had resigned; and no person hereafter elected to any office of honor, profit or trust, civil or military, (members of the Legislature excepted) shall, until the Legislature shall otherwise provide and direct, enter on the execution of his office, or be in any respect competent to discharge the duties thereof, until he shall, in like manner, have taken a similar oath; and no juror shall be impaneled in any of the Courts of this State, in any cause in which shall be in question this Ordinance, or any act of the Legislature passed in pursuance thereof, unless he shall first, in addition to the usual oath, have taken an oath that he will well and truly obey, execute, and enforce this Ordinance, and such act or acts of the Legislature as may be passed to carry the same into operation and effect, according to the true intent and meaning thereof.

And we, the People of South Carolina, to the end that it may be fully understood by the Government of the United States, and the people of the co-States, that we are determined to maintain this, our Ordinance and Declaration, at every hazard, Do further Declare, that we will not submit to the application of force, on the part of the Federal Government, to reduce this State to obedience; but that we will consider the passage, by Congress, of any act authorizing the employment of a military or naval force against the State of South Carolina, her constituted authorities or citizens, or any act abolishing or closing the ports of this State, or any of them, or otherwise obstructing the free ingress of vessels to and from the said ports, or any other act, on the part of the Federal Government, to coerce the State, shut up her ports, destroy or harass her commerce, or to enforce the acts hereby declared to be null and void, otherwise than through the civil tribunals of the country, as inconsistent with the longer continuance of South Carolina in the Union; and that the People of this State will thenceforth hold themselves absolved from all further obligation to maintain or preserve their political connexion with the people of the other States, and will forthwith proceed to organize a separate Government, and to do all other acts and things which sovereign and independent States may of right do.

23

Daniel Webster, *The Constitution Is Not a Compact*

February 16, 1833*

Mr. President,—The gentleman from South Carolina has admonished us to be mindful of the opinions of those who shall come after us. We must take our chance, Sir, as to the light in which posterity will regard us. I do not decline its judgment, nor withhold myself from its scrutiny. Feeling that I am performing my public duty with singleness of heart and to the best of my ability, I fearlessly trust myself to the country, now and hereafter, and leave both my motives and my character to its decision.

The gentleman has terminated his speech in a tone of threat and defiance towards this bill, even should it become a law of the land, altogether unusual in the halls of Congress. But I shall not suffer myself to be excited into warmth by his denunciation of the measure which I support. Among the feelings which at this moment fill my breast, not the least is that of regret at the position in which the gentleman has placed himself. Sir, he does himself no justice. The cause which he has espoused finds no basis in the Constitution, no succor from pub-

*Edwin P. Whipple, *Great Speeches and Orations of Daniel Webster, with an Essay on Daniel Webster as a Master of English Style* (Boston: Little, Brown, 1886), 273. [Webster's speech responded to that of Sen. Calhoun, who had previously submitted a set of resolutions declaring, "*Resolved*, That the people of the several States composing these United States are united as parties to a constitutional compact, to which the people of each State acceded as a separate sovereign community, each binding itself by its own particular ratification; and that the union, of which the said compact is the bond, is a union *between the States* ratifying the same." See *Register of Debates*, 22nd Cong., 2nd Sess., 191–92 (Jan. 22, 1833) (Calhoun's resolutions); *Register of Debates*, 22nd Cong., 2nd Sess., 520 (Feb. 15, 1833) (Speech of Sen. Calhoun); *Register of Debates*, 22nd Cong., 2nd Sess., 553 (Feb. 16, 1833) (Speech of Sen. Webster). —Ed.]

lic sympathy, no cheering from a patriotic community. He has no foothold on which to stand while he might display the powers of his acknowledged talents. Every thing beneath his feet is hollow and treacherous. He is like a strong man struggling in a morass: every effort to extricate himself only sinks him deeper and deeper. And I fear the resemblance may be carried still farther; I fear that no friend can safely come to his relief, that no one can approach near enough to hold out a helping hand, without danger of going down himself, also, into the bottomless depths of this Serbonian bog.

The honorable gentleman has declared, that on the decision of the question now in debate may depend the cause of liberty itself. I am of the same opinion; but then, Sir, the liberty which I think is staked on the contest is not political liberty, in any general and undefined character, but our own well-understood and long-enjoyed *American* liberty.

Sir, I love Liberty no less ardently than the gentleman himself, in whatever form she may have appeared in the progress of human history. As exhibited in the master states of antiquity, as breaking out again from amidst the darkness of the Middle Ages, and beaming on the formation of new communities in modern Europe, she has, always and everywhere, charms for me. Yet, Sir, it is our own liberty, guarded by constitutions and secured by union, it is that liberty which is our paternal inheritance, it is our established, dear-bought, peculiar American liberty, to which I am chiefly devoted, and the cause of which I now mean, to the utmost of my power, to maintain and defend.

Mr. President, if I considered the constitutional question now before us as doubtful as it is important, and if I supposed that its decision, either in the Senate or by the country, was likely to be in any degree influenced by the manner in which I might now discuss it, this would be to me a moment of deep solicitude. Such a moment has once existed. There has been a time, when, rising in this place, on the same question, I felt, I must confess, that something for good or evil to the Constitution of the country might depend on an effort of mine. But circumstances are changed. Since that day, Sir, the public opinion has become awakened to this great question; it has grasped it; it has reasoned upon it, as becomes an intelligent and patriotic community, and has settled it, or now seems in the progress of settling it, by an authority which none can disobey, the authority of the people themselves.

I shall not, Mr. President, follow the gentleman, step

by step, through the course of his speech. Much of what he has said he has deemed necessary to the just explanation and defence of his own political character and conduct. On this I shall offer no comment. Much, too, has consisted of philosophical remark upon the general nature of political liberty, and the history of free institutions; and upon other topics, so general in their nature as to possess, in my opinion, only a remote bearing on the immediate subject of this debate.

But the gentleman's speech made some days ago, upon introducing his resolutions, those resolutions themselves, and parts of the speech now just concluded, may, I presume, be justly regarded as containing the whole South Carolina doctrine. That doctrine it is my purpose now to examine, and to compare it with the Constitution of the United States. I shall not consent, Sir, to make any new constitution, or to establish another form of government. I will not undertake to say what a constitution for these United States ought to be. That question the people have decided for themselves; and I shall take the instrument as they have established it, and shall endeavor to maintain it, in its plain sense and meaning, against opinions and notions which, in my judgment, threaten its subversion.

The resolutions introduced by the gentleman were apparently drawn up with care, and brought forward upon deliberation. I shall not be in danger, therefore, of misunderstanding him, or those who agree with him, if I proceed at once to these resolutions, and consider them as an authentic statement of those opinions upon the great constitutional question by which the recent proceedings in South Carolina are attempted to be justified.

These resolutions are three in number.

The third seems intended to enumerate, and to deny, the several opinions expressed in the President's proclamation, respecting the nature and powers of this government. Of this third resolution, I propose, at present, to take no particular notice.

The first two resolutions of the honorable member affirm these propositions, viz.:—1. That the political system under which we live, and under which Congress is now assembled, is a *compact*, to which the people of the several States, as separate and sovereign communities, are *the parties*.

2. That these sovereign parties have a right to judge, each for itself, of any alleged violation of the Constitution by Congress; and, in case of such violation, to choose, each for itself, its own mode and measure of redress.

It is true, Sir, that the honorable member calls this a "constitutional" compact; but still he affirms it to be a compact between sovereign States. What precise meaning, then, does he attach to the term *constitutional*? When applied to compacts between sovereign States, the term *constitutional* affixes to the word *compact* no definite idea. Were we to hear of a constitutional league or treaty between England and France, or a constitutional convention between Austria and Russia, we should not understand what could be intended by such a league, such a treaty, or such a convention. In these connections, the word is void of all meaning; and yet, Sir, it is easy, quite easy, to see why the honorable gentleman has used it in these resolutions. He cannot open the book, and look upon our written frame of government, without seeing that it is called a *constitution*. This may well be appalling to him. It threatens his whole doctrine of compact, and its darling derivatives, nullification and secession, with instant confutation. Because, if he admits our instrument of government to be a *constitution*, then, for that very reason, it is not a compact between sovereigns; a constitution of government and a compact between sovereign powers being things essentially unlike in their very natures, and incapable of ever being the same. Yet the word *constitution* is on the very front of the instrument. He cannot overlook it. He seeks, therefore, to compromise the matter, and to sink all the substantial sense of the word, while he retains a resemblance of its sound. He introduces a new word of his own, viz. *compact*, as importing the principal idea, and designed to play the principal part, and degrades *constitution* into an insignificant, idle epithet, attached to *compact*. The whole then stands as a "*constitutional compact*"! And in this way he hopes to pass off a plausible gloss, as satisfying the words of the instrument. But he will find himself disappointed. Sir, I must say to the honorable gentleman, that, in our American political grammar, CONSTITUTION is a noun substantive; it imports a distinct and clear idea of itself; and it is not to lose its importance and dignity, it is not to be turned into a poor, ambiguous, senseless, unmeaning adjective, for the purpose of accommodating any new set of political notions. Sir, we reject his new rules of syntax altogether. We will not give up our forms of political speech to the grammarians of the school of nullification. By the Constitution, we mean, not a "constitutional compact," but, simply and directly, the Constitution, the fundamental law; and if there be one word in the language which the people of the United States understand, this is that word. We know no more of a constitutional compact between sovereign powers, than we know of a *constitutional* indenture of copartnership, a *constitutional* deed of conveyance, or a *constitutional* bill of exchange. But we know what the *Constitution* is; we know what the plainly written fundamental law is; we know what the bond of our Union and the security of our liberties is; and we mean to maintain and to defend it, in its plain sense and unsophisticated meaning.

The sense of the gentleman's proposition, therefore, is not at all affected, one way or the other, by the use of this word. That proposition still is, that our system of government is but a *compact* between the people of separate and sovereign States.

Was it Mirabeau, Mr. President, or some other master of the human passions, who has told us that words are things? They are indeed things, and things of mighty influence, not only in addresses to the passions and high-wrought feelings of mankind, but in the discussion of legal and political questions also; because a just conclusion is often avoided, or a false one reached, by the adroit substitution of one phrase, or one word, for another. Of this we have, I think, another example in the resolutions before us.

The first resolution declares that the people of the several States *"acceded"* to the Constitution, or to the constitutional compact, as it is called. This word "accede," not found either in the Constitution itself, or in the ratification of it by any one of the States, has been chosen for use here, doubtless, not without a well-considered purpose.

The natural converse of *accession* is *secession*; and, therefore, when it is stated that the people of the States acceded to the Union, it may be more plausibly argued that they may secede from it. If, in adopting the Constitution, nothing was done but acceding to a compact, nothing would seem necessary, in order to break it up, but to secede from the same compact. But the term is wholly out of place. *Accession*, as a word applied to political associations, implies coming into a league, treaty, or confederacy, by one hitherto a stranger to it; and *secession* implies departing from such league or confederacy. The people of the United States have used no such form of expression in establishing the present government. They do not say that they *accede* to a league, but they declare that they *ordain* and *establish* a Constitution, Such are the very words of the instrument itself; and in all the States, without an exception, the language used by their conventions was, that they *"ratified the*

Constitution"; some of them employing the additional words "assented to" and "adopted," but all of them "ratifying."

There is more importance than may, at first sight, appear, in the introduction of this new word, by the honorable mover of these resolutions. Its adoption and use are indispensable to maintain those premises from which his main conclusion is to be afterwards drawn. But before showing that, allow me to remark, that this phraseology tends to keep out of sight the just view of a previous political history, as well as to suggest wrong ideas as to what was actually done when the present Constitution was agreed to. In 1789, and before this Constitution was adopted, the United States had already been in a union, more or less close, for fifteen years. At least as far back as the meeting of the first Congress, in 1774, they had been in some measure, and for some national purposes, united together. Before the Confederation of 1781, they had declared independence jointly, and had carried on the war jointly, both by sea and land; and this not as separate States, but as one people. When, therefore, they formed that Confederation, and adopted its articles as articles of perpetual union, they did not come together for the first time; and therefore they did not speak of the States as *acceding* to the Confederation, although it was a league, and nothing but a league, and rested on nothing but plighted faith for its performance. Yet, even then, the States were not strangers to each other; there was a bond of union already subsisting between them; they were associated, United States; and the object of the Confederation was to make a stronger and better bond of union. Their representatives deliberated together on these proposed Articles of Confederation, and, being authorized by their respective States, finally *"ratified and confirmed"* them. Inasmuch as they were already in union, they did not speak of *acceding* to the new Articles of Confederation, but of *ratifying and confirming* them; and this language was not used inadvertently, because, in the same instrument, *accession* is used in its proper sense, when applied to Canada, which was altogether a stranger to the existing union. "Canada," says the eleventh article, *"acceding* to this Confederation, and joining in the measures of the United States, shall be admitted into the Union."

Having thus used the terms *ratify* and *confirm*, even in regard to the old Confederation, it would have been strange indeed, if the people of the United States, after its formation, and when they came to establish the present Constitution, had spoken of the States, or the people of the States, as *acceding* to this Constitution. Such language would have been ill-suited to the occasion. It would have implied an existing separation or disunion among the States, such as never has existed since 1774. No such language, therefore, was used. The language actually employed is, *adopt, ratify, ordain, establish.*

Therefore, Sir, since any State, before she can prove her right to dissolve the Union, must show her authority to undo what has been done, no State is at liberty to *secede*, on the ground that she and other States have done nothing but *accede*. She must show that she has a right to *reverse* what has been *ordained*, to *unsettle* and *overthrow* what has been *established*, to *reject* what the people have *adopted*, and to *break up* what they have *ratified*; because these are the terms which express the transactions which have actually taken place. In other words, she must show her right to make a revolution.

If, Mr. President, in drawing these resolutions, the honorable member had confined himself to the use of constitutional language, there would have been a wide and awful *hiatus* between his premises and his conclusion. Leaving out the two words *compact* and *accession*, which are not constitutional modes of expression, and stating the matter precisely as the truth is, his first resolution would have affirmed that *the people of the several States ratified this Constitution, or form of government.* These are the very words of South Carolina herself, in her act of ratification. Let, then, his first resolution tell the exact truth; let it state the fact precisely as it exists; let it say that the people of the several States ratified a constitution, or form of government, and then, Sir, what will become of his inference in his second resolution, which is in these words, viz. "that, as in all other cases of compact among sovereign parties, each has an equal right to judge for itself, as well of the infraction as of the mode and measure of redress"? It is obvious, is it not, Sir? that this conclusion requires for its support quite other premises; it requires premises which speak of *accession* and of *compact* between sovereign powers; and, without such premises, it is altogether unmeaning.

Mr. President, if the honorable member will truly state what the people did in forming this Constitution, and then state what they must do if they would now undo what they then did, he will unavoidably state a case of revolution. Let us see if it be not so. He must state, in the first place, that the people of the several States adopted and ratified this Constitution, or form of government; and, in the next place, he must state that they have a right to undo this; that is to say, that they

have a right to discard the form of government which they have adopted, and to break up the Constitution which they have ratified. Now, Sir, this is neither more nor less than saying that they have a right to make a revolution. To reject an established government, to break up a political constitution, is revolution.

I deny that any man can state accurately what was done by the people, in establishing the present Constitution, and then state accurately what the people, or any part of them, must now do to get rid of its obligations, without stating an undeniable case of the overthrow of government. I admit, of course, that the people may, if they choose, overthrow the government. But, then, that is revolution. The doctrine now contended for is, that, by *nullification*, or *secession*, the obligations and authority of the government may be set aside or rejected, without revolution. But that is what I deny; and what I say is, that no man can state the case with historical accuracy, and in constitutional language, without showing that the honorable gentleman's right, as asserted in his conclusion, is a revolutionary right merely; that it does not and cannot exist under the Constitution, or agreeably to the Constitution, but can come into existence only when the Constitution is overthrown.

. . .

And now, Sir, against all these theories and opinions, I maintain,—

1. That the Constitution of the United States is not a league, confederacy, or compact between the people of the several States in their sovereign capacities; but a government proper, founded on the adoption of the people, and creating direct relations between itself and individuals.

2. That no State authority has power to dissolve these relations; that nothing can dissolve them but revolution; and that, consequently, there can be no such thing as secession without revolution.

3. That there is a supreme law, consisting of the Constitution of the United States, and acts of Congress passed in pursuance of it, and treaties; and that, in cases not capable of assuming the character of a suit in law or equity, Congress must judge of, and finally interpret, this supreme law so often as it has occasion to pass acts of legislation; and in cases capable of assuming, and actually assuming, the character of a suit, the Supreme Court of the United States is the final interpreter.

4. That an attempt by a State to abrogate, annul, or nullify an act of Congress, or to arrest its operation within her limits, on the ground that, in her opinion,

such law is unconstitutional, is a direct usurpation on the just powers of the general government, and on the equal rights of other States; a plain violation of the Constitution, and a proceeding essentially revolutionary in its character and tendency.

. . .

There is no language in the whole constitution applicable to a confederation of States. If the States be parties, as States, what are their rights, and what their respective covenants and stipulations? And where are their rights, covenants, and stipulations expressed? The States engage for nothing, they promise nothing. In the Articles of Confederation they did make promises, and did enter into engagements, and did plight the faith of each State for their fulfillment; but in the Constitution there is nothing of that kind. The reason is, that, in the Constitution, it is the people who speak and not the States. The people ordain the Constitution, and therein address themselves to the States, and to the legislatures of the States, in the language of injunction and prohibition. The Constitution utters its behests in the name and by the authority of the people, and it does not exact from States any plighted public faith to maintain it. On the contrary, it makes its own preservation depend on individual duty and individual obligation. Sir, the States cannot omit to appoint Senators and electors. It is not a matter resting in State discretion or State pleasure. The Constitution has taken better care of its own preservation. It lays its hand on individual duty and individual conscience. It incapacitates any man to sit in the Legislature of a State, who shall not first have taken his solemn oath to support the Constitution of the United States. From the obligation of this oath, no State power can discharge him.

. . .

The second proposition, Sir, which I propose to maintain, is, that no State authority can dissolve the relations subsisting between the government of the United States and individuals; that nothing can dissolve these relations but revolution; and that, therefore, there can be no such thing as *secession* without revolution. All this follows, as it seems to me, as a just consequence, if it be first proved that the Constitution of the United States is a government proper, owing protection to individuals, and entitled to their obedience.

The people, Sir, in every State, live under two governments. They owe obedience to both. These governments, though distinct, are not adverse. Each has its separate sphere, and its peculiar powers and duties. It

is not a contest between two sovereigns for the same power, like the wars of the rival houses in England; nor is it a dispute between a government *de facto* and a government *de jure*. It is the case of a division of powers between two governments, made by the people, to whom both are responsible. Neither can dispense with the duty which individuals owe to the other; neither can call itself master of the other: the people are masters of both. This division of power, it is true, is in a great measure unknown in Europe. It is the peculiar system of America; and, though new and singular, it is not incomprehensible. The State constitutions are established by the people of the States. This Constitution is established by the people of all the States. How, then, can a State secede? How can a State undo what the whole people have done? How can she absolve her citizens from their obedience to the laws of the United States? How can she annul their obligations and oaths? How can the members of her legislature renounce their own oaths? Sir, secession, as a revolutionary right, is intelligible; as a right to be proclaimed in the midst of civil commotions, and asserted at the head of armies, I can understand it. But as a practical right, existing under the Constitution, and in conformity with its provisions, it seems to me to be nothing but a plain absurdity; for it supposes resistance to government, under the authority of government itself; it supposes dismemberment, without violating the principles of union; it supposes opposition to law, without crime; it supposes the violation of oaths, without responsibility; it supposes the total overthrow of government, without revolution.

The Constitution, Sir, regards itself as perpetual and immortal. It seeks to establish a union among the people of the States, which shall last through all time. Or, if the common fate of things human must be expected at some period to happen to it, yet that catastrophe is not anticipated.

The instrument contains ample provisions for its amendment, at all times; none for its abandonment, at any time. It declares that new States may come into the Union, but it does not declare that old States may go out. The Union is not a temporary partnership of States. It is the association of the people, under a constitution of government, uniting their power, joining together their highest interests, cementing their present enjoyments, and blending, in one indivisible mass, all their hopes for the future. Whatsoever is steadfast in just political principles; whatsoever is permanent in the structure of human society; whatsoever there is which can derive an enduring character from being founded on deep-laid principles of constitutional liberty and on the broad foundations of the public will, — all these unite to entitle this instrument to be regarded as a permanent constitution of government.

In the next place, Mr. President, I contend that there is a supreme law of the land, consisting of the Constitution, acts of Congress passed in pursuance of it, and the public treaties. This will not be denied, because such are the very words of the Constitution. But I contend, further, that it rightfully belongs to Congress, and to the courts of the United States, to settle the construction of this supreme law, in doubtful cases. This is denied; and here arises the great practical question, *Who is to construe finally the Constitution of the United States?* We all agree that the Constitution is the supreme law; but who shall interpret that law? In our system of the division of powers between different governments, controversies will necessarily sometimes arise, respecting the extent of the powers of each. Who shall decide these controversies? Does it rest with the general government, in all or any of its departments, to exercise the office of final interpreter? Or may each of the States, as well as the general government, claim this right of ultimate decision? The practical result of this whole debate turns on this point. The gentleman contends that each State may judge for itself of any alleged violation of the Constitution, and may finally decide for itself, and may execute its own decisions by its own power. All the recent proceedings in South Carolina are founded on this claim of right. Her convention has pronounced the revenue laws of the United States unconstitutional; and this decision she does not allow any authority of the United States to overrule or reverse. Of course she rejects the authority of Congress, because the very object of the ordinance is to reverse the decision of Congress; and she rejects, too, the authority of the courts of the United States, because she expressly prohibits all appeal to those courts. It is in order to sustain this asserted right of being her own judge, that she pronounces the Constitution of the United States to be but a compact, to which she is a party, and a sovereign party. If this be established, then the inference is supposed to follow, that, being sovereign, there is no power to control her decision; and her own judgment on her own compact is, and must be, conclusive.

I have already endeavored, Sir, to point out the practical consequences of this doctrine, and to show how utterly inconsistent it is with all ideas of regular government, and how soon its adoption would involve the whole country in revolution and absolute anarchy. I hope it is easy now to show, Sir, that a doctrine bringing such consequences with it is not well founded; that it has nothing to stand on but theory and assumption; and that it is refuted by plain and express constitutional provisions. I think the government of the United States does possess, in its appropriate departments, the authority of final decision on questions of disputed power. I think it possesses this authority, both by necessary implication and by express grant.

It will not be denied, Sir, that this authority naturally belongs to all governments. They all exercise it from necessity, and as a consequence of the exercise of other powers. The State governments themselves possess it, except in that class of questions which may arise between them and the general government, and in regard to which they have surrendered it, as well by the nature of the case as by clear constitutional provisions. In other and ordinary cases, whether a particular law be in conformity to the constitution of the State is a question which the State legislature or the State judiciary must determine. We all know that these questions arise daily in the State governments, and are decided by those governments; and I know no government which does not exercise a similar power.

Upon general principles, then, the government of the United States possesses this authority; and this would hardly be denied were it not that there are other governments. But since there are State governments, and since these, like other governments, ordinarily construe their own powers, if the government of the United States construes its own powers also, which construction is to prevail in the case of opposite constructions? And again, as in the case now actually before us, the State governments may undertake, not only to construe their own powers, but to decide directly on the extent of the powers of Congress. Congress has passed a law as being within its just powers; South Carolina denies that this law is within its just powers, and insists that she has the right so to decide this point, and that her decision is final. How are these questions to be settled?

In my opinion, Sir, even if the Constitution of the United States had made no express provision for such cases, it would yet be difficult to maintain, that, in a Constitution existing over four-and-twenty States, with equal authority over all, *one* could claim a right of construing it for the whole. This would seem a manifest impropriety; indeed, an absurdity. If the Constitution is a government existing over all the States, though with limited powers, it necessarily follows, that, to the extent of those powers, it must be supreme. If it be not superior to the authority of a particular State, it is not a national government. But as it is a government, as it has a legislative power of its own, and a judicial power coextensive with the legislative, the inference is irresistible that this government, thus created *by* the whole and *for* the whole, must have an authority superior to that of the particular government of any one part. Congress is the legislature of all the people of the United States; the judiciary of the general government is the judiciary of all the people of the United States. To hold, therefore, that this legislature and this judiciary are subordinate in authority to the legislature and judiciary of a single State, is doing violence to all common sense, and overturning all established principles. Congress must judge of the extent of its own powers so often as it is called on to exercise them, or it cannot act at all; and it must also act independent of State control, or it cannot act at all.

The right of State interposition strikes at the very foundation of the legislative power of Congress. It possesses no effective legislative power, if such right of State interposition exists; because it can pass no law not subject to abrogation. It cannot make laws for the Union, if any part of the Union may pronounce its enactments void and of no effect. Its forms of legislation would be an idle ceremony, if, after all, any one of four-and-twenty States might bid defiance to its authority. Without express provision in the Constitution, therefore, Sir, this whole question is necessarily decided by those provisions which create a legislative power and a judicial power. If these exist in a government intended for the whole, the inevitable consequence is, that the laws of this legislative power and the decisions of this judicial power must be binding on and over the whole. No man can form the conception of a government existing over four-and-twenty States, with a regular legislative and judicial power, and of the existence at the same time of an authority, residing elsewhere, to resist, at pleasure or discretion, the enactments and the decisions of such a government. I maintain, therefore, Sir, that, from the nature of the case, and as an inference wholly unavoidable, the acts of Congress and the decisions of the national courts must be of higher authority than State laws and State decisions. If this be not so, there is, there can be, no general government.

But, Mr. President, the Constitution has not left this cardinal point without full and explicit provisions. First,

as to the authority of Congress. Having enumerated the specific powers conferred on Congress, the Constitution adds, as a distinct and substantive clause, the following, viz.: "To make all laws which shall be necessary and proper for carrying into execution the foregoing powers, and all other powers vested by this Constitution in the government of the United States, or in any department or officer thereof." If this means any thing, it means that Congress may judge of the true extent and just interpretation of the specific powers granted to it, and may judge also of what is necessary and proper for executing those powers. If Congress is to judge of what is necessary for the execution of its powers, it must, of necessity, judge of the extent and interpretation of those powers.

And in regard, Sir, to the judiciary, the Constitution is still more express and emphatic. It declares that the judicial power shall extend to all *cases* in law or equity arising under the Constitution, laws of the United States, and treaties; that there shall be *one* Supreme Court, and that this Supreme Court shall have appellate jurisdiction of all these cases, subject to such exceptions as Congress may make. It is impossible to escape from the generality of these words. If a case arises under the Constitution, that is, if a case arises depending on the construction of the Constitution, the judicial power of the United States extends to it. It reaches *the case, the question*; it attaches the power of the national judicature to the *case* itself, in whatever court it may arise or exist; and in this *case* the Supreme Court has appellate jurisdiction over all courts whatever. No language could provide with more effect and precision than is here done, for subjecting constitutional questions to the ultimate decision of the Supreme Court. And, Sir, this is exactly what the Convention found it necessary to provide for, and intended to provide for. It is, too, exactly what the people were universally told was done when they adopted the Constitution. One of the first resolutions adopted by the Convention was in these words, viz.: "That the jurisdiction of the national judiciary shall extend to cases which respect *the collection of the national revenue*, and questions which involve the national peace and harmony." Now, Sir, this either had no sensible meaning at all, or else it meant that the jurisdiction of the national judiciary should extend to these questions, *with a paramount authority*. It is not to be supposed that the Convention intended that the power of the national judiciary should extend to these questions, and that the power of the judicatures of the States should also extend to them, *with equal power of final decision*. This would be to defeat the whole object of the provision. There were thirteen judicatures already in existence. The evil complained of, or the danger to be guarded against, was contradiction and repugnance in the decisions of these judicatures. If the framers of the Constitution meant to create a fourteenth, and yet not to give it power to revise and control the decisions of the existing thirteen, then they only intended to augment the existing evil and the apprehended danger by increasing still further the chances of discordant judgments. Why, Sir, has it become a settled axiom in politics that every government must have a judicial power coextensive with its legislative power? Certainly, there is only this reason, namely, that the laws may receive a uniform interpretation and a uniform execution. This object cannot be otherwise attained. A statute is what it is judicially interpreted to be; and if it be construed one way in New Hampshire, and another way in Georgia, there is no uniform law. One supreme court, with appellate and final jurisdiction, is the natural and only adequate means, in any government, to secure this uniformity. The Convention saw all this clearly; and the resolution which I have quoted, never afterwards rescinded, passed through various modifications, till it finally received the form which the article now bears in the Constitution.

It is undeniably true, then, that the framers of the Constitution intended to create a national judicial power, which should be paramount on national subjects. And after the Constitution was framed, and while the whole country was engaged in discussing its merits, one of its most distinguished advocates, Mr. Madison, told the people that it *was true, that, in controversies relating to the boundary between the two jurisdictions, the tribunal which is ultimately to decide is to be established under the general government.* Mr. Martin, who had been a member of the Convention, asserted the same thing to the legislature of Maryland, and urged it as a reason for rejecting the Constitution. Mr. Pinckney, himself also a leading member of the Convention, declared it to the people of South Carolina. Everywhere it was admitted, by friends and foes, that this power was in the Constitution. By some it was thought dangerous, by most it was thought necessary; but by all it was agreed to be a power actually contained in the instrument. The Convention saw the absolute necessity of some control in the national government over State laws. Different modes of establishing this control were suggested and considered. At one time, it was proposed that the laws of the States should, from time to time,

be laid before Congress, and that Congress should possess a negative over them. But this was thought inexpedient and inadmissible; and in its place, and expressly as a substitute for it, the existing provision was introduced; that is to say, a provision by which the federal courts should have authority to overrule such State laws as might be in manifest contravention of the Constitution. The writers of the Federalist, in explaining the Constitution, while it was yet pending before the people, and still unadopted, give this account of the matter in terms, and assign this reason for the article as it now stands. By this provision Congress escaped the necessity of any revision of State laws, left the whole sphere of State legislation quite untouched, and yet obtained a security against any infringement of the constitutional power of the general government. Indeed, Sir, allow me to ask again, if the national judiciary was not to exercise a power of revision on constitutional questions over the judicatures of the States, why was any national judicature erected at all? Can any man give a sensible reason for having a judicial power in this government, unless it be for the sake of maintaining a uniformity of decision on questions arising under the Constitution and laws of Congress, and insuring its execution? And does not this very idea of uniformity necessarily imply that the construction given by the national courts is to be the prevailing construction? How else, Sir, is it possible that uniformity can be preserved?

Gentlemen appear to me, Sir, to look at but one side of the question. They regard only the supposed danger of trusting a government with the interpretation of its own powers. But will they view the question in its other aspect? Will they show us how it is possible for a government to get along with four-and-twenty interpreters of its laws and powers? Gentlemen argue, too, as if, in these cases, the State would be always right, and the general government always wrong. But suppose the reverse, — suppose the State wrong (and, since they differ, some of them must be wrong), — are the most important and essential operations of the government to be embarrassed and arrested, because one State holds the contrary opinion? Mr. President, every argument which refers the constitutionality of acts of Congress to State decision appeals from the majority to the minority; it appeals from the common interest to a particular interest; from the counsels of all to the counsel of one; and endeavors to supersede the judgment of the whole by the judgment of a part.

...

My fourth and last proposition, Mr. President, was, that any attempt by a State to abrogate or nullify acts of Congress is a usurpation on the powers of the general government and on the equal rights of other States, a violation of the Constitution, and a proceeding essentially revolutionary. This is undoubtedly true, if the preceding propositions be regarded as proved. If the government of the United States be trusted with the duty, in any department, of declaring the extent of its own powers, then a State ordinance, or act of legislation, authorizing resistance to an act of Congress, on the alleged ground of its unconstitutionally, is manifestly a usurpation upon its powers. If the States have equal rights in matters concerning the whole, then for one State to set up her judgment against the judgment of the rest, and to insist on executing that judgment by force, is also a manifest usurpation on the rights of other States. If the Constitution of the United States be a government proper, with authority to pass laws, and to give them a uniform interpretation and execution, then the interposition of a State, to enforce her own construction, and to resist, as to herself, that law which binds the other States, is a violation of the Constitution.

If that be revolutionary which arrests the legislative, executive, and judicial power of government, dispenses with existing oaths and obligations of obedience, and elevates another power to supreme dominion, then nullification is revolutionary. Or if that be revolutionary the natural tendency and practical effect of which are to break the Union into fragments, to sever all connection among the people of the respective States, and to prostrate this general government in the dust, then nullification is revolutionary.

Nullification, Sir, is as distinctly revolutionary as secession; but I cannot say that the revolution which it seeks is one of so respectable a character. Secession would, it is true, abandon the Constitution altogether; but then it would profess to abandon it. Whatever other inconsistencies it might run into, one, at least, it would avoid. It would not belong to a government, while it rejected its authority. It would not repel the burden, and continue to enjoy the benefits. It would not aid in passing laws which others are to obey, and yet reject their authority as to itself. It would not undertake to reconcile obedience to public authority with an asserted right of command over that same authority. It would not be in the government, and above the government, at the same time. But though secession may be a more respectable mode of attaining the object than nullification, it is not

more truly revolutionary. Each, and both, resist the constitutional authorities; each, and both, would sever the Union and subvert the government.

...

Mr. President, if the friends of nullification should be able to propagate their opinions, and give them practical effect, they would, in my judgment, prove themselves the most skillful "architects of ruin," the most effectual extinguishers of high-raised expectation, the greatest blasters of human hopes, that any age has produced. They would stand up to proclaim, in tones which would pierce the ears of half the human race, that the last great experiment of representative government had failed. They would send forth sounds, at the hearing of which the doctrine of the divine right of kings would feel, even in its grave, a returning sensation of vitality and resuscitation. Millions of eyes, of those who now feed their inherent love of liberty on the success of the American example, would turn away from beholding our dismemberment, and find no place on earth whereon to rest their gratified sight. Amidst the incantations and orgies of nullification, secession, disunion, and revolution, would be celebrated the funeral rites of constitutional and republican liberty.

But, Sir, if the government do its duty, if it act with firmness and with moderation, these opinions cannot prevail. Be assured, Sir, be assured, that, among the political sentiments of this people, the love of union is still uppermost. They will stand fast by the Constitution, and by those who defend it. I rely on no temporary expedients, on no political combination; but I rely on the true American feeling, the genuine patriotism of the people, and the imperative decision of the public voice. Disorder and confusion, indeed, may arise; scenes of commotion and contest are threatened, and perhaps may come. With my whole heart, I pray for the continuance of the domestic peace and quiet of the country. I desire, most ardently, the restoration of affection and harmony to all its parts. I desire that every citizen of the whole country may look to this government with no other sentiments than those of grateful respect and attachment. But I cannot yield even to kind feelings the cause of the Constitution, the true glory of the country, and the great trust which we hold in our hands for succeeding ages. If the Constitution cannot be maintained without meeting these scenes of commotion and contest, however unwelcome, they must come. We cannot, we must not, we dare not, omit to do that which, in our judgment, the safety of the Union requires. Not regardless of consequences, we must yet meet consequences; seeing the hazards which surround the discharge of public duty, it must yet be discharged. For myself, Sir, I shun no responsibility justly devolving on me, here or elsewhere, in attempting to maintain the cause. I am bound to it by indissoluble ties of affection and duty, and I shall cheerfully partake in its fortunes and its fate. I am ready to perform my own appropriate part, whenever and wherever the occasion may call on me, and to take my chance among those upon whom blows may fall first and fall thickest. I shall exert every faculty I possess in aiding to prevent the Constitution from being nullified, destroyed, or impaired; and even should I see it fall, I will still, with a voice feeble, perhaps, but earnest as ever issued from human lips, and with fidelity and zeal which nothing shall extinguish, call on the PEOPLE to come to its rescue.

24

James Madison to Daniel Webster

March 15, 1833[*]

I return my thanks for the copy of your late very powerful Speech in the Senate of the United S. It crushes "nullification" and must hasten the abandonment of "Secession." But this dodges the blow by confounding the claim to secede at will, with the right of seceding from intolerable oppression. The former answers itself, being a violation, without cause, of a faith solemnly pledged. The latter is another name only for revolution, about which there is no theoretic controversy. Its double aspect, nevertheless, with the countenance recd from certain quarters, is giving it a popular currency here which may influence the approaching elections both for Congress & for the State Legislature. It has gained some advantage also, by mixing itself with the question whether the Constitution of the U.S. was formed by the people or by the States, now under a theoretic discussion by animated partizans.

It is fortunate when disputed theories, can be decided by undisputed facts. And here the undisputed fact is, that the Constitution was made by the people, but as

[*] James Madison, *Letters and Other Writings of James Madison* (Philadelphia: J. B. Lippincott, 1865), 4:293–94.

embodied into the several states, who were parties to it and therefore made by the States in their highest authoritative capacity. They might, by the same authority & by the same process have converted the Confederacy into a mere league or treaty; or continued it with enlarged or abridged powers; or have embodied the people of their respective States into one people, nation or sovereignty; or as they did by a mixed form make them one people, nation, or sovereignty, for certain purposes, and not so for others.

The Constitution of the U.S. being established by a Competent authority, by that of the sovereign people of the several States who were the parties to it, it remains only to inquire what the Constitution is; and here it speaks for itself. It organizes a Government into the usual Legislative Executive & Judiciary Departments; invests it with specified powers, leaving others to the parties to the Constitution; it makes the Government like other Governments to operate directly on the people; places at its Command the needful Physical means of executing its powers; and finally proclaims its supremacy, and that of the laws made in pursuance of it, over the Constitutions & laws of the States; the powers of the Government being exercised, as in other elective & responsible Governments, under the controul of its Constituents, the people & legislatures of the States, and subject to the Revolutionary Rights of the people in extreme cases.

It might have been added, that whilst the Constitution, therefore, is admitted to be in force, its operation, in every respect must be precisely the same, whether its authority be derived from that of the people, in the one or the other of the modes, in question; the authority being equally Competent in both; and that, without an annulment of the Constitution itself its supremacy must be submitted to.

The only distinctive effect, between the two modes of forming a Constitution by the authority of the people, is that if formed by them as embodied into separate communities, as in the case of the Constitution of the U.S. a dissolution of the Constitutional Compact would replace them in the condition of separate communities, that being the Condition in which they entered into the compact; whereas if formed by the people as one community, acting as such by a numerical majority, a dissolution of the compact would reduce them to a state of nature, as so many individual persons. But whilst the Constitutional compact remains undissolved, it must be executed according to the forms and provisions specified in the compact. It must not be forgotten, that compact, express or implied is the vital principle of free Governments as contradistinguished from Governments not free; and that a revolt against this principle leaves no choice but between anarchy and despotism.

25

Barron v. Baltimore

32 U.S. 243 (1833)

Mr. Chief Justice MARSHALL delivered the opinion of the court.

The judgment brought up by this writ of error having been rendered by the court of a State, this tribunal can exercise no jurisdiction over it unless it be shown to come within the provisions of the 25th section of the Judiciary Act.

The plaintiff in error contends that it comes within that clause in the Fifth Amendment to the Constitution which inhibits the taking of private property for public use without just compensation. He insists that this amendment, being in favor of the liberty of the citizen, ought to be so construed as to restrain the legislative power of a state, as well as that of the United States. If this proposition be untrue, the court can take no jurisdiction of the cause.

The question thus presented is, we think, of great importance, but not of much difficulty.

The Constitution was ordained and established by the people of the United States for themselves, for their own government, and not for the government of the individual States. Each State established a constitution for itself, and in that constitution provided such limitations and restrictions on the powers of its particular government as its judgment dictated. The people of the United States framed such a government for the United States as they supposed best adapted to their situation and best calculated to promote their interests. The powers they conferred on this government were to be exercised by itself, and the limitations on power, if expressed in general terms, are naturally, and we think necessarily, applicable to the government created by the instrument. They are limitations of power granted in the instrument itself, not of distinct governments framed by different persons and for different purposes.

If these propositions be correct, the fifth amendment must be understood as restraining the power of the General Government, not as applicable to the States. In their several Constitutions, they have imposed such restrictions on their respective governments, as their own wisdom suggested, such as they deemed most proper for themselves. It is a subject on which they judge exclusively, and with which others interfere no further than they are supposed to have a common interest.

The counsel for the plaintiff in error insists that the Constitution was intended to secure the people of the several States against the undue exercise of power by their respective State governments, as well as against that which might be attempted by their General Government. It support of this argument he relies on the inhibitions contained in the tenth section of the first article.

We think that section affords a strong, if not a conclusive, argument in support of the opinion already indicated by the court.

The preceding section contains restrictions which are obviously intended for the exclusive purpose of restraining the exercise of power by the departments of the General Government. Some of them use language applicable only to Congress, others are expressed in general terms. The third clause, for example, declares, that "no bill of attainder or ex post facto law shall be passed." No language can be more general, yet the demonstration is complete that it applies solely to the Government of the United States. In addition to the general arguments furnished by the instrument itself, some of which have been already suggested, the succeeding section, the avowed purpose of which is to restrain State legislation, contains in terms the very prohibition. It declares, that "no State shall pass any bill of attainder or ex post facto law." This provision, then, of the ninth section, however comprehensive its language, contains no restriction on State legislation.

The ninth section having enumerated, in the nature of a bill of rights, the limitations intended to be imposed on the powers of the General Government, the tenth proceeds to enumerate those which were to operate on the State legislatures. These restrictions are brought together in the same section, and are by express words applied to the States. "No State shall enter into any treaty," &c. Perceiving, that in a constitution framed by the people of the United States, for the government of all, no limitation of the action of government on the people would apply to the State government, unless expressed in terms, the restrictions contained in the tenth section are in direct words so applied to the States.

It is worthy of remark, too, that these inhibitions generally restrain State legislation on subjects intrusted to the General Government, or in which the people of all the States feel an interest.

A State is forbidden to enter into any treaty, alliance or confederation. If these compacts are with foreign nations, they interfere with the treaty-making power, which is conferred entirely on the General Government; if with each other, for political purposes, they can scarcely fail to interfere with the general purpose and intent of the Constitution. To grant letters of marque and reprisal, would lead directly to war, the power of declaring which is expressly given to Congress. To coin money is also the exercise of a power conferred on Congress. It would be tedious to recapitulate the several limitations on the powers of the States which are contained in this section. They will be found generally to restrain State legislation on subjects intrusted to the government of the Union, in which the citizens of all the States are interested. In these alone were the whole people concerned. The question of their application to States is not left to construction. It is averred in positive words.

If the original Constitution, in the ninth and tenth sections of the first article, draws this plain and marked line of discrimination between the limitations it imposes on the powers of the General Government and on those of the State; if, in every inhibition intended to act on State power, words are employed which directly express that intent; some strong reason must be assigned for departing from this safe and judicious course in framing the amendments before that departure can be assumed.

We search in vain for that reason.

Had the people of the several States, or any of them, required changes in their Constitutions, had they required additional safeguards to liberty from the apprehended encroachments of their particular governments, the remedy was in their own hands, and could have been applied by themselves. A convention could have been assembled by the discontented State, and the required improvements could have been made by itself. The unwieldy and cumbrous machinery of procuring a recommendation from two-thirds of Congress and the assent of three-fourths of their sister States could never have occurred to any human being as a mode of doing that which might be effected by the State itself. Had the framers of these amendments intended them to be limitations on the powers of the State governments, they would have imitated the framers of the original Constitution, and have expressed that intention. Had Congress engaged in the extraordinary occupation of improving the Constitutions of the several States by affording the people additional protection from the exercise of power by their own governments in matters which concerned themselves alone, they would have declared this purpose in plain and intelligible language.

But it is universally understood, it is a part of the history of the day, that the great revolution which established the Constitution of the United States was not effected without immense opposition. Serious fears were extensively entertained that those powers which the patriot statesmen who then watched over the interests of our country deemed essential to union, and to the attainment of those invaluable objects for which union was sought, might be exercised in a manner dangerous to liberty. In almost every convention by which the Constitution was adopted, amendments to guard against the abuse of power were recommended. These amendments demanded security against the apprehended encroachments of the General Government—not against those of the local governments.

In compliance with a sentiment thus generally expressed, to quiet fears thus extensively entertained, amendments were proposed by the required majority in Congress and adopted by the States. These amendments contain no expression indicating an intention to apply them to the State governments. This court cannot so apply them.

We are of opinion that the provision in the Fifth Amendment to the Constitution declaring that private property shall not be taken for public use without just compensation is intended solely as a limitation on the exercise of power by the Government of the United States, and is not applicable to the legislation of the States. We are therefore of opinion that there is no repugnancy between the several acts of the general assembly of Maryland, given in evidence by the defendants at the trial of this cause, in the court of that State, and the Constitution of the United States. This court, therefore, has no jurisdiction of the cause, and it is dismissed.

This cause came on to be heard on the transcript of the record from the Court of Appeals for the Western Shore of the State of Maryland, and was argued by counsel. On consideration whereof, it is the opinion of this

Court that there is no repugnancy between the several acts of the General Assembly of Maryland given in evidence by the defendants at the trial of this cause in the court of that State and the Constitution of the United States; whereupon it is ordered and adjudged by this court that this writ of error be, and the same is hereby, dismissed for the want of jurisdiction.

26

Joseph Story, *Commentaries on the Constitution*

1833[*]

NATURE OF THE CONSTITUTION — WHETHER A COMPACT

§ 306. Having thus sketched out a general history of the origin and adoption of the constitution of the United States, and a summary of the principal objections and difficulties, which it had to encounter, we are at length arrived at the point at which it may be proper to enter upon the consideration of the actual structure, organization, and powers, which belong to it. Our main object will henceforth be to unfold in detail all its principal provisions, with such commentaries, as may explain their import and effect, and with such illustrations, historical and otherwise, as will enable the reader fully to understand the objections, which have been urged against each of them respectively; the amendments, which have been proposed to them; and the arguments, which have sustained them in their present form.

§ 307. Before doing this, however, it seems necessary, in the first place, to bestow some attention upon several points, which have attracted a good deal of discussion, and which are preliminary in their own nature; and in the next place to consider, what are the true rules of interpretation belonging to the instrument.

§ 308. In the first place, what is the true nature and import of the instrument? Is it a treaty, a convention, a league, a contract, or a compact? Who are the parties to it? By whom was it made? By whom was it ratified? What are its obligations? By whom, and in what manner may it be dissolved? Who are to determine its validity and construction? Who are to decide upon the supposed infractions and violations of it? These are questions often asked, and often discussed, not merely for the purpose of theoretical speculation; but as matters of practical importance, and of earnest and even of vehement debate. The answers given to them by statesmen and jurists are often contradictory, and irreconcilable with each other; and the consequences, deduced from the views taken of some of them, go very deep into the foundations of the government itself, and expose it, if not to utter destruction, at least to evils, which threaten its existence, and disturb the just operation of its powers.

§ 309. It will be our object to present in a condensed form, some of the principal expositions, which have been insisted on at different times, as to the nature and obligations of the constitution, and to offer some of the principal objections, which have been suggested against those expositions. To attempt a minute enumeration would, indeed, be an impracticable task; and considering the delicate nature of others, which are still the subject of heated controversy, where the ashes are scarcely yet cold, which cover the concealed fires of former political excitements, it is sufficiently difficult to detach some of the more important from the mass of accidental matter, in which they are involved.

§ 310. It has been asserted by a learned commentator,[1] that the constitution of the United States is an original, written, federal, and social compact, freely, voluntarily, and solemnly entered into by the several states, and ratified by the people thereof respectively; whereby the several states, and the people thereof, respectively have bound themselves to each other, and to the federal government of the United States, and by which the federal government is bound to the several states and to every citizen of the United States. The author proceeds to expound every part of this definition at large. It is (says he) a compact, by which it is distinguished from a charter or grant, which is either the act of a superior to an inferior, or is founded upon some consideration moving from one of the parties to the other, and operates as an exchange or sale.[2] But were the contracting parties, whether considered as states in their political capacity and character, or as individuals, are all equal; nor is there any thing granted from one to another; but

[*] Joseph Story, *Commentaries on the Constitution of the United States*, 1st ed. (Boston: Hilliard, Gray, 1833), 1:§§306–72. [Footnote numbers have been changed for this collection. —Ed.]

1. 1 Tucker's Black. Comm. App. note D, p. 140 et seq.
2. 1 Tucker's Black. Comm. App. note D. p. 141.

each stipulates to part with, and receive the same thing precisely without any distinction or difference between any of the parties.

§ 311. It is a federal compact.[3] Several sovereign and independent states may unite themselves together by a perpetual confederation, without each ceasing to be a perfect state. They will together form a federal republic. The deliberations in common will offer no violence to each member, though they may in certain respects put some constraint on the exercise of it in virtue of voluntary engagements. The extent, modifications, and objects of the federal authority are mere matters of discretion.[4] So long as the separate organization of the members remains; and, from the nature of the compact, must continue to exist both for local and domestic, and for federal purposes, the union is in fact, as well as in theory, an association of states, or a confederacy.

§ 312. It is, also, to a certain extent, a social compact. In the act of association, in virtue of which a multitude of men form together a state or nation, each individual is supposed to have entered into engagements with all, to procure the common welfare; and all are supposed to have entered into engagements with each other, to facilitate the means of supplying the necessities of each individual, and to protect and defend him.[5] And this is what is ordinarily meant by the original contract of society. But a contract of this nature actually existed in a visible form between the citizens of each state in their several constitutions. It might, therefore, be deemed somewhat extraordinary, that in the establishment of a federal republic, it should have been thought necessary to extend its operation to the persons of individuals, as well as to the states composing the confederacy.

3. Mr. Jefferson asserts, that the constitution of the United States is a compact between the states. "They entered into a compact," says he (in a paper designed to be adopted by the legislature of Virginia, as a solemn protest,) "which is called the Constitution of the United States of America, by which they agreed to unite in a single government, as to their relations with each, and with foreign nations, and as to certain other articles particularly specified." [4 Jefferson's Corresp. 415.] It would, I imagine, be very difficult to point out when, and in what manner, any such compact was made. The constitution was neither made, nor ratified by the states, as sovereignties, or political communities. It was framed by a convention, proposed to the people of the states for their adoption by congress; and was adopted by state conventions,—the immediate representatives of the people.
4. 1 Tucker's Black. Comm. App. note D. p. 141.
5. Id. p. 144.

§ 313. It may be proper to illustrate the distinction between federal compacts and obligations, and such as are social, by one or two examples.[6] A federal compact, alliance, or treaty, is an act of the state or body politic, and not of an individual. On the contrary, a social compact is understood to mean the act of individuals about to create, and establish a state or body politic among themselves. If one nation binds itself by treaty to pay a certain tribute to another; or if all the members of the same confederacy oblige themselves to furnish their quotas of a common expense, when required; in either of these cases, the state or body politic only, and not the individual, is answerable for this tribute or quota. This is, therefore, a federal obligation. But, where by any compact, express or implied, a number of persons are bound to contribute their proportions of the common expenses, or to submit to all laws made by the common consent; and where in default of compliance with these engagements the society is authorized to levy the contribution, or to punish the person of the delinquent; this seems to be understood to be more in the nature of a social, than a federal obligation.[7]

§ 314. It is an original compact. Whatever political relation existed between the American colonies antecedent to the Revolution, as constituent parts of the British empire, or as dependencies upon it, that relation was completely dissolved, and annihilated from that period. From the moment of the Revolution they became severally independent and sovereign states, possessing all the lights, jurisdictions, and authority, that other sovereign states, however constituted, or by whatever title denominated, possess; and bound by no ties, but of their own creation, except such, as all other civilized nations are equally bound by, and which together constitute the customary law of nations.

§ 315. It is a written compact. Considered as a federal compact or alliance between the states, there is nothing new or singular in this circumstance, as all national compacts since the invention of letters have probably been reduced to that form. But considered in the light of an original social compact, the American Revolution seems to have given birth to this new political phenomenon. In every state a written constitution was framed, and adopted by the people both in their individual and sovereign capacity and character.[8]

6. Id. 145.
7. 1 Tucker's Black. Comm. App. note D. p. 145.
8. 1 Tucker's Black. Comm. App. note D. p. 153.

§ 316. It is a compact freely, voluntarily, and solemnly entered into by the several states, and ratified by the people thereof respectively; freely, there being neither external nor internal force or violence to influence, or promote the measure; the United States being at peace with all the world and in perfect tranquility in each state; voluntarily, because the measure had its commencement in the spontaneous acts of the state legislatures, prompted by a due sense of the necessity of some change in the existing confederation; and solemnly, as having been discussed, not only in the general convention, which proposed and framed it; but afterwards in the legislatures of the several states; and finally in the conventions of all the states, by whom it was adopted and ratified.[9]

§ 317. It is a compact, by which the several states and the people thereof respectively have bound themselves to each other, and to the federal government. The constitution had its commencement with the body politic of the several states; and its final adoption and ratification was by the several legislatures referred to, and completed by conventions especially, called and appointed for that purpose in each state. The acceptance of the constitution was not only an act of the body politic of each state, but of the people thereof respectively in their sovereign character and capacity. The body politic was competent to bind itself, so far as the constitution of the state permitted.[10] But not having power to bind the people in cases beyond their constitutional authority, the assent of the people was indispensably necessary to the validity of the compact, by which the rights of the people might be diminished, or submitted to a new jurisdiction, or in any manner affected. From hence, not only the body politic of the several states, but every citizen thereof, may be considered as parties to the compact, and to have bound themselves reciprocally to each other for the due observance of it; and also to have bound themselves to the federal government, whose authority has been thereby created and established.[11]

§ 318. Lastly. It is a compact, by which the federal government is bound to the several states, and to every citizen of the United States. Although the federal government can in no possible view be considered as a party to a compact made anterior to its existence, and by which

it was in fact created; yet, as the creature of that compact, it must be bound by it to its creators, the several states in the union, and the citizens thereof. Having no existence, but under the constitution, nor any rights, but such as that instrument confers; and those very rights being, in fact duties, it can possess no legitimate power, but such as is absolutely necessary for the performance of a duty prescribed, and enjoined by the constitution.[12] Its duties then became the exact measure of its powers; and whenever it exerts a power for any other purpose, than the performance of a duty prescribed by the constitution, it transgresses its proper limits, and violates the public trust. Its duties being moreover imposed for the general benefit and security of the several states in their political character, and of the people, both in their sovereign and individual capacity, if these objects be not obtained, the government does not answer the end of its creation. It is, therefore, bound to the several states respectively, and to every citizen thereof, for the due execution of those duties, and the observance of this obligation is enforced under the solemn sanction of an oath from those, who administer the government.

§ 319. Such is a summary of the reasoning of the learned author, by which he has undertaken to vindicate his views of the nature of the constitution. That reasoning has been quoted at large, and for the most part in his own words; not merely as his own, but as representing, in a general sense, the opinions of a large body of statesmen and jurists in different parts of the Union, avowed and acted upon in former times; and recently revived under circumstances, which have given them increased importance, if not a perilous influence.[13]

9. Id. 155, 156.
10. Id. 169.
11. 1 Tucker's Black. Comm. note D. p. 170.

12. Id. 170.
13. Many traces of these opinions will be found in the public debates in the state legislatures and in Congress at different periods. In the resolutions of Mr. Taylor in the Virginia legislature in 1798, it was resolved, "that this assembly doth explicitly and peremptorily declare, that it views the powers of the federal government as resulting from the compact, *to which the states are parties*."—See Dane's Appendix, p 17. The original resolution had the word "*alone*" after "states," which was struck out upon the motion of the original mover, it having been asserted in the debate, that the *people* were parties also, and by some of the speakers, that the people were exclusively parties.

The Kentucky Resolutions of 1797, which were drafted by Mr. Jefferson, declare, "that to this compact [the federal constitution] each state acceded as a state, and is an integral party." North American Review, Oct. 1830, p. 501, 545. In the resolutions of the senate of South Carolina, in Nov. 1817, it is declared, "that the constitution of the United States is a compact between the

§ 320. It is wholly beside our present purpose to engage in a critical commentary upon the different parts of this exposition. It will be sufficient for all the practical objects we have in view, to suggest the difficulties of maintaining its leading positions, to expound the objections, which have been urged against them, and to bring into notice those opinions, which rest on a very different basis of principles.

§ 321. The obvious deductions, which may be, and indeed have been, drawn from considering the constitution as a compact between the states, are, that it operates as a mere treaty, or convention between them, and has an obligatory force upon each state no longer than suits its pleasure, or its consent continues; that each state has a right to judge for itself in relation to the nature, extent, and obligations. Of the instrument, without being at all bound by the interpretation of the federal government, or by that of any other state; and that each retains the power to withdraw from the confederacy and to dissolve the connexion, when such shall be its choice; and may suspend the operations of the federal government, and nullify its acts within its own territorial limits, whenever, in its own opinion, the exigency of the case may require.[14] These conclusions may

not always be avowed; but they flow naturally from the doctrines, which we have under consideration.[15] They go to the extent of reducing the government to a mere confederacy during pleasure; and of thus presenting the extraordinary spectacle of a nation existing only at the will of each of its constituent parts.

§ 322. If this be the true interpretation of the instrument, it has wholly failed to express the intentions of its framers, and brings back, or at least may bring back, upon us all the evils of the old confederation, from which we were supposed to have had a safe deliverance. For the power to operate upon individuals, instead of operating merely on states, is of little consequence, though yielded by the constitution, if that power is to depend for, its exercise upon the continual consent of all the members upon every emergency. We have already seen, that the framers of the instrument contemplated no such dependence. Even under the confederation it was deemed a gross heresy to maintain, that a party to a compact has a right to revoke that compact; and the possibility of a question of this nature was deemed to prove the necessity of laying the foundations of our na-

_____

people of the different states with each other, as separate and independent sovereignties." In Nov. 1799 the Kentucky legislature passed a resolution, declaring, that the federal states had a right to judge of any infraction of the constitution, and, that a nullification by those sovereignties of all unauthorized acts done under color of that instrument is the rightful remedy. North American Review, Id. 503. Mr. Madison, in the Virginia Report of 1800, reasserts the right of the states, as parties, to decide upon the unconstitutionality of any measure. Report. p. 6, 7, 8, 9. The Virginia legislature, in 1829, passed a resolution, declaring, that "the constitution of the United States being a federative compact between sovereign states, in construing which no common arbiter is known, each state has the right to construe the compact for itself." [3 American Annual Register; Local History, 131.] Mr. Vice President Calhoun's letter to Gov. Hamilton of Aug. 28, 1832, contains a very elaborate exposition of this among other doctrines.

14. Virginia, in the resolutions of her legislature on the tariff, in Feb. 1829, declared, "that there is no common arbiter to construe the constitution; *being a federative compact between sovereign states*, each state has a right to construe the compact for itself." 9 Dane's Abridg. ch. 187, art. 20, § 14, p. 589. See also North American Review, Oct. 1830, p. 488 to 528. The resolutions of Kentucky of 1798 contain a like declaration, that "to this compact [the constitution] each state acceded as a state, and is an integral party; that the government created by this compact was not made the exclusive, or final judge of the powers

delegated to itself, &c.; but that, as in all other cases of compact among parties having no common judge, each party has an equal right to judge for itself, *as well of infractions, as of the mode and measure of redress.*" North American Review, Oct. 1830, p. 501. The Kentucky resolutions of 1799 go further, and assert, "that the several states, who formed that instrument, [the constitution] being sovereign and independent, have the unquestionable right to judge of its infraction; and that a nullification by those sovereignties of all unauthorized acts done under colour of that instrument is the rightful remedy." North American Review, Id. 503; 4 Elliot's Debates, 315, 322. In Mr. Madison's Report in the Virginia legislature, in January, 1800, it is also affirmed, that the states are parties to the constitution; but by *states* he here means (as the context explains) the people of the states. That report insists, that the states are in the last resort the ultimate judges of the infractions of the constitution. p. 6, 7, 8, 9.

15. I do not mean to assert that all those who held these doctrines have adopted the conclusions drawn from them. There are eminent exceptions; and among them the learned commentator on Blackstone's Commentaries seems properly numbered. See 1 Tucker's Black. App. 170, 171, § 8. See the Debates in the senate on Mr. Foot's Resolution in 1830, and Mr. Dane's Appendix, and his Abridgment and Digest, 9th Vol. ch. 187, art. 20, § 13 to 22, p. 588 et seq.; North American Review for Oct. 1830, on the Debates on the Public Lands, p. 481 to 486, 488 to 528; 4 Elliot's Debates, 315 to 330; Madison's Virginia Report, Jan. 1800, p. 6, 7, 8, 9; 4 Jefferson's Correspondence, 415; Vice President Calhoun's Letter to Gov. Hamilton, Aug. 28, 1832.

tional government deeper, than in the mere sanction of delegated authority.[16] "A compact between independent sovereigns, founded on acts of legislative authority, can pretend to no higher validity, than a league or treaty between the parties. It is an established doctrine on the subject of treaties, that all the articles are mutually conditions of each other; that a breach of any one article is a breach of the whole treaty; and that a breach committed by either of the parties absolves the others, and authorizes them, if they please, to pronounce the compact violated and void." Consequences like these, which place the dissolution of the government in the hands of a single state, and enable it at will to defeat, or suspend the operation of the laws of the union, are too serious, not to require us to scrutinize with the utmost care and caution the principles, from which they flow, and by which they are attempted to be justified.

. . .

§ 332. Admitting, therefore, for the sake of argument, that the institution of a government is to be deemed, in the restricted sense already suggested, an original compact or contract between each citizen and the whole community, is it to be construed, as a continuing contract after its adoption, so as to involve the notion of there being still distinct and independent parties to the instrument, capable, and entitled, as matter of right, to judge and act upon its construction, according, to their own views of its import and obligations? to resist the enforcement of the powers delegated to the government at the good pleasure of each? to dissolve all connexion with it, whenever there is a supposed breach of it on the other side? These are momentous questions, and go to the very foundation of every government founded on the voluntary choice of the people; and they should be seriously investigated, before we admit the conclusions, which may be drawn from one aspect of them.[17]

16. The Federalist, No. 22; Id. No. 43; see also Mr. Patterson's Opinion in the Convention, 4 Elliot's Debates, 74, 75; and Yates's Minutes.

17. Mr. Woodeson (Elements of Jurisp. p. 22,) says, "However the historical fact may be of a social compact, government ought to be, and is generally considered as founded on consent, tacit or express, or a real, or quasi compact. This theory is a material basis of political rights; and as a theoretical point, is not difficult to be maintained, &c. &c. Not that such consent is subsequently revokable at the will, even of all the subjects of the state, for that would be making a part of the community equal in power to the whole originally, and superior to the rulers thereof after their establishment." However questionable this

§ 333. Take, for instance, the constitution of Massachusetts, which in its preamble contains the declaration already quoted, that government "is a social compact, by which the whole people covenants with each citizen, and each citizen with the whole government;" are we to construe that compact, after the adoption of the constitution, as still a contract, in which each citizen is still a distinct party, entitled to his remedy for any breach of its obligations, and authorized to separate himself from the whole society, and to throw off all allegiance, whenever he supposes, that any of the fundamental principles of that compact are infringed, or misconstrued? Did the people intend, that it should be thus in the power of any individual to dissolve the whole government at his pleasure, or to absolve himself from all obligations and duties thereto, at his choice, or upon his own interpretation of the instrument? If such a power exists, where is the permanence or security of the government? In what manner are the rights and property of the citizens to be maintained or enforced? Where are the duties of allegiance or obedience? May one withdraw his consent to-day, and re-assert it to-morrow? May one claim the protection and assistance of the laws and institutions to-day, and to-morrow repudiate them? May one declare war against all the others for a supposed infringement of the constitution? If he may, then each one has the same right in relation to all others; and anarchy and confusion, and not order and good government and obedience, are the ingredients, which are mainly at work in all free institutions, founded upon the will, and choice, and compact of the people. The existence of the government, and its peace, and its vital interests will, under such circumstances, be at the mercy and even at the caprice of a single individual. It would not only be vain, but unjust to punish him for disturbing society, when it is but by a just exercise of the original rights reserved to him by the compact. The maxim, that in every government the will of the majority shall, and ought to govern the rest, would be thus subverted; and society would, in effect, be reduced to its original elements. The association would be temporary and fugitive, like those voluntary meetings among barbarous and savage communities, where each acts for himself, and submits only, while it is his pleasure.

———

latter position may be, (and it is open to many objections, [See 1 Wilson's 417, 418, 419, 420.]) it is certain, that a right of the minority to withdraw from the government, and to overthrow its powers, has no foundation in any just reasoning.

§ 334. It can readily be understood, in what manner contracts, entered into by private persons, are to be construed, and enforced under the regular operations of an organized government. Under such circumstances, if a breach is insisted on by either side, the proper redress is administered by the sovereign power, through the medium of its delegated functionaries, and usually by the judicial department, according to the principles established by the laws, which compose the jurisprudence of that country. In such a case no person supposes, that each party is at liberty to insist absolutely and positively upon his own construction, and to redress himself accordingly by force or by fraud. He is compellable to submit the decision to others, not chosen by himself, but appointed by the government, to secure the rights, and redress the wrongs of the whole community. In such cases the doctrine prevails, *inter leges silent arma*. But the reverse maxim would prevail upon the doctrine, of which we are speaking, *inter arma silent leges*. It is plain, that such a resort is not contemplated by any of our forms of government, by a suit of one citizen against the whole for a redress of his grievances, or for a specific performance of the obligations of the constitution. He may have, and doubtless in our forms of administering justice has, a complete protection of his rights secured by the constitution, when they are invaded by any other citizen. But that is in a suit by one citizen against another; and not against the body politic, upon the notion of contract.

§ 335. It is easy, also, to understand, how compacts between independent nations are to be construed, and violations of them redressed. Nations, in their sovereign character, are all upon an equality; and do not acknowledge any superior, by whose decrees they are bound, or to whose opinions they are obedient. Whenever, therefore, any differences arise between them, as to the interpretation of a treaty, or of the breach of its terms, there is no common arbiter, whom they are bound to acknowledge, having authority to decide them. There are but three modes, in which these differences can be adjusted; first, by new negotiations, embracing and settling the matters in dispute; secondly, by referring the same to some common arbiter, *pro hac vice*, whom they invest with such power; or thirdly, by a resort to arms, which is the *ultima ratio regum*, or the last appeal between sovereigns.

§ 336. It seems equally plain, that in our forms of government, the constitution cannot contemplate either of these modes of interpretation or redress. Each citizen is not supposed to enter into the compact, as a sovereign with all the others as sovereign, retaining an independent and coequal authority to Judge, and decide for himself. He has no authority reserved to institute new negotiations; or to suspend the operations of the constitution, or to compel the reference to a common arbiter; or to declare war against the community, to which he belongs.

§ 337. No such claim has ever (at least to our knowledge) been asserted by any jurist or statesman, in respect to any of our state constitutions. The understanding is general, if not universal, that, having been adopted by the majority of the people, the constitution of the state binds the whole community *proprio vigore*; and is unalterable, unless by the consent of the majority of the people, or at least of the qualified voters of the state, in the manner prescribed by the constitution, or otherwise provided for by the majority. No right exists, or is supposed to exist, on the part of any town, or county, or other organized body within the state, short of a majority of the whole people of the state, to alter, suspend, resist, or dissolve the operations of that constitution, or to withdraw themselves from its jurisdiction. Much less is the compact supposed liable to interruption, or suspension, or dissolution, at the will of any private citizen upon his own notion of its obligations, or of any infringements of them by the constituted authorities. The only redress for any such infringements, and the only guaranty of individual rights and property, are understood to consist in the peaceable appeal to the proper tribunals constituted by the government for such purposes; or if these should fail, by the ultimate appeal to the good sense, and integrity, and justice of the majority of the people. And this, according to Mr. Locke, is the true sense of the original compact, by which every individual has surrendered to the majority of the society the right permanently to control, and direct the operations of government therein.

§ 338. The true view to be taken of our state constitutions is, that they are forms of government, ordained and established by the people in their original sovereign capacity to promote their own happiness, and permanently to secure their rights, property, independence, and common welfare. The language of nearly all these state constitutions is, that the people do ordain and establish this constitution; and where these terms are not expressly used, they are necessarily implied in the very substance of the frame of government. They may be deemed compacts, (though not generally declared so on their face,) in the sense of their being founded on the voluntary consent or agreement of a majority of the qualified voters of the state. But they are not treated as contracts and conventions between independent individuals and communities, having no common umpire. The language of these instruments is not the usual or appropriate language for mere matters resting, and forever to rest in contract. In general the import is, that the people "ordain and establish," that is, in their sovereign capacity, meet and declare, what shall be the fundamental LAW for the government of themselves and their posterity. Even in the constitution of Massachusetts, which, more than any other, wears the air of contract, the compact is declared to be a "mere constitution of civil government," and the people "do agree on, ordain, and establish the following declaration of rights, and frame of government, as the constitution of government." In this very bill of rights, the people are declared "to have the sole and exclusive right of governing themselves, as a free, sovereign, and independent state"; and that "they have an incontestable, unalienable, and indefeasible right to institute government, and to reform, alter, or totally change the same, when their protection, safety, prosperity, and happiness require it." It is, and accordingly has always been, treated as a fundamental law, and not as a mere contract of government, during the good pleasure of all the persons; who were originally bound by it, or assented to it.

§ 339. A constitution is in fact a fundamental law or basis of government, and falls strictly within the definition of law, as given by Mr. Justice Blackstone. It is a rule of action, prescribed by the supreme power in a state, regulating the rights and duties of the whole community. It is a rule, as contradistinguished from a temporary or sudden order; permanent, uniform, and universal. It is also called a rule, to distinguish it from a compact, or agreement; for a compact (he adds) is a promise proceeding from us; law is a command directed to us. The language of a compact is, I will, or will not do this; that of a law is, Thou shalt, or shalt not do it. "In compacts we ourselves determine and promise, what shall be done, before we are obliged to do it. In laws, we are obliged to act without ourselves determining, or promising any thing at all." It is a rule prescribed; that is, it is laid down, promulgated, and established. It is prescribed by the supreme power in a state, that is, among us, by the people, or a majority of them in their original sovereign capacity. Like the ordinary munici-

pal laws, it may be founded upon our consent, or that of our representatives; but it derives its ultimate obligatory force, as a law, and not as a compact.

§ 340. And it is in this light, that the language of the constitution of the United States manifestly contemplates it; for it declares (article 6th), that this constitution and the laws, &c. and treaties made under the authority of the United States, "shall be the supreme LAW of the land." This (as has been justly observed by the Federalist) results from the very nature of political institutions. A law, by the very meaning of the terms, includes supremacy.[18] If individuals enter into a state of society, the laws of that society must be the supreme regulator of their conduct. If a number of political societies enter into a larger political society, the laws, which the latter may enact, pursuant to the powers entrusted to it by its constitution, must be supreme over those societies, and the individuals, of whom they are composed. It would otherwise be a mere treaty, dependent on the good faith of the parties, and not a government, which is only another word for political power and supremacy.[19] A state constitution is then in a just and appropriate sense, not only a law, but a supreme law, for the government of the whole people, within the range of the powers actually contemplated, and the rights secured by it. It would, indeed, be an extraordinary use of language to consider a declaration of rights in a constitution, and especially of rights, which it proclaims to be "unalienable and indefeasible," to be a matter of contract, and resting, on such a basis, rather than a solemn recognition and admission of those rights, arising from the law of nature, and the gift of Providence, and incapable of being, transferred or surrendered.

. . .

§ 349. The subject has been, thus far, considered chiefly in reference to the point, how far government is to be considered as a compact, in the sense of a contract, as contradistinguished from an act of solemn acknowledgment or assent; and how far our state constitutions are to be deemed such contracts, rather than fundamental laws, prescribed by the sovereign power. The conclusion, to which we have arrived, is, that a state constitution is no farther to be deemed a compact, than that it is a matter of consent by the people, binding them to obedience to its requisitions; and that its proper char-

18. The Federalist, No. 33. See also, No. 15.
19. The Federalist, No. 33.

acter is that of a fundamental law, prescribed by the will of the majority of the people of the state, (who are entitled to prescribe it,) for the government and regulation of the whole people. It binds them, as a supreme compact, ordained by the sovereign power, and not merely as a voluntary contract, entered into by parties capable of contracting and binding, themselves by such terms, as they choose to select. If this be a correct view of the subject, it will enable us to enter upon the other parts of the proposed discussion with principles to guide us in the illustration of the controversy.

§ 350. In what light, then, is the constitution of the United States to be regarded? Is it a mere compact, treaty, or confederation of the states composing the Union, or of the people thereof, whereby each of the several states, and the people thereof, have respectively bound themselves to each other? Or is it a form of government, which, having been ratified by a majority of the people in all the states, is obligatory upon them, as the prescribed rule of conduct of the sovereign power, to the extent of its provisions?

§ 351. Let us consider, in the first place, whether it is to be deemed a compact? By this, we do not mean an act of solemn assent by the people to it, as a form of government, (of which there is no room for doubt;) but a contract imposing mutual obligations, and contemplating the permanent subsistence of parties having an independent right to construe, control, and judge of its obligations. If in this latter sense it is to be deemed a compact, it must be, either because it contains on its face stipulations to that effect, or because it is necessarily implied from the nature and objects of a frame of government.

§ 352. There is nowhere found upon the face of the constitution any clause, intimating it to be a compact, or in anywise providing for its interpretation, as such. On the contrary, the preamble emphatically speaks of it, as a solemn ordinance and establishment of government. The language is, "We, the people of the United States, do ordain and establish this constitution for the United States of America." The people do ordain and establish, not contract and stipulate with each other. The people of the United States, not the distinct people of a particular state with the people of the other states. The people ordain and establish a "constitution," not a "confederation." The distinction between a constitution and a confederation is well known and understood. The latter, or at least a pure confederation, is a mere treaty or league between independent states, and binds no

longer, than during, the good pleasure of each.[20] It rests forever in articles of compact, where each is, or may be the supreme judge of its own rights and duties. The former is a permanent form of government, where the powers, once given, are irrevocable, and cannot be resumed or withdrawn at pleasure. Whether formed by a single people, or by different societies of people, in their political capacity, a constitution, though originating in consent, becomes, when ratified, obligatory, as a fundamental ordinance or law.[21] The constitution of a confederated republic, that is, of a national republic formed of several states, is, or at least may be, not less an irrevocable form of government, than the constitution of a state formed and ratified by the aggregate of the several counties of the state.[22]

§ 353. If it had been the design of the framers of the constitution or of the people, who ratified it, to consider it a mere confederation, resting on treaty stipulations, it is difficult to conceive, that the appropriate terms should not have been found in it. The United States were no strangers to compacts of this nature.[23] They had subsisted to a limited extent before the revolution. The articles of confederation, though in some few respects national, were mainly of a pure federative character, and were treated as stipulations between states for many purposes independent and sovereign.[24] And yet (as has been already seen) it was deemed a political heresy to maintain, that under it any state had a right to

20. The Federalist, No. 9, 15, 17, 18, 33; Webster's Speeches, 1830; Dane's App. § 2, p. 11, § 14, p. 25, &c.; Id. § 10, p. 21; Mr. Martin's Letter, 3 Elliot, 53; 1 Tucker's Black. Comm. App. 146.

21. 1 Wilson's Lectures, 417.

22. See The Federalist, No. 9; Id. No. 15, 16; Id. No. 33; Id. No. 39.

23. New-England Confederacy of 1643; 3 Kent. Comm. 190, 191, 192; Rawle on Const. Introduct. p. 24, 25. — In the ordinance of 1787, for the government of the territory northwest of the Ohio, certain articles were expressly declared to be "articles of *compact* between the original states, [i. e. the United States,] and the people and states [states *in futuro*, for none were then in being] in the said territory." But to guard against any possible difficulty, it was declared, that these articles should "forever remain unalterable, unless by *common consent*." So, that though a compact, neither party was at liberty to withdraw from it at its pleasure, or to absolve itself from its obligations. Why was not the constitution of the United States declared to be articles of compact, if that was the intention of the framers?

24. The Federalist, No. 15, 22, 39, 40, 43; Ogden v. Gibbons, 9 Wheaton's R. 1, 187.

withdraw from it at pleasure, and repeal its operation; and that a party to the compact had a right to revoke that compact.[25] The only places, where the terms, confederation or compact, are found in the constitution, apply to subjects of an entirely different nature, and manifestly in contradistinction to constitution. Thus in the tenth section of the first article it is declared, that "no state shall enter into any treaty, alliance, or confederation;" "no state shall, without the consent of congress, &c. enter into any agreement or compact with another state, or with a foreign power." Again, in the sixth article it is declared, that "all debts contracted, and engagements entered into, before the adoption of this constitution, shall be as valid against the United States under this constitution, as under the confederation." Again, in the tenth amendment it is declared, that "the powers not delegated by the constitution, nor prohibited by it to the states, are reserved to the states respectively, or to the people." A contract can in no just sense be called a delegation of powers.

§ 354. But that, which would seem conclusive on the subject, (as has been already stated,) is, the very language of the constitution itself, declaring it to be a supreme fundamental law, and to be of judicial obligation, and recognition in the administration of justice. "This constitution," says the sixth article, "and the laws of the United States, which shall be made in pursuance thereof, and all treaties made, or which shall be made under the authority of the United States, shall be the supreme law of the land; and the judges in every state shall be bound thereby, any thing in the constitution or law of any state to the contrary notwithstanding." If it is the supreme law, how can the people of any state, either by any form of its own constitution, or laws, or other proceedings, repeal, or abrogate, or suspend it?

§ 355. But, if the language of the constitution were less explicit and irresistible, no other inference could be correctly deduced from a view of the nature and objects of the instrument. The design is to establish a form of government. This, of itself, imports legal obligation, permanence, and uncontrollability by any, but the authorities authorized to alter, or abolish it. The object was to secure the blessings of liberty to the people, and to their posterity. The avowed intention was to supercede the old confederation, and substitute in its place a new form of government. We have seen, that the inefficiency of the old confederation forced the states to surrender

the league then existing, and to establish a national constitution.[26] The convention also, which framed the constitution, declared this in the letter accompanying it. "It is obviously impracticable in the federal government of these states," says that letter, "to secure all rights of independent sovereignty to each, and yet provide for the interest and safety of all. Individuals entering into society must give up a share of liberty to preserve the rest."[27] "In all our deliberations on this subject, we kept steadily in our view that, which appeared to us the greatest interest of every true American, the consolidation of our Union, in which is involved our prosperity, felicity, safety, perhaps our national existence." Could this be attained consistently with the notion of an existing treaty or confederacy, which each at its pleasure was at liberty to dissolve?[28]

§ 356. It is also historically known, that one of the objections taken by the opponents of the constitution was, "that it is not a confederation of the states, but a government of individuals."[29] It was, nevertheless, in the solemn instruments of ratification by the people of the several states, assented to, as a constitution. The language of those instruments uniformly is, "We, &c. do as-

25. The Federalist, No. 22; Id. No. 43.

26. The very first resolution adopted by the convention (six states to two states) was in the following words: "Resolved, that it is the opinion of this committee, that a national government ought to be established of a supreme legislative, judiciary, and executive;" [Journal of Convention, p. 83, 134, 139, 207; 4 Elliot's Debates, 49. See also 2 Pitkin's History, 232.] plainly showing, that it was a national government, not a compact, which they were about to establish; a supreme legislative, judiciary, and executive, and not a mere treaty for the exercise of dependent powers during the good pleasure of all the contracting parties.

27. Journal of Convention, p. 367, 368.

28. The language of the Supreme Court in Gibbons v. Ogden, (9 Wheat. R. 1, 187,) is very expressive on this subject:

As preliminary to the very able discussions of the constitution, which we have heard from the bar, and as having some influence on its construction, reference has been made to the political situation of these states, anterior to its formation. It has been said, that they were sovereign, were completely independent, and were connected with each other only by a league. This is true. But, when these allied sovereigns converted their league into a government, when they converted their Congress of Ambassadors, deputed to deliberate on their common concerns, and to recommend measures of general utility, into a legislature, empowered to enact laws on the most interesting subjects, the whole character, in which the states appear, underwent a change, the extent of which must be determined by a fair consideration of the instrument, by which that change was effected.

29. The Federalist, No. 38, p. 247; Id. No. 39, p. 256.

sent to, and ratify the said constitution."[30] The forms of the convention of Massachusetts and New Hampshire are somewhat peculiar in their language. "The convention, &c. acknowledging, with grateful hearts, the goodness of the Supreme Ruler of the Universe in affording the people of the United States, in the course of his providence, an opportunity, deliberately and peaceably, without force or surprise, of entering into an explicit and solemn compact with each other, by assenting to, and ratifying a new constitution, &c. do assent to, and ratify the said constitution."[31] And although many declarations of rights, many propositions of amendments, and many protestations of reserved powers are to be found accompanying the ratifications of the various conventions, sufficiently evincive of the extreme caution and jealousy of those bodies, and of the people at large, it is remarkable, that there is nowhere to be found the slightest allusion to the instruments as a confederation or compact of states in their sovereign capacity, and no reservation of any right, on the part of any state, to dissolve its connexion, or to abrogate its assent, or to suspend the operations of the constitution, as to itself. On the contrary, that of Virginia, which speaks most pointedly to the topic, merely declares, "that the powers granted under the constitution, being derived from the people of the United States, may be resumed by them [not by any one of the states] whenever the same shall be perverted to their injury or oppression."[32]

§ 357. So that there is very strong negative testimony against the notion of its being a compact or confederation, of the nature of which we have spoken, founded upon the known history of the times, and the acts of ratification, as well as upon the antecedent articles of confederation. The latter purported on their face to be a mere confederacy. The language of the third article was, "The said states hereby severally enter into a firm league of friendship with each other for their common defence, &c. binding themselves to assist each other." And the ratification was by delegates of the state legislatures, who solemnly plighted and engaged the faith of their respective constituents, that they should abide by the determination of the United States in congress as-

sembled on all questions, which, by the said confederation, are submitted to them; and that the articles thereof should be inviolably observed by the states they respectively represented.[33]

§ 358. It is not unworthy of observation, that in the debates of the various conventions called to examine and ratify the constitution, this subject did not pass without discussion. The opponents, on many occasions, pressed the objection, that it was a consolidated government, and contrasted it with the confederation.[34] None of its advocates pretended to deny, that its design was to establish a national government, as contradistinguished from a mere league or treaty, however they might oppose the suggestions, that it was a consolidation of the states.[35] In the North Carolina debates, one of the members laid it down, as a fundamental principle of every safe and free government, that "a government is a compact between the rulers and the people." This was most strenuously denied on the other side by gentlemen of great eminence. They said, "A compact cannot be annulled, but by the consent of both parties. Therefore, unless the rulers are guilty of oppression, the people, on the principles of a compact, have no right to new-model their government. This is held to be the principle of some monarchical governments in Europe. Our government is founded on much nobler principles. The people are known with certainty to have originated it themselves. Those in power are their servants and agents. And the people, without their consent, may new-model the government, whenever they think proper, not merely because it is oppressively exercised, but because they think another form will be more conducive to their welfare."[36]

34. I do not say, that the manner of stating the objection was just, but the fact abundantly appears in the printed debates. For instance, in the Virginia debates, (2 Elliot's Deb. 47,) Mr. Henry said, "That this is a consolidated government is demonstrably clear." "The language [is] 'We, the people,' instead of, 'We, the states.' States are the characteristics and soul of a confederation. If the states be not the agents of this compact, it must be one great consolidated national government of the people of all the states." The like suggestion will be found in various places in Mr. Elliot's Debates in other states. See 1 Elliot's Debates, 91, 92, 110. See also 3 Amer. Museum, 422; 2 Amer. Museum, 540, 546; Mr. Martin's Letter, 4 Elliot's Debates, p. 53.

30. See the forms in the Journals of the Convention, &c. (1819), p. 390 to 465.

31. Journals of the Convention, &c. (1819), p. 401, 402, 412.

32. Id. p. 416.—Of the right of a majority of the whole people to change their constitution, at will, there is no doubt. See 1 Wilson's Lectures, 418; 1 Tucker's Black. Comm. 165.

33. Articles of Confederation, 1781, art. 13.

35. 3 Elliot's Debates, 145, 257, 201; The Federalist, No. 32, 33, 39, 44, 45; 3 Amer. Museum, 422, 424.

36. Mr. Iredell, 3 Elliot's Debates, 24, 25; Id. 200, Mr. McClure, Id. 25; Mr. Spencer, Id. 26, 27; Id. 139. See also 3 Elliot's Debates, 156; See also Chisholm v. Georgia, 3 Dall, 419; 2 Condensed Rep.

§ 359. Nor should it be omitted, that in the most elaborate expositions of the constitution by its friends, its character, as a permanent form of government, as a fundamental law, as a supreme rule, which no state was at liberty to disregard, suspend, or annul, was constantly admitted, and insisted on, as one of the strongest reasons, why it should be adopted in lieu of the confederation.[37] It is matter of surprise, therefore, that a learned commentator should have admitted the right of any state, or of the people of any state, without the consent of the rest, to secede from the Union at its own pleasure.[38] The people of the United States have a right to abolish, or alter the constitution of the United States; but that the people of a single state have such a right, is a proposition requiring some reasoning beyond the suggestion, that it is implied in the principles, on which our political systems are founded. It seems, indeed, to have its origin in the notion of all governments being founded in compact, and therefore liable to be dissolved by the parties, or either of them; a notion, which it has been our purpose to question, at least in the sense, to which the objection applies.

§ 360. To us the doctrine of Mr. Dane appears far better founded, that "the constitution of the United States is not a compact or contract agreed to by two or more parties, to be construed by each for itself, and here to stop for the want of a common arbiter to revise the construction of each party or state. But that it is, as the people have named and called it, truly a Constitution; and they properly said, 'We, the people of the United States, do ordain and establish this constitution,' and not, we, the people of each state."[39] And this

exposition has been sustained by opinions of some of our most eminent statesmen and judges.[40] It was truly remarked by the Federalist,[41] that the constitution was the result neither from the decision of a majority of the people of the union, nor from that of a majority of the states. It resulted from the unanimous assent of the several states that are parties to it, differing no otherwise from their ordinary assent, than its being expressed, not by the legislative authority but by that of the people themselves.

§ 361. But if the constitution could in the sense, to which we have alluded, be deemed a compact, between whom is it to be deemed a contract? We have already seen, that the learned commentator on Blackstone, deems it a compact with several aspects, and first between the states, (as contradistinguished from the people of the states) by which the several states have bound themselves to each other, and to the federal government.[42] The Virginia Resolutions of 1798, assert, that "Virginia views the powers of the federal government, as resulting from the compact, to which the states are parties." This declaration was, at the time, matter of much debate and difference of opinion among the ablest representatives in the legislature. But when it was subsequently expounded by Mr. Madison in the celebrated Report of January, 1800, after admitting, that the term "states" is used in different senses, and among

635, 667, 668. See also in Penn. Debates, Mr. Wilson's denial, that the constitution was a compact; 3 Elliot's Debates, 286, 287. See also McCulloch v. Maryland, 4 Wheaton, 316, 404.

37. The Federalist, No. 15 to 20, 38, 39, 44; North Amer. Review, Oct. 1827, p. 265, 266.

38. Rawle on the Constitution, ch. 32, p. 295, 296, 297, 302, 305.

39. Mr. (afterwards Mr. Justice) Wilson, who was a member of the Federal Convention, uses, in the Pennsylvania Debates, the following language: "We were told, &c. that the convention no doubt thought they were forming a compact or contract of the greatest importance. It was matter of surprise to see the great lending principles of this system still so very much misunderstood. I cannot answer for what every member thought; but I believe it cannot be said, they thought they were making a contract, because I cannot discover the least trace of a compact in that system. There can be no compact, unless there are more parties than one. It is a new doctrine, that one can make

a compact with himself. 'The convention were forming contracts! with whom? I know no bargains, that were there made, I am unable to conceive, who the parties could be. The state governments make a bargain with each other. That is the doctrine, that is endeavoured to be established by gentlemen in the opposition; their state sovereignties wish to be represented. But far other were the ideas of the convention. *This is not a government founded upon compact. It is founded upon the power of the people.* They express in their name and their authority, we, the people, do ordain and establish," &c. 3 Elliot's Debates, 286, 287. He adds (Id. 288) "This system is not a compact or contract. The system tells you, what it is; it is an ordinance and establishment of the people." 9 Dane's Abridg. ch. 187, art. 20, § 15, p. 589, 590; Dane's App. § 10, p. 21, § 50, p. 69.

40. See Ware v. Hylton, 3 Dall. 199; I Cond. Rep. 99, 112; Chisholm v. Georgia, 2 Dall. 419; 2 Cond. R. 668, 671; Elliot's Debates, 72; 2 Elliot's Debates, 47; Webster's Speeches, p. 410; The Federalist, No. 22, 33, 39; 2 Amer. Museum, 536, 516; Virginia Debates in 1798, on the Alien Laws, p. 111, 136, 138, 140; North Amer. Rev. Oct. 1830, p. 437, 444.

41. No. 39.

42. 1 Tuck. Black. Comm. 169; Haynes's Speech in the Senate, in 1830; 4 Elliot's Debates, 315, 316.

others, that it sometimes means the people composing a political society in their highest sovereign capacity, he considers the resolution unobjectionable, at least in this last sense, because in that sense the constitution was submitted to the "states"; in that sense the "states" ratified it; and in that sense the states are consequently parties to the compact, from which the powers of the federal government result.[43] And that is the sense, in which he considers the states parties in his still later and more deliberate examinations.[44]

§ 362. This view of the subject is, however, wholly at variance with that, on which we are commenting; and which, having no foundation in the words of the constitution, is altogether a gratuitous assumption, and therefore inadmissible. It is no more true, that a state is a party to the constitution, as such, because it was framed by delegates chosen by the states, and submitted by the legislatures thereof to the people of the states for ratification, and that the states are necessary agents to give effect to some of its provisions, than that for the same reasons the governor, or senate, or house of representatives, or judges, either of a state or of the United States, are parties thereto. No state, as such, that is the body politic, as it was actually organized, had any power to establish a contract for the establishment of any new government over the people thereof, or to delegate the powers of government in whole, or in part to any other sovereignty. The state governments were framed by the people to administer the state constitutions, such as they were, and not to transfer the administration thereof to any other persons, or sovereignty. They had no authority to enter into any compact or contract for such a purpose. It is no where given, or implied in the state constitutions; and consequently, if actually entered into, (as it was not,) would have had no obligatory force. The people, and the people only, in their original sovereign capacity, had a right to change their form of government, to enter into a compact, and to transfer any sovereignty to the national government.[45] And the states never, in fact, did in their political capacity, as contradistinguished from the people thereof, ratify the constitution. They were not called upon to do it by congress; and were not contemplated, as essential to give validity to it.[46]

§ 363. The doctrine, then, that the states are parties is a gratuitous assumption. In the language of a most

———

may quote the reasoning of the Supreme Court in the case of McCulloch v. Maryland, (4 Wheaton's R 316,) in answer to the very argument.

"The powers of the general government, it has been said, are delegated by the states, who alone are truly sovereign; and must be exercised in subordination to the states, who alone possess supreme dominion.

"It would be difficult to sustain this proposition. The convention, which framed the constitution, was indeed elected by the state legislatures. But the instrument, when it came from their hands, was a mere proposal, without obligation, or pretensions to it. It was reported to the then existing congress of the United States, with a request, that it might be submitted to a convention of delegates, chosen in each state by the people thereof, under the recommendation of its legislature, for their assent and ratification. This mode of proceeding was adopted; and by the convention, by congress, and by the state legislatures, the instrument was submitted to the people. They acted upon it in the only manner, in which they can act safely, effectively, and wisely, on such a subject, by assembling in convention. It is true, they assembled in their several states—and where else should they have assembled? No political dreamer was ever wild enough to think of breaking down the lines, which separate the states, and of compounding the American people into one common mass. Of consequence, when they act, they act in their states. But the measures they adopt do not, on that account, cease to be the measures of the people themselves, or become the measures of the state governments.

"From these conventions the constitution derives its whole authority. The government proceeds directly from the people; is 'ordained and established' in the name of the people; and is declared to be ordained, 'in order to form a more perfect union, establish justice, ensure domestic tranquility, and secure the blessings of liberty to themselves and to their posterity.' The assent of the states, in their sovereign capacity, is implied in calling a convention, and thus submitting that instrument to the people. But the people were at perfect liberty to accept or reject it; and their act was final. It required not the affirmance, and could not be negatived, by the state governments. The constitution, when thus adopted, was of complete obligation, and bound the state sovereignties.

"It has been said, that the people had already surrendered all their powers to the state sovereignties, and had nothing more to give. But, surely, the question, whether they may resume and modify the power granted to government, does not remain to be settled in this country. Much more might the legitimacy of the general government be doubted, had it been created by the states. The powers delegated to the state sovereignties were to be exercised by themselves, not by a distinct and independent sovereignty, created by themselves. To the formation of a league, such as was the confederation, the state sovereignties

43. Resolutions of 1800, p. 5, 6.
44. North American Review Oct. 1830, p. 537, 544.
45. 4 Wheaton, 404.
46. The Federalist, No 39.—In confirmation of this view, we

distinguished statesman,[47] "the constitution itself in its very front refutes that. It declares, that it is ordained and established by the PEOPLE of the United States. So far from saying, that it is established by the governments of the several states, it does not even say, that it is established by the people of the several states. But it pronounces, that it is established by the people of the United States in the aggregate. Doubtless the people of the several states, taken collectively, constitute the people of the United States. But it is in this their collective capacity, it is as all the people of the United States, that they establish the constitution."[48]

§ 364. But if it were admitted, that the constitution is a compact between the states, "the inferences deduced from it," as has been justly observed by the same statesman,[49] "are warranted by no just reason. Because,

———

were certainly competent. But when, 'in order to form a more perfect union,' it was deemed necessary to change this alliance into an effective government, possessing great and sovereign powers, and acting directly on the people, the necessity of referring it to the people, and of deriving its power directly from them, was felt and acknowledged by all.

"The government of the Union, then, (whatever may be the influence of this fact on the case,) is, emphatically, and truly, a government of the people. In form and in substance it emanates from them. Its powers are granted by them, and are to be exercised directly on them, and for their benefit.

"This government is acknowledged by all to be one of enumerated powers. The principle, that it can exercise only the powers granted to it, would seem too apparent to have required to be enforced by all those arguments, which its enlightened friends, while it was depending before the people, found it necessary to urge. That principle is now universally admitted. But the question respecting the extent of the powers actually granted, is perpetually arising, and will probably continue to arise, as long as our system shall exist."

47. Webster's Speeches, 1830, p. 431; 4 Elliot's Debates, 326.

48. Mr. Dane reasons to the same effect, though it is obvious, that he could not, at the time, have had any knowledge of the views of Mr. Webster. [9 Dane's Abridg. ch. 189, art. 20, § 15, p. 589, 590; Dane's App. 40, 41, 42.] He adds, "If a contract, when and how did the Union become a party to it? If a compact, why is it never so denominated, but often and invariably in the instrument itself, and in its amendments, styled, *this* constitution? and if a contract, why did the framers and people call it the supreme law." [Dane's Abridg. 590.] In Martin v. Hunter, (1 Wheat. R. 304, 324,) the supreme court expressly declared, that "the constitution was ordained and established," not by the states in their sovereign capacity, but emphatically, as the preamble of the constitution declares, "by the people of the United States."

49. Webster's Speeches, 429; 4 Elliot's Debates, 324.

if the constitution be a compact between the states, still that constitution or that compact has established a government with certain powers; and whether it be one of these powers, that it shall construe and interpret for itself the terms of the compact in doubtful cases, can only be decided by looking to the compact, and inquiring, what provisions it contains on that point. Without any inconsistency with natural reason, the government even thus created might be trusted with this power of construction. The extent of its powers must, therefore, be sought in the instrument itself." "If the constitution were the mere creation of the state governments, it might be modified, interpreted, or construed according to their pleasure. But even in that case, it would be necessary, that they should agree. One alone could not interpret it conclusively. One alone could not construe it. One alone could not modify it." "If all the states are parties to it, one alone can have no right to fix upon it her own peculiar construction."[50]

§ 365. Then, is it a compact between the people of the several states, each contracting with all the people of the other states?[51] It may be admitted, as was the early exposition of its advocates, "that the constitution is founded on the assent and ratification of the people of America, given by deputies elected for the special purpose; but that this assent and ratification is to be given by the whole people, not as individuals, composing one entire nation, but as composing the distinct and independent states, to which they respectively belong. It is to be the assent and ratification of the several states,

50. Even under the confederation, which was confessedly, in many respects, a mere league or treaty, though in other respects national, congress unanimously resolved, that it was not within the competency of any state to pass acts for interpreting, explaining, or construing a national treaty, or any part or clause of it. Yet in that instrument there was no express judicial powers given to the general government to construe it. It was, however, deemed an irresistible and exclusive authority in the general government, from the very nature of the other powers given to them; and especially from the power to make war and peace, and to form treaties. Journals of Congress, April 13, 1787, p. 32, &c.; Rawle on Const. App. 2, p. 316, 320.

51. In the resolutions passed by the senate of South-Carolina in December, 1827, it was declared, that "the constitution of the United States is a compact between the people of the different states with each other, as separate and independent sovereignties." Mr. Grimke filed a protest founded on different views of it. See Grimke's Address and Resolutions in 1828, (edition, 1829, at Charleston,) where his exposition of the constitution is given at large, and maintained in a very able speech.

derived from the supreme authority in each state, the authority of the people themselves. The act, therefore, establishing the constitution will not be [is not to be] a national, but a federal act."[52] "It may also be admitted," in the language of one of its most enlightened commentators, that "it was formed, not by the governments of the component states, as the federal government, for which it was substituted, was formed. Nor was it formed by a majority of the people of the United States, as a single community, in the manner of a consolidated government. It was formed by the states, that is, by the people in each of the states acting in their highest sovereign capacity; and formed consequently by the same authority, which formed the state constitutions."[53] But this would not necessarily draw after it the conclusion, that it was to be deemed a compact, (in the sense, to which we have so often alluded,) by which each state was still, after the ratification, to act upon it, as a league or treaty, and to withdraw from it at pleasure. A government may originate in the voluntary compact or assent of the people of several states, or of a people never before united, and yet when adopted and ratified by them, be no longer a matter resting in compact; but become an executed government or constitution, a fundamental law, and not a mere league. But the difficulty in asserting it to be a compact between the people of each state, and all the people of the other states is, that the constitution itself contains no such expression, and no such designation of parties. We, "the people of the United States, &c. do ordain, and establish this constitution," is the language; and not we, the people of each state, do establish this compact between ourselves, and the people of all the other states. We are obliged to depart from the words of the instrument, to sustain the other interpretation; an interpretation, which can serve no better purpose, than to confuse the mind in relation to a subject otherwise clear. It is for this reason, that we should prefer an adherence to the words of the constitution, and to the judicial exposition of these words according to their plain and common import.[54]

52. The Federalist, No. 39; see Sturges v. Crowninshield, 4 Wheat. R. 122, 193.

53. Mr. Madison's Letter in North American Review, October, 1830, p. 537, 538.

54. Chisholm v. Georgia, 2 Dall. 419; 2 Cond. Rep. 668, 671; Martin v. Hunter, 1 Wheat. R. 304, 324; Dane's App. p. 22, 24, 29, 30, 37, 39, 40, 41, 42, 43, 51.

This subject is considered with much care by President Monroe in his Exposition, accompanying his Message, of the

§ 366. But supposing, that it were to be deemed such a compact among the people of the several states, let

———

4th of May, 1822. It is due to his memory to insert the following passages which exhibits his notion of the supremacy of the Union.

"The constitution of the United States being ratified by the people of the several states, became, of necessity, to the extent of its powers, the paramount authority of the Union. On sound principles, it can be viewed in no other light. The people, the highest authority known to our system, from whom all our institutions spring, and on whom they depend, formed it. Had the people of the several states thought proper to incorporate themselves into one community under one government, they might have done it. They had the power, and there was nothing then, nor is there any thing now, should they be so disposed, to prevent it. They wisely stopped, however, at a certain point, extending the incorporation to that point, making the national government, thus far, a consolidated government, and preserving the state government, without that limit, perfectly sovereign and independent of the national government. Had the people of the several states incorporated themselves into one community, they must have remained such; their constitution becoming then, like the constitutions of the several states, incapable of change, until altered by the will of the majority. In the institution of a state government by the citizens of a state, a compact is formed, to which all and every citizen are equal parties. They are also the sole parties; and may amend it at pleasure. In the institution of the government of the United States, by the citizens of every state, a compact was formed between the whole American people, which has the same force, and partakes of all the qualities, to the extent, of its powers, as a compact between the citizens of a state, in the formation of their own constitution. It cannot be altered, except by those who formed it, or in the mode prescribed by the parties to the compact itself.

"This constitution was adopted for the purpose of remedying all the defects of the confederation; and in this, it has succeeded, beyond any calculation, that could have been formed of any human institution. By binding the states together, the constitution performs the great office of the confederation, but it is in that sense only, that it has any of the properties of that compact, and in that it is more effectual, to the purpose, as it holds them together by a much stronger bond, and in all other respects, in which the confederation failed, the constitution has been blessed with complete success. The confederation was a compact between separate and independent states; the execution of whose articles, in the powers which operated internally, depended on the state governments. But the great office of the constitution, by incorporating the people of the several states, to the extent of its powers, into one community, and enabling it to act directly on the people, was to annul the powers of the state government to that extent, except in cases where they were concurrent, and to preclude their agency in us see what the enlightened statesman, who vindicates that opinion, holds as the appropriate deduction from it. "Being thus derived (says he) from the same source, as the constitutions of the states, it has, within each state, the same authority, as the constitution of the state; and is as much a constitution within the strict sense of the term, within its prescribed sphere, as the constitutions of the states are, within their respective spheres. But with this obvious and essential difference, that being a compact among the states in their highest sovereign capacity, and constituting the people thereof one people for certain purposes, it cannot be altered, or annulled at the will of the states individually, as the constitution of a state may be at its individual will."[55]

—————

giving effect to those of the general government. The government of the United States relies on its own means for the execution of its powers, as the state governments do for the execution of theirs; both governments having, a common origin, or sovereign, the people; the state governments, the people of each state, the national government, the people of every state; and being amenable to the power, which created it. It is by executing its functions as a government, thus originating and thus acting, that the constitution of the United States holds the states together, and performs the office of a league. It is owing to the nature of its powers, and the high source, from whence they are derived, the people, that it performs that office better than the confederation, or any league, whichever existed, being a compact, which the state governments did not form, to which they are not parties, and which executes its own powers independently of them."

55. Mr. Madison's Letter, North American Review, Oct. 1830, p. 538.—Mr. Paterson (afterwards Mr. Justice Paterson) in the convention, which framed the constitution, held the doctrine, that under the confederation no state had a right to withdraw from the Union without the consent of all. "The confederation (said he) is in the nature of a compact; and can any state, unless by the consent of the whole, either in politics or law, withdraw their powers? Let it be said by Pennsylvania and the other large states, that they, for the sake of peace, assented to the confederation; can she now resume her original right without the consent of the donee?" [Yates's debates, 4 Elliot's Debates, 75.] Mr. Dane unequivocally holds the same language in respect to the constitution. "It is clear (says he) the people of any one state alone never can take, or withdraw power from the United States, which was granted to it by all, as the people of all the states can do rightfully in a justifiable revolution, or as the people can do in the manner their constitution prescribes." Dane's App. § 10, p. 21.

The ordinance of 1787, for the government of the western territory, contains (as we have seen) certain articles declared to be "articles of compact;" but they are also declared to "remain forever unalterable, except by common consent." So, that there

§ 367. The other branch of the proposition, we have been considering, is, that it is not only a compact between the several states, and the people thereof, but also a compact between the states and the federal government; and *e converso* between the federal government, and the several states, and every citizen of the United States.[56] This seems to be a doctrine far more involved, and extraordinary, and incomprehensible, than any part of the preceding. The difficulties have not escaped the observation of those, by whom it has been advanced. "Although (says the learned commentator) the federal government can, in no possible view, be considered as a party to a compact made anterior to its existence; yet, as the creature of that compact, it must be bound by it to its creators, the several states in the Union, and the citizens thereof."[57] If by this, no more were meant than to state, that the federal government cannot lawfully exercise any powers, except those conferred on it by the constitution, its truth could not admit of dispute. But it is plain, that something more was in the author's mind. At the same time, that he admits, that the federal government could not be a party to the compact of the constitution "in any possible view," he still seems to insist upon it, as a compact, by which the federal government is bound to the several states, and to every citizen; that is, that it has entered into a contract with them for the due execution of its duties.

§ 368. And a doctrine of a like nature, viz. that the federal government is a party to the compact, seems to have been gravely entertained on other solemn occasions.[58] The difficulty of maintaining it, however, seems absolutely insuperable. The federal government is the result of the constitution, or (if the phrase is deemed by any person more appropriate) the creature of the compact. How, then, can it be a party to that compact, to which it owes its own existence?[59] How can it be said, that it has entered into a contract, when at the time it had no capacity to conduct; and was not even *in esse*? If any provision was made for the general government's becoming a party, and entering into a compact, after it was brought into existence, where is that provision to be

—————

may be a compact and yet by the stipulations neither party may be at liberty to withdraw from it, or absolve itself from its obligations. Ante, p. 209.

56. 1 Tucker's Black. Comm. 169, 170.

57. 1 Tucker's Black. Comm. 170.

58. Debates in the Senate, in 1830, on Mr. Foot's Resolution, 4 Elliot's Debates, 315 to 331.

59. Webster's Speeches, 429; 4 Elliot's Debates, 324.

found? It is not to be found in the constitution itself. Are we at liberty to imply such a provision, attaching to no power given in the constitution? This would be to push the doctrine of implication to an extent truly alarming; to draw inferences, not from what is, but from what is not, stated in the instrument. But, if any such implication could exist, when did the general government signify its assent to become such a party? When did the people authorize it to do so? Could the government do so, without the express authority of the people? These are questions, which are more easily asked, than answered.

§ 369. In short, the difficulties attendant upon all the various theories under consideration, which treat the constitution of the United States, as a compact, either between the several states, or between the people of the several states, or between the whole people of the United States, and the people of the several states, or between each citizen of all the states, and all other citizens, are, if not absolutely insuperable, so serious, and so wholly founded upon mere implication, that it is matter of surprise, that they should have been so extensively adopted, and so zealously propagated. These theories, too, seem mainly urged with a view to draw conclusions, which are at war with the known powers, and reasonable objects of the constitution; and which, if successful, would reduce the government to a mere confederation. They are objectionable, then, in every way; first, because they are not justified by the language of the constitution; secondly, because they have a tendency to impair, and indeed to destroy, its express powers and objects; and thirdly, because they involve consequences, which, at the will of a single state, may overthrow the constitution itself. One of the fundamental rules in the exposition of every instrument is, so to construe its terms, if possible, as not to make them the source of their own destruction, or to make them utterly void, and nugatory. And if this be generally true, with how much more force does the rule apply to a constitution of government, framed for the general good, and designed for perpetuity? Surely, if any implications are to be made beyond its terms, they are implications to preserve, and not to destroy it.[60]

60. The following strong language is extracted from Instruction given to some Representatives of the state of Virginia by their constituents in 1787, with reference to the confederation: "Government without coercion is a proposition at once so absurd and self contradictory, that the idea creates a con-

§ 370. The cardinal conclusion, for which this doctrine of a compact has been, with so much ingenuity and ability, forced into the language of the constitution, (for the language no where alludes to it,) is avowedly to establish, that in construing the constitution, there is no common umpire; but that each state, nay each department of the government of each state, is the supreme judge for itself, of the powers, and rights, and duties, arising under that instrument.[61] Thus, it has been solemnly asserted on more than one occasion, by some of the state legislatures, that there is no common arbiter, or tribunal, authorized to decide in the last resort, upon the powers and the interpretation of the constitution. And the doctrine has been recently revived with extraordinary zeal, and vindicated with uncommon vigour.[62] A majority of the states, however, have never assented to this doctrine; and it has been, at different

———

fusion of the understanding. It is form without substance; at best a body without a soul. If men would act right, government of all kinds would be useless. If states or nations, who are but assemblages of men, would do right, there would be no wars or disorders in the universe. Bad as individuals are, states are worse. Clothe men with public authority, and almost universally they consider themselves, as liberated from the obligations of moral rectitude, because they are no longer amenable to justice." 1 Amer. Mus. 290.

61. Madison's Virginia Report, January, 1800, p. 6, 7, 8, 9; Webster's Speeches, 407 to 409, 410, 411, 419 to 421.

62. The legislature of Virginia, in 1829, resolved, "that there is no common arbiter to construe the constitution of the United States; the constitution being a federative compact between sovereign states, each state has a right to construe the compact for itself." Georgia and South-Carolina have recently maintained the same doctrine; and it has been asserted in the senate of the United States, with an uncommon display of eloquence and pertinacity. It is not a little remarkable, that in 1810, the legislature of Virginia thought very differently, and then deemed the supreme court a fit and impartial tribunal. Pennsylvania at the same time, though she did not deny the court to be, under the constitution, the appropriate tribunal, was desirous of substituting some other arbiter. The recent resolutions of her own legislature (in March, 1831) show, that she now approves of the supreme court, as the true and common arbiter. One of the expositions of the doctrine is, that if a single state denies a power to exist under the constitution, that power is to be deemed defunct, unless three-fourths of the states shall afterwards reinstate that power by an amendment to the constitution. What, then, is to be done, where ten states resolve, that a power exists, and one, that it does not exist? See Mr. Vice-President Calhoun's Letter of 28th August, 1832, to Gov. Hamilton.

times, resisted by the legislatures of several of the states, in the most formal declarations.

§ 371. But if it were admitted, that the constitution is a compact, the conclusion, that there is no common arbiter, would neither be a necessary, nor natural conclusion from that fact standing alone. To decide upon the point, it would still behove us to examine the very terms of the constitution, and the delegation of powers under it. It would be perfectly competent even for confederated states to agree upon, and delegate authority to construe the compact to a common arbiter. The people of the United States had an unquestionable right to confide this power to the government of the United States, or to any department thereof, if they chose so to do. The question is, whether they have done it. If they have, it becomes obligatory and binding upon all the states.

§ 372. It is not, then, by artificial reasoning founded upon theory, but upon a careful survey of the language of the constitution itself, that we are to interpret its powers, and its obligations. We are to treat it, as it purports on its face to be, as a CONSTITUTION of government; and we are to reject all other appellations, and definitions of it, such, as that it is a compact, especially as they may mislead us into false constructions and glosses, and can have no tendency to instruct us in its real objects.

27

William Yates, *Rights of Colored Men*

1838*

---

2. CITIZENSHIP OF PERSONS OF COLOR.
In regard to citizenship, this is a subject of great importance—an exclusion from suffrage is a withholding of political rights only, but the question of citizenship strikes deeper; deny a man this, and his personal rights are not safe. He may be hindered from going into a State—or, if he enters it, he may be expelled, or treated as an alien. On this principle Missouri attempted to prohibit free colored men from coming into, or settling in the State, on any pretext whatever. And Connecticut

*William Yates, *Rights of Colored Men to Suffrage, Citizenship and Trial by Jury: Being a Book of Facts, Arguments and Authorities, Historical Notices and Sketches of Debates—with Notes* (Philadelphia: Merrihew and Gunn, 1838), 36–38.

undertook to deprive those of the benefits of a school, who came for the laudable purpose of education.

. . .

"The citizens of each State shall be entitled to all the privileges and immunities of citizens in the several States."
Const. U. S. Art. iv. *Sec.* 2, *clause* 1.

These are important and valuable privileges.
"Do they belong to free persons of color?
If they were *white* it is conceded they would. The point then turns on a distinction of *color*.

But such a distinction, as the basis of fundamental rights, is not recognized by the common law of England, or the principles of the British constitution; nor by our own declaration of independence.

Free persons of color are human beings, natives of the country—for such of we speak—and owe the same obligations to the State, and to its government as white citizens." They have an equal right to liberty—to the enjoyment and security of home and family—and of a good name and character as white men; so, to all the rights of conscience—to read, write, and print—to speak, teach, and debate—to preach, and worship God according to its dictates—their title as the same as that of white men. They have the same right to the rewards of their industry, as white men.—They may buy, hold, or sell real or personal estate, the same—and they are as fully entitled to the protection of the law—have a right to sue—to jury trial—to a verdict and judgment—to execution—to *habeas corpus*, and in some of the States to the writ of *homine replegiando*, or writ of personal replevin, as white men.—For them all our courts, from the highest to the lowest, are as open, and the officers as much bound to issue, to obey, and execute process, as for white men; and they equally, as white citizens, enjoy the advantages of the public mail.[1]

"Thus we see the colored man is not of an intermediate class—his relations to society are the same as others; his absolute and relative rights; his rights of persons and to things; his acquisitions of property by contract, and by inheritance; and even the soil which no alien inherits, are the same. Every favor or right conferred on the citizens by general legislation, reaches *him*, and every requisition demands his obedience.

1. *Note.*—Colored persons, it is believed, are not allowed to carry the mail.

In all the writers on public law there is one ancient and universal classification of the people of a country; all who are born within the jurisdiction of a State are natives, and all others are aliens. This classification grows out of the doctrine of natural allegiance, a tie created by birth. All writers agree in the foundation of allegiance, and in its obligations while it exists; some holding that it can never be thrown off, and some that it may be under legislative enactments, but all agreeing that while the residence of the citizen continues in the State of his birth, allegiance demands obedience from the citizen, and protection from the government. Allegiance is not peculiar to any one government or country, but it is held to exist in every country and every government where there are pretensions to social order and civil institutions. It reaches the man of one complexion as much as that of another. It is the ordinance of the great parent of all society, fairly inferable from the nature and necessity of human government. If allegiance is due from our colored population, its correlative is due from the government, viz.: protection and equal laws. If allegiance is an ordinance of Heaven, it reaches, and binds, and confers rights upon every man within its range and rightful sway. Here the free man of color may take his position, and upon the immutable principles of justice and truth, demand his political rights from that government which he is bound to aid and to defend. *He is not a citizen to obey, and an alien to demand protection.*

But it may be objected, that although they enjoy all the absolute and relative rights, and all personal rights, the same as a white man, yet they are not citizens, because they do not vote. To this it is replied, that in many of the States they do vote.

But the right of voting is *not* the criterion of citizenship; the one has no natural or necessary connexion with the other; cases may exist where persons may vote who are not citizens, and where persons are citizens and do not vote. The right of suffrage is no where universal and absolute."

...

Again, it is objected that slaves are not citizens. The reason why slaves are not citizens, is, because they are held as *property*, and not men; and hence have not freedom of choice or action. The reason does not reach free colored men.

28

Women's Rights Convention, Seneca Falls, NY, Declaration of Sentiments

July 19, 1848*

When, in the course of human events, it becomes necessary for one portion of the family of man to assume among the people of the earth a position different from that which they have hitherto occupied, but one to which the laws of nature and of nature's God entitle them, a decent respect to the opinions of mankind requires that they should declare the causes that impel them to such a course.

We hold these truths to be self-evident: that all men and women are created equal; that they are endowed by their Creator with certain inalienable rights; that among these are life, liberty, and the pursuit of happiness; that to secure these rights governments are instituted, deriving their just powers from the consent of the governed. Whenever any form of government becomes destructive of these ends, it is the right of those who suffer from it to refuse allegiance to it, and to insist upon the institution of a new government, laying its foundation on such principles, and organizing its powers in such form, as to them shall seem most likely to effect their safety and happiness. Prudence, indeed, will dictate that governments long established should not be changed for light and transient causes; and accordingly all experience hath shown that mankind are more disposed to suffer. while evils are sufferable, than to right themselves by abolishing the forms to which they are accustomed. But when a long train of abuses and usurpations, pursuing invariably the same object, evinces a design to reduce them under absolute despotism, it is their duty to throw off such government, and to provide new guards for their future security. Such has been the patient sufferance of the women under this government, and such is now the necessity which constrains them to demand the equal station to which they are entitled. The history of mankind is a history of repeated injuries and usurpa-

*Elizabeth Cady Stanton, *History of Woman Suffrage* (Rochester, NY: Fowler and Wells, 1889), 1:70–71.

tions on the part of man toward woman, having in direct object the establishment of an absolute tyranny over her. To prove this, let facts be submitted to a candid world.

The history of mankind is a history of repeated injuries and usurpations on the part of man toward woman, having in direct object the establishment of an absolute tyranny over her. To prove this, let facts be submitted to a candid world.

He has never permitted her to exercise her inalienable right to the elective franchise.

He has compelled her to submit to laws, in the formation of which she had no voice.

He has withheld from her rights which are given to the most ignorant and degraded men—both natives and foreigners.

Having deprived her of this first right of a citizen, the elective franchise, thereby leaving her without representation in the halls of legislation, he has oppressed her on all sides.

He has made her, if married, in the eye of the law, civilly dead.

He has taken from her all right in property, even to the wages she earns.

He has made her, morally, an irresponsible being, as she can commit many crimes with impunity, provided they be done in the presence of her husband. In the covenant of marriage, she is compelled to promise obedience to her husband, he becoming, to all intents and purposes, her master—the law giving him power to deprive her of her liberty, and to administer chastisement.

He has so framed the laws of divorce, as to what shall be the proper causes, and in case of separation, to whom the guardianship of the children shall be given, as to be wholly regardless of the happiness of women—the law, in all cases, going upon a false supposition of the supremacy of man, and giving all power into his hands.

After depriving her of all rights as a married woman, if single, and the owner of property, he has taxed her to support a government which recognizes her only when her property can be made profitable to it.

He has monopolized nearly all the profitable employments, and from those she is permitted to follow, she receives but a scanty remuneration. He closes against her all the avenues to wealth and distinction which he considers most honorable to himself. As a teacher of theology, medicine, or law, she is not known.

He has denied her the facilities for obtaining a thorough education, all colleges being closed against her.

He allows her in church, as well as state, but a subordinate position, claiming apostolic authority for her exclusion from the ministry, and, with some exceptions, from any public participation in the affairs of the church.

He has created a false public sentiment by giving to the world a different code of morals for men and women, by which moral delinquencies which exclude women from society, are not only tolerated, but deemed of little account in man.

He has usurped the prerogative of Jehovah himself, claiming it as his right to assign for her a sphere of action, when that belongs to her conscience and to her God.

He has endeavored, in every way that he could, to destroy her confidence in her own powers, to lessen her self-respect, and to make her willing to lead a dependent and abject life.

Now, in view of this entire disfranchisement of one-half the people of this country, their social and religious degradation—in view of the unjust laws above mentioned, and because women do feel themselves aggrieved, oppressed, and fraudulently deprived of their most sacred rights, we insist that they have immediate admission to all the rights and privileges which belong to them as citizens of the United States.

29

Luther v. Borden

48 U.S. 1 (1849)

Mr. Chief Justice TANEY delivered the opinion of the court.

This case has arisen out of the unfortunate political differences which agitated the people of Rhode Island in 1841 and 1842.

It is an action of trespass brought by Martin Luther, the plaintiff in error, against Luther M. Borden and others, the defendants, in the Circuit Court of the United States for the District of Rhode Island, for breaking and entering the plaintiff's house. The defendants justify upon the ground that large numbers of men were assembled in different parts of the State for the purpose of overthrowing the government by military force, and were actually levying war upon the State; that, in order to defend itself from this insurrection, the State was declared by competent authority to be under martial law; that the plaintiff was engaged in the insurrection; and that the defendants, being in the military service of the State, by command of their superior officer, broke and entered the house and searched the rooms for the plaintiff, who was supposed to be there concealed, in order to arrest him, doing as little damage as possible. The plaintiff replied, that the trespass was committed by the defendants of their own proper wrong, and without any such cause; and upon the issue joined on this replication, the parties proceeded to trial.

The evidence offered by the plaintiff and the defendants is stated at large in the record; and the questions decided by the Circuit Court, and brought up by the writ of error, are not such as commonly arise in an action of trespass. The existence and authority of the government under which the defendants acted was called in question; and the plaintiff insists, that, before the acts complained of were committed, that government had been displaced and annulled by the people of Rhode Island, and that the plaintiff was engaged in supporting the lawful authority of the State, and the defendants themselves were in arms against it.

This is a new question in this court, and certainly a very grave one; and at the time when the trespass is alleged to have been committed it had produced a general and painful excitement in the State, and threatened to end in bloodshed and civil war.

The evidence shows that the defendants, in breaking into the plaintiff's house and endeavoring to arrest him, as stated in the pleadings, acted under the authority of the government which was established in Rhode Island at the time of the Declaration of Independence, and which is usually called the charter government. For when the separation from England took place, Rhode Island did not, like the other States, adopt a new constitution, but continued the form of government established by the charter of Charles the Second in 1663; making only such alterations, by acts of the legislature, as were necessary to adapt it to their condition and rights as an independent State. It was under this form of government that Rhode Island united with the other States in the Declaration of Independence, and afterwards ratified the Constitution of the United States and became a member of this Union; and it continued to be the established and unquestioned government of the State until the difficulties took place which have given rise to this action.

In this form of government no mode of proceeding

was pointed out by which amendments might be made. It authorized the legislature to prescribe the qualification of voters, and in the exercise of this power the right of suffrage was confined to freeholders, until the adoption of the constitution of 1843.

...

We do not understand from the argument that the constitution under which the plaintiff acted is supposed to have been in force after the constitution of May, 1843, went into operation. The contest is confined to the year preceding. The plaintiff contends that the charter government was displaced, and ceased to have any lawful power, after the organization, in May, 1842, of the government which he supported, and although that government never was able to exercise any authority in the State, nor to command obedience to its laws or to its officers, yet he insists that it was the lawful and established government, upon the ground that it was ratified by a large majority of the male people of the State of the age of twenty-one and upwards, and also by a majority of those who were entitled to vote for general officers under the then existing laws of the State. The fact that it was so ratified was not admitted; and at the trial in the Circuit Court he offered to prove it by the production of the original ballots, and the original registers of the persons voting, verified by the oaths of the several moderators and clerks of the meetings, and by the testimony of all the persons so voting, and by the said constitution; and also offered in evidence, for the same purpose, that part of the census of the United States for the year 1840 which applies to Rhode Island; and a certificate of the secretary of state of the charter government, showing the number of votes polled by the freemen of the State for the ten years then last past.

The Circuit Court rejected this evidence, and instructed the jury that the charter government and laws under which the defendants acted were, at the time the trespass is alleged to have been committed, in full force and effect as the form of government and paramount law of the State, and constituted a justification of the acts of the defendants as set forth in their pleas.

It is this opinion of the Circuit Court that we are now called upon to review. It is set forth more at large in the exception, but is in substance as above stated; and the question presented is certainly a very serious one: For, if this court is authorized to enter upon this inquiry as proposed by the plaintiff, and it should be decided that the charter government had no legal existence during the period of time above mentioned, if it had been annulled by the adoption of the opposing government,- then the laws passed by its legislature during that time were nullities; its taxes wrongfully collected; its salaries and compensation to its officers illegally paid; its public accounts improperly settled; and the judgments and sentences of its courts in civil and criminal cases null and void, and the officers who carried their decisions into operation answerable as trespassers, if not in some cases as criminals. When the decision of this court might lead to such results, it becomes its duty to examine very carefully its own powers before it undertakes to exercise jurisdiction.

Certainly, the question which the plaintiff proposed to raise by the testimony he offered has not heretofore been recognized as a judicial one in any of the State courts. In forming the constitutions of the different States, after the Declaration of Independence, and in the various changes and alterations which have since been made, the political department has always determined whether the proposed constitution or amendment was ratified or not by the people of the State, and the judicial power has followed its decision. In Rhode Island, the question has been directly decided. Prosecutions were there instituted against some of the persons who had been active in the forcible opposition to the old government. And in more than one of the cases evidence was offered on the part of the defence similar to the testimony offered in the Circuit Court, and for the same purpose; that is, for the purpose of showing that the proposed constitution had been adopted by the people of Rhode Island, and had, therefore, become the established government, and consequently that the parties accused were doing nothing more than their duty in endeavouring to support it.

But the courts uniformly held that the inquiry proposed to be made belonged to the political power and not to the judicial; that it rested with the political power to decide whether the charter government had been displaced or not; and when that decision was made, the judicial department would be bound to take notice of it as the paramount law of the State, without the aid of oral evidence or the examination of witnesses; that, according to the laws and institutions of Rhode Island, no such change had been recognized by the political power; and that the charter government was the lawful and established government of the State during the period in contest, and that those who were in arms against it were insurgents, and liable to punishment. This doctrine is clearly and forcibly stated in the opinion of the Supreme Court of the State in the trial of Thomas W. Dorr, who was the governor elected under the opposing constitution, and headed the armed force which endeavoured to maintain its authority. Indeed, we do not see how the question could be tried and judicially decided in a State court. Judicial power presupposes an established government capable of enacting laws and enforcing their execution, and of appointing judges to expound and administer them. The acceptance of the judicial office is a recognition of the authority of the government from which it is derived. And if the authority of that government is annulled and overthrown, the power of its courts and other officers is annulled with it. And if a State court should enter upon the inquiry proposed in this case, and should come to the conclusion that the government under which it acted had been put aside and displaced by an opposing government, it would cease to be a court, and be incapable of pronouncing a judicial decision upon the question it undertook to try. If it decides at all as a court, it necessarily affirms the existence and authority of the government under which it is exercising judicial power.

. . .

Moreover, the Constitution of the United States, as far as it has provided for an emergency of this kind, and authorized the general government to interfere in the domestic concerns of a State, has treated the subject as political in its nature, and placed the power in the hands of that department.

The fourth section of the fourth article of the Constitution of the United States provides that the United States shall guarantee to every State in the Union a republican form of government, and shall protect each of them against invasion; and on the application of the legislature or of the executive (when the legislature cannot be convened) against domestic violence.

Under this article of the Constitution it rests with Congress to decide what government is the established one in a State. For as the United States guarantee to each State a republican government, Congress must necessarily decide what government is established in the State before it can determine whether it is republican or not. And when the senators and representatives of a State are admitted into the councils of the Union, the authority of the government under which they are appointed, as well as its republican character, is recognized by the proper constitutional authority. And its decision is binding on every other department of the government, and could not be questioned in a judicial tribunal. It is true that the contest in this case did not last long enough to bring the matter to this issue; and as no senators or representatives were elected under the authority of the government of which Mr. Dorr was the head, Congress was not called upon to decide the controversy. Yet the right to decide is placed there, and not in the courts.

So, too, as relates to the clause in the above-mentioned article of the Constitution, providing for cases of domestic violence. It rested with Congress, too, to determine upon the means proper to be adopted to fulfil this guarantee. They might, if they had deemed it most advisable to do so, have placed it in the power of a court to decide when the contingency had happened which required the federal government to interfere. But Congress thought otherwise, and no doubt wisely; and by the act of February 28, 1795, provided, that, "in case of an insurrection in any State against the government thereof, it shall be lawful for the President of the United States, on application of the legislature of such State or of the executive (when the legislature cannot be convened), to call forth such number of the militia of any other State or States, as may be applied for, as he may judge sufficient to suppress such insurrection."

By this act, the power of deciding whether the exigency had arisen upon which the government of the United States is bound to interfere, is given to the President. He is to act upon the application of the legislature or of the executive, and consequently he must determine what body of men constitute the legislature, and who is the governor, before he can act. The fact that both parties claim the right to the government cannot alter the case, for both cannot be entitled to it. If there is an armed conflict, like the one of which we are speaking, it is a case of domestic violence, and one of the parties must be in insurrection against the lawful government. And the President must, of necessity, decide which is the government, and which party is unlawfully arrayed against it, before he can perform the duty imposed upon him by the act of Congress.

. . .

It is said that this power in the President is dangerous to liberty, and may be abused. All power may be abused if placed in unworthy hands. But it would be difficult, we think, to point out any other hands in which this power would be more safe, and at the same time equally effectual.

When citizens of the same State are in arms against each other, and the constituted authorities unable to execute the laws, the interposition of the United States must be prompt, or it is of little value. The ordinary course of proceedings in courts of justice would be utterly unfit for the crisis. And the elevated office of the President, chosen as he is by the people of the United States, and the high responsibility he could not fail to feel when acting in a case of so much moment, appear to furnish as strong safeguards against a willful abuse of power as human prudence and foresight could well provide. At all events, it is conferred upon him by the Constitution and laws of the United States, and must therefore be respected and enforced in its judicial tribunals.

. . .

The remaining question is whether the defendants, acting under military orders issued under the authority of the government, were justified in breaking and entering the plaintiff's house. In relation to the act of the legislature declaring martial law, it is not necessary in the case before us to inquire to what extent, nor under what circumstances, that power may be exercised by a State. Unquestionably a military government, established by the permanent government of the State, would not be a republican government, and it would be the duty of Congress to overthrow it. But the law of Rhode Island evidently contemplated no such government. It was intended merely for the crisis, and to meet the peril in which the existing government was placed by the armed resistance to its authority. It was so understood and construed by the State authorities. And, unquestionably, a State may use its military power to put down an armed insurrection, too strong to be controlled by the civil authority. The power is essential to the existence of every government, essential to the preservation of order and free institutions, and is as necessary to the States of this Union as to any other government. The State itself must determine what degree of force the crisis demands. And if the government of Rhode Island deemed the armed opposition so formidable, and so ramified throughout the State, as to require the use of its military force and the declaration of martial law, we see no ground upon which this court can question its authority.

It was a state of war; and the established government resorted to the rights and usages of war to maintain itself, and to overcome the unlawful opposition. And in that state of things the officers engaged in its military service might lawfully arrest any one, who, from the information before them, they had reasonable grounds to believe was engaged in the insurrection; and might order a house to be forcibly entered and searched, when there were reasonable grounds for supposing he might be there concealed. Without the power to do this, martial law and the military array of the government would be mere parade, and rather encourage attack than repel it. No more force, however, can be used than is necessary to accomplish the object. And if the power is exercised for the purposes of oppression, or any injury wilfully done to person or property, the party by whom, or by whose order, it is committed would undoubtedly be answerable.

...

Upon the whole, we see no reason for disturbing the judgment of the Circuit Court. The admission of evidence to prove that the charter government was the established government of the State was an irregularity, but is not material to the judgment. A Circuit Court of the United States sitting in Rhode Island is presumed to know the constitution and law of the State. And in order to make up its opinion upon that subject, it seeks information from any authentic and available source, without waiting for the formal introduction of testimony to prove it, and without confining itself to the process which the parties may offer. But this error of the Circuit Court does not affect the result. For whether this evidence was or was not received, the Circuit Court, for the reasons herein before stated, was bound to recognize that government as the paramount and established authority of the State.

Much of the argument on the part of the plaintiff turned upon political rights and political questions, upon which the court has been urged to express an opinion. We decline doing so. The high power has been conferred on this court of passing judgment upon the acts of the State sovereignties, and of the legislative and executive branches of the federal government, and of determining whether they are beyond the limits of power marked out for them respectively by the Constitution of the United States. This tribunal, therefore, should be the last to overstep the boundaries which limit its own jurisdiction. And while it should always be ready to meet any question confided to it by the Constitution, it is equally its duty not to pass beyond its appropriate sphere of action, and to take care not to involve itself in discussions which properly belong to other forums. No one, we believe, has ever doubted the proposition, that, according to the institutions of this country, the sovereignty in every State resides in the people of the State, and that they may alter and change their form of government at their own pleasure. But whether they have

changed it or not by abolishing an old government, and establishing a new one in its place, is a question to be settled by the political power. And when that power has decided, the courts are bound to take notice of its decision, and to follow it.

The judgment of the Circuit Court must therefore be affirmed.

30

John C. Calhoun, *A Discourse on the Constitution* (I)

1851*

Ours is a system of government, compounded of the separate governments of the several States composing the Union, and of one common government of all its members, called the Government of the United States. The former preceded the latter, which was created by their agency. Each was framed by written constitutions; those of the several States by the people of each, acting separately, and in their sovereign character; and that of the United States, by the same, acting in the same character,—but jointly instead of separately.... The entire powers of government are divided between the two; those of a more general character being specifically delegated to the United States; and all others not delegated, being reserved to the several States in their separate character. Each, within its appropriate sphere, possesses all the attributes, and performs all the functions of government. Neither is perfect without the other. The two combined, form one entire perfect government....

The Government of the United States was formed by the Constitution of the United States;—and ours is a democratic, federal republic.

It is democratic, in contradistinction to aristocracy and monarchy.... It has for its fundamental principle, the great cardinal maxim, that the people are the source of all power; that the governments of the several States and of the United States were created by them, and for them; that the powers conferred on them are not sur-

* John C. Calhoun, *A Disquisition on Government and a Discourse on the Constitution and Government of the United States*, ed. Richard K. Cralle (Charleston, SC: Walker & James, 1851), 111–301.

rendered, but delegated; and, as such, are held in trust, and not absolutely; and can be rightfully exercised only in furtherance of the objects for which they were delegated.

It is federal as well as democratic. *Federal*, on the one hand, in contradistinction to *national*, and, on the other, to a confederacy.

…

To express it more concisely, it is federal and not national, because it is the government of a community of States, and not the government of a single State or nation.

…

That the States, when they formed and ratified the constitution, were distinct, independent, and sovereign communities, has already been established. That the people of the several States, acting in their separate, independent, and sovereign character, adopted their separate State constitutions, is a fact uncontested and incontestable; but it is not more certain than that, acting in the same character, they ratified and adopted the constitution of the United States; with this difference only, that in making and adopting the one, they acted without concert of agreement; but, in the other, with concert in making, and mutual agreement in adopting it. That the delegates who constituted the convention which framed the constitution, were appointed by the several States, each on its own authority; that they voted in the convention by States; and that their votes were counted by States, — are recorded and unquestionable facts. So, also, the facts that the constitution, when framed, was submitted to the people of the several States for their respective ratification; that it was ratified by them, each for itself; and that it was binding on each, only in consequence of its being so ratified by it. Until then, it was but the plan of a constitution, without any binding force. It was the act of ratification which established it as a constitution between the States ratifying it; and only between *them*, on the condition that not less than nine of the thirteen States should concur in the ratification; — as is expressly provided by its seventh and last article…. If additional proof be needed to show that it was only binding on the States that ratified it, it may be found in the fact, that two States, North Carolina and Rhode Island, refused, at first, to ratify; and were, in consequence, regarded in the interval as foreign States, without obligation, on their parts to respect it, or, on the part of their citizens, to obey it. Thus far, there can be no difference of opinion. The facts are too recent and too

well established, — and the provision of the constitution too explicit, to admit of doubt.

That the States, then, retained, after the ratification of the constitution, the distinct, independent, and sovereign character in which they formed and ratified it, is certain; unless they divested themselves of it by the act of ratification, or by some provision of the constitution. If they have not, the constitution must be federal, and not national; for it would have, in that case, every attribute necessary to constitute it federal, and not one to make it national. On the other hand, if they have divested themselves, then it would necessarily lose its federal character, and become national. Whether, then, the government is federal or national, is reduced to a single question; whether the act of ratification, of itself, or the constitution, by some one, or all of its provisions, did, or did not, divest the several States of their character of separate, independent, and sovereign communities, and merge them all in one great community or nation, called the American people?

Before entering on the consideration of this important question, it is proper to remark, that, on its decision, the character of the government, as well as the constitution, depends. The former must, necessarily, partake of the character of the latter, as it is but its agent, created by it, to carry its powers into effect. Accordingly, then, as the constitution is federal or national, so must the government be; and I shall, therefore, use them indiscriminately in discussing the subject.

Of all the questions which can arise under our system of government, this is by far the most important. It involves many others of great magnitude; and among them, that of allegiance of the citizen; or, in other words, the question to whom allegiance and obedience are ultimately due…. For it is clear, if the States still retain their sovereignty as separate and independent communities, the allegiance and obedience of the citizens of each would be due to their respective States; and that the government of the United States and those of the several States would stand as equals and co-ordinates in their respective spheres; and, instead of being united socially, their citizens would be politically connected through their respective States. On the contrary, if they have, by ratifying the constitution, divested themselves of their individuality and sovereignty, and merged themselves into one great community or nation, it is equally clear, that the sovereignty would reside in the whole, — or what is called the American people; and that allegiance and obedience would be due to them. Nor is it less so, that the government of the several States would, in such a case, stand to that of the United States, in the relation of inferior and subordinate, to superior and paramount; and that the individuals of the several States, thus fused, as it were, into one general mass, would be united *socially*, and not *politically*. So great a change of condition would have involved a thorough and radical revolution, both socially and politically,—a revolution much more radical, indeed, than that which followed the Declaration of Independence.

...

The process preparatory to ratification, and the acts by which it was done, prove, beyond the possibility of a doubt, that it was ratified by the several States, through conventions of their delegates, chosen in each State by the people thereof; and acting, each in the name and by the authority of its State: and, as all the States ratified it,—"We, the people of the United States," mean,— We, the people of the several States of the Union. The inference is irresistible. And when it is considered that the States of the Union were then members of the confederacy,—and that, by the express provision of one of its articles, "each State retains its sovereignty, freedom, and independence," the proof is demonstrative, that,— "We, the people of the United States of America," mean the people of the several States of the Union acting as free, independent, and sovereign States.

...

Taken altogether, it follows, from what has been stated, that the constitution was ordained and established *by* the several States, as *distinct, sovereign communities*; and that it was ordained and established by them for *themselves*—for their common welfare and safety, as *distinct and sovereign communities*.

...

Having now established that the constitution is federal throughout, in contradistinction to national; and that the several States still retain their sovereignty and independence unimpaired, one would suppose that the conclusion would follow, irresistibly, in the judgment of all, that the government is also federal. But such is not the case. There are those, who admit the *constitution* to be entirely federal, but insist that the *government* is partly federal, and partly national. They rest their opinion on the authority of the "Federalist." That celebrated work comes to this conclusion, after explicitly admitting that the constitution was ratified and adopted by the people of the several States, and not by them as

individuals composing one entire nation;—that the act establishing the constitution is, itself, a federal, and not a national act;—that it resulted neither from the act of a majority of the people of the union, nor from a majority of the States; but from the unanimous assent of the several States;—differing no otherwise from their ordinary assent than as being given, not by their legislatures, but by the people themselves;—that they are parties to it;—that each State, in ratifying it, was considered as a sovereign body, independent of all others, and is bound only by its own voluntary act;—that, in consequence, the constitution itself is federal and not national;—that, if it had been formed by the people as one nation or community, the will of the majority of the whole people of the Union would have bound the minority;—that the idea of a national government involves in it, not only authority over individual citizens, but an infinite supremacy over all persons and things, so far as they are objects of lawful government;—that among the people consolidated into one nation, this supremacy is completely vested in the government; that the State governments, and all local authorities, are subordinate to it, and may be controlled, directed, or abolished by it at pleasure;—and, finally, that the States are regarded, by the constitution, as distinct, independent, and sovereign.[1]

How strange, after all these admissions, is the conclusion that the government is partly federal and partly national! It is the constitution which determines the character of the government. It is impossible to conceive how the constitution can be *exclusively* federal, (as it is admitted, and has been clearly proved to be,) and the government *partly* federal and *partly* national. It would be just as easy to conceive how a constitution can be exclusively monarchical, and the government partly monarchical, and partly aristocratic or popular; and *vice versa....* What can be more contradictious? This, of itself, is sufficient to destroy the authority of the work on this point,—as celebrated as it is,—without showing, as might be done, that the admissions it makes throughout, are, in like manner, in direct contradiction to the conclusions, to which it comes.

...

From what has been stated, the conclusion follows, irresistibly, that the constitution and the government, regarding the latter apart from the former, rest, throughout, on the principle of the concurrent majority;

1. See *Federalist*, Nos. 39 and 40.

and that it is, of course, a Republic;—a constitutional democracy, in contradistinction to an absolute democracy; and that, the theory which regards it as a government of the mere numerical majority, rests on a gross and groundless misconception. So far is this from being the case, the numerical majority was entirely excluded as an element, throughout the whole process of forming and ratifying the constitution: and, although admitted as one of the two elements, in the organization of the government, it was with the important qualification, that it should be the numerical majority of the population of the *several States*, regarded in the corporate character, and not of the whole Union, regarded as one community.

. . .

The question, then, is,—what provision has the constitution of the United States made to preserve the division of powers among the several departments of the government? And this involves another; whether the departments are so constituted, that each has, within itself, the power of self-protection; the power, by which, it may prevent the others from encroaching on, and absorbing the portion vested in it, by the constitution? Without such power, the strongest would, in the end, inevitably absorb and concentrate the powers of the others in itself, as has been fully shown in the preliminary discourse;—where, also, it is shown that there is but one mode in which this can be prevented; and that is, by investing each division of power, or the representative and organ of each, with a veto, or something tantamount, in one form or another.

. . .

The question is one of the first magnitude;—and deserves the most serious and deliberate consideration. I shall begin with considering,—what means the government of a State possesses, to prevent the government of the United States from encroaching on its reserved powers? I shall, however, pass over the right of remonstrating against its encroachments; of adopting resolutions against them, as unconstitutional; of addressing the governments of its co-States, and calling on them to unite and co-operate in opposition to them; and of instructing its Senators in Congress, and requesting its members of the House of Representatives, to oppose them,—and other means of like character; not because they are of no avail, but because they are utterly impotent to arrest the strong and steady tendency of the government of the United States to encroach on the reserved powers; however much they may avail, in par-

ticular instances. . . . Nothing short of a negative, absolute or in effect, on the part of the government of a State, can possibly protect it against the encroachments of the government of the United States, whenever their powers come in conflict. That there is, in effect, a mutual negative on the part of each, in such cases, is what I next propose to show.

. . .

[I]t may be affirmed as true, that governments, in full possession of all the powers appertaining to government, have the right to enforce their decisions as to the extent of their powers, against all opposition. But the case is different in a system of government like ours,—where the powers appertaining to government are divided,—a portion being delegated to one government, and a portion to another;—and the residue retained by those who ordained and established both. In such case, neither can have the right to enforce its decisions, as to the extent of its powers, when a conflict occurs between them in reference to it; because it would be, in the first place, inconsistent with the relation in which they stand to each other as co-ordinates. The idea of co-ordinates, excludes that of superior and subordinate, and, necessarily, implies that of equality. But to give either the right, not only to judge of the extent of its own powers, but, also, of that of its co-ordinate, and to enforce its decision against it, would be, not only to destroy the equality between them, but to deprive one of an attribute,—appertaining to all governments,—to judge, in the first instance, of the extent of its powers. . . . If one, then, possess the right to enforce its decision, so, also, must the other. But to assume that both possess it, would be to leave the umpirage, in case of conflict, to mere brute force; and thus to destroy the equality, clearly implied by the relation of co-ordinates, and the division between the two governments. . . . As the one or the other might prove the stronger, consolidation or disunion would, inevitably, be the consequence.

. . .

It follows, from what has been stated, that the people of the several States, regarded as parties to the constitutional compact, have imposed restrictions on the exercise of their sovereign power, by entering into a solemn obligation to do no act inconsistent with its provisions, and to uphold and support it within their respective limits. To this extent the restrictions go,—but no further. As parties to the constitutional compact, they retain the right, unrestricted, which appertains to such a relation in all cases where it is not surrendered, to judge as to the extent of the obligation imposed by the agreement or compact,—in the first instance, where there is a higher authority; and, in the last resort, where there is none. The principle on which this assertion rests, is essential to the nature of contracts; and is in accord with universal practice. But the right to judge as to the extent of the obligation imposed, necessarily involves the right of pronouncing whether an act of the federal government, or any of its departments, be, or be not, in conformity to the provisions of the constitutional compact; and, if decided to be inconsistent, or pronouncing it to be unauthorized by the constitution, and, therefore, null, void, and of no effect. If the constitution be a compact, and the several States, regarded in their sovereign character, be parties to it, all the rest follow as necessary consequences.

...

These conclusions follow irresistibly from incontestable facts and well established principles. But the possession of a right is one thing, and the exercise of it another. Rights, themselves, must be exercised with prudence and propriety: when otherwise exercised, they often cease to be rights, and become wrongs. The more important the right, and the more delicate its character, the higher the obligation to observe, strictly, the rules of prudence and propriety. But, of all the rights appertaining to the people of the several States, as members of the common Union, the one in question, is by far the most important and delicate; and, of course, requires, in its exercise, the greatest caution and forbearance. As parties to the compact which constitutes the Union, they are under obligations to observe its provisions, and prevent their infraction. In exercising the right in question, they are bound to take special care that they do not themselves, violate this, the most sacred of obligations. To avoid this, prudence and propriety require that they should abstain from interposing their authority, to arrest an act of their common government, unless the case, in their opinion, involve a clear and palpable infraction of the instrument. They are bound to go further,—and to forbear from interposing, even when it is clear and palpable, unless it be, at the same time, highly dangerous in its character, and apparently admitting of no other remedy; and for the plain reason, that prudence and propriety require, that a right so high and delicate should be called into exercise, only in cases of great magnitude and extreme urgency.

...

[In such a case], it is the duty of the federal government to invoke the action of the amending power, by proposing a declaratory amendment affirming the power it claims, according to the forms prescribed in the constitution; and, if it fail, to abandon the power.

On the other hand, should it succeed in obtaining the amendment, the act of the government of the separate State which caused the conflict, and operated as a negative on the act of the federal government, would, in all cases, be overruled; and the latter become operative within its limits. But the result is, in some respects, different,—were a State, acting in her sovereign character, and as a party to the constitutional compact, has interposed, and declared an act of the federal government to be unauthorized by the constitution,—and, therefore, null and void. In this case, if the act of the latter be predicated on a power consistent with the character of the constitution, the ends for which it was established, and the nature of our system of government;—or, more briefly, if it come fairly within the scope of the amending power, the State is bound to acquiesce, by the solemn obligation which it contracted, in ratifying the constitution. But if it transcends the limits of the amending power,—be inconsistent with the character of the constitution and the ends for which it was established,—or with the nature of the system,—the result is different. In such case, the State is not bound to acquiesce. It may choose whether it will, or whether it will not secede from the Union.... That a State, as a party to the constitutional compact, has the right to secede,—acting in the same capacity in which it ratified the constitution,—cannot, with any show of reason, be denied by any one who regards the constitution as a compact,—if a power should be inserted by the amending power, which would radically change the character of the constitution, or the nature of the system; or if the former should fail to fulfill the ends for which it was established.

31

Campbell v. Georgia

11 Ga. 353 (1852)

By the Court.—LUMPKIN, J. delivering the opinion.

James Campbell, convicted of manslaughter in the Superior Court of Richmond County, sues out a writ of error to reverse the judgment of the Court below, in refusing him a new trial. His application for a re-hearing, was based upon two grounds: 1st. Because the *dying declarations* of Alfred Mays, the person killed, were permitted to go in evidence to the Jury, contrary to the provision in the 6th amendment of the Constitution of the United States, entitling the accused to be confronted with the witnesses against him. And 2dly. Because these *declarations* were not admissible, for the reason, that they were not made under the consciousness of immediate death.

The first point submitted in the argument is, that deathbed declarations in cases of homicide, cannot be given in evidence, because their admission would contravene the 6th article of the amendments to the Constitution of the United States, entitling the accused in all criminal prosecutions, to be confronted with the witnesses against him.

The answer given to this objection is, that the article in question, applies to the United States government only, and was not intended to control the laws of the several States.

That this amendment, like the other nine adopted at the same time, was primarily introduced for the purpose of preventing an abuse of power by the Federal Government, is readily conceded. Grasping, however, as the National Judiciary is supposed to be, and studious to accumulate power in the central government, it may well be questioned, whether the limitations and restrictions imposed by these amendments, were necessary. The rights which they were designed to protect, were too sacred to be violated by any republican tribunal, legislative or judicial. A disregard of them, was mainly instrumental in overturning the Stuart dynasty in England; depriving one monarch of his head, and another of his crown. And no Court, probably, in this free country, would have ventured to enforce practices so arbitrary, unjust, and oppressive, as those inhibited by these amendments; practices condemned by Magna Charta—the Petition of Right—the Bill of Rights—and more especially, by the Act of Settlement, in Britain.

The principles embodied in these amendments, for better securing the lives, liberties, and property of the people, were declared to be the "birthright" of our ancestors, several centuries previous to the establishment of our government. It is not likely, therefore, that any Court could be found in America of sufficient hardihood to deprive our citizens of these invaluable safe-

guards. Still, our patriotic forefathers, out of abundant caution, super-added these amendments to the Constitution, so as to place the matter beyond doubt or cavil, misconstruction or abuse.

And the question to be decided now is, not whether these amendments were intended to operate as a restriction upon the government of the United States, but whether it is competent for a State Legislature, by virtue of its inherent powers, to pass an Act directly impairing the great principles of protection to person and property, embraced in these amendments?

That the power to pass any law infringing on these principles is taken from the Federal Government, no one denies. But is it a part of the reserved rights of a State to do this? May the Legislature of a State, for example, unless restrained by its own Constitution, pass a law "respecting an establishment of religion, or prohibiting the free exercise thereof; or abridging the freedom of speech or of the press; or the right of the people peaceably to assemble and petition the government for a redress of grievances?" If so, of what avail, I ask, is the negation of these powers to the General Government? Our revolutionary sires wisely resolved that religion should be purely voluntary in this country; that it should subsist by its own omnipotence, or come to nothing. Hence, they solemnly determined that there should be no church established by law, and maintained by the secular power. Now, the doctrine is, that Congress may not exercise this power, but that each State Legislature may do so for itself. As if a National religion and State religion, a National press and State press, were quite separate and distinct from each other; and that the one might be subject to control, but the other not!

Such logic, I must confess, fails to commend itself to my judgment. For let it constantly be borne in mind, that notwithstanding we may have different governments, a nation within a nation, *imperium in imperio*, we have but *one* people; and that the same people which, divided into separate communities, constitute the respective State governments, comprise in the aggregate, the United States Government; and that it is in vain to shield them from a blow aimed by the Federal arm, if they are liable to be prostrated by one dealt with equal fatality by their own.

But I deem it unnecessary to pursue this line of argument and of illustration, any farther. When it can be demonstrated that an individual or a government has the *right* to do *wrong*, contrary to the old adage, that one person's *rights* cannot be another person's *wrongs*, then, and not before, will it be yielded that it is a part and parcel of the original jurisdiction of the State governments, reserved to them in the distribution of power under the Constitution, to enact laws, to deprive the citizen of the right to keep and bear arms; to quarter soldiers in time of peace, in any house, without the consent of the owner; to subject the people to unreasonable search and seizure, in their persons, houses, papers and effects; to hold a person to answer for a capital, or otherwise infamous crime, without presentment or indictment, to be twice put in jeopardy of life or limb for the same offence; to compel him, in a criminal case, to be a witness against himself; to deprive him of life, liberty or property, without due course of law; to take private property for public use, without just compensation; to deprive the accused in all criminal trials, of the right to a speedy and public trial, by an impartial Jury; to be informed of the nature and cause of the accusation; *to be confronted with the witnesses against him*; to have compulsory process for obtaining witnesses in his favor, and to have the assistance of counsel for his defence; to enact laws requiring excessive bail, imposing oppressive and ruinous fines, and inflicting cruel and unusual punishments!

From such *State rights*, good Lord deliver us! I utterly repudiate them from the creed of my political faith!

It was not because it was supposed that legislation over the subjects here enumerated might be better and more safely entrusted to the State governments, that it was prohibited to Congress. It was to *declare* to the world the fixed and unalterable determination of our people, that these invaluable rights which had been established at so great a cost of blood and treasure, should never be disturbed by *any* government. They feared no interference from their own local Legislatures. They determined to fetter the hands of the Federal authority, the only quarter from which danger was apprehended.

One of the reasons set forth in the preamble to these amendments, for their adoption was, that it would "extend thereby, the ground of public confidence in the government, and thus best secure the beneficent ends of its institution." *Marbury & Crawford's Digest*, 660. What confidence will be reposed in a *State* government, whose legislation should be characterized by acts which disgrace the most tyrannical epoch of the British monarchy? A free people would instantly and indignantly reject it and its authors.

The famous indictment preferred by the Grand In-

quest of 1776, against George the Third, charged him, among other things, with "quartering large bodies of armed troops among the people;" and with depriving the provinces, in many cases, of "the benefits of trial by Jury;" two of the articles expressly forbidden by the amendments. It further alleged, that he had "*abolished the free system of English law in a neighboring province*, establishing therein an arbitrary government, and enlarging its boundaries so as to render it at once an example and fit instrument for introducing the same *absolute rule* into these colonies." To uphold this "free system of English law," was the great end and object of the whole of the ten amendments—but for the apparent irreverence, I would say *commandments*—which were added to the Constitution. If the foregoing acts justly branded this trans-Atlantic Prince as a tyrant, and rendered him unfit to be the ruler of a free people, republican legislators will beware how they tread in his footsteps.

While this Court yields to none in its devotion to State *rights*, and would be the first to *resist* all attempts at Federal usurpation, it feels itself called on by the blood of the many martyrs, who nobly died to maintain the great principles of civil liberty contained in these amendments—*our American Magna Charta*—to stand by, support and defend the rights which they guarantee, against all encroachments, whether proceeding from the National or State governments.

The Chancellor who delivered the opinion of the Court of Errors, in *Barker vs. The People*, (3 *Cow.* 686,) one of the cases cited in support of the position which I am combating, notices the fact, that in the Constitutions established by the different States, since the adoption of the amendments in question, provisions are inserted in reference to the same subjects embraced in the amendments. And the inference is, that the States which imposed the same restraints upon their own governments, which were contained in these amendments, gave conclusive evidence that they conceived that they were at liberty to do so or not; and that the Constitution of the Union imposed no restraint upon the State governments; and that to consider these amendments as operative upon the several States, would be to render nugatory the like provisions in the Constitutions of many of the States.

There is plausibility in this proposition. It is a curious circumstance, however, and one worthy of remark, that the States in framing their Constitutions, have done things more strange and unaccountable than this. Many of them have imposed restraints by their Constitutions, on certain powers, over which the States are expressly forbidden to legislate, by the Federal Constitution. By the latter, for instance, it is provided that no State shall pass any *ex post facto* law. The same prohibition is contained in the Constitution of Georgia, Massachusetts, Pennsylvania, Delaware, Maryland, North and South Carolina, Kentucky, and I believe, of every State in the Union. Did these States conceive that they had the power to pass an *ex post facto* law, or not? Let this example, one only of many which might be adduced, suffice to show how utterly unsatisfactory is the course of reasoning adopted by the Court of Errors of New York.

Other precedents are cited to sustain the proposition, that none of these amendments extend to the State governments, but were intended for Congress and the United States Courts. *James vs. The Commonwealth*, 12 *Serg. & Rawl.* 220. *The Mayor and City Council of Baltimore*, 7 *Peters* 243. I will not stop to examine these cases, or to array the conflicting opinions of Courts and Jurists, equally eminent, on the other side.

The question, I am aware, is still regarded as an unsettled one; but in this country, the weight of authority will be found in favor of the doctrine, that governments are not clothed with absolute and despotic power; but that independently of written constitutions, there are restrictions upon the legislative power, growing out of the nature of the civil compact and the natural rights of man. And that, when certain boundaries are overleaped and a law passed subversive of the great principles of republican liberty and natural justice—as for instance, taking away without cause, and for no offence, the liberty of the citizen—that it would become the imperative duty of the Courts, to pronounce such a statute inoperative and void.

In *Fletcher vs. Peck*, (6 *Cranch* 87,) Chief Justice *Marshall* himself says, "It may well be doubted whether the nature of society and of government, does not prescribe *some* limits to legislative power."

In *Terrell vs. Taylor*, (9 *Cranch* 43,) the Court say, "We know of no case in which a legislative act to transfer the property of A to B, without his consent, has ever been held a constitutional exercise of power in any State in the Union. On the contrary, it has been constantly resisted, as *inconsistent with first principles*."

In *Green vs. Biddle*, (8 *Wheat.* 1,) Mr. Justice *Washington*, in delivering the opinion of the Court, speaks of *"the universal law of all free governments."*

In *Wilkinson vs. Leland*, (2 *Peters* 654,) the Supreme Court say, "that government can scarcely be deemed free, where the rights of property are left solely dependent upon the will of the legislative body, without any restraint. *The fundamental maxims of a free government seem to require, that the rights of personal liberty and private property, should be held sacred.*"

In *Bonaparte vs. The Camden & Amboy R. R. Co.* (1 *Baldwin's C. C. R.* 223,) it was adjudged, that the Legislature has not the power to take the property of a man, for private purposes, without his consent; that if a law was clearly open to that objection, it would be a fatal one.

Now, all of these adjudications, with numerous others, to the same effect, proceed upon the fundamental principles of natural justice, independent of any constitutional restriction.

In the case of *The Regents of the University of Maryland vs. Williams* (9 *Gill. & Johnson* 365,) the Court is still more explicit. After deciding that the Act of the Legislature of Maryland, which took away the vested rights of the Regents, was void, as being in collision with the Constitution of the United States; Chief Justice *Buchanan* adds, "but the objection to the validity of the Act of 1825, does not rest alone for support upon the Constitution of the United States."

"Independent of that instrument, and of any express restriction in the Constitution of the State, there is a fundamental principle of right and justice, inherent in the nature and spirit of the social compact (in this country at least,) the character and genius of our governments, the causes from which they sprang, and the purposes for which they were established, that rises above the restraints and sets bounds to the power of legislation, which the Legislature cannot pass, without exceeding its lawful authority. It is that principle which protects the life, liberty, and property of the citizen, from violation, in the unjust exercise of legislative power."

The Constitution of New York confers upon the Legislature of that State, the broad grant *to pass all laws* which they deem necessary and proper for the good of the State, and which shall not be repugnant to the paramount law. And yet, in *Taylor vs. Porter*, (4 *Hill's R.* 146,) Mr. Justice *Bronson* says, "under our form of government, the Legislature is not supreme. It is only one of the organs of that absolute sovereignty which resides in the whole body of the people." And notwithstanding the general grant of power to pass *all* constitutional laws, he denied that it reached to the unwarrantable extent of taking the property of A and giving it to B, with or without compensation. "Neither life, liberty, nor property," says the learned Judge, "except when forfeited for crime, or when the latter is taken for public use, falls within the scope of this power."

It is for this reason, that the power of the Legislature, independent of any constitutional restrictions, to pass retrospective laws which shall have a *retroactive* effect, has been uniformly denied. 2 *Gallison*, 139; 1 *N. H. R.* 213; 16 *Mass.* 215; 7 *Johns. R.* 477.

But we do not intend to put our opinion in this case, upon this foundation, however solid it may be. For while we have denied the omnipotence of the Legislature, the tendency of our administration, nevertheless has been, to side with those who refused to declare an Act of the Legislature void, because it conflicts with the Court's views of reason, expediency or justice; and who recommend an appeal to the ballot-box as the only remedy for *unwise* legislation. And one of the strongest arguments against Judicial interposition in such cases is, that apart from a *written Constitution*, our ideas of natural justice are vague and uncertain, regulated by no fixed standard; the ablest and best men differing widely upon this, as well as all other subjects.

But as to questions arising under these amendments, there is nothing indefinite. The people of the several States, by adopting these amendments, have defined accurately and recorded permanently their opinion, as to the great principles which they embrace; and to make them more emphatic and enduring, have had them incorporated into the Constitution of the Union—the permanent law of the land. Admit, therefore, that the Legislature of a State may be absolute and without control over all other subjects, where its authority is not restrained by the Constitution of the State or of the United States; still, viewing these amendments as we do, as intended to establish justice—to secure the blessings of liberty—to protect person and property from violence; and that these were the very purposes for which this government was established, we hold that they constitute a limit to all legislative power, Federal or State, beyond which it cannot go; that these vital truths lie at the foundation of our free, republican institutions; that without this security for personal liberty and private property, our social compact could not exist. No Court should ever presume that it was the design of the people to entrust their representatives with the power to take away or impair these securities. Such an assumption would be against all reason. The very genius, nature and spirit of our institutions amount to a prohibition of such acts of legislation, and will overrule and forbid them.

I admit, that all criminal jurisdiction rightfully belonging to any independent community, is vested in our State governments, except where, to promote the general welfare, it has been expressly delegated to the national government. To paraphrase the language of a distinguished Justiciary, the Legislature may enjoin, permit, forbid and punish; they may declare new crimes; they may, in a word, *command* what is right, and *prohibit* what is wrong, in the broadest sense; but they cannot commit political suicide, or rather *parricide*, by violating or destroying the great first principles of American civil liberty, as set forth and declared in the ten amendments of the Constitution—a legal decalogue for every civilized society, in all time to come.

No such attempt would be considered a rightful exercise of legislative authority. To maintain that our Federal or State Legislature possess such a power, is, in our opinion, a political heresy, altogether inadmissible. The British Parliament dare not, at this day, with all its transcendental power, commit such an outrage. For such monstrosity in legislation we must go to semi-imperial France, or semi-barbarous Russia. Any attempt in this country, at this day, to establish religion; to curtail the freedom of speech or of the press; to deprive a party of the privilege of appearing personally, or by counsel; to inflict cruel or unusual punishments; to immure a prisoner without trial, in a dungeon for life; to subject a citizen to a star-chamber proceeding instead of a public trial; would shock not only the common sense, but sense of justice of the teeming millions in this free and happy country! Shame! shame! upon such legislation, would be indignantly uttered by ten thousand tongues!

No republican Legislature, I am persuaded, will ever be so forgetful or regardless of moral rectitude as to incur so severe a rebuke. Our law-makers are too deeply penetrated with a sense of duty and of justice; too profoundly imbued with moral and religious principle; too much interested in the enjoyment of that security to person and property, (the fruit of our free institutions) which these amendments provide; too indelibly impressed with the worth of these principles, by a consideration of their cost, deliberately to trample them under foot. Should the Legislature, through haste or inadvertence, pass an act at war with the spirit, object and design of our social system, as manifested in this charter, it would become the imperative duty of the Courts, however delicate the task, to vindicate the rights of the citizen, by pronouncing such a Statute invalid. This Court has been compelled more than once since its organization, reluctantly to perform this painful function.

Holding then, as we do, that the inviolability of the rule must be preserved, which, in all criminal prosecutions entitles the accused to be confronted with the witnesses against him, does it abrogate the Common Law principle, that the declarations *in extremis* of a murdered person, as to the homicide, are admissible in evidence? The right of a party accused of a crime, to meet the witnesses against him, face to face, is no new principle. It is coeval with the Common Law. Its recognition in the Constitution was intended for the two-fold purposes of giving it prominence and permanence. The argument for the exclusion of the testimony, proceeds upon the idea that the deceased is the witness, when in fact it is the individual who swears to the statements of the deceased, who is the witness. And it is as to *him* that the privileges of an oral and cross examination are secured.

The admission of dying declarations in evidence, was never supposed, in England, to violate the well-established principles of the Common Law, that the witnesses against the accused should be examined in his presence. The two rules have co-existed there certainly, since the trial of Ely, in 1720, and are considered of equal authority.

The constant and uniform practice of all the Courts of this country, before and since the revolution, and since the adoption of the Federal Constitution, and of the respective State Constitutions, containing a similar provision, has been to receive in evidence, *in cases of homicide*, declarations properly made, *in articulo mortis.*

It constitutes one of the exceptions to the rule which rejects *hearsay evidence.* It is founded in the necessity of the case; and for the reason, that the sanction under which these declarations are made, in view of impending death and judgment, when the last hope of life is extinct, and when the retributions of eternity are at hand, is of equal solemnity as that of statements made on oath. With the policy of the rule which was been so ingeniously assailed by counsel for the accused, we have nothing to do. I will not deny but that it may be justified by that urgent necessity, which is a sufficient ground for dispensing with any rule. Chief Justice *Tilghman* thought there could not be a stronger case of necessity, than that which requires the declarations of

the dying victim of secret assassination to be received, in order to the detection and punishment of his murderer. Moreover, he supposed that its allowance, and the knowledge that upon it, the culprit might be condemned, would have a saving and protecting influence upon society. Still it must be admitted that great caution should be observed in the use of this kind of evidence; and that were the point, *res integra*, much might be said against the practice.

Without dwelling longer upon this exception, we consider it settled, that *in case of homicide*, declarations by one mortally wounded and who is conscious of his condition, are admissible in evidence, both as to who was the perpetrator of the injury and the facts which attended the transaction.

The only remaining ground of objection is, that the evidence does not sufficiently show that the deceased knew or thought that his end was *near*; and that the declarations testified to were made with the belief of death present to the mind of the declarant. That declarations, to be admissible in evidence, must be made under apprehension of immediate death, is unquestionable. The facts disclosed by the record satisfied the mind of the presiding Judge, as they do ours, that the statements were made at a time when the deceased was without hope of life, and in expectation of approaching dissolution.

The wounds were inflicted on Saturday night, the 19th of January, 1851; one of which was so severe as to cause a protrusion of the membranes of the intestines from the abdomen; and in this state the deceased lay, so exposed to the bitter cold of winter, until next morning. When found, he was completely torpid, and he continued in this condition until he died—before sun-rise Tuesday morning—no re-action having taken place in his system.

John Evans testifies that he was with him a great deal during his illness, spending three hours or more at one time, on Sabbath evening. He heard him say he was very bad off; he was cut all to pieces, and he believed he should die. John J. Flournoy swears, that on Monday afternoon, about 4 o'clock, he saw Mays. He found him very weak, and very much depressed in feeling. He stated that certain persons (naming them) who had inflicted the wounds, had threatened to kill him; and that they had done it—or nearly done it. William Goodwin called on the deceased, on Sunday and Monday evenings, and staid some hours with him. He was in great pain, and said he would never get over it; that he was cut all to pieces; and that he wanted Mr. Evans to attend to having these people arrested, if he died. Seaborn Skinner, a neighbor of the deceased, and known to him as a member and a class-leader of the Church, called on him on Monday. He told witness he thought he would die; and when he bid him good bye, Mays said to witness, he never expected to see him in this world again, and asked him to pray for him.

This testimony, embracing as it does, separate conversations. held with different persons, at various times, at their respective interviews with the deceased, would seem to be conclusive as to the belief of the party, that he was a dying man; and that, consequently what he said to the witnesses on these occasions was properly submitted to the Jury by the Court, and with equal propriety, regarded by them as the *dying declarations* of Alfred Mays, in the full view of death and eternity as just at hand.

Is it the province of the Judge or of the Jury to decide whether the deceased thought himself dying or not, when he made the declarations inculpating the defendant?

His Honor Judge *Starnes*, after giving to this case, as he does all others which come before him, the most careful and scrupulous attention, and bringing to bear upon it that clear and discriminating judgment, patient and thorough research, which characterises all of his decisions, *held*, that the proper course to be pursued was this: that a *prima facie* case of the moral consciousness required, should be exhibited to the Court in the first instance, as preliminary to the admission of the testimony. This done, the evidence should be received and left for the Jury to determine whether the deceased was really under the apprehension of death when the declarations were made, which they might infer either from circumstances or the expressions used.

All the analogies of the law, as to proof of books, handwriting, &c., would seem to sanction this practice; and it is certainly in accordance with the symmetry of our Judicial system. Up to the time of Woodstock's case, decided in England in 1789, the whole subject seems to have been left to the Jury, under the direction of the Court, as a mixed question of law and fact. Since that period, it has been held there, to be the peculiar and exclusive duty of the Court, to decide whether the decedent made the declarations under the consciousness of inevitable death.

Affirming then, as we do, the doctrine of the Circuit Judge, that the condition of the deceased is to be determined by the Jury, by his statements, and by the character and nature of the injury, his appearance, conduct, &c. why should this *issue of fact* be placed upon a different footing from any other? And if there be evidence to warrant the verdict, why should it be disturbed by this or any other Court?

For myself, I must say, that the testimony satisfies me, that Alfred Mays *felt* that his departure was at hand; that he was going the way of all flesh; that he was fully sensible of the hopelessness of his condition.

On the whole, therefore, our conclusions are clearly against the prisoner, on all the grounds on which he seeks a reversal.

Judgment affirmed.

32

Address of the Colored National Convention to the People of the United States, Rochester, NY

July 6–8, 1853*

Fellow-Citizens: Met in convention as delegates, representing the Free Colored people of the United States; charged with the responsibility of inquiring into the general condition of our people, and of devising measures which may, with the blessing of God, tend to our mutual improvement and elevation; conscious of entertaining no motives, ideas, or aspirations, but such as are in accordance with truth and justice, and are compatible with the highest good of our country and the world, with a cause as vital and worthy as that for which (nearly eighty years ago) your fathers and our fathers bravely contended, and in which they gloriously triumphed— we deem it proper, on this occasion, as one method of promoting the honorable ends for which we have met, and of discharging our duty to those in whose name we speak, to present the claims of our common cause to your candid, earnest, and favorable consideration.

. . .

* Printed at the Office of Frederick Douglass's Paper (Rochester, NY, 1853). Available online at https://omeka.coloredconventions.org/items/show/458.

The great truths of moral and political science, upon which we rely, and which we press upon your consideration, have been evolved and enunciated by you. We point to your principles, your wisdom, and to your example as the full justification of our course this day. That "ALL MEN ARE CREATED EQUAL": THAT "LIFE, LIBERTY AND THE PURSUIT OF HAPPINESS" ARE THE RIGHT OF ALL; THAT "TAXATION AND REPRESENTATION" SHOULD GO TOGETHER; THAT GOVERNMENTS ARE TO PROTECT, NOT TO DESTROY, THE RIGHTS OF MANKIND; THAT THE CONSTITUTION OF THE UNITED STATES WAS FORMED TO ESTABLISH JUSTICE, PROMOTE THE GENERAL WELFARE, AND SECURE THE BLESSING OF LIBERTY TO ALL THE PEOPLE OF THIS COUNTRY; THAT RESISTANCE TO TYRANTS IS OBEDIENCE TO GOD—are American principles and maxims, and together they form and constitute the constructive elements of the American government.

. . .

We are Americans, and as Americans, we would speak to Americans. We address you not as aliens nor as exiles, humbly asking to be permitted to dwell among you in peace; but we address you as American citizens asserting their rights on their own native soil. Neither do we address you as enemies, (although the recipients of innumerable wrongs;) but in the spirit of patriotic good will. In assembling together as we have done, our object is not to excite pity for ourselves, but to command respect for our cause, and to obtain justice for our people. . . .

We ask that in our native land, we shall not be treated as strangers, and worse than strangers.

We ask that, being friends of America, we should not be treated as enemies of America.

We ask that, speaking the same language and being of the same religion, worshipping the same God, owing our redemption to the same Savior, and learning our duties from the same Bible, we shall not be treated as barbarians.

We ask that, having the same physical, moral, mental, and spiritual wants, common to other members of the human family, we shall have the same means which are granted and secured to others, to supply those wants.

We ask that the doors of the school-house, the workshop, the church, the college, shall be thrown open as freely to our children as to the children of other members of the community.

We ask that the American government shall be administered as that beneath the broad shield of the Constitution, the colored seaman, shall be secure in his life, liberty and property, in every State in the Union.

We ask that as justice knows no rich, no poor, no black, no white, but, like the government of God, renders alike to every man reward or punishment, according to his works shall be—the white and black man may stand upon an equal footing before the laws of the land.

We ask that (since the right of trial by jury is a safeguard to liberty, against the encroachments of power, only as it is a trial by impartial men, drawn indiscriminately from the country) colored men shall not, in every instance, be tried by white persons; and that colored men shall not be either by custom or enactment excluded from the jury-box.

We ask that (inasmuch as we are, in common with other American citizens, supporters of the State, subject to its laws, interested in its welfare liable to be called upon to defend it in time of war, contributors to its wealth in times of peace) the complete and unrestricted right of suffrage, which is essential to the dignity even of the white man, be extended to the Free Colored man also.

. . .

To be still more explicit: we would, first of all, be understood to range ourselves no lower among our fellow-countrymen than is implied in the high appellation of "citizen."

Notwithstanding the impositions and deprivations which have fettered us—notwithstanding the disabilities and liabilities, pending and impending—notwithstanding the cunning, cruel, and scandalous efforts to blot out that right, we declare that we are, and of right we ought to be *American citizens*. We claim this right, and we claim all the rights and privileges, and duties which, properly, attach to it.

It may, and it will, probably, be disputed that we are citizens. We may, and, probably, shall be denounced for this declaration, as making an inconsiderate, impertinent and absurd claim to citizenship; but a very little reflection will vindicate the position we have assumed, from so unfavorable a judgment. . . .

By birth, we are American citizens; by the principles of the Declaration of Independence, we are American citizens; within the meaning of the United States Constitution, we are American citizens; by the facts of history, and the admissions of American statesmen, we are American citizens; by the hardships and trials endured; by the courage and fidelity displayed by our ancestors in defending the liberties and in achieving the independence of our land, we are American citizens. . . .

The Constitution of the United States declares "that the citizens of each State shall be entitled to all the privileges and immunities of citizens in the "United States."

There is in this clause of the Constitution, nothing whatever, of that watchful malignity which has manifested itself lately in the insertion of the word "*white*," before the term "*citizen*." The word "*white*," was unknown to the framers of the Constitution of the United States in such connections—unknown to the signers of the Declaration of Independence—unknown to the brave men at *Bunker Hill, Ticonderoga* and at *Red Bank*. It is a modern word, brought into use by modern legislators, despised in revolutionary times....

In conclusion, fellow-citizens, while conscious of the immense disadvantages which beset our pathway, and fully appreciating our own weakness, we are encouraged to persevere in efforts adapted to our improvement, by a firm reliance upon God, and a settled conviction, as immovable as the everlasting hills, that all the truths in the whole universe of God are allied to our cause.

    Frederick Douglass,
    J. M. Whitfield,
    H. O. Wagoner,
    Rev. A. N. Freeman,
    George B. Vashon.

33

John Bingham, Speech Opposing the Admission of Oregon

February 11, 1859*

Mr. BINGHAM. Mr. Speaker, I am constrained to oppose this bill for the admission of Oregon as a State, with the constitution presented by the People of that Territory.

. . .

In my judgment, sir, this constitution, framed by the people of Oregon, is repugnant to the Federal Constitution, and violative of the rights of citizens of the United States.

. . .

The Oregon constitution, in its first section, second article, violates a law of the United States; unless, indeed, your proposed act of admission, being inconsistent with a preexisting law of the United States, be a repeal of that law. I shall not consider the question of the repeal of the naturalization laws at this time. I take it for granted that gentlemen who insist on the passage of this bill, and the establishment thereby of this Oregon constitution as the fundamental law of that Territory, do not advocate a repeal of the naturalization laws of the United States. The second section of the second article of the Oregon constitution contains these words:

> "In all elections not otherwise provided for in this constitution," * * * * "every white male of foreign birth, of the age of twenty-one years and upwards, who shall have resided in the United States one year, and shall have resided in this State during the six months immediately preceding such election, and shall have declared his intention to become a citizen of the United States one year preceding such election," * * * * "shall be entitled to vote at all elections authorized by law."

Now, sir, this is simply a provision that aliens, upon one year's residence, after a mere declaration of intention to become a citizen of the United States, may vote at all general elections, for all Federal and State officers; that aliens, by reason of one year's residence after a declaration of intention, may elect your Representatives in Congress and select the State Legislature to choose your United States Senators, and elect presidential electors for the purpose of choosing a President and Vice President of the United States. I do not hesitate to say that this presents the question, whether a State may transfer the sovereignty of the ballot, which is the ultimate sovereignty of the country, to aliens, on one year's residence, and a mere declaration of intention to become citizens of the United States when it suits them, and not before. If there were no other objection to this constitution, I might surrender my individual judgment to bad precedents in the cases of the admission of Michigan, Wisconsin, and, more recently, of Minnesota. I think such concessions to new States most pernicious in policy and of doubtful constitutionality.

. . .

It has always been well understood amongst jurists in this country, that the citizens of each State constitute the body politic of each community, called the people of the State; and that the citizens of each State in the

---

Cong. Globe, 35th Cong., 2nd Sess., 981–85 (Feb. 11, 1859).

Union are *ipso facto* citizens of the United States. (Story on the Constitution, vol. 3, p. 565).

Who are the citizens of the United States? Sir, they are those, and those only, who owe allegiance to the Government of the United States; not the base allegiance imposed upon the Saxon by the Conqueror, which required him to meditate in solitude and darkness at the sound of the curfew; but the allegiance which requires the citizen not only to obey, but to support and defend, if need be with his life, the Constitution of his country. All free persons born and domiciled within the jurisdiction of the United States, are citizens of the United States from birth; all aliens become citizens of the United States only by act of naturalization, under laws of the United States. What I have said on this question of United States citizenship, and the words "the people," as used in the Constitution of the United States, is sustained by jurists and the decisions of the courts, Federal and State.

Rawle writes as follows:

"The citizens of each State constituted the citizens of the United States when the Constitution was adopted. The rights which appertain to them as citizens of those respective Commonwealths accompanied them in the formation of the great compound Commonwealth which ensued. They became citizens of the latter, without ceasing to be citizens of the former; and he who was subsequently born a citizen of a State, became, at the moment of his birth, a citizen of the United States."—*Rawle on the Constitution*, page 86.

Chancellor Kent says:

"If a slave, born in the United States, be manumitted, or otherwise lawfully discharged from bondage, or if a black man born within the United States, and born free, he becomes thenceforward a citizen." 2 *Kent's Com.*, 4th ed., page 257—Note.

. . .

The Congress of the United States should not consent that the sovereignty of the ballot, which is the sovereignty of America, should be transferred by its act to those who may use it to aid treason, and who may themselves levy war upon us, and give aid and comfort to the enemy without any legal responsibility for their acts.

. . .

If I am right in this, sir, then I submit that the elective franchise for the election of Federal officers, either directly or indirectly, should be confined to, and exercised exclusively by, citizens of the United States resident within the several States. That the several States have, by the terms of the Federal Constitution, the exclusive power to regulate and control the exercise of the elective franchise in all general elections, Federal and State, is conceded; but I do deny that any State can rightfully, under the Federal Constitution, transfer this great political privilege, in whole or in part, from the citizens of the United States, native and naturalized, to aliens, who owe no allegiance to our Constitution, who are not obliged to bear arms in defense of our country, and who cannot be held to answer for treason if they give aid and comfort to the public enemy, or if they themselves levy war against us.

. . .

Between myself and gentlemen there is a perfect agreement in this, that the several States may determine who, amongst the citizens of the United States resident within their respective limits, may exercise the elective franchise; they may prescribe the age of majority requisite to the exercise of this right; the term of residence within the State; whether citizens, male or female, shall vote; whether a tax or property qualification shall be required; but I deny that any State may rightfully transfer this political right from the citizen to the alien, and it may be, to the open and avowed enemy of the country and the Constitution!

. . .

Sir, what are the distinctive political rights of citizens of the United States? The great right to choose (under the laws of the States) severally, as I remarked before, either directly by ballot or indirectly through their duly-constituted agents, all the officers of the Federal Government, legislative, executive, and judicial, and through these to make all constitutional laws for their own government, and to interpret and enforce them; the right, also, to hold and exercise, upon election thereto, the several offices of honor, of power, and of trust, under the Constitution and Government of the United States. It is worthy of remark that every political right guarantied by the Constitution of the United States is limited by the words people or citizen, or by an official oath, to those who owe allegiance to the Constitution.

. . .

And in further illustration of my position I invite attention to the significant fact that natural or inherent rights, which belong to all men irrespective of all conventional regulations, are by this constitution guarantied by the broad and comprehensive word "person," as contradistinguished from the limited term citizen—as in the fifth article of amendments, guarding those sacred rights which are as universal and indestructible as the human race, that "no person shall be deprived of life, liberty, or property but by due process of law, nor shall private property be taken without just compensation." And this guarantee applies to all citizens within the United States. That these wise and beneficent guarantees of political rights to the citizens of the United States, as such, and of natural rights to all persons, whether citizens or strangers, may not be infringed, it is further in this national Constitution provided:

> "That this Constitution and the laws of the United States which shall be made in pursuance thereof, and all treaties made, or which shall be made, under the authority of the United States, shall be the supreme law of the land, and the judges in every State shall be bound thereby, anything in the Constitution or laws of any State to the contrary notwithstanding."—*Article six of Amendments.*

There, sir, is the limitation upon State sovereignty—simple, clear and strong. No State may rightfully, by constitution or statute law, impair any of these guarantied rights, either political or natural. They may not rightfully or lawfully declare that the strong citizens may deprive the weak citizens of their rights, natural or political; and if the State should do so by enacting statutes to that effect, there stands the limitation of the Constitution of the United States, sanctioned by the strong averment assented to and ratified by all the people and all the States—this Constitution shall be the supreme law; and the judges in every State shall be bound thereby.

...

But, sir, there is a still more objectionable feature than alien suffrage in this Oregon constitution. That is the provision of the schedule, which declares that large numbers of the citizens of the United States shall not, after the admission of the proposed State of Oregon, come or be within said State; that they shall hold no property there; and that they shall not prosecute any suits in any of the courts of that State; and that the Legislature shall, by statute, make it a penal offense for any person to harbor any of the excluded class of their fellow-citizens who may thereafter come or be within the State. This provision seems to me, in its spirit and letter, to be injustice and oppression incarnate. This provision, sir, excludes from the State of Oregon eight hundred thousand of the native-born citizens of the other States. I grant you that a State may restrict the exercise of the elective franchise to certain classes of citizens of the United States, to the exclusion of others; but I deny that any State may exclude a law abiding citizen of the United States from coming within its Territory, or abiding therein, or acquiring and enjoying property therein, or from the enjoyment therein of the "privileges and immunities" of a citizen of the United States. What says the Constitution:

> "The citizens of each State shall be entitled to all privileges and immunities of citizens in the several States." *Article* 4, *section* 2.

Here is no qualification, as in the clause guarantying suffrage or an elective representation to the people; here is no room for that refined construction, that each State may exclude all or any of the citizens of the United States from its territory. The citizens of each State, all the citizens of each State, being citizens of the United States, shall be entitled to "all privileges and immunities of citizens in the several States." Not to the rights and immunities of the several States; not to those constitutional rights and immunities which result exclusively from State authority or State legislation; but to "all privileges and immunities" of citizens of the United States in the several States. There is an ellipsis in the language employed in the Constitution, but its meaning is self-evident that it is "the privileges and immunities of citizens of the United States in the several States" that it guaranties.

This guaranty of the Constitution of the United States is senseless and a mockery, if it does not limit State sovereignty and restrain each and every State from closing its territory and its courts of justice against citizens of the United States. Lest it may be said that I have overstated the odious provisions of this Oregon constitution, I read the entire provisions of this section of the schedule, and which is expressly declared to be "a part of this constitution:"

> "Sec. 4. No free negro or mulatto, not residing in this State at the time of the adoption of this constitution, shall ever come, reside or be, within this State, or hold any real estate, or make any contract, or maintain any suit therein; and the Legislative Assembly shall provide by penal laws for the removal by public officers of all such free negroes and mulattoes, and for their effectual exclusion from the State, and

for the punishment of persons who shall bring them into the State, or employ or harbor them therein."
—*Oregon Constitution, Mis. Doc., No.* 38, page 20.

...

Sir, if the persons thus excluded from the right to maintain any suit in the courts of Oregon were not citizens of the United States; if they were not natives born of free parents within the limits of the Republic, I should oppose this bill; because I say that a State which, in its fundamental law, denies to any person, or to a large class of persons, a hearing in her courts of justice, ought to be treated as an outlaw, unworthy a place in the sisterhood of the Republic. A suit is a legal demand of one's right, and the denial of this right by the judgment of the American Congress is to be sanctioned as law! But sir, I maintain that the persons thus excluded from the State by this section of the Oregon constitution, are citizens by birth of the several States, and therefore are citizens of the United States, and as such are entitled to all the privileges and immunities of citizens of the United States, amongst which are the rights of life and liberty and property, and their due protection in the enjoyment thereof by law; and therefore I hold this section for their exclusion from that State and its courts, to be an infraction of that wise and essential provision of the national Constitution to which I before referred, to wit:

"The citizens of each State shall be entitled to all privileges and immunities of citizens IN THE SEVERAL STATES."

Who, sir, are citizens of the United States? First, all free persons born and domiciled within the United States—not all free white persons, but all free persons. You will search in vain, in the Constitution of the United States, for that word *white*; it is not there. You will look in vain for it in that first form of national Government—the Articles of Confederation; it is not there. The omission of this word—this phrase of caste—from our national charter, was not accidental, but intentional.

...

Inasmuch as black men helped to make the Constitution, as well as to achieve the independence of the country by the terrible trial by battle, it is not surprising that the Constitution of the United States does not exclude them from the body politic, and the privileges and immunities of citizens of the United States.... This Government rests upon the absolute equality of natural rights amongst men. There is not, and cannot be, any equality in the enjoyment of political or conventional rights, because that is impossible.

The franchise of the office of a Representative in Congress is a political right. It cannot be exercised by all; it is therefore limited to those who possess the qualifications of citizenship, age, and residence, prescribed by the Constitution, and are duly elected by the majority of the people of any State or district entitled so to elect. So the elective franchise is a political right, which all cannot exercise, and is therefore limited to some citizens to the exclusion of others. An infant in its cradle, the child of a citizen of the United States, is also a citizen of the United States, but has not the capacity to exercise this political right, and is therefore excluded from it. Practically, political rights are exercised only by a majority of the male population, and are subject to just such limitations as the majority see fit to impose. To this I have, and can have, no objection. Gentlemen need not trouble themselves, therefore, about the demagogue cry of "the political equality of the negro." Nobody proposes or dreams of political equality any more than of physical or mental equality. It is as impossible for men to establish equality in these respects as it is for "the Ethiopian to change his skin." Who would say that all men are equal in stature, in weight, and in physical strength; or that all are equal in natural mental force, or in intellectual acquirements? Who, on the other hand, will be bold enough to deny that all persons are equally entitled to the enjoyment of the rights of life and liberty and property; and that no one should be deprived of life or liberty, but as punishment for crime; nor of his property, against his consent and without due compensation?

...

All free persons, then, born and domiciled in any State of the Union, are citizens of the United States; and, although not equal in respect of political rights, are equal in respect of natural rights. Allow me, sir, to disarm prejudice and silence the demagogue cry of "negro suffrage," and "negro political equality," by saying, that no sane man ever seriously proposed political equality to all, for the reason that it is impossible. Political rights are conventional, not natural; limited, not universal; and are, in fact, exercised only by the majority of the qualified electors of any State, and by the minority only nominally.

While, therefore, I recognize the obligation of the majority to extend political privileges, so far as consistent with the stability of good government, to the largest number of the citizens, I as fully recognize the fact that all political privileges are, and ought to be, under the absolute control of the majority in a republican government; and their will is, and should be, the law. But sir, while this is cheerfully conceded, I cannot, and will not, consent that the majority of any republican State may, in any way, rightfully restrict the humblest citizen of the United States in the free exercise of any one of his natural rights; those rights common to all men, and to protect which, not to confer, all good governments are instituted; and the failure to maintain which inviolate furnishes, at all times, a sufficient cause for the abrogation of such government; and, I may add, imposes a necessity for such abrogation, and the reconstruction of the political fabric on a juster basis, with surer safeguards.

. . .

I ask no change of the law as it is written in the Federal Constitution. I leave the States as that constitution leaves them, free to regulate the elective franchise among citizens of the United States; to extend it to or to withhold it at their pleasure from all colored citizens, or only some of them; from all minors, white or black; and, if they see fit, from the best portion of the citizens of the United States—from all the free intelligent women of the land. But I protest against the attempt to mar that great charter of our rights, almost divine in its conception and in its spirit of equality, by the interpolation into it of any word of caste, such as white, or black, male or female; for no such word is in that great instrument now, and, by my act, or word, or vote, never shall be.

The equality of all to the right to live; to the right to know; to argue and to utter, according to conscience; to work and enjoy the product of their toil, is the rock on which that Constitution rests—its sure foundation and defense. Take this away, and that beautiful and wise and just structure, so full of the goodness and truth of our fathers, falls. The charm of that Constitution lies in the great democratic idea which it embodies, that all men, before the law, are equal in respect to those rights of person which God gives and no man or State may rightfully take away, except as a forfeiture for crime. Before your constitution, sir, as it is, as I trust it ever will be, all men are sacred, whether white or black, rich or poor, strong or weak, wise or simple.

. . .

I cannot consent to mutilate and destroy that great instrument, the Constitution of my country, by supporting a bill which, on its face, gives effect to a State constitution which denies to citizens of the United States the right of a fair trial in the courts of justice for the enforcement of a right or the redress of a wrong. In opposing this bill, sir, I am doing what I can to maintain the Constitution and the honor of my country.*

* [On February 14, 1859, Congress voted to accept the proposed state constitution and admit Oregon into the Union. See George Minot and George P. Sanger, eds., *United States Statutes at Large* (Boston: Little, Brown, 1859), 11:383. —Ed.]

C. SLAVERY: ANTEBELLUM LAW AND POLITICS

Introduction to Part 1C

A horrific and divisive institution from the earliest days of the republic (doc. 1), American slavery guaranteed an ever-widening legal and cultural divide between the Northern and Southern states. In antebellum America, slavery's shadow fell across almost every aspect of national law and politics. From the shape of the federal Constitution (docs. 6 and 7) and debates over congressional power and the autonomy of the states (docs. 8–10) to the administration of the territories (doc. 12) and the basic freedoms of religion, speech, and press (docs. 16–19, 21, 23), all were distorted by the gravitational pull of slavery and its advocates.

The divisions between the opponents and supporters of slavery can be seen in the text of the Constitution itself—a document that simultaneously refused to name the "peculiar institution" while also temporarily allowing the importation of slaves and ensuring the dominance of Southern slaveholding states in presidential politics (doc. 7). The thinly woven seam of constitutional compromise that bound together the free North and the slaveholding South became increasingly frayed as abolitionists demanded immediate, uncompensated abolition (doc. 24), and Southern states demanded that the North suppress abolitionist speech and insisted on the right to carry slavery into the territories (docs. 16, 19, 21, and 34). As a presidential candidate, when Abraham Lincoln guaranteed states the right to maintain slavery within their boundaries but opposed the extension of slavery into the territories, his election precipitated Southern secession and civil war (section D, doc. 1).

The documents in this section are not meant to present American slavery in all its manifold dimensions and effects. Numerous excellent historical collections relating to slavery already do so. This section means only to acquaint the reader with the basic legal aspects of American slavery and illuminate its role in major antebellum legal and constitutional debates.

The English court's decision in *Sommersett's Case* (doc. 2) declared that because slavery was in conflict with natural law, the institution could be maintained only by an act of positive law. If American courts followed the same approach, this would effectively deny Southern slave owners the right to recover slaves who had escaped to Northern free states. Bowing to pressure from the Southern states, the members of the Philadelphia Constitutional Convention agreed to add a clause declaring that "no person held to service or labour in one state, under the laws thereof, escaping into another, shall, in consequence of any law or regulation therein, be discharged from such service or labour, but shall be delivered up on claim of the party to whom such service or labour may be due" (doc. 7). The federal Fugitive Slave Acts (docs. 10 and 30) attempted to enforce this clause, though with mixed effects (docs. 22, 27, 33, and 36–39).

The original Constitution also gave slaveholding states an electoral advantage by counting slaves as three-fifths of a person for purposes of determining representation in the House of Representatives and the electoral college (docs. 6 and 7). Although somewhat counterintuitive, it was the *opponents* of slavery who resisted counting slaves as full persons and the *slaveholding* states who demanded that their "property" be treated as persons for the purposes of determining congressional representation (doc. 6).

Northern states moved toward abolition even before the adoption of the Constitution (doc. 3). Even in the South, influential statesmen questioned the justice and sustainability of slavery—or at least did so prior to the rise of state laws prohibiting the public criticism of slavery. Constitutional treatise writer and influential Virginia judge St. George Tucker, for example, published his *Dissertation on Slavery* in 1796 (doc. 11), calling for the gradual abolition of slavery and decrying slavery's denial of the natural rights of life and liberty. Southern slave owners were not beyond questioning the justice of the institution, at least in these early years. But the racialized nature of slavery in the United States infected the thinking of even those otherwise committed to the principles of human freedom. Thomas Jefferson's *Notes on the State of Virginia* (1785) (doc. 4), for example, contains a painfully racist account of what Jefferson viewed as the physical and mental differences between whites and blacks. The remarks are all the more jarring given Jefferson's call for the gradual abolition of slavery and his prescient warning: "I tremble for my country when I reflect that God is just: that his justice cannot sleep forever."

Opposition to slavery evolved in a variety of ways between the nation's founding and the passage of the Thirteenth Amendment. The preconstitutional Northwest Ordinance banned slavery in the territory that ultimately became the states of Ohio, Indiana, Illinois, Michigan, Wisconsin, and part of Minnesota (doc. 5). Early critics of slavery like Thomas Jefferson and St. George Tucker (docs. 4 and 11) advocated gradual emancipation and colonization outside the United States. As Northern opposition to slavery grew, abolitionists such as Wendell Phillips and William Lloyd Garrison and the members of the American Anti-Slavery Society favored immediate emancipation and called for the abandonment of what they viewed as a proslavery Constitution—or, as Garrison put it, "a covenant with death and agreement with hell" (doc. 24). Other abolitionists insisted that slavery was inconsistent with a proper reading of the Constitution. Lysander Spooner and Joel Tiffany, for example, developed detailed legal arguments refuting the "Constitution as pro-slavery" position of both Garrisonian abolitionists and the defenders of slavery (docs. 26 and 29). Women's rights groups joined the abolitionist movement, with Susan B. Anthony encouraging her fellow travelers to "Make the Slave's Case Our Own" (doc. 35). One of the most influential voices in the abolitionist movement, the statesman and former slave Frederick Douglass abandoned his earlier Garrisonian views and ultimately decided that Spooner and Tiffany were correct: the Constitution, properly interpreted, could not be reconciled with the institution of chattel slavery (doc. 40). This view came to dominate Republican politics. The 1843 Liberty Party platform insisted that the inalienable rights of life, liberty, and property enshrined in the Declaration of Independence had been constitutionalized through the adoption of the Fifth Amendment, which demanded that *no person* be denied life, liberty, or property without due process of law (doc. 23). According to this view, although constitutional federalism allowed the states to maintain the practice of slavery within their borders, the federal government was duty-bound to resist the extension of slavery into any territory within its control. This idea was embraced by the Free Soil Party (doc. 28) and, eventually, the Republican Party (section D, doc. 2).

Throughout the antebellum period, the debates over slavery dangerously stretched the constitutional garment that patched together the interests of Northern and Southern states. Regional divisions over the status of slaves in the proposed state of Missouri (doc. 12) alarmed Thomas Jefferson, who reacted to the debates as if he had heard "a fire bell in the night" (doc. 13). Northern abolitionism took on an increasingly radical tone. In addition to Garrison's public burning of the Constitution as an "agreement with hell" (doc. 33), the black abolitionist author David Walker in his *Appeal* encouraged slaves to engage in violent resistance against slave owners (doc. 15). The growing abolitionist movement in the North infuriated Southern politicians and triggered a successful effort to cleanse the national mail of abolitionist literature (doc. 18) and temporarily suspend the right to petition Congress for the eradication of slavery (doc. 21). Northern politicians investigating illegal incarceration of free blacks in Southern ports were greeted by mobs and hounded from the state (doc. 25). In its effort to bring the rule of law to bear on sectional differences, the Supreme Court upheld the constitutionality of the Fugitive Slave Act in *Prigg v. Pennsylvania* (doc. 22) and, in *Dred Scott v. Sandford*, closed the federal courts to blacks, declaring that white slave owners had a constitutional right to carry their "property" into the territories (doc. 34). On the other hand, once the Supreme Court ruled in *Prigg* that states had no obligation to assist in the return of runaway slaves (doc. 22), Northern states passed numerous "personal liberty" laws protecting their black residents from Southern "slavecatch-

ers" (doc. 33). Some states openly defied the Supreme Court's decision in *Prigg* and insisted that Congress had no power to enforce the fugitive slave clause (docs. 36–38). Other Northern states denied slave owners the right to bring their "property" with them as they traveled from one state to another (doc. 39). The collective acts of Northern opposition and intransigence convinced a growing number of slave-state politicians that neither slavery nor the Southern economy could be sustained if they remained in the Union (doc. 31).

One dangerously destabilizing factor in the debates over slavery was the unresolved question of who had the final word in constitutional disputes between the states and the national government. If the Constitution represented a compact between still-sovereign states and the new national government, neither party to that compact had a superior right to determine the proper *interpretation* of that compact. According to James Madison in his Report of 1800, it was "essential to the nature of compacts; that where resort can be had to no tribunal superior to the authority of the parties, the parties themselves must be the rightful judges in the last resort, whether the bargain made, has been pursued or violated" (section B, doc. 12). The Northern Federalists at the Hartford Convention agreed: "When emergencies occur which are either beyond the reach of the judicial tribunals, or too pressing to admit of the delay incident to their forms, States, which have no common umpire, must be their own judges, and execute their own decisions" (section B, doc. 15). During the Nullification Crisis of the 1830s, John C. Calhoun wrote that "[t]he right of judging, in such cases, is an essential attribute of sovereignty, of which the States cannot be divested without losing their sovereignty itself" (section B, doc. 20). Calhoun carried this idea to its logical conclusion in his 1851 *Discourse*, where he argued that states retained the unilateral right to secede from the Union if they concluded there had been "a clear and palpable infraction of the instrument" (section B, doc. 30). The North's policy regarding slavery, Calhoun insisted, represented such an infraction and left the South "no alternative, but to resist, or sink down into a colonial condition" (doc. 31). The most radical of the Northern state governments agreed that local governments retained the right to reject the decisions of the US Supreme Court. The Wisconsin state legislature, for example, resolved "[t]hat the government formed by the constitution of the United States was not made the exclusive or final judge of the extent of the powers delegated to itself; but that as in all other cases of compact among parties having no common judge, each party has an equal right to judge for itself, as well of infractions as of the mode and measure of redress" (doc. 38).

With free states in the North and slaves states in the South both insisting on the right of nullification and secession, dissolution of the Union increasingly seemed inevitable.

1

Virginia, *An Act concerning Servants and Slaves*

October 1705[*]

I. *Be it enacted, by the governor, council, and burgesses, of this present general assembly, and it is hereby enacted, by the authority of the same*, That all servants brought into this country without indenture, if the said servants be christians, and of christian parentage, and above nineteen years of age, shall serve but five years; and if under nineteen years of age, 'till they shall become twenty-four years of age, and no longer.

II. *Provided always*, That every such servant be carried to the county court, within six months after his or her arrival into this colony, to have his or her age adjudged by the court, otherwise shall be a servant no longer than the accustomary five years, although much under the age of nineteen years; and the age of such servant being adjudged by the court, within the limitation aforesaid shall be entered upon the records of the said court, and be accounted, deemed, and taken, for the true age of the said servant, in relation to the time of service aforesaid.

III. *And also be it enacted, by the authority aforesaid, and it is hereby enacted*, That when any servant sold for the custom, shall pretend to have indentures, the master or owner of such servant, for discovery of the truth thereof, may bring the said servant before a justice of the peace; and if the said servant cannot produce the indenture then, but shall still pretend to have one, the

said justice shall assign two months time for the doing thereof; in which time, if the said servant shall not produce his or her indenture, it shall be taken for granted that there never was one, and shall be a bar to his or her claim of making use of one afterwards, or taking any advantage by one.

IV. *And also be it enacted, by the authority aforesaid, and it is hereby enacted*, That all servants imported and brought into this country, by sea or land, who were not christians in their native country, (except Turks and Moors in amity with her majesty, and others that can make due proof of their being free in England, or any other christian country, before they were shipped, in order to transportation hither) shall be accounted and be slaves, and such be here bought and sold notwithstanding a conversion to christianity afterwards.

V. *And be it enacted, by the authority aforesaid, and it is hereby enacted*, That if any person or persons shall hereafter import into this colony, and here sell as a slave, any person or persons that shall have been a freeman in any christian country, island, or plantation, such importer or seller as aforesaid, shall forfeit and pay, to the party from whom the said freeman shall recover his freedom, double the sum for which the said freeman was sold. To be recovered, in any court of record within this colony, according to the course of the common law, wherein the defendant shall not be admitted to plead in bar, any act or statute for limitation of actions.

VI. *Provided always*, That a slave's being in England, shall not be sufficient to discharge him of his slavery, without other proof of his being manumitted there.

VII. *And also be it enacted, by the authority aforesaid, and it is hereby enacted*, That all masters and owners of servants, shall find and provide for their servants, wholesome and competent diet, clothing, and lodging, by the discretion of the county court; and shall not, at any time, give immoderate correction; neither shall, at any time, whip a christian white servant naked, without an order from a justice of the peace: And if any, notwithstanding this act, shall presume to whip a christian white servant naked, without such order, the person so offending, shall forfeit and pay for the same, forty shillings sterling to the party injured: To be recovered, with costs, upon petition, without the formal process of an action, as in and by this act is provided for servants complaints to be heard; provided complaint be made within six months after such whipping.

VIII. *And also be it enacted, by the authority aforesaid, and it is hereby enacted*, That all servants, (not

---

[*]William Waller Hening, ed., *The Statutes at Large; Being a Collection of All the Laws of Virginia from the First Session of the Legislature, in the Year 1619* (Philadelphia: R. & W. & G. Bartow, 1823), 3:447–63.

being slaves,) whether imported, or become servants of their own accord here, or bound by any court or church-wardens, shall have their complaints received by a justice of the peace, who, if he find cause, shall bind the master over to answer the complaint at court; and it shall be there determined: And all complaints of servants, shall and may, by virtue hereof, be received at any time, upon petition, in the court of the county wherein they reside, without the formal process of an action; and also full power and authority is hereby given to the said court, by their discretion, (having first summoned the masters or owners to justify themselves, if they think fit,) to adjudge, order, and appoint what shall be necessary, as to diet, lodging, clothing, and correction: And if any master or owner shall not thereupon comply with the said court's order, the said court is hereby authorised and impowered, upon a second just complaint, to order such servant to be immediately sold at an outcry, by the sheriff, and after charges deducted, the remainder of what the said servant shall be sold for, to be paid and satisfied to such owner.

IX. *Provided always, and be it enacted*, That if such servant be so sick and lame, or otherwise rendered so uncapable, that he or she cannot be sold for such value, at least, as shall satisfy the fees, and other incident charges accrued, the said court shall then order the church-wardens of the parish to take care of and provide for the said servant, until such servant's time, due by law to the said master, or owner, shall be expired, or until such servant, shall be so recovered, as to be sold for defraying the said fees and charges: And further, the said court, from time to time, shall order the charges of keeping the said servant, to be levied upon the goods and chattels of the master or owner of the said servant, by distress.

X. *And be it also enacted*, That all servants, whether, by importation, indenture, or hire here, as well feme coverts, as others, shall, in like manner, as is provided, upon complaints of misusage, have their petitions received in court, for their wages and freedom, without the formal process of an action; and proceedings, and judgment, shall, in like manner, also, be had thereupon.

XI. And for a further christian care and usage of all christian servants, *Be it also enacted, by the authority aforesaid, and it is hereby enacted*, That no negros, mulattos, or Indians, although christians, or Jews, Moors, Mahometans, or other infidels, shall, at any time, purchase any christian servant, nor any other, except of their own complexion, or such as are declared slaves by

this act: And if any negro, mulatto, or Indian, Jew, Moor, Mahometan, or other infidel, or such as are declared slaves by this act, shall, notwithstanding, purchase any christian white servant, the said servant shall, ipso facto, become free and acquit from any service then due, and shall be so held, deemed, and taken: And if any person, having such christian servant, shall intermarry with any such negro, mulatto, or Indian, Jew, Moor, Mahometan, or other infidel, every christian white servant of every such person so intermarrying, shall, ipso facto, become free and acquit from any service then due to such master or mistress so intermarrying, as aforesaid.

. . .

XV. *And also be it enacted, by the authority aforesaid, and it is hereby enacted*, That no person whatsoever shall, buy, sell, or receive of, to, or from, any servant, or slave, any coin or commodity whatsoever, without the leave, licence, or consent of the master or owner of the said servant, or slave: And if any person shall, contrary hereunto, without the leave or licence aforesaid, deal with any servant, or slave, he or she so offending, shall be imprisoned one calender month, without bail or main-prize; and then, also continue in prison, until he or she shall find good security, in the sum of ten pounds current money of Virginia, for the good behaviour for one year following; wherein, a second offence shall be a breach of the bond; and moreover shall forfeit and pay four times the value of the things so bought, sold, or received, to the master or owner of such servant, or slave: To be recovered, with costs, by action upon the case, in any court of record in this her majesty's colony and dominion, wherein no essoin, protection, or wager of law, or other than one imparlance, shall be allowed.

XVI. *Provided always, and be it enacted*, That when any person or persons convict for dealing with a servant, or slave, contrary to this act, shall not immediately give good and sufficient security for his or her good behaviour, as aforesaid: then in such case, the court shall order thirty-nine lashes, well laid on, upon the bare back of such offender, at the common whipping-post of the county, and the said offender to be thence discharged of giving such bond and security.

. . .

XVIII. . . . And if any woman servant shall have a bastard child by a negro, or mulatto, over and above the years service due to her master or owner, she shall immediately, upon the expiration of her time to her then present master or owner, pay down to the church-wardens of the parish wherein such child shall be born, for the use of the said parish, fifteen pounds current money of Virginia, or be by them sold for five years, to the use aforesaid: And if a free christian white woman shall have such bastard child, by a negro, or mulatto, for every such offence, she shall, within one month after her delivery of such bastard child, pay to the church-wardens for the time being, of the parish wherein such child shall be born, for the use of the said parish fifteen pounds current money of Virginia, or be by them sold for five years to the use aforesaid: And in both the said cases, the church-wardens shall bind the said child to be a servant, until it shall be of thirty one years of age.

XIX. And for a further prevention of that abominable mixture and spurious issue, which hereafter may increase in this her majesty's colony and dominion, as well by English, and other white men and women intermarrying with negroes or mulattos, as by their unlawful coition with them, *Be it enacted, by the authority aforesaid, and it is hereby enacted,* That whatsoever English, or other white man or woman, being free, shall intermarry with a negro or mulatto man or woman, bond or free, shall, by judgment of the county court, be committed to prison, and there remain, during the space of six months, without bail or mainprize; and shall forfeit and pay ten pounds current money of Virginia, to the use of the parish, as aforesaid.

XX. *And be it further enacted,* That no minister of the church of England, or other minister, or person whatsoever, within this colony and dominion, shall hereafter wittingly presume to marry a white man with a negro or mulatto woman; or to marry a white woman with a negro or mulatto man, upon pain of forfeiting and paying, for every such marriage the sum of ten thousand pounds of tobacco; one half to our sovereign lady the Queen, her heirs and successors, for and towards the support of the government, and the contingent charges thereof; and the other half to the informer; To be recovered, with costs, by action of debt, bill, plaint, or information, in any court of record within this her majesty's colony and dominion, wherein no essoin, protection, or wager of law, shall be allowed....

XXIII. And for encouragement of all persons to take up runaways, *Be it enacted, by the authority aforesaid, and it is hereby enacted,* That for the taking up of every servant, or slave, if ten miles, or above, from the house or quarter where such servant, or slave was kept, there shall be allowed by the public, as a reward to the taker-up, two hundred pounds of tobacco; and if above five miles, and under ten, one hundred pounds of tobacco:

Which said several rewards of two hundred, and one hundred pounds of tobacco, shall also be paid in the county where such taker-up shall reside, and shall be again levied by the public upon the master or owner of such runaway, for re-imbursement of the same to the public. And for the greater certainty in paying the said rewards and re-imbursement of the public, every justice of the peace before whom such runaway shall be brought, upon the taking up, shall mention the proper-name and sur-name of the taker-up, and the county of his or her residence, together with the time and place of taking up the said runaway; and shall also mention the name of the said runaway, and the proper-name and sur-name of the master or owner of such runaway, and the county of his or her residence, together with the distance of miles, in the said justice's judgment, from the place of taking up the said runaway, to the house or quarter where such runaway was kept.

XXIV. *Provided,* That when any negro, or other runaway, that doth not speak English, and cannot, or through obstinacy will not, declare the name of his or her masters or owner, that then it shall be sufficient for the said justice to certify the same, instead of the name of such runaway, and the proper name and sur-name of his or her master or owner, and the county of his or her residence and distance of miles, as aforesaid; and in such case, shall, by his warrant, order the said runaway to be conveyed to the public gaol, of this country, there to be continued prisoner until the master or owner shall be known; who, upon paying the charges of the imprisonment, or giving caution to the prison-keeper for the same, together with the reward of two hundred or one hundred pounds of tobacco, as the case shall be, shall have the said runaway restored.

XXV. And further, the said justice of the peace, when such runaway shall be brought before him, shall, by his warrant commit the said runaway to the next constable, and therein also order him to give the said runaway so many lashes as the said justice shall think fit, not exceeding the number of thirty-nine; and then to be conveyed from constable to constable, until the said runaway shall be carried home, or to the country gaol, as aforesaid, every constable through whose hands the said runaway shall pass, giving a receipt at the delivery; and every constable failing to execute such warrant according to the tenor thereof, or refusing to give such receipt, shall forfeit and pay two hundred pounds of tobacco to the church-wardens of the parish wherein such failure shall be, for the use of the poor of the said parish: To be recovered, with costs, by action of debt, in any court of record in this her majesty's colony and dominion, wherein no essoin, protection or wager of law, shall be allowed. And such corporal punishment shall not deprive the master or owner of such runaway of the other satisfaction here in this act appointed to be made upon such servant's running away.

...

XXIX. *And be it enacted, by the authority aforesaid, and it is hereby enacted,* That if any constable, or sheriff, into whose hands a runaway servant or slave shall be committed, by virtue of this act, shall suffer such runaway to escape, the said constable or sheriff shall be liable to the action of the party agrieved, for recovery of his damages, at the common law with costs.

...

XXXII. *And also be it enacted, by the authority aforesaid, and it is hereby enacted,* That no master, mistress, or overseer of a family, shall knowingly permit any slave, not belonging to him or her, to be and remain upon his or her plantation, above four hours at any one time, without the leave of such slave's master, mistress, or overseer, on penalty of one hundred and fifty pounds of tobacco to the informer; cognizable by a justice of the peace of the county wherein such offence shall be committed.

...

XXXIV. And if any slave resist his master, or owner, or other person, by his or her order, correcting such slave, and shall happen to be killed in such correction, it shall not be accounted felony; but the master, owner, and every such other person so giving correction, shall be free and acquit of all punishment and accusation for the same, as if such incident had never happened: And also, if any negro, mulatto, or Indian, bond or free, shall at any time, lift his or her hand, in opposition against any christian, not being negro, mulatto, or Indian, he or she so offending shall, for every such offence, proved by the oath of the party, receive on his or her bare back, thirty lashes, well laid on; cognizable by a justice of the peace for that county wherein such offence shall be committed.

XXXV. *And also be it enacted, by the authority aforesaid, and it is hereby enacted,* That no slave go armed with gun, sword, club, staff, or other weapon, nor go from off the plantation and seat of land where such slave shall be appointed to live, without a certificate of leave in writing, for so doing, from his or her master, mistress, or overseer: And if any slave shall be found of-fending herein, it shall be lawful for any person or persons to apprehend and deliver such slave to the next constable or head-borough, who is hereby enjoined and required, without further order or warrant, to give such slave twenty lashes on his or her bare back, well laid on, and so send him or her home: And all horses, cattle, and hogs, now belonging, or that hereafter shall belong to any slave, or of any slaves mark in this her majesty's colony and dominion, shall be seised and sold by the church-wardens of the parish, wherein such horses, cattle, or hogs shall be, and the profit thereof applied to the use of the poor of the said parish: And also, if any damage shall be hereafter committed by any slave living at a quarter where there is no christian overseer, the master or owner of such slave shall be liable to action for the trespass and damage, as if the same had been done by him or herself.

XXXVI. *And also it is hereby enacted and declared,* That baptism of slaves doth not exempt them from bondage; and that all children shall be bond or free, according to the condition of their mothers, and the particular direction of this act.

XXXVII. And whereas, many times, slaves run away and lie out, hid or lurking in swamps, woods, and other obscure places, killing hogs, and committing other injuries to the inhabitants of this her majesty's colony and dominion, *Be it therefore enacted, by the authority aforesaid, and it is hereby enacted,* That in all such cases, upon intelligence given of any slaves lying out, as aforesaid, any two justices (Quorum unus) of the peace of the county wherein such slave is supposed to lurk or do mischief, shall be and are impowered and required to issue proclamation against all such slaves, reciting their names, and owners names, if they are known, and thereby requiring them, and every of them, forthwith to surrender themselves; and also impowering the sheriff of the said county, to take such power with him, as he shall think fit and necessary, for the effectual apprehending such out-lying slave or slaves, and go in search of them: Which proclamation shall be published on a Sabbath day, at the door of every church and chapel, in the said county, by the parish clerk, or reader, of the church, immediately after divine worship: And in case any slave, against whom proclamation hath been thus issued, and once published at any church or chapel, as aforesaid, stay out, and do not immediately return home, it shall be lawful for any person or persons whatsoever, to kill and destroy such slaves by such ways and means as he, she, or they shall think fit, without accusation or impeachment of any crime for the same: And if any slave, that hath run away and lain out as aforesaid, shall be apprehended by the sheriff, or any other person, upon the application of the owner of the said slave, it shall and may be lawful for the county court, to order such punishment to the said slave, either by dismembring, or any other way, not touching his life, as they in their discretion shall think fit, for the reclaiming any such incorrigible slave, and terrifying others from the like practices.

XXXVIII. *Provided always, and it is further enacted,* That for every slave killed, in pursuance of this act, or put to death by law, the master or owner of such slave shall be paid by the public:

2

Sommersett's Case

20 Howell's State Trials 1 (K.B. 1772)

Lord *Mansfield.*—On the part of Sommersett, the case which we gave notice should be decided this day, the Court now proceeds to give its opinion. I shall recite the return to the writ of Habeas Corpus, as the ground of our determination; omitting only words of form. The captain of the ship on board of which the negro was taken, makes his return to the writ in terms signifying that there have been, and still are, slaves to a great number in Africa; and that the trade in them is authorized by the laws and opinions of Virginia and Jamaica; that they are goods and chattels; and, as such, saleable and sold. That James Sommersett is a negro of Africa, and long before the return of the king's writ was brought to be sold, and was sold to Charles Steuart, esq. then in Jamaica, and has not been manumitted since; that Mr. Steuart, having occasion to transact business, came over hither, with an intention to return; and brought Sommersett to attend and abide with him, and to carry him back as soon as the business should be transacted. That such intention has been, and still continues; and that the negro did remain till the time of his departure in the service of his master Mr. Steuart, and quitted it without his consent; and thereupon, before the return of the king's writ, the said Charles Steuart did commit the slave on board the Anne and Mary, to safe custody, to be kept till he should set sail, and then to be taken with him to Jamaica, and

there sold as a slave. And this is the cause why he, captain Knowles, who was then and now is, commander of the above vessel, then and now lying in the river of Thames, did the said negro, committed to his custody, detain; and on which he now renders him to the orders of the Court. We pay all due attention to the opinion of sir Philip Yorke, and lord chancellor Talbot, whereby they pledged themselves to the British planters, for all the legal consequences of slaves coming over to this kingdom or being baptized, recognized by lord Hardwicke, sitting as chancellor on the 19th of October, 1749, that trover would lie: that a notion had prevailed, if a negro came over, or became a Christian, he was emancipated, but no ground in law: that he and lord Talbot, when attorney and solicitor-general, were of opinion, that no such claim for freedom was valid; that though the statute of tenures had abolished villeins regardant to a manor, yet he did not conceive but that a man might still become a villein in gross, by confessing himself such in open court. We are so well agreed, that we think there is no occasion of having it argued (as I intimated an intention at first,) before all the judges, as is usual, for obvious reasons, on a return to a Habeas Corpus. The only question before us is, whether the cause on the return is sufficient? If it is, the negro must be remanded; if it is not, he must be discharged. Accordingly, the return states, that the slave departed and refused to serve; whereupon he was kept, to be sold abroad. So high an act of dominion must be recognized by the law of the country where it is used. The power of a master over his slave has been extremely different, in different countries. The state of slavery is of such a nature, that it is incapable of being introduced on any reasons, moral or political, but only by positive law, which preserves its force long after the reasons, occasion, and time itself from whence it was created, is erased from memory. It is so odious, that nothing can be suffered to support it, but positive law. Whatever inconveniences, therefore, may follow from the decision, I cannot say this case is allowed or approved by the law of England; and therefore the black must be discharged.

3

Pennsylvania, *An Act for the Gradual Abolition of Slavery*

March 1, 1780*

Section 1. WHEN we contemplate our abhorrence of that condition to which the arms and tyranny of Great Britain were exerted to reduce us; when we look back on the variety of dangers to which we have been exposed, and how miraculously our wants in many instances have been supplied, and our deliverances wrought, when even hope and human fortitude have become unequal to the conflict; we are unavoidably led to a serious and grateful sense of the manifold blessings which we have undeservedly received from the hand of that Being from whom every good and perfect gift cometh. Impressed with these ideas, we conceive that it is our duty, and we rejoice that it is in our power to extend a portion of that freedom to others, which hath been extended to us; and a release from that state of thraldom to which we ourselves were tyrannically doomed, and from which we have now every prospect of being delivered. It is not for us to enquire why, in the creation of mankind, the inhabitants of the several parts of the earth were distinguished by a difference in feature or complexion. It is sufficient to know that all are the work of an Almighty Hand. We find in the distribution of the human species, that the most fertile as well as the most barren parts of the earth are inhabited by men of complexions different from ours, and from each other; from whence we may reasonably, as well as religiously, infer, that He who placed them in their various situations, hath extended equally his care and protection to all, and that it becometh not us to counteract his mercies. We esteem it a peculiar blessing granted to us, that we are enabled this day to add one more step to universal civilization, by removing as much as possible the sorrows of those who have lived in undeserved bondage, and from which, by the assumed authority of the kings of Great Britain, no effectual, legal relief could be obtained. Weaned by a long course of experience from

those narrower prejudices and partialities we had imbibed, we find our hearts enlarged with kindness and benevolence towards men of all conditions and nations; and we conceive ourselves at this particular period extraordinarily called upon, by the blessings which we have received, to manifest the sincerity of our profession, and to give a substantial proof of our gratitude.

SECT. 2. And whereas the condition of those persons who have heretofore been denominated Negro and Mulatto slaves, has been attended with circumstances which not only deprived them of the common blessings that they were by nature entitled to, but has cast them into the deepest afflictions, by an unnatural separation and sale of husband and wife from each other and from their children; an injury, the greatness of which can only be conceived by supposing that we were in the same unhappy case. In justice therefore to persons so unhappily circumstanced, and who, having no prospect before them whereon they may rest their sorrows and their hopes, have no reasonable inducement to render their service to society, which they otherwise might; and also in grateful commemoration of our own happy deliverance from that state of unconditional submission to which we were doomed by the tyranny of Britain.

SECT. 3. Be it enacted, and it is hereby enacted, by the representatives of the freeman of the commonwealth of Pennsylvania, in general assembly met, and by the authority of the same, That all persons, as well Negroes and Mulattoes as others, who shall be born within this state from and after the passing of this act, shall not be deemed and considered as servants for life, or slaves; and that all servitude for life, or slavery of children, in consequence of the slavery of their mothers, in the case of all children born within this state, from and after the passing of this act as aforesaid, shall be, and hereby is utterly taken away, extinguished and forever abolished.

SECT. 4. Provided always, and be it further enacted by the authority aforesaid, That every Negro and Mulatto child born within this state after the passing of this act as aforesaid (who would, in case this act had not been made, have been born a servant for years, or life, or a slave) shall be deemed to be and shall be by virtue of this act the servant of such person or his or her assigns, who would in such case have been entitled to the service of such child, until such child shall attain unto the age of twenty eight years, in the manner and on the conditions whereon servants bound by indenture for four years are or may be retained and holder; and

*Henry Flanders and James Mitchell, *The Statutes at Large of Pennsylvania from 1682–1801* (Harrisburg, PA: State Printers, 1896), 10 *Pa. Stat.* 67–73.

shall be liable to like correction and punishment, and entitled to like relief in case he or she be evilly treated by his or her master or mistress, and to like freedom dues and other privileges as servants bound by indenture for four years are or may be entitled, unless the person to whom the service of any such child shall belong shall abandon his or her claim to the same; in which case the overseers of the poor of the city, township or district respectively, where such child shall be so abandoned, shall by indenture bind out every child so abandoned, as an apprentice for a time not exceeding the age herein before limited for the service of such children.

SECT. 5. And be it further enacted by the authority aforesaid, That every person, who is or shall be the owner of any Negro or Mulatto slave or servant for life or till the age of thirty one years, now within this state, or his lawful attorney, shall on or before the said first day of November next deliver or cause to be delivered in writing to the clerk of the peace of the county, or to the clerk of the court of record of the city of Philadelphia, in which he or she shall respectively inhabit, the name and surname and occupation or profession of such owner, and the name of the county and township, district or ward wherein he or she resideth; and also the name and names of any such slave and slaves, and servant and servants for life or till the age of thirty one years, together with their ages and sexes severally and respectively set forth and annexed, by such person owned or statedly employed and then being within this state, in order to ascertain and distinguish the slaves and servants for life, and till the age of thirty one years, within this state, who shall be such on the said first day of November next, from all other persons; which particulars shall by said clerk of the sessions asked clerk of the said city court be entered in books to be provided for that purpose by the said clerks; and that no Negro or Mulatto, now within this state, shall from and after the said first day of November, be deemed a slave or servant for life, or till the age of thirty one years, unless his or her name shall be entered as aforesaid on such record, except such Negro and Mulatto slaves and servants as are herein after excepted; the said clerk to be entitled to a fee of two dollars for each slave or servant so entered as aforesaid from the treasurer of the county, to be allowed to him in his accounts.

SECT. 6. Provided always, That any person, in whom the ownership or right to the service of any Negro or Mulatto shall be vested at the passing of this act, other than such as are herein before excepted, his or her heirs, ex-

ecutors, administrators and assigns, and all and every of them severally shall be liable to the overseers of the poor of the city, township or district to which any such Negro or Mulatto shall become chargeable, for such necessary expence, with costs of suit thereon, as such overseers may be put to, through the neglect of the owner, master or mistress of such Negro or Mulatto; notwithstanding the name and other descriptions of such Negro or Mulatto shall not be entered and recorded as aforesaid; unless his or her master or owner shall before such slave or servant attain his or her twenty eighth year execute and record in the proper county a deed or instrument, securing to such slave or servant his or her freedom.

SECT. 7. And be it further enacted by the authority aforesaid, That the offences and crimes of Negroes and Mulattoes, as well slaves and servants as freemen, shall be enquired of, adjudged, corrected and punished in like manner as the offences and crimes of the other inhabitants of this state are and shall be enquired of, adjudged, corrected and punished, and not otherwise; except that a slave shall not be admitted to bear witness against a freeman.

SECT. 8. And be it further enacted by the authority aforesaid, That in all cases wherein sentence of death shall be pronounced against a slave, the jury before whom he or she shall be tried, shall appraise and declare the value of such slave; and in case such sentence be executed, the court shall make an order on the state treasurer, payable to the owner for the same and for the costs of prosecution; but case of remission or mitigation, for the costs only.

SECT. 9. And be it further enacted by the authority aforesaid, That the reward for taking up runaway and absconding Negro and Mulatto slaves and servants, and the penalties for enticing away, dealing with, or harbouring, concealing or employing Negro and Mulatto slaves and servants, shall be the same, and shall be recovered in like manner as in case of servants bound for four years.

SECT. 10. And be it further enacted by the authority aforesaid, That no man or woman of any nation or colour, except the Negroes or Mulattoes who shall be registered as aforesaid, shall at any time hereafter be deemed, adjudged, or holden within the territories of this commonwealth as slaves or servants for life, but as free men and free women; except the domestic slaves attending upon delegates in congress from the other American states, foreign ministers and consuls, and persons passing through or sojourning in this state, and not becoming resident therein; and seamen employed in ships not belonging to any inhabitant of this state, nor employed in any ship owned by any such inhabitant. Provided such domestic slaves be not aliened or sold to any inhabitants nor (except in the case of members of congress, foreign ministers and consuls) retained in this state longer than six months.

SECT. 11. Provided always; And be it further enacted by the authority aforesaid, That this act or any thing in it contained shall not give any relief or shelter to any absconding or runaway Negro or Mulatto slave or servant, who has absented himself or shall absent himself from his or her owner, master or mistress residing in any other state or country, but such owner, master or mistress shall have like right and aid to demand, claim and take away his slave or servant, as he might have had in case this act had not been made: And that all Negro and Mulatto slaves now owned and heretofore resident in this state, who have absented themselves, or been clandestinely carried away, or who may be employed abroad as seamen and have not returned or been brought back to their owners, masters or mistresses, before the passing of this act, may within five years be registered as effectually as is ordered by this act concerning those who are now within the state, on producing such slave before any two justices of the peace, and satisfying the said justices by due proof of the former residence, absconding, taking away, or absence of such slaves as aforesaid; who thereupon shall direct and order the said slave to be entered on the record as aforesaid.

SECT. 12. And whereas attempts may be made to evade this act, by introducing into this state Negroes and Mulatoes bound by covenant to serve for long and unreasonable terms of years, if the same be not prevented:

SECT. 13. Be it therefore enacted by the authority aforesaid, That no covenant of personal servitude or apprenticeship whatsoever shall be valid or binding on a Negro or Mulatto for a longer time than seven years, unless such servant or apprentice were at the commencement of such servitude or apprenticeship under the age of twenty one years; in which case such Negro or Mulatto may be holden as a servant or apprentice respectively, according to the covenant, as the case shall be, until he or she shall attain the age of twenty eight years, but no longer.

SECT. 14. And be it further enacted by the authority aforesaid, That an act of assembly of the province of Pennsylvania, passed in the year one thousand

seven hundred and five, entitled, "an Act for the trial of Negroes;" and another act of assembly of the said province, passed in the year one thousand seven hundred and twenty five, entitled, "An Act for the better regulating of Negroes in this province;" and another act of assembly of the said province, passed in the year one thousand seven hundred and sixty one, entitled, "An Act for laying a duty on Negro and Mulatto slaves imported into this province;" and also another act of assembly of the said province, passed in the year one thousand seven hundred and seventy three, entitled, "An Act making perpetual an Act laying a duty on Negro and Mulatto slaves imported into this province, and for laying an additional duty said slaves," shall be and are hereby repealed, annulled and made void.

JOHN BAYARD, SPEAKER

Enabled into a law at Philadelphia, on Wednesday, the first day of March, A.D. 1780

4

Thomas Jefferson, *Notes on the State of Virginia*

1785*

QUERY VIII

The number of its inhabitants?

...

Under the mild treatment our slaves experience, and their wholesome, though coarse, food, this blot in our country increases as fast, or faster, than the whites. During the regal government, we had at one time obtained a law, which imposed such a duty on the importation of slaves, as amounted nearly to a prohibition, when one inconsiderate assembly, placed under a peculiarity of circumstance, repealed the law. This repeal met a joyful sanction from the then sovereign, and no devices, no expedients, which could ever after be attempted by subsequent assemblies, and they seldom met without attempting them, could succeed in getting the royal assent to a renewal of the duty. In the very first session held under the republican government, the assembly passed a law for the perpetual prohibition of the im-

* *Thomas Jefferson: Writings*, ed. Merrill D. Peterson (New York: Library of America, 1984), 214, 256, 263–70, 288–89.

portation of slaves. This will in some measure stop the increase of this great political and moral evil, while the minds of our citizens may be ripening for a complete emancipation of human nature.

QUERY XIV
The administration of justice and
description of the laws?

...

Many of the laws which were in force during the monarchy being relative merely to that form of government, or inculcating principles inconsistent with republicanism, the first assembly which met after the establishment of the commonwealth, appointed a committee to revise the whole code, to reduce it into proper form and volume, and report it to the assembly. This work has been executed by three gentlemen, and reported; but probably will not be taken up till a restoration of peace shall leave to the legislature leisure to go through such a work.

The plan of the revisal was this. The common law of England, by which is meant that part of the English law which was anterior to the date of the oldest statutes extant, is made the basis of the work. It was thought dangerous to attempt to reduce it to a text: it was therefore left to be collected from the usual monuments of it. Necessary alterations in that, and so much of the whole body of the British statutes, and of acts of assembly, as were thought proper to be retained, were digested into 126 new acts, in which simplicity of style was aimed at, as far as was safe. The following are the most remarkable alterations proposed:

To change the rules of descent, so as that the lands of any person dying intestate shall be divisible equally among all his children, or other representatives, in equal degree.

To make slaves distributable among the next of kin, as other movables.

To have all public expences, whether of the general treasury, or of a parish or county, (as for the maintenance of the poor, building bridges, court-houses, &c.,) supplied by assessments on the citizens, in proportion to their property.

To hire undertakers for keeping the public roads in repair, and indemnify individuals through whose lands new roads shall be opened.

To define with precision the rules whereby aliens should become citizens, and citizens make themselves aliens.

To establish religious freedom on the broadest bottom.

To emancipate all slaves born after passing the act. The bill reported by the revisers does not itself contain this proposition; but an amendment containing it was prepared, to be offered to the legislature whenever the bill should be taken up, and further directing, that they should continue with their parents to a certain age, then be brought up, at the public expence, to tillage, arts, or sciences, according to their geniusses, till the females should be eighteen, and the males twenty-one years of age, when they should be colonized to such place as the circumstances of the time should render most proper, sending them out with arms, implements of household and of the handicraft arts, seeds, pairs of the useful domestic animals, &c. to declare them a free and independant people, and extend to them our alliance and protection, till they shall have acquired strength; and to send vessels at the same time to other parts of the world for an equal number of white inhabitants; to induce whom to migrate hither, proper encouragements were to be proposed. It will probably be asked, Why not retain and incorporate the blacks into the state, and thus save the expence of supplying by importation of white settlers, the vacancies they will leave? Deep rooted prejudices entertained by the whites; ten thousand recollections, by the blacks, of the injuries they have sustained; new provocations; the real distinctions which nature has made; and many other circumstances will divide us into parties, and produce convulsions, which will probably never end but in the extermination of the one or the other race.—To these objections, which are political, may be added others, which are physical and moral. The first difference which strikes us is that of colour. Whether the black of the negro resides in the reticular membrane between the skin and scarfskin, or in the scarfskin itself; whether it proceeds from the colour of the blood, the colour of the bile, or from that of some other secretion, the difference is fixed in nature, and is as real as if its seat and cause were better known to us. And is this difference of no importance? Is it not the foundation of a greater or less share of beauty in the two races? Are not the fine mixtures of red and white, the expressions of every passion by greater or less suffusions of colour in the one, preferable to that eternal monotony, which reigns in the countenances, that immovable veil of black which covers all the emotions of the other race? Add to these, flowing hair, a more elegant symmetry of form, their own judgment in favour of the whites, declared by their preference of them as uniformly as is the preference of the Oranootan for the black woman over those of his own species. The circumstance of superior beauty, is thought worthy attention in the propagation of our horses, dogs, and other domestic animals; why not in that of man? Besides those of colour, figure, and hair, there are other physical distinctions proving a difference of race. They have less hair on the face and body. They secrete less by the kidnies, and more by the glands of the skin, which gives them a very strong and disagreeable odour. This greater degree of transpiration, renders them more tolerant of heat, and less so of cold than the whites. Perhaps too a difference of structure in the pulmonary apparatus, which a late ingenious experimentalist has discovered to be the principal regulator of animal heat, may have disabled them from extricating, in the act of inspiration, so much of that fluid from the outer air, or obliged them in expiration, to part with more of it. They seem to require less sleep. A black after hard labour through the day, will be induced by the slightest amusements to sit up till midnight or later, though knowing he must be out with the first dawn of the morning. They are at least as brave, and more adventuresome. But this may perhaps proceed from a want of forethought, which prevents their seeing a danger till it be present. When present, they do not go through it with more coolness or steadiness than the whites. They are more ardent after their female; but love seems with them to be more an eager desire, than a tender delicate mixture of sentiment and sensation. Their griefs are transient. Those numberless afflictions, which render it doubtful whether heaven has given life to us in mercy or in wrath, are less felt, and sooner forgotten with them. In general, their existence appears to participate more of sensation than reflection. To this must be ascribed their disposition to sleep when abstracted from their diversions, and unemployed in labour. An animal whose body is at rest, and who does not reflect, must be disposed to sleep of course. Comparing them by their faculties of memory, reason, and imagination, it appears to me that in memory they are equal to the whites; in reason much inferior, as I think one could scarcely be found capable of tracing and comprehending the investigations of Euclid: and that in imagination they are dull, tasteless, and anomalous. It would be unfair to follow them to Africa for this investigation. We will consider them here, on the same stage with the whites, and where the facts are not apochryphal on which a judgment is to be formed. It will be right to make great allowances for the difference of condition, of education, of conversation, of the sphere in which they move. Many millions of them have been brought to, and born in America. Most of them, indeed, have been confined to tillage, to their own homes, and their own society: yet many have been so situated, that they might have availed themselves of the conversation of their masters; many have been brought up to the handicraft arts, and from that circumstance have always been associated with the whites. Some have been liberally educated, and all have lived in countries where the arts and sciences are cultivated to a considerable degree, and have had before their eyes samples of the best works from abroad. The Indians, with no advantages of this kind, will often carve figures on their pipes not destitute of design and merit. They will crayon out an animal, a plant, or a country, so as to prove the existence of a germ in their minds which only wants cultivation. They astonish you with strokes of the most sublime oratory; such as prove their reason and sentiment strong, their imagination glowing and elevated. But never yet could I find that a black had uttered a thought above the level of plain narration; never seen even an elementary trait of painting or sculpture. In music they are more generally gifted than the whites, with accurate ears for tune and time, and they have been found capable of imagining a small catch. Whether they will be equal to the composition of a more extensive run of melody, or of complicated harmony, is yet to be proved. Misery is often the parent of the most affecting touches in poetry.—Among the blacks is misery enough, God knows, but no poetry. Love is the peculiar œstrum of the poet. Their love is ardent, but it kindles the senses only, not the imagination. Religion, indeed, has produced a Phyllis Whately; but it could not produce a poet. The compositions published under her name are below the dignity of criticism. The heroes of the Dunciad are to her, as Hercules to the author of that poem. Ignatius Sancho has approached nearer to merit in composition; yet his letters do more honour to the heart than the head. They breathe the purest effusions of friendship and general philanthropy, and show how great a degree of the latter may be compounded with strong religious zeal. He is often happy in the turn of his compliments, and his style is easy and familiar, except when he affects a Shandean fabrication of words. But his imagination is wild and extravagant, escapes incessantly from every restraint of reason and taste, and, in the course of its vagaries, leaves a tract of thought as incoherent and eccentric, as is the course of a meteor through the sky. His subjects should often have led him to a process of sober reasoning; yet we find him always substituting sentiment for demonstration. Upon the whole, though we admit him to the first place among those of his own color who have presented themselves to the public judgment, yet when we compare him with the writers of the race among whom he lived and particularly with the epistolary class in which he has taken his own stand, we are compelled to enroll him at the bottom of the column. This criticism supposes the letters published under his name to be genuine, and to have received amendment from no other hand; points which would not be of easy investigation. The improvement of the blacks in body and mind, in the first instance of their mixture with the whites, has been observed by every one, and proves that their inferiority is not the effect merely of their condition of life. We know that among the Romans, about the Augustan age especially, the condition of their slaves was much more deplorable than that of the blacks on the continent of America. The two sexes were confined in separate apartments, because to raise a child cost the master more than to buy one. Cato, for a very restricted indulgence to his slaves in this particular, took from them a certain price. But in this country the slaves multiply as fast as the free inhabitants. Their situation and manners place the commerce between the two sexes almost without restraint.—The same Cato, on a principle of economy, always sold his sick and superannuated slaves. He gives it as a standing precept to a master visiting his farm, to sell his old oxen, old waggons, old tools, old and diseased servants, and everything else become useless. 'Vendat boves vetulos, plaustrum vetus, feramenta vetera, servum senem, servum morbosum, si quid aliud supersit vendat.' Cato de re rusticâ, c. 2. The American slaves cannot enumerate this among the injuries and insults they receive. It was the common practice to expose in the island Æsculapius, in the Tyber, diseased slaves whose cure was like to become tedious. The Emperor Claudius, by an edict, gave freedom to such of them as should recover, and first declared that if any person chose to kill rather than to expose them, it should be deemed homicide. The exposing them is a crime of which no instance has existed with us; and were it to be followed by death, it would be punished capitally. We are told of a certain Vedius Pollio, who, in the presence of Augustus, would have given a slave as food to his fish, for having broken a glass. With the Romans, the regular method of taking the evidence of their slaves was under torture. Here it has been thought better never to resort to their evidence. When a master was murdered, all his slaves, in the same house, or within hearing, were condemned to death. Here punishment falls on the guilty only, and as precise proof is required against him as against a freeman. Yet notwithstanding these and other discouraging circumstances among the Romans, their slaves were often their rarest artists. They excelled too in science, insomuch as to be usually employed as tutors to their master's children. Epictetus, Terence, and Phædrus, were slaves. But they were of the race of whites. It is not their condition then, but nature, which has produced the distinction.—Whether further observation will or will not verify the conjecture, that nature has been less bountiful to them in the endowments of the head, I believe that in those of the heart she will be found to have done them justice. That disposition to theft with which they have been branded, must be ascribed to their situation, and not to any depravity of the moral sense. The man in whose favour no laws of property exist, probably feels himself less bound to respect those made in favour of others. When arguing for ourselves, we lay it down as a fundamental, that laws, to be just, must give a reciprocation of right: that, without this, they are mere arbitrary rules of conduct, founded in force, and not in conscience; and it is a problem which I give to the master to solve, whether the religious precepts against the violation of property were not framed for him as well as his slave? And whether the slave may not as justifiably take a little from one who has taken all from him, as he may slay one who would slay him? That a change in the relations in which a man is placed should change his ideas of moral right and wrong, is neither new, nor peculiar to the colour of the blacks. Homer tells us it was so 2600 years ago.

Ἥμισυ, γὰρ τ' ἀρετῆς ἀποαίνυται εὐρύοπα Ζεὺ
Ἀφνερος, ευτ' ἄν μιν κατὰ δουλιον ἥμαρ ἕλησιν.

Jove fix'd it certain, that whatever day
Makes man a slave, takes half his worth away.
—Od. 17, 323.

But the slaves of which Homer speaks were whites. Notwithstanding these considerations which must weaken their respect for the laws of property, we find among them numerous instances of the most rigid integrity, and as many as among their better instructed masters, of benevolence, gratitude, and unshaken fidelity. The opinion that they are inferior in the faculties of reason and imagination, must be hazarded with great diffidence. To justify a general conclusion, requires many observations, even where the subject may be submitted to the Anatomical knife, to Optical glasses, to analysis by fire or by solvents. How much more then where it is a faculty, not a substance, we are examining; where it eludes the research of all the senses; where the conditions of its existence are various and variously combined; where the effects of those which are present or absent bid defiance to calculation; let me add too, as a circumstance of great tenderness, where our conclusion would degrade a whole race of men from the rank in the scale of beings which their Creator may perhaps have given them. To our reproach it must be said, that though for a century and a half we have had under our eyes the races of black and of red men, they have never yet been viewed by us as subjects of natural history. I advance it, therefore, as a suspicion only, that the blacks, whether originally a distinct race, or made distinct by time and circumstances, are inferior to the whites in the endowments both of body and mind. It is not against experience to suppose that different species of the same genus, or varieties of the same species, may possess different qualifications. Will not a lover of natural history then, one who views the gradations in all the races of animals with the eye of philosophy, excuse an effort to keep those in the department of man as distinct as nature has formed them? This unfortunate difference of colour, and perhaps of faculty, is a powerful obstacle to the emancipation of these people. Many of their advocates, while they wish to vindicate the liberty of human nature, are anxious also to preserve its dignity and beauty. Some of these, embarrassed by the question, 'What further is to be done with them?' join themselves in opposition with those who are actuated by sordid avarice only. Among the Romans emancipation required but one effort. The slave, when made free, might mix with, without staining the blood of his master. But with us a second is necessary, unknown to history. When freed, he is to be removed beyond the reach of mixture.

...

QUERY XVIII

The peculiar customs and manners that may happen to be received in that state?

It is difficult to determine on the standard by which the manners of a nation may be tried, whether catholic or particular. It is more difficult for a native to bring to that standard the manners of his own nation, familiarized

to him by habit. There must doubtless be an unhappy influence on the manners of our people produced by the existence of slavery among us. The whole commerce between master and slave is a perpetual exercise of the most boisterous passions, the most unremitting despotism on the one part, and degrading submissions on the other. Our children see this, and learn to imitate it; for man is an imitative animal. This quality is the germ of all education in him. From his cradle to his grave he is learning to do what he sees others do. If a parent could find no motive either in his philanthropy or his self-love, for restraining the intemperance of passion towards his slave, it should always be a sufficient one that his child is present. But generally it is not sufficient. The parent storms, the child looks on, catches the lineaments of wrath, puts on the same airs in the circle of smaller slaves, gives a loose to the worst of passions, and thus nursed, educated, and daily exercised in tyranny, cannot but be stamped by it with odious peculiarities. The man must be a prodigy who can retain his manners and morals undepraved by such circumstances. And with what execrations should the statesman be loaded, who permitting one half the citizens thus to trample on the rights of the other, transforms those into despots, and these into enemies, destroys the morals of the one part, and the amor patriæ of the other. For if a slave can have a country in this world, it must be any other in preference to that in which he is born to live and labour for another: in which he must lock up the faculties of his nature, contribute as far as depends on his individual endeavours to the evanishment of the human race, or entail his own miserable condition on the endless generations proceeding from him. With the morals of the people, their industry also is destroyed. For in a warm climate, no man will labour for himself who can make another labour for him. This is so true, that of the proprietors of slaves a very small proportion indeed are ever seen to labour. And can the liberties of a nation be thought secure when we have removed their only firm basis, a conviction in the minds of the people that these liberties are of the gift of God? That they are not to be violated but with his wrath? Indeed I tremble for my country when I reflect that God is just: that his justice cannot sleep forever: that considering numbers, nature and natural means only, a revolution of the wheel of fortune, an exchange of situation, is among possible events: that it may become probable by supernatural interference! The Almighty has no attribute which can take side with us in such a contest. — But it is impossible to be temperate and to pursue this subject through the various considerations of policy, of morals, of history natural and civil. We must be contented to hope they will force their way into every one's mind. I think a change already perceptible, since the origin of the present revolution. The spirit of the master is abating, that of the slave rising from the dust, his condition mollifying, the way I hope preparing, under the auspices of heaven, for a total emancipation, and that this is disposed, in the order of events, to be with the consent of the masters, rather than by their extirpation.

5

The Northwest Ordinance

July 13, 1787[*]

Art. 6. There shall be neither slavery nor involuntary servitude in the said territory, otherwise than in the punishment of crimes whereof the party shall have been duly convicted: Provided, always, That any person escaping into the same, from whom labor or service is lawfully claimed in any one of the original States, such fugitive may be lawfully reclaimed and conveyed to the person claiming his or her labor or service as aforesaid.

6

Debates in the Philadelphia Constitutional Convention

June, July, August 1787[†]

ARTICLE I, SECTION 2, CLAUSE 3:
THE THREE-FIFTHS RATIO
Madison, Wednesday July 11. In Convention[‡]
Mr. Randolph's motion requiring the Legislre. to take a periodical census for the purpose of redressing inequalities in the Representation was resumed.

[*] Tansill, *Documents*, 47–54.
[†] Max Farrand, ed., *The Records of the Federal Convention of 1787*, rev. ed., 4 vols. (New Haven, CT: Yale University Press, 1937).
[‡] Farrand, *Records*, 1:578–81, 586–88.

Mr. Sherman was agst. shackling the Legislature too much. We ought to choose wise & good men, and then confide in them.

Mr. Mason. The greater the difficulty we find in fixing a proper rule of Representation, the more unwilling ought we to be, to throw the task from ourselves, on the Genl. Legislre. He did not object to the conjectural ratio which was to prevail in the outset; but considered a Revision from time to time according to some permanent & precise standard as essential to ye. fair representation required in the 1st. branch. According to the present population of America, the Northn. part of it had a right to preponderate, and he could not deny it. But he wished it not to preponderate hereafter when the reason no longer continued. From the nature of man we may be sure, that those who have power in their hands will not give it up while they can retain it. On the Contrary we know they will always, when they can, rather increase it. If the S. States therefore should have 3/4 of the people of America within their limits, the Northern will hold fast the majority of Representatives. 1/4 will govern the 3/4. The S. States will complain: but they may complain from generation to generation without redress. Unless some principle therefore which will do justice to them hereafter shall be inserted in the Constitution, disagreeable as the declaration was to him, he must declare he could neither vote for the system here nor support it, in his State. Strong objections had been drawn from the danger to the Atlantic interests from new Western States. Ought we to sacrifice what we know to be right in itself, lest it should prove favorable to States which are not yet in existence? If the Western States are to be admitted into the Union as they arise, they must, he wd. repeat, be treated as equals, and subjected to no degrading discriminations. They will have the same pride & other passions which we have, and will either not unite with or will speedily revolt from the Union, if they are not in all respects placed on an equal footing with their brethren. It has been said they will be poor, and unable to make equal contributions to the general Treasury. He did not know but that in time they would be both more numerous & more wealthy than their Atlantic brethren. The extent & fertility of their soil, made this probable; and though Spain might for a time deprive them of the natural outlet for their productions, yet she will, because she must, finally yield to their demands. He urged that numbers of inhabitants; though not always a precise standard of wealth was sufficiently so for every substantial purpose.

Mr. Williamson was for making it the duty of the Legislature to do what was right & not leaving it at liberty to do or not do it. He moved that Mr. Randolph's proposition be postponed, in order to consider the following "that in order to ascertain the alterations that may happen in the population & wealth of the several States, a census shall be taken of the free white inhabitants and 3/5ths of those of other descriptions on the 1st year after this Government shall have been adopted and every —— year thereafter; and that the Representation be regulated accordingly."

Mr. Randolph agreed that Mr. Williamson's proposition should stand in the place of his. He observed that the ratio fixt for the 1st. meeting was a mere conjecture, that it placed the power in the hands of that part of America, which could not always be entitled to it, that this power would not be voluntarily renounced; and that it was consequently the duty of the Convention to secure its renunciation when justice might so require; by some constitutional provisions. If equality between great & small States be inadmissible, because in that case unequal numbers of Constituents wd. be represented by equal number of votes; was it not equally inadmissible that a larger & more populous district of America should hereafter have less representation, than a smaller & less populous district. If a fair representation of the people be not secured, the injustice of the Govt. will shake it to its foundations. What relates to suffrage is justly stated by the celebrated Montesquieu, as a fundamental article in Republican Govts. If the danger suggested by Mr. Govr. Morris be real, of advantage being taken of the Legislature in pressing moments, it was an additional reason, for tying their hands in such a manner that they could not sacrifice their trust to momentary considerations. Congs. have pledged the public faith to New States, that they shall be admitted on equal terms. They never would nor ought to accede on any other. The census must be taken under the direction of the General Legislature. The States will be too much interested to take an impartial one for themselves.

Mr. Butler & Genl. Pinkney insisted that blacks be included in the rule of Representation, equally with the Whites: and for that purpose moved that the words "three fifths" be struck out.

Mr. Gerry thought that 3/5 of them was to say the least the full proportion that could be admitted.

Mr. Ghorum. This ratio was fixed by Congs. as a rule of taxation. Then it was urged by the Delegates representing the States having slaves that the blacks were still more inferior to freemen. At present when the ratio of representation is to be established, we are assured that they are equal to freemen. The arguments on the former occasion had convinced him that 3/5 was pretty near the just proportion and he should vote according to the same opinion now.

Mr. Butler insisted that the labour of a slave in S. Carola. was as productive & valuable as that of a freeman in Massts., that as wealth was the great means of defence and utility to the Nation they were equally valuable to it with freemen; and that consequently an equal representation ought to be allowed for them in a Government which was instituted principally for the protection of property, and was itself to be supported by property.

Mr. Mason. could not agree to the motion, notwithstanding it was favorable to Virga. because he thought it unjust. It was certain that the slaves were valuable, as they raised the value of land, increased the exports & imports, and of course the revenue, would supply the means of feeding & supporting an army, and might in cases of emergency become themselves soldiers. As in these important respects they were useful to the community at large, they ought not to be excluded from the estimate of Representation. He could not however regard them as equal to freemen and could not vote for them as such. He added as worthy of remark, that the Southern States have this peculiar species of property, over & above the other species of property common to all the States.

Mr. Williamson reminded Mr. Ghorum that if the Southn. States contended for the inferiority of blacks to whites when taxation was in view, the Eastern States on the same occasion contended for their equality. He did not however either then or now, concur in either extreme, but approved of the ratio of 3/5.

On Mr. Butlers motion for considering blacks as equal to Whites in the apportionmt. of Representation

Massts. no. Cont. no. (N. Y. not on floor.) N. J. no. Pa. no. Del. ay. Md. no. Va no N. C. no. S. C. ay. Geo. ay. [Ayes—3; noes—7.]

. . .

the next clause as to 3/5 of the negroes considered

Mr. King. being much opposed to fixing numbers as the rule of representation, was particularly so on account of the blacks. He thought the admission of them along with Whites at all, would excite great discontents among the States having no slaves. He had never said as to any particular point that he would in no event acquiesce in & support it; but he wd. say that if in any case such a declaration was to be made by him, it would be in this. He remarked that in the temporary allotment of Representatives made by the Committee, the Southern States had received more than the number of their white & three fifths of their black inhabitants entitled them to.

Mr. Sherman. S. Carola. had not more beyond her proportion than N. York & N. Hampshire, nor either of them more than was necessary in order to avoid fractions or reducing them below their proportion. Georgia had more; but the rapid growth of that State seemed to justify it. In general the allotment might not be just, but considering all circumstances, he was satisfied with it.

Mr. Ghorum. supported the propriety of establishing numbers as the rule. He said that in Massts. estimates had been taken in the different towns, and that persons had been curious enough to compare these estimates with the respective numbers of people; and it had been found even including Boston, that the most exact proportion prevailed between numbers & property. He was aware that there might be some weight in what had fallen from his colleague, as to the umbrage which might be taken by the people of the Eastern States. But he recollected that when the proposition of Congs for changing the 8th. art: of Confedn. was before the Legislature of Massts. the only difficulty then was to satisfy them that the negroes ought not to have been counted equally with whites instead of being counted in the ratio of three fifths only.

Mr. Wilson did not well see on what principle the admission of blacks in the proportion of three fifths could be explained. Are they admitted as Citizens? Then why are they not admitted on an equality with White Citizens? Are they admitted as property? then why is not other property admitted into the computation? These were difficulties however which he thought must be overruled by the necessity of compromise. He had some apprehensions also from the tendency of the blending of the blacks with the whites, to give disgust to the people of Pena. as had been intimated by his colleague (Mr. Govr. Morris). But he differed from him in thinking numbers of inhabts. so incorrect a measure of wealth. He had seen the Western settlemts. of Pa. and on a comparison of them with the City of Philada. could discover little other difference, than that property was more unequally divided among individuals here than there. Taking the same number in the aggregate in the

two situations he believed there would be little difference in their wealth and ability to contribute to the public wants.

Mr. Govr. Morris was compelled to declare himself reduced to the dilemma of doing injustice to the Southern States or to human nature, and he must therefore do it to the former. For he could never agree to give such encouragement to the slave trade as would be given by allowing them a representation for their negroes, and he did not believe those States would ever confederate on terms that would deprive them of that trade.

On Question for agreeing to include 3/5 of the blacks
Masts. no. Cont. ay N. J. no. Pa. no. Del. no. Md. no. Va. ay. N. C. ay. S. C. no. Geo. ay [Ayes—4; noes—6.]
...

Madison, Thursday, July 12. In Convention[*]

Mr. Govr. Morris moved to add to the clause empowering the Legislature to vary the Representation according to the principles of wealth & number of inhabts. a "proviso that taxation shall be in proportion to Representation".

Mr Butler contended again that Representation sd. be according to the full number of inhabts. including all the blacks; admitting the justice of Mr. Govr. Morris's motion.

Mr. Mason also admitted the justice of the principle, but was afraid embarrassments might be occasioned to the Legislature by it. It might drive the Legislature to the plan of Requisitions.

Mr. Govr. Morris, admitted that some objections lay agst. his motion, but supposed they would be removed by restraining the rule to direct taxation. With regard to indirect taxes on exports & imports & on consumption, the rule would be inapplicable. Notwithstanding what had been said to the contrary he was persuaded that the imports & consumption were pretty nearly equal throughout the Union.

General Pinkney liked the idea. He thought it so just that it could not be objected to. But foresaw that if the revision of the census was left to the discretion of the Legislature, it would never be carried into execution. The rule must be fixed, and the execution of it enforced by the Constitution. He was alarmed at what was said yesterday, concerning the Negroes. He was now again alarmed at what had been thrown out concerning the

[*] Farrand, *Records*, 1:591.

taxing of exports. S. Carola. has in one year exported to the amount of £600,000 Sterling all which was the fruit of the labor of her blacks. Will she be represented in proportion to this amount? She will not. Neither ought she then to be subject to a tax on it. He hoped a clause would be inserted in the system restraining the Legislature from a taxing Exports.

Mr. Wilson approved the principle, but could not see how it could be carried into execution; unless restrained to direct taxation.

Mr. Govr. Morris having so varied his motion by inserting the word "direct". It passd. nem. con. as follows—"provided always that direct taxation ought to be proportioned to representation".

Mr. Davie, said it was high time now to speak out. He saw that it was meant by some gentlemen to deprive the Southern States of any share of Representation for their blacks. He was sure that N. Carola. would never confederate on any terms that did not rate them at least as 3/5. If the Eastern States meant therefore to exclude them altogether the business was at an end.

Dr. Johnson, thought that wealth and population were the true, equitable rule of representation; but he conceived that these two principles resolved themselves into one; population being the best measure of wealth. He concluded therefore that ye. number of people ought to be established as the rule, and that all descriptions including blacks equally with the whites, ought to fall within the computation. As various opinions had been expressed on the subject, he would move that a Committee might be appointed to take them into consideration and report thereon.

Mr. Govr. Morris. It has been said that it is high time to speak out. As one member, he would candidly do so. He came here to form a compact for the good of America. He was ready to do so with all the States: He hoped & believed that all would enter into such a Compact. If they would not he was ready to join with any States that would. But as the Compact was to be voluntary, it is in vain for the Eastern States to insist on what the Southn States will never agree to. It is equally vain for the latter to require what the other States can never admit; and he verily believed the people of Pena. will never agree to a representation of Negroes. What can be desired by these States more than has been already proposed; that the Legislature shall from time to time regulate Representation according to population & wealth.

Gen. Pinkney desired that the rule of wealth should

be ascertained and not left to the pleasure of the Legislature; and that property in slaves should not be exposed to danger under a Govt. instituted for the protection of property.

The first clause in the Report of the first Grand Committee was postponed.

Mr. Elseworth. In order to carry into effect the principle established, moved to add to the last clause adopted by the House the words following "and that the rule of contribution by direct taxation for the support of the Government of the U. States shall be the number of white inhabitants, and three fifths of every other description in the several States, until some other rule that shall more accurately ascertain the wealth of the several States can be devised and adopted by the Legislature."

Mr. Butler seconded the motion in order that it might be committed.

Mr. Randolph was not satisfied with the motion. The danger will be revived that the ingenuity of the Legislature may evade or pervert the rule so as to perpetuate the power where it shall be lodged in the first instance. He proposed in lieu of Mr. Elseworth's motion, "that in order to ascertain the alterations in Representation that may be required from time to time by changes in the relative circumstances of the States, a census shall be taken within two years from the 1st. meeting of the Genl. Legislature of the U. S., and once within the term of every year afterwards, of all the inhabitants in the manner & according to the ratio recommended by Congress in their resolution of the 18th day of Apl. 1783; (rating the blacks at 3/5 of their number) and that the Legislature of the U. S. shall arrange the Representation accordingly."—He urged strenuously that express security ought to be provided for including slaves in the ratio of Representation. He lamented that such a species of property existed. But as it did exist the holders of it would require this security. It was perceived that the design was entertained by some of excluding slaves altogether; the Legislature therefore ought not to be left at liberty.

Mr. Elseworth withdraws his motion & seconds that of Mr. Randolph.

Mr. Wilson observed that less umbrage would perhaps be taken agst. an admission of the slaves into the Rule of representation, if it should be so expressed as to make them indirectly only an ingredient in the rule, by saying that they should enter into the rule of taxation: and as representation was to be according to taxation, the end would be equally attained. He accordingly moved & was 2ded so to alter the last clause adopted by the House, that together with the amendment proposed the whole should read as follows—provided always that the representation ought to be proportioned according to direct taxation, and in order to ascertain the alterations in the direct taxation which may be required from time to time by the changes in the relative circumstances of the States. Resolved that a census be taken within two years from the first meeting of the Legislature of the U. States, and once within the term of every years afterwards of all the inhabitants of the U. S. in the manner and according to the ratio recommended by Congress in their Resolution of April 18 1783; and that the Legislature of the U. S. shall proportion the direct taxation accordingly."

Mr. King. Altho' this amendment varies the aspect somewhat, he had still two powerful objections agst. tying down the Legislature to the rule of numbers. 1. they were at this time an uncertain index of the relative wealth of the States. 2. if they were a just index at this time it can not be supposed always to continue so. He was far from wishing to retain any unjust advantage whatever in one part of the Republic. If justice was not the basis of the connection it could not be of long duration. He must be short sighted indeed who does not foresee that whenever the Southern States shall be more numerous than the Northern, they can & will hold a language that will awe them into justice. If they threaten to separate now in case injury shall be done them, will their threats be less urgent or effectual, when force shall back their demands. Even in the intervening period there will no point of time at which they will not be able to say, do us justice or we will separate.

He urged the necessity of placing confidence to a certain degree in every Govt. and did not conceive that the proposed confidence as to a periodical readjustment of the representation exceeded that degree.

Mr. Pinkney moved to amend Mr. Randolph's motion so as to make "blacks equal to the whites in the ratio of representation". This he urged was nothing more than justice. The blacks are the labourers, the peasants of the Southern States: they are as productive of pecuniary resources as those of the Northern States. They add equally to the wealth, and considering money as to the sinew of war, to the strength of the nation. It will also be politic with regard to the Northern States as taxation is to keep pace with Representation.

Genl. Pinkney moves to insert 6 years instead of two,

as the period computing from 1st meeting of ye Legis— within which the first census should be taken. On this question for inserting six instead of "two" in the proposition of Mr. Wilson, it passed in the affirmative

Masts. no. Ct. ay. N. J. ay. Pa. ay. Del. divd. Mayd. ay. Va. no. N. C. no. S. C. ay. Geo. no. [Ayes—5; noes—4; divided—1.]

On a question for filling the blank for ye. periodical census with 20 years, (it passed in the negative)

Masts. no. Ct. ay. N. J. ay. P. ay. Del. no. Md. no. Va. no. N. C. no. S. C. no. Geo. no. [Ayes—3; noes—7.]

On a question for 10 years, (it passed in the affirmative.)

Mas. ay. Cont. no. N. J. no. P. ay. Del. ay. Md. ay. Va. ay. N. C. ay. S. C. ay. Geo. ay. [Ayes—8; noes—2.]

On Mr. Pinkney's motion for rating blacks as equal to whites instead of as 3/5.

Mas. no. Cont. no. (Dr Johnson ay) N. J. no. Pa. no. (3 agst. 2) Del. no. Md. no. Va. no. N. C. no. S. C. ay. Geo—ay. [Ayes—2; noes—8.]

Mr. Randolph's proposition as varied by Mr. Wilson being read for question on the whole.

Mr. Gerry, urged that the principle of it could not be carried into execution as the States were not to be taxed as States. With regard to taxes in imports, he conceived they would be more productive—Where there were no slaves than where there were; the consumption being greater—

Mr. Elseworth. In case of a poll tax there wd. be no difficulty. But there wd. probably be none. The sum allotted to a State may be levied without difficulty according to the plan used by the State in raising its own supplies. On the question on ye. whole proposition; (as proportioning representation to direct taxation & both to the white & 3/5 of black inhabitants, & requiring a census within six years—& within every ten years afterwards.)

Mas. divd. Cont. ay. N. J. no. Pa. ay. Del. no. Md. ay. Va. ay. N. C. ay. S. C. divd. Geo. ay. [Ayes—6; noes—2; divided—2.]

. . .

Madison, Friday, July 13. In Convention[*]

Mr. Gerry, moved to add as an amendment to the last clause agreed to by the House "That from the first meeting of the Legislature of the U. S. till a census shall be taken all monies to be raised for supplying the public Treasury by direct taxation, shall be assessed on the in-

[*] Farrand, *Records*, 1:600.

habitants of the several States, according to the number of their Representatives respectively in the 1st branch." He said this would be as just before as after the Census: according to the general principle that taxation & Representation ought to go together.

Mr. Williamson feared that N. Hampshire will have reason to complain. 3 members were allotted to her as a liberal allowance for this reason among others, that she might not suppose any advantage to have been taken of her absence. As she was still absent, and had no opportunity of deciding whether she would chuse to retain the number on the condition, of her being taxed in proportion to it, he thought the number ought to be reduced from three to two, before the question on Mr. G's motion.

Mr. Read could not approve of the proposition. He had observed he said in the Committee a backwardness in some of the members from the large States, to take their full proportion of Representatives. He did not then see the motive. He now suspects it was to avoid their due share of taxation. He had no objection to a just & accurate adjustment of Representation & taxation to each other.

Mr. Govr. Morris & Mr. Madison answered that the charge itself involved an acquittal, since notwithstanding the augmentation of the number of members allotted to Masts. & Va. the motion for proportioning the burdens thereto was made by a member from the former State & was approved by Mr. M from the latter who was on the Come. Mr. Govr. Morris said that he thought Pa. had her due share in 8 members; and he could not in candor ask for more. Mr. M. said that having always conceived that the difference of interest in the U. States lay not between the large & small, but the N. & Southn. States, and finding that the number of members allotted to the N. States was greatly superior, he should have preferred, an addition of two members to the S. States, to wit one to N & 1 to S. Carla. rather than of one member to Virga. He liked the present motion, because it tended to moderate the views both of the opponents & advocates for rating very high, the negroes.

Mr. Elseworth hoped the proposition would be withdrawn. It entered too much into detail. The general principle was already sufficiently settled. As fractions can not be regarded in apportioning the no. of representatives, the rule will be unjust until an actual census shall be made. after that taxation may be precisely proportioned according to the principle established, to the number of inhabitants.

Mr. Wilson hoped the motion would not be withdrawn. If it shd. it will be made from another quarter. The rule will be as reasonable & just before, as after a Census. As to fractional numbers, the Census will not destroy, but ascertain them. And they will have the same effect after as before the Census: for as he understands the rule, it is to be adjusted not to the number of inhabitants, but of Representatives.

Mr. Sherman opposed the motion. He thought the Legislature ought to be left at liberty: in which case they would probably conform to the principles observed by Congs.

Mr. Mason did not know that Virga. would be a loser by the proposed regulation, but had some scruple as to the justice of it. He doubted much whether the conjectural rule which was to precede the census, would be as just, as it would be rendered by an actual census.

Mr. Elseworth & Mr. Sherman moved to postpone the motion (of Mr. Gerry), on ye. question, it passed in the negative.

Mas. no. Cont. ay. N. J. ay. Pa. no. Del. ay. Md. ay. Va. no. N. C. no. S. C. no. Geo. no. [Ayes—4; noes—6.]

Question on Mr. Gerry's motion, (it passed in the negative, the States being equally divided.)

Mas. ay. Cont. no. N. J. no. Pa. ay. Del. no. Md. no. Va. no. N. C. ay. S. C. ay. Geo. ay. [Ayes—5; noes—5.]

Mr. Gerry finding that the loss of the question had proceeded from an objection with some, to the proposed assessment of direct taxes on the *inhabitants* of the States, which might restrain the legislature to a poll tax, moved his proposition again, but so varied as to authorize the assessment on the States, which wd. leave the mode to the Legislature (viz "that from the 1st meeting of the Legislature of the U. S. until a census shall be taken, all monies for supplying the public Treasury by direct taxation shall be raised from the several States according to the number of their representatives respectively in the 1st branch)"

(On this varied question it passed in the affirmative)

Mas. ay. Cont. no. N. J. no. Pa. divd. Del. no. Md. no. Va. ay. N. C. ay. S. C. ay. Geo. ay. [Ayes—5; noes—4; divided—1.]

On the motion of Mr. Randolph, the vote of Saturday last authorizing the Legislre. to adjust from time to time, the representation upon the principles of *wealth* & numbers of inhabitants was reconsidered by common consent in order to strike out "Wealth" and adjust the resolution to that requiring periodical revisions according to the number of whites & three fifths of the blacks: the motion was in the words following—"But as the present situation of the States may probably alter in the number of their inhabitants, that the Legislature of the U. S. be authorized from time to time to apportion the number of representatives: and in case any of the States shall hereafter be divided or any two or more States united or new States created within the limits of the U. S. the Legislature of U. S. shall possess authority to regulate the number of Representatives in any of the foregoing cases, upon the principle of their number of inhabitants; according to the provisions hereafter mentioned."

Mr. Govr. Morris opposed the alteration as leaving still an incoherence. If Negroes were to be viewed as inhabitants, and the revision was to proceed on the principle of numbers of inhabts. they ought to be added in their entire number, and not in the proportion of 3/5. If as property, the word wealth was right, and striking it out would produce the very inconsistency which it was meant to get rid of.—The train of business & the late turn which it had taken, had led him he said, into deep meditation on it, and He wd. candidly state the result. A distinction had been set up & urged, between the Nn. & Southn. States. He had hitherto considered this doctrine as heretical. He still thought the distinction groundless. He sees however that it is persisted in; and that the Southn. Gentleman will not be satisfied unless they see the way open to their gaining a majority in the public Councils. The consequence of such a transfer of power from the maritime to the interior & landed interest will he foresees be such an oppression of commerce, that he shall be obliged to vote for ye. vicious principle of equality in the 2d. branch in order to provide some defence for the N. States agst. it. But to come now more to the point, either this distinction is fictitious or real: if fictitious let it be dismissed & let us proceed with due confidence. If it be real, instead of attempting to blend incompatible things, let us at once take a friendly leave of each other. There can be no end of demands for security if every particular interest is to be entitled to it. The Eastern States may claim it for their fishery, and for other objects, as the Southn. States claim it for their peculiar objects. In this struggle between the two ends of the Union, what part ought the Middle States in point of policy to take: to join their Eastern brethren according to his ideas. If the Southn. States get the power into their hands, and be joined as they will be with the interior Country they will inevitably bring on a war with Spain for the Mississippi. This language is already held.

The interior Country having no property nor interest exposed on the sea, will be little affected by such a war. He wished to know what security the Northn. & middle States will have agst. this danger. It has been said that N. C. S. C. and Georgia only will in a little time have a majority of the people of America. They must in that case include the great interior Country, and every thing was to be apprehended from their getting the power into their hands.

Mr. Butler. The security the Southn. States want is that their negroes may not be taken from them which some gentlemen within or without doors, have a very good mind to do. It was not supposed that N. C. S. C & Geo. would have more people than all the other States, but many more relatively to the other States than they now have. The people & strength of America are evidently bearing Southwardly & S. westwdly.

Mr. Wilson. If a general declaration would satisfy any gentleman he had no indisposition to declare his sentiments. Conceiving that all men wherever placed have equal rights and are equally entitled to confidence, he viewed without apprehension the period when a few States should contain the superior number of people. The majority of people wherever found ought in all questions to govern the minority. If the interior Country should acquire this majority they will not only have the right, but will avail themselves of it whether we will or no. This jealousy misled the policy of G. Britain with regard to America. The fatal maxims espoused by her were that the Colonies were growing too fast, and that their growth must be stinted in time. What were the consequences? first. enmity on our part, then actual separation. Like consequences will result on the part of the interior settlements, if like jealousy & policy be pursued on ours. Further, if numbers be not a proper rule, why is not some better rule pointed out. No one has yet ventured to attempt it. Congs. have never been able to discover a better. No State as far as he had heard, has suggested any other. In 1783, after elaborate discussion of a measure of wealth all were satisfied then as they are now that the rule of numbers, does not differ much from the combined rule of numbers & wealth. Again he could not agree that property was the sole or the primary object of Governt. & Society. The cultivation & improvement of the human mind was the most noble object. With respect to this object, as well as to other personal rights, numbers were surely the natural & precise measure of Representation. And with respect to property, they could not vary much from the precise measure. In no point of view however could the establishmt. of numbers as the rule of representation in the 1st. branch vary his opinion as to the impropriety of letting a vicious principle into the 2d. branch.—On the question to strike out wealth & to make the change as moved by Mr. Randolph, (it passed in the affirmative—)

Mas. ay. Cont. ay. N. J. ay. Pa. ay. Del. divd. Md. ay. Va. ay. N. C. ay. S. C. ay. Geo. ay. [Ayes—9; noes—0; divided—1.]

…

Madison, Monday, July 23. In Convention*

Genl. Pinkney reminded the Convention that if the Committee should fail to insert some security to the Southern States agst. an emancipation of slaves, and taxes on exports, he shd. be bound by duty to his State to vote agst. their Report.—The appt. of a Come. as moved by Mr. Gerry. Agd. to nem. con.

…

Madison, Monday, August 6. In Convention†

…

Mr. Rutlidge (delivered in) the Report of the Committee of detail as follows;

…

VII

…

Sect. 3. The proportions of direct taxation shall be regulated by the whole number of white and other free citizens and inhabitants, of every age, sex and condition, including those bound to servitude for a term of years, and three fifths of all other persons not comprehended in the foregoing description, (except Indians not paying taxes) which number shall, within six years after the first meeting of the Legislature, and within the term of every ten years afterwards, be taken in such manner as the said Legislature shall direct.

…

Madison, Wednesday, Augst. 8. In Convention‡

…

(The 3. Sect. of Art: IV was then agreed to.)

Art: IV. Sect. 4. taken up.

Mr. Williamson moved to strike out "according to the provisions hereinafter made" and to insert (the) words

"according "to the rule hereafter to be provided for direct taxation"—

See Art VII. sect. 3.

On the question for agreeing to Mr. Williamson's amendment

N. H—ay. Mas. ay. Ct. ay. N. J. no. Pa. ay. Del. no. Md. ay. Va ay. N. C. Ay. S. C. ay. Geo. ay. [Ayes—9; noes—2.]

Mr. King wished to know what influence the vote just passed was meant have on the succeeding part of the Report, concerning the admission of slaves into the rule of Representation. He could not reconcile his mind to the article if it was to prevent objections to the latter part. The admission of slaves was a most grating circumstance to his mind, & he believed would be so to a great part of the people of America. He had not made a strenuous opposition to it heretofore because he had hoped that this concession would have produced a readiness which had not been manifested, to strengthen the Genl. Govt. and to mark a full confidence in it. The Report under consideration had by the tenor of it, put an end to all these hopes. In two great points the hands of the Legislature were absolutely tied. The importation of slaves could not be prohibited—exports could not be taxed. Is this reasonable? What are the great objects of the Genl. System? 1. defence agst. foreign invasion. 2. agst. internal sedition. Shall all the States then be bound to defend each; & shall each be at liberty to introduce a weakness which will render defence more difficult? Shall one part of the U. S. be bound to defend another part, and that other part be at liberty not only to increase its own danger, but to withhold the compensation for the burden? If slaves are to be imported shall not the exports produced by their labor, supply a revenue the better to enable the Genl. Govt. to defend their Masters?—There was so much inequality & unreasonableness in all this, that the people of the Northern States could never be reconciled to it. No candid man could undertake to justify it to them. He had hoped that some accommodation wd. have taken place on this subject; that at least a time wd. have been limited for the importation of slaves. He never could agree to let them be imported without limitation & then be represented in the Natl. Legislature. Indeed he could so little persuade himself of the rectitude of such a practice, that he was not sure he could assent to it under any circumstances. At all events, either slaves should not be represented, or exports should be taxable.

Mr. Sherman regarded the slave-trade as iniquitous; but the point of representation having been Settled after

---

* Farrand, *Records*, 2:87, 95.

† Farrand, *Records*, 2:177, 181–83.

‡ Farrand, *Records*, 2:215, 219.

much difficulty & deliberation, he did not think himself bound to make opposition; especially as the present article as amended did not preclude any arrangement whatever on that point in another place of the Report.

Mr. Madison objected to 1 for every 40,000 inhabitants as a perpetual rule. The future increase of population if the Union shd. be permanent, will render the number of Representatives excessive.

Mr. Ghorum. It is not to be supposed that the Govt will last so long as to produce this effect. Can it be supposed that this vast Country including the Western territory will 150 years hence remain one nation?

Mr. Elseworth. If the Govt. should continue so long, alterations may be made in the Constitution in the manner proposed in a subsequent article.

Mr. Sherman & Mr. Madison moved to insert the words "not exceeding" before the words "1 for every 40,000, which was agreed to nem. con.

Mr. Govr. Morris moved to insert "free" before the word "inhabitants." Much he said would depend on this point. He never would concur in upholding domestic slavery. It was a nefarious institution—It was the curse of heaven on the States where it prevailed. Compare the free regions of the Middle States, where a rich & noble cultivation marks the prosperity & happiness of the people, with the misery & poverty which overspread the barren wastes of Va. Maryd. & the other States having slaves. (Travel thro' ye whole Continent & you behold the prospect continually varying with the appearance & disappearance of slavery. The moment you leave ye E. Sts. & enter N. York, the effects of the institution become visible; Passing thro' the Jerseys and entering Pa— every criterion of superior improvement witnesses the change. Proceed Southwdly, & every step you take thro' ye great regions of slaves, presents a desert increasing with ye increasing proportion of these wretched beings.)

Upon what principle is it that the slaves shall be computed in the representation? Are they men? Then make them Citizens & let them vote? Are they property? Why then is no other property included? The Houses in this City (Philada.) are worth more than all the wretched slaves which cover the rice swamps of South Carolina. The admission of slaves into the Representation when fairly explained comes to this: that the inhabitant of Georgia and S. C. who goes to the Coast of Africa, and in defiance of the most sacred laws of humanity tears away his fellow creatures from their dearest connections & damns them to the most cruel bondages, shall have more votes in a Govt. instituted for protection of the rights of mankind, than the Citizen of Pa or N. Jersey who views with a laudable horror, so nefarious a practice. He would add that Domestic slavery is the most prominent feature in the aristocratic countenance of the proposed Constitution. The vassalage of the poor has ever been the favorite offspring of Aristocracy. And what is the proposed compensation to the Northern States for a sacrifice of every principle of right, of every impulse of humanity. They are to bind themselves to march their militia for the defence of the S. States; for their defence agst those very slaves of whom they complain. They must supply vessels & seamen, in case of foreign Attack. The Legislature will have indefinite power to tax them by excises, and duties on imports: both of which will fall heavier on them than on the Southern inhabitants; for the bohea tea used by a Northern freeman, will pay more tax than the whole consumption of the miserable slave, which consists of nothing more than his physical subsistence and the rag that covers his nakedness. On the other side the Southern States are not to be restrained from importing fresh supplies of wretched Africans, at once to increase the danger of attack, and the difficulty of defence; nay they are to be encouraged to it by an assurance of having their votes in the Natl Govt increased in proportion. and are at the same time to have their exports & their slaves exempt from all contributions for the public service. Let it not be said that direct taxation is to be proportioned to representation. It is idle to suppose that the Genl Govt. can stretch its hand directly into the pockets of the people scattered over so vast a Country. They can only do it through the medium of exports imports & excises. For what then are all these sacrifices to be made? He would sooner submit himself to a tax for paying for all the Negroes in the U. States. than saddle posterity with such a Constitution.

Mr. Dayton 2ded. the motion. He did it he said that his sentiments on the subject might appear whatever might be the fate of the amendment.

Mr. Sherman. did not regard the admission of the Negroes into the ratio of representation, as liable to such insuperable objections. It was the freemen of the Southn. States who were in fact to be represented according to the taxes paid by them, and the Negroes are only included in the Estimate of the taxes. This was his idea of the matter.

Mr. Pinkney, considered the fisheries & the Western frontier as more burdensome to the US than the slaves—He thought this could be demonstrated if the occasion were a proper one.

Mr Wilson. thought the motion premature—An agreement to the clause would be no bar to the object of it.

Question On Motion to insert "free" before "inhabitants."

N. H—no. Mas. no. Ct. no. N. J. ay. Pa. no. Del. no. Md. no. Va. no. N C. no. S. C. no. Geo. no. [Ayes—1; noes—10.]

On the suggestion of Mr. Dickenson (the words), "provided that each State shall have one representative at least."—were added nem. con.

Art. IV. sect. 4. as amended was Agreed to nem. con.

…

THE IMPORTATION OF SLAVES

Madison, Tuesday August 21. In Convention[*]

Mr. L—Martin, proposed to vary the sect: 4. art VII so as to allow a prohibition or tax on the importation of slaves. 1. As five slaves are to be counted as 3 free men in the apportionment of Representatives; such a clause wd. leave an encouragement to this traffic. 2 slaves weakened one part of the Union which the other parts were bound to protect: the privilege of importing them was therefore unreasonable—3. it was inconsistent with the principles of the revolution and dishonorable to the American character to have such a feature in the Constitution.

Mr. Rutlidge did not see how the importation of slaves could be encouraged by this section. He was not apprehensive of insurrections and would readily exempt the other States from the obligation to protect the Southern against them.—Religion & humanity had nothing to do with this question—Interest alone is the governing principle with Nations—The true question at present is whether the Southn. States shall or shall not be parties to the Union. If the Northern States consult their interest, they will not oppose the increase of Slaves which will increase the commodities of which they will become the carriers.

Mr. Elseworth was for leaving the clause as it stands. let every State import what it pleases. The morality or wisdom of slavery are considerations belonging to the States themselves—What enriches a part enriches the whole, and the States are the best judges of their particular interest. The old confederation had not meddled with this point, and he did not see any greater necessity for bringing it within the policy of the new one:

Mr. Pinkney. South Carolina can never receive the plan if it prohibits the slave trade. In every proposed extension of the powers of Congress, that State has expressly & watchfully excepted that of meddling with the importation of negroes. If the States be all left at liberty on this subject, S. Carolina may perhaps by degrees do of herself what is wished, as Virginia & Maryland have already done.

…

Madison, Wednesday August 22nd 1787.[†]

Art. VII sect 4. resumed. Mr. Sherman was for leaving the clause as it stands. He disapproved of the slave trade: yet as the States were now possessed of the right to import slaves, as the public good did not require it to be taken from them, & as it was expedient to have as few objections as possible to the proposed scheme of Government, he thought it best to leave the matter as we find it. He observed that the abolition of slavery seemed to be going on in the U. S. & that the good sense of the several States would probably by degrees complete it. He urged on the Convention the necessity of despatching its business.

Col. Mason. This infernal traffic originated in the avarice of British Merchants. The British Govt. constantly checked the attempts of Virginia to put a stop to it. The present question concerns not the importing States alone but the whole Union. The evil of having slaves was experienced during the late war. Had slaves been treated as they might have been by the Enemy, they would have proved dangerous instruments in their hands. But their folly dealt by the slaves, as it did by the Tories. He mentioned the dangerous insurrections of the slaves in Greece and Sicily; and the instructions given by Cromwell to the Commissioners sent to Virginia, to arm the servants & slaves, in case other means of obtaining its submission should fail. Maryland & Virginia he said had already prohibited the importation of slaves expressly. N. Carolina had done the same in substance. All this would be in vain if S. Carolina & Georgia be at liberty to import. The Western people are already calling out for slaves for their new lands; and will fill that Country with slaves if they can be got thro' S. Carolina & Georgia. Slavery discourages arts & manufactures. The poor despise labor when performed by slaves. They prevent the immigration of Whites, who really enrich & strengthen a Country. They produce the most pernicious effect on manners. Every master of slaves is born

[*] Farrand, *Records*, 2:355, 364.

[†] Farrand, *Records*, 2:366, 369.

a petty tyrant. They bring the judgment of heaven on a Country. As nations can not be rewarded or punished in the next world they must be in this. By an inevitable chain of causes & effects providence punishes national sins, by national calamities. He lamented that some of our Eastern brethren had from a lust of gain embarked in this nefarious traffic. As to the States being in possession of the Right to import, this was the case with many other rights, now to be properly given up. He held it essential in every point of view, that the Genl. Govt. should have power to prevent the increase of slavery.

Mr. Elsworth. As he had never owned a slave could not judge of the effects of slavery on character. He said however that if it was to be considered in a moral light we ought to go farther and free those already in the Country.—As slaves also multiply so fast in Virginia & Maryland that it is cheaper to raise than import them, whilst in the sickly rice swamps foreign supplies are necessary, if we go no farther than is urged, we shall be unjust towards S. Carolina & Georgia—Let us not intermeddle. As population increases; poor laborers will be so plenty as to render slaves useless. Slavery in time will not be a speck in our Country. Provision is already made in Connecticut for abolishing it. And the abolition has already taken place in Massachusetts. As to the danger of insurrections from foreign influence, that will become a motive to kind treatment of the slaves.

Mr. Pinkney—If slavery be wrong, it is justified by the example of all the world. He cited the case of Greece Rome & other antient States; the sanction given by France England, Holland & other modern States. In all ages one half of mankind have been slaves. If the S. States were let alone they will probably of themselves stop importations. He wd. himself as a Citizen of S. Carolina vote for it. An attempt to take away the right as proposed will produce serious objections to the Constitution which he wished to see adopted.

General Pinkney declared it to be his firm opinion that if himself & all his colleagues were to sign the Constitution & use their personal influence, it would be of no avail towards obtaining the assent of their Constituents. S. Carolina & Georgia cannot do without slaves. As to Virginia she will gain by stopping the importations. Her slaves will rise in value, & she has more than she wants. It would be unequal to require S. C. & Georgia to confederate on such unequal terms. He said the Royal assent before the Revolution had never been refused to S. Carolina as to Virginia. He contended that the importation of slaves would be for the interest of the whole Union. The more slaves, the more produce to employ the carrying trade; The more consumption also, and the more of this, the more of revenue for the common treasury. He admitted it to be reasonable that slaves should be dutied like other imports, but should consider a rejection of the clause as an exclusion of S. Carola from the Union.

Mr. Baldwin had conceived national objects alone to be before the Convention, not such as like the present were of a local nature. Georgia was decided on this point. That State has always hitherto supposed a Genl Governmt to be the pursuit of the central States who wished to have a vortex for every thing—that her distance would preclude her from equal advantage—& that she could not prudently purchase it by yielding national powers. From this it might be understood in what light she would view an attempt to abridge one of her favorite prerogatives. If left to herself, she may probably put a stop to the evil. As one ground for this conjecture, he took notice of the sect of which he said was a respectable class of people, who carried their ethics beyond the mere *equality of men*, extending their humanity to the claims of the whole animal creation.

Mr. Wilson observed that if S. C. & Georgia were themselves disposed to get rid of the importation of slaves in a short time as had been suggested, they would never refuse to Unite because the importation might be prohibited. As the Section now stands all articles imported are to be taxed. Slaves alone are exempt. This is in fact a bounty on that article.

Mr. Gerry thought we had nothing to do with the conduct of the States as to Slaves, but ought to be careful not to give any sanction to it.

Mr. Dickenson considered it as inadmissible on every principle of honor & safety that the importation of slaves should be authorized to the States by the Constitution. The true question was whether the national happiness would be promoted or impeded by the importation, and this question ought to be left to the National Govt. not to the States particularly interested. If Engd. & France permit slavery, slaves are at the same time excluded from both those Kingdoms. Greece and Rome were made unhappy by their slaves. He could not believe that the Southn. States would refuse to confederate on the account apprehended; especially as the power was not likely to be immediately exercised by the Genl. Government.

Mr. Williamson stated the law of N. Carolina on the subject, to wit that it did not directly prohibit the importation of slaves. It imposed a duty of £5. on each slave imported from Africa. £10. on each from elsewhere, & £50 on each from a State licensing manumission. He thought the S. States could not be members of the Union if the clause should be rejected, and that it was wrong to force any thing down, not absolutely necessary, and which any State must disagree to.

Mr. King thought the subject should be considered in a political light only. If two States will not agree to the Constitution as stated on one side, he could affirm with equal belief on the other, that great & equal opposition would be experienced from the other States. He remarked on the exemption of slaves from duty whilst every other import was subjected to it, as an inequality that could not fail to strike the commercial sagacity of the Northn. & middle States.

Mr. Langdon was strenuous for giving the power to the Genl. Govt. He cd. not with a good conscience leave it with the States who could then go on with the traffic, without being restrained by the opinions here given that they will themselves cease to import slaves.

Genl. Pinkney thought himself bound to declare candidly that he did not think S. Carolina would stop her importations of slaves in any short time, but only stop them occasionally as she now does. He moved to commit the clause that slaves might be made liable to an equal tax with other imports which he thought right & wch. wd. remove one difficulty that had been started.

Mr. Rutlidge. If the Convention thinks that N. C; S. C. & Georgia will ever agree to the plan, unless their right to import slaves be untouched, the expectation is vain. The people of those States will never be such fools as to give up so important an interest. He was strenuous agst. striking out the Section, and seconded the motion of Genl. Pinkney for a commitment.

Mr. Govr. Morris wished the whole subject to be committed including the clauses relating to taxes on exports & to a navigation act. These things may form a bargain among the Northern & Southern States.

Mr. Butler declared that he never would agree to the power of taxing exports.

Mr. Sherman said it was better to let the S. States import slaves than to part with them, if they made that a sine qua non. He was opposed to a tax on slaves imported as making the matter worse, because it implied they were *property*. He acknowledged that if the power of prohibiting the importation should be given to the Genl. Government that it would be exercised. He thought it would be its duty to exercise the power.

Mr. Read was for the commitment provided the clause concerning taxes on exports should also be committed.

Mr. Sherman observed that that clause had been agreed to & therefore could not committed.

Mr. Randolph was for committing in order that some middle ground might, if possible, be found. He could never agree to the clause as it stands. He wd. sooner risk the constitution—He dwelt on the dilemma to which the Convention was exposed. By agreeing to the clause, it would revolt the Quakers, the Methodists, and many others in the States having no slaves. On the other hand, two States might be lost to the Union. Let us then, he said, try the chance of a commitment.

On the question for committing the remaining part of Sect 4 & 5. of art: 7. N. H. no. Mas. abst. Cont. ay N. J. ay Pa. no. Del. no Maryd ay. Va ay. N. C. ay S. C. ay. Geo. ay. [Ayes—7; noes—3; absent—1.]

. . .

Madison, Saturday August. 25. 1787—In Convention[*]
Genl. Pinkney moved to strike out the words "the year eighteen hundred" as the year limiting the importation of slaves, and to insert the words "the year eighteen hundred and eight" Mr. Ghorum 2ded. the motion

Mr. Madison. Twenty years will produce all the mischief that can be apprehended from the liberty to import slaves. So long a term will be more dishonorable to the National character than to say nothing about it in the Constitution.

On the motion; which passed in the affirmative.

N—H—ay. Mas. ay—Ct. ay. N. J. no. Pa. no. Del—no. Md. ay. Va. no. N—C. ay. S—C. ay. Geo. ay. [Ayes—7; noes—4.]

Mr. Govr. Morris was for making the clause read at once, "importation of slaves into N. Carolina, S—Carolina & Georgia shall not be prohibited &c." This he said would be most fair and would avoid the ambiguity by which, under the power with regard to naturalization, the liberty reserved to the States might be defeated. He wished it to be known also that this part of the Constitution was a compliance with those States. If the change of language however should be objected to by the members from those States, he should not urge it.

Col. Mason was not against using the term "slaves" but agst naming N—C—S—C. & Georgia, lest it should give offence to the people of those States.

[*] Farrand, *Records*, 2:412, 415.

Mr. Sherman liked a description better than the terms proposed, which had been declined by the old Congs & were not pleasing to some people. Mr. Clymer concurred with Mr. Sherman

Mr. Williamson said that both in opinion & practice he was, against slavery; but thought it more in favor of humanity, from a view of all circumstances, to let in S—C & Georgia on those terms, than to exclude them from the Union—

Mr. Govr. Morris withdrew his motion.

Mr. Dickenson wished the clause to be confined to the States which had not themselves prohibited the importation of slaves, and for that purpose moved to amend the clause so as to read "The importation of slaves into such of the States as shall permit the same shall not be prohibited by the Legislature of the U—S—until the year 1808".—which was disagreed to nem: cont:

The first part of the report was then agreed to, amended as follows. "The migration or importation of such persons as the several States now existing shall think proper to admit, shall not be prohibited by the Legislature prior to the year 1808."

N. H. Mas. Con. Md. N. C. S. C: Geo: ay

N. J. Pa. Del. Virga: no

[Ayes—7; noes—4.]

Mr. Baldwin in order to restrain & more explicitly define "the average duty" moved to strike out of the 2d. part the words "average of the duties laid on imports" and insert "common impost on articles not enumerated" which was agreed to nem: cont:

Mr. Sherman was agst. this 2d. part, as acknowledging men to be property, by taxing them as such under the character of slaves.

Mr. King & Mr. Langdon considered this as the price of the 1st. part.

Genl. Pinkney admitted that it was so.

Col: Mason. Not to tax, will be equivalent to a bounty on the importation of slaves.

Mr. Ghorum thought that Mr. Sherman should consider the duty, not as implying that slaves are property, but as a discouragement to the importation of them.

Mr. Govr. Morris remarked that as the clause now stands it implies that the Legislature may tax freemen imported.

Mr. Sherman in answer to Mr. Ghorum observed that the smallness of the duty shewed revenue to be the object, not the discouragement of the importation.

Mr. Madison thought it wrong to admit in the Constitution the idea that there could be property in men.

The reason of duties did not hold, as slaves are not like merchandize, consumed, &c

Col. Mason (in answr. to Govr. Morris) the provision as it stands was necessary for the case of Convicts in order to prevent the introduction of them.

It was finally agreed nem: contrad: to make the clause read "but a tax or duty may be imposed on such importation not exceeding ten dollars for each person," and then the 2d. part as amended was agreed to.

Sect 5. art. VII was agreed to nem: con: as reported.

. . .

FUGITIVE SLAVES
Madison, Tuesday August 28, 1787—In Convention[*]
Mr. Butler and Mr Pinkney moved "to require fugitive slaves and servants to be delivered up like criminals."

Mr. Wilson. This would oblige the Executive of the State to do it, at the public expence.

Mr Sherman saw no more propriety in the public seizing and surrendering a slave or servant, than a horse.

Mr. Butler withdrew his proposition in order that some particular provision might be made apart from this article.

Art XV as amended was then agreed to nem: con:

Journal, Wednesday August 29, 1787.[†]

It was moved and seconded to agree to the following proposition to be inserted after the 15 article

"If any Person bound to service or labor in any of the United States shall escape into another State, He or She shall not be discharged from such service or labor in consequence of any regulations subsisting in the State to which they escape; but shall be delivered up to the person justly claiming their service or labor" which passed in the affirmative [Ayes—11; noes—0.]

Committee of Style[‡]
. . .

No person legally held to service or labour in one state, escaping into another, shall in consequence of regulations subsisting therein be discharged from such service or labor, but shall be delivered up on claim of the party to whom such service or labour may be due.

[*] Farrand, *Records*, 2:437, 443.
[†] Farrand, *Records*, 2:445, 446.
[‡] Farrand, *Records*, 2:577, 601.

*Madison, Saturday, Sepr 15th. In Convention**

...

Art. IV. sect 2, parag: 3. the term "legally" was struck out, and "under the laws thereof" inserted (after the word "State,") in compliance with the wish of some who thought the term (legal) equivocal, and favoring the idea that slavery was legal in a moral view—

IMPORTATION OF SLAVES AND THE AMENDING OF THE CONSTITUTION
Madison, Monday Sepr. 10. 1787. In Convention[†]

Mr. Gerry moved to reconsider art XIX. viz, "On the application of the Legislatures of two thirds of the States in the Union, for an amendment of this Constitution, the Legislature of the U. S. shall call a Convention for that purpose." (see Aug. 6)

This Constitution he said is to be paramount to the State Constitutions. It follows, hence, from this article that two thirds of the States may obtain a Convention, a majority of which can bind the Union to innovations that may subvert the State-Constitutions altogether. He asked whether this was a situation proper to be run into—

Mr. Hamilton 2ded. the motion, but he said with a different view from Mr. Gerry—He did not object to the consequences stated by Mr. Gerry—There was no greater evil in subjecting the people of the U. S. to the major voice than the people of a particular State—It had been wished by many and was much to have been desired that an easier mode for introducing amendments had been provided by the articles of Confederation. It was equally desirable now that an easy mode should be established for supplying defects which will probably appear in the new System. The mode proposed was not adequate. The State Legislatures will not apply for alterations but with a view to increase their own powers—The National Legislature will be the first to perceive and will be most sensible to the necessity of amendments, and ought also to be empowered, whenever two thirds of each branch should concur to call a Convention—There could be no danger in giving this power, as the people would finally decide in the case.

Mr. Madison remarked on the vagueness of the terms, "call a Convention for the purpose." as sufficient reason for reconsidering the article. How was a Conven-

tion to be formed? by what rule decide? what the force of its acts?

On the motion of Mr. Gerry to reconsider

N. H. divd. Mas. ay—Ct. ay. N. J.—no. Pa ay. Del. ay. Md. ay. Va. ay. N—C. ay. S. C. ay. Geo. ay. [Ayes—9; noes—1; divided—1.]

Mr. Sherman moved to add to the article "or the Legislature may propose amendments to the several States for their approbation, but no amendments shall be binding until consented to by the several States."

Mr. Gerry 2ded. the motion

Mr. Wilson moved to insert "two thirds of" before the words "several States"—on which amendment to the motion of Mr. Sherman

N. H. ay. Mas. no Ct. no. N. J. no Pa. ay—Del—ay Md. ay. Va. ay. N. C. no. S. C. no. Geo. no. [Ayes—5; noes—6.]

Mr. Wilson then moved to insert "three fourths of" before "the several Sts" which was agreed to nem: con:

Mr. Madison moved to postpone the consideration of the amended proposition in order to take up the following,

"The Legislature of the U—S—whenever two thirds of both Houses shall deem necessary, or on the application of two thirds of the Legislatures of the several States, shall propose amendments to this Constitution, which shall be valid to all intents and purposes as part thereof, when the same shall have been ratified by three fourths at least of the Legislatures of the several States, or by Conventions in three fourths thereof, as one or the other mode of ratification may be proposed by the Legislature of the U. S:"

Mr. Hamilton 2ded. the motion.

Mr. Rutledge said he never could agree to give a power by which the articles relating to slaves might be altered by the States not interested in that property and prejudiced against it. In order to obviate this objection, these words were added to the proposition: "provided that no amendments which may be made prior to the year 1808. shall in any manner affect the 4 & 5 sections of the VII article"—The postponement being agreed to,

On the question on the proposition of Mr. Madison & Mr. Hamilton as amended

N. H. divd. Mas. ay. Ct. ay. N. J. ay. Pa. ay. Del. no. Md. ay. Va ay. N. C. ay S. C. ay. Geo. ay. [Ayes—9; noes—1; divided—1.]

---

[*] Farrand, *Records*, 2:622, 628.
[†] Farrand, *Records*, 2:557.

7

Constitutional Provisions Relating to Slavery

1787

ARTICLE. I.

Section 2

Representatives and direct Taxes shall be apportioned among the several States which may be included within this Union, according to their respective Numbers, which shall be determined by adding to the whole Number of free Persons, including those bound to Service for a Term of Years, and excluding Indians not taxed, three fifths of all other Persons.

Section 9

The Migration or Importation of such Persons as any of the States now existing shall think proper to admit, shall not be prohibited by the Congress prior to the Year one thousand eight hundred and eight, but a Tax or duty may be imposed on such Importation, not exceeding ten dollars for each Person.

ARTICLE. IV.

Section 2.

. . .

No Person held to Service or Labour in one State, under the Laws thereof, escaping into another, shall, in Consequence of any Law or Regulation therein, be discharged from such Service or Labour, but shall be delivered up on Claim of the Party to whom such Service or Labour may be due.

ARTICLE. V.

The Congress, whenever two thirds of both Houses shall deem it necessary, shall propose Amendments to this Constitution, or, on the Application of the Legislatures of two thirds of the several States, shall call a Convention for proposing Amendments, which, in either Case, shall be valid to all Intents and Purposes, as Part of this Constitution, when ratified by the Legislatures of three fourths of the several States, or by Conventions in three fourths thereof, as the one or the other Mode of Ratification may be proposed by the Congress; Provided that no Amendment which may be made prior to the Year One thousand eight hundred and eight shall in any Manner affect the first and fourth Clauses in the Ninth Section of the first Article; and that no State, without its Consent, shall be deprived of its equal Suffrage in the Senate.

8

Charles C. Pinckney, South Carolina House of Representatives, The Three-Fifths Clause

January 18, 1788*

General Pinckney then observed . . . Every member who attended the Convention was, from the beginning, sensible of the necessity of giving greater powers: to the federal government. This was the very purpose for which they were convened. The delegations of Jersey and Delaware were, at first, averse to this organization; but they afterwards acquiesced in it; and the conduct of their delegates has been so very agreeable to the people of these states, that their respective conventions have unanimously adopted the Constitution. As we have found it necessary to give very extensive powers to the federal government both over the persons and estates of the citizens, we thought it right to draw one branch of the legislature immediately from the people, and that both wealth and numbers should be considered in the representation. We were at a loss, for some time, for a rule to ascertain the proportionate wealth of the states. At last we thought that the productive labor of the inhabitants was the best rule for ascertaining their wealth. In conformity to this rule, joined to a spirit of concession, we determined that representatives should be apportioned among the several states, by adding to the whole number of free persons three fifths of the slaves. We thus obtained a representation for our property; and I confess I did not expect that we had conceded too much to the Eastern States, when they allowed us a representation for a species of property which they have not among them.

* *Elliot's Debates*, 281, 283.

9

Debates in the Virginia Ratifying Convention (Article I, Section 9, Clause 1)

June 15, 1788[*]

(The first clause, of the ninth section, read)

Mr. George Mason.—Mr. Chairman.—This is a fatal section, which has created more dangers than any other.—The first clause allows the importation of slaves for twenty years. Under the royal government, this evil was looked upon as a great oppression, and many attempts were made to prevent it; but the interest of the African merchants prevented its prohibition. No sooner did the revolution take place, than it was thought of. It was one of the great causes of our separation from Great Britain. Its exclusion has been a principal object of this state, and most of the states in the Union. The augmentation of slaves weakens the states; and such a trade is diabolical in itself, and disgraceful to mankind; yet, by this Constitution, it is continued for twenty years. As much as I value a union of all the states, I would not admit the Southern States into the Union unless they agree to the discontinuance of this disgraceful trade, because it would bring weakness, and not strength, to the Union. And, though this infamous traffic be continued, we have no security for the property of that kind which we have already. There is no clause in this Constitution to secure it; for they may lay such a tax as will amount to manumission. And should the government be amended, still this detestable kind of commerce cannot be discontinued till after the expiration of twenty years; for the 5th article, which provides for amendments, expressly excepts this clause. I have ever looked upon this as a most disgraceful thing to America. I cannot express my detestation of it. Yet they have not secured us the property of the slaves we have already. So that "they have done what they ought not to have done, and have left undone what they ought to have done."

Mr. *Madison.*—Mr. Chairman.—I should conceive this clause to be impolitic, if it were one of those things which could be excluded without encountering greater evils. The Southern States would not have entered into the Union of America without the temporary permission of that trade; and if they were excluded from the Union, the consequences might be dreadful to them and to us. We are not in a worse situation than before. That traffic is prohibited by our laws, and we may continue the prohibition. The Union in general is not in a worse situation. Under the Articles of Confederation, it might be continued forever; but, by this clause, an end may be put to it after twenty years. There is, therefore, an amelioration of our circumstances. A tax may be laid in the mean time; but it is limited; otherwise Congress might lay such a tax as would amount to a prohibition. From the mode of representation and taxation, Congress cannot lay such a tax on slaves as will amount to manumission. Another clause secures us that property which we now possess. At present, if any slave elopes to any of those states where slaves are free, he becomes emancipated by their laws; for the laws of the states are uncharitable to one another in this respect. But in this Constitution, "no person held to service or labor in one state, under the laws thereof, escaping into another, shall, in consequence of any law or regulation therein, be discharged from such service or labor; but shall be delivered up on claim of the party to whom such service or labor shall be due." This clause was expressly inserted, to enable owners of slaves to reclaim them. This is a better security than any that now exists. No power is given to the general government to interpose with respect to the property in slaves now held by the states. The taxation of this state being equal only to its representation, such a tax cannot be laid as he supposes. They cannot prevent the importation of slaves for twenty years; but after that period, they can. The gentlemen from South Carolina and Georgia argued in this manner: "We have now liberty to import this species of property, and much of the property now possessed had been purchased, or otherwise acquired, in contemplation of improving it by the assistance of imported slaves. What would be the consequence of hindering us from it? The slaves of Virginia would rise in value, and we should be obliged to go to your markets." I need not expatiate on this subject. Great as the evil is, a dismemberment of the Union would be worse. If those states should disunite from the other states for not indulging them in the temporary continuance of this traffic, they might solicit and obtain aid from foreign powers.

[*]John P. Kaminski and Gaspare J. Saladino, eds., *Documentary History of the Ratification of the Constitution; Ratification of the Constitution by the States, Virginia* (Madison: Wisconsin Historical Society, 1993), 10:1338.

10

Fugitive Slave Act

1 Stat. 302, February 12, 1793*

AN ACT RESPECTING FUGITIVES FROM
JUSTICE, AND PERSONS ESCAPING FROM
THE SERVICE OF THEIR MASTERS.

Section 1. *Be it enacted by the Senate and House of Representatives of the United States of America in Congress Assembled,* That, whenever the Executive authority of any State in the Union, or of either of the Territories Northwest or South of the river Ohio, shall demand any person as a fugitive from justice, of the Executive authority of any such State or Territory to which such person shall have fled, and shall moreover produce the copy of an indictment found, or an affidavit made before a magistrate of any state or territory as aforesaid, charging the person so demanded with having committed treason, felony, or other crime, certified as authentic by the governor or chief magistrate of the state or territory from whence the person so charged fled, it shall be the duty of the executive authority of the State or Territory to which such person shall have fled, to cause him or her to be arrested and secured, and notice of the arrest to be given to the executive authority making such demand, or to the agent of such authority appointed to receive the fugitive, and to cause the fugitive to be delivered to such agent when he shall appear: But if no such agent shall appear within six months from the time of the arrest, the prisoner may be discharged. And all costs or expenses incurred in the apprehending, securing, and transmitting such fugitive to the state or territory making such demand, shall be paid by such state or territory.

Sec. 2. *And be it further enacted,* That any agent, appointed as aforesaid, who shall receive the fugitive into his custody, shall be empowered to transport him or her to the state or territory from which he or she shall have fled. And if any person or persons shall by force set at liberty, or rescue the fugitive from such agent while transporting, as aforesaid, the person or persons so offending shall, on conviction, be fined not exceeding five hundred dollars, and be imprisoned not exceeding one year.

Sec. 3. *And be it also enacted,* That when a person held to labor in any of the United States, or in either of the territories on the northwest or south of the river Ohio, under the laws thereof, shall escape into any other part of the said states or territory, the person to whom such labor or service may be due, his agent or attorney, is hereby empowered to seize or arrest such fugitive from labor, and to take him or her before any judge of the circuit or district courts of the United States, residing or being within the state, or before any magistrate of a county, city, or town corporate, wherein such seizure or arrest shall be made, and upon proof to the satisfaction of such Judge or magistrate, either by oral testimony or affidavit taken before and certified by a magistrate of any such state or territory, that the person so seized or arrested, doth, under the laws of the state or territory from which he or she fled, owe service or labor to the person claiming him or her, it shall be the duty of such judge or magistrate to give a certificate thereof to such claimant, his agent, or attorney, which shall be sufficient warrant for removing the said fugitive from labor to the state or territory from which he or she fled.

Sec. 4. *And be it further enacted,* That any person who shall knowingly and willingly obstruct or hinder such claimant, his agent, or attorney, in so seizing or arresting such fugitive from labour, or shall rescue such fugitive from such claimant, his agent or attorney, when so arrested pursuant to the authority herein given and declared; or shall harbor or conceal such person after notice that he or she was a fugitive from labour, as aforesaid, shall, for either of the said offences, forfeit and pay the sum of five hundred dollars. Which penalty may be recovered by and for the benefit of such claimant, by action of debt, in any court proper to try the same, saving moreover to the person claiming such labor or service, his right of action for or on account of the said injuries or either of them.

Approved, February 12, 1793.

*Peters, *Statutes at Large,* 1:302.

11

St. George Tucker,

A Dissertation on Slavery

May 20, 1796*

In the preceding inquiry into the absolute rights of the citizens of united America, we must not be understood as if those rights were equally and universally the privilege of all the inhabitants of the United States, or even of all those, who may challenge this land of freedom as their native country. Among the blessings which the Almighty hath showered down on these states, there is a large portion of the bitterest draught that ever flowed from the cup of affliction. Whilst America hath been the land of promise to Europeans, and their descendants, it hath been the vale of death to millions of the wretched sons of Africa. The genial light of liberty, which hath here shone with unrivalled lustre on the former, hath yielded no comfort to the latter, but to them hath proved a pillar of darkness, whilst it hath conducted the former to the most enviable state of human existence. Whilst we were offering up vows at the shrine of liberty, and sacrificing hecatombs upon her altars; whilst we swore irreconcilable hostility to her enemies, and hurled defiance in their faces; whilst we adjured the God of Hosts to witness our resolution to live free, or die, and imprecated curses on their heads who refused to unite with us in establishing the empire of freedom; we were imposing upon our fellow men; who differ in complexion from us, a slavery, ten thousand times more cruel than the utmost extremity of those grievances and oppressions, of which we complained. Such are the inconsistencies of human nature; such the blindness of those who pluck not the beam out of their own eyes, whilst they can espy a moat, in the eyes of their brother; such that partial system of morality which confines rights and injuries, to particular complexions; such the effect of that self-love which justifies, or condemns, not according to principle, but to the agent. Had we turned our eyes inwardly when we supplicated the Father of Mercies to aid the injured and oppressed; when we in-

voked the Author of Righteousness to attest the purity of our motives, and the justice of our cause; and implored the God of Battles to aid our exertions in its defence, should we not have stood more self convicted than the contrite publican! Should we not have left our gift upon the altar, that we might be first reconciled to our brethren whom we held in bondage? should we not have loosed their chains, and broken their fetters? Or if the difficulties and dangers of such an experiment prohibited the attempt during the convulsions of a revolution, is it not our duty to embrace the first moment of constitutional health and vigour, to effectuate so desirable an object, and to remove from us a stigma, with which our enemies will never fail to upbraid us, nor our consciences to reproach us? To form a just estimate of this obligation, to demonstrate the incompatibility of a state of slavery with the principles of our government, and of that revolution upon which it is founded, and to elucidate the practicability of its total, though gradual abolition, it will be proper to consider the nature of slavery, its properties, attendants, and consequences in general; it's rise, progress, and present state, not only in this commonwealth, but in such of our sister states as have either perfected, or commenced the great work of its extirpation; with the means they have adopted to effect it, and those which the circumstances and situation of our country may render it most expedient for us to pursue, for the attainment of the same noble and important end.

. . .

I. When a nation is, from any external cause, deprived of the right of being governed by its own laws, only, such a nation may be considered as in a state of political slavery. Such is the state of conquered countries, and, generally, of colonies, and other dependent governments. Such was the state of united America before the revolution. In this case the personal rights of the subject may be so far secured by wholesome laws, as that the individual may be esteemed free, whilst the state is subject to a higher power: this subjection of one nation, or people, to the will of another, constitutes the first species of slavery, which, in order to distinguish it from the other two, I have called political; inasmuch as it exists only in respect to the governments, and not to the individuals of the two countries. Of this it is not our business to speak, at present.

II. Civil liberty, according to judge Blackstone, being no other than natural liberty so far restrained by human

*Tucker, *Blackstone's Commentaries*, Appendix, 31–32, 35–43, 54–55, 68–69, 74–81.

laws, and no farther, as is necessary and expedient for the general advantage of the public, whenever that liberty is, by the laws of the state, further restrained than is necessary and expedient for the general advantage, a state of civil slavery commences immediately: this may affect the whole society, and every description of persons in it, and yet the constitution of the state be perfectly free. And this happens whenever the laws of a state respect the form, or energy of the government, more than the happiness of the citizen; as in Venice, where the most oppressive species of civil slavery exists; extending to every individual in the state, from the poorest gondolier to the members of the senate, and the doge himself.

This species of slavery also exists whenever there is an inequality of rights, or privileges, between the subjects or citizens of the same state, except such as necessarily results from the exercise of a public office; for the pre-eminence of one class of men must be founded and erected upon the depression of another; and the measure of exaltation in the former, is that of the slavery of the latter. In all governments, however constituted, or by what description soever denominated, wherever the distinction of rank prevails, or is admitted by the constitution, this species of slavery exists. It existed in every nation, and in every government in Europe before the French revolution. It existed in the American colonies before they became independent states; and notwithstanding the maxims of equality which have been adopted in their several constitutions, it exists in most, if not all, of them, at this day, in the persons of our free negroes and mulattoes; whose civil incapacities are almost as numerous as the civil rights of our free citizens. A brief enumeration of them, may not be improper before we proceed to the third head.

Free negroes and mulattoes are by our constitution excluded from the right of suffrage, and by consequence, I apprehend, from office too: they were formerly incapable of serving in the militia, except as drummers or pioneers, but of late years I presume they were enrolled in the lists of those that bear arms, though formerly punishable for presuming to appear at a musterfield. During the revolutionary war many of them were enlisted as soldiers in the regular army. Even slaves were not rejected from military service at that period, and such as served faithfully during the period of their enlistment, were emancipated by an act passed after the conclusion of the war. An act of justice to which they were entitled upon every principle. All but housekeepers, and persons residing upon the frontiers, are prohibited from keeping, or carrying any gun, powder, shot, club, or other weapon offensive or defensive: Resistance to a white person, in any case, was, formerly, and now, in any case, except a wanton assault on the negroe or mulattoe, is punishable by whipping. No negroe or mulattoe can be a witness in any prosecution, or civil suit in which a white person is a party. Free negroes, together with slaves, were formerly denied the benefit of clergy in cases where it was allowed to white persons; but they are now upon an equal footing as to the allowance of clergy. Emancipated negroes may be sold to pay the debts of their former master contracted before their emancipation; and they may be hired out to satisfy their taxes where no sufficient distress can be had. Their children are to be bound out apprentices by the overseers of the poor. Free negroes have all the advantages in capital cases, which white men are entitled to, except a trial by a jury of their own complexion: and a slave suing for his freedom shall have the same privilege. Free negroes residing, or employed to labour in any town, must be registered; the same thing is required of such as go at large in any county. The penalty in both cases is a fine upon the person employing, or harbouring them, and imprisonment of the negroe. The migration of free negroes or mulattoes to this state is also prohibited; and those who do migrate hither may be sent back to the place from whence they came. Any person, not being a negroe, having one-fourth or more negroe blood in him, is deemed a mulattoe. The law formerly made no other distinction between negroes and mulattoes, whether slaves or freemen. But now the act of 1796, c. 2, which abolishes the punishment of death, except in case of murder, in all cases where any free person may be convicted, creates a most important distinction in their favour; slaves not being entitled to the same benefit. These incapacities and disabilities are evidently the fruit of the third species of slavery, of which it remains to speak; or, rather, they are scions from the same common stock: which is,

III. That condition in which one man is subject to be directed by another in all his actions, and this constitutes a state of domestic slavery; to which state all the incapacities and disabilities of civil slavery are incident, with the weight of other numerous calamities superadded thereto. And here it may be proper to make a short inquiry into the origin and foundation of domestic slavery in other countries, previous to its fatal introduction into this.

Slaves, says Justinian, are either born such or become so. They are born slaves when they are children of bond women; and they become slaves, either by the law of nations, that is, by captivity; for it is the practice of our generals to sell their captives, being accustomed to preserve, and not to destroy them: or by the civil law, which happens when a free person, above the age of twenty, suffers himself to be sold for the sake of sharing the price given for him. The author of the Commentaries on the Laws of England thus combats the reasonableness of all these grounds: "The conqueror," says he, "according to the civilians, had a right to the life of his captive; and having spared that, has a right to deal with him as he pleases. But it is an untrue position, when taken generally, that by the law of nature or nations, a man may kill his enemy: he has a right to kill him only in particular cases; in cases of absolute necessity for self-defence; and it is plain that this absolute necessity did not subsist, since the victor did not actually kill him, but made him prisoner. War itself is justifiable only on principles of self-preservation; and therefore it gives no other right over prisoners but merely to disable them from doing harm to us, by confining their persons: much less can it give a right to kill, torture, abuse, plunder, or even to enslave, an enemy, when the war is over. Since, therefore, the right of making slaves by captivity, depends on a supposed right of slaughter, that foundation failing, the consequence drawn from it must fail likewise. But, secondly, it is said slavery may begin jure civili; when one man sells himself to another. This, if only meant of contracts to serve, or work for, another, is very just: but when applied to strict slavery, in the sense of the laws of old Rome or modern Barbary, is also impossible. Every sale implies a price, a quid pro quo, an equivalent given to the seller, in lieu of what he transfers to the buyer; but what equivalent can be given for life and liberty, both of which, in absolute slavery, are held to be in the master's disposal? His property, also, the very price he seems to receive, devolves, ipso facto, to his master, the instant he becomes a slave. In this case, therefore, the buyer gives nothing, and the seller receives nothing: of what validity then can a sale be, which destroys the very principles upon which all sales are founded? Lastly we are told, that besides these two ways by which slaves are acquired, they may also be hereditary; 'servi nascuntur;' the children of acquired slaves are, 'jure naturae,' by a negative kind of birthright, slaves also.... But this, being built on the two former rights, must fall together with them. If neither captivity, nor the sale of one's self, can by the law of nature and reason reduce the parent to slavery, much less can they reduce the offspring." Thus by the most clear, manly, and convincing reasoning does this excellent author refute every claim, upon which the practice of slavery is founded, or by which it has been supposed to be justified, at least, in modern times. But were we even to admit, that a captive taken in a just war, might by his conqueror be reduced to a state of slavery, this could not justify the claim of Europeans to reduce the natives of Africa to that state: it is a melancholy, though well-known fact, that in order to furnish supplies of these unhappy people for the purposes of the slave trade, the Europeans have constantly, by the most insidious (I had almost said infernal) arts, fomented a kind of perpetual warfare among the ignorant and miserable people of Africa; and instances have not been wanting, where, by the most shameful breach of faith, they have trepanned and made slaves of the sellers as well as the sold. That such horrid practices have been sanctioned by a civilized nation; that a nation ardent in the cause of liberty, and enjoying its blessings in the fullest extent, can continue to vindicate a right established upon such a foundation; that a people who have declared, "That all men are by nature equally free and independent," and have made this declaration the first article in the foundation of their government, should in defiance of so sacred a truth, recognized by themselves in so solemn a manner, and on so important an occasion, tolerate a practice incompatible therewith, is such an evidence of the weakness and inconsistency of human nature, as every man who hath a spark of patriotic fire in his bosom must wish to see removed from his own country. If ever there was a cause, if ever an occasion, in which all hearts should be united, every nerve strained, and every power exerted, surely the restoration of human nature to its unalienable right, is such. Whatever obstacles, therefore, may hitherto have retarded the attempt, he that can appreciate the honour and happiness of his country, will think it time that we should attempt to surmount them.

. . .

Civil, or rather social rights, we may remember, are reducible to three primary heads; the right of personal security; the right of personal liberty; and the right of private property. In a state of slavery the two last are wholly abolished, the person of the slave being at the absolute disposal of his master; and property, what he is incapable, in that state, either of acquiring, or holding, to his own use. Hence it will appear how perfectly irreconcilable a state of slavery is to the principles of a democracy, which, form the basis and foundation of our government. For our bill of rights, declares, "that all men are, by nature equally free, and independent, and have certain rights of which they cannot deprive or divest their posterity . . . namely, the enjoyment of life and liberty, with the means of acquiring and possessing property." This is, indeed, no more than a recognition of the first principles of the law of nature, which teaches us this equality, and enjoins every man, whatever advantages he may possess over another, as to the various qualities or endowments of body or mind, to practise the precepts of the law of nature to those who are in these respects his inferiors, no less than it enjoins his inferiors to practise them towards him. Since he has no more right to insult them, than they have to injure him. Nor does the bare unkindness of nature, or of fortune condemn a man to a worse condition than others, as to the enjoyment of common privileges. It would be hard to reconcile reducing the negroes to a state of slavery to these principles, unless we first degrade them below the rank of human beings, not only politically, but also physically and morally. . . . The Roman lawyers look upon those only properly as persons, who are free, putting slaves into the rank of goods and chattels; and the policy of our legislature, as well as the practise of slave-holders in America in general, seems conformable to that idea: but surely it is time we should admit the evidence of moral truth, and learn to regard them as our fellow men, and equals, except in those particulars where accident, or possibly nature, may have given us some advantage; a recompence, for which they, perhaps, enjoy in other respects.

. . .

The extirpation of slavery from the United States, is a task equally arduous and momentous. To restore the blessings of liberty to near a million of oppressed individuals, who have groaned under the yoke of bondage, and to their descendants, is an object, which those who trust in Providence, will be convinced would not be unaided by the Divine Author of our being, should we invoke his blessing upon our endeavors. Yet human prudence forbids that we should precipitately engage in a work of such hazard as a general and simultaneous emancipation. The mind of a man must in some measure be formed for his future condition. The early impressions of obedience and submission, which slaves have received among us, and the no less habitual arrogance and assumption of superiority, among the whites,

contribute, equally, to unfit the former for freedom, and the latter for equality.

. . .

"But why not retain and "incorporate the blacks into the state?" This question has been well answered by Mr. Jefferson, and who is there so free from prejudices among us, as candidly to declare that he has none against such a measure? The recent scenes transacted in the French colonies in the West Indies are enough to make one shudder with the apprehension of realizing similar calamities in this country. Such probably would be the event of an attempt to smother those prejudices which have been cherished for a period of almost two centuries. Many persons who regret domestic slavery, contend that in abolishing it, we must also abolish that scion from it, which I have denominated civil slavery. That there must be no distinction of rights; that the descendants of Africans, as men, have an equal claim to all civil rights, as the descendants of Europeans; and upon being delivered from the yoke of bondage have a right to be admitted to all the privileges of a citizen. . . . But have not men when they enter into a state of society, a right to admit, or exclude any description of persons, as they think proper? If it be true, as Mr. Jefferson seems to suppose, that the Africans are really an inferior race of mankind, will not sound policy advise their exclusion from a society in which they have not yet been admitted to participate in civil rights; and even to guard against such admission, at any future period, since it may eventually depreciate the whole national character? And if prejudices have taken such deep root in our minds, as to render it impossible to eradicate this opinion, ought not so general an error, if it be one, to be respected? Shall we not relieve the necessities of the naked diseased beggar, unless we will invite him to a seat at our table; nor afford him shelter from the inclemencies of the night air, unless we admit him also to share our bed! To deny that we ought to abolish slavery, without incorporating the Negroes into the state, and admitting them to a full participation of all our civil and social rights, appears to me to rest upon a similar foundation. The experiment so far as it has been already made among us, proves that the emancipated blacks are not ambitious of civil rights. To prevent the generation of such an ambition, appears to comport with sound policy; for if it should ever rear its head, its partizans, as well as its opponents, will be enlisted by nature herself, and always ranged in formidable array against each other. We must therefore endeavour to find some middle course, between the tyrannical and iniquitous policy which holds so many human creatures in a state of grievous bondage, and that which would turn loose a numerous, starving, and enraged banditti, upon the innocent descendants of their former oppressors. Nature, time and sound policy must co-operate with each other to produce such a change: if either be neglected, the work will be incomplete, dangerous, and not improbably destructive.

The plan therefore which I would presume to propose for the consideration of my countrymen is such, as the number of slaves, the difference of their nature, and habits, and the state of agriculture, among us, might render it expedient, rather than desirable to adopt: and would partake partly of that proposed by Mr. Jefferson, and adopted in other states; and partly of such cautionary restrictions, as a due regard to situation and circumstances, and even to general prejudices, might recommend to those, who engage in so arduous, and perhaps unprecedented an undertaking.

1. Let every female born after the adoption of the plan, be free, and transmit freedom to all the descendants, both male and female.

2. As a compensation to those persons, in whose families such females, or their descendants may be born, for the expence and trouble of their maintenance during infancy, let them serve such persons until the age of twenty-eight years: let them then receive twenty dollars in money, two suits of clothes, suited to the season, a hat, a pair of shoes, and two blankets. If these things be not voluntarily done, let the county courts enforce the performance, upon complaint.

3. Let all negro children be registered with the clerk of the county or corporation court, where born, within one month after their birth: let the person in whose family they are born, take a copy of the register, and deliver it to the mother, or if she die, to the child, before it is of the age of twenty-one years. Let any negro claiming to be free, and above the age of puberty, be considered as of the age of twenty-eight years, if he or she be not registered as required.

4. Let all the negro servants be put on the same footing as white servants and apprentices now are, in respect to food, raiment, correction, and the assignment of their service from one to another.

5. Let the children of negroes and mulattoes, born in the families of their parents, be bound to service by the overseers of the poor, until they shall attain the age of twenty-one years. Let all above that age, who are not house-keepers, nor have voluntarily bound themselves to service for a year before the first day of February annually, be then bound for the remainder of the year by the overseers of the poor. To stimulate the overseers of the poor to perform their duty, let them receive fifteen per cent. of their wages, from the person hiring them, as a compensation for their trouble, and ten per cent. per annum out of the wages of such as they may bind apprentices.

6. If at the age of twenty-seven years, the master of a negro or mulattoe servant be unwilling to pay his freedom dues, above mentioned, at the expiration of the succeeding year, let him bring him into the county court, clad and furnished with necessaries as before directed, and pay into court five dollars, for the servant, and thereupon let the court direct him to be hired by the overseers of the poor for the succeeding year, in the manner before directed.

7. Let no negro or mulatto be capable of taking, holding, or exercising, any public office, freehold, franchise, or privilege, or any estate in lands or tenements, other than a lease not exceeding twenty-one years. . . . Nor of keeping, or bearing arms, unless authorised so to do by some act of the general assembly, whose duration shall be limited to three years. Nor of contracting matrimony with any other than a negro or mulattoe; nor be an attorney; nor be a juror; nor a witness in any court of judicature, except against, or between negroes and mulattoes. Nor be an executor or administrator; nor capable of making any will or testament; nor maintain any real action; nor be a trustee of lands or tenements himself, nor any other person to be a trustee to him or to his use.

8. Let all persons born after the passing of the act, be considered as entitled to the same mode of trial in criminal cases, as free negroes and mulattoes are now entitled to.

The restrictions in this plan may appear to savour strongly of prejudice: whoever proposes any plan for the abolition of slavery must either encounter, or accommodate himself, to prejudice. . . . I have preferred the latter; not that I pretend to be wholly exempt from it, but that I might avoid as many obstacles as possible to the completion of so desirable a work, as the abolition of slavery. Though I am opposed to the banishment of the negroes, I wish not to encourage their future residence among us. By denying them the most valuable privileges which civil government affords, I wish to render it their inclination and their interest to seek those privileges in some other climate. There is an immense unsettled territory on this continent more congenial to their natural constitutions than ours, where they may perhaps be received upon more favourable terms than we can permit them to remain with us. Emigrating in small numbers, they will be able to effect settlements more easily than in large numbers; and without the expence or danger of numerous colonies. By releasing them from the yoke of bondage, and enabling them to seek happiness wherever they can hope to find it, we surely confer a benefit, which no one can sufficiently appreciate, who has not tasted of the bitter curse of compulsory servitude. By excluding them from offices, we may hope that the seeds of ambition would be buried too deep, ever to germinate: by disarming them, we may calm our apprehensions of their resentments arising from past sufferings; by incapacitating them from holding lands, we should add one inducement more to emigration, and effectually remove the foundation of ambition, and party-struggles. Their personal rights, and their property, though limited, would, whilst they remain among us, be under the protection of the laws; and their condition not at all inferior to that of the labouring poor in most other countries. Under such an arrangement we might reasonably hope, that time would either remove from us a race of men, whom we wish not to incorporate with us, or obliterate those prejudices, which now form an obstacle to such incorporation.

But it is not from the want of liberality to the emancipated race of blacks that I apprehend the most serious objections to the plan I have ventured to suggest. ... Those slave holders (whose numbers I trust are few) who have been in the habit of considering their fellow creatures as no more than cattle, and the rest of the brute creation, will exclaim that they are to be deprived of their property, without compensation. Men who will shut their ears against this moral truth, that all men are by nature free, and equal, will not even be convinced that they do not possess a property in an unborn child: they will not distinguish between allowing to unborn generations the absolute and unalienable rights of human nature, and taking away that which they now possess; they will shut their ears against truth, should you tell them, the loss of the mother's labour for nine months, and the maintenance of a child for a dozen or fourteen years, is amply compensated by the service of that child for as many years more, as he has been an expence to them. But if the voice of reason, justice, and humanity, be not stifled by sordid avarice, or unfeeling tyranny, it would be easy to convince even those who have entertained such erroneous notions, that the right of one man over another is neither founded in nature, nor in sound policy. That it cannot extend to those not in being; that no man can in reality be deprived of what he doth not possess: that fourteen years labour by a young person in the prime of life, is an ample compensation for a few months of labour lost by the mother, and for the maintenance of a child, in that coarse homely manner that negroes are brought up: and lastly, that a state of slavery is not only perfectly incompatible with the principles of government, but with the safety and security of their masters. History evinces this. At this moment we have the most awful demonstrations of it. Shall we then neglect a duty, which every consideration, moral, religious, political, or selfish, recommends? Those who wish to postpone the measure, do not reflect that every day renders the task more arduous to be performed. We have now 300,000 slaves among us. Thirty years hence we shall have double the number. In sixty years we shall have 1,200,000: and in less than another century from this day, even that enormous number will be doubled. Milo acquired strength enough to carry an ox, by beginning with the ox while he was yet a calf. If we complain that the calf is too heavy for our shoulders, what will the ox be?

12

US Congress, Debate on the Tallmadge Amendment

February 15 and March 2, 1819[*]

FEBRUARY 15, 1819, HOUSE
OF REPRESENTATIVES

The House having again resolved itself into a Committee of the Whole, (Mr. SMITH of Maryland in the chair,) on the bill to authorize the people of the Missouri Territory to form a constitution and State government, and for the admission of the same into the Union—

The question being on the proposition of Mr. TALLMADGE to amend the bill by adding to it the following proviso:

[*] *Annals of Congress*, 15th Cong., 2nd Sess., 1170–93, 1436–37 (Feb. 15, Mar. 2, 1819).

"*And provided*, That the further introduction of slavery or involuntary servitude be prohibited, except for the punishment of crimes, whereof the party shall have been fully convicted; and that all children born within the said State, after the admission thereof into the Union, shall be free at the age of twenty-five years:"

...

Mr. TAYLOR, of New York, spoke as follows:

Mr. Chairman, if the few citizens who now inhabit the Territory of Missouri were alone interested in the decision of this question, I should content myself with voting in favor of the amendment, without occupying for a moment the attention of the Committee. But the fact is far otherwise: those whom we shall authorize to set in motion the machine of free government beyond the Mississippi, will, in many respects, decide the destiny of millions.

...

First. Has Congress power to require of Missouri a Constitutional prohibition against the further introduction of slavery, as a condition of her admission into the Union?

Second. If the power exist, is it wise to exercise it?

Congress has no power unless it be expressly granted by the Constitution, or necessary to the execution of some power clearly delegated. What, then, are the grants made to Congress in relation to the Territories? The third section of the fourth article declares, that "the Congress shall have power to dispose of and make all needful rules and regulations respecting the territory, or other property, belonging to the United States." It would be difficult to devise a more comprehensive grant of power. The whole subject is put at the disposal of Congress, as well the right of judging what regulations are proper to be made, as the power of making them, is clearly granted. Until admitted into the Union, this political society is a territory; all the preliminary steps relating to its admission are territorial regulations. Hence, in all such cases, Congress has exercised the power of determining by whom the constitution should be made, how its framers should be elected, when and where they should meet, and what propositions should be submitted to their decision. After its formation, the Congress examine its provisions, and, if approved, admit the State into the Union, in pursuance of a power delegated by the same section of the Constitution, in the following words: "New States may be admitted by the Congress into the Union." This grant of power is evidently alternative; its exercise is committed to the sound discretion of Congress; no injustice is done by declining it. But if Congress has the power of altogether refusing to admit new States, much more has it the power of prescribing such conditions of admission as may be judged reasonable. The exercise of this power, until now, has never been questioned. The act of 1802, under which Ohio was admitted into the Union, prescribed the condition that its constitution should not be repugnant to the ordinance of 1787. The sixth article of that ordinance declares, "there shall be neither slavery nor involuntary servitude in the said Territory, otherwise than in the punishment of crimes whereof the party shall have been duly convicted." The same condition was imposed by Congress on the people of Indiana and Illinois. These States have all complied with it, and framed constitutions excluding slavery. Missouri lies in the same latitude. Its soil, productions, and climate are the same, and the same principles of government should be applied to it.

But it is said that, by the treaty of 1803, with the French Republic, Congress is restrained from imposing this condition. The third article is quoted as containing the prohibition. It is in the following words: "The inhabitants of the ceded territory shall be incorporated in the Union of the United States, and admitted as soon as possible, according to the principles of the Federal Constitution, to the enjoyment of all the rights, advantages and immunities of citizens of the United States, and, in the meantime, they shall be maintained and protected in the free enjoyment of their liberty, property, and the religion which they profess." The inhabitants of the ceded territory, when transferred from the protection of the French Republic, in regard to the United States, would have stood in the relation of aliens. The object of the article doubtless was to provide for their admission to the rights of citizens, and their incorporation into the American family. The treaty made no provision for the erection of new States in the ceded territory. That was a question of national policy, properly reserved for the decision of those to whom the Constitution had committed the power. The framers of the treaty well knew that the President and Senate could not bind Congress to admit new States into the Union. The unconstitutional doctrine had not then been broached, that the President and Senate could not only purchase a West India island or an African principality, but also impose upon Congress an obligation to make it an independent State, and admit it into the Union. If the President and Senate can, by treaty, change the Constitution of the United States, and rob Congress of a power clearly delegated, the doctrine may be true, but otherwise, it is false. The treaty, therefore, has no operation on the question in debate.

...

Mr. FULLER, of Massachusetts, said, . . . [S]ir, the amendment proposed by the gentleman from New York, Mr. TALLMADGE, merely requires that slavery shall be prohibited in Missouri. Does this imply anything more than that its constitution shall be republican? The existence of slavery in any State is so far a departure from republican principles. The Declaration of Independence, penned by the illustrious statesman then and at this time a citizen of a State which admits slavery, defines the principle on which our National and State Constitutions are all professedly founded. The second paragraph of that instrument begins thus: "We hold these truths to be self-evident—that all men are created equal—that they are endowed by their Creator with certain inalienable rights—that among these are life, liberty, and the pursuit of happiness." Since, then, it cannot be denied that slaves are men, it follows that they are in a purely republican government born free, and are entitled to liberty and the pursuit of happiness. [Mr. F. was here interrupted by several gentlemen, who thought it improper to question in debate the republican character of the slaveholding States, which had also a tendency, as one gentleman (Mr. COLSTON, of Virginia) said, to deprive those States of the right to hold slaves as property, and he adverted to the probability that there might be slaves in the gallery listening to the debate.] Mr. F. assured the gentleman that nothing was further from his thoughts than to question on that floor the right of Virginia and other States, which held slaves when the Constitution was established, to continue to hold them. With that subject the National Legislature could not interfere, and ought not to attempt it. But, Mr. F. continued, if gentlemen will be patient, they will see that my remarks will neither derogate from the Constitutional rights of the States, nor from a due respect to their several forms of government. Sir, it is my wish to allay, not to excite local animosities; but I shall never refrain from advancing such arguments in debate as my duty requires, nor do I believe that the reading of our Declaration of Independence, or a discussion of republican principles on any occasion, can endanger the rights, or merit the disapprobation of any portion of the Union.

My reason, Mr. Chairman, for recurring to the Declaration of our Independence, was to draw from an authority admitted in all parts of the Union a definition of the basis of republican government. If, then, all men have equal rights it can no more comport with the principles of a free Government to exclude men of a certain color from the enjoyment of "liberty and the pursuit of happiness," than to exclude those who have not attained a certain portion of wealth, or a certain stature of body; or to found the exclusion on any other capricious or accidental circumstance. Suppose Missouri, before her admission as a State, were to submit to us her constitution, by which no person could elect, or be elected to any office, unless he possessed a clear annual income of twenty thousand dollars; and suppose we had ascertained that only five, or a very small number of persons had such an estate; would this be anything more or less than a real aristocracy, under a form nominally republican? Election and representation, which some contend are the only essential principles of republics, would exist only in name—a shadow without substance, a body without a soul. But if all the other inhabitants were to be made slaves, and mere property of the favored few, the outrage on principle would be still more palpable. Yet, sir, it is demonstrable that the exclusion of the black population from all political freedom, and making them the property of the whites, is an equally palpable invasion of right and abandonment of principle. If we do this in the admission of new States, we violate the Constitution, and we have not now the excuse which existed when our National Constitution was established. Then, to effect a concert of interests, it was proper to make concessions. The States where slavery existed not only claimed the right to continue it, but it was manifest that a general emancipation of slaves could not be asked of them. Their political existence would have been in jeopardy; both masters and slaves must have been involved in the most fatal consequences.

To guard against such intolerable evils, it is provided in the Constitution "that the migration or importation of such persons, as any of the existing States think proper to admit, shall not be prohibited till 1808." Art. 1, sec. 9. And it is provided elsewhere, that persons held to service by the laws of any State, shall be given up by other States to which they may have escaped, &c. Art. 4. sec. 2.

These provisions effectually recognised the right in the States, which, at the time of framing the Constitution, held the blacks in slavery, to continue so to hold them, until they should think proper to meliorate their condition. The Constitution is a compact among all the States then existing, by which certain principles of government are established for the whole and for each individual State. The predominant principle, in both respects, is, that all men are free, and have an equal right to liberty, and all other privileges; or, in other words, the predominant principle is republicanism, in its largest sense.

...

Mr. P.P. BARBOUR, of Virginia, said that, as he was decidedly opposed to the amendment which had been offered, he asked the indulgence of the House whilst he made some remarks in addition to those which had fallen from the Speaker, for the purpose of showing the impropriety of its adoption.

The effect of the proposed amendment is to prohibit the further introduction of slaves into the new State of Missouri, and to emancipate, at the age of twenty-five years, the children of all those slaves who are now within its limits. The first objection, said he, which meets us at the very threshold of the discussion, is this, that we have no Constitutional right to enact the proposed provision. Our power, in relation to this subject, is derived from the first clause of the third section of the fourth article of the Constitution, which is in these words: "New States may be admitted, by the Congress, into this Union." Now, sir, although, by the next succeeding clause of the same section, "Congress has the power to make all needful rules and regulations respecting the territory of the United States;" and although, therefore, whilst the proposed State continued a part of our territory, upon the footing of a Territorial government, it would have been competent for us, under the power expressly given, to make needful rules and regulations—to have established the principle now proposed; yet, the question assumes a totally different aspect when that principle is intended to apply to a State. This term State has a fixed and determinate meaning; in itself, it imports the existence of a political community, free and independent, and entitled to exercise all the rights of sovereignty, of every description whatever. As it stands in the Constitution, it is to be defined with some limitation upon that principle of construction which has reference to the subject-matter. The extent of the limitation, according to this rule, is obviously this, that it shall enjoy all those rights of sovereignty which belong to the original States which composed the Federal family, and into an union with which it is to be admitted. Now, sir,

although the original States are shorn of many of their beams of sovereignty—such, for example, as that of declaring war, of regulating commerce, &c.; yet we know that, even by an express amendment to the Constitution, all powers not expressly delegated are reserved to the States respectively; and of course the power in question, of deciding whether slavery shall or shall not exist. Gentlemen had said that slavery was prohibited in many of the original States. Does not the House, said Mr. B., at the first glance, perceive the answer to this remark? It is an argument from fact to principle, and in this its utter fallacy consists. It is true that slavery does not exist in many of the original States; but why does it not? Because they themselves, in the exercise of their legislative power, have willed that it shall be so. But, though it does not now exist, it is competent for them, by a law of their own enactment, to authorize it—to call it into existence whenever they shall think fit. Sir, how different would be the situation of Missouri, if the proposed amendment be adopted. We undertake to say that slavery never shall be introduced into that State. The State of Missouri, then, would obviously labor under this disadvantage in relation to the other States: that, though for the time being the fact might be the same in it as in them—that is to say, slavery might be alike prohibited, and not at all exist, yet, as the prohibition of it in other States was repealable at their own will, it might be altered whensoever they chose; whereas, if this prohibition were enacted by Congress, and were required as a *sine qua non* to their admission into the Union, that State could not repeal it, unless, indeed, another opinion was correct, which had been advanced, that, though we did require this provision in their constitution, as indispensable to their admission, yet they might forthwith change their constitution, and get rid of the difficulty. If that be the case, sir, as has been justly remarked, we were doing worse than nothing to legislate upon the subject. But, sir, this provision would be in violation of another principle of the Constitution, to be found in the first clause of the second section of the fourth article; by which it is declared that "the citizens of each State shall be entitled to all privileges and immunities of citizens in the several States." Now, he would ask, whether a citizen of the State of Missouri, who (if this amendment prevail) cannot hold a slave, could, in the language of the section which he had just quoted, be said to enjoy the same privileges with a citizen of Virginia who now may hold a slave, or even with a citizen of Pennsylvania, who, though he cannot now hold one, yet may be permitted by the Legislature of his own State? Sir, it would be a solecism in language, a contradiction in terms. This part of the Constitution, then, also forbids the adoption of the amendment under discussion.

...

Mr. LIVERMORE spoke as follows: Mr. Chairman, I am in favor of the proposed amendment. The object of it is to prevent the extension of slavery over the territory ceded to the United States by France. It accords with the dictates of reason, and the best feelings of the human heart; and is not calculated to interrupt any legitimate right arising either from the Constitution or any other compact. I propose to show what slavery is, and to mention a few of the many evils which follow in its train; and I hope to evince that we are not bound to tolerate the existence of so disgraceful a state of things beyond its present extent, and that it would be impolitic, and very unjust, to let it spread over the whole face of our Western territory. Slavery in the United States is the condition of man subjected to the will of a master, who can make any disposition of him short of taking away his life. In those States where it is tolerated, laws are enacted, making it penal to instruct slaves in the art of reading, and they are not permitted to attend public worship, or to hear the Gospel preached. Thus the light of science and of religion is utterly excluded from the mind, that the body may be more easily bowed down to servitude. The bodies of slaves may, with impunity, be prostituted to any purpose, and deformed in any manner by their owners. The sympathies of nature in slaves are disregarded; mothers and children are sold and separated; the children wring their little hands and expire in agonies of grief, while the bereft mothers commit suicide in despair. How long will the desire of wealth render us blind to the sin of holding both the bodies and souls of our fellow men in chains! But, sir, I am admonished of the Constitution, and told that we cannot emancipate slaves. I know we may not infringe that instrument, and therefore do not propose to emancipate slaves. The proposition before us goes only to prevent our citizens from making slaves of such as have a right to freedom. In the present slaveholding States let slavery continue, for our boasted Constitution connives at it; but do not, for the sake of cotton and tobacco, let it be told to future ages that, while pretending to love liberty, we have purchased an extensive country to disgrace it with the foulest reproach of nations. Our Constitution requires no such thing of us. The ends for which that supreme law was made are succinctly stated in its preface.

They are, first, to form a more perfect union, and insure domestic tranquillity. Will slavery effect this? Can we, sir, by mingling bond with free, black spirits with white, like Shakspeare's witches in Macbeth, form a more perfect union, and insure domestic tranquillity? Secondly, to establish justice. Is justice to be established by subjecting half mankind to the will of the other half? Justice, sir, is blind to colors, and weighs in equal scales the rights of all men, whether white or black. Thirdly, to provide for the common defence and secure the blessings of liberty. Does slavery add anything to the common defence? Sir, the strength of a Republic is in the arm of freedom. But, above all things, do the blessings of liberty consist in slavery? If there is any sincerity in our profession, that slavery is an ill, tolerated only from necessity, let us not, while we feel that ill, shun the cure which consists only in an honest avowal that liberty and equal rights are the end and aim of all our institutions, and that to tolerate slavery beyond the narrowest limits prescribed for it by the Constitution, is a perversion of them all.

Slavery, sir, I repeat, is not established by our Constitution; but a part of the States are indulged in the commission of a sin from which they could not at once be restrained, and which they would not consent to abandon. But, sir, if we could, by any process of reasoning, be brought to believe it justifiable to hold others to involuntary servitude, policy forbids that we should increase it. Even the present slaveholding States have an interest, I think, in limiting the extent of involuntary servitude; for, should slaves become much more numerous and, conscious of their strength, draw the sword against their masters, it will be to the free States that the masters must resort for an efficient power to suppress servile insurrection. But we have made a treaty with France, which, we are told can only be preserved by the charms of slavery.

Sir, said Mr. L., until the ceded territory shall have been made into States, and the new States admitted into the Union, we can do what we will with it. We can govern it as a province, or sell it to any other nation. A part of it is probably at this time sold to Spain, and the inhabitants of it may soon not only enjoy the comforts of slavery, but the blessings of the holy inquisition along with them. The question is on the admission of Missouri as a State into the Union. Surely it will not be contended that we are bound by the treaty to admit it. The treaty-making power does not extend so far. Can the President and Senate, by a treaty with Great Britain, make the province of Lower Canada a State of this Union? To be received as a State into this Union, is a privilege which no country can claim as a right. It is a favor to be granted or not, as the United States may choose. When the United States think proper to grant a favor, they may annex just and reasonable terms: and what can be more reasonable than for these States to insist that a new territory, wishing to have the benefits of freedom extended to it, should renounce a principle that militates with justice, morality, religion, and every essential right of mankind? Louisiana was admitted into the Union on terms. The conditions, I admit, were not very important; but still they recognise the principles for which I contend.

An opportunity is now presented, if not to diminish, at least to prevent, the growth of a sin which sits heavy on the soul of every one of us. By embracing this opportunity, we may retrieve the national character, and, in some degree, our own. But if we suffer it to pass unimproved, let us at least be consistent, and declare that our Constitution was made to impose slavery, and not to establish liberty.

MARCH 2, 1819, HOUSE OF REPRESENTATIVES
Missouri State

. . .

Mr. COBB observed that he did not rise for the purpose of detaining the attention of the House for any length of time. He was too sensible of the importance of each moment which yet remained of the session, to obtrude many remarks upon their patience. But, upon a measure involving the important consequences that this did, he felt it to be an imperious duty to express his sentiments, and to enter his most solemn protest against the principle proposed for adoption by the amendment. Were gentlemen aware of what they were about to do? Did they foresee no evil consequences likely to result out of the measure if adopted? Could they suppose that the Southern States would submit with patience to a measure, the effect of which would be to exclude them from all enjoyment of the vast region purchased by the United States beyond the Mississippi, and which belonged equally to them as to the Northern States? He ventured to assure them that they would not. The people of the slaveholding States, as they are called, know their rights, and will insist upon the enjoyment of them. He should not now attempt to go over ground already occupied by others, with much more ability, and attempt to show that, by the treaty with France, the people of that territory were secured in the enjoyment of the prop-

erty which they held in their slaves. That the proposed amendment was an infraction of this treaty, had been most clearly shown. Nor would he attempt to rescue from slander the character of the people of the Southern States in their conduct towards, and treatment of, their black population. That had also been done, with a degree of force and eloquence to which he could pretend no claim, by the gentleman from Virginia, (Mr. BARBOUR) and the honorable Speaker. He was, however, clearly of opinion that Congress possessed no power under the Constitution to adopt the principle proposed in the amendment. He called upon the advocates of it to point out, and lay their finger upon, that clause of the Constitution of the United States which gives to this body the right to legislate upon the subject. Could they show in what clause or section this right was expressly given, or from which it could be inferred? Unless this authority could be shown, Congress would be assuming a power, if the amendment prevailed, not delegated to them, and most dangerous in its exercise. What is the end and tendency of the measure proposed? It is to impose upon the State of Missouri conditions not imposed upon any other State. It is to deprive her of one branch of sovereignty not surrendered by any other State in the Union, not even those beyond the Ohio; for all of them had legislated upon this subject: all of them had decided for themselves whether slavery should be tolerated at the time they framed their several constitutions. He would not now discuss the propriety of admitting slavery. It is not now a question whether it is politic or impolitic to tolerate slavery in the United States, or in a particular State. It was a discussion into which he would not permit himself to be dragged. Admit, however, its moral impropriety: yet there was a vast difference between moral impropriety and political sovereignty. The people of New York or Pennsylvania may deem it highly immoral and politically improper to permit slavery, but yet, they possess the sovereign right and power to permit it, if they choose. They can to-morrow so alter their constitutions and laws as to admit it, if they were so disposed. It is a branch of sovereignty which the old thirteen States never surrendered in the adoption of the Federal Constitution. Now the bill proposes that the new State shall be admitted upon an equal footing with the other States of the Union. It is in this way only that she can be admitted, under the Constitution. These words can have no other meaning than that she shall be required to surrender no more of her rights of sovereignty, than the other States, into a union with which she is about to be admitted, have surrendered. But if the proposed amendment is adopted, will not this new State be shorn of one branch of her sovereignty, one right, which the other States may and have exercised, (whether properly or not, is immaterial) and do now exercise whenever they think fit?

Mr. C. observed that he did conceive the principle involved in the amendment pregnant with danger. It was one he repeated, to which he believed the people of the region of country which he represented would not quietly submit. He might perhaps subject himself to ridicule for attempting the display of a spirit of prophecy which he did not possess, or of zeal and enthusiasm for which he was entitled to little credit. But he warned the advocates of this measure against the certain effects which it must produce. Effects destructive of the peace and harmony of the Union. He believed that they were kindling a fire which all the waters of the ocean could not extinguish. It could be extinguished only in blood!

13

Thomas Jefferson to John Holmes ("A fire bell in the night")

April 22, 1820*

Monticello, Apr. 22, 1820

I thank you, Dear Sir, for the copy you have been so kind as to send me of the letter to your constituents on the Missouri question. It is a perfect justification to them. I had for a long time ceased to read the newspapers or pay any attention to public affairs, confident they were in good hands, and content to be a passenger in our bark to the shore from which I am not distant. But this momentous question, like a fire bell in the night, awakened and filled me with terror. I considered it at once as the knell of the Union. It is hushed, indeed, for the moment. But this is a reprieve only, not a final sentence. A geographical line, coinciding with a marked principle, moral and political, once conceived and held up to the angry passions of men, will never be obliterated; and every new irritation will mark it deeper and deeper. I can say with conscious truth that there is not a man on earth who would sacrifice more than I would, to

* Jefferson, *Writings*, 1433–35.

relieve us from this heavy reproach, in any *practicable* way. The cession of that kind of property, for so it is misnamed, is a bagatelle which would not cost me in a second thought, if, in that way, a general emancipation and *expatriation* could be effected: and, gradually, and with due sacrifices, I think it might be. But, as it is, we have the wolf by the ear, and we can neither hold him, nor safely let him go. Justice is in one scale, and self-preservation in the other. Of one thing I am certain, that as the passage of slaves from one state to another would not make a slave of a single human being who would not be so without it, so their diffusion over a greater surface would make them individually happier and proportionally facilitate the accomplishment of their emancipation, by dividing the burthen on a greater number of co-adjutors. An abstinence too from this act of power would remove the jealousy excited by the undertaking of Congress, to regulate the condition of the different descriptions of men composing a state. This certainly is the exclusive right of every state, which nothing in the constitution has taken from them and given to the general government. Could Congress, for example, say that the non-freemen of Connecticut, shall be freemen, or that they shall not emigrate into any other state?

I regret that I am now to die in the belief that the useless sacrifice of themselves, by the generation of 1776, to acquire self-government and happiness to their country, is to be thrown away by the unwise and unworthy passions of their sons, and that my only consolation is to be that I live not to weep over it. If they would but dispassionately weigh the blessings they will throw away against an abstract principle more likely to be effected by union than by scission, they would pause before they would perpetrate this act of suicide on themselves and of treason against the hopes of the world. To yourself as the faithful advocate of union I tender the offering of my high esteem and respect.

14

State v. Mann

13 N.C. 263 (1829)

The Defendant was indicted for an assault and battery upon Lydia, the slave of one Elizabeth Jones.

On the trial it appeared that the Defendant had hired

the slave for a year—that during the term, the slave had committed some small offence, for which the Defendant undertook to chastise her—that while in the act of so doing, the slave ran off, whereupon the Defendant called upon her to stop, which being refused, he shot at and wounded her.

His honor Judge DANIEL charged the Jury, that if they believed the punishment inflicted by the Defendant was cruel and unwarrantable, and disproportionate to the offence committed by the slave, that in law the Defendant was guilty, as he had only a special property in the slave.

A verdict was returned for the State, and the Defendant appealed.

No Counsel appeared for the Defendant.

The Attorney-General contended, that no difference existed between this case and that of the State v. Hall, (2 Hawks, 582.) In this case the weapon used was one calculated to produce death. He assimilated the relation between a master and a slave, to those existing between parents and children, masters and apprentices, and tutors and scholars, and upon the limitations to the right of the superiors in these relations, he cited Russell on Crimes, 866.

RUFFIN, Judge.

A Judge cannot but lament, when such cases as the present are brought into judgment. It is impossible that the reasons on which they go can be appreciated, but where institutions similar to our own, exist and are thoroughly understood. The struggle, too, in the Judge's own breast between the feelings of the man, and the duty of the magistrate is a severe one, presenting strong temptation to put aside such questions, if it be possible. It is useless however, to complain of things inherent in our political state. And it is criminal in a Court to avoid any responsibility which the laws impose. With whatever reluctance therefore it is done, the Court is compelled to express an opinion upon the extent of the dominion of the master over the slave in North-Carolina.

The indictment charges a battery on Lydia, a slave of Elizabeth Jones. Upon the face of the indictment, the case is the same as the State v. Hall. (2 Hawks 582.)—No fault is found with the rule then adopted; nor would be, if it were now open. But it is not open; for the question, as it relates to a battery on a slave by a stranger, is considered as settled by that case. But the evidence makes this a different case. Here the slave had been hired by the Defendant, and was in his possession; and the battery was committed during the period of hiring. With the liabilities of the hirer to the general owner, for an injury permanently impairing the value of the slave, no rule now laid down is intended to interfere. That is left upon the general doctrine of bailment. The enquiry here is, whether a cruel and unreasonable battery on a slave, by the hirer, is indictable. The Judge below instructed the Jury, that it is. He seems to have put it on the ground, that the Defendant had but a special property. Our laws uniformly treat the master or other person having the possession and command of the slave, as entitled to the same extent of authority. The object is the same—the services of the slave; and the same powers must be confided. In a criminal proceeding, and indeed in reference to all other persons but the general owner, the hirer and possessor of a slave, in relation to both rights and duties, is, for the time being, the owner. This opinion would, perhaps dispose of this particular case; because the indictment, which charges a battery upon the slave of Elizabeth Jones, is not supported by proof of a battery upon Defendant's own slave; since different justifications may be applicable to the two cases. But upon the general question, whether the owner is answerable criminaliter, for a battery upon his own slave, or other exercise of authority or force, not forbidden by statute, the Court entertains but little doubt.—That he is so liable, has never yet been decided; nor, as far as is known, been hitherto contended. There have been no prosecutions of the sort. The established habits and uniform practice of the country in this respect, is the best evidence of the portion of power, deemed by the whole community, requisite to the preservation of the master's dominion. If we thought differently, we could not set our notions in array against the judgment of every body else, and say that this, or that authority, may be safely lopped off. This has indeed been assimilated at the bar to the other domestic relations; and arguments drawn from the well established principles, which confer and restrain the authority of the parent over the child, the tutor over the pupil, the master over the apprentice, have been pressed on us. The Court does not recognise their application. There is no likeness between the cases. They are in opposition to each other, and there is an impassable gulf between them.—The difference is that which exists between freedom and slavery—and a greater cannot be imagined. In the one, the end in view is the happiness of the youth, born to equal rights with that governor, on whom the duty devolves of training the young to usefulness, in a station which he is afterwards to assume among freemen. To such an end, and with such a subject, moral and intellectual instruction seem the natural means; and for the most part, they are found to suffice. Moderate force is superadded, only to make the others effectual. If that fail, it is better to leave the party to his own headstrong passions, and the ultimate correction of the law, than to allow it to be immoderately inflicted by a private person. With slavery it is far otherwise. The end is the profit of the master, his security and the public safety; the subject, one doomed in his own person, and his posterity, to live without knowledge, and without the capacity to make any thing his own, and to toil that another may reap the fruits. What moral considerations shall be addressed to such a being, to convince him what, it is impossible but that the most stupid must feel and know can never be true—that he is thus to labour upon a principle of natural duty, or for the sake of his own personal happiness, such services can only be expected from one who has no will of his own; who surrenders his will in implicit obedience to that of another. Such obedience is the consequence only of uncontrolled authority over the body. There is nothing else which can operate to produce the effect. The power of the master must be absolute, to render the submission of the slave perfect. I most freely confess my sense of the harshness of this proposition, I feel it as deeply as any man can. And as a principle of moral right, every person in his retirement must repudiate it. But in the actual condition of things, it must be so. There is no remedy. This discipline belongs to the state of slavery. They cannot be disunited, without abrogating at once the rights of the master, and absolving the slave from his subjection. It constitutes the curse of slavery to both the bond and free portions of our population. But it is inherent in the relation of master and slave.

That there may be particular instances of cruelty and deliberate barbarity, where, in conscience the law might properly interfere, is most probable. The difficulty is to determine, where a Court may properly begin. Merely in the abstract it may well be asked, which power of the master accords with right. The answer will probably sweep away all of them. But we cannot look at the matter in that light. The truth is, that we are forbidden to enter upon a train of general reasoning on the subject. We cannot allow the right of the master to be brought into discussion in the Courts of Justice. The slave, to remain a slave, must be made sensible, that there is no appeal from his master; that his power is in no instance, usurped; but is conferred by the laws of man at least, if

not by the law of God. The danger would be great indeed, if the tribunals of justice should be called on to graduate the punishment appropriate to every temper, and every dereliction of menial duty. No man can anticipate the many and aggravated provocations of the master, which the slave would be constantly stimulated by his own passions, or the instigation of others to give; or the consequent wrath of the master, prompting him to bloody vengeance, upon the turbulent traitor—a vengeance generally practised with impunity, by reason of its privacy. The Court therefore disclaims the power of changing the relation. in which these parts of our people stand to each other.

We are happy to see, that there is daily less and less occasion for the interposition of the Courts. The protection already afforded by several statutes, that all powerful motive, the private interest of the owner, the benevolences towards each other, seated in the hearts of those who have been born and bred together, the frowns and deep execrations of the community upon the barbarian, who is guilty of excessive and brutal cruelty to his unprotected slave, all combined, have produced a mildness of treatment, and attention to the comforts of the unfortunate class of slaves, greatly mitigating the rigors of servitude, and ameliorating the condition of the slaves. The same causes are operating, and will continue to operate with increased action, until the disparity in numbers between the whites and blacks, shall have rendered the latter in no degree dangerous to the former, when the police now existing may be further relaxed. This result, greatly to be desired, may be much more rationally expected from the events above alluded to, and now in progress, than from any rash expositions of abstract truths, by a Judiciary tainted with a false and fanatical philanthropy, seeking to redress an acknowledged evil, by means still more wicked and appalling than even that evil.

I repeat, that I would gladly have avoided this ungrateful question. But being brought to it, the Court is compelled to declare, that while slavery exists amongst us in its present state, or until it shall seem fit to the Legislature to interpose express enactments to the contrary, it will be the imperative duty of the Judges to recognise the full dominion of the owner over the slave, except where the exercise of it is forbidden by statute. And this we do upon the ground, that this dominion is essential to the value of slaves as property, to the security of the master, and the public tranquillity, greatly dependent upon their subordination; and in fine, as most effectually securing the general protection and comfort of the slaves themselves.

PER CURIAM.—Let the judgment below be reversed, and judgment entered for the Defendant.

15

Walker's Appeal

September 28, 1829*

My dearly beloved Brethren and Fellow Citizens:

Having travelled over a considerable portion of these United States, and having, in the course of my travels taken the most accurate observations of things as they exist—the result of my observations has warranted the full and unshakened conviction, that we, (colored people of these United States) are the most degraded, wretched, and abject set of beings that ever lived since the world began, and I pray God, that none like us ever may live again until time shall be no more. They tell us of the Israelites in Egypt, the Helots in Sparta, and of the Roman Slaves, which last, were made up from almost every nation under heaven, whose sufferings under those ancient and heathen nations were, in comparison with ours, under this enlightened and Christian nation, no more than a cypher—or in other words, those heathen nations of antiquity, had but little more among them than the name and form of slavery, while wretchedness and endless miseries were reserved, apparently in a phial, to be poured out upon our fathers, ourselves and our children by Christian Americans!

These positions, I shall endeavour, by the help of the Lord, to demonstrate in the course of this appeal, to the satisfaction of the most incredulous mind—and may God Almighty who is the father of our Lord Jesus Christ, open your hearts to understand and believe the truth.

The causes, my brethren, which produce our

wretchedness and miseries, are so very numerous and aggravating, that I believe the pen only of a Josephus or a Plutarch, can well enumerate and explain them. Upon subjects, then, of such incomprehensible magnitude, so impenetrable, and so notorious, I shall be obliged to omit a large class of, and content myself with giving you an exposition of a few of those, which do indeed rage to such an alarming pitch, that they cannot but be a perpetual source of terror and dismay to every reflecting mind.

I am fully aware, in making this appeal to my much afflicted and suffering brethren, that I shall not only be assailed by those whose greatest earthly desires are, to keep us in abject ignorance and wretchedness, and who are of the firm conviction that heaven has designed us and our children to be slaves and beasts of burden to them and their children.—I say, I do not only expect to be held up to the public as an ignorant, impudent and restless disturber of the public peace, by such avaricious creatures, as well as a mover of insubordination—and perhaps put in prison or to death, for giving a superficial exposition of our miseries, and exposing tyrants. But I am persuaded, that many of my brethren, particularly those who are ignorantly in league with slave-holders or tyrants, who acquire their daily bread by the blood and sweat of their more ignorant brethren—and not a few of those too, who are too ignorant to see an inch beyond their noses, will rise up and call me cursed—Yea, the jealous ones among us will perhaps use more abject subtlety by affirming that this work is not worth perusing; that we are well situated and there is no use in trying to better our condition, for we cannot. I will ask one question here.—Can our condition be any worse?—Can it be more mean and abject? If there are any changes, will they not be for the better, though they may appear for the worse at first? Can they get us any lower? Where can they get us? They are afraid to treat us worse, for they know well, the day they do it they are gone. But against all accusations which may or can be preferred against me, I appeal to heaven for my motive in writing—who knows that my object is, if possible, to awaken in the breasts of my afflicted, degraded and slumbering brethren, a spirit of enquiry and investigation respecting our miseries and wretchedness in this Republican Land of Liberty!!!!!

The sources from which our miseries are derived and on which I shall comment, I shall not combine in one, but shall put them under distinct heads and expose them in their turn; in doing which, keeping truth

* *Walker's Appeal in Four Articles together with a Preamble to the Colored Citizens of the World, but in Particular and very expressly to those of the United States of America* (Boston: Printed for the author, 1829), http://archive.org/stream/walkersapp ealinf1829walk#mode/2up. [See also Henry Highland Garnet, *Walker's Appeal, with a Brief Sketch of His Life* (New York: J. H. Tobitt, 1848), http://www.gutenberg.org/files/16516/16516 -h/16516-h.htm. —Ed.]

on my side, and not departing from the strictest rules of morality, I shall endeavor to penetrate, search out, and lay them open for your inspection. If you cannot or will not profit by them, I shall have done my duty to you, my country and my God.

...

ARTICLE 1.
Our wretchedness in consequence of slavery.
...

I have been for years troubling the pages of historians to find out what our fathers have done to the white Christians of America, to merit such condign punishment as they have inflicted on them, and do continue to inflict on us their children. But I must aver, that my researches have hitherto been to no effect. I have therefore come to the immovable conclusion, that they (Americans) have, and do continue to punish us for nothing else, but for enriching them and their country. For I cannot conceive of any thing else. Nor will I ever believe otherwise until the Lord shall convince me.

The world knows, that slavery as it existed among the Romans, (which was the primary cause of their destruction) was, comparatively speaking, no more than a cypher, when compared with ours under the Americans. Indeed, I should not have noticed the Roman slaves, had not the very learned and penetrating Mr. Jefferson said, "When a master was murdered, all his slaves in the same house or within hearing, were condemned to death."—Here let me ask Mr. Jefferson, (but he is gone to answer at the bar of God, for the deeds done in his body while living,) I therefore ask the whole American people, had I not rather die, or be put to death than to be a slave to any tyrant, who takes not only my own, but my wife and children's lives by the inches? Yea, would I meet death with avidity far! far!! in preference to such servile submission to the murderous hands of tyrants. Mr. Jefferson's very severe remarks on us have been so extensively argued upon by men whose attainments in literature, I shall never be able to reach, that I would not have meddled with it, were it not to solicit each of my brethren, who has the spirit of a man, to buy a copy of Mr. Jefferson's "Notes on Virginia," and put it in the hand of his son. For let no one of us suppose that the refutations which have been written by our white friends are enough—they are whites—we are blacks. We, and the world wish to see the charges of Mr. Jefferson refuted by the blacks themselves, according to their chance: for we must remember that what the whites have written respecting this subject, is other men's labors and did not emanate from the blacks. I know well, that there are some talents and learning among the coloured people of this country, which we have not a chance to develop, in consequence of oppression; but our oppression ought not to hinder us from acquiring all we can.—For we will have a chance to develop them by and by. God will not suffer us, always to be oppressed. Our sufferings will come to an end, in spite of all the Americans this side of eternity. Then we will want all the learning and talents among ourselves, and perhaps more, to govern ourselves.—"Every dog must have its day," the American's is coming to an end.

But let us review Mr. Jefferson's remarks respecting us some further. Comparing our miserable fathers, with the learned philosophers of Greece, he says:

"Yet notwithstanding these and other discouraging circumstances among the Romans, their slaves were often their rarest artists. They excelled too in science, insomuch as to be usually employed as tutors to their master's children; Epictetus, Terence and Phædrus, were slaves,—but they were of the race of whites. It is not their condition then, but nature, which has produced the distinction."

See this, my brethren!! Do you believe that this assertion is swallowed by millions of the whites? Do you know that Mr. Jefferson was one of as great characters as ever lived among the whites? See his writings for the world, and public labors for the United States of America. Do you believe that the assertions of such a man, will pass away into oblivion unobserved by this people and the world? If you do you are much mistaken—See how the American people treat us—have we souls in our bodies? are we men who have any spirits at all? I know that there are many swell-bellied fellows among us whose greatest object is to fill their stomachs. Such I do not mean—I am after those who know and feel, that we are men as well as other people; to them, I say, that unless we try to refute Mr. Jefferson's arguments respecting us, we will only establish them.

But the slaves among the Romans. Every body who has read history, knows, that as soon as a slave among the Romans obtained his freedom, he could rise to the greatest eminence in the State, and there was no law instituted to hinder a slave from buying his freedom. Have not the Americans instituted laws to hinder us from obtaining our freedom? Do any deny this charge? Read the laws of Virginia, North Carolina, &c. Further: have not the Americans instituted laws to prohibit a man of colour from obtaining and holding any office whatever, under the government of the United States of America? Now, Mr. Jefferson tells us that our condition is not so hard, as the slaves were under the Romans!!!!

It is time for me to bring this article to a close. But before I close it, I must observe to my brethren that at the close of the first Revolution in this country with Great Britain, there were but thirteen States in the Union, now there are twenty-four, most of which are slave-holding States, and the whites are dragging us around in chains and hand-cuffs to their new States and Territories to work their mines and farms, to enrich them and their children, and millions of them believing firmly that we being a little darker than they, were made by our creator to be an inheritance to them and their children forever—the same as a parcel of brutes!!

Are we men!!—I ask you, O my brethren! are we MEN? Did our creator make us to be slaves to dust and ashes like ourselves? Are they not dying worms as well as we? Have they not to make their appearance before the tribunal of heaven, to answer for the deeds done in the body, as well as we? Have we any other master but Jesus Christ alone? Is he not their master as well as ours?—What right then, have we to obey and call any other master, but Himself? How we could be so submissive to a gang of men, whom we cannot tell whether they are as good as ourselves or not, I never could conceive. However, this is shut up with the Lord and we cannot precisely tell—but I declare, we judge men by their works.

The whites have always been an unjust, jealous, unmerciful, avaricious and blood thirsty set of beings, always seeking after power and authority.—We view them all over the confederacy of Greece, where they were first known to be any thing, (in consequence of education) we see them there, cutting each other's throats—trying to subject each other to wretchedness and misery, to effect which they used all kinds of deceitful, unfair and unmerciful means. We view them next in Rome, where the spirit of tyranny and deceit raged still higher.—We view them in Gaul, Spain and in Britain—in fine, we view them all over Europe, together with what were scattered about in Asia and Africa, as heathens, and we see them acting more like devils than accountable men. But some may ask, did not the blacks of Africa, and the mulattoes of Asia, go on in the same way as did the whites of Europe. I answer no—they never were half so avaricious, deceitful and unmerciful as the whites, according to their knowledge.

But we will leave the whites or Europeans as heathens and take a view of them as Christians, in which capacity we see them as cruel, if not more so than ever. In fact, take them as a body, they are ten times more cruel avaricious and unmerciful than ever they were; for while they were heathens they were bad enough it is true, but it is positively a fact that they were not quite so audacious as to go and take vessel loads of men, women and children, and in cold blood and through devilishness, throw them into the sea, and murder them in all kind of ways. While they were heathens, they were too ignorant for such barbarity. But being Christians, enlightened and sensible, they are completely prepared for such hellish cruelties. Now suppose God were to give them more sense, what would they do? If it were possible would they not dethrone Jehovah and seat themselves upon his throne? I therefore, in the name and fear of the Lord God of heaven and of earth, divested of prejudice either on the side of my colour or that of the whites, advance my suspicion of them, whether they are as good by nature as we are or not. Their actions, since they were known as a people, have been the reverse, I do indeed suspect them, but this, as I before observed, is shut up with the Lord, we cannot exactly tell, it will be proved in succeeding generations.—The whites have had the essence of the gospel as it was preached by my master and his apostles—the Ethiopians have not, who are to have it in its meridian splendor—the Lord will give it to them to their satisfaction. I hope and pray my God, that they will make good use of it, that it may be well with them.

ARTICLE 2.
Our wretchedness in consequence of ignorance.
Ignorance, my brethren, is a mist, low down into the very dark and almost impenetrable abyss of which, our fathers for many centuries have been plunged. The christians, and enlightened of Europe, and some of Asia, seeing the ignorance and consequent degradation of our fathers, instead of trying to enlighten them, by teaching them that religion and light with which God had blessed them, they have plunged them into wretchedness ten thousand times more intolerable, than if they had left them entirely to the Lord, and to add to their miseries, deep down into which they have plunged them, tell them, that they are an inferior and distinct race of beings, which they will be glad enough to recall and swallow by and by. Fortune and misfortune, two inseparable companions, lay rolled up in the

wheel of events, which have from the creation of the world, and will continue to take place among men until God shall dash worlds together.

. . .

To show the force of degraded ignorance and deceit among us some further, I will give here an extract from a paragraph, which may be found in the Columbian Centinel of this city, for September 9, 1829, on the first page of which the curious may find an article, headed

"AFFRAY AND MURDER."

"Portsmouth, (Ohio) Aug. 22, 1829.

"A most shocking outrage was committed in Kentucky, about eight miles from this place, on the 14th inst. A negro driver, by the name of Gordon, who had purchased in Maryland about sixty negroes, was taking them, assisted by an associate named Allen and the wagoner who conveyed the baggage, to the Mississippi. The men were hand-cuffed and chained together, in the usual manner for driving these poor wretches, while the women and children were suffered to proceed without incumbrance. It appears that, by means of a file the negroes unobserved had succeeded in separating the irons which bound their hands, in such a way as to be able to throw them off at any moment. About 8 o'clock in the morning, while proceeding on the state road leading from Greenup to Vanceburg, two of them dropped their shackles and commenced a fight, when the wagoner (Petit) rushed in with his whip to compel them to desist. At this moment, every negro was found to be perfectly at liberty; and one of them seizing a club, gave Petit a violent blow on the head and laid him dead at his feet; and Allen, who came to his assistance, met a similar fate from the contents of a pistol fired by another of the gang. Gordon was then attacked, seized and held by one of the negroes, whilst another fired twice at him with a pistol, the ball of which each time grazed his head, but not proving effectual, he was beaten with clubs, and left for dead They then commenced pillaging the wagon and with an axe split open the trunk of Gordon and rifled it of the money, about $2,490. Sixteen of the negroes then took to the woods; Gordon, in the mean time, not being materially injured was enabled, by the assistance of one of the women, to mount his horse and flee; pursued, however, by one of the gang on another horse, with a drawn pistol;

fortunately he escaped with his life, barely arriving at a plantation, as the negro came in sight; who then turned about and retreated.

"The neighborhood was immediately rallied, and a hot pursuit given—which, we understand, has resulted in the capture of the whole gang and the recovery of the greatest part of the money.—Seven of the negro men and one woman, it is said were engaged in the murder, and will be brought to trial at the next court in Greenupsburg."

Here my brethren, I want you to notice particularly in the above article, the ignorant and deceitful actions of this colored woman. I beg you to view it carefully, as for eternity!!! Here a notorious wretch, with two other confederates had sixty of them in a gang, driving them like brutes—the men all in chains and hand-cuffs, and by the help of God they got their chains and hand-cuffs thrown off and caught two of the wretches and put them to death, and beat the other until they thought he was dead, and left him for dead; however he deceived them, and rising from the ground, this servile woman helped him upon his horse and he made his escape. Brethren what do you think of this? Was it the natural fine feelings of this woman, to save such a wretch alive? I know that the blacks, take them half enlightened and ignorant, are more humane and merciful than the most enlightened and refined Europeans that can be found in all the earth. Let no one say that I assert this because I am prejudiced on the side of my color, and against the whites or Europeans. For what I write, I do it candidly, for my God and the good of both parties: Natural observations have taught me these things; there is a solemn awe in the hearts of the blacks, as it respects murdering men: whereas the whites (though they are great cowards) where they have the advantage, or think that there are any prospects of getting it, they murder all before them, in order to subject men to wretchedness and degradation under them. This is the natural result of pride and avarice.—But I declare, the actions of this black woman are really insupportable. For my own part, I cannot think it was any thing but servile deceit, combined with the most gross ignorance: for we must remember that humanity, kindness and the fear of the Lord, does not consist in protecting devils. Here is a set of wretches, who had sixty of them in a gang, driving them around the country like brutes, to dig up gold and silver for them, (which they will get enough of yet.)

Should the lives of such creatures be spared? Is God and Mammon in league? What has the Lord to do with a gang of desperate wretches, who go sneaking about the country like robbers—light upon his people wherever they can get a chance, binding them with chains and hand-cuffs, beat and murder them as they would rattle-snakes? Are they not the Lord's enemies? Ought they not to be destroyed? Any person who will save such wretches from destruction, is fighting against the Lord, and will receive his just recompense. The black men acted like blockheads. Why did they not make sure of the wretch? He would have made sure of them if he could. It is just the way with black men—eight white men can frighten fifty of them; whereas, if you can only get courage into the blacks, I do declare it, that one good black man can put to death six white men; and I give it as a fact, let twelve black men get well armed for battle, and they will kill and put to flight fifty whites. The reason is, the blacks, once you get them started, they glory in death. The whites have had us under them for more than three centuries, murdering, and treating us like brutes; and, as Mr. Jefferson wisely said, they have never found us out—they do not know, indeed, that there is an unconquerable disposition in the breasts of the blacks, which when it is fully awakened and put in motion, will be subdued, only with the destruction of the animal existence. Get the blacks started, and if you do not have a gang of lions and tigers to deal with, I am a deceiver of the blacks and the whites. How sixty of them could let that wretch escape unkilled, I cannot conceive—they will have to suffer as much for the two whom they secured, as if they had put one hundred to death: if you commence, make sure work—do not trifle, for they will not trifle with you—they want us for their slaves, and think nothing of murdering us in order to subject us to that wretched condition—therefore, if there is an attempt made by us, kill or be killed.

16

North Carolina, *An Act to Prevent the Circulation of Seditious Publications*

1830*

CHAPTER V

An act to prevent the circulation of seditious publications, and for other purposes.

Be it enacted by the General Assembly of the State of North Carolina, and it is hereby enacted by the authority of the same,

That if any person shall knowingly bring into this State, with an intent to circulate, or knowingly circulate or publish within this State, or shall aid or abet the bringing into this State, or the circulation or publication within this State, any written or printed pamphlet or paper, whether written or printed in or out of the State, the evident tendency whereof would be to excite insurrection, conspiracy or resistance in the slaves or free negroes and persons of colour within the State, or which shall advise or persuade slaves or free persons of colour to insurrection, conspiracy or resistance, such person so offending shall be deemed guilty of felony, and on conviction thereof in any court having jurisdiction thereof, shall for the first offense be imprisoned not less than one year and be put into the pillory and whipped, at the discretion of the court; and for the second offense shall suffer death without benefit of clergy.

* North Carolina: Acts Passed by the General Assembly of the State of North Carolina at the Session of 1830–31 (Raleigh, 1831), 10.

17

American Anti-Slavery Society, Declaration of Sentiments

December 6, 1833*

The Convention assembled in the city of Philadelphia, to organize a National Anti-Slavery Society, promptly seize the opportunity to promulgate the following Declaration of Sentiments, as cherished by them in relation to the enslavement of one-sixth portion of the American people.

More than fifty-seven years have elapsed, since a band of patriots convened in this place, to devise measures for the deliverance of this country from a foreign yoke. The cornerstone upon which they founded the Temple of Freedom was broadly this—"that all men are created equal; that they are endowed by their Creator with certain inalienable rights; that among these are life, LIBERTY, and the pursuit of happiness." At the sound of their trumpet-call, three millions of people rose up as from the sleep of death, and rushed to the strife of blood; deeming it more glorious to die instantly as freemen, than desirable to live one hour as slaves. They were few in number—poor in resources; but the honest conviction that Truth, Justice and Right were on their side, made them invincible.

We have met together for the achievement of an enterprise, without which that of our fathers is incomplete; and which, for its magnitude, solemnity, and probable results upon the destiny of the world, as far transcends theirs as moral truth does physical force.

In purity of motive, in earnestness of zeal, in decision of purpose, in intrepidity of action, in steadfastness of faith, in sincerity of spirit, we would not be inferior to them.

Their principles led them to wage war against their oppressors, and to spill human blood like water, in order to be free. Ours forbid the doing of evil that good may come, and lead us to reject, and to entreat the oppressed to reject, the use of all carnal weapons for deliverance from bondage; relying solely upon those which

*William Lloyd Garrison, *Selections from the Writings and Speeches of William Lloyd Garrison* (Boston: R. F. Wallcut, 1852), 66.

are spiritual, and mighty through God to the pulling down of strong holds.

Their measures were physical resistance—the marshalling in arms—the hostile array—the mortal encounter. Ours shall be such only as the opposition of moral purity to moral corruption—the destruction of error by the potency of truth—the overthrow of prejudice by the power of love—and the abolition of slavery by the spirit of repentance.

Their grievances, great as they were, were trifling in comparison with the wrongs and sufferings of those for whom we plead. Our fathers were never slaves—never bought and sold like cattle—never shut out from the light of knowledge and religion—never subjected to the lash of brutal taskmasters.

But those, for whose emancipation we are striving—constituting at the present time at least one-sixth part of our countrymen—are recognized by law, and treated by their fellow-beings, as marketable commodities, as goods and chattels, as brute beasts; are plundered daily of the fruits of their toil without redress; really enjoy no constitutional nor legal protection from licentious and murderous outrages upon their persons; and are ruthlessly torn asunder—the tender babe from the arms of its frantic mother—the heart-broken wife from her weeping husband—at the caprice or pleasure of irresponsible tyrants. For the crime of having a dark complexion, they suffer the pangs of hunger, the infliction of stripes, the ignominy of brutal servitude. They are kept in heathenish darkness by laws expressly enacted to make their instruction a criminal offence.

These are the prominent circumstances in the condition of more than two millions of our people, the proof of which may be found in thousands of indisputable facts, and in the laws of the slaveholding States.

Hence we maintain—that, in view of the civil and religious privileges of this nation, the guilt of its oppression is unequalled by any other on the face of the earth; and, therefore, that it is bound to repent instantly, to undo the heavy burdens, and to let the oppressed go free.

We further maintain—that no man has a right to enslave or imbrute his brother—to hold or acknowledge him, for one moment, as a piece of merchandise—to keep back his hire by fraud—or to brutalize his mind, by denying him the means of intellectual, social and moral improvement.

The right to enjoy liberty is inalienable. To invade it is to usurp the prerogative of Jehovah. Every man has a right to his own body—to the products of his own labor—to the protection of law—and to the common advantages of society. It is piracy to buy or steal a native African, and subject him to servitude. Surely, the sin is as great to enslave an American as an African.

Therefore we believe and affirm—that there is no difference, in principle, between the African slave trade and American slavery:

That every American citizen, who detains a human being in involuntary bondage as his property, is, according to Scripture, (Ex. xxi. 16,) a man-stealer:

That the slaves ought instantly to be set free, and brought under the protection of law:

That if they had lived from the time of Pharaoh down to the present period, and had been entailed through successive generations, their right to be free could never have been alienated, but their claims would have constantly risen in solemnity:

That all those laws which are now in force, admitting the right of slavery, are therefore, before God, utterly null and void; being an audacious usurpation of the Divine prerogative, a daring infringement on the law of nature, a base over-throw of the very foundations of the social compact, a complete extinction of all the relations, endearments and obligations of mankind, and a presumptuous transgression of all the holy commandments; and that therefore they ought instantly to be abrogated.

We further believe and affirm—that all persons of color, who possess the qualifications which are demanded of others, ought to be admitted forthwith to the enjoyment of the same privileges, and the exercise of the same prerogatives, as others; and that the paths of preferment, of wealth, and of intelligence, should be opened as widely to them as to persons of a white complexion.

We maintain that no compensation should be given to the planters emancipating their slaves:

Because it would be a surrender of the great fundamental principle, that man cannot hold property in man:

Because slavery is a crime, and therefore is not an article to be sold:

Because the holders of slaves are not the just proprietors of what they claim; freeing the slave is not depriving them of property, but restoring it to its rightful owner; it is not wronging the master, but righting the slave—restoring him to himself:

Because immediate and general emancipation would only destroy nominal, not real property; it would not amputate a limb or break a bone of the slaves, but by infusing motives into their breasts, would make them doubly valuable to the masters as free laborers; and

Because, if compensation is to be given at all, it should be given to the outraged and guiltless slaves, and not to those who have plundered and abused them.

We regard as delusive, cruel and dangerous, any scheme of expatriation which pretends to aid, either directly or indirectly, in the emancipation of the slaves, or to be a substitute for the immediate and total abolition of slavery.

We fully and unanimously recognise the sovereignty of each State, to legislate exclusively on the subject of the slavery which is tolerated within its limits; we concede that Congress, under the present national compact, has no right to interfere with any of the slave States, in relation to this momentous subject:

But we maintain that Congress has a right, and is solemnly bound, to suppress the domestic slave trade between the several States, and to abolish slavery in those portions of our territory which the Constitution has placed under its exclusive jurisdiction.

We also maintain that there are, at the present time, the highest obligations resting upon the people of the free States to remove slavery by moral and political action, as prescribed in the Constitution of the United States. They are now living under a pledge of their tremendous physical force, to fasten the galling fetters of tyranny upon the limbs of millions in the Southern States; they are liable to be called at any moment to suppress a general insurrection of the slaves; they authorize the slave owner to vote for three-fifths of his slaves as property, and thus enable him to perpetuate his oppression; they support a standing army at the South for its protection and they seize the slave, who has escaped into their territories, and send him back to be tortured by an enraged master or a brutal driver. This relation to slavery is criminal, and full of danger: IT MUST BE BROKEN UP.

These are our views and principles—these our designs and measures. With entire confidence in the overruling justice of God, we plant ourselves upon the Declaration of our Independence and the truths of Divine Revelation, as upon the Everlasting Rock.

We shall organize Anti-Slavery Societies, if possible, in every city, town and village in our land.

We shall send forth agents to lift up the voice of remonstrance, of warning, of entreaty, and of rebuke.

We shall circulate, unsparingly and extensively, anti-slavery tracts and periodicals.

We shall enlist the pulpit and the press in the cause of the suffering and the dumb.

We shalt aim at a purification of the churches from all participation in the guilt of slavery.

We shall encourage the labor of freemen rather than that of slaves, by giving a preference to their productions: and

We shall spare no exertions nor means to bring the whole nation to speedy repentance.

Our trust for victory is solely in God. We may be personally defeated, but our principles never. Truth, Justice, Reason, Humanity, must and will gloriously triumph. Already a host is coming up to the help of the Lord against the mighty, and the prospect before us is full of encouragement.

Submitting this Declaration to the candid examination of the people of this country, and of the friends of liberty throughout the world, we hereby affix our signatures to it; pledging ourselves that, under the guidance and by the help of Almighty God, we will do all that in us lies, consistently with this Declaration of our principles, to overthrow the most execrable system of slavery that has ever been witnessed upon earth; to deliver our land from its deadliest curse; to wipe out the foulest stain which rests upon our national escutcheon; and to secure to the colored population of the United States, all the rights and privileges which belong to them as men, and as Americans—come what may to our persons, our interests, or our reputation—whether we live to witness the triumph of Liberty, Justice and Humanity, or perish untimely as martyrs in this great, benevolent, and holy cause.

18

Letter of Postmaster General Amos Kendall Regarding the Delivery of Antislavery Literature, *Richmond Whig* (VA)

August 11, 1835, p. 1

The postmaster at Richmond has obligingly furnished us with a copy of a letter from the postmaster general to the postmaster at Charleston, which as an interesting paper, we lay before the public.

Post Office Department,
5th August, 1835.

Sir: My views in relation to the subject of your letter of the 3d inst. May be learnt from the enclosed copy of a letter to the postmaster at Charleston S.C. dated 4th inst.

Very respectfully, your obedient servant,

Amos Kendall

Edm'd Anderson,
Asst. P.M., Richmond, Va.

Post Office Department,
August 4th, 1835.
P.M. Charleston, S.C.

Sir: In your letter of the 29th ult. just received, you inform me that by the steamboat mail from New York your office had been filled with pamphlets and tracts upon slavery; that the public mind was highly excited upon the subject; that you doubted the safety of the mail itself out of your possession; that you had determined, as the wisest course, to detain these papers; and you now ask instructions from the department.

Upon a careful examination of the law, I am satisfied that the postmaster general has no legal authority to exclude newspapers from the mail, nor prohibit their carriage or delivery on account of their character or tendency, real or supposed. Probably, it was not thought safe to confer on the head of an executive department a power over the press, which might be perverted and abused.

But I am not prepared to direct you to forward or deliver the papers of which you speak. The post office department was created to serve the people of *each* and *all* of the *United States,* and not to be used as the instrument of their *destruction.* None of the papers detained have been forwarded to me, and I cannot judge for myself of their character and tendency; but you inform me, that they are, in character, "the most inflammatory and incendiary—and insurrectionary in the highest degree."

By no act, or direction of mine, official or private, could I be induced to aid, knowingly, in giving circulation to papers of this description, directly or indirectly. We owe an obligation to the laws, but a higher one to the communities in which we live, and if the *former* be perverted to destroy the *latter,* it is patriotism to disregard them. Entertaining these views, I cannot sanction, and will not condemn the step you have taken.

Your justification must be looked for in the character of the papers detained, and the circumstances by which you are surrounded.

19

South Carolina, Resolutions on Abolitionist Propaganda

December 16, 1835[*]

1. Resolved, That the formation of the abolition societies, and the acts and doings of certain fanatics, calling themselves abolitionists, in the non-slaveholding states of this confederacy, are in direct violation of the obligations of the compact of the union, dissocial, and incendiary in the extreme.

2. Resolved, That no state having a just regard for her own peace and security can acquiesce in a state of things by which such conspiracies are engendered within the limits of a friendly state, united to her by the bonds of a common league of political association, without either surrendering or compromising her most essential rights.

3. Resolved, That the Legislature of South Carolina, having every confidence in the justice and friendship of the non-slaveholding states, announces to her co-states her confident expectation, and she earnestly requests that the governments of these states will promptly and effectually suppress all those associations within their respective limits, purporting to be abolition societies, and that they will make it highly penal to print, publish, and distribute newspapers, pamphlets, tracts and pictorial representations calculated and having an obvious tendency to excite the slaves of the southern states to insurrection and revolt.

4. Resolved, That, regarding the domestic slavery of the southern states as a subject exclusively within the control of each of the said states, we shall consider every interference, by any other state of the general government, as a direct and unlawful interference, to be resisted at once, and under every possible circumstance.

5. Resolved, In order that a salutary negative may be put on the mischievous and unfounded assumption of some of the abolitionists—the non-slaveholding states are requested to disclaim by legislative declaration, all right, either on the part of themselves or the government of the United States, to interfere in any manner with domestic slavery, either in the states, or in the territories where it exists.

6. Resolved, That we should consider the abolition of slavery in the District of Columbia, as a violation of the rights of the citizens of that District, derived from the implied conditions on which that territory was ceded to the general government, and as an usurpation to be at once resisted as nothing more than the commencement of a scheme of much more extensive and flagrant injustice.

7. Resolved, That the legislature of South Carolina, regards with decided approbation, the measures of security adopted by the Post Office Department of the United States, in relation to the transmission of incendiary tracts. But if this highly essential and protective policy, be counteracted by Congress, and the United States mail becomes a vehicle for the transmission of the mischievous documents, with which it was recently freighted we, in this contingency, expect that the Chief Magistrate of our State, will forthwith call the legislature together, that timely measures may be taken to prevent its traversing our territory.

(Resolutions of transmission.)

20

Commonwealth v. Aves

35 Mass. 193 (1836)

SHAW C. J. delivered the opinion of the Court.

The question now before the Court arises upon a return to a habeas corpus, originally issued in vacation by Mr. Justice Wilde, for the purpose of bringing up the person of a colored child named Med, and instituting a legal inquiry into the fact of her detention, and the causes for which she was detained. By the provisions of the revised code, the practice upon habeas corpus is somewhat altered. In case the party complaining, or in behalf of whom complaint is made, on the ground of unlawful imprisonment, is not in the custody of an officer, as of a sheriff or deputy, or corresponding officer of the United States, the writ is directed to the sheriff, requiring him or his deputy to take the body of the person thus complaining, or in behalf of whom complaint is thus made, and have him before the court or magistrate issuing the writ, and to summon the party alleged

[*] Henry Steele Commager, ed., *Documents of American History* (New York: Appleton-Century-Crofts, 1963), 1:280.

to have or claim the custody of such person, to appear at the same time, and show the cause of the detention. The person thus summoned is to make a statement under oath, setting forth all the facts fully and particularly; and in case he claims the custody of such party, the grounds of such claim must be fully set forth. This statement is in the nature of a return to the writ, as made under the former practice, and will usually present the material facts upon which the questions arise. Such return, however, is not conclusive of the facts stated in it, but the court is to proceed and inquire into all the alleged causes of detention, and decide upon them in a summary manner. But the court may, if occasion require it, adjourn the examination, and in the mean time bail the party, or commit him to a general or special custody, as the age, health, sex, and other circumstances of the case may require. It is further provided, that when the writ is issued by one judge of the court in vacation, and in the mean time, before a final decision, the court shall meet in the same county, the proceedings may be adjourned into the court, and there be conducted to a final issue, in the same manner as if they had been originally commenced by a writ issued from the court. I have stated these provisions the more minutely, because there have been as yet but few proceedings under the Revised Statutes, and the practice is yet to be established.

Upon the return of this writ before Mr. Justice Wilde, a statement was made by Aves, the respondent; the case was then postponed. It has since been fully and very ably argued before all the judges, and is now transferred to and entered in court, and stands here for judgment, in the same manner as if the writ had been originally returnable in court. Notice having been given to Mr. and Mrs. Slater, an appearance has been entered for them, and in this state of the case and of the parties, the cause has been heard. The statement on oath is now to be considered in the same aspect as if made by Mr. Slater. It is made in fact by Aves, claiming the custody of the slave in right of Slater, and that claim is sanctioned by Slater, who appears by his attorney to maintain and enforce it. He claims to have the child as master, and carry her back to New Orleans, and whether the claim has been made in terms or not, to hold and return her as a slave, that intent is manifest, and the argument has very properly placed the claim upon that ground.

The case presents an extremely interesting question, not so much on account of any doubt or difficulty attending it, as on account of its important consequences to those who may be affected by it, either as masters or slaves.

The precise question presented by the claim of the respondent is, whether a citizen of any one of the United States, where negro slavery is established by law, coming into this State, for any temporary purpose of business or pleasure, staying some time, but not acquiring a domicil here, who brings a slave with him as a personal attendant, may restrain such slave of his liberty during his continuance here, and convey him out of this State on his return, against his consent. It is not contended that a master can exercise here any other of the rights of a slave owner, than such as may be necessary to retain the custody of the slave during his residence, and to remove him on his return.

Until this discussion, I had supposed that there had been adjudged cases on this subject in this Commonwealth; and it is believed to have been a prevalent opinion among lawyers, that if a slave is brought voluntarily and unnecessarily within the limits of this State, he becomes free, if he chooses to avail himself of the provisions of our laws; not so much because his coming within our territorial limits, breathing our air, or treading on our soil, works any alteration in his status, or condition, as settled by the law of his domicil, as because by the operation of our laws, there is no authority on the part of the master, either to restrain the slave of his liberty, whilst here, or forcibly to take him into custody in order to his removal. There seems, however, to be no decided case on the subject reported.

It is now to be considered as an established rule, that by the constitution and laws of this Commonwealth, before the adoption of the constitution of the United States, in 1789, slavery was abolished, as being contrary to the principles of justice, and of nature, and repugnant to the provisions of the declaration of rights, which is a component part of the constitution of the State.

. . .

Without pursuing this inquiry farther, it is sufficient for the purposes of the case before us, that by the constitution adopted in 1780, slavery was abolished in Massachusetts, upon the ground that it is contrary to natural right and the plain principles of justice. The terms of the first article of the declaration of rights are plain and explicit. "All men are born free and equal, and have certain natural, essential, and unalienable rights, which are, the right of enjoying and defending their lives and liberties, that of acquiring, possessing, and protecting property." It would be difficult to select words more precisely adapted to the abolition of negro slavery. According to the laws prevailing in all the States, where slavery is upheld, the child of a slave is not deemed to be born free, a slave has no right to enjoy and defend his own liberty, or to acquire, possess, or protect property. That the description was broad enough in its terms to embrace negroes, and that it was intended by the framers of the constitution to embrace them, is proved by the earliest contemporaneous construction, by an unbroken series of judicial decisions, and by a uniform practice from the adoption of the constitution to the present time. The whole tenor of our policy, of our legislation and jurisprudence, from that time to the present, has been consistent with this construction, and with no other.

Such being the general rule of law, it becomes necessary to inquire how far it is modified or controlled in its operation; either,

1. By the law of other nations and states, as admitted by the comity of nations to have a limited operation within a particular state; or

2. By the constitution and laws of the United States.

In considering the first, we may assume that the law of this State is analogous to the law of England, in this respect; that while slavery is considered as unlawful and inadmissible in both, and this because contrary to natural right and to laws designed for the security of personal liberty, yet in both, the existence of slavery in other countries is recognized, and the claims of foreigners, growing out of that condition, are, to a certain extent, respected. Almost the only reason assigned by Lord Mansfield in Sommersett's case was, that slavery is of such a nature, that it is incapable of being introduced on any reasons moral or political, but only by positive law; and, it is so odious, that nothing can be suffered to support it but positive law.

The same doctrine is clearly stated in the full and able opinion of Marshall C. J., in the case of the Antelope, 10 Wheat. 120. He is speaking of the slave trade, but the remark itself shows that it applies to the state of slavery. "That it is contrary to the law of nature will scarcely be denied. That every man has a natural right to the fruits of his own labor, is generally admitted, and that no other person can rightfully deprive him of those fruits, and appropriate them against his will, seems to be the necessary result of the admission."

But although slavery and the slave trade are deemed contrary to natural right, yet it is settled by the judicial decisions of this country and of England, that it is not contrary to the law of nations. The authorities are cited in the case of the Antelope, and that case is itself an authority directly in point. The consequence is, that each independent community, in its intercourse with every other, is bound to act on the principle, that such other country has a full and perfect authority to make such laws for the government of its own subjects, as its own judgment shall dictate and its own conscience approve, provided the same are consistent with the law of nations; and no independent community has any right to interfere with the acts or conduct of another state, within the territories of such state, or on the high seas, which each has an equal right to use and occupy; and that each sovereign state, governed by its own laws, although competent and well authorized to make such laws as it may think most expedient to the extent of its own territorial limits, and for the government of its own subjects, yet beyond those limits, and over those who are not her own subjects, has no authority to enforce her own laws, or to treat the laws of other states as void, although contrary to its own views of morality.

This view seems consistent with most of the leading cases on the subject.

...

Upon a general review of the authorities, and upon an application of the well established principles upon this subject, we think they fully maintain the point stated, that though slavery is contrary to natural right, to the principles of justice, humanity and sound policy, as we adopt them and found our own laws upon them, yet not being contrary to the laws of nations, if any other state or community see fit to establish and continue slavery by law, so far as the legislative power of that country extends, we are bound to take notice of the existence of those laws, and we are not at liberty to declare and hold an act done within those limits, unlawful and void, upon our views of morality and policy, which the sovereign and legislative power of the place has pronounced to be lawful. If, therefore, an unwarranted interference and wrong is done by our citizens to a foreigner, acting under the sanction of such laws, and within their proper limits, that is, within the local limits of the power by whom they are thus established, or on the high seas, which each and every nation has a right in common with all others to occupy, our laws would no doubt afford a remedy against the wrong done. So, in pursuance of a well known maxim, that in the construction of contracts, the lex loci contractus shall govern, if a person, having in other respects a right to sue in our courts, shall bring an action against another, liable in other respects to be sued in our courts, upon a contract made upon the subject of slavery in a state where slavery is allowed by law, the law here would give it effect. As if a note of hand made in New Orleans were sued on here, and the defence should be, that it was on a bad consideration, or without consideration, because given for the price of a slave sold, it may well be admitted, that such a defence could not prevail, because the contract was a legal one by the law of the place where it was made.

This view of the law applicable to slavery, marks strongly the distinction between the relation of master and slave, as established by the local law of particular states, and in virtue of that sovereign power and independent authority which each independent state concedes to every other, and those natural and social relations, which are everywhere and by all people recognized, and which, though they may be modified and regulated by municipal law, are not founded upon it, such as the relation of parent and child, and husband and wife. Such also is the principle upon which the general right of property is founded, being in some form universally recognized as a natural right, independently of municipal law.

This affords an answer to the argument drawn from the maxim, that the right of personal property follows the person, and therefore, where by the law of a place a person there domiciled acquires personal property, by the comity of nations the same must be deemed his property everywhere. It is obvious, that if this were true, in the extent in which the argument employs it, if slavery exists anywhere, and if by the laws of any place a property can be acquired in slaves, the law of slavery must extend to every place where such slaves may be carried. The maxim, therefore, and the argument can apply only to those commodities which are everywhere, and by all nations, treated and deemed subjects of property. But it is not speaking with strict accuracy to say, that a property can be acquired in human beings, by local laws each state may, for its own convenience, declare that slaves shall be deemed property, and that the relations and laws of personal chattels shall be deemed to apply to them; as, for instance, that they may be bought and sold, delivered, attached, levied upon, that trespass will lie for an injury done to them, or trover for converting them. But it would be a perversion of terms to say, that

such local laws do in fact make them personal property generally; they can only determine, that the same rules of law shall apply to them as are applicable to property, and this effect will follow only so far as such laws proprio vigore can operate.

…

The conclusion to which we come from this view of the law is this:

That by the general and now well established law of this Commonwealth, bond slavery cannot exist, because it is contrary to natural right, and repugnant to numerous provisions of the constitution and laws, designed to secure the liberty and personal rights of all persons within its limits and entitled to the protection of the laws.

That though by the laws of a foreign state, meaning by "foreign," in this connection, a state governed by its own laws, and between which and our own there is no dependence one upon the other, but which in this respect are as independent as foreign states, a person may acquire a property in a slave, such acquisition, being contrary to natural right, and effected by the local law, is dependent upon such local law for its existence and efficacy, and being contrary to the fundamental laws of this State, such general right of property cannot be exercised or recognized here.

That, as a general rule, all persons coming within the limits of a state, become subject to all its municipal laws, civil and criminal, and entitled to the privileges which those laws confer; that this rule applies as well to blacks as whites, except in the case of fugitives, to be afterwards considered; that if such persons have been slaves, they become free, not so much because any alteration is made in their status, or condition, as because there is no law which will warrant, but there are laws, if they choose to avail themselves of them, which prohibit, their forcible detention or forcible removal.

That the law arising from the comity of nations cannot apply; because if it did, it would follow as a necessary consequence, that all those persons, who, by force of local laws, and within all foreign places where slavery is permitted, have acquired slaves as property, might bring their slaves here, and exercise over them the rights and power which an owner of property might exercise, and for any length of time short of acquiring a domicil; that such an application of the law would be wholly repugnant to our laws, entirely inconsistent with our policy and our fundamental principles, and is therefore inadmissible.

Whether, if a slave, voluntarily brought here and with his own consent returning with his master, would resume his condition as a slave, is a question which was incidentally raised in the argument, but is one on which we are not called on to give an opinion in this case, and we give none. From the principle above stated, on which a slave brought here becomes free, to wit, that he becomes entitled to the protection of our laws, and there is no law to warrant his forcible arrest and removal, it would seem to follow as a necessary conclusion, that if the slave waives the protection of those laws, and returns to the state where he is held as a slave, his condition is not changed.

In the case of The Slave, Grace, 2 Haggard's Adm. R. 94, this question was fully considered by Sir William Scott, in the case of a slave brought from the West Indies to England, and afterwards voluntarily returning to the West Indies; and he held that she was reinstated in her condition of slavery.

A different decision, I believe, has been made of the question in some of the United States; but for the reasons already given, it is not necessary to consider it further here. The question has thus far been considered as a general one, and applicable to cases of slaves brought from any foreign state or country; and it now becomes necessary to consider how far this result differs, where the person is claimed as a slave by a citizen of another State of this Union. As the several States, in all matters of local and domestic jurisdiction are sovereign, and independent of each other, and regulate their own policy by their own laws, the same rule of comity applies to them on these subjects as to foreign states, except so far as the respective rights and duties of the several States, and their respective citizens, are affected and modified by the constitution and laws of the United States.

In art. 4, § 2, the constitution declares that no person held to service or labor in one State, under the laws thereof, escaping into another, shall in consequence of any law or regulation therein, be discharged from such service or labor, but shall be delivered up on claim of the party to whom such service or labor may be due.

The law of congress made in pursuance of this article provides, that when any person held to labor in any of the United States, &c. shall escape into any other of the said States or Territories, the person entitled, &c. is empowered to arrest the fugitive, and upon proof made that the person so seized, under the law of the State from which he or she fled, owes service, &c. Act of February 12, 1793, c. 7, § 3.

In regard to these provisions, the Court are of opinion, that as by the general law of this Commonwealth, slavery cannot exist, and the rights and powers of slave owners cannot be exercised therein; the effect of this provision in the constitution and laws of the United States, is to limit and restrain the operation of this general rule, so far as it is done by the plain meaning and obvious intent and import of the language used, and no further. The constitution and law manifestly refer to the case of a slave escaping from a State where he owes service or labor, into another State or Territory. He is termed a fugitive from labor; the proof to be made is, that he owed service or labor, under the laws of the State or Territory from which he fled, and the authority is given to remove such fugitive to the State from which he fled. This language can, by no reasonable construction, be applied to the case of a slave who has not fled from the State, but who has been brought into the State by his master.

. . .

The constitution and laws of the United States, then, are confined to cases of slaves escaping from other States and coming within the limits of this State without the consent and against the will of their masters, and cannot by any sound construction extend to a case where the slave does not escape and does not come within the limits of this State against the will of the master, but by his own act and permission. The provision is to be construed according to its plain terms and import, and cannot be extended beyond this, and where the case is not that of an escape, the general rule shall have its effect. It is upon these grounds we are of opinion, that an owner of a slave in another State where slavery is warranted by law, voluntarily bringing such slave into this State, has no authority to detain him against his will, or to carry him out of the State against his consent, for the purpose of being held in slavery.

This opinion is not to be considered as extending to a case where the owner of a fugitive slave, having produced a certificate according to the law of the United States, is bonâ fide removing such slave to his own domicil, and in so doing passes through a free State; where the law confers a right or favor, by necessary implication it gives the means of enjoying it. Nor do we give any opinion upon the case, where an owner of a slave in one State is bona fide removing to another State where slavery is allowed, and in so doing necessarily passes through a free State, or where by accident or necessity he is compelled to touch or land therein, remaining no longer than necessary. Our geographical position exempts us from the probable necessity of considering such a case, and we give no opinion respecting it.

The child who is the subject of this habeas corpus, being of too tender years to have any will or give any consent to be removed, and her mother being a slave and having no will of her own and no power to act for her child, she is necessarily left in the custody of the law. The respondent having claimed the custody of the child, in behalf of Mr. and Mrs. Slater, who claim the right to carry her back to Louisiana, to be held in a state of slavery, we are of opinion that his custody is not to deemed by the Court a proper and lawful custody.

Under a suggestion made in the outset of this inquiry, that a probate guardian would probably be appointed, we shall for the present order the child into temporary custody, to give time for an application to be made to the judge of probate.

21

US House of Representatives, The "Gag" Rules

May 26, 1836*

The House resumed the consideration of the report of Mr. PINCKNEY, from the select committee on the subject of abolition.

. . .

The preamble and third resolution were then read as follows:

> And whereas it is extremely important and desirable that the agitation of this subject should be finally arrested, for the purpose of restoring tranquility to the public mind, your committee respectfully recommend the adoption of the following additional resolution, viz:
>
> *Resolved*, That all petitions, memorials, resolutions, propositions, or papers, relating in any way, or to any extent whatever, to the subject of slavery, or the abolition of slavery, shall, without being either printed or referred, be laid upon the table, and that no further action whatever shall be had thereon.

* *Cong. Globe*, 24th Cong., 1st Sess., 505–6 (May 26, 1836).

Mr. PHILLIPS rose to make a point of order, and was proceeding to state the same, when

Mr. HAWES called him to order, on the ground that he was making an argument.

The CHAIR requested the gentleman from Massachusetts to reduce his point of order to writing.

The hour of eleven having arrived, the Chair announced the special order of the day.

Mr. PATTON moved to suspend the rule, for the purpose of disposing of the subject before the House, which was agreed to—ayes 126, noes not counted.

Mr. PHILLIPS then sent to the Chair the following point of order:

> Can a committee, specially instructed to report two resolutions, the form of which was given by the House, report another resolution, changing the rules and orders of the House in regard to the management of its business, and depriving citizens of the privilege of obtaining the usual consideration of petitions on subjects other than those referred to the committee?

The CHAIR stated, that it was not within the competency of the Speaker to draw within the vortex of order the question raised by the gentleman from Massachusetts. Questions relating to the jurisdiction of the committee of the House, or whether they had or had not exceeded that jurisdiction, or transcended the authority conferred upon them by the House, were for the House, and not the Speaker, to determine. If gentlemen were of opinion that committees, in their reports, had exceeded the authority given them by the House, there were other modes of correcting what they had done; as, for example, the report may be recommitted with instructions; or the House on that, as well as other grounds, may refuse to concur in their report.

The point now raised could not, therefore, be considered as a point of order to be decided by the Chair. It was in some respects analogous to the case of inconsistent amendments proposed, in which case it was well settled, that "if an amendment be proposed inconsistent with one already agreed to, it is a fit ground for its rejection by the House; but not within the competence of the Speaker to suppress, as if it were against order; for were he permitted to draw questions of consistence within the vortex of order, he might usurp a negative on important modifications, and suppress, instead of subserving the legislative will."

So in this case, if the House shall be satisfied that the

committee were not clothed with authority, by the order of the House under which they were appointed, to report this resolution, "it may be a fit ground for its rejection by the House, but not within the competence of the Speaker to suppress, as if it were against order."

Mr. PHILLIPS then moved to lay the preamble and third resolution on the table.

Mr. GRENNELL asked for the yeas and nays, which were ordered, and the motion to lay on the table was negatived—yeas 69, nays 118.

The question recurring upon the adoption of the preamble and third resolution, the Clerk proceeded to call the roll.

When the name of Mr. ADAMS was called, that gentleman rose and said: I hold the resolution to be a direct violation of the Constitution of the United States, the rules of this House, and the rights of my constituents. Mr. A. resumed his seat amid loud cries of "Order!" from all parts of the Hall.

The third resolution was then agreed to—yeas 117, nays 68.

22

Prigg v. Pennsylvania

41 U.S. 549 (1842)

Mr. Justice STORY delivered the opinion of the Court.

This is a writ of error to the Supreme Court of Pennsylvania, brought under the 25th section of the judiciary act of 1789, ch. 20, for the purpose of revising the judgment of that Court, in a case involving the construction of the Constitution and laws of the United States.

The facts are briefly these: The plaintiff in error was indicted in the Court of Oyer and Terminer for York county, for having, with force and violence, taken and carried away from that county to the state of Maryland, a certain negro woman, named Margaret Morgan, with a design and intention of selling and disposing of, and keeping her as a slave or servant for life, contrary to a statute of Pennsylvania, passed on the 26th of March, 1826. That statute in the first section, in substance, provides, that if any person or persons shall from and after the passing of the act, by force and violence take and carry away, or cause to be taken and carried away, and shall by fraud or false pretense,

seduce, or cause to be seduced, or shall attempt to take, carry away, or seduce any negro or mulatto from any part of that commonwealth, with a design and intention of selling and disposing of, or causing to be sold, or of keeping and detaining, or of causing to be kept and detained, such negro or mulatto as a slave or servant for life, or for any term whatsoever; every such person or persons, his or their aiders or abettors, shall, on conviction thereof, be deemed guilty of a felony, and shall forfeit and pay a sum not less than five hundred, nor more than one thousand dollars; and moreover, shall be sentenced to undergo a servitude for any term or terms of years, not less than seven years nor exceeding twenty-one years; and shall be confined and kept to hard labour, &c. There are many other provisions in the statute which is recited at large in the record, but to which it is in our view unnecessary to advert upon the present occasion.

The plaintiff in error pleaded not guilty to the indictment; and at the trial the jury found a special verdict, which, in substance, states, that the negro woman, Margaret Morgan, was a slave for life, and held to labour and service under and according to the laws of Maryland, to a certain Margaret Ashmore a citizen of Maryland; that the slave escaped and fled from Maryland into Pennsylvania in 1832; that the plaintiff in error, being legally constituted the agent and attorney of the said Margaret Ashmore, in 1837, caused the said negro woman to be taken and apprehended as a fugitive from labour by a state constable, under a warrant from a Pennsylvania magistrate; that the said negro woman was thereupon brought before the said magistrate, who refused to take further cognisance of the case; and thereupon the plaintiff in error did remove, take, and carry away the said negro woman and her children out of Pennsylvania into Maryland, and did deliver the said negro woman and her children into the custody and possession of the said Margaret Ashmore. The special verdict further finds, that one of the children was born in Pennsylvania, more than a year after the said negro woman had fled and escaped from Maryland.

Upon this special verdict, the Court of Oyer and Terminer of York county, adjudged that the plaintiff in error was guilty of the offence charged in the indictment. A writ of error was brought from that judgment to the Supreme Court of Pennsylvania, where the judgment was, pro forma, affirmed. From this latter judgment, the present writ of error has been brought to this Court.

...

Few questions which have ever come before this Court involve more delicate and important considerations; and few upon which the public at large may be presumed to feel a more profound and pervading interest. We have accordingly given them our most deliberate examination; and it has become my duty to state the result to which we have arrived, and the reasoning by which it is supported.

Before, however, we proceed to the points more immediately before us, it may be well—in order to clear the case of difficulty—to say, that in the exposition of this part of the Constitution, we shall limit ourselves to those considerations which appropriately and exclusively belong to it, without laying down any rules of interpretation of a more general nature. It will, indeed, probably, be found, when we look to the character of the Constitution itself, the objects which it seeks to attain, the powers which it confers, the duties which it enjoins, and the rights which it secures, as well as the known historical fact that many of its provisions were matters of compromise of opposing interests and opinions; that no uniform rule of interpretation can be applied to it which may not allow, even if it does not positively demand, many modifications in its actual application to particular clauses. And, perhaps, the safest rule of interpretation after all will be found to be to look to the nature and objects of the particular powers, duties, and rights, with all the lights and aids of contemporary history; and to give to the words of each just such operation and force, consistent with their legitimate meaning, as may fairly secure and attain the ends proposed.

There are two clauses in the Constitution upon the subject of fugitives, which stand in juxtaposition with each other, and have been thought mutually to illustrate each other. They are both contained in the second section of the fourth article, and are in the following words: "A person charged in any state with treason, felony, or other crime, who shall flee from justice, and be found in another state, shall, on demand of the executive authority of the state from which he fled, be delivered up, to be removed to the state having jurisdiction of the crime."

"No person held to service or labour in one state under the laws thereof, escaping into another, shall in consequence of any law or regulation therein, be discharged from such service or labour; but shall be delivered up, on claim of the party to whom such service or labour may be due."

The last clause is that, the true interpretation whereof is directly in judgment before us. Historically, it is well known, that the object of this clause was to secure to the citizens of the slaveholding states the complete right and title of ownership in their slaves, as property, in every state in the Union into which they might escape from the state where they were held in servitude. The full recognition of this right and title was indispensable to the security of this species of property in all the slaveholding states; and, indeed, was so vital to the preservation of their domestic interests and institutions, that it cannot be doubted that it constituted a fundamental article, without the adoption of which the Union could not have been formed. Its true design was to guard against the doctrines and principles prevalent in the non-slaveholding states, by preventing them from intermeddling with, or obstructing, or abolishing the rights of the owners of slaves.

By the general law of nations, no nation is bound to recognise the state of slavery, as to foreign slaves found within its territorial dominions, when it is in opposition to its own policy and institutions, in favour of the subjects of other nations where slavery is recognised. If it does it, it is as a matter of comity, and not as a matter of international right. The state of slavery is deemed to be a mere municipal regulation, founded upon and limited to the range of the territorial laws. This was fully recognised in Somerset's Case, Lofft's Rep. 1; S.C., 11 State Trials by Harg. 340; S.C., 20 Howell's State Trials, 79; which was decided before the American revolution. It is manifest from this consideration, that if the Constitution had not contained this clause, every non-slaveholding state in the Union would have been at liberty to have declared free all runaway slaves coming within its limits, and to have given them entire immunity and protection against the claims of their masters; a course which would have created the most bitter animosities, and engendered perpetual strife between the different states. The clause was, therefore, of the last importance to the safety and security of the southern states; and could not have been surrendered by them without endangering their whole property in slaves. The clause was accordingly adopted into the Constitution by the unanimous consent of the framers of it; a proof at once of its intrinsic and practical necessity.

How, then, are we to interpret the language of the clause? The true answer is, in such a manner, as, consistently with the words, shall fully and completely effectuate the whole objects of it. If by one mode of interpretation the right must become shadowy and unsubstantial, and without any remedial power adequate to the end; and by another mode it will attain its just end and secure its manifest purpose; it would seem, upon principles of reasoning, absolutely irresistible, that the latter ought to prevail: No Court of justice can be authorized so to construe any clause of the Constitution as to defeat its obvious ends, when another construction, equally accordant with the words and sense thereof, will enforce and protect them.

The clause manifestly contemplates the existence of a positive, unqualified right on the part of the owner of the slave, which no state law or regulation can in any way qualify, regulate, control, or restrain. The slave is not to be discharged from service or labour, in consequence of any state law or regulation. Now, certainly, without indulging in any nicety of criticism upon words, it may fairly and reasonably be said, that any state law or state regulation, which interrupts, limits, delays, or postpones the right of the owner to the immediate possession of the slave, and the immediate command of his service and labour, operates, pro tanto, a discharge of the slave therefrom. The question can never be, how much the slave is discharged from; but whether he is discharged from any, by the natural or necessary operation of state laws or state regulations. The question is not one of quantity or degree, but of withholding, or controlling the incidents of a positive and absolute right.

We have said that the clause contains a positive and unqualified recognition of the right of the owner in the slave, unaffected by any state law or regulation whatsoever, because there is no qualification or restriction of it to be found therein; and we have no right to insert any which is not expressed, and cannot be fairly implied; especially are we estopped from so doing, when the clause puts the right to the service or labour upon the same ground and to the same extent in every other state as in the state from which the slave escaped, and in which he was held to the service or labour. If this be so, then all the incidents to that right attach also; the owner must, therefore, have the right to seize and repossess the slave, which the local laws of his own state confer upon him as property; and we all know that this right of seizure and recaption is universally acknowledged in all the slaveholding states. Indeed, this is no more than a mere affirmance of the principles of the common law applicable to this very subject. Mr. Justice Blackstone (3 Bl. Comm. 4) lays it down as unquestionable doctrine. "Recaption or reprisal (says he) is another species of remedy by the mere act of the party injured.

This happens when any one hath deprived another of his property in goods or chattels personal, or wrongfully detains one's wife, child, or servant; in which case the owner of the goods, and the husband, parent, or master may lawfully claim and retake them, wherever he happens to find them, so it be not in a riotous manner, or attended with a breach of the peace." Upon this ground we have not the slightest hesitation in holding, that, under and in virtue of the Constitution, the owner of a slave is clothed with entire authority, in every state in the Union, to seize and recapture his slave, whenever he can do it without any breach of the peace, or any illegal violence. In this sense, and to this extent this clause of the Constitution may properly be said to execute itself; and to require no aid from legislation, state or national.

But the clause of the Constitution does not stop here; nor indeed, consistently with its professed objects, could it do so. Many cases must arise in which, if the remedy of the owner were confined to the mere right of seizure and recaption, he would be utterly without any adequate redress. He may not be able to lay his hands upon the slave. He may not be able to enforce his rights against persons who either secrete or conceal, or withhold the slave. He may be restricted by local legislation as to the mode of proofs of his ownership; as to the Courts in which he shall sue, and as to the actions which he may bring; or the process he may use to compel the delivery of the slave. Nay, the local legislation may be utterly inadequate to furnish the appropriate redress, by authorizing no process in rem, or no specific mode of repossessing the slave, leaving the owner, at best, not that right which the Constitution designed to secure—a specific delivery and repossession of the slave, but a mere remedy in damages; and that perhaps against persons utterly insolvent or worthless. The state legislation may be entirely silent on the whole subject, and its ordinary remedial process framed with different views and objects; and this may be innocently as well as designedly done, since every state is perfectly competent, and has the exclusive right to prescribe the remedies in its own judicial tribunals, to limit the time as well as the mode of redress, and to deny jurisdiction over cases, which its own policy and its own institutions either prohibit or discountenance.

If, therefore, the clause of the Constitution had stopped at the mere recognition of the right, without providing or contemplating any means by which it might be established and enforced in cases where it did not execute itself, it is plain that it would have, in a great variety of cases, a delusive and empty annunciation. If it did not contemplate any action either through state or national legislation, as auxiliaries to its more perfect enforcement in the form of remedy, or of protection, then, as there would be no duty on either to aid the right, it would be left to the mere comity of the states to act as they should please; and would depend for its security upon the changing course of public opinion, the mutations of public policy, and the general adaptations of remedies for purposes strictly according to the lex fori.

And this leads us to the consideration of the other part of the clause, which implies at once a guaranty and duty. It says, "But he (the slave) shall be delivered up on claim of the party to whom such service or labour may be due." Now, we think it exceedingly difficult, if not impracticable, to read this language and not to feel that it contemplated some farther remedial redress than that which might be administered at the hands of the owner himself. A claim is to be made. What is a claim? It is, in a just juridical sense, a demand of some matter as of right made by one person upon another, to do or to forbear to do some act or thing as a matter of duty. A more limited, but at the same time an equally expressive definition was given by Lord Dyer as cited in Stowell v. Zouch, Plowden, 359; and it is equally applicable to the present case: that "a claim is a challenge by a man of the propriety or ownership of a thing, which he has not in possession, but which is wrongfully detained from him." The slave is to be delivered up on the claim. By whom to be delivered up? In what mode to be delivered up? How, if a refusal takes place, is the right of delivery to be enforced? Upon what proofs? What shall be the evidence of a rightful recaption or delivery? When and under what circumstances shall the possession of the owner, after it is obtained, be conclusive of his right, so as to preclude any further inquiry or examination into it by local tribunals or otherwise, while the slave, in possession of the owner, is in transitu to the state from which he fled?

These, and many other questions, will readily occur upon the slightest attention to the clause; and it is obvious that they can receive but one satisfactory answer. They require the aid of legislation to protect the right, to enforce the delivery, and to secure the subsequent possession of the slave. If, indeed, the Constitution guarantees the right, and if it requires the delivery upon the claim of the owner, (as cannot well be doubted,) the natural inference certainly is, that the national government is clothed with the appropriate authority and

functions to enforce it. The fundamental principle applicable to all cases of this sort, would seem to be, that where the end is required, the means are given; and where the duty is enjoined, the ability to perform it is contemplated to exist on the part of the functionaries to whom it is entrusted. The clause is found in the national Constitution, and not in that of any state. It does not point out any state functionaries, or any state action to carry its provisions into effect. The states cannot, therefore, be compelled to enforce them; and it might well be deemed an unconstitutional exercise of the power of interpretation, to insist that the states are bound to provide means to carry into effect the duties of the national government, nowhere delegated or intrusted to them by the Constitution. On the contrary, the natural, if not the necessary conclusion is, that the national government, in the absence of all positive provisions to the contrary, is bound, through its own proper departments, legislative, judicial, or executive, as the case may require, to carry into effect all the rights and duties imposed upon it by the Constitution. The remark of Mr. Madison, in the Federalist, (No. 43,) would seem in such cases to apply with peculiar force. "A right (says he) implies a remedy; and where else would the remedy be deposited, than where it is deposited by the Constitution?" meaning, as the context shows, in the government of the United States.

It is plain, then, that where a claim is made by the owner, out of possession, for the delivery of a slave, it must be made, if at all, against some other person; and inasmuch as the right is a right of property capable of being recognised and asserted by proceedings before a Court of justice, between parties adverse to each other, it constitutes, in the strictest sense, a controversy between the parties, and a case "arising under the Constitution" of the United States; within the express delegation of judicial power given by that instrument. Congress, then, may call that power into activity for the very purpose of giving effect to that right; and if so, then it may prescribe the mode and extent in which it shall be applied, and how, and under what circumstances the proceedings shall afford a complete protection and guaranty to the right.

Congress has taken this very view of the power and duty of the national government. As early as the year 1791, the attention of Congress was drawn to it, (as we shall hereafter more fully see,) in consequence of some practical difficulties arising under the other clause, respecting fugitives from justice escaping into other states. The result of their deliberations, was the passage of the act of the 12th of February, 1793, ch. 51, (7,) which, after having, in the first and second sections, provided for the case of fugitives from justice by a demand to be made of the delivery through the executive authority of the state where they are found. proceeds, in the third section, to provide, that when a person held to labour or service in any of the United States, shall escape into any other of the states or territories, the person to whom such labour or service may be due, his agent or attorney, is hereby empowered to seize or arrest such fugitive from labour, and take him or her before any judge of the Circuit or District Courts of the United States, residing or being within the state, or before any magistrate of a county, city, or town corporate, wherein such seizure or arrest shall be made; and upon proof to the satisfaction of such judge or magistrate, either by oral evidence or affidavit, &c., that the person so seized or arrested, doth, under the laws of the state or territory from which he or she fled, owe service or labour to the person claiming him or her, it shall be the duty of such judge or magistrate, to give a certificate thereof to such claimant, his agent or attorney, which shall be sufficient warrant for removing the said fugitive from labour, to the state or territory from which he or she fled. The fourth section provides a penalty against any person who shall knowingly and willingly obstruct or hinder such claimant, his agent, or attorney, in so seizing or arresting such fugitive from labour, or rescue such fugitive from the claimant, or his agent, or attorney when so arrested, or who shall harbour or conceal such fugitive after notice that he is such; and it also saves to the person claiming such labour or service, his right of action for or on account of such injuries.

In a general sense, this act may be truly said to cover the whole ground of the Constitution, both as to fugitives from justice, and fugitive slaves; that is, it covers both the subjects, in its enactments; not because it exhausts the remedies which may be applied by Congress to enforce the rights, if the provisions of the act shall in practice be found not to attain the object of the Constitution; but because it points out fully all the modes of attaining those objects, which Congress, in their discretion, have as yet deemed expedient or proper to meet the exigencies of the Constitution. If this be so, then it would seem, upon just principles of construction, that the legislation of Congress, if constitutional, must supersede all state legislation upon the same subject; and by necessary implication prohibit it. For if Congress

have a constitutional power to regulate a particular subject, and they do actually regulate it in a given manner, and in a certain form, it cannot be that the state legislatures have a right to interfere; and, as it were, by way of complement to the legislation of Congress, to prescribe additional regulations, and what they may deem auxiliary provisions for the same purpose. In such a case, the legislation of Congress, in what it does prescribe, manifestly indicates that it does not intend that there shall be any farther legislation to act upon the subject-matter. Its silence as to what it does not do, is as expressive of what its intention is as the direct provisions made by it. This doctrine was fully recognised by this Court, in the case of Houston v. Moore, 5 Wheat. Rep. 1, 21, 22; where it was expressly held, that where Congress have exercised a power over a particular subject given them by the Constitution, it is not competent for state legislation to add to the provisions of Congress upon that subject; for that the will of Congress upon the whole subject is as clearly established by what it had not declared, as by what it has expressed.

But it has been argued, that the act of Congress is unconstitutional, because it does not fall within the scope of any of the enumerated powers of legislation confided to that body; and therefore it is void. Stripped of its artificial and technical structure, the argument comes to this, that although rights are exclusively secured by, or duties are exclusively imposed upon the national government, yet, unless the power to enforce these rights, or to execute these duties can be found among the express powers of legislation enumerated in the Constitution, they remain without any means of giving them effect by any act of Congress; and they must operate solely proprio vigore, however defective may be their operation; nay, even although, in a practical sense, they may become a nullity from the want of a proper remedy to enforce them, or to provide against their violation. If this be the true interpretation of the Constitution, it must, in a great measure, fail to attain many of its avowed and positive objects as a security of rights, and a recognition of duties. Such a limited construction of the Constitution has never yet been adopted as correct, either in theory or practice. No one has ever supposed that Congress could, constitutionally, by its legislation, exercise powers, or enact laws beyond the powers delegated to it by the Constitution; but it has, on various occasions, exercised powers which were necessary and proper as means to carry into effect rights expressly given, and duties expressly enjoined thereby. The end being required, it has been deemed a just and necessary implication, that the means to accomplish it are given also; or, in other words, that the power flows as a necessary means to accomplish the end.

...

We hold the act to be clearly constitutional in all its leading provisions, and, indeed, with the exception of that part which confers authority upon state magistrates, to be free from reasonable doubt and difficulty upon the grounds already stated. As to the authority so conferred upon state magistrates, while a difference of opinion has existed, and may exist still on the point, in different states, whether state magistrates are bound to act under it; none is entertained by this Court that state magistrates may, if they choose, exercise that authority, unless prohibited by state legislation.

The remaining question is, whether the power of legislation upon this subject is exclusive in the national government, or concurrent in the states, until it is exercised by Congress. In our opinion it is exclusive; and we shall now proceed briefly to state our reasons for that opinion. The doctrine stated by this Court, in Sturgis v. Crowninshield, 4 Wheat. Rep. 122, 193, contains the true, although not the sole rule or consideration, which is applicable to this particular subject. "Wherever," said Mr. Chief Justice Marshall, in delivering the opinion of the Court, "the terms in which a power is granted to Congress, or the nature of the power require that it should be exercised exclusively by Congress, the subject is as completely taken from the state legislatures, as if they had been forbidden to act." The nature of the power, and the true objects to be attained by it, are then as important to be weighed, in considering the question of its exclusiveness, as the words in which it is granted.

In the first place, it is material to state, (what has been already incidentally hinted at,) that the right to seize and retake fugitive slaves, and the duty to deliver them up, in whatever state of the Union they may be found, and of course the corresponding power in Congress to use the appropriate means to enforce the right and duty, derive their whole validity and obligation exclusively from the Constitution of the United States; and are there, for the first time, recognised and established in that peculiar character. Before the adoption of the Constitution, no state had any power whatsoever over the subject, except within its own territorial limits, and could not bind the sovereignty or the legislation of other states. Whenever the right was acknowledged or the duty enforced in any state, it was as a matter of comity and favour, and not as a matter of strict moral, political, or international obligation or duty. Under the Constitution it is recognised as an absolute, positive, right and duty, pervading the whole Union with an equal and supreme force, uncontrolled and uncontrollable by state sovereignty or state legislation. It is, therefore, in a just sense a new and positive right, independent of comity, confined to no territorial limits, and bounded by no state institutions or policy. The natural inference deducible from this consideration certainly is, in the absence of any positive delegation of power to the state legislatures, that it belongs to the legislative department of the national government, to which it owes its origin and establishment. It would be a strange anomaly, and forced construction, to suppose that the national government meant to rely for the due fulfilment of its own proper duties and the rights which it intended to secure, upon state legislation; and not upon that of the Union. A fortiori, it would be more objectionable to suppose that a power, which was to be the same throughout the Union, should be confided to state sovereignty, which could not rightfully act beyond its own territorial limits.

In the next place, the nature of the provision and the objects to be attained by it, require that it should be controlled by one and the same will, and act uniformly by the same system of regulations throughout the Union. If, then, the states have a right, in the absence of legislation by Congress, to act upon the subject, each state is at liberty to prescribe just such regulations as suit its own policy, local convenience, and local feelings. The legislation of one state may not only be different from, but utterly repugnant to and incompatible with that of another. The time, and mode, and limitation of the remedy; the proofs of the title, and all other incidents applicable thereto, may be prescribed in one state, which are rejected or disclaimed in another. One state may require the owner to sue in one mode, another in a different mode. One state may make a statute of limitations as to the remedy, in its own tribunals, short and summary; another may prolong the period, and yet restrict the proofs; nay, some states may utterly refuse to act upon the subject at all; and others may refuse to open its Courts to any remedies in rem, because they would interfere with their own domestic policy, institutions, or habits. The right, therefore, would never, in a practical sense be the same in all the states. It would have no unity of purpose, or uniformity of operation. The duty might be enforced in some states; retarded, or limited in others; and denied, as compulsory in many, if not in all. Consequences like these must have been foreseen as very likely to occur in the non-slaveholding states; where legislation, if not silent on the subject, and purely voluntary, could scarcely be presumed to be favourable to the exercise of the rights of the owner.

It is scarcely conceivable that the slaveholding states would have been satisfied with leaving to the legislation of the non-slaveholding states, a power of regulation, in the absence of that of Congress, which would or might practically amount to a power to destroy the rights of the owner. If the argument, therefore, of a concurrent power in the states to act upon the subject-matter in the absence of legislation by Congress, be well founded; then, if Congress had never acted at all; or if the act of Congress should be repealed without providing a substitute, there would be a resulting authority in each of the states to regulate the whole subject at its pleasure; and to dole out its own remedial justice, or withhold it at its pleasure and according to its own views of policy and expediency. Surely such a state of things never could have been intended, under such a solemn guarantee of right and duty. On the other hand, construe the right of legislation as exclusive in Congress, and every evil, and every danger vanishes. The right and the duty are then co-extensive and uniform in remedy and operation throughout the whole Union. The owner has the same security, and the same remedial justice, and the same exemption from state regulation and control, through however many states he may pass with his fugitive slave in his possession, in transitu, to his own domicile. But, upon the other supposition, the moment he passes the state line, he becomes amenable to the laws of another sovereignty, whose regulations may greatly embarrass or delay the exercise of his rights; and even be repugnant to those of the state where he first arrested the fugitive. Consequences like these show that the nature and objects of the provision imperiously require, that, to make it effectual, it should be construed to be exclusive of state authority. We adopt the language of this Court in Sturgis v. Crowninshield, 4 Wheat. Rep. 193, and say, that "it has never been supposed that the concurrent power of legislation extended to every possible case in which its exercise by the states has not been expressly prohibited. The confusion of such a practice would be endless." And we know no case in which the confusion and public inconvenience and mischiefs thereof, could be more completely exemplified than the present.

These are some of the reasons, but by no means all, upon which we hold the power of legislation on this subject to be exclusive in Congress. To guard, however, against any possible misconstruction of our views, it is proper to state, that we are by no means to be understood in any manner whatsoever to doubt or to interfere with the police power belonging to the states in virtue of their general sovereignty. That police power extends over all subjects within the territorial limits of the states; and has never been conceded to the United States. It is wholly distinguishable from the right and duty secured by the provision now under consideration; which is exclusively derived from and secured by the Constitution of the United States, and owes its whole efficacy thereto. We entertain no doubt whatsoever, that the states, in virtue of their general police power, possess full jurisdiction to arrest and restrain runaway slaves, and remove them from their borders, and otherwise to secure themselves against their depredations and evil example, as they certainly may do in cases of idlers, vagabonds, and paupers. The rights of the owners of fugitive slaves are in no just sense interfered with, or regulated by such a course; and in many cases, the operations of this police power, although designed essentially for other purposes, for the protection, safety, and peace of the state, may essentially promote and aid the interests of the owners. But such regulations can never be permitted to interfere with or to obstruct the just rights of the owner to reclaim his slave, derived from the Constitution of the United States; or with the remedies prescribed by Congress to aid and enforce the same.

Upon these grounds, we are of opinion that the act of Pennsylvania upon which this indictment is founded, is unconstitutional and void. It purports to punish as a public offence against that state, the very act of seizing and removing a slave by his master, which the Constitution of the United States was designed to justify and uphold. The special verdict finds this fact, and the State Courts have rendered judgment against the plaintiff in error upon that verdict. That judgment must, therefore, be reversed, and the cause remanded to the Supreme Court of Pennsylvania; with directions to carry into effect the judgment of this Court rendered upon the special verdict in favour of the plaintiff in error.

Mr. Chief Justice TANEY.

I concur in the opinion pronounced by the Court, that the law of Pennsylvania, under which the plaintiff in error was indicted, is unconstitutional and void; and that the judgment against him must be reversed. But as the questions before us arise upon the construction of the Constitution of the United States, and as I do not assent to all the principles contained in the opinion just delivered, it is proper to state the points on which I differ.

I agree entirely in all that is said in relation to the right of the master, by virtue of the third clause of the second section of the fourth article of the Constitution of the United States, to arrest his fugitive slave in any state wherein he may find him. He has a right, peaceably, to take possession of him and carry him away without any certificate or warrant from a judge of the District or Circuit Court of the United States, or from any magistrate of the state; and whoever resists or obstructs him, is a wrongdoer: and every state law which proposes directly or indirectly to authorize such resistance or obstruction is null and void, and affords no justification to the individual or the officer of the state who acts under it. This right of the master being given by the Constitution of the United States, neither Congress nor a state legislature can by any law or regulation impair it, or restrict it.

I concur also in all that is contained in the opinion concerning the power of Congress to protect the citizens of the slaveholding states, in the enjoyment of this right; and to provide by law an effectual remedy to enforce it, and to inflict penalties upon those who shall violate its provisions; and no state is authorized to pass any law, that comes in conflict in any respect with the remedy provided by Congress.

The act of February 12th, 1793, is a constitutional exercise of this power; and every state law which requires the master, against his consent, to go before any state tribunal or officer, before he can take possession of his property; or which authorizes a state officer to interfere with him, when he is peaceably removing it from the state, is unconstitutional and void.

But, as I understand the opinion of the Court, it goes further, and decides that the power to provide a remedy for this right is vested exclusively in Congress; and that all laws upon the subject passed by a state, since the adoption of the Constitution of the United States, are null and void; even although they were intended, in good faith, to protect the owner in the exercise of his rights of property, and do not conflict in any degree with the act of Congress.

I do not consider this question as necessarily involved in the case before us; for the law of Pennsylvania, under which the plaintiff in error was prosecuted, is clearly in conflict with the Constitution of the United States, as well as with the law of 1793. But as the ques-

tion is discussed in the opinion of the Court, and as I do not assent either to the doctrine or the reasoning by which it is maintained, I proceed to state very briefly my objections.

The opinion of the Court maintains that the power over this subject is so exclusively vested in Congress, that no state, since the adoption of the Constitution, can pass any law in relation to it. In other words, according to the opinion just delivered, the state authorities are prohibited from interfering for the purpose of protecting the right of the master and aiding him in the recovery of his property. I think the states are not prohibited; and that, on the contrary, it is enjoined upon them as a duty to protect and support the owner when he is endeavouring to obtain possession of his property found within their respective territories.

The language used in the Constitution does not, in my judgment, justify the construction given to it by the Court. It contains no words prohibiting the several states from passing laws to enforce this right. They are in express terms forbidden to make any regulation that shall impair it. But there the prohibition stops. And according to the settled rules of construction for all written instruments, the prohibition being confined to laws injurious to the right, the power to pass laws to support and enforce it, is necessarily implied. And the words of the article which direct that the fugitive "shall be delivered up," seem evidently designed to impose it as a duty upon the people of the several states to pass laws to carry into execution, in good faith, the compact into which they thus solemnly entered with each other. The Constitution of the United States, and every article and clause in it, is a part of the law of every state in the Union; and is the paramount law. The right of the master, therefore, to seize his fugitive slave, is the law of each state; and no state has the power to abrogate or alter it. And why may not a state protect a right of property, acknowledged by its own paramount law? Besides, the laws of the different states, in all other cases, constantly protect the citizens of other states in their rights of property, when it is found within their respective territories; and no one doubts their power to do so. And in the absence of any express prohibition, I perceive no reason for establishing, by implication, a different rule in this instance; where, by the national compact, this right of property is recognised as an existing right in every state of the Union.

I do not speak of slaves whom their masters voluntarily take into a non-slaveholding state. That case is not before us. I speak of the case provided for in the Constitution; that is to say, the case of a fugitive who has escaped from the service of his owner, and who has taken refuge and is found in another state.

23

Liberty Party Platform

August 30, 1843[*]

RESOLVED, That human brotherhood is a cardinal principle of true democracy, as well as of pure Christianity, which spurns all inconsistent limitations; and neither the political party which repudiates it, nor the political system which is not based upon it, can be truly democratic or permanent.

RESOLVED, That the Liberty party, placing itself upon this broad principle, will demand the absolute and unqualified divorce of the general government from slavery, and also the restoration of equality of rights among men in every state where the party exists, or may exist.

RESOLVED, That the Liberty party has not been organized for any temporary purpose by interested politicians, but has arisen from among the people in consequence of a conviction, hourly gaining ground, that no other party in the country represents the true principles of American liberty, or the true spirit of the constitution of the United States.

RESOLVED, That the Liberty party has not been organized merely for the overthrow of slavery; its first decided effort must, indeed, be directed against slaveholding as the grossest and most revolting manifestation of despotism, but it will also carry out the principle of equal rights into all its practical consequences and applications, and support every just measure conducive to individual and social freedom.

RESOLVED, That the Liberty party is not a sectional party but a national party; was not originated in a desire to accomplish a single object, but in a comprehensive regard to the great interests of the whole country; is not a new party, nor a third party, but is the party of 1776, reviving the principles of that memorable era, and striving to carry them into practical application.

[*] Reinhard O. Johnson, *The Liberty Party, 1840–1848: Antislavery Third Party Politics in the United States* (Baton Rouge: Louisiana State University Press, 2009), 317.

RESOLVED, That it was understood in the times of the declaration and the constitution, that the existence of slavery in some of the states was in derogation of the principles of American liberty, and a deep stain upon the character of the country, and the implied faith of the states and the nation was pledged that slavery should never be extended beyond its then existing limits, but should be gradually, and yet, at no distant day, wholly abolished by state authority.

RESOLVED, That the faith of the states and the nation thus pledged, was most nobly redeemed by the voluntary abolition of slavery in several of the states, and by the adoption of the ordinance of 1787, for the government of the territory northwest of the river Ohio, then the only territory in the United States, and consequently the only territory subject in this respect to the control of Congress, by which ordinance slavery was forever excluded from the vast regions which now compose the states of Ohio, Indiana, Illinois, Michigan, and the territory of Wisconsin, and an incapacity to bear up any other than freemen was impressed on the soil itself.

RESOLVED, That the faith of the states and the nation thus pledged, has been shamefully violated by the omission, on the part of many of the states, to take any measures whatever for the abolition of slavery within their respective limits; by the continuance of slavery in the District of Columbia, and in the territories of Louisiana and Florida; by the legislation of Congress; by the protection afforded by national legislation and negotiation of slaveholding in American vessels, on the high seas, employed in the coastwise Slave Traffic; and by the extension of slavery far beyond its original limits, by acts of Congress admitting new slave states into the Union.

RESOLVED, That the fundamental truths of the Declaration of Independence, that all men are endowed by their Creator with certain inalienable rights, among which are life, liberty, and the pursuit of happiness, was made the fundamental law of our national government, by that amendment of the constitution which declares that no person shall be deprived of life, liberty, or property, without due process of law.

RESOLVED, That we recognize as sound the doctrine maintained by slaveholding jurists, that slavery is against natural rights, and strictly local, and that its existence and continuance rests on no other support than state legislation, and not on any authority of Congress.

RESOLVED, That the general government has, under the constitution, no power to establish or continue slavery anywhere, and therefore that all treaties and acts of Congress establishing, continuing or favoring slavery in the District of Columbia, in the territory of Florida, or on the high seas, are unconstitutional, and all attempts to hold men as property within the limits of exclusive national jurisdiction ought to be prohibited by law.

RESOLVED, That the provisions of the constitution of the United States which confer extraordinary political powers on the owners of slaves, and thereby constituting the two hundred and fifty thousand slaveholders in the slave states a privileged aristocracy; and the provision for the reclamation of fugitive slaves from service, are anti-republican in their character, dangerous to the liberties of the people, and ought to be abrogated.

RESOLVED, That the practical operation of the second of these provisions is seen in the enactment of the act of Congress respecting persons escaping from their masters, which act, if the construction given to it by the Supreme Court of the United States in the case of Prigg v. Pennsylvania be correct, nullifies the habeas corpus acts of all the states, takes away the whole legal security of personal freedom, and ought, therefore, to be immediately repealed.

RESOLVED, That the peculiar patronage and support hitherto extended to slavery and slaveholding, by the general government, ought to be immediately withdrawn, and the example and influence of national authority ought to be arrayed on the side of liberty and free labor.

RESOLVED, That the practice of the general government, which prevails in the slave states, of employing slaves upon the public works, instead of free laborers, and paying aristocratic masters, with a view to secure or reward political services, is utterly indefensible and ought to be abandoned.

RESOLVED, That freedom of speech and of the press, and the right of petition, and the right of trial by jury, are sacred and inviolable; and that all rules, regulations and laws, in derogation of either, are oppressive, unconstitutional, and not to be endured by a free people.

RESOLVED, That we regard voting, in an eminent degree, as a moral and religious duty, which, when exercised, should be by voting for those who will do all in their power for immediate emancipation.

RESOLVED, That this convention recommend to the friends of liberty in all those free states where any inequality of rights and privileges exists on account of color, to employ their utmost energies to remove all such remnants and effects of the slave system.

RESOLVED, The constitution of these United States is a series of agreements, covenants or contracts between the people of the United States, each with all, and all with each; and,

WHEREAS, It is a principle of universal morality, that the moral laws of the Creator are paramount to all human laws; or, in the language of an Apostle, that "we ought to obey God rather than men;" and

WHEREAS, The principle of common law—that any contract, covenant, or agreement, to do an act derogatory to natural right, is vitiated and annulled by its inherent immorality—has been recognized by one of the justices of the Supreme Court of the United States, who in a recent case expressly holds that "any contract that rests upon such a basis is void;" and

WHEREAS, The third clause of the second section of the fourth article of the constitution of the United States, when construed as providing for the surrender of a fugitive slave, does "rest upon such a basis," in that it is a contract to rob a man of a natural right—namely, his natural right to his own liberty—and is therefore absolutely void. Therefore,

RESOLVED, That we hereby give it to be distinctly understood by this nation and the world, that, as abolitionists, considering that the strength of our cause lies in its righteousness, and our hope for it in our conformity to the laws of God, and our respect for the rights of man, we owe it to the Sovereign Ruler of the Universe, as a proof of our allegiance to Him, in all our civil relations and offices, whether as private citizens, or public functionaries sworn to support the constitution of the United States, to regard and to treat the third clause of the fourth article of that instrument, whenever applied to the case of a fugitive slave, as utterly null and void, and consequently as forming no part of the constitution of the United States, whenever we are called upon or sworn to support it.

RESOLVED, That the power given to Congress by the constitution, to provide for calling out the militia to suppress insurrection, does not make it the duty of the government to maintain slavery by military force, much less does it make it the duty of the citizens to form a part of such military force; when freemen unsheathe the sword it should be to strike for liberty, not for despotism.

RESOLVED, That to preserve the peace of the citizens, and secure the blessings of freedom, the legislature of each of the free states ought to keep in force suitable statutes rendering it penal for any of its inhabitants to transport, or aid in transporting from such state, any person sought to be thus transported, merely because subject to the slave laws of any other state; this remnant of independence being accorded to the free states by the decision of the Supreme Court in the case of Prigg v. the state of Pennsylvania.

24

Wendell Phillips, *The Constitution: A Pro-slavery Compact*

1844*

INTRODUCTION.

Every one knows that the "Madison Papers" contain a Report, from the pen of James Madison, of the Debates in the Old Congress of the Confederation, and in the Convention which formed the Constitution of the United States. We have extracted from them, in these pages, all the Debates on those clauses of the Constitution which relate to slavery. To these we have added all that is found, on the same topic, in the Debates of the several State Conventions which ratified the Constitution: together with so much of the speech of Luther Martin before the Legislature of Maryland, and of the Federalist, as relate to our subject; with some extracts, also, from the Debates of the first Federal Congress on slavery. These are all printed without alteration, except that, in some instances, we have inserted in brackets, after the name of a speaker, the name of the State from which he came. The notes and italics are those of the original, but the editor has added one note on page 30th, which is marked as his, and we have taken the liberty of printing in capitals one sentiment of Rufus King's, and two of James Madison's—a distinction which the importance of the statements seemed to demand—otherwise we have reprinted exactly from the originals.

These extracts develop most clearly all the details of that "compromise," which was made between freedom and slavery, in 1787; granting to the slaveholder distinct privileges and protection for his slave property, in return for certain commercial concessions on his part

*Wendell Phillips, *The Constitution: A Pro-slavery Compact; or, Selections from the Madison Papers*, 1st ed. (New York: American Anti-Slavery Society, 1844), 3.

toward the North. They prove also that the Nation at large were fully aware of this bargain at the time, and entered into it willingly and with open eyes.

. . .

The clauses of the Constitution to which we refer as of a pro-slavery character are the following:—

Art. 1, Sect. 2. Representatives and direct taxes shall be apportioned among the several States, which may be included within this Union, according to their respective numbers, which shall be determined by adding to the whole number of free persons, including those bound to service for a term of years, and excluding Indians not taxed, three fifths of all other persons.

Art. 1, Sect. 8. Congress shall have power . . . to suppress insurrections.

Art. 1, Sect. 9. The migration or importation of such persons as any of the States now existing shall think proper to admit, shall not be prohibited by the Congress prior to the year one thousand eight hundred and eight: but a tax or duty may be imposed on such importation, not exceeding ten dollars for each person.

Art. 4, Sect. 2. No person, held to service or labor in one State, under the laws thereof, escaping into another, shall, in consequence of any law or regulation therein, be discharged from such service or labor; but shall be delivered up on claim of the party to whom such service or labor may be due.

Art. 4, Sect. 4. The United States shall guarantee to every State in this Union a republican form of government; and shall protect each of them against invasion; and, on application of the legislature, or of the executive, (when the legislature cannot be convened,) against domestic violence.

The first of these clauses, relating to representation, confers on a slaveholding community additional political power for every slave held among them, and thus tempts them to continue to uphold the system: the second and the last, relating to insurrection and domestic violence, perfectly innocent in themselves, yet being made with the fact directly in view that slavery exists among us, do deliberately pledge the whole national force against the unhappy slave if he imitate our fathers and resist oppression—thus making us partners in the guilt of sustaining slavery: the third, relating to the slave trade, disgraces the nation by a pledge not to abolish that traffic till after twenty years, without obliging Congress to do so even then, and thus the slave trade may be legalized to-morrow if Congress choose: the fourth is a promise on the part of the whole nation to return fugitive slaves to their masters, a deed which God's law expressly condemns, and which every noble feeling of our nature repudiates with loathing and contempt.

These are the articles of the "Compromise," so much talked of between the North and South.

We do not produce the extracts which make up these pages to show what is the meaning of the clauses above cited. For no man or party, of any authority in such matters, has ever pretended to doubt to what subject they all relate. If indeed they were ambiguous in their terms, a resort to the history of those times would set the matter at rest forever. A few persons, to be sure, of late years, to serve the purposes of a party, have tried to prove that the Constitution makes no compromise with slavery. Notwithstanding the clear light of history;—the unanimous decision of all the courts in the land, both State and Federal;—the action of Congress and the State Legislature;—the constant practice of the Executive in all its branches;—and the deliberate acquiescence of the whole people for half a century, still they contend that the nation does not know its own meaning, and that the Constitution does not tolerate slavery! Every candid mind, however, must acknowledge that the language of the Constitution is clear and explicit.

Its terms are so broad, it is said, that they include many others besides slaves, and hence it is wisely (!) inferred that they cannot include the slaves themselves! Many persons besides slaves in this country doubtless are "held to service and labor under the laws of the States," but that does not at all show that slaves are not "held to service;" many persons beside the slaves may take part "in insurrections," but that does not prove that when the slaves rise, the National Government is not bound to put them down by force. Such a thing has been heard of before as one description including a great variety of persons,—and this is the case in the present instance.

But granting that the terms of the Constitution are ambiguous—that they are susceptible of two meanings—if the unanimous, concurrent, unbroken practice of every department of the Government, judicial, legislative, and executive, and the acquiescence of the whole people for fifty years, do not prove which is the true construction, then how and where can such a question ever be settled? If the people and the courts of the land do not know what they themselves mean, who has authority to settle their meaning for them?

If, then, the people and the courts of a country are to be allowed to determine what their own laws mean, it follows that at this time, and for the last half century, the Constitution of the United States has been, and still is, a pro-slavery instrument, and that any one who swears to support it, swears to do pro-slavery acts, and violates his duty both as a man and an abolitionist. What the Constitution may become a century hence, we know not; we speak of it as it is, and repudiate it as it is.

But the purpose, for which we have thrown these pages before the community, is this. Some men, finding the nation unanimously deciding that the Constitution tolerates slavery, have tried to prove that this false construction, as they think it, has been foisted into the instrument by the corrupting influence of slavery itself, tainting all it touches. They assert that the known antislavery spirit of revolutionary times never could have consented to so infamous a bargain as the Constitution is represented to be, and has in its present hands become. Now these pages prove the melancholy fact, that willingly, with deliberate purpose, our fathers bartered honesty for gain, and became partners with tyrants, that they might share in the profits of their tyranny.

And in view of this fact, will it not require a very strong argument to make any candid man believe, that the bargain which the fathers tell us they meant to incorporate into the Constitution, and which the sons have always thought they found there incorporated, does not exist there, after all? Forty of the shrewdest men and lawyers in the land assemble to make a bargain, among other things, about slaves. After months of anxious deliberation, they put it into writing, and sign their names to the instrument. Fifty years roll away,—twenty millions, at least, of their children pass over the stage of life,—courts sit and pass judgment,—parties arise and struggle fiercely; still, all concur in finding in the instrument just that meaning which the fathers tell us they intended to express:—must not he be a desperate man, who, after all this, sets out to prove that the fathers were bunglers and the sons fools, and that slavery is not referred to at all?

Besides, the advocates of this new theory of the Antislavery character of the Constitution quote some portions of the Madison Papers in support of their views,—and this makes it proper that the community should hear *all* that these Debates have to say on the subject. The further we explore them, the clearer becomes the fact, that the Constitution was meant to be, what it has always been esteemed, a compromise between slavery and freedom.

If, then, the Constitution be, what these Debates

show that our fathers intended to make it, and what, too, their descendants, this nation, say they did make it and agree to uphold,—then we affirm that it is "a covenant with death and an agreement with hell," and ought to be immediately annulled. No abolitionist can consistently take office under it, or swear to support it.

But if, on the contrary, our fathers failed in their purpose, and the Constitution is all pure and untouched by slavery,—then, Union itself is impossible, without guilt. For it is undeniable that the fifty years passed under this (anti-slavery) Constitution show us the slaves trebling in numbers;—slaveholders monopolizing the offices and dictating the policy of the Government;—prostituting the strength and influence of the nation to the support of slavery here and elsewhere;—trampling on the rights of the free States, and making the courts of the country their tools. To continue this disastrous alliance longer is madness. The trial of fifty years with the best of men and the best of Constitutions, on this supposition, only proves that it is impossible for free and slave States to unite on any terms, without all becoming partners in the guilt, and responsible for the sin of slavery. We dare not prolong the experiment, and with double earnestness we repeat our demand upon every honest man to join in the outcry of the American Anti-Slavery Society,

NO UNION WITH SLAVEHOLDERS.

25

South Carolina, Resolutions Relating to the Exclusion of Samuel Hoar, *Charleston Courier*

December 7, 1844, p. 2

STATE OF SOUTH CAROLINA.
In the House of Representatives,
The Committee on Federal Relations, to whom was referred the communication of his Excellency the Governor, transmitting a letter addressed to him by Samuel Hoar, an agent of the State of Massachusetts for certain purposes, submit the following Report:

By an Act passed on the 19th day of December, 1835, the General Assembly endeavored to guard against the introduction of free negroes and persons of color into this State, upon principles of public policy affecting her

safety and her most vital interests. The right of excluding from her territory conspirators against the public peace, and disaffected persons whose presence may be dangerous to her safety, is essential to every government. It is every where exercised by Independent States, and there is nothing in the Constitution of the United States which forbids to South Carolina the right, or relieves from this Legislature the duty of providing for the public safety.

Massachusetts has seen fit to contest this right, and has sent an agent to reside in the midst of us, whose avowed object is to defeat a police regulation essential to our peace. This agent comes here, not as a citizen of the United States, but as the emissary of a Foreign Government, hostile to our domestic institutions, and with the sole purpose of subverting our internal police. We should be insensible to every dictate of prudence, if we consented to the residence of such a missionary, or shut our eyes to the consequences of this interference with our domestic concerns.

The Union of these States was formed for the purpose, among other things, of ensuring domestic tranquility and providing for the common defense; and in consideration thereof, this State yielded the right to keep troops, or ships of war, in time of peace, without the consent of Congress; but while thus consenting to be disarmed, she has in no part of the constitutional compact, surrendered her right of internal government and police, and on the contrary thereof has expressly reserved all powers not delegated to the United States, nor prohibited by it to the States.

The State of Massachusetts denominates as citizens those persons for whose protection her tender solicitude has devised this extraordinary mission. Yet if it were admitted that they are not citizens of that State, your Committee cannot suppose that she will challenge for them greater rights, immunities and privileges, within our territories, than are enjoyed by persons of the same class in South-Carolina. But your Committee deny that they are citizens within the meaning of the Constitution; nor did Massachusetts herself, treat as citizens persons of this class residing within her limits, either at the adoption of the Constitution, or since; but, on the contrary, they have been subjected to various disabilities from which her other inhabitants are exempt.

Your Committee cannot but regard this extraordinary movement as part of a deliberate and concerted scheme to subvert the domestic institutions of the Southern States, in plain violation of the terms of the

National compact, and of the good faith which ought to subsist between the parties thereto, and to which they stand solemnly pledged.

Your Committee recommend the adoption of the following Resolutions:

Resolved 1st, That the right to exclude from their Territories, seditious persons, or others, whose presence may be dangerous to their peace, is essential to every Independent State.

Resolved 2d, That free negroes and persons of color are not citizens of the United States, within the meaning of the Constitution, which confers upon the citizens of one State, the privileges and immunities of the citizens of the several States.

Resolved 3d, That the emissary sent by the State of Massachusetts, to the State of South-Carolina, with the avowed purpose of interfering with her institutions and disturbing her peace, is to be regarded, in the character he has assumed and to be treated accordingly.

Resolved 4th, That His Excellency the Governor, be requested to expel from our Territory the said agent, after due notice to depart, and that the Legislature will sustain the Executive authority in any measure it may adopt for the purpose aforesaid.

The foregoing Report and Resolutions were this day agreed to by the House of Representatives, and were concurred in by the Senate.

W. E. MARTIN,
Clerk of the Senate.

26

Lysander Spooner,

The Unconstitutionality of Slavery

1845[*]

CHAPTER II.

Written Constitutions.

Taking it for granted that it has now been shown that no rule of civil conduct, that is inconsistent with the natural rights of men, can be rightfully established by government, or consequently be made obligatory as law, either upon the people, or upon judicial tribunals—let

[*] Lysander Spooner, *The Unconstitutionality of Slavery* (Boston: Bela Marsh, 1845), 18–23, 42–45, 65–67, 135–37.

us now proceed to test the legality of slavery by those written constitutions of government, which judicial tribunals actually recognize as authoritative.

In making this examination, however, I shall not insist upon the principle of the preceding chapter, that there can be no law contrary to natural right; but shall admit, for the sake of the argument, that there may be such laws. I shall only claim that in the interpretation of all statutes and constitutions, the ordinary legal rules of interpretation be observed. The most important of these rules, and the one to which it will be necessary constantly to refer, is the one that all language must be construed "strictly" in favor of natural right. The rule is laid down by the Supreme Court of the United States in these words, to wit:

"Where rights are infringed, where fundamental principles are overthrown, where the general system of the laws is departed from, the legislative intention must be expressed with irresistible clearness, to induce a court of justice to suppose a design to effect such objects."

It will probably appear from this examination of the written constitutions, that slavery neither has, nor ever had any constitutional existence in this country; that it has always been a mere abuse, sustained, in the first instance, merely by the common consent of the strongest party, without any law on the subject, and, in the second place, by a few unconstitutional enactments, made in defiance of the plainest provisions of their fundamental law.

. . .

CHAPTER V.

The Declaration of Independence.

Admitting, for the sake of the argument, that prior to the revolution, slavery had a constitutional existence, (so far as it is possible that crime can have such an existence,) was it not abolished by the declaration of independence?

The declaration was certainly the constitutional law of this country for certain purposes. For example, it absolved the people from their allegiance to the English crown. It would have been so declared by the judicial tribunals of this country, if an American, during the revolutionary war, or since, had been tried for treason to the crown. If, then, the declaration were the constitutional law of the country for that purpose, was it not also constitutional law for the purpose of recognizing and establishing, as law, the natural and inalienable right of individuals to life, liberty, and the pursuit of happiness? The lawfulness of the act of absolving themselves from their allegiance to the crown, was avowed by the people of the country—and that too in the same instrument that declared the absolution—to rest entirely upon, and to be only a consequence of the natural right of all men to life, liberty, and the pursuit of happiness. If, then, the act of absolution was lawful, does it not necessarily follow that the principles that legalized the act, were also law? And if the country ratified the act of absolution, did they not also necessarily ratify and acknowledge the principles which they declared legalized the act?

It is sufficient for our purpose, if it be admitted that this principle was the law of the country at that particular time, (1776)—even though it had continued to be the law for only a year, or even a day. For if it were the law of the country even for a day, it freed every slave in the country—(if there were, as we say there were not, any legal slaves then in the country.) And the burden would then be upon the slaveholder to show that slavery had since been constitutionally established. And to show this, he must show an express constitutional designation of the particular individuals, who have since been made slaves. Without such particular designation of the individuals to be made slaves, (and not even the present constitutions of the slave States make any such designation,) all constitutional provisions, purporting to authorize slavery, are indefinite, and uncertain in their application, and for that reason void.

But again. The people of this country—in the very instrument by which they first announced their independent political existence, and first asserted their right to establish governments of their own—declared that the natural and inalienable right of all men to life, liberty, and the pursuit of happiness, was a "self-evident truth."

Now, all "self-evident truths," except such as may be explicitly, or by necessary implication, denied, (and no government has a right to deny any of them,) enter into, are taken for granted by, and constitute an essential part of all constitutions, compacts, and systems of government whatsoever. Otherwise it would be impossible for any systematic government to be established; for it must obviously be impossible to make an actual enumeration of all the "self-evident truths," that are to be taken into account in the administration of such a government. This is more especially true of governments founded, like ours, upon contract. It is clearly impossible, in a contract of government, to enumerate all the "self-evident truths" which must be acted upon in the administration of law. And therefore they are all taken for granted unless particular ones be plainly denied.

This principle, that all "self-evident truths," though not enumerated, make a part of all laws and contracts, unless clearly denied, is not only indispensable to the very existence of civil society, but it is even indispensable to the administration of justice in every individual case or suit, that may arise, out of contract or otherwise, between individuals. It would be impossible for individuals to make contracts at all, if it were necessary for them to enumerate all the "self-evident truths," that might have a bearing upon their construction before a judicial tribunal. All such truths are therefore taken for granted.

And it is the same in all compacts of government, unless particular truths are plainly denied. And governments, no more than individuals, have a right to deny them in any case. To deny, in any case, that "self-evident truths" are a part of the law, is equivalent to asserting that "self-evident falsehood" is law.

If, then, it be a "self-evident truth," that all men have a natural and inalienable right to life, liberty, and the pursuit of happiness, that truth constitutes a part of all our laws and all our constitutions, unless it have been unequivocally and authoritatively denied.

It will hereafter be shown that this "self-evident truth" has never been denied by the people of this country, in their fundamental constitution, or in any other explicit or authoritative manner. On the contrary, it has been reiterated, by them, annually, daily and hourly, for the last sixty-nine years, in almost every possible way, and in the most solemn possible manner. On the 4th of July, '76, they collectively asserted it, as their justification and authority for an act the most momentous and responsible of any in the history of the country. And this assertion has never been retracted by us as a people. We have virtually reasserted the same truth in nearly every state constitution since adopted. We have virtually reasserted it in the national constitution. It is a truth that lives on the tongues and in the hearts of all. It is true we have, in our practice, been so unjust as to withhold the benefits of this truth from a certain class of our fellowmen. But even in this respect, this truth has but shared the common fate of other truths. They are generally allowed but a partial application. Still, this truth itself, as a truth, has never been denied by us, as a people, in any authentic form, or otherwise than impliedly by our practice in particular cases. If it have, say when and where. If it have not, it is still law; and courts are bound to administer it, as law, impartially to all.

Our courts would want no other authority than this truth, thus acknowledged, for setting at liberty any individual, other than one having negro blood, whom our governments, state or national, should assume to authorize another individual to enslave. Why then, do they not apply the same law in behalf of the African? Certainly not because it is not as much the law of his case, as of others. But it is simply because they will not. It is because the courts are parties to an understanding, prevailing among the white race, but expressed in no authentic constitutional form, that the negro may be deprived of his rights at the pleasure of avarice and power. And they carry out this unexpressed understanding in defiance of, and suffer it to prevail over, all our constitutional principles of government—all our authentic, avowed, open and fundamental law.

…

CHAPTER VIII.

The Constitution of the United States.

We come now to the period commencing with the adoption of the constitution of the United States.

We have already seen that slavery had not been authorized or established by any of the fundamental constitutions or charters that had existed previous to this time; that it had always been a mere abuse sustained by the common consent of the strongest party, in defiance of the avowed constitutional principles of their governments. And the question now is, whether it was constitutionally established, authorized or sanctioned by the constitution of the United States?

It is perfectly clear, in the first place, that the constitution of the United States did not, of itself, create or establish slavery as a new institution; or even give any authority to the state governments to establish it as a new institution.—The greatest sticklers for slavery do not claim this. The most they claim is, that it recognized it as an institution already legally existing, under the authority of the State governments; and that it virtually guaranteed to the States the right of continuing it in existence during their pleasure. And this is really the only question arising out of the constitution of the United States on this subject, viz., whether it did thus recognize and sanction slavery as an existing institution?

This question is, in reality, answered in the negative by what has already been shown; for if slavery had no constitutional existence, under the State constitutions, prior to the adoption of the constitution of the United States, then it is absolutely certain that the constitution of the United States did not recognize it as a constitutional institution; for it cannot, of course, be pretended that the United States constitution recognized, as constitutional, any State institution that did not constitutionally exist.

Even if the constitution of the United States had intended to recognize slavery, as a constitutional State institution, such intended recognition would have failed of effect, and been legally void, because slavery then had no constitutional existence to be recognized.

Suppose, for an illustration of this principle, that the constitution of the United States had, by implication, plainly taken it for granted that the State legislatures had power—derived from the State constitutions—to order arbitrarily that infant children, or that men without the charge of crime, should be maimed—deprived, for instance, of a hand, a foot, or an eye. This intended recognition, on the part of the constitution of the United States, of the legality of such a practice, would obviously have failed of all legal effect—would have been mere surplusage—if it should appear, from an examination of the State constitutions themselves, that they had really conferred no such power upon the legislatures. And this principle applies with the same force to laws that would arbitrarily make men or children slaves, as to laws that should arbitrarily order them to be maimed or murdered.

We might here safely rest the whole question—for no one, as has already been said, pretends that the constitution of the United States, by its own authority, created or authorized slavery as a new institution; but only that it intended to recognize it as one already established by authority of the State constitutions. This intended recognition—if there were any such—being founded on an error as to what the State constitutions really did authorize, necessarily falls to the ground, a defunct intention.

We make a stand, then, at this point, and insist that the main question—the only material question—is already decided against slavery; and that it is of no consequence what recognition or sanction the constitution of the United States may have intended to extend to it.

The constitution of the United States, at its adoption, certainly took effect upon, and made citizens of all "the people of the United States," who were not slaves under the State constitutions. No one can deny a proposition so self-evident as that. If, then, the State constitutions, then existing, authorized no slavery at all, the constitution of the United States took effect upon, and made citizens of all "the people of the United States," without discrimination. And if all "the people of the United States" were made citizens of the United States, by the United States constitution, at its adoption, it was then forever too late for the State governments to reduce any of them to slavery. They were thenceforth citizens of a higher government, under a constitution that was "the supreme law of the land," "anything in the constitution or laws of the States to the contrary notwithstanding." If the State governments could enslave citizens of the United States, the State constitutions, and not the constitution of the United States, would be the "supreme law of the land"—for no higher act of supremacy could be exercised by one government over another, than that of taking the citizens of the latter out of the protection of their government, and reducing them to slavery.

. . .

CHAPTER IX.

The Intentions of the Convention.

The intentions of the framers of the constitution, (if we could have, as we cannot, any *legal* knowledge of them, except from the words of the constitution,) have nothing to do with fixing the legal meaning of the constitution. That convention were not delegated to adopt or establish a constitution; but only to consult, devise and recommend. The instrument, when it came from their hands, was a mere proposal, having no legal force or authority. It finally derived all its validity and obligation, as a frame of government, from its adoption by the people at large. Of course the intentions of the people at large are the only ones, that are of any importance to be regarded in determining the legal meaning of the instrument. And their intentions are to be gathered entirely from the words, which they adopted to express them. And their intentions must be presumed to be just what, and only what the words of the instrument legally express. In adopting the constitution, the people acted as legislators, in the highest sense in which that word can be applied to human lawgivers. They were establishing a law that was to govern both themselves and their government. And their intentions, like those of other legislators, are to be gathered from the words of their enactments. Such is the dictate of both law and common sense. The instrument had been reported by their committee, the convention. But the people did not ask this committee what was the legal meaning of the instrument reported. They adopted it, judging for themselves of its legal meaning, as any other legislative body would

have done. The people at large had not even an opportunity of consultation with the members of the convention, to ascertain their opinions. And even if they had consulted them, they would not have been bound at all by their opinions. But being unable to consult them, they were compelled to adopt or reject the instrument, on their own judgment of its meaning, without any reference to the opinions of the convention. The instrument, therefore, is now to be regarded as expressing the intentions of the people at large; and not the intentions of the convention, if the convention had any intentions differing from the meaning which the law gives to the words of the instrument.

But why do the partisans of slavery resort to the debates of the convention for evidence that the constitution sanctions slavery? Plainly for no other reason than because the words of the instrument do not sanction it. But can the intentions of that convention, attested only by a mere skeleton of its debates, and not by any impress upon the instrument itself, add anything to the words, or to the legal meaning of the words of the constitution? Plainly not. Their intentions are of no more consequence, in a legal point of view, than the intentions of any other equal number of the then voters of the country. Besides, as members of the convention, they were not even parties to the instrument; and no evidence of their intentions, at that time, is applicable to the case. They became parties to it only by joining with the rest of the people in its subsequent adoption; and they themselves, equally with the rest of the people, must then be presumed to have adopted its legal meaning, and that alone—notwithstanding anything they may have previously said. What absurdity then is it to set up the opinions expressed in the convention, and by a few only of its members, in opposition to the opinions expressed by the whole people of the country, in the constitution itself.

But notwithstanding the opinions expressed in the convention by some of the members, we are bound, as a matter of law, to presume that the convention itself, in the aggregate, had no intention of sanctioning slavery—and why? Because, after all their debates, they agreed upon an instrument that did not sanction it. This was confessedly the result in which all their debates terminated. This instrument is also the only authentic evidence of their intentions. It is subsequent in its date to all the other evidence. It comes to us, also, as none of the other evidence does, signed with their own hands. And is this to be set aside, and the constitution itself to be impeached and destroyed, and free government overturned, on the authority of a few meagre snatches of argument, intent or opinion, uttered by a few only of the members; jotted down by one of them, (Mr. Madison,) merely for his own convenience, or from the suggestions of his own mind; and only reported to us fifty years afterwards by a posthumous publication of his papers? If anything could excite the utter contempt of the people of this nation for the miserable subterfuges, to which the advocates of slavery resort, it would seem that their offering such evidence as this in support of their cause, must do it. And yet these, and such as these mere fragments of evidence, all utterly inadmissible and worthless in their kind, for any legal purpose, constitute the warp and the woof, the very *sine qua non* of the whole argument for slavery.

27

Pennsylvania, Personal Liberty Act
March 3, 1847*

AN ACT

To prevent kidnapping, preserve the public peace, prohibit the exercise of certain powers heretofore exercised by Judges, Justices of the Peace, Aldermen, and Jailors in this Commonwealth and to repeal certain slave laws.

Section 1. *Be it enacted by the Senate and House of Representatives of the Commonwealth of Pennsylvania, in General Assembly met, and it is hereby enacted by the authority of the same,* That if any person or persons shall, from and after the passage of this act, by force or violence take and carry away, and cause to be taken or carried away, and shall by fraud or false pretence entice or caused to be enticed, or shall attempt so to take, carry away or entice any free negro or mulatto, from any part or parts of this Commonwealth to any other place whatsoever out of this Commonwealth, with a design and intention of selling and disposing of or of causing to be kept and detained, such free negro or mulatto as a slave or servant for life, or for any term

*Laws of the General Assembly of the Commonwealth of Pennsylvania Passed at the Session of 1847 (Harrisburg, 1847), 206–8.

whatsoever, every such person or persons, his or their aiders and abettors, shall be deemed guilty of high misdemeanor, and on conviction thereof, in any Court of Quarter Sessions of this Commonwealth, having competent jurisdiction, shall be sentenced to pay, at the discretion of the Court passing the sentence, any sum not less than five hundred nor more than two thousand dollars; one half whereof shall be paid to the persons or persons who shall prosecute for the same, and the other half to this Commonwealth, and moreover, shall be sentenced to undergo a punishment by solitary confinement in the proper penitentiary, at hard labor, for a period not less than five years, nor exceeding twelve years; and on conviction of the second offence of the kind, the person so offending shall be sentenced to pay like fine, and undergo a punishment, by solitary confinement in the penitentiary, for twenty-one years.

Section 2. That if any person or persons shall hereafter knowingly sell, transfer or assign, or purchase, take a transfer or assignment of any free negro or mulatto, for the purpose of fraudulently removing, exporting, or carrying such free negro or mulatto out of this State, with the design or intent, by fraud or false pretences, of making him or her a slave or servant for life, or for any term whatsoever, every person so offending shall be deemed guilty of a high misdemeanor, and on conviction thereof, in any Court of Quarter Sessions of this Commonwealth, shall be sentenced by such Court to pay a fine of not less than five hundred dollars, nor more than two thousand dollars; one half whereof shall be paid to the person or persons who shall prosecute for the same, and the other half to this Commonwealth; and moreover, shall be sentenced at the discretion of the court to undergo a punishment by solitary confinement, at hard labor, in the proper penitentiary, for a period not less than five years nor exceeding twelve years.

Section 3. That no Judge of any of the Courts of this Commonwealth, nor any Alderman or Justice of the Peace of said Commonwealth shall have jurisdiction or take cognizance of the case of any fugitive from labor from any of the United States or Territories, under a certain act of Congress, passed on the twelfth day of February, one thousand seven hundred and ninety three, entitled, "An Act respecting fugitives from justice and persons escaping from the service of their masters," nor shall any Judge, Alderman, or Justice of the Peace of this Commonwealth, issue or grant any certificate or warrant of removal of any such fugitive from labor, under the said act of Congress, or under any other law, authority or act of the Congress of the United States, and if any Alderman, or Justice of the Peace of this Commonwealth, shall take cognizance or jurisdiction of the case of any such fugitive, or shall grant or issue any such certificate of removal as aforesaid, then, and in either case, he shall be deemed guilty of a misdemeanor in office, and shall on conviction thereof, be sentenced to pay at the discretion of the Court, any sum not less than five hundred dollars, nor exceeding one thousand dollars, the one half to the party prosecution for the same, and the other half to the use of this Commonwealth.

Section 4. That if any person or persons claiming any negro or mulatto, as fugitive from servitude or labor, shall under any pretence or authority, whatsoever, violently and tumultuously seize upon and carry away to any place, or attempt to seize and carry away in riotous, violent, tumultuous and unreasonable manner, and so as to disturb or endanger the public peace, any negro or mulatto within this Commonwealth, either with or without the intention of taking such Negro or mulatto before any district or circuit judge, the person or persons so offending against the peace of this Commonwealth, shall be sentenced by such Court to pay a fine of not less than one hundred dollars, nor more than one thousand dollars, with costs of prosecution, and further, to be committed to the county jail for any period, at the discretion of the court, not exceeding three months.

Section 5. That nothing in this act shall be constructed to take away what is hereby declared to be invested in the Judges of this Commonwealth, the right, power and authority, at all times, on application made, to issue the writ of habeas corpus, and to inquire into the causes and legality of the arrest or imprisonment of any human being within this Commonwealth.

Section 6. It shall not be lawful to use any jail or prison of this Commonwealth, for the detention of any person claimed as a fugitive from servitude or labor, except where jurisdiction may lawfully be taken by any Judge, under the provisions of this act, and any jailor or keeper of any prison, or other persons who shall offend against the provisions of this section, shall, on conviction thereof, pay a fine of five hundred dollars, one-half thereof for the use of the Commonwealth and the other half to the person who prosecutes, and shall moreover, thenceforth be removed from office, and be incapable of holding such office of jailor or keeper of a prison, at any time during his natural lifetime.

Section 7. That so much of the act of the General Assembly entitled "An Act for the gradual abolition of slavery," passed the first day of March, one thousand seven hundred and eighty, as authorizes the masters or owners of slaves to bring and retain such slaves within this Commonwealth, for the period of six months, in involuntary servitude, or for any period of time whatsoever, and so much of said act as prevents a slave from giving testimony against any person whatsoever, be and the same is hereby repealed:

Section 8. That the act passed March twenty-fifth, eighteen hundred and twenty-six, and all laws of this Commonwealth, which are hereby altered, be and the same is hereby repealed.

28
Free Soil Party Platform
August 9–10, 1848*

We have assembled in convention as a union of free men, for the sake of freedom, forgetting all past political differences, in a common resolve to maintain the rights of free labor against the aggression of the slave power, and to secure free soil to a free people; and

Whereas, The political conventions recently assembled at Baltimore and Philadelphia—the one stifling the voice of a great constituency entitled to be heard in its deliberations, and the other abandoning its distinctive principles for mere availability—have dissolved the national party organization heretofore existing, by nominating for the chief magistracy of the United States, under the slaveholding dictation, candidates neither of whom can be supported by the opponents of slavery extension without a sacrifice of consistency, duty and self-respect; and

Whereas, These nominations so made furnish the occasion and demonstrate the necessity of the union of the people under the banner of free democracy, in a solemn and formal declaration of their independence of the slave power, and of their fixed determination to rescue the federal government from its control,

1. *Resolved, Therefore*, that we, the people here assembled, remembering the example of our fathers in the

*Kirk H. Porter and Donald Bruce Johnson, eds., *National Party Platforms*, 2nd ed. (Urbana: University of Illinois Press, 1961), 13.

days of the first Declaration of Independence, putting our trust in God for the triumph of our cause, and invoking his guidance in our endeavors to advance it, do now plant ourselves upon the national platform of freedom, in opposition to the sectional platform of slavery.

2. *Resolved*, That slavery in the several states of this Union which recognize its existence depends upon the state law alone, which cannot be repealed or modified by the federal government, and for which laws that government is not responsible. We therefore propose no interference by Congress with slavery within the limits of any state.

3. *Resolved*, That the proviso of Jefferson, to prohibit the existence of slavery after 1800 in all the territories of the United States, southern and northern; the votes of six states and sixteen delegates in the Congress of 1784 for the proviso, to three states and seven delegates against it; the actual exclusion of slavery from the Northwestern Territory, by the Ordinance of 1787, unanimously adopted by the states in Congress, and the entire history of that period, clearly show that it was the settled policy of the nation not to extend, nationalize, or encourage, but to limit, localize, and discourage slavery; and to this policy, which should never have been departed from, the government ought to return.

4. *Resolved*, That our fathers ordained the Constitution of the United States in order, among other great national objects, to establish justice, promote the general welfare, secure the blessings of liberty; but expressly denied to the federal government, which they created, a constitutional power to deprive any person of life, liberty, or property, without due legal process.

5. *Resolved*, That in the judgment of this convention Congress has no more power to make a slave than to make a king; no more power to institute or establish slavery than to institute or establish a monarchy. No such power can be found among those specifically conferred by the Constitution, or derived by just implication from them.

6. *Resolved*, That it is the duty of the federal government to relieve itself from all responsibility for the existence or continuance of slavery wherever the government possesses constitutional power to legislate on that subject, and is thus responsible for its existence.

7. *Resolved*, That the true and, in the judgment of this convention, the only safe means of preventing the extension of slavery into territory now free is to prohibit its extension in all such territory by an act of Congress.

8. *Resolved*, That we accept the issue which the slave power has forced upon us; and to their demand for more slave states and more slave territory, our calm but final answer is: No more slave states and no more slave territory. Let the soil of our extensive domain be kept free for the hardy pioneers of our own land and the oppressed and banished of other lands seeking homes of comfort and fields of enterprise in the new world.

9. *Resolved*, That the bill lately reported by the committee of eight in the Senate of the United States was no compromise, but an absolute surrender of the rights of the non-slaveholders of the states; and while we rejoice to know that a measure which, while opening the door for the introduction of slavery into the territories now free, would also have opened the door to litigation and strife among the future inhabitants thereof, to the ruin of their peace and prosperity, was defeated in the House of Representatives, its passage in hot haste by a majority, embracing several Senators who voted in open violation of the known will of their constituents, should warn the people to see to it that their representatives be not suffered to betray them. There must be no more compromises with slavery; if made, they must be repealed.

10. *Resolved*, That we demand freedom and established institutions for our brethren in Oregon now exposed to hardships, peril, and massacre, by the reckless hostility of the slave power to the establishment of free government for free territories; and not only for them, but for our brethren in California and New Mexico.

11. *Resolved*, It is due not only to this occasion, but to the whole people of the United States, that we should also declare ourselves on certain other questions of national policy; therefore,

12. *Resolved*, That we demand cheap postage for the people; a retrenchment of the expenses and patronage of the federal government; the abolition of all unnecessary offices and salaries; and the election by the people of all civil officers in the service of the government so far as the same may be practicable.

13. *Resolved*, That river and harbor improvements, when demanded by the safety and convenience of commerce with foreign nations, or among the several states, are objects of national concern, and that it is the duty of Congress, in the exercise of its constitutional power, to provide therefor.

14. *Resolved*, That the free grant to actual settlers, in consideration of the expenses they incur in making settlements in the wilderness, which are usually fully equal to their actual cost, and of the public benefits re-

sulting therefrom, of reasonable portions of the public lands under suitable limitations, Is a wise and just measure of public policy, which will promote, in various ways, the interest of all the states of this Union; and we therefore recommend it to the favorable consideration of the American people.

15. *Resolved*, That the obligations of honor and patriotism require the earliest practical payment of the national debt, and we are therefore in favor of such a tariff of duties as will raise revenue adequate to defray the expenses of the federal government, and to pay annual installments of our debt, and the interest thereon.

16. *Resolved*, That we inscribe on our banner, "Free Soil, Free Speech, Free Labor, and Free Men," and under it we will fight on, and fight forever, until a triumphant victory shall reward our exertions.

29

Joel Tiffany, *A Treatise on the Unconstitutionality of American Slavery*

1849*

CHAPTER IV.
The universality, sacredness, and inalienability of Human Rights
The existence of human slavery is an antagonism in any government, not based upon physical force. It cannot be reconciled with the fundamental principles upon which our government rests.

All men are possessed of the same natural rights, secured by the same natural guarantys—held by the same tenure—their title is derived from the same source. Now, if this title is not good in all, and each, it is not good in any. If it is defective as to any, it is defective as to all. And the same Court that decides against the inalienability of the natural rights of a single individual, decides against the inalienability, of the rights of every human being; and by its own judgment makes its own members proper subjects of slavery.

To illustrate this, we will suppose that all the people of

* Joel Tiffany, *A Treatise on the Unconstitutionality of American Slavery: Together with the Powers and Duties of the Federal Government in Relation to That Subject* (Cleveland, OH: J. Calyer, 1849), 23–37, 45–52, 53–58, 61–62, 67–78, 84–114, 117–30, 138.

the city of New York hold their title to their real estate in the city through a single individual. Suppose all the several conveyances from the original proprietor, down to the present holders, to be regular, and in due form, that is, they have each and all derived their titles from the same source, secured by the same guarantys, and held by the same tenure. Now if the title of any of these fail, it must be because the title of the original proprietor is defective. And if the title is defective, then the title of all the others must be defective; and the same Court that awards judgment against one, virtually awards judgment against all who have derived title from that source.

We come, then, to this: Has man an inalienable right to life, liberty, &c.,? or are these rights dependent upon the amount of *physical force* he can wield in their defence; and when overpowered, do these *rights cease*, and the individual stand forth a *naked human chattel*, divested of all right? Was this the sentiment of our Revolutionary Fathers? Is this the spirit of the immortal Declaration of Independence? Was the war of the Revolution fought to establish such a principle as this? Yet the doctrine that the States in their sovereign character, can make any class of men slaves, asserts all this. And they who assent to it, are guilty of sustaining the principle upon which all despotism rests.

If the doctrine of the *inalienability* of man's natural rights be true, then each man's claim to these rights is good against any, and all mankind; and he has a right to assert and maintain them, before any tribunal that recognizes the doctrine; and no man, or body of men, can lawfully resist his claim, or deny to him that which is *rightfully* his own.

But it is claimed that governments can lawfully enslave their subjects. By virtue of what right, or authority can they do so. They can have no rightful power, not delegated to them by the people: and the *people* can delegate to them no power which they, as individuals, do not possess. As individuals they have no rightful power to enslave their fellow men. Hence they can have no such right, in their governmental character. And it is as much an unlawful usurpation of power, on the part of government, to enslave an individual, as it would be for a single individual to do so. A has no right to enslave his fellow. B has no right to do it, neither has C, D, E or F. Then by what rule of reasoning is it, that A, B, C, D, E and F, together have that right? It is not so. They cannot possess it. The right of the Pirate in his slave-ship, to his human cargo, is as full and perfect, as the whole world can make it. Every nation on earth, may by special enactment, declare that he is the rightful owner of his cargo of human beings; yet he thereby acquires no additional right, and the poor victims loose none. *Rights are not things that men can make, or mar.*

Therefore our conclusion is, that men cannot rightfully make human beings *chattels*, by virtue of any authority which they possess; nor can they delegate any such authority; and if they attempt it, nothing is conveyed by the pretended grant.

Deny these truths, and you destroy the foundation upon which society is based. Violate them, and you are at war with yourself, with Man and God. Admit that any human government can rightfully take a slave, and you have given up the only ground upon which you can defend *your own liberties*, and the liberty of your *wives* and *children,*—

But as legislatures can pass no laws, that will chattelize man because no one can confer on them such authority, therefore whenever they make any such enactments, they are of no validity, for the same reason that all other acts of theirs transcending their authority, are null and void; and all courts are bound so to declare then. Hence the principle, recognized as sound law in all civilized countries, "that the law of nature—*natural justice*, (as Justinian has it,) is superior in obligation to every other law. It is binding all over the globe, in all countries, at all times. No human laws are of any validity, if contrary. And all such as are valid, derive all their force and authority from the original." (Bla. Con. vol. 1, 41.) Also *Chief Justice Hobert* has said, "that even an act of Parliament, made against natural justice, is void." This doctrine has, however, been denied in England, on the ground, that *Absolute Despotic* power is vested in Parliament, and there is no other power under the British Constitution to control it. But it is also there held, that the court will not *construe* an act of parliament to be against natural justice, if by any possible means, they can avoid it. That "they will make no *construction* to do wrong."

If Parliament will enact a law that conflicts with natural justice, it shall make known its intentions, by language as clear, explicit, and unequivocal, as to leave no room for *construction*. And, were it not for the *absolute, despotic power* of Parliament, that holds itself above, and independent of the people, the English judiciary would go the full length of the doctrine, that all laws which conflict with the claims of natural justice are void. As it is, this is the spirit of the British Administration, and so far as their precedents are of any just

force, and authority, in this country, they would authorize our courts to go the entire doctrine.—For *here* we do not recognize the existence of *absolute, despotic power*, either in the Government or people. All civil and political power, in this country, is limited by the inalienability of man's natural rights.

CHAPTER V.
The Nation are estopped from sanctioning or guaranteeing human Slavery, by the Declaration of Independence.

When a man or body of men, in their individual, or associated capacity, deny the existence of certain rights and powers in others, circumstance like themselves, and base all of their own individual or governmental action upon the truth of those positions, if they afterwards attempt to assume those rights, and exercise those powers, in acting upon the rights of others, their actions and assumptions, in all such matters, are confessedly without authority and void.

Hence the affirmation of the *American Colonies*, as to the existence of certain great fundamental principals, described as *self-evident truths*, puts it forever out of their power, rightfully, to establish, or maintain human slavery.

It has been said by MR. PHILLIPS, in his review of MR. SPOONER, "that the DECLARATION OF INDEPENDENCE had nothing to do with slavery." That, "that paper dissolved the political bands that bound the Colonies to England, and that was all it did, and all it intended to do."

What had the affirmation of those great, self-evident truths to do with dissolving the political bands that bound the Colonies to Great Britain? What had the doctrine, that governments "derived all their *just* powers from the consent of the governed," to do with sundering such bands? What had the declaration, "that when a long train of abuses and usurpations, pursuing invariably the same object evinces a design," (on the part of the government,) "to reduce" [the subjects,] "under absolute despotism, it is their right it is *their duty* to throw off such government, and provide new guards for their future security," to do with declaring themselves independent? The plain answer is, these truths were uttered as the *foundation of their right*, thus to dissolve those "political bands," and establish a government for themselves, "laying its foundations on such principals, and organizing its powers in such forms, as to them seemed most likely to secure their happiness and safety." These truths were uttered as the great law of God, which arose in authority, above all political constitutions, and governmental powers, and guaranteed to them, as men, the authority by which they were about to act.

And they claimed no peculiar rights above their fellows. They set up no pretence, that any special grant had been made to them. They predicated their authority upon the equal, common rights of man. They claimed all their powers by virtue of their common humanity, and, by that claim, accorded to all other men the same rights and powers.

By denying to the government of Great Britain, the rightful power to violate these privileges in their own persons, they denied to *themselves* the rightful power to violate them in the persons of others; and by this solemn act of theirs, they are forever estopped from setting up such claim. The Declaration of Independence was a solemn deed of acquittance, of all rightful power to violate the natural and inalienable rights of man, acknowledged before God, in the presence of the world. That deed of acquittance contained the following covenants.

1st. That life, liberty and the pursuit of happiness, are gifts from God to man, and therefore the natural and *inalienable* right of all.

2nd. That governments "derive all their *just* powers from the consent of the governed," and are established for the protection of these natural rights.

3rd. That when governments become destructive of these ends, for which they are established, they act without authority, and the people are at liberty to resist, and throw them off.

4th. That when the government evinces a design to disregard the ends of justice, and reduce her subjects under absolute despotism, *it is their duty* to overthrow such government, and establish new guards for their future security.

Who were they that thus executed this great deed of acquittance? For, and in whose behalf was it thus executed?

They were the representatives of the THIRTEEN UNITED COLONIES in general congress assembled; and they assumed to do it in the name, and by the authority of the good people of those colonies. They were the chosen Embassadors of all the States; emphatically the leading minds of the nation. They were such men as Jefferson, Hancock, Adams, Garry, Wythe, Carrol, Sherman, Morris, Rush, Franklin, and Lee. They were men selected by the people for their wisdom, virtue, prudence, patriotism; and empowered to speak and decide for their respective nations. They were men whose sentiments were known, and approved by the people. They were to utter forth the PEOPLE's determinations.

This was no sudden, or rash act of theirs. For years they had witnessed the steady encroachments of the British Government upon their rights and liberties. They had become familiar with the great doctrines they were about promulgating to the world, as the basis of their action. Reflection, Reason, Judgment, Consciousness had demonstrated their eternal truths; history and experience had taught their necessity; and humanity had proclaimed their value, and taught them to exclaim "*Liberty or Death.*"

They were not uttered under the influence of passion, as the outburst of a transient enthusiasm. They knew they must be prepared to vindicate these truths, at the expense of blood, and treasure. The step they were about to take was a final one, from which there was no retreat It would necessarily involve them in a conflict with the most powerful Nation on earth,—with a nation, who was master of the Ocean,—a nation in whose hands were even then, the strong defences of their own country; and lastly, a nation of fathers and brothers:— A country they had even been proud to call their mother, and to which they were bound by the strongest ties of sympathy and affection. This then was not the effect of haste, but the work of cool heads and strong resolute, and brave hearts. They were inspired by all that was noble, great and true; and as those venerable men sat in that Hall, and one by one, executed that deed for freedom, the sacred stillness of that hour betokened the audience of angels. Then they rose above the mortal *and uttered forth the Law of God.*

And did their constituents repudiate these doctrines? No! They flew to arms, and for seven long years endured toil, privation, exposure, and eminent peril, fighting, in vindication of those truths. There was not a town, or a hamlet in the land, that was not made vocal with the ratifying shout. The *Declaration of Independence*, was read in Churches, in Court-houses, in Work-shops, in the field, and by the way and one long, universal amen went pealing up to heaven in ratification of that Deed. The day on which it was published, became an era in the worlds history. There was no battle fought, or victory won, by the force of arms; but it was a day made holy by the advent of the great doctrines of *Universal Freedom*—

Thus we have seen, that the *Inalienable Right* of all

men to liberty, was proclaimed by the representatives of the thirteen, united colonies, in congress assembled, in the name and by the authority of the good people of those colonies: that the people ratified the proclamation in the most earnest and solemn manner; and that by so doing they have denied to themselves the power to trample upon the rights and liberties of their follow men-

According to their views, there must be a true source of all political power, and there must necessarily be a *limit* to all political power, in all just governments. This source of power was the people; the limit of that power was the inalienability of the rights of man. Hence they repudiated the dogma that government possessed absolute, despotic power, or could possess any such power, for the people had no such powers to delegate. Government could never legitimately trample on the rights of man, for the two-fold reason, first, because it could never rightfully acquire any such authority, and secondly, such action would be destructive of the ends for which government was created and would re-invest the people with all their original authority.

Let this then be remembered, in construing the constitution formed by these men, who, for themselves and the people they represented, disclaimed all such authority, and we shall find that no language found in that instrument no force of circumstances, no historical proof not even all combined, can make that instrument legally recognize, sanction, or guaranty human slavery.

CHAPTER VI.
The limit and extent of Constitutional and Legislature authority.

It seems unnecessary in this work, to devote any time to the consideration of rules of *interpretation* and *construction*. The provisions of the Constitution, relating to this subject, are so simple and easy to be understood, that no interpretation or construction seems necessary. We can indulge the friends of slavery, with an unwarrantable degree of latitude in the construction or interpretation of that instrument, and still defend it, from the gross scandal of supporting slavery. In truth, the greatest latitudinarian in the country, would find it difficult, with the aid of his loosest and most liberal rules of Construction, to extort from it, by a connected train of reasoning, any argument in support of slavery.

Still it may not be amiss, to offer a few thoughts on the subject of these rules, for the purpose of showing the pro-slavery interpreter how utterly without founda-

tion he is, in his effort to engraft slavery upon the Constitution of the United States.

It is a fundamental principle of our government, that natural rights, such as life, liberty &c., are inalienable and supreme, and above the authority of all governments. That governments are institutions of the people, for the *protection* of these rights and liberties; and that it is incompetent for them to enact laws for their destruction. Hence the presumption always is, in cases of doubtful interpretation, that the legislature intended to do, or require nothing contrary to natural right and justice,—and unless the language of the enactment is so clear and explicit, that it is impossible to avoid the contrary conclusion, the courts are bound so to interpret them; or to use the language of the Supreme Court of the United States, in the case of United States v. Fisher, 2 Cranch, 390: "Where rights are infringed, where fundamental principles are overthrown, where the general System of the law is departed from, the legislative intention must be expressed with irresistible clearness, to induce a court of justice, to suppose a design to effect such objects."

But, it has been supposed by some, that when, that legislative intention, to infringe rights, overthrow fundamental principles, and depart from the general system of the law, was expressed with irresistible clearness, the courts were bound, to enforce that intention; and MR. PHILIPS, in his review of MR. SPOONER, *denys* that, in this country, courts are at liberty to disregard such enactments; and in remarking upon the subject, says: "This question is not to be confounded with one somewhat similar to it, and which, has sometimes, been discussed, especially in England, whether a judge there, may disregard an unjust statute. Our question is different; for it should be remembered, that in England, there is no written constitution. Even if a judge had such power there, (which he has not) it would by no means follow, that he had the same under our form of government. There, the judge, swears to bear true allegiance to the king. It might therefore, with some plausibility, be argued that having no test to which to bring acts of Parliament, except the rule of natural justice, judges were authorized to declare them void, when inconsistent with those rules."

The distinction, which Mr. Philips has made between the character of the British and American Government, is such, as would lead us to directly the opposite conclusion, and is a distinction necessary to be made, in determining the *force* of English precedent.

The British government has no written constitution. The legitimate powers of parliament, are not restricted by any written or unwritten law. And in theory, and practice Parliament is absolute, supreme, uncontrollable, and irresponsible. In the language of Lord Coke, "It hath sovereign, and uncontrollable authority, in the making, confirming, enlarging, restraining, abrogating, repealing, revising and expounding of laws, concurring matters of all possible denominations, ecclesiastical, or temporal; civil, military, maritime, or criminal; this being the place where that absolute, despotic power, which must, in all government, reside somewhere, is invested by the Constitution of the Kingdom." Here we have a full key, to those English precedents which say, "if Parliament will enact laws that are against natural justice &c, the courts are not at liberty to disregard them" &c.

In the theory, of the founders of that government, absolute, despotic power, is a necessary incident to all governments; and in theirs, that power is vested in Parliament, and there is no power under that government, authorized to control it. They hold that the right of government, is derived directly from God, not through the people, and therefore, they are not responsible to them. That what they do for the people, is a matter of "grace" &c. Hence, English precedents go far to sustain the doctrine of Mr. Philips. But even under this high, all commanding power of the British Parliament, to authorize, or sanction a wrong, the language must be clear, explicit, and unequivocal, for "the law will not make a construction to do wrong."

But the theory of the institutions of this country, is entirely different. It is no part of our doctrine, that *absolute, despotic power* resides anywhere, not even in the people, much less in the legislature. They denounced this doctrine in their Declaration of Independence. They defined the nature, source and object, of all political power, and affixed limits, beyond which it could not rightfully pass. It is our theory, that all governmental power emanates from the people, and is delegated to be used for the protection of the natural and inalienable rights of man; that this power, coming from the people, can never rise above, or become independent of them. It is our theory, that when governments become destructive of the ends of justice, and right, it is the *duty* of the people to overthrow them.

It is our theory, that the legislative department of our Federal Government, is the creature of the National Constitution, and has no powers not delegated therein;

and that it is only supreme in the legitimate, and constitutional exercise of those powers. It is the theory of our government, that the judiciary is independent of the legislative department, and is as supreme in the exercise of its legitimate functions, as is the legislature. That it is the prerogative of the judiciary to sit in judgment upon the enactments of the legislature, and to declare such laws void, as they shall think transcend the scope of legislative authority, or conflict with the general objects and designs of the government. It is the theory of our government, that men possess certain, natural rights, which cannot be *alienated* by themselves, or others; that no government can have the rightful power to disregard and trample upon them. Hence, Courts in the United States have full authority to declare all laws null and void, which violate the fundamental principles of natural right and justice. And in this respect they are entirely independent of the legislative departments. So then, the conclusion is, that however much the judiciary of Great Britain may feel themselves bound to give force and effect to unjust and wicked laws, enacted by Parliament, it is not so in this country. And as our National Government was ordained by the people, for the purpose of establishing justice, and securing the blessings of liberty, &c., it becomes the duty of the judiciary, if they find the legislative going beyond their legitimate sphere of action, by enacting laws destructive of liberty and justice, to declare all their improper action void. At all events to hold, that the legislature can have no authority to do, or require, that which is wrong, or destructive to liberty and natural justice, by virtue of any implied power. That if they *will* sanction that which is unjust and wrong, they shall be compelled, not only to show clear and unequivocal *authority, expressly given* for so doing, but shall also express *their intention* in language so clear and positive as to admit of no other interpretation.

. . .

CHAPTER VII.
Rules of Construction and Interpretation.
The Supreme Court of the United States, in construing certain parts of the Constitution, have, on several occasions, referred to, "Historical evidence of the meaning of certain provisions of that instrument. It may be proper, in this place to examine the question how far they are at liberty to travel out of the record into the uncertain, indefinite history of the times, to ascertain the meaning of certain provisions of the organic law of the

land." The practice is certainly a novel one, and the propriety of it should be fully investigated and settled, before it finally grows into settled law. If there is any thing in the nature of the institutions of our country which requires such a rule of interpretation to be adopted let it be known, and if the nature of the difficulty be such, that it cannot be obviated without the introduction of so uncertain and dangerous a method of construction we must submit. But we are confident that nothing short of the most urgent necessity will ever obtain from the profession their consent to the introduction of so strange and anomalous a rule.

If we are to depart from the letter and spirit of a written instrument, and search for the intentions of the makers thereof, in the journals, newspapers, debates, and partisan representations of the sayings and doings of those who participated in the making of the instrument, it will become necessary to re-moddle certain other rules of interpretation which hitherto have been considered good and necessary, and also to determine what histories shall be considered authentic, and upon what subjects they shall be considered conclusive, &c., &c.

The rules of construction laid down by Blackstone, and referred to by *Mr. Story*, are simply these.—Says Blackstone, "The fairest and most rational method of interpreting the will of the legislator is, by exploring his intentions at the time the law was made, by signs the most natural and probable; and these signs are either the *words*, the *context*, the *subject matter*, the *effect* and *consequences*, and the *spirit and reason of the law*."

…

But even if the courts could indulge any such latitude in the construction of statutes, the case would be entirely different in the exposition of a fundamental law, like the constitution of the United States. It is all important that such an instrument should be strictly construed. For if a loose construction be allowed, there will be no limit to the implied powers which a fertile imagination, or an ambitious, or designing administration may not graft upon it. Powers never intended to be granted by the people, will be assumed. In all governmental bodies, there is always a strong tendency to usurp power. Hence written constitutions were adopted to hold them in check. But these have not always been successful. The doctrines of latitudinarian construction readily form a ladder by which all constitutional bulwarks are scaled; and history has demonstrated that there is no safety in allowing courts, or legislatures to

go beyond the plan, palpable meaning of the grant, in construing written constitutions,—and more especially should our courts and legislatures be kept within the plain letter of the grant, if the power sought to be grafted on by implication is one in conflict with natural right and justice, and opposed to the general object and professed designs of the instrument. The maxim that "The law will make no construction to do wrong," should apply with peculiar force.

It is admitted that the supreme court of the United States have gone farther, in travelling out of the record, to ascertain the meaning and give a particular construction to parts of the constitution, than any other judicial tribunal in any civilized country; and it is also admitted, that their practice has been altogether unwarranted by any known rules of law common sense, or justice. And that even they themselves, have not any fixed or uniform rule on the subject, except to make such rules as the particular emergencies of each case seem to require. Hence they often given conflicting rules of interpretation. Some times they intimate that they only intend applying certain rules to the *particular* case at bar, as in the case of Prigg vs Penn. In other words they assume the authority to go in any, and all directions for light, and aid when they please; and then shut themselves up in the prison of the letter when they please.

But it is said "That precise, legal maxims are not applicable to a constitution of government. In relation to such a subject, the natural and obvious meaning of its provisions, apart from technical rules, is the true criterion of its construction." But by examining all authorities on that subject, we can find no intimation that the instrument itself is to be abandoned to the vague teachings of "Collateral History, or National Circumstances."

It is fully admitted that, in the construction of that instrument, "Great regard should be paid to the spirit and intention thereof." But that *spirit* and *intention* should be gathered from the instrument itself. It is an instrument purporting to delegate sovereign power, to be exercised over a variety of subjects, affecting the lives, liberty and property of the whole people. It is entrusting the dearests, and most vital interests of community to the hands of men who may be disposed to abuse their trust, unless held within strict bounds.

Great latitude of construction would easily graft upon it powers which might be fatal to the liberties of the people. Give government general license to construe such an instrument by such "Collateral aids," as they might please to call in, and there is no power which ambitious, and designing men might not attach. If we are to go out of that instrument to look for aid, in the journals, newspapers, publications, debates and histories of any particular time, who is to limit the extent of that judicial wandering? Who to determine what histories are to be consulted, on what particular portions are to be taken as true? Who is to say, "thus far, and no farther?" Every court would be at liberty to call in such exterior aid, and from such sources as they should think proper. Your constitution would no longer be the simple, plain spoken instrument, adopted by the people; but it would be what the debates, journals, histories and idle rumors of the day would make it. You could no longer look to the plain, obvious meaning of the language employed; for, under some apparently blooming plant of liberty, would lurk a basalisk, concealed by dubious words and doubtful implications, to be developed into a fatal power, by the aid of "Collateral history," and "National Circumstances."

But this is not so. The constitution can be submitted to no such test. It is enough that the court may engraft upon it such implied powers as are obviously necessary to carry into effect the powers therein expressively granted. If, after doing this, it should be found that other powers are needed, it is safer to call upon the people to surrender, in express terms, the further powers, by amending their constitution, than to let in a flood of powers by implication against which no future barriers could be erected; and which is the same thing in effect, if by the ordinary rules of interpretation, the meaning of certain words and phrases are still doubtful, so that it cannot definitely be told what grant was intended, it is better to leave the doubtful power undeveloped, until the people, by amendment, can develop it, than to resort to such rules of interpretation for the purpose of developing it, as, when applied to other parts of the instrument and to other instruments of a like kind, put an end to all certainty and stability, and thereby break down all barriers against governmental usurpations.

...

CHAPTER VIII.
Our Government, its origin, nature, objects, and powers.
...

The Constitution of the United States, is not a compact between the several states in their sovereign state capacity, but the Constitution of *the people* of all the states, acting in their capacity as individuals. Hence the powers delegated by that instrument, did not come,

second handed, though the states, but came directly from the people, with all the power and vigor of virgin sovereignty; and the contract was between each individual, and all the people of the Union; and between all and each. Not between communities of people, but between individuals. Hence the ordaining, and establishing the fundamental law looked to securing the objects mentioned in its preamble, against the petty despotisms of factions or states,—against the selfishness, or arrogance of any man, or set of men. The whole people stood up in their original, sovereign capacity; and, by virtue of the authority vested in them by the Almighty, declared what powers should belong to the national government, and what should be denied to the states. They made such grants of power, and imposed such restrictions as they thought proper, making the Federal Government supreme in all matters within the sphere of its action; and when they had finished their work, they reserved to themselves and to the states, respectively the powers not delegated in that instrument.

Hence, when we find a restriction imposed upon the federal government, we must remember it was imposed by the people, not by the States; and when we find a prohibition imposed upon the states, we must remember that it was imposed by the people, not by the Federal Government.

Again the National Government, is peculiar in this respect; it is a government of delegated powers, established for specific and limited purposes. It possesses no power to act upon any subject, unless that power has been delegated in express terms, or by necessary implication. The constitution of the United States is their charter, defining their powers, and enjoining their duties, and no department of the National Government is at liberty to go beyond the limits prescribed in that instrument: and should they do, so, their entire action beyond it, would be of no binding force, or validity.

The state governments differ from the National Government in this respect. They do not derive their power to act, from state constitutions. The objects of those instruments are rather to define the manner of acting, by pointing out the method of organizing and maintaining their state governments and imposing such restrictions upon the exercise of their governmental powers as wisdom and prudence dictate. The Federal Government can do nothing except what they are authorized to do by the National Constitution. The state governments can do every thing within the legitimate sphere of government, which they are not restrained from doing, by their

Constitutions, or which power has not been delegated to the National Government. The Constitution of [the] United States is one, delegating power. The Constitution of the State is one restraining power: and this difference must be kept in mind in construing those instruments.

The *object* of the National Government was to protect the rights of each individual citizen against oppression at home and abroad. Against the encroachments of foreign nations, and domestic states: against lawless violence, exercised under the forms of governmental authority. Protection, in the enjoyment of their natural, and *inalienable* rights, was the great paramount object of the institution of the National Government. Hence they declare, "that they *ordain* and *establish* that government, *to establish justice, insure domestic tranquility, provide for the common defence, promote the general welfare, and secure the blessings of liberty*" &c. Without the National government, a state, or a portion of it, might be invaded by a foreign enemy. The people might be robed of their property, deprived of their liberty, and be reduced under absolute despotism, without sufficient power to defend themselves. Also a state might assume the authority to rob a portion of her citizens of their dearest rights. But by the formation of the National Government, they constituted themselves citizens of a Government that had *power* to defend them, individually and collectively, against all such encroachments. And it will be found on a careful examination of the Constitution of the United States, that ample provision was therein made for the guaranty of all these rights to every individual, against the encroachments of Nations from abroad, or from the despotism of states at home.

Then as citizens of the United States, we stand mutually pledged to each other, to see that all the rights, privileges, and immunities, granted by the constitution of the United States, are extended to all, if need be, by the force of the whole Union.

What is it, then, to be a citizen of the United States? It is to be *invested* with a *title* to *life*, *liberty*, and the *pursuit* of *happiness*, and to be *protected* in the *enjoyment thereof*, by the guaranty of twenty millions of people. It is, or should be, a panoply of defence equal, at least, to the ancient cry, "*I am a Roman Citizen.*" And when understood, and respected in the true spirit of the immortal founders of our government, it will prove a perfect bulwark against all oppression.

We are fully aware of the objection which is taken to this view of the subject. It is thought this view would lead to the extreme doctrine of consolidation. We have not taken this view from any feeling of necessity on our part, to maintain the argument that the Federal Government is not authorized by the Constitution, to encourage, support or sanction slavery. We do not need it; and make no use of it, except in the consideration of certain positive guarantys of the Constitution.

We hold that under the constitution, the Federal Government has full power to put an end to the institution of slavery, and that it is the duty of the government to exercise that power without delay: and we maintain this position without calling in aid, any of the positive guarantys of the Constitution for liberty.

We therefore say to those who object to this view of the objects and designs of the establishment of the Federal Government, you may reject it entirely: the argument is complete without it.

But before rejecting this doctrine, we would suggest a few considerations. Under the constitution of the United States, we all become citizens of the National Government by birth or naturalization; and as such citizens are entitled to the benefits of all these guaranties for personal security and liberty.

The states can have no authority to deprive us of those benefits; for the guarantys are a part of the supreme organic law of the land, made by a compact of all with each and each with all.

We do not hold that the Federal Government is bound to enact laws, to see that those rights are observed between citizen and citizen in the same state. It is peculiarly the province of the state governments to do that; and they will be presumed to have performed that duty, except in those cases where, by positive enactments, they have authorized a violation of these rights.

Our position then is this; that whenever a state shall by its legislation, attempt to deprive a citizen of the United States of those rights and privileges which are guaranteed to him by the Federal Constitution, as such citizen, such legislation of the state is void. And that it is the duty of the federal judiciary to take cognizance of such violations, whenever any of the citizens of the United States are thus injured by state legislation.

This doctrine is not obnoxious to the charge of consolidation on the one hand, nor of state rights and nullification on the other.

With this view of the guarantys of the Federal Constitution the right of citizenship is valuable to us while residing within the jurisdiction of the Federal Government. But the other view renders the National Government valueless to all citizens while at home. If its guarantys were only intended to protect the citizen against its own despotism, a vast majority of the citizens would have been more secure without a union government, than with it.

...

CHAPTER X.

Our Constitution neither sanctions,
legalizes, nor guarantys Slavery

We now proceed to enquire into all those provisions of the Constitution, of the United States, which are said to favor slavery; and shall maintain the following propositions:

1st.—The constitution nowhere guarantys the existence of slavery, in any part of the Union, for a *single hour.*

2nd.—It nowhere sanctions slavery directly or indirectly.

3rd.—It nowhere recognizes the legal existence of slavery, in a single state the Union.

4th.—It nowhere restrains the Federal Government from extending to all men, black and white, all the guarantys of that instrument, for the personal security, and liberty of the citizens of the United States.

5th.—Under the general provisions of that instrument the Federal Government have *full* and *complete* power to put an end to slavery in the United States at pleasure; and it can never fulfil the designs of its creation and satisfy the anticipations awakened until it does so.

We shall argue these propositions from the letter and spirit of the constitution; applying the most liberal rules of construction, and shall fortify their correctness by referring to the history of the formation of that instrument. It will be admitted that slaves, and slavery were referred to, in every clause of that instrument, where the pro-slavery interpreters insist they are especially referred to.

...

CHAPTER XI.

The Fugitive Clause.

The next clause of the constitution that claims our particular attention is the 3d clause of the 2d sec. of the 4th art. which is: "No person held to service, or labor in one State, under the laws thereof, escaping into another, shall, in consequence of any law or regulation therein be discharged from such service, or labor, but shall be delivered up on claim of the party to whom such service or labor may be due."

Slavery is so odious in the eye of the law, that it can only exist *"in invitum."* A man can only be considered a slave while he remains within the jurisdiction of the authority that makes him such. The moment he escapes beyond that jurisdiction, his legal chains fall off, and he assumes his native, original manhood. We mean by this, he becomes a freeman in the eye of the law. This was the case with the thirteen colonial states. Each had their own regulations, chattleizing men. But they were of no force, or validity beyond the limits of their respective jurisdictions. Consequently if a slave from Virginia, escaped into Pennsylvania, he thereby became free in the eye of the law, unless by a comity between Pennsylvania and Virginia it was agreed that he should still be considered as subject to the jurisdiction that made him a slave. This comity existed between the original thirteen states, prior to the formation of the Federal Constitution, as all of them were slave states, and each sovereign, having full power to enter into alliance with each other, for all matters of comity, &c. These states, or rather the people composing these states, were about to enter into a union government, into which a portion of their original sovereignty was to be merged: among other things the right to enter into any treaties, alliances, or confederations with each other, aside from the general union was to be given up. Besides, the feeling in many of the states was such, that the people were indisposed to continue slavery among themselves, or tolerate it, in others: and there was very little inclination among a portion of the states, to continue the old line of comity by which the slave laws of one state were to be recognized in other States.

With the exception of South Carolina and Georgia, there was no serious objection to discontinuing that practice. But these States, insisted upon it, and refused to come into the union, unless this comity was continued. Now it is worthy of notice that these states apprehended no danger from the action of the *General Government*, at least expressed no such apprehension. It was only against the action of the *States*, they wished to guard. Hence, the clause, which they sought to insert into the constitution, contained no restriction upon the Federal Government, nor did it enjoin any duty upon them. It was only restrictive of state action.

There was much opposition to the introduction of this and other clauses, relating to the subject of slavery. It was the feeling and determination of a large portion of the convention framing the Constitution, that slavery, as such, should receive no favor or support at their hands even for the shortest period. And, as has before been observed, they would not admit into the constitution any word, or phrase, which by any legal rule of construction, could be made to mean slavery. This was not owing to carelessness or neglect. It was not because they had not suitable and proper language to express slavery; but it was the result of an open deliberate and expressed design on their part.

Keeping these things in mind we will now proceed to examine this, so called, "fugitive clause" "No person held to service or labor in one state, under the laws thereof, escaping into another, shall, in consequence of any law or regulation therein, be discharged from such labor or service" &.

The plain English of this, is, that the state into which the fugitive escapes shall make no law, or adopt no regulation, by which to prevent the master, or owner from reclaiming his slave. But this clause imposes no restriction upon the action of the Federal Government. It leaves that Government as free to act, as though that clause had not been introduced into the constitution. And the truth is, it was not *intended* to impose any restriction upon the action of the Union Government. Then, so far as this clause is concerned, if the constitution has, in any of its other clauses, imposed any duties upon the National Government, inconsistent with the continuance of slavery, this clause can never be used to restrain its action.

But it is said, "They shall be delivered up on claim." Who shall deliver them up? Who is compelled at the sound of the slave hunters horn, to start in pursuit of the panting fugitive? The Federal Government? The state government? or the Citizen? Who are bound, by this clause, to become the human blood hounds! The plain simple answer is, no one. He is to "be delivered up on claim." That claim can be preferred against no one who has not the fugitive in his custody, or his control. The simple meaning is, if the fugitive is brought before the authorities of the state, "by Habeas Corpus," or otherwise, suing for his liberty, and the owner or master establishes his legal claim to his labor or service, under the laws of the state from which he escaped, that the court shall not discharge the fugitive, but shall deliver him over to the claimant, and that is all it does mean. It is all the duty, or restriction it imposes on any government, or any person.

But it is said that the *Supreme court* of the United States have decided this question, and declared this to be the legal meaning of the clause, that the Federal Government should make such laws and adopt such regulations as were necessary to carry into effect, the effort of the master, to reclaim his fugitive slave.

In reference to the above it may be remarked in the first place, even if the Supreme Court have made such a decision, it by no means follows that such is the law. Decisions of Courts are not, necessarily law. Precedents, at most, are but evidence of what the law has been held to be, on certain points; but they are liable to be overruled by the same, or other courts, and are never considered conclusive.

. . .

Again it is in pursuance of the professed objects, and designs of the Constitution, for the government to provide for the apprehension and punishment of criminals, as being necessary to guard the rights and liberties of the citizen but it is contrary to the professed design of the constitution, and entirely foreign to the objects for which the Government was instituted, to employ its functionaries to hunt down men panting for liberty, and fleeing from oppression. Therefore we say, this clause of the constitution does not, purport to delegate any power to the Federal Government, either expressly, or by any necessary implication; nor does it restrain that Government, in the exercise of any powers, otherwise delegated. It imposes no duty upon them. It merely restrains the States from passing any laws or making any regulations interfering with the ascertained rights of the claimant. The truth really is, this clause never contemplated any other action by the National Government, than that the principles of citizenship, given by the Constitution, should be secured to all within its jurisdiction; and no other powers can be exercised by them, on this subject, without trampling in the dust, other provisions of the constitution, adopted for "establishing justice" and securing the "blessings of liberty."

In this view of the case, the [Fugitive Slave] act of 1793, is undeniably, unconstitutional and void.

. . .

CHAPTER XII.
Citizenship.

What is it to be a citizen of the United States, and what are the necessary incidents to citizenship?

. . .

What, then, are the privileges and immunities which the American citizen has a right to demand of the Federal Government? The answer is, he has a right to demand, and have full and ample protection in the enjoyment of his personal security, personal liberty, and private property; protection against the oppression of individuals, communities and nations; and the Nation stands pledged to him, as he to them, to defend him in the enjoyment of these rights. His civil obligations to defend his country are based upon his country's obligation to defend him. Were it not for our relations growing out of his National Government, the citizens of Ohio would be under no legal obligation to defend the citizens of New York, should they need our assistance. But under the Federal Union we have become citizens of one, and the same government. We have a National relation to each other, which is of a higher character; and into which state relations, for certain purposes, are merged; and to which, when in conflict, state regulations must yield. As a citizen of the United States, residing in Ohio, we are bound to protect and defend the citizen of the United States residing in New York; and in this obligation, is to be found the immunity of an American citizen, When the liberties of a citizen are invaded, either by a domestic, or a foreign force, we are all bound in our National character to afford them protection. We are bound to secure to all the benefits of a "Republican form of Government," thus protecting the citizen against the despotism of a State. And when we look over the guarantys of the Federal Constitution for personal security, liberty and property, and remember that they are the standing guarantys of a Nation, numbering twenty millions, why should not the American citizen feel that his liberties are safe, especially if he can rely upon the integrity and good faith of the government in enforcing those guarantys?

This then is the conclusion; to be a citizen of the United States, is to be brought within the protection of twenty millions of people, each of whom stand pledged under the constitutional government of the Union to defend all, and each in the enjoyment of those natural and inalienable rights which the Declaration of Independence asserted, the war of the Revolution maintained, and the adoption of the Federal Constitution secured.

The next question very naturally suggested is, *how do men become citizens of the United States?*

1st. The answer is, all persons who had a legal residence in the country at the time of the Revolution, and at the adoption of the Federal Constitution, and who were not, by that instrument excepted, became citizens of the United States. Story Com. Con. 3v.571.

2nd. All persons, born within the jurisdiction of the United States, since the adoption of the Federal Constitution, became citizens by birth.

. . .

Hence, then we must conclude that all persons residing in the United States, at the time of the American Revolution, and the formation of the National Government, known under state laws as slaves, and all who have since been born within the jurisdiction of the United States, are Citizens thereof. Is it objected that a colored person cannot become a citizen of the United States, by naturalization? That may be true of all colored persons who have been brought within the jurisdiction of the United States, from foreign countries, since congress have passed any laws on the subject of naturalization. That is, those who were aliens to the National Government, at the time congress passed their first naturalization laws, may be aliens still. For Congress by the first section of the act passed in relation to the Naturalization of aliens, provided that "any alien, being a free white person, may be admitted to become a citizen of the United States or any of them" &c. So that any *alien*, who is not a "*free white person*," cannot be admitted to the benefits of citizenship, under the rules and regulations of congress.

But this act of congress does not exclude from the benefits of citizenship those colored persons who, prior to that, had ceased to be aliens either to the National or State Governments. Neither does it affect the rights of those who were born within the jurisdiction of the Federal Government, and who consequently, never were aliens, and stand in no need of naturalization; and inasmuch as all are citizens or natural born subjects, who are not aliens, hence all colored persons. who are born in the United States, whether their parents are citizens or aliens, become citizens by birth; and there is no Constitutional power any where, to declare or treat them as aliens. They are not born under the protection of any foreign power, and they owe no allegiance to any; consequently they cannot be required to take any oath of renunciation of allegiance.

But further, that colored persons are citizens of the United States, if born within its jurisdiction is in proof from the practice of our State and National Governments. In several of the States, where slavery has been abolished the colored man has been admitted to the privileges of an elector, of both the State and Nation. In the States of New York and Massachusetts the colored man, who was once a slave, by the laws and practice of the States, now stands, not only a free citizen, but an elector of the nation; and every state in the Union possess the power to cloth all their natural born, colored subjects with the franchise of an elector of the National Government, which they could not do, if these colored men were not citizens.

The right to establish uniform rules of naturalization belongs, under the constitution exclusively to congress. The States have now no authority to say who may, or who may not be citizens of the United States. But the people left it with the *state* governments to say what class of citizens, residing within their state jurisdictions, should be clothed with the franchise of an elector; and different states have adopted different regulations on that subject. In certain states a property qualification is necessary to entitle a citizen to the franchise of an elector. In others a particular color of the skin. In others both these are deemed essential: and in others, neither &c. Hence, it will be observed, that the *right of suffrage* is not a necessary incident to citizenship. A large portion of the citizens of Rhode Island were disfranchised under the old charter; but nevertheless they were citizens of the United States. So also in Virginia, or South Carolina, an alien may be naturalized, and thereby become a citizen of the United States. Yet not possessing the requisite amount of property to entitle him to vote, he may nevertheless be deprived of the right of suffrage. No one can deny that Kentucky has the power to abolish slavery within her limits, and then admit all the emancipated to the right of suffrage. This she could not do unless they were already citizens of the United States.

Thus upon every principle of reasoning, all colored persons, as well as others, who have been born within the jurisdiction of the United States, whether they have been deemed slaves, or free men, are citizens thereof, and as such, under our National constitution, *entitled to all the privileges and immunities of Citizenship.*

But is it still affirmed that colored men, and slaves are not citizens? If they are not, what prevents them from becoming citizens? Their color?—are they not persons? Does the constitution of the United States say any thing about the color of its citizens? or any thing from which the color thereof can be legally inferred? They are citizens unless excluded by State legislation. But state legislation cannot exclude any person from the rights and benefits of citizenship. The constitution has committed that power to the Federal Government to determine what persons, being aliens, can become citizens, and *how* they can become so.

The States can pass no laws that shall deprive a person of the right of citizenship. Nor can they pass any law that shall in any manner conflict with that right. There is nothing in the Constitution of the United States, nor in any law passed by the authority of that instrument, that excludes, or can exclude any person from the right of citizenship, who is born within our National jurisdiction; and for this reason, that class of persons made slaves, "*de facto*" by state governments, are nevertheless citizens of the United States.

If they are not citizens it is because certain state laws have made them slaves, and thereby deprived them of the right of citizenship. But if state legislatures have a right to deprive one class of persons of the right of citizenship, they have the same power to deny it to all classes; at least there is no rule or limitation beyond which they cannot go. For the constitution gives none, either expressly or impliedly: and it gives no other test than that of natural born, or naturalized citizens.

A state law, therefore, which would conflict with the rights of citizenship, is necessarily unconstitutional and void. If making a man a slave, withholds from him citizenship, or is inconsistent with his privileges, and immunities as a citizen, then it is unlawful to make a man a slave, in the United States. But if the slave is a citizen (and that he is we have no doubt) then is he entitled to all the privileges and immunities of citizenship, which are guaranteed in the Federal Constitution for personal security, personal liberty, and private property. And the whole Nation, individually and collectively, stand pledged to protect and defend him in the enjoyment of those rights.

CHAPTER XIII.
The Writ of Habeas Corpus.
What are the privileges, and immunities of citizenship, of the United States?

We have already seen that to be a citizen of the United States is to be entitled to the benefits of all the guarantys of the Federal Constitution for personal security, personal liberty and private property. That the whole nation stands individually pledged, to all and each, to abide by and enforce those guarantys. And every citizen who is wantonly robbed of any of these rights, by the express or tacit permission of the Government of the United States, is a swift witness against us all, that we have violated our pledge to him, and thereby released him from his obligation to us. The permitting a single citizen to be crushed, and destroyed unjustly by any despotic power at home or abroad, without calling to his aid, if need be, the whole force of the Nation is at once aiming a death blow at the vitality of the Union.

Let it be known that the Federal Government will stand by and permit one of its citizens to be thus robed without calling to his aid the needful assistance, and it will no longer command respect; for it will be of no value. The end for which it was created will have failed. If the exclamation, *"I am an American Citizen,"* will not enshield us at home and abroad, and secure to us those rights which are inalienably ours, let us stand humbled and subdued by the memory of the ancient Romans, or arm ourselves again, for the establishment of a government that will afford us that protection. England has taught the world that it is of some value to be an English subject. Spain will never forget the lesson. The wanton destruction of a humble British subject by Spanish authority brought the whole power of England upon their coast, and *compelled* restitution. The British flag, in the port of Charleston, South Carolina, protects her subjects, from that oppression which the American flag has hitherto failed to do. Is it less a privilege to be an American Citizen, than a British subject? Let American citizens answer, and by that answer let them vindicate themselves before the world.

If all American citizens are not protected where lies the fault? in the nature and character of the government? or in those who are entrusted with the administration of it? Let the defect be known and remedied. If our government is fundamentally defective, give us *change* or *revolution*. If those who administer it are faithless, *hurl them from power*! Give us a government that will afford protection to its citizens, *equal* at least, to the ancient Roman government, or the present British. With nothing short of that, should the American Citizen be satisfied.

But what further guarantys, for personal security and liberty, could a government provide, than the constitution of the United States has already provided? It has secured the right of petition,—the right to keep and bear arms, the right to be secure from all unwarrantable seizures and searches, the right to demand, and have a presentment, or indictment found by a grand jury before he shall be held to answer to any criminal charge, the right to be informed beforehand of the nature and cause of accusation against him, the right to a public and, speedy trial by an impartial jury of his peers, the right to confront those who testify against him, the right to have compulsory process to bring in his witnesses, the right to demand and have counsel for his defence,

the right to be exempt from excessive bail, or fines, &e., from cruel and unusual punishments, or from being twice jeopardized for the same offence; and the right to the privileges of the *great writ of Liberty, the Habeas Corpus*. And all these guarantys preceded by the *express* declaration, that they are given to *establish justice, provide for the common defence*, and *secure the blessings of liberty*. But, it is said the Federal Government has not power to enforce these guarantees? We answer in the language of the Supreme Court of the United States, it has. For say they, in the case of Prigg vs. Pennsylvania, "if the constitution guarantys a right, the natural inference certainly is, that the National Government is clothed with appropriate authority to enforce it."

...

Here then we have, in clear and unequivocal terms the guaranty of the privileges of this writ of liberty, placed above the authority of State and National legislation, by the voice of the people themselves; unrestricted in its application to any human being within our Federal jurisdiction; an authority entrusted in the hands of the highest functionaries of our National Government to maintain and enforce the privileges of that writ, and a positive duty enjoined upon them to do so. Now what becomes of slavery in the United States? What becomes of the State laws, and constitutions, denying to *three million American Citizens* the *"privileges"* of this writ? Again we say, "Well said Mr. Christian, Slavery can exist in no country, where the privileges of this writ are secured."

But it has been objected that this clause of the constitution was only restrictive of the action of the Federal Government; or rather of Congress. But it must mean something more than that; for the Constitution, and the laws made in pursuance thereof &c, are to be the supreme law of the land, anything in State laws, or constitutions to the contrary notwithstanding. It was designed by it to secure to every individual in the Union the benefits of this great writ of liberty, against both State and Federal legislation. For in the first place the Federal Government, being a government of only delegated power, and being authorized to do only that which the constitution, by express grant, or necessary implication authorized it to do, had no power to suspend the privileges of that writ. In the next place the people were there securing to themselves the privileges of that writ, by making it one of the guaranties of the supreme organic law of the land; and it was to secure to themselves the privileges of this writ, which was then called *"the great writ of Liberty,"* against all legislation, state and National, that this restriction was imposed.

Again, it would have been a matter of little consequence to restrain the National Government from depriving a citizen of the benefits of this writ, while the States could have done so, at pleasure. There was far less danger to be apprehended from the limited power and action of the National Government than from the, so called, sovereign States. When a restriction is thus put in general terms, upon a subject equally affecting all the people, it is safe to infer that it applies to all, and is restrictive of both the State and National Government.

Thus, "No person shall be deprived of life, liberty, or property, without due process of law. No person shall be held to answer to a capital or otherwise infamous crime, but upon presentment or indictment &c. No person shall be twice put in jeopardy of life, or limb, &c., &c., &c., all these, and such like guaranties are National in their character, and binding upon the State, as well as the National Government.

CHAPTER XIV.
"A Republican form of Government."
We find in the 4th section, of the 4th article of the Constitution of the United States, the following guaranty.—"The United States shall guaranty to every State in this Union, a Republican form of Government, and shall protect each of them against invasion; and, on application of the legislature, or of the Executive, when the legislature cannot be convened, against domestic violence."

Here we find a guaranty of a Republican form of Government to every State in the Union. This clause has generally been understood to guaranty to every State in the Union, as such State, that each of their sister States should sustain a Republican form of Government, and that it was the right of each State, under the Federal Constitution to demand that the government of every other state in the Union, should be Republican in form. But this is not the real meaning of that clause, although the effect of it will be to secure to each State a Republican form of Government. It has a meaning more vital to the cause of human freedom, and one that bears more directly upon the sacred immunities of the American citizen, than such a construction could possibly give to it.

We must again recur to the question who made the Constitution of the United States? The answer is, the people. Who made the several guaranties therein con-

tained? The people. With whom were they made? With one another, each with all, and all with each; they are the mutual guaranties of all and each. For what purposes were they made? "To establish justice, ensure domestic tranquility, provide for the common defence, and secure the blessings of Liberty to themselves and their posterity." All these guaranties are joint, and several in their character. Let it, then, be constantly kept in mind, that the people of the United States, in their original, sovereign capacity, as individuals, were the only parties to this instrument. That as such, they, in the exercise of their native sovereignty, formed this Constitution, and made with each other the guaranties therein contained, for their *mutual* and *individual* protection.

The States, as such were no parties to that instrument, although through the people, they were all parties to it. To the States, as such, no guaranties were made, although through the people, composing the States, all the guaranties were made to them. Let these things be kept in mind in fixing the meaning and force of this guaranty of a Republican form of government, to every State.

. . .

All the ends sought to be accomplished by the formation of the National Government are better secured by considering this guaranty as made with all the people of the several States, securing to each the benefits of a Republican form of Government, and pledging to them the faith and power of the Nation, that their relation to the state government shall ever be that of free citizens, for whose benefit, and by whose authority, in common with their fellow citizens, that government was established, and to be administered. By giving this construction to that clause, we not only secure to each individual the benefits of a Republican form of Government, but we secure the same to each State, and also to all the States, that every State in the Union shall possess a government—Republican in form.

. . .

What then is our conclusion from this guaranty? It is this, that all the citizens of the United States stand pledged to each citizen, that the State government under which he lives shall be to *him* Republican. That the relation which he shall sustain to that government shall be that of one of the *free, independent sovereigns*, by whose consent the government was established, and for whose protection it shall be maintained. And if there be a single citizen who is, or has been robbed of full and ample protection in the enjoyment of his natural and inherent rights, by the authority, or permission of the State in which he lives, this solemn guaranty has been violated, and the plighted faith of the nation demands that his wrongs shall be redressed, if need be, by the overthrow of that government that thus oppresses him. Let this be the construction of that guaranty, (and it should be nothing less) and let the Nation see to it, that it is enforced, and who could boast of immunity, like an American citizen! Then, indeed, could she be called "the land of the free and the home of the brave."

...

CHAPTER XVI.
The Right to bear arms: Due process of Law.
Militia.

The 2d article of the amendments to the constitution provides "a well regulated militia being necessary to the security of a free state, the right of the people to keep and bear arms shall not be infringed."

Here is another of the immunities of a citizen of the United States, which is guaranteed by the supreme, organic law of the land. This is one of the subordinate rights, mentioned by Blackstone, as belonging to every Englishman. It is called *"subordinate"* in reference to the great, absolute rights of man; and is accorded to every subject for the purpose of *protecting and defending himself*, if need be, in the enjoyment of his Absolute rights to life, liberty and property. And this guaranty is to all without any exception; for there is none, either expressed or implied. And our courts have already decided, that in such cases we have no right to make any exceptions. It is hardly necessary to remark that this guaranty is absolutely inconsistent with permitting a portion of our citizens to be enslaved. The colored citizen, under our constitution, has now as full and perfect a right to keep and bear arms as any other; and no State law, or State regulation has authority to deprive him of that right.

But there is another thing implied in this guaranty; and that is the *right of self defence*. For the right to keep and bear arms, also implies the right to use them if necessary in self defence; without this right to use the guaranty would have hardly been worth the paper it consumed.

But again this right of self-defence also implies that the citizen has a right to himself, that is to, his own personal security, liberty, property, &c.,—all of which is herein and hereby guaranteed.

And this right to personal security is more fully and directly guaranteed in the *4th art. of the amendments*, to wit, "the right of the people to be secure in their persons," &c., "shall not be violated;" "and no warrants shall be issued but upon probable cause supported by oath, or affirmation, and particularly describing the person to be seized." Now these are among the guaranties of the people of the United States, made to each and every citizen, and are even held applicable to those who are not citizens. The warrant to arrest an alien must contain all the requisites of a warrant to arrest a citizen. His personal security and liberty are under the care and protection of the government while he resides within her jurisdiction.

Now by what authority can any State pass a law setting at naught these positive guaranties of the constitution in the face of this provision? "This constitution and the laws of the United States made in pursuance thereof," &o., "shall be the supreme law of the land, and the judges in every State shall be bound thereby; any thing in the constitution, or laws of any State to the contrary notwithstanding."

Who does not know that these guaranties in the Federal Constitution, were made for the express and only purpose, of securing to every citizen full and perfect immunity in the enjoyment of his natural and inalienable rights? That no exceptions, or limitations were made or designed to be made, by which these guaranties were to be modified. We have before shown that at the time this constitution was adopted the feeling of the country was strongly *against* slavery. That the leading members of the convention denounced it, and refused to admit into the constitution any word, which could, by any legal rules of interpretation, be made to mean slave or slavery,—at the same time declaring that they would not admit the idea that man could be the subject of property. We have also shown, that at this time, the most that was asked was for time, so to arrange their circumstances as to put an end to slavery, with the least possible loss and inconvenience. That it was the express understanding that slavery was circumscribed, and limited, by the Ordinance of '87 &c., and that within a few years it would cease in the United States. That it was supposed, the death blow had already been given to it, from which it could never recover. That there were then no apologists for slavery, no advocates for slavery extension, or perpetuation, but all desired to see some way devised by which it should be speedily terminated. It was with feelings and expectations of this kind that the constitution was adopted, and the Government of the United States went into operation. The constitution was framed, and all the guaranties for freedom, made as though there were none but freemen in the country; and nothing but this tacit understanding, that slavery should be abolished at the earliest practical day caused it to survive that period. And it was this understanding and expectation that restrained the full and speedy operation of those guaranties for freedom. But that understanding has been violated, and those expectations have most signally failed. The entire policy of the slaveholding portion of this Government has been changed. Instead of confining slavery to its then limits, and abolishing it with all convenient dispatch, they have extended it over territories as large as the original thirteen states. They have brought nine new slaveholding states into the Union, and are now concentrating their whole power to extend it further, and gain a permanent dominion in this Government; and there is now no alternative left, but to stand by the guaranties of the National Constitution, and extend the blessings of liberty to all within the United States.

Due Process of Law.

But there are other guaranties for freedom, to be found in that instrument, which cannot be realized while slavery is permitted in the Union. Nevertheless, they stand there, as fresh and imperative as they did the day they were made. Among others, is to be found the following; in the latter clause of the 5th article of the amendments to the constitution, "No person shall be deprived of life, liberty, or property, without due process of law."

It cannot be claimed that the word "*person*" does not include the so called slave. In all the clauses of the constitution where it is claimed that this class are referred to, they are denominated "*persons.*" As for example, in the 3d clause of the 2d sec. of the 1st article of the constitution, slaves are said to be intended by the expression "three fifths of all other *persons;*" again in the 1st clause of the 9th sec., "The migration and importation of such persons," &c., is said to mean slaves!—and again in the 3d clause of the 3d sec., of the 4th article, "No *person* held to service or labor" &e., is translated slave. Then by what authority can any one affirm that in the clause under consideration the term *person* does not also include that class known under State laws as slaves. They cannot be excluded by any known, legal rule of interpretation, and whoever presumes to exclude them is guilty of an arbitrary assumption, dangerous to the liberties of the American people. For the same authority that can exclude one class from the benefits of that guaranty, can with equal propriety excluded any, and any other classes. But they cannot be denied the benefits of that guaranty. Can a colored man, or a slave even, be tried for a capital, or otherwise infamous crime, unless upon a presentment, or indictment of a grand jury? It is universally admitted that they cannot. That they are within the provisions of that guaranty. Can they, or either of them be twice put in jeopardy of life or limb for the same offence? Certainly not. What would be a good plea, in bar, for any white citizen, would also be good for them. Can a colored man or slave, be lawfully compelled to be a witness against himself? By no means: in that respect, he is within the meaning of the constitution. How is it then that the colored man and slave, are understood to be within the meaning of all the provisions of the 5th article of the amendments of the constitution except that which extends to life and liberty? By what rule of shuffling and double interpreting is it, that the same person to whom these several guaranties are made in that section is excluded from this latter clause, when on examination it will be found that the person to whom these other guaranties are made is the same to whom the latter is made also? It is not true that the colored man is excluded from the benefits of this guaranty. Nor is there any constitutional power in either the National or State Governments to exclude him. And any law passed either by congress or any of the State legislatures that denies to him the full benefits of that guaranty, is flatly and palpably in violation of this provision of the National Constitution.

But what is to be understood by "due process of law?" The fact that we have a law upon our statute books punishing murder, theft, burglary &c., is no warrant for arresting a man supposed to be guilty of any of those crimes, without legal process: that is, the law itself is no process authorizing an arrest, and detention. That is technically called the "*process*" which the Government puts into the hands of its officer, authorizing him to do the particular thing, which the law requires to be done; and we have already seen that no warrants of seizure shall issue against any person, but on probable cause supported by oath, or affirmation; and that a warrant to authorize the seizure must so particularly describe the person, to be seized, as to leave no room for mistake. All processes which can authorize any person to seize and detain another, must be issued by the proper officer, authorized by law to issue such process, under his hand and the seal of his office. And that process must set out upon its face, such facts as will, under the law justify its execution. The man that has been guilty of murder, cannot be arrested and detained without process. The officer who seeks to bring him to justice must have his process issued by the proper authority of the state. The Jailor must have his process of commitment, to detain him in jail; and the Sheriff must have his warrant of execution, before he can inflict the fatal penalty. Thus from the beginning of the arrest to the end of the execution, the process of law must be constantly in the hands of the officer, to warrant the detention of the criminal—and under our Federal Constitution there is no authority in any department of any government to dispense with such process. And this guaranty is as broad as the Union. It extends to every human being, be he citizen or alien, black or white-bond or free. It is as valuable as is the good faith and integrity of the American Nation. It is as sacred as our National honor as strong as our National power.

By what legal process, we then inquire, are the three million slaves held in bondage, *"deprived of liberty?"* Go into the infamous slave pens in our National Capitol, and inquire by what *legal process* that wife is torn from her husband! That mother from her babe? Follow up that coffle of slaves, hand cuffed and manacled,— driven through the streets of Washington, under the stars and stripes which float from the dome of the Capitol, and inquire by what "legal process" they have been thus stripped of their God-given rights and hurled down from the high eminence of humanity, to a level with the brute? Think of this, American Citizens, and then seriously tell us, what you think the solemn guaranty of the American Nation is worth. Think of this, and then, in the presence of a holy and righteous Judge, tell us, if you think his *"wrath can sleep forever."*

CHAPTER XVII.
The power of the Federal Government over the Territories of the United States.

The new doctrine started by the apologists and advocates of Slavery, that Congress has no power to legislate for the Territories of the United States, is now being advocated with so much apparent earnestness, that it demands a passing notice.

. . .

Since the establishment of the Federal government, the Nation has exercised legislative judicial and executive jurisdiction over these Territories. Crimes against the United States could as well be committed and punished in the Territories as in the States. It was as much piracy to import slaves into the Territories as into the States. The Act of 1800 prohibiting the Slave Trade, applied to all citizens of the United States, whether residing in the Territories or States. By the act of 1798 it was made a penal offence to bring slaves into the territory of Mississippi from without the United States. In 1804 certain classes of slaves were forbidden to be brought into the territory of New Orleans. In 1819 congress legislated on the subject of Slavery in Florida. In 1820 the famous Missouri compromise was made excluding slavery north of 36° 30'.

All territorial governments which have been established since the formation of the Union, have been established by the authority of congress, and they have always reserved to themselves or the President, the authority to appoint and control the civil action of the Governors of these Territories They have always reserved to themselves the power, and not unfrequently exercised it, to supervise the action of these territorial legislatures. Congress frequently has determined the qualifications of the electors of both Houses in the Territories. No law of the Territories is valid until approved by the Governor who receives his appointment and is also removable by the President of the United States, and when any law is approved by such Governor, it may be annulled by congress or the President.

We might go on and instance many specific cases, proving that the National government, since its first organization, has continued to exercise full and exclusive jurisdiction over all HER territories, legislative judicial and executive. But it is unnecessary.

Our conclusion then is, that the Federal government has full and exclusive jurisdiction over all the Territories of the United States; and that the native inhabitants of those Territories are citizens of the United States and subject to HER jurisdiction. That they are enshielded by the Federal Constitution and entitled to all the privileges and immunities guaranteed by that instrument to persons and citizens of the Union.

From the foregoing we, therefore, infer, that whatever may be the dispute between consolidationists, and the states right men as to the meaning and extent of the guaranties of the Constitution of the United States in regard to citizens of State governments, there can be none, as to citizens of the Territories of the United States.

All territorial governments in the Union are established by the direct action and authority of the United

States, under the Federal Constitution; and all citizens residing under those governments are entitled to all the privileges and immunities guaranteed by the Constitution of the United States for the personal liberty and security of the subject.

No law affecting the liberty or security of the territorial citizen can be passed except by the authority of the National government. Consequently no law can be passed that will be of any binding effect, which contravenes any of the provisions of the Federal Constitution.

If the Constitution of the United States does not authorize Congress to enslave men by legislative enactment, they cannot delegate the power to others to do so; nor can that power be exercised by any one, while the subject is a citizen of the United States, and entitled to the benefit of the positive guaranties of the Constitution for personal liberty and security.

But the Constitution of the United States knows men only as persons and citizens. This question was so decided by the Supreme court in the celebrated Mississippi case. Consequently the Constitution knows no class of persons residing in the territories of the United States, who are not entitled to all the immunities, guaranteed to persons in that instrument.

But the privileges and immunities guaranteed to citizens and persons in that instrument are absolutely inconsistent with slavery. Consequently these guaranties make it impossible legally to treat men as slaves in the territories of the United States.

But if slavery cannot legally exist in the Territories of the United States, because of the guarantys of the federal Constitution for liberty. These territories can not legally be converted into slave holding States. For if all persons residing in the Territories up to the time they are converted into States, are entitled to liberty under the Federal Constitution, they are in the eye of the supreme law of the land free; and cannot be legally enslaved by any authority whatever. For the Constitution of the United States &c., is the supreme law of the land; and no State constitution or State law which has been framed and enacted since the time of its adoption, and which conflicts with any of the provisions of that instrument, or tends directly to deprive any citizen or person of the United States of any of the privileges or immunities guaranteed to him by it, is of any legal force or validity whatever.

The person who has once been free under the American eagle, can never again be enslaved. When he has once been within the reach of these constitutional guaranties, there is no legal power in the United States, which can deprive him of their protection. Consequently if a master shall voluntarily permit a slave to go beyond the jurisdiction that enslaved him, and beyond the reach of slaveholding comity, his slave becomes a free man. The legal shackles fall off, and there is no legal power in the Union which can again put them on him.

This then is the conclusion! Before a Territory of the United States is erected into a State, the citizens of that Territory are citizens of the United States, and of the United States only. That no laws but those passed, by the authority of the United States can effect their rights. That no laws passed by the National Legislature or by their authority, which conflict with either the letter or spirit of the Federal constitution are of any binding force. Consequently slavery cannot exist under Territorial Governments, and therefore all persons residing within the National Territories are necessarily free in the eye of the law.

But if they are free under the Territorial Government, they cannot be enslaved by any government of a State which can be formed out of such Territory. For any State Constitution or law which would enslave them, would be void as being in conflict with the supreme law of the land, under which they could not be enslaved.

In this view, all the States which have been formed out of the Territories of the United States since the adoption of the Federal Constitution, can have no authority to establish slavery, and all such State Constitutions and all laws made in pursuance of such constitutions tending to establish slavery therein are void; and all persons held in bondage by virtue of such Constitutions and laws, are in contemplation of law free.

...

CHAPTER XIX.
What would insure the availability of these Guaranties?
...

The only thing wanting for the protection of every individual in the full enjoyment of his natural and Constitutional rights, is a disposition, on the part of the people, to enforce the guaranties of the constitution. Let them no longer plead that they *would* do it if they *could*. They have the full power, but lack the disposition to exercise it.

...

Let no American citizen think to throw this responsibility upon others, while he is silent, or idle. Let no choice of evils excuse him from the honest, firm, out spoken, and out acted duty, which for years he has owed to the slave.

But this is not all. Since the formation of our National Government, nine new Slave States have been brought in to this Union. The blighting curse of slavery has, by the faithlessness of the American citizen, been extended protected, and perpetuated over territories, equal in size to the original thirteen States. All this the American citizen had full power to prevent. Before they were admitted, Congress had power to abolish their slavery and to secure perfect immunity to the slave. Let the American citizen, if he would learn the crushing weight of his responsibilities, look to the fruit of his work in Florida, Alabama, Mississippi, Louisiana, Tennessee, Kentucky Missouri, Arkansas, Texas, and perhaps, now to be added, New-Mexico and California. If he thinks the cup of Divine wrath is not yet full, let the latter come in, as Slave States and there can be little doubt that it will then overflow the very brim. Be it known that, as American citizens, we have had the full power in our hands for years, to control, and put an end to all these evils, and nothing *but the lack of a disposition*, has prevented us from the exercise of that power—so that before God, and the world, the whole guilt of slavery rests upon our heads—the blood of six millions of slaves is now in our skirts; and nothing but the most bitter tears of repentance, producing, in us, the appropriate and necessary fruits, can remove that sinking burden from our souls. Else, like the ghost of Ann, to Richard, the boding cry of all these murdered slaves will come and say "let me sit heavy on thy soul" in Judgment.

THE END.

30

Fugitive Slave Act

9 Stat. 462, September 18, 1850*

Be it enacted by the Senate and House of Representatives of the United States of America in congress assembled, That the persons who have been, or may hereafter be, appointed commissioners, in virtue of any act of Congress, by the Circuit Courts of the United States, and

*George Minot, ed., *United States Statutes at Large* (Boston: Little, Brown, 1862), 9:462.

Who, in consequence of such appointment, are authorized to exercise the powers that any justice of the peace, or other magistrate of any of the United States, may exercise in respect to offenders for any crime or offense against the United States, by arresting, imprisoning, or bailing the same under and by the virtue of the thirty-third section of the act of the twenty-fourth of September seventeen hundred and eighty-nine, entitled "An Act to establish the judicial courts of the United States" shall be, and are hereby, authorized and required to exercise and discharge all the powers and duties conferred by this act.

Sec. 2. And be it further enacted, That the Superior Court of each organized Territory of the United States shall have the same power to appoint commissioners to take acknowledgments of bail and affidavits, and to take depositions of witnesses in civil causes, which is now possessed by the Circuit Court of the United States; and all commissioners who shall hereafter be appointed for such purposes by the Superior Court of any organized Territory of the United States, shall possess all the powers, and exercise all the duties, conferred by law upon the commissioners appointed by the Circuit Courts of the United States for similar purposes, and shall moreover exercise and discharge all the powers and duties conferred by this act.

Sec. 3. *And be it further enacted*, That the Circuit Courts of the United States shall from time to time enlarge the number of the commissioners, with a view to afford reasonable facilities to reclaim fugitives from labor, and to the prompt discharge of the duties imposed by this act.

Sec. 4. *And be it further enacted*, That the commissioners above named shall have concurrent jurisdiction with the judges of the Circuit and District Courts of the United States, in their respective circuits and districts within the several States, and the judges of the Superior Courts of the Territories, severally and collectively, in term-time and vacation; shall grant certificates to such claimants, upon satisfactory proof being made, with authority to take and remove such fugitives from service or labor, under the restrictions herein contained, to the State or Territory from which such persons may have escaped or fled.

Sec. 5. *And be it further enacted*, That it shall be the duty of all marshals and deputy marshals to obey and execute all warrants and precepts issued under the provisions of this act, when to them directed; and should any marshal or deputy marshal refuse to receive such warrant, or other process, when tendered, or to use all proper means diligently to execute the same, he shall, on conviction thereof, be fined in the sum of one thousand dollars, to the use of such claimant, on the motion of such claimant, by the Circuit or District Court for the district of such marshal; and after arrest of such fugitive, by such marshal or his deputy, or whilst at any time in his custody under the provisions of this act, should such fugitive escape, whether with or without the assent of such marshal or his deputy, such marshal shall be liable, on his official bond, to be prosecuted for the benefit of such claimant, for the full value of the service or labor of said fugitive in the State, Territory, or District whence he escaped: and the better to enable the said commissioners, when thus appointed, to execute their duties faithfully and efficiently, in conformity with the requirements of the Constitution of the United States and of this act, they are hereby authorized and empowered, within their counties respectively, to appoint, in writing under their hands, any one or more suitable persons, from time to time, to execute all such warrants and other process as may be issued by them in the lawful performance of their respective duties; with authority to such commissioners, or the persons to be appointed by them, to execute process as aforesaid, to summon and call to their aid the bystanders, or posse comitatus of the proper county, when necessary to ensure a faithful observance of the clause of the Constitution referred to, in conformity with the provisions of this act; and all good citizens are hereby commanded to aid and assist in the prompt and efficient execution of this law, whenever their services may be required, as aforesaid, for that purpose; and said warrants shall run, and be executed by said officers, any where in the State within which they are issued.

Sec. 6. *And be it further enacted*, That when a person held to service or labor in any State or Territory of the United States, has heretofore or shall hereafter escape into another State or Territory of the United States, the person or persons to whom such service or labor may be due, or his, her, or their agent or attorney, duly authorized, by power of attorney, in writing, acknowledged and certified under the seal of some legal officer or court of the State or Territory in which the same may be executed, may pursue and reclaim such fugitive person, either by procuring a warrant from some one of the courts, judges, or commissioners aforesaid, of the proper circuit, district, or county, for the apprehension of such fugitive from service or labor, or by seizing and arresting such fugitive, where the same can be done without process, and by taking, or causing such person to be taken, forthwith before such court, judge, or commissioner, whose duty it shall be to hear and determine the case of such claimant in a summary manner; and upon satisfactory proof being made, by deposition or affidavit, in writing, to be taken and certified by such court, judge, or commissioner, or by other satisfactory testimony, duly taken and certified by some court, magistrate, justice of the peace, or other legal officer authorized to administer an oath and take depositions under the laws of the State or Territory from which such person owing service or labor may have escaped, with a certificate of such magistracy or other authority, as aforesaid, with the seal of the proper court or officer thereto attached, which seal shall be sufficient to establish the competency of the proof, and with proof, also by affidavit, of the identity of the person whose service or labor is claimed to be due as aforesaid, that the person so arrested does in fact owe service or labor to the person or persons claiming him or her, in the State or Territory from which such fugitive may have escaped as aforesaid, and that said person escaped, to make out and deliver to such claimant, his or her agent or attorney, a certificate setting forth the substantial facts as to the service or labor due from such fugitive to the claimant, and of his or her escape from the State or Territory in which he or she was arrested, with authority to such claimant, or his or her agent or attorney, to use such reasonable force and restraint as may be necessary, under the circumstances of the case, to take and remove such fugitive person back to the State or Territory whence he or she may have escaped as aforesaid. In no trial or hearing under this act shall the testimony of such alleged fugitive be admitted in evidence; and the certificates in this and the first [fourth] section mentioned, shall be conclusive of the right of the person or persons in whose favor granted, to remove such fugitive to the State or Territory from which he escaped, and shall prevent all molestation of such person or persons by any process issued by any court, judge, magistrate, or other person whomsoever.

Sec. 7. *And be it further enacted*, That any person who shall knowingly and willingly obstruct, hinder, or prevent such claimant, his agent or attorney, or any person or persons lawfully assisting him, her, or them, from arresting such a fugitive from service or labor, either with or without process as aforesaid, or shall rescue, or attempt to rescue, such fugitive from service or labor, from the custody of such claimant, his or her agent or attorney, or other person or persons lawfully assisting as aforesaid, when so arrested, pursuant to the authority herein given and declared; or shall aid, abet, or assist such person so owing service or labor as aforesaid, directly or indirectly, to escape from such claimant, his agent or attorney, or other person or persons legally authorized as aforesaid; or shall harbor or conceal such fugitive, so as to prevent the discovery and arrest of such person, after notice or knowledge of the fact that such person was a fugitive from service or labor as aforesaid, shall, for either of said offences, be subject to a fine not exceeding one thousand dollars, and imprisonment not exceeding six months, by indictment and conviction before the District Court of the United States for the district in which such offence may have been committed, or before the proper court of criminal jurisdiction, if committed within any one of the organized Territories of the United States; and shall moreover forfeit and pay, by way of civil damages to the party injured by such illegal conduct, the sum of one thousand dollars for each fugitive so lost as aforesaid, to be recovered by action of debt, in any of the District or Territorial Courts aforesaid, within whose jurisdiction the said offence may have been committed.

Sec. 8. *And be it further enacted*, That the marshals, their deputies, and the clerks of the said District and Territorial Courts, shall be paid, for their services, the like fees as may be allowed for similar services in other cases; and where such services are rendered exclusively in the arrest, custody, and delivery of the fugitive to the claimant, his or her agent or attorney, or where such supposed fugitive may be discharged out of custody for the want of sufficient proof as aforesaid, then such fees are to be paid in whole by such claimant, his or her agent or attorney; and in all cases where the proceedings are before a commissioner, he shall be entitled to a fee of ten dollars in full for his services in each case, upon the delivery of the said certificate to the claimant, his agent or attorney; or a fee of five dollars in cases where the proof shall not, in the opinion of such commissioner, warrant such certificate and delivery, inclusive of all services incident to such arrest and examination, to be paid, in either case, by the claimant, his or her agent or attorney. The person or persons authorized to execute the process to be issued by such commissioner for the arrest and detention of fugitives from service or labor as aforesaid, shall also be entitled to a fee of five dollars each for each person he or they may

arrest, and take before any commissioner as aforesaid, at the instance and request of such claimant, with such other fees as may be deemed reasonable by such commissioner for such other additional services as may be necessarily performed by him or them; such as attending at the examination, keeping the fugitive in custody, and providing him with food and lodging during his detention, and until the final determination of such commissioners; and, in general, for performing such other duties as may be required by such claimant, his or her attorney or agent, or commissioner in the premises, such fees to be made up in conformity with the fees usually charged by the officers of the courts of justice within the proper district or county, as near as may be practicable, and paid by such claimants, their agents or attorneys, whether such supposed fugitives from service or labor be ordered to be delivered to such claimant by the final determination of such commissioner or not.

Sec. 9. *And be it further enacted*, That, upon affidavit made by the claimant of such fugitive, his agent or attorney, after such certificate has been issued, that he has reason to apprehend that such fugitive will be rescued by force from his or their possession before he can be taken beyond the limits of the State in which the arrest is made, it shall be the duty of the officer making the arrest to retain such fugitive in his custody, and to remove him to the State whence he fled, and there to deliver him to said claimant, his agent, or attorney. And to this end, the officer aforesaid is hereby authorized and required to employ so many persons as he may deem necessary to overcome such force, and to retain them in his service so long as circumstances may require. The said officer and his assistants, while so employed, to receive the same compensation, and to be allowed the same expenses, as are now allowed by law for transportation of criminals, to be certified by the judge of the district within which the arrest is made, and paid out of the treasury of the United States.

Sec. 10. *And be it further enacted*, That when any person held to service or labor in any State or Territory, or in the District of Columbia, shall escape therefrom, the party to whom such service or labor shall be due, his, her, or their agent or attorney, may apply to any court of record therein, or judge thereof in vacation, and make satisfactory proof to such court, or judge in vacation, of the escape aforesaid, and that the person escaping owed service or labor to such party. Whereupon the court shall cause a record to be made of the matters so proved, and also a general description of the person so escaping, with such convenient certainty as may be; and a transcript of such record, authenticated by the attestation of the clerk and of the seal of the said court, being produced in any other State, Territory, or district in which the person so escaping may be found, and being exhibited to any judge, commissioner, or other office, authorized by the law of the United States to cause persons escaping from service or labor to be delivered up, shall be held and taken to be full and conclusive evidence of the fact of escape, and that the service or labor of the person escaping is due to the party in such record mentioned. And upon the production by the said party of other and further evidence if necessary, either oral or by affidavit, in addition to what is contained in the said record of the identity of the person escaping, he or she shall be delivered up to the claimant, And the said court, commissioner, judge, or other person authorized by this act to grant certificates to claimants or fugitives, shall, upon the production of the record and other evidences aforesaid, grant to such claimant a certificate of his right to take any such person identified and proved to be owing service or labor as aforesaid, which certificate shall authorize such claimant to seize or arrest and transport such person to the State or Territory from which he escaped: Provided, That nothing herein contained shall be construed as requiring the production of a transcript of such record as evidence as aforesaid. But in its absence the claim shall be heard and determined upon other satisfactory proofs, competent in law.

Approved, September 18, 1850.

31

John C. Calhoun, *A Discourse on the Constitution* (II)

1851*

When the government of the United States was established, the two sections were nearly equal in respect to the two elements of which it is composed; a fact which, doubtless, had much influence, in determining the con-

*John C. Calhoun, *A Disquisition on Government and a Discourse on the Constitution and Government of the United States*, ed. Richard K. Cralle (Charleston, SC: Walker & James, 1851), 388–91.

vention to select them as the basis of its construction. Since then, their equality in reference to both, has been destroyed, mainly through the action of the government established for their mutual benefit. The first step towards it occurred under the old Congress of the confederation. It was among its last acts. It took place while the convention, which formed the present constitution and government, was in session, and may be regarded as contemporaneous with it. I refer to the ordinance of 1787; which, among other things, contained a provision excluding slavery from the North-Western Territory; that is, from the whole region lying between the Ohio and Mississippi rivers. The effect of this was, to restrict the Southern States, in that quarter, to the country lying south of it; and to extend the Northern over the whole of that great and fertile region. It was literally to restrict the one and extend the other.

. . .

The South received no equivalent for this magnificent cession, except a pledge inserted in the ordinance, similar to that contained in the constitution of the United States, to deliver up fugitive slaves. It is probable that there was an understanding among the parties, that it should be inserted in both instruments;—as the old Congress and the convention were then in session in the same place; and that it contributed much to induce the southern members of the former to agree to the ordinance. But be this as it may, both, in practice, have turned out equally worthless. Neither have, for many years, been respected. Indeed, the act itself was unauthorized. The articles of confederation conferred not a shadow of authority on Congress to pass the ordinance,—as is admitted by Mr. Madison; and yet this unauthorized, one-sided act (as it has turned out to be), passed in the last moments of the old confederacy, was relied on, as a precedent, for excluding the South from two thirds of the territory acquired from France by the Louisiana treaty, and the whole of the Oregon territory; and is now relied on to justify her exclusion from all the territory acquired by the Mexican war,—and all that may be acquired,—in any manner, hereafter. The territory from which she has already been excluded, has had the effect to destroy the equilibrium between the sections as it originally stood; and to concentrate, permanently, in the northern section the two majorities of which the government of the United States is composed. Should she be excluded from the territory acquired from Mexico, it will give to the Northern States an overwhelming preponderance in the government.

In the meantime, in the spirit of fanaticism, which had been long lying dormant, was roused into action by the course of the government,—as has been explained. It aims, openly and directly, at destroying the existing relations between the races in the southern section; on which depend its peace, prosperity and safety. To effect this, exclusion from the territories is an important step; and, hence, the union between the abolitionists and the advocates of exclusion, to effect objects so intimately connected.

All of this has brought about a state of things hostile to the continuance of the union, and the duration of the government. Alienation is succeeding to attachment, and hostile feelings to alienation; and these, in turn, will be followed by revolution, or a disruption of the Union, unless timely prevented. But this cannot be done by restoring the government to its federal character;—however necessary that may be as a first step. What has been done cannot be undone. The equilibrium between the two sections has been permanently destroyed by the measures above stated. The northern section, in consequence, will ever concentrate within itself the two majorities of which the government is composed; and should the southern be excluded from all territories, now acquired, or to be hereafter acquired, it will soon have so decided a preponderance in the government and the Union, as to be able to mould the constitution to its pleasure. Against this, the restoration of the federal character of the government can furnish no remedy. So long as it continues, there can be no safety for the weaker section. It places in the hands of the stronger and hostile section, the power to crush her and her institution; and leaves her no alternative, but to resist, or sink down into a colonial condition.

32

"No Union with Slaveholders,"
Liberator (Boston, MA)
July 7, 1854, vol. 24, no. 27, p. 106

NO UNION WITH SLAVEHOLDERS
The Meeting at Framingham
On the Fourth of July, (Tuesday last,) was of almost unprecedented numbers, and great unanimity and enthusiasm.

. . .

Mr. Garrison said he should now proceed to perform an action which would be the testimony of his own soul to all present, of the estimation in which he held the pro-slavery laws and deeds of the nation. Producing a copy of the *Fugitive Slave Law*, he set fire to it, and burnt it to ashes. Using an old and well-known phrase, he said, 'And let all the people say, *Amen;*' and a unanimous cheer and shout of '*Amen*' burst from the vast audience. In like manner, Mr. Garrison burned the decision of Edward G. Loring in the case of Anthony Burns, and the late charge of Judge Benjamin R. Curtis to the United States Grand Jury in reference to the 'treasonable' assault upon the Court House for the rescue of the fugitive—the multitude ratifying the fiery immolation with shouts of applause. Then holding up the U.S. Constitution, he branded it as the source and patent of all the other atrocities,—'a covenant with death, and an agreement with hell,'—and consumed it to ashes on the spot, exclaiming, 'So perish all compromises with tyranny! 'And let all the people say, Amen!' A tremendous shout of 'Amen!' went up to heaven in ratification of the deed, mingled with a few hisses and wrathful exclamations from some who were evidently in a rowdyish state of mind, but who were at once cowed by the popular feeling.

33

Massachusetts, Personal Liberty Act
May 21, 1855*

Be it enacted by the Senate and House of Representatives, in General Court assembled, and by the authority of the same, as follows:

Sect. 3. The writ of habeas corpus may be issued by the supreme judicial court, the court of common pleas, by any justice's court or police court of any town or city, by any court of record, or by any justice of either of said courts, or by any judge of probate; and it may be issued by any justice of the peace, if no magistrate above named is known to said justice of the peace to be within five miles of the place where the party is im-

* *Acts and Resolves Passed by the General Court of Massachusetts* (Boston, 1855), 924.

prisoned or restrained, and it shall be returnable before the supreme judicial court, or any one of the justices thereof, whether the court may be in session or not, and in term time or vacation.

. . .

Sect. 6. If any claimant shall appear to demand the custody or possession of the person for whose benefit such writ is sued out, such claimant shall state in writing the facts on which he relies, with precision and certainty; and neither the claimant of the alleged fugitive, nor any person interested in his alleged obligation to service or labor, nor the alleged fugitive, shall be permitted to testify at the trial of the issue; and no confessions, admissions or declarations of the alleged fugitive against himself shall be given in evidence. Upon every question of fact involved in the issue, the burden of proof shall be on the claimant, and the facts alleged and necessary to be established, must be proved by the testimony of at least two credible witnesses, or other legal evidence equivalent thereto, and by the rules of evidence known and secured by the common law; and no ex parte deposition or affidavit shall be received in proof in behalf of the claimant, and no presumption shall arise in favor of the claimant from any proof that the alleged fugitive or any of his ancestors had actually been held as a slave, without proof that such holding was legal.

Sect. 7. If any person shall remove from the limits of this Commonwealth, or shall assist in removing therefrom, or shall come into the Commonwealth with the intention of removing or of assisting in the removing therefrom, or shall procure or assist in procuring to be so removed, any person being in the peace thereof who is not "held to service or labor" by the "party" making "claim," or who has not "escaped" from the "party" making "claim," within the meaning of those words in the constitution of the United States, on the pretence that such person is so held or has so escaped, or that his "service or labor" is so "due," or with the intent to subject him to such "service or labor," he shall be punished by a fine of not less than one thousand, nor more than five thousand dollars, and by imprisonment in the State Prison not less than one, nor more than five years.

. . .

Sect. 9. No person, while holding any office of honor, trust, or emolument, under the laws of this Commonwealth, shall, in any capacity, issue any warrant or other process, or grant any certificate, under or by virtue of an act of congress, approved the twelfth day of February, in the year one thousand seven hundred and ninety-

three, entitled "An Act respecting fugitives from justice and persons escaping from the service of their masters," or under or by virtue of an act of congress, approved the eighteenth day of September, in the year one thousand eight hundred and fifty, entitled "An Act to amend, and supplementary to, 'An Act respecting fugitives from justice and persons escaping from the service of their masters.'" or shall in any capacity, serve any such warrant or other process.

Sect. 10. Any person who shall grant any certificate under or by virtue of the acts of congress, mentioned in the preceding section, shall be deemed to have resigned any commission from the Commonwealth which he may possess, his office shall be deemed vacant, and he shall be forever thereafter ineligible to any office of trust, honor or emolument under the laws of this Commonwealth.

Sect. 11. Any person who shall act as counsel or attorney for any claimant of any alleged fugitive from service or labor, under or by virtue of the acts of congress mentioned in the ninth section of this act, shall be deemed to have resigned any commission from the Commonwealth that he may possess, and he shall be thereafter incapacitated from appearing as counsel or attorney in the courts of this Commonwealth.

. . .

Sect. 14. Any person holding any judicial office under the constitution or laws of this Commonwealth, who shall continue, for ten days after the passage of this act, to hold the office of United States commissioner, or any office under the laws of the United States which qualifies him to issue any warrant or other process, or grant of any certificate under the acts of Congress named in the ninth section of this act, shall be deemed to have violated good behavior, to have given reason for the loss of public confidence, and furnished sufficient ground either for impeachment or for removal by address.

Sect. 15. Any sheriff, deputy sheriff, jailer, coroner, constable, or other officer of this Commonwealth, or the police of any city or town, or any district, county, city or town officer, or any officer or other member of the volunteer militia of this Commonwealth, who shall hereafter arrest, imprison, detain or return, or aid in arresting, imprisoning, detaining or returning, any person for the reason that he is claimed or adjudged to be a fugitive from service or labor, shall be punished by fine not less than one thousand dollars, and by imprisonment in the State Prison for not less than one, nor more than two, years.

Sect. 16. The volunteer militia of the Commonwealth shall not act in any manner in the seizure, detention or rendition of any person for the reason that he is claimed or adjudged to be a fugitive from service or labor.

...

Sect. 19. No jail, prison, or other place of confinement belonging to, or used by, either the Commonwealth of Massachusetts or any county therein, shall be used for the detention or imprisonment of any person accused or convicted of any offence created by either of the said acts of congress mentioned in the ninth section of this act, or accused or convicted of obstructing or resisting any process, warrant, or order issued under either of said acts, or of rescuing, or attempting to rescue, any person arrested or detained under any of the provisions of either of the said acts.

...

Sect. 20. All the provisions of law as to the writ of *habeas corpus*, heretofore existing and in force, so far as applicable, and so far as not hereby changed, shall apply to the cases arising under this act.

34

Dred Scott v. Sandford

60 U.S. 393 (1856)

Mr. Chief Justice TANEY delivered the opinion of the court.

This case has been twice argued. After the argument at the last term, differences of opinion were found to exist among the members of the court; and as the questions in controversy are of the highest importance, and the court was at that time much pressed by the ordinary business of the term, it was deemed advisable to continue the case, and direct a re-argument on some of the points, in order that we might have an opportunity of giving to the whole subject a more deliberate consideration. It has accordingly been again argued by counsel, and considered by the court; and I now proceed to deliver its opinion.

There are two leading questions presented by the record:

1. Had the Circuit Court of the United States jurisdiction to hear and determine the case between these parties? And

2. If it had jurisdiction, is the judgment it has given erroneous or not?

The plaintiff in error, who was also the plaintiff in the court below, was, with his wife and children, held as slaves by the defendant, in the State of Missouri; and he brought this action in the Circuit Court of the United States for that district, to assert the title of himself and his family to freedom. The declaration is in the form usually adopted in that State to try questions of this description, and contains the averment necessary to give the court jurisdiction; that he and the defendant are citizens of different States; that is, that he is a citizen of Missouri, and the defendant a citizen of New York. The defendant pleaded in abatement to the jurisdiction of the court, that the plaintiff was not a citizen of the State of Missouri, as alleged in his declaration, being a negro of African descent, whose ancestors were of pure African blood, and who were brought into this country and sold as slaves. To this plea the plaintiff demurred, and the defendant joined in demurrer. The court overruled the plea, and gave judgment that the defendant should answer over. And he thereupon put in sundry pleas in bar, upon which issues were joined; and at the trial the verdict and judgment were in his favor. Whereupon the plaintiff brought this writ of error.

Before we speak of the pleas in bar, it will be proper to dispose of the questions which have arisen on the plea in abatement. That plea denies the right of the plaintiff to sue in a court of the United States, for the reasons therein stated. If the question raised by it is legally before us, and the court should be of opinion that the facts stated in it disqualify the plaintiff from becoming a citizen, in the sense in which that word is used in the Constitution of the United States, then the judgment of the Circuit Court is erroneous, and must be reversed.

...

[Although the United States] is sovereign and supreme in its appropriate sphere of action, yet it does not possess all the powers which usually belong to the sovereignty of a nation. Certain specified powers, enumerated in the Constitution, have been conferred upon it; and neither the legislative, executive, nor judicial departments of the Government can lawfully exercise any authority beyond the limits marked out by the Constitution. And in regulating the judicial department, the cases in which the courts of the United States shall have jurisdiction are particularly and specifically enumerated and defined; and they are not authorized to take cognizance of any case which does not come within the description therein specified. Hence, when a plaintiff sues in a court of the United States, it is necessary that he should show, in his pleading, that the suit he brings is within the jurisdiction of the court, and that he is entitled to sue there. And if he omits to do this, and should, by any oversight of the Circuit Court, obtain a judgment in his favor, the judgment would be reversed in the appellate court for want of jurisdiction in the court below.

...

[I]t becomes, therefore, our duty to decide whether the facts stated in the plea are or are not sufficient to show that the plaintiff is not entitled to sue as a citizen in a court of the United States.

This is certainly a very serious question, and one that now for the first time has been brought for decision before this court. But it is brought here by those who have a right to bring it, and it is our duty to meet it and decide it.

The question is simply this: Can a negro, whose ancestors were imported into this country, and sold as slaves, become a member of the political community formed and brought into existence by the Constitution of the United States, and as such become entitled to all the rights, and privileges, and immunities, guaranteed by that instrument to the citizen? One of which rights is the privilege of suing in a court of the United States in the cases specified in the Constitution.

It will be observed, that the plea applies to that class of persons only whose ancestors were negroes of the African race, and imported into this country, and sold and held as slaves. The only matter in issue before the court, therefore, is, whether the descendants of such slaves, when they shall be emancipated, or who are born of parents who had become free before their birth, are citizens of a State, in the sense in which the word citizen is used in the Constitution of the United States. And this being the only matter in dispute on the pleadings, the court must be understood as speaking in this opinion of that class only, that is, of those persons who are the descendants of Africans who were imported into this country, and sold as slaves.

The situation of this population was altogether unlike that of the Indian race. The latter, it is true, formed no part of the colonial communities, and never amalgamated with them in social connections or in government. But although they were uncivilized, they were yet a free and independent people, associated together in nations or tribes, and governed by their own laws. Many of these political communities were situated in territo-

ries to which the white race claimed the ultimate right of dominion. But that claim was acknowledged to be subject to the right of the Indians to occupy it as long as they thought proper, and neither the English nor colonial Governments claimed or exercised any dominion over the tribe or nation by whom it was occupied, nor claimed the right to the possession of the territory, until the tribe or nation consented to cede it. These Indian Governments were regarded and treated as foreign Governments, as much so as if an ocean had separated the red man from the white; and their freedom has constantly been acknowledged, from the time of the first emigration to the English colonies to the present day, by the different Governments which succeeded each other. Treaties have been negotiated with them, and their alliance sought for in war; and the people who compose these Indian political communities have always been treated as foreigners not living under our Government. It is true that the course of events has brought the Indian tribes within the limits of the United States under subjection to the white race; and it has been found necessary, for their sake as well as our own, to regard them as in a state of pupilage, and to legislate to a certain extent over them and the territory they occupy. But they may, without doubt, like the subjects of any other foreign Government, be naturalized by the authority of Congress, and become citizens of a State, and of the United States; and if an individual should leave his nation or tribe, and take up his abode among the white population, he would be entitled to all the rights and privileges which would belong to an emigrant from any other foreign people.

We proceed to examine the case as presented by the pleadings.

The words "people of the United States" and "citizens" are synonymous terms, and mean the same thing. They both describe the political body who, according to our republican institutions, form the sovereignty, and who hold the power and conduct the Government through their representatives. They are what we familiarly call the "sovereign people," and every citizen is one of this people, and a constituent member of this sovereignty. The question before us is, whether the class of persons described in the plea in abatement compose a portion of this people, and are constituent members of this sovereignty? We think they are not, and that they are not included, and were not intended to be included, under the word "citizens" in the Constitution, and can therefore claim none of the rights and privileges which that instrument provides for and secures to citizens of the United States. On the contrary, they were at that time considered as a subordinate and inferior class of beings, who had been subjugated by the dominant race, and, whether emancipated or not, yet remained subject to their authority, and had no rights or privileges but such as those who held the power and the Government might choose to grant them.

It is not the province of the court to decide upon the justice or injustice, the policy or impolicy, of these laws. The decision of that question belonged to the political or law-making power; to those who formed the sovereignty and framed the Constitution. The duty of the court is, to interpret the instrument they have framed, with the best lights we can obtain on the subject, and to administer it as we find it, according to its true intent and meaning when it was adopted.

In discussing this question, we must not confound the rights of citizenship which a State may confer within its own limits, and the rights of citizenship as a member of the Union. It does not by any means follow, because he has all the rights and privileges of a citizen of a State, that he must be a citizen of the United States. He may have all of the rights and privileges of the citizen of a State, and yet not be entitled to the rights and privileges of a citizen in any other State. For, previous to the adoption of the Constitution of the United States, every State had the undoubted right to confer on whomsoever it pleased the character of citizen, and to endow him with all its rights. But this character of course was confined to the boundaries of the State, and gave him no rights or privileges in other States beyond those secured to him by the laws of nations and the comity of States. Nor have the several States surrendered the power of conferring these rights and privileges by adopting the Constitution of the United States. Each State may still confer them upon an alien, or any one it thinks proper, or upon any class or description of persons; yet he would not be a citizen in the sense in which that word is used in the Constitution of the United States, nor entitled to sue as such in one of its courts, nor to the privileges and immunities of a citizen in the other States. The rights which he would acquire would be restricted to the State which gave them. The Constitution has conferred on Congress the right to establish an uniform rule of naturalization, and this right is evidently exclusive, and has always been held by this court to be so. Consequently, no State, since the adoption of the Constitution, can by naturalizing an alien invest him with the rights and privileges

secured to a citizen of a State under the Federal Government, although, so far as the State alone was concerned, he would undoubtedly be entitled to the rights of a citizen, and clothed with all the rights and immunities which the Constitution and laws of the State attached to that character.

It is very clear, therefore, that no State can, by any act or law of its own, passed since the adoption of the Constitution, introduce a new member into the political community created by the Constitution of the United States. It cannot make him a member of this community by making him a member of its own. And for the same reason it cannot introduce any person, or description of persons, who were not intended to be embraced in this new political family, which the Constitution brought into existence, but were intended to be excluded from it.

The question then arises, whether the provisions of the Constitution, in relation to the personal rights and privileges to which the citizen of a State should be entitled, embraced the negro African race, at that time in this country, or who might afterwards be imported, who had then or should afterwards be made free in any State; and to put it in the power of a single State to make him a citizen of the United States, and endue him with the full rights of citizenship in every other State without their consent? Does the Constitution of the United States act upon him whenever he shall be made free under the laws of a State, and raised there to the rank of a citizen, and immediately clothe him with all the privileges of a citizen in every other State, and in its own courts?

The court think the affirmative of these propositions cannot be maintained. And if it cannot, the plaintiff in error could not be a citizen of the State of Missouri, within the meaning of the Constitution of the United States, and, consequently, was not entitled to sue in its courts.

It is true, every person, and every class and description of persons, who were at the time of the adoption of the Constitution recognized as citizens in the several States, became also citizens of this new political body; but none other; it was formed by them, and for them and their posterity, but for no one else. And the personal rights and privileges guaranteed to citizens of this new sovereignty were intended to embrace those only who were then members of the several State communities, or who should afterwards by birthright or otherwise become members, according to the provisions of the Constitution and the principles on which it was founded. It was the union of those who were at that time members of distinct and separate political communities into one political family, whose power, for certain specified purposes, was to extend over the whole territory of the United States. And it gave to each citizen rights and privileges outside of his State which he did not before possess, and placed him in every other State upon a perfect equality with its own citizens as to rights of person and rights of property; it made him a citizen of the United States.

It becomes necessary, therefore, to determine who were citizens of the several States when the Constitution was adopted. And in order to do this, we must recur to the Governments and institutions of the thirteen colonies, when they separated from Great Britain and formed new sovereignties, and took their places in the family of independent nations. We must inquire who, at that time, were recognized as the people or citizens of a State, whose rights and liberties had been outraged by the English Government; and who declared their independence, and assumed the powers of Government to defend their rights by force of arms.

In the opinion of the court, the legislation and histories of the times, and the language used in the Declaration of Independence, show, that neither the class of persons who had been imported as slaves, nor their descendants, whether they had become free or not, were then acknowledged as a part of the people, nor intended to be included in the general words used in that memorable instrument.

It is difficult at this day to realize the state of public opinion in relation to that unfortunate race, which prevailed in the civilized and enlightened portions of the world at the time of the Declaration of Independence, and when the Constitution of the United States was framed and adopted. But the public history of every European nation displays it in a manner too plain to be mistaken.

They had for more than a century before been regarded as beings of an inferior order, and altogether unfit to associate with the white race, either in social or political relations; and so far inferior, that they had no rights which the white man was bound to respect; and that the negro might justly and lawfully be reduced to slavery for his benefit. He was bought and sold, and treated as an ordinary article of merchandise and traffic, whenever a profit could be made by it. This opinion was at that time fixed and universal in the civilized portion of the white race. It was regarded as an axiom in morals as well as in politics, which no one thought of

disputing, or supposed to be open to dispute; and men in every grade and position in society daily and habitually acted upon it in their private pursuits, as well as in matters of public concern, without doubting for a moment the correctness of this opinion.

And in no nation was this opinion more firmly fixed or more uniformly acted upon than by the English Government and English people. They not only seized them on the coast of Africa, and sold them or held them in slavery for their own use; but they took them as ordinary articles of merchandise to every country where they could make a profit on them, and were far more extensively engaged in this commerce than any other nation in the world.

The opinion thus entertained and acted upon in England was naturally impressed upon the colonies they founded on this side of the Atlantic. And, accordingly, a negro of the African race was regarded by them as an article of property, and held, and bought and sold as such, in every one of the thirteen colonies which united in the Declaration of Independence, and afterwards formed the Constitution of the United States. The slaves were more or less numerous in the different colonies, as slave labor was found more or less profitable. But no one seems to have doubted the correctness of the prevailing opinion of the time.

The legislation of the different colonies furnishes positive and indisputable proof of this fact.

It would be tedious, in this opinion, to enumerate the various laws they passed upon this subject. It will be sufficient, as a sample of the legislation which then generally prevailed throughout the British colonies, to give the laws of two of them; one being still a large slaveholding State, and the other the first State in which slavery ceased to exist.

The province of Maryland, in 1717, (ch. 13, s. 5,) passed a law declaring "that if any free negro or mulatto intermarry with any white woman, or if any white man shall intermarry with any negro or mulatto woman, such negro or mulatto shall become a slave during life, excepting mulattoes born of white women, who, for such intermarriage, shall only become servants for seven years, to be disposed of as the justices of the county court, where such marriage so happens, shall think fit; to be applied by them towards the support of a public school within the said county. And any white man or white woman who shall intermarry as aforesaid, with any negro or mulatto, such white man or white woman shall become servants during the term of seven years, and shall be disposed of by the justices as aforesaid, and be applied to the uses aforesaid."

The other colonial law to which we refer was passed by Massachusetts in 1705, (chap. 6.) It is entitled "An act for the better preventing of a spurious and mixed issue," &c.; and it provides, that "if any negro or mulatto shall presume to smite or strike any person of the English or other Christian nation, such negro or mulatto shall be severely whipped, at the discretion of the justices before whom the offender shall be convicted."

And "that none of her Majesty's English or Scottish subjects, nor of any other Christian nation, within this province, shall contract matrimony with any negro or mulatto; nor shall any person, duly authorized to solemnize marriage, presume to join any such in marriage, on pain of forfeiting the sum of fifty pounds; one moiety thereof to her Majesty, for and towards the support of the Government within this province, and the other moiety to him or them that shall inform and sue for the same, in any of her Majesty's courts of record within the province, by bill, plaint, or information."

We give both of these laws in the words used by the respective legislative bodies, because the language in which they are framed, as well as the provisions contained in them, show, too plainly to be misunderstood, the degraded condition of this unhappy race. They were still in force when the Revolution began, and are a faithful index to the state of feeling towards the class of persons of whom they speak, and of the position they occupied throughout the thirteen colonies, in the eyes and thoughts of the men who framed the Declaration of Independence and established the State Constitutions and Governments. They show that a perpetual and impassable barrier was intended to be erected between the white race and the one which they had reduced to slavery, and governed as subjects with absolute and despotic power, and which they then looked upon as so far below them in the scale of created beings, that intermarriages between white persons and negroes or mulattoes were regarded as unnatural and immoral, and punished as crimes, not only in the parties, but in the person who joined them in marriage. And no distinction in this respect was made between the free negro or mulatto and the slave, but this stigma, of the deepest degradation, was fixed upon the whole race.

We refer to these historical facts for the purpose of showing the fixed opinions concerning that race, upon which the statesmen of that day spoke and acted. It is necessary to do this, in order to determine whether the general terms used in the Constitution of the United States, as to the rights of man and the rights of the people, was intended to include them, or to give to them or their posterity the benefit of any of its provisions.

The language of the Declaration of Independence is equally conclusive:

It begins by declaring that, "when in the course of human events it becomes necessary for one people to dissolve the political bands which have connected them with another, and to assume among the powers of the earth the separate and equal station to which the laws of nature and nature's God entitle them, a decent respect for the opinions of mankind requires that they should declare the causes which impel them to the separation."

It then proceeds to say: "We hold these truths to be self-evident: that all men are created equal; that they are endowed by their Creator with certain unalienable rights; that among them is life, liberty, and the pursuit of happiness; that to secure these rights, Governments are instituted, deriving their just powers from the consent of the governed."

The general words above quoted would seem to embrace the whole human family, and if they were used in a similar instrument at this day would be so understood. But it is too clear for dispute, that the enslaved African race were not intended to be included, and formed no part of the people who framed and adopted this declaration; for if the language, as understood in that day, would embrace them, the conduct of the distinguished men who framed the Declaration of Independence would have been utterly and flagrantly inconsistent with the principles they asserted; and instead of the sympathy of mankind, to which they so confidently appealed, they would have deserved and received universal rebuke and reprobation.

Yet the men who framed this declaration were great men—high in literary acquirements—high in their sense of honor, and incapable of asserting principles inconsistent with those on which they were acting. They perfectly understood the meaning of the language they used, and how it would be understood by others; and they knew that it would not in any part of the civilized world be supposed to embrace the negro race, which, by common consent, had been excluded from civilized Governments and the family of nations, and doomed to slavery. They spoke and acted according to the then established doctrines and principles, and in the ordinary language of the day, and no one misunderstood them. The unhappy black race were separated from the white by indelible marks, and laws long before established, and were never thought of or spoken of except as property, and when the claims of the owner or the profit of the trader were supposed to need protection.

This state of public opinion had undergone no change when the Constitution was adopted, as is equally evident from its provisions and language.

The brief preamble sets forth by whom it was formed, for what purposes, and for whose benefit and protection. It declares that it is formed by the *people* of the United States; that is to say, by those who were members of the different political communities in the several States; and its great object is declared to be to secure the blessings of liberty to themselves and their posterity. It speaks in general terms of the *people* of the United States, and of *citizens* of the several States, when it is providing for the exercise of the powers granted or the privileges secured to the citizen. It does not define what description of persons are intended to be included under these terms, or who shall be regarded as a citizen and one of the people. It uses them as terms so well understood, that no further description or definition was necessary.

But there are two clauses in the Constitution which point directly and specifically to the negro race as a separate class of persons, and show clearly that they were not regarded as a portion of the people or citizens of the Government then formed.

One of these clauses reserves to each of the thirteen States the right to import slaves until the year 1808, if it thinks proper. And the importation which it thus sanctions was unquestionably of persons of the race of which we are speaking, as the traffic in slaves in the United States had always been confined to them. And by the other provision the States pledge themselves to each other to maintain the right of property of the master, by delivering up to him any slave who may have escaped from his service, and be found within their respective territories. By the first above-mentioned clause, therefore, the right to purchase and hold this property is directly sanctioned and authorized for twenty years by the people who framed the Constitution. And by the second, they pledge themselves to maintain and uphold the right of the master in the manner specified, as long as the Government they then formed should endure. And these two provisions show, conclusively, that neither the description of persons therein referred to, nor their descendants, were embraced in any of the other provisions of the Constitution; for certainly these

two clauses were not intended to confer on them or their posterity the blessings of liberty, or any of the personal rights so carefully provided for the citizen.

No one of that race had ever migrated to the United States voluntarily; all of them had been brought here as articles of merchandise. The number that had been emancipated at that time were but few in comparison with those held in slavery; and they were identified in the public mind with the race to which they belonged, and regarded as a part of the slave population rather than the free. It is obvious that they were not even in the minds of the framers of the Constitution when they were conferring special rights and privileges upon the citizens of a State in every other part of the Union.

Indeed, when we look to the condition of this race in the several States at the time, it is impossible to believe that these rights and privileges were intended to be extended to them.

. . .

The legislation of the States therefore shows, in a manner not to be mistaken, the inferior and subject condition of that race at the time the Constitution was adopted, and long afterwards, throughout the thirteen States by which that instrument was framed; and it is hardly consistent with the respect due to these States, to suppose that they regarded at that time, as fellow-citizens and members of the sovereignty, a class of beings whom they had thus stigmatized; whom, as we are bound, out of respect to the State sovereignties, to assume they had deemed it just and necessary thus to stigmatize, and upon whom they had impressed such deep and enduring marks of inferiority and degradation; or, that when they met in convention to form the Constitution, they looked upon them as a portion of their constituents, or designed to include them in the provisions so carefully inserted for the security and protection of the liberties and rights of their citizens. It cannot be supposed that they intended to secure to them rights, and privileges, and rank, in the new political body throughout the Union, which every one of them denied within the limits of its own dominion. More especially, it cannot be believed that the large slaveholding States regarded them as included in the word citizens, or would have consented to a Constitution which might compel them to receive them in that character from another State. For if they were so received, and entitled to the privileges and immunities of citizens, it would exempt them from the operation of the special laws and from the police regulations which they considered to be necessary for their own safety. It would give to persons of the negro race, who were recognized as citizens in any one State of the Union, the right to enter every other State whenever they pleased, singly or in companies, without pass or passport, and without obstruction, to sojourn there as long as they pleased, to go where they pleased at every hour of the day or night without molestation, unless they committed some violation of law for which a white man would be punished; and it would give them the full liberty of speech in public and in private upon all subjects upon which its own citizens might speak; to hold public meetings upon political affairs, and to keep and carry arms wherever they went. And all of this would be done in the face of the subject race of the same color, both free and slaves, and inevitably producing discontent and insubordination among them, and endangering the peace and safety of the State.

...

And even as late as 1820, (chap. 104, sec. 8,) in the charter to the city of Washington, the corporation is authorized "to restrain and prohibit the nightly and other disorderly meetings of slaves, free negroes, and mulattoes," thus associating them together in its legislation; and after prescribing the punishment that may be inflicted on the slaves, proceeds in the following words: "And to punish such free negroes and mulattoes by penalties not exceeding twenty dollars for any one offence; and in case of the inability of any such free negro or mulatto to pay any such penalty and cost thereon, to cause him or her to be confined to labor for any time not exceeding six calendar months." And in a subsequent part of the same section, the act authorizes the corporation "to prescribe the terms and conditions upon which free negroes and mulattoes may reside in the city."

This law, like the laws of the States, shows that this class of persons were governed by special legislation directed expressly to them, and always connected with provisions for the government of slaves, and not with those for the government of free white citizens. And after such an uniform course of legislation as we have stated, by the colonies, by the States, and by Congress, running through a period of more than a century, it would seem that to call persons thus marked and stigmatized, "citizens" of the United States, "fellow-citizens," a constituent part of the sovereignty, would be an abuse of terms, and not calculated to exalt the character of an American citizen in the eyes of other nations.

The conduct of the Executive Department of the Government has been in perfect harmony upon this subject with this course of legislation. The question was brought officially before the late William Wirt, when he was the Attorney General of the United States, in 1821, and he decided that the words "citizens of the United States" were used in the acts of Congress in the same sense as in the Constitution; and that free persons of color were not citizens, within the meaning of the Constitution and laws; and this opinion has been confirmed by that of the late Attorney General, Caleb Cushing, in a recent case, and acted upon by the Secretary of State, who refused to grant passports to them as "citizens of the United States."

But it is said that a person may be a citizen, and entitled to that character, although he does not possess all the rights which may belong to other citizens; as, for example, the right to vote, or to hold particular offices; and that yet, when he goes into another State, he is entitled to be recognized there as a citizen, although the State may measure his rights by the rights which it allows to persons of a like character or class resident in the State, and refuse to him the full rights of citizenship.

This argument overlooks the language of the provision in the Constitution of which we are speaking.

Undoubtedly, a person may be a citizen, that is, a member of the community who form the sovereignty, although he exercises no share of the political power, and is incapacitated from holding particular offices. Women and minors, who form a part of the political family, cannot vote; and when a property qualification is required to vote or hold a particular office, those who have not the necessary qualification cannot vote or hold the office, yet they are citizens.

So, too, a person may be entitled to vote by the law of the State, who is not a citizen even of the State itself. And in some of the States of the Union foreigners not naturalized are allowed to vote. And the State may give the right to free negroes and mulattoes, but that does not make them citizens of the State, and still less of the United States. And the provision in the Constitution giving privileges and immunities in other States, does not apply to them.

Neither does it apply to a person who, being the citizen of a State, migrates to another State. For then he becomes subject to the laws of the State in which he lives, and he is no longer a citizen of the State from which he removed. And the State in which he resides may then, unquestionably, determine his *status* or condition, and place him among the class of persons who are not recognized as citizens, but belong to an inferior and subject race; and may deny him the privileges and immunities enjoyed by its citizens.

But so far as mere rights of person are concerned, the provision in question is confined to citizens of a State who are temporarily in another State without taking up their residence there. It gives them no political rights in the State, as to voting or holding office, or in any other respect. For a citizen of one State has no right to participate in the government of another. But if he ranks as a citizen in the State to which he belongs, within the meaning of the Constitution of the United States, then, whenever he goes into another State, the Constitution clothes him, as to the rights of person, with all the privileges and immunities which belong to citizens of the State. And if persons of the African race are citizens of a State, and of the United States, they would be entitled to all of these privileges and immunities in every State, and the State could not restrict them; for they would hold these privileges and immunities under the paramount authority of the Federal Government, and its courts would be bound to maintain and enforce them, the Constitution and laws of the State to the contrary notwithstanding. And if the States could limit or restrict them, or place the party in an inferior grade, this clause of the Constitution would be unmeaning, and could have no operation; and would give no rights to the citizen when in another State. He would have none but what the State itself chose to allow him. This is evidently not the construction or meaning of the clause in question. It guaranties rights to the citizen, and the State cannot withhold them. And these rights are of a character and would lead to consequences which make it absolutely certain that the African race were not included under the name of citizens of a State, and were not in the contemplation of the framers of the Constitution when these privileges and immunities were provided for the protection of the citizen in other States.

The case of Legrand v. Darnall (2 Peters, 664) has been referred to for the purpose of showing that this court has decided that the descendant of a slave may sue as a citizen in a court of the United States; but the case itself shows that the question did not arise and could not have arisen in the case.

. . .

This case, however, strikingly illustrates the consequences that would follow the construction of the Constitution which would give the power contended for to a State. It would in effect give it also to an individual. For if the father of young Darnall had manumitted him in his lifetime, and sent him to reside in a State which recognized him as a citizen, he might have visited and sojourned in Maryland when he pleased, and as long as he pleased, as a citizen of the United States; and the State officers and tribunals would be compelled, by the paramount authority of the Constitution, to receive him and treat him as one of its citizens, exempt from the laws and police of the State in relation to a person of that description, and allow him to enjoy all the rights and privileges of citizenship, without respect to the laws of Maryland, although such laws were deemed by it absolutely essential to its own safety.

The only two provisions which point to them and include them, treat them as property, and make it the duty of the Government to protect it; no other power, in relation to this race, is to be found in the Constitution; and as it is a Government of special, delegated, powers, no authority beyond these two provisions can be constitutionally exercised. The Government of the United States had no right to interfere for any other purpose but that of protecting the rights of the owner, leaving it altogether with the several States to deal with this race, whether emancipated or not, as each State may think justice, humanity, and the interests and safety of society, require. The States evidently intended to reserve this power exclusively to themselves.

No one, we presume, supposes that any change in public opinion or feeling, in relation to this unfortunate race, in the civilized nations of Europe or in this country, should induce the court to give to the words of the Constitution a more liberal construction in their favor than they were intended to bear when the instrument was framed and adopted. Such an argument would be altogether inadmissible in any tribunal called on to interpret it. If any of its provisions are deemed unjust, there is a mode prescribed in the instrument itself by which it may be amended; but while it remains unaltered, it must be construed now as it was understood at the time of its adoption. It is not only the same in words, but the same in meaning, and delegates the same powers to the Government, and reserves and secures the same rights and privileges to the citizen; and as long as it continues to exist in its present form, it speaks not only in the same words, but with the same meaning and intent with which it spoke when it came from the hands of its framers, and was voted on and adopted by the people of the United States. Any other rule of construction would abrogate the judicial character of this court, and make it the mere reflex of the popular opinion or passion of the day. This court was not created by the Constitution for such purposes. Higher and graver trusts have been confided to it, and it must not falter in the path of duty.

What the construction was at that time, we think can hardly admit of doubt. We have the language of the Declaration of Independence and of the Articles of Confederation, in addition to the plain words of the Constitution itself; we have the legislation of the different States, before, about the time, and since, the Constitution was adopted; we have the legislation of Congress, from the time of its adoption to a recent period; and we have the constant and uniform action of the Executive Department, all concurring together, and leading to the same result. And if anything in relation to the construction of the Constitution can be regarded as settled, it is that which we now give to the word 'citizen' and the word 'people.'

And upon a full and careful consideration of the subject, the court is of opinion, that, upon the facts stated in the plea in abatement, Dred Scott was not a citizen of Missouri within the meaning of the Constitution of the United States, and not entitled as such to sue in its courts; and, consequently, that the Circuit Court had no jurisdiction of the case, and that the judgment on the plea in abatement is erroneous.

We are aware that doubts are entertained by some of the members of the court, whether the plea in abatement is legally before the court upon this writ of error; but if that plea is regarded as waived, or out of the case upon any other ground, yet the question as to the jurisdiction of the Circuit Court is presented on the face of the bill of exception itself, taken by the plaintiff at the trial; for he admits that he and his wife were born slaves, but endeavors to make out his title to freedom and citizenship by showing that they were taken by their owner to certain places, hereinafter mentioned, where slavery could not by law exist, and that they thereby became free, and upon their return to Missouri became citizens of that State.

Now, if the removal of which he speaks did not give them their freedom, then by his own admission he is still a slave; and whatever opinions may be entertained in favor of the citizenship of a free person of the African race, no one supposes that a slave is a citizen of the State or of the United States. If, therefore, the acts done by his owner did not make them free persons, he is still a slave, and certainly incapable of suing in the character of a citizen.

The principle of law is too well settled to be disputed, that a court can give no judgment for either party, where it has no jurisdiction; and if, upon the showing of Scott himself, it appeared that he was still a slave, the case ought to have been dismissed, and the judgment against him and in favor of the defendant for costs, is, like that on the plea in abatement, erroneous, and the suit ought to have been dismissed by the Circuit Court for want of jurisdiction in that court.

But, before we proceed to examine this part of the case, it may be proper to notice an objection taken to the judicial authority of this court to decide it; and it has been said, that as this court has decided against the jurisdiction of the Circuit Court on the plea in abatement, it has no right to examine any question presented by the exception; and that anything it may say upon that part of the case will be extra-judicial, and mere obiter dicta.

This is a manifest mistake; there can be no doubt as to the jurisdiction of this court to revise the judgment of a Circuit Court, and to reverse it for any error apparent on the record, whether it be the error of giving judgment in a case over which it had no jurisdiction, or any other material error; and this, too, whether there is a plea in abatement or not.

The objection appears to have arisen from confounding writs of error to a State court, with writs of error to a Circuit Court of the United States. Undoubtedly, upon a writ of error to a State court, unless the record shows a case that gives jurisdiction, the case must be dismissed for want of jurisdiction in *this court*. And if it is dismissed on that ground, we have no right to examine and decide upon any question presented by the bill of exceptions, or any other part of the record. But writs of error to a State court, and to a Circuit Court of the United States, are regulated by different laws, and stand upon entirely different principles. And in a writ of error to a Circuit Court of the United States, the whole record is before this court for examination and decision; and if the sum in controversy is large enough to give jurisdiction, it is not only the right, but it is the judicial duty of the court, to examine the whole case as presented by the record; and if it appears upon its face that any material error or errors have been committed by the court below, it is the duty of this court to reverse the judgment, and remand the case. And certainly an error in passing a judgment upon the merits in favor of either party, in a case which it was not authorized to try, and over which it had no jurisdiction, is as grave an error as a court can commit.

The plea in abatement is not a plea to the jurisdiction of this court, but to the jurisdiction of the Circuit Court. And it appears by the record before us, that the Circuit Court committed an error, in deciding that it had jurisdiction, upon the facts in the case, admitted by the pleadings. It is the duty of the appellate tribunal to correct this error; but that could not be done by dismissing the case for want of jurisdiction here—for that would leave the erroneous judgment in full force, and the injured party without remedy. And the appellate court therefore exercises the power for which alone appellate courts are constituted, by reversing the judgment of the court below for this error. It exercises its proper and appropriate jurisdiction over the judgment and proceedings of the Circuit Court, as they appear upon the record brought up by the writ of error.

The correction of one error in the court below does not deprive the appellate court of the power of examining further into the record, and correcting any other material errors which may have been committed by the inferior court. There is certainly no rule of law—nor any practice—nor any decision of a court—which even questions this power in the appellate tribunal. On the contrary, it is the daily practice of this court, and of all appellate courts where they reverse the judgment of an inferior court for error, to correct by its opinions whatever errors may appear on the record material to the case; and they have always held it to be their duty to do so where the silence of the court might lead to misconstruction or future controversy, and the point has been relied on by either side, and argued before the court.

In the case before us, we have already decided that the Circuit Court erred in deciding that it had jurisdiction upon the facts admitted by the pleadings. And it appears that, in the further progress of the case, it acted upon the erroneous principle it had decided on the pleadings, and gave judgment for the defendant, where, upon the facts admitted in the exception, it had no jurisdiction.

We are at a loss to understand upon what principle of law, applicable to appellate jurisdiction, it can be supposed that this court has not judicial authority to correct the last-mentioned error, because they had before corrected the former; or by what process of reasoning it can be made out, that the error of an inferior court in actually pronouncing judgment for one of the parties, in a case in which it had no jurisdiction, cannot be looked into or corrected by this court, because we have decided a similar question presented in the pleadings.

The last point is distinctly presented by the facts contained in the plaintiff's own bill of exceptions, which he himself brings here by this writ of error. It was the point which chiefly occupied the attention of the counsel on both sides in the argument—and the judgment which this court must render upon both errors is precisely the same. It must, in each of them, exercise jurisdiction over the judgment, and reverse it for the errors committed by the court below; and issue a mandate to the Circuit Court to conform its judgment to the opinion pronounced by this court, by dismissing the case for want of jurisdiction in the Circuit Court. This is the constant and invariable practice of this court, where it reverses a judgment for want of jurisdiction in the Circuit Court.

It can scarcely be necessary to pursue such a question further. The want of jurisdiction in the court below may appear on the record without any plea in abatement. This is familiarly the case where a court of chancery has exercised jurisdiction in a case where the plaintiff had a plain and adequate remedy at law, and it so appears by the transcript when brought here by appeal. So also where it appears that a court of admiralty has exercised jurisdiction in a case belonging exclusively to a court of common law. In these cases there is no plea in abatement. And for the same reason, and upon the same principles, where the defect of jurisdiction is patent on the record, this court is bound to reverse the judgment, although the defendant has not pleaded in abatement to the jurisdiction of the inferior court.

The cases of Jackson *v.* Ashton and of Capron *v.* Van Noorden, to which we have referred in a previous part of this opinion, are directly in point. In the last-mentioned case, Capron brought an action against Van Noorden in a Circuit Court of the United States, without showing, by the usual averments of citizenship, that the court had jurisdiction. There was no plea in abatement put in, and the parties went to trial upon the merits. The court gave judgment in favor of the defendant with costs. The plaintiff thereupon brought his writ of error, and this court reversed the judgment given in favor of the defendant, and remanded the case with directions to dismiss it, because it did not appear by the transcript that the Circuit Court had jurisdiction.

The case before us still more strongly imposes upon this court the duty of examining whether the court below has not committed an error, in taking jurisdiction and giving a judgment for costs in favor of the defendant; for in Capron *v.* Van Noorden the judgment was reversed, because it did *not appear* that the parties were citizens of different States. They might or might not be. But in this case it *does appear* that the plaintiff was born a slave; and if the facts upon which he relies have not made him free, then it appears affirmatively on the record that he is not a citizen, and consequently his suit against Sandford was not a suit between citizens of different States, and the court had no authority to pass any judgment between the parties. The suit ought, in this view of it, to have been dismissed by the Circuit Court, and its judgment in favor of Sandford is erroneous, and must be reversed.

It is true that the result either way, by dismissal or by a judgment for the defendant, makes very little, if any, difference in a pecuniary or personal point of view to either party. But the fact that the result would be very nearly the same to the parties in either form of judgment, would not justify this court in sanctioning an error in the judgment which is patent on the record, and which, if sanctioned, might be drawn into precedent, and lead to serious mischief and injustice in some future suit.

We proceed, therefore, to inquire whether the facts relied on by the plaintiff entitled him to his freedom. The case, as he himself states it, on the record brought here by his writ of error, is this:

The plaintiff was a negro slave, belonging to Dr. Emerson, who was a surgeon in the army of the United States. In the year 1834, he took the plaintiff from the State of Missouri to the military post at Rock Island, in the State of Illinois, and held him there as a slave until the month of April or May, 1836. At the time last mentioned, said Dr. Emerson removed the plaintiff from said military post at Rock Island to the military post at Fort Snelling, situate on the west bank of the Mississippi river, in the Territory known as Upper Louisiana, acquired by the United States of France, and situate north of the latitude of thirty-six degrees thirty minutes north, and north of the State of Missouri. Said Dr. Emerson held the plaintiff in slavery at said Fort Snelling, from said last-mentioned date until the year 1838.

In the year 1835, Harriet, who is named in the second count of the plaintiff's declaration, was the negro slave of Major Taliaferro, who belonged to the army of the United States. In that year, 1835, said Major Taliaferro took said Harriet to said Fort Snelling, a military post, situated as hereinbefore stated, and kept her there as a slave until the year 1836, and then sold and delivered her as a slave, at said Fort Snelling, unto the said Dr. Emerson hereinbefore named. Said Dr. Emerson held said Harriet in slavery at said Fort Snelling until the year 1838.

In the year 1836, the plaintiff and Harriet intermarried, at Fort Snelling, with the consent of Dr. Emerson, who then claimed to be their master and owner. Eliza and Lizzie, named in the third count of the plaintiff's declaration, are the fruit of that marriage. Eliza is about fourteen years old, and was born on board the steamboat Gipsey, north of the north line of the State of Missouri, and upon the river Mississippi. Lizzie is about seven years old, and was born in the State of Missouri, at the military post called Jefferson Barracks.

In the year 1838, said Dr. Emerson removed the plaintiff and said Harriet, and their said daughter Eliza, from said Fort Snelling to the State of Missouri, where they have ever since resided.

Before the commencement of this suit, said Dr. Emerson sold and conveyed the plaintiff, and Harriet, Eliza, and Lizzie, to the defendant, as slaves, and the defendant has ever since claimed to hold them, and each of them, as slaves.

In considering this part of the controversy, two questions arise: 1. Was he, together with his family, free in Missouri by reason of the stay in the territory of the United States hereinbefore mentioned? And 2. If they were not, is Scott himself free by reason of his removal to Rock Island, in the State of Illinois, as stated in the above admissions?

We proceed to examine the first question.

The act of Congress, upon which the plaintiff relies, declares that slavery and involuntary servitude, except as a punishment for crime, shall be forever prohibited in all that part of the territory ceded by France, under the name of Louisiana, which lies north of thirty-six degrees thirty minutes north latitude, and not included within the limits of Missouri. And the difficulty which meets us at the threshold of this part of the inquiry is, whether Congress was authorized to pass this law under any of the powers granted to it by the Constitution; for if the authority is not given by that instrument, it is the duty of this court to declare it void and inoperative, and incapable of conferring freedom upon any one who is held as a slave under the laws of any one the States.

The counsel for the plaintiff has laid much stress upon that article in the Constitution which confers on Congress the power 'to dispose of and make all needful rules and regulations respecting the territory or other property belonging to the United States;' but, in the judgment of the court, that provision has no bearing on the present controversy, and the power there given, whatever it may be, is confined, and was intended to be confined, to the territory which at that time belonged to, or was claimed by, the United States, and was within their boundaries as settled by the treaty with Great Britain, and can have no influence upon a territory afterwards acquired from a foreign Government. It was a special provision for a known and particular territory, and to meet a present emergency, and nothing more.

...

Whether, therefore, we take the particular clause in question, by itself, or in connection with the other provisions of the Constitution, we think it clear, that it applies only to the particular territory of which we have spoken, and cannot, by any just rule of interpretation, be extended to territory which the new Government might afterwards obtain from a foreign nation. Consequently, the power which Congress may have lawfully exercised in this Territory, while it remained under a Territorial Government, and which may have been sanctioned by judicial decision, can furnish no justification and no argument to support a similar exercise of power over territory afterwards acquired by the Federal Government. We put aside, therefore, any argument, drawn from precedents, showing the extent of the power which the General Government exercised over slavery in this Territory, as altogether inapplicable to the case before us.

...

This brings us to examine by what provision of the Constitution the present Federal Government, under its delegated and restricted powers, is authorized to acquire territory outside of the original limits of the United States, and what powers it may exercise therein over the person or property of a citizen of the United States, while it remains a Territory, and until it shall be admitted as one of the States of the Union.

There is certainly no power given by the Constitution to the Federal Government to establish or maintain colonies bordering on the United States or at a distance, to be ruled and governed at its own pleasure; nor to enlarge its territorial limits in any way, except by the admission of new States. That power is plainly given; and if a new State is admitted, it needs no further legislation by Congress, because the Constitution itself defines the relative rights and powers, and duties of the State, and the citizens of the State, and the Federal Government. But no power is given to acquire a Territory to be held and governed permanently in that character.

And indeed the power exercised by Congress to acquire territory and establish a Government there, according to its own unlimited discretion, was viewed with great jealousy by the leading statesmen of the day. And in the Federalist, (No. 38,) written by Mr. Madison, he speaks of the acquisition of the Northwestern Territory by the confederated States, by the cession from Virginia, and the establishment of a Government there, as an exercise of power not warranted by the Articles of Confederation, and dangerous to the liberties of the people. And he urges the adoption of the Constitution as a security and safeguard against such an exercise of power.

We do not mean, however, to question the power of Congress in this respect. The power to expand the territory of the United States by the admission of new States is plainly given; and in the construction of this power by all the departments of the Government, it has been held to authorize the acquisition of territory, not fit for admission at the time, but to be admitted as soon as its population and situation would entitle it to admission. It is acquired to become a State, and not to be held as a colony and governed by Congress with absolute authority; and as the propriety of admitting a new State is committed to the sound discretion of Congress, the power to acquire territory for that purpose, to be held by the United States until it is in a suitable condition to become a State upon an equal footing with the other States, must rest upon the same discretion. It is a question for the political department of the Government, and not the judicial; and whatever the political department of the Government shall recognize as within the limits of the United States, the judicial department is also bound to recognize, and to administer in it the laws of the United States, so far as they apply, and to maintain in the Territory the authority and rights of the Government, and also the personal rights and rights of property of individual citizens, as secured by the Constitution. All we mean to say on this point is, that, as there is no express regulation in the Constitution defining the power which the General Government may exercise over the person or property of a citizen in a Territory thus acquired, the court must necessarily look to the provisions and principles of the Constitution, and its distribution of powers, for the rules and principles by which its decision must be governed.

Taking this rule to guide us, it may be safely assumed that citizens of the United States who migrate to a Territory belonging to the people of the United States, cannot be ruled as mere colonists, dependent upon the will of the General Government, and to be governed by any laws it may think proper to impose. The principle upon which our Governments rest, and upon which alone they continue to exist, is the union of States, sovereign and independent within their own limits in their internal and domestic concerns, and bound together as one people by a General Government, possessing certain enumerated and restricted powers, delegated to it by the people of the several States, and exercising supreme authority within the scope of the powers granted to it, throughout the dominion of the United States. A power, therefore, in the General Government to obtain and hold colonies and dependent territories, over which they might legislate without restriction, would be inconsistent with its own existence in its present form. Whatever it acquires, it acquires for the benefit of the people of the several States who created it. It is their trustee acting for them, and charged with the duty of promoting the interests of the whole people of the Union in the exercise of the powers specifically granted.

At the time when the Territory in question was obtained by cession from France, it contained no population fit to be associated together and admitted as a State; and it therefore was absolutely necessary to hold possession of it, as a Territory belonging to the United States, until it was settled and inhabited by a civilized community capable of self-government, and in a condition to be admitted on equal terms with the other States as a member of the Union. But, as we have before said, it was acquired by the General Government, as the representative and trustee of the people of the United States, and it must therefore be held in that character for their common and equal benefit; for it was the people of the several States, acting through their agent and representative, the Federal Government, who in fact acquired the Territory in question, and the Government holds it for their common use until it shall be associated with the other States as a member of the Union.

But until that time arrives, it is undoubtedly necessary that some Government should be established, in order to organize society, and to protect the inhabitants in their persons and property; and as the people of the United States could act in this matter only through the Government which represented them, and the through which they spoke and acted when the Territory was obtained, it was not only within the scope of its powers, but it was its duty to pass such laws and establish such a Government as would enable those by whose authority they acted to reap the advantages anticipated from its acquisition, and to gather there a population which would enable it to assume the position to which it was destined among the States of the Union. The power to acquire necessarily carries with it the power to preserve and apply to the purposes for which it was acquired. The form of government to be established necessarily rested in the discretion of Congress. It was their duty to establish the one that would be best suited for the protection and security of the citizens of the United States, and other inhabitants who might be authorized to take up their abode there, and that must always depend upon the existing condition of the Territory, as to the number and character of its inhabitants, and their situation in the Territory. In some cases a Government, consisting of persons appointed by the Federal Government, would best subserve the interests of the Territory, when the inhabitants were few and scattered, and new to one another. In other instances, it would be more advisable to commit the powers of self-government to the people who had settled in the Territory, as being the most competent to determine what was best for their own interests. But some form of civil authority would be absolutely necessary to organize and preserve civilized society, and prepare it to become a State; and what is the best form must always depend on the condition of the Territory at the time, and the choice of the mode must depend upon the exercise of a discretionary power by Congress, acting within the scope of its constitutional authority, and not infringing upon the rights of person or rights of property of the citizen who might go there to reside, or for any other lawful purpose. It was acquired by the exercise of this discretion, and it must be held and governed in like manner, until it is fitted to be a State.

But the power of Congress over the person or property of a citizen can never be a mere discretionary power under our Constitution and form of Government. The powers of the Government and the rights and privileges of the citizen are regulated and plainly defined by the Constitution itself. And when the Territory becomes a part of the United States, the Federal Government enters into possession in the character impressed upon it by those who created it. It enters upon it with its powers over the citizen strictly defined, and limited by the Constitution, from which it derives its own existence, and by virtue of which alone it continues to exist and act as a Government and sovereignty. It has no power of any kind beyond it; and it cannot, when it enters a Territory of the United States, put off its character, and assume discretionary or despotic powers which the Constitution has denied to it. It cannot create for itself a new character separated from the citizens of the United States, and the duties it owes them under the provisions of the Constitution. The Territory being a part of the United States, the Government and the citizen both enter it under the authority of the Constitution, with their respective rights defined and marked out; and the Federal Government can exercise no power over his person or property, beyond what that instrument confers, nor lawfully deny any right which it has reserved.

A reference to a few of the provisions of the Constitution will illustrate this proposition.

For example, no one, we presume, will contend that Congress can make any law in a Territory respecting the establishment of religion, or the free exercise thereof, or abridging the freedom of speech or of the press, or the right of the people of the Territory peaceably to assemble, and to petition the Government for the redress of grievances.

Nor can Congress deny to the people the right to keep and bear arms, nor the right to trial by jury, nor compel any one to be a witness against himself in a criminal proceeding.

These powers, and others, in relation to rights of person, which it is not necessary here to enumerate, are, in express and positive terms, denied to the General Government; and the rights of private property have been guarded with equal care. Thus the rights of property are united with the rights of person, and placed on the same ground by the fifth amendment to the Constitution, which provides that no person shall be deprived of life, liberty, and property, without due process of law. And an act of Congress which deprives a citizen of the United States of his liberty or property, merely because he came himself or brought his property into a particular Territory of the United States, and who had committed no offence against the laws, could hardly be dignified with the name of due process of law.

So, too, it will hardly be contended that Congress could by law quarter a soldier in a house in a Territory without the consent of the owner, in time of peace; nor in time of war, but in a manner prescribed by law. Nor could they by law forfeit the property of a citizen in a Territory who was convicted of treason, for a longer period than the life of the person convicted; nor take private property for public use without just compensation.

The powers over person and property of which we speak are not only not granted to Congress, but are in express terms denied, and they are forbidden to exercise them. And this prohibition is not confined to the States, but the words are general, and extend to the whole territory over which the Constitution gives it power to legislate, including those portions of it remaining under Territorial Government, as well as that covered by States. It is a total absence of power everywhere within the dominion of the United States, and places the citizens of a Territory, so far as these rights are concerned, on the same footing with citizens of the States, and guards them as firmly and plainly against any inroads which the General Government might attempt, under the plea of implied or incidental powers. And if Congress itself cannot do this—if it is beyond the powers conferred on the Federal Government—it will be admitted, we presume, that it could not authorize a Territorial Government to exercise them. It could confer no power on any local Government, established by its authority, to violate the provisions of the Constitution.

It seems, however, to be supposed, that there is a difference between property in a slave and other property, and that different rules may be applied to it in expounding the Constitution of the United States. And the laws and usages of nations, and the writings of eminent jurists upon the relation of master and slave and their mutual rights and duties, and the powers which Governments may exercise over it, have been dwelt upon in the argument.

But in considering the question before us, it must be borne in mind that there is no law of nations standing between the people of the United States and their Government, and interfering with their relation to each other. The powers of the Government, and the rights of the citizen under it, are positive and practical regulations plainly written down. The people of the United States have delegated to it certain enumerated powers, and forbidden it to exercise others. It has no power over the person or property of a citizen but what the citizens of the United States have granted. And no laws or usages of other nations, or reasoning of statesmen or jurists upon the relations of master and slave, can enlarge the powers of the Government, or take from the citizens the rights they have reserved. And if the Constitution recognizes the right of property of the master in a slave, and makes no distinction between that description of property and other property owned by a citizen, no tribunal, acting under the authority of the United States, whether it be legislative, executive, or judicial, has a right to draw such a distinction, or deny to it the benefit of the provisions and guarantees which have been provided for the protection of private property against the encroachments of the Government.

Now, as we have already said in an earlier part of this opinion, upon a different point, the right of property in a slave is distinctly and expressly affirmed in the Constitution. The right to traffic in it, like an ordinary article of merchandise and property, was guarantied to the citizens of the United States, in every State that might desire it, for twenty years. And the Government in express terms is pledged to protect it in all future time, if the slave escapes from his owner. This is done in plain words—too plain to be misunderstood. And no word can be found in the Constitution which gives Congress a greater power over slave property, or which entitles property of that kind to less protection that property of any other description. The only power conferred is the power coupled with the duty of guarding and protecting the owner in his rights.

Upon these considerations, it is the opinion of the court that the act of Congress which prohibited a citizen from holding and owning property of this kind in the territory of the United States north of the line therein mentioned, is not warranted by the Constitution, and is therefore void; and that neither Dred Scott himself, nor any of his family, were made free by being carried into this territory; even if they had been carried there by the owner, with the intention of becoming a permanent resident.

We have so far examined the case, as it stands under the Constitution of the United States, and the powers thereby delegated to the Federal Government.

But there is another point in the case which depends on State power and State law. And it is contended, on the part of the plaintiff, that he is made free by being taken to Rock Island, in the State of Illinois, independently of his residence in the territory of the United States; and being so made free, he was not again reduced to a state of slavery by being brought back to Missouri.

Our notice of this part of the case will be very brief; for the principle on which it depends was decided in this court, upon much consideration, in the case of Strader et al. *v.* Graham, reported in 10th Howard, 82. In that case, the slaves had been taken from Kentucky to Ohio, with the consent of the owner, and afterwards brought back to Kentucky. And this court held that their *status* or condition, as free or slave, depended upon the laws of Kentucky, when they were brought back into that State, and not of Ohio; and that this court had no jurisdiction to revise the judgment of a State court upon its own laws. This was the point directly before the court, and the decision that this court had not jurisdiction turned upon it, as will be seen by the report of the case.

So in this case. As Scott was a slave when taken into the State of Illinois by his owner, and was there held as such, and brought back in that character, his *status*, as free or slave, depended on the laws of Missouri, and not of Illinois.

It has, however, been urged in the argument, that by the laws of Missouri he was free on his return, and that this case, therefore, cannot be governed by the case of Strader et al. *v.* Graham, where it appeared, by the laws of Kentucky, that the plaintiffs continued to be slaves on their return from Ohio. But whatever doubts or opinions may, at one time, have been entertained upon this subject, we are satisfied, upon a careful examination of all the cases decided in the State courts of Missouri referred to, that it is now firmly settled by the decisions of the highest court in the State, that Scott and his family upon their return were not free, but were, by the laws of Missouri, the property of the defendant; and that the Circuit Court of the United States had no jurisdiction, when, by the laws of the State, the plaintiff was a slave, and not a citizen.

Moreover, the plaintiff, it appears, brought a similar action against the defendant in the State court of Missouri, claiming the freedom of himself and his family upon the same grounds and the same evidence upon which he relies in the case before the court. The case was carried before the Supreme Court of the State; was fully argued there; and that court decided that neither the plaintiff nor his family were entitled to freedom, and were still the slaves of the defendant; and reversed the judgment of the inferior State court, which had given a different decision. If the plaintiff supposed that this judgment of the Supreme Court of the State was erroneous, and that this court had jurisdiction to revise and reverse it, the only mode by which he could legally bring it before this court was by writ of error directed to the Supreme Court of the State, requiring it to transmit the record to this court. If this had been done, it is too plain for argument that the writ must have been dismissed for want of jurisdiction in this court. The case of Strader and others *v.* Graham is directly in point; and, indeed, independent of any decision, the language of the 25th section of the act of 1789 is too clear and precise to admit of controversy.

But the plaintiff did not pursue the mode prescribed by law for bringing the judgment of a State court before this court for revision, but suffered the case to be remanded to the inferior State court, where it is still continued, and is, by agreement of parties, to await the judgment of this court on the point. All of this appears on the record before us, and by the printed report of the case.

And while the case is yet open and pending in the inferior State court, the plaintiff goes into the Circuit Court of the United States, upon the same case and the same evidence, and against the same party, and proceeds to judgment, and then brings here the same case from the Circuit Court, which the law would not have permitted him to bring directly from the State court. And if this court takes jurisdiction in this form, the result, so far as the rights of the respective parties are concerned, is in every respect substantially the same as if it had in open violation of law entertained jurisdiction over the judgment of the State court upon a writ of error, and revised and reversed its judgment upon the ground that its opinion upon the question of law was erroneous. It would ill become this court to sanction such an attempt to evade the law, or to exercise an appellate power in this circuitous way, which it is forbidden to exercise in the direct and regular and invariable forms of judicial proceedings.

Upon the whole, therefore, it is the judgment of this court, that it appears by the record before us that the plaintiff in error is not a citizen of Missouri, in the sense in which that word is used in the Constitution; and that the Circuit Court of the United States, for that reason, had no jurisdiction in the case, and could give no judgment in it. Its judgment for the defendant must, consequently, be reversed, and a mandate issued, directing the suit to be dismissed for want of jurisdiction.

Mr. Justice CAMPBELL.

I concur in the judgment pronounced by the Chief Justice, but the importance of the cause, the expectation and interest it has awakened, and the responsibility involved in its determination, induce me to file a separate opinion.

...

It is a settled doctrine of this court, that the Federal Government can exercise no power over the subject of slavery within the States, nor control the intermigration of slaves, other than fugitives, among the States. Nor can that Government affect the duration of slavery within the States, other than by a legislation over the foreign slave trade. The power of Congress to adopt the section of the act above cited must therefore depend upon some condition of the Territories which distinguishes them from States, and subjects them to a control more extended. The third section of the fourth article of the Constitution is referred to as the only and all-sufficient grant to support this claim. It is, that 'new States may be admitted by the Congress to this Union; but no new State shall be formed or erected within the jurisdiction of any other State, nor any State be formed by the junction of two or more States, or parts of State, without the consent of the Legislatures of the States concerned, as well as of the Congress. The Congress shall have power to dispose of and make all needful rules and regulations respecting the territory or other property belonging to the United States; and nothing in this Constitution shall be so construed as to prejudice any claims of the United States, or of any particular State.'

It is conceded, in the decisions of this court, that Congress may secure the rights of the United States in the public domain, provide for the sale or lease of any part of it, and establish the validity of the titles of the purchasers, and may organize Territorial Governments, with powers of legislation. (3 How., 212; 12 How., 1; 1 Pet., 511; 13 Pet., 436; 16 H., 164)

But the recognition of a plenary power in Congress to dispose of the public domain, or to organize a Government over it, does not imply a corresponding authority to determine the internal polity, or to adjust the domestic relations, or the persons who may lawfully inhabit the territory in which it is situated.

...

[The acquisition of Louisiana, in 1803] gave rise to jealous inquiries, as to the influence it would exert in determining the men and States that were to be "the arbiters and rulers" of the destinies of the Union; and unconstitutional opinions, having for their aim to promote sectional divisions, were announced and developed. "Something," said an eminent statesman, "something has suggested to the members of Congress the policy of acquiring geographical majorities. This is a very direct step towards disunion, for it must foster the geographical enmities by which alone it can be effected. This something must be a contemplation of particular advantages to be derived from such majorities; and is it not notorious that they consist of nothing else but usurpations over persons and property, by which they can regulate the internal *wealth and prosperity of States and individuals?*"

The most dangerous of the efforts to employ a geographical political power, to perpetuate a geographical preponderance in the Union, is to be found in the deliberations upon the act of the 6th of March, 1820, before cited. The attempt consisted of a proposal to exclude Missouri from a place in the Union, unless her people would adopt a Constitution containing a prohibition upon the subject of slavery, according to a prescription of Congress. The sentiment is now general, if not universal, that Congress had no constitutional power to impose the restriction. This was frankly admitted at the bar, in the course of this argument. The principles which this court have pronounced condemn the pretension then made on behalf of the legislative department. In Groves *v.* Slaughter, (15 Pet.,) the Chief Justice said: "The power over this subject is exclusively with the several States, and each of them has a right to decide for itself whether it will or will not allow persons of this description to be brought within its limits." Justice McLean said: "The Constitution of the United States operates alike in all the States, and one State has the same power over the subject of slavery as every other State." In Pollard's Lessee *v.* Hagan, (3 How., 212) the court say: "The United States have no constitutional capacity to exercise municipal jurisdiction, sovereignty, or eminent domain, within the limits of a State or elsewhere, except in cases where it is delegated, and the court denies the faculty of the Federal Government to add to its powers by treaty or compact."

This is a necessary consequence, resulting from the nature of the Federal Constitution, which is a federal compact among the States, establishing a limited Government, with powers delegated by the people of distinct and independent communities, who reserved to their State Governments, and to themselves, the powers they did not grant. This claim to impose a restriction upon the people of Missouri involved a denial of the constitutional relations between the people of the States and Congress, and affirmed a concurrent right for the latter, with their people, to constitute the social and political system of the new States. A successful maintenance of this claim would have altered the basis of the Constitution. The new States would have become members of a Union defined in part by the Constitution and in part by Congress. They would not have been admitted to "this Union." Their sovereignty would have been restricted by Congress as well as the Constitution. The demand was unconstitutional and subversive, but was prosecuted with an energy, and aroused such animosities among the people, that patriots, whose confidence had not failed during the Revolution, began to despair for the Constitution. Amid the utmost violence of this extraordinary contest, the expedient contained in the eighth section of this act was proposed, to moderate it, and to avert the catastrophe it menaced. It was not seriously debated, nor were its constitutional aspects severely scrutinized by Congress. For the first time, in the history of the country, has its operation been embodied in a case at law, and been presented to this court for their judgment. The inquiry is, whether there are conditions in the Constitutions of the Territories which subject the capacity and *status* of persons within their limits to the direct action of Congress. Can Congress determine the condition and *status* of persons who inhabit the Territories?

The Constitution permits Congress to dispose of and to make all needful rules and regulations respecting the territory or other property belonging to the United States. This power applies as well to territory belonging to the United States within the States, as beyond them. It comprehends all the public domain, wherever it may be. The argument is, that the power to make "ALL needful rules and regulations" "is a power of legislation," "a full legislative power;" "that it includes all subjects of legislation in the territory," and is without any limitations, except the positive prohibitions which affect all the powers of Congress. Congress may then regulate or prohibit slavery upon the public domain within the new States, and such a prohibition would permanently affect the capacity of a slave, whose master might carry him to it. And why not? Because no power has been conferred on Congress. This is a conclusion universally admitted. But the power to "make rules and regulations respecting the territory" is not restrained by State lines, nor are there any constitutional prohibitions upon its exercise in the domain of the United States within the States; and whatever rules and regulations respecting territory Congress may constitutionally make are supreme, and are not dependent on the *situs* of "the territory."

The author of the Farmer's Letters, so famous in the ante-revolutionary history, thus states the argument made by the American loyalists in favor of the claim of the British Parliament to legislate in all cases whatever over the colonies: "It has been urged with great vehemence against us," he says, "and it seems to be thought their FORT by our adversaries, that a power of regulation is a power of legislation; and a power of legislation, if constitutional, must be universal and supreme, in the utmost sense of the word. It is therefore concluded that the colonies, by acknowledging the power of regulation, acknowledged every other power."

This sophism imposed upon a portion of the patriots of that day. Chief Justice Marshall, in his life of Washington, says "that many of the best-informed men in Massachusetts had perhaps adopted the opinion of the parliamentary right of internal government over the colonies;" "that the English statute book furnishes many instances of its exercise;" "that in no case recollected, was their authority openly controverted;" and "that the General Court of Massachusetts, on a late occasion, openly recognized the principle." (Marsh. Wash., v. 2, p. 75, 76.)

But the more eminent men of Massachusetts rejected it; and another patriot of the time employs the instance to warn us of "the stealth with which oppression approaches," and "the enormities towards which precedents travel." And the people of the United States, as we have seen, appealed to the last argument, rather than acquiesce in their authority. Could it have been the purpose of Washington and his illustrious associates, by the use of ambiguous, equivocal, and expansive words, such as "rules," "regulations," "territory," to re-establish in the Constitution of their country that *fort* which had been prostrated amid the toils and with the sufferings and sacrifices of seven years of war? Are these words to be understood as the Norths, the Grenvilles, Hillsboroughs, Hutchinsons, and Dunmores—in a word, as George III would have understood them—or are we to look for their interpretation to Patrick Henry or Samuel Adams, to Jefferson, and Jay, and Dickinson; to the sage Franklin, or to Hamilton, who from his early manhood was engaged in combating British constructions of such words? We know that the resolution of Congress of 1780 contemplated that the new States to be formed under their recommendation were to have the same rights of sovereignty, freedom, and independence, as the old. That every resolution, cession, compact, and ordinance, of the States, observed the same liberal principle. That the Union of the Constitution is a union formed of equal States; and that new States, when admitted, were to enter "this Union." Had another union been proposed in 'any pointed manner,' it would have encountered not only "strong" but successful opposition. The disunion between Great Britain and her colonies originated in the antipathy of the latter to 'rules and regulations' made by a remote power respecting their internal policy. In forming the Constitution, this fact was ever present in the minds of its authors. The people were assured by their most trusted statesmen "that the jurisdiction of the Federal Government is limited to certain enumerated objects, which concern all members of the republic," and "that the local or municipal authorities form distinct portions of supremacy, no more subject within their respective spheres to the general authority, than the general authority is subject to them within its own sphere."

Still, this did not content them. Under the lead of Hancock and Samuel Adams, of Patrick Henry and George Mason, they demanded an explicit declaration that no more power was to be exercised than they had delegated. And the ninth and tenth amendments to the Constitution were designed to include the reserved rights of the States, and the people, within all the sanctions of that instrument, and to bind the authorities, State and Federal, by the judicial oath it prescribes, to their recognition and observance. Is it probable, therefore, that the supreme and irresponsible power, which is now claimed for Congress over boundless territories, the use of which cannot fail to react upon the political system of the States, to its subversion, was ever within the contemplation of the statesmen who conducted the counsels of the people in the formation of this Constitution? When the questions that came to the surface upon the acquisition of Louisiana were presented to the mind of Jefferson, he wrote: "I had rather ask an enlargement of power from the nation, where it is found necessary, than to assume it by a construction which would make our powers boundless. Our peculiar security is in the possession of a written Constitution. Let us not make it blank paper by construction. I say the same as to the opinion of those who consider the grant of the treaty-making power as boundless. If it is, then we have no Constitution. If it has bounds, they can be no others than the definitions of the powers which that instrument gives. It specifies and delineates the operations permitted to the Federal Government, and gives the powers necessary to carry them into execution." The publication of the journals of the Federal Convention in 1819, of the debates reported by Mr. Madison in 1840, and the mass of private correspondence of the early statesmen before and since, enable us to approach the discussion of the aims of those who made the Constitution, with some insight and confidence.

I have endeavored, with the assistance of these, to find a solution for the grave and difficult question involved in this inquiry. My opinion is, that the claim for

Congress of supreme power in the Territories, under the grant to "dispose of and make all needful rules and regulations respecting *territory*," is not supported by the historical evidence drawn from the Revolution, the Confederation, or the deliberations which preceded the ratification of the Federal Constitution. The ordinance of 1787 depended upon the action of the Congress of the Confederation, the assent of the State of Virginia, and the acquiescence of the people who recognized the validity of that plea of necessity which supported so many of the acts of the Governments of that time; and the Federal Government accepted the ordinance as a recognized and valid engagement of the Confederation.

. . .

Upon this record, it is apparent that this is not a controversy between citizens of different States; and that the plaintiff, at no period of the life which has been submitted to the view of the court, has had a capacity to maintain a suit in the courts of the United States. And in so far as the argument of the Chief Justice upon the plea in abatement has a reference to the plaintiff or his family, in any of the conditions or circumstances of their lives, as presented in the evidence, I concur in that portion of his opinion. I concur in the judgment which expresses the conclusion that the Circuit Court should not have rendered a general judgment.

The capacity of the plaintiff to sue is involved in the pleas in bar, and the verdict of the jury discloses an incapacity under the Constitution. Under the Constitution of the United States, his is an incapacity to sue in their courts, while, by the laws of Missouri, the operation of the verdict would be more extensive. I think it a safe conclusion to enforce the lesser disability imposed by the Constitution of the United States, and leave to the plaintiff all his rights in Missouri. I think the judgment should be affirmed, on the ground that the Circuit Court had no jurisdiction, or that the case should be reversed and remanded, that the suit may be dismissed.

. . .

Mr. Justice McLEAN dissenting.

. . .

But it is said, if the court, on looking at the record, shall clearly perceive that the Circuit Court had no jurisdiction, it is a ground for the dismissal of the case. This may be characterized as rather a sharp practice, and one which seldom, if ever, occurs. No case was cited in the argument as authority, and not a single case precisely in point is recollected in our reports. The pleadings do not show a want of jurisdiction. This want of jurisdiction can only be ascertained by a judgment on the demurrer to the special plea. No such case, it is believed, can be cited. But if this rule of practice is to be applied in this case, and the plaintiff in error is required to answer and maintain as well the points ruled in his favor, as to show the error of those ruled against him, he has more than an ordinary duty to perform. Under such circumstances, the want of jurisdiction in the Circuit Court must be so clear as not to admit of doubt. Now, the plea which raises the question of jurisdiction, in my judgment, is radically defective. The gravamen of the plea is this: "That the plaintiff is a negro of African descent, his ancestors being of pure African blood, and were brought into this country, and sold as negro slaves."

There is no averment in this plea which shows or conduces to show an inability in the plaintiff to sue in the Circuit Court. It does not allege that the plaintiff had his domicil in any other State, nor that he is not a free man in Missouri. He is averred to have had a negro ancestry, but this does not show that he is not a citizen of Missouri, within the meaning of the act of Congress authorizing him to sue in the Circuit Court. It has never been held necessary, to constitute a citizen within the act, that he should have the qualifications of an elector. Females and minors may sue in the Federal courts, and so may any individual who has a permanent domicil in the State under whose laws his rights are protected, and to which he owes allegiance.

Being born under our Constitution and laws, no naturalization is required, as one of foreign birth, to make him a citizen. The most general and appropriate definition of the term citizen is 'a freeman.' Being a freeman, and having his domicil in a State different from that of the defendant, he is a citizen within the act of Congress, and the courts of the Union are open to him.

. . .

In the argument, it was said that a colored citizen would not be an agreeable member of society. This is more a matter of taste than of law. Several of the States have admitted persons of color to the right of suffrage, and in this view have recognized them as citizens; and this has been done in the slave as well as the free States. On the question of citizenship, it must be admitted that we have not been very fastidious. Under the late treaty with Mexico, we have made citizens of all grades, combinations, and colors. The same was done in the admission of Louisiana and Florida. No one ever doubted, and no court ever held, that the people of these Territories did not become citizens under the treaty. They have exercised all the rights of citizens, without being naturalized under the acts of Congress.

There are several important principles involved in this case, which have been argued, and which may be considered under the following heads:

1. The locality of slavery, as settled by this court and the courts of the States.

2. The relation which the Federal Government bears to slavery in the States.

3. The power of Congress to establish Territorial Governments, and to prohibit the introduction of slavery therein.

4. The effect of taking slaves into a new State or Territory, and so holding them, where slavery is prohibited.

5. Whether the return of a slave under the control of his master, after being entitled to his freedom, reduces him to his former condition.

6. Are the decisions of the Supreme Court of Missouri, on the questions before us, binding on this court, within the rule adopted.

In the course of my judicial duties, I have had occasion to consider and decide several of the above points.

1. As to the locality of slavery. The civil law throughout the Continent of Europe, it is believed, without an exception, is, that slavery can exist only within the territory where it is established; and that, if a slave escapes, or is carried beyond such territory, his mater cannot reclaim him, unless by virtue of some express stipulation. (Grotius, lib. 2, chap. 15, 5, 1; lib. 10, chap. 10, 2, 1; Wicqueposts Ambassador, lib. 1, p. 418; 4 Martin, 385; Case of the Creole in the House of Lords, 1842; 1 Phillimore on International Law, 316, 335.)

There is no nation in Europe which considers itself bound to return to his master a fugitive slave, under the civil law or the law of nations. On the contrary, the slave is held to be free where there is no treaty obligation, or compact in some other form, to return him to his master. The Roman law did not allow freedom to be sold. An ambassador or any other public functionary could not take a slave to France, Spain, or any other country of Europe, without emancipating him. A number of slaves escaped from a Florida plantation, and were received on board of ship by Admiral Cochrane; by the King's Bench, they were held to be free. (2 Barn. and Cres., 440.)

In the great and leading case of Prigg v. The State of Pennsylvania, (16 Peters, 594; 14 Curtis, 421,) this court

say that, by the general law of nations, no nation is bound to recognize the state of slavery, as found within its territorial dominions, where it is in opposition to its own policy and institutions, in favor of the subjects of other nations where slavery is organized. If it does it, it is as a matter of comity, and not as a matter of international right. The state of slavery is deemed to be a mere municipal regulation, founded upon and limited to the range of the territorial laws. This was fully recognized in Somersett's case, (Lafft's Rep., 1; 20 Howell's State Trials, 79,) which was decided before the American Revolution.

There was some contrariety of opinion among the judges on certain points ruled in Prigg's case, but there was none in regard to the great principle, that slavery is limited to the range of the laws under which it is sanctioned.

No case in England appears to have been more thoroughly examined than that of Somersett. The judgment pronounced by Lord Mansfield was the judgment of the Court of King's Bench. The cause was argued at great length, and with great ability, by Hargrave and others, who stood among the most eminent counsel in England. It was held under advisement from term to term, and a due sense of its importance was felt and expressed by the Bench.

In giving the opinion of the court, Lord Mansfield said: "The state of slavery is of such a nature that it is incapable of being introduced on any reasons, moral or political, but only by positive law, which preserves its force long after the reasons, occasion, and time itself, from whence it was created, is erased from the memory; it is of a nature that nothing can be suffered to support it but positive law."

He referred to the contrary opinion of Lord Hardwicke, in October, 1749, as Chancellor: "That he and Lord Talbot, when Attorney and Solicitor General, were of opinion that no such claim, as here presented, for freedom, was valid."

The weight of this decision is sought to be impaired, from the terms in which it was described by the exuberant imagination of Curran. The words of Lord Mansfield, in giving the opinion of the court, were such as were fit to be used by a great judge, in a most important case. It is a sufficient answer to all objections to that judgment, that it was pronounced before the Revolution, and that it was considered by this court as the highest authority. For near a century, the decision in Somersett's case has remained the law of England. The case of the slave Grace, decided by Lord Stowell in 1827, does not, as has been supposed, overrule the judgment of Lord Mansfield. Lord Stowell held that, during the residence of the slave in England, "No dominion, authority, or coercion, can be exercised over him." Under another head, I shall have occasion to examine the opinion in the case of Grace.

To the position, that slavery can only exist except under the authority of law, it is objected, that in few if in any instances has it been established by statutory enactment. This is no answer to the doctrine laid down by the court. Almost all the principles of the common law had their foundation in usage. Slavery was introduced into the colonies of this country by Great Britain at an early period of their history, and it was protected and cherished, until it became incorporated into the colonial policy. It is immaterial whether a system of slavery was introduced by express law, or otherwise, if it have the authority of law. There is no slave State where the institution is not recognized and protected by statutory enactments and judicial decisions. Slaves are made property by the laws of the slave States, and as such are liable to the claims of creditors; they descend to heirs, are taxed, and in the South they are a subject of commerce.

In the case of Rankin *v.* Lydia, (2 A. K. Marshall's Rep.,) Judge Mills, speaking for the Court of Appeals of Kentucky, says: "In deciding the question, (of slavery,) we disclaim the influence of the general principles of liberty, which we all admire, and conceive it ought to be decided by the law as it is, and not as it ought to be. Slavery is sanctioned by the laws of this State, and the right to hold slaves under our municipal regulations is unquestionable. But we view this as a right existing by positive law of a municipal character, without foundation in the law of nature, or the unwritten and common law."

I will now consider the relation which the Federal Government bears to slavery in the States:

Slavery is emphatically a State institution. In the ninth section of the first article of the Constitution, it is provided "that the migration or importation of such persons as any of the States now existing shall think proper to admit, shall not be prohibited by the Congress prior to the year 1808, but a tax or duty may be imposed on such importation, not exceeding ten dollars for each person."

In the Convention, it was proposed by a committee of eleven to limit the importation of slaves to the year 1800, when Mr. Pinckney moved to extend the time to the year 1808. This motion was carried—New Hampshire, Massachusetts, Connecticut, Maryland, North Carolina, South Carolina, and Georgia, voting in the affirmative; and New Jersey, Pennsylvania, and Virginia, in the negative. In opposition to the motion, Mr. Madison said: "Twenty years will produce all the mischief that can be apprehended from the liberty to import slaves; so long a term will be more dishonorable to the American character than to say nothing about it in the Constitution." (Madison Papers.)

The provision in regard to the slave trade shows clearly that Congress considered slavery a State institution, to be continued and regulated by its individual sovereignty; and to conciliate that interest, the slave trade was continued twenty years, not as a general measure, but for the 'benefit of such States as shall think proper to encourage it.'

In the case of Groves v. Slaughter, (15 Peters, 499; 14 Curtis, 137,) Messrs. Clay and Webster contended that, under the commercial power, Congress had a right to regulate the slave trade among the several States; but the court held that Congress had no power to interfere with slavery as it exists in the States, or to regulate what is called the slave trade among them. If this trade were subject to the commercial power, it would follow that Congress could abolish or establish slavery in every State of the Union.

The only connection which the Federal Government holds with slaves in a State, arises from that provision of the Constitution which declares that "No person held to service or labor in one State, under the laws thereof, escaping into another, shall, in consequence of any law or regulation therein, be discharged from such service or labor, but shall be delivered up, on claim of the party to whom such service or labor may be due."

This being a fundamental law of the Federal Government, it rests mainly for its execution, as has been held, on the judicial power of the Union; and so far as the rendition of fugitives from labor has become a subject of judicial action, the Federal obligation has been faithfully discharged.

In the formation of the Federal Constitution, care was taken to confer no power on the Federal Government to interfere with this institution in the States. In the provision respecting the slave trade, in fixing the ratio of representation, and providing for the reclamation of fugitives from labor, slaves were referred to as persons, and in no other respect are they considered in the Constitution.

We need not refer to the mercenary spirit which introduced the infamous traffic in slaves, to show the degradation of negro slavery in our country. This system was imposed upon our colonial settlements by the mother country, and it is due to truth to say that the commercial colonies and States were chiefly engaged in the traffic. But we know as a historical fact, that James Madison, that great and good man, a leading member in the Federal Convention, was solicitous to guard the language of that instrument so as not to convey the idea that there could be property in man.

I prefer the lights of Madison, Hamilton, and Jay, as a means of construing the Constitution in all its bearings, rather than to look behind that period, into a traffic which is now declared to be piracy, and punished with death by Christian nations. I do not like to draw the sources of our domestic relations from so dark a ground. Our independence was a great epoch in the history of freedom; and while I admit the Government was not made especially for the colored race, yet many of them were citizens of the New England States, and exercised the rights of suffrage when the Constitution was adopted, and it was not doubted by any intelligent person that its tendencies would greatly ameliorate their condition.

Many of the States, on the adoption of the Constitution, or shortly afterward, took measures to abolish slavery within their respective jurisdictions; and it is a well-known fact that a belief was cherished by the leading men, South as well as North, that the institution of slavery would gradually decline, until it would become extinct. The increased value of slave labor, in the culture of cotton and sugar, prevented the realization of this expectation. Like all other communities and States, the South were influenced by what they considered to be their own interests.

But if we are to turn our attention to the dark ages of the world, why confine our view to colored slavery? On the same principles, white men were made slaves. All slavery has its origin in power, and is against right.

The power of Congress to establish Territorial Governments, and to prohibit the introduction of slavery therein, is the next point to be considered.

...

The sovereignty of the Federal Government extends to the entire limits of our territory. Should any foreign power invade our jurisdiction, it would be repelled. There is a law of Congress to punish our citizens for crimes committed in districts of country where there is no organized Government. Criminals are brought to certain Territories or States, designated in the law, for punishment. Death has been inflicted in Arkansas and in Missouri, on individuals, for murders committed beyond the limit of any organized Territory or State; and no one doubts that such a jurisdiction was rightfully exercised. If there be a right to acquire territory, there necessarily must be an implied power to govern it. When the military force of the Union shall conquer a country, may not Congress provide for the government of such country? This would be an implied power essential to the acquisition of new territory. This power has been exercised, without doubt of its constitutionality, over territory acquired by conquest and purchase.

And when there is a large district of country within the United States, and not within any State Government, if it be necessary to establish a temporary Government to carry out a power expressly vested in Congress—as the disposition of the public lands—may not such Government be instituted by Congress? How do we read the Constitution? Is it not a practical instrument?

...

The prohibition of slavery north of thirty-six degrees thirty minutes, and of the State of Missouri, contained in the act admitting that State into the Union, was passed by a vote of 134, in the House of Representatives, to 42. Before Mr. Monroe signed the act, it was submitted by him to his Cabinet, and they held the restriction of slavery in a Territory to be within the constitutional powers of Congress. It would be singular, if in 1804 Congress had power to prohibit the introduction of slaves in Orleans Territory from any other part of the Union, under the penalty of freedom to the slave, if the same power, embodied in the Missouri compromise, could not be exercised in 1820.

But this law of Congress, which prohibits slavery north of Missouri and of thirty-six degrees thirty minutes, is declared to have been null and void by my brethren. And this opinion is founded mainly, as I understand, on the distinction drawn between the ordinance of 1787 and the Missouri compromise line. In what does the distinction consist?

...

When Dred Scott, his wife and children, were removed from Fort Snelling to Missouri, in 1838, they were free, as the law was then settled, and continued for fourteen years afterwards, up to 1852, when the above decision was made. Prior to this, for nearly thirty years, as Chief Justice Gamble declares, the residence of a master with his slave in the State of Illinois, or in the Territory north of Missouri, where slavery was prohibited by the act called the Missouri compromise, would manumit the slave as effectually as if he had executed a deed of emancipation; and that an officer of the army who takes his slave into that State or Territory, and holds him there as a slave, liberates him the same as any other citizen—and down to the above time it was settled by numerous and uniform decisions, and that on the return of the slave to Missouri, his former condition of slavery did not attach. Such was the settled law of Missouri until the decision of Scott and Emerson.

...

But there is no pretense that the case of Dred Scott *v.* Emerson turned upon the construction of a Missouri statute; nor was there any established rule of property which could have rightfully influenced the decision. On the contrary, the decision overruled the settled law for near thirty years.

This is said by my brethren to be a Missouri question; but there is nothing which gives it this character, except that it involves the right to persons claimed as slaves who reside in Missouri, and the decision was made by the Supreme Court of that State. It involves a right claimed under an act of Congress and the Constitution of Illinois, and which cannot be decided without the consideration and construction of those laws. But the Supreme Court of Missouri held, in this case, that it will not regard either of those laws, without which there was no case before it; and Dred Scott, having been a slave, remains a slave. In this respect it is admitted this is a Missouri question—a case which has but one side, if the act of Congress and the Constitution of Illinois are not recognized.

...

But there is another ground which I deem conclusive, and which I will re-state.

The Supreme Court of Missouri refused to notice the act of Congress or the Constitution of Illinois, under which Dred Scott, his wife and children, claimed that they are entitled to freedom.

This being rejected by the Missouri court, there was no case before it, or least it was a case with only one side. And this is the case which, in the opinion of this court, we are bound to follow. The Missouri court disregards the express provisions of an act of Congress and the Constitution of a sovereign State, both of which laws for twenty-eight years it had not only regarded, but carried into effect.

If a State court may do this, on a question involving the liberty of a human being, what protection do the laws afford? So far from this being a Missouri question, it is a question, as it would seem, within the twenty-fifth section of the judiciary act, where a right to freedom being set up under the act of Congress, and the decision being against such right, it may be brought for revision before this court, from the Supreme Court of Missouri.

I think the judgment of the court below should be reversed.

Mr. Justice CURTIS dissenting.

...

If it can be shown, by anything in the Constitution itself, that when it confers on Congress the power to make *all* needful rules and regulations respecting the territory belonging to the United States, the exclusion or the allowance of slavery was excepted; or if anything in the history of this provision tends to show that such an exception was intended by those who framed and adopted the Constitution to be introduced into it, I hold it to be my duty carefully to consider, and to allow just weight to such considerations in interpreting the positive text of the Constitution. But where the Constitution has said *all* needful rules and regulations, I must find something more than theoretical reasoning to induce me to say it did not mean all.

...

For these reasons, I am of opinion that so much of the several acts of Congress as prohibited slavery and involuntary servitude within that part of the Territory of Wisconsin lying north of thirty-six degrees thirty minutes north latitude, and west of the river Mississippi, were constitutional and valid laws.

35
Susan B. Anthony, *Make the Slave's Case Our Own*
1859[*]

We are assembled here this evening for the purpose of discussing the question of American Slavery. The star-

[*] John Witte Jr. and Frank S. Alexander, eds., *The Teachings of Modern Protestantism on Law, Politics, and Human Nature* (New York: Columbia University Press, 2007), 130–31.

tling fact that there are in these United States, under the sanction of this professedly Christian, Republican government, nearly four millions of human beings now clanking in the chains of slavery. Four millions of men and women and children, who are owned like horses and cattle, and bought and sold in the market. Four millions of thinking, acting, conscious beings, like ourselves, driven to unpaid toil, from the rising to the setting of the sun, through the weary days and years of their wretched life times.

Let us, my friends, for the passing hour, make the slave's case our own. As much as in us lies, let us feel that it is ourselves, and our kith and kin who are despoiled of our inalienable rights to life, liberty and the pursuit of happiness, that it is our backs that are bared to the slave driver's lash. That it is our own flesh that is lacerated and torn. That it is our own life blood that is poured out.

Let us feel that it is our own children, that are ruthlessly torn from our yearning mother hearts, and driven in the "coffle gang," through burning suns, and drenching rains, to be sold on the auction block to the highest bidder, and worked up, body and soul, on the cotton, sugar and rice plantations of the more remote south.

That it is our own loved sister and daughter, who are shamelessly exposed to the public market, and whose beauty of face, delicacy of complexion, symmetry of form, and grace of motion, do but enhance their monied value, and more surely victimize them to the unbridled passions and lust of their proud purchasers.

Could we, my friends, but make the slave's case our own—could we but feel for the slave, as bound with him (Heb 13:3)—could we but make the slave our neighbor, and "love him as ourself" (Mt 22:39), and do unto him as we would that he should do unto us (Lk 6:31)—how very easy would be the task of converting us all to Abolitionism.

36

In re Booth

3 Wis. (1854)

SMITH, J.

The facts in these two cases are essentially the same, and any observations which I feel called upon to make will apply to both cases alike, and, therefore, for the sake of convenience, mention will be made of the petition of Rycraft only.

It is, perhaps, needless to say, that the subject matter of this petition has been considered with all the deep anxiety and careful deliberation which the time would permit, and the occasion so imperiously required. Justly appreciating the delicacy of the position of the court, and, as we thought, actuated by a due regard to the representatives of the United States court and government, we postponed the hearing of the application from Tuesday till Friday, and ordered that formal notice be served upon the district attorney of the United States for the district of Wisconsin, of the pendency of the petition and of the time of hearing; although it was apparent that he was not unadvised of the proceedings. He did not see fit to appear, and the government of the United States was not formally represented, except by the marshal, as will appear by reference to his return to the writ issued to and served upon him, contained in the statement of the case. The sheriff of Milwaukee county also made return to the writ issued by him, together with the day and cause of the caption and detention of the petitioner, and thus all the parties (including the legal representatives of the government of the United States) as well as the subject matter of the writ, together with all the questions which the case presented, were properly and regularly before the court.

It is also proper here to remark, that the authority of this court to issue the writ of habeas corpus in this case, is not derived from the revised statutes, or any other enactment of the legislature, but from the constitution of the state: That the jurisdiction of the supreme court, of this writ, and to hear and determine the same, is coextensive with the territorial limits of the state, and that the legislature cannot if they would, restrict the exercise of this power, conferred upon the court, not by legislative enactment, but by the constitution itself. A judge in vacation, or an officer authorized by the legislature to issue, hear and determine the writ, may perhaps be limited to the provisions of the statute. Not so the supreme court in term, whose jurisdiction is coextensive with the state in this behalf, which no legislative enactment can circumscribe or impair, which penetrates the remotest corners of the state, and is competent, on petition, to inquire into the condition of every citizen whose liberty is assailed.

On the application of Sherman M. Booth at the last term of this court for a writ of habeas corpus, no copy of the indictment was presented, but only a copy of the warrant upon which he had been arrested, which recited merely, that he had been indicted under the act of congress of 1850, for aiding the escape of one Joshua Glover, etc. This was an ordinary bench warrant, to bring in a defendant to answer to an indictment found in the district court of the United States; and it appeared to us, that we ought not (and indeed, without an inspection of the indictment, a copy of which was not presented, we could not) interfere with the regular action of that court, but were bound to presume, that if the indictment, when at the proper time it should be brought up for examination, failed to present a case of which that court had jurisdiction, or charged no offense at all, the court in which it was found would so decide, and to leave all such questions preliminarily within the proper scope of the power of that court. But now, the case is different. All those questions have been properly and timely urged, and without avail; and the petitioner comes before us and shows by the return of the officer that he has been pressed on to a conviction, and sentenced to imprisonment, and is now actually imprisoned, within this state, and that the sole authority therefor, is a transcript of the record of such conviction.

The first, the fundamental question which the case presents, is: Has this court the power to inquire into the legality of the authority by which it is claimed, the prisoner is, and ought to be held in custody?

It seems to me that the solution of this question is to be found in a few simple elementary propositions, which require little or no proof or argument to sustain them. It is the duty of the government to protect and secure the just rights of its citizens, whose support and allegiance it commands, among which is the right to personal liberty. This duty of the government is to be measured only by the extent of the individual right, and it is bound to provide means adequate to its full and complete performance. If the government be complex, the means may be distributed, and the obligations of duty divided, but not so as to come short in the whole, of the object to be accomplished.

Ours is a complex system, with powers distributed to each of its parts, but all of its parts together constituting an entire sovereignty, and so, of course, in duty bound, as a whole, to furnish complete protection. Whatever powers and duties are not delegated or assigned to one department or branch of the entire sovereignty, must remain in the other; the federal and state organizations together constituting a complete government, endowed with all the attributes properly pertaining to a sovereign state.

If one be made up of delegated, and the other of reserved powers, the duties assigned to the former can only be coextensive with the powers delegated, and the duties of the latter must remain commensurate with the powers reserved or not delegated, and these powers adequate to every emergency not within the scope of the former.

The federal government is one of delegated powers, the state government is one of inherent or reserved powers; the former competent to act only within the sphere prescribed by the constitution; the latter exercising all the functions of sovereignty not delegated or relinquished by that instrument.

The power to guard and protect the liberty of the individual citizen is inherent in every government; one which it cannot relinquish, which was reserved to the states, which was never granted to the federal government, has never been claimed by it or for it, but has always been conceded to the states, without which they could not exist, because it is obvious that they could claim no allegiance or support from their citizens whom they had not the power to protect.

If, therefore, it is the duty of the state to guard and protect the liberty of its citizens, it must necessarily have the right and power to inquire into any authority by which that liberty is attempted to be taken away. But the power to inquire, includes the power to decide. The right of the sovereign to demand by what authority such imprisonment is attempted, implies the obligation and duty of the person imprisoning to respond; the right to demand such authority on the one hand, implies on the other the duty to exhibit it.

The states and people thereof have delegated to the federal government the power to imprison the citizen in certain cases, but in none other. So far, then, as that government acts upon the power thus delegated, the states cannot interfere to protect its citizen, but in every other case they not only have the power, but it is their solemn duty to interpose their authority. As the power by which the federal government can imprison, is a delegated power, it must necessarily appear, in every case where it imprisons, that it is acting in conformity with some power delegated. It must be "nominated in the bond." Its jurisdiction is never presumed, but must always affirmatively appear. 1 Wheat., 304, 380.

The constitution of the United States is the deed of grant, so to speak, expressing in written terms all the powers delegated to the federal government, and prohibited to the states. The states respectively retain all else of sovereignty, limited only by the local constitutions prescribed by the people of each. Therefore, to me it is plain, that when the federal government assumes to act in a given case, it is bound to exhibit a case within its prescribed powers; for a denial of this proposition involves the assumption of inherent powers, derived from a source other than the states and their respective people, transcending the constitution itself.

As, therefore, the STATES delegated, and the federal government took power, limited in character and extent, the latter is at all times answerable to the former, and may be required to exhibit the constitutional warrant by which it claims to do, or refuses to perform, any given act, when so required by the primary original authority, in conformity with the modes lawfully established.

In the constitution of the United States, sound policy required the incorporation of a function by which the government thus created might be such in fact, by executing its own constitutional laws and decrees, and to that end be enabled to act upon individuals in all of the creative, constituent sovereignties. This could only be accomplished by the creation of a judicial department, supreme and independent within its prescribed sphere, whose process should extend to every citizen. But in giving up so much of this vital element of sovereignty as was deemed essential to the system, the states, or the people thereof respectively, carefully guarded it, hedged it about with provisions which, it was supposed, would be impassable. They prescribed its extent (that is of the judicial power of the United States), by words most carefully selected, whose import could, as was believed, scarcely be mistaken, and beyond which it was supposed, no venturesome mind would rush.

"The judicial power" (of the United States) "shall extend to all cases in law or equity, arising under this constitution, the laws and treaties made or which shall be made under their authority," etc. Const. U. S., Act 3, § 2. Martin v. Hunter's Lessees, 4 Munf. 1 (Vir. Rep). The words "extend to," might, perhaps, on the theory of liberal or latitudinarian construction, be held to be exclusive in their import, in behalf of the judicial power of the United States, were it not for another provision of that instrument which will presently be noticed. But the very selection of the words "extend to," when we consider the extreme caution observed by the members of the national convention which framed the constitution, is

too significant to be overlooked, and ought to admonish us against a rash assumption of exclusive jurisdiction of the subjects therein mentioned. That which merely "extends to" a particular subject or class of subjects, cannot, upon any legitimate mode of interpretation, be considered as comprising the whole of such subject or class of subjects, to the exclusion of every other power. Several powers may "extend to" a given class of subjects; but one can comprehend them all. The extension of a power to a subject by no means merges it exclusively within such power.

But we are relieved from the necessity of criticism upon these words, by another provision of the same instrument, which is in the following words: "This constitution and the laws of the United States which shall be made in pursuance thereof, and all treaties made, or which shall be made, under the authority of the United States, shall be the supreme law of the land; and the judges in every state shall be bound thereby, etc." Const. U. S., art. 6.

Here is a distinct recognition of the power and duty of state judges, not to be bound by all the acts of congress, or by the judgments and decrees of the supreme federal court, or by their interpretation of the constitution and acts of congress, but by "this constitution," "and the laws made in pursuance thereof." The requirement is, that the state judges shall conform to the constitution, and decide upon all questions which may arise within their jurisdiction under the same, as well as the laws of the United States "made in pursuance thereof."

It will be seen that the state judges and courts are by no means alien to that instrument, but bound by it in the same manner as are the federal courts and judges. If the words "extend to," in a former provision were intended to vest sole, exclusive and ultimate power of that class of subjects, in the federal courts and judges, why should the duty and obligation, of construction, obedience and conformity be imposed under the solemn obligation of an official oath, upon the state judges? To bind the judicial conscience, and exclude the judgment from consideration, is an absurdity too flagrant to be attributed to the members of the convention which framed our national constitution. Why are the constitution and the laws of the United States "made in pursuance thereof," proclaimed as the supreme law of the land, and hence the paramount law of every state, and the judges of every state bound thereby, unless those subjects were addressed to the judicial mind and conscience of those officers? and why that careful phrase, "laws made in pursuance thereof" unless those officers were required to determine whether or not the acts of congress subject to their consideration and commanding their obedience, are made in pursuance of, or are repugnant to the constitution?

It would seem obvious that if certain powers and attributes of sovereignty were reserved to the states, they must necessarily have the right to protect them. It would have been stupendous folly to insist upon an express amendment to the constitution, that all powers not delegated to the United States, nor prohibited to the states, are reserved to the states respectively, or to the people," if, among these powers was not reserved that of protecting them. If to the federal government were granted the sole power to decide what powers were reserved and what were not, and to enforce its decision upon the states, the incorporation of this amendment would be a mere empty sounding announcement, placing the governments of original, inherent and reserved powers at the mere forbearance of the federal government. This would indeed be "bringing the machine to the field after the battle is over." The very idea of division is inseparable from that of control of the parts distributed or retained to, or by each agent in the process. That part of the organization which operates upon delegated power, must have the right to control, modify and protect such power; that which operates by virtue of the powers reserved and inherent must have a like right in respect of the powers so reserved. As regards individuals, there is a superior, not to one of the parties only, but to both, to determine between them. Not so as to divided sovereignty, unless an umpire outside of either is expressly provided, which would be incompatible with the sovereignty of either. The deposition of the power of final arbitrament in the one or the other of the parties, is nothing less than placing one at the mercy or forbearance of the other.

But it may be said, if this be so, our system is not perfect, and there can be no uniform will to guide its operations. So indeed is the truth. But, it should be remembered that where one will rules, there can be no freedom for the many. The imposition of uniformity is but another name or process for usurpation or tyranny. It was never intended that there should be one uniform will to administer this government. The object of delegating judicial power to the federal government, was two fold; to enable the government to protect the powers delegated by the direct execution of them through its own instrumentalities; and also to operate as a check upon

the other departments, the executive and legislative. Each is independent and coördinate. In like manner, and for a like purpose, were certain powers delegated to the federal government as a whole, while other powers were reserved to the states, and among these reserved to the state governments was the judicial power, being as essential to the states for the protection of their reserved powers, as it is to the federal government for the protection of its delegated powers. It is equally essential to both. Without it, neither would be a government. It being equally necessary to both, it is obvious that one cannot be subjected to the other without endangering the very object of its institution and endowment. Consequently, both are coequal and coordinate; as much so as are the several departments of each government coëqual and coördinate with each other.

It has been said, and repeated with emphasis, that if state courts are permitted to call in question the jurisdiction of an inferior court of the United States (as the district courts of the United States must be considered in reference to the supreme court of the United States and of the respective states, however they may be regarded in reference to the technical term "inferior courts" as used in the judicial system of England), there must necessarily result great confusion in the interpretation of the constitution, and different rules of interpretation prevail in different states; that the execution of the judgments of the United States courts may be arrested by the state courts, and "revolution or dissolution must soon follow." But a glance at the practical working of our system of government shows these assertions not only to be unfounded in truth, but most vicious in their tendency. One among the objects in distributing the powers and elements of complete sovereignty, was expressed in the preamble to the federal constitution, "to secure the blessings of liberty," etc., and the theory is apparent, viz.: to provide such a distribution of powers, as to make one branch or department operate as a check upon another, and to preclude the possibility of any one branch or department from assuming or exercising the whole or those of another, and to make each independent of the other, but all ultimately responsible to the primary source of all power.

The principle of this objection applies as well to the different departments of the federal government, as to the courts or other functionaries of the respective states. The federal courts may be of the opinion that a penal statute of congress is constitutional, and pass sentence upon one convicted of its violation. The federal executive may deem the statute unconstitutional, and remit the execution of the penalty. Is not the course of justice as much frustrated in this case, as though a state court had interfered to protect a citizen from the usurpation of two departments of the federal government—the legislative and judicial? Again, the United States courts may adopt rules of practice which congress may regard as an assumption of legislative power, and repeal them or forbid their observance; or congress may prescribe certain rules of practice for the courts, such, for example, as the manner of selecting and empannelling jurors, which the courts will disregard; the courts persist, congress persists. Here is confusion, indeed!—"collision," and all its attendant evils. We may go on and suppose a thousand cases in which the harmony of government may be disturbed, which would be as idle as their suggestion in support of unlimited power is reprehensible. It is enough to say, that all history, as well as philosophy, teach us, that individual liberty is never safe where the power of the rulers is unrestricted, and that every guaranty of personal liberty is liable to abuse. The former condition has always resulted in despotism intolerable, the latter may expand into license, and license whirl into anarchy.

Such, however, is not the tendency of our system, nor can it occur, until the officers of the government shall become faithless to the grants and covenants of the constitution, and the people unworthy of the liberty which their constitution was designed, and is competent to secure.

It seems to me that the provision of the constitution before referred to, is an express recognition of the judicial power of the states, as extending to all laws of the United States, and a requisition of obedience on the part of the state judges, to all laws of the United States, provided they are made in pursuance of the constitution, and not otherwise.

...

The states never yielded to the federal government the guardianship of the liberties of their people. In a few carefully specified instances they delegated to that government the power to punish, and so far, and so far only, withdrew their protection. In all else they reserved the power to prescribe the rules of civil conduct, and continued upon themselves the duty and obligation to protect and secure the rights of their citizens declared to be inalienable, viz: "Life, liberty and the pursuit of happiness."

It will readily be conceded, that the main provision which the people have made in the organization of their governments, for the protection of these rights, in them individually, is found in the judicial department. That is the arm of sovereignty whose aid the citizen invokes when these rights are individually invaded. The courts are open to receive his complaint, and to afford him the redress which the constitution and laws entitle him to demand. Every citizen has the right to appeal to the fundamental charter of both sovereignties to which he owes allegiance, to test the validity of the authority by which his right to liberty is denied. It follows, therefore, that the power which he has the right to invoke in his behalf, must possess the right to inquire into the conformity of the authority to set up over his natural rights, with the fundamental law. As the state judiciary is the power to which the guardianship of individual liberty is intrusted, it follows that it must have the right to inquire into such conformity, unrestricted by, and independent of, the power which demands his imprisonment.

It would seem obvious that this power to inquire into the condition of the citizen, and to be informed of the causes of his imprisonment or restraint, has never been surrendered or relinquished by the states. It is one of the highest attributes of sovereignty. We look in vain among the various provisions of the constitution to find it delegated to the United States government or any department thereof. Nor is the relinquishment of this power found among any of those prohibited to the states. Without the tenth amendment it would be clearly reserved to the states, because it is original and inherent in every government. If so, then the appropriate means and instrumentalities are alike reserved, inherent and original. Among such instrumentalities the writ of habeas corpus is especially recognized by the federal constitution, and a positive inhibition upon the power of the government to interfere with its scope and functions, except in specified cases, is carefully inserted. As if it were not enough to restrict the general government to its specifically delegated powers, but to render the power of the states more conspicuous, certain and efficacious, for the protection of individual liberty and for the resistance of unauthorized, unconstitutional power, all power on the part of congress to suspend even the benefit of the writ of habeas corpus is expressly denied, "except in cases of rebellion or invasion." Art. 1, § 9, clause 2, Const. U. S.

Therefore, so far as the proceeding under this writ is concerned, it is original, and from the necessity of the case the jurisdiction of it is original in the states, and as the government of the United States cannot suspend its benefits, it cannot abridge the power and jurisdiction of the state judiciary in regard to any or all questions which the case of the writ may present—that of federal jurisdiction among the number; and that to no one can be granted exemption from the obligation of obedience to its mandates; and it clearly follows, that every individual within the state, no matter by whatsoever authority he may claim to act, is bound to obey the writ when issued by the proper state authority, because the highest earthly power which might otherwise at times be lost sight of, has expressly commanded such obedience, and inhibited the exercise of any power which might thwart its purposes. No person can be exempt from obedience to its mandate, and every act of the national or state legislature which directly or indirectly abrogates or even suspends its benefits (except in the case of rebellion or invasion), is, in so far, absolutely null and void; and its execution will be enforced by all the power of the state and the union, so long as their functionaries are faithful to their duties and oaths.

...

The obligations of the state and federal governments are herein perceived to be mutual and reciprocal. The one to abstain from all interference, whenever it perceives the subject matter to be within the attached jurisdiction of the other, and that other to show that the authority which it claims to exercise is within the powers delegated, and one which it may rightfully exercise. There is little danger of troublesome collision, so long as each shall be willing to measure its functions by the standard created for the guide of both. But, if to avoid collision, an absolute unquestioning submission on the one hand is requisite, and on the other, a perfect immunity to claim and usurp all powers, and to be the sole and ultimate judge of the extent and validity of its own claims; and to enforce its decisions upon the states, then collision is the preferable alternative, because collision invokes the arbitrament of the people themselves, the ultimate source of political power, whose judgments and decrees are made and pronounced through the peaceful and constitutional modes and means which they had the wisdom and foresight to provide in the organization of the present system of government. "Collisions" of this kind are by no means new in this government. They have occurred from time to time as the supposed exigencies of the country have called into exercise new powers, or have seemed to require the adoption of new measures. They are the rightful and healthful operations of those necessary checks and bal-

ances which are indispensable in a government of divided or distributed powers. But such "collisions" have, all along our history, found their appropriate remedy in the awakening of inquiry, in a recurrence to primary and fundamental principles, and in a return of the erring to the constitutional sphere. And so will it ever be, until one or another shall repudiate these constitutional checks and balances, and rashly and madly rush on to extremities, in defiance of constitutional obligations and remedies.

The state judges and courts are as much bound to support the Constitution and laws of the United States, as are the federal courts and judges. I cannot yield to the assumption that the former will be less mindful of their oaths and obligations than the latter; though I can readily perceive why the state judges may be naturally more mindful of the exact lines of demarkation between delegated and reserved powers, because they are under the additional obligation to support the constitution and rights of the states.

If these views be correct, how stands the present case? It is clearly our duty to grant this writ, to inquire into the cause of the prisoner's caption and detention. The return of the respondent sets out the cause. Our next duty is to inquire into the return, in order to ascertain whether the prisoner is held by virtue of any legal authority. It will be conceded that the only rightful authority by which he can be imprisoned must be exercised either by the government of this state or by that of the United States. No other earthly power can rightfully interfere with his right to liberty.

But it is conceded that he is not held by the authority of this state. The next step in the inquiry is to ascertain whether he is held by any constitutional authority of the federal government. Whatever such authority may be, to be of any validity whatever, must clearly appear to be within the powers delegated by the constitution and laws of the United States made in pursuance thereof. Any other power attempted to be exercised by any department of the federal government, would be a manifest usurpation and of no binding validity. The national convention that framed the constitution was exceedingly cautious about conferring criminal jurisdiction upon the national government, so much so that an enumeration of the crimes for which punishment could be provided was carefully made. Congress has, however, provided for the definition and punishment of numerous other crimes and offenses, as necessarily incident to the due execution of powers expressly granted. But all agree that the federal courts can exercise no criminal jurisdiction except in cases specifically prescribed by act of congress.

Every act of congress must be conformable to the constitution, that is, either the exercise of some power expressly granted, or necessary to the execution of some express power.

I have on another occasion attempted to show that the act of congress, approved September 18, 1850, commonly called the fugitive slave act, was not within the constitutional power of congress. I have no time now to enlarge upon the views there presented. But I may be permitted to say, that after careful research, and much reflection, I have not been able to perceive any reason to recede from the positions then taken, but on the contrary it is clear to my mind, that the contrary doctrine is dangerous to the sovereignty and independence of the states, destructive to the peace and harmony of the union, and ultimately subversive of the very end and aim contemplated by that enactment.

I cannot discharge my duty without again affirming the conclusions to which I then arrived. I cannot hang my conscience upon the suggestions or opinions dictated by the conscience of others. They must judge and act for themselves. So must I. I must be faithful to my trust as others doubtless are to theirs. But believing as I do, that congress had no power to pass the act of 1850, that the duties and obligations declared by the constitution in that respect by the 3d clause of sec. 2 of art. 4 of the constitution, were imposed upon the states, and all power in relation thereto reserved to the states and the people, I am compelled to hold that the act is unconstitutional and void, and can confer no authority upon the federal courts.

This doctrine goes to the jurisdiction of the court which attempted to try and sentence this petitioner, which jurisdiction is always subject to inquiry and decision in any other court in which its proceeding may come in question collaterally or otherwise. This is true of courts of general original jurisdiction, and much more is it true in regard to the jurisdiction of courts of inferior, special and limited jurisdiction.

The second clause of the ninth section of the first article of the constitution of the United States, provides: "The privileges of the writ of habeas corpus shall not be suspended, unless, when in case of rebellion or invasion, the public safety may require it." The insertion of this clause in the constitution clearly indicates the extreme caution which was exercised by the members of the national convention, and also the apprehension which they felt lest the power of the states might prove too much for that of the federal government. While on the one hand, they obviously intended to leave to the state governments the jurisdiction and control of this high prerogative writ, in all ordinary circumstances, and on all ordinary occasions, on the other, they granted to congress the power to suspend its privileges whenever there should be manifest an open rebellion against the federal authority, or an invasion of the national or state territory. The suspension of the privileges of the writ here referred to, could not be held as applying only to the power of the United States courts to issue it, because such power could not be made to extend to but few cases, and more palpably, because it could hardly be conceived that the national judiciary would ever be found disposed to use the writ in aid of the subversion of the very authority upon the existence of which our own functions depended. Hence it is apparent that the inhibition and the exception therefrom, have reference to the state functionaries, and the clause must be regarded as restrictive upon the power of congress to interfere with the authority of the state judges and courts to issue, hear and determine the writ.

This clause may then be regarded in two aspects, the one as an express reservation to the states of the power and jurisdiction over the writ of habeas corpus in all cases whatsoever, except in cases of rebellion or invasion, when the public safety might require its suspension, and in such cases, as an implied grant of power to congress to suspend its privileges. But these cases must be declared by congress before any suspension can be ordered. All this goes to show that the framers of the constitution not only recognized in the states the general absolute control of the writ, but by the provisions cited, absolutely required obedience to it, on all occasions, and by all persons and functionaries, whether state or federal, unless congress should declare the existence of the emergencies wherein it might and should suspend its privileges, and to secure the states and people against the exercise of any power, which might possibly override or evade its authority.

In view of this remarkable provision of the constitution, it is not a little surprising, that a claim is lately set up in behalf of federal officers even of the lowest grade, of entire immunity from any obligation to regard the writ when emanating from the state authority, and that jurisdiction of this writ is pertly questioned by inferior ministerial officers, even when issued from the highest judicial tribunal of a sovereign state. However regardless a people may be of encroachments upon the power to which alone they have confided their liberties, it would seem that such pretensions from such sources, could hardly fail to invite inquiry in regard, not to the rights of sovereignty originally reserved, but in regard to what yet remain, not yet frittered away by thoughtless acquiescence in assumptions of power on the one hand, or voluntary surrender on the other.

But it seems to me unnecessary to pursue this subject further. The whole tenor and scope of the federal constitution, indicate most clearly that the state judges, and indeed all state officers, were essential to its maintenance and support, and accordingly the very last clause in the instrument requires such officers to be bound by oath or affirmation to support it.

Yet the course of reasoning sometimes resorted to, in order to oust the state judiciary of jurisdiction of a constitutional question, is based on the assumption that state judges must necessarily be reckless of such obligation, and that fidelity in official duty is only to be expected from federal officers. But this assumption goes too far. It is a weapon with a double edge. The same hypothesis presupposes that federal judges are utterly unmindful of the restrictions which the constitution imposes upon federal power, and that they are willing, for the sake of "uniformity," as they say, to administer all power, both state and national. Neither assumption is true. The earnest desire of all, or nearly all, is, to ascertain the true line of duty, and to act accordingly.

That errors upon both sides must necessarily be committed, is only admitting that the agencies by which each government is administered, are human. But those who suppose that error upon the one side or the other must necessarily lead to insurrection, revolution and anarchy, have studied the temper of our people and officers to little purpose. Time, reason, reflection, discussion, forbearance, patriotism, will now, as they have done heretofore, prove that the wisdom and intelligence of the parties interested, and especially of the ultimate authority will be found competent for the emergencies which call for their exercise, and equal to the fortune which may put them to the test.

I agree fully with the course of reasoning of my brother Crawford, upon the second branch of this case, viz: that the record of conviction here returned does not show an offense within the jurisdiction of the federal court, even admitting the act of 1850 to be constitutional; and even on that ground alone I should agree to discharge the prisoner. I am permitted and desire to adopt his course of reasoning in that respect, which is so clear and conclusive that further suggestions would be entirely superfluous. I will only say, that whatever the congress may have designed by the 7th section of the act of 1850, such design can only be discovered from the words of the statute. If they failed to designate the offense as they intended to do, their defect cannot be supplied by any legislation of a judicial tribunal. By their own language must their enactment be construed, and if their intentions may be thwarted in consequence of a failure accurately to express them, congress has the same power to amend that it originally had to enact the statute.

I have deemed it my duty on this occasion to express my views upon a question which I deem vital to the system on which our government is based. The foundation of my action is broader and deeper than the mere purport of the indictment, though that alone would be sufficient for the present occasion.

But the question suggests, and indeed upon the argument have been raised questions involving the powers of the federal and state governments; questions not confined to the particular subject matter of the act of 1850, but questions pervading the entire scope of the two governments, in all of their departments, upon other subjects which may from time to time arise. And firmly believing that the beneficent designs of the union can only be realized, and the union itself only preserved by maintaining the independence and sovereignty of the states intact, in all respects, except where they have clearly delegated power, and by confining the federal government to powers clearly conferred, I have felt called upon to place my views upon our records, in order that I may discharge my full duty, and that my reasons for the decision to which I have been impelled, may be fully known, and not misapprehended.

37

Ableman v. Booth

62 U.S. 506 (1859)

Mr. Chief Justice TANEY delivered the opinion of the court.

The plaintiff in error in the first of these cases is the marshal of the United States for the district of Wisconsin, and the two cases have arisen out of the same transaction, and depend, to some extent, upon the same principles. On that account, they have been argued and considered together; and the following are the facts as they appear in the transcripts before us:

Sherman M. Booth was charged before Winfield Smith, a commissioner duly appointed by the District Court of the United States for the district of Wisconsin, with having, on the 11th day of March, 1854, aided and abetted, at Milwaukee, in the said district, the escape of a fugitive slave from the deputy marshal, who had him in custody under a warrant issued by the district judge of the United States for that district, under the act of Congress of September 18, 1850.

Upon the examination before the commissioner, he was satisfied that an offence had been committed as charged, and that there was probable cause to believe that Booth had been guilty of it; and thereupon held him to bail to appear and answer before the District Court of the United States for the district of Wisconsin, on the first Monday in July then next ensuing. But on the 26th of May his bail or surety in the recognisance delivered him to the marshal, in the presence of the commissioner, and requested the commissioner to recommit Booth to the custody of the marshal; and he having failed to recognise again for his appearance before the District Court, the commissioner committed him to the custody of the marshal, to be delivered to the keeper of the jail until he should be discharged by due course of law.

Booth made application on the next day, the 27th of May, to A. D. Smith, one of the justices of the Supreme Court of the State of Wisconsin, for a writ of *habeas corpus*, stating that he was restrained of his liberty by Stephen V. R. Ableman, marshal of the United States for that district, under the warrant of commitment hereinbefore mentioned; and alleging that his imprisonment was illegal, because the act of Congress of September 18, 1850, was unconstitutional and void; and also that the warrant was defective, and did not describe the offence created by that act, even if the act were valid.

Upon this application, the justice, on the same day, issued the writ of *habeas corpus*, directed to the marshal, requiring him forthwith to have the body of Booth before him, (the said justice,) together with the time and cause of his imprisonment. The marshal thereupon, on the day above mentioned, produced Booth, and made his return, stating that he was received into his custody as marshal on the day before, and held in custody by virtue of the warrant of the commissioner above mentioned, a copy of which he annexed to and returned with the writ.

To this return Booth demurred, as not sufficient in law to justify his detention. And upon the hearing the justice decided that his detention was illegal, and ordered the marshal to discharge him and set him at liberty, which was accordingly done.

Afterwards, on the 9th of June, in the same year, the marshal applied to the Supreme Court of the State for a *certiorari*, setting forth in his application the proceedings hereinbefore mentioned, and charging that the release of Booth by the justice was erroneous and unlawful, and praying that this proceedings might be brought before the Supreme Court of the State for revision.

The *certiorari* was allowed on the same day; and the writ was accordingly issued on the 12th of the same month, and returnable on the third Tuesday of the month; and on the 20th the return was made by the justice, stating the proceedings, as hereinbefore mentioned.

The case was argued before the Supreme Court of the State, and on the 19th of July it pronounced its judgment, affirming the decision of the associate justice discharging Booth from imprisonment, with costs against Ableman, the marshal.

Afterwards, on the 26th of October, the marshal sued out a writ of error, returnable to this court on the first Monday of December, 1854, in order to bring the judgment here for revision; and the defendant in error was regularly cited to appear on that day; and the record and proceedings were certified to this court by the clerk of the State court in the usual form, in obedience to the writ of error. And on the 4th of December, Booth, the defendant in error, filed a memorandum in writing in this court, stating that he had been cited to appear here in this case, and that he submitted it to the judgment of this court on the reasoning in the argument and opinions in the printed pamphlets therewith sent.

After the judgment was entered in the Supreme Court of Wisconsin, and before the writ of error was sued out, the State court entered on its record, that, in the final judgment it had rendered, the validity of the act of Congress of September 18, 1850, and of February 12, 1793, and the authority of the marshal to hold the defendant in his custody, under the process mentioned in his return to the writ of *habeas corpus*, were respectively drawn in question, and the decision of the court in the final judgment was against their validity, respectively.

This certificate was not necessary to give this court jurisdiction, because the proceedings upon their face show that these questions arose, and how they were decided; but it shows that at that time the Supreme Court of Wisconsin did not question their obligation to obey the writ of error, nor the authority of this court to re-examine their judgment in the cases specified. And the certificate is given for the purpose of placing distinctly on the record the points that were raised and decided in that court, in order that this court might have no difficulty in exercising its appellate power, and pronouncing its judgment upon all of them.

We come now to the second case. At the January term of the District Court of the United States for the district of Wisconsin, after Booth had been set at liberty, and after the transcript of the proceedings in the case above mentioned had been returned to and filed in this court, the grand jury found a bill of indictment against Booth for the offence with which he was charged before the commissioner, and from which the State court had discharged him. The indictment was found on the 4th of January, 1855. On the 9th a motion was made, counsel on behalf of the accused, to quash the indictment, which was overruled by the court; and he thereupon pleaded not guilty, upon which issue was joined. On the 10th a jury was called and appeared in court, when he challenged the array; but the challenge was overruled and the jury empanelled. The trial, it appears, continued from day to day, until the 13th, when the jury found him guilty in the manner and form in which he stood indicted in the fourth and fifth counts. On the 16th he moved for a new trial and in arrest of judgment, which motions were argued on the 20th, and on the 23d the court overruled the motions, and sentenced the prisoner to be imprisoned for one month, and to pay a fine of $1,000 and the costs of prosecution; and that he remain in custody until the sentence was complied with.

We have stated more particularly these proceedings, from a sense of justice to the District Court, as they show that every opportunity of making his defence was afforded him, and that his case was fully heard and considered.

On the 26th of January, three days after the sentence was passed, the prisoner by his counsel filed his petition in the Supreme Court of the State, and with his petition filed a copy of the proceedings in the District Court, and also affidavits from the foreman and one other member of the jury who tried him, stating that their verdict was, guilty on the fourth and fifth counts, and not guilty on the other three; and stated in his petition that his imprisonment was illegal, because the fugitive slave law was unconstitutional; that the District Court had no jurisdiction to try or punish him for the matter charged against him, and that the proceedings and sentence of that court were absolute nullities in law. Various other objections to the proceedings are alleged, which are unimportant in the questions now before the court, and need not, therefore, be particularly stated. On the next day, the 27th, the court directed two writs of *habeas corpus* to be issued—one to the marshal, and one to the sheriff of Milwaukee, to whose actual keeping the prisoner was committed by the marshal, by order of the District Court. The *habeas corpus* directed each of them to produce the body of the prisoner, and make known the cause of his imprisonment, immediately after the receipt of the writ.

On the 30th of January the marshal made his return, not acknowledging the jurisdiction, but stating the sentence of the District Court as his authority; that the prisoner was delivered to, and was then in the actual keeping of the sheriff of Milwaukee county, by order of the court, and he therefore had no control of the body of the prisoner; and if the sheriff had not received him, he should have so reported to the District Court, and should have conveyed him to some other place or prison, as the court should command.

On the same day the sheriff produced the body of Booth before the State court, and returned that he had been committed to his custody by the marshal, by virtue of a transcript, a true copy of which was annexed to his return, and which was the only process or authority by which he detained him.

This transcript was a full copy of the proceedings and sentence in the District Court of the United States, as hereinbefore stated. To this return the accused, by his counsel, filed a general demurrer.

The court ordered the hearing to be postponed until the 2d of February, and notice to be given to the district attorney of the United States. It was accordingly heard on that day, and on the next, (February 3d,) the court decided that the imprisonment was illegal, and ordered and adjudged that Booth be, and he was by that judgment, forever discharged from that imprisonment and restraint, and he was accordingly set at liberty.

On the 21st of April next following, the Attorney General of the United States presented a petition to the Chief Justice of the Supreme Court, stating briefly the facts in the case, and at the same time presenting an exemplification of the proceedings hereinbefore stated, duly certified by the clerk of the State court, and averring in his petition that the State court had no jurisdiction in the case, and praying that a writ of error might issue to bring its judgment before this court to correct the error. The writ of error was allowed and issued, and, according to the rules and practice of the court, was returnable on the first Monday of December, 1855, and a citation for the defendant in error to appear on that day was issued by the Chief Justice at the same time.

No return having been made to this writ, the Attorney General, on the 1st of February, 1856, filed affidavits, showing that the writ of error had been duly served on the clerk of the Supreme Court of Wisconsin, at his office, on the 30th of May, 1855, and the citation served on the defendant in error on the 28th of June, in the same year. And also the affidavit of the district attorney of the United States for the district of Wisconsin, setting forth that when he served the writ of error upon the clerk, as above mentioned, he was informed by the clerk, and has also been informed by one of the justices of the Supreme Court, which released Booth, *"that the court had directed the clerk to make no return to the writ of error, and to enter no order upon the journals or records of the court concerning the same."* And, upon these proofs, the Attorney General moved the court for an order upon the clerk to make return to the writ of error, on or before the first day of the next ensuing term of this court. The rule was accordingly laid, and on the 22d of July, 1856, the Attorney General filed with the clerk of this court the affidavit of the marshal of the district of Wisconsin, that he had served the rule on the clerk on the 7th of the month above mentioned; and no return having been made, the Attorney General, on the 27th of February, 1857, moved for leave to file the certified copy of the record of the Supreme Court of Wisconsin, which he had produced with his application for the writ of error, and to docket the case in this court, in conformity with a motion to that effect made at the last term. And the court thereupon, on the 6th of March, 1857, ordered the copy of the record filed by the Attorney General to be received and entered on the docket of this court, to have the same effect and legal operation as if returned by the clerk with the writ of error, and that the case stand for argument at the next ensuing term, without further notice to either party.

The case was accordingly docketed, but was not reached for argument in the regular order and practice of the court until the present term.

This detailed statement of the proceedings in the different courts has appeared to be necessary in order to form a just estimate of the action of the different tribunals in which it has been heard, and to account for the delay in the final decision of a case, which, from its character, would seem to have demanded prompt action. The first case, indeed, was reached for trial two terms ago. But as to two cases are different portions of the same prosecution for the same offence, they unavoidably, to some extent, involve the same principles of law, and it would hardly have been proper to hear and decide the first before the other was ready for hearing and decision. They have accordingly been argued together, by the Attorney General of the United States, at the present term. No counsel has in either case appeared for the defendant in error. But we have the pamphlet arguments filed and referred to by Booth in the first case, as hereinbefore mentioned, also the opinions and arguments of the Supreme Court of Wisconsin, and of the judges who compose it, in full, and are enabled, therefore, to see the grounds on which they rely to support their decisions.

It will be seen, from the foregoing statement of facts, that a judge of the Supreme Court of the State of Wisconsin in the first of these cases, claimed and exercised the right to supervise and annul the proceedings of a commissioner of the United States, and to discharge a prisoner, who had been committed by the commissioner for an offence against the laws of this Government, and that this exercise of power by the judge was afterwards sanctioned and affirmed by the Supreme Count of the State.

In the second case, the State Court has gone a step further, and claimed and exercised jurisdiction over the proceedings and judgment of a District Court of the United States, and upon a summary and collateral proceeding, by *habeas corpus*, has set aside and annulled its judgment, and discharged a prisoner who had been tried and found guilty of an offence against the laws of the United States, and sentenced to imprisonment by the District Court.

And it further appears that the State court have not only claimed and exercised this jurisdiction, but have also determined that their decision is final and conclusive upon all the courts of the United States, and ordered their clerk to disregard and refuse obedience to the writ of error issued by this court, pursuant to the act of Congress of 1789, to bring here for examination and revision the judgment of the State court.

These propositions are new in the jurisprudence of the United States, as well as of the States; and the supremacy of the State courts over the courts of the United States, in cases arising under the Constitution and laws of the United States, is now for the first time asserted and acted upon in the Supreme Court of a State.

The supremacy is not, indeed, set forth distinctly and broadly, in so many words, in the printed opinions of the judges. It is intermixed with elaborate discussions of different provisions in the fugitive slave law, and of the privileges and power of the writ of *habeas corpus*. But the paramount power of the State court lies at the foundation of these decisions; for their commentaries upon the provisions of that law, and upon the privileges and power of the writ of *habeas corpus*, were out of place, and their judicial action upon them without authority of law, unless they had the power to revise and control the proceedings in the criminal case of which they were speaking; and their judgments, releasing the prisoner, and disregarding the writ of error from this court, can rest upon no other foundation.

If the judicial power exercised in this instance has been reserved to the States, no offence against the laws of the United States can be punished by their own courts, without the permission and according to the judgment of the courts of the State in which the party happens to be imprisoned; for, if the Supreme Court of Wisconsin possessed the power it has exercised in relation to offences against the act of Congress in question, it necessarily follows that they must have the same judicial authority in relation to any other law of the United States; and, consequently, their supervising and controlling power would embrace the whole criminal code of the United States, and extend to offences against our revenue laws, or any other law intended to guard the different departments of the General Government from fraud or violence. And it would embrace all crimes, from the highest to the lowest; including felonies, which are punished with death, as well as misdemeanors, which are punished by imprisonment. And, moreover, if the power is possessed by the Supreme Court of the State of Wisconsin, it must belong equally to every other State in the Union, when the prisoner is within its territorial limits; and it is very certain that the State courts would not always agree in opinion; and it would often happen, that an act which was admitted to be an offence, and justly punished, in one State, would be regarded as innocent, and indeed as praiseworthy, in another.

It would seem to be hardly necessary to do more than state the result to which these decisions of the State courts must inevitably lead. It is, of itself, a sufficient and conclusive answer; for no one will suppose that a Government which has now lasted nearly seventy years, enforcing its laws by its own tribunals, and preserving the union of the States, could have lasted a single year, or fulfilled the high trusts committed to it, if offences against its laws could not have been punished without the consent of the State in which the culprit was found.

. . .

In the case before the Supreme Court of Wisconsin, a right was claimed under the Constitution and laws of the United States, and the decision was against the right claimed; and it refuses obedience to the writ of error, and regards its own judgment as final. It has not only reversed and annulled the judgment of the District Court of the United States, but it has reversed and annulled the provisions of the Constitution itself, and the act of Congress of 1789, and made the superior and appellate tribunal the inferior and subordinate one.

We do not question the authority of State court, or judge, who is authorized by the laws of the State to issue the writ of *habeas corpus*, to issue it in any case where the party is imprisoned within its territorial limits, provided it does not appear, when the application is made, that the person imprisoned is in custody under the authority of the United States. The court or judge has a right to inquire, in this mode of proceeding, for what cause and by what authority the prisoner is confined within the territorial limits of the State sovereignty. And it is the duty of the marshal, or other person having the custody of the prisoner, to make known to the judge or court, by a proper return, the authority by which he holds him in custody. This right to inquire by process of *habeas corpus*, and the duty of the officer to make a return, grows, necessarily, out of the complex character of our Government, and the existence of two distinct and separate sovereignties within the same territorial space, each of them restricted in its powers, and each within its sphere of action, prescribed by the Constitution of the United States, independent of the other. But, after the return is made, and the State judge or court judicially apprized that the party is in custody under the authority of the United States, they can proceed no further.

. . .

Neither this Government, nor the powers of which we are speaking, were forced upon the States. The Constitution of the United States, with all the powers conferred by it on the General Government, and surrendered by the States, was the voluntary act of the people of the several States, deliberately done, for their own protection and safety against injustice from one another. And their anxiety to preserve it in full force, in all its powers, and to guard against resistance to or evasion of its authority, on the part of a State, is proved by the clause which requires that the members of the State Legislatures, and all executive and judicial officers of the several States, (as well as those of the General Government,) shall be bound, by oath or affirmation, to support this Constitution. This is the last and closing clause of the Constitution, and inserted when the whole frame of Government, with the powers hereinbefore specified, had been adopted by the Convention; and it was in that form, and with these powers, that the Constitution was submitted to the people of the several States, for their consideration and decision.

Now, it certainly can be no humiliation to the citizen of a republic to yield a ready obedience to the laws as administered by the constituted authorities. On the contrary, it is among his first and highest duties as a citizen, because free government cannot exist without it. Nor can it be inconsistent with the dignity of a sovereign State to observe faithfully, and in the spirit of sincerity and truth, the compact into which it voluntarily entered when it became a State of this Union. On the contrary, the highest honor of sovereignty is untarnished faith.

. . .

We are sensible that we have extended the examination of these decisions beyond the limits required by any intrinsic difficulty in the questions. But the decisions in question were made by the supreme judicial tribunal of the State; and when a court so elevated in its position has pronounced a judgment which, if it could be maintained, would subvert the very foundations of this Government, it seemed to be the duty of this court, when exercising its appellate power, to show plainly the grave errors into which the State court has fallen, and the consequences to which they would inevitably lead.

But it can hardly be necessary to point out the errors which followed their mistaken view of the jurisdiction they might lawfully exercise; because, if there was any defect of power in the commissioner, or in his mode of proceeding, it was for the tribunals of the United States to revise and correct it, and not for a State court. And as regards the decision of the District Court, it had exclusive and final jurisdiction by the laws of the United States; and neither the regularity of its proceedings nor the validity of its sentence could be called in question

in any other court, either of a State or the United States, by *habeas corpus* or any other process.

But although we think it unnecessary to discuss these questions, yet, as they have been decided by the State court, and are before us on the record, and we are not willing to be misunderstood, it is proper to say that, in the judgment of this court, the act of Congress commonly called the fugitive slave law is, in all of its provisions, fully authorized by the Constitution of the United States; that the commissioner had lawful authority to issue the warrant and commit the party, and that his proceedings were regular and conformable to law. We have already stated the opinion and judgment of the court as to the exclusive jurisdiction of the District Court, and the appellate powers which this court is authorized and required to exercise. And if any argument was needed to show the wisdom and necessity of this appellate power, the cases before us sufficiently prove it, and at the same time emphatically call for its exercise.

The judgment of the Supreme Court of Wisconsin must therefore be reversed in each of the cases now before the court.

38

Wisconsin, Resolutions in Defiance of *Ableman v. Booth*

March 16, 1859*

Whereas, The supreme court of the United States has assumed appellate jurisdiction in the matter of the petition of Sherman M. Booth for a writ of habeas corpus presented and prosecuted to final judgment in the supreme court of this state, and has, without process or any of the forms recognized by law, assumed the power to render that judgment in a matter involving the personal liberty of the citizen, asserted by and adjudged to him in the regular course of judicial proceedings upon the great writ of liberty, secured to the people of each state by the Constitution of the United States; and

Whereas: Such assumption of power and authority by the supreme court of the United States to become the final arbiter of the liberty of the citizen, and to override

State of Wisconsin Assembly Journal, Mar. 16, 1859 (Madison, 1859), 863–64.

and nullify the judgment of the state courts declarative thereof, is in direct conflict with that provision of the constitution of the United States which secures to the people the benefits of the writ of habeas corpus; therefore

Resolved, the Senate concurring, That we regard the action of the supreme court of the United States, in assuming jurisdiction in the case before mentioned, as an arbitrary act of power, unauthorized by the constitution, and virtually superceding the benefit of the writ of habeas corpus, and prostrating the rights and liberties of the people, at the foot of unlimited power.

Resolved, That this assumption of jurisdiction by the federal judiciary, in the said case and without process, is an act of undelegated power, and therefore without authority, void, and of no force.

Resolved, That the government formed by the constitution of the United States was not made the exclusive or final judge of the extent of the powers delegated to itself; but that as in all other cases of compact among parties having no common judge, each party has an equal right to judge for itself, as well of infractions as of the mode and measure of redress.

Resolved, That the principle and construction contended for by the party which now rules in the councils of the nation, that the general government is the exclusive judge of the powers delegated to it, stop nothing short of despotism; since the *discretion* of those who administer the government, and not the *constitution* would be the measure of their powers; that the several states which formed that instrument being sovereign and independent, have the unquestionable right to judge of its infraction, and that a *positive defiance* by those sovereignties of all unauthorized acts done, or attempted to be done, under color of that instrument is the right remedy.

39

Lemmon v. People

6 E.P. Smith 562; 20 N.Y. 562 (1860)

DENIO, J.

The petition upon which the writ of *habeas corpus* was issued, states that the colored persons sought to be discharged from imprisonment were, on the preceding night, taken from the steamer City of Richmond, in the harbor of New York, and at the time of presenting the petition, were confined in a certain house in Carlisle street in that city. The writ is directed to the appellant by the name of "Lemmings," as the person having in charge "eight colored persons lately taken from the steamer City of Richmond, and to the man in whose house in Carlisle street they were confined." The return is made by Lemmon, the appellant, and it speaks of the colored persons who are therein alleged to be slaves, and the property of Juliet Lemmon, as "the eight slaves or persons named in the said writ of habeas corpus." It alleges that they were taken out of the possession of Mrs. Lemmon, while in transit between Norfolk, in Virginia, and the State of Texas, and that both Virginia and Texas are slaveholding States; that she had no intention of bringing the slaves into this State to remain therein, or in any manner except on their transit as aforesaid through the port of New York; that she was compelled by necessity to touch or land, but did not intend to remain longer than necessary, and that such landing was for the purpose of passage and transit and not otherwise, and that she did not intend to sell the slaves. It is also stated that she was compelled by "necessity or accident" to take passage from Norfolk in the above mentioned steamship, and that Texas was her ultimate place of destination.

I understand the effect of these statements to be that Mrs. Lemmon, being the owner of these slaves, desired to take them from her residence in Norfolk to the State of Texas; and, as a means of effecting that purpose, she embarked, in the steamship mentioned, for New York, with a view to secure a passage from thence to her place of destination. As nothing is said of any stress of weather, and no marine casualty is mentioned, the necessity of landing, which is spoken of, refers, no doubt, to the exigency of that mode of prosecuting her journey. If the ship in which she arrived was not bound for the Gulf of Mexico, she would be under the necessity of landing at New York to reëmbark in some other vessel sailing for that part of the United States; and this, I suppose, is what it was intended to state. The necessity or accident which is mentioned as having compelled her to embark at Norfolk in the City of Richmond, is understood to refer to some circumstance which prevented her making a direct voyage from Virginia to Texas. The question to be decided is whether the bringing the slaves into this State under these circumstances entitled them to their freedom.

The intention, and the effect, of the statutes of this State bearing upon the point are very plain and unequivocal. By an act passed in 1817, it was declared that no person held as a slave should be imported, introduced or brought into this State on any pretence whatever, except in the cases afterwards mentioned in the act, and any slave brought here contrary to the act was declared to be free. Among the excepted cases was that of a person, not an inhabitant of the State, passing through it, who was allowed to bring his slaves with him; but they were not to remain in the State longer than nine months. (Laws of 1817, ch. 137, §§ 9, 15.) The portions of this act which concern the present question were reenacted at the revision of the laws in 1830. The first and last sections of the title are in the following language:

"§ 1. No person held as a slave shall be imported, introduced or brought into this State on any pretence whatsoever, except in the cases hereinafter specified. Every such person shall be free. Every person held as a slave who hath been introduced or brought in this State contrary to the laws in force at the time, shall be free."

"§ 16. Every person born in this State, whether white or colored, is free. Every person who shall hereafter be born within this State shall be free; and every person brought into this State as a slave, except as authorized by this title, shall be free." (R. S., part 1, ch 20, tit. 7.)

The intermediate sections, three to seven inclusive, contain the exceptions. Section 6 is as follows: "Any person, not being an inhabitant of this State, who shall be traveling to or from, or passing through this State, may bring with him any person lawfully held in slavery, and may take such person with him from this State; but the person so held in slavery shall not reside or continue in this State more than nine months; if such residence be continued beyond that time such person shall be free." In the year 1841, the Legislature repealed this section, together with the four containing other exceptions to the general provisions above mentioned. (Ch. 247.) The effect of this repeal was to render the 1st and 16th sections absolute and unqualified. If any doubt of this could be entertained upon the perusal of the part of the title left un-repealed, the rules of construction would oblige us to look at the repealed portions in order to ascertain the sense of the residue. (Bussey v. Story, 4 Barn. & Adolph., 98.) Thus examined, the meaning of the statute is as plain as though the Legislature had declared in terms that if any person should introduce a

slave into this State, in the course of a journey to or from it, or in passing through it, the slave shall be free.

If, therefore, the Legislature had the constitutional power to enact this statute, the law of the State precisely meets the case of the persons who were brought before the judge on the writ of habeas corpus, and his order discharging them from constraint was unquestionably correct. Every sovereign State has a right to determine by its laws the condition of all persons who may at any time be within its jurisdiction; to exclude therefrom those whose introduction would contravene its policy, or to declare the conditions upon which they may be received, and what subordination or restraint may lawfully be allowed by one class or description of persons over another. Each State has, moreover, the right to enact such rules as it may see fit respecting the title to property, and to declare what subjects shall, within the State, possess the attributes of property, and what shall be incapable of a proprietary right. These powers may of course be variously limited or modified by its own constitutional or fundamental laws; but independently of such restraints (and none are alleged to exist affecting this case) the legislative authority of the State over these subjects is without limit or control, except so far as the State has voluntarily abridged her jurisdiction by arrangements with other States. There are, it is true, many cases where the conditions impressed upon persons and property by the laws of other friendly States may and ought to be recognized within our own jurisdiction.

These are defined, in the absence of express legislation, by the general assent and by the practice and usage of civilized countries, and being considered as incorporated into the municipal law, are freely administered by the courts. They are not, however, thus allowed on account of any supposed power residing in another State to enact laws which should be binding on our tribunals, but from the presumed assent of the law-making power to abide by the usages of other civilized States. Hence it follows that where the Legislature of the State, in which a right or privilege is claimed on the ground of comity, has by its laws spoken upon the subject of the alleged right, the tribunals are not at liberty to search for the rule of decision among the doctrines of international comity, but are bound to adopt the directions laid down by the political government of their own State. We have not, therefore, considered it necessary to inquire whether by the law of nations, a country where negro slavery is established has generally a right to claim of a neighboring State, in which it is not allowed, the right to have that species of property recognized and protected in the course of a lawful journey taken by the owner through the last mentioned country, as would undoubtedly be the case with a subject recognized as property everywhere; and it is proper to say that the counsel for the appellant has not urged that principle in support of the claim of Mrs. Lemmon.

What has been said as to the right of a sovereign State to determine the status of persons within its jurisdiction applies to the States of this Union, except as it has been modified or restrained by the Constitution of the United States (Groves v. Slaughter, 15 Pet., 419; Moore v. The People of Illinois, 14 How., 13; City of New York v. Miln, 11 Pet., 131, 139.) There are undoubtedly reasons, independently of the provisions of the Federal Constitution, for conciliatory legislation on the part of the several States, towards the polity, institutions and interests of each other, of a much more persuasive character than those which prevail even between the most friendly States unconnected by any political union; but these are addressed exclusively to the political power of the respective States; so that whatever opinion we might entertain as to the reasonableness, or policy, or even of the moral obligation of the non-slaveholding States to establish provisions similar to those which have been stricken out of the Revised Statutes, it is not in our power, while administering the laws of this State in one of its tribunals of justice, to act at all upon those sentiments, when we see, as we cannot fail to do, that the Legislature has deliberately repudiated them.

The power which has been mentioned as residing in the States is assumed by the Constitution itself to extend to persons held as slaves by such of the States as allow the condition of slavery, and to apply also to a slave in the territory of another State, which did not allow slavery, even unaccompanied with an intention on the part of the owner to hold him in a state of slavery in such other State. The provision respecting the return of fugitives from service contains a very strong implication to that effect. It declares that no person held to service or labor in one State, under the laws thereof, escaping into another, shall in consequence of any law or regulation therein, be discharged from such service or labor, &c. There was at least one State which at the adoption of the Constitution did not tolerate slavery; and in several of the other States the number of slaves was so small and the prevailing sentiment in favor of emancipation so strong, that it was morally certain that slavery would be speedily abolished. It was assumed by the authors of the Constitution, that the fact of a Federative Union would not of itself create a duty on the part of the States which should abolish slavery to respect the rights of the owners of slaves escaping thence from the States where it continued to exist.

The apprehension was not that any of the States would establish rules or regulations looking primarily to the emancipation of fugitives from labor, but that the abolition of slavery in any State would draw after it the principle that a person held in slavery would immediately become free on arriving, in any manner, within the limits of such State. That principle had then recently been acted upon in England in a case of great notoriety, which could not fail to be well known to the cultivated and intelligent men who were the principal actors in framing the Federal Constitution. A Virginia gentleman of the name of Stewart had occasion to make a voyage from his home in that Colony to England, on his own affairs, with the intention of returning as soon as they were transacted; and he took with him as his personal servant his negro slave, Somerset, whom he had purchased in Virginia and was entitled to hold in a state of slavery by the laws prevailing there. While they were in London, the negro absconded from the service of his master, but was re-taken and put on board a vessel lying in the Thames bound to Jamaica, where slavery also prevailed, for the purpose of being there sold as a slave. On application to Lord MANSFIELD, Chief Justice of the King's Bench, a writ of habeas corpus was issued to Knowles as master of the vessel, whose return to the writ disclosed the foregoing facts. Lord MANSFIELD referred the case to the decision of the Court of King's Bench, where it was held, by the unanimous opinion of the judges, that the restraint was illegal, and the negro was discharged. (The Negro Case, 11 Harg. S. T., 340; Somerset v. Stewart, Lofft, 1.) It was the opinion of the court that a state of slavery could not exist except by force of positive law, and it being considered that there was no law to uphold it in England, the principles of the law respecting the writ of habeas corpus immediately applied themselves to the case, and it became impossible to continue the imprisonment of the negro. The case was decided in 1772, and from that time it became a maxim that slaves could not exist in England. The idea was reiterated in the popular literature of the language, and fixed in the public mind by a striking metaphor which attributed to the atmosphere of the British Islands a quality which caused the shackles of the slave to fall off. The laws of England respecting personal rights were in general the laws of the Colonies, and they continued the same system after the Revolution by provisions in their Constitutions, adopting the common law subject to alterations by their own statutes. The literature of the Colonies was that of the mother country.

The aspect in which the case of fugitive slaves was presented to the authors of the Constitution therefore was this: A number of the States had very little interest in continuing the institution of slavery, and were likely soon to abolish it within their limits. When they should do so, the principle of the laws of England as to personal rights and the remedies for illegal imprisonment, would immediately prevail in such States. The judgment in Somerset's case and the principles announced by Lord MANSFIELD, were standing admonitions that even a temporary restraint of personal liberty by virtue of a title derived under the laws of slavery, could not be sustained where that institution did not exist by positive law, and where the remedy by habeas corpus, which was a cherished institution of this country as well as in England, was established. Reading the provision for the rendition of fugitive slaves, in the light which these considerations afford, it is impossible not to perceive that the Convention assumed the general principle to be that the escape of a slave from a State in which he was lawfully held to service into one which had abolished slavery would ipso facto transform him into a free man. This was recognized as the legal consequence of a slave going into a State where slavery did not exist, even though it were without the consent and against the will of the owner. A fortiori he would be free if the master voluntarily brought him into a free State for any purpose of his own. But the provision in the Constitution extended no further than the case of fugitives. As to such cases, the admitted general consequence of the presence of a slave in a free State was not to prevail, but he was by an express provision in the federal compact to be returned to the party to whom the service was due. Other cases were left to be governed by the general laws applicable to them. This was not unreasonable, as the owner was free to determine whether he would voluntarily permit his slave to go within a jurisdiction which did not allow him to be held in bondage. That was within his own power, but he could not always prevent his slaves from escaping out of the State in which

their servile condition was recognized. The provision was precisely suited to the exigency of the case, and it went no further.

In examining other arrangements of the Constitution, apparently inserted for purposes having no reference to slavery, we ought to bear in mind that when passing the fugitive slave provision the Convention was contemplating the future existence of States which should have abolished slavery, in a political union with other States where the institution would still remain in force. It would naturally be supposed that if there were other cases in which the rights of slave owners ought to be protected in the States which should abolish slavery, they would be adjusted in connection with the provision looking specially to that case, instead of being left to be deduced by construction from clauses intended primarily for cases to which slavery had no necessary relation. It has been decided that the fugitive clause does not extend beyond the case of the actual escape of a slave from one State to another. (Ex parte Simmons, 4 Wash. C. C. R., 396.) But the provision is plainly so limited by its own language.

The Constitution declares that the citizens of each State shall be entitled to all privileges and immunities of citizens in the several States. (Art. 4, § 2.) No provision in that instrument has so strongly tended to constitute the citizens of the United States one people as this. Its influence in that direction cannot be fully estimated without a consideration of what would have been the condition of the people if it or some similar provision had not been inserted. Prior to the adoption of the Articles of Confederation, the British colonies on this continent had no political connection, except that they were severally dependencies of the British crown. Their relation to each other was the same which they respectively bore to the other English colonies, whether on this continent or in Europe or Asia. When, in consequence of the Revolution, they severally became independent and sovereign States, the citizens of each State would have been under all the disabilities of alienage in every other, but for a provision in the compacts into which they entered whereby that consequence was avoided. The articles adopted during the Revolution formed essentially a league for mutual protection against external force; but in passing them it was felt to be necessary to secure a community of intercourse which would not necessarily obtain even among closely allied States. This was effected by the fourth article of that instrument, which declared that the free inhabitants of each of the

States (paupers, vagabonds, and fugitives from justice excepted) should be entitled to all privileges and immunities of free citizens in the several States, and that the people of each State should have free ingress and egress to and from any other State, and should enjoy therein all the privileges of trade and commerce, subject to the same duties, impositions and restrictions as the inhabitants thereof, respectively. The Constitution organized a still more intimate Union, constituting the States, for all external purposes and for certain enumerated domestic objects, a single nation; but still the principle of State sovereignty was retained as to all subjects, except such as were embraced in the delegations of power to the General Government or prohibited to the States. The social status of the people, and their personal and relative rights as respects each other, the definition and arrangements of property, were among the reserved powers of the States.

The provision conferring rights of citizenship upon the citizens of every State in every other State, was inserted substantially as it stood in the Articles of Confederation. The question now to be considered is, how far the State jurisdiction over the subjects just mentioned is restricted by the provision we are considering; or, to come at once to the precise point in controversy, whether it obliges the State governments to recognize, in any way, within their own jurisdiction, the property in slaves which the citizens of States in which slavery prevails may lawfully claim within their own States—beyond the case of fugitive slaves. The language is that they shall have the privileges and immunities of citizens in the several States. In my opinion the meaning is, that in a given State, every citizen of every other State shall have the same privileges and immunities—that is, the same rights—which the citizens of that State possess. In the first place, they are not to be subjected to any of the disabilities of alienage. They can hold property by the same titles by which every other citizen may hold it, and by no other. Again, any discriminating legislation which should place them in a worse situation than a proper citizen of the particular State would be unlawful. But the clause has nothing to do with the distinctions founded on domicile. A citizen of Virginia, having his home in that State, and never having been within the State of New York, has the same rights under our laws which a native born citizen, domiciled elsewhere, would have, and no other rights. Either can be the proprietor of property here, but neither can claim any rights which under our laws belong only to residents of

the State. But where the laws of the several States differ, a citizen of one State asserting rights in another, must claim them according to the laws of the last mentioned State, not according to those which obtain in his own.

The position that a citizen carries with him, into every State into which he may go, the legal institutions of the one in which he was born, cannot be supported. A very little reflection will show the fallacy of the idea. Our laws declare contracts depending upon games of chance or skill, lotteries, wagering policies of insurance, bargains for more than 7 per cent per annum of interest, and many others, void. In other States such contracts, or some of them, may be lawful. But no one would contend that if made within this State by a citizen of another State where they would have been lawful, they would be enforced in our courts. Certain of them, if made in another State and in conformity with the laws there, would be executed by our tribunals upon the principles of comity; and the case would be the same if they were made in Europe or in any other foreign country. The clause has nothing to do with the doctrine of international comity. That doctrine, as has been remarked, depends upon the usage of civilized nations and the presumed assent of the legislative authority of the particular State in which the right is claimed; and an express denial of the right by that authority is decisive against the claim. How then, is the case of the appellant aided by the provision under consideration?

The Legislature has declared, in effect, that no person shall bring a slave into this State, even in the course of a journey between two slaveholding States, and that if he does, the slave shall be free. Our own citizens are of course bound by this regulation. If the owner of these slaves is not in like manner bound it is because, in her quality of citizen of another State, she has rights superior to those of any citizen of New York, and because, in coming here, or sending her slaves here for a temporary purpose, she has brought with her, or sent with them, the laws of Virginia, and is entitled to have those laws enforced in the courts, notwithstanding the mandate of our own laws to the contrary. But the position of the appellant proves too much. The privileges and immunities secured to the citizens of each State by the Constitution are not limited by time, or by the purpose for which, in a particular case, they may be desired, but are permanent and absolute in their character. Hence, if the appellant can claim exemption from the operation of the statute on which the respondent relies, on the ground that she is a citizen of a State where slavery is allowed, and that our courts are obliged to respect the title which those laws confer, she may retain slaves here during her pleasure; and, as one of the chief attributes of property is the power to use it, and to sell or dispose of it, I do not see how she could be debarred of these rights within our jurisdiction as long as she may choose to exercise them. She could not, perhaps, sell them to a citizen of New York, who would at all events be bound by our laws, but any other citizen of a slave State—who would equally bring with him the immunities and privileges of his own State—might lawfully traffic in the slave property. But my opinion is that she has no more right to the protection of this property than one of the citizens of this State would have upon bringing them here under the same circumstances, and that the clause of the Constitution referred to has no application to the case.

I concede that this clause gives to citizens of each State entire freedom of intercourse with every other State, and that any law which should attempt to deny them free ingress or egress would be void. But it is citizens only who possess these rights, and slaves certainly are not citizens. Even free negroes, as is well known, have been alleged not to possess that quality. In Moore v. The State of Illinois, already referred to, the Supreme Court of the United States, in its published opinion, declared that the States retained the power to forbid the introduction into their territory of paupers, criminals or fugitive slaves. The case was a conviction under a statute of Illinois, making it penal to harbor or secrete any negro, mulatto or person of color being a slave or servant owing service or labor to any other person. The indictment was for secreting a fugitive slave who had fled from his owner in Missouri. The owner had not intervened to reclaim him so as to bring the fugitive law into operation, and the case was placed by the court on the ground that it was within the legitimate power of State legislation, in the promotion of its policy, to exclude an unacceptable population. I do not at all doubt the right to exclude a slave as I do not consider him embraced under the provision securing a common citizenship; but it does not seem to me clear that one who is truly a citizen of another State can be thus excluded, though he may be a pauper or a criminal, unless he be a fugitive from justice. The fourth article of confederation contained an exception to the provision for a common citizenship, excluding from its benefits paupers and vagabonds as well as fugitives from justice; but this exception was omitted in the corresponding provision of the Constitution. If a slave attempting to come into a State of his own accord can be excluded on the ground mentioned, namely, because as a slave he is an unacceptable inhabitant, as it is very clear he may be, it would seem to follow that he might be expelled if accompanied by his master. It might, it is true, be less mischievous to permit the residence of such a person when under the restraint of his owner; but of this the Legislature must judge. But it is not the right of the slave but of the master which is supposed to be protected under the clause respecting citizenship. The answer to the claim in that aspect has been already given. It is that the owner cannot lawfully do anything which our laws do not permit to be done by one of our own citizens, and as a citizen of this State cannot bring a slave within its limits except under the condition that he shall immediately become free, the owner of these slaves could not do it without involving herself in the same consequences.

. . .

We will concede, for the purpose of the argument, that the transportation of slaves from one slaveholding State to another is an act of inter-state commerce, which may be legally protected and regulated by federal legislation. Acts have been passed to regulate the coasting trade, so that if these slaves had been in transitu between Virginia and Texas, in a coasting vessel, at the time the habeas corpus was served, they could not have been interfered with while passing through the navigable waters of a free State by the authority of a law of such State. But they were not thus in transit at that time. Congress has not passed any act to regulate commerce between the States when carried on by land, or otherwise than in coasting vessels. . . . I repeat the remark, that the law of the State under consideration has no aspect which refers directly to commerce among the States. It would have a large and important operation upon cases falling within its provisions, and having no connection with any commercial enterprise. It is then, so far as the commercial clause is concerned, generally valid; but in the case of supposable federal legislation, under the power conferred upon Congress to regulate commerce, circumstances might arise where its execution, by freeing a slave cargo landed on our shores, in the course of an inter-state voyage, would interfere with the provisions of an act of Congress. The present state of federal legislation however, does not, in my opinion, raise any conflict between it and the laws of this State under consideration.

Upon the whole case, I have come to the conclusion

that there is nothing in the National Constitution or the laws of Congress to preclude the State judicial authorities from declaring these slaves thus introduced into the territory of this State, free, and setting them at liberty, according to the direction of the statute referred to.

40

Frederick Douglass, *The Constitution of the United States: Is It Pro-slavery or Anti-slavery?*

March 26, 1860*

I proceed to the discussion. And first a word about the question. Much will be gained at the outset if we fully and clearly understand the real question under discussion. Indeed, nothing is or can be understood. Things are often confounded and treated as the same, for no better reason than that they resemble each other, even while they are in their nature and character totally distinct and even directly opposed to each other. This jumbling up things is a sort of dust-throwing which is often indulged in by small men who argue for victory rather than for truth. Thus, for instance, the American Government and the American Constitution are spoken of in a manner which would naturally lead the hearer to believe that one is identical with the other; when the truth is, they are distinct in character as is a ship and a compass. The one may point right and the other steer wrong. A chart is one thing, the course of the vessel is another. The Constitution may be right, the Government is wrong. If the Government has been governed by mean, sordid, and wicked passions, it does not follow that the Constitution is mean, sordid, and wicked. What, then, is the question? I will state it. But first let me state what is not the question. It is not whether slavery existed in the United States at the time of the adoption of the Constitution; it is not whether slaveholders took part in the framing of the Constitution; it is not whether those slaveholders, in their hearts, intended to secure certain advantages in that instrument for slav-

*Frederick Douglass: Selected Speeches and Writing, ed. Philip S. Foner, abridged and adapted by Yuval Taylor (Chicago: Lawrence Hill Books, 1999), 380–90.

ery; it is not whether the American Government has been wielded during seventy-two years in favour of the propagation and permanence of slavery; it is not whether a pro-slavery interpretation has been put upon the Constitution by the American Courts—all these points may be true or they may be false, they may be accepted or they may be rejected, without in any wise affecting the real question in debate. The real and exact question between myself and the class of persons represented by the speech at the City Hall may be fairly stated thus:—1st, Does the United States Constitution guarantee to any class or description of people in that country the right to enslave, or hold as property, any other class or description of people in that country? 2nd, Is the dissolution of the union between the slave and free States required by fidelity to the slaves, or by the just demands of conscience? Or, in other words, is the refusal to exercise the elective franchise, and to hold office in America, the surest, wisest, and best way to abolish slavery in America?

To these questions the Garrisonians say Yes. They hold the Constitution to be a slaveholding instrument, and will not cast a vote or hold office, and denounce all who vote or hold office, no matter how faithfully such persons labour to promote the abolition of slavery. I, on the other hand, deny that the Constitution guarantees the right to hold property in man, and believe that the way to abolish slavery in America is to vote such men into power as will use their powers for the abolition of slavery. This is the issue plainly stated, and you shall judge between us. Before we examine into the disposition, tendency, and character of the Constitution, I think we had better ascertain what the Constitution itself is. Before looking for what it means, let us see what it is. Here, too, there is much dust to be cleared away. What, then, is the Constitution? I will tell you. It is not even like the British Constitution, which is made up of enactments of Parliament, decisions of Courts, and the established usages of the Government. The American Constitution is a written instrument full and complete in itself. No Court in America, no Congress, no President, can add a single word thereto, or take a single word thereto. It is a great national enactment done by the people, and can only be altered, amended, or added to by the people. I am careful to make this statement here; in America it would not be necessary. It would not be necessary here if my assailant had shown the same desire to be set before you the simple truth, which he manifested to make out a good case for himself and friends. Again, it should be borne in mind that the mere text, and only the text, and not any commentaries or creeds written by those who wished to give the text a meaning apart from its plain reading, was adopted as the Constitution of the United States. It should also be borne in mind that the intentions of those who framed the Constitution, be they good or bad, for slavery or against slavery, are so respected so far, and so far only, as we find those intentions plainly stated in the Constitution. It would be the wildest of absurdities, and lead to endless confusion and mischiefs, if, instead of looking to the written paper itself, for its meaning, it were attempted to make us search it out, in the secret motives, and dishonest intentions, of some of the men who took part in writing it. It was what they said that was adopted by the people, not what they were ashamed or afraid to say, and really omitted to say. Bear in mind, also, and the fact is an important one, that the framers of the Constitution sat with doors closed, and that this was done purposely, that nothing but the result of their labours should be seen, and that that result should be judged of by the people free from any of the bias shown in the debates. It should also be borne in mind, and the fact is still more important, that the debates in the convention that framed the Constitution, and by means of which a pro-slavery interpretation is now attempted to be forced upon that instrument, were not published till more than a quarter of a century after the presentation and the adoption of the Constitution.

These debates were purposely kept out of view, in order that the people should adopt, not the secret motives or unexpressed intentions of any body, but the simple text of the paper itself. Those debates form no part of the original agreement. I repeat, the paper itself, and only the paper itself, with its own plainly written purposes, is the Constitution. It must stand or fall, flourish or fade, on its own individual and self-declared character and objects. Again, where would be the advantage of a written Constitution, if, instead of seeking its meaning in its words, we had to seek them in the secret intentions of individuals who may have had something to do with writing the paper? What will the people of America a hundred years hence care about the intentions of the scriveners who wrote the Constitution? These men are already gone from us, and in the course of nature were expected to go from us. They were for a generation, but the Constitution is for ages. Whatever we may owe to them, we certainly owe it to ourselves, and to mankind, and to God, to maintain the truth of our own language, and to allow no villainy, not even the villainy of holding men as slaves—which Wesley says is the sum of all villainies—to shelter itself under a fair-seeming and virtuous language. We owe it to ourselves to compel the devil to wear his own garments, and to make wicked laws speak out their wicked intentions. Common sense, and common justice, and sound rules of interpretation all drive us to the words of the law for the meaning of the law. The practice of the Government is dwelt upon with much fervour and eloquence as conclusive as to the slaveholding character of the Constitution. This is really the strong point and the only strong point, made in the speech in the City Hall. But good as this argument is, it is not conclusive. A wise man has said that few people have been found better than their laws, but many have been found worse. To this last rule America is no exception. Her laws are one thing, her practice is another thing. We read that the Jews made void the law by their tradition, that Moses permitted men to put away their wives because of the hardness of their hearts, but that this was not so at the beginning. While good laws will always be found where good practice prevails, the reverse does not always hold true. Far from it. The very opposite is often the case. What then? Shall we condemn the righteous law because wicked men twist it to the support of wickedness? Is that the way to deal with good and evil? Shall we blot out all distinction between them, and hand over to slavery all that slavery may claim on the score of long practice? Such is the course commended to us in the City Hall speech. After all, the fact that men go out of the Constitution to prove it pro-slavery, whether that going out is to the practice of the Government, or to the secret intentions of the writers of the paper, the fact that they do go out is very significant. It is a powerful argument on my side. It is an admission that the thing for which they are looking is not to be found where only it ought to be found, and that is in the Constitution itself. If it is not there, it is nothing to the purpose, be it wheresoever else it may be. But I shall have no more to say on this point hereafter.

The very eloquent lecturer at the City Hall doubtless felt some embarrassment from the fact that he had literally to *give* the Constitution a pro-slavery interpretation; because upon its face it of itself conveys no such meaning, but a very opposite meaning. He thus sums up what he calls the slaveholding provisions of the Constitution. I quote his own words:—"Article 1, section 9, provides for the continuance of the African slave trade for the 20 years, after the adoption of the Constitution. Art. 4, section 9, provides for the recovery from the other States of fugitive slaves. Art. 1, section 2, gives the slave States a representation of the three-fifths of all the slave population; and Art. 1, section 8, requires the President to use the military, naval, ordnance, and militia resources of the entire country for the suppression of slave insurrection, in the same manner as he would employ them to repel invasion." Now any man reading this statement, or hearing it made with such a show of exactness, would unquestionably suppose that the speaker or writer had given the plain written text of the Constitution itself. I can hardly believe that he intended to make any such impression. It would be a scandalous imputation to say he did. And yet what are we to make of it? How can we regard it? How can he be screened from the charge of having perpetrated a deliberate and point-blank misrepresentation? That individual has seen fit to place himself before the public as my opponent, and yet I would gladly find some excuse for him. I do not wish to think as badly of him as this trick of his would naturally lead me to think. Why did he not read the Constitution? Why did he read that which was not the Constitution? He pretended to be giving chapter and verse, section and clause, paragraph and provision. The words of the Constitution were before him. Why then did he not give you the plain words of the Constitution? Oh, sir, I fear that the gentleman knows too well why he did not. It so happens that no such words as "African slave trade," no such words as "slave insurrections," are anywhere used in that instrument. These are the words of that orator, and not the words of the Constitution of the United States. Now you shall see a slight difference between my manner of treating this subject and that which my opponent has seen fit, for reasons satisfactory to himself, to pursue. What he withheld, that I will spread before you: what he suppressed, I will bring to light: and what he passed over in silence, I will proclaim: that you may have the whole case before you, and not be left to depend upon either his, or upon my inferences or testimony. Here then are several provisions of the Constitution to which reference has been made. I read them word for word just as they stand in the paper, called the United States Constitution, Art. I, sec. 2. "Representatives and direct taxes shall be apportioned among the several States which may be included in this Union, according to their respective numbers, which shall be determined by adding to the whole number of free persons, including those bound to service for a term years,

and excluding Indians not taxed, three-fifths of all other persons; Art. I, sec. 9. The migration or importation of such persons as any of the States now existing shall think fit to admit, shall not be prohibited by the Congress prior to the year one thousand eight hundred and eight, but a tax or duty may be imposed on such importation, not exceeding ten dollars for each person; Art. 4, sec. 2. No person held to service or labour in one State, under the laws thereof, escaping into another shall, in consequence of any law or regulation therein, be discharged from service or labour; but shall be delivered up on claim of the party to whom such service or labour may be due; Art. I, sec. 8. To provide for calling for the militia to execute the laws of the Union, suppress insurrections, and repel invasions." Here then, are those provisions of the Constitution, which the most extravagant defenders of slavery can claim to guarantee a right of property in man. These are the provisions which have been pressed into the service of the human flesh-mongers of America. Let us look at them just as they stand, one by one. Let us grant, for the sake of the argument, that the first of these provisions, referring to the basis of representation and taxation, does refer to slaves. We are not compelled to make that admission, for it might fairly apply to aliens—persons living in the country, but not naturalized. But giving the provisions the very worst construction, what does it amount to? I answer—It is a downright disability laid upon the slave-holding States; one which deprives those States of two-fifths of their natural basis of representation. A black man in a free State is worth just two-fifths more than a black man in a slave State, as a basis of political power under the Constitution. Therefore, instead of encouraging slavery, the Constitution encourages freedom by giving an increase of "two-fifths" of political power to free over slave States. So much for the three-fifths clause; taking it at its worst, it still leans to freedom, not slavery; for, be it remembered that the Constitution nowhere forbids a coloured man to vote. I come to the next, that which it is said guaranteed the continuance of the African slave trade for twenty years. I will also take that for just what my opponent alleges it to have been, although the Constitution does not warrant any such conclusion. But, to be liberal, let us suppose it did, and what follows? Why, this—that this part of the Constitution, so far as the slave trade is concerned, became a dead letter more than 50 years ago, and now binds no man's conscience for the continuance of any slave trade whatsoever. Mr. Thompson is just 52 years too late in dissolving the Union on account of this clause. He might as well dissolve the British Government, because Queen Elizabeth granted to Sir John Hawkins to import Africans into the West Indies 300 years ago! But there is still more to be said about this abolition of the slave trade. Men, at that time, both in England and in America, looked upon the slave trade as the life of slavery. The abolition of the slave trade was supposed to be the certain death of slavery. Cut off the stream, and the pond will dry up, was the common notion at the time.

Wilberforce and Clarkson, clear-sighted as they were, took this view; and the American statesmen, in providing for the abolition of the slave trade, thought they were providing for the abolition of the slavery. This view is quite consistent with the history of the times. All regarded slavery as an expiring and doomed system, destined to speedily disappear from the country. But, again, it should be remembered that this very provision, if made to refer to the African slave trade at all, makes the Constitution anti-slavery rather than for slavery; for it says to the slave States, the price you will have to pay for coming into the American Union is, that the slave trade, which you would carry on indefinitely out of the Union, shall be put an end to in twenty years if you come into the Union. Secondly, if it does apply, it expired by its own limitation more than fifty years ago. Thirdly, it is anti-slavery, because it looked to the abolition of slavery rather than to its perpetuity. Fourthly, it showed that the intentions of the framers of the Constitution were good, not bad. I think this is quite enough for this point. I go to the "slave insurrection" clause, though, in truth, there is no such clause. The one which is called so has nothing whatever to do with slaves or slaveholders any more than your laws for suppression of popular outbreaks has to do with making slaves of you and your children. It is only a law for suppression of riots or insurrections. But I will be generous here, as well as elsewhere, and grant that it applies to slave insurrections. Let us suppose that an anti-slavery man is President of the United States (and the day that shall see this the case is not distant) and this very power of suppressing slave insurrections would put an end to slavery. The right to put down an insurrection carries with it the right to determine the means by which it shall be put down. If it should turn out that slavery is a source of insurrection, that there is no security from insurrection while slavery lasts, why, the Constitution would be best obeyed by putting an end to slavery, and an anti-slavery Congress would do the very same thing. Thus, you see, the so-called slave-

holding provisions of the American Constitution, which a little while ago looked so formidable, are, after all, no defence or guarantee for slavery whatever. But there is one other provision. This is called the "Fugitive Slave Provision." It is called so by those who wish to make it subserve the interest of slavery in America, and the same by those who wish to uphold the views of a party in this country. It is put thus in the speech at the City Hall:—"Let us go back to 1787, and enter Liberty Hall, Philadelphia, where sat in convention the illustrious men who framed the Constitution—with George Washington in the chair. On the 27th of September, Mr. Butler and Mr. Pinckney, two delegates from the State of South Carolina, moved that the Constitution should require that fugitive slaves and servants should be delivered up like criminals, and after a discussion on the subject, the clause, as it stands in the Constitution, was adopted. After this, in the conventions held in the several States to ratify the Constitution, the same meaning was attached to the words. For example, Mr. Madison (afterwards President), when recommending the Constitution to his constituents, told them that the clause would secure them their property in slaves." I must ask you to look well to this statement. Upon its face, it would seem a full and fair statement of the history of the transaction it professes to describe and yet I declare unto you, knowing as I do the facts in the case, my utter amazement at the downright untruth conveyed under the fair seeming words now quoted. The man who could make such a statement may have all the craftiness of a lawyer, but who can accord to him the candour of an honest debater? What could more completely destroy all confidence in his statements? Mark you, the orator had not allowed his audience to hear read the provision of the Constitution to which he referred. He merely characterized it as one to "deliver up fugitive slaves and servants like criminals," and tells you that this was done "after discussion." But he took good care not to tell you what was the nature of that discussion. He would have spoiled the whole effect of his statement had he told you the whole truth. Now, what are the facts connected with this provision of the Constitution? You shall have them. It seems to take two men to tell the truth. It is quite true that Mr. Butler and Mr. Pinckney introduced a provision expressly with a view to the recapture of fugitive slaves: it is quite true also that there was some discussion on the subject—and just here the truth shall come out. These illustrious kidnappers were told promptly in that discussion that no such idea as property in man should be admitted into the Constitution. The speaker in question might have told you, and he would have told you but the simple truth, if he had told you that the proposition of Mr. Butler and Mr. Pinckney—which he leads you to infer was adopted by the convention that framed the Constitution—was, in fact, promptly and indignantly rejected by that convention. He might have told you, had it suited his purpose to do so, that the words employed in the first draft of the fugitive slave clause were such as applied to the condition of slaves, and expressly declared that persons held to "servitude" should be given up; but that the word "servitude" was struck from the provision, for the very reason that it applied to slaves. He might have told you that the same Mr. Madison declared that the word was struck out because the convention would not consent that the idea of property in men should be admitted into the Constitution. The fact that Mr. Madison can be cited on both sides of this question is another evidence of the folly and absurdity of making the secret intentions of the framers the criterion by which the Constitution is to be construed. But it may be asked—if this clause does not apply to slaves, to whom does it apply?

I answer, that when adopted, it applies to a very large class of persons—namely, redemptioners—persons who had come to America from Holland, from Ireland, and other quarters of the globe—like the Coolies to the West Indies—and had, for a consideration duly paid, become bound to "serve and labour" for the parties to whom their service and labour was due. It applies to indentured apprentices and others who have become bound for a consideration, under contract duly made, to serve and labour, to such persons this provision applies, and only to such persons. The plain reading of this provision shows that it applies, and that it can only properly and legally apply, to persons "bound to service." Its object plainly is, to secure the fulfillment of contracts for "service and labour." It applies to indentured apprentices, and any other persons from whom service and labour may be due. The legal condition of the slave puts him beyond the operation of this provision. He is not described in it. He is a simple article of property. He does not owe and cannot owe service. He cannot even make a contract. It is impossible for him to do so. He can no more make such a contract than a horse or an ox can make one. This provision, then, only respects persons who owe service, and they only can owe service who can receive an equivalent and make a bargain. The slave cannot do that, and is therefore exempted from the operation of this fugitive provision. In all matters where laws are taught to be made the means of oppression, cruelty, and wickedness, I am for strict construction. I will concede nothing. It must be shown that it is so nominated in the bond. The pound of flesh, but not one drop of blood. The very nature of law is opposed to all such wickedness, and makes it difficult to accomplish such objects under the forms of law. Law is not merely an arbitrary enactment with regard to justice, reason, or humanity. Blackstone defines it to be a rule prescribed by the supreme power of the State commanding what is right and forbidding what is wrong. The speaker at the City Hall laid down some rules of legal interpretation. These rules send us to the history of the law for its meaning. I have no objection to such a course in ordinary cases of doubt. But where human liberty and justice are at stake, the case falls under an entirely different class of rules. There must be something more than history—something more than tradition. The Supreme Court of the United States lays down this rule, and it meets the case exactly—"Where rights are infringed—where the fundamental principles of the law are overthrown—where the general system of the law is departed from, the legislative intention must be expressed with irresistible clearness." The same court says that the language of the law must be construed strictly in favour of justice and liberty. Again, there is another rule of law. It is—Where a law is susceptible of two meanings, the one making it accomplish an innocent purpose, and the other making it accomplish a wicked purpose, we must in all cases adopt that which makes it accomplish an innocent purpose. Again, the details of a law are to be interpreted in the light of the declared objects sought by the law. I set these rules down against those employed at the City Hall. To me they seem just and rational. I only ask you to look at the American Constitution in the light of them, and you will see with me that no man is guaranteed a right of property in man, under the provisions of that instrument. If there are two ideas more distinct in their character and essence than another, those ideas are "persons" and "property," "men" and "things." Now, when it is proposed to transform persons into "property" and men into beasts of burden, I demand that the law that completes such a purpose shall be expressed with irresistible clearness. The thing must not be left to inference, but must be done in plain English. I know how this view of the subject is treated by the class represented at the City Hall. They are in the habit of treating the Negro as an exception to general rules. When their own liberty is in question they will avail themselves of all rules of law which protect and defend their freedom; but when the black man's rights are in question they concede everything, admit everything for slavery, and put liberty to the proof. They reserve the common law usage, and presume the Negro a slave unless he can prove himself free. I, on the other hand, presume him free unless he is proved to be otherwise. Let us look at the objects for which the Constitution was framed and adopted, and see if slavery is one of them. Here are its own objects as set forth by itself:—"We, the people of these United States, in order to form a more perfect union, establish justice, ensure domestic tranquility, provide for the common defense, promote the general welfare, and secure the blessings of liberty to ourselves and our posterity, do ordain and establish this Constitution of the United States of America." The objects here set forth are six in number: union, defence, welfare, tranquility, justice, and liberty. These are all good objects, and slavery, so far from being among them, is a foe of them all. But it has been said that Negroes are not included within the benefits sought under this declaration. This is said by the slaveholders in America—it is said by the City Hall orator—but it is not said by the Constitution itself. Its language is "we the people;" not we the white people, not even we the citizens, not we the privileged class, not we the high, not we the low, but we the people; not we the horses, sheep, and swine, and wheel-barrows, but we the people, we the human inhabitants; and, if Negroes are people, they are included in the benefits for which the Constitution of America was ordained and established. But how dare any man who pretends to be a friend to the Negro thus gratuitously concede away what the Negro has a right to claim under the Constitution? Why should such friends invent new arguments to increase the hopelessness of his bondage? This, I undertake to say, as the conclusion of the whole matter, that the constitutionality of slavery can be made out only by disregarding the plain and common-sense reading of the Constitution itself; by discrediting and casting away as worthless the most beneficent rules of legal interpretation; by ruling the Negro outside of these beneficent rules; by claiming that the Constitution does not mean what it says, and that it says what it does not mean; by disregarding the written Constitution, and interpreting it in the light of a secret understanding. It is in this mean, contemptible, and underhand method that the American Constitution is pressed into the service of slavery. They go every-

where else for proof that the Constitution declares that no person shall be deprived of life, liberty, or property without due process of law; it secures to every man the right of trial by jury, the privilege of the writ of habeas corpus—the great writ that put an end to slavery and slave-hunting in England—and it secures to every State a republican form of government. Anyone of these provisions in the hands of abolition statesmen, and backed up by a right moral sentiment, would put an end to slavery in America. The Constitution forbids the passing of a bill of attainder: that is, a law entailing upon the child the disabilities and hardships imposed upon the parent. Every slave law in America might be repealed on this very ground. The slave is made a slave because his mother is a slave. But to all this it is said that the practice of the American people is against my view. I admit it. They have given the Constitution a slaveholding interpretation. I admit it. They have committed innumerable wrongs against the Negro in the name of the Constitution. Yes, I admit it all; and I go with him who goes farthest in denouncing these wrongs. But it does not follow that the Constitution is in favour of these wrongs because the slaveholders have given it that interpretation. To be consistent in his logic, the City Hall speaker must follow the example of some of his brothers in America—he must not only fling away the Constitution, but the Bible. The Bible must follow the Constitution, for that, too, has been interpreted for slavery by American divines. Nay, more, he must not stop with the Constitution of America, but make war with the British Constitution, for, if I mistake not, the gentleman is opposed to the union of Church and State. In America he called himself a Republican. Yet he does not go for breaking down the British Constitution, although you have a Queen on the throne, and bishops in the House of Lords.

My argument against the dissolution of the American Union is this: It would place the slave system more exclusively under the control of the slaveholding States, and withdraw it from the power in the Northern States which is opposed to slavery. Slavery is essentially barbarous in its character. It, above all things else, dreads the presence of an advanced civilisation. It flourishes best where it meets no reproving frowns, and hears no condemning voices. While in the Union it will meet with both. Its hope of life, in the last resort, is to get out of the Union. I am, therefore, for drawing the bond of the Union more completely under the power of the Free States. What they most dread, that I most desire. I have much confidence in the instincts of the slaveholders.

They see that the Constitution will afford slavery no protection when it shall cease to be administered by slaveholders. They see, moreover, that if there is once a will in the people of America to abolish slavery, this is no word, no syllable in the Constitution to forbid that result. They see that the Constitution has not saved slavery in Rhode Island, in Connecticut, in New York, or Pennsylvania; that the Free States have only added three to their original number. There were twelve Slave States at the beginning of the Government: there are fifteen now. The dissolution of the Union would not give the North a single advantage over slavery, but would take from it many. Within the Union we have a firm basis of opposition to slavery. It is opposed to all the great objects of the Constitution. The dissolution of the Union is not only an unwise but a cowardly measure—15 millions running away from three hundred and fifty thousand slaveholders. Mr. Garrison and his friends tell us that while in the Union we are responsible for slavery. He and they sing out "No Union with slaveholders," and refuse to vote. I admit our responsibility for slavery while in the Union but I deny that going out of the Union would free us from that responsibility. There now clearly is no freedom from responsibility for slavery to any American citizen short to the abolition of slavery. The American people have gone quite too far in this slaveholding business now to sum up their whole business of slavery by singing out the cant phrase, "No union with slaveholders." To desert the family hearth may place the recreant husband out of the presence of his starving children, but this does not free him from responsibility. If a man were on board of a pirate ship, and in company with others had robbed and plundered, his whole duty would not be performed simply by taking the longboat and singing out, "No union with pirates." His duty would be to restore the stolen property. The American people in the Northern States have helped to enslave the black people. Their duty will not have been done till

they give them back their plundered rights. Reference was made at the City Hall to my having once held other opinions, and very different opinions to those I have now expressed. An old speech of mine delivered fourteen years ago was read to show—I know not what. Perhaps it was to show that I am not infallible. If so, I have to say in defence, that I never pretended to be. Although I cannot accuse myself of being remarkably unstable, I do not pretend that I have never altered my opinion both in respect to men and things. Indeed, I have been very much modified both in feeling and opinion within the last fourteen years. When I escaped from slavery, and was introduced to the Garrisonians, I adopted very many of their opinions, and defended them just as long as I deemed them true. I was young, had read but little, and naturally took some things on trust. Subsequent experience and reading have led me to examine for myself. This had brought me to other conclusions. When I was a child, I thought and spoke as a child. But the question is not as to what were my opinions fourteen years ago, but what they are now. If I am right now, it really does not matter what I was fourteen years ago. My position now is one of reform, not of revolution. I would act for the abolition of slavery through the Government—not over its ruins. If slaveholders have ruled the American Government for the last fifty years, let the anti-slavery men rule the nation for the next fifty years. If the South has made the Constitution bend to the purposes of slavery, let the North now make that instrument bend to the cause of freedom and justice. If 350,000 slaveholders have, by devoting their energies to that single end, been able to make slavery the vital and animating spirit of the American Confederacy for the last 72 years, now let the freemen of the North, who have the power in their own hands, and who can make the American Government just what they think fit, resolve to blot out for ever the foul and haggard crime, which is the blight and mildew, the curse and the disgrace of the whole United States.

D. SECESSION AND CIVIL WAR

Introduction to Part 1D

By the end of the 1850s, Southern politicians openly discussed secession as a response to the election of any US president opposing slavery in the territories (section C, doc. 31). Relying on decisions like *Dred Scott*, proslavery advocates insisted that banning slavery in the territories was unconstitutional and violated the equal rights of the slaveholding states. The antislavery platform of the new Republican Party, on the other hand, rejected slavery in the territories but nevertheless embraced the principle of federalism and the equal right of every state, whether North or South, to decide the issue for itself (doc. 2). The national debate ultimately focused on a fundamental question of constitutional law: Was slavery so inextricably fused into the terms of the federal Constitution as to make its preservation and extension an essential part of the original compact? If so, then banning slavery in the territories and refusing to vigorously enforce the fugitive slave laws in free states could be viewed as a breach of the original compact and justification for a *constitutional* decision to secede.

Abraham Lincoln perceptively analyzed the growing national crisis over slavery in his 1860 *Cooper Union Address* (doc. 1). Summarizing the disputes over slavery in the territories since America's founding, Lincoln in-

sisted that the South would not be appeased until slavery became legal throughout the nation and all were forced to approve of the institution or remain silent. Speaking to his critics in the South, Lincoln condemned the growing threats of secession: "But you will not abide the election of a Republican president! In that supposed event, you say, you will destroy the Union; and then, you say, the great crime of having destroyed it will be upon us!"

As a moderate Republican, Lincoln shared the general federalist approach to the issue of slavery announced in the 1860 Republican Party platform: although states had the right to permit slavery, nothing prevented federal opposition to the institution in the territories (doc. 2). In their 1860 platform, a divided Democratic Party took no specific position on slavery in the territories but instead promised to "abide by the decision of the Supreme Court of the United States upon these questions of Constitutional Law" (doc. 3).

On November 6, 1860, Abraham Lincoln was elected the sixteenth president of the United States. As Lincoln had predicted, politicians in Southern slaveholding states called for immediate secession from the Union. On November 10, South Carolina's Senator James Chestnut Jr. resigned from Congress, and that same day, the South Carolina legislature called for a convention to vote on seceding from the Union. Other slaveholding states prepared to follow suit. Because Lincoln would not take office until after the first of the year, outgoing president James Buchanan was forced to deal with the secession crisis.

In his annual message to Congress, delivered on December 3, 1860, Buchanan insisted that Lincoln's election did not justify "dissolving the Union," and he rejected secession as an unnecessary and revolutionary act (doc. 4). Relying on Madison's Report of 1800, Buchanan insisted secession was justified only in cases involving "deliberate, palpable and dangerous exercise" of powers not granted by the Constitution rather than as a mere reaction to a presidential election. Quoting Madison's letter to Edward Everett (section B, doc. 21), Buchanan denied that secession was a constitutional remedy reserved to the states. Rather than attempting to leave the Union, Southern states were encouraged by Buchanan to join efforts to add an "explanatory amendment" to the Constitution that would establish both the right to slavery and the right of slave owners to carry their slaves into the territories. Should that effort fail, and should the Southern states then decide to secede, there was nothing Congress could do to stop them. In Buchanan's words, "After much serious reflection I have arrived at the conclusion that no such power has been delegated to Congress or to any other department of the Federal Government."

On December 24, 1860, South Carolina became the first state to announce its exit from the Union (doc. 5). Self-consciously adopting the style and language of the Declaration of Independence, the South Carolina *Declaration of the Causes Which Justify Secession* asserted that the people had the right to "alter or abolish" any government "destructive of the ends for which it was established." In this case, South Carolina was one of "free and independent states" announced by the Declaration that had entered into a compact with its sister states under conditions of mutual obligation. Northern states, however, had breached their obligations by ignoring the fugitive slave clause and by refusing slave owners the right of interstate travel with their "property." More recently, the Northern states had "united in the election of a man to the high office of President of the United States whose opinions and purposes are hostile to slavery" and who had declared that "[g]overnment cannot endure permanently half slave, half free."

When the Republican Party took control of the government, declared the document, "[t]he guaranties of the Constitution will no longer exist; the equal rights of the States will be lost. The slaveholding States will no longer have the power of self-government, or self-protection, and the Federal Government will have become their enemy."

In his farewell speech to the United States Senate, Louisiana senator Judah Benjamin presented the constitutional case for secession (doc. 6). Citing the Declaration of Independence as well as the Virginia and Kentucky Resolutions, Benjamin insisted that the rights of secession were among the reserved rights and powers left to the people in the several states under the Ninth and Tenth Amendments. As James Madison had explained decades before, each state had the right to decide for itself whether the original compact had been irrevocably broken. Benjamin concluded with a warning: "[Y]ou must acknowledge the independence of the seceding State, or reduce her to subjection by war.... We desire, we beseech you, let this parting be in peace." Soon afterward, Benjamin resigned his seat and accepted the position of Attorney General in the Confederate Cabinet of Jefferson Davis.

Desperate to stop the continued flow of seceding states, Congress considered passing a constitutional amendment guaranteeing Southern states the right to maintain slavery. On March 2, 1861, two days before Abraham Lincoln took the oath of office, Congress passed an amendment drafted by Ohio representative Thomas Corwin, which declared, "No amendment shall be made to the Constitution which will authorize or give to Congress the power to abolish or interfere, within any State, with the domestic institutions thereof, including that of persons held to labor or service by the laws of said State" (doc. 7).

The Corwin Amendment not only constitutionally protected state-established slavery but, if ratified, would also make slavery an unamendable part of the federal Constitution. A number of states quickly ratified the proslavery amendment, including Kentucky, Ohio, Rhode Island, Maryland, and Illinois.[1]

Two days after Congress's action on the Corwin Amendment, incoming president Abraham Lincoln

1. See, generally, Daniel W. Crofts, *Lincoln and the Politics of Slavery: The Other Thirteenth Amendment and the Struggle to Save the Union* (Chapel Hill: University of North Carolina Press, 2016), 15.

delivered his first inaugural address (doc. 8). Lincoln assured the slaveholding states that his election was not a threat to their peculiar institution. Echoing the Republican platform, Lincoln accepted "the rights of the states" over their "domestic institutions." What he could not allow, however, was secession. "[T]he Union of these States is perpetual," Lincoln declared, and "no State upon its own mere volition can lawfully get out of the Union." Although the right of revolution might be triggered should the majority deprive a minority of "any clearly written constitutional right," the existence of slavery in the territories remained a disputed matter not clearly resolved by any constitutional text. On the other hand, states had the reserved right to allow slavery within their borders. Lincoln therefore had "no objection" to proposals, like the Corwin Amendment, which made state authority over slavery "express and irrevocable." As far as a potential civil war was concerned, the Union would protect all federal property, but it would not initiate hostilities with the seceding states. "In your hands, my dissatisfied fellow-countrymen, and not mine, is the momentous issue of civil war.... We are not enemies, but friends. We must not be enemies." One month later, South Carolina fired on Fort Sumter, and the Civil War began.

Believing themselves now legally independent of the Union, the Confederate States proceeded to draft their own constitution (doc. 9). Although closely following the structure of the original Constitution, among the Confederate Constitution's few changes was a provision in Article IV expressly guaranteeing slave owners "the right of transit and sojourn in any State of this Confederacy, with their slaves and other property." The Ninth and Tenth Amendments were moved to the end of Article VI and their language altered to clarify that the "people" who reserved both rights and powers were the "people of the several states."

The North, meanwhile, found itself grappling with an exquisitely complicated set of issues relating to the legal status of the rebel governments. Was secession constitutionally permitted, and if not, why? If the people of the Northern states were about to commit their blood and treasure to force the rebel states back into the Union, it was incumbent on the incoming president to explain the legal grounds for going to war. On July 4, 1861, in a message calling on Congress to pass legislation funding and manning military action against the seceding states, Lincoln presented the case for military action (doc. 10). This was a rebellion, Lincoln insisted,

not a revolution—and certainly not a constitutionally authorized "secession." Echoing the antebellum nationalist theories of Joseph Story and Daniel Webster, Lincoln insisted that the Union had preceded the states. *Constitutional* secession was impossible, since "[t]he States have their status in the Union, and they have no other legal status."

Having initially attempted to stave off secession with an offer to constitutionally entrench the practice of slavery, Union policy as the conflict wore on turned increasingly to abolition. In April of 1862, Lincoln signed a federal bill emancipating slaves in the District of Columbia (and compensating their former owners; doc. 11). Sponsored by Massachusetts senator Henry Wilson (who would also help draft the Thirteenth Amendment), the Compensated Emancipation Act immediately emancipated slaves, compensated the owners up to $300, and secured funds for transferring willing freedmen to countries such as Haiti or Liberia. Soon after publicly declaring himself committed to abolition only so far as it served to help save the Union (doc. 12), on January 1, 1863, President Lincoln signed the Emancipation Proclamation. The proclamation freed all persons held as slaves in rebel-controlled territory and allowed freedmen to enroll in the armed forces of the Union. Though limited in its scope—it did not apply to slaves held in loyal border states or in those parts of the Confederacy that had come under the Union army's control—the proclamation transformed the conflict into a struggle to advance the cause of human freedom. In his 1863 *Gettysburg Address* (doc. 15), Lincoln declared that "[o]ur fathers" had "brought forth on this continent a new nation, conceived in liberty and dedicated to the proposition that all men are created equal." In his April 1864 letter to Albert Hodges (using language that would be repeated by Republicans in the Thirty-Eighth Congress), Lincoln declared, "If slavery is not wrong, nothing is wrong." Lincoln ended his letter with a thought that he would expand upon in his second inaugural address: "If God now wills the removal of a great wrong, and wills also that we of the North as well as you of the South, shall pay fairly for our complicity in that wrong, impartial history will find therein new cause to attest and revere the justice and goodness of God" (doc. 16).

In advance of the 1864 presidential election, Republicans committed their party to securing an uncompromised military victory over the rebellion, applauding Lincoln's Emancipation Proclamation and the receipt of freedmen into the Union army (doc. 17). Had the Union military not secured important victories in advance of the elections that fall (particularly in Atlanta), the country might well have given the presidency to a man who had promised a negotiated peace—Democratic candidate General George McClellan.[2]

Instead, Lincoln was reelected, and he delivered his second inaugural address on March 4, 1865 (doc. 18). In this remarkable speech, Lincoln named slavery as the cause of this "terrible war" and, on behalf of a shattered country, bowed before the righteous judgment of God:

> If we shall suppose that American slavery is one of those offenses which, in the providence of God, must needs come, but which, having continued through His appointed time, He now wills to remove, and that He gives to both North and South this terrible war as the woe due to those by whom the offense came, shall we discern therein any departure from those divine attributes which the believers in a living God always ascribe to Him? Fondly do we hope, fervently do we pray, that this mighty scourge of war may speedily pass away. Yet, if God wills that it continue until all the wealth piled by the bondsman's two hundred and fifty years of unrequited toil shall be sunk, and until every drop of blood drawn with the lash shall be paid by another drawn with the sword, as was said three thousand years ago, so still it must be said "the judgments of the Lord are true and righteous altogether."

One month later, Confederate general Robert E. Lee surrendered to Union general Ulysses S. Grant at Appomattox Court House (doc. 19). Not with a bang but with the stiff cordiality of an exchange of letters by two military titans did the Civil War end. The need to avoid additional loss of life, to which both generals referred, was but a melancholy nod to the approximately 620,000 soldiers killed as a result of the bloody conflict—roughly 2 percent of the nation's population.

The North now faced the daunting task of reconstructing the Union. Doing so would require the addition of three critical amendments to the Constitution: one abolishing slavery, another establishing the conditions for the return of the rebel states, and a third granting black males the right to participate in the elective franchise.

2. See James M. McPherson, *Battle Cry of Freedom: The Civil War Era* (New York: Oxford University Press, 1988), 718.

1

Abraham Lincoln, Address at the Cooper Institute

February 27, 1860[*]

Mr. President and fellow citizens of New York:

The facts with which I shall deal this evening are mainly old and familiar; nor is there anything new in the general use I shall make of them. If there shall be any novelty, it will be in the mode of presenting the facts, and the inferences and observations following that presentation.

In his speech last autumn, at Columbus, Ohio, as reported in "The New-York Times," Senator Douglas said:

"Our fathers, when they framed the Government under which we live, understood this question just as well, and even better, than we do now."

I fully indorse this, and I adopt it as a text for this discourse. I so adopt it because it furnishes a precise and an agreed starting point for a discussion between Republicans and that wing of the Democracy headed by Senator Douglas. It simply leaves the inquiry: *"What was the understanding those fathers had of the question mentioned?"*

What is the frame of government under which we live?

The answer must be: "The Constitution of the United States." That Constitution consists of the original, framed in 1787, (and under which the present government first went into operation,) and twelve subsequently framed amendments, the first ten of which were framed in 1789.

Who were our fathers that framed the Constitution? I suppose the "thirty-nine" who signed the original instrument may be fairly called our fathers who framed that part of the present Government. It is almost exactly true to say they framed it, and it is altogether true to say they fairly represented the opinion and sentiment of the whole nation at that time. Their names, being familiar to nearly all, and accessible to quite all, need not now be repeated.

[*] *Abraham Lincoln, Speeches and Writings, 1859–1865*, ed. Don E. Fehrenbacher (New York: Library of America, 1989), 2:111.

I take these "thirty-nine," for the present, as being "our fathers who framed the Government under which we live."

What is the question which, according to the text, those fathers understood "just as well, and even better than we do now?"

It is this: Does the proper division of local from federal authority, or anything in the Constitution, forbid *our Federal Government* to control as to slavery in *our Federal Territories*?

Upon this, Senator Douglas holds the affirmative, and Republicans the negative. This affirmation and denial form an issue; and this issue—this question—is precisely what the text declares our fathers understood "better than we."

Let us now inquire whether the "thirty-nine," or any of them ever acted upon this question; and if they did, how they acted upon it—how they expressed that better understanding?

In 1784, three years before the Constitution—the United States then owning the Northwestern Territory, and no other, the Congress of the Confederation had before them the question of prohibiting slavery in that Territory; and four of the "thirty-nine" who afterward framed the Constitution, were in that Congress, and voted on that question. Of these, Roger Sherman, Thomas Mifflin, and Hugh Williamson voted for the prohibition, thus showing that, in their understanding, no line dividing local from federal authority, nor anything else, properly forbade the Federal Government to control as to slavery in federal territory. The other of the four—James M'Henry—voted against the prohibition, showing that, for some cause, he thought it improper to vote for it.

In 1787, still before the Constitution, but while the Convention was in session framing it, and while the Northwestern Territory still was the only territory owned by the United States, the same question of prohibiting slavery in the territory again came before the Congress of the Confederation; and two more of the "thirty-nine" who afterward signed the Constitution, were in that Congress, and voted on the question. They were William Blount and William Few; and they both voted for the prohibition—thus showing that, in their understanding, no line dividing local from federal authority, nor anything else, properly forbids the Federal Government to control as to slavery in Federal territory. This time the prohibition became a law, being part of what is now well known as the Ordinance of '87.

The question of federal control of slavery in the territories, seems not to have been directly before the Convention which framed the original Constitution; and hence it is not recorded that the "thirty-nine," or any of them, while engaged on that instrument, expressed any opinion on that precise question.

In 1789, by the first Congress which sat under the Constitution, an act was passed to enforce the Ordinance of '87, including the prohibition of slavery in the Northwestern Territory. The bill for this act was reported by one of the "thirty-nine," Thomas Fitzsimmons, then a member of the House of Representatives from Pennsylvania. It went through all its stages without a word of opposition, and finally passed both branches without yeas and nays, which is equivalent to a unanimous passage. In this Congress there were sixteen of the thirty-nine fathers who framed the original Constitution. They were John Langdon, Nicholas Gilman, Wm. S. Johnson, Roger Sherman, Robert Morris, Thos. Fitzsimmons, William Few, Abraham Baldwin, Rufus King, William Paterson, George Clymer, Richard Bassett, George Read, Pierce Butler, Daniel Carroll, James Madison.

This shows that, in their understanding, no line dividing local from federal authority, nor anything in the Constitution, properly forbade Congress to prohibit slavery in the federal territory; else both their fidelity to correct principle, and their oath to support the Constitution, would have constrained them to oppose the prohibition.

Again, George Washington, another of the "thirty-nine," was then President of the United States, and, as such approved and signed the bill; thus completing its validity as a law, and thus showing that, in his understanding, no line dividing local from federal authority, nor anything in the Constitution, forbade the Federal Government, to control as to slavery in federal territory.

. . .

The remaining sixteen of the "thirty-nine," so far as I have discovered, have left no record of their understanding upon the direct question of federal control of slavery in the federal territories. But there is much reason to believe that their understanding upon that question would not have appeared different from that of their twenty-three compeers, had it been manifested at all.

For the purpose of adhering rigidly to the text, I have purposely omitted whatever understanding may have been manifested by any person, however distinguished, other than the thirty-nine fathers who framed the original Constitution; and, for the same reason, I have also omitted whatever understanding may have been manifested by any of the "thirty-nine" even, on any other phase of the general question of slavery. If we should look into their acts and declarations on those other phases, as the foreign slave trade, and the morality and policy of slavery generally, it would appear to us that on the direct question of federal control of slavery in federal territories, the sixteen, if they had acted at all, would probably have acted just as the twenty-three did. Among that sixteen were several of the most noted anti-slavery men of those times—as Dr. Franklin, Alexander Hamilton and Gouverneur Morris—while there was not one now known to have been otherwise, unless it may be John Rutledge, of South Carolina.

The sum of the whole is, that of our thirty-nine fathers who framed the original Constitution, twenty-one—a clear majority of the whole—certainly understood that no proper division of local from federal authority, nor any part of the Constitution, forbade the Federal Government to control slavery in the federal territories; while all the rest probably had the same understanding. Such, unquestionably, was the understanding of our fathers who framed the original Constitution; and the text affirms that they understood the question "better than we."

But, so far, I have been considering the understanding of the question manifested by the framers of the original Constitution. In and by the original instrument, a mode was provided for amending it; and, as I have already stated, the present frame of "the Government under which we live" consists of that original, and twelve amendatory articles framed and adopted since. Those who now insist that federal control of slavery in federal territories violates the Constitution, point us to the provisions which they suppose it thus violates; and, as I understand, that all fix upon provisions in these amendatory articles, and not in the original instrument. The Supreme Court, in the Dred Scott case, plant themselves upon the fifth amendment, which provides that no person shall be deprived of "life, liberty or property without due process of law;" while Senator Douglas and his peculiar adherents plant themselves upon the tenth amendment, providing that "the powers not delegated to the United States by the Constitution" "are reserved to the States respectively, or to the people."

Now, it so happens that these amendments were framed by the first Congress which sat under the Constitution—the identical Congress which passed the act already mentioned, enforcing the prohibition of slavery in the Northwestern Territory. Not only was it the same Congress, but they were the identical, same individual men who, at the same session, and at the same time within the session, had under consideration, and in progress toward maturity, these Constitutional amendments, and this act prohibiting slavery in all the territory the nation then owned. The Constitutional amendments were introduced before, and passed after the act enforcing the Ordinance of '87; so that, during the whole pendency of the act to enforce the Ordinance, the Constitutional amendments were also pending.

The seventy-six members of that Congress, including sixteen of the framers of the original Constitution, as before stated, were pre-eminently our fathers who framed that part of "the Government under which we live," which is now claimed as forbidding the Federal Government to control slavery in the federal territories.

Is it not a little presumptuous in any one at this day to affirm that the two things which that Congress deliberately framed, and carried to maturity at the same time, are absolutely inconsistent with each other? And does not such affirmation become impudently absurd when coupled with the other affirmation from the same mouth, that those who did the two things, alleged to be inconsistent, understood whether they really were inconsistent better than we—better than he who affirms that they are inconsistent?

It is surely safe to assume that the thirty-nine framers of the original Constitution, and the seventy-six members of the Congress which framed the amendments thereto, taken together, do certainly include those who may be fairly called "our fathers who framed the Government under which we live." And so assuming, I defy any man to show that any one of them ever, in his whole life, declared that, in his understanding, any proper division of local from federal authority, or any part of the Constitution, forbade the Federal Government to control as to slavery in the federal territories. I go a step further. I defy any one to show that any living man in the whole world ever did, prior to the beginning of the present century, (and I might almost say prior to the beginning of the last half of the present century,) declare that, in his understanding, any proper division of local from federal authority, or any part of the Constitution, forbade the Federal Government to control as to slavery in the federal territories. To those who now so declare, I give, not only "our fathers who framed the Government under which we live," but with them all other living men within the century in which it was framed,

315

among whom to search, and they shall not be able to find the evidence of a single man agreeing with them.

Now, and here, let me guard a little against being misunderstood. I do not mean to say we are bound to follow implicitly in whatever our fathers did. To do so, would be to discard all the lights of current experience—to reject all progress—all improvement. What I do say is, that if we would supplant the opinions and policy of our fathers in any case, we should do so upon evidence so conclusive, and argument so clear, that even their great authority, fairly considered and weighed, cannot stand; and most surely not in a case whereof we ourselves declare they understood the question better than we.

If any man at this day sincerely believes that a proper division of local from federal authority, or any part of the Constitution, forbids the Federal Government to control as to slavery in the federal territories, he is right to say so, and to enforce his position by all truthful evidence and fair argument which he can. But he has no right to mislead others, who have less access to history, and less leisure to study it, into the false belief that "our fathers who framed the Government under which we live" were of the same opinion—thus substituting falsehood and deception for truthful evidence and fair argument. If any man at this day sincerely believes "our fathers who framed the Government under which we live," used and applied principles, in other cases, which ought to have led them to understand that a proper division of local from federal authority or some part of the Constitution, forbids the Federal Government to control as to slavery in the federal territories, he is right to say so. But he should, at the same time, brave the responsibility of declaring that, in his opinion, he understands their principles better than they did themselves; and especially should he not shirk that responsibility by asserting that they "understood the question just as well, and even better, than we do now."

But enough! *Let all who believe that "our fathers, who framed the Government under which we live, understood this question just as well, and even better, than we do now," speak as they spoke, and act as they acted upon it. This is all Republicans ask—all Republicans desire—in relation to slavery. As those fathers marked it, so let it be again marked, as an evil not to be extended, but to be tolerated and protected only because of and so far as its actual presence among us makes that toleration and protection a necessity. Let all the guarantees those fathers gave it, be, not grudgingly, but fully and fairly, main-*tained.* For this Republicans contend, and with this, so far as I know or believe, they will be content.

And now, if they would listen—as I suppose they will not—I would address a few words to the Southern people.

I would say to them:—You consider yourselves a reasonable and a just people; and I consider that in the general qualities of reason and justice you are not inferior to any other people. Still, when you speak of us Republicans, you do so only to denounce us as reptiles, or, at the best, as no better than outlaws. You will grant a hearing to pirates or murderers, but nothing like it to "Black Republicans." In all your contentions with one another, each of you deems an unconditional condemnation of "Black Republicanism" as the first thing to be attended to. Indeed, such condemnation of us seems to be an indispensable prerequisite—license, so to speak—among you to be admitted or permitted to speak at all. Now, can you, or not, be prevailed upon to pause and to consider whether this is quite just to us, or even to yourselves? Bring forward your charges and specifications, and then be patient long enough to hear us deny or justify.

You say we are sectional. We deny it. That makes an issue; and the burden of proof is upon you. You produce your proof; and what is it? Why, that our party has no existence in your section—gets no votes in your section. The fact is substantially true; but does it prove the issue? If it does, then in case we should, without change of principle, begin to get votes in your section, we should thereby cease to be sectional. You cannot escape this conclusion; and yet, are you willing to abide by it? If you are, you will probably soon find that we have ceased to be sectional, for we shall get votes in your section this very year. You will then begin to discover, as the truth plainly is, that your proof does not touch the issue. The fact that we get no votes in your section, is a fact of your making, and not of ours. And if there be fault in that fact, that fault is primarily yours, and remains until you show that we repel you by some wrong principle or practice. If we do repel you by any wrong principle or practice, the fault is ours; but this brings you to where you ought to have started—to a discussion of the right or wrong of our principle. If our principle, put in practice, would wrong your section for the benefit of ours, or for any other object, then our principle, and we with it, are sectional, and are justly opposed and denounced as such. Meet us, then, on the question of whether our principle, put in practice, would wrong your section; and so meet it as if it were possible that something may be said on our side. Do you accept the challenge? No! Then you really believe that the principle which "our fathers who framed the Government under which we live" thought so clearly right as to adopt it, and indorse it again and again, upon their official oaths, is in fact so clearly wrong as to demand your condemnation without a moment's consideration.

Some of you delight to flaunt in our faces the warning against sectional parties given by Washington in his Farewell Address. Less than eight years before Washington gave that warning, he had, as President of the United States, approved and signed an act of Congress, enforcing the prohibition of slavery in the Northwestern Territory, which act embodied the policy of the Government upon that subject up to and at the very moment he penned that warning; and about one year after he penned it, he wrote LaFayette that he considered that prohibition a wise measure, expressing in the same connection his hope that we should at some time have a confederacy of free States.

Bearing this in mind, and seeing that sectionalism has since arisen upon this same subject, is that warning a weapon in your hands against us, or in our hands against you? Could Washington himself speak, would he cast the blame of that sectionalism upon us, who sustain his policy, or upon you who repudiate it? We respect that warning of Washington, and we commend it to you, together with his example pointing to the right application of it.

But you say you are conservative—eminently conservative—while we are revolutionary, destructive, or something of the sort. What is conservatism? Is it not adherence to the old and tried, against the new and untried? We stick to, contend for, the identical old policy on the point in controversy which was adopted by "our fathers who framed the Government under which we live;" while you with one accord reject, and scout, and spit upon that old policy, and insist upon substituting something new. True, you disagree among yourselves as to what that substitute shall be. You are divided on new propositions and plans, but you are unanimous in rejecting and denouncing the old policy of the fathers. Some of you are for reviving the foreign slave trade; some for a Congressional Slave-Code for the Territories; some for Congress forbidding the Territories to prohibit Slavery within their limits; some for maintaining Slav-ery in the Territories through the judiciary; some for the "gur-reat pur-rinciple" that "if one man would enslave another, no third man should object," fantastically called "Popular Sovereignty;" but never a man among you is in favor of federal prohibition of slavery in federal territories, according to the practice of "our fathers who framed the Government under which we live." Not one of all your various plans can show a precedent or an advocate in the century within which our Government originated. Consider, then, whether your claim of conservatism for yourselves, and your charge or destructiveness against us, are based on the most clear and stable foundations.

Again, you say we have made the slavery question more prominent than it formerly was. We deny it. We admit that it is more prominent, but we deny that we made it so. It was not we, but you, who discarded the old policy of the fathers. We resisted, and still resist, your innovation; and thence comes the greater prominence of the question. Would you have that question reduced to its former proportions? Go back to that old policy. What has been will be again, under the same conditions. If you would have the peace of the old times, re-adopt the precepts and policy of the old times.

. . .

But you will break up the Union rather than submit to a denial of your Constitutional rights.

That has a somewhat reckless sound; but it would be palliated, if not fully justified, were we proposing, by the mere force of numbers, to deprive you of some right, plainly written down in the Constitution. But we are proposing no such thing.

When you make these declarations, you have a specific and well-understood allusion to an assumed Constitutional right of yours, to take slaves into the federal territories, and to hold them there as property. But no such right is specifically written in the Constitution. That instrument is literally silent about any such right. We, on the contrary, deny that such a right has any existence in the Constitution, even by implication.

Your purpose, then, plainly stated, is that you will destroy the Government, unless you be allowed to construe and enforce the Constitution as you please, on all points in dispute between you and us. You will rule or ruin in all events.

This, plainly stated, is your language. Perhaps you will say the Supreme Court has decided the disputed Constitutional question in your favor. Not quite so. But waiving the lawyer's distinction between dictum and decision, the Court have decided the question for you in a sort of way. The Court have substantially said, it is your Constitutional right to take slaves into the federal territories, and to hold them there as property. When I say the decision was made in a sort of way, I mean it was made in a divided Court, by a bare majority of the Judges, and they not quite agreeing with one another in the reasons for making it; that it is so made as that its avowed supporters disagree with one another about its meaning, and that it was mainly based upon a mistaken statement of fact—the statement in the opinion that "the right of property in a slave is distinctly and expressly affirmed in the Constitution."

An inspection of the Constitution will show that the right of property in a slave is not "*distinctly* and *expressly* affirmed" in it. Bear in mind, the Judges do not pledge their judicial opinion that such right is *impliedly* affirmed in the Constitution; but they pledge their veracity that it is "*distinctly* and *expressly*" affirmed there—"distinctly," that is, not mingled with anything else—"expressly," that is, in words meaning just that, without the aid of any inference, and susceptible of no other meaning.

If they had only pledged their judicial opinion that such right is affirmed in the instrument by implication, it would be open to others to show that neither the word "slave" nor "slavery" is to be found in the Constitution, nor the word "property" even, in any connection with language alluding to the things slave, or slavery; and that wherever in that instrument the slave is alluded to, he is called a "person;"—and wherever his master's legal right in relation to him is alluded to, it is spoken of as "service or labor which may be due,"—as a debt payable in service or labor. Also, it would be open to show, by contemporaneous history, that this mode of alluding to slaves and slavery, instead of speaking of them, was employed on purpose to exclude from the Constitution the idea that there could be property in man.

To show all this, is easy and certain.

When this obvious mistake of the Judges shall be brought to their notice, is it not reasonable to expect that they will withdraw the mistaken statement, and reconsider the conclusion based upon it?

And then it is to be remembered that "our fathers, who framed the Government under which we live"—the men who made the Constitution—decided this same Constitutional question in our favor, long ago—decided it without division among themselves, when

making the decision; without division among themselves about the meaning of it after it was made, and, so far as any evidence is left, without basing it upon any mistaken statement of facts.

Under all these circumstances, do you really feel yourselves justified to break up this Government unless such a court decision as yours is, shall be at once submitted to as a conclusive and final rule of political action? But you will not abide the election of a Republican president! In that supposed event, you say, you will destroy the Union; and then, you say, the great crime of having destroyed it will be upon us! That is cool. A highwayman holds a pistol to my ear, and mutters through his teeth, "Stand and deliver, or I shall kill you, and then you will be a murderer!"

To be sure, what the robber demanded of me—my money—was my own; and I had a clear right to keep it; but it was no more my own than my vote is my own; and the threat of death to me, to extort my money, and the threat of destruction to the Union, to extort my vote, can scarcely be distinguished in principle.

A few words now to Republicans. *It is exceedingly desirable that all parts of this great Confederacy shall be at peace, and in harmony, one with another. Let us Republicans do our part to have it so. Even though much provoked, let us do nothing through passion and ill temper. Even though the southern people will not so much as listen to us, let us calmly consider their demands, and yield to them if, in our deliberate view of our duty, we possibly can.* Judging by all they say and do, and by the subject and nature of their controversy with us, let us determine, if we can, what will satisfy them.

Will they be satisfied if the Territories be unconditionally surrendered to them? We know they will not. In all their present complaints against us, the Territories are scarcely mentioned. Invasions and insurrections are the rage now. Will it satisfy them, if, in the future, we have nothing to do with invasions and insurrections? We know it will not. We so know, because we know we never had anything to do with invasions and insurrections; and yet this total abstaining does not exempt us from the charge and the denunciation.

The question recurs, what will satisfy them? Simply this: We must not only let them alone, but we must somehow, convince them that we do let them alone. This, we know by experience, is no easy task. We have been so trying to convince them from the very beginning of our organization, but with no success. In all our platforms and speeches we have constantly protested our purpose to let them alone; but this has had no tendency to convince them. Alike unavailing to convince them, is the fact that they have never detected a man of us in any attempt to disturb them.

These natural, and apparently adequate means all failing, what will convince them? This, and this only: cease to call slavery *wrong*, and join them in calling it *right*. And this must be done thoroughly—done in *acts* as well as in *words*. Silence will not be tolerated—we must place ourselves avowedly with them. Senator Douglas' new sedition law must be enacted and enforced, suppressing all declarations that slavery is wrong, whether made in politics, in presses, in pulpits, or in private. We must arrest and return their fugitive slaves with greedy pleasure. We must pull down our Free State constitutions. The whole atmosphere must be disinfected from all taint of opposition to slavery, before they will cease to believe that all their troubles proceed from us.

I am quite aware they do not state their case precisely in this way. Most of them would probably say to us, "Let us alone, *do* nothing to us, and *say* what you please about slavery." But we do let them alone—have never disturbed them—so that, after all, it is what we say, which dissatisfies them. They will continue to accuse us of doing, until we cease saying.

I am also aware they have not, as yet, in terms, demanded the overthrow of our Free-State Constitutions. Yet those Constitutions declare the wrong of slavery, with more solemn emphasis, than do all other sayings against it; and when all these other sayings shall have been silenced, the overthrow of these Constitutions will be demanded, and nothing be left to resist the demand. It is nothing to the contrary, that they do not demand the whole of this just now. Demanding what they do, and for the reason they do, they can voluntarily stop nowhere short of this consummation. Holding, as they do, that slavery is morally right, and socially elevating, they cannot cease to demand a full national recognition of it, as a legal right, and a social blessing.

Nor can we justifiably withhold this, on any ground save our conviction that slavery is wrong. If slavery is right, all words, acts, laws, and constitutions against it, are themselves wrong, and should be silenced, and swept away. If it is right, we cannot justly object to its nationality—its universality; if it is wrong, they cannot justly insist upon its extension—its enlargement. All they ask, we could readily grant, if we thought slavery right; all we ask, they could as readily grant, if they thought it wrong. Their thinking it right, and our think-

ing it wrong, is the precise fact upon which depends the whole controversy. Thinking it right, as they do, they are not to blame for desiring its full recognition, as being right; but, thinking it wrong, as we do, can we yield to them? Can we cast our votes with their view, and against our own? In view of our moral, social, and political responsibilities, can we do this?

Wrong as we think slavery is, we can yet afford to let it alone where it is, because that much is due to the necessity arising from its actual presence in the nation; but can we, while our votes will prevent it, allow it to spread into the National Territories, and to overrun us here in these Free States? If our sense of duty forbids this, then let us stand by our duty, fearlessly and effectively. Let us be diverted by none of those sophistical contrivances wherewith we are so industriously plied and belabored—contrivances such as groping for some middle ground between the right and the wrong, vain as the search for a man who should be neither a living man nor a dead man—such as a policy of "don't care" on a question about which all true men do care—such as Union appeals beseeching true Union men to yield to Disunionists, reversing the divine rule, and calling, not the sinners, but the righteous to repentance—such as invocations to Washington, imploring men to unsay what Washington said, and undo what Washington did.

Neither let us be slandered from our duty by false accusations against us, nor frightened from it by menaces of destruction to the Government nor of dungeons to ourselves. LET US HAVE FAITH THAT RIGHT MAKES MIGHT, AND IN THAT FAITH, LET US, TO THE END, DARE TO DO OUR DUTY AS WE UNDERSTAND IT.

2

Republican Party Platform

May 17, 1860[*]

Resolved, That we, the delegated representatives of the Republican electors of the United States in Convention assembled, in discharge of the duty we owe to our constituents and our country, unite in the following declarations:

[*] Commager, *Documents*, 1:363–65.

1. That the history of the nation during the last four years, has fully established the propriety and necessity of the organization and perpetuation of the Republican party, and that the causes which called it into existence are permanent in their nature, and now, more than ever before, demand its peaceful and constitutional triumph.

2. That the maintenance of the principles promulgated in the Declaration of Independence and embodied in the Federal Constitution, "That all men are created equal; that they are endowed by their Creator with certain inalienable rights; that among these are life, liberty and the pursuit of happiness; that to secure these rights, governments are instituted among men, deriving their just powers from the consent of the governed," is essential to the preservation of our Republican institutions; and that the Federal Constitution, the Rights of the States, and the Union of the States must and shall be preserved.

3. That to the Union of the States this nation owes its unprecedented increase in population, its surprising development of material resources, its rapid augmentation of wealth, its happiness at home and its honor abroad; and we hold in abhorrence all schemes for disunion, come from whatever source they may. And we congratulate the country that no Republican member of Congress has uttered or countenanced the threats of disunion so often made by Democratic members, without rebuke and with applause from their political associates; and we denounce those threats of disunion, in case of a popular overthrow of their ascendency as denying the vital principles of a free government, and as an avowal of contemplated treason, which it is the imperative duty of an indignant people sternly to rebuke and forever silence.

4. That the maintenance inviolate of the rights of the states, and especially the right of each state to order and control its own domestic institutions according to its own judgment exclusively, is essential to that balance of powers on which the perfection and endurance of our political fabric depends; and we denounce the lawless invasion by armed force of the soil of any state or territory, no matter under what pretext, as among the gravest of crimes.

5. That the present Democratic Administration has far exceeded our worst apprehensions, in its measureless subserviency to the exactions of a sectional interest, as especially evinced in its desperate exertions to force the infamous Lecompton Constitution upon the protesting people of Kansas; in construing the personal relations between master and servant to involve an unqualified property in persons; in its attempted enforcement everywhere, on land and sea, through the intervention of Congress and of the Federal Courts of the extreme pretensions of a purely local interest; and in its general and unvarying abuse of the power intrusted to it by a confiding people.

6. That the people justly view with alarm the reckless extravagance which pervades every department of the Federal Government; that a return to rigid economy and accountability is indispensable to arrest the systematic plunder of the public treasury by favored partisans; while the recent startling developments of frauds and corruptions at the Federal metropolis, show that an entire change of administration is imperatively demanded.

7. That the new dogma that the Constitution, of its own force, carries slavery into any or all of the territories of the United States, is a dangerous political heresy, at variance with the explicit provisions of that instrument itself, with contemporaneous exposition, and with legislative and judicial precedent; is revolutionary in its tendency, and subversive of the peace and harmony of the country.

8. That the normal condition of all the territory of the United States is that of freedom: That, as our Republican fathers, when they had abolished slavery in all our national territory, ordained that "no persons should be deprived of life, liberty or property without due process of law," it becomes our duty, by legislation, whenever such legislation is necessary, to maintain this provision of the Constitution against all attempts to violate it; and we deny the authority of Congress, of a territorial legislature, or of any individuals, to give legal existence to slavery in any territory of the United States.

9. That we brand the recent reopening of the African slave trade, under the cover of our national flag, aided by perversions of judicial power, as a crime against humanity and a burning shame to our country and age; and we call upon Congress to take prompt and efficient measures for the total and final suppression of that execrable traffic.

10. That in the recent vetoes, by their Federal Governors, of the acts of the legislatures of Kansas and Nebraska, prohibiting slavery in those territories, we find a practical illustration of the boasted Democratic principle of Non-Intervention and Popular Sovereignty, embodied in the Kansas-Nebraska Bill, and a demonstration of the deception and fraud involved therein.

11. That Kansas should, of right, be immediately admitted as a state under the Constitution recently formed and adopted by her people, and accepted by the House of Representatives.

12. That, while providing revenue for the support of the general government by duties upon imports, sound policy requires such an adjustment of these imports as to encourage the development of the industrial interests of the whole country; and we commend that policy of national exchanges, which secures to the working-men liberal wages, to agriculture remunerative prices, to mechanics and manufacturers an adequate reward for their skill, labor, and enterprise, and to the nation commercial prosperity and independence.

13. That we protest against any sale or alienation to others of the public lands held by actual settlers, and against any view of the free-homestead policy which regards the settlers as paupers or suppliants for public bounty; and we demand the passage by Congress of the complete and satisfactory homestead measure which has already passed the House.

14. That the Republican party is opposed to any change in our naturalization laws or any state legislation by which the rights of citizens hitherto accorded to immigrants from foreign lands shall be abridged or impaired; and in favor of giving a full and efficient protection to the rights of all classes of citizens, whether native or naturalized, both at home and abroad.

15. That appropriations by Congress for river and harbor improvements of a national character, required for the accommodation and security of an existing commerce, are authorized by the Constitution, and justified by the obligation of Government to protect the lives and property of its citizens.

16. That a railroad to the Pacific Ocean is imperatively demanded by the interests of the whole country; that the federal government ought to render immediate and efficient aid in its construction; and that, as preliminary thereto, a daily overland mail should be promptly established.

17. Finally, having thus set forth our distinctive principles and views, we invite the co-operation of all citizens, however differing on other questions, who substantially agree with us in their affirmance and support.

3
Democratic Party Platform
June 18, 1860[*]

1. Resolved, That we, the Democracy of the Union in Convention assembled, hereby declare our affirmance of the resolutions unanimously adopted and declared as a platform of principles by the Democratic Convention at Cincinnati, in the year 1856, believing that Democratic principles are unchangeable in their nature, when applied to the same subject matters; and we recommend, as the only further resolutions, the following:

2. Inasmuch as difference of opinion exists in the Democratic party as to the nature and extent of the powers of a Territorial Legislature, and as to the powers and duties of Congress, under the Constitution of the United States, over the institution of slavery within the Territories,

Resolved, That the Democratic party will abide by the decision of the Supreme Court of the United States upon these questions of Constitutional Law.

3. Resolved, That it is the duty of the United States to afford ample and complete protection to all its citizens, whether at home or abroad, and whether native or foreign born.

4. Resolved, That one of the necessities of the age, in a military, commercial, and postal point of view, is speedy communications between the Atlantic and Pacific States; and the Democratic party pledge such Constitutional Government aid as will insure the construction of a Railroad to the Pacific coast, at the earliest practicable period.

5. Resolved, that the Democratic party are in favor of the acquisition of the Island of Cuba on such terms as shall be honorable to ourselves and just to Spain.

6. Resolved, That the enactments of the State Legislatures to defeat the faithful execution of the Fugitive Slave Law, are hostile in character, subversive of the Constitution, and revolutionary in their effect.

7. Resolved, That it is in accordance with the interpretation of the Cincinnati platform, that during the existence of the Territorial Governments the measure of re-

[*]Commager, *Documents*, 1:365-66.

striction, whatever it may be, imposed by the Federal Constitution on the power of the Territorial Legislature over the subject of the domestic relations, as the same has been, or shall hereafter be finally determined by the Supreme Court of the United States, should be respected by all good citizens, and enforced with promptness and fidelity by every branch of the general government.

4

President James Buchanan, Fourth Annual Message, *New York Herald*

December 5, 1860, p. 1*

FELLOW-CITIZENS OF THE SENATE AND HOUSE OF REPRESENTATIVES:

Throughout the year since our last meeting the country has been eminently prosperous in all its material interests. The general health has been excellent, our harvests have been abundant, and plenty smiles throughout the laud. Our commerce and manufactures have been prosecuted with energy and industry, and have yielded fair and ample returns. In short, no nation in the tide of time has ever presented a spectacle of greater material prosperity than we have done until within a very recent period.

Why is it, then, that discontent now so extensively prevails, and the Union of the States, which is the source of all these blessings, is threatened with destruction? The long-continued and intemperate interference of the Northern people with the question of slavery in the Southern States has at length produced its natural effects. The different sections of the Union are now arrayed against each other, and the time has arrived, so much dreaded by the Father of his Country, when hostile geographical parties have been formed.

. . .

It cannot be denied that for five and twenty years the agitation at the North against slavery has been incessant. In 1835 pictorial handbills and inflammatory appeals were circulated extensively throughout the South of a character to excite the passions of the slaves, and, in the language of General Jackson, "to stimulate them

* [President Buchanan delivered his address on December 3, 1860. —Ed.]

to insurrection and produce all the horrors of a servile war." This agitation has ever since been continued by the public press, by the proceedings of State and county conventions and by abolition sermons and lectures. The time of Congress has been occupied in violent speeches on this never-ending subject, and appeals, in pamphlet and other forms, indorsed by distinguished names, have been sent forth from this central point and spread broadcast over the Union.

How easy would it be for the American people to settle the slavery question forever and to restore peace and harmony to this distracted country!

They, and they alone, can do it. All that is necessary to accomplish the object, and all for which the slave States have ever contended, is to be let alone and permitted to manage their domestic institutions in their own way. As sovereign States, they, and they alone, are responsible before God and the world for the slavery existing among them. For this the people of the North are not more responsible and have no more right to interfere than with similar institutions in Russia or in Brazil. Upon their good sense and patriotic forbearance I confess I still greatly rely. Without their aid it is beyond the power of any President, no matter what may be his own political proclivities, to restore peace and harmony among the States. Wisely limited and restrained as is his power under our Constitution and laws, he alone can accomplish but little for good or for evil on such a momentous question.

And this brings me to observe that the election of any one of our fellow-citizens to the office of President does not of itself afford just cause for dissolving the Union. This is more especially true if his election has been effected by a mere plurality, and not a majority of the people, and has resulted from transient and temporary causes, which may probably never again occur. In order to justify a resort to revolutionary resistance, the Federal Government must be guilty of "a deliberate, palpable, and dangerous exercise" of powers not granted by the Constitution. The late Presidential election, however, has been held in strict conformity with its express provisions. How, then, can the result justify a revolution to destroy this very Constitution? Reason, justice, a regard for the Constitution, all require that we shall wait for some overt and dangerous act on the part of the President elect before resorting to such a remedy.

It is said, however, that the antecedents of the President-elect have been sufficient to justify the fears of the South that he will attempt to invade their constitutional rights. But are such apprehensions of contingent danger in the future sufficient to justify the immediate destruction of the noblest system of government ever devised by mortals? From the very nature of his office and its high responsibilities he must necessarily be conservative. The stern duty of administering the vast and complicated concerns of this Government affords in itself a guaranty that he will not attempt any violation of a clear constitutional right.

After all, he is no more than the chief executive officer of the Government. His province is not to make but to execute the laws. And it is a remarkable fact in our history that, notwithstanding the repeated efforts of the antislavery party, no single act has ever passed Congress, unless we may possibly except the Missouri compromise, impairing in the slightest degree the rights of the South to their property in slaves; and it may also be observed, judging from present indications, that no probability exists of the passage of such an act by a majority of both Houses, either in the present or the next Congress. Surely under these circumstances we ought to be restrained from present action by the precept of Him who spake as man never spoke, that "sufficient unto the day is the evil thereof." The day of evil may never come unless we shall rashly bring it upon ourselves.

It is alleged as one cause for immediate secession that the Southern States are denied equal rights with the other States in the common Territories. But by what authority are these denied? Not by Congress, which has never passed, and I believe never will pass, any act to exclude slavery from these Territories; and certainly not by the Supreme Court, which has solemnly decided that slaves are property, and, like all other property, their owners have a right to take them into the common Territories and hold them there under the protection of the Constitution.

So far then, as Congress is concerned, the objection is not to anything they have already done, but to what they may do hereafter. It will surely be admitted that this apprehension of future danger is no good reason for an immediate dissolution of the Union. It is true that the Territorial legislature of Kansas, on the 23d February, 1860, passed in great haste an act over the veto of the governor declaring that slavery "is and shall be forever prohibited in this Territory." Such an act, however, plainly violating the rights of property secured by the Constitution, will surely be declared void by the judiciary whenever it shall be presented in a legal form.

Only three days after my inauguration the Supreme Court of the United States solemnly adjudged that this power did not exist in a Territorial legislature. Yet such has been the factious temper of the times that the correctness of this decision has been extensively impugned before the people, and the question has given rise to angry political conflicts throughout the country. Those who have appealed from this judgment of our highest constitutional tribunal to popular assemblies would, if they could, invest a Territorial legislature with power to annul the sacred rights of property. This power Congress is expressly forbidden by the Federal Constitution to exercise. Every State legislature in the Union is forbidden by its own constitution to exercise it. It cannot be exercised in any State except by the people in their highest sovereign capacity, when framing or amending their State constitution. In like manner it can only be exercised by the people of a Territory represented in a convention of delegates for the purpose of framing a constitution preparatory to admission as a State into the Union. Then, and not until then, are they invested with power to decide the question whether slavery shall or shall not exist within their limits. This is an act of sovereign authority, and not of subordinate Territorial legislation. Were it otherwise, then indeed would the equality of the States in the Territories be destroyed, and the rights of property in slaves would depend not upon the guaranties of the Constitution, but upon the shifting majorities of an irresponsible Territorial legislature. Such a doctrine, from its intrinsic unsoundness, can not long influence any considerable portion of our people, much less can it afford a good reason for a dissolution of the Union.

The most palpable violations of constitutional duty which have yet been committed consist in the acts of different State legislatures to defeat the execution of the fugitive-slave law. It ought to be remembered, however, that for these acts neither Congress nor any President can justly be held responsible. Having been passed in violation of the Federal Constitution, they are therefore null and void. All the courts, both State and national, before whom the question has arisen have from the beginning declared the fugitive-slave law to be constitutional. The single exception is that of a State court in Wisconsin, and this has not only been reversed by the proper appellate tribunal, but has met with such universal reprobation that there can be no danger from it as a precedent.

The validity of this law has been established over and over again by the Supreme Court of the United

States with perfect unanimity. It is rounded upon an express provision of the Constitution, requiring that fugitive slaves who escape from service in one State to another shall be "delivered up" to their masters. Without this provision it is a well-known historical fact that the Constitution itself could never have been adopted by the Convention.... The fugitive-slave law has been carried into execution in every contested case since the commencement of the present Administration, though often, it is to be regretted, with great loss and inconvenience to the master and with considerable expense to the Government. Let us trust that the State legislatures will repeal their unconstitutional and obnoxious enactments. Unless this shall be done without unnecessary delay, it is impossible for any human power to save the Union.

The Southern States, standing on the basis of the Constitution, have right to demand this act of justice from the States of the North. Should it be refused, then the Constitution, to which all the States are parties, will have been willfully violated by one portion of them in a provision essential to the domestic security and happiness of the remainder. In that event the injured States, after having first used all peaceful and constitutional means to obtain redress, would be justified in revolutionary resistance to the Government of the Union.

I have purposely confined my remarks to revolutionary resistance, because it has been claimed within the last few years that any State, whenever this shall be its sovereign will and pleasure, may secede from the Union in accordance with the Constitution and without any violation of the constitutional rights of the other members of the Confederacy; that as each became parties to the Union by the vote of its own people assembled in convention, so any one of them may retire from the Union in a similar manner by the vote of such a convention.

In order to justify secession as a constitutional remedy, it must be on the principle that the Federal Government is a mere voluntary association of States, to be dissolved at pleasure by any one of the contracting parties. If this be so, the Confederacy is a rope of sand, to be penetrated and dissolved by the first adverse wave of public opinion in any of the States. In this manner our thirty-three States may resolve themselves into as many petty, jarring, and hostile republics, each one retiring from the Union without responsibility whenever any sudden excitement might impel them to such a course. By this process a Union might be entirely broken into fragments in a few weeks which cost our forefathers many years of toil, privation, and blood to establish.

Such a principle is wholly inconsistent with the history as well as the character of the Federal Constitution. After it was framed with the greatest deliberation and care it was submitted to conventions of the people of the several States for ratification. Its provisions were discussed at length in these bodies, composed of the first men of the country. Its opponents contended that it conferred powers upon the Federal Government dangerous to the rights of the States, whilst its advocates maintained that under a fair construction of the instrument there was no foundation for such apprehensions. In that mighty struggle between the first intellects of this or any other country it never occurred to any individual, either among its opponents or advocates, to assert or even to intimate that their efforts were all vain labor, because the moment that any State felt herself aggrieved she might secede from the Union. What a crushing argument would this have proved against those who dreaded that the rights of the States would be endangered by the Constitution! The truth is that it was not until many years after the origin of the Federal Government that such a proposition was first advanced. It was then met and refuted by the conclusive arguments of General Jackson, who in his message of the 16th of January, 1833, transmitting the nullifying ordinance of South Carolina to Congress, employs the following language: "The right of the people of a single State to absolve themselves at will and without the consent of the other States from their most solemn obligations, and hazard the liberties and happiness of the millions composing this Union, cannot be acknowledged. Such authority is believed to be utterly repugnant both to the principles upon which the General Government is constituted and to the objects which it is expressly formed to attain."

It is not pretended that any clause in the Constitution gives countenance to such a theory. It is altogether rounded upon inference; not from any language contained in the instrument itself, but from the sovereign character of the several States by which it was ratified. But is it beyond the power of a State, like an individual, to yield a portion of its sovereign rights to secure the remainder? In the language of Mr. Madison, who has been called the father of the constitution, "it was formed by the States—that is, by the people in each of the States— acting in their highest sovereign capacity, and formed, consequently, by the same authority which formed the State constitutions.

"Nor is the government of the United States, created by the constitution, less a government, in the strict sense of the term, within the sphere of its powers than the governments created by the constitutions of the States are within their several spheres. It is, like them, organized into legislative, executive, and judiciary departments. It operates, like them directly on persons and things, and, like them, it has at command a physical force for executing the powers committed to it."*

It was intended to be perpetual, and not to be annulled at the pleasure of any one of the contracting parties. The old Articles of Confederation were entitled "Articles of Confederation and Perpetual Union between the States," and by the thirteenth article it is expressly declared that "the articles of this Confederation shall be inviolably observed by every State, and the Union shall be perpetual." The preamble to the Constitution of the United States, having express reference to the Articles of Confederation, recites that it was established "in order to form a more perfect union." And yet it is contended that this "more perfect union" does not include the essential attribute of perpetuity.

But that the Union was designed to be perpetual appears conclusively from the nature and extent of the powers conferred by the Constitution on the Federal Government. These powers embrace the very highest attributes of national sovereignty. They place both the sword and the purse under its control. Congress has power to make war and to make peace, to raise and support armies and navies, and to conclude treaties with foreign governments. It is invested with the power to coin money and to regulate the value thereof, and to regulate commerce with foreign nations and among the several States. It is not necessary to enumerate the other high powers which have been conferred upon the Federal Government. In order to carry the enumerated powers into effect, Congress possesses the exclusive right to lay and collect duties on imports, and, in common with the States, to lay and collect all other taxes.

But the constitution has not only conferred these high powers upon Congress, but it has adopted effectual means to restrain the States from interfering with their exercise.

. . .

In short, the government created by the Constitution, and deriving its authority from the sovereign people of

each of the several States, has precisely the same right to exercise its power over the people of all these States in the enumerated cases that each one of them possesses over subjects not delegated to the United States, but "reserved to the States respectively or to the people."

To the extent of the delegated powers the Constitution of the United States is as much a part of the constitution of each State and is as binding upon its people as though it had been textually inserted therein.

. . .

It may be asked, then, are the people of the States without redress against the tyranny and oppression of the Federal Government? By no means. The right of resistance on the part of the governed against the oppression of their governments cannot be denied. It exists independently of all constitutions, and has been exercised at all periods of the world's history. Under it old governments have been destroyed and new ones have taken their place. It is embodied in strong and express language in our own Declaration of Independence. But the distinction must ever be observed that this is revolution against an established government, and not a voluntary secession from it by virtue of an inherent constitutional right. In short, let us look the danger fairly in the face. Secession is neither more nor less than revolution. It may or it may not be a justifiable revolution, but still it is revolution.

What, in the meantime, is the responsibility and true position of the Executive?

. . .

Apart from the execution of the laws, so far as this may be practicable, the Executive has no authority to decide what shall be the relations between the federal government and South Carolina. He has been invested with no such discretion. He possesses no power to change the relations heretofore existing between them, much less to acknowledge the independence of that State. This would be to invest a mere executive officer with the power of recognizing the dissolution of the confederacy among our thirty-three sovereign States. It bears no resemblance to the recognition of a foreign de facto government, involving no such responsibility. Any attempt to do this would, on his part, be a naked act of usurpation. It is therefore my duty to submit to Congress the whole question in all its bearings. The course of events is so rapidly hastening forward that the emergency may soon arise when you may be called upon to decide the momentous question whether you possess the power by force of arms to compel a State to remain in the Union. I

* [James Madison to Edward Everett, Aug. 28, 1830. See this volume, 1B, doc. 21. —Ed.]

should feel myself recreant to my duty were I not to express an opinion on this important subject.

The question fairly stated is, Has the constitution delegated to Congress the power to coerce a State into submission which is attempting to withdraw or has actually withdrawn from the Confederacy? If answered in the affirmative, it must be on the principle that the power has been conferred upon Congress to declare and to make war against a State. After much serious reflection I have arrived at the conclusion that no such power has been delegated to Congress or to any other department of the Federal Government.

...

Without descending to particulars, it may be safely asserted that the power to make war against a State is at variance with the whole spirit and intent of the constitution. Suppose such a war should result in the conquest of a State; how are we to govern it afterwards? Shall we hold it as a province and govern it by despotic power? In the nature of things, we could not by physical force control the will of the people and compel them to elect Senators and Representatives to Congress and to perform all the other duties depending upon their own volition and required from the free citizens of a free State as a constituent member of the Confederacy.

But if we possessed this power, would it be wise to exercise it under existing circumstances? The object would doubtless be to preserve the Union. War would not only present the most effectual means of destroying it, but would vanish all hope of its peaceable reconstruction. Besides, in the fraternal conflict a vast amount of blood and treasure would be expended, rendering future reconciliation between the States impossible. In the meantime, who can foretell what would be the sufferings and privations of the people during its existence?

The fact is that our Union rests upon public opinion, and can never be cemented by the blood of its citizens shed in civil war. If it cannot live in the affections of the people, it must one day perish. Congress possesses many means of preserving it by conciliation, but the sword was not placed in their hand to preserve it by force.

...

It is not every wrong—nay, it is not every grievous wrong—which can justify a resort to such a fearful alternative. This ought to be the most desperate remedy of a despairing people, after every other constitutional means of conciliation had been exhausted. We should reflect that under this free government there is an incessant ebb and flow of public opinion. The slavery question, like everything human, will have its day. I firmly believe that it has already reached and passed the culminating point. But if, in the midst of the existing excitement, the Union shall perish, the evil may then become irreparable. Congress can contribute much to avert it by proposing and recommending to the Legislatures of the several States the remedy for existing evils, which the constitution itself has provided for its own preservation.

...

In this connection, I shall merely call attention to a few sentences in Mr. Madison's justly celebrated report, in 1799, to the Legislature of Virginia.* In this he ably and conclusively defended the resolutions of the preceding Legislature against the strictures of several other State Legislatures. These were mainly founded upon the protest of the Virginia Legislature against the "Alien and Sedition acts," as "palpable and alarming infractions of the constitution." In pointing out the peaceful and constitutional remedies—and he referred to none other—to which the States were authorized to resort on such occasions, he concludes by saying "that the Legislatures of the States might have made a direct representation to Congress with a view to obtain a rescinding of the two offensive acts, or they might have represented to their respective Senators in Congress their wish that two-thirds thereof would propose an explanatory amendment to the Constitution; or two-thirds of themselves, if such had been their option, might by an application to Congress have obtained a convention for the same object."

This is the very course which I earnestly recommend in order to obtain an "explanatory amendment" of the Constitution on the subject of slavery. This might originate with Congress or the State legislatures, as may be deemed most advisable to attain the object. The explanatory amendment might be confined to the final settlement of the true construction of the Constitution on three special points:

1. An express recognition of the right of property in slaves in the States where it now exists or may hereafter exist.

2. The duty of protecting this right in all the common Territories throughout their Territorial existence, and until they shall be admitted as States into the Union,

---

* [See James Madison, *Report on the Virginia Resolutions*, this volume, 1B, doc. 12. —Ed.]

with or without slavery, as their constitutions may prescribe.

3. A like recognition of the right of the master to have his slave who has escaped from one State to another restored and "delivered up" to him, and of the validity of the fugitive-slave law enacted for this purpose, together with a declaration that all State laws impairing or defeating this right are violations of the Constitution, and are consequently null and void.

It may be objected that this construction of the Constitution has already been settled by the Supreme Court of the United States, and what more ought to be required? The answer is that a very large proportion of the people of the United States still contest the correctness of this decision, and never will cease from agitation and admit its binding force until clearly established by the people of the several States in their sovereign character. Such an explanatory amendment would, it is believed, forever terminate the existing dissensions, and restore peace and harmony among the States.

It ought not to be doubted that such an appeal to the arbitrament established by the constitution itself would be received with favor by all the States of the confederacy. In any event, it ought to be tried in a spirit of conciliation before any of these States shall separate themselves from the Union.

...

JAMES BUCHANAN

5

South Carolina, Declaration of the Causes Which Justify Secession

December 24, 1860*

DECLARATION OF THE IMMEDIATE CAUSES WHICH INDUCE AND JUSTIFY THE SECESSION OF SOUTH CAROLINA FROM THE FEDERAL UNION:
The people of the State of South Carolina, in Convention assembled, on the 26th day of April, A.D., 1852, declared that the frequent violations of the Constitution of the United States, by the Federal Government, and its encroachments upon the reserved rights of the States,

*Frank Moore, ed., *The Rebellion Record, Part II (Documents)* (New York: G. P. Putnam, 1861), 1:3–4.

fully justified this State in then withdrawing from the Federal Union; but in deference to the opinions and wishes of the other slaveholding States, she forbore at that time to exercise this right. Since that time, these encroachments have continued to increase, and further forbearance ceases to be a virtue.

And now the State of South Carolina having resumed her separate and equal place among nations, deems it due to herself, to the remaining United States of America, and to the nations of the world, that she should declare the immediate causes which have led to this act.

In the year 1765, that portion of the British Empire embracing Great Britain, undertook to make laws for the government of that portion composed of the thirteen American Colonies. A struggle for the right of self-government ensued, which resulted, on the 4th of July, 1776, in a Declaration, by the Colonies, "that they are, and of right ought to be, FREE AND INDEPENDENT STATES; and that, as free and independent States, they have full power to levy war, conclude peace, contract alliances, establish commerce, and to do all other acts and things which independent States may of right do."

They further solemnly declared that whenever any "form of government becomes destructive of the ends for which it was established, it is the right of the people to alter or abolish it, and to institute a new government." Deeming the Government of Great Britain to have become destructive of these ends, they declared that the Colonies "are absolved from all allegiance to the British Crown, and that all political connection between them and the State of Great Britain is, and ought to be, totally dissolved."

In pursuance of this Declaration of Independence, each of the thirteen States proceeded to exercise its separate sovereignty; adopted for itself a Constitution, and appointed officers for the administration of government in all its departments—Legislative, Executive and Judicial. For purposes of defense, they united their arms and their counsels; and, in 1778, they entered into a League known as the Articles of Confederation, whereby they agreed to entrust the administration of their external relations to a common agent, known as the Congress of the United States, expressly declaring, in the first Article "that each State retains its sovereignty, freedom and independence, and every power, jurisdiction and right which is not, by this Confederation, expressly delegated to the United States in Congress assembled."

Under this Confederation the war of the Revolution was carried on, and on the 3rd of September, 1783, the contest ended, and a definite Treaty was signed by Great Britain, in which she acknowledged the independence of the Colonies in the following terms: "ARTICLE 1— His Britannic Majesty acknowledges the said United States, viz: New Hampshire, Massachusetts Bay, Rhode Island and Providence Plantations, Connecticut, New York, New Jersey, Pennsylvania, Delaware, Maryland, Virginia, North Carolina, South Carolina and Georgia, to be FREE, SOVEREIGN AND INDEPENDENT STATES; that he treats with them as such; and for himself, his heirs and successors, relinquishes all claims to the government, propriety and territorial rights of the same and every part thereof."

Thus were established the two great principles asserted by the Colonies, namely: the right of a State to govern itself; and the right of a people to abolish a Government when it becomes destructive of the ends for which it was instituted. And concurrent with the establishment of these principles, was the fact, that each Colony became and was recognized by the mother Country a FREE, SOVEREIGN AND INDEPENDENT STATE.

In 1787, Deputies were appointed by the States to revise the Articles of Confederation, and on 17th September, 1787, these Deputies recommended for the adoption of the States, the Articles of Union, known as the Constitution of the United States.

The parties to whom this Constitution was submitted, were the several sovereign States; they were to agree or disagree, and when nine of them agreed the compact was to take effect among those concurring; and the General Government, as the common agent, was then invested with their authority.

If only nine of the thirteen States had concurred, the other four would have remained as they then were— separate, sovereign States, independent of any of the provisions of the Constitution. In fact, two of the States did not accede to the Constitution until long after it had gone into operation among the other eleven; and during that interval, they each exercised the functions of an independent nation.

By this Constitution, certain duties were imposed upon the several States, and the exercise of certain of their powers was restrained, which necessarily implied their continued existence as sovereign States. But to remove all doubt, an amendment was added, which declared that the powers not delegated to the United States by the Constitution, nor prohibited by it to the States, are reserved to the States, respectively, or to the people. On the 23d May, 1788, South Carolina, by a Convention of her People, passed an Ordinance assenting to this Constitution, and afterwards altered her own Constitution, to conform herself to the obligations she had undertaken.

Thus was established, by compact between the States, a Government with definite objects and powers, limited to the express words of the grant. This limitation left the whole remaining mass of power subject to the clause reserving it to the States or to the people, and rendered unnecessary any specification of reserved rights.

We hold that the Government thus established is subject to the two great principles asserted in the Declaration of Independence; and we hold further, that the mode of its formation subjects it to a third fundamental principle, namely: the law of compact. We maintain that in every compact between two or more parties, the obligation is mutual; that the failure of one of the contracting parties to perform a material part of the agreement, entirely releases the obligation of the other; and that where no arbiter is provided, each party is remitted to his own judgment to determine the fact of failure, with all its consequences.

In the present case, that fact is established with certainty. We assert that fourteen of the States have deliberately refused, for years past, to fulfill their constitutional obligations, and we refer to their own Statutes for the proof.

The Constitution of the United States, in its fourth Article, provides as follows: "No person held to service or labor in one State, under the laws thereof, escaping into another, shall, in consequence of any law or regulation therein, be discharged from such service or labor, but shall be delivered up, on claim of the party to whom such service or labor may be due."

This stipulation was so material to the compact, that without it that compact would not have been made. The greater number of the contracting parties held slaves, and they had previously evinced their estimate of the value of such a stipulation by making it a condition in the Ordinance for the government of the territory ceded by Virginia, which now composes the States north of the Ohio River.

The same article of the Constitution stipulates also for rendition by the several States of fugitives from justice from the other States.

The General Government, as the common agent,

passed laws to carry into effect these stipulations of the States. For many years these laws were executed. But an increasing hostility on the part of the non-slaveholding States to the institution of slavery, has led to a disregard of their obligations, and the laws of the General Government have ceased to effect the objects of the Constitution. The States of Maine, New Hampshire, Vermont, Massachusetts, Connecticut, Rhode Island, New York, Pennsylvania, Illinois, Indiana, Michigan, Wisconsin and Iowa, have enacted laws which either nullify the Acts of Congress or render useless any attempt to execute them. In many of these States the fugitive is discharged from service or labor claimed, and in none of them has the State Government complied with the stipulation made in the Constitution. The State of New Jersey, at an early day, passed a law in conformity with her constitutional obligation; but the current of anti-slavery feeling has led her more recently to enact laws which render inoperative the remedies provided by her own law and by the laws of Congress. In the State of New York even the right of transit for a slave has been denied by her tribunals; and the States of Ohio and Iowa have refused to surrender to justice fugitives charged with murder, and with inciting servile insurrection in the State of Virginia. Thus the constituted compact has been deliberately broken and disregarded by the non-slaveholding States, and the consequence follows that South Carolina is released from her obligation.

The ends for which the Constitution was framed are declared by itself to be "to form a more perfect union, establish justice, insure domestic tranquility, provide for the common defence, promote the general welfare, and secure the blessings of liberty to ourselves and our posterity."

These ends it endeavored to accomplish by a Federal Government, in which each State was recognized as an equal, and had separate control over its own institutions. The right of property in slaves was recognized by giving to free persons distinct political rights, by giving them the right to represent, and burthening them with direct taxes for three-fifths of their slaves; by authorizing the importation of slaves for twenty years; and by stipulating for the rendition of fugitives from labor.

We affirm that these ends for which this Government was instituted have been defeated, and the Government itself has been made destructive of them by the action of the non-slaveholding States. Those States have assume the right of deciding upon the propriety of our domestic institutions; and have denied the rights of property established in fifteen of the States and recognized by the Constitution; they have denounced as sinful the institution of slavery; they have permitted open establishment among them of societies, whose avowed object is to disturb the peace and to eloign the property of the citizens of other States. They have encouraged and assisted thousands of our slaves to leave their homes; and those who remain, have been incited by emissaries, books and pictures to servile insurrection.

For twenty-five years this agitation has been steadily increasing, until it has now secured to its aid the power of the common Government. Observing the forms of the Constitution, a sectional party has found within that Article establishing the Executive Department, the means of subverting the Constitution itself. A geographical line has been drawn across the Union, and all the States north of that line have united in the election of a man to the high office of President of the United States, whose opinions and purposes are hostile to slavery. He is to be entrusted with the administration of the common Government, because he has declared that that "Government cannot endure permanently half slave, half free," and that the public mind must rest in the belief that slavery is in the course of ultimate extinction.

This sectional combination for the submersion of the Constitution, has been aided in some of the States by elevating to citizenship, persons who, by the supreme law of the land, are incapable of becoming citizens; and their votes have been used to inaugurate a new policy, hostile to the South, and destructive of its beliefs and safety.

On the 4th day of March next, this party will take possession of the Government. It has announced that the South shall be excluded from the common territory, that the judicial tribunals shall be made sectional, and that a war must be waged against slavery until it shall cease throughout the United States.

The guaranties of the Constitution will then no longer exist; the equal rights of the States will be lost. The slaveholding States will no longer have the power of self-government, or self-protection, and the Federal Government will have become their enemy.

Sectional interest and animosity will deepen the irritation, and all hope of remedy is rendered vain, by the fact that public opinion at the North has invested a great political error with the sanction of more erroneous religious belief.

We, therefore, the People of South Carolina, by our

delegates in Convention assembled, appealing to the Supreme Judge of the world for the rectitude of our intentions, have solemnly declared that the Union heretofore existing between this State and the other States of North America, is dissolved, and that the State of South Carolina has resumed her position among the nations of the world, as a separate and independent State; with full power to levy war, conclude peace, contract alliances, establish commerce, and to do all other acts and things which independent States may of right do.

Adopted December 24, 1860

6

US Senate, Speech of Judah P. Benjamin Defending the Secession of South Carolina

December 31, 1860*

Mr. BENJAMIN. Mr. President, when I took the floor at our last adjournment I stated that I expected to address the Senate to-day in reference to the critical issue now before the country. I had supposed that by this time there would have been some official communication to the Senate in reference to the fact now known to all of the condition of affairs in South Carolina. I will assume, for the purposes of the remarks that I have to make, that those facts have been officially communicated, and address myself to them. And, Mr. President, probably never has a deliberative assembly been called upon to determine a question calculated to awaken a more solemn sense of responsibility than those that now address themselves to our consideration. We are brought at last, sir, directly forced, to meet promptly an issue produced by an irresistible course of events whose inevitable results some of us, at least, have foreseen for years. Nor, sir, have we failed in our duty of warning the Republicans that they were fast driving us to a point where the very instincts of self-preservation would impose upon us the certain necessity of separation. We repeated those warnings with a depth of conviction, with an earnestness of assertion that inspired the hope that we should succeed in imparting at least some faint as-

surance of our sincerity to those by whose aid alone could the crisis be averted. But, sir, our assertions were derided; our predictions were scoffed at; all our honest and patriotic efforts to save the Constitution and the Union sneered at and maligned, as dictated, not by love of country, but by base ambition for place and power.

Mr. President, it has been justly said that this is no time for crimination; and, sir, it is in no such spirit, but with the simple desire to free myself personally, as a public servant, from all responsibility for the present condition of affairs, that I desire to recall to the Senate some remarks made by me in debate more than four years ago, in which I predicted the precise state of public feeling now, and pointed out the two principal causes that were certain to produce that state. The first was the incessant attack of the Republicans, not simply on the interests, but on the feelings and sensibilities of a high-spirited people by the most insulting language, and the most offensive epithets; the other was their fatal success in persuading their followers that these constant aggressions could be continued and kept up with no danger; that the South was too weak and too conscious of weakness to dare resistance. Sir, on the 2d of May, 1856, after reviewing this subject at some length, I said:

"Now, Mr. President, when we see these two interests contrasted—the North struggling for the possession of a power to which she has no legitimate claim under the Constitution, for the sole purpose of abusing that power—the South struggling for property, honor, safety—all that is dear to man—tell me if the history of the world exhibits an example of a people occupying a more ennobling attitude than the people of the South? To vituperation they oppose calm reason. To menaces and threats of violence, and insulting assumptions of superiority, they disdain reply. To direct attacks on their rights or their honor, they appeal to the guarantees of the Constitution; and when those guarantees shall fail, and not till then, will the injured, outraged South throw her sword into the scale of her rights, and appeal to the God of battles to do her justice. I say her sword, because I am not one of those who believe in the possibility of a peaceful disruption of the Union. It can not come until all possible means of conciliation have been exhausted; it cannot come until every angry passion shall have been roused; it cannot come until brotherly feeling shall have been converted into

* *Cong. Globe*, 36th Cong., 2nd Sess., 212–17 (Dec. 31, 1860).

deadly hate; and then, sir, with feelings embittered by the consciousness of injustice, or passions high-wrought and inflamed, dreadful will be the internecine war that must ensue.

"Mr. President, among what I consider to be the most prominent dangers that now exist, is the fact that the leaders of the Republican party at the North have succeeded in persuading the masses of the North that there is no danger. They have finally so wrought upon the opinion of their own people at home by the constant iteration of the same false statements and the same false principles, that the people of the North cannot be made to believe that the South is in earnest, notwithstanding its calm and resolute determination which produces the quiet so ominous of evil if ever the clouds shall burst. The people of the North are taught to laugh at the danger of dissolution. One honorable Senator is reported to have said, with exquisite amenity, that the South could not be kicked out of the Union. The honorable Senator from New York says:

"'The slaveholders, in spite of all their threats, are bound to it by the same bonds, and they are bound to it also by a bond *peculiarly their own — that of dependence on it for their own safety. Three million slaves are a hostile force constantly in their presence, in their very midst.* The servile war is always the most fearful form of war. *The world without sympathizes with the servile enemy.* Against that war the American Union is the only defense of the slaveholders — their *only* protection. If ever they shall, in a season of madness, recede from that Union, and provoke that war, they will — soon come back again.'

"The honorable Senator from Massachusetts [Mr. WILSON] indulges in the repetition of a figure of rhetoric that seems peculiarly to please his ear and tickle his fancy. He represents the southern mother as clasping her infant with convulsive and closer embrace, because the black avenger, with uplifted dagger, would be at the door, and he tells us that is a bond of Union which we dare not violate."

Mr. President, no man can deny that the words uttered four years and a half ago form a faithful picture of the state of things that we see around us now. Would to God, sir, that I could believe that the apprehensions of civil war, then plainly expressed, were but the vain imaginations of a timorous spirit. Alas, sir, the feelings and sentiments expressed since the commencement of this session, on the opposite side of this floor, almost force the belief that a civil war is their desire; and that the day is full near when American citizens are to meet each other in hostile array; and when the hands of brothers will be reddened with the blood of brothers.

Mr. President, the State of South Carolina, with a unanimity scarcely with parallel in history, has dissolved the union which connects her with the other States of the confederacy, and declared herself independent. We, the representatives of those remaining States, stand here to-day, bound either to recognize that independence, or to over-throw it; either to permit her peaceful secession from the confederacy, or to put her down by force of arms. That is the issue. That is the sole issue. No artifice can conceal it. No attempts by men to disguise it from their own consciences, and from an excited or alarmed public, can suffice to conceal it. Those attempts are equally futile and disingenuous. As for the attempted distinction between coercing a State, and forcing all the people of the State, by arms, to yield obedience to an authority repudiated by the sovereign will of the State, expressed in its most authentic form, it is as unsound in principle as it is impossible of practical application. Upon that point, however, I shall have something to say a little further on.

If we elevate ourselves, Mr. President, to the height from which we are bound to look in order to embrace all the vast consequence that must result from our decision, we are not permitted to ignore the fact that our determination does not involve the State of South Carolina alone. Next week, Mississippi, Alabama, and Florida, will have declared themselves independent; the week after, Georgia; and a little later, Louisiana; soon, very soon, to be followed by Texas and Arkansas. I confine myself purposely to these eight States, because I wish to speak only of those whose action we know with positive certainty, and which no man can for a moment pretend to controvert. I designedly exclude others, about whose action I feel equally confident, although others may raise a cavil.

Now, sir, shall we recognize the fact that South Carolina has become an independent State, or shall we wage war against her? And first as to her right. I do not agree with those who think it idle to discuss that right. In a great crisis like this, when the right asserted by a sovereign State is questioned, a decent respect for the opinions of mankind at least requires that those who maintain that right, and mean to act upon it, should state the reasons upon which they maintain it. If, in the discussion of this question, I shall refer to familiar principles, it is not that I deem it at all necessary to call the attention of members here to them; but because they naturally fall within the scope of my argument, which might otherwise prove unintelligible.

From the time that this people declared its independence of Great Britain, the right of the people to self-government in its fullest and broadest extent has been a cardinal principle of American liberty. None deny it. And in that right, to use the language of the Declaration itself, is included the right whenever a form of government becomes destructive of their interests or their safety, "to alter or to abolish it, and to institute a new government, laying its foundation on such principles and organizing its powers in such form as to them shall seem most likely to effect their safety and happiness." I admit that there is a principle that modifies this power, to which I shall presently advert; but leaving that principle for a moment out of view, I say that there is no other modification which, consistently with our liberty, we can admit, and that the right of the people of one generation, in convention duly assembled, to alter the institutions bequeathed by their fathers is inherent, inalienable, not susceptible of restriction; that by the same power under which one Legislature can repeal the act of a former Legislature, so can one convention of the people duly assembled, repeal the acts of a former convention of the people duly assembled; and that it is in strict and logical deduction from this fundamental principle of American liberty, that South Carolina has adopted the form in which she has declared her independence. She has in convention duly assembled in 1860, repealed an ordinance passed by her people in convention duly assembled in 1788. If no interests of third parties were concerned, if no question of compact intervened, all must admit the inherent power—the same inherent power which authorizes a Legislature to repeal a law, subject to the same modifying principle, that where the rights of others than the people who passed the law are concerned, those rights must be respected and cannot be infringed by those who descend from the first Legislature or who succeed them. If a law be passed by a Legislature impairing a contract, that law is void, not because the Legislature under ordinary circumstances would not have the power to repeal a law of its predecessor but because by repealing a law of its predecessor involving a contract, it exercises rights in which third persons are interested, and over which they

are entitled to have an equal control. So in the case of a convention of the people assuming to act in repeal of an ordinance which showed their adherence to the Constitution of the United States, the power is inherently in them, subject only to this modification: that they are bound to exercise it with due regard to the obligations imposed upon them by the compact with others.

Authorities, on points like this, are perfectly idle; but I fear that I may not have expressed the ideas which I entertain so well as I find them expressed by Mr. Webster in his celebrated argument in the Rhode Island case. He says:

> "First and chief, no man makes a question that the people are the source of all political power. Government is instituted for their good, and its members are their agents and servants. He who would argue against this, must argue without an adversary. And who thinks there is any peculiar merit in asserting a doctrine like this, it the midst of twenty million people, when nineteen million nine hundred and ninety-nine thousand nine hundred and ninety-nine of them hold it, as well as himself? There is no other doctrine of government here; and no man imputes to another, and no man should claim for himself, any particular merit for asserting what everybody knows to be true, and nobody denies."
> —*Works of Daniel Webster*, vol. 6, p. 221.

But he says in this particular case an attempt is made to establish the validity of the action of the people, organized in convention, without their having been called into convention by the exercise of any constituted authority of the State; and against the exercise of such a right of the people as that he protests. He says:

> "Is it not obvious enough that men cannot get together and count themselves, and say they are so many hundreds and so many thousands, and judge of their own qualifications, and call themselves the people and set up a government? Why, another set of men forty miles off, on the same day, with the same propriety, with as good qualifications, and in as large numbers, may meet and set up another government; one may meet at Newport and another at Chepachet, and both may call themselves the people." *Ibid.*, p. 226.

Therefore, he says, it is not a mere assemblage of the people, gathered together *sua sponte*, that forms that meeting of the people authorized to act in behalf of the people; but he says that—

"Another American principle growing out of this, and just as important and well settled as is the truth that the people are the source of power, is, that, when in the course of events it becomes necessary to ascertain the will of the people on a new exigency, or a new state of things or of opinion, the legislative power provides for that ascertainment by an ordinary act of legislation."

* * * * * * * * * * * * * *

"All that is necessary here is, that the will of the people should be ascertained by some regular rule of proceeding prescribed by previous law. But when ascertained, that will is as sovereign as the will of a despotic prince, of the Czar of Muscovy, or the Emperor of Austria himself, though not quite so easily made known. A ukase or an edict signifies at once the will of a despotic prince; but that will of the people, which is here as sovereign as the will of such a prince, is not so quickly ascertained or known; and hence arises the necessity for suffrage, which is the mode whereby each man's power is made to tell upon the Constitution of the Government, and in the enactment of laws."

He concludes—

"We see, therefore, from the commencement of the Government under which we live, down to this late act of the State of New York"—

To which he had just referred—

"one uniform current of law, of precedent, and of practice, all going to establish the point that changes in government are to be brought about by the will of the people, assembled under such legislative provisions as may be necessary to ascertain that will truly and authentically."—*Ibid.*, pp. 227, 229.

We have then, sir, in the case of South Carolina, so far as the duly organized convention is concerned, the only body that could speak the will of this generation in repeal of the ordinance passed by their fathers in 1788; and I say again, if no third interests intervened by a compact binding upon their faith, their power to do so is inherent and complete. But, sir, there is a compact, and no man pretends that the generation of to-day is not bound by the compacts of the fathers; but, to use the language of Mr. Webster, a bargain broken on one side is a bargain broken on all; and the compact is binding upon the generation of to-day only if the other parties to the compact have kept their faith.

This is no new theory, nor is practice upon it without precedent. I say that it was precisely upon this principle that this Constitution was formed. I say that the old Articles of Confederacy provided in express terms that they should be perpetual; that they should never be amended or altered without the consent of all the States. I say that the delegates of States unwilling that that Confederation should be altered or amended, appealed to that provision in the convention which formed the Constitution, and said: "If you do not satisfy us by the new provisions, we will prevent your forming your new government, because your faith is plighted, because you have agreed that there shall be no change in it unless with the consent of all." This was the argument of Luther Martin, it was the argument of Paterson, of New Jersey, and of large numbers of other distinguished members of the convention. Mr. Madison answered it. Mr. Madison said, in reply to that:

"It has been alleged that the Confederation having been formed by unanimous consent, could be dissolved by unanimous consent only. Does this doctrine result from the nature of compacts? Does it arise from any particular stipulation in the Articles of Confederation? If we consider the Federal Union as analogous to the fundamental compact by which individuals compose one society, and which must, in its theoretic origin at least, have been the unanimous act of the component members, it cannot be said that no dissolution of the compact can be effected without unanimous consent. A breach of the fundamental principles of the compact, by a part of the society would certainly absolve the other part from their obligations to it."

* * * * * * * * * * * * * *

"If we consider the Federal Union as analogous, not to the social compacts among individual men, but to the conventions among individual States, what is the doctrine resulting from these conventions? Clearly, according to the expositors of the law of nations, that a breach of any one article, by any one party, leaves all the other parties at liberty to consider the whole convention as dissolved, unless they choose rather to compel the delinquent party to repair the breach. In some treaties, indeed, it is expressly stipulated that a violation of particular articles shall not have this consequence, and even that particular articles shall remain in force during war, which is, in general, understood to dissolve all subsisting treaties. But are there any exceptions of this sort to the Articles of Confederation? So far from it, that there is not even an express stipulation that force shall be used to compel an offending member of the Union to discharge its duty."—*Madison Papers of Debates in the Federal Convention*, vol. 5., pp. 206, 207.

I need scarcely ask, Mr. President, if anybody has found in the Constitution of the United States any article providing, by express stipulation, that force shall be used to compel an offending member of the Union to discharge its duty. Acting on that principle, nine States of the Confederation seceded from the Confederation, and formed a new Government. They formed it upon the express ground that some of the States had violated their compact. Immediately after, two other States seceded and joined them. They left two alone, Rhode Island and North Carolina; and here is my answer to the Senator from Wisconsin, [Mr. DOOLITTLE,] who asked me the other day, if thirty-three States could expel one, inasmuch as one had the right to leave thirty-three: I point him to the history of our country, to the acts of the fathers, as a full answer upon that subject. After this Government had been organized; after every department had been in full operation for some time; after you had framed your navigation laws, and provided what should be considered as ships and vessels of the United States, North Carolina and Rhode Island were still foreign nations, and so treated by you, so treated by you in your laws; and in September, 1789, Congress passed an act authorizing the citizens of the States of North Carolina and Rhode Island to enjoy all the benefits attached to owners of ships and vessels of the United States up to the 1st of the following January—gave them that much more time to come into the new Union, if they thought proper; if not, they were to remain as foreign nations. Here is the history of the formation of this Constitution, so far as it involves the power of the States to secede from a Confederation, and to form new confederacies to suit themselves.

Now, Mr. President, there is a difficulty in this matter, which was not overlooked by the framers of the Constitution. One State may allege that the compact has been broken, and others may deny it: who is to judge? When pecuniary interests are involved, so that a case can be brought up before courts of justice, the Constitution has provided a remedy within itself. It has declared that no act of a State, either in convention or by Legislature, or in any other manner, shall violate the Constitution of the United States, and it has provided for a supreme judiciary to determine cases arising in law or equity which may involve the construction of the Constitution or the construction of such laws.

But, sir, suppose infringements on the Constitution in political matters, which from their very nature cannot be brought before the court? That was a difficulty not unforeseen; it was debated upon propositions that were made to meet it. Attempts were made to give power to this Federal Government in all its departments, one after the other, to meet that precise case, and the convention sternly refused to admit any. It was proposed to enable the Federal Government, through the action of Congress, to use force. That was refused. It was proposed to give to the President of the United States the nomination of State Governors, and to give them a veto on State laws, so as to preserve the supremacy of the Federal Government. That was refused. It was proposed to make the Senate the judge of difficulties that might arise between States and the General Government. That was refused. It was finally proposed to give Congress a negative on State legislation interfering with the powers of the Federal Government. That was refused. At last, at the very last moment, it was proposed to give that power to Congress by a vote of two thirds of each branch; and that, too, was denied.

Now, sir, I wish to show, with some little detail—as briefly as I possibly can and do justice to the subject—what was said by the leading members of the convention on these propositions to subject the States, in their political action, to any power of the General Government, whether of Congress, of the judiciary, or of the Executive, and by any majorities whatever. The first proposition was made by Mr. Randolph, on the 29th of May, 1787; and it was, that power should be given to Congress—

"To negative all laws passed by the several States contravening in the opinion of the National Legislature, the articles of Union, or any treaty subsisting under the authority of the Union; and to call forth the force or the Union against any member of the Union failing to fulfil its duty under the articles thereof."

To negative all laws violative of the articles of Union, and to employ force to constrain a State to perform its duty. Mr. Pinckney's proposition on the same day was:

"And to render these prohibitions effectual, the Legislature of the United States shall have the power to revise the laws of the several States that may be supposed to infringe the powers exclusively delegated by this Constitution to Congress, and to negative and annul such as do."

The proposition giving a power to negative the laws of the States, passed at first hurriedly, without consideration; but upon further examination, full justice was done to it. Upon the subject of force, Mr. Madison said, moving to postpone the proposition to authorize force:

"Mr. Madison observed, that the more he reflected on the use of force, the more he doubted the practicability, the justice, and the efficacy of it, when applied to people collectively, and not individually. A union of the States containing such an ingredient, seemed to provide for its own destruction. The use of force against a State would look more like a declaration of war than an infliction of punishment, and would probably be considered by the party attacked as a dissolution of all previous compacts by which it might be bound. He hoped that such a system would be framed as might render this resource unnecessary, and moved that the clause be postponed."—*Madison Papers—Debates in the Federal Convention*, vol. 5, p. 140.

Mr. Mason, the ancestor of our own distinguished colleague from Virginia, said:

"The most jarring elements of nature, fire and water, themselves, are not more incompatible than such a mixture of civil liberty and military execution. Will the militia march from one State into another in order to collect the arrears of taxes from the delinquent members of the Republic? Will they maintain an army for this purpose? Will not the citizens of the invaded States assist one another, till they rise as one man, and shake off the Union altogether?"

...

But, sir, strong as these gentlemen were against giving the power to exert armed force against the States, some of the best and ablest members of the convention were in favor of giving Congress control over State action by a negative. Mr. Madison himself was strongly in favor

of that; and if that power had been granted, the first of the personal liberty bills that were passed would have been the last, for Congress would at once have annulled it, and the other States would have taken warning by that example. Mr. Pinckney's proposition was brought up, that "the national Legislature should have authority to negative all laws which they should judge to be improper."

...

Mr. Rutledge said:

"If nothing else, this alone would damn, and ought to damn the Constitution. Will any State ever agree to be bound hand and foot in this manner? It is worse than making mere corporations of them, whose by-laws would not be subject to this shackle."

And thereupon Mr. Pinckney withdrew his proposition, and all control was abandoned.

There was then to be no control on the part of the General Government over State legislation, otherwise than in the action of the Federal judiciary upon such pecuniary controversies as might be properly brought before them.

Notwithstanding all this jealousy, when this Constitution came to be discussed in the conventions of the States, it met formidable opposition, upon the ground that the States were not sufficiently secure. Its advocates by every possible means endeavored to quiet the alarms of the friends of State rights. Mr. Madison, in Virginia, against Patrick Henry; Mr. Hamilton and Chief Justice Jay, in New York, against the opponents there; in all the States, eminent men used every exertion in their power to induce the adoption of the Constitution. They failed, until they proposed to accompany their ratifications with amendments that should prevent its meaning from being perverted, and prevent it from being falsely construed; and in two of the States especially— the States of Virginia and New York, the ratification was preceded by a statement of what their opinion of its true meaning was, and a statement that, on that construction, and under that impression, they ratified it. Some of the members of the Convention were for asking for these amendments in advance of ratification; but they were told it was unnecessary. In the Virginia convention, Mr. Randolph, who was General Washington's Attorney General, and Judge Nicholas, both expressed the opinion that it was not necessary, and that the ratification would be conditional upon that construction. Mr. Randolph said:

"If it be not considered too early, as ratification has not yet been spoken of, I beg to speak of it. If I did believe, with the honorable gentleman, that all power not expressly retained was given up by the people, I would detest this Government.

"But I never thought so; nor do I now. If, in the ratification, we put words to this purpose, 'And that all authority not given is retained by the people, and may be resumed when perverted to their oppression; and that no right can be canceled, abridged, or restrained, by the Congress, or any officer of the United States'—I say if we do this, I conceive that, as this style of ratification would manifest the principles on which Virginia adopted it, we should be at liberty to consider as a violation of the Constitution every exercise of a power not expressly delegated therein. I see no objection to this."

And Mr. Nicholas said the same thing:

"Mr. Nicholas contended that the language of the proposed ratification would secure everything which gentlemen desired, as it declared that all powers vested in the Constitution were derived from the people, and might be resumed by them whensoever they should be perverted to their injury and oppression; and that every power not granted thereby remained at their will. No danger whatever could arise; for [says he] these expressions will become a part of the contract. The Constitution cannot be binding on Virginia but with these conditions. If thirteen individuals are about to make a contract, and one agrees to it, but at the same time declares that he understands its meaning, signification, and intent to be (what the words of the contract plainly and obviously denote) that it is not to be construed so as to impose any supplementary condition on him, and that he is to be exonerated from it whensoever any such imposition shall be attempted, I ask whether, in this case, these conditions on which he has assented to it would not be binding on the other twelve? In like manner these conditions will be binding on Congress. They can exercise no power that is not expressly granted them."

So, sir, we find that not alone in these two conventions, but by the common action of the States, there was an important addition made to the Constitution by which it was expressly provided that it should not

be construed to be a General Government over all the people, but that it was a Government of States, which delegated powers to the General Government. The language of the ninth and tenth amendments to the Constitution is susceptible of no other construction:

"The enumeration in the Constitution of certain rights shall not be construed to deny or disparage others retained by the people."

"The powers not delegated to the United States."

Gentlemen are fond of using the words "surrendered," abandoned, given up. That is the constant language on the other side. The language of the amendment intended to fix the meaning of the Constitution says that these powers were not abandoned by the State, not surrendered, not given up, but "delegated," and therefore subject to resumption:

"The powers not delegated to the United States by the Constitution, nor prohibited by it to the States, are reserved to the States respectively, or to the people."

Now, Mr. President, if we admit, as we must, that there are certain political rights guarantied to the States of this Union by the terms of the Constitution itself—rights political in their character, and not susceptible of judicial decision—if any State is deprived of any of those rights, what is the remedy? For it is idle to talk to us at this day in a language which shall tell us we have rights and no remedies. For the purpose of illustrating the argument upon this subject, let us suppose a clear, palpable case of violation of the Constitution. Let us suppose that the State of South Carolina having sent two Senators to sit upon this floor, had been met by a resolution of the majority here that, according to her just weight in the Confederacy, one was enough, and that we had directed our Secretary to swear in but one, and to call but one name on our roll as the yeas and nays are called for voting. The Constitution says that each State shall be entitled to two Senators, and each Senator shall have one vote. What power is there to force the dominant majority to repair that wrong? Any court? Any tribunal? Has the Constitution provided any recourse whatever? Has it not remained designedly silent on the subject of that recourse? And yet, what man will stand up in this Senate and pretend that if, under these circumstances, the State of South Carolina had declared, "I entered into a Confederacy or a compact by which I was to have my rights guarantied by the constant presence of two Senators upon your floor; you allow me but one; you refuse to repair the injustice; I withdraw;" what man would dare say that that was a violation of the Constitution on the part of South Carolina? Who would say that that was a revolutionary remedy? Who would deny the plain and palpable proposition that it was the exercise of a right inherent in her under the very principles of the Constitution, and necessarily so inherent for self-defense?

Why, sir, the North, if it has not a majority here to-day, will have it very soon. Suppose these gentlemen from the North with the majority think that it is no more than fair, inasmuch as we represent here States in which there are large numbers of slaves, that the northern States should have each three Senators: what are we to do? They swear them in. No court has the power of prohibition, of *mandamus* over this body in the exercise of its political powers. It is the exclusive judge of the elections, the qualifications, and the returns of its own members, a judge without appeal. Shall the whole fifteen southern States submit to that, and be told that they are guilty of revolutionary excess if they say, we will not remain with you on these terms; we never agreed to it? Is that revolution, or is it the exercise of clear constitutional right?

Suppose this violation occurs under circumstances where it does not appear so plain to you, but where it does appear equally plain to South Carolina: then you are again brought back to the irrevocable point, who is to decide? South Carolina says, "You forced me to the expenditure of my treasure, you forced me to the shedding of the blood of my people, by a majority vote, and with my aid you acquired territory; now I have a constitutional right to go into that territory with my property, and to be there secured by your laws against its loss." You say, no, she has not. Now there is this to be said: that right is not put down in the Constitution in quite so clear terms as the right to have two Senators; but it is a right which she asserts with the concurrent opinion of the entire South. It is a right which she asserts with the concurrent opinion of one third or two fifths of your own people interested in refusing it. It is a right that she asserts, at all events, if not in accordance with the decision—as you may say no decision was rendered—in accordance with the opinion expressed by the Supreme Court of the United States; but yet there is no tribunal for the assertion of that political right. Is she without a remedy under the Constitution? If not, then what tribunal? If none is provided, then natural law and the law

of nations tell you that she and she alone, from the very necessity of the ease, must be the judge of the infraction and of the mode and measure of redress.

This is no novel doctrine; but it is as old as the law of nations, coeval in our system with the foundation of the Constitution; clearly announced over and over again in our political history. A very valued friend from New York did me the favor to send me an extract, which he has written out, from an address delivered by John Quincy Adams before the New York Historical Society in 1839, at the jubilee of the Constitution. His language is this:

"Nations acknowledge no judge between them upon earth, and their Governments, from necessity, must, in their intercourse with each other, decide when the failure of one party to a contract to perform its obligations absolves the other from the reciprocal fulfillment of its own. But this last of earthly powers is not necessary to the freedom or independence of the States, connected together by the immediate action of the people, of whom they consist. To the people alone is there reserved, as well the dissolving as the constituent power, and that power can be exercised by them only under the tie of conscience, binding them to the retributive justice of heaven.

"With these qualifications, we may admit the same right as vested in the people of every State in the Union, with reference to the General Government, which was exercised by the people of the United Colonies with reference to the supreme head of the British Empire, of which they formed a part; and, under these limitations, have the people of each State in the Union a right to secede from the confederated Union itself?

"Thus stands the RIGHT. But the indissoluble link of union between the people of the several States of this confederated nation is, after all, not in the *right*, but in the *heart*. If the day should ever come (may Heaven avert it!) when the affections of the people of these States shall be alienated from each other; when the fraternal spirit shall give way to cold indifference, or collisions of interest shall fester into hatred, the bands of political association will not long hold together parties no longer attracted by the magnetism of conciliated interests and kindly sympathies; and far better will it be for the people of the *disunited* States to part in friendship from each other, than to be held together by constraint. Then will be the time for reverting to the precedent, which occurred at the formation and adoption of the Constitution, to form again a more perfect Union, by dissolving that which could no longer bind, and to leave the separated parts to be reunited by the law of political gravitation, to the center."

I am compelled to refer also, for the purpose of completing my argument, to the very familiar Virginia and Kentucky resolutions. They cannot, however, be too often repeated or held too reverently in memory. The first, drawn by Mr. Jefferson, is:

"Resolved, That the several States composing the United States of America are not united on the principle of unlimited submission to their General Government; but that, by compact, under the style and title of a Constitution for the United States, and of amendments thereto, they constituted a General Government for special purposes, delegated to that Government certain definite powers, reserving each State to itself the residuary mass of right to their own self-government; and that whensoever the General Government assumes undelegated powers its acts are unauthoritative, void, and of no force; that to this compact each State acceded as a State, and is an integral party; that this Government, created by this compact, was not made the exclusive or final judge of the extent of the powers delegated to itself, since that would have made its discretion, and not the Constitution, the measure of its power; but that, as in all other cases of compact among parties having no common judge, each party has an equal right to judge for itself as well of infractions as of the mode and measure of redress."

These resolutions of Virginia were submitted to all the States. They were commented upon; they were answered generally with contempt and disdain, because the people of the northern States never seem to have comprehended that the States had any rights at all. They have always gone astray in the heresy that this was one consolidated Government, governing subjects to the Federal Government, and not controlling States, and individuals in the States. These resolutions were returned in many cases with terms of contempt and contumely. They were, therefore, referred to Mr. Madison for further consideration and defense, and he produced upon that subject the best considered, the most perfect,

the most compact argument upon the constitutional rights of the States of this Union, that has ever been delivered. It has never been answered to this day in any of its positions. No man can answer it. The proof is such that conviction is forced home upon the mind as by the enunciation of an axiom. A single passage I desire to quote. It has been often quoted, but I must read it again:

"It appears to your committee to be a plain principle, founded in common sense, illustrated by common practice, and essential to the nature of compacts, that, where resort can be had to no tribunal superior to the authority of the parties, the parties themselves must be the rightful judges in the last resort, whether the bargain made has been pursued or violated. The Constitution of the United States was formed by the sanction of the States, given by each in its sovereign capacity. It adds to the stability and dignity, as well as to the authority, of the Constitution, that it rests on this legitimate and solid foundation. The States then, being the parties to the constitutional compact, and in their sovereign capacity, it follows, of necessity, that there can be no tribunal, above their authority, to decide, in the last resort, whether the compact made by them be violated, and consequently, that, as the parties to it, they must themselves decide, in the last resort, such questions as may be of sufficient magnitude to require their interposition."

He goes on to state, not limitations upon the power, but considerations in regard to the mode of exercising it. He says:

"The resolution has, accordingly, guarded against any misapprehension of its object, by expressly requiring, for such an interposition, 'the case of a deliberate, palpable, and dangerous breach of the Constitution, by the exercise of powers not granted by it.' It must be a case not of light and transient nature, but of a nature dangerous to the great purposes for which the Constitution was established."

Mr. Madison, in the debates in the Virginia convention, seemed to take it for granted that any State had a right to secede at any time, without any condition or limitation. His later, well-considered report, qualifies that doctrine, as I have just shown; but at the time the debates occurred in the Virginia convention about adopting the Constitution, it was taken for granted on all sides that Virginia could withdraw whenever she pleased; nobody seems to have disputed that. After defending the grant of power in relation to the militia, Mr. Madison said:

> "An observation fell from a gentleman on the same side with myself, which deserves to be attended to. If we be dissatisfied with the National Government, if we should choose to renounce it, this is an additional safeguard to our defense." — *Elliot's Debates*, vol. 3, p. 414.

Apparently taking it for granted that any State could renounce it when it pleased, and that the militia would already be organized as a safeguard for its defense. I do not state this as any particularly pertinent authority, but to show the impressions that generally prevailed at the time of the adoption of the Constitution; but when the question was subsequently discussed in 1798 and 1799, upon the alien and sedition laws, not only did Mr. Madison make this report, but I have a reference here to a letter of Mr. Jefferson, which I have not on the table, and which I will annex to my speech when printed, showing that he deliberately examined this whole question, and came to the same conclusion.

But, Mr. President, the President of the United States tells us that he does not admit this right to be constitutional; that it is revolutionary. I have endeavored thus far to show that it results from the nature of the compact itself; that it must necessarily be one of those reserved powers which was not abandoned by it, and therefore grows out of the Constitution, and is not in violation of it. If I am asked how I will distinguish this from revolutionary abuse, the answer is prompt and easy. These States, parties to the compact, have a right to withdraw from it, by virtue of its own provisions, when those provisions are violated by the other parties to the compact, when either powers not granted are usurped, or rights are refused that are especially granted to the States. But, sir, there is a large class of powers granted by this Constitution, in the exercise of which a discretion is vested in the General Government, and, in the exercise of that discretion, these admitted powers might be so perverted and abused as to give cause of complaint, and finally, to give the right to revolution; for under those circumstances there would be no other remedy. Now, taking again the supposition of a dominant northern majority in both branches, and of a sectional President and Vice President, the Congress of the United States then, in the exercise of its admitted powers, and the President to back them, could spend the entire revenue of the Confederation in that section which had control, without violating the words or the letter of the Constitution; they could establish forts, light-houses, arsenals, magazines, and all public buildings of every character in the northern States alone, and utterly refuse any to the South. The President, with the aid of his sectional Senate, could appoint all officers of the Navy and of the Army, all the civil officers of the Government, all the judges, attorneys, and marshals, all collectors and revenue officers, all postmasters — the whole host of public officers he might, under the forms and powers vested by the Constitution, appoint exclusively from the northern States, and quarter them in the southern States, to eat out the substance of our people, and assume an insulting superiority over them. All that might be done in the exercise of admitted constitutional power; and it is just that train of evils, of outrages, of wrongs, of oppressions long continued, that the Declaration of Independence says a people preserves the inherent right of throwing off by destroying their government by revolution. I say, therefore, that I distinguish the rights of the States under the Constitution into two classes: one resulting from the nature of their bargain; if the bargain is broken by the sister States, to consider themselves freed from it on the ground of breach of compact; if the bargain be not broken, but the powers be perverted to their wrong and their oppression, then, whenever that wrong and oppression shall become sufficiently aggravated, the revolutionary right — the last inherent right of man to preserve freedom, property, and safety — arises, and must be exercised, for none other will meet the case.

But, Mr. President, suppose South Carolina to be altogether wrong in her opinion that this compact has been violated to her prejudice; and that she has, therefore, a right to withdraw; take that for granted: what then? You still have the same issue to meet face to face. You must permit her to withdraw in peace, or you must declare war. That is, you must coerce the State itself, or you must permit her to depart in peace. There is nothing whatever that can render for an instant tenable the attempted distinction between coercing a State itself, and coercing all the individuals in the manner now proposed. Let me read a few lines upon that subject. First, Vattel, in speaking of States, and of their rights, and the rights of their citizens, uses this language;

> "Every nation that governs itself, under what form soever, without dependence on any foreign Power, is a *sovereign State*. Its rights are naturally the same

as those of any other State. Such are the moral persons who live together in a natural society, subject to the law of nations. To give a nation a right to make an immediate figure in this grand society, it is sufficient that it be really sovereign and independent; that is, that it govern itself by its own authority and laws."

Then, he speaks of those qualifications that may exist in relation to this sovereignty; and he says:

"Several sovereign and Independent States may unite themselves together by a perpetual confederacy, without ceasing to be, each individually, a perfect State. They will together constitute a federal republic: their joint deliberations will not impair the sovereignty of each member, though they may, in certain respects, put some restraint on the exercise of it, in virtue of voluntary engagements. A person does not cease to be free and independent when he is obliged to fulfill engagements which he has voluntarily contracted." — *Vattel's Law of Nations*, book I, chap. 1.

Here, then, we see that, under the law of nations, the State of South Carolina is a sovereign State, independently of all considerations drawn from the language of the Constitution itself, and as such is entitled to be treated, and as such has a right to protect and shield her citizens from all the consequences of obedience to her acts. The honorable Senator from Illinois [Mr. TRUMBULL] put to my friend from Virginia [Mr. MASON] the question what rebellion was, and put it with a triumphant air, as if he supposed that in case of rebellion the laws of war did not apply; that then it was a mere question of hanging traitors; that there could be no independence of the State of South Carolina, but a mere rebellion of the body of its citizens. Suppose it to be so; what does the law of nations say in that very case?

"When a party is formed in a State who no longer obey the sovereign, and are possessed of sufficient strength to oppose him or when, in a Republic, the nation is divided into two opposite factions, and both sides take up arms — this is called a *civil war*. Some writers confine this term to a just insurrection of the subjects against their sovereign, to distinguish that lawful resistance from *rebellion*, which is an open and unjust resistance. But what appellation will they give to a war which arises in a republic torn by two factions — or in a monarchy, between

two competitors for the crown? Custom appropriates the term 'civil war' to every war between the members of one and the same political society. If it be between part of the citizens on the one side, and the sovereign, with those who continue in obedience to him, on the other, provided the malcontents have any reason for taking up arms, nothing further is required to entitle such disturbance to the name of civil war, and not to that of *rebellion*. This latter term is applied only to such an insurrection against lawful authority as is void of all appearance of justice. The sovereign, indeed, never fails to bestow the appellation of *rebels* on all such of his subjects as openly resist him; but when the latter have acquired sufficient strength to give him effectual opposition, and oblige him to carry on the war against them according to the established rules, he must necessarily submit to the use of the term '*civil war*.'"

...

[I]t is a principle of the law of nations, that the citizen owes obedience to the command of his sovereign, and he cannot enter into the question whether the sovereign's order is lawful or unlawful, except at his peril. If his sovereign engages in war — if his State declares her independence — he is bound by the action of his State, and has no authority to control it. Why, Mr. President, how idle and absurd would be any other proposition! How idle and absurd to suppose that you can, in principle and in practice, separate each particular individual of a State and make him responsible for the collective act of his Government — each agent in turn. The honorable Senator from Ohio, [Mr. PUGH,] who delivered to us the other day so magnificent and patriotic an appeal, read you the language of the different Presidents of the United States upon that subject, and cited to you the language of Mr. Adams, in which he said that he had been forced to avoid making use of the power of the Federal Government, in the State of Georgia, against certain surveyors acting in defiance of the Federal authority, because he understood that they were ordered so to act by their State government, and believed themselves bound to obey the order.

Sir, if there was anything in this idea in theory, you might reduce it to practice; but what can be more absurd, more vague, more fanciful, than the suggestions put out by gentlemen here? You are going now, observe, to declare no war and to coerce no State; you are simply going to execute the laws of the United States against individuals in the State of South Carolina. That is your proposition. Is it serious? One gentleman says he will hang for treason. Ah, where is the marshal to seize, and where is the court to try, where is the district attorney to prosecute, and where is the jury to convict? Are you going to establish all these by arms? Perhaps you tell me you will remove him elsewhere for trial. Not so; our fathers have not left our liberties so unguarded and so unprotected as that. The Constitution originally provided that no man could be brought to trial for an offense out of the State where he committed it. The fathers were not satisfied with it, and they added an amendment that he should not be brought to trial out of the district even in which he had committed it. You cannot take him out of the district. You have got no judge, no marshal, no attorney, no jurors, there; and suppose you had: who is to adjudge, who is to convict? His fellow-citizens, unanimous in opinion with him, determine that he has done his duty, and has committed no guilt. That is the way you are going to execute the laws against treason!

What next? Oh, no, says the Senator from Ohio, [Mr. WADE,] that is what we will do; we will execute the laws to collect revenue by blockading your ports, and stopping them up. At first blush this seems a very amusing mode of collecting revenue in South Carolina, by allowing no vessels to come in on which revenue can be collected. It is the strangest of all possible fancies that that is the way of collecting revenue there, of enforcing the laws in the State against individuals. But first you are to have no war. And what is blockade? Does any man suppose that blockade can exist by a nation at peace with another; that it is a peace power; that it can be exercised on any other ground than that you are at war with the party whose ports you blockade, and that you make proclamation to all the Governments of the earth that their vessels shall not be authorized to enter into these ports, because you are reducing your enemy by the use of regular constituted, recognized, warlike means? Oh, but perhaps it is not a blockade that you will have; you will have an embargo, that is what you mean. We are guarded here again. The Constitution heads you off at every step in this Quixotic attempt to go into a State to exercise your laws against her whole citizens without declaring war or coercing the State. You cannot embargo the ports of one State without embargoing all your ports; you cannot shut up one without shutting up all; the Constitution of the United States expressly forbids it. If your blockade or your embargo were a peace-ful measure, you are prohibited by the very words of the Constitution itself from forcing a vessel bound to or from one State to enter or clear or pay duties in another, or from making any regulations of commerce whatever, giving any preference to the ports of one State over the ports of another; and you have no more right to blockade or close the ports of South Carolina by embargo, even by act of Congress, than you have to declare that a sovereign State shall have no right to have more than one Senator on this floor. Your blockade is impracticable, unconstitutional, out of the power of the President.

What is this idea of executing the laws by armed force against individuals? Gentlemen seem to suppose—and they argue upon the supposition—that it is possible, under the Constitution of the United States, for the President to determine when laws are not obeyed and to force obedience by the sword, without the interposition of courts of justice. Does any man have such an idle conceit as that? Does he suppose that, by any possible construction, the power of the Federal Congress to call out the militia, and to use the Army and the Navy to suppress insurrection and to execute the laws, means that the President is to do it of his own volition and without the intervention of the civil power? The honorable Senator from Tennessee, [Mr. JOHNSON,] the other day, called upon us to look at the example of Washington, who put down rebellion in Pennsylvania. He said well that he was no lawyer, when he cited that General Washington called forth the militia of Pennsylvania and of other States to aid in executing the laws, upon a requisition by a judge of the Supreme Court of the United States certifying to him that the marshal was unable to carry out the judgments of the court.

Mr. JOHNSON, of Tennessee. I understood that very well.

Mr. BENJAMIN. Then what on earth do you mean by saying that you will go into a State and execute the laws of the United States against individuals, without a judge or jury there, without a marshal or attorney, with nobody to declare the violation of law, or to order its execution before you attempt to enforce it? The Senator may not have intended to assume such a position. He has been unfortunate in the impressions that he has produced upon the country.

But, sir, other means are suggested. We cannot go to war; we are not going to war; we are not going to coerce a State. "Why," says the Senator from Illinois "who talks of coercing a State; you are attempting to breed confusion in the public mind; you are attempting to impose upon people by perverting the question; we only mean to execute the laws against individuals." Again, I say, where will be the civil process which must precede the action of the military force? Surely, surely it is not at this day that we are to argue that neither the President, nor the President and Congress combined, are armed with the powers of a military despot to carry out the laws, without the intervention of the courts, according to their own caprice and their own discretion, to judge when laws are violated, to convict for the violation, to pronounce sentence, and to execute it. You can do nothing of the kind with your military force.

...

This whole scheme, this whole fancy, that you can treat the act of a sovereign State, issued in an authoritative form, and in her collective capacity as a State, as being utterly out of existence; that you can treat the State as still belonging collectively to the Confederacy, and that you can proceed, without a solitary Federal officer in the State, to enforce your laws against private individuals, is as vain, as idle, and delusive, as any dream that ever entered into the head of man. The thing cannot be done. It is only asserted for the purpose of covering up the true question, than which there is no other: you must acknowledge the independence of the seceding State, or reduce her to subjection by war.

...

You, Senators of the Republican party, assert, and your people whom you represent assert, that under a just and fair interpretation of the Federal Constitution, it is right that you deny that our slaves, which directly and indirectly involve a value of more than four thousand million dollars, are property at all, or entitled to protection in Territories owned by the common Government. You assume the interpretation that it is right to encourage, by all possible means, directly and indirectly, the robbery of this property, and to legislate so as to render its recovery as difficult and dangerous as possible; that it is right and proper and justifiable, under the Constitution, to prevent our mere transit across a sister State, to embark with our property on a lawful voyage, without being openly despoiled of it. You assert, and practice upon the assertion, that it is right to hold us up to the ban of man-kind in speech, writing, and print, with every possible appliance of publicity—as thieves, robbers, murderers, villains, and criminals of the blackest dye, because we continue to own property which we owned at the time that we all signed the compact; that

it is right that we should be exposed to spend our treasure in the purchase, or shed our blood in the conquest, of foreign territory, with no right to enter it for settlement without leaving behind our most valuable property, under penalty of its confiscation. You practically interpret this instrument to me that it is eminently in accordance with the assurance that our tranquillity and welfare were to be preserved and promoted; that our sister States should combine to prevent our growth and development; that they should surround us with a cordon of hostile communities, for the express and avowed purpose of accumulating in dense masses, and within restricted limits, a population which you believe to be dangerous, and thereby force the sacrifice of property nearly sufficient in value to pay the public debt of every nation in Europe.

This is the construction of the instrument that was to preserve our security, promote our welfare, and which we only signed on your assurance that that was its object. You tell us that this is a fair construction—not all, some say one thing, some another; but you act, or your people do, upon this principle. You do not propose to enter into our States, you say, and what do we complain of? You do not pretend to enter into our States to kill or destroy our institutions by force. Oh, no. You imitate the faith of Rhadamistus: you propose simply to close us in an embrace that will suffocate us. You do not propose to fell the tree; you promised not. You merely propose to girdle it, that it dies. And then, when we tell you that we did not understand this bargain this way, that your acting upon it in this spirit releases us from the obligations that accompany it; that under no circumstances can we consent to live together under that interpretation, and say: "we will go from you; let us go in peace;" we are answered by your leading spokesmen: "Oh, no; you cannot do that; we have no objection to it personally, but we are bound by our oaths; if you attempt it, your people will be hanged for treason. We have examined this Constitution thoroughly; we have searched it out with a fair spirit, and we can find warrant in it for releasing ourselves from the obligation of giving you any of its benefits, but our oaths force us to tax you; we can dispense with everything else; but our consciences, we protest upon our souls, will be sorely worried if we do not take your money." [Laughter.] That is the proposition of the honorable Senator from Ohio, in plain language. He can avoid everything else under the Constitution, in the way of secession; but how is he to get rid of the duty of taking our money he cannot see. [Laughter.]

Now, Senators, this picture is not placed before you with any idea that it will act upon any one of you, or change your views, or alter your conduct. All hope of that is gone. Our committee has reported this morning that no possible scheme of adjustment can be devised by them all combined. The day for the adjustment has passed. If you would give it now, you are too late.

And now, Senators, within a few weeks we part to meet as Senators in one common council chamber of the nation no more forever. We desire, we beseech you, let this parting be in peace. I conjure you to indulge in no vain delusion that duty or conscience, interest or honor, imposes upon you the necessity of invading our States or shedding the blood of our people. You have no possible justification for it. I trust it is in no craven spirit, and with no sacrifice of the honor or dignity of my own State, that I make this last appeal, but from far higher and holier motives. If, however, it shall prove vain, if you are resolved to pervert the Government framed by the fathers for the protection of our rights into an instrument for subjugating and enslaving us, then, appealing to the Supreme Judge of the universe for the rectitude of our intentions, we must meet the issue that you force upon us as best becomes freemen defending all that is dear to man.

What may be the fate of this horrible contest, no man can tell, none pretend to foresee; but this much I will say: the fortunes of war may be adverse to our arms; you may carry desolation into our peaceful land, and with torch and fire you may set our cities in flames; you may even emulate the atrocities of those who, in the war of the Revolution, hounded on the blood-thirsty savage to attack upon the defenseless frontier; you may, under the protection of your advancing armies, give shelter to the furious fanatics who desire, and profess to desire, nothing more than to add all the horrors of a servile insurrection to the calamities of civil war; you may do all this—and more, too, if more there be—but you never can subjugate us; you never can convert the free sons of the soil into vassals, paying tribute to your power; and you never, never can degrade them to the level of an inferior and servile race. Never! Never! [Loud applause in the galleries.]

Mr. MASON. I demand that the galleries be cleared instantly.

Mr. FOOT. I second that demand.

The PRESIDING OFFICER, (Mr. BRIGHT) The Chair will make that order, that the galleries on the right of the Chair be cleared.

Mr. FOOT. And that they be cleared forthwith. [Hisses in the galleries.]

The Sergeant-at-Arms proceeded to execute the order of the Presiding Officer.

7

US Congress, The "Corwin Amendment"

12 Stat. 251, March 2, 1861*

No amendment shall be made to the Constitution which will authorize or give to Congress the power to abolish or interfere, within any State, with the domestic institutions thereof, including that of persons held to labor or service by the laws of said State.

Approved, March 2, 1861

8

Abraham Lincoln, First Inaugural Address

March 4, 1861†

Fellow-Citizens of the United States:

In compliance with a custom as old as the Government itself, I appear before you to address you briefly and to take in your presence the oath prescribed by the Constitution of the United States to be taken by the President before he enters on the execution of this office.

I do not consider it necessary at present for me to discuss those matters of administration about which there is no special anxiety or excitement.

Apprehension seems to exist among the people of the Southern States that by the accession of a Republi-

---

* George P. Sanger, ed., *United States Statutes at Large* (Boston: Little, Brown, 1866), 12:251. [Named after its author, Representative Thomas Corwin (R-OH), the "Corwin" amendment was signed by President Buchanan and sent to the states for ratification. The ratification process ended with the initiation of the Civil War. —Ed.]

† Lincoln, *Speeches and Writings*, 2:215–24.

can Administration their property and their peace and personal security are to be endangered. There has never been any reasonable cause for such apprehension. Indeed, the most ample evidence to the contrary has all the while existed and been open to their inspection. It is found in nearly all the published speeches of him who now addresses you. I do but quote from one of those speeches when I declare that "I have no purpose, directly or indirectly, to interfere with the institution of slavery in the States where it exists. I believe I have no lawful right to do so, and I have no inclination to do so." Those who nominated and elected me did so with full knowledge that I had made this and many similar declarations and had never recanted them; and more than this, they placed in the platform for my acceptance, and as a law to themselves and to me, the clear and emphatic resolution which I now read:

Resolved, That the maintenance inviolate of the rights of the States, and especially the right of each State to order and control its own domestic institutions according to its own judgment exclusively, is essential to that balance of power on which the perfection and endurance of our political fabric depend; and we denounce the lawless invasion by armed force of the soil of any State or Territory, no matter what pretext, as among the gravest of crimes.

I now reiterate these sentiments, and in doing so I only press upon the public attention the most conclusive evidence of which the case is susceptible that the property, peace, and security of no section are to be in any wise endangered by the now incoming Administration. I add, too, that all the protection which, consistently with the Constitution and the laws, can be given will be cheerfully given to all the States when lawfully demanded, for whatever cause—as cheerfully to one section as to another.

There is much controversy about the delivering up of fugitives from service or labor. The clause I now read is as plainly written in the Constitution as any other of its provisions:

"No person held to service or labor in one State, under the laws thereof, escaping into another, shall in consequence of any law or regulation therein be discharged from such service or labor, but shall be delivered up on claim of the party to whom such service or labor may be due."

It is scarcely questioned that this provision was intended by those who made it for the reclaiming of what we call fugitive slaves; and the intention of the lawgiver is the law. All members of Congress swear their support to the whole Constitution—to this provision as much as to any other. To the proposition, then, that slaves whose cases come within the terms of this clause "shall be delivered up" their oaths are unanimous. Now, if they would make the effort in good temper, could they not with nearly equal unanimity frame and pass a law by means of which to keep good that unanimous oath?

There is some difference of opinion whether this clause should be enforced by national or by State authority, but surely that difference is not a very material one. If the slave is to be surrendered, it can be of but little consequence to him or to others by which authority it is done. And should anyone in any case be content that his oath shall go unkept on a merely unsubstantial controversy as to how it shall be kept?

Again: In any law upon this subject ought not all the safeguards of liberty known in civilized and humane jurisprudence to be introduced, so that a free man be not in any case surrendered as a slave? And might it not be well at the same time to provide by law for the enforcement of that clause in the Constitution which guarantees that "the citizens of each State shall be entitled to all privileges and immunities of citizens in the several States?"

I take the official oath to-day with no mental reservations and with no purpose to construe the Constitution or laws by any hypercritical rules; and while I do not choose now to specify particular acts of Congress as proper to be enforced, I do suggest that it will be much safer for all, both in official and private stations, to conform to and abide by all those acts which stand unrepealed than to violate any of them trusting to find impunity in having them held to be unconstitutional.

It is seventy-two years since the first inauguration of a President under our National Constitution. During that period fifteen different and greatly distinguished citizens have in succession administered the executive branch of the Government. They have conducted it through many perils, and generally with great success. Yet, with all this scope of precedent, I now enter upon the same task for the brief constitutional term of four years under great and peculiar difficulty. A disruption of the Federal Union, heretofore only menaced, is now formidably attempted.

I hold that in contemplation of universal law and of the Constitution the Union of these States is perpetual. Perpetuity is implied, if not expressed, in the fundamental law of all national governments. It is safe to assert that no government proper ever had a provision in its organic law for its own termination. Continue to execute all the express provisions of our National Constitution, and the Union will endure forever—it being impossible to destroy it except by some action not provided for in the instrument itself.

Again, if the United States be not a government proper, but an association of States in the nature of contract merely, can it, as a contract, be peaceably unmade by less than all the parties who made it? One party to a contract may violate it—break it, so to speak—but does it not require all to lawfully rescind it?

Descending from these general principles, we find the proposition that in legal contemplation the Union is perpetual confirmed by the history of the Union itself. The Union is much older than the Constitution. It was formed, in fact, by the Articles of Association in 1774. It was matured and continued by the Declaration of Independence in 1776. It was further matured, and the faith of all the then thirteen States expressly plighted and engaged that it should be perpetual, by the Articles of Confederation in 1778. And finally, in 1787, one of the declared objects for ordaining and establishing the Constitution was *"to form a more perfect Union."*

But if destruction of the Union by one or by a part only of the States be lawfully possible, the Union is less perfect than before the Constitution, having lost the vital element of perpetuity.

It follows from these views that no State upon its own mere motion can lawfully get out of the Union; that resolves and ordinances to that effect are legally void, and that acts of violence within any State or States against the authority of the United States are insurrectionary or revolutionary, according to circumstances.

I therefore consider that in view of the Constitution and the laws the Union is unbroken, and to the extent of my ability, I shall take care, as the Constitution itself expressly enjoins upon me, that the laws of the Union be faithfully executed in all the States. Doing this I deem to be only a simple duty on my part, and I shall perform it so far as practicable unless my rightful masters, the American people, shall withhold the requisite means or in some authoritative manner direct the contrary. I trust this will not be regarded as a menace, but only as the declared purpose of the Union that it will constitutionally defend and maintain itself.

In doing this there needs to be no bloodshed or violence, and there shall be none unless it be forced upon the national authority. The power confided to me will be used to hold, occupy, and possess the property and places belonging to the Government and to collect the duties and imposts; but beyond what may be necessary for these objects, there will be no invasion, no using of force against or among the people anywhere. Where hostility to the United States in any interior locality shall be so great and universal as to prevent competent resident citizens from holding the Federal offices, there will be no attempt to force obnoxious strangers among the people for that object. While the strict legal right may exist in the Government to enforce the exercise of these offices, the attempt to do so would be so irritating and so nearly impracticable withal that I deem it better to forego for the time the uses of such offices.

The mails, unless repelled, will continue to be furnished in all parts of the Union. So far as possible the people everywhere shall have that sense of perfect security which is most favorable to calm thought and reflection. The course here indicated will be followed unless current events and experience shall show a modification or change to be proper, and in every case and exigency my best discretion will be exercised, according to circumstances actually existing and with a view and a hope of a peaceful solution of the national troubles and the restoration of fraternal sympathies and affections.

That there are persons in one section or another who seek to destroy the Union at all events and are glad of any pretext to do it I will neither affirm nor deny; but if there be such, I need address no word to them. To those, however, who really love the Union may I not speak?

Before entering upon so grave a matter as the destruction of our national fabric, with all its benefits, its memories, and its hopes, would it not be wise to ascertain precisely why we do it? Will you hazard so desperate a step while there is any possibility that any portion of the ills you fly from have no real existence? Will you, while the certain ills you fly to are greater than all the real ones you fly from, will you risk the commission of so fearful a mistake?

All profess to be content in the Union if all constitutional rights can be maintained. Is it true, then, that any right plainly written in the Constitution has been denied? I think not. Happily, the human mind is so constituted that no party can reach to the audacity of doing this. Think, if you can, of a single instance in which a plainly written provision of the Constitution has ever been denied. If by the mere force of numbers a majority should deprive a minority of any clearly written constitutional right, it might in a moral point of view justify revolution; certainly would if such right were a vital one. But such is not our case. All the vital rights of minorities and of individuals are so plainly assured to them by affirmations and negations, guaranties and prohibitions, in the Constitution that controversies never arise concerning them. But no organic law can ever be framed with a provision specifically applicable to every question which may occur in practical administration. No foresight can anticipate nor any document of reasonable length contain express provisions for all possible questions. Shall fugitives from labor be surrendered by national or by State authority? The Constitution does not expressly say. May Congress prohibit slavery in the Territories? The Constitution does not expressly say. Must Congress protect slavery in the Territories? The Constitution does not expressly say.

From questions of this class spring all our constitutional controversies, and we divide upon them into majorities and minorities. If the minority will not acquiesce, the majority must, or the Government must cease. There is no other alternative, for continuing the Government is acquiescence on one side or the other. If a minority in such case will secede rather than acquiesce, they make a precedent which in turn will divide and ruin them, for a minority of their own will secede from them whenever a majority refuses to be controlled by such minority. For instance, why may not any portion of a new confederacy a year or two hence arbitrarily secede again, precisely as portions of the present Union now claim to secede from it? All who cherish disunion sentiments are now being educated to the exact temper of doing this.

Is there such perfect identity of interests among the States to compose a new union as to produce harmony only and prevent renewed secession?

Plainly the central idea of secession is the essence of anarchy. A majority held in restraint by constitutional checks and limitations, and always changing easily with deliberate changes of popular opinions and sentiments, is the only true sovereign of a free people. Whoever rejects it does of necessity fly to anarchy or to despotism. Unanimity is impossible. The rule of a minority, as a permanent arrangement, is wholly inadmissible; so that, rejecting the majority principle, anarchy or despotism in some form is all that is left.

I do not forget the position assumed by some that constitutional questions are to be decided by the Supreme Court, nor do I deny that such decisions must be

binding in any case upon the parties to a suit as to the object of that suit, while they are also entitled to very high respect and consideration in all parallel cases by all other departments of the Government. And while it is obviously possible that such decision may be erroneous in any given case, still the evil effect following it, being limited to that particular case, with the chance that it may be overruled and never become a precedent for other cases, can better be borne than could the evils of a different practice. At the same time, the candid citizen must confess that if the policy of the Government upon vital questions affecting the whole people is to be irrevocably fixed by decisions of the Supreme Court, the instant they are made in ordinary litigation between parties in personal actions the people will have ceased to be their own rulers, having to that extent practically resigned their Government into the hands of that eminent tribunal. Nor is there in this view any assault upon the court or the judges. It is a duty from which they may not shrink to decide cases properly brought before them, and it is no fault of theirs if others seek to turn their decisions to political purposes.

One section of our country believes slavery is *right* and ought to be extended, while the other believes it is *wrong* and ought not to be extended. This is the only substantial dispute. The fugitive slave clause of the Constitution and the law for the suppression of the foreign slave trade are each as well enforced, perhaps, as any law can ever be in a community where the moral sense of the people imperfectly supports the law itself. The great body of the people abide by the dry legal obligation in both cases, and a few break over in each. This, I think, can not be perfectly cured, and it would be worse in both cases *after* the separation of the sections than before. The foreign slave trade, now imperfectly suppressed, would be ultimately revived without restriction in one section, while fugitive slaves, now only partially surrendered, would not be surrendered at all by the other.

Physically speaking, we can not separate. We can not remove our respective sections from each other nor build an impassable wall between them. A husband and wife may be divorced and go out of the presence and beyond the reach of each other, but the different parts of our country can not do this. They can not but remain face to face, and intercourse, either amicable or hostile, must continue between them. Is it possible, then, to make that intercourse more advantageous or more satisfactory after separation than before? Can aliens make treaties easier than friends can make laws? Can treaties be more faithfully enforced between aliens than laws can among friends? Suppose you go to war, you can not fight always; and when, after much loss on both sides and no gain on either, you cease fighting, the identical old questions, as to terms of intercourse, are again upon you.

This country, with its institutions, belongs to the people who inhabit it. Whenever they shall grow weary of the existing Government, they can exercise their *constitutional* right of amending it or their *revolutionary* right to dismember or overthrow it. I can not be ignorant of the fact that many worthy and patriotic citizens are desirous of having the National Constitution amended. While I make no recommendation of amendments, I fully recognize the rightful authority of the people over the whole subject, to be exercised in either of the modes prescribed in the instrument itself; and I should, under existing circumstances, favor rather than oppose a fair opportunity being afforded the people to act upon it. I will venture to add that to me the convention mode seems preferable, in that it allows amendments to originate with the people themselves, instead of only permitting them to take or reject propositions originated by others, not especially chosen for the purpose, and which might not be precisely such as they would wish to either accept or refuse. I understand a proposed amendment to the Constitution—which amendment, however, I have not seen—has passed Congress, to the effect that the Federal Government shall never interfere with the domestic institutions of the States, including that of persons held to service. To avoid misconstruction of what I have said, I depart from my purpose not to speak of particular amendments so far as to say that, holding such a provision to now be implied constitutional law, I have no objection to its being made express and irrevocable.

The Chief Magistrate derives all his authority from the people, and they have referred none upon him to fix terms for the separation of the States. The people themselves can do this if also they choose, but the Executive as such has nothing to do with it. His duty is to administer the present Government as it came to his hands and to transmit it unimpaired by him to his successor.

Why should there not be a patient confidence in the ultimate justice of the people? Is there any better or equal hope in the world? In our present differences, is either party without faith of being in the right? If the Almighty Ruler of Nations, with His eternal truth and justice, be on your side of the North, or on yours of the South, that truth and that justice will surely prevail by the judgment of this great tribunal of the American people.

By the frame of the Government under which we live this same people have wisely given their public servants but little power for mischief, and have with equal wisdom provided for the return of that little to their own hands at very short intervals. While the people retain their virtue and vigilance no Administration by any extreme of wickedness or folly can very seriously injure the Government in the short space of four years.

My countrymen, one and all, think calmly and well upon this whole subject. Nothing valuable can be lost by taking time. If there be an object to hurry any of you in hot haste to a step which you would never take deliberately, that object will be frustrated by taking time; but no good object can be frustrated by it. Such of you as are now dissatisfied still have the old Constitution unimpaired, and, on the sensitive point, the laws of your own framing under it; while the new Administration will have no immediate power, if it would, to change either. If it were admitted that you who are dissatisfied hold the right side in the dispute, there still is no single good reason for precipitate action. Intelligence, patriotism, Christianity, and a firm reliance on Him who has never yet forsaken this favored land are still competent to adjust in the best way all our present difficulty.

In your hands, my dissatisfied fellow-countrymen, and not in mine, is the momentous issue of civil war. The Government will not assail you. You can have no conflict without being yourselves the aggressors. You have no oath registered in heaven to destroy the Government, while I shall have the most solemn one to "preserve, protect, and defend it."

I am loath to close. We are not enemies, but friends. We must not be enemies. Though passion may have strained it must not break our bonds of affection. The mystic chords of memory, stretching from every battlefield and patriot grave to every living heart and hearthstone all over this broad land, will yet swell the chorus of the Union, when again touched, as surely they will be, by the better angels of our nature.

9

Constitution of the Confederate States of America

March 11, 1861[*]

We, the people of the Confederate States, each State acting in its sovereign and independent character, in order to form a permanent federal government, establish justice, insure domestic tranquillity, and secure the blessings of liberty to ourselves and our posterity invoking the favor and guidance of Almighty God do ordain and establish this Constitution for the Confederate States of America.

ARTICLE I

Sec. 1. All legislative powers herein delegated shall be vested in a Congress of the Confederate States, which shall consist of a Senate and House of Representatives.

Sec. 2. (1) The House of Representatives shall be composed of members chosen every second year by the people of the several States; and the electors in each State shall be citizens of the Confederate States, and have the qualifications requisite for electors of the most numerous branch of the State Legislature; but no person of foreign birth, not a citizen of the Confederate States, shall be allowed to vote for any officer, civil or political, State or Federal.

(2) No person shall be a Representative who shall not have attained the age of twenty-five years, and be a citizen of the Confederate States, and who shall not when elected, be an inhabitant of that State in which he shall be chosen.

(3) Representatives and direct taxes shall be apportioned among the several States, which may be included within this Confederacy, according to their respective numbers, which shall be determined by adding to the whole number of free persons, including those bound to service for a term of years, and excluding Indians not taxed, three-fifths of all slaves. The actual enumeration shall be made within three years after the first meeting of the Congress of the Confederate States, and within every subsequent term of ten years, in such man-

ner as they shall by law direct. The number of Representatives shall not exceed one for every fifty thousand, but each State shall have at least one Representative; and until such enumeration shall be made, the State of South Carolina shall be entitled to choose six; the State of Georgia ten; the State of Alabama nine; the State of Florida two; the State of Mississippi seven; the State of Louisiana six; and the State of Texas six.

(4) When vacancies happen in the representation from any State the executive authority thereof shall issue writs of election to fill such vacancies.

(5) The House of Representatives shall choose their Speaker and other officers; and shall have the sole power of impeachment; except that any judicial or other Federal officer, resident and acting solely within the limits of any State, may be impeached by a vote of two-thirds of both branches of the Legislature thereof.

Sec. 3. (1) The Senate of the Confederate States shall be composed of two Senators from each State, chosen for six years by the Legislature thereof, at the regular session next immediately preceding the commencement of the term of service; and each Senator shall have one vote.

(2) Immediately after they shall be assembled, in consequence of the first election, they shall be divided as equally as may be into three classes. The seats of the Senators of the first class shall be vacated at the expiration of the second year; of the second class at the expiration of the fourth year; and of the third class at the expiration of the sixth year; so that one-third may be chosen every second year; and if vacancies happen by resignation, or other wise, during the recess of the Legislature of any State, the Executive thereof may make temporary appointments until the next meeting of the Legislature, which shall then fill such vacancies.

(3) No person shall be a Senator who shall not have attained the age of thirty years, and be a citizen of the Confederate States; and who shall not, then elected, be an inhabitant of the State for which he shall be chosen.

(4) The Vice President of the Confederate States shall be president of the Senate, but shall have no vote unless they be equally divided.

(5) The Senate shall choose their other officers; and also a president pro tempore in the absence of the Vice President, or when he shall exercise the office of President of the Confederate states.

(6) The Senate shall have the sole power to try all impeachments. When sitting for that purpose, they shall

[*]Commager, *Documents*, 1:376–84.

be on oath or affirmation. When the President of the Confederate States is tried, the Chief Justice shall preside; and no person shall be convicted without the concurrence of two-thirds of the members present.

(7) Judgment in cases of impeachment shall not extend further than to removal from office, and disqualification to hold any office of honor, trust, or profit under the Confederate States; but the party convicted shall, nevertheless, be liable and subject to indictment, trial, judgment, and punishment according to law.

Sec. 4. (1) The times, places, and manner of holding elections for Senators and Representatives shall be prescribed in each State by the Legislature thereof, subject to the provisions of this Constitution; but the Congress may, at any time, by law, make or alter such regulations, except as to the times and places of choosing Senators.

(2) The Congress shall assemble at least once in every year; and such meeting shall be on the first Monday in December, unless they shall, by law, appoint a different day.

Sec. 5. (1) Each House shall be the judge of the elections, returns, and qualifications of its own members, and a majority of each shall constitute a quorum to do business; but a smaller number may adjourn from day to day, and may be authorized to compel the attendance of absent members, in such manner and under such penalties as each House may provide.

(2) Each House may determine the rules of its proceedings, punish its members for disorderly behavior, and, with the concurrence of two-thirds of the whole number, expel a member.

(3) Each House shall keep a journal of its proceedings, and from time to time publish the same, excepting such parts as may in their judgment require secrecy; and the yeas and nays of the members of either House, on any question, shall, at the desire of one-fifth of those present, be entered on the journal.

(4) Neither House, during the session of Congress, shall, without the consent of the other, adjourn for more than three days, nor to any other place than that in which the two Houses shall be sitting.

Sec. 6. (1) The Senators and Representatives shall receive a compensation for their services, to be ascertained by law, and paid out of the Treasury of the Confederate States. They shall, in all cases, except treason, felony, and breach of the peace, be privileged from arrest during their attendance at the session of their respective Houses, and in going to and returning from

the same; and for any speech or debate in either House, they shall not be questioned in any other place.

(2) No Senator or Representative shall, during the time for which he was elected, be appointed to any civil office under the authority of the Confederate States, which shall have been created, or the emoluments whereof shall have been increased during such time; and no person holding any office under the Confederate States shall be a member of either House during his continuance in office. But Congress may, by law, grant to the principal officer in each of the Executive Departments a seat upon the floor of either House, with the privilege of discussing any measures appertaining to his department.

Sec. 7. (1) All bills for raising revenue shall originate in the House of Representatives; but the Senate may propose or concur with amendments, as on other bills.

(2) Every bill which shall have passed both Houses, shall, before it becomes a law, be presented to the President of the Confederate States; if he approve, he shall sign it; but if not, he shall return it, with his objections, to that House in which it shall have originated, who shall enter the objections at large on their journal, and proceed to reconsider it. If, after such reconsideration, two-thirds of that House shall agree to pass the bill, it shall be sent, together with the objections, to the other House, by which it shall likewise be reconsidered, and if approved by two-thirds of that House, it shall become a law. But in all such cases, the votes of both Houses shall be determined by yeas and nays, and the names of the persons voting for and against the bill shall be entered on the journal of each House respectively. If any bill shall not be returned by the President within ten days (Sundays excepted) after it shall have been presented to him, the same shall be a law, in like manner as if he had signed it, unless the Congress, by their adjournment, prevent its return; in which case it shall not be a law. The President may approve any appropriation and disapprove any other appropriation in the same bill. In such case he shall, in signing the bill, designate the appropriations disapproved; and shall return a copy of such appropriations, with his objections, to the House in which the bill shall have originated; and the same proceedings shall then be had as in case of other bills disapproved by the President.

(3) Every order, resolution, or vote, to which the concurrence of both Houses may be necessary (except on a question of adjournment) shall be presented to the

President of the Confederate States; and before the same shall take effect, shall be approved by him; or, being disapproved by him, shall be repassed by two-thirds of both Houses, according to the rules and limitations prescribed in case of a bill.

Sec. 8. The Congress shall have power—

(1) To lay and collect taxes, duties, imposts, and excises for revenue, necessary to pay the debts, provide for the common defense, and carry on the Government of the Confederate States; but no bounties shall be granted from the Treasury; nor shall any duties or taxes on importations from foreign nations be laid to promote or foster any branch of industry; and all duties, imposts, and excises shall be uniform throughout the Confederate States.

(2) To borrow money on the credit of the Confederate States.

(3) To regulate commerce with foreign nations, and among the several States, and with the Indian tribes; but neither this, nor any other clause contained in the Constitution, shall ever be construed to delegate the power to Congress to appropriate money for any internal improvement intended to facilitate commerce; except for the purpose of furnishing lights, beacons, and buoys, and other aids to navigation upon the coasts, and the improvement of harbors and the removing of obstructions in river navigation; in all which cases such duties shall be laid on the navigation facilitated thereby as may be necessary to pay the costs and expenses thereof.

(4) To establish uniform laws of naturalization, and uniform laws on the subject of bankruptcies, throughout the Confederate States; but no law of Congress shall discharge any debt contracted before the passage of the same.

(5) To coin money, regulate the value thereof, and of foreign coin, and fix the standard of weights and measures.

(6) To provide for the punishment of counterfeiting the securities and current coin of the Confederate States.

(7) To establish post offices and post routes; but the expenses of the Post Office Department, shall be paid out of its own revenues.

(8) To promote the progress of science and useful arts, by securing for limited times to authors and inventors the exclusive right to their respective writings and discoveries.

(9) To constitute tribunals inferior to the Supreme Court.

(10) To define and punish piracies and felonies committed on the high seas, and offenses against the law of nations.

(11) To declare war, grant letters of marque and reprisal, and make rules concerning captures on land and water.

(12) To raise and support armies; but no appropriation of money to that use shall be for a longer term than two years.

(13) To provide and maintain a navy.

(14) To make rules for the government and regulation of the land and naval forces.

(15) To provide for calling forth the militia to execute the laws of the Confederate States, suppress insurrections, and repel invasions.

(16) To provide for organizing, arming, and disciplining the militia, and for governing such part of them as may be employed in the service of the Confederate States; reserving to the States, respectively, the appointment of the officers, and the authority of training the militia according to the discipline prescribed by Congress.

(17) To exercise exclusive legislation, in all cases whatsoever, over such district (not exceeding ten miles square) as may, by cession of one or more States and the acceptance of Congress, become the seat of the Government of the Confederate States; and to exercise like authority over all places purchased by the consent of the Legislature of the State in which the same shall be, for the erection of forts, magazines, arsenals, dockyards, and other needful buildings; and

(18) To make all laws which shall be necessary and proper for carrying into execution the foregoing powers, and all other powers vested by this Constitution in the Government of the Confederate States, or in any department or officer thereof.

Sec. 9. (1) The importation of negroes of the African race from any foreign country other than the slaveholding States or Territories of the United States of America, is hereby forbidden; and Congress is required to pass such laws as shall effectually prevent the same.

(2) Congress shall also have power to prohibit the introduction of slaves from any State not a member of, or Territory not belonging to, this Confederacy.

(3) The privilege of the writ of habeas corpus shall not be suspended, unless when in cases of rebellion or invasion the public safety may require it.

(4) No bill of attainder, ex post facto law, or law denying or impairing the right of property in negro slaves shall be passed.

(5) No capitation or other direct tax shall be laid, unless in proportion to the census or enumeration hereinbefore directed to be taken.

(6) No tax or duty shall be laid on articles exported from any State, except by a vote of two-thirds of both Houses.

(7) No preference shall be given by any regulation of commerce or revenue to the ports of one State over those of another.

(8) No money shall be drawn from the Treasury, but in consequence of appropriations made by law; and a regular statement and account of the receipts and expenditures of all public money shall be published from time to time.

(9) Congress shall appropriate no money from the Treasury except by a vote of two-thirds of both Houses, taken by yeas and nays, unless it be asked and estimated for by some one of the heads of departments and submitted to Congress by the President; or for the purpose of paying its own expenses and contingencies; or for the payment of claims against the Confederate States, the justice of which shall have been judicially declared by a tribunal for the investigation of claims against the Government, which it is hereby made the duty of Congress to establish.

(10) All bills appropriating money shall specify in Federal currency the exact amount of each appropriation and the purposes for which it is made; and Congress shall grant no extra compensation to any public contractor, officer, agent, or servant, after such contract shall have been made or such service rendered.

(11) No title of nobility shall be granted by the Confederate States; and no person holding any office of profit or trust under them shall, without the consent of the Congress, accept of any present, emolument, office, or title of any kind whatever, from any king, prince, or foreign state.

(12) Congress shall make no law respecting an establishment of religion, or prohibiting the free exercise thereof; or abridging the freedom of speech, or of the press; or the right of the people peaceably to assemble and petition the Government for a redress of grievances.

(13) A well-regulated militia being necessary to the security of a free State, the right of the people to keep and bear arms shall not be infringed.

(14) No soldier shall, in time of peace, be quartered in any house without the consent of the owner; nor in time of war, but in a manner to be prescribed by law.

(15) The right of the people to be secure in their persons, houses, papers, and effects, against unreasonable searches and seizures, shall not be violated; and no warrants shall issue but upon probable cause, supported by oath or affirmation, and particularly describing the place to be searched and the persons or things to be seized.

(16) No person shall be held to answer for a capital or otherwise infamous crime, unless on a presentment or indictment of a grand jury, except in cases arising in the land or naval forces, or in the militia, when in actual service in time of war or public danger; nor shall any person be subject for the same offense to be twice put in jeopardy of life or limb; nor be compelled, in any criminal case, to be a witness against himself; nor be deprived of life, liberty, or property without due process of law; nor shall private property be taken for public use, without just compensation.

(17) In all criminal prosecutions the accused shall enjoy the right to a speedy and public trial, by an impartial jury of the State and district wherein the crime shall have been committed, which district shall have been previously ascertained by law, and to be informed of the nature and cause of the accusation; to be confronted with the witnesses against him; to have compulsory process for obtaining witnesses in his favor; and to have the assistance of counsel for his defense.

(18) In suits at common law, where the value in controversy shall exceed twenty dollars, the right of trial by jury shall be preserved; and no fact so tried by a jury shall be otherwise reexamined in any court of the Confederacy, than according to the rules of common law.

(19) Excessive bail shall not be required, nor excessive fines imposed, nor cruel and unusual punishments inflicted.

(20) Every law, or resolution having the force of law, shall relate to but one subject, and that shall be expressed in the title.

Sec. 10. (1) No State shall enter into any treaty, alliance, or confederation; grant letters of marque and reprisal; coin money; make anything but gold and silver coin a tender in payment of debts; pass any bill of attainder, or ex post facto law, or law impairing the obligation of contracts; or grant any title of nobility.

(2) No State shall, without the consent of the Congress, lay any imposts or duties on imports or exports, except what may be absolutely necessary for executing its inspection laws; and the net produce of all duties and imposts, laid by any State on imports, or exports, shall be for the use of the Treasury of the Confederate States;

and all such laws shall be subject to the revision and control of Congress.

(3) No State shall, without the consent of Congress, lay any duty on tonnage, except on seagoing vessels, for the improvement of its rivers and harbors navigated by the said vessels; but such duties shall not conflict with any treaties of the Confederate States with foreign nations; and any surplus revenue thus derived shall, after making such improvement, be paid into the common treasury. Nor shall any State keep troops or ships of war in time of peace, enter into any agreement or compact with another State, or with a foreign power, or engage in war, unless actually invaded, or in such imminent danger as will not admit of delay. But when any river divides or flows through two or more States they may enter into compacts with each other to improve the navigation thereof.

ARTICLE II

Section 1. (1) The executive power shall be vested in a President of the Confederate States of America. He and the Vice President shall hold their offices for the term of six years; but the President shall not be reeligible. The President and Vice President shall be elected as follows:

(2) Each State shall appoint, in such manner as the Legislature thereof may direct, a number of electors equal to the whole number of Senators and Representatives to which the State may be entitled in the Congress; but no Senator or Representative or person holding an office of trust or profit under the Confederate States shall be appointed an elector.

(3) The electors shall meet in their respective States and vote by ballot for President and Vice President, one of whom, at least, shall not be an inhabitant of the same State with themselves; they shall name in their ballots the person voted for as President, and in distinct ballots the person voted for as Vice President, and they shall make distinct lists of all persons voted for as President, and of all persons voted for as Vice President, and of the number of votes for each, which lists they shall sign and certify, and transmit, sealed, to the seat of the Government of. the Confederate States, directed to the President of the Senate; the President of the Senate shall, in the presence of the Senate and House of Representatives, open all the certificates, and the votes shall then be counted; the person having the greatest number of votes for President shall be the President, if such number be a majority of the whole number of electors appointed; and if no person have such majority, then from

the persons having the highest numbers, not exceeding three, on the list of those voted for as President, the House of Representatives shall choose immediately, by ballot, the President. But in choosing the President the votes shall be taken by States, the representation from each State having one vote; a quorum for this purpose shall consist of a member or members from two-thirds of the States, and a majority of all the States shall be necessary to a choice. And if the House of Representatives shall not choose a President, whenever the right of choice shall devolve upon them, before the 4th day of March next following, then the Vice President shall act as President, as in case of the death, or other constitutional disability of the President.

(4) The person having the greatest number of votes as Vice President shall be the Vice President, if such number be a majority of the whole number of electors appointed; and if no person have a majority, then, from the two highest numbers on the list, the Senate shall choose the Vice President; a quorum for the purpose shall consist of two-thirds of the whole number of Senators, and a majority of the whole number shall be necessary to a choice.

(5) But no person constitutionally ineligible to the office of President shall be eligible to that of Vice President of the Confederate States.

(6) The Congress may determine the time of choosing the electors, and the day on which they shall give their votes; which day shall be the same throughout the Confederate States.

(7) No person except a natural-born citizen of the Confederate States, or a citizen thereof at the time of the adoption of this Constitution, or a citizen thereof born in the United States prior to the 20th of December, 1860, shall be eligible to the office of President; neither shall any person be eligible to that office who shall not have attained the age of thirty-five years, and been fourteen years a resident within the limits of the Confederate States, as they may exist at the time of his election.

(8) In case of the removal of the President from office, or of his death, resignation, or inability to discharge the powers and duties of said office, the same shall devolve on the Vice President; and the Congress may, by law, provide for the case of removal, death, resignation, or inability, both of the President and Vice President, declaring what officer shall then act as President; and such officer shall act accordingly until the disability be removed or a President shall be elected.

(9) The President shall, at stated times, receive for

his services a compensation, which shall neither be increased nor diminished during the period for which he shall have been elected; and he shall not receive within that period any other emolument from the Confederate States, or any of them.

(10) Before he enters on the execution of his office he shall take the following oath or affirmation:

Sec. 2. (1) The President shall be Commander-in-Chief of the Army and Navy of the Confederate States, and of the militia of the several States, when called into the actual service of the Confederate States; he may require the opinion, in writing, of the principal officer in each of the Executive Departments, upon any subject relating to the duties of their respective offices; and he shall have power to grant reprieves and pardons for offenses against the Confederate States, except in cases of impeachment.

(2) He shall have power, by and with the advice and consent of the Senate, to make treaties; provided two-thirds of the Senators present concur; and he shall nominate, and by and with the advice and consent of the Senate shall appoint, ambassadors, other public ministers and consuls, judges of the Supreme Court, and all other officers of the Confederate States whose appointments are not herein otherwise provided for, and which shall be established by law; but the Congress may, by law, vest the appointment of such inferior officers, as they think proper, in the President alone, in the courts of law, or in the heads of departments.

(3) The principal officer in each of the Executive Departments, and all persons connected with the diplomatic service, may be removed from office at the pleasure of the President. All other civil officers of the Executive Departments may be removed at any time by the President, or other appointing power, when their services are unnecessary, or for dishonesty, incapacity. inefficiency, misconduct, or neglect of duty; and when so removed, the removal shall be reported to the Senate, together with the reasons therefor.

(4) The President shall have power to fill all vacancies that may happen during the recess of the Senate, by granting commissions which shall expire at the end of their next session; but no person rejected by the Senate shall be reappointed to the same office during their ensuing recess.

Sec. 3. (1) The President shall, from time to time, give to the Congress information of the state of the Confederacy, and recommend to their consideration such measures as he shall judge necessary and expedient; he

may, on extraordinary occasions, convene both Houses, or either of them; and in case of disagreement between them, with respect to the time of adjournment, he may adjourn them to such time as he shall think proper; he shall receive ambassadors and other public ministers; he shall take care that the laws be faithfully executed, and shall commission all the officers of the Confederate States.

Sec. 4. (1) The President, Vice President, and all civil officers of the Confederate States, shall be removed from office on impeachment for and conviction of treason, bribery, or other high crimes and misdemeanors.

ARTICLE III

Section 1. (1) The judicial power of the Confederate States shall be vested in one Supreme Court, and in such inferior courts as the Congress may, from time to time, ordain and establish. The judges, both of the Supreme and inferior courts, shall hold their offices during good behavior, and shall, at stated times, receive for their services a compensation which shall not be diminished during their continuance in office.

Sec. 2. (1) The judicial power shall extend to all cases arising under this Constitution, the laws of the Confederate States, and treaties made, or which shall be made, under their authority; to all cases affecting ambassadors, other public ministers and consuls; to all cases of admiralty and maritime jurisdiction; to controversies to which the Confederate States shall be a party; to controversies between two or more States; between a State and citizens of another State, where the State is plaintiff; between citizens claiming lands under grants of different States; and between a State or the citizens thereof, and foreign states, citizens, or subjects; but no State shall be sued by a citizen or subject of any foreign state.

(2) In all cases affecting ambassadors, other public ministers and consuls, and those in which a State shall be a party, the Supreme Court shall have original jurisdiction. In all the other cases before mentioned, the Supreme Court shall have appellate jurisdiction both as to law and fact, with such exceptions and under such regulations as the Congress shall make.

(3) The trial of all crimes, except in cases of impeachment, shall be by jury, and such trial shall be held in the State where the said crimes shall have been committed; but when not committed within any State, the trial shall be at such place or places as the Congress may by law have directed.

Sec. 3. (1) Treason against the Confederate States

shall consist only in levying war against them, or in adhering to their enemies, giving them aid and comfort. No person shall be convicted of treason unless on the testimony of two witnesses to the same overt act, or on confession in open court.

(2) The Congress shall have power to declare the punishment of treason; but no attainder of treason shall work corruption of blood, or forfeiture, except during the life of the person attainted.

ARTICLE IV

Section 1. (1) Full faith and credit shall be given in each State to the public acts, records, and judicial proceedings of every other State; and the Congress may, by general laws, prescribe the manner in which such acts, records, and proceedings shall be proved, and the effect thereof.

Sec. 2. (1) The citizens of each State shall be entitled to all the privileges and immunities of citizens in the several States; and shall have the right of transit and sojourn in any State of this Confederacy, with their slaves and other property; and the right of property in said slaves shall not be thereby impaired.

(2) A person charged in any State with treason, felony, or other crime against the laws of such State, who shall flee from justice, and be found in another State, shall, on demand of the executive authority of the State from which he fled, be delivered up, to be removed to the State having jurisdiction of the crime.

(3) No slave or other person held to service or labor in any State or Territory of the Confederate States, under the laws thereof, escaping or lawfully carried into another, shall, in consequence of any law or regulation therein, be discharged from such service or labor; but he shall be delivered up on claim of the party to whom such service or labor may be due.

Sec. 3. (1) Other States may be admitted into this Confederacy by a vote of two-thirds of the whole House of Representatives and two-thirds of the Senate, the Senate voting by States; but no new State shall be formed or erected within the jurisdiction of any other State, nor any State be formed by the junction of two or more States, or parts of States, without the consent of the Legislatures of the States concerned, as well as of the Congress.

(2) The Congress shall have power to dispose of and make all needful rules and regulations concerning the property of the Confederate States, including the lands thereof.

(3) The Confederate States may acquire new territory; and Congress shall have power to legislate and provide governments for the inhabitants of all territory belonging to the Confederate States, lying without the limits of the several States; and may permit them, at such times, and in such manner as it may by law provide, to form States to be admitted into the Confederacy. In all such territory the institution of negro slavery, as it now exists in the Confederate States, shall be recognized and protected by Congress and by the Territorial government; and the inhabitants of the several Confederate States and Territories shall have the right to take to such Territory any slaves lawfully held by them in any of the States or Territories of the Confederate States.

(4) The Confederate States shall guarantee to every State that now is, or hereafter may become, a member of this Confederacy, a republican form of government; and shall protect each of them against invasion; and on application of the Legislature (or of the Executive when the Legislature is not in session,) against domestic violence.

ARTICLE V

Section 1. (1) Upon the demand of any three States, legally assembled in their several conventions, the Congress shall summon a convention of all the States, to take into consideration such amendments to the Constitution as the said States shall concur in suggesting at the time when the said demand is made; and should any of the proposed amendments to the Constitution be agreed on by the said convention, voting by States, and the same be ratified by the Legislatures of two-thirds of the several States, or by conventions in two-thirds thereof, as the one or the other mode of ratification may be proposed by the general convention, they shall thenceforward form a part of this Constitution. But no State shall, without its consent, be deprived of its equal representation in the Senate.

ARTICLE VI

1. The Government established by this Constitution is the successor of the Provisional Government of the Confederate States of America, and all the laws passed by the latter shall continue in force until the same shall be repealed or modified; and all the officers appointed by the same shall remain in office until their successors are appointed and qualified, or the offices abolished.

2. All debts contracted and engagements entered into before the adoption of this Constitution shall be as

valid against the Confederate States under this Constitution, as under the Provisional Government.

3. This Constitution, and the laws of the Confederate States made in pursuance thereof, and all treaties made, or which shall be made, under the authority of the Confederate States, shall be the supreme law of the land; and the judges in every State shall be bound thereby, anything in the constitution or laws of any State to the contrary notwithstanding.

4. The Senators and Representatives before mentioned, and the members of the several State Legislatures, and all executive and judicial officers, both of the Confederate States and of the several States, shall be bound by oath or affirmation to support this Constitution; but no religious test shall ever be required as a qualification to any office or public trust under the Confederate States.

5. The enumeration, in the Constitution, of certain rights shall not be construed to deny or disparage others retained by the people of the several States.

6. The powers not delegated to the Confederate States by the Constitution, nor prohibited by it to the States, are reserved to the States, respectively, or to the people thereof.

ARTICLE VII

1. The ratification of the conventions of five States shall be sufficient for the establishment of this Constitution between the States so ratifying the same.

2. When five States shall have ratified this Constitution, in the manner before specified, the Congress under the Provisional Constitution shall prescribe the time for holding the election of President and Vice President; and for the meeting of the Electoral College; and for counting the votes, and inaugurating the President. They shall, also, prescribe the time for holding the first election of members of Congress under this Constitution, and the time for assembling the same. Until the assembling of such Congress, the Congress under the Provisional Constitution shall continue to exercise the legislative powers granted them; not extending beyond the time limited by the Constitution of the Provisional Government.

Adopted unanimously by the Congress of the Confederate States of South Carolina, Georgia, Florida, Alabama, Mississippi, Louisiana, and Texas, sitting in convention at the capitol, the city of Montgomery, Ala., on the eleventh day of March, in the year eighteen hundred and Sixty-one.

10

Abraham Lincoln, Message to Congress in Special Session

July 4, 1861*

Fellow Citizens of the Senate and House of Representatives:

Having been convened on an extraordinary occasion, as authorized by the Constitution, your attention is not called to any ordinary subject of legislation.

At the beginning of the present presidential term, four months ago, the functions of the Federal government were found to be generally suspended within the several states of South Carolina, Georgia, Alabama, Mississippi, Louisiana, and Florida, excepting only those of the Post Office Department.

Within these states all the Forts, arsenals, dockyards, customhouses, and the like, including the movable and stationary property in and about them, had been seized and were held in open hostility to this government, excepting only Forts Pickens, Taylor, and Jefferson, on and near the Florida coast, and Fort Sumter, in Charleston Harbor, South Carolina. The Forts thus seized had been put in improved condition, new ones had been built, and armed forces had been organized and were organizing, all avowedly with the same hostile purpose.

The Forts remaining in the possession of the Federal government in and near those states were either besieged or menaced by warlike preparations, and especially Fort Sumter was nearly surrounded by well-protected hostile batteries, with guns equal in quality to the best of its own and outnumbering the latter as perhaps ten to one.

. . .

As had been intended in this contingency, it was also resolved to notify the governor of South Carolina that he might expect an attempt would be made to provision the Fort, and that if the attempt should not be resisted there would be no effort to throw in men, arms, or ammunition without further notice, or in case of an attack upon the Fort. This notice was accordingly given, whereupon the fort was attacked and bombarded to its

---

*Lincoln, *Speeches and Writings*, 2:246–61.

fall, without even awaiting the arrival of the provisioning expedition.

It is thus seen that the assault upon and reduction of Fort Sumter was in no sense a matter of self-defense on the part of the assailants. They well knew that the garrison in the fort could by no possibility commit aggression upon them. They knew—they were expressly notified—that the giving of bread to the few brave and hungry men of the garrison was all which would on that occasion be attempted, unless themselves, by resisting so much, should provoke more. They knew that this government desired to keep the garrison in the fort, not to assail them but merely to maintain visible possession, and thus to preserve the Union from actual and immediate dissolution, trusting, as hereinbefore stated, to time, discussion, and the ballot box for final adjustment; and they assailed and reduced the fort for precisely the reverse object—to drive out the visible authority of the Federal Union, and thus force it to immediate dissolution.

That this was their object the executive well understood; and having said to them in the inaugural address, "You can have no conflict without being yourselves the aggressors," he took pains not only to keep this declaration good but also to keep the case so free from the power of ingenious sophistry as that the world should not be able to misunderstand it. By the affair at Fort Sumter, with its surrounding circumstances, that point was reached. Then and thereby the assailants of the government began the conflict of arms, without a gun in sight or in expectancy to return their fire, save only the few in the fort, sent to that harbor years before for their own protection, and still ready to give the protection in whatever was lawful. In this act, discarding all else, they have forced upon the country the distinct issue: "Immediate dissolution or blood."

And this issue embraces more than the fate of the United States. It presents to the whole family of man the question whether a constitutional republic, or democracy—a government of the people by the same people—can or cannot maintain its territorial integrity against its own domestic foes. It presents the question whether discontented individuals, too few in numbers to control administration according to organic law in any case, can always, upon the pretenses made in this case, or on any other pretenses, or arbitrarily without any pretense, break up their government and thus practically put an end to free government upon the earth. It forces us to ask—Is there in all republics this inherent

and fatal weakness? Must a government of necessity be too strong for the liberties of its own people, or too weak to maintain its own existence?

So viewing the issue, no choice was left but to call out the war power of the government and so to resist force employed for its destruction by force for its preservation.

. . .

It might seem at first thought to be of little difference whether the present movement at the South be called "secession" or "rebellion." The movers, however, well understand the difference. At the beginning they knew they could never raise their treason to any respectable magnitude by any name which implies *violation* of law. They knew their people possessed as much of moral sense, as much of devotion to law and order, and as much pride in and reverence for the history and government of their common country as any other civilized and patriotic people. They knew they could make no advancement directly in the teeth of these strong and noble sentiments. Accordingly, they commenced by an insidious debauching of the public mind. They invented an ingenious sophism, which, if conceded, was followed by perfectly logical steps through all the incidents to the complete destruction of the Union. The sophism itself is that any state of the Union may *consistently* with the national Constitution, and therefore *lawfully* and *peacefully*, withdraw from the Union without the consent of the Union or of any other state. The little disguise that the supposed right is to be exercised only for just cause, themselves to be the sole judge of its justice, is too thin to merit any notice.

With rebellion thus sugarcoated, they have been drugging the public mind of their section for more than thirty years, and until at length they have brought many good men to a willingness to take up arms against the government the day after some assemblage of men have enacted the farcical pretense of taking their state out of the Union who could have been brought to no such thing the day *before*.

This sophism derives much, perhaps the whole, of its currency from the assumption that there is some omnipotent and sacred supremacy pertaining to a *State*—to each State of our Federal Union. Our states have neither more nor less power than that reserved to them in the Union by the Constitution, no one of them ever having been a State *out* of the Union. The original ones passed into the Union even *before* they cast off their British colonial dependence, and the new ones each came into the Union directly from a condition of dependence, excepting Texas; and even Texas, in its temporary independence, was never designated a State. The new ones only took the designation of States on coming into the Union, while that name was first adopted for the old ones in and by the Declaration of Independence. Therein the "United Colonies" were declared to be "Free and Independent States"; but even then the object plainly was not to declare their independence of *one another* or of the *Union*, but directly the contrary, as their mutual pledge and their mutual action before, at the time, and afterward abundantly show.

The express plighting of faith by each and all of the original thirteen in the Articles of Confederation, two years later, that the Union shall be perpetual is most conclusive. Having never been States, either in substance or in name, *outside* of the Union, whence this magical omnipotence of "State rights," asserting a claim of power to lawfully destroy the Union itself? Much is said about the "sovereignty" of the States, but the word even is not in the national Constitution, nor, as is believed, in any of the State constitutions. What is a "sovereignty" in the political sense of the term? Would it be far wrong to define it "a political community without a political superior"? Tested by this, no one of our States, except Texas, ever was a sovereignty; and even Texas gave up the character on coming into the Union, by which act she acknowledged the Constitution of the United States and the laws and treaties of the United States made in pursuance of the Constitution to be for her the supreme law of the land. The States have their *status* IN the Union, and they have no other *legal status*. If they break from this, they can only do so against law and by revolution. The Union, and not themselves separately, procured their independence and their liberty. By conquest or purchase the Union gave each of them whatever of independence and liberty it has. The Union is older than any of the States, and, in fact, it created them as States. Originally some dependent colonies made the Union, and in turn the Union threw off their old dependence for them and made them States, such as they are. Not one of them ever had a State constitution independent of the Union. Of course it is not forgotten that all the new States framed their constitutions before they entered the Union, nevertheless dependent upon and preparatory to coming into the Union.

Unquestionably the States have the powers and rights reserved to them in and by the national Constitution; but among these surely are not included all conceivable powers, however mischievous or destructive, but at most such only as were known in the world at the time as governmental powers; and certainly a power to destroy the government itself had never been known as a governmental—as a merely administrative—power. This relative matter of national power and State rights, as a principle, is no other than the principle of *generality* and *locality*. Whatever concerns the whole should be confided to the whole—to the general government—while whatever concerns only the state should be left exclusively to the State. This is all there is of original principle about it. Whether the national Constitution in defining boundaries between the two has applied the principle with exact accuracy is not to be questioned. We are all bound by that defining without question.

What is now combated is the position that secession is consistent with the Constitution—is *lawful* and *peaceful*. It is not contended that there is any express law for it, and nothing should ever be implied as law which leads to unjust or absurd consequences.

. . .

The seceders insist that our Constitution admits of secession. They have assumed to make a national constitution of their own, in which of necessity they have either *discarded* or *retained* the right of secession, as they insist it exists in ours. If they have discarded it, they thereby admit that on principle it ought not to be in ours. If they have retained it, by their own construction of ours they show that to be consistent they must secede from one another whenever they shall find it the easiest way of settling their debts or effecting any other selfish or unjust object. The principle itself is one of disintegration and upon which no government can possibly endure.

If all the States save one should assert the power to drive that one out of the Union, it is presumed the whole class of seceder politicians would at once deny the power and denounce the act as the greatest outrage upon State rights. But suppose that precisely the same act, instead of being called "driving the one out," should be called "the seceding of the others from that one," it would be exactly what the seceders claim to do, unless, indeed, they make the point that the one, because it is a minority, may rightfully do what the others, because they are a majority, may not rightfully do. These politicians are subtle and profound on the rights of minorities. They are not partial to that power which made the Constitution and speaks from the Preamble, calling itself "We, the people."

It may well be questioned whether there is today a majority of the legally qualified voters of any State, except, perhaps, South Carolina, in favor of disunion. There is much reason to believe that the Union men are the majority in many, if not in every other one, of the so-called seceded States. The contrary has not been demonstrated in any one of them. It is ventured to affirm this even of Virginia and Tennessee; for the result of an election held in military camps, where the bayonets are all on one side of the question voted upon, can scarcely be considered as demonstrating popular sentiment. At such an election all that large class who are at once *for* the Union and *against* coercion would be coerced to vote against the Union.

…

This is essentially a People's contest. On the side of the Union it is a struggle for maintaining in the world that form and substance of government whose leading object is to elevate the condition of men; to lift artificial weights from all shoulders; to clear the paths of laudable pursuit for all; to afford all an unfettered start and a fair chance in the race of life. Yielding to partial and temporary departures, from necessity, this is the leading object of the government for whose existence we contend.

…

Our popular government has often been called an experiment. Two points in it our people have already settled—the successful *establishing* and the successful *administering* of it. One still remains: its successful *maintenance* against a formidable internal attempt to overthrow it. It is now for them to demonstrate to the world that those who can fairly carry an election can also suppress a rebellion; that ballots are the rightful and peaceful successors of bullets, and that when ballots have fairly and constitutionally decided, there can be no successful appeal back to bullets; that there can be no successful appeal except to ballots themselves at succeeding elections. Such will be a great lesson of peace, teaching men that what they cannot take by an election neither can they take it by a war; teaching all the folly of being the beginners of a war.

Lest there be some uneasiness in the minds of candid men as to what is to be the course of the government, toward the Southern States, *after* the rebellion shall have been suppressed, the Executive deems it proper to say it will be his purpose then, as ever, to be guided by the Constitution and the laws, and that he probably will have no different understanding of the powers and duties of the Federal government relatively to the rights of the States and the people under the Constitution than that expressed in the inaugural address.

He desires to preserve the government, that it may be administered for all as it was administered by the men who made it. Loyal citizens everywhere have the right to claim this of their government, and the government has no right to withhold or neglect it. It is not perceived that in giving it there is any coercion, any conquest, or any subjugation in any just sense of those terms.

The Constitution provides, and all the States have accepted the provision, that "the United States shall guarantee to every State in this Union a republican form of government." But if a State may lawfully go out of the Union, having done so it may also discard the republican form of government, so that to prevent its going out is an indispensable means to the end of maintaining the guaranty mentioned; and when an end is lawful and obligatory, the indispensable means to it are also lawful and obligatory.

It was with the deepest regret that the executive found the duty of employing the war power in defense of the government forced upon him. He could but perform this duty or surrender the existence of the government. No compromise by public servants could in this case be a cure; not that compromises are not often proper, but that no popular government can long survive a marked precedent that those who carry an election can only save the government from immediate destruction by giving up the main point upon which the people gave the election. The people themselves, and not their servants, can safely reverse their own deliberate decisions. As a private citizen the executive could not have consented that these institutions shall perish; much less could he in betrayal of so vast and so sacred a trust as these free people had confided to him. He felt that he had no moral right to shrink, not even to count the chances of his own life, in what might follow. In full view of his great responsibility he has so far done what he has deemed his duty. You will now, according to your own judgment, perform yours. He sincerely hopes that your views and your action may so accord with his as to assure all faithful citizens who have been disturbed in their rights of a certain and speedy restoration to them under the Constitution and the laws.

And having thus chosen our course, without guile and with pure purpose, let us renew our trust in God and go forward without fear and with manly hearts.

July 4, 1861.

11

District of Columbia, Compensated Emancipation Act

12 Stat. 376, April 16, 1862[*]

AN ACT FOR THE RELEASE OF CERTAIN
PERSONS HELD TO SERVICE OR LABOR
IN THE DISTRICT OF COLUMBIA

Be it enacted by the Senate and House of Representatives of the United States of America in Congress assembled, That all persons held to service or labor within the District of Columbia by reason of African descent are hereby discharged and freed of and from all claim to such service or labor; and from and after the passage of this act neither slavery nor involuntary servitude, except for crime, whereof the party shall be duly convicted, shall hereafter exist in said District.

Sec. 2. *And be it further enacted*, That all persons loyal to the United States, holding claims to service or labor against persons discharged therefrom by this act, may, within ninety days from the passage thereof, but not thereafter, present to the commissioners hereinafter mentioned their respective statements or petitions in writing, verified by oath or affirmation, setting forth the names, ages, and personal description of such persons, the manner in which said petitioners acquired such claim, and any facts touching the value thereof, and declaring his allegiance to the Government of the United States, and that he has not borne arms against the United States during the present rebellion, nor in any way given aid or comfort thereto: *Provided*, That the oath of the party to the petition shall not be evidence of the facts therein stated.

Sec. 3. *And be it further enacted*, That the President of the United States, with the advice and consent of the Senate, shall appoint three commissioners, residents of the District of Columbia, any two of whom shall have power to act, who shall receive the petitions above mentioned, and who shall investigate and determine the validity and value of the claims therein presented, as aforesaid, and appraise and apportion, under the proviso hereto annexed, the value in money of the several claims by them found to be valid: *Provided, however*,

[*] Sanger, *Statutes at Large*, 12:376.

That the entire sum so appraised and apportioned shall not exceed in the aggregate an amount equal to three hundred dollars for each person shown to have been so held by lawful claim: *And provided, further*, That no claim shall be allowed for any slave or slaves brought into said District after the passage of this act, nor for any slave claimed by any person who has borne arms against the Government of the United States in the present rebellion, or in any way given aid or comfort thereto, or which originates in or by virtue of any transfer heretofore made, or which shall hereafter be made by any person who has in any manner aided or sustained the rebellion against the Government of the United States.

Sec. 4. *And be it further enacted*, That said commissioners shall, within nine months from the passage of this act, make a full and final report of their proceedings, findings, and appraisement, and shall deliver the same to the Secretary of the Treasury, which report shall be deemed and taken to be conclusive in all respects, except as hereinafter provided; and the Secretary of the Treasury shall, with like exception, cause the amounts so apportioned to said claims to be paid from the Treasury of the United States to the parties found by said report to be entitled thereto as aforesaid, and the same shall be received in full and complete compensation: *Provided*, That in cases where petitions may be filed presenting conflicting claims, or setting up liens, said commissioners shall so specify in said report, and payment shall not be made according to the award of said commissioners until a period of sixty days shall have elapsed, during which time any petitioner claiming an interest in the particular amount may file a bill in equity in the Circuit Court of the District of Columbia, making all other claimants defendants thereto, setting forth the proceedings in such case before said commissioners and their actions therein, and praying that the party to whom payment has been awarded may be enjoined from receiving the same; and if said court shall grant such provisional order, a copy thereof may, on motion of said complainant, be served upon the Secretary of the Treasury, who shall thereupon cause the said amount of money to be paid into said court, subject to its orders and final decree, which payment shall be in full and complete compensation, as in other cases.

Sec. 5. *And be it further enacted*, That said commissioners shall hold their sessions in the city of Washington, at such place and times as the President of the United States may direct, of which they shall give due and public notice. They shall have power to subpoena and compel the attendance of witnesses, and to receive testimony and enforce its production, as in civil cases before courts of justice, without the exclusion of any witness on account of color; and they may summon before them the persons making claim to service or labor, and examine them under oath; and they may also, for purposes of identification and appraisement, call before them the persons so claimed. Said commissioners shall appoint a clerk, who shall keep files and [a] complete record of all proceedings before them, who shall have power to administer oaths and affirmations in said proceedings, and who shall issue all lawful process by them ordered. The Marshal of the District of Columbia shall personally, or by deputy, attend upon the sessions of said commissioners, and shall execute the process issued by said clerk.

Sec. 6. *And be it further enacted*, That said commissioners shall receive in compensation for their services the sum of two thousand dollars each, to be paid upon the filing of their report; that said clerk shall receive for his services the sum of two hundred dollars per month; that said marshal shall receive such fees as are allowed by law for similar services performed by him in the Circuit Court of the District of Columbia; that the Secretary of the Treasury shall cause all other reasonable expenses of said commission to be audited and allowed, and that said compensation, fees, and expenses shall be paid from the Treasury of the United States.

Sec. 7. *And be it further enacted*, That for the purpose of carrying this act into effect there is hereby appropriated, out of any money in the Treasury not otherwise appropriated, a sum not exceeding one million of dollars.

Sec. 8. *And be it further enacted*, That any person or persons who shall kidnap, or in any manner transport or procure to be taken out of said District, any person or persons discharged and freed by the provisions of this act, or any free person or persons with intent to re-enslave or sell such person or person into slavery, or shall re-enslave any of said freed persons, the person or persons so offending shall be deemed guilty of a felony, and on conviction thereof in any court of competent jurisdiction in said District, shall be imprisoned in the penitentiary not less than five nor more than twenty years.

Sec. 9. *And be it further enacted*, That within twenty days, or within such further time as the commissioners herein provided for shall limit, after the passage of this act, a statement in writing or schedule shall be filed with the clerk of the Circuit court for the District of Colum-bia, by the several owners or claimants to the services of the persons made free or manumitted by this act, setting forth the names, ages, sex, and particular description of such persons, severally; and the said clerk shall receive and record, in a book by him to be provided and kept for that purpose, the said statements or schedules on receiving fifty cents each therefor, and no claim shall be allowed to any claimant or owner who shall neglect this requirement.

Sec. 10. *And be it further enacted*, That the said clerk and his successors in office shall, from time to time, on demand, and on receiving twenty-five cents therefor, prepare, sign, and deliver to each person made free or manumitted by this act, a certificate under the seal of said court, setting out the name, age, and description of such person, and stating that such person was duly manumitted and set free by this act.

Sec. 11. *And be it further enacted*, That the sum of one hundred thousand dollars, out of any money in the Treasury not otherwise appropriated, is hereby appropriated, to be expended under the direction of the President of the United States, to aid in the colonization and settlement of such free persons of African descent now residing in said District, including those to be liberated by this act, as may desire to emigrate to the Republics of Hayti or Liberia, or such other country beyond the limits of the United States as the President may determine: *Provided*, The expenditure for this purpose shall not exceed one hundred dollars for each emigrant.

Sec. 12. *And be it further enacted*, That all acts of Congress and all laws of the State of Maryland in force in said District, and all ordinances of the cities of Washington and Georgetown, inconsistent with the provisions of this act, are hereby repealed.

Approved, April 16, 1862.

12

Abraham Lincoln to Horace Greeley
August 22, 1862[*]

Dear Sir

I have just read yours of the 19th, addressed to myself through the New-York Tribune. If there be in it any

[*] Lincoln, *Speeches and Writings*, 2:357–58.

statements, or assumptions of fact, which I may know to be erroneous, I do not, now and here, controvert them. If there be in it any inferences which I may believe to be falsely drawn, I do not now and here, argue against them. If there be perceptable in it an impatient and dictatorial tone, I waive it in deference to an old friend, whose heart I have always supposed to be right.

As to the policy I "seem to be pursuing" as you say, I have not meant to leave any one in doubt.

I would save the Union. I would save it the shortest way under the Constitution. The sooner the national authority can be restored; the nearer the Union will be "the Union as it was." If there be those who would not save the Union unless they could at the same time *save* slavery, I do not agree with them. If there be those who would not save the Union unless they could at the same time *destroy* slavery, I do not agree with them. My paramount object in this struggle *is* to save the Union, and is *not* either to save or destroy slavery. If I could save the Union without freeing *any* slave, I would do it, and if I could save it by freeing *all* the slaves, I would do it; and if I could save it by freeing some and leaving others alone, I would also do that. What I do about slavery and the colored race, I do because I believe it helps to save the Union, and what I forbear, I forbear because I do *not* believe it would help to save the Union. I shall do *less* whenever I shall believe what I am doing hurts the cause, and I shall do *more* whenever I shall believe doing more will help the cause. I shall try to correct errors when shown to be errors; and I shall adopt new views so fast as they shall appear to be true views.

I have here stated my purpose according to my view of *official* duty, and I intend no modification of my oft-expressed *personal* wish that all men, every where, could be free.

Yours,

A. LINCOLN.

13

Attorney General Edward Bates, on Citizenship

November 29, 1862*

Who is a citizen? What constitutes a citizen of the United States? I have often been pained by the fruitless search in our law books and the records of our courts for a clear and satisfactory definition of the phrase citizen of the United States. I find no such definition, no authoritative establishment of the meaning of the phrase, neither by a course of judicial decision in our courts nor by the continued and consentaneous action of the different branches of our political government. For aught I see to the contrary, the subject is now as little understood in its details and elements, and the question as open to argument and to speculative criticism, as it was at the beginning of the government. Eighty years of practical enjoyment of citizenship, under the Constitution, have not sufficed to teach us either the exact meaning of the word or the constituent elements of the thing we prize so highly.

In most instances, within my knowledge, in which the matter of citizenship has been discussed, the argument has not turned upon the existence and intrinsic qualities of citizenship itself, but upon the claim of some right or privilege as belonging to and inhering in the character of citizen. In this way, we are easily led into errors of fact and principle. We see individuals, who are known to be citizens, in the actual enjoyment of certain rights and privileges, and in the exercise of certain powers, social and political, and we, inconsiderately, and without any regard to legal and logical consequences, attribute to those individuals, and to all of their class, the enjoyment of those powers as incidents to their citizenship, and belonging to them only in their quality of citizens.

In such cases it often happens that the rights enjoyed and the powers exercised have no relation whatever to

---

*Edward Bates, *On Citizenship* (Washington, DC: Government Printing Office, 1862). [Excerpt from a letter to Secretary of the Treasury S. P. Chase, in response to Chase's letter soliciting Bates's opinion on whether colored men can be citizens of the United States. —Ed.]

the quality of citizen, and might be as perfectly enjoyed and exercised by known aliens.

...

[W]ith regard to the right of suffrage, that is, the right to choose officers of the government, there is a very common error to the effect that the right to vote for public officers is one of the constituent elements of American citizenship, the leading faculty indeed of the citizen, the test at once of his legal right, and the sufficient proof of his membership in the body politic. No error can be greater than this, and few more injurious to the right understanding of our constitutions and the actual working of our political governments. It is not only not true in law or fact, in principle or in practice, but the reverse is conspicuously true; for I make bold to affirm that, viewing the nation as a whole, or viewing States separately, there is no district in the nation in which a majority of the known and recognized citizens are not excluded by law from the right of suffrage. Besides those who are excluded specially on account of some personal defect, such as paupers, idiots, lunatics and men convicted of infamous crimes, and, in some States, soldiers, all females and all minor males are also excluded; and yet, I think no one will venture to deny that women and children, and lunatics, and even convict felons, may be citizens of the United States.

...

The Constitution of the United States does not declare who are and who are not citizens, nor does it attempt to describe the constituent elements of citizenship. It leaves that quality where it found it, resting upon the fact of home-birth, and upon the laws of the several States.

...

From all this it is manifest that American citizenship does not necessarily depend upon nor coexist with the legal capacity to hold office and the right of suffrage, either or both of them. The Constitution of the United States, as I have said, does not define citizenship; neither does it declare who may vote, nor who may hold office, except in regard to a few of the highest national functionaries. And the several States, as far as I know, in exercising that power act independently and without any controlling authority over them, and hence it follows that there is no limit to their power in that particular but their own prudence and discretion; and therefore we are not surprised to find that these faculties of voting and holding office are not uniform in the different States, but are made to depend upon a variety of factors, purely discretionary, such as age, sex, race, color,

property, residence in a particular place, and length of residence there.

...

I am aware that some of our most learned lawyers and able writers have allowed themselves to speak upon this subject in loose and indeterminate language. They speak of "all the rights, privileges, and immunities guaranteed by the Constitution to the citizen" without telling us what they are. They speak of a man's citizenship as defective and imperfect, because he is supposed not to have "all the civil rights," (all the *jura civitatis*, as expressed by one of my predecessors,) without telling what particular rights they are nor what relation they have, if any, with citizenship. And they suggest, without affirming, that there may be different grades of citizenship of higher or lower degree in point of legal virtue and efficacy; one grade "in the sense of the Constitution," and another inferior grade made by a State and not recognized by the Constitution.

In my opinion the Constitution uses the word citizen only to express the political quality of the individual in his relations to the nation; to declare that he is a member of the body politic, and bound to it by the reciprocal obligation of allegiance on the one side and protection on the other. And I have no knowledge of any other kind of political citizenship, higher or lower, statal or national; or of any other sense in which the word has been used in the Constitution, or can be used properly in the laws of the United States.

...

We have *natural born* citizens (Constitution, article 2, 5,) not made by law or otherwise, but *born*. And this class is the large majority; in fact, the mass of our citizens; for all others are exceptions specially provided for by law. And they became citizens in the natural way, *by birth*, so they remain citizens during their natural lives, unless, by virtue of their own voluntary act, they expatriate themselves and become citizens or subjects of another nation. For we have no law (as the French have) to *decitizenize* a citizen, who has become such either by natural process of birth, or by the legal process of adoption. And in this connection the Constitution says not one word, and furnishes not one hint, in relation to the color or to the ancestral race of the "natural born citizen." Whatever may have been said, in the opinion of lawyers and judges, and in State statutes, about negroes, mulattoes, and persons of color, the Constitution is wholly silent upon that subject. The Constitution itself does not make the citizens, (it is, in fact, made by them.) It only intends and recognizes such of them as are natural—home-born—and provides for the naturalization of such of them as were alien—foreign-born—making the latter, as far as nature will allow, like the former.

And I am not aware of any provision in our laws to warrant us in presuming the existence in this country, of a class of persons intermediate between citizens and aliens. In England there is such a class, clearly defined by law, and called *denizens.*

. . .

If this be a true principle, and I do not doubt it, it follows that every person born in the country is, at the moment of their birth, *prima facia* a citizen; and he who would deny it must take upon himself the burden of proving some great disenfranchisement strong enough to override the *"natural born"* right as recognized by the Constitution in terms of the most simple and comprehensive, and without any reference to race or color, or any other accidental circumstances.

. . .

2. *Color.*—It is strenuously insisted by some that 'persons of color,' though born in the country, are not capable of being citizens of the United States. As far as the Constitution is concerned, this is a naked assumption; for the Constitution contains not one word upon the subject. The exclusion, if it exists, must then rest upon some fundamental fact which, in the reason and nature of things, is so inconsistent with citizenship that the two cannot coexist in the same person. Is mere *color* such a fact? Let those who assert it prove that it is so. It has never been so understood nor put into practice in the nation from which we derive our language, laws, and institutions, and our very morals and modes of thought; and, as far as I know, there is not a single nation in Christendom which does not regard the new-found idea with incredulity, if not disgust. What can there be in the mere color of a man (we are speaking now not of *race*, but of *color* only) to disqualify him for bearing true and faithful allegiance to his native country, and for demanding the protection of that country? And these two, allegiance and protection, constitute the sum of the duties and rights of a "natural born citizen of the United States."

. . .

As to the objection (not in law, but sentiment only) that if a negro can be a citizen of the United States, he might, possibly, become President, the legal inference is true. There would be such a legal possibility. But those who make such that objection are not arguing upon the Constitution as it is, but upon what, in their own minds and feelings, they think ought to be.

. . .

Finally, the celebrated case of Scott *vs.* Sandford, 19 Howard's Reports, 393, is sometimes cited as a direct authority against the capacity of free persons of color to be citizens of the United States. That is an entire mistake. The case, as it stands of record, does not determine, nor purport to determine, that question.

. . .

In this argument I raise no question upon the legal validity of the judgement in Scott *vs.* Sandford. I only insist that the judgement in that case is limited in law, as it is, in fact, limited on the face of the record, to the plea in abatement; and, consequently, that whatever was said in the long course of the case, as reported, (240 pages,) respecting the legal merits of the case, and respecting any supposed legal disability resulting from the mere fact of color, though entitled to all the respect which is due to the learned and upright sources from which the opinions come, was *"dehors the record,"* and of no authority as a judicial decision.

. . .

And now, upon the whole matter, I give it as my opinion that the *free man of color*, mentioned in your letter, if born in the United States, is a citizen of the United States, and, if otherwise qualified, is competent, according to the acts of Congress, to be master of a vessel engaged in the coasting trade.

All of which is respectfully submitted by your obedient servant,

EDWARD BATES
Attorney General.

14

Abraham Lincoln, Emancipation Proclamation

January 1, 1863*

Whereas, on the twenty-second day of September, in the year of our Lord one thousand eight hundred and sixty-two, a proclamation was issued by the President of

* Lincoln, *Speeches and Writings*, 2:424–25.

the United States, containing, among other things, the following, to wit:

"That on the first day of January, in the year of our Lord one thousand eight hundred and sixty-three, all persons held as slaves within any State or designated part of a State, the people whereof shall then be in rebellion against the United States, shall be then, thenceforward, and forever free; and the Executive Government of the United States, including the military and naval authority thereof, will recognize and maintain the freedom of such persons, and will do no act or acts to repress such persons, or any of them, in any efforts they may make for their actual freedom.

"That the Executive will, on the first day of January aforesaid, by proclamation, designate the States and parts of States, if any, in which the people thereof, respectively, shall then be in rebellion against the United States; and the fact that any State, or the people thereof, shall on that day be, in good faith, represented in the Congress of the United States by members chosen thereto at elections wherein a majority of the qualified voters of such State shall have participated, shall, in the absence of strong countervailing testimony, be deemed conclusive evidence that such State, and the people thereof, are not then in rebellion against the United States."

Now, therefore I, Abraham Lincoln, President of the United States, by virtue of the power in me vested as Commander-in-Chief, of the Army and Navy of the United States in time of actual armed rebellion against the authority and government of the United States, and as a fit and necessary war measure for suppressing said rebellion, do, on this first day of January, in the year of our Lord one thousand eight hundred and sixty-three, and in accordance with my purpose so to do publicly proclaimed for the full period of one hundred days, from the day first above mentioned, order and designate as the States and parts of States wherein the people thereof respectively, are this day in rebellion against the United States, the following, to wit:

Arkansas, Texas, Louisiana, (except the Parishes of St. Bernard, Plaquemines, Jefferson, St. John, St. Charles, St. James Ascension, Assumption, Terrebonne, Lafourche, St. Mary, St. Martin, and Orleans, including the City of New Orleans) Mississippi, Alabama, Florida, Georgia, South Carolina, North Carolina, and Virginia,

(except the forty-eight counties designated as West Virginia, and also the counties of Berkley, Accomac, Northampton, Elizabeth City, York, Princess Ann, and Norfolk, including the cities of Norfolk and Portsmouth), and which excepted parts, are for the present, left precisely as if this proclamation were not issued.

And by virtue of the power, and for the purpose aforesaid, I do order and declare that all persons held as slaves within said designated States, and parts of States, are, and henceforward shall be free; and that the Executive government of the United States, including the military and naval authorities thereof, will recognize and maintain the freedom of said persons.

And I hereby enjoin upon the people so declared to be free to abstain from all violence, unless in necessary self-defence; and I recommend to them that, in all cases when allowed, they labor faithfully for reasonable wages.

And I further declare and make known, that such persons of suitable condition, will be received into the armed service of the United States to garrison forts, positions, stations, and other places, and to man vessels of all sorts in said service.

And upon this act, sincerely believed to be an act of justice, warranted by the Constitution, upon military necessity, I invoke the considerate judgment of mankind, and the gracious favor of Almighty God.

In witness whereof, I have hereunto set my hand and caused the seal of the United States to be affixed.

Done at the City of Washington, this first day of January, in the year of our Lord one thousand eight hundred and sixty three, and of the Independence of the United States of America the eighty-seventh.

By the President: ABRAHAM LINCOLN
WILLIAM H. SEWARD, Secretary of State.

15

Abraham Lincoln, Address at Gettysburg, PA

November 19, 1863*

Four score and seven years ago our fathers brought forth on this continent a new nation, conceived in lib-

*Lincoln, *Speeches and Writings*, 2:536.

erty and dedicated to the proposition that all men are created equal.

Now we are engaged in a great civil war, testing whether that nation or any nation so conceived and so dedicated can long endure. We are met on a great battle-field of that war. We have come to dedicate a portion of that field as a final resting-place for those who here gave their lives that that nation might live. It is altogether fitting and proper that we should do this.

But in a larger sense, we cannot dedicate, we cannot consecrate, we cannot hallow this ground. The brave men, living and dead who struggled here have consecrated it far above our poor power to add or detract. The world will little note nor long remember what we say here, but it can never forget what they did here. It is for us the living rather to be dedicated here to the unfinished work which they who fought here have thus far so nobly advanced. It is rather for us to be here dedicated to the great task remaining before us—that from these honored dead we take increased devotion to that cause for which they gave the last full measure of devotion—that we here highly resolve that these dead shall not have died in vain, that this nation under God shall have a new birth of freedom, and that government of the people, by the people, for the people shall not perish from the earth.

16

Abraham Lincoln to Albert G. Hodges
April 4, 1864*

My dear Sir: You ask me to put in writing the substance of what I verbally said the other day, in your presence, to Governor Bramlette and Senator Dixon. It was about as follows:

"I am naturally anti-slavery. If slavery is not wrong, nothing is wrong. I can not remember when I did not so think, and feel. And yet I have never understood that the Presidency conferred upon me an unrestricted right to act officially upon this judgment and feeling. It was in the oath I took that I would, to the best of my ability, preserve, protect, and defend the Constitution of the United States. I could not take the office without

*Lincoln, *Speeches and Writings*, 2:585–86.

taking the oath. Nor was it my view that I might take an oath to get power, and break the oath in using the power. I understood, too, that in ordinary civil administration this oath even forbade me to practically indulge my primary abstract judgment on the moral question of slavery. I had publicly declared this many times, and in many ways. And I aver that, to this day, I have done no official act in mere deference to my abstract judgment and feeling on slavery. I did understand however, that my oath to preserve the constitution to the best of my ability, imposed upon me the duty of preserving, by every indispensable means, that government—that nation—of which that constitution was the organic law. Was it possible to lose the nation, and yet preserve the constitution? By general law life *and* limb must be protected; yet often a limb must be amputated to save a life; but a life is never wisely given to save a limb. I felt that measures, otherwise unconstitutional, might become lawful, by becoming indispensable to the preservation of the constitution, through the preservation of the nation. Right or wrong, I assumed this ground, and now avow it. I could not feel that, to the best of my ability, I had even tried to preserve the constitution, if, to save slavery, or any minor matter, I should permit the wreck of government, country, and Constitution all together. When, early in the war, Gen. Fremont attempted military emancipation, I forbade it, because I did not then think it an indispensable necessity. When a little later, Gen. Cameron, then Secretary of War, suggested the arming of the blacks, I objected, because I did not yet think it an indispensable necessity. When, still later, Gen. Hunter attempted military emancipation, I again forbade it, because I did not yet think the indispensable necessity had come. When, in March, and May, and July 1862 I made earnest, and successive appeals to the border states to favor compensated emancipation, I believed the indispensable necessity for military emancipation, and arming the blacks would come, unless averted by that measure. They declined the proposition; and I was, in my best judgment, driven to the alternative of either surrendering the Union, and with it, the Constitution, or of laying strong hand upon the colored element. I chose the latter. In choosing it, I hoped for greater gain than loss; but of this, I was not entirely confident. More than a year of trial now shows no loss by it in our foreign relations, none in our home popular sentiment, none in our white military force,—no loss by it any how or any where. On the contrary, it shows a gain of quite a hundred and thirty thousand soldiers, seamen, and laborers. These are palpable facts, about which, as facts, there can be no cavilling. We have the men; and we could not have had them without the measure.

"And now let any Union man who complains of the measure, test himself by writing down in one line that he is for subduing the rebellion by force of arms; and in the next, that he is for taking these hundred and thirty thousand men from the Union side, and placing them where they would be but for the measure he condemns. If he can not face his case so stated, it is only because he can not face the truth."

I add a word which was not in the verbal conversation. In telling this tale I attempt no compliment to my own sagacity. I claim not to have controlled events, but confess plainly that events have controlled me. Now, at the end of three years struggle the nation's condition is not what either party, or any man devised, or expected. God alone can claim it. Whither it is tending seems plain. If God now wills the removal of a great wrong, and wills also that we of the North as well as you of the South, shall pay fairly for our complicity in that wrong, impartial history will find therein new cause to attest and revere the justice and goodness of God. Yours truly,

A. Lincoln

17

Republican (Union) Party Platform

June 7, 1864[*]

1. *Resolved*, That it is the highest duty of every American citizen to maintain against all their enemies the integrity of the Union and the paramount authority of the Constitution and laws of the United States; and that, laying aside all differences of political opinion, we pledge ourselves, as Union men, animated by a common sentiment and aiming at a common object, to do everything in our power to aid the Government in quelling by force of arms the Rebellion now raging against its authority, and in bringing to the punishment due to their crimes the Rebels and traitors arrayed against it.

2. *Resolved*, That we approve the determination of the Government of the United States not to compromise

[*] Commager, *Documents*, 1:435.

with Rebels, or to offer them any terms of peace, except such as may be based upon an unconditional surrender of their hostility and a return to their just allegiance to the Constitution and laws of the United States, and that we call upon the Government to maintain this position and to prosecute the war with the utmost possible vigor to the complete suppression of the Rebellion, in full reliance upon the self-sacrificing patriotism, the heroic valor and the undying devotion of the American people to the country and its free institutions.

3. *Resolved*, That as slavery was the cause, and now constitutes the strength of this Rebellion, and as it must be, always and everywhere, hostile to the principles of Republican Government, justice and the National safety demand its utter and complete extirpation from the soil of the Republic; and that, while we uphold and maintain the acts and proclamations by which the Government, in its own defense, has aimed a deathblow at this gigantic evil, we are in favor, furthermore, of such an amendment to the Constitution, to be made by the people in conformity with its provisions, as shall terminate and forever prohibit the existence of Slavery within the limits of the jurisdiction of the United States.

4. *Resolved*, That the thanks of the American people are due to the soldiers and sailors of the Army and Navy, who have periled their lives in defense of the country and in vindication of the honor of its flag; that the nation owes to them some permanent recognition of their patriotism and their valor, and ample and permanent provision for those of their survivors who have received disabling and honorable wounds in the service of the country; and that the memories of those who have fallen in its defense shall be held in grateful and everlasting remembrance.

5. *Resolved*, That we approve and applaud the practical wisdom, the unselfish patriotism and the unswerving fidelity to the Constitution and the principles of American liberty, with which ABRAHAM LINCOLN has discharged, under circumstances of unparalleled difficulty, the great duties and responsibilities of the Presidential office; that we approve and indorse, as demanded by the emergency and essential to the preservation of the nation and as within the provisions of the Constitution, the measures and acts which he has adopted to defend the nation against its open and secret foes; that we approve, especially, the Proclamation of Emancipation, and the employment as Union soldiers of men heretofore held in slavery; and that we have full confidence in his determination to carry these and all

other Constitutional measures essential to the salvation of the country into full and complete effect.

6. *Resolved*, That we deem it essential to the general welfare that harmony should prevail in the National Councils, and we regard as worthy of public confidence and official trust those only who cordially indorse the principles proclaimed in these resolutions, and which should characterize the administration of the government.

7. *Resolved*, That the Government owes to all men employed in its armies, without regard to distinction of color, the full protection of the laws of war—and that any violation of these laws, or of the usages of civilized nations in time of war, by the Rebels now in arms, should be made the subject of prompt and full redress.

8. *Resolved*, That foreign immigration, which in the past has added so much to the wealth, development of resources and increase of power to the nation, the asylum of the oppressed of all nations, should be fostered and encouraged by a liberal and just policy.

9. *Resolved*, That we are in favor of the speedy construction of the railroad to the Pacific coast.

10. *Resolved*, That the National faith, pledged for the redemption of the public debt, must be kept inviolate, and that for this purpose we recommend economy and rigid responsibility in the public expenditures, and a vigorous and just system of taxation; and that it is the duty of every loyal state to sustain the credit and promote the use of the National currency.

11. *Resolved*, That we approve the position taken by the Government that the people of the United States can never regard with indifference the attempt of any European Power to overthrow by force or to supplant by fraud the institutions of any Republican Government on the Western Continent and that they will view with extreme jealousy, as menacing to the peace and independence of their own country, the efforts of any such power to obtain new footholds for Monarchical Government, sustained by foreign military force, in near proximity to the United States.

18

Abraham Lincoln, Second Inaugural Address

March 4, 1865*

Fellow-Countrymen:

At this second appearing to take the oath of the Presidential office there is less occasion for an extended address than there was at the first. Then a statement somewhat in detail of a course to be pursued seemed fitting and proper. Now, at the expiration of four years, during which public declarations have been constantly called forth on every point and phase of the great contest which still absorbs the attention and engrosses the energies of the nation, little that is new could be presented. The progress of our arms, upon which all else chiefly depends, is as well known to the public as to myself, and it is, I trust, reasonably satisfactory and encouraging to all. With high hope for the future, no prediction in regard to it is ventured.

On the occasion corresponding to this four years ago all thoughts were anxiously directed to an impending civil war. All dreaded it, all sought to avert it. While the inaugural address was being delivered from this place, devoted altogether to *saving* the Union without war, insurgent agents were in the city seeking to *destroy* it without war—seeking to dissolve the Union and divide effects by negotiation. Both parties deprecated war, but one of them would *make* war rather than let the nation survive, and the other would *accept* war rather than let it perish, and the war came.

One-eighth of the whole population were colored slaves, not distributed generally over the Union, but localized in the southern part of it. These slaves constituted a peculiar and powerful interest. All knew that this interest was somehow the cause of the war. To strengthen, perpetuate, and extend this interest was the object for which the insurgents would rend the Union even by war, while the Government claimed no right to do more than to restrict the territorial enlargement of it. Neither party expected for the war the magnitude or the duration which it has already attained. Neither anticipated that the *cause* of the conflict might cease with or

*Lincoln, *Speeches and Writings*, 2:686–87.

even before the conflict itself should cease. Each looked for an easier triumph, and a result less fundamental and astounding. Both read the same Bible and pray to the same God, and each invokes His aid against the other. It may seem strange that any men should dare to ask a just God's assistance in wringing their bread from the sweat of other men's faces, but let us judge not, that we be not judged. The prayers of both could not be answered. That of neither has been answered fully. The Almighty has His own purposes. "Woe unto the world because of offenses; for it must needs be that offenses come, but woe to that man by whom the offense cometh." If we shall suppose that American slavery is one of those offenses which, in the providence of God, must needs come, but which, having continued through His appointed time, He now wills to remove, and that He gives to both North and South this terrible war as the woe due to those by whom the offense came, shall we discern therein any departure from those divine attributes which the believers in a living God always ascribe to Him? Fondly do we hope, fervently do we pray, that this mighty scourge of war may speedily pass away. Yet, if God wills that it continue until all the wealth piled by the bondsman's two hundred and fifty years of unrequited toil shall be sunk, and until every drop of blood drawn with the lash shall be paid by another drawn with the sword, as was said three thousand years ago, so still it must be said "the judgments of the Lord are true and righteous altogether."

With malice toward none, with charity for all, with firmness in the right as God gives us to see the right, let us strive on to finish the work we are in, to bind up the nation's wounds, to care for him who shall have borne the battle and for his widow and his orphan, to do all which may achieve and cherish a just and lasting peace among ourselves and with all nations.

19

"Union Victory! Peace! The Correspondence between Grant and Lee," *New York Times*

April 10, 1865, p. 1

April 7, 1865.

To Gen. R. E. LEE, *Commanding C. S. A.*:

GENERAL: The result of the last week must convince you of the hopelessness of further resistance on the part of the Army of Northern Virginia in this struggle. I feel that it is so, and regard it as my duty to shift from myself the responsibility of any further effusion of blood, by asking of you the surrender of that portion of the Confederate States army known as the Army of Northern Virginia.

Very respectfully, your obedient servant,

U. S. GRANT, *Lieut. Gen.,*
Commanding Armies of the United States

—

To Lieut. Gen. GRANT, *Commanding Armies of the United States*

GENERAL: I have received your note of this date. Though not entirely of the opinion you express of the hopelessness of the further resistance on the part of the Army of Northern Virginia, I reciprocate your desire to avoid a useless effusion of blood, and therefore before considering your proposition I ask the terms you will offer on the condition of surrender.

R. E. LEE, *General*

—

April 8, 1865.

To Gen. R. E. LEE, *Commanding C. S. A.*:

GENERAL: Your note of last evening, in reply to mine of same date, asking conditions on which I will accept the surrender of the Army of Northern Virginia, is just received.

In reply I would say that peace being my first desire, there is but one condition I insist upon, viz: That the men surrendered shall be disqualified for taking up arms against the Government of the United States, until properly exchanged. I will meet you, or designate officers to meet any officers you may name, for the same purpose, at any point agreeable to you, for the purpose of arranging definitely the terms upon which the surrender of the Army of Northern Virginia will be received.

Very respectfully, your obedient servant,

U. S. GRANT, *Lieut. Gen.,*
Commanding Armies of the United States

—

April 8, 1865.

To Lieut. Gen. GRANT, *Commanding Armies U.S.A.*

GENERAL: I received, at a late hour, your note of to-day, in answer to mine of yesterday. I did not intend to propose the surrender of the Army of Northern Virginia, but to ask the terms of your proposition. To be frank, I do not think the emergency has arisen to call for the surrender of this army; but as the restoration of peace should be the sole object of all, I desire to know whether your proposal would tend to that end. I cannot, therefore, meet you with a view to surrender the Army of Northern Virginia; but as far as your proposition may affect the Confederate States forces under my command, and tend to the restoration of peace, I should be pleased to meet you at 10 A. M. to-morrow, on the old state road to Richmond, between the picket lines of the two armies.

Very respectfully, your obedient servant,

R. E. LEE, *General*

—

April 9, 1865.

To Gen. R. E. LEE, *Commanding C. S. A.:*

GENERAL: Your note of yesterday is received. As I have no authority to treat on the subject of peace, the meeting proposed for 10 A. M. to-day could lead to no good. I will state, however, General, that I am equally anxious for peace with yourself, and the whole North entertain the same feeling.

The terms upon which peace can be had are well understood. By the South laying down their arms they will hasten that most desirable event, save thousands of human lives, and hundreds of millions of property not yet destroyed. Sincerely hoping that all our difficulties may be settled without the loss of another life. I subscribe myself, very respectfully, your obedient servant,

U. S. GRANT, *Lieut. Gen., U.S.A.*

—

April 9, 1865.

To Lieut. Gen. GRANT, *Com'g U.S. Armies.*

GENERAL: I received your note this morning on the picket line, whither I had come to meet you and as-

certain definitely what terms were embraced in your proposition as of yesterday with reference to the surrender of this army. I now request an interview in accordance with the offer contained in your letter of yesterday for that purpose.

Very respectfully, your obedient servant,

R. E. LEE, *General*

—

April 9.

To Gen. R. E. LEE, *Commanding C. S. A.:*

Your note of this date is but this moment (11.50 A. M.) received, in consequence of my having passed from the Lynchburg road to the Farmville and Lynchburg road. I am at this writing about four miles west of Walter's Church; and will push forward to the front for the purpose of meeting you.

Notice sent to me on this road where you wish the interview to take place, will meet me.

Very respectfully, your obedient servant,

U. S. GRANT, *Lieut. Gen., U.S.A.*
Commanding Armies of the United States

—

APPOMATTOX C.H. April 9, 1865.

To Gen. R. E. LEE, *Commanding C. S. A.:*

GENERAL: In accordance with the substance of my letter to you of the 8th instant, I propose to receive the surrender of the Army of Northern Virginia on the following terms, to wit:

Rolls of all the officers and men to be made in duplicate, one copy to be given to an officer designated by me, the other to be retained by such officer or officers as you may designate.

The officers to give their individual paroles not to take up arms against the Government of the United States until properly exchanged, and each company or regimental commander sign a like parole for the men of their commands. The arms, artillery, and public property to be parked and stacked, and turned over to the officers appointed by me to receive them. This will not embrace the side-arms of officers, nor their private horses or baggage.

This done, each officer and man will be allowed to return to their homes, not to be disturbed by United States authority so long as they observe their parole and the laws in force where they may reside.

Very respectfully,

U. S. GRANT, *Lieut. Gen.*

—

HEADQ'RS ARMY OF NORTHERN VIRGINIA
April 9, 1865.
Lieut. Gen. U.S. GRANT, *Com'g U.S. Armies*
GENERAL: I have received your letter of this date containing the terms of surrender of the Army of Northern Virginia, as proposed by you. As they are substantially the same as those expressed in your letter of the 8th instant, they are accepted. I will proceed to designate the proper officer to carry the stipulations into effect.

Very respectfully, your obedient servant,
R. E. LEE, *General**

* [The other Rebel armies subsequently surrendered on substantially the same terms. —Ed.]

PART 2

The Thirteenth Amendment

A. DRAFTING

Introduction to Part 2A

The Thirty-Eighth Congress drafted the Thirteenth Amendment in the midst of a civil war. The congressional assembly first met on December 7, 1863, one month after President Lincoln's dedication of the cemetery at Gettysburg, Pennsylvania. It had been a bloody year: the battle of Stones River had yielded 18,459 casualties; Chancellorsville, 22,114; and Gettysburg, 34,680.[1]

1. David J. Eicher, *The Longest Night: A Military History of the Civil War* (New York: Simon & Schuster, 2001), 428–88.

All told, about 620,000 soldiers would perish by the end of the war.[2] In his *Gettysburg Address*, Lincoln invited the American people to resolve that "these dead shall not have died in vain." Fulfilling that resolve would take more than military power—it would require the enactment of law.

On December 14, 1863, Ohio representative James Ashley proposed an amendment "prohibiting slavery or involuntary servitude" (doc. 2). On the same day, Iowa representative James Wilson introduced a joint resolution calling for the adoption of a two-section amendment declaring that slavery was "forever prohibited in the United States" and granting Congress power to enforce the amendment "by appropriate legislation" (doc. 2). Both proposals were submitted to the House Committee on the Judiciary, which Wilson chaired. One month later, on January 11, 1864, Missouri senator John Brooks Henderson introduced a proposed abolition amendment, which was submitted to the Senate Judiciary Committee (doc. 3). On February 8, 1864, Massachusetts senator Charles Sumner introduced his own proposed amendment, which declared that "all persons are equal before the law, so that no person can hold another as a slave" (doc. 5). Ultimately, Congress chose a version of Henderson's proposed amendment to send to the states for ratification (doc. 31). Reaching that point, however, took months of debate, the amendment's initial failure, an intervening presidential election, and a last-minute vote by a lame-duck Congress.

In deciding whether to constitutionally abolish slavery, members of Congress struggled with issues of high constitutional theory, wartime strategy, political ambitions, and their own racist assumptions about enslaved blacks. The Constitution had been untouched for almost sixty years; was it appropriate to alter its provisions during a civil war and in the absence of representatives from states that the North insisted were still in the Union? If ratifying the original Constitution had required a compromise with the slaveholding states, then wasn't banning slavery a revolutionary act beyond the proper scope of the amendment process laid out in Article V of the Constitution? If the South was fighting to preserve slavery, then would abolishing slavery prolong the war by removing any incentive for the South to enter into peace negotiations? Since Republicans increasingly embraced abolition as an essential aspect of their party platform, could the Democratic members of Congress

support abolition without losing the support of their party and constituents? Finally, as of 1863, there were approximately four million slaves in the United States, primarily in the seceded Southern states but also in the Union border states of Maryland, Delaware, Kentucky, and Missouri. Would abolition not punish the loyal slave owners in these Union states? And what would become of the millions of freed slaves? Would they remain in the South? Would they remain in the United States? Would they be destitute and unable to care for themselves? Would they demand equal social and political rights? The cumulative impact of these concerns was enough to defeat the slavery amendment when the House first voted on June 15, 1864. That vote would change in the aftermath of the 1864 presidential election.

When Congress began debating the amendment in early 1864, it did so with the encouragement of Northern abolitionist groups and affiliated associations that had long called for the end of slavery. On January 25, Susan B. Anthony and Elizabeth Cady Stanton began a petition drive on behalf of the Women's Loyal National League calling for a law abolishing slavery (doc. 4). On February 9, Charles Sumner presented this petition to the Senate with its first one hundred thousand signatures.[3] Sumner was committed to securing the passage of a broad, equality-based abolition amendment, and he attempted to have his own proposal sent to the Committee on Slavery and Freedmen, which he himself chaired (doc. 5). Senator Lyman Trumbull headed off the attempt and had Sumner's proposal, along with other proposed amendments, sent to the Senate Judiciary Committee, headed by Trumbull (doc. 6).

From March through June 1864, first the Senate and then the House debated the abolition amendment. The debates were divided along party lines, with Republicans supporting the amendment and Democrats generally (though not uniformly) opposed. The Senate acted first, passing the amendment on April 8, 1864 (doc. 16). When the House finally voted on June 15, 1864, although a majority favored the amendment, the vote fell short of the two-thirds majority required by Article V of the Constitution (doc. 21). The House revisited the issue after the fall presidential elections, however, and passed the amendment on January 31, 1865 (doc. 31).

Supporters of an abolition amendment insisted that slavery violated the foundational principles of the country articulated in the Declaration of Independence

---

2. Eicher, *Longest Night*, 17.

3. *Cong. Globe*, 38th Cong., 1st Sess., 536 (Feb. 9, 1864).

(see docs. 8, 9, 16, and 18) and the due process clause of the Fifth Amendment (see doc. 16). Although America's founding generation expected slavery to quickly die out, inventions like the cotton gin allowed the institution to flourish in the South and become an increasing source of sectional friction (doc. 15). In their efforts to preserve and extend slavery, the slave states had increasingly violated the essential rights of American citizens, including the rights of speech, press, assembly, and petition (see especially docs. 8, 9, 10, 12, and 14). Summing up the Republican case for abolition, John Farnsworth declared that slavery had led the South to secede and caused a bloody civil war. Should Congress not act, slavery would cause another war in the future. Because Congress either lacked or did not clearly possess the constitutional power to end slavery, an amendment was the best option (doc. 21).

Supporters were not completely uniform in their arguments. Some Republicans, for example, insisted that Congress lacked the power to abolish slavery absent an amendment (doc. 9). Others believed that Congress already had the power to abolish slavery, but nevertheless, they supported the amendment as a matter of policy (doc. 16). Supporters also differed over the *sufficiency* of mere abolition. Charles Sumner, for example, wanted to not only end slavery but also constitutionally guarantee that "all persons are equal before the law" (doc. 16). This language reflected the broader equal civil rights goals of the radical Republicans—indeed, Sumner's suggested language of equality would be drafted into the 1864 platform of the Radical Democracy Party, of which Sumner was a member (doc. 17). Others resisted Sumner's attempt to ensure both freedom and equal civil rights. According to Senator Henderson, "We give him no right except his freedom, and leave the rest to the States" (doc. 15).

Those Democrats opposed to constitutional abolition insisted that slavery was an essential aspect of the original Constitution that could not constitutionally be removed. Kentucky senator Garrett Davis, for example, claimed that the federalist nature of the Constitution forever guaranteed the right of states to decide this matter for themselves and that any effort to alter this aspect of the Constitution was not legal but "revolutionary" and must be treated as "null and void, notwithstanding it might be formally adopted" (doc. 11; see also doc. 21). It was not slavery that triggered a civil war but rather the inflammatory actions of abolitionists and the refusal of Northern states to enforce the fugitive slave clause (doc.

11). Even if the amendment procedure of Article V could be used to address the issue of slavery, it was wrong to pursue the matter during wartime, when so many states remained unrepresented. Delaware's Willard Saulsbury, for example, argued that the amendment "would not be binding on any State whose interest was affected by it" if their representatives were not present to vote on the matter (doc. 12). Such a violation of the original compact would fatally undermine state sovereignty and the federalist nature of the Constitution as declared in the Ninth and Tenth Amendments (doc. 21). Others expressed concerns about the impact of taking the "property" of loyal slave owners (doc. 21). As did many other Democrats, Pennsylvania's Alexander Coffroth initially worried that abolishing slavery might prolong the war, since the South would have little reason to lay down arms if doing so meant economic ruin.

On April 8, 1864, just prior to the Senate's vote, Charles Sumner raised a number of objections to the wording of the amendment, stating, "I must be pardoned if I venture to doubt the expediency of perpetuating in the Constitution language which, if it have any signification, seems to imply that 'slavery or involuntary servitude' may be provided 'for the punishment of crime.' There was a reason for that language when it was first employed, but that reason no longer exists. If my desires could prevail, I would put aside the ordinance on this occasion, and find another form" (doc. 16).

Sumner's last-minute effort to rewrite the proposed amendment with his preferred language ("all persons are equal before the law") threatened to derail what otherwise appeared would be a favorable Senate vote and was met with a rebuke from Lyman Trumbull, who insisted the amendment's proposed language represented a compromise among committee members (doc. 16). Jacob Howard criticized Sumner's suggested language, which had been taken from "French codes," and praised the amendment's use of Thomas Jefferson's language from the 1787 Northwest Ordinance, as "an expression which has been adjudicated upon repeatedly, which is perfectly well understood both by the public and by judicial tribunals" (doc. 16). The Senate then voted 38–6 in favor of the amendment, thus meeting the two-thirds majority vote required by Article V of the Constitution (doc. 16).

The amendment faced stiffer winds in the House of Representatives. In the Senate, Republicans outnumbered Democrats thirty-three to ten (the remaining nine senators being from other parties). In the House, their majority over the Democrats was only eighty-five to seventy-two (with twenty-seven members being from other parties).[4] The Senate also included influential Democrats like Reverdy Johnson, who spoke in favor of the amendment (doc. 13). No equally influential Democrat supported the amendment in the House. A successful vote would require Republicans to convince a significant number of Democrats to support the amendment or at least abstain from voting. The task became even more difficult when, a week before the House voted, the national Republican Party adopted a platform calling for an amendment abolishing slavery (doc. 19). Two days later, President Lincoln declared his support for such an amendment (doc. 20). These announcements left potentially supportive House Democrats in the awkward position of seeming to support the Republican Party if they voted in favor of the abolition amendment.

On June 15, the House voted ninety-three to sixty-five (with twenty-three abstentions) in favor of the amendment, with only four Democrats voting in support (doc. 22).[5] Since this was thirteen votes shy of the two-thirds majority required by Article V of the Constitution, the proposal failed. Once it was clear the amendment would not pass, Representative Ashley "changed his vote from the affirmative to the negative" in order to preserve an opportunity to move for future reconsideration (doc. 21).

The fate of the abolition amendment now rested with the outcome of the fall presidential election, a fact duly noted by the *New York Times* (doc. 22). Major victories by the Union army that summer (particularly the fall of Atlanta) fueled public support for the war and helped pave the way for Lincoln's victory on November 8, 1864.[6] Lincoln lost only three Union states: Kentucky, Delaware, and New Jersey. The Republicans, meanwhile, gained fifty congressional seats—a number that seemed to guarantee passage of the Thirteenth Amendment should the matter come to a vote in the Thirty-Ninth Congress (doc. 23).

Republicans and abolitionists interpreted the election results as signaling the people's desire to end slavery

(doc. 24). The only question was whether constitutional abolition should be left to the incoming Thirty-Ninth Congress or revisited during the final weeks of the outgoing Thirty-Eighth. President Lincoln encouraged immediate reconsideration (doc. 25). Republican leaders in the House agreed, and on January 6, 1865, James Ashley of Ohio moved for reconsideration of the abolition amendment (doc. 26).

Although the same members were voting on the same proposed amendment, the political ground had shifted in a number of ways since the previous summer. First, by returning Lincoln and an even greater number of Republicans to national office, the addition of an abolition amendment by the next Congress seemed guaranteed. Second, Union victory now seemed inevitable, making it less necessary to offer the preservation of slavery as an incentive for the South to come to the peace table. Third, the few Union slaveholding states were themselves embracing abolition without waiting for an amendment: Maryland abolished slavery just prior to the national election,[7] and Missouri did the same in the middle of the second round of congressional debates (doc. 28). On January 14, 1865, just days before the second House vote on the Thirteenth Amendment, Vice President elect Andrew Johnson's home state of Tennessee passed a resolution calling for the abolition of slavery (doc. 30). Finally, a number of Democrats had lost their reelection bid and, during this lame-duck session, were less subject to political pressure by the public and their peers.

On January 6, 1865, Representative James Ashley of Ohio opened reconsideration of the amendment by quoting Lincoln's declaration: "If slavery is not wrong, nothing is wrong" (doc. 26). In his speech, Ashley denounced "the terrible barbarism and indescribable villainy of slavery" and its decades-long suppression of constitutional liberties such as freedom of speech, press, and religious exercise. As they had the prior summer, Democratic opponents of the amendment stressed the revolutionary nature of the proposal and what they viewed as its betrayal of the founders' understanding of federalism and the sovereign right of states to regulate "domestic matters" as they saw fit. Democrat Andrew Rogers of New Jersey, for example, warned that the amendment would open the door to federal interference with everything from "the right of licensing hotels"

---

4. *Party Divisions of the House of Representatives, 1789–Present*, United States House of Representatives, http://history.house .gov/Institution/Party-Divisions/Party-Divisions/.

5. Joseph Bailey (D-PA), John A. Griswold (D-NY), Moses F. Odell (D-NY), and Ezra Wheeler (D-WI).

6. McPherson, *Battle Cry*, 718, 774–76.

7. See Art. 24 of the Maryland Declaration of Rights of the Maryland Constitution of 1864 (Nov. 1, 1864).

to "the right of making private contracts" (doc. 26). To Rogers, it was ludicrous to claim that the framers of the Declaration of Independence, "when they said that all men were born equal and had certain inalienable rights, intended to include slaves." Hadn't the members read the *Dred Scott* decision? Finally, slavery had not caused the Civil War. It was "the abolitionists of the North" who were "responsible for all this bloodshed which is now wetting American soil" (doc. 26).

Radical Republicans like James Ashley scoffed at the state sovereignty claims of Democrats. Echoing the nationalist theories of Daniel Webster and Abraham Lincoln, Ashley insisted that the nation "preexisted" the states—indeed, he maintained, "the unity of the people antedates the Revolution." Ashley's reading of history rendered claims of state sovereignty and "confederation" as absurdities "too transparent for serious argument" (see also doc. 29). Rather than constitutionally entrenching slavery, the founders had provided for its removal through the use of Article V. Nor was it necessary that the absent Southern states be allowed to debate the proposal or vote for its ratification. It was enough that "whenever three fourths of the States *now* represented in Congress give their consent to this proposition it will legally become a part of the national Constitution." According to Ashley, "States in rebellion have no constitutional governments" and thus no longer legally existed until such a time as they were recognized by the existing Congress.

More moderate Republicans insisted that abolishing slavery could be reconciled with the original federalist Constitution of James Madison and the founders. According to John Baldwin of Massachusetts, Madison's words had been twisted by Calhoun and radical states' rights theorists into doctrines of nullification and secession (doc. 29). New Hampshire's James Patterson explained that Article V represented the "wisdom of the Founders" by providing for "the right of gradual and peaceful revolution . . . so as to obviate forever the necessity for violent and bloody revolutions" (doc. 31). Although the Ninth and Tenth Amendments originally guarded the autonomy of the states, those amendments themselves were added through the process of Article V and were subject to later amendments using the same process (doc. 31). Surprisingly, one of the most significant voices supporting the Republican view of Article V came from a Democrat: Samuel Cox of Ohio. Cox opposed the abolition amendment, but in an extended speech later reported in the *New York Herald*, Cox laid

out historical evidence establishing that the framers and ratifiers of the original Constitution believed that there were no limitations on the use of Article V other than those limits expressly listed in the Constitution (docs. 26 and 27). Cox's speech seriously undercut arguments by other Democrats that the proposed amendment was a revolutionary and unconstitutional use of Article V.

For a number of lame-duck Democrats, the changed political circumstances were enough to move them from opposition to support—or at least to provide them with political cover for doing so. Kentucky representative George Yeaman had not supported the amendment when it first came before the House. Now, "[b]eing among those who were defeated at the last presidential election," Yeaman no longer faced political pressure and so could reevaluate the issue free from "compulsion." (doc. 26). In an extended speech, Yeaman announced that "[a]fter much hesitation and earnest reflection," he had "concluded to vote for the resolution submitting to the people of the States the proposed amendment to the Constitution, which, if successful, will forever settle the vexed and distressing question of slavery." "[S]lavery is doomed," Yeaman declared, "[a]nd since it is settled that slavery must die, and that this amendment will pass in a few months, if not now, why keep the country in turmoil, or have any fierce contest over it, contending about that which is practically settled?" Yeaman rejected the argument that the Constitution could not be amended to prohibit slavery, characterizing that position as "based on the extremest point of State rights, State sovereignty, compact, league, &c." Yeaman believed instead that "the original compact" had sprung "from the source of all power, the people" and that if they wished to amend the compact and abolish the institution, they were free to do so.

Missouri's James Rollins paraphrased Lincoln's letter to Horace Greeley and declared, "Sir, if I could save this Constitution and this Union by preserving the institution of slavery in its present status in the various States I would do it most cheerfully" (doc. 29). Rollins had considered this the case when he voted against the amendment the prior summer, and those views had subsequently led him to oppose Lincoln in the election. Thinking about the matter now, however, Rollins was "inclined to doubt whether, under all the circumstances, the people have not at last acted more wisely than I did." Rollins was particularly moved by the news that, just two days earlier, his state of Missouri "had adopted an amendment to our present State constitution for the immediate emancipation of all the slaves in the state." In light of such news, Rollins demurred, saying, "I very gracefully yield to the public sentiment." As far as federalism was concerned, Rollins rejected the claim that Article V could not be used to abolish slavery: "Congress has the right and power to propose any amendment to be adopted or rejected by the States themselves"—at least, so long as a "proposed amendment [came] within the scope of the preamble" and did not "destroy the very object and purposes for which the Constitution was established." Just before the vote, Democrat Anson Herrick from New York announced that he no longer opposed the amendment and was instead convinced that this was "a desirable opportunity for the Democracy to rid itself at once and forever of the incubus of slavery" (doc. 31).

It is important to remember that these debates took place while the Civil War continued to rage only miles away from the halls of Congress. Although the tide of the war had clearly turned in favor of the North, the possibility of an early end to hostilities remained a powerful incentive against any strategy that might prevent peace. In the first half of 1864, Democrats could plausibly claim that the possibility of holding onto the institution of slavery might bring the South to the negotiating table and potentially restore the Union. By 1865, however, it was clear that the South would pursue peace only on the condition of retaining their full independence—a condition unacceptable to the Union. Southern intransigence on this point was enough to convince Democrats like Archibald McAllister that it was pointless to maintain slavery in the hopes of negotiating an early end to the war (doc. 31). For the same reason, however, rumors that a Confederate peace commission had entered the city to negotiate terms with Union officials briefly caused a "sensation" (docs. 26 and 27).

On January 31, 1865, after a final round of speeches and debates, Ashley called the question, and the House clerk prepared to call the roll and record the vote. In June, the House vote had been ninety-three to sixty-five, a mere thirteen votes shy of the needed two-thirds majority. Although a number of Democrats had announced they would change their earlier votes and support the amendment, even now no one knew if there would be enough votes to pass the amendment. Everyone knew the vote would be close. When Democrats realized some of their members were absent (including the stridently antiabolitionist Andrew Rogers), they made a desperate, last-second effort to delay the vote

until the next day (doc. 31). Ashley refused their request, and the roll was called.

The House was packed for the occasion. The galleries above the chamber floor were filled with spectators both black and white. As the vote proceeded, every time a previously undeclared member voted "Aye," Republicans and the gallery erupted into "considerable applause." The honor of the final vote went to the Speaker of the House, Schuyler Colfax, who voted "Aye." The final tally was 119 to 56—two votes more than needed for passage. In the end, eleven Democrats changed their prior votes and supported the amendment, and eight members did not vote at all.[8] When the clerk announced the result, the chamber erupted into joyous cheering and applause. As reported in the *Congressional Globe*, the official record of congressional debates:

> The announcement was received by the House and by the spectators with an outburst of enthusiasm. The members on the Republican side of the House instantly sprung to their feet, and, regardless of parliamentary rules, applauded with cheers and clapping of hands. The example was followed by the male spectators in the galleries, which were crowded to excess, who waved their hats and cheered loud and long, while the ladies, hundreds of whom were present, rose in their seats and waved their handkerchiefs, participating in and adding to the general excitement and intense interest of the scene. This lasted for several minutes.[9]

The celebration was captured by an artist who was present for the vote (doc. 32). Unable to calm the crowd and proceed with any business, Congress adjourned. The next day, the amendment was sent to President Lincoln, who, though not required to do so, signed the proposed amendment (doc. 33). It was now up to the states—states still engaged in a civil war—to ratify the Thirteenth Amendment.

8. Democrats who changed their vote: Augustus C. Baldwin, Alexander Coffroth, James English, John Ganson, Anson Herrick, Wells Hutchins, Austin King, Archibald McAllister, William G. Brown, James S. Rollins, William Radford—11. Democrats who did not vote the first time but supported the amendment on the second vote: Homer Nelson and George Yeaman—2.

9. *Cong. Globe*, 38th Cong., 2nd Sess., 531.

1

The Thirty-Eighth Congress, Membership

1863–1865[*]

ALABAMA
Senators
Vacant
Representatives
Vacant

ARKANSAS
Senators
Vacant
Representatives
Vacant[1]

CALIFORNIA
Senators
James A. McDougall, *San Francisco*
John Conness, *Sacramento*
Representatives
Thomas B. Shannon, *Quincy*
William Higby, *Mokelumne Hill*
Cornelius Cole, *Santa Cruz*

CONNECTICUT
Senators
La Fayette S. Foster, *Norwich*
James Dixon, *Hartford*
Representatives
Henry C. Deming, *Hartford*
James E. English, *New Haven*
Augustus Brandegee, *New London*
John H. Hubbard, *Litchfield*

DELAWARE
Senators
James A. Bayard,[2] *Wilmington*
George R. Riddle,[3] *Wilmington*
Willard Saulsbury, *Georgetown*
Representatives
William Temple,[4] *Smyrna*
Nathaniel B. Smithers,[5] *Dover*

FLORIDA
Senators
Vacant
Representative at Large
Vacant

GEORGIA
Senators
Vacant
Representatives
Vacant

ILLINOIS
Senators
Lyman Trumbull, *Alton*
William A. Richardson, *Quincy*
Representatives
Isaac N. Arnold, *Chicago*
John F. Farnsworth, *St. Charles*
E.B. Washburne, *Galena*
Charles M. Harris, *Oquawka*
Owen Lovejoy,[6] *Princeton*
Ebon C. Ingersoll,[7] *Peoria*
Jesse O. Norton, *Joliet*
John R. Eden, *Sullivan*
John T. Stuart, *Springfield*
Lewis W. Ross, *Lewistown*
Anthony L. Knapp, *Jerseyville*
James C. Robinson, *Waterloo*
William J. Allen, *Marion*
At Large—James C. Allen, *Palestine*

[*] *Biographical Directory of the United States Congress, 1774–2005* (United States Congress, 2005), 166–69.

1. James M. Johnson, T.M. Jacks, and Anthony A.C. Rogers presented credentials as Members-elect, but their claims were not finally disposed of. By resolution of March 3, 1865, each was allowed the sum of $2,000 for "compensation, expenses, and mileage."

2. Resigned January 29, 1864.

3. Elected to fill vacancy caused by resignation of James A. Bayard, and took his seat February 2, 1864.

4. Died May 28, 1863, before Congress assembled.

5. Elected to fill vacancy caused by death of William Temple, and took his seat December 7, 1863.

6. Died March 25, 1864.

7. Elected to fill vacancy caused by the death of Owen Lovejoy, and took his seat May 20, 1864.

INDIANA

Senators

Henry S. Lane, *Crawfordsville*

Thomas A. Hendricks, *Indianapolis*

Representatives

John Law, *Evansville*

James A. Cravens, *Hardinsburg*

H.W. Harrington, *Madison*

William S. Holman, *Aurora*

George W. Julian, *Centerville*

Ebenezer Dumont, *Indianapolis*

Daniel W. Voorhees, *Terre Haute*

Godlove S. Orth, *La Fayette*

Schuyler Colfax, *South Bend*

Joseph K. Edgerton, *Fort Wayne*

James F. McDowell, *Marion*

IOWA

Senators

James Harlan, *Mount Pleasant*

James W. Grimes, *Burlington*

Representatives

James F. Wilson, *Fairfield*

Hiram Price, *Davenport*

J.B. Grinnell,[8] *Grinnell*

John A, Kasson, *Des Moines*

A.W. Hubbard, *Sioux City*

KANSAS

Senators

Samuel C. Pomeroy, *Atchison*

James H. Lane, *Lawrence*

Representatives

A. Carter Wilder, *Lawrence*

KENTUCKY

Senators

Lazarus W. Powell, *Henderson*

Garrett Davis, *Paris*

Representatives

Lucien Anderson, *Mayfield*

George H. Yeaman,[9] *Owensboro*

Henry Grider, *Bristol*

Aaron Harding, *Greensburg*

Robert Mallory, *La Grange*

Green Clay Smith, *Covington*

Brutus J. Clay, *Paris*

William H. Randall, *London*

William H. Wadsworth, *Maysville*

LOUISIANA

Senators

Vacant

Representatives

Vacant

MAINE

Senators

William Pitt Fessenden,[10] *Portland*

Nathan A. Farwell,[11] *Rockland*

Lot M. Morrill, *Augusta*

Representatives

L.D.M. Sweat, *Portland*

Sidney Perham, *Paris*

James G. Blaine, *Augusta*

John H. Rice, *Foxcroft*

F.A. Pike, *Calais*

MARYLAND

Senators

Thomas H. Hicks,[12] *Cambridge*

Reverdy Johnson, *Baltimore*

Representatives

John A.J. Creswell, *Elkton*

Edwin H. Webster, *Bel Air*

Henry Winter Davis, *Baltimore*

Francis Thomas, *Frankville*

Benjamin G. Harris, *Leonardtown*

MASSACHUSETTS

Senators

Charles Sumner, *Boston*

Henry Wilson, *Natick*

Representatives

Thomas D. Eliot, *New Bedford*

Oakes Ames, *North Easton*

Alexander H. Rice,[13] *Boston*

Samuel Hooper, *Boston*

John B. Alley, *Lynn*

10. Resigned July 1, 1864 to become Secretary of the Treasury.

11. Appointed to fill vacancy caused by resignation of William Pitt Fessenden, and took his seat December 5, 1864; subsequently elected.

12. Died February 12, 1865.

13. Election unsuccessfully contested by John S. Sleeper.

8. Election unsuccessfully contested by Hugh M. Martin.

9. Election unsuccessfully contested by John H. McHenry, Jr.

Daniel W. Gooch, *Melrose*
George S. Boutwell, *Groton*
John D. Baldwin, *Worcester*
William B. Washburn, *Greenfield*
Henry L. Dawes, *Pittsfield*

MICHIGAN
Senators
Zachariah Chandler, *Detroit*
Jacob M. Howard, *Detroit*
Representatives
F.C. Beaman, *Adrian*
Charles Upson, *Coldwater*
John W. Longyear, *Lansing*
Francis W. Kellogg, *Grand Rapids*
Augustus C. Baldwin, *Pontiac*
John F. Driggs, *East Saginaw*

MINNESOTA
Senators
Morton S. Wilkinson, *Mankato*
Alexander Ramsey, *St. Paul*
Representatives
William Windom, *Winona*
Ignatius Donnelly, *Nininger*

MISSISSIPPI
Senators
Vacant
Representatives
Vacant

MISSOURI
Senators
John B. Henderson, *Louisiana*
Robert Wilson, *St. Joseph*
B. Gratz Brown,[14] *St. Louis*
Representatives
F.P. Blair, Jr.,[15] *St. Louis*
Samuel Knox,[16] *St. Louis*

Henry T. Blow, *St. Louis*
John W. Noell,[17] *Perryville*
John G. Scott,[18] *Irondale*
Sempronius H. Boyd, *Springfield*
Joseph W. McClurg,[19] *Linn Creek*
Austin A. King, *Richmond*
Benjamin, F. Loan,[20] *St. Joseph*
William A. Hall, *Huntsville*
James S. Rollins, *Columbia*

NEVADA[21]
Senators
William M. Stewart,[22] *Virginia City*
James W. Nye,[23] *Carson City*
Representatives
Henry G. Worthington,[24] *Austin*

NEW HAMPSHIRE
Senators
John P. Hale, *Dover*
Daniel Clark, *Manchester*
Representatives
Daniel Marcy, *Portsmouth*
E.H. Rollins, *Concord*
James W. Patterson, *Hanover*

NEW JERSEY
Senators
John C. Ten Eyck, *Mount Holly*
William Wright, *Newark*
Representatives
John F. Starr, *Camden*
George Middleton, *Allentown*
William G. Steele, *Somerville*
Andrew J. Rogers, *Newton*
Nehemiah Perry, *Newark*

14. Elected on November 13, 1863, to fill vacancy caused by expulsion of Waldo Porter Johnson in preceding Congress, and took his seat December 14, 1863; Robert Wilson, Senator-designate in previous Congress, attended on December 7, 1863, but the following day was declared not entitled to a seat.

15. Served until June 10, 1864; succeeded by Samuel Knox, who contested his election.

16. Successfully contested the election of F.P. Blair Jr. and took his seat June 15, 1864.

17. Died March 14, 1863.

18. Elected to fill vacancy caused by the death of John W. Noell, and took his seat December 7, 1863; election unsuccessfully contested by James Lindsay.

19. Election unsuccessfully contested by Thomas L. Price.

20. Election unsuccessfully contested by John P. Bruce.

21. Admitted as a state into the Union October 31, 1864.

22. Took his seat February 1, 1865; term to expire, as determined by lot, March 3, 1869.

23. Took his seat February 1, 1865; term to expire, as determined by lot, March 3. 1867.

24. Took his seat December 21, 1864.

NEW YORK

Senators

Ira Harris, *Albany*

Edwin D. Morgan, *New York City*

Representatives

H.G. Stebbins,[25] *New Brighton*

Dwight Townsend,[26] *Clifton*

Martin Kalbfleisch, *Brooklyn*

M.F. Odell, *Brooklyn*

Benjamin Wood, *New York City*

Fernando Wood, *New York City*

Elijah Ward, *New York City*

John W. Chanler, *New York City*

James Brooks, *New York City*

Anson Herrick, *New York City*

William Radford, *Yonkers*

Charles H. Winfield, *Goshen*

Homer A. Nelson, *Poughkeepsie*

John B. Steele, *Kingston*

Erastus Corning,[27] *Albany*

John V.L. Pruyn,[28] *Albany*

John A. Griswold, *Troy*

Orlando Kellogg, *Elizabethtown*

C.T. Hulburd, *Brasher Falls*

James M. Marvin, *Saratoga Springs*

Samuel F. Miller, *Franklin*

A.W. Clark, *Watertown*

Francis Kernan, *Utica*

De Witt C. Littlejohn, *Oswego*

Thomas T. Davis, *Syracuse*

T.M. Pomeroy, *Auburn*

Daniel Morris, *Penn Yan*

Giles W. Hotchkiss, *Binghamton*

Robert B. Van Valkenburg, *Bath*

Freeman Clarke, *Rochester*

Augustus Ganson, *Buffalo*

Reuben E. Fenton,[29] *Frewsburg*

NORTH CAROLINA

Senators

Vacant

Representatives

Vacant

OHIO

Senators

Benjamin F. Wade, *Jefferson*

John Sherman, *Mansfield*

Representatives

George H. Pendleton, *Cincinnati*

A. Long, *Cincinnati*

Robert C. Schenck, *Dayton*

J.F. McKinney, *Piqua*

F.C. Le Blond, *Celina*

Chilton A. White, *Georgetown*

Samuel S. Cox, *Columbus*

William Johnston, *Mansfield*

Warren P. Noble, *Tiffin*

James M. Ashley, *Toledo*

Wells A. Hutchins, *Portsmouth*

William E. Finck, *Somerset*

John O'Neill, *Zanesville*

George Bliss, *Wooster*

James R. Morris, *Woodsfield*

Joseph W. White, *Cambridge*

E.R. Eckley, *Carrollton*

Rufus P. Spalding, *Cleveland*

James A. Garfield, *Hiram*

OREGON

Senators

James W. Nesmith, *Salem*

Benjamin F. Harding, *Salem*

Representative at Large

J.R. McBride, *Lafayette*

PENNSYLVANIA

Senators

Edgar Cowan, *Greensburg*

Charles R. Buckalew, *Bloomsburg*

Representatives

Samuel J. Randall, *Philadelphia*

Charles O'Neill, *Philadelphia*

Leonard Myers,[30] *Philadelphia*

William D. Kelley, *Philadelphia*

25. Resigned October 24, 1864.

26. Elected to fill vacancy caused by resignation of H.G. Stebbins, and took his seat December 5, 1864.

27. Resigned October 5, 1863, before Congress assembled.

28. Elected to fill vacancy caused by the resignation of Erastus Corning, and took his seat December 7, 1863.

29. Resigned effective December 20, 1864.

30. Election unsuccessfully contested by John Kline.

M. Russell Thayer,[31] *Chestnut Hill*

John D. Stiles, *Allentown*

John M. Broomall, *Media*

S.E. Ancona, *Reading*

Thaddeus Stevens, *Lancaster*

Myer Strouse, *Pottsville*

Philip Johnson, *Easton*

Charles Denison, *Wilkes-Barre*

Henry W. Tracy, *Standing Stone*

William H. Miller, *Harrisburg*

Joseph Bailey, *Newport*

Alexander H. Coffroth, *Somerset*

A. McAllister, *Springfield Furnace*

James T. Hale, *Bellefonte*

Glenni W. Schofield, *Warren*

Amos Myers, *Clarion*

John L. Dawson, *Brownsville*

James K. Moorhead, *Pittsburg*

Thomas Williams, *Pittsburg*

Jesse Lazear, *Waynesburg*

RHODE ISLAND

Senators

Henry B. Anthony, *Providence*

William Sprague, *Providence*

Representatives

Thomas A. Jenckes, *Providence*

Nathan F. Dixon, *Westerly*

SOUTH CAROLINA

Senators

Vacant

Representatives

Vacant

TENNESSEE

Senators

Vacant

Representatives

Vacant

TEXAS

Senators

Vacant

Representatives

Vacant

VERMONT

Senators

Solomon Foot, *Rutland*

Jacob Collamer, *Woodstock*

Representatives

F.E. Woodbridge, *Vergennes*

Justin S. Morrill, *Strafford*

Portus Baxter, *Derby Line*

VIRGINIA

Senators

John S. Carlile, *Clarksburg*

Lemuel J. Bowden,[32] *Williamsburg*

Representatives

Vacant[33]

WEST VIRGINIA[34]

Senators

Peter G. Van Winkle,[35] *Parkersburg*

Waitman T. Willey,[36] *Morgantown*

Representatives

Jacob B. Blair,[37] *Parkersburg*

William G. Brown,[38] *Kingwood*

Kellian V. Whaley,[39] *Point Pleasant*

WISCONSIN

Senators

James R. Doolittle, *Racine*

31. Election unsuccessfully contested by Charles W. Carrigan.

32. Died January 2, 1864. On February 17, 1865, the credential of Joseph E. Segar, to fill vacancy caused by the death of Lemuel J. Bowden, were presented but were ordered to lie on the table; no further action taken. State unrepresented on this class from this date to October 20, 1869.

33. Joseph E. Segar, from the first district, Lucius H. Chandler, from the second district, and Bethuel M. Kitchen, from the seventh district, presented credentials. They were declared not entitled to seats, the first two by resolution of May 17, 1864; the last named by resolution of April 16, 1864. Lewis McKenzie also claimed to have been elected from the seventh district, and was declared not entitled to the seat by resolution of February 26, 1864. The first three claimants were subsequently allowed mileage and pay to the dates of the adoption of the resolutions.

34. Formed form a portion of the state of Virginia and admitted into the Union June 19, 1863.

35. Took his seat December 7, 1863; term to expire, as determined by lot, March 3, 1869.

36. Took his seat December 7, 1863; term to expire, as determined by lot, March 3, 1865.

37. Took his seat December 7, 1863.

38. Took his seat December 7, 1863.

39. Took his seat December 7, 1863.

Timothy O. Howe, *Green Bay*
Representatives
James S. Brown, *Milwaukee*
I.C. Sloan, *Janesville*
Amasa Cobb, *Mineral Point*
Charles A. Eldridge, *Fond du Lac*
Ezra Wheeler, *Berlin*
Walter D. McIndoe, *Wausau*

TERRITORY OF ARIZONA[40]
Delegate
Charles D. Poston,[41] *Tubac*

TERRITORY OF COLORADO
Delegate
Hiram P. Bennet, *Denver*

TERRITORY OF DAKOTA
Delegate
William Jayne,[42] *Yankton*
John B.S. Todd,[43] *Yankton*

TERRITORY OF IDAHO[44]
Delegate
William H. Wallace,[45] *Lewiston*

TERRITORY OF MONTANA[46]
Delegate
Samuel McLean,[47] *Bannack*

TERRITORY OF NEBRASKA
Delegate
Samuel G. Daily, *Peru*

TERRITORY OF NEVADA[48]
Delegate
Gordon N. Mott,[49] *Carson City*

TERRITORY OF NEW MEXICO
Delegate
Francisco Perea,[50] *Bernalillo*

TERRITORY OF UTAH
Delegate
John F. Kinney, *Salt Lake City*

TERRITORY OF WASHINGTON
Delegate
George E. Cole, *Walla Walla*

2

US House of Representatives, Proposed Abolition Amendments (Ashley, Wilson) and Abolition Bill (Lovejoy)

December 14, 1863[*]

AMENDMENT OF THE CONSTITUTION

Mr. ASHLEY also introduced a bill to provide for the submission to the several States of a proposition to amend the national Constitution prohibiting slavery, or involuntary servitude, in all of the States and Territories now owned or which may be hereby acquired by the United States; which was read a first and second time.

Mr. W. J. ALLEN. Read the bill.

The clerk read the bill *in extenso*.

[A Bill to provide for submitting to the several States a proposition to amend the National Constitution prohibiting slavery or involuntary servitude in all the States, and in the Territories now owned, or which may hereafter be acquired, by the United States.

40. Formed from a portion of the Territory of New Mexico and granted a Delegate in Congress by act of February 24, 1863.

41. Took his seat December 5, 1864.

42. Served until June 17, 1864; succeeded by John B.S. Todd who contested his election.

43. Successfully contested the election of William Jayne, and took his seat June 17, 1864.

44. Formed from a portion of the territory ceded to the United States by France by treaty of April 30, 1803, and granted a Delegate in Congress by an act of March 3, 1863.

45. Took his seat February 1, 1864.

46. Formed from a portion of the territory ceded to the United States by France by treaty of April 30, 1803, and granted a Delegate in Congress by act of May 26, 1864.

47. Took his seat January 6, 1865.

48. Granted statehood October 31, 1864.

49. Served until October 31, 1864, when the Territory of Nevada was granted statehood.

50. Election unsuccessfully contested by José Manuel Gallegos.

[*] *Cong. Globe*, 38th Cong., 1st Sess., 19–21 (Dec. 14, 1863).

Be it enacted by the Senate and House of Representatives of the United States of America in Congress assembled, (two-thirds of both houses concurring,) That the following article be submitted by Congress to the legislatures of the several States as an amendment to the Constitution of the United States, which amendment, when approved by three-fourths of said legislatures, shall become a part of said Constitution.

ARTICLE —. Slavery or involuntary servitude, except in punishment of crime, whereof the party shall have been duly convicted, is hereby forever prohibited in all the States of this Union, and in all Territories now owned, or which may hereafter be acquired by the United States.]*

...

The Bill was referred to the Judiciary Committee.

...

RIGHTS OF COLORED MEN
Mr. LOVEJOY introduced a bill to give effect to the Declaration of Independence, and also to certain provisions of the Constitution of the United States.

Mr. HOLMAN. I demand the reading of the bill.

The bill was read. It recites that all men were created equal, and were endowed by the Creator with the inalienable right to life, liberty, and the fruits of honest toil; that the Government of the United States was instituted to secure those rights; that the Constitution declares that no person shall be deprived of liberty without due process of law, and also provides—article 5, clause 2—that "this Constitution, and the laws of the United States made in pursuance thereof, shall be the supreme law of the land, and the judges in each State shall be bound thereby, anything in the constitution and laws of any State to the contrary notwithstanding;" that it is now demonstrated by the rebellion that slavery is absolutely incompatible with the union, peace, and general welfare, for which Congress is to provide. It therefore enacts that all persons heretofore held in slavery in any of the States or Territories of the United States are declared free men, and are forever released from slavery or involuntary servitude, except as pun-

*[The text of Rep. Ashley's proposed amendment is not quoted in the *Congressional Globe*, but it can be found in *Bills and Resolutions*, House of Representatives, 38th Cong., 1st Sess., 14 (Dec. 14, 1863). —Ed.]

ishment for crime, on due conviction. The second section enacts that all persons declared free by the first section shall be protected, as all other free citizens are protected, from unreasonable search and seizure, and shall be allowed to sue and be sued, and to testify in cases in the courts of the United States. The third section enacts that if any person shall hereafter seize or arrest, or cause to be seized or arrested and imprisoned, any slave declared free by the act, with intent to reduce such slave to involuntary servitude or bondage, every person so offending shall be guilty of a high misdemeanor, and shall be subject to indictment and trial in any court of the United States having competent jurisdiction, and, on conviction thereof, shall be punished by imprisonment for not less than one year or more than five years, and by fine of not less than $1,000 or more than $5,000.

The bill was read a first and second time.

Mr. MALLORY. Will the Chair entertain a motion to lay that bill on the table?

The SPEAKER. That motion is not in order. It can be made when the bill is reported back.

Mr. LOVEJOY. I am informed that there is to be a special committee—

Mr. SPEAKER. Debate is not in order.

Mr. LOVEJOY. Then let the bill go to the Committee on the Judiciary.

It was so referred.

...

PROHIBITION OF SLAVERY
Mr. WILSON introduced a joint resolution submitting to the Legislatures of the several States a proposition to amend the Constitution of the United States.

Mr. F. WOOD called for the reading of the joint resolution,

The joint resolution was read. It provides for submitting, in the usual form, to the Legislatures of the several States the following amendments to the Constitution of the United States:

Sec. 1. Slavery, being incompatible with a free government, is forever prohibited in the United States; and involuntary servitude shall be permitted only as a punishment for crime.

Sec. 2. Congress shall have power to enforce the foregoing section of this article by appropriate legislation.

The joint resolution was read a second time, and referred to the Committee on the Judiciary.

3

US Senate, Proposed Abolition Amendment (Henderson)

January 11, 1864[*]

Mr. HENDERSON asked, and by unanimous consent obtained, leave to introduce a joint resolution (S. No. 16) proposing amendments to the Constitution of the United States; which was read twice by its title, and referred to the Committee on the Judiciary.

4

Women's Loyal National League, Petition for a Law Abolishing Slavery

January 25, 1864[†]

OFFICE OF THE WOMEN'S LOYAL NATIONAL LEAGUE,
Room No. 20, Cooper Institute
New York, January 25, 1864.

THE WOMEN'S LOYAL NATIONAL LEAGUE,
TO THE WOMEN OF THE REPUBLIC:

We ask you to sign and circulate this petition for the ENTIRE ABOLITION OF SLAVERY. We have now ONE HUNDRED THOUSAND signatures, but we want a MILLION before Congress adjourns. Remember the President's Proclamation reaches only the Slaves of Rebels. The jails of LOYAL Kentucky are to-day "crammed" with Georgia, Mississippi and Alabama slaves, adver-

tised to be sold for their jail fees "According to LAW," precisely as before the war!!! While slavery exists ANYWHERE there can be freedom NOWHERE. THERE MUST BE A LAW ABOLISHING SLAVERY. We have undertaken to canvass the Nation for freedom. Women, you cannot vote or fight for your country. Your only way to be a power in the Government is through the exercise of this one, sacred, *Constitutional* "RIGHT OF PETITION;" and we ask you to use it NOW to the utmost. Go to the rich, the poor, the high, the low, the soldier, the civilian, the white, the black—gather up the names of all who *hate* slavery—all who love LIBERTY, and would have it the LAW of the land and lay them at the feet of Congress, your silent but potent vote for human freedom guarded by the law.

You have shown true courage and self-sacrifice from the beginning of the war. You have been angels of mercy to our sick and dying soldiers in camp and hospital, and on the battle-field. But let it not be said that the women of the Republic, absorbed in ministering to the outward alone, saw not the philosophy of the revolution through which they passed; understood not the moral struggle that convulsed the nation—the irrepressible conflict between liberty and slavery. Remember the angels of mercy and justice are twin sisters, and ever walk hand in hand. While you give yourselves so generously to the Sanitary and Freedmen's Commissions, forget not to hold up the eternal principles on which our Republic rests. Slavery once abolished, our brothers, husbands and sons will never again, for ITS SAKE, be called on to die on the battle-field, starve in rebel prisons, or return to us crippled for life; but our country free from the one blot that has always marred its fair escutcheon, will be an example to all the world that "RIGHTEOUSNESS EXALTETH A NATION."

THE GOD OF JUSTICE IS WITH US, AND OUR WORD, OUR WORK—OUR PRAYER FOR FREEDOM—WILL NOT, CANNOT BE IN VAIN.

E. CADY STANTON
President.
SUSAN B. ANTHONY,
Secretary W.L.N. League,
Room 20, Cooper Institute,
New York.

[*] *Cong. Globe*, 38th Cong., 1st Sess., 145 (Jan. 25, 1864).

[†] Copy on file, National Archives. [According to Wendy Venet, "The first 6000 petition forms, bearing 100,000 signatures, were glued end to end, rolled into a bundle and mailed to [Sen. Charles] Sumner in a trunk." Venet reports that on February 9, 1864, "two black men entered the Senate Chamber and carried the first installment of League petitions to the desk of Charles Sumner." Wendy H. Venet, *Neither Ballots nor Bullets: Women Abolitionists and the Civil War* (Charlottesville: University of Virginia Press, 1991), 120. —Ed.]

5

US Senate, Proposed Abolition Amendment (Sumner), Debates

February 8, 1864[*]

Mr. SUMNER asked, and by unanimous consent obtained, leave to introduce a joint resolution (S. No. 24) to provide for submitting to the several States an amendment of the Constitution of the United States; which was read twice by its title.

Mr. SUMNER. I move that it be referred to the committee on slavery and freedmen.

Mr. TRUMBULL. I suppose the proper committee to which to refer bills to change the Constitution would be the Judiciary Committee. There are already several propositions before that committee in reference to amendments to the Constitution, and I submit to the Senator whether that is not the proper committee to have charge of these subjects.

Mr. SUMNER. Let the amendment be read, and then perhaps the Senate can determine best.

The VICE PRESIDENT. The joint resolution will be read.

The Secretary read it, as follows:

Be it resolved, &c., That the following article be proposed to the Legislatures of the several States as an amendment to the Constitution of the United States, which, when ratified, shall become a part of the Constitution, to wit:

Article —. Everywhere within the limits of the United States, and of each State or Territory thereof, all persons are equal before the law, so that no person can hold another as a slave.

The VICE PRESIDENT. The question is on referring this joint resolution to the committee on slavery and freedmen.

Mr. TRUMBULL. I will state to the Senator from Massachusetts that at a very early stage of the session the Senator from Missouri [Mr. HENDERSON] introduced a proposition to change the Constitution of the United States so as to prohibit slavery everywhere within its territorial limits. That proposition has been under

consideration, and has been somewhat discussed and considered by the Committee on the Judiciary. This is a proposition in another form on the same subject. I submit to the Senator from Massachusetts whether the appropriate committee for all propositions to change the Constitution is not the Judiciary Committee. It seems to me that would be the proper committee. At any rate we are considering that very subject, and these propositions had best all go together. If the Senator from Massachusetts and the Senate should think that the proper committee to consider amendments to the Constitution is the committee on freedmen and slavery, the Committee on the Judiciary had better be discharged from all these propositions which are pending before it in regard to amendments of that character or relating in any way to the subject of slavery.

Mr. FESSENDEN (to Mr. TRUMBULL.) Move to amend the motion so as to substitute the Committee on the Judiciary.

Mr. TRUMBULL. I submit it to the Senator from Massachusetts; I thought probably he would give it that direction.

Mr. SUMNER. I am obliged to the Senator from Illinois for his remarks. He will remember that only a few days ago he reported from the Committee on the Judiciary the petitions relating to the fugitive slave law with a recommendation that they be referred to the committee on slavery. Now, on general grounds, indeed, on the grounds suggested by the Senator, that subject should properly go before the Committee on the Judiciary; but the Committee on the Judiciary have thought otherwise, and it has now been referred to the committee on slavery. Still further, there are propositions which have already been referred to the committee on slavery relating to an amendment of the Constitution so far as to prohibit slavery throughout the United States. I presume the reason for that reference was that the committee on slavery was specially constituted to take into consideration that subject and what should be done with reference to it, whether great or small, whether with regard to the treatment of the freedmen, or amendments in the laws of the land, or even in the Constitution. The language of the resolution under which the committee has been raised is broad enough to cover every proposition relating to slavery; and I simply follow the lead of my distinguished friend, who the other day moved the reference of all papers relating to the fugitive slave law to that committee, when I propose to refer this proposition to the same committee. If the Senator wishes to

[*] *Cong. Globe*, 38th Cong., 1st Sess., 521–23 (Feb. 8, 1864).

take charge of it I certainly shall not object; but I understand that already the same question is now pending before the committee on slavery, as the Senator says it is pending before the Committee on the Judiciary. If the Senator desires, after this statement, that this joint resolution which I introduce to-day be referred to the committee of which he is the honored head, I shall consent with the greatest pleasure.

Mr. SAULSBURY. I move that the further consideration of this resolution be indefinitely postponed; and on that motion I ask for the yeas and nays.

Mr. TRUMBULL. Does that question have precedence of a reference? However, it is immaterial. Either is open to discussion, and I only wish to say a word in reply.

The VICE PRESIDENT. It has precedence.

Mr. TRUMBULL. I only wish to say a word in reply to the Senator from Massachusetts. Personally, I have no desire to take charge of this proposition which the Senator submits. It is only because I supposed that the Judiciary Committee was the proper committee to consider amendments to the Constitution. The Senator remarks that the Committee on the Judiciary the other day were discharged from the consideration of certain petitions relating to the fugitive slave law and asked that they be referred to the special committee on the subject of freedmen and slavery. That is true, sir. That was deemed by the Committee on the Judiciary to be the appropriate committee to consider all these propositions in reference to a change in the law; but none of the petitions which the Committee on the Judiciary asked to be discharged from related to an amendment of the Constitution. If petitions have been referred to the committee on freedmen and slavery asking for a change of the Constitution, it has been inadvertently done, I presume, so far as the Senate is concerned. I had not observed it and was not aware that petitions of that character had gone to the committee on freedmen and slavery. Certain it is that petitions of that character and a resolution to amend the Constitution in that respect were referred to the Committee on the Judiciary at a very early day in the session. I have certainly no personal desire to take charge of this matter because I happen to be on the Committee on the Judiciary. It is for the Senate to determine which are the appropriate committees for the business that is presented. It seemed to me that the appropriate committee for all propositions to change the Constitution was the Judiciary Committee. If the Senate is of a different opinion I shall certainly acquiesce in any

disposition of it. It is only because I thought, as this subject was pending before the Judiciary Committee, they had best be together that I made the suggestion.

Mr. DOOLITTLE. I never heard before in my life that an amendment to the Constitution was ever referred to any other committee than the Judiciary Committee. It seems to me this is one of those cases that cannot admit of any serious question as to where this proposition should go. I shall not take up time in discussing the subject, but clearly it ought to go to the Judiciary Committee.

Mr. SUMNER. I am perfectly willing to follow the suggestion of the Senator from Illinois. I only hope the committee will take charge of it and act upon it soon.

. . .

Mr. ANTHONY asked, and by unanimous consent obtained, leave to introduce a joint resolution (S. No. 25) repealing a joint resolution to amend the Constitution of the United States; which was read twice by its title.

Mr. ANTHONY. I ask to have the resolution referred to the Committee on the Judiciary. It proposes to repeal a joint resolution approved March 2, 1861, and as that resolution is short I ask to have it read.

The Secretary read, as follows:

> A joint resolution to amend the
> Constitution of the United States.
> *Resolved, &c.*, That the following article be proposed to the Legislatures of the several States as an amendment to the Constitution of the United States which, when ratified by three fourths of said Legislatures, shall be valid to all intents and purposes as part of the said Constitution, namely:
> ART. XIII. No amendment shall be made to the Constitution which will authorize or give to Congress the power to abolish or interfere within any State with the domestic institutions thereof, including that of persons held to labor or service by the laws of said State.
> Approved March 2, 1861

Mr. ANTHONY. Mr. President, I voted, as did two thirds of the members present of both Houses of the Thirty-Sixth Congress, for this resolution. I would have gone much further than this in any reasonable and proper effort to avert the evils of civil war and, to assure the people who had been disaffected by the misrepresentations of demagogues, and made to believe that the Republican party meditated the invasion of their constitutional rights. But the offer was spurned by those whom it was intended to conciliate. So far from accepting it in the spirit in which it was tendered, they threw off their allegiance to the Government and organized rebellion, with the avowed purpose of preventing a Republican Administration from doing what it solemnly avowed it had no purpose of doing, and what they had the power, in a perfectly constitutional manner, to prevent it from doing. Not only was the revolt made upon a false pretext, but even if the pretext had been true there was abundant remedy by peaceable means and within the Constitution.

It does not consist with the dignity of the Government to continue this offer after it has been so received; and it is no longer proper that such a restriction should be put upon the power of Congress, or should be kept upon the power of Congress, even if those to whom it was tendered should be willing to accept it. The grand events of the last two years have altered the whole aspect of the question, and have advanced public opinion to a point which it would not have attained in scores of peaceful years. The policy that then would have been only the affirmation of a political truism would now be an outrage upon the sense of the country and a shame in the face of the civilized world. The true policy now is to strike at slavery wherever it can be reached. So far from adding new guarantees to its existence and its safety, so far from reaffirming the old ones, the true policy is to remove by legal measures the securities that now protect it. The amendment which the Constitution requires on the subject of slavery is quite in the other direction. It has been indicated by the Senator from Massachusetts, [Mr. SUMNER,] and the Senator from Missouri, [Mr. HENDERSON,] in their propositions so to amend the Constitution as to give to Congress the power to abolish slavery, and thus to secure the public tranquillity by removing the disloyal cause of the troubles which afflict the land, to secure the sympathy of the world by placing our institutions upon the basis of progressive civilization, to invoke the favor of Heaven by ceasing to violate its laws. This proposition comes most appropriately from a Senator from that State which declared that slavery was inconsistent with the Declaration of Independence and the Bill of Rights, and from the Senator of a State that has felt the curse of slavery and the terrible evils of the rebellion that slavery has inaugurated. Wisely has Missouri, wisely has West Virginia, wisely has Maryland determined to remove that curse, and wisely will Congress and the States determine when they shall

resolve that the curse shall never be restored where it has been removed by the people, or where it has been practically abolished by its own suicidal revolt against the Government.

It may be argued that to confer upon Congress the power to abolish slavery may be an implication that the power already exercised in that direction and the larger exercise of it contemplated are not legitimate. The inference is not a necessary one. And the States where the slaves are emancipated by the President's proclamation or by acts of Congress directed against rebels and the source of rebel supply may reenact slavery as soon as the pressure is removed. It is necessary to guard against that; it is necessary not only to proclaim and to establish freedom, but to secure it.

Nor is such a policy inconsistent with the declarations of the Republicans, that originally they had no design of interfering with slavery in the States where the people chose to retain it. We had no such design. It is not we, it is they who have opened the way to freedom, and have made it our duty to tread in the path before us. Slavery in the States never was stronger than it was on the 4th of March, 1861. The election which had pronounced its downfall in the Territories and in this District had affirmed its accursed rights in the States. But God maketh the wrath of man to praise Him, and the remainder of wrath He restraineth. What the Republican party could not do, what no election could do, what no peaceable movement would have been likely to accomplish in many years, slavery has done of itself and to itself. It has sealed its own doom; it has made its existence incompatible with the safety of the Republic, with the continuance of the Union. It has committed suicide. If we had been asked a few years ago, Do you purpose to invade Virginia? do you intend to blockade Mobile? do you mean to batter down the walls of Sumter? no one will doubt the sincerity with which we should have answered, No. Yet we have done all this and much more of the same character, and the only complaint is that we have not done enough of it nor with sufficient vigor. Equally sincere was our denial of the intention to interfere with slavery in the States. But they who have made it necessary that we should invade Virginia, that we should blockade Mobile, that we should batter down Sumter, have equally made it necessary that we should strike at slavery, the primal cause, the sustaining power of the rebellion. The responsibility, so far as their own interests are affected, is theirs; the duty is ours; the benefit will be to the country, to the world.

6

US Senate, Notice of Two-Sectioned Abolition Amendment (Trumbull)

February 10, 1864[*]

Mr. TRUMBULL. The Committee on the Judiciary, to whom were referred various petitions from different parts of the country, praying for an amendment of the Constitution of the United States so as to incorporate a provision prohibiting slavery in all the States and Territories of the Union, and also a joint resolution (S. No. 16) proposing amendments to the Constitution of the United States, and: a joint resolution (S. No. 24) to provide for submitting to the several States an amendment of the Constitution of the United States, instruct me to report back an amendment to the Senate of the joint resolution No. 16, in the way of a substitute. I will state that the amendment, as recommended by the Committee on the Judiciary, provides for submitting to the Legislatures of the several States a proposition to amend the Constitution of the United States so that neither slavery nor involuntary servitude, except as a punishment for crime, whereof a party shall have been duly convicted, shall exist within the United States, or any place subject to their jurisdiction; and also that Congress shall have power to enforce this article by proper legislation. I desire to give notice to the Senate that I shall, at an early day, call for the consideration of this resolution.

7

US Senate, Notice of Amended Proposal (S. No. 16) (Trumbull), Notice of Abolition Amendment (Sumner)

February 17, 1864[†]

Mr. TRUMBULL. I move to take up the joint resolution (S. No. 16) with a view to make it the special order for a future day.

The motion was agreed to.

Mr. TRUMBULL. I will state to the Senate that this is the joint resolution introduced at an early day of the session by the Senator from Missouri, [Mr. HENDERSON] and to which the Committee on the Judiciary have proposed an amendment, to amend the Constitution of the United States so as to prohibit slavery throughout the United States, and in all places within its jurisdiction. I move that the resolution be made the special order for Monday next at one o'clock.

The motion was agreed to by a two-thirds vote.

Mr. SUMNER subsequently said: I ask the consent of the Senate to offer an amendment, which I propose to move on Monday next to the joint resolution to amend the Constitution which was made the order of the day for that day at one o'clock, and I desire to have it printed.

The VICE PRESIDENT. The amendment will be received and the order to print will be made, if there be no objection.

---

[*] *Cong. Globe*, 38th Cong., 1st Sess., 553 (Feb. 10, 1864).

[†] *Cong. Globe*, 38th Cong., 1st Sess., 694 (Feb. 17, 1864).

8

US House of Representatives, Speech of James Wilson (R-IA) Introducing Abolition Amendment

March 19, 1864[*]

Mr. WILSON. Mr. Chairman, on the first day of the present session of Congress I gave notice of my intention to introduce a joint resolution submitting to the Legislatures of the several States a proposition to amend the Constitution of the United States. On a subsequent day, in pursuance of the notice thus given, I introduced and had referred to the Committee on the Judiciary the following joint resolution:

Be it resolved by the Senate and House of Representatives of the United States of America in Congress assembled, (two thirds of both Houses concurring,) That the following article be proposed to the Legislatures of the several States as an amendment to the Constitution of the United States, which, when ratified by three fourths of said Legislatures shall be valid, to all intents and purposes, as a part of said Constitution, namely:

Article XIII.

Sec. 1. Slavery, being incompatible with a free Government, is forever prohibited in the United States; and involuntary servitude shall be permitted only as a punishment for crime.

Sec. 2. Congress shall have power to enforce the foregoing section of this article by appropriate legislation.

I am well aware, sir, that a proposition in the Congress of the United States to so amend the Constitution of the Republic as to weaken or destroy slavery is a novel thing. With bills, resolutions, and propositions to amend the Constitution to more firmly establish, extend, and perpetuate slavery the country has been perfectly familiar. It was long the custom in this body, whenever slavery became excited and angry, to try to appease its wrath by offering it some new hold on the

* *Cong. Globe*, 38th Cong., 1st Sess., 1199–204 (Mar. 19, 1864).

life of the nation, some greater advantage over free government and human liberty. When slavery cried "Give, give," by force of habit and loss of conscience we always responded by offering more than it demanded of us. We were the slaves of the slave power.

When slavery became a political power, and held in its hands the rewards which ambition covets, the nation became its most cringing, fawning, stupidly debased slave; and a most cruel task-master it proved. Its political career was an incessant, unrelenting, aggressive warfare upon the principles of the Government, the objects for which the Constitution was ordained, the rights of the people, the development of national resources, the advancement of education, the establishment of public morals, and the purity of religion. It touched everything, defiled everything. And we submitted quietly, tamely, cowardly, while the work of destruction and death was carried on by this insatiable enemy of all that is lovely, desirable, just, and sacred. No political power, whether found in republics or despotisms, ever wielded so baneful an influence on the affairs of nations or men as the one to which we so passively submitted, and under whose shadow we so fearfully dwarfed. Its progress was a constant, crushing dead march over everything which stood in the way of its own aggrandizement; and everything desirable to a free people stood in its way. The nation grew stupid under the manipulations of slavery, and seemed to know but little, and to care less, of the danger which threatened the free institutions of the country with destruction.

The public opinion now existing in this country, in opposition to this power is the result of slavery overleaping itself, rather than of the determination of freemen to form it. But, however formed, thank God it is formed, and is our priceless possession of real, active, national life, never to be surrendered. We must hold all we have gained, and add to the strength of public opinion by daring to do our duty as if in the immediate presence of Him who directs the destinies of nations. We may now talk of freedom, act for it, legislate for it, and above all other acts we may place one which shall stamp universal freedom on our national Constitution, never to be erased, never to die while the Republic lives. To accomplish this great end I introduced the joint resolution to which I have alluded, and I believe its passage is desired by the truly loyal people of the country almost without an exception.

In preparing the resolution I was careful to present but one issue, the incompatibility of slavery with a free Government. This issue is no reflection on the wise and good men who laid the firm foundations and fashioned the sublime architecture of our Constitution. They entertained not the remotest idea that they were tolerating a tenant in the grand structure which would, when warmed into life and developed into the form of a political power, endeavor to tear down the altars of liberty, and erect in their stead a throne of absolutism and death. The oft-expressed and universally understood views of the fathers fully attest that they regarded this tenant as the thing to be tolerated only because it promised speedy dissolution. They found it in the house they were erecting for the protection of themselves and their children, looked upon it with horror, and left it to die, never suspecting the dreadful power it embodied. Surrounded by the grand teachings of a successful war, based upon principles utterly destructive of slavery if enforced, they looked forward to the death of the latter by the mere development and power of the former. They believed in the incompatibility of slavery with a free Government; but they regarded the latter to be the stronger, not yet having had experience with slavery as a political power. These reasons will account in great part for the absence from the Constitution of a section prohibiting slavery. It is impossible to believe that the master-workmen who gave to us this best of human Governments in the least degree suspected that they were transmitting with it the seeds of dissolution. They believed their work secure from molestation by this tolerated thing which all good men loathed and expected to see pass speedily away. In this they were mistaken, as we have discovered to our deepest sorrow and infinite cost. But their wisdom provided the means for overruling the disastrous consequences of their mistake. The Constitution which they formed, and which the people ordained and established, contains ample provisions for accomplishing the destruction of that power which so long disturbed the tranquillity of the nation, and finally enveloped us in the whirling, leaping, encircling red flame of war. The fifth article of the Constitution of the United States reads as follows:

> "Congress, whenever two thirds of both Houses shall deem it necessary, shall propose amendments to this Constitution or, on the application of the Legislatures of two thirds of the several States, shall call a convention for proposing amendments, which, in either case shall be valid to all intents and purposes, as part of this Constitution, when rati-

fied by the Legislatures of three fourths of the several States by conventions in three fourths thereof, as the one or the other mode of ratification may be proposed by Congress: *Provided*, That no amendment which may be made prior to the year 1808 shall in any manner affect the first and fourth clauses in the ninth section of the first article; and that no State, without its consent, shall be deprived of its equal suffrage in the Senate."

This highly practical section of the Constitution, free from all conditions and limitations since the year 1808, with regard to the subjects concerning which amendments may be adopted, with the single exception of the suffrage of the States in the Senate, was provided as a means for adapting the fundamental law of the Republic to the changes incident to the development of the nation. It is the safety-valve of the Constitution, so constructed and guarded as to prevent hasty and inconsiderate action, and utterly destructive of every pretense for forcible revolution. It is impossible to justify a resort to force as a remedy for wrongs imaginary or real, while this recognition of the great doctrine that "Governments derive their just powers from the consent of the governed" remains a part of our organic law; and it would be equally difficult to justify the existence of anything in the Government destructive of the inalienable, rights of "life, liberty, and the pursuit of happiness," without, at least, an earnest and determined effort to remove it. When the people established the Constitution, embracing the section which I have quoted, they agreed upon the means whereby the consent of the governed should be determined, and by the same act placed upon themselves and upon us the responsibility attached to those things which interfere with the inalienable rights of man, or which tend to the destruction of free government. Amendments proposed by Congress, or by a convention called for that purpose, and adopted or rejected by the Legislatures of the several States, are the mediums through which the consent of the governed is to be determined concerning all things not now provided for in the Constitution. It was a fair agreement, placing upon each and every citizen, and upon the several States, all of the risks and responsibilities incident thereto, for "we, the people of the United States;" made it. It was expected that the nation would develop into grander proportions, its interests become more varied, its wants and necessities increase, and that it might be beset by dangers not occurring to the minds which molded the form of the organic law. It was agreed and expressly provided that the Constitution should grow to meet all of these new demands, keeping within the bounds of its ordination "to form a more perfect Union, establish justice, insure domestic tranquillity, provide for the common defense, promote the general welfare, and secure the blessings of liberty to ourselves and our posterity."

This section of the Constitution is my authority for introducing the joint resolution which I have read; and it also imposes upon this House the responsibility of meeting the question fairly and with a view to the promotion of the best interests of the nation, by releasing it from the thralldoms of a hostile power which has entwined itself around the heart and life of the Republic. The proposition introduces no intricate question of constitutional law for discussion. It simply submits a question of fact for our determination, upon which the past and present throw such a flood of light that not even willfulness can lead us astray. Is slavery incompatible with a free Government? This is the true question involved; and no artful summonings of cunningly devised side issues, or of the ghosts of dead expediencies, can release any member of this body from passing upon this single issue. It is all there is in the case. The contest is squarely between slavery and free government, and in this light is to be conducted to the end. Let us follow it, and see how it will end.

Slavery is defined to be "the state of entire subjection of one person to the will of another." This is despotism, pure and simple. It is true that this definition concerns more the relations existing between master and slave than it does those between the system of slavery and the Government. But we need not hope to find a system purely despotic acting in harmony with a Government wholly, or even partially, republican. An antagonism exists between the two which can never be reconciled. This our experiences with the principles involved have taught us is a truism from which indifference will not enable us to escape, nor dissimulation release us. But when we connect with the despotism of the slave system of this country the immense land and money power embraced in it, and reflect how thoroughly it had become interwoven with the entire social fabric of nearly one half of the States, we can more readily understand and fully comprehend how and why this antagonism took upon itself the form of political organization through which for many years it controlled the nation, and through which it insisted on the death of the Re-

public when it could control no longer. We can also understand why the system of which this antagonism is the active life took possession of every department of the local governments of the States where it existed, and hedged itself about with laws which were not only violations of the fundamental principles of our national Constitution but disgraceful to civilization and destructive of free Government. No man, whose conscience has vitality sufficient to make him honest, can read the slave codes of the southern States without admitting that they are utterly repugnant to the genius of our free institutions and irreconcilably opposed to the theory of our Government. And yet every one knows that these tyrannical, hostile, and barbarous codes were absolutely necessary for the preservation of the slave system, even in those dark days of slavery's rule which existed before the present war awakened to its true and real life the moral sense of the nation, and forced its ever-enduring light into the beclouded minds of the bondmen of this land, quickening their perception into that keen appreciation of every man's right to "life, liberty, and the pursuit of happiness," which bids defiance to slave codes, and effectively asserts and maintains the right of every man to own himself. The system, being a pure despotism, was forced to resort to despotic laws for support, defense, and perpetuation.

It was perfectly natural for the comparatively few men who held four million human beings in a bondage which puts to shame all other kindred systems which ever cursed man for their mildness, not only to resort to cruel and despotic laws for aid in their diabolical act, but also to seek refuge in the anti-republican dogma that "the right to govern resides in a very small minority; the duty to obey is inherent in the great mass of mankind." Domestic slavery, backed by immense capital and political power, knitted its lethargic web closely and firmly around statesmen and parties, and soon forged fetters for holding the mass of the people in governmental slavery. The minority commanded, and flew to arms to destroy the Government when the mass of the people refused to obey; and the war which is now so severely taxing the energies of our people, and drawing so exhaustively on the resources of the country, is the legitimate offspring of the attempt of a reckless, insolent, and depraved slaveholding oligarchy to mold this Government into a political counterpart of that barbaric domestic despotism which asserts the right of property in man. "The state of entire subjection of one person to the will of another" struck hands with "the right to govern resides in a very small minority; the duty to obey is inherent in the great mass of mankind." Domestic slavery and political slavery were joined in unholy wedlock in the temple of the Republic, amid their infernal progeny are now trying to demolish the grand edifice in which their incestuous parents plighted their criminal vows. The entire combination, from minutest nefarious particle to its aggregated atrocity, is an antirepublican, despotic whole, the sworn enemy of all that is good, the bane of all that is just.

Mr. Chairman, we can cast our eyes upon no page of this nation's history whereon it is not written, "Slavery is incompatible with a free Government." We have tried to close our eyes against this constantly repeated and self-evident truth. We have tried to reason it away, to practice arts which should carry us around it, or over it, or under it. We have failed to accomplish the desired result. As immutable at the laws of God stands the declaration, "Slavery is incompatible with a free Government." Decked with the habiliments of death, surrounded by all the dread scenes of war, this incompatibility is thundering at the gates of the citadel of the Republic, demanding recognition. The loyal inmates command us to obey the summons. But we have not yet had enough of sorrow, desolation, and death. We must stop and reason, while the national treasure pours out in streams of increasing volume, while the life-blood flows from other hearts, while graves in untold numbers are preparing, and the ashes of desolation are cast upon unnumbered hearthstones. We must not act rashly. We must be calm, discreet, dignified. We must inquire why this great thunderer is thus disturbing our old traditions and confusing our conservative ideas. Well, let us examine this demand, and ascertain upon what facts it is supported.

In order to understand perfectly the objects which the people had in view when they ordained the Constitution of the United States, we must turn to the preamble which introduces us to that instrument. When we give it our attention we find it a very plain-spoken guide, void of guile or dissimulation. It discloses to us, first, that the Constitution is the work of the people; and this at once develops the thoroughly republic-democratic character of the Government established. It was a grand creation of the people for their own security in the possession of the great objects expressed in the preamble. All of the powers embraced in the Constitution were placed there for the sole purpose of putting these objects above interference from any source and beyond

the hazard of loss. These objects are not only compatible with, but absolutely necessary to, the existence and enjoyment of a free Government. No one of them can be destroyed without detriment to the whole; and anything which by its nature is incompatible with either stands in the same relation to all the rest, and must, if permitted to acquire supremacy, ultimately subvert the tree principles of the Government itself. How does the account stand between slavery and these great objects? Let us give our attention to this question for a few minutes, for it is one of transcendent importance.

The first object of the people was "to form a more perfect Union." What has been and is now the attitude of slavery toward this primary object of the Constitution? When slavery, in the natural threatening and disturbing course of its development, assumed the character and form of a political power, its first act was a denial that the *people* had formed a "more perfect Union," coupled with the assertion that the Union was a mere compact between the several *States*, which might be dissolved at the pleasure of any party thereto. This position was selected as most likely to terrify the people into submission while their power was being transferred to the hands of the few, and as affording a plausible pretext for the destruction of the Union in the event freedom should prove too strong for slavery and the people should refuse to surrender their power into the hands of those who would destroy their liberties. Shrewd calculators were the men who selected and intrenched this position. For many years the terrors which they exhibited to the people from this cunningly masked battery of error held the mass in check. But, when it was almost too late, the people discovered their danger, regained their power, resolved to enforce the grand principles and traditions of justice and liberty, and stood up in their majesty masters of the situation. Slavery flew to its last resort, sought to enforce by strife and battle its doctrine of a compact of States, and the right to dissolve the same at pleasure, and for three long and bloody years has been by the dread power and fearful engineries of war seeking the destruction of the Union of the people.

The second object of the people was "to establish justice." How could slavery stand otherwise than opposed to this? Slavery is injustice. The establishment of justice would destroy slavery. Both cannot live together in peace. In the very nature of things a state of strife, contention, war, will and must exist unceasingly between these two irreconcilable enemies until one shall succumb to the other. Justice is "the virtue which consists in giving to every one what is his due; practical conformity to the laws and to the principles of rectitude in the dealings of men with each other." Slavery is the direct, perfect, absolute opposite of this. Must not the house in which these two antagonisms exist be divided against itself? Can such a house stand? Is it possible to establish justice and maintain slavery? The long, dark, terrible record written on the pages of all incessant strife, first in unhealthy, feverish, exhausting political excitements, and finally in the best, truest, and bravest blood of the nation, and now culminating amid the awful scenes of a war unprecedented in proportions and unequaled in the matchless glory of its promised results, furnishes to us and to the world an unquestionable negative to the queries I have submitted. Slavery challenged the people in their endeavors to establish justice, and resorted to the ordeal of battle against them in their efforts to maintain a Government founded upon this divine attribute. The ordeal of battle is not yet closed. The contest is in the full tide of its power. All around the combatants the nations of the world as spectators press with an eagerness and intensity of interest never before prepared for the pages of history, while the spirits of the fathers of our republican system look down from their bright and blest abode, hoping for the triumph of justice, and appeal to God who has gathered them to Himself to strengthen the arms which strike for the right. We know, the peoples of the earth know, the spirits of the fathers know, that this grand struggle for victory can be terminated only by the triumph of justice and the death of slavery, or by the success of slavery and the death of the Republic. No compromise can be made, no truce can be adjusted, no silver-tongued appeals for peace can be heard amid the din of this fierce conflict. We must establish justice upon the tomb of slavery, or have it not at all. We must establish it or acknowledge the Republic a failure. We will establish it by destroying, in the manner and form prescribed by our Constitution, that which stands in our way—slavery.

Another object to be accomplished by the adoption of the Constitution was to "insure domestic tranquillity." This was the voice of the people. How stands the account between the Republic and slavery concerning this grand purpose of the people? When, since slavery assumed political proportions, has it subserved the great end of domestic tranquillity? It has been powerful, but what are the fruits of its power? The long line of political, legislative, judicial history of this nation presents not a page which is not disfigured by some blot

placed upon it by the aggressive, intolerant, exacting, and despotic spirit of slavery. From school-book to statute-book, from hearthstone opinions to decisions of the Supreme Court of the United States, from political hustings to the sacred desk, from town meetings to Congress, no bright spot appears without a blemish from the hands of the restless, meddling, disturbing genius of slavery. Everywhere its footprints appear, always tending toward a disturbance of our domestic tranquillity. We had no national repose, for constant pro-slavery agitation kept a continual fever in the national system, consuming its energies and its life. This was the condition of the nation in the so-called times of peace, and before the good guns of Sumter answered the war summons of slavery. Since that time our domestic tranquility, always disturbed, has been enveloped in the dark, dense, impenetrable cloud of war thrown over it and around it by the spirit which discharged the first shot against the flag of the Union, and commenced the present deplorable trial by battle. Instead of insuring domestic tranquillity slavery has been an irrepressible disturber of the nation's repose. It accorded to us no rest in our miscalled day of peace. Steadily it pressed us toward despotism or war. We declined to advance further upon either of these dread alternatives, and turned our faces back to the position which the fathers had occupied. No sooner was our gaze turned in that direction than slavery's shrill bugle-blast aroused the people to the fearful realities of the most gigantic, wicked, and causeless civil war that ever cursed the earth or disturbed the repose of nations. Summoning to its standard panoplied hosts of deceived, misguided, ignorant men, keeping step under the flag of death to the music of disunion, it has forced from the shops and offices and stores and fields of the loyal and freedom-loving North hundreds of thousands of the brave, true, intelligent, patriotic sons of the Republic to sterner work than the enjoyment of domestic tranquility—to the battlefield, to death, and the grave. Mourning households, broken hearth-circles, bleeding hearts, everywhere bear witness that slavery is the destroyer and not a promoter of domestic tranquillity.

"To provide for the common defense" was another declared purpose of the people when they ordained the Constitution. The common defense of a republic can never be insured by nurturing within it its implacable enemy. The elements on which a republic relies for that concentration of resources and strength necessary to effective common defense must be homogeneous. Anything which prevents this is inimical to the prosperity and success of the Government. Doctrines of government, systems of labor, social organizations, commercial and manufacturing interests, religious, moral, and educational purposes, all must be so connectedly harmonious "as to create a chain of mutual dependencies," each relying on its fellows for support, while all work in unison for the accomplishment of a common end. Interrupt this harmony and the rule which enforces the resulting discord is arbitrary, and consequently at war with free government. And we must remember that the common defense which the people declared for, and which our security demands, is not merely that which shall meet and overcome the assaults of foreign Powers, but has quite as direct reference to the preservation of the equipoise of our republican system in opposition to all hostile efforts and influences originating among ourselves. Very little good would result from a mere maintenance of our territorial proportions in opposition to outward assailants, if we should fail to preserve our republican forms, our Christian principles, our true moral and social characteristics, from internal efforts to destroy them. We have long had, and now have, a wily, aggressive, restless domestic enemy, which has to a greater extent imperiled the nation than have all other foes combined. It has interfered with every element of national strength, by aggressing upon our doctrines of government, forcing collision between systems of labor, distracting our social organizations, disturbing our commercial relations, injuring our manufacturing interests, dividing our religious communities, debauching the public morals, preventing universality of education, and forcing discord into every fiber of the Republic. Slavery has done this, and now wages war for the purpose of completing the destruction of the nation. These are the contributions of slavery to the common defense.

Following naturally and logically in the chain of objects declared by the people we find the next is to "promote the general welfare." In opposition to this slavery has stood as a wall of brass. For the aggrandizement of a privileged class, the upbuilding of an aristocracy, and the debasement of the masses, slavery has been the chief instrument. But all these ends are opposed to the general welfare. That must rest upon things quite different—upon equality, democracy, and the elevation of the masses. There can be no true development of those qualities which make a nation great and prosperous unless its energies are so diffused as to reach all classes, all interests, all sources of power, and embrace them all

in its grand march of progress. Who ever measured the mighty resources of this nation before the present war broke the spell which slavery had cast over the people, and set the national mind and conscience free? Three years, marked by the bloody footprints of war, surcharged with the griefs of a hundred battle-fields, have done more for the development of the powers and resources of this nation than half a century accomplished when slavery controlled the national mind. When slavery ruled, the energies of the people were comparatively dormant. What little of vigor worked its way up to and through the incrusted surface was made captive by the interminable political agitations with which slavery disturbed the country and checked the progress of the Republic. Underlying these agitations were false principles of political economy, unsound doctrines of government, erroneous theories of trade and commerce, ruinous systems of public policy, unjust systems of labor—everything which was calculated to retard the true advancement of the nation. These agitations dominated over everything. The brain-force of the country was subject to them. They everywhere overshadowed the material interests of the country, directed its legislation, overawed its executive agents, controlled its courts, corrupted its religion, debased its morals, vitiated its literature, beclouded and benumbed everything upon which a people must rely for greatness, prosperity, happiness, and the promotion of the general welfare. They kept the public mind in a constant state of unhealthy excitement, and infused their poison into every vein and artery of the body-politic.

Sir, this is the past as molded by slavery. Shall the future be its harmonious counterpart? Shall we pass through this horrid political nightmare again to be awakened therefrom by the bugle-blast and cannon-roar of another war, or shall we secure a permanent peace to ourselves and our children by firmly establishing the general welfare upon the tomb of slavery? We cannot postpone these grave questions for posterity to answer. With us they abide, and we are to answer them. We must answer them, and do it faithfully for freedom, if we would have this war pass into the history of past events, and not "drag its slow length along" the pages of the future. No avenue is presented for our escape except that which leads over the dead body of slavery. This great fact is recognized by the nation. Its immense proportions have attracted the attention of the civilized world. Shall we alone close our eyes to it and attempt to avoid its grave responsibilities? We cannot succeed in this if we should try. We ought not to try, for the general welfare of the nation forbids it.

The last, the grandest, the most sublime of the objects declared by the people in the ordination of the Constitution is, "to secure the blessings of liberty to ourselves and our posterity." Of this great object of the people, Story, in his Commentaries on the Constitution, says:

"Surely no object could be more worthy of the wisdom and ambition of the best men in any age. If there be anything which may justly challenge the admiration of all mankind, it is that sublime patriotism which, looking beyond its own times and its own fleeting pursuits, aims to secure the permanent happiness of posterity by laying the broad foundations of Government upon immovable principles of justice. Our affections, indeed, may naturally be presumed to outlive the brief limits of our own lives, and to repose with deep sensibility upon our own immediate descendants. But there is a noble disinterestedness in that forecast which disregards present objects for the sake of *all mankind* and erects structures to protect, support, and bless the most distant generations."

Let us not overlook that portion of this well-expressed and better-bestowed praise which rests upon the fact that the glorious work of the people was for "the sake of all mankind." Let it bring afresh to our minds that important question propounded by Jefferson:

"Can the liberties of a nation be thought secure when we have removed their only firm basis, a conviction in the minds of the people that these liberties are the gift of God; that they are not to be violated but with His wrath?"

Has not slavery denied that this great work of the people was intended for the "safety of all mankind," and brought upon us the just chastisement of God, who intended "these liberties" for all of His creatures? What are the thunders of this war but the voice of God calling upon this nation to return from the evil paths, made rough by errors and misfortunes, blunders and crimes, made slippery by the warm, smoking blood of our brothers and friends, to the grand highway of national thrift, prosperity, happiness, glory, and peace, in which He planted the feet of the fathers? Cannot we hear amid the wild rushing roar of this war storm the voice of Him who rides upon the winds and rules the tempest saying unto us, "You cannot have peace until you secure liberty to all who are subject to your laws?" Sir, this declaration must be heeded. It has been whispered into the ears of this nation since first we pronounced life, liberty, and the pursuit of happiness to be the inalienable rights of all men, and now it rolls in upon as like the voice of the ocean, tendering peace or war to our election. Which shall we elect? Shall it be peace? How can it be peace while liberty and slavery dwell together in our midst? These are enemies. These are ideas which cannot dwell together in harmony. How can we have peace? Let slavery die. Let its death be written in our Constitution. Let the Constitution "proclaim liberty throughout the land to all the inhabitants thereof." This is the way to peace—firm, enduring peace, embracing all mankind, and reaching to the most distant generations. In this way only can we secure liberty to ourselves and our posterity.

But, sir, slavery has not contented itself with manifesting its incompatibility with our free Government by opposing the great objects for securing which the people ordained and established the Constitution. It has confronted the Constitution itself, and prevented the enforcement of its most vital provisions. Section two of article six of the Constitution says:

"This Constitution, and the laws of the United States which shall be made in pursuance thereof, and all treaties made, or which shall be made, under the authority of the United States, shall be the supreme law of the land; and the judges in every State shall be bound thereby, anything in the constitution or laws of any State to the contrary notwithstanding."

Of the many provisions of the Constitution devised for the protection of the unity of the nation, this one stands first in importance. Without it the bond of union would be as weak as an invalid between whom and the grave but a breath intervenes. The supremacy of the Constitution, the laws and treaties of the United States, are necessary to our existence as a nation. Our unity can be preserved in no other way. This was the belief of those who ordained the Constitution, and our experience accords therewith. But, sir, slavery planted itself in opposition to this provision of the Constitution, and declared that it should not be enforced. Do you ask for proof? We need not go far to find it. Turn to the Constitution and take as a guide the words:

"The citizens of each State shall be entitled to all the privileges and immunities of citizens of the several States."

To what extent has this been regarded as the supreme law of the land in States where slavery controlled legislation, presided in the courts, directed the Executives, and commanded the mob? It is a provision of most vital importance to every citizen. We could not be a nation of equals without it. It is the peerage title of our people. How has it been observed? What has been the conduct of slavery toward it? Let us turn again to the Constitution for practical aid in the solution of these questions. In the first article of the Amendments to the Constitution we find this language:

> "Congress shall make no law respecting an establishment of religion, or prohibiting the free exercise thereof; or abridging the freedom of speech, or of the press; or the right of the people peaceably to assemble, and to petition the Government for a redress of grievances."

The great rights here enumerated were regarded by the people as too sacred and too essential to the preservation of their liberties to be trusted with no firmer defense than the rule that "Congress can exercise no power which is not delegated to it." Around this negative protection was erected the positive barrier of absolute prohibition. Freedom of religious opinion, freedom of speech and press, and the right of assemblage for the purpose of petition belong to every American citizen, high or low, rich or poor, wherever he may be within the jurisdiction of the United States. With these rights no State may interfere without breach of the bond which holds the Union together. How have these rights essential to liberty been respected in those sections of the Union where slavery held the reins of local authority and directed the thoughts, prejudices, and passions of the people? The bitter, cruel, relentless persecutions of the Methodists in the South, almost as void of pity as those which were visited upon the Huguenots in France, tell how utterly slavery disregards the right to a free exercise of religion. No religion which recognizes God's eternal attribute of justice and breathes that spirit of love which applies to all men the sublime commandment, "Whatsoever ye would that men should do unto you, do ye even so to them," can ever be allowed free exercise where slavery curses men and defies God. No religious denomination can flourish or even be tolerated where slavery rules without surrendering the choicest jewels of its faith into the keeping of that infidel power which withholds the Bible from the poor. Religion, "consisting in the performance of all known duties to God and our fellow-men," never has been and never will be allowed free exercise in any community where slavery dwarfs the consciences of men. The Constitution may declare the right, but slavery ever will, as it ever has, trample upon the Constitution and prevent the enjoyment of the right.

How much better has free discussion fared at the hands of the black censor who guards the interests of slavery against the expression of the thoughts of freemen? On what rood of this Republic cursed by slavery have men been free to declare their approval of the divine doctrines of the Declaration of Independence? Where, except in the free States of this Union, have the nation's toiling millions been permitted to assert their great protective doctrine, "The laborer is worthy of his hire?" What member of our great free labor force, North or South, could stand up in the presence of the despotism which owns men and combat the atrocious assertion that "Slavery is the natural and normal condition of the laboring man, whether white or black," with the noble declaration that "Labor being the sure foundation of the nation's prosperity should be performed by free men, for they alone have an interest in the preservation of free government," with any assurance that his life would not be exacted as the price of his temerity? In all this broad land not one could be found. The press has been padlocked, and men's lips have been sealed. Constitutional defense of free discussion by speech or press has been a rope of sand south of the line which marked the limit of dignified free labor in this country. South of that line an organized element of death was surely sapping the foundations of our free institutions, reversing the theory of our Government, dwarfing our civilization, contracting the national conscience, compassing the destruction of everything calculated to preserve the republican character of our Constitution; and no man in the immediate presence of this rapidly accumulating ruin dared to raise a voice of warning. Submission and silence were inexorably exacted. Such, sir, is the free discussion which slavery tolerates. Such is its observance of the high constitutional rights of the citizen. Its past will be repeated in its future if the people permit it to curse the world with a continued existence.

"The right of the people peaceably to assemble and to petition the Government for a redress of grievances," has been as completely disregarded as the other rights I have mentioned by the terrorism which guards the citadel of slavery. If slavery persecuted religionists, denied the privilege of free discussion, prevented free elections, trampled upon all of the constitutional guarantees belonging to the citizen, peaceable assemblages of the people to consider these grievances with a view to petition the Government for redress could not be held. If non-slaveholding whites became alarmed at the bold announcement that "slavery is the natural and normal condition of the laboring man, whether white or black," seeing therein the commencement of an effort intended to result in the enslavement of labor instead of the mere enslavement of the African race, they were not privileged to peaceably assemble and petition the Government in regard thereto, or to discuss the barbarism and to arouse the people in opposition to it. Slavery held political and social power sufficient to crush all such attempts on the part of the injured people. Slavery could hold its assemblages, discuss, resolve, petition, threaten, disregard its constitutional obligations, trample upon the rights of labor, do anything its despotic disposition might direct; but freedom and freemen must be deaf, dumb, and blind. Throughout all the dominions of slavery republican government, constitutional liberty, the blessings of our free institutions were mere fables. An aristocracy enjoyed unlimited power, while the people were pressed to the earth and denied the inestimable privileges which by right they should have enjoyed in all the fullness designed by the Constitution.

Sir, I might enumerate many other constitutional rights of the citizen which slavery has disregarded and practically destroyed, but I have enough to illustrate my proposition: that slavery disregards the supremacy of the Constitution and denies to the citizens of each State the privileges and immunities of citizens in the several States.

The proposition needs no argument. We all know that for many years before the commencement of the gigantic rebellion now in progress the supporters of slavery enforced this disregard of the supremacy of the Constitution and of the privileges and immunities of the citizen by every power and influence known to the communities cursed by the presence of a slave. Legislatures, courts, Executives, almost every person holding political or social power and position in the southern States, were all arrayed on the side of slavery, and what they could not accomplish was turned over to the mob, which, without law, with abuse, indignities, cruelties, and hempen halters, did its work with fearful accuracy and terrible exactness. Twenty million free men in the free States were practically reduced to the condition

of semi-citizens of the United States; for the enjoyment of their rights, privileges, and immunities as citizens depended upon a perpetual residence north of Mason and Dixon's line. South of that line the rights which I have mentioned, and many more which I might mention, could be enjoyed only when debased to the uses of slavery. Slave-holders and their supporters alone were free to think and print, to do and say what seemed to them best on both sides of that line. They could think, read, talk, discuss with perfect freedom in each and every State, and fearfully they used this advantage to destroy the liberties of this country. It is quite time, sir, for the people of the free States to look these facts squarely in the face and provide a remedy which shall make the future safe for the rights of each and every citizen. Had slavery not possessed this advantage, civil war, freighted with sorrow, desolation, and death, would not have visited this nation. But since it has come, the people of the free States should insist on ample protection to their rights, privileges, and immunities, which are none other than those which the Constitution was designed to secure to all citizens alike, and see to it that the power which caused the war shall cease to exist, to the end that the curse of civil war may never be visited upon us again, and that the citizen whose home is in the North shall be as free to assert his opinions and enjoy all of his constitutional rights in the sunny South as he whose roof-tree is the magnolia shall to the same ends be free amid the mountains of New England and the sparkling lakes of the North and the West. An equal and exact observance of the constitutional rights of each and every citizen, in each and every State, is the end to which we should cause the lessons of this war to carry us. Whatever stands between us and the accomplishment of this great end should be removed. Can we reach this end and save slavery? Can we reconcile the antagonisms which have produced this war? Can we mix the oil and water of despotism and republicanism? Can we harmonize the contending elements of absolutism and free government? No, sir; it is not given to human power to accomplish these results. What, then, shall we do? Abolish slavery. How? By amending our national Constitution. Why? Because slavery is incompatible with free government. Peace, prosperity, national harmony, progress, civilization, Christianity, all admonish us that our only safety lies in universal freedom.

Sir, I have endeavored to show that slavery stands arrayed against every object for the attainment of which the people ordained and established the Constitution; that it is seeking the destruction of the Union, is opposed to the establishment of justice, has disturbed our domestic tranquillity, makes war upon us instead of providing for the common defense, promotes widespread desolation and ruin instead of advancing the general welfare, and seeks to withhold from us and our posterity the blessings of liberty. I have endeavored to show that it has disregarded the Constitution and trampled upon the most sacred rights of the citizen. But the case is so nearly self-evident that it is difficult to argue it. The antagonism is so marked, and the incompatibility so glaringly apparent, that they overshadow proof and argument. The conscience of the nation is so sensitively active concerning the questions to which I have spoken that it arrives at conclusions with the rapidity by which thought measures distance. Argument cannot travel so fast. At best it is but the baggage-train of the grand army of ideas and aspirations which is now leading this nation to that higher and purer civilization that forms the silver lining of the dark war cloud which overhangs the Republic.

Mr. Chairman, the position which this nation maintains to-day in relation to the true character of slavery is more perfect than that which the founders of the Government occupied. They believed that slavery was so directly opposed to justice, so distinctly arrayed against divine law, so utterly depraved and desperately wicked, that its own aggregation of enormities would speedily accomplish its dissolution. We recognize their faith as most correct, except in its conclusion. We see that the death can only be accomplished by an executioner. Slavery will not kill itself. The decree of death has been enrolled. The death-warrant was sealed by the first shot which struck Fort Sumter. But condemned culprits do not execute themselves, and slavery is no exception to the rule.

I admit that the progress of the war has accomplished much toward giving effect to the decree. In our harvest of blood we have gathered great compensatory results. The spirit of patriotism has returned to us clothed with a resurrectional brightness like unto that which shall light the heirs of glory to the abode of the eternal Father. Manhood, as it stood proudly erect in the grand, colossal, symmetrical proportions known to the early days of the Republic, again gives sublimity to American character. An acknowledged dependence on Him who guides the planets and notices the fall of a sparrow is once more the sure defense of our people. An awakened, invigorated, concentrated national conscience re-

vivifies our observance of justice. Fear of God and love of country blend and course from heart to extremities of the earnest masses who struggle amid the awful terrors and black woes of war for that sublime end, a true peace. These happy results have effected many of the preliminaries to the final death of the condemned disturber of our repose. Already the glowing fruits of ultimate victory gather around and about us. Thousands of human beings who were slaves at the commencement of this accursed rebellion are now enjoying the freedom which God designed for all of His creatures. The limits of slavery have been contracted by State action, and other States are directing their efforts to the further compression of the dominion of the black power which wars upon all that is good. Congress has not failed to provide a way through which men may march from bondage to freedom. The President has nobly performed his duty by striking the chains of slavery from millions of men. Public opinion, the conqueror of men and parties, the maker of Presidents and Congresses, has flung its banner to the breeze, inscribed with the glorious words, "Liberty and Union." Providence has opened up the way to that higher civilization and purer Christianity which the Republic is to attain. The very atmosphere which surrounds us is filled with the spirit of emancipation. Every throb of the popular heart sends coursing to the very extremities of national life the warm blood of freedom. These things all cheer the hearts of the true sons of the Republic. Our Red Sea passage promises to be as propitious as was that of God's chosen people when the waters parted and presented the sea-bed for their escape from the hosts upon whom these waters closed and effected the burial appointed by Him who had declared, "Let my people go." The bow of promise now arches the heavens, but the end is not yet. We have advanced, but promise signifies future. We hope for the end, but it is not yet abiding with us; for hope pertains to that which we do not possess. We feel that we have gained much during the terrible trial to which the Republic has been subjected, and we know that at far too great price have the people purchased the position of which they are now the masters to permit it to pass again into the possession of the enemies of free government. The position must be fortified and the lines advanced. What freedom has gained must be intrenched by the strong arm of the Constitution. The life and treasure which the loyal citizens of the Union have expended, in amount unprecedented and with cheerfulness almost incomprehensible, must be made to secure something more durable than a lull of the storm, a delusive hope, and a deceitful peace. Security for the future must be the result of the great demands to which our people have so nobly responded. The price paid is ample, and its returns must be worthy of the grand patriotism which rose, as if by the command of God, all panoplied for war, and equal to all of the exactions of the awful conflict whose birth was announced by the roar of rebel cannon over the bay of Charleston.

Sir, let us not be misled by delusive hopes, nor deceived by artful words. Let no siren song divert us from the path which the events of our fancied days of peace and the lessons of this war have marked out for us with more unerring exactness than that with which the magnetic needle points the course of the mariner on the trackless ocean. There was a lurking devil in the words of the gentleman from New York [Mr. BROOKS] when he told us that he accepted "the abolition of slavery as a fact accomplished." He knows, the world knows, that none of the acts hostile to slavery which I have mentioned have gone beyond the fact of making men affected by them free; that no one of them has reached the root of slavery and prepared for the destruction of the system. We have made some men free, but the system yet lives, and has its thousands of active tongues all over this land, hissing its defense and seeking to benumb the public conscience by covering it over with the slime of death. One of these tongues, forked and slimy, speaks from the mouth of the man who holds in his hands the reigns of the executive power of the Empire State the words—

"If it is true that slavery must be abolished to save this Union, then the people of the South should be allowed to withdraw themselves from that Government which cannot give them the protection guarantied by its terms."

This man does not believe that the abolition of slavery is a "fact accomplished;" and he has a numerous, active, crafty, unscrupulous party at his back, every member of which accepts the teachings of this master. In this Hall busy tongues paraphrase this guilty declaration, and cry aloud for the "Union as it was," with the great, black crime of slavery "as it was," or "peace on any terms."

From the other end of this Capitol a senatorial tongue has hissed upon the records of the country these defiant words in behalf of slavery:

"By your acts you attempt to free slaves. You will not have them among you. You leave them where they are. Then what is to be the result? I presume that local State governments will be preserved. If they are, if the people have a right to make their own laws and to govern themselves, they will not only reenslave every person you attempt to set free, but they will reenslave the whole race."

And a tongue in this body answers, "If you destroy slavery, you destroy our free institutions." These are the tongues which are to be the oracles of the convention that is to meet at Chicago on the 4th day of next July to organize the elements of a powerful party in the interests of slavery.

Sir, is it not madness to act upon the idea that slavery is dead? We hold it as a condemned, unexecuted culprit, and know that it is not dead. Why shall we not recognize the fact and provide for the execution? We must do so, or go on digging graves and pouring sorrow into the loyal homes of the people; for the systems and ideas which flash their lightning among the clouds of this war will never cease from strife until from hilltop to mountain-top, from valley to plain, from ocean to ocean, from the lakes to the Gulf, the swelling tide of the nation's acclaim announces to the people of the earth that American slavery is to be known to the future only through the history of the past. To us is this great work intrusted. How shall we perform it? There lies no difficulty in our way if we will but do our duty.

The Committee on the Judiciary have authorized me to report to the House the proposed amendment of the Constitution of the United States, with a recommendation that it be passed by this body and submitted to the Legislatures of the several States for their acceptance. A concurrence in this recommendation is the plain road over which we may escape from the difficulties which now beset us. A submission of this proposition to the several States will at once remove from Congress the question of slavery. No further agitation of this vexatious question need disturb our deliberations if we concur in this recommendation, and we shall be far advanced toward a lasting, ever-enduring peace. Send this proposition to the States, trust it to the people, fix it as a center around which public opinion may gather its potent agencies, and we shall have accomplished more for the future tranquillity of the Republic than ever was effected by Congress before. The people are now convinced of the incompatibility of slavery with free government. Let us impart to them an opportunity to give effect to their conviction. If we refuse, our successors will be more obedient; for the people have decreed that slavery shall die, and that its death shall be recorded in the Constitution. We are to construct the machinery which shall execute the decree or give place to those who will perform the bidding of the people. We cannot evade the responsibility which rests upon us by declaring that we "accept the abolition of slavery as a fact accomplished." The nation knows that this enunciation is a mere lachrymose, diplomatic intrigue employed by slavery to arrest the grand volcanic action that is upheaving the great moral ideas which underlie the Republic. The nation demands more, its faith embraces more; its acute appreciation of the true nature of the disease which preys upon its heartstrings assures it that the work of death cannot be arrested until the fact of slavery's dissolution is accomplished; and that this may not be until, by amendment of the Constitution, we assert the ultimate triumph of liberty over slavery, democracy over aristocracy, free government over absolutism.

9

US Senate, Speech of Lyman Trumbull (R-IL) Reporting Amended Version of Abolition Amendment

March 28, 1864[*]

The Senate, as in Committee of the Whole, proceeded to consider the joint resolution (S. No. 16) proposing amendments to the Constitution of the United States.

The joint resolution, as originally introduced by Mr. HENDERSON, proposed the following articles as amendments to the Constitution of the United States, which, when adopted by the Legislatures of three fourths of the several States, shall be valid, to all intents and purposes, as part of the Constitution:

ART. 1. Slavery or involuntary servitude, except as a punishment for crime, shall not exist in the United States.

ART. 2. The Congress, whenever a majority of the members elected to each House shall deem it necessary, may propose amendments to the Constitution, or, on the application of the Legislatures of a

majority of the several States, shall call a convention for proposing amendments, which in either case shall be valid, to all intents and purposes, as part of the Constitution, when ratified by the Legislatures of two thirds of the several States, or by conventions in two thirds thereof; as the one or the other mode of ratification may be proposed by Congress.

The Committee on the Judiciary proposed an amendment to strike out all after the resolving clause and insert the following:

(Two thirds of both Houses concurring,) That the following article be proposed to the Legislatures of the several States as an amendment to the Constitution of the United States, which, when ratified by three fourths of said Legislatures, shall be valid, to all intents and purposes, as a part of the said Constitution, namely:

Article XIII.

Sec. 1. Neither slavery nor involuntary servitude, except as a punishment for crime, whereof the party shall have been duly convicted, shall exist within the United States, or any place subject to their jurisdiction.

Sec. 2. Congress shall have power to enforce this article by appropriate legislation.

Mr. TRUMBULL. Mr. President, as the organ of the Committee on the Judiciary which has reported this resolution to the Senate, I desire to present briefly some of the considerations which induced me, at least, to give it my support. It is a proposition so to amend the Constitution of the United States as forever to prohibit slavery within its jurisdiction, and authorize the Congress of the United States to pass such laws as may be necessary to carry this provision into effect.

Without stopping to inquire into all the causes of our troubles, and of the distress, desolation, and death which have grown out of this atrocious rebellion, I suppose it will be generally admitted that they sprung from slavery. If a large political party in the North attribute these troubles to the impertinent interference of northern philanthropists and fanatics with an institution in the southern States with which they had no right to interfere, I reply, if there had been no such institution there could have been no such alleged impertinent interference; if there had been no slavery in the South, there could have been no abolitionists in the North to interfere with it. If, upon the other hand, it be said that

[*] *Cong. Globe*, 38th Cong., 1st Sess., 1313–14 (Mar. 28, 1864).

this rebellion grows out of the attempt on the part of those in the interest of slavery to govern this country so as to perpetuate and increase the slaveholding power, and failing in this that they have endeavored to overthrow the Government and set up an empire of their own, founded upon slavery as its chief corner-stone, I reply, if there had been no slavery there could have been no such foundation on which to build. If the freedom of speech and of the press, so dear to freemen everywhere, and especially cherished in this time of war by a large party in the North who are now opposed to interfering with slavery, has been denied us all our lives in one half the States of the Union, it was by reason of slavery.

If these Halls have resounded from our earliest recollections with the strifes and contests of sections, ending sometimes in blood, it was slavery which almost always occasioned them. No superficial observer, even, of our history North or South, or of any party, can doubt that slavery lies at the bottom of our present troubles. Our fathers who made the Constitution regarded it as an evil, and looked forward to its early extinction. They felt the inconsistency of their position, while proclaiming the equal rights of all to life, liberty, and happiness, they denied liberty, happiness, and life itself to a whole race, except in subordination to them. It was impossible, in the nature of things, that a Government based on such antagonistic principles could permanently and peacefully endure, nor did its founders expect it would. They looked forward to the not distant, nor as they supposed uncertain period when slavery should be abolished, and the Government become in fact, what they made it in name, one securing the blessings of liberty to all. The history of the last seventy years has proved that the founders of the Republic were mistaken in their expectations; and slavery, so far from gradually disappearing as they had anticipated, had so strengthened itself that in 1860 its advocates demanded the control of the nation in its interests, failing in which they attempted its overthrow. This attempt brought into hostile collision the slaveholding aristocracy, who made the right to live by the toil of others the chief article of their faith, and the free laboring masses of the North, who believed in the right of every man to eat the bread his own hands had earned.

In the earlier stages of the war there was an indisposition on the part of the executive authority to interfere with slavery at all. For a long time slaves who escaped from their rebel owners and came within our lines were driven back. Congress, however, at an early day took action upon this subject, and at the very first session which met after the rebellion broke out, the special session of July, 1861, a law was passed declaring free all slaves who were permitted by their masters to take any part in the rebellion. Under the provisions of that act, had it been efficiently executed, a great many slaves must necessarily have obtained their freedom. The constitutionality of the act would seem to be clear. I do not suppose that even my honorable friend from Kentucky [Mr. DAVIS] would deny the proposition that if we captured a slave engaged, by consent of his master, in constructing rebel works and fortifications, we might set him free.

That act, however, has not been executed. So far as I am advised not a single slave has been set at liberty under it. Subsequently, at the regular session of Congress which convened in December, 1861, an act of a more comprehensive character was passed—a law providing for the freedom of all slaves who should come within the lines of our armies, who should be deserted by their masters, or who should be found in regions of country which had been occupied by rebel troops and afterwards came within our possession, and who belonged to rebel masters. It is under the provisions of this law that most of the slaves made free have been emancipated. This act also authorized the President of the United States to organize and employ as many persons of African descent as he should think proper to aid in the suppression of the rebellion. But it was a long time before this law was put in operation. Although it was an act called for by the public sentiment of the country, and although it was the duty of those charged with the execution of the laws to see that it was faithfully executed, it was more than a year after its enactment before any considerable number of persons of African descent were organized and armed; and even at this day a much smaller number are in the service than would have been by an efficient execution of the law. It was not until after the passage of this act that our officers, especially in the West, ceased to expel slaves who came within the lines of our Army; and so persistently was this practice persevered in that Congress had to interfere by positive enactment, and declare that any officer of the Army or Navy who aided in restoring a slave to his master should be dismissed from the public service, before it could be stopped.

But, sir, had these laws, all of them, been efficiently executed they would not wholly have extirpated slavery. They were only aimed at the slaves of rebels. Congress never undertook to free the slaves of loyal men; no act has ever passed for that purpose.

At a later period, the President by proclamation undertook to free the slaves in certain localities. Notice of this proclamation was given in September, 1862, and it was to become effective in January, 1863. Unlike the acts of Congress, which undertook to free the slaves of rebels only, and of such as came under our control, the President's proclamation excepted from its provisions the regions of country subject to our authority, and declared free the slaves only who were in regions of country from which the authority of the United States was expelled, enjoining upon the persons proposed to be made free to abstain from all violence unless in necessary self-defense, and recommending them in all cases, when allowed, to labor faithfully for reasonable wages.

The force and effect of this proclamation are understood very differently by its advocates and opponents. The former insist that it is and was within the constitutional power of the President, as Commander-in-Chief, to issue such a proclamation; that it is the noblest act of his life or the age; and that by virtue of its provisions all slaves within the localities designated become *ipso facto* free; while others declare that it was issued without competent authority, and has not and cannot effect the emancipation of a single slave. These latter insist that the most the President could do, as commander of the armies of the United States, would be, in the absence of legislation, to seize and free the slaves which came within the control of the Army; that the power exercised by a commander-in-chief, as such, must be a power exercised in fact, and that beyond his lines where his armies cannot go his orders are mere *brutum fulmen*, and can neither work a forfeiture of property nor freedom of slaves; that the power of Fremont and Hunter, commanders-in-chief for a certain time in their departments, who assumed to free the slaves within their respective commands, was just as effective within the boundaries of their commands as that of the Commander-in-Chief of all the departments, who as commander could not draw to himself any of his presidential powers; and that neither had or could have any force except within the lines and where the Army actually had the power to execute the order; that to that extent the previous acts of Congress would free the slaves of rebels, and if the President's proclamation had any effect it would only be to free the slaves of loyal men, for which the laws of the land did not provide. I will not undertake to say which of these opinions is correct, nor

is it necessary for my purposes to decide. It is enough for me to show that any and all these laws and proclamations, giving to each the largest effect claimed by its friends, are ineffectual to the destruction of slavery. The laws of Congress if faithfully executed would leave remaining the slaves belonging to loyal masters, which, considering how many are held by children and females not engaged in the rebellion, would be no inconsiderable number, and the President's proclamation excepts from its provisions all of Delaware, Maryland, Kentucky, Tennessee, Missouri, and a good portion of Louisiana and Virginia—almost half the slave States.

If then we are to get rid of the institution, we must have some more efficient way of doing it than by the proclamations that have been issued or the acts of Congress which have been passed.

Some, however, say that we may pass an act of Congress to abolish slavery altogether, and petitions are sent to Congress asking it to pass such a law. I am as anxious to get rid of slavery as any person; but has Congress authority to pass a law abolishing slavery everywhere, freeing the slaves of the loyal, the slaves of the friends of the Government as well as the slaves of the disloyal and of the enemies of the Government? Why, sir, it has been an admitted axiom from the foundation of this Government, among all parties, that Congress had no authority to interfere with slavery in the States where it existed. But it is said this was in a time of peace, and we are now at war, and Congress has authority to carry on war, and in carrying on war we may free the slaves. Why so? Because it is necessary; for no other reason. If we can do it by act of Congress it must be because it is a necessity to the prosecution of the war. We have authority to put down the enemies of the country; we have the right to slay them in battle; we have authority to confiscate their property; but, mark you, does that give any authority to slay the friends of the country, to confiscate the property of the friends of the country, or to free the slaves of the friends of the country?

But it is said that freeing slaves would aid us in raising troops; that slaves are unwilling to volunteer and enter the public service unless other slaves are made free, and that we could raise troops better, sooner, and have a more efficient army if slavery were declared abolished. Suppose that were so, is it a necessity? Can we not raise an army without doing this? Has not the Congress of the United States unlimited authority to provide for the raising of armies by draft, by force to put any and every man capable of bearing arms into its service? Have we not already passed a law compelling men to enter the service of the Government in its defense and for the putting down this rebellion? Then there is no necessity to free the slaves in order to raise an army.

But it is a convenience, perhaps some will say. Sir, it is not because a measure would be convenient that Congress has authority to adopt it. The measure must be appropriate and needful to carry into effect some granted power, or we have no authority to adopt it. I can imagine a thousand things that would aid us to raise troops which no one would contend Congress had authority to do. We now find that it is costing us a large sum of money to carry on this war. There are apprehensions in some quarters that the finances of the country will not be sufficient to prosecute it to the end. A measure that would enable us to carry on the war cheaper would certainly be one in aid of this war power. In consequence of the prosperity which prevails in the country, wages at this time are very high. Men are unwilling to enlist without large bounties and large pay, because they get high wages at home. Suppose we introduce a bill that no man shall be paid in any manufacturing establishment, at any mechanic art, or for his daily labor, more than ten cents a day, and we visit with penalties and punishment any man who shall give to his employ more than that sum; do you not think that would hold out an additional inducement to volunteer? But who would contend that Congress had any such authority? Manifestly it has not. Nor can I find the constitutional authority to abolish slavery everywhere by act of Congress as a necessity to prosecuting the war.

Then, sir, in my judgment, the only effectual way of ridding the country of slavery, and so that it cannot be resuscitated, is by an amendment of the Constitution forever prohibiting it within the jurisdiction of the United States. This amendment adopted, not only does slavery cease, but it can never be reestablished by State authority, or in any other way than by again amending the Constitution. Whereas, if slavery should now be abolished by act of Congress or proclamation of the President, assuming that either has the power to do it, there is nothing in the Constitution to prevent any State from reestablishing it. This change of the Constitution will also relieve us of all difficulty in the restoration to the Union of the rebel States when our brave soldiers shall have reduced them to obedience to the laws.

To secure its passage requires, in the first instance, a vote of two thirds in its favor in each branch of Congress, and its ratification subsequently by three fourths of the States of the Union. Can these majorities be ob-

tained? It is very generally conceded, I believe, by men of all political parties, that slavery is gone; that the value of slavery is destroyed by the rebellion. What objection, then, can there be on the part of any one, in the present state of public feeling in the country, to giving the people an opportunity to pass upon this question? I would appeal to Senators upon the opposite side of the Chamber, and ask them—for I expect some of them to support this measure, and I trust all of them will—what objection they have to submitting this question to the people and letting them pass upon it? Do any of you deny that slavery lies at the bottom of this rebellion? Do you believe that we should have had this terrible war upon us had there been no slavery in the land? I repeat, then, why not afford an opportunity to the people to pass upon this amendment? I trust I do not assume too much when I assume that it will receive the requisite vote of two thirds of each branch of Congress.

Having obtained that, the question then arises, is it probable that it can have the ratification of three fourths of the States? We have now thirty-five States, and bills have passed both branches of Congress and been approved by the President for the creation of two more, Colorado and Nevada, which will make thirty-seven. When these States are admitted it will require the concurring vote of twenty-eight States in order to adopt this amendment.

If Nebraska should be admitted, for the admission of which a bill is now pending, that would make the number of States thirty-eight, and the votes of twenty-nine States would then be requisite to adopt the amendment. But the admission of Nebraska would not probably affect the result, as, if admitted, she would most probably vote for the amendment.

Of the thirty-seven States, twenty-one are free States, including Colorado and Nevada, and I assume that all those States would vote for this constitutional amendment. There are, then, the States of Maryland, West Virginia, Missouri, Arkansas, Tennessee, and Louisiana, all of which have taken initiatory steps for the abolition of slavery within their borders; and I think we might confidently count that they would unite with the free States to pass this amendment. Those six added to the twenty-one free States would make twenty-seven. Then there is the State of Delaware, with hardly slaves enough in it to count, which would be left standing alone with free States all around her. Although she has not yet, so far as I am aware, taken any legislative steps for the abolition of slavery, though the question is agitated among her people, I cannot think she would stand alone in such a locality, resisting a constitutional amendment which would forever give us peace on this question.

I have assumed that all the free States will adopt the amendment. It is now very generally conceded that slavery is not a divine institution. The few in the northern or free States who attempt to uphold it do so on constitutional grounds, denying the authority of the Government to interfere with it; but none of these persons deny or can deny the power of the people to amend the Constitution in the mode prescribed by the instrument itself. If, then, they shall oppose an amendment for the abolition of slavery, it will not be because to abolish it in that form is unconstitutional, but because it is not right, or, if right, not expedient.

I think, then, it is reasonable to suppose that if this proposed amendment passes Congress, it will within a year receive the ratification of the requisite number of States to make it a part of the Constitution. That accomplished, and we are forever freed of this troublesome question. We accomplish then what the statesmen of this country have been struggling to accomplish for years. We take this question entirely away from the politics of the country. We relieve Congress of sectional strifes, and, what is better than all, we restore to a whole race that freedom which is theirs by the gift of God, but which we for generations have wickedly denied them.

I know that the passage of this measure will not end this rebellion. I do not claim that for it. There is but one way to do that; and that is by the power of our brave soldiers. We can never have the Union restored, the authority of the Constitution recognized, and its laws obeyed and respected, until our armies shall overcome and vanquish the rebel armies. We must look to our soldiers, to our patriotic Army, to put down the rebellion. But, sir, when they shall have accomplished that, this measure will secure to us future peace. That is what I claim for it. I trust that within a year, in less time than it will take to make this constitutional amendment effective, our armies will have put to flight the rebel armies. I think it ought long ago to have been done; and I think but for the indecision, the irresolution, the want of plan, and the scattering of our forces, it would have been done long ago. Hundreds of millions of treasure and a hundred thousand lives would have been saved had the power of this Republic been concentrated under one mind and hurled in masses upon the main rebel armies. This is what our patriotic soldiers have wanted, and what I trust is now soon to be done.

But instead of looking back and mourning over the errors of the past, let us remember them only for the lessons they teach for the future. Forgetting the things which are past, let us press forward to the accomplishment of what is before. We have at last placed at the head of our armies a man in whom the country has confidence, a man who has won victories wherever he has been, and I trust that his mind is to be permitted uninterfered with to unite our forces, never before so formidable as to-day, in one or two grand armies and hurl them upon the rebel force. Let him put to fight the main rebel army which has threatened the capital for the last three years, and the small rebel armies will quickly succumb. I look for that result during the coming campaign, and with that result, if we civilians do our duty, we shall have the authority of the Constitution vindicated, constitutional liberty reestablished, the Union restored, and freedom everywhere proclaimed.

10

US Senate, Speech of Henry Wilson (R-MA)

March 28, 1864[*]

Mr. WILSON.

...

Why is it, Mr. President, that this magnificent continental Republic is now rent, torn, dissevered, by civil war? Why is it that the land resounds with the measured tread of a million of armed men? Why is it that our bright waters are stained and our green fields reddened with fraternal blood? Why is it that the young men of America, in the pride and bloom of early manhood, are summoned from homes, from the mothers who bore them, from the wives and sisters who love them, to the fields of bloody strife? Why is it that millions of the men and the women of Christian America are sorrowing with aching hearts and tearful eyes for the absent, the loved, and the lost? Why is it that the heart of loyal America throbs heavily oppressed with anxiety and gloom for the future of the country?

Sir, this gigantic crime against the peace, the unity,

[*] *Cong. Globe*, 38th Cong., 1st Sess., 1319, 1320–22 (Mar. 28, 1864).

and the life of the nation is to make eternal the hateful dominion of man over the souls and bodies of his fellow-men. These sacrifices of property, of health, and of life, these appalling sorrows and agonies now upon us, are all the merciless inflictions of slavery in its gigantic effort to found its empire and make its hateful power forever dominant in Christian America. Yes, slavery is the conspirator that conceived and organized this mighty conspiracy against the unity and existence of the Republic. Slavery is the traitor that madly plunged the nation into the fire and blood and darkness of civil war. Slavery is the criminal whose hands are dripping with the blood of our murdered sons. Yes, sir, slavery is the conspirator, the traitor, the criminal that is reddening the sods of Christian America with the blood of fathers and husbands, sons and brothers, and bathing them with the bitter tears of mothers, wives, and sisters.

Sir, slavery—bold, proud, domineering, with hate in its heart, scorn in its eye, defiance in its mien—has pronounced against the existence of republican institutions in America, against the supremacy of the Government, the unity and life of the nation. Slavery, hating the cherished institutions that tend to secure the rights and enlarge the privileges of mankind; despising the toiling masses as mudsills and white slaves; defying the Government, its Constitution and its laws, has openly pronounced itself the mortal and unappeasable enemy of the Republic. Slavery stands to-day the only clearly pronounced foe our country has on the globe. Therefore every word spoken, every line written, every act performed, that keeps the breath of life in slavery for a moment is against the existence of democratic institutions, against the dignity of the toiling millions, against the liberty, the peace, the honor, time renown, and the life of the nation. In the lights of to-day that flash upon us from camp and battle-field, the loyal eye, heart, and brain of America sees and feels and realizes that the death of slavery is the life of the nation! The loyal voice of patriotism pronounces, in clear accents, that American slavery must die that the American Republic may live!

...

Slaves were held in the District of Columbia, and slave pens and the slave trade polluted and dishonored the national capital under the color of laws for which the people of America were responsible in the forum of nations and before the throne of Almighty God. Christian men and women, oppressed with the sin and shame, humbly petitioned Congress to relieve them from that sin and shame by making the national capital free. Slavery bade its tools—its Pattons, its Pinckney, and its Athertons—violate the constitutional right of petition, and willing majorities hastened to register its decree. Slavery arraigned before the bar of the House of Representatives John Quincy Adams, the illustrious champion of the right of petition and the freedom of speech and it expelled the fearless and faithful Giddings for the offense of daring to construe the Constitution of his country and interpret the law of nations. Slavery stepped upon the decks of Massachusetts ships in the harbor of Charleston, seized colored seamen, citizens of the Commonwealth, and consigned them to prisons, to be fined, to be lashed, and to be sold into perpetual bondage. Massachusetts, mindful of the rights of all her citizens, sent Samuel Hoar, one of her most honored sons, to test the constitutional rights of her imprisoned citizens in the judicial tribunals. Slavery cast him violently from South Carolina, and enacted that whoever should attempt to defend the rights of colored seamen in the courts of that Commonwealth should suffer the ignominy of imprisonment.

...

To the full comprehension of every man in America whose heart, brain, and soul have not been poisoned by its seductive arts and malign influence slavery is the cause, the whole cause, of this foul, wicked, and bloody rebellion. Every loyal American whose reason is unclouded sees that slavery is the prolific mother of all these nameless woes—these sumless agonies of civil war. He sees that every loyal soldier upon the cot of sickness, of wounds, and of death, was laid there by slavery; that every wounded and maimed soldier hobbling along our streets was wounded and maimed by slavery; that the lowly grave of every loyal soldier fallen in defense of the country was dug by slavery; that mourning wives and sorrowing children were made widows and orphans by slavery. Before the tribunal of mankind of the present and of coming ages, before the bar of the ever-living God, the loyal heart of America holds slavery responsible for every dollar sacrificed, for every drop of blood shed, for every pang of toil, of agony, and of death, for every tear wrung from suffering or affection, in this godless rebellion now upon us. For these treasonable deeds, for these crimes against freedom, humanity, and the life of the nation, slavery should be doomed by the loyal people of America to a swift, utter, and ignominious annihilation.

But slavery, Mr. President, should not only be doomed to an ignominious death, to perish utterly from the face of the country, for the treasonable crime of levying war upon the Government, but the safety if not the existence of the nation demands its extermination. The experience of nearly three years of civil war has demonstrated to the full comprehension of every loyal and intelligent man in America that slavery is the motive-power, the heart and soul and brain of the rebellion. Slavery fills the hearts of the southern people with its sweltered venom, with its dark and malignant hatred of the free States, and with its bitter scorn and contempt for the toiling masses for the policy that cares for their rights and interests, and for the institutions that improve and elevate them. Slavery instinctively feels that the achieved institutions of twenty million free people, their free speech, free presses, their political, moral, and religious convictions, their permanent interests, all forbid that its policy should continue to control the national Government. Slavery realizes, too, that every enduring element of the Constitution, every permanent principle of national policy and interest, is and must continue to be hostile to the ascendency of its principles and its policy. Slavery, hating, scorning, despising the toiling millions of the Republic, conscious that it cannot longer retain the permanent control of the national Government, consolidates the public opinion of the South against the people and Government, and fires southern ambition and interest with the idea of a splendid slaveholding empire, sitting on the shores of the Mexican Gulf, and extending its imperial sway over Cuba, Mexico, and Central America.

Sir, slavery not only fires the southern heart, brain, and soul, and nerves the southern arm in council-hall and on the battle-field with its malignant hate and bitter scorn of Yankee laborers and Yankee institutions, its lofty contempt for the principles and policy of freedom, its haughty defiance of the authority of the national Government, and its gorgeous visions of the future power of the southern confederacy, commanding the commerce of the world by its tropical productions and its millions of slaves, but it uses the bones and sinews of more than three millions of the bondmen of rebel masters in support of the rebellion. These slaves of rebel masters sow and reap, plant and gather the harvests that support rebel masters and feed rebel armies. By their ceaseless, unpaid toil, these millions of bondmen enable their traitorous masters and the poor white men of the rebel States to leave their fields and shops and rush to the battle-field to shed the blood of our loyal countrymen, of our neighbors and friends and brothers

and sons. These bondmen throw up fortifications, dig trenches and rifle-pits, make roads and bridges, fell forests and build barracks, drive teams, and relieve in many ways the toil of rebel soldiers, thus making more efficient the rebel armies. It is as clear as the track of the sun across the heavens that these slaves of rebel masters are as efficient instruments for the overthrow of the authority of the Federal Government, for the dismemberment of the Republic, and the establishment of the rebel empire, as are rebel soldiers in camp or on battle-field. The spade and hoe of the slaves of rebels support the rifle and bayonet of rebel soldiers. Slavery is not only the motive-power, the heart and soul of the rebellion, but it is the arm also. Therefore the preservation of the life of the country, and the lives of our brave soldiers battling for national existence, as well as the just punishment of conspiracy and treason, demand that the loyal men of the Republic shall swear by Him who liveth evermore that slavery in America shall die.

Not only the punishment of its appalling crimes, not only the lives of our countrymen and the preservation of the life of the nation, demand the utter extermination of slavery, but the future repose of the country also demands it. Slavery has poisoned the very fountains of existence in the South; it has entered into the blood and bone and marrow and the soul of our southern countrymen. It has filled their bosoms with bitter, fierce, unreasoning hate toward their countrymen of the North, and the institutions, the Government, and the flag of their country. So long as slavery shall live, it will infuse its deadly and fatal poison into the southern brain, heart, and soul. Then let slavery die a felon's death, and sink into a traitor's grave, amid the curses of a loyal nation.

11

US Senate, Speech of Garrett Davis (U-KY)

March 30, 1864*

Mr. DAVIS said:

Mr. PRESIDENT: There is no more important business to be transacted by the people of the United States than

*Cong. Globe, 38th Cong., 1st Sess., Appendix, 104–8 (Mar. 30, 1864).

the amendment of their Federal Constitution, the fundamental law of their Government. The general reason assigned by the chairman of the Committee on the Judiciary, who reported this resolution, and supported it in a very able speech, why the proposed amendment should be adopted, struck me as being very unsound and altogether fallacious. He assumed that slavery was the cause of the rebellion: in substance, that whether the immediate and proximate cause was in the purpose of the rebels to establish a southern confederacy, consisting exclusively of slave States, and based upon the institution of slavery, or whether that immediate and proximate cause was the interference of the northern fanatics and abolitionists with the institution—in either state of case, slavery was the cause of the war, and therefore should be abolished. If my honorable friend should devote himself to the general policy of abolishing all causes that directly or indirectly lead to wars, with the purpose and hope to prevent them, I think he will adopt one of the most utopian and impracticable notions that has ever yet engaged the mind of a statesman and a legislator.

Sir, what produced the war of the Revolution? The apparent cause was the encroachment of the mother country upon the rights of the colonies. The immediate and proximate cause was the imposition of the stamp tax and duties on the importation of teas and other articles into the colonies. This was taxation without representation. According to the logic of this day, as taken up and enforced by the honorable chairman of the Committee on the Judiciary, the wise and proper mode of treating that difficulty at the time would have been to prohibit such transactions as required stamps and the importation of articles upon which duties had been or were likely to be imposed by act of Parliament. Taxation of the colonies by the Parliament of England without being represented in it was unquestionably the proximate cause of that war; and according to the reasoning of the Senator, the abrogation of all property, commerce, and transactions in the colonies upon which the mother country could levy taxes would have made their imposition impossible, and have thus removed the cause of the impending war, and that policy should have been adopted by the colonies as well to prevent the then impending as future wars.

...

Mr. President, if I was asked to point out the most operative single cause of the pending war, I should certainly name the intermeddling of Massachusetts with the institution of slavery. I suppose other Senators, and especially those from the northern portion of the free States, would associate South Carolina as being equally probably a greater sinner than Massachusetts. From this equality of delinquency and guilt I should certainly dissent. But I would be disposed to compromise the matter by conceding "bad eminence" to both of these States, and in relation to both I would be perfectly willing to adopt the remedy of the honorable Senator from Illinois and inflexibly to put it in execution. I would abolish both of the States; and if that *abolition* could have occurred twenty or thirty years ago I feel entire confidence that this deplorable war would never have occurred. I only regret that it has not been within the scope of providential events or within the actual and executed policy of the Government and people of the United States that these two pestiferous States had been wiped out in the past generation. Sir, it would have been a demolition, but it would have produced incalculable good to the whole country.

But, sir, I am opposed to the pending proposition to amend the Constitution of the United States for several reasons intrinsic to the subject. In the first place it strikes at one of the most essential principles of our commingled system of national and of State governments. When the Declaration of Independence was promulgated and when the Constitution of the United States was adopted, there were thirteen States. According to the present boundary of these thirteen States, the area of territory of the United States is now more than five times as much as the aggregate of those States, and the number of States will be, if the Union is restored, before many years multiplied to more than fourfold of the original thirteen. Those States had existed as independent communities. While they were colonies, they were independent of each other; dependent only upon the Government of the mother country. When the colonies assumed their independence, they took that condition as separate and distinct sovereignties, and the attributes of independence, in its essential nature, of each of the States was not destroyed or parted with by the old Articles of Confederation. All the substantial powers of sovereignty, of separate political independence, subsisted and were exercised by the various States after the adoption of the Articles of Confederation. According to my recollection, the Articles of Confederation were not finally adopted by all the States until 1778. They were offered for the adoption of the colonies in 1776, and a considerable time elapsed before they were adopted by several of them.

The people of all the colonies had been habituated from their first settlement each for itself, by its own will and by its own legislative body, to manage its own domestic and local concerns. There consequently was no proposition that these domestic concerns of the States should be surrendered to a common national Government, either when the Articles of Confederation or the present Constitution of the United States was formed. If such a proposition had been made, it would not have been entertained one moment, either in the Congress that formed the Articles of Confederation or the Convention that framed the Constitution. But if such an extensive jurisdiction had been surrendered by the States to the General Government, its exercise would have been impossible under the Articles of Confederation and impracticable under the Constitution, as well from the generally limited and restricted powers of the United States Government under both, as from the incompetency of our central Government to wisely and safely manage all the local affairs of so many States, varying in climate, soil, pursuits, productions, natural and artificial, education, opinions, and religious faith; and each for itself having always previously had the exclusive management of all these concerns. They were never intended to be, and are not in fact, confided to the General Government; but by an express provision of the Constitution are with jealous forethought reserved to the States.

If that was the state of things when there were but thirteen States and comparatively so small a territory, with what accumulated force does it present itself now, when we are about to have thirty-eight or thirty-nine States, and many others will soon be thronging into the Union and it has already overleaped the distant Rocky and Coast mountains, and is washed by the billows of both the Atlantic and Pacific oceans?

If we are to have union, liberty, and peace, the indispensable condition is that the great fundamental principle, that the States are to have the entire and exclusive control of their own local and domestic institutions and affairs, must be held inviolable by the General Government. The opposite would result in intolerable despotism and misgovernment, soon to be overthrown by general consent or violence.

Sir, to this objection it may be answered, "This amendment is restricted to a single subject, and that subject slavery." But the proposed amendment carries a general principle which is as hostile to other peculiarly local and State institutions and interests as to slavery.

When the war of the Revolution commenced every State in the Union held slaves, and it was the normal condition of the colonies. It continued to be the normal condition of the States from their Declaration of Independence until after its acknowledgment by the treaty of 1783. The States that adhered to slavery and continued that institution had more reason and juster grounds of complaint against the States which abolished it than these States had against those that continued it. If all the States that held to slavery at the close of the war of the Revolution had continued it to the present time, the subsequent mischievous agitation by the people of some of the States of slavery in other States, and the present convulsion would never have been heard of. Slavery would not have been even an imputed cause of any war or trouble among the States. The States that abolished slavery themselves departed from the homogeneous condition of the colonies and original States. They had no power or reason to claim more than the right to control that institution within their own borders, to abolish it or to continue it, as seemed to them best; and they ought scrupulously to have abstained from intermeddling with it in other States who chose to continue it. The plainest policy and the commonest good faith required this forbearance.

The right of Kentucky to continue slavery was as perfect and absolute as was the right of Massachusetts to abolish it. She had no more just ground to insist that the other slave States should abolish slavery than they had that she should continue it. But Senators seem to lose sight of this great feature in our blended system of government. To maintain it, to hold it in its harmonious and perfect action, it is as essential that the existence of the authority and powers of the States within their reserved-sovereignty should be upheld, maintained, and preserved as it is that the limited and delegated powers and sovereignty of the General Government should exist, be supported, defended, and exercised. Sir, our complex system of government was so fashioned and understood by those who made it. I will read from the thirty-ninth number of the Federalist, which was written by Mr. Madison in support of this important principle. He is discussing the character of the Government and its mixed features, and he says:

"But if the Government be national, with regard to the *operation* of its powers, It changes its aspect again when we contemplate it in relation to the *extent* of its powers. The idea of a national Government involves in it, not only an authority over the individual citizens, but an indefinite supremacy over all persons and things, so far they are objects of lawful government. Among a people consolidated into one nation this supremacy is completely vested in the national legislature. Among communities united for particular purposes it is vested partly in the general and partly in the municipal legislatures. In the former case all local authorities are subordinate to the supreme, and may be controlled, directed, or abolished by it at pleasure. In the latter the local or municipal authorities form distinct and independent portions of the supremacy, no more subject, within their respective spheres, to the general authority than the general authority is subject to them within its own sphere. In this relation, then, the proposed Government cannot be deemed a *national* one, since its jurisdiction extends to certain enumerated objects only, and leaves to the several States a residuary and inviolable sovereignty over all other objects."*

The men who framed the Constitution were preeminently wise, experienced, and patriotic statesmen. Its contemporaneous expounders understood it well, and the presentation and argument of its leading principles in the numbers of the Federalist, for ability and truth never was exceeded by commentary or gloss on any Government. If those who have charge of and administer the Government now and in the future would learn from them, maladministration could be but rare and of no great or abiding mischief. In no treatise which I have read can as much be learned in the same space of the true nature and principles of our Government as in number thirty-nine of the Federalist. In this paragraph the sovereignty delegated by the people of the States to the Federal Government and that retained to themselves and their governments respectively is clearly stated. In the first "its jurisdiction extends to *certain enumerated objects only*, and leaves to the several States a *residuary and inviolable sovereignty over all other objects.*" The Government of the United States and of the States have separate and distinct portions of the aggregate mass of all political sovereignty, and each government is of paramount and supreme authority within its proper jurisdiction. To make war upon the United States or any States when they are respectively in the exercise

of their constitutional powers or to resist by armed force the execution of their laws is equally treason; and if this war or resistance is made by officers of the United States against a State, or by officers of any State government against the United States, it is no less treason against the State or the United States respectively than it would be if the delinquents were unofficial persons. The President may commit treason against a State and a Governor of any State against the United States by the same acts that would be treason if done by private individuals. No position of office or authority, whether under the United States or a State, gives any immunity whatever for acts of treason against either.

Mr. HOWE. As the Senator and I seem to be agreed upon one point, and I wish to know how far I am committed—

Mr. DAVIS. I do not hold you committed at all.

Mr. HOWE. In reference to that I should like to ask him a single question. I ask him whether the Army of the United States commit treason in making war against the laws of South Carolina? Does he hold that that is one of the States whose laws limit the action of the Army of the United States?

Mr. DAVIS. No, I do not hold that, but I lay down my position thus: that when a State is in the performance of its duty in conformity to the Federal Constitution, that State is entitled to the same immunity from infraction of its laws and sovereignty by the President of the United States and all officers of the General Government, civil and military, as from its own citizens, and as the United States and their Government are from the Governor and other officers of the State. That is my position. The absorption of the sovereignty not delegated by the Constitution to the General Government, and consequently reserved to the States, or any portion of it, by the President or Congress, would be revolutionary and destructive of our system, as would be the absorption by the States of the sovereignty, or any portion of it, delegated to the Government of the United States. The encroachment of either upon the other would be equally unauthorized and criminal, and the persons engaged in making it punishable for parallel offenses by their respective judicial tribunals. There is a common and reciprocal duty and right between the Government of the United States and the States, to respect the powers and rights of each other and to defend their own. It is the highest obligation of every citizen to support and defend both against all assailants, though they be the officers of the other, and with its colorable authority. Mr.

* [*Federalist*, No. 39 (Madison), this volume, 1B, doc. 3. —Ed.]

President, [Mr. POWELL in the chair,] it is clearly and imperatively the duty of you and myself to defend the reserved rights and sovereignty of Kentucky against the encroachments of Abraham Lincoln and his party, as it is to defend the limited sovereignty of the United States against the assaults of the rebels. To fail in either would be equally delinquent and criminal.

. . .

But to the objection that the proposed amendment of the Constitution would infringe the right of the States to manage their local and domestic affairs, it may also be answered that slavery concerns all the States as well as those in which it exists. If there be truth in this position, it may be replied that there is no important property interest, pursuit, or institution in any State that does not, directly or indirectly, concern the people of every other State; and that argument would require the Constitution of the United States to be so amended as to give the Federal Government power over all of them, which would establish a perfectly consolidated Government and virtually annihilate the States.

There are many matters, the control of which is left by our Government wholly and exclusively with the States, and over which the people would not have confided to Congress and the President a particle of power when the Constitution was formed, that much more closely and momentously concern all the States than the continuance of slavery in some of them. Religious faith is one. There is intrinsic antagonism between Romanism and Protestantism. For the first half century after the colonies became a nation the former was so weak in comparison with the latter that any great disturbance by conflict between them was impossible. But in the last thirty years Romanism has made great increase on Protestantism in the United States, both by immigration and propagandism. In Europe the fiercest and most implacable contests that man ever made with man as often occurred between these professors of the same Christian religion, and about it. There is no reason to hope that they will not be reproduced both on that continent and in the United States. The Federal Government has no power to interfere in any way with the subject of religion, although it has recently by its military officers made such interference, in violation of the express prohibition of the Constitution. The *entailment* of real and personal property, the principle of *primogeniture*, a system of railroads and other internal improvements in the several States connecting with the systems of other States—all these are subjects of domestic and local concern within every State, of which it has the exclusive management; and yet each one more nearly, and with larger interest and greater sympathy, would concern the people of all the other States than does slavery in the slave States the people of the free States.

The commerce, the social intercourse, and the material prosperity of the people of each State require that its mediums of travel and commerce should connect with those of all the adjacent States. Our general system of government is based upon the principles of popular equality and the equal distribution of property, upon the death of its owner, among all his children and heirs. The whole people of the United States have an indirect but essential interest in the maintenance of these principles in all the States; and a policy of self-isolation, or the establishment of entails or primogeniture in one, and especially in many, of the States, would be seriously hostile to those principles, and very repugnant to the people of the other States. The questions of the religious faith of the people of each State, whether all phases shall be tolerated, whether Romanism or Protestantism shall dominate, whether any and what form shall be recognized by law and have exclusive privileges as the religion of the State, whether Mormonism, Deism, or Atheism shall be established and exist in one or many States, and other modes of intercommunication and trade in each State to connect with those of all the others, are matters of much more real interest to the whole people of the United States than the continuance of slavery in the slave States can be to the people of the free States. The matter of religion is more apt to grapple strongly the passions and the imaginations of mankind, and the other subjects their selfishness and prejudices, than the existence of slavery in communities of which they are not members. Slavery, in this day and generation, has for the people of the United States a factitious but an absorbing interest; in the future, under altered circumstances, the others, and especially religion, may still more strongly possess them. If this proposed alteration of the Constitution be accepted it will be a precedent, and may establish a principle that may carry those other domestic concerns, and still others not now thought of, into the domain of an encroaching and centralized despotism, and which would be a very great stride.

If it were conceded that the power to amend the Constitution, as established and regulated by the fifth article, would by its terms and letter authorize the proposed change, it would be in fatal conflict with its intent and spirit, and therefore, according to a universal

412

rule of construction, void and of no effect. It never was the purpose of those who made it to subject many of its great principles to be expunged by the exercise of this power of amendment. The power to amend is but the power to improve, and any alteration to be legitimate should be an amendment. To this it may be said that as there is no certain test by which this question of amendment can be tried it is necessarily decided by the amending power. Granting this argument to be sound, still there is another and very important question connected with this power of amendment. Does it import the power of revolution? Of making such essential change in the nature, form, powers, and limitations of the Government as would be revolutionary of it—of its important structure, of its characteristic principles, of the great and essential rights and liberties assured by it to the citizen? The true and precise question is, does the proposed change, or *amendment*, carry a revolutionary principle and power? I hold that the framers of the Constitution did not intend it to be, and that it is not in its nature or in fact, a revolutionary power; that there is a boundary between the power of revolution and the power of amendment, which the latter, as established in our Constitution, cannot pass; and that if the proposed change is revolutionary it would be null and void, notwithstanding it might be formally adopted. It would not be a part of the Constitution, and would consequently have no effect. An amendment proposing to abolish all the popular elective features of our Government, or that Representatives should hold their offices for life; that the place of Senator should be hereditary, coupled with a title and the privileges of nobility; that the President should be a king, and transmit his crown and throne as in England, would be revolutionary, and out of the power of the pale of amendment. Neither the legislative, executive, nor judicial branch of the Government could be swept away under the guise of the exercise of this power of amendment. The States and their governments are as essential and indispensable parts of our compound system of Government, as the United States and the Federal Government, and could not be expunged by this power of amendment. The retention by the States of their exclusive rights, and the right to ordain, manage, and control them, independent of all control or interference by the United States Government any more than of a foreign Power, is a great and essential feature of our system, and it cannot be revolutionized, destroyed, by this power of amendment. If it can take cognizance of slavery, it may of every other local and domestic con-

cern of the States. That would be revolutionary, and is therefore out of the domain of amendment. The power of amendment can only be made to embrace the forms and the provisions and principles of secondary importance.

. . .

Nor, sir, is the present condition of the country and the people at all propitious or fit to enter upon the most grave and important work of amending, altering the Constitution of our Government, the paramount law which regulates and controls within its orbit the constitutions, laws, and administrations of all the States and every official act of Congress, the President, and of every other officer of the United States. The revision of the work of the preeminently great and patriotic men who put together that wonderful political structure, so admirably adjusted and balanced, so novel yet so complete, so free and yet possessed of all the necessary and proper powers and vigor, is one of the most delicate and important tasks which those who are to perform it can possibly undertake. They ought to be free from all sectional prejudice and excitement, and bring to it calm and unperturbed reason and broad and true patriotism and statesmanship. The condition of the country should be fixed, that of settled and stable repose, that any changes and modifications might be safely and wisely adapted to its permanent relations, interests, and tranquillity. Who can foresee how materially different its situation may be at the earliest day when the proposed amendment would take effect from what it now is? Changes that might now be innoxious or proper and salutary may then be *malapropos* and mischievous. Such might be their nature and consequences in the circumstances of the country when the war closes.

. . .

But, sir, if the country and the people were in a suitable condition to enter upon this work of revising and altering, with the purpose to improve, a constitutional Government made by the great men, so ripe in experience, and wisdom, so broad and unselfish in patriotism, and so truly devoted to liberty regulated by law, and yet so diffident of their competency to the task, the mode adopted is not the best one. The principles and points that would demand consideration will not be one, but many. Their proper examination and settlement would require the freest and most unreserved interchange of opinions and views of the wisest and most virtuous men of each and all the States selected for this special work, and meeting together in common convention for its performance. Casual Congresses, assuming and presuming to initiate and lay out this work in single and separate patch-pieces, would promise but little of wisdom or good; and the simple acceptance or rejection of their recommended propositions, by as many local Legislatures or conventions as there are States, representing the sectional interests, opinions, prejudices, aversions, partialities, and all the weaknesses and errors of their several States, would hardly eviscerate from such assemblies any additions to the Constitution formed by Washington and his compeers that could be truthfully denominated *amendments*.

The best mode of reaching truth and principle, policy and safety, in any changes of the Constitution would be a convention, in which every State and all its leading interests should be represented; and the presentation of important facts, opinions, and views that concern them all, should be made to the entire representation of the people of the United States. The assembling of men together, face to face, who are local representatives, to unfold directly to each other matters of so much importance, that have close connections, and necessarily extensive antagonism, and that ought as near as possible to be satisfactorily compromised, harmonized, and settled, is unquestionably the best mode. If the Senators and Representatives of each State were to be isolated and convened in them, and without any comparison of views with those of all the other States were to act on all subjects of legislation, it could not bear any comparison with the existing mode. It is true that in the continuing and never-ending business of making laws for the United States, those objections would apply with a vastly increased force. But in the momentous and most difficult task of altering the Constitution in this perturbed and fearful time, and adapting it to an extent and condition of country and a trial and laboring of the Government that was not anticipated by the men who framed it, the same considerations ought to have the effect utterly to forbid this single or any other amendments in the proposed form.

Another objection of overruling weight is that no revision of the Constitution in any form ought to be undertaken under the auspices of the party in power. Its leaders have always been hostile to the compromises on the subject of slavery, and the protection which it guaranties to the owners of that property. . . . Mr. Lincoln had been an extreme abolitionist from early life; and it was that consideration that procured him the nomination of the Chicago convention. When he and

the chiefs of his party in Congress, at the commencement of the war, unanimously declared that their purpose and policy were not to attack slavery, or any other rights or institutions of the insurgent States, but only to vindicate the authority and laws of the United States over the rebels, they were dissembling, and then lying in wait to make an onset on slavery. They knew that their purpose could be effected only by breaking over constitutional guarantees, and by the power of the Army to subdue all opposition to their scheme. There is no right of person or property that the President and Congress has not outrageously infracted and trampled out, under and by the agency of the iron heel of military despotism, to subjugate or awe every person disposed to offer even legal and peaceful resistance to their flagrant abuses and usurpations of power. As they progressed, and met with impunity in their nefarious work, their objects were enlarged. They determined not only to consummate the destruction of slavery, so that it could never be restored, but also to continue themselves and their party in place and power. The first they consider substantially as an accomplished fact; and they are, and have been for more than a year, moving with increasing energy and boldness toward the other as their now paramount object. They affect to adhere to the forms of the Constitution, while they utterly disregard not only its spirit but also its express provisions and all the liberty and protection which it assures to the citizen. They have devised the boldest and most revolutionary measures under the guise of law and executive administration as the machinery of their operations. The first in time was the erection of West Virginia into a new State, and her admission into the Union in palpable violation of the Constitution, so admitted and avowed by many of their leaders both in and out of Congress; and attempted to be justified by them on the ground that the country was in a state of rebellion and revolution, and the Constitution of no obligation whatever. The President took the official opinion of the Attorney General, which was that the measure was without constitutional authority, and yet he approved it.

. . .

But Mr. Lincoln has long since imbibed other views and projects of personal ambition. A desire for reelection has seized upon him. It now possesses all the mind and heart and soul that he has. He is no statesman, but a mere political charlatan. He has inordinate vanity and conceit. He is a consummate dissembler and an adroit and sagacious demagogue.

...

Our own Government has become so abused and perverted, so unjust and oppressive to all who will not bow to those who administer it in unquestioning submission, so fruitful and general a source of evil and practical despotism, that hundreds of thousands and millions of the most loyal people of the United States are in doubt whether it as administered or the rebellion is the greatest national scourge. The assaults, wrongs, and oppressions of both on the border slave States is such as to be passing them, as it were, between the upper and nether millstone. The greatest good that could now fall to the lot of the people of those States would be the speediest suppression of the rebellion by all constitutional measures and means, and by the expulsion from power of the party that has possession of the Government and is ruling the country and so recklessly rushing both upon ruin. I look for the consummation of the first to the continued efforts of our brave and numerous soldiery and the submission of the rebels. For the second I still rely upon the peaceful remedy of the ballot-box, applied by the sovereign power of the United States; and if it were applied so as to produce that great change, I believe that the cessation of the war, the submission and reconciliation of the rebels, the reconstruction of the Union, and the vindication of the laws and Constitution, with renewed guarantees and strength, would all speedily ensue. But if the dominant party can continue their power and rule, either by the will or acquiescence of the people or the exercise of the formidable powers which it has usurped, I am not able to see any termination of the present and still growing ills short of the ordeal of general and bloody anarchy.

12

US Senate, Debate on Abolition Amendment

March 31, 1864*

The Senate, as in Committee of the Whole, resumed the consideration of the joint resolution (S. No. 16) proposing amendments to the Constitution of the United States.

* *Cong. Globe*, 38th Cong., 1st Sess., 1364–69 (Mar. 31, 1864).

The joint resolution, as originally introduced by Mr. HENDERSON, proposed the following articles as amendments to the Constitution of the United States, which, when adopted by the Legislatures of three fourths of the several States, shall be valid, to all intents and purposes, as part of the Constitution:

ART. 1. Slavery or involuntary servitude, except as a punishment for crime, shall not exist in the United States.

ART. 2. The Congress, whenever a majority of the members elected to each House shall deem it necessary, may propose amendments to the Constitution, or, on the application of the Legislature of a majority of the several States, shall call a convention for proposing amendments, which in either case shall be valid, to all intents and purposes, as part of the Constitution, when ratified by the Legislatures of two thirds of the several States, or by conventions in two thirds thereof, as the one or the other mode of ratification may be proposed by Congress.

The Committee of the Judiciary proposed an amendment to strike out all after the resolving clause and insert the following:

(Two thirds of both Houses concurring,) That the following article be proposed to the Legislatures of the several States as an amendment to the Constitution of the United States, which, when ratified by three fourths of said Legislatures, shall be valid, to all intents and purposes, as a part of the said Constitution, namely:

Article XIII.
Sec. 1. Neither slavery nor involuntary servitude, except as a punishment for crime, whereof the party shall have been duly convicted, shall exist within the United States, or any place subject to their jurisdiction.
Sec. 2. Congress shall have power to enforce this article by appropriate legislation.

Yesterday Mr. DAVIS moved to amend the amendment by striking out all after the word "that," and inserting:

The States of Maine, New Hampshire and Vermont are formed into and shall constitute one State of the United States, to be called North New England; and the States of Massachusetts, Connecticut, and Rhode Island, including the Providence Planta-

415

tions, are formed into and constitute one State, to be called South New England; and Congress shall pass all laws necessary and proper to give full effect to this amendment of the Constitution.

Mr. SAULSBURY.

…

Mr. President, the question before the Senate is whether the resolution proposed by the Committee of the Judiciary shall be adopted by this body and the proposed constitutional amendments be submitted to the States. I may be about to announce a heresy, but if it be heresy I firmly believe in the truth of it, that if the Senate of the United States were to adopt this joint resolution, and were to submit it to all the States of this Union, and if three fourths of the States should ratify the amendment, it would not be binding on any State whose interest was affected by it if that State protested against it. I know the popular doctrine is, that if a convention is called by two thirds of the States and proposes any amendments whatever to the Constitution, which amendments are ratified by three fourths of the States, such amendments then become the supreme law of the land, and are binding on each and every State—those who had not assented to them as well as those who had. Such is not the opinion which I entertain of this matter. I maybe in error; I know my view is against the popular opinion; but let us test it and see who is right and who is wrong. Who framed this Constitution. Who made it?

The preamble to the Constitution commences, "We, the people of the United States," and hence some say that this is a popular Government; and they would have you believe that it has the same effect as though the people in mass meeting had framed it. Sir, that clause of the Constitution is susceptible of a rendering perfectly legitimate which would do away with this idea, even if the preamble to the Constitution could govern its provisions, and that is, "We, the people of the States united," who are but the people of the United States. Sir, that Constitution was framed by the States, by the people of the States, who elected delegates to their conventions or Legislatures. It was submitted separately to each State. It never was submitted to the people of the United States as an aggregate body. It was not even submitted to the Congress of the United States elected by the people from the particular States. It was not submitted to a general convention of delegates elected in the different States, but it was submitted directly and immediately to the States themselves. It was to bind no

State, and had no effect in any State except those States which, in their independent and separate character, ratified it.

Our seceding fathers withdrew not *en masse* from the old Articles of Confederation. The State which I have the honor in part to represent, although now one of the least populous in the Union, was the first seceder. New Jersey, Pennsylvania, and other States followed, until finally New Hampshire made secession complete from the other States by ratifying that Constitution. New York, Virginia, North Carolina, and Rhode Island were left to determine the great issue of peaceable separation or forcible opposition to it. They were left to try the power of military coercion or to exclaim that their wayward sisters might depart in peace. New York and Virginia soon seceded from the old Confederation and came in, and finally North Carolina; but Rhode Island would not whip them back again.

I am not going to discuss the question of the power of the Federal Government to coerce States back into the Union. This is not the time to discuss any such question. It has been discussed heretofore. We are now engaged in war, and we must look to the great and momentous issues of war and to the circumstances by which we are surrounded. I do not propose to enter into any discussion of that character; but I will say this, as a historical and legal truth, that there was as much authority in Rhode Island and these other States, when the nine left them, to coerce them back and make them live up to their plighted faith, for the preservation of this "perpetual Union," to which their honors were plighted, as there is in the Federal Government to coerce any of the seceded States back again. Those, however, were practical days. Practical men lived in those days. They pursued a different plan, and a "more perfect Union" was formed than that created by the Articles of Confederation. If out of all this terrible war and the struggles between the several States a more perfect Union shall be formed, a Union in which the rights of the citizen and of the States shall be respected, and in which civil liberty shall be preserved, no one will be more rejoiced than myself.

But, sir, I denied the proposition that it was competent for three fourths or the States by an amendment of the Constitution to say to any dissenting State, "This shall be your Constitution, and you shall live in this Union notwithstanding we have interfered with your independent control over your domestic rights."

…

But, sir, I hold that if you adopt this amendment, and you could get three fourths of the States to ratify it, it would not be obligatory upon the others for another reason; and that is, that you cannot propose this amendment to all the States, as contemplated by the Constitution of the United States. There are confessedly some eight or nine of these States now out of the Union, over which the Federal Government does not pretend to exercise control. What is the meaning of the clause that the Congress of the United States may propose amendments, which, when ratified by three fourths of the States, shall become a part of the Constitution? It means that you shall propose those amendments, not to a portion of the States, but to all the States, so that all the States may have the power to act upon them. I ask you, suppose we were at peace to-day; suppose this revolution had never occurred, and it had been considered proper and necessary by a majority of the people of the United States to change their fundamental law by making amendments to the Constitution; suppose, in reference to this matter or in reference to any other matter, you had adopted a joint resolution proposing those amendments, and you submitted them to three fourths of the States, and not to the other one fourth, and that they had been ratified by three fourths of the States, would you tell me that they would be a part and parcel of the Constitution because they were ratified by three fourths of the States?

Hence occurs the principle with which I started, that the Constitution of the United States is the same as any other contract. It is a contract between the States, who, in the language of Mr. Madison, are parties to it, and the plain, evident, honest import of this clause of the Constitution giving the power of ratification to three fourths of the States is and must be so understood by all right-thinking men, that all the States shall have the power of passing upon that proposed amendment, of ratifying or rejecting it, and that if any State is denied that privilege, if your amendment is not proposed to any State, it cannot operate upon that State, because it would be in violation of the just terms and fair interpretation of the Constitution. The correctness of this principle would not be denied at all in reference to a contract between parties in a court.

Then I say you cannot propose to or have your proposition acted on by a portion of the States, because you have actually declared them a hostile power, and are engaged in a war with them. You have recognized as between you and those very States belligerent rights. This only shows the impropriety of this proposition at the present time. If you wish to make an amendment to the Constitution of the United States which shall be binding and obligatory in all future time upon the parties to that Constitution, why not wait till peace is restored; why not wait till passion ceases to inflame the breast and madness to warp the judgment and craze the brain of men? The fundamental law of a great people should never be changed amid the shock of arms. Reason should sit calmly on her throne; judgment should be brought to the "line" before acting on such a question.

But, sir, I oppose this proposed amendment on another ground. It is impossible for it to be ratified by a vote of three fourths of the States. The Senator from Illinois, the chairman of the Committee on the Judiciary, said it would require twenty-eight States, and he named the States which he supposed would vote to ratify it. He included all the adhering States with the exception of my own, and he thought she could not stand against it. Let me tell the honorable Senator that if the resolution is passed, I do not suppose my State will be in the way of it; not because she will approve of it; not because the majority of her people will not be honestly opposed to it and would not vote against it, but because you do not intend that they shall ever act upon it. The Senator said that Maryland had inaugurated this policy, and she would be in favor of it. I have some acquaintance with the people of that State. She will agree to it, just as the Senator, if met by a highwayman, solitary, alone, and unarmed, presenting a pistol at his head and demanding his purse, would agree to give it up.

But he expects to receive accessions from Arkansas, Tennessee, North Carolina, and Louisiana in favor of this proposed amendment. I appeal to the honorable Senator, would he have an amendment to the Constitution and get up in his place in the Senate of the United States and declare that that was an amendment adopted by the people of Arkansas, Tennessee, North Carolina, or Louisiana, if the election were to be held at the present time? Does the Senator believe that if the people of those States were free to act, and could pass upon his proposed amendment according to their wish or judgment, there would be one man in ten who would vote to ratify it? It is impossible for the Senator so to believe.

What is your government in Arkansas, in Louisiana, and in Tennessee? Take away your soldiers, and there would be scarcely one man in fifty in either of those States that would either approve your amendment or recognize your authority. And yet the Senator would affect the rights of nearly one half of what was once this Union by going through—I say it in no disrespect to the honorable Senator, but I say it because I believe it and think it—going through the farce of an election under military control and restraint, and then come in the presence of the Senate of the United States and before the people of the country and of the world, and proclaim that the people of three fourths of the States of the Union, in the spirit which their fathers intended them to act and in the free exercise of their judgments and their opinions as guarantied to them by their fathers, have agreed to amend their Constitution and forever hereafter wipe out the foul blot of slavery!

Mr. President, nothing is to be gained by this except one thing, and that you may accomplish. You may succeed by such an amendment as this, by an election—no, not by an election, but by a farce enacted in the border States and by a worse farce enacted in some of the seceded States—you may succeed in abolishing slavery in the States of Delaware, Maryland, Kentucky, and Missouri. That is what you can do. You can succeed in injuring those who never tried to injure you; but unless you conquer the South, unless you subjugate them, unless you make them pass under the yoke as you avow your purpose to do, unless you take bodily hold of their slaves and draw them within your lines and keep them there, you have accomplished nothing. You have regarded them as belligerents, and consequently the slave you take to-day from them and put your uniform upon, if he is recaptured by them, is not free, though proclamations and legislative enactments may so declare, but is a slave still, and not only a slave by reason of the fact that he is in possession of his original master, but, by a sound principle of the law of nations, the *jus postliminii*, he reverts to his original owner.

...

Mr. CLARK.

...

Mr. President, I would amend the Constitution and banish slavery from the United States for that. She has spread herself since the formation of the Constitution over millions of square miles and among millions of people. She has excluded from that territory free schools and those institutions of learning which are accessible to the poor, and thus kept the people in comparative ignorance. She has degraded labor and increased poverty and vice. She has reared an aristocracy and trampled down the masses. She has denied oftentimes in those States to citizens of other States

their rights under the Constitution. She has shut up to them the liberty of speech and the press. She has assaulted them, imprisoned them, lynched them, expatriated them, murdered them, for no crime, but because they testified against her. She has debarred from that territory most of the improvements which mark a free people. She has perverted knowledge. She has opened in parts of it the foreign slave trade, and obstructed the punishment of the kidnapper and the pirate. In other parts she has degraded the people to the infamous business of raising negroes for sale, and living upon their increase. She has practiced concubinage, destroyed the sanctity of marriage, and sundered and broken the domestic ties. She has bound men, women, and children, robbed them, beat them, bruised and mangled them, burned and otherwise murdered them. To their cries she has turned a deaf ear, to their complaints shut the courts, and taken from them the power to testify against their oppressors. She has compelled them to submit in silence and labor in tears. She has forbidden their instruction, and mocked them with the pretense she was christianizing them through suffering.

She has devised and set up the doctrine of State rights, denying that her people owed allegiance to the national Government, thus weakening their attachment to it and sapping its foundations.

She has claimed to nullify the acts of Congress and to yield obedience to those only which she chose to obey.

She agreed to a division of the national domain by the line of 36° 30′, abided by it till she had appropriated the part assigned to her, then abrogated it, and filled Kansas with fraud, violence, and blood to secure the rest.

She stole into Texas, caused it to rebel against Mexico, and then erected it into a slave State in the Union, and made the nation pay the debts of the adventure.

She made war again on Mexico for more territory; and when California, a part of the territory obtained by the war, asked to be admitted as a free State, she refused her assent until appeased by new compromises.

She went into the court, and,

"Squat like a toad,"

she whispered into the ear of the Chief Magistrate that the negro lad no "rights which the white man was bound to respect." She caused the court to deny him the rights of a citizen, and, breaking down the old landmarks, drive him from the justice-hall a castaway without aid and without hope. Failing to elect a President agreeable to herself, she prepared to revolt. She set assassins to murder the Chief Magistrate-elect on his way to the capital. She emptied the Treasury; she sent away the Army and the Navy; she transferred arms from the North to the southern arsenals, and stole them when they reached there; she beleaguered and assaulted and captured the fortifications of the United States; she threatened the capital; she burned bridges to obstruct the arrival of succor; she shot down Union soldiers in the streets of Baltimore; she has set armies in the field, and she now seeks the nation's life and the destruction of the Government. To this end she has waged this war of rebellion three long years, and will continue to wage it till subdued by superior force and arms.

Mr. President, this rebellion is slavery in arms; and slavery is the ward if not the child of the Constitution. Right well has the guardian discharged the trust. But the creature thus protected and warmed into life has stolen to the bosom of its protector and aimed its dagger at the life of the Government. Sir, it is time this disastrous relation should cease.

13

US Senate, Speech of Reverdy Johnson (D-MD)

April 5, 1864[*]

The Senate, as in Committee of the Whole, resumed the consideration of the joint resolution (S. No. 16) proposing amendments to the Constitution of the United States.

Mr. JOHNSON. Mr. President, I am fully conscious, in rising to address the Senate, of the great importance of the measure to which I am about to speak. Indeed, in that respect it cannot be exaggerated. To manumit at once nearly four million slaves, who have been in bondage by hereditary descent during their whole lives, and who, because they were in bondage, and as one of the consequences of the condition in which they were placed, have been kept in a state of almost absolute ignorance, is an event of which the world's history furnishes no parallel. Whether if it succeeds it will be attended by weal or by woe, the future must decide.

That it will not be followed by unmixed good or by unmixed evil, is perhaps almost certain; and the only question in my view that presents itself to statesmen is, first, whether the measure itself be right, independent of its consequences; and secondly, whether those consequences may be such as render it inexpedient, because inhuman in other particulars, to do what is right.

There was a period in our own time when there was but one opinion upon the question of right, or almost but one opinion upon that question. The men who fought through the Revolution, those who survived its peril and shared in its glory, and who were called to the Convention by which the Constitution of the United States was drafted and recommended to the adoption of the American people, almost without exception thought that slavery was not only an evil to any people among whom it might exist, but that it was an evil of the highest character, which it was the duty of all Christian people, if possible, to remove, because it was a sin as well as an evil.

I think the history of those times will bear me out in the statement that if the men by whom that Constitution was framed, and the people by whom it was adopted, had anticipated the times in which we live, they would have provided by constitutional enactment that that evil and that sin should at some comparatively unremote day be removed. During our colonial dependence, and immediately preceding the epoch when our fathers found it necessary to claim for themselves the freedom which was their right, one of their complaints against the Government from which they were about to disengage themselves was that that Government had, by its own power, and against the will of the colonies, brought Africans as slaves and settled them in the United States; and from the period that their numbers increased so as to promise a still greater increase, almost every man of reflection at that time who looked to the future was satisfied that sooner or later the country would, because of it, be involved in trouble; and they also fondly looked to the period, not only with hope, but evidently with confidence, when, from a conviction of the danger as well as from a conviction of the sin of the institution, it would be removed. Without recurring to authority, the writings, public or private, of the men of that day, it is sufficient for my purpose to state what the facts will justify me in saying, that every man of them who largely shared in the dangers of the revolutionary struggle, and who largely participated in the deliberations of the Convention by which the Constitution was

[*] *Cong. Globe*, 38th Cong., 1st Sess., 1419–24 (Apr. 5, 1864).

adopted, earnestly desired, not only upon grounds of political economy, not only upon reasons material in their character, but upon grounds of morality and religion, that sooner or later the institution should terminate. Its recognition in the Constitution, therefore, (for it is idle, as I think, to deny that it is there recognized,) the authority given by implication to a trade which might lead to its increase by immigration, was not because a large majority of the members of the Convention, and a large majority of the people of the United States in the mass favored the institution, but because they believed that without provisions of that description it would be difficult to have a Union adopted. Whether they were right or wrong, it is now useless to inquire. Judging by what was occurring at the time, it is possible, and perhaps even more than probable, that they were right; but if they made a mistake as to that fact, if the Union could have been adopted without the recognition of the institution in the Government which formed it, if its gradual extirpation could have been provided for, no one who is a spectator of the scenes around us will now fail to regret that it had not been done.

The opinion that I have, Mr. President, (and I only ask permission of the Senate to recur to it, not because it can have any influence except for the purpose of showing that that opinion has been uniform,) the opinion that I have of it now I have entertained ever since I was capable in my own belief of forming a judgment upon human rights. But in the public situations in which I have been placed heretofore as well as in the one in which I now stand, I have deemed it my duty to recognize the binding and paramount authority of the Constitution, to yield my moral convictions to the obligation of that instrument, and not to esteem myself as excusable or justified in construing it by any views of morality which I might entertain, or in construing out of it any provisions that might be found in it inconsistent with such views. I have therefore in the past when the subject has been before me for official action steadily maintained to the extent of whatever ability I might possess the binding authority of that instrument; and in what I am about to urge now in support of the measure which is upon your table, I am not departing from the conviction that that authority should be implicitly acquiesced in. I am about appealing to the authority of the Constitution itself as a justification for the vote which I shall give upon this measure.

A word or two further by way of preliminary remark. My honorable friend who now presides over the body

(Mr. CLARK in the chair) thought proper, and with it I find no fault, to charge nearly all the calamities which the nation has sustained in the past, whatever these may have been, upon this institution. However, in my judgment, the present war might have been avoided by a different course of public policy and of popular sentiment from that which has prevailed, and however satisfied I may be or am that at least during our times, the existence of the present generation, it might have been avoided if a different policy had been adopted, I am satisfied now, and I was satisfied throughout all the contests in which that question has been presented, that sooner or later the present condition of things was inevitable or something nearly like that. If there be justice in God's providence, if we are at liberty to suppose that He will abandon man and his rights to their own fate, and suffer their destiny to be worked out by their own means and with their own lights, I never doubted that the day must come when human slavery would be exterminated by a convulsive effort on the part of the bondsmen, unless that other and better reason and influence which might bring it about should be successful—the mild though powerful influences of that higher and elevated morality which the Christian religion teaches. I concurred and concur still in the judgment of the great apostle of American liberty, the author of that Declaration which is to live through all time as the Magna Charta of human rights, that in a contest between the slave to throw off his thralldom and the master who holds him to it, the God of justice could take no part in favor of the latter. And as I have said to the Senate already, and alluded to it on a former occasion, my opinion upon the institution is not now for the first time announced.

. . .

The honorable member from Ohio, [Mr. SHERMAN], if I understood him correctly, in the speech made some weeks since to which we all listened with so much pleasure, and for myself with so much instruction, seemed to consider it as within the power of Congress by virtue of its legislative authority. There are many well-judging men, with the President at their head, who seem to suppose that it is within the reach of the Executive; while, on the contrary, there are some among us who express the opinion that it is not within the scope of either executive or legislative authority or of constitutional amendment. In my judgment, it can only be effected in the latter mode;

. . .

The honorable member from Kentucky [Mr. DAVIS] if I understood him correctly, in the very elaborate speech which he delivered upon the subject a few days since, full of all the learning which belongs to the question and pregnant with a very ingenious application of that learning, seems to think that there is something in the admitted sovereignty of the States which is inconsistent with the authority of the people of the United States to amend the Constitution so as to trench at all upon the existing authority of the States. The honorable member from Delaware [Mr. SAULSBURY] takes another ground, and that is, that as slaves are made property by the laws of the States, that property, like every other description of property, is not the subject of Government interference, except as that interference may be necessary for its protection. Now, a word or two upon each objection.

The honorable member from Kentucky is right in saying that in a certain sense the States are sovereign; but if he means by that to say that the United States in another sense are not equally sovereign, he is mistaken. The school of which Mr. Calhoun was the head, and the antecedent school by whose teachings he professed to be governed, that which had for its head Mr. Madison, seemed to have been under the impression, and unfortunately succeeded in inculcating it upon the public mind too strongly for the peace of the country, the safety and prosperity of his own section, that the only sovereignty was that which belonged to the States. There never was a greater political heresy. The States in the first place were never disunited. As one they declared independence. As one they fought and conquered the independence so declared. As one, in order to make that independence fruitful of all the blessings which they anticipated from it, they made the Constitution of the United States. The Articles of Confederation suddenly prepared were found during the war, and for three or four years subsequent to the war, to be not only not suited to the purposes of the men by whom those Articles were agreed upon, but to be destructive of the very purposes for which our fathers fought and bled and triumphed in establishing their independence. They met in convention, they adopted the Constitution in convention, and recommended it not to the States in the capacity of States, not to the governments of the States as governments, but to the people of the States for their adoption; and they could have submitted it in no other way. Any other mode of laying it before the country would have been inconsistent with the preamble to the instrument, which states that it is the work of the

people as contradistinguished from the States. How the people were to assemble, where they were to assemble, what influences were to govern them in deciding for or against the Constitution, is immaterial. When they once decided in its favor, the people of each State agreed as a people with the people of every other State that that should be the form of Government. They consented in adopting the Constitution as a people that the Constitution, if adopted by the people of nine States, should be the Constitution of the people of those States in the aggregate.

So said the Supreme Court of the United States in the case of McCulloch vs. The State of Maryland in the opinion given by Mr. Chief Justice Marshall. So said the same court in the opinion given, and it was the unanimous opinion, in the case of Booth vs. The United States by the present Chief Justice. They both announced as the clear operation of the Constitution and as a fact ever to be borne in mind in construing the Constitution of the United States, that it was the adoption of the people of the United States, and that the sovereignty of the United States to the extent of the powers conferred upon the Government of the United States and the sovereignty conferred upon the governments of the States by the people of the States respectively, was precisely the same and no more than it would have been if they had been framed and adopted at the same time. That is to say, each State, except so far as the people as a people had gone with other people in depriving themselves of the powers with which they were antecedently clothed, had no authority, as long as that other Constitution remained, to take any step inconsistent with powers conferred by that Constitution; or, in the language of the court, that each, within the sphere of the authority with which it was clothed, was supreme. There was no absolute sovereignty; that is to say, there was no sovereignty coextensive with the whole scope of political power belonging to the government of either; but each was invested with a portion of the sovereignty which the people might create, and each therefore within the extent of the portion allowed it was to the extent of that portion supreme.

That being the case, what is there in the objection suggested by the honorable member from Kentucky that the States are sovereign? The answer to it is, so is the United States, and so were the people of the United States when they adopted the Constitution of the United States. What they have done is, except in the mode pointed out by the Constitution, irrevocably done, unless there should occur a state of things in which that other and paramount right, never recognized by constitutions of government, comes into existence, the right of vindicating the rights conferred by the existing Government against oppression and tyranny—the right of revolution. There is a letter—I have it not by me now—written in 1833 by Mr. Madison to Mr. Webster,* found in the first volume of Mr. Webster's works, the edition by Mr. Everett, and in the biography prefixed to that edition, which states, as I think very clearly, as he ever stated any proposition before him, the character of the two Governments. Mr. Calhoun professed to follow the teachings of 1798 and Madison as at the head of the school by whom the doctrines of 1798 were taught. Madison, however, the founder of the school, so to speak, denounced the conduct of South Carolina as utterly inconsistent with the principles of the school of 1798, and in the letter to which I allude complimented Mr. Webster upon his speech in answer to Mr. Calhoun, as a triumphant vindication of the true nature of the Government, and as demolishing, in his judgment, forever the frightful and unconstitutional heresy of nullification and secession.

Mr. President, if the people of the United States when they assembled together in their several States and adopted the Constitution of the United States were supreme, then it was their right and nobody else's right to provide how long the Government should last, whether it should be changed at all, and if changed how changed. They did provide. They were too wise not to know in advance that the circumstances of the country might change; the Constitution as it was then, admirably suited in their judgment to the wants of the people as they were, might prove inadequate to its cherished end; and they therefore provided by the fifth article of the Constitution for the amendment of the instrument itself, and placed the whole instrument subject to the power of amendment with exceptions, the exception as to the abolition of the slave trade until 1808, and the exception as to the taxing and representative clauses; but everything else was made subject to amendment in the way pointed out by the article, and the article goes on to declare that when amended in the mode so pointed out the amendment shall to all intents and purposes be a part of the Constitution, and of course be as valid as if, instead of coming into the Constitution hereafter by

*[James Madison to Daniel Webster, Mar. 15, 1833. See this volume, 1B, doc. 24. —Ed.]

way of amendment, it was incorporated in the Constitution itself as it was originally adopted.

Now, a word or two in answer to the honorable member from Delaware. He says that this measure cannot be constitutionally adopted, because the subject with which it deals, if I understand him, is not a subject for political action. That would be singular.

Mr. SAULSBURY. The Senator will pardon me for interrupting him. He will find no such remark in anything that I said as that the subject was not a subject of political government. I admit that it is a very proper subject for State political government; but I deny the authority of three fourths of the States to take action to abolish slavery in the remaining States, or to destroy property, to say what shall or what shall not be property, because that does not come within the scope, purposes, and objects that the framers of the Constitution, and those who formed the Union, had in making the Constitution. That is the position I have taken.

Mr. JOHNSON. I may have expressed myself inaccurately for the purpose of conveying my own understanding of what the honorable member said; but I did understand him precisely as he has stated now. He says that, with reference to the Constitution of the United States, the institution of slavery is not within the amendatory clause, because, with reference to the Government of the United States, it is not a subject for political interference. Let me ask the honorable member, and he can answer it hereafter if he thinks proper, could human slavery have been abolished by the Constitution originally? I suppose no one will doubt that. If the framers of the Constitution had put a clause in it that slavery should not exist, that it should go out of existence at once, or go out of existence at any period thereafter, instantaneously or gradually, would anybody doubt that it would have been legally operative? Certainly not. If it would have been within the power of the people of the United States, acting precisely in the mode in which they acted in adopting the Constitution as it is, to have provided by an express article for the termination of human slavery, why is it that it cannot be done by them now under the clause which gives to the people of the United States the authority to amend the Constitution? It can only be, not that human slavery is not in itself an object of government; that the honorable member admits not to be the case; it is not because it was not an object of government in 1789; but that it has been taken entirely out of the scope of governmental power, the scope of the political power of the people, because it was not abolished by the Constitution. Why, Mr. President, what says the preamble to the Constitution?

Remember, now the question is, can that institution which deals with humanity as property, which claims to shackle the mind, the soul, and the body, which brings to the level of the brute a portion of the race of man, cease to be within time reach of the political power of the people of the United States, not because it was not at one time within their power, but because at that time they did not exert the power? What says the preamble? How pregnant with a conclusive answer is the preamble to the proposition that slavery cannot be abolished! What does that preamble state to have been the chief objects that the great and wise and good men had at heart in recommending this Constitution with that preamble to the adoption of the American people? That justice might be established; that tranquillity might be preserved; that the common defense and general welfare might be maintained; and, last and chief of all, that liberty might be secured. Is there no justice in putting an end to human slavery? Is there no danger to the tranquillity of the country in its existence? May it not interfere with the common defense and general welfare? And, above all, is it consistent with any notion which the mind of man can conceive of human liberty? The very clause under which we seek to put an end to the institution, the amendatory clause, may have been and in all probability was inserted into the instrument from a conviction that the time would come when justice would call so loudly for the extinction of the institution that her call could not be disobeyed, when the peace and tranquillity of the land would demand in thunder tones the destruction of the institution as inconsistent with such peace and tranquillity and when the sentiment of the world would become shocked with the existence of a condition of things in the only free Government upon the face of the globe as far as the white man is concerned, and founded upon principles utterly inconsistent with any other form of government than a Government which secures freedom—when the sentiment of the world would be shocked by the continuing existence of human bondage and we should become the scoff and scorn of Christendom.

I am not to be told, Mr. President, that our fathers looked to this race merely because they differed in color from ourselves as not entitled to the rights which for themselves they declared to be inalienable. There was not one of them, from the most humble, intellectually and morally—if there were any humble in that great

body which formed the Convention that recommended the Constitution of the United States to the adoption of the American people—who would not have been shocked if he had been told that there was a right to make a slave of any human being. The advocates of slavery now in our midst—I do not mean here, but in the South and in some of the pulpits at the North—say that slavery of the black race is of divine origin. Scriptural authority for its existence and its perpetual existence from time to time, till, as I think, the moral mind has become nauseated by the declaration, has been vouched for its sanctity and its perpetual existence. The Saviour of mankind did not put an end to it by physical power or by the declaration of any existing illegality in word. His mission upon earth was not to propagate His doctrines by force. He came to save, not to conquer. His purpose was not to march armed legions throughout the habitable globe, securing the allegiance of those for whose safety He was striving. He warred by other influences. He aimed at the heart principally. He inculcated his doctrines, more ennobling than any that the world, enlightened as the world was before His advent upon earth, had been able to discover. He taught to man the obligation of brotherhood. He announced that the true duty of man was to do to others as he would have others do to him, to all men the world over; and unless some convert to the modern doctrine that slavery itself finds not only a guarantee for its existence but for its legal existence in the Scripture, excepts out of the operation of the influences which His morality brought to bear on the mind of the Christian world the black man, and shows that it was not intended to apply to black men, then it is not true, it cannot be true, that He designed His doctrine not to be equally applicable to the black and to the white, to the race of man as he then existed, or as he might exist in all after-time.

Is it to be supposed, because of the present condition of this degraded population, that they are not proper subjects for the enjoyment of human freedom? Are they by nature, and in spite of whatever education tyranny may have left them, so mentally and morally deficient that they do not know what are the blessings of human freedom? What do we see? Wherever the flag of the United States, the symbol of human liberty, now goes, under it from their hereditary bondage are to be found men, women, and children assembling and craving its protection. Is it because they expect greater physical comfort, and that they obtain it? The mere physical condition of the man, in many cases, while under the control of a master, was better than that which he received after coming under the protection of our flag; but in the one the iron of oppression had pierced his soul, and in the other he is gladdened by the light of liberty. It is idle to deny, we feel it in our own persons, how with reference to that sentiment all men are brethren. Look to the illustrations which the times now afford, how in the illustration of that sentiment do we differ from the black man? He is willing to incur every personal danger which promises to result in throwing down his shackles and making him tread the earth which God has created for all as a man and not as a slave. It is an instinct of the soul. Tyranny may oppress it for ages and centuries; the pall of despotism may hang over it; but the sentiment is ever there; it kindles into a flame in the very furnace of affliction, and it avails itself of the first opportunity that offers promising the least chance of escape, and wades through blood and slaughter to achieve it, and whether it succeeds or fails demonstrates, vindicates in the very effort the inextinguishable right to liberty.

...

The only practical mischief of the measure is the condition of the slaves. They are uneducated. If there was nothing in the teachings of morality which as I think belong to an unadulterated moral constitution, showing the wickedness of this institution, showing how inconsistent it is with such principles and with religion, it might be shown by appealing to the conduct of the slave-owners themselves. Why are these poor creatures kept in a state of absolute ignorance? Why is education, the most humble, denied them? Why are the Holy Scriptures kept from their hovels? Why? Call there be but one answer: that if they knew what knowledge imparts, if they knew what the gospel of our Saviour inculcates, they would be freemen, or sooner or later die in the effort to obtain it?

Mr. President, I feel that I have taken up much more of the time of the Senate than I had a right to exact, and I conclude with saying, not a truth which every Senator here does not feel as strongly as I feel, but with saying what is indelibly engraved upon my soul, that we owe it not only to ourselves and to those who are to follow us, but to humanity, to bring this war to a successful result. All other considerations should, for a time, be forgotten. One single object should ever be before us—the restoration of the Union; and when it shall be restored, as I trust in Providence it will be, and unquestionably can be, if the power of the Government is exerted as it may be, we shall be restored, I trust, with a Government, na-

tional and State, in which human bondage has no place, and when we shall be able to say to the world, "However late we were in carrying out the principles of our institutions, we have at last accomplished it. The Union is restored, and slavery is terminated."

14

US Senate, Abolition Amendment, Amended Language Approved for Debate

April 6, 1864*

Mr. HARLAN.

...

Some of the incidents of slavery may be stated as follows: it necessarily abolishes the conjugal relation. This, I take it, needs no argument for its support of the floor of the Senate. We have the result of the fruits of the accumulated experience and wisdom of the people of the slave States for a period of three fourths of a century before us in the character of their laws. Here may be found the cumulation of their wisdom, the fruits of their ripened judgment. The honorable Senator from Maryland, [Mr. JOHNSON,] a few days since, when discussing this subject, stated that in none of the slave States was this relation tolerated in opposition to the will of the slave-owner; and that in many of them, I think he said a majority of them, it was prohibited absolutely by their statute laws. This, I take it then, is the matured, ripened opinion of the people of those States. In their opinion the prohibition of the conjugal relation is a necessary incident of slavery, and that slavery would not be maintained in the absence of such a regulation.

The existence of this institution therefore requires the existence of a law that annuls the law of God establishing the relation of man and wife, which is taught by the churches to be a sacrament as holy in its nature and its designs as the eucharist itself. If informed that in these Christian States of the Union men were prohibited by positive statute law from partaking of the emblems of the broken body and shed blood of the Savior, what

* Cong. Globe, 38th Cong., 1st Sess., 1439–40, 1447 (Apr. 6, 1864).

Senator could hesitate to vote for their repeal and future inhibition? And yet here one of those holy sacraments that we are taught to regard with the most sacred feelings, equally holy, instituted by the Author of our being, deemed to be necessary for the preservation of virtue in civil society, is absolutely inhibited by the statute laws of the States where slavery exists.

. . .

Another incident is the abolition practically of the parental relation, robbing the offspring of the care and attention of his parents, severing a relation which is universally cited as the emblem of the relation sustained by the Creator to the human family.

. . .

But again, it abolishes necessarily the relation of person to property. It declares the slave to be incapable of acquiring and holding property, and that this disability shall extend to his offspring from generation to generation throughout the coming ages.

. . .

But it also necessarily, as an incident of its continuance, deprives all those held to be slaves of a status in court. Having no rights to maintain and no legal wrongs to redress, they are held to be incapable of bringing a suit in the courts of the United States; a disability as it seems to me that ought to shock the moral sensibilities of any Christian statesman. Robbed of all their rights, and then robbed of their capacity to complain of wrong; robbed of the power to appear before impartial tribunals for redress of any grievances, however severe!

. . .

And then another incident of this institution is the suppression of the freedom of speech and of the press, not only among these down-trodden people themselves but among the white race. Slavery cannot exist where its merits can be freely discussed; hence in the slave States it becomes a crime to discuss its claims for protection or the wisdom of its continuance. Its continuance also requires the perpetuity of the ignorance of its victims. It is therefore made a felony to teach slaves to read and write.

. . .

If, then, none of these necessary incidents of slavery are desirable, how can an American Senator cast a vote to justify its continuance for a single hour, or withhold a vote necessary for its prohibition?

. . .

The question recurred on the amendment reported by the Committee on the Judiciary, which was to strike out all of the original resolution after the resolving clause, and insert the following:

(Two thirds of both Houses concurring,) That the following article be proposed to the Legislatures of the several States as an amendment to the Constitution of the United States, which, when ratified by three fourths of said Legislatures, shall be valid to all intents and purposes as a part of the said Constitution, namely:

Article XIII.

Sec. 1. Neither slavery nor involuntary servitude, except as a punishment for crime whereof the party shall have been duly convicted, shall exist within the United States, or any place subject to their jurisdiction.

Sec. 2. Congress shall have power to enforce this article by appropriate legislation.

The amendment was agreed to.

The joint resolution was reported to the Senate as amended.

15

US Senate, Debate on Abolition Amendment

April 7, 1864[*]

The PRESIDING OFFICER. The joint resolution (S. No. 16) proposing amendments to the Constitution of the United States is now before the Senate, and the question is on concurring, in the Senate, with the amendment made as in Committee of the Whole.

Mr. HENDRICKS.

. . .

Is the Senator right sure that it is going to add to the happiness and prosperity of those people in the South? Is he sure that the four millions who, at the commencement of this war, had masters to take care of them, if turned loose and made dependent upon their own efforts for their subsistence and their prosperity, will be happier after that state of things than they were when

---

[*] *Cong. Globe*, 38th Cong., 1st Sess., 1456–57, 1459–65 (Apr. 7, 1864).

they were taken care of by their masters in the South? I am not sure that it is going to be so.

The Senator contemplates that they will be free, that they will go when and where they please; but when they come into the northern States among a people not accustomed to them, and commence to crowd the free white labor of the North, these unfortunate people will come in contact with a northern prejudice that will be hard upon them and upon their prosperity. But, sir, with all the calamities and misfortunes that have befallen twenty-six million white people, the Senator is gratified when he contemplates the happiness that may possibly by chance come upon four million negroes.

Does the history of the last year and a half justify the Senator's exultation and joy? Let him go along the Mississippi, and instead of finding the negroes there happy and industrious, he will find them without protection, and, as the reports are, without provision and almost without clothing, and a large number of them prematurely dead. The Senator from Kentucky [Mr. DAVIS] suggests to me that at least two hundred thousand of them have already perished prematurely. And yet with this state of facts before the Senator he expects a good time for these unfortunate people yet to come!

Are they to remain among us? I can say to the Senator that they never will associate with the white people of this country upon terms of equality. It may be preached; it may be legislated for; it may be prayed for; but there is that difference between the two races that renders it impossible. If they are among us as a free people, they are among us as an inferior people. The Senator from Delaware [Mr. SAULSBURY] most happily expressed it, that this difference between the races is not chargeable upon us; it is not chargeable upon our institutions; it is not chargeable upon the condition in which these people have been kept for many generations past; it was the pleasure of God to mark that difference upon the races; a difference in intellect, in tastes, in all the qualities that enable a race to go upward and onward, which God himself has made and impressed upon them.

...

Mr. President, I will not vote for the resolution that is before the body. I do not intend to discuss the merits or demerits of the proposition of general emancipation. That question has been sufficiently discussed, perhaps, by other Senators. In the first place, I will not vote for the resolution because I think the times are not auspicious. It is not a favorable time for us to lay our hand upon the work of the fathers. Our Constitution was made after the war of the Revolution was closed, when peace had returned, when there was but little party prejudice and strife in the country—a time most favorable for laying the foundations of government. Our fathers were statesmen, taught in the scenes of the Revolution. They laid the foundations of government; and, for myself, I am not willing to disturb them in these times of excitement and strife.

Ought not the people deliberately to consider any proposition for an amendment of the Constitution? Ought it not to be considered more deliberately than any ordinary measure of government or of administration? Sir, what is our condition? We are in a state of war. The minds of the people are greatly excited. They come to conclusions now not so much upon reflection and argument and reason as they do upon the passions of the hour. I ask Senators whether a time like this is favorable to consider amendments of the organic law?

Besides that, there are many of the States that are especially in no condition to consider amendments to the Constitution. Three fourths of the States must agree by their Legislatures or by conventions to this amendment before it shall become a part of the organic law. Let me ask the attention of Senators to the condition of a few of the States that must assent to it before this measure can become a part of the Constitution. It may be that twenty-one States could deliberately consider this question. It may be that California, Connecticut, Illinois, Indiana, Iowa, Kansas, Maine, Maryland, Massachusetts, Michigan, Minnesota, New Hampshire, New Jersey, New York, Ohio, Oregon, Pennsylvania, Rhode Island, Vermont, Wisconsin, and Western Virginia may be in something of a condition to consider the proposed amendment of the Constitution. Those are twenty-one States, not two thirds, much less three fourths. I ask Senators, then, in what condition are Alabama, Arkansas, Delaware, Florida, Georgia, Kentucky, Louisiana, Mississippi, Missouri, Tennessee, Texas, and Virginia to consider amendments to the Constitution? Is this to be their Constitution as well as ours? Is this to be a Constitution for Louisiana as well as Indiana, for Florida as well as New Hampshire? Then, sir, if it is to be their great law, to which they will owe allegiance and render obedience, shall they not be in a condition to consider so important an amendment before it is proposed to them?

Mr. HOWARD. Will the Senator from Indiana allow me to ask him a question on this particular point?

Mr. HENDRICKS. Yes, sir.

Mr. HOWARD. If those States to which he refers are

not in a condition to participate in the amendment of the Constitution, as is contemplated by this joint resolution, whose fault will it be? Can a party in that attitude take advantage of his own fault, of his own wrong?

Mr. HENDRICKS. I will ask the Senator before I answer his question, whether it be a fault or no fault, can this Constitution be amended unless three fourths of the thirty-five States agree to it? Three fourths of the thirty-five States must agree to it, and it is not a matter of so much importance when we come to the question I am now discussing whose fault it is. I have said whose fault it was. I have said that these States had no just and sufficient cause for secession. I repudiate the act. I am against it, and from the first have condemned it. But I ask the Senator, is it not to be their Constitution as well as ours; and must not this amendment be considered by them and acted upon by them, so as to secure three fourths of the thirty-five States, before it becomes a part of the Constitution?

Mr. HOWARD. I will answer the Senator. It is their duty to take it into consideration when submitted to them; but if, in violation of that constitutional duty, they have placed themselves in such an attitude that they will not participate in it, it is their fault and not the fault of the other States. They have an opportunity to-day, the same opportunity possessed by other States, and may with just as much ease as other States participate in the amendment of the Constitution. Nothing but their own stubborn wills, nothing but their own rebellious spirits, nothing but their open treason prevents them from doing so, if it can be said that those causes prevent them, which I deny.

Mr. HENDRICKS. I shall now insist upon the Senator answering my question. The question which I asked him is, can this proposed amendment become a part of the Constitution of the United States unless as much as three fourths of the States agree to it?

Mr. HOWARD. Of course, I suppose, there must be a concurrence of the constitutional number of States, which number would be three fourths of the States of the Union, or, in the language of the Constitution, in the Union.

…

Mr. HENDERSON.

…

This war has wrought a wonderful change in the opinions of Union men in the slaveholding States. Heretofore a majority of the people of the North have been opposed to interfering with the institution of slavery where it existed. They opposed it because they believed the South desired to retain the institution—and that seems to be the opinion of my friend from Indiana—and so long as this desire lasted they properly held it to be a breach of faith to disturb it. So strong was this feeling that even after the commencement of practical secession northern Representatives, anti-slavery in their sentiments, with almost entire unanimity in both branches of Congress adopted and presented for acceptance by the States a constitutional amendment, irrepealable in its character, whereby the power of interference was to be forever removed. By it no State could be deprived of the privilege of slaveholding except with its own consent. In January, February, and March, 1861, such an amendment to the organic law would have received the sanction of perhaps every non-slaveholding State in the Union. The South would not accept it.

The only great idea of an anti-slavery character that triumphed, if anything anti-slavery triumphed at all, in the canvass of 1860, was founded on the purpose to exclude slavery from the Territories, and this exclusion was only to last while they were Territories. It did not deny the right of the people, after their Territory had been admitted as a State, to adopt the institution of slavery. The corruptions of Mr. Buchanan's administration gave success to the Republican party. The opposition to slavery, even at the outbreak of the rebellion, had not become so radical as to deny that a slaveholding State might be republican in its form of government. It was admitted that a State might either institute or abolish slavery; that whatever might be the true boundary line between State rights and Federal authority this subject was one of local control, and Congress could not legitimately interfere. To what extent this disinclination to meddle with the institution yet pervades the non-slaveholding States, I, of course, do not know. It cannot be doubted by any rational and reflecting mind that our forefathers, in the adoption of the Constitution, whatever may have been their individual opinions, determined to leave the subject of slavery with the several States. They found it then, as we have ever found it since, a dangerous and impracticable question. The importance of union was then paramount. Union could not be secured except by remitting the whole subject to State authority, Congress retaining only the power to enforce the surrender of slaves escaping from one State to another.

This view of the Constitution, though not conceded to be correct by what has been called the abolition party, was accepted, however, by a large majority of the people in the North. Remembering the compromises of the Constitution, they remembered their duty under them, and wished to comply with the bond. Whatever their individual convictions as to the immorality and impolicy of slavery, they have generally discarded the dogma that the obligations of moral law were superior to those of the municipal law, or that the whisperings of conscience could excuse the violation of the statute. I care not what may now be the prejudices against this institution of slavery or how ignoble this former obedience to law on the part of the northern people may appear at a time when our passions are aroused by the war that party ambition, in the name of slavery, is waging against us, the cooler judgment of the more peaceful future, whenever it comes, will again approve their conduct as essentially patriotic. Governments are not moral codes. They cannot be such. Each individual upon entering into society must agree to yield something of his own opinions to the opinions of others. If any one man's opinions be the law, the Government is a monarchy; if the opinions of a few shall govern, it is an aristocracy or oligarchy; if the opinion of each is a law unto himself, it cannot be other than anarchy. Hence the mass of opinion, in a Government republican in form, must control. That opinion, expressed according to the forms of law, must be the rule of action. He that yields to that expression and obeys the law, so long as it stands unrepealed, is not only the best citizen but the most effective promoter of public morals and also the best teacher of private virtue.

A simple adherence to this principle would have prevented the present rebellion; indeed, it must eventually drive out every heresy in government and establish the right. To deny this proposition is to deny the virtue of self-government. If human slavery be wrong, human reason, under the operation of this principle, is left free to combat it, and slavery must die so soon as reason can obtain expression under the forms of law. It cannot die sooner, for the achievements of the sword, if against reason, last generally no longer than while the sword is drawn. When it is sheathed, reason takes the place of force. Ideas of private interest and considerations of public good combined with convictions of religious duty, unintimidated by fear, are left free again to shape governmental policy.

The people of the non-slaveholding States generally were willing to trust the solution of slavery to peaceful times. They, like the founders of the Republic, generally hoped for its ultimate extinction. They did not believe that the desolations of war would ever be required to show its injustice, or that war should be waged for its extermination. They had found it within certain limits, and there they left it. It was local, and they who lived in its midst were left to its enjoyment and held responsible for its existence. They felt it to be their duty to leave it alone. They would aid us to rid ourselves of the blighting influences when we might wish to remove it, but until then we must keep it, with all its good, if any it had, and all its evil. This, sir, was right, and under similar circumstances their conduct should be the same as heretofore. But things have now materially changed.

A few words only in reference to the causes and effects of that change. For three quarters of a century this feeling of comity, this reverence of the letter and spirit of the organic law, this overpowering desire to preserve the national unity, had, notwithstanding the existence of slavery, given us peace and prosperity, both public and private, unparalleled in the growth of nations. The genius and industry of the North gave value to the great southern production in the discovery of the cotton-gin and the erection of improved machinery to convert this production into useful fabrics. The northerners were early thrown upon their own exertions, and, taught to rely upon those exertions, they became an active, industrious, inquiring, intelligent people. The southerners, I mean the more favored, enjoying a monopoly in the cotton culture, and finding that slave labor not only brought them large profit but that exemption from toil which, however coveted by men, never fails to corrupt them, soon abandoned themselves to pleasure and the lighter accomplishments of life. These frivolous accomplishments obtained in preference, because easily obtained, to the more solid acquirements, combined with this exemption from labor, soon created a feeling of superiority. They imagined themselves rich, and powerful, and like all people under similar circumstances, they became first proud of themselves and then proud of their ancestry. They invested their Cavalier fathers with the same heroic virtues and nobility of soul that Virgil in the palmy days of Roman greatness ascribed to the founders of the imperial city. In both cases perhaps much unreal greatness was thrust upon the dead that the pride of the living might be exalted.

The first difficulty that presented itself to the southern people was to satisfy themselves that slavery is morally right; and the second was to satisfy the people of the North that they could not legally interfere with it except in their own States, and further that the Constitution imposed on them the duty to protect the South in the enjoyment of it. It was southern statesmen who in the earlier periods of our history had most fiercely assailed the institution. It was Washington, Jefferson, Madison, Marshall, Mason, Martin, Williamson, and others in their own land who had stamped slavery with the most decided disapprobation. But a change was to be wrought in some way. These denunciations of the institution were to be put aside and a new dispensation proclaimed. Through the influence of South Carolina and Georgia alone, slavery had secured a footing in the compromises of the Constitution, and upon these compromises the South relied for legal protection. To calm the conscience, religious denominations ransacked the Scriptures, and finding the institution upheld under the Jewish theocracy, and not assailed by Christ and His apostles under the Christian dispensation, this was readily accepted as sufficient. The Senator from Delaware thinks it sufficient even yet. As the production of cotton increased, the conviction of the morality of slavery increased in the same ratio. Its divine character was inculcated in religion, in politics, and in morals. The justice of slavery, its economy, and harmony with republican institutions, were the first impressions stamped upon the youthful mind. The southern people are not the only people who are blind to truth because of the prejudices of early education.

To accomplish the other end, that is to quiet northern men on the subject, to satisfy them that they, not being responsible for its existence, could not legally interfere with it, and ought to protect the South in its enjoyment, required much argument. But southern men attempted to furnish it. They had nothing else to do. While the slaves produced cotton their masters discussed politics. The whole South was turned into a debating society. Every man was a politician. Every court-house and cross-roads became an arena for political gladiators. The alpha and omega of every discussion was slavery, and everybody was on the same side. If some old fogy, some believer in the doctrines of the past, happened to express doubts of the sacredness of the institution, suddenly many voices were joined to greet him as Paul was greeted at Ephesus. While the northern people built manufactories, railroads, bridges, and canals, erected cities, opened farms, constructed ships, and founded institutions of learning, the South was discussing the negro question. As in all attempts to vindicate error, they fell into the most glaring contradictions, seen by everybody except themselves. They claimed to

be fiercely democratic. Holding one half of the population of their States in abject slavery, they clamored loudly for the largest liberty. The privilege of the writ of *habeas corpus* denied to every man held by them in bondage, they insisted that republican government would be instantly lost if the writ were suspended for a moment in the case of a white man. Claiming that the institution was local, deriving its vitality from the States, and that Congress could exercise no power over it at all, they yet insisted that Congress should plant it upon all the national domain. Adopting a false theory of State rights, originally designed for the protection of slavery, which rendered the Constitution powerless on all other subjects, they yet found authority within its grants of power to establish and perpetuate slavery against the will of the local government. Looking only to the preservation of that one institution, they adopted any and every theory that seemed available for the purpose. They advocated the Missouri Compromise, and afterwards ostracized as abolitionists all who did not favor its repeal. They opened the Territories to popular sovereignty, and so soon as it failed to bring a slave State into the Union, the doctrine was discarded, and he who did not at once repudiate it became unto them the heathen and the publican.

In the mean time the northern people, thoroughly convinced of the immorality and inutility of slavery, began to take its denunciations into the pulpit and the schoolroom. At this point the divergence between the North and the South commenced. Congregations of Christians who had formerly worshiped at the same altar met and quarreled and separated. Then commenced this idea of two distinct civilizations, this notion that the two races, the one inhabiting the North, the other the South, were not the same; that they were different in origin, different in manners, different in pursuits, and different in ideas of government. Extreme men on both sides urged these reasons in favor of political separation and the establishment of separate governments. The one extreme said the Union could not, must not subsist with slavery; with the other slavery was the *sine qua non* of Union. Politicians at once seized upon this state of feeling, and, instead of pouring oil on the troubled waters, for selfish purposes they added to the agitation. They who became the representatives of the people seemed to look rather to the promotion of party interests than to the substantial welfare of the country. In other words, too many of our statesmen became demagogues. Falsehood was admitted and acted upon simply because the pioneers in reformation are seldom honored; they scarcely ever get to Congress.

The country finally became divided into two great parties. The true cause of division, with a majority on each side, is to be found, no doubt, in the construction given by them respectively to the Constitution, the one confining the powers of Congress to expressly delegated grants, leaving the States sovereign in all other respects; the other finding in the instrument warrant for the exercise of powers deemed necessary "for the common defense and general welfare" of the United States.

The southern people being an agricultural people, looking chiefly to a foreign market for the sale of their surplus productions, not engaged in the carrying trade, believing free trade to be beneficial to their interests, and not feeling the same necessity with the people of the North for improving the lakes, rivers, and harbors of the South, very generally accepted the limited, or what has always been termed the strict, construction of the Constitution. From precisely the opposite considerations sprang the party of liberal or latitudinarian construction. It is plain to see that the pro-slavery men of the South would naturally fall into the ranks of the former party, because the theory of strict construction furnished the best protection for the institution. If Congress could not attack it, it might, in their opinion, retreat from State to State, if attacked by local authority, and thus gain time to fortify its defenses. For the opposite reason, again, the zealous anti-slavery men of the North joined the other party. In the latitude of construction, their assaults upon the institution might be made effective; from State action they had no hope.

As it has always been—and it is as much so now perhaps as ever—extreme men on either side gave tone to party action. The more moderate were controlled by them. They seemed to have no power of resistance. They drifted like floats upon the current. They knew what is right, but they had not the moral courage to pursue the right. In a short time, party platforms became a mere string of dogmas on the subject of slavery. A foreigner seeing them would naturally suppose that we had no other interests in this country than slavery.

But why is it that the extreme men in this case, as they have done in others, succeeded in controlling their respective parties? I ascribe it to the fact that extreme men generally start with an undeniable truth. They boldly challenge refutation of that truth. They seek controversy, and controversy gives them strength. Truth needs

but be repeated, and the assent of reason is finally given. The anti-slavery men asserted the proposition that slavery is wrong; that it is condemned in morals, and anti-republican in its very nature; that it is unjust to the slave and prejudicial to his master; that it is corrupting in its social relations, and deeply injurious to the economical interests of the country. This proposition could not be denied. To oppose it but established it the more firmly. The history of the country itself brought new arguments to its support. The great disparity in the material development of the two sections as time passed on gradually strengthened the convictions of anti-slavery men, and struck down the arguments of their opponents. The earnest men of the anti-slavery party who stuck to the one idea of their faith, and demanded its recognition in political platforms, as well as in religious creeds, though branded as zealots, abolitionists, disturbers of the public peace, yet stood upon the one truth, and challenged its denial. If this truth had been acknowledged and acted on by the other side we should have had no war. While they were obtaining the almost universal recognition of this truth, however, in the northern States, and its partial recognition in the South, the fiery conflict through which they were passing unfortunately aroused the fiercest passions. Religion and politics brought their influences to inflame. Many of them became maddened as with frenzy, and struck at slavery without skill, as the wounded gladiator strikes at his adversary.

The arguments used to satisfy others that slavery is wrong had satisfied themselves that no law, human or divine, standing in the way of its destruction, was obligatory on the citizen. The extremist of the South, too, was not without his truth—an equally undeniable truth—for the erection of his party. His truth was the one to which I have already alluded. It was that, however indefensible slavery might be as an abstract proposition, the very bond of Union, the Constitution, left it under the exclusive control of the States interested; that Congress could not abolish it; and that every act of interference with it where it existed was without authority. He claimed, and truthfully, too, that unless its existence had been left free from congressional legislation no Union could have been formed. This became his controlling idea. It was his strong point, his fortress; and to it he retreated when the moral question was urged. He must have it inserted in every platform of principle. Those of the South who looked forward to the final extinction of slavery soon lost courage to assert the truth which lay behind this, and were constantly driven to the assertion of political tenets that stood in the way of such consummation.

Upon this truth sophistry built a thousand errors. Threats of interference by northern extremists helped to stimulate southern pride, in which the injustice of slavery was to be forgotten. From this vantage-ground taken by pro-slavery men of the South, and resolutely adhered to, they gradually put forward and developed the principles of that new faith which asserted the divinity of slavery, taught the doctrine of State supremacy, and enforced the heresy of nullification and secession.

The northern Democracy never believed in these heresies. They adopted the strict construction theory of the Government without reference to slavery. If the application of what was thought to be a sound principle of construction inured to the protection of the institution, they yet would not abandon the principle. They did not believe slavery to be ordained of God or productive of human good; indeed, they believe it a curse. They acted with the southern Democracy for two reasons: first, they condemned what they termed the fanatical heresies of the abolitionists, who, they thought, in their pursuit of a moral principle would rush to anarchy; and secondly, their respect for the great constitutional truth to which I have alluded dominated their moral convictions against the institution. Hence, when secession came, the northern Democracy were found on the side of the Government. They have given their blood and their treasure to the prosecution of war, intended for the restoration of the Union. At this point it may be suggested that the difficulty of amending the Constitution added seriously, in my judgment, to our troubles. Why was the power of amendment inserted at all? It was to utilize the experience of the future, to correct error in the Government. The Senator from Indiana is very much mistaken when he says that the Constitution cannot be constitutionally amended in reference to slavery. It is provided that it shall not be amendable in only one particular, and that is, "that no State, without its consent, shall be deprived of its equal suffrage in the Senate." In no other respect is there now any limitation whatever upon the power of amendment. Up to 1808 there were two other clauses in the Constitution that could not be amended, the one in regard to the importation of Africans into this country, and the other in regard to capitation or other direct taxes. The power to amend was a part of the contract; it was a part of the bond of each State when we entered

into the Union; and we have clearly and indisputably the power to amend it in reference to slavery.

As I have said, the power to amend was inserted to enable us to utilize the experience of the future and correct error. It was designed to let deliberate and matured convictions of public policy take a place in the organic law. It was to be the safety-valve of our institutions. Ours was to be a Government of the people. Their opinions are the motive-power. When I speak of opinions I mean the satisfied judgment, not the mere sentiment or passion of the hour. If these opinions, rarefied and expanded by the heat of truth, are confined, explosion comes. It had become the settled conviction of three fourths of the people that slavery is wrong. That conviction could find no place in legislation, because it would conflict with the Constitution. It could not find place in the Constitution, because the ratification of three fourths of the States could not be obtained. With thirty-five States in the Union it requires twenty seven to carry this amendment. It matters not what may be their population, one tenth or one twentieth of the whole, the remaining eight may exclude it. This may be a wise provision, but I have been led to doubt it, and hence my proposition as introduced originally was to remove a part of this difficulty in future cases, to facilitate amendments to the Constitution. I am aware of the danger on the other side, but the recent experience of our own and that of the English Government for centuries, inclines me to think that the greater danger lies in damming up public sentiment until it gathers force to break away its barriers and desolate the country. Indeed, if ministers would leave their posts in our Government then public opinion condemns them, the change would be for the better. The Judiciary Committee, however, have disagreed to this proposition, and to their better judgment I submit.

...

The war is upon us. The Union is severed in the name of slavery. The civilized world regards slavery as the remote or proximate cause of the war. I discard the question of who is responsible for it—whether the North or the South. I look at things as they are, and ask what is now our duty? Nine tenths, perhaps, of the loyal men of the country conscientiously believe that slavery is morally wrong and an evil in government. If they were to-day constructing a new Government, they would prohibit slavery. This I assume to be an admitted proposition. The rebels on the other hand assert its morality, and have established a government whose foundation-stone is slavery. In the interest of slavery they claimed the right to sever the Union. They have done so, to the extent of their power. We have denied this assumed right, and the issue is involved in the pending war. The rebels declare that slavery cannot longer exist under our Government; that the two things, slavery and the Federal Union, have become incompatible. In this alleged belief was found the motive for secession, and in it today consists the strength of secession.

But while so large a majority of our people believe slavery to be wrong, perhaps but a small number, comparatively, believe that Congress possesses the power to abolish it. In other words, they confess that the moral law condemns it, but that the Constitution tolerates it. As an original proposition they think it should never have existed, but being in existence when the Government was framed, they think our forefathers may have adopted the wisest policy in regard to it, if its adoption had been followed by peace.

The sum total of our present position is that a great wrong, in a moral and social point of view, was admitted into the organic law, under a supposed necessity for union. Those opposed to slavery were willing to bear its evils in consideration of the blessings to be derived from a union of the States. If those evils had continued to be compensated by the blessings of peace, prosperity, and repose, which union would have given, the same reasons that influenced the framers of the Government originally might now be urged in its defense with some show of propriety.

But the friends of slavery in its name have destroyed our peace and given us war; they have taken away our prosperity and given us debt and taxes; they have broken our repose and given us the calamities of a civil strife; in fine, they have rudely severed the bond that bound them to the Union, and now defiantly mock the faith that once gave them protection.

Mr. President, all will admit that if slavery be responsible for our condition, there are but few circumstances of mitigation to be urged in its favor. With bloody hands and devilish visage it craves no mercy yet, but points to new fields of carnage and destruction. Its friends have been appalled at its wickedness. The predictions of its enemies have been verified as fully as were the prophecies of Elisha in regard to the future cruelties of the Persian minister.

Then we all admit that slavery is wrong, and that its friends have driven the country to unnecessary war. If they made war once, they may make it again. We cannot

remove anti-slavery convictions. Therefore the restoration of slavery is a restoration of political strife. History will repeat itself. New wars will come. The innocent will suffer again. Shall we then leave slavery to fester again in the public vitals? Even its foolish fears have well-nigh ruined the nation. They have sent to untimely graves thousands of men, yea, hundreds of thousands. They have clothed the country in the weeds of mourning, and inflicted burdens under which far distant generations must toil and groan. If slavery has committed this great iniquity once, what guarantee can it give of future forbearance and peace? It has none to give; and if it had a thousand guarantees, it would not give one. The friends of slavery staked its existence upon the result of this rebellion. If rebellion fails, the most sanguine of those friends expect slavery to cease. They do not thank their old Democratic associates of the North for this clamor which demands "the Union as it was, the Constitution as it is." They would not have either. If so, why this rebellion? They had them both before it commenced. They might have had them to-day, but they cast them aside, making a constitution and a union for themselves, differing from the old only in that it builded on slavery. In support of their position they have staked their lives, and never have they asked for peace on any terms that do not involve a dissolution of the Union.

. . .

If slavery be not antagonistic to our institutions, why was it not safe under the Constitution? If not safe before the war it cannot be safe hereafter. If mere apprehension of attack was sufficient in times of profound peace and prosperity to drive its friends to war upon their Government, the now quickened prejudices against it will render them still more restless and uneasy in case the Union with slavery be restored. If the moral conflict proved to be unceasing before the war, it will be truly irresistible hereafter if slavery remains. Opposition to slavery will die when slavery itself dies. It will not die sooner, for, slavery being a wrong, the moral sentiments are in constant revolt against it. It is prejudicial to the public interests, and therefore considerations of public good condemn it. A majority of the people, whatever may be the fact, believe it is responsible for the sufferings of the present war, and the desire to punish it as the chief architect of ruin is natural enough. In all its relations, it heretofore conflicted with our ideas of justice. It now stands associated with barbarity and all uncharitableness. Therefore, humanity and reason and instinct tell us to reject it.

It is sometimes said the Republican party is dead, and the Democracy can restore peace to the country by bringing back the old regime. As an organization the Republican party may be dead, but the principle of anti-slavery is not dead. A deep conviction of the injustice and impolicy of slavery yet lives. That conviction is now stronger than ever. It has been made so by the many crimes recently committed in the name of the institution. In my honest judgment, Mr. President, slavery and rebellion, by the action of parties, by the course of events which none of us can now control, have become so closely and intimately allied that they must share the same fate. If the rebellion succeeds, slavery for many years may be a cherished institution in the South. If it fails, the rebels themselves will be found too honorable to ask its continuance. If my positions, then, be correct, the following propositions are true: first, slavery, being detrimental to public and private interests, anti-republican in its tendencies, and subversive of good government, should now be abolished; second, the Constitution as it now stands confers upon Congress no power to abolish it; and third, to attain the ends which are essential to the establishment and maintenance of peace, a change in the Constitution, the peaceful and effective mode of governmental reform wisely provided by our ancestors for throwing off such evils as now afflict us and for utilizing the experience of history as developed in national progress, should at once be made.

Our ancestors acknowledged the truth when they proclaimed the inalienable right of liberty unto all men. That declaration gave *them* liberty. It fired the world and enlisted the sympathies of civilization. So soon as they obtained it for themselves, however, the false counsels of expediency came to refuse it to others. When the test of practical government was to be applied, they were content to declare in the preamble of the Constitution one of its objects to be "to secure the blessings of liberty" to themselves and their posterity. In the body of the instrument the liberty of the African is not secured. His return to slavery is enjoined. In this contradiction is the element of strife. Truth and error cannot be reconciled. Right and wrong cannot dwell together in peace. This effort to reconcile antagonisms was vain. It first brought political convulsions; it then brought war. In the kingdom of nature, volcanic disturbances follow the union of fire and combustible material. From various causes the disturbances may be unfelt for many years, but eventually they return, and cease not till the material is consumed. This thing of slavery is a heresy. The fire of truth is upon it, and the moral world will be convulsed until it is consumed. The strong desire for peace may induce some new concession in its favor. This might smother the flames for a few years. Such peace would not be permanent. In process of time our cities would again be blasted by its upheavings; our fields again scorched by its burning lava.

Mr. President, the country may not yet be prepared for the announcement, but I am free to say but two alternatives in this matter present themselves to my mind. There are but two sides to the question. The one is Union without slavery; the other is the immediate and unconditional acknowledgment of the southern confederacy. To this end must it come at last. For the expression of this sentiment I shall be called a fanatic. I cannot help it; it is my opinion, and it is my duty to say it. If it be fanaticism, it is only that species of fanaticism that springs from conviction. It results not from any sudden abhorrence of slavery, for I have been in its midst all my life. It does not spring from hatred of slaveholders, for whether in honor or shame, I am a slaveholder to-day.

. . .

But I have not time nor inclination to pursue this subject further. I have perhaps said enough. Let this amendment be adopted, and let slavery agitation, with all its errors and its consequent curses to the country, cease. That agitation has brought upon us untold miseries. It has given us a war which we cannot bear to have repeated. It may be that the money to be expended by us must equal the amount wrung from the sinews of the slave; it may be that the anguish and tears of this war must equal the anguish and tears of the African in his long captivity. If the measure of our iniquity was full, let us hope the measure of our retribution is also full. Let the iniquity be cast away. The cup of misery may be at once withdrawn. It can be no worse. I confess I see no probability of restoring the Union with the institution of slavery remaining. I wish the Union restored, but I confess also I do not desire the perpetuation of slavery. I will not be intimidated by the fears of negro equality. The negro may possess mental qualities entitling him to a position beyond our present belief. If so, I shall put no obstacle in the way of his elevation. There is nothing in me that despises merit or envies its rewards. Whether he shall be a citizen of any one of the States is a question for that State to determine. If New York or Massachusetts or Louisiana shall confer on him the elective franchise, it is a matter of policy with which I have nothing to do. The qualification of voters for members of Congress is a question under the exclusive control of the respective States. Whatever qualifications are prescribed by the States for electors of the lower branch of the State Legislatures, the same are constitutionally prescribed for electors of members of Congress. Senators are chosen by the State Legislatures, and the people of each State determine the qualifications of voters for both branches of the Legislature. The manner of choosing presidential electors is left to the Legislatures of the States. So in passing this amendment we do not confer upon the negro the right to vote. We give him no right except his freedom, and leave the rest to the States.

16

US Senate, Debate and Passage of Abolition Amendment

April 8, 1864[*]

The PRESIDING OFFICER, (Mr. FOOT.)

The special order of the day, which is the joint resolution (S. No. 16) proposing amendments to the Constitution of the United States, is now before the Senate, and the question is on concurring in the amendment made as in Committee of the Whole. That amendment is in the form of a substitute for the original resolution, and is open to amendment before the question of concurrence is taken. After the Senate shall have concurred, if they do concur, in that amendment, the text of the joint resolution, the amendment itself being in the form of a substitute, will not be open to amendment. Amendments then can only be offered in the form of provisos or additional sections to the amendment. The Chair deems it proper to make this announcement in advance, that no misapprehension may be entertained.

Mr. SUMNER. Mr. President, if an angel from the skies or a stranger from another planet were permitted to visit this earth, and to examine its surface, who can doubt that his eyes would rest with astonishment upon the outstretched extent and exhaustless resources of this Republic of the New World, young in years but already rooted beyond any dynasty in history? In proportion as he considered and understood all those things

[*] *Cong. Globe*, 38th Cong., 1st Sess., 1479–83, 1487–90 (Apr. 8, 1864).

among us which enter into and constitute the national life, his astonishment would increase, for he would find a numerous people, powerful beyond precedent, without a king or a noble, but with the schoolmaster instead. And yet the astonishment which he confessed, as all these things appeared before him, would swell into marvel as he learned that in this Republic, which had arrested his admiration, where there was neither king nor noble, but the schoolmaster instead, there were four million human beings in abject bondage, degraded to be chattels, under the pretense of property in man, driven by the lash like beasts, despoiled of all rights, even the right to knowledge and the sacred right of family; so that the relation of husband and wife was impossible and no parent could claim his own child; while all were condemned to brutish ignorance. Startled by what he beheld, the stranger would naturally inquire by what authority, under what sanction, and through what terms of law or Constitution, this fearful inconsistency, so shocking to human nature itself, continued to be upheld. But his growing astonishment would know no bounds, when he was pointed to the Constitution of the United States, as the final guardian and conservator of this peculiar and many-headed wickedness.

"And is it true," the stranger would exclaim, "that, in laying the foundations of this Republic, dedicated to human rights, all these wrongs have been positively established?" He would ask to see that Constitution and to know the fatal words by which the sacrifice was commanded. The trembling with which he began its perusal would be succeeded by joy as he finished it; for he would find nothing in that golden text, not a single sentence, phrase, or word, even, to serve as origin, authority, or apology for the outrage. And then his astonishment, already knowing no bounds, would break forth anew, as he exclaimed, "Shameful and irrational as is slavery, it is not more shameful or irrational than that unsupported interpretation which undertakes to make your Constitution the final guardian and conservator of this terrible and unpardonable denial of human rights."

. . .

There are three things which he would observe: first and foremost, that the dismal words "slave" and "slavery" do not appear in the Constitution; so that if the unnatural pretension of property in man lurk anywhere in that text, it is under a feigned name or an *alias*, which of itself is cause of suspicion, while an imperative rule renders its recognition impossible. Next, he would consider the preamble, which is the key to open the whole succeeding instrument; but here no single word can be found which does not open the Constitution to freedom and close it to slavery. The object of the Constitution is announced to be "in order to form a more perfect union, establish justice, insure domestic tranquillity, provide for the common defense, promote the general welfare, and secure the blessings of *liberty* to ourselves and our posterity;" all of which, in every particular, is absolutely inconsistent with slavery. And thirdly he would observe those time-honored, most efficacious, chain-breaking words in the Amendments: "*No person shall be deprived of life, liberty, or property, without due process of law.*" Scorning all false interpretations and glosses which may have been fastened upon the Constitution as a support of slavery, and with these three things before him, he would naturally declare that there was nothing in the original text on which this hideous wrong could be founded anywhere within the sphere of its operation.

. . .

3. There is still another clause: "The United States shall guaranty to every State in this Union a *republican form of government.*" There again is a plain duty. But the question recurs, what is a republican form of government?

. . .

[T]he guarantee of a republican form of government must have a meaning congenial with the purposes of the Constitution. If a Government like that of Turkey, or even like that of Venice, could come within the scope of this guarantee, it would be of little value. It would be words and nothing more. Evidently it must be construed so as to uphold the Constitution according to all the promises of its preamble, and Mr. Madison has left a record, first published to the Senate by the distinguished Senator from Vermont, [Mr. COLLAMER,] the chairman of the Committee on the Library, showing that this clause was originally suggested in part by the fear of slavery. The record is important, disclosing the real intention of this guarantee. But no American need be at a loss to designate some of the distinctive elements of a republic according to the idea of American institutions. These will be found, first, in the Declaration of Independence, by which it is solemnly announced "that all men are endowed by their Creator with certain unalienable rights; that among these are life, liberty, and the pursuit of happiness." And they will be found, secondly, in that other guarantee and prohibition of the Constitution, in harmony with the Declaration of Independence; "*no person* shall be deprived of life, *liberty*,

or property *without due process of law.*" Such are some of the essential elements of a "republican form of government," which cannot be disowned by us without disowning the very muniments of our liberties; and it is there which the United States are bound to guaranty. But all these make slavery impossible. It is idle to say that this result was not anticipated. It would be, then, only another illustration that our fathers "builded wiser than they knew."

4. But, independent of the clause of guarantee, there is the clause just quoted, which in itself is a source of power: "*no person* shall be deprived of life, *liberty*, or property *without due process of law.*" This was a part of the amendments to the Constitution proposed by the First Congress, under the popular demand for a Bill of Rights. Brief as it is, it is in itself alone a whole Bill of Rights. Liberty can be lost only by "due process of law," words borrowed from the old liberty-loving common law, illustrated by our master in law, Lord Coke, but best explained by the late Mr. Justice Bronson, of New York, in a judicial opinion where he says:

> "The meaning of the section then seems to be, that *no member of the State shall be disenfranchised or deprived of any of his rights or privileges* unless the matter shall be adjudged against him upon trial had according to the course of common law. The words 'due process of law' in this place cannot mean less than a prosecution or suit instituted and conducted according to the prescribed forms and solemnities for ascertaining guilt or determining the title to property." — 4 *Hill's Reports*, 146.

Such is the protection which is thrown by the Constitution over every "person," without distinction of race or color, class or condition. There can be no doubt about the universality of this protection. All, without exception, come within its scope. Its natural meaning is plain; but there is an incident of history which makes it plainer still, excluding all possibility of misconception. A clause of this character was originally recommended as an amendment by two slave States, North Carolina and Virginia, but it was restrained by them to *freemen*, thus: "No *freemen* ought to be deprived of his life, *liberty*, or property but by the *law of the land.*" But when the recommendation came before Congress the word "person" was substituted for "freeman," and the more searching phrase "due process of law" was substituted for "the law of the land." In making this change, rejecting the recommendation of two slave States, the authors of this amendment revealed their purpose, that *no person* wearing the human form should be deprived of *liberty* without due process of law; and the proposition was adopted by the votes of Congress and then of the States as a part of the Constitution. Clearly on its face it is an express guarantee of personal liberty and an express prohibition against its invasion anywhere.

In the face of this guarantee and prohibition—for it is both—how can any "person" be held as a slave? But it is sometimes said that this provision must be restrained to places within the exclusive jurisdiction of the national Government. Let me say frankly that such formerly was my own impression, often avowed in this Chamber; but I never doubted its complete efficacy to render slavery unconstitutional in all such places, so that "no person" could be held as a slave at the national capital or in any national territory. Constitutionally slavery has always been an outlaw where ever that provision of the Constitution was applicable. Nobody doubted that it was binding on the national courts, and yet it was left unexecuted—a dead letter, killed by the predominant influence of slavery, until at last Congress was obliged by legislative act to do what the courts had failed to do, and to put an end to slavery in the national capital and national territories.

But there are no words in this guarantee and prohibition by which they are restrained to any exclusive jurisdiction. They are broad and general as the Constitution itself; and since they are in support of human rights they cannot be restrained by any interpretation. There is no limitation in them, and nobody now can supply any such limitation, without encountering the venerable maxim of law, *Impius ac crudelis qui libertati non favet*—"Impious and cruel is he who does not favor liberty." Long enough courts and Congress have merited this condemnation. The time has come when they should merit it no longer. The Constitution should become a living letter under the Predominant influence of freedom.

. . .

Putting aside, then, all objections that have been interposed, whether proceeding from open opposition or from lukewarm support, the great question recurs, that question which dominates this whole debate, How shall slavery be overthrown? The answer is threefold: first, by the courts, declaring and applying the true principles of the Constitution; secondly, by Congress, in the exercise of powers which belong to it; and, thirdly, by the people, through an amendment to the Constitution.

Courts, Congress, people, all may be invoked, and the occasion will justify the appeal.

1. Let the appeal be made to the courts. But alas! one of the saddest chapters in our history has been the conduct of judges, who have lent themselves to the support of slavery.

. . .

2. But unhappily the courts will not perform the duty of the hour, and we must look elsewhere. An appeal must be made to Congress; and here, as has been fully developed, the powers are ample, unless in their interpretation you surrender in advance to slavery. By a single brief statute, Congress may sweep slavery out of existence. Patrick Henry saw that in the maintenance of "the general welfare" and under the influence of a growing detestation of slavery this could be done, even without resort to those capacious war powers which proclaim trumpet-tongued that it can be done.

Of course we encounter here again the "execrable" pretension of property in man, and the claim of "just compensation" for the renunciation of Heaven-defying wrongs. But this pretension is no more applicable to abolition by act of Congress than to abolition by an amendment of the Constitution; so that if the pretension of "just compensation" can be discarded in one case it can be in the other. But the votes that have already been taken in the Senate on the latter proposition testify that it is discarded. Sir, let the "execrable" pretension never again be named, except for condemnation, no matter how or when it appears or what the form it may take.

But even if Congress be not prepared for that single decisive measure which shall promptly put an end to this whole question and strike slavery to death, there are other measures by which this end may be hastened. The towering Upas may be girdled, even if it may not be felled at once to the earth.

The fugitive slave bill, conceived in iniquity and imposed upon the North as a badge of subjugation, may be repealed.

The coastwise slave trade may be deprived of all support in the statute-book.

The traffic in human beings, as an article of "commerce among States," may be extirpated.

And, above all, that odious rule of evidence, so injurious to justice and discreditable to the country, excluding the testimony of colored persons in national courts, may be abolished.

Let these things be done. In themselves they will be

much. But they will be more as the assurance of the overthrow sure to follow.

3. But all these will not be enough. The people must be summoned to confirm the whole work. It is for them to put the cap-stone upon the sublime structure. An amendment of the Constitution may do what courts and Congress decline to do, or, even should they act, it may cover their action with its panoply. Such an amendment in any event will give completeness and permanence to emancipation, and bring the Constitution into avowed harmony with the Declaration of Independence. Happy day, long wished for, destined to gladden those beatified spirits who have labored on earth to this end, but died without the sight.

…

Happily, in our case the way is easy, for it is only necessary to carry the Republic back to its baptismal vows, and the declared sentiments of its origin. There is the Declaration of Independence: let its solemn promises be redeemed. There is the Constitution: let it speak, according to the promises of the Declaration.

But the immediate question now before us is on the proposition to prohibit slavery by constitutional amendment; and here I hope to be indulged for a moment with regard to the form which it should take. A new text of the Constitution cannot be considered too carefully even in this respect, especially when it embodies a new article of freedom. Here for a moment we are performing something of that duty which belongs to the *conditores imperii*, placed foremost by Lord Bacon among the actors in human affairs. From the magnitude of the task we may naturally borrow circumspection, and I approach this part of the question with suggestion rather than argument.

Let me say frankly that I should prefer a form of expression different from that which has the sanction of the committee. They have selected what was intended for the old Jeffersonian ordinance, sacred in our history, although, let me add, they have not imitated it closely. But I must be pardoned if I venture to doubt the expediency of perpetuating in the Constitution language which, if it have any signification, seems to imply that "slavery or involuntary servitude" may be provided "for the punishment of crime." There was a reason for that language when it was first employed, but that reason no longer exists. If my desires could prevail, I would put aside the ordinance on this occasion, and find another form.

I know nothing better than these words:

All persons are equal before the law, so that no person can hold another as a slave; and the Congress shall have power to make all laws necessary and proper to carry the declaration into effect everywhere within the United States and the jurisdiction thereof.

The words in the latter part supersede all questions as to the applicability of the declaration to States. But the distinctive words in this clause assert the *equality of all persons before the law*. The language may be new in our country, but it is already well known in history. And here let me show how it has grown to its present place of authority. We must repair for a moment to France.

The first constitution adopted by France, September, 1791, in the throes of revolution, was preceded by a Declaration of Rights, which after setting forth that "ignorance, forgetfulness, or contempt of the rights of man are the sole causes of public evils and of the corruption of Governments," undertakes to announce "the natural rights of man, inalienable and sacred, to the end that this Declaration, constantly present to all the members of the social system, may without cessation recall their rights and duties; to the end that the acts of the legislative power and those of the executive power capable at each instant of being compared with the object of every political institution, may be more respected; to the end that the claims of citizens, founded on simple and incontestable principles, may turn always to the maintenance of the constitution, and the happiness of all." After this too elaborate preamble the Declaration begins with the following article:

"ART. 1. Men are born and continue free and *equal in rights.*"

Here is a generality of expression not unlike that of our own Declaration of Independence.

Next came the constitution of June, 1793, which, after a preamble, sets forth a series of articles, beginning with three, as follows:

"ART. 1. The object of society is the common happiness. Government is instituted to guaranty to man the enjoyment of his natural and imprescriptible rights.

"2. These rights are equality, liberty, security, property.

"3. *All men are equal* by nature and *before the law.*"

Here this declaration begins to show itself.

This same constitution concludes with what is called a guarantee of rights, in the following article:

"ART. 122. The Constitution guaranties to all Frenchmen equality, liberty, security, property, the public debt, the free exercise of worship, common instruction, public assistance, the indefinite liberty of the press, the right of petition, the right to assemble in public meetings, the enjoyment of all the rights of men."

Then came the constitutional charter of June, 1814, following the restoration of the Bourbons, which begins with the following article:

"ART. 1. *Frenchmen are equal before the law*, whatever may be otherwise their title and ranks."

This is followed by another, as follows:

"ART. 4. Their individual liberty is equally guarantied, so that nobody can be prosecuted or arrested, except in cases provided for by the law, and in the form which it prescribes."

The constitutional charter of August, 1830, at the installation of Louis Philippe as king, with La Fayette by his side, contains the articles already quoted from that of Louis XVIII, in the same words, placing the declaration of *equality before the law* in the front.

And this article has been adopted in the charters of Belgium, Italy, Greece; so that it is now a well-known expression of a commanding principle of human rights.

It will be felt at once that this expression, "*equality before the law,*" gives precision to that idea of human rights which is enunciated in our Declaration of Independence. The sophistries of Calhoun, founded on the obvious inequalities of body and mind, are all overthrown by this simple statement, which, though borrowed latterly from France, is older than French history. The curious student will find in the ancient Greek of Herodotus a single word which supplies the place of this phrase, when he tells us that "the government of the many has the most beautiful name of [isonomy]" or *equality before the law*. (Book 3, p. 80.) The father of history was right. The name is most beautiful; but it is not a little singular that, in an age when *equality before the law* was practically unknown, the Greek language, so remarkable for its flexibility and comprehensiveness, supplied a single word, not to be found in modern tongues, to express an idea which has been authoritatively recognized only in modern times. Such a word in our own language to express that equality of rights which is claimed for all mankind might have superseded some of the criticism to which this Declaration has been exposed.

Enough has been said to explain the origin of the words which are now proposed. It will be for the Senate to determine if it will adopt them.

Should the Senate not incline to this form, there is still another which I would suggest, as follows:

Slavery shall not exist anywhere within the United States or the jurisdiction thereof; and the Congress shall have power to make all laws necessary and proper to carry this prohibition into effect.

This is simple, and avoids all language which is open to question. The word "slavery" is explicit, and describes precisely what it is proposed to blast.

But if the Senate is determined to adhere to the Jeffersonian ordinance, then I prefer that it should be the ordinance actually, and not as reported by the committee. And I would complete the work by expelling from the Constitution all those words which have been the apology for slavery, by an amendment as follows:

There shall be neither slavery nor involuntary servitude anywhere in the United States, or within the jurisdiction thereof, otherwise than in the punishment of crimes, whereof the party shall have been duly convicted; and the Congress may make all laws which shall be necessary and proper to enforce this prohibition.

But while desirous of seeing the great rule of freedom which we are about to ordain embodied in a text which shall be like the precious casket to the more precious treasure, yet I confess that I feel humbled by my own endeavors. And whatever way be the judgment of the Senate, I am consoled by the thought that the most homely text containing such a rule will be more beautiful far than any words of poetry or eloquence, and that it will endure to be read with gratitude when the rising dome of this Capitol, with the statue of Liberty which surmounts it, has crumbled to dust.

The VICE PRESIDENT. The question is on concurring in the amendment which was made as in Committee of the Whole.

Mr. SUMNER. I move to amend the amendment by striking out the words of the proposed article, and inserting the following:

All persons are equal before the law, so that no person can hold another as a slave; and the Congress may make all laws necessary and proper to carry this article into effect everywhere within the United States and the jurisdiction thereof.

...

The VICE PRESIDENT. The-question before the Senate is on agreeing to the amendment proposed by the Senator from Massachusetts.

Mr. SUMNER. I merely wish to have Senators understand that amendment, and, as I have said, I make it rather in the form of suggestion than proposition. If I understand from my friend the chairman of the Judiciary Committee that he is strongly inclined against it, I certainly have no desire to press it. If the Chair will be good enough, I should like to have it read for the information of the Senate.

The VICE PRESIDENT. It will be read.

The Secretary read the amendment, to strike out the first and second sections of article thirteen as reported, by the committee, and to insert:

Sec. 1. All persons are free [equal] before the law, so that no person can hold another as a slave; and the Congress may make all laws necessary and proper to carry this article into effect everywhere within the United States and the jurisdiction thereof.

Mr. SUMNER. Now, Mr. President, the state of the question is this. The Senator from Missouri [Mr. HENDERSON] offered a proposition in this form:

ART. 1. Slavery or involuntary servitude, except as a punishment for crime, shall not exist in the United States.

ART. 2. The Congress, whenever a majority of the members elected to each House shall deem it necessary, may propose amendments to the Constitution, or, on the application of the Legislatures of a majority of the several States, shall call a convention for proposing amendments, which in either case shall be valid, to all intents and purposes, as part of the Constitution, when ratified by the Legislatures of two thirds of the several States, or by conventions in two thirds thereof, as the one or the other mode of ratification may be proposed by Congress

It will be observed that this proposition of the Senator from Missouri is twofold: the first article applies to the matter which has been under discussion in this de-

bate, the prohibition of slavery; the second, to a proposition which is not necessarily associated with it. I believe, from what has occurred, the Senate is agreed in confining what we do now to the first proposition. I must say I accept that idea completely. I think the first proposition should be acted upon absolutely by itself alone, and therefore however much I may be tempted by other propositions, as I must confess I was by one or two of the propositions of the Senator from Kentucky [Mr. POWELL] the other day, yet I was not disposed to be diverted or turned aside from that great original proposition which it should be now our object to introduce into the Constitution.

I make this comment on the first proposition which we have before us, that of the Senator from Missouri, in order to explain why I should be against that in the form in which it stands; but if we should go to the first article of the proposition of the Senator from Missouri, I am free to say that in some respects I think it better than the article proposed by the committee. It is as follows:

Slavery or involuntary servitude, except as a punishment for crime, shall not exist in the United States.

It is simpler than the proposition of the committee, to which I now come. That is as follows:

ART. 13, Sec. 1.—

It will be observed that it is in two sections—

Neither slavery nor involuntary servitude, except as a punishment for crime, whereof the party shall have been duly convicted—

Which I must say I think here is verbiage entirely. There is no need of having it in a constitutional proposition—

shall exist within the United States, or any place subject to their jurisdiction.

Sec. 2. Congress shall have power to enforce this article by appropriate legislation.

On the face of that article I object to it, first, inasmuch as it is in two sections when I think it ought to be in one.

...

But then my objection to it is, further, if this amendment in this first particular, which is comparatively unimportant, be secured, it seems to me the language is not happy. I do not know that I shall have the concurrence of other Senators in the criticism which I make upon it; but I understand that it starts with the idea of reproducing the Jeffersonian ordinance. I doubt the expediency of reproducing that ordinance. It performed an excellent work in its day; but there are words in it which are entirely inapplicable to our time. That ordinance I will read. It is as follows:

> "There shall be neither slavery nor involuntary servitude in the said Territory otherwise than in the punishment of crimes whereof the party shall have been duly convicted."

This ordinance, in precisely these words, was reproduced at a later day, in the very important act by which Missouri was admitted into the Union, containing the well-known prohibition which afterwards caused such debate.

There are words here, I have said, which are entirely inapplicable to our time. They are the limitation, "otherwise than in the punishment of crimes whereof the party shall have been duly convicted." Now, unless I err, there is an implication from those words that men may be enslaved as a punishment of crimes whereof they shall have been duly convicted. There was a reason, I have said, for that at the time, for I understand that it was the habit in certain parts of the country to convict persons or to doom them as slaves for life as a punishment for crime, and it was not proposed to prohibit this habit. But slavery in our day is something distinct, perfectly well known, requiring no words of distinction outside of itself. Why, therefore, add "nor involuntary servitude otherwise than in the punishment of crimes whereof the party shall have been duly convicted?" To my mind they are entirely surplusage. They do no good there, but they absolutely introduce a doubt.

In placing a new and important text into our Constitution, it seems to me we cannot be too careful in the language we adopt. We should consider well that the language that we adopt here in this Chamber to-day will in all probability be adopted in the other House, and it must be adopted, also, by three fourths of the Legislatures of the States. Once having passed this body, it is substantially beyond correction. Therefore, it seems to me, we have every motive, the strongest inducement in the world, to make that language as perfect as possible.

I say, therefore, that I object to the Jeffersonian ordinance even if it were presented here in its original text. But now I am brought to the point that the proposition of the committee is not the Jeffersonian ordinance, except in its bad feature. In other respects, it discards the

language of the Jeffersonian ordinance and also its collocation of words. The language of the committee is as follows:

> Neither slavery nor involuntary servitude, except as a punishment for crime, whereof the party shall have been duly convicted, shall exist within the United States, or any place subject to their jurisdiction.

The Senate will observe what to my ear is a discord, the introduction of those two "shalls" so near together; but that is not of great importance.

Mr. DOOLITTLE. They are both in the Jeffersonian ordinance.

Mr. SUMNER. But they are further apart, and the whole effect is entirely different. As I have said already, the language of the ordinance is, "There shall be." Mark the beginning as compared with that of the committee. The committee say, "Neither slavery nor involuntary servitude," &c. The ordinance says, "There shall be"— the word of prohibition coming first, at the outset— "neither slavery nor involuntary servitude in the said Territory otherwise than in the punishment of crimes whereof the party shall have been duly convicted;" whereas the committee say, "Neither slavery nor involuntary servitude, except as a punishment for crime, whereof the party shall have been duly convicted, shall exist within the United States, or anyplace subject to their jurisdiction."

If Senators desire the Jeffersonian ordinance, I say let us take it in its original form as it appears in that ordinance, and was subsequently reproduced in the Missouri statute; do not let us take it in this modified form, which, while pretending to be the Jeffersonian ordinance, is not the Jeffersonian ordinance except in that feature which I think, if Senators apply their minds to it, they will see is clearly objectionable. I refer to the words "except as a punishment for crimes whereof the party shall have been duly convicted." I have already said that for myself I should prefer the form which I have sent to the Chair, and on which the question is now to be taken; but I offer it as a suggestion, and if Senators do not incline to it, I have no desire to press it.

Mr. TRUMBULL. Mr. President, at an early stage of the session, the Senator from Missouri introduced a proposition to amend the Constitution of the United States so as forever to prohibit slavery. That resolution was referred to the Committee on the Judiciary. At a later day, a month or two afterwards, the Senator from

Massachusetts also introduced a proposition to prohibit slavery. The committee had both those propositions before them. They considered them. There was some difference of opinion in the committee as to the language to be used; and it was upon discussion and an examination of both these propositions, the one originally introduced by the Senator from Missouri, and subsequently by the Senator from Massachusetts, that the committee came to the conclusion to adopt the form which is reported here. I do not know that I should have adopted these precise words, but a majority of the committee thought they were the best words; they accomplish the object; and I cannot see why the Senator from Massachusetts should be so pertinacious about particular words. The words that we have adopted will accomplish the object. If every member of the Senate is to select the precise words in which a law shall be clothed, and will be satisfied with none other, we shall have very little legislation.

Mr. SUMNER. I have already said I shall be perfectly satisfied with what the Senate do. I am making a sincere effort now to contribute as much as I can to improve the proposition in form.

Mr. TRUMBULL. Undoubtedly in the opinion of the Senator from Massachusetts it would improve the proposition. If I had had my precise way in the committee, very likely it would have improved the proposition to have had the language as I wanted it; but a majority of the committee agreed upon these words; and although the Senator from Massachusetts may satisfy himself that the words he has suggested, copied from the French Revolution, are the best words for us to adopt, I am not at all sure of it. I think there is nothing historical about them, nothing in the source from whence they come to commend them particularly to us. I would not go to the French Revolution to find the proper words for a constitution. We all know that their constitutions were failures, while ours, we trust, will be permanent. I therefore am not inclined to accept the gentleman's suggestions, and I hope he will withdraw them and let the Senate come to a vote upon this subject.

Mr. DOOLITTLE. If the Senator from Illinois will allow me for a single moment, it is said that men's first impressions are sometimes the best, and it seems that the Senator from Massachusetts when he introduced his proposition used in it the very words of which he now makes such complaint, "otherwise than in the punishment of crime whereof the party shall have been duly convicted."

Mr. SUMNER. I beg the Senator's pardon. The first proposition I introduced was a month or six weeks before that; but after the committee made their report, when I examined it and found that they had undertaken to give us the Jeffersonian ordinance, and I saw that it was not the Jeffersonian ordinance, I then prepared that proposition with a view to embody the Jeffersonian ordinance precisely.

Mr. TRUMBULL. I was very much tempted to reply to some of the remarks that have been made in opposition to this proposed amendment, and am strongly tempted also to reply to some of the remarks which have fallen from the Senator from Massachusetts, who in an elaborate argument has attempted to show that no amendment of the Constitution is necessary; but, sir, if we can have a vote on this subject I will forego making any reply to what has been said, and will content myself with the passage of the resolution, which is the object I have in view, to abolish slavery and prevent its existence hereafter. The language as reported by the committee will accomplish these objects; and although it may not be the best possible form to the mind of every Senator here, I wish him to reflect that it is impossible for us all to agree upon the language. We have discussed this matter in committee. As to its being now embodied in two sections that is a matter of taste; there is no importance in it. Perhaps it would be just as well in one.

Mr. SUMNER. Why not alter it in that way?

Mr. TRUMBULL. No, sir, I will not alter it. I cannot alter it. The committee considered this subject and deliberately agreed upon this form. I have no authority to consent to an alteration of it. The Senate can alter it. If each Senator thinks he can find better words and proceeds to offer other words, it will be for the Senate to determine what words they will adopt.

Mr. HOWARD. I believe the proposition now before the Senate is the amendment offered by the Senator from Massachusetts, and on that question I have one word to say.

Mr. SUMNER. The Senator will allow me to make a remark. I cannot resist the appeal of my friend, the chairman of the committee, and therefore shall not pursue any of the propositions, and I wish to withdraw them. I merely wish to put myself right with my friends. I offered them sincerely with a desire to make a contribution to perfect the measure. I now withdraw them.

Mr. HOWARD. I must object to the withdrawal of the amendment, as I have the floor. I desire, as I said before, to say one word on this subject of the amendment offered by the Senator from Massachusetts. The language of it is this, that all persons are free before the law.

Mr. SUMNER. "All persons are equal."

Mr. HOWARD. Will the Secretary be good enough to read it?

The Secretary read, as follows:

Sec. 1. All persons are free before the law, so that no person can hold another as a slave, &c.

Mr. SUMNER. That is a mistake. It is "equal."

Mr. HOWARD. It is written in the handwriting of the Senator from Massachusetts.

Mr. SUMNER. It is "equal," and not "free."

Mr. HOWARD. I regard it as very immaterial whether the word "free" or "equal" is used in that connection. What I insist upon is this, that in a legal and technical sense that language is utterly insignificant and meaningless as a clause of the Constitution. I should like the Senator from Massachusetts, if he is able, to state what effect this would have in law in a court of justice. What significance is given to the phrase "equal" or "free" before the law in a common-law court? It is not known at all.

Besides, the proposition speaks of all men being equal. I suppose before the law a woman would be equal to a man, a woman would be as free as a man. A wife would be equal to her husband and as free as her husband before the law.

The learned Senator from Massachusetts, I apprehend, has made a very radical mistake in regard to the application of this language of the French constitution. The purpose for which this language was used in the original constitution of its French republic of 1791, was to abolish nobility and privileged classes. It was a mere political reformation relating to the political rights of Frenchmen, and nothing else. It was to enable all Frenchmen to reach positions of eminence and honor in the French Government, and was intended for no other purpose whatever. It was never intended there as a means of abolishing slavery at all. The Convention of 1794 abolished slavery by another and separate decree expressly putting an end to slavery within the dominions of the French republic and all its colonies.

Now, sir, I wish as much as the Senator from Massachusetts in making this amendment to use significant language, language that cannot be mistaken or misunderstood; but I prefer to dismiss all reference to French constitutions or French codes, and go back to the good old Anglo-Saxon language employed by our fathers in the ordinance of 1787, an expression which has been adjudicated upon repeatedly, which is perfectly well understood both by the public and by judicial tribunals, a phrase, I may say further, which is peculiarly near and dear to its people of the Northwestern Territory, from whose soil slavery was excluded by it. I think it is well understood, well comprehended by the people of the United States, and that no court of justice, no magistrate, no person, old or young, can misapprehend the meaning and effect of that clear, brief, and comprehensive clause. I hope we shall stand by the report of the committee.

Mr. SUMNER. My proposition is withdrawn, the Chair understands.

. . .

The VICE PRESIDENT. The question is on the passage of the joint resolution, upon which the yeas and nays have been ordered.

The Secretary proceeded to call the roll.

Mr. HENDRICKS, (when Mr. BUCKALEW's name was called.) I desire to say that Mr. BUCKALEW is not able to be in his seat to-day, and he expressed a wish that I should say that if he were present he would vote against the proposition.

The call of the roll having concluded, the result was announced—yeas 38, nays 6; as follows:

YEAS—Messrs. Anthony, Brown, Chandler, Clark, Collamer, Conness, Cowan, Dixon, Doolittle, Fessenden, Foot, Foster, Grimes, Hale, Harding, Harlan, Harris, Henderson, Howard, Howe, Johnson, Lane of Indiana, Lane of Kansas, Morgan, Morrill, Nesmith, Pomeroy, Ramsey, Sherman, Sprague, Sumner, Ten Eyck, Trumbull, Van Winkle, Wade, Wilkinson, Willey, and Wilson—38.

NAYS—Messrs. Davis, Hendricks, McDougall, Powell, Riddle, and Saulsbury—6.

The VICE PRESIDENT announced that the joint resolution, having received the concurrence of two thirds of the Senators present, was passed. Its title was amended to read: A joint resolution submitting to the Legislatures of the several States a proposition to amend the Constitution of the United States.

Mr. SAULSBURY. I rise simply to say that I now bid farewell to any hope of the reconstruction of the American Union.

Mr. MCDOUGALL. I desire to ask a question for the purpose of understanding a ruling of the Chair. The ruling, I understand, is that the vote as it stands now has no relation to the States not represented on the floor. I think our vote now being a final vote should have relation to all the States as recognized under the Constitution.

The VICE PRESIDENT. The Chair rules that a majority of all the Senators is a quorum, and two thirds of the number voting, provided a quorum votes, is sufficient to pass any resolution proposing an amendment to the Constitution.

Mr. McDOUGALL. I only desire the privilege of saying that such is not the opinion I entertain.

17

Radical Democracy Party Platform, Cleveland, OH

May 31, 1864[*]

Mr. Carroll, Chairman of the Committee on Resolutions, reported the following resolutions:

1. That the Federal Union shall be preserved.

2. That the Constitution and laws of the United States must be observed and obeyed.

3. That the rebellion must be suppressed by force of arms, and without compromise.

4. That the rights of free speech, free press, and the *habeas corpus* be held inviolate, save in districts where martial law has been proclaimed.

5. That the rebellion has destroyed slavery, and the Federal Constitution should be amended to prohibit its reestablishment, and to secure to all men absolute equality before the law.

6. That integrity and economy are demanded at all times in the administration of the Government; and that in time of war the want of them is criminal.

7. That the right of asylum, except for crime and subject to law, is a recognized principle of American liberty; that any violation of it cannot be overlooked, and must not go unrebuked.

8. That the national policy known as the "Monroe doctrine" has become a recognized principle, and that the establishment of an anti-republican Government on this continent by any foreign power cannot be tolerated.

9. That the gratitude and support of the nation are due to the faithful soldiers and the earnest leaders of the Union army and navy for their heroic achievements and deathless valor in defense of our imperiled country and of civil liberty.

10. That the one-term policy for the Presidency, adopted by the people, is strengthened by the force of the existing crisis, and should be maintained by constitutional amendments.

11. That the Constitution should be so amended that the President and Vice President shall be elected by a direct vote of the people.

12. That the question of the reconstruction of the rebellious States belongs to the people, through their representatives in Congress, and not to the Executive.

13. That the confiscation of the lands of the rebels, and their distribution among the soldiers and actual settlers, is a measure of justice.

18

US House of Representatives, Debates on Abolition Amendment

May 31, 1864[†]

Joint resolution (S. No. 16) submitting to the Legislatures of the several States a proposition to amend the Constitution of the United States.

. . .

The joint resolution is as follows:

That the following article be proposed to the Legislatures of the several States as an amendment to the Constitution of the United States, which, when ratified by three fourths of said Legislatures, shall be valid, to all intents and purposes, as a part of the said Constitution, namely:

Article XIII.

Sec. 1. Neither slavery nor involuntary servitude, except as a punishment for crime whereof the party shall have been duly convicted, shall exist within the United States, or any place subject to their jurisdiction.

[*] Thomas Valentine Cooper, ed., *American Politics (Nonpartisan) from Beginning to Date, Embodying a History of All the Political Parties, with Their Views and Records on All Important Questions* (Chicago: C. R. Brodix, 1883), 44.

[†] *Cong. Globe*, 38th Cong., 1st Sess., 2612, 2613–17 (May 31, 1864).

Sec. 2. Congress shall have power to enforce this article by appropriate legislation.

...

Mr. MORRIS, of New York. Mr. Speaker, the questions which now engross so much of the public attention as to the status of the several states in rebellion, and just what disposition shall be made of them when finally subdued, are increasing in interest. Upon these points loyal men are known to differ; hence an examination and a discussion of them may be profitable.

...

But to the question, what is the status of the States in rebellion? Are they really in or are they actually out of the Union? Paradoxical as it may seem, I hold they are neither, and yet are they both. Suppose the officers and crew of any Federal vessel should mutiny and run out a piratical flag, would this act absolve the mutineers from allegiance to the Government? When the malcontents are subdued, should they be restored to command? May they insist upon the control of the recaptured vessel? By their acts they have forfeited this privilege, and yet they are amenable to the laws. They owe the fealty of a citizen without a citizen's rights. There can be no question as to the status of the vessel. Why should there be as to who shall command it? Should this be done by piratical outlaws, or by men of unquestioned loyalty? A highwayman by transgression does not absolve himself from obedience to the law he has trampled upon and defied. As far as allegiance, duty, and obligation are concerned his condition is unchanged, but he has no voice at the ballot-box, he may not hold an office of trust, nor can he participate as a witness or juror in any of our courts. He is a felon, he wears the taint and the disabilities of a felon. No one complains of this except the transgressor.

...

These States, while they may not claim the prerogatives of loyal constituents of the Union, yet are they as actually subject to its dominion and power as if they never had rebelled. I go further; a State can no more secede from the Union than can the arm from the natural body. The arm may be severed by force, but irreparable disaster would follow. A State may be separated from the body-politic of which it is a member by revolution, but peacefully, rightfully, never. The efficiency and completeness of the corporate whole would be destroyed by the act.

...

[T]he founders of our Government adopted and we indorse the cardinal truths:

"That all men are created equal; that they are endowed by their Creator with certain unalienable rights; that among these are life, liberty, and the pursuit of happiness. That, to secure these rights, governments are instituted among men, deriving their just powers from the consent of the governed; that, whenever any form of government becomes destructive of these ends it is the right of the people to alter or to abolish it, and to institute a new government, laying its foundation on such principles, and organizing its powers in such form, as to them shall seem most likely to effect their safety and happiness."

Under this authority some have strangely sought to justify the rebellion of the southern States. It should be borne in mind that the power conferred by this instrument is upon an entire, not an integral part of a people, and its exercise is limited expressly to the altering or the abolishing of a Government that has become destructive of certain enumerated rights. I find no warrant in this for the secession of a State, but on the contrary I find authority directing the people (the Federal Government) to alter and abolish any law or constitution whenever the public interests demand it. We sometimes err in supposing that our Government and the people are distinct entities. Hence we hear of the Government's exactions and tyranny. The truth is, the Government and the people are identical.

The Executive of the nation, the Legislature, and the Judiciary, are not severally nor are they jointly the Government; they are only servants. They represent and act for the sovereign people, and to them must yield obedience and render an account. This common error is a source of much mischief. Many suppose they may assail the Government and embarrass its action with impunity, not reflecting that by so doing they injure their own interests.

...

[O]ur fathers permitted slavery from a supposed necessity. This was their first error. They expected it would become extinct under the workings of the Constitution. This was a second error. Others followed, and since the formation of our Government millions have been enslaved. An entire race has been deprived of all social rank, barred our schools, shut out from the gospel, and then held to be inferior for not rising in spite of their hindrances to an equality with the Saxon in the enjoyment of each of these privileges. Under our Government the African is a nondescript; he is not a man, nor yet is he a brute; he has not the rights nor the protection of either; he has no resting place, no refuge within this land of liberty and Christianity, and yet he is the only innocent party within its entire boundaries. Tell me where he may rear the home altar and enjoy unmolested the companionship of wife and children. Up to this hour, such is the force of prejudice, that if, rising above and forgetting the inhuman treatment of our Government, the colored man enters our armies and imperils his life in its defense, he is denied not only the pay but the protection of a soldier. And yet we crave Heaven's blessing.

. . .

Sir, this is not a mere struggle between the North and the South; it is a conflict between two systems; a controversy between right and wrong. This is not a war between the Puritan and the Cavalier; freedom begat the former and slavery the latter. They are only instruments in the hands of their respective creators.

Mr. Speaker, the present American Congress occupies a position at this moment of greater responsibility than has devolved upon a like body since the year 1776. The events of an entire century transpire in a year. The United States have made more history in the three years last past than can be written out in an ordinary lifetime. Our action upon this question will adorn or forever sully one of its pages. Our action this day will give perpetuity to a nation of freemen or of slaves. By our action at this time shall we be honored or execrated by the millions who shall people the continent of the West. The eyes of a world are upon us; the hopes of the oppressed, the interests of freedom in every land hang upon our decision, and the blessings or the cursings of Almighty God await our final proceedings.

. . .

Mr. HERRICK. Mr. Speaker, as I intend to vote against this proposition to tamper with the Constitution of our fathers, which I have been taught to reverence as a masterpiece of wisdom in statesmanship, and as being the foundation of the most perfect system of human government ever devised by man, it is but proper that I should state to the House and the country some of the reasons which impel me to make the record I intend upon the question of the passage of this important resolution.

. . .

Sir, this resolution is nothing else than a disunion measure. It means nothing else than eternal disunion and a continuous war. Its design could have been only to widen the existing breach between the Union and the slave States now in rebellion, and to render peace upon any acceptable terms to the South unapproachable. It will give the rebel leaders a new pretext for continuing in arms, for it is virtually a formal declaration of Congress and the northern people that submission to the Federal authority and a renewal in good faith of their allegiance to the Government will profit them nothing in the way of securing to themselves and their posterity the rights which the Constitution, as their fathers and our fathers made it, guaranties to all the States. I mean the right to regulate their own internal affairs, to determine their own system of labor, to control their own social institutions, to have slavery or leave it alone, to fix the status of their inhabitants severally, and to give or withhold the rights of citizenship and suffrage as they may see fit, and to exercise the attributes of absolute sovereignty in all matters not especially delegated to the General Government.

. . .

Sir, the assumption that slavery is the cause of this war, and that there can be no union of these States while slavery is tolerated in any of them, is a position which the facts do not warrant or justify. The Union, according to my understanding, was established upon the idea that a free Government could exist when composed of independent States, of various geographical positions, and possessing altogether different systems of social organization, for common purposes; and the assumption of the Republicans, to which I refer, is an argument not only against the rights of States to govern themselves, but it is a concession that the great principle contended for in the Revolution of 1776, after a trial of eighty years has proved a failure, and that we are now carrying on a gigantic civil war to establish a consolidated central Government upon a homogeneity of interests. Success in this undertaking would only undo what our fathers accomplished in 1776. But, sir, in my judgment this can never be accomplished.

. . .

Nobody, Mr. Speaker, will pretend to say, even at this day, that the Union could have been formed in the first place if the Constitution had not recognized and protected the slave institution. Sir, does anybody believe that if the representatives of a majority of the States in the Convention which framed the Constitution had insisted upon incorporating into that instrument the resolution now upon your table our Union could have been consummated? No, sir. Had New England then insisted upon the abolition of slavery we all know that the Constitution would have failed and there would have been no Union for the rebels of the present day to destroy or for us to save. This country then would have been split up into sundry confederacies, or perhaps each of the States would have been left to "go it alone."

Now, sir, the truth is that the protection which the Constitution threw around the slavery system of the South, and the guarantee it gave to the African slave trade for a period of twenty years, was in fact the very bond of our Union; for it is manifest that no Union could have been formed if those, in these days, horrid provisions had been omitted! What a terrible idea for our negro-worshiping friends on the other side of the House to contemplate!

In this view of our governmental compact—denominated by the abolitionists "an agreement with hell"—and its provisions establishing the tenure of slave property, the rights of the people of the slaveholding States in such property cannot be equitably or honestly abrogated without their consent. It is not, however, my intention to argue this point, for I am sure that I should never be able to convince the majority of this House that they have not the right by some "higher law" to abrogate every species of property belonging to a slaveholder, and to tinker the Constitution to suit themselves, and then say to the people of the South, "This shall be your Constitution; submit to it without a murmur, or we will exterminate your whole race from the face of the earth and parcel out your lands to your negroes in forty-acre lots!"

In this spirit they have conducted the war from its beginning—as full of venomous persecution toward slaveholders for the sin of slavery as was Saul of Tarsus when he made that memorable journey from Jerusalem to Damascus, breathing threatenings and slaughter against the saints! But, sir, Paul on that occasion saw a great light and heard a loud voice; and I am hopeful that before our once happy land is utterly ruined—say in the month of November next—the relentless career of the fanatics in power will in like manner be arrested by the mighty voice of the people at the polls.

19

National Union (Republican) Party Convention, Baltimore, MD

June 7, 1864[*]

The National Union Convention which assembled at Baltimore on Tuesday of last week, gave expression to the wishes of the loyal people of this country by nominating Abraham Lincoln for President and Andrew Johnson for Vice President. The proceedings were more than ordinarily harmonious, and the nominations were made with the utmost unanimity.

The resolutions adopted by the Convention are as follows:

Mr. Raymond, of New York, from the Committee on Resolutions, reported the following:

Resolved, That as slavery was the cause, and now constitutes the strength of this rebellion, and as it must be, always and everywhere hostile to the principles of republican government, justice and the national safety demand its utter and complete extirpation from the soil of the Republic, [applause,] and that we uphold and maintain the acts and proclamations by which the Government, in its own defence, has aimed a deathblow at this gigantic evil. We are in favor, furthermore, of such an amendment to the Constitution to be made by the people in conformity with its provisions, as shall terminate and forever prohibit the existence of Slavery within the limits of the jurisdiction of the United States. [Applause]

Resolved, That the thanks of the American people are due to the soldiers and sailors of the army and navy, [applause,] who have periled their lives in defense of their country and in vindication of the honor of the flag; that the nation owes to them some permanent recognition of their patriotism and their valor, and ample and permanent provision for those of their survivors who have received disabling and honorable wounds in the service of the country; and that the memories of those who have fallen in its defense shall be held in grateful and everlasting remembrance. [Loud applause.]

Resolved, That we approve and applaud the practical wisdom, the unselfish patriotism and the unswerv-

[*] *Washington Reporter* (PA), June 15, 1864, 2.

ing fidelity to the Constitution, and the principles of American liberty with which Abraham Lincoln has discharged, under circumstances of unparalleled difficulty, the great duties and responsibilities of the Presidential office; that we approve and indorse, as demanded by the emergency, and essential to the preservation of the nation and as within the provisions of the Constitution, the measures and acts which he has adopted to defend the nation against its open and secret foes. That we approve, especially, the Proclamation of Emancipation, and the employment as Union soldiers of men heretofore held in slavery. [Applause] That we have full confidence in his determination to carry these and all other constitutional measures essential to the salvation of the country into full and complete effect.

...

Resolved, That the Government owes to all men employed in its armies without regard to distinction of color, the full protection of the laws of war, [applause.] and that any violation of these laws, or of the usages of civilized nations in time of war, by the rebels now in arms, should be made the subject of full and prompt redress. [Prolonged applause.]

20

Abraham Lincoln, Letter to the National Union Convention

June 9, 1864[*]

Gentlemen of the Committee: I will neither conceal my gratification, nor restrain the expression of my gratitude, that the Union people, through their convention, in their continued effort to save, and advance the nation, have deemed me not unworthy to remain in my present position.

I know no reason to doubt that I shall accept the nomination tendered; and yet perhaps I should not declare definitely before reading and considering what is called the Platform.

I will say now, however, I approve the declaration in favor of so amending the Constitution as to prohibit slavery throughout the nation. When the people in revolt, with a hundred days of explicit notice, that they

could, within those days, resume their allegiance, without the overthrow of their institution, and that they could not so resume it afterwards, elected to stand out, such amendment of the Constitution as now proposed, became a fitting, and necessary conclusion to the final success of the Union cause. Such alone can meet and cover all cavils. Now, the unconditional Union men, North and South, perceive its importance, and embrace it. In the joint names of Liberty and Union, let us labor to give it legal form, and practical effect.

21

US House of Representatives, Debates and Failed Vote on Abolition Amendment

June 14–15, 1864[†]

JUNE 14, 1864

The SPEAKER stated that the first business in order was the special order, being Senate joint resolution No. 16, proposing amendments to the Constitution of the United States, on which the gentleman from California [Mr. HIGBY] was entitled to the floor.

Mr. PRUYN. By an arrangement with the gentleman from California he has agreed to let me precede him.

...

Mr. PRUYN. For the first time in our history it is now proposed to make a change in the Constitution which, if effected, will interfere with the reserved rights of the States. This question is presented in the midst of a great struggle which demands all the power and energies and thought of the country, and when a large number of the States, and those most deeply to be affected by the contemplated change, are not represented in either House of Congress.

...

I admit that the Constitution should be liberally construed for the purposes for which it was established, but I deny that it can be constructively enlarged, or that under the pretense of amending it, we can go outside of the terms and of the spirit of the grant and draw within

---

[*] Lincoln, *Speeches and Writings*, 2:597–98.

[†] *Cong. Globe*, 38th Cong., 1st Sess., 2939–62, 2977–95 (June 14–15, 1864).

its grasp subjects with which it does not deal, and which have been expressly declared to be beyond its reach. This is not the legitimate meaning of the power to amend; such a power would be one to originate—to create—to establish. The right remained with the States severally to regulate their internal affairs each in its own way, and according to its own views of right and duty.

...

Twelve amendments to the Constitution have been made, the first ten almost simultaneously with its adoption. They are declaratory and restrictive, containing the great principles of the Bill of Rights. The eleventh and twelfth amendments were adopted a few years subsequently. The eleventh, as to the judicial powers, is also restrictive. The twelfth prescribes more definitely than before the mode of casting the electoral vote and of conducting the election for President and Vice President under the provisions of the Constitution. All these amendments, it will be observed, are in substance declaratory and restrictive, or regulate the exercise of powers already granted, and do not enlarge the powers of the General Government. Since the last of them was adopted sixty years have passed, during which time the instrument has not been touched.

...

If three fourths of the States can take away rights now clearly reserved to their associates, what is to prevent the absorption of their territory by other States? If one right can be taken away, several can be—all can be. If one principle can be swept away, all can be. Under such a doctrine States may be annihilated and a monarchy built up. These it may be said are extreme cases, but they are legitimate results from the power to amend now claimed. The right to amend is not a right to *extend and enlarge* the power granted under the Constitution. It was only intended through its instrumentality to provide for the better and more convenient exercise of the powers expressly granted, in case defects should be found to exist in the practical working of the system. The amendment as to the manner of electing the President and Vice President illustrates this view.

To construe the Constitution as authorizing three fourths of the States to impose upon the residue terms and conditions of Union not agreed upon or assented to by them, would be a wide departure from its spirit, aid a monstrous usurpation of power; and this it is which we are now called upon to do; to take a further step to alienate the feelings of the South, and to embarrass and

impede their return to the Union. No matter what the question may be, whether that of slavery or of any other domestic institution or right reserved to the States; so long as it is reserved, Congress has no right to interfere with it in any way.

...

Mr. FERNANDO WOOD. Mr. Speaker, this is a proposition to provide by an amendment to the Constitution for the abolition of slavery without compensation in all of the States in the Union. It will be, if adopted, a change in the fundamental law—a material alteration in the Constitution of the United States as formed by the founders of the Government. It is, therefore, a proposition which involves considerations and reflections such as belong to the gravest questions which can come before the American people for determination. It is whether we shall alter the whole structure and theory of government by changing the basis upon which it rests.

My first difficulty in assenting to the resolution is that this is no time for any alteration in the organic law. We are now in the midst of a fearful civil war. The horrid din of this conflict, the groans of the wounded and dying, the sad evidences of death and destruction are all around us. Until recently, even at the very doors of this capital, the armed enemy has presented his threatening hostility. The whole people of America are involved directly or indirectly in this dreadful conflict. Reason, judgment, and that cautious investigation and comparison of interests, opinions, end prejudices necessary to a proper adjustment of a nation's welfare have been banished by the graver realities of war. This is no time to make or alter constitutions. Those who are enveloped in the elemental strifes of the tempest or the earthquake, and involved in the ruin thus created, cannot judge of the cause or measure the extent of the calamity. So it is with the historical convulsions which have desolated vast regions and swept myriads to the grave. The spectator who is himself in the midst of the horrors of war has seldom the coolness to discriminate and decide, with any reasonable degree of accuracy, as to the impelling cause of the struggle.

...

But if a change *can* be made, is this such a one as *should* be made? It is sought through this amendment to abolish at once and summarily the system of domestic servitude existing in one third of the States which came into the Union with the Government and which have remained with it until now. The effects of such a revulsion in such an interest will be of the most widespread and radical character. It will, of course, add to the existing sectional hostilities, and if possible make the pending conflict yet more intense and deadly.

. . .

Our Union was made for the *political* government of the parties to it, for certain specified objects of a very general character, all of them *political*, and none of them relating to or affecting in any manner individual or personal interests in those things which touch the domestic concerns. There is no feature or principle of it giving to the Federal power authority over them. These were reserved and left exclusively to the jurisdiction of the States and "the people thereof." Of this character are the marital relations, the religious beliefs, the right of eminent domain within the territorial limits of the States, other private property, and all matters purely social. Slavery where it exists is a system of domestic labor; it is not the creature of law. It existed without law before this Government was established. It is incorporated into the organization of society as part of the existing domestic regulations. It cannot be brought within constitutional jurisdiction any more than can any or either of the other private and personal interests referred to.

. . .

But, sir, the most important aspect of this question is whether it is not a violation of the plighted faith of the States who shall aid in foisting this amendment into the Constitution. That the States in establishing the Constitution performed it as a *federal* act has been shown in the Federalist by an argument as indisputable as any mathematical demonstration. Mr. Madison says on this subject:

> "Each State in ratifying the Constitution is considered as a sovereign body independent of all others, and only to be bound by its own voluntary act. In this relation, then, the new Constitution will, if established, be a *federal*, and not a *national* Constitution."*

It is true that the common Government which resulted presents national characteristics, especially in this respect, that its operation is exerted immediately upon citizens within the scope of the powers delegated to it in their individual capacities. The State sovereign-

ties were by no means quenched by the act of federation, but by it certain functions were delegated by the sovereign power in each State to a common depository, to be used in certain cases, and to be exercised over the citizens respectively of each and every State by virtue of the sovereignty of their several States. The obligation, however, of the citizen of the State of New York to obey the Federal laws or authorities results from the powers imparted to the Federal Legislature or Executive by the act of New York, and derives no additional strength from other States entering into the Union. The citizen is bound to obey the Constitution and laws of the United States, because his State is a party to the Federal compact, and for no other reason. The State has delegated a portion of her authority (not of her sovereignty, which is, in its very nature, indivisible as that of individual personality) to a common agency, who may thus within the scope of such procuration require obedience to its requirements. The Government of the Union has this extent and no more, and allegiance, loyalty, and nationality are the new-fangled catch-words of the exploded dogmas of the old Federal party. Allegiance is due to the law, and derives its sanction from the sovereignty of each individual State.

The Democratic party has always maintained the doctrine that the Constitution was a compact from the times of Jefferson, and has for more than sixty years declared this as the foundation of its political faith. It is laid down most distinctly in the Kentucky and Virginia resolutions, the corner-stone of Democracy.

> "That the several States composing the United States of America are not united on the principles of unlimited submission to the General Government, but that by compact, under the style and title of a Constitution for the United States and of amendments thereto, they constituted a General Government for special purposes, delegated to that Government certain definitive powers, reserving each State to itself the residuary mass of right to their own self-government and that whensoever the General Government assumes undelegated powers its acts are unauthoritative, void, and of no force; that to this compact each State acceded as a State and is an integral party; that this Government, created by this compact, was not made the exclusive or final judge of the extent of the powers delegated to itself, since that would have made its discretion, and not

* [*Federalist*, No. 39 (Madison). See this volume, 1B, doc. 3. —Ed.]

the Constitution, the measure of its powers; but that, as in all other cases of compact among parties having no common judge, each party has an equal right to judge for itself, as well of infractions as of the mode and measures of redress."

Such is the language of Mr. Jefferson in the Kentucky Resolutions. In the Virginia Resolutions, the author of which was Mr. Madison, it is declared—

"That in case of a deliberate, palpable, and dangerous exercise of other powers not granted by the said compact, the States who are parties thereto have the right, and are in duty bound, to interpose, for arresting the progress of the evil, and for maintaining within their respective limits the authorities, rights, and liberties appertaining to them."

. . .

Now, the very nature of a compact requires that there be contracting parties, and mutual obligations and considerations. The States and the people of those States in their sovereign capacity are the parties, and must be held answerable for any breach of good faith in not observing the terms of the contract, or in attempting to change them in any particular which destroys or alters essential and material portions. There was an implied and solemn understanding that the local and domestic institutions of the States should not be attempted to be interfered with in any manner so as to be drawn within the sphere of Federal authority.

. . .

The control over slavery, and the domestic and social relations of the people of the respective States, was not and never was intended to be delegated to the United States, and cannot now be delegated except by the consent of all the States. Articles nine and ten of the Amendments to the Constitution are conclusive on this point. These articles are the general rules for the construction and interpretation of the entire instrument. Powers already granted may be modified, enlarged, or taken away by an amendment, but those which are retained by the people, or reserved to them or to the States, cannot be delegated to the United States, except by the unanimous consent of all the States. This is the only reasonable construction of those articles, in accordance with the plain sense and meaning of the words. The entire subject of slavery in the States has been reserved by them, and the right been retained by the people.

. . .

This identical proposition was laid down in the fourth resolution of the Chicago platform, *once* deemed so sacred in the eyes of the President and the gentlemen on the other side of the House, which asserts—

"That the maintenance inviolate of the rights of the States, and especially the right of each State to order and control its own domestic institutions according to its own judgment exclusively, is essential to that balance of power on which the perfection and endurance of our political faith depend."*

Where now will be the right of each State to order and control its domestic institutions if the institutions of one fourth of the States are to be subjected to the will of the people of three fourths by amending the Constitution so as to make them belong to and under the control of a majority in Congress, or to wipe them out altogether?

. . .

The proposal of this amendment arraigns the President as having violated the Constitution in his emancipation proclamation, and stamps it as a nullity and void. It is an implied confession, that the Administration, carrying on an aggressive war on States and State institutions, had this design in view from the commencement—that the war was not for the purpose of sustaining the Government, preserving the Union, and maintaining the supremacy of the Constitution, but was directed against the sovereignties of the States, and to destroy such of their domestic institutions as were obnoxious to the views of the party controlling the Government for the time.

. . .

Mr. HIGBY. Before speaking to the resolution embracing the proposition to amend, I refer to the fifth article of the Constitution of the United States, which makes ample provision and explains the way by which an amendment may be made. The article reads as follows:

. . .

There is nowhere contemplated in the Constitution of the United States any action by Congress that more completely acknowledges and recognizes State sovereignty than this very provision of the Constitution explaining how it may be amended. Our people are looking with anxiety to the action of Congress with reference to this subject. And now let me put a question

* [See Republican Party Platform, 1860, this volume, 1D, doc. 2. —Ed.]

to gentlemen on the other side of the House. They have belabored this side often and long with denunciations that State rights are not regarded, that State sovereignty by our action is unheeded, and that we are aiding the national Government to absorb all powers which legitimately belong to the States under and by virtue of the Constitution. I appeal to them when a proposition does come from this side of the House that acknowledges and recognizes State sovereignty in full, whether they dare submit that proposition to the several States; whether they have faith in State sovereignty so great that when the Constitution makes a provision so ample as it has in this case, and so safe too, requiring the Legislatures of three fourths of the States to ratify, that they dare allow their different States to act upon this subject.

. . .

The member from New York who has just taken his seat [Mr. FERNANDO WOOD] has had the hardihood to promulge to this nation that the ninth and tenth articles of the Amendments to the Constitution do away and make a nullity of the article to which I have directed attention and quoted. Can he find anywhere in the Constitution a provision by which it may be amended in so indirect a way, and the portions amended be left as dead matter to cumber the living body? He would search in vain for such a provision. Why, sir, he would trample the Constitution under his feet. And if we follow out his argument and act upon it we will become violators of that instrument.

I regard the fifth article as a part of the Constitution just as full of vitality as it was the day our fathers established it as a part of the Constitution of this country; and, sir, the gentleman from New York, if he has a particle of honesty, himself will ignore every word which he has said upon that one subject.

. . .

Mr. SHANNON.

. . .

It will not, I trust, be necessary in this, the fourth year of our struggle, to press upon this House proof that slavery is alone responsible for this war. No man who has read carefully the history of the past eighty years, whatever may, be his political bias, will, I think, differ with this opinion. It is now our province to inquire whether that curse can be perpetuated with safety to American freedom and national unity, and if we find that it cannot, it will then become our duty to see to it that for the future it shall not exist as an element of disruption and disintegration in our midst.

Sir, the apothegm "liberty regulated by law" expresses my idea of the spirit of American institutions. It is that condition of the people wherein each is at liberty to regulate his own domestic affairs according to his own judgment or caprice, only being careful that those laws which protect the rights of his neighbor from infringement must not be violated. Slavery is inconsistent with this condition; it makes the many subject to the few, makes the laborer the mere tool of the capitalist, and centralizes the political power of the nation. Yet, sir, this centralization is not such as that which gave Russia her solidity and despotic greatness; it is that cheaper article from which "petty lords and feudal despots" spring. It draws around the slave-owning nabob all the petty trappings of the feudal system, and does not hesitate to assume like political powers. Its slaves are numbered as people to be represented, yet considered before the law as soulless beasts of burden. The man who owns five hundred slaves figures in the tables of representation as the equal of three hundred non-slaveholders.

. . .

It has been asserted, and even in some cases by divines otherwise respectable, that this thing, slavery, was of divine origin. I shall not stop, nor have I patience to discuss those texts in holy writ which are said to favor this view, but shall content myself with remembering the one great test by which the divinity of all doctrines must be weighed: "By their fruits ye shall know them." Who will dare make, in this enlightened age, the assertion that the fruits of slavery are divine? What divinity, pray, in that condition of affairs where men and women are compelled to labor illy fed, more illy clothed, and unpaid, to the end that one, no better before God, should live in ease and without labor? What divinity in whipping women for protesting when their virtue is assailed? What divinity in tearing from the mother's arms the sucking child, and selling them to different and distant owners? Where is there one fruit of this tree that any man will dare to call divine?

Mr. Speaker, I have no respect for clergymen who so far forget the sacredness of their high calling as to give utterance to such a dogma.

. . .

Now, sir, what is this institution of slavery that has sought to assume the reins of Government in this land of freedom? What is slavery, sir? It is "the sum total of all villainies." It is the destroyer of every virtue, public as well as private, because it encourages promiscuous and unbridled licentiousness, and renders null the marriage relation. It is the enemy of all religion, insomuch as it has caused to be enacted in every slave State laws making it a felony to teach men and women whose skins are black to read even the Bible, and places restrictions about their assembling themselves together to worship God. It destroys all thrift, energy, and good citizenship among the ruling classes, teaching them to depend upon the labor of others for support when God has ordained to man that by the sweat of his brow he should eat his bread. Slavery is paganism refined, brutality vitiated, dishonesty corrupted; and, sir, we are asked to retain this curse, to protect it after it has corrupted our sons, dishonored our daughters, subverted our institutions, and shed rivers of the best blood of our countrymen.

Sir, the time has passed for concessions to the slave power. Slavery has risked all to gain all, and now it must abide by the cast of its own die; and to us there is but one issue, dissolution and a recognition of the confederacy, or the utter and immediate abolition of slavery. There is now no middle ground.

. . .

Members upon this floor who fear that their constituency will not sustain them in voting for this measure should remember that they have a constituency coming after those whom they now represent, a constituency who will hold them to a more strict account of their stewardship than will the partial friends of to-day, and the execrations of that constituency will be heaped upon the man who now hesitates to aid in wiping out this stain and curse that has disgraced us so long. We want no timid men now. Our brothers and sons have poured out their blood upon fields made memorable by their bravery, and shall fear that some of us will not be returned to seats in this House lead us to hesitate in doing justice to our country in this the crisis of her destiny?

. . .

Sir, I can never bring myself calmly to contemplate the possibility of a reunion with the South which shall tolerate the further existence of slavery, much less one that shall restore it to its former assumed privileges. No, sir, we must either abolish slavery, or consent to see the Union of our fathers destroyed, its hitherto proud name become a hissing and a reproach, and its people no longer free.

. . .

Mr. COFFROTH. Mr. Speaker, when I entered this Hall at the opening of the session, I had determined not to participate in any general debate. It was my in-

tention to be a listener and not a talker. This resolve would have been faithfully kept had it not been for the extraordinary legislation that has been pressed upon the House—legislation, in my opinion, which is not only subversive of the interests of the people, but which erects an insurmountable barrier to the restoration of the Union. The resolution before us proposes to amend the Constitution, made by the patriots of the Revolution, so as to abolish slavery throughout the United States. It proposes to set free four million ignorant and debased negroes to swarm the country with pestilential effect. It is to carry out the design of the bad and wicked men whose fanatical teaching has produced the terrible bloodshed and destruction of life through which we are now passing.

Sir, we should pause before proceeding any further in this unconstitutional and censurable legislation. The mere abolition of slavery is not my cause of complaint. I care not whether slavery is retained or abolished by the people of the States in which it exists—the only rightful authority. The question to me is, has Congress a right to take from the people of the South their property; or, in other words, having no pecuniary interest therein, are we justified in freeing the slave property of others? Can we abolish slavery in the loyal State of Kentucky against her will? If this resolution should pass, and be ratified by three fourths of the States—States already free—and Kentucky refuses to ratify it, upon what principle of right or law would we be justified in taking this slave property of the people of Kentucky? Would it be less than stealing?

This legislation has a tendency not only to create discord among the people of the North, but has a power so immense the mind cannot calculate its weight in giving strength and force to the rebellion. It fulfills all the prophecies of the South concerning the North. They have been bolstering up and maintaining their Army by asserting that the people of the North intended to confiscate their homes and rob them of their slave property. The one has already been put in force by an unconstitutional enactment, and you now propose to do the other by the same process of illegality. These acts constitute the propelling power which has filled southern armies. The fanatical legislation of this Congress has been of more value to the South, in giving them large armies, than all the conscriptions they have passed or bounties they have paid. Men who were attached to the old Union, but placed under circumstances to be of little service to it, and who have been waiting with beating hearts to be again sheltered under the old flag, are now forced, not only into sympathy with the rebellion, but into hearty co-operation. They have no other resort. To remain idle now is to lose all they have. In their opinion, to sustain the rebellion retains to them their property.

If slavery is to be abolished, allow it to be done according to the principles of common justice. Allow the people in each State the inalienable right, through their legally constituted authorities, to control their own domestic institutions in their own way. This was the doctrine held by statesmen whose passions and prejudices did not blind them to a correct idea of right.

...

Mr. ROSS.

...

Mr. Speaker, the life of the nation is in imminent peril; the agonizing throes and death-rattle admonish us of approaching dissolution; but while there is life there is still hope. As the ship-wrecked mariner seizes with dying hope to the last floating spar, so let the people rally around and cling to the Constitution as the sheet-anchor of our hope. Their duties and responsibilities are fearfully great and cannot be ignored. They owe it to their sires, the wives of their bosoms, the innocent prattlers that dandle upon their knees, to unborn generations, and to their own manhood, to preserve free government and transmit constitutional liberty as the most invaluable legacy. The Federal Constitution with all its limitations and just balances must be maintained; the reserved rights of the States and the people protected; the union of the States must be preserved and perpetuated; the personal rights and liberties of the citizen must be upheld and defended; free speech, a free press, and a free ballot, cannot be surrendered by a free people; these inalienable, clearly-defined, expressly guaranteed constitutional rights, invaluable to freemen, formidable only to tyrants, must be protected, maintained, and defended from any and every assault, from whatever source or under whatever pretext made, by every lawful means, peaceably if they can, but forcibly if they must.

...

This side of the House is powerless to give relief to our bleeding, dying country. Its destinies for weal or woe, with all its glorious memories of the past and precious hopes of the future, hang tremblingly in the balance in your hands. Will you save us our liberties, and preserve us our blood-bought inheritance? This boon we demand at your hands; we demand it in behalf of thirty million free-born Anglo-Saxons, whose throbbing hearts implore and wistful eyes are anxiously turned toward this capital. This you can still do. Will you do it? We do not expect you to relieve us from the burdens of the $3,000,000,000 of national debt created by this war; this is not in your power. You cannot expiate for nor breathe new life into the two hundred and fifty thousand brave men wantonly sacrificed, I fear, by your war policy. You cannot restore them to their stricken and disconsolate friends, nor fill the aching void that palls these bereft and desolate hearthstones. You cannot close the gaping wounds nor ease the piercing agony of a hundred thousand brave men languishing on the field and in the hospitals. You cannot bind up the broken heart nor stay the gushing tear of the inconsolable widow. You cannot meliorate the piteous condition, soothe the plaintive wail, nor hush the unbid sob of the moaning, heart-stricken orphan.

These things you cannot do. But you can yet give us back a free, independent judiciary, the writ of *habeas corpus*, a free ballot, free speech, and a free press. Give us back the old Constitution of our fathers, with all its sacred memories and cherished associations; though torn and rent and perverted as it has been, we love it still; strong arms will uphold and warm hearts cluster and nestle around it. Give us back as it was the old Union of our fathers, without a star erased or stricken from the bright galaxy of its effulgent constellation, with the old flag of our fathers with all its ample folds still floating proudly in triumph above us.

Mr. HOLMAN. Mr. Speaker, I am reluctant to occupy the attention of the House at this late moment, but I desire to present briefly my views on the pending question. This bill, having passed the Senate by a constitutional majority, only awaits the approval of this House. It proposes to introduce into the political contest of the present year a measure of great public concern. It presents the question, shall the Constitution of the United States be amended? In view, sir, of the present condition of the country, no graver question has ever challenged the attention of the American Congress. The merits of the amendment are of comparatively little moment. The more serious question is, shall the Constitution be amended at all? Are the times propitious for the consideration of such a question? Is it a time to weaken in the public mind, already in a state of revolution, the authority of established principles by innovation and change? I cannot but express my earnest regret that this new element of discord has been forced upon the country. Of all of the measures of this disastrous Administration, each in its turn producing new calamities, this attempt to tamper with the Constitution threatens the most permanent injury. I speak, sir, without reference to the merits of the amendment. If it were ever so wise in the abstract the present condition of the country would demand its postponement.

. . .

But as to the merits of the proposed amendment. You propose to invade the domestic policy of States so solemnly guaranteed by the Constitution and, without which the Union would never have been formed, and abolish African slavery, a subject foreign to the Constitution, for it has no relation to domestic concerns of a State. Its purpose was to unite the States, while each as to domestic government was still a sovereign, as parts of one nation each subordinate to the Federal head. You now propose to abolish African slavery throughout the United States. I am, sir, a firm advocate of the rights of the States. I would maintain these rights with the same fidelity that I would the rights of Federal Government. I am neither the advocate nor the apologist of slavery. In a war for the Constitution and the Union I would not have slavery weigh a feather against the progress of our arms. If it went down in such a struggle, even the loyal men of the South could not complain. But, sir, the Federal Constitution is in no sense responsible for slavery. It is not for slavery nor against slavery, as it is not for or against any other domestic institution of the States. It has not the remotest connection with such questions, and even the clause for the return of fugitives from justice and labor is but a measure of comity to preserve the friendly relations of the States. The change you propose is a fundamental change of your Government never contemplated by is founders.

But, sir, what are you to gain by the amendment? In Maryland, Missouri, and Virginia, at least to the extent of the recognized powers of these States, slavery is already abolished. The President's proclamation, solemnly indorsed by yourselves and the validity of which you assert, has declared slavery abolished in every State in rebellion except Tennessee. Tennessee, then, a State full of loyal citizens, and the loyal State of Kentucky, with sixty thousand Union soldiers in the field, are the only States to be affected, according to your own theory. The slaves of the disloyal in those States have already been impressed into your employment, so that upon your own theory this provision will only affect loyal citizens who, through every misfortune, have adhered to the cause of their country. Sir, will this act of violence, this usurpation of a majority under the spur of party organization, increase the loyalty of those whose rights you impair? Is your condition such, after the terrible effects of your policy on this subject, to justify you in still further impairing your cause in the southern States? Are you so strong and irresistible, laying aside all questions of justice and good faith, that you can afford to provoke new and permanent causes of hostility on the part of men now loyal to the Union? So far as this measure affects the interests of your citizens in the slaveholding States it can only provoke indignation and bitterness. If Kentucky wishes to abolish African slavery it is well. I should rejoice to know that she regarded such to be her true policy. It is her own domestic institution; in good faith and justice it is a measure beyond your power. If consummated, it is but an act of violence. If in the reckless arrogance of political power you assume to annul rights guaranteed by your fathers and enjoyed for ages—the rights of domestic government—and provoke to a just indignation a loyal people, the result of the folly should fall upon your own heads;

. . .

But, sir, the amendment goes further. It confers on Congress the power to invade any State to enforce the freedom of the African in war or peace. What is the meaning of all that? Is freedom the simple exemption from personal servitude? No, sir; in the language of America it means the right to participate in government, the freedom for which our fathers resisted the British empire. Mere exemption from servitude is a miserable idea of freedom. A pariah in the State, a subject, but not a citizen, holding any right at the will of the governing power. What is this but slavery? It exists in my own noble State. Then, sir, this amendment has some significance. Your policy, directed in its main purpose to the enfranchisement of a people who have looked with indifference on your struggle, who have given their strength to your enemies, and then the constitutional power to force them into freedom, to citizenship. If such be your purpose, why deceive a noble and confiding people?

. . .

JUNE 15, 1864

The House then resumed the consideration of joint resolution of the Senate (No. 16) submitting to the Legislatures of the several States a proposition to amend the Constitution of the United States.

Mr. FARNSWORTH.

...

Another objection to this proposition, made by my colleague, [Mr. ROSS,] and also by the gentleman from New York, [Mr. FERNANDO WOOD,] and by the other gentleman from New York, [Mr. PRUYN,] is that it strikes at property; that it interferes with the vested rights of the people of States in property. What constitutes property? I know it is said by some gentlemen on the other side that what the statute makes property is property. I deny it. What vested right has any man or State in property in man?

...

Mr. Speaker, at the time of the organization of this Government there were but about fifty thousand slaves within the limits of the United States. When our fathers rose out of the clouds of the Revolution and formed this Constitution, which I trust we are about to amend, no one of them dreamed that slavery in this land would continue until this time.

This fact may be gathered from the writings of the men who wrote and from the speeches of the men who spoke in that day. Why, sir, immediately after the Revolution, Congress issued an address to the people in which occur these memorable words:

"Let it be remembered, finally, that it has ever been the boast and pride of America that the rights for which she contended are the RIGHTS OF HUMAN NATURE."

This language was deliberately adopted and addressed to the people of the United States. This was after the Declaration of Independence, wherein they had declared as self-evident facts that all men were created equal, and endowed with the inalienable rights of life, liberty, and the pursuit of happiness. And when they followed this by the adoption of the Constitution the greatest care was taken that no words should be incorporated into that instrument which would imply that "man could hold property in man." I use the very language of James Madison, a member of the Convention which framed the Constitution. He objected to incorporating the word "slave" or "slavery" into the Constitution, for the reason, as he said, that he would have nothing put into it which would recognize the right of a man to hold property in man. And you may search through the Constitution from the beginning to the conclusion of it, and no stranger to the fact that slavery has existed in the United States would believe for a moment that slavery could exist under it.

Let that Constitution go before a court which is a stranger to the fact that slavery has existed here, and let it be construed as courts are required to construe written instruments, by itself, without looking to the facts of contemporaneous history, and no judge thus construing the Constitution would say that slavery could exist under it.

Our fathers were thus careful in framing the Constitution so that when slavery should be entirely abolished, and when their posterity should come to look in there, they could find nothing to mar its beautiful symmetry. That was the object, that when future generations came to look at that sacred instrument they should not find anything in it to indicate or imply that slavery ever existed in this land. Why, sir, they believed that slavery was going to die out speedily. Already steps had been taken in several of the States toward the abolition of slavery, and several of the States abolished it soon afterwards. There were, as I said before, but fifty thousand slaves in the Union. The raising of slaves for market was unprofitable. The old fathers who made the Constitution, the men who fought the battles of the Revolution, fought for the rights of *human nature*, and they believed that slavery was at war with the rights of *human nature*. Of course such men, who had just gone through the fires of a seven years' war for those principles, and who framed the Constitution upon such a base, believed that slavery would die, and that speedily. Mr. Jefferson, in his Notes on Virginia, says:

"In the very first session held under the republican Government the assembly [of Virginia] passed a law for the perpetual prohibition of the importation of slaves. This will in some measure stop the increase of this great *political and moral evil*, while the minds of our citizens may be ripening for a COMPLETE EMANCIPATION OF HUMAN NATURE."

...

I refer to these things for the purpose of showing the doctrine which prevailed in that day, "in the early and better days of the Republic." But, sir, alas! it happened we took our departure from these landmarks. Men became greedy and avaricious. The invention of the cotton-gin, the cultivation of cotton made it profitable to raise men and women for the southern market. The price of slaves was enhanced; from being worth $250 they went up to $1,200 and $1,300. Then the greed for power took possession of the slaveholders, and the avarice of these men overleaped itself and they became clamorous for the extension of slavery. The bounds were too narrow for them. They became ambitious of a nation that should be founded upon the "corner-stone of slavery."

Then it was, Mr. Speaker, that the slave power got the control of the Government, of the executive, legislative, and judicial departments. Then it was that they got possession of the high place of society. They took possession of the churches. They took possession of the lands. Then it became criminal for a man to open his lips in denunciation of the evil and sin of slaveholding. Then followed those scenes of riot and bloodshed in the North, the dragging of Garrison through the streets of Boston with a rope around his neck to be hanged; the issuing of a message by the Governor of Massachusetts, Edward Everett, declaring that the men agitating the slavery question were indictable at common law; the indictment in southern States of men in the North for anti-slavery publications in the city of New York. Then came requisitions upon the Governors of the North to surrender the bodies of these men to be taken South to be tried; the offering rewards for the heads of northern men; the murder of Lovejoy at Alton; the thrusting of that old patriot, Joshua R. Giddings, out of Congress; the attempt to expel John Quincy Adams; the throttling of the right of petition; suppressing the freedom of the press; the suppression of the freedom of the mails; all these things followed the taking possession of the Government and lands by the slave power, until we were the slaves of slaves, being chained to the car of this slave Juggernaut. Both the great political parties of the country wore its yoke and were prostrate before its power. But, thank God, there were men in the land who stood shoulder to shoulder and declared that they would not be slaves, that they would still make their voice and action felt.

...

I thank God that the Republic has at last recognized the manhood of the negro. Gentlemen may call us "miscegenists," and they may talk of equal rights. I do not know of any man in the party to which I belong who is fearful of coming into competition with the negro. I know there are many men of the party of my colleague who spoke last evening, [Mr. ROSS,] who do feel that the negro is their natural competitor and rival, and they do fear, and fear with some reason, too, that the negroes will outstrip them if we give them a fair chance. I have heard gentlemen talk about their fears that negroes might become Representatives upon this floor. Well, I am inclined to think that the country would not suffer by such a change *in some instances*. Oh! they, are afraid of "negro equality" and "miscegenation." You must not unchain the slave and allow him the fruits of his own toil and permit him to fight for the Republic for fear of *negro equality and miscegenation*. Can the head or heart of man conceive of anything more mean and despicable?

...

Mr. Speaker, I am not afraid of *"miscegenation."* If my colleague over the way is afraid of it, if he requires the restraining influences of a penal statute to keep him and his party from running into miscegenation, I will willingly vote it to them. But we do not want it; we do not practice miscegenation; we do not belong to that school; that is a Democratic institution; that goes hand in hand with slavery. Why, sir, some of the very best blood of the Democracy of Virginia may be found in the contraband village at Arlington today; the blood of the Masons, the Hunters, the Garnetts, the Carters, and the Haxalls; their lineal though natural descendants are among the contrabands.

I said I thank God that this nation at last has recognized the manhood of the negro. It did that when it put on him the uniform of a soldier of the Republic, and put him into the field to defend the country. His rights and his manhood were recognized, and nobly does he vindicate himself.

...

Mr. ROSS. I desire to ask the gentleman whether he thinks the white man is equal to the negro.

Mr. FARNSWORTH. Mr. Speaker, that is a silly question which it is useless to answer. I think some white men are better than some other white men. I think some white men are better than some negroes, and that some negroes are better than some white men, especially those of the copperhead persuasion.

Mr. Speaker, upon every battle-field where the black troops have had any chance to show their gallantry and bravery, they have vindicated the high estimation which has been placed upon them and the confidence imposed in them in elevating them to the position of soldiers. I know it used to be said when the idea of arming the blacks was first broached that white soldiers would not fight by the side of black men. Go to the Army to-day and witness the charge of a black brigade, and then come back and tell me whether the white soldier is not willing that the black man shall fight by his side. Witness the shouts and plaudits and cheers which ring out from the throats of the white soldiers as the black men march steadily up to the serried lines of the rebels, and then come back and tell me if the white man is not willing that the black man shall help him to fight the battles of his country.

. . .

Mr. THAYER. Mr. Speaker, it is not my intention to detain the House at this late period of the present discussion with any protracted expression of my views in regard to the measure now before the House. I rise merely to make one or two suggestions in reply to the line of argument which was pursued yesterday upon this question by gentlemen on the opposite side of the House, and to give my reasons why I believe it to be the duty of every man who has the welfare of his country at heart to vote for the joint resolution now before the House. With that class of thinkers who agree with the member from the fifth congressional district of New York [Mr. FERNANDO WOOD] that slavery is the best possible condition for the negro race, or for any race, I do not intend at the present time to enter into argument. Sir, I would consider it derogatory to the representatives of a free people to enter into a deliberate argument to refute a proposition so monstrous and so barbarous as that enunciated by the gentleman from New York. Humanity and civilization revolt against a sentiment so inhuman in itself, and so debasing to the mind that holds it, as the sentiment which we listened to yesterday, that slavery is the best possible condition of the negro race.

Mr. FERNANDO WOOD. I reaffirm it.

Mr. THAYER. I am willing that he shall reaffirm it. Let that record which he here reaffirms to-day go down to posterity in the history of this country, and let those who act with the gentleman from New York assume the responsibility of that sentiment before the country if they dare.

Sir, the gentleman from New York has a right to his sentiments. He has a right to express them. While I find no fault with his expression of them I can only say that for myself I would not hold or avow a sentiment so barbarous, so cruel, and so inhuman in its character as that for all the wealth and honor that are embraced within the four quarters of the world.

. . .

Sir, this is a matter for the people of the United States. We are not amending the Constitution. We do not propose to amend the Constitution. We propose by this joint resolution to afford the people the opportunity of amending their Constitution if they see proper to exercise that power. When the Legislatures of the several States shall act upon the amendment proposed to them by Congress in accordance with the provisions of the Constitution, they will act as the representatives of the people. The votes which they will give for or against any such amendment are the votes of the representatives of the people. Their voices are the voice of the people. If then, sir, the people have an unlimited right of amendment of their Constitution except in so far as they have chosen in the fundamental law to restrain themselves from the exercise of that right, the only question which remains is whether it is proper at the present time to afford the people the opportunity of so amending the Constitution of the United States, if they shall see proper so to do, as to prohibit slavery forever within the territory of the United States.

. . .

Mr. MALLORY.

Sir, when you compare the pigmies who undertake to trifle with the Constitution and the legislation of this land upon this floor to-day with the great men who framed and expounded that Constitution in the earlier and better days of the Republic, it is like comparing Hyperion to a satyr.

No, Mr. Speaker, this is not the time for changing the Constitution of the United States. When men return to their reason, or when reason returns to men, when passion has subsided, when this civil war has ended, and peace spreads her wings over this land, will be time, if there be a necessity for it, to consider this great system and attach to it such amendments as the calm wisdom of that day shall adjudge proper. Does the gentleman from Pennsylvania [Mr. THAYER] feel that he is competent to examine and analyze and alter and amend this great instrument? Has he the conscious power?

Mr. THAYER. In this particular I think that we are all fitted.

Mr. MALLORY. In this particular! Why, sir, in *this particular* you are less fitted to act than in any other particular that can be imagined. You cannot reason about the institution of slavery. You cannot judge about it. You run a "muck" whenever the question is introduced into this Hall. No word of reason, no word of judgment, and no word of sense scarcely falls from your lips when the subject is mooted. Yet in this particular you feel your-selves competent to do better than the great men who framed this Government have done!

The provisions of that great instrument in relation to the subject of slavery were the result of compromise, without which this Government never could have been framed. To that Constitution, with that and other com-promises embraced in it, every State in the Union gave not only an implied but a direct and express assent. We are informed by the best writers on the science of government, at least they have consented to the truth of the aphorism, that "all government derives its just powers from the consent of the governed." Even now in this time of war, in this time of passion and excite-ment, to change the Constitution on a vital point, when eleven States are not here to consult and act with us, and when their assent to this altered Constitution is not expressed and cannot be implied by any sort of forced construction, and say that they shall be subjected to it, is in utter violation of this great and just principle. They do not compose a foreign country and a foreign Gov-ernment, as so many on that side of the House have as-serted. They are States of the Union yet, who have for-mally given their assent to the Constitution which you now propose to amend. If you change it in their absence what right have you to declare that they shall abide by it? If all Governments derive their just powers from the consent of the governed, when you have amended this Constitution what right have you to say to those States in revolt, who are not here to-day to engage in your de-liberations, that they are bound by that Constitution to which they have given neither assent or dissent?

...

You say that slavery is incompatible with peace, and fealty and allegiance to the Constitution dangerous to the Union. Sir, did the existence of slavery in Kentucky, Missouri, and Maryland lead those States into rebellion against the General Government? Did it induce them to follow the lead of South Carolina into rebellion? Yet slav-ery existed there. It exists in those States now. How then can you, in the face of this proof, say that slavery can-not exist in States and those States be loyal? Why persist in the declaration that it is impossible to preserve the Union and let slavery exist? In making this declaration you give the lie to your President and his prime minister. Seward, in his letters to Dayton and Adams, says, "Slav-ery will remain whether the rebellion succeeds or fails." Ah, Mr. Speaker, slavery is not properly a ground or a cause for a dissolution of this Union, for civil war, or for

disturbance. But I am very much afraid that the party upon the other side of the House, aided by the present Administration of the General Government, may make slavery the cause for the disruption of this Union. You have changed your whole policy in regard to the war. You have converted it from a war to preserve the Union, as you acknowledge and boldly declare, into a war for the abolition of slavery, because you say that is the only way to preserve the Union.

...

The President strikes down the writ of *habeas corpus*, the safeguard of personal liberty, and says that is in-dispensable and is right. And you support him in it. He abolishes trial by jury, and says that it is indispensable to do it in order to get at traitors; and you say so, too, and that he has a right to do it, because he deemed it indis-pensable. He has arrested without "warrant" and con-demned without "due process of law" hundreds of our citizens, and confined them in prisons and forts, who have been ascertained to be guiltless of any crime, and you approve it. He has subjected hundreds of free citi-zens not in military service to be tried by military tri-bunals, and punished by martial law, and you indorse it. He struck down slavery, as he himself acknowledges, in defiance of the rights of the States to control their own domestic institutions. He says it was in violation of the Constitution, and that he knew it when he did it. You say it was indispensable as a war measure, and, constitutional or unconstitutional, it is right. Very well; why, then, do you want to tamper with the Constitution? Why do you want to change the Constitution? Why do you want to exercise this power through the Constitu-tion to accomplish that which you say the President has already done with your consent, in spite of and in viola-tion of the Constitution? The Constitution is no impedi-ment to the President or to you.

...

Now, let me ask you a practical question. What do you intend to do with the slaves you propose to set free? What are you going to do with the elephant when you get him? [Laughter.] Has anybody attempted to fur-nish a solution of this question? Yes, sir, a solution has been attempted; I will examine it. They propose to put those of them capable of rendering military service into the Army to fight the battles of the country. They have been placed in the Army to the number of one hundred and thirty or one hundred and fifty thousand. Where, in your armies, have you placed these men? Have you placed them as a shield between the enemy and your white troops? A gentleman in this House in the last Congress declared he was willing a black soldier should stand as a shield between his son and the bullets of the enemy. No, sir; these black men have not been placed in that position; they have been placed behind fortifications and out of the reach of the guns of the enemy. You make them equal to white soldiers in pay, clothing, rations, and position; you make them superior in position to white soldiers by saving them from danger and wounds and death. You degrade the white private soldier to a level with or below the negro; but the officers you make a privileged class. You make the black private soldiers equal to the white, but you will not allow your white officers to be degraded by allowing the negro to become his equal in position as an officer in the Army of the United States.

. . .

What do you propose to do with those you cannot use in the Army—the women and children and worn-out men? Three years ago I asked that question in this House, and the answer by the leading abolitionists then was, "We will colonize them." I stated then that this would not be done, that the country would never consent to add to its debt twelve or fifteen hundred million dollars for such a purpose. I said truly. You have abandoned the idea of colonization. Numbers of the free States by law prohibit their immigration within their limits. You are afraid as yet to resist the exercise of this right in despite of that prohibition, although you dispute it. You cannot send them into those States; but you propose to leave them where they are freed, and protect them in their right to remain there. You do not intend, however, to leave them to the tender mercies of those States. You propose by a most flagrant violation of their rights to hold the control of this large class in these various States in your own hands. The abolitionists of New England, by means of a majority which they hope to secure in Congress and an Administration they expect to retain in office in some way, intend to govern thousands of these creatures in my State and the other border slave States, and exempt them from the operation of the laws of those States. They intend to establish an "*imperium in imperio*" in all those States. Do you expect that the States will submit quietly to this outrage? You are not so infatuated. Do you expect then to force obedience to your will, to coerce obedience to the regulations of the "Freedmen's Bureau" by means of negro soldiers to be garrisoned in these States to overawe the people? Do you intend to "quarter a standing army on

us without our consent?" Our history teaches a lesson on this subject which I commend to your consideration.

. . .

Mr. KELLEY.

. . .

We were asked this morning whether we are wiser than the framers of our Government. I utter no word, I think no thought of disparagement of those great men. They were good men and were wise in their day and generation, but all wisdom did not die with them, and we are expiating in blood and agony and death and bereavement one of their errors—the unwise compromise they made with wrong in providing for the toleration and perpetuation of human slavery. The Convention which framed the Constitution unwisely compromised with wrong, and the bill before the House proposes to submit their work to the people through the States for revisal in this particular. It was not unknown to many of them that evil must result from their action. They knew and said while in the Convention that right and wrong were in eternal conflict, and that the avenging God was ever on the side of right.

. . .

The gentleman from Kentucky also said that we do not use our colored soldiers to fight, but pet and save them at the expense of our white soldiers. Did we save them at Fort Pillow? And let me pause to ask who crucified the men at Fort Pillow, and why was it done? But that your infernal institutions had taught the people of the South to look upon men, women, and children as cattle, soulless beings, things to be scourged as you would scourge an unruly and dangerous animal, that horrible chapter would never have disgraced American history.

. . .

What, asks the gentleman, are you going to do with the freed negroes? I will tell that gentleman a secret confidentially. Above us all there is a God—slave-owners have not generally known the fact—who will take care of His children. I will trust the freed negroes to the care of God, under our beneficent republican institutions.

. . .

Mr. EDGERTON.

. . .

I shall notice in general terms some of the cardinal objections to the joint resolution.

1. It proposes a revolutionary change in the Government. It seeks to draw within the authority of the Federal Constitution and the Federal Congress a question

of local or internal policy belonging exclusively to the slaveholding States.... In its present form the resolution is aimed at slavery; but it might, with equal propriety, be aimed at any other local law or institution of a State. It might as well propose that freedom of religious opinion should be abolished, and one form of religious worship only prevail in all the States; or that marriage should not take place except between certain classes and at certain ages and otherwise define marital rights, or be extended to regulate the relations of parent and child, or the canons of property, or the elective franchise.

...

Mr. Speaker, I have no desire to discuss the right or policy of slavery at this time. It may be a sin; it may be impolitic; it may be unprofitable. Arguments on both sides have been and can be made, and radical differences of opinion exist on the subject, and neither the power of a political majority nor the power of war can determine the abstract right or wrong of the opposing opinions. I am not the apologist nor friend of slavery, but no abstract or theoretical opinions about slavery determine my vote on the question before the House. If so be that slavery is dead, as the result of civil war, as many say, not of the emancipation proclamation, which the author of it has himself aptly termed *brutem fulmen*, I have no regrets for it; no tears to shed over its grave; its own advocates have done their part to slay it; let them reap as they have sown; I have no desire to revive or restore it. If, however, slavery be wounded nigh unto death, but not slain, I for one will not, for the sake of giving it its death-blow, either swear to or admit the right to abolish it by executive edict, or introduce into the Constitution of my country, by way of amendment, a principle and a precedent that may in an evil hour of excited passion like the present put the dagger to the heart of the freedom and independence of my own State, and make me the serf of a despotism. Better, sir, for our country, better for man, that negro slavery exist a thousand years than that American white men lose their constitutional liberty in the extinction of the constitutional sovereignty of the Federal States of this Union. Slavery is the creature of the States alone, not of the Federal Union; they made it, let them unmake it. If the States wherein slavery still lives, a mangled, bleeding, prostrate form, see fit to give it the final blow that shall make it a thing of the past, let them do it in their own time and way. If, however, they see fit to nurse it into a further brief vitality, let them do it; it is their ward, not yours nor mine.

...

Mr. ARNOLD.

...

This constitutional amendment has passed the Senate, long regarded the citadel of the slave power; how strange if it should fail in the popular branch of Congress! The people and the States are eager and impatient to ratify it. Will those who claim to represent the ancient Democracy refuse to give the people an opportunity to vote upon it? Is this your confidence in the loyal masses?

The passage of this resolution will strike the rebellion at the heart. I appeal to border State men and Democrats of the free States; look over your country; see the bloody footsteps of slavery; see the ruin and desolation which it has brought upon our once happy land; and I ask, why stay the hand now ready to strike down to death the cause of all these evils? Why seek to prolong the life, to restore to vigor, the institution of slavery, now needing but this last act to doom it to everlasting death and damnation?

Gentlemen may flatter themselves with a restoration of the slave power in this country. "The Union as it was!" It is a dream, never again to be realized. The America of the past is gone forever. A new nation is to be born from the agony through which the people are now passing. This new nation is to be wholly free. Liberty, *equality before the law* is to be the great corner-stone.

...

Mr. INGERSOLL.

...

For eighty years the bogus aristocracy of slavery have left nothing undone to corrupt and demoralize the people and their Representatives. For eighty years they have attempted to clothe this monster in the radiance of divinity, when in reality it should only be draped in the blackness of its own enormity.

...

The eloquent and scholarly SUMNER may be knocked down in the United States Senate by a southern ruffian and blackguard: northern doughfaces say, "Served him right." A Giddings and an Adams may be censured in the House of Representatives because they have the manhood to raise their voices in behalf of liberty and justice: northern doughfaces cry out again, "Served them right." The incorruptible Parker, Codding, and Garrison may be mobbed, stoned, and imprisoned, for daring to give utterance to the sublime and eternal principles of truth, and liberty, and justice, and these same northern doughfaces rise up and cry out, "Served them right." A northern man imbued with the spirit of liberty may, within the limits of a slave State, have the effrontery to raise his voice against oppression, and say, "Your system of slavery is wrong, and you ought to abolish it:" a coat of tar and feathers or the halter may be administered as a corrective of such heretical expressions, and the northern doughfaces again cry out, "Served him right." A minister of the gospel may find it to be his duty to say to his people, "It is right that you should do unto others as you would they should do unto you;" that you ought to let the bondman go free; and he is immediately denounced as an abolition agitator, and the varnished hypocrites of his church call upon him at once and say they cannot tolerate the expression of such opinions in the pulpit, as they are calculated to irritate the South, and he must stop them or they will withdraw their support. Consequently the poor, good preacher must close his lips to such divine and heaven-born truths or starve, and this, too, in a free State; and again the northern doughfaces say, "Served him right." To crown all this record of infamy, the martyr, Elijah P. Lovejoy, is mobbed and murdered on the free, broad prairies of Illinois, simply for the crime of publishing a paper dedicated to the advocacy of the rights of mankind; and again these northern doughfaces cry out, "Away with him," "Served him right." O liberty! where is thy power? O justice! where is thy strength? But thank God, that day is gone, and gone forever. Let us take courage; the world is better; their sufferings and their trials were not in vain; liberty is stronger; justice is surer; and the idols of oppression, ignorance, and prejudice, which have been worshiped so long, are crumbling to dust. And so the good work goes bravely on. It is as irresistible as the avalanche and as grand as the Alps.

Sir, I am in favor in the fullest sense of personal liberty. I am in favor of the freedom of speech. The freedom of speech that I am in favor of is the freedom which guaranties to the citizen of Illinois, in common with the citizen of Massachusetts, the right to proclaim the eternal principles of liberty, truth, and justice in Mobile, Savannah, or Charleston with the same freedom and security as though he were standing at the foot of Bunker Hill monument; and if this proposed amendment to the Constitution is adopted and ratified, the day is not far distant when this glorious privilege will be accorded to every citizen of the Republic. I am in favor of the adoption of this amendment because it will secure to the oppressed slave his natural and God-given rights. I believe that the black man has certain inalienable rights, which are as sacred in the sight of Heaven as those of any other

race. I believe he has a right to live, and live in a state of freedom. He has a right to breathe the free air and enjoy God's free sunshine. He has a right to till the soil, to earn his bread by the sweat of his brow, and enjoy the rewards of his own labor. He has a right to the endearments and enjoyment of family ties; and no white man has any right to rob him of or infringe upon any of these blessings.

. . .

Mr. PENDLETON. I desire, before proceeding with any remarks upon this joint resolution, to submit an amendment.

The SPEAKER. One amendment is pending offered yesterday by the gentleman from Wisconsin, [Mr. WHEELER.]

Mr. PENDLETON. Is not an amendment to the amendment in order?

The SPEAKER. If it is germane to the amendment of the gentleman from Wisconsin.

Mr. PENDLETON. What I propose is to strike out that portion of the bill which submits the amendment of the Constitution to the Legislatures of the several States, and to insert a provision submitting it to the conventions of the several States, so that the ratification, if at all, shall be by conventions of three fourths of the States.

The SPEAKER. The gentleman can only introduce his amendment to accomplish that purpose by moving a substitute for the entire resolution.

Mr. PENDLETON. I offer my amendment, then, in the shape of a substitute.

Mr. ARNOLD. Will the gentleman yield to me for five minutes?

Mr. PENDLETON. I will.

Mr. ARNOLD. I desire to ask the gentleman from Ohio whether with that amendment he will vote for the resolution?

Mr. PENDLETON. I will not. There is no difficulty in answering that question; but I desire, if gentlemen intend to submit a proposition of this kind to the States for ratification, that they shall submit it to conventions which are elected for the sole purpose of passing on it, and not to Legislatures already elected upon other and different issues.

. . .

The gentleman from Ohio [Mr. GARFIELD] has spoken of "the pestilent doctrine of State rights;" and the gentleman from Massachusetts [Mr. BALDWIN] has said "State sovereignty never was anything more than a dream of theorists." I confront them with Hamilton:

"The State governments, by their original constitutions are invested with complete sovereignty." * * *

"An entire consolidation of the States into one corporate national sovereignty would imply an entire subordination of the parts; and whatever powers might remain in them would be altogether dependent on the general will. But as the plan of the Convention aims only at a partial union or consolidation, the State governments would clearly retain all the rights of sovereignty which they before had and which were not by that act exclusively delegated to the United States." * * * "The rule that all the authorities of which the States are not explicitly divested in favor of the Union remain with them in full vigor, is not only a theoretical consequence of that division (i.e., of sovereign power,) but is clearly admitted by the whole tenor of the instrument which contains the articles of the proposed Constitution." *Federalist*, Nos. 31, 32.

I confront them with Madison:

"In this relation, then, the proposed Government cannot be considered a national one, since its jurisdiction extends to certain enumerated articles only, and leaves to the several States a residuary and inviolable sovereignty over all other objects." *Federalist*, No. 39.

. . .

The Constitution was adopted by the States, not by the people as a nation, nor yet by the people of the States, but by the States themselves:

"Each State in ratifying the Constitution is considered as a sovereign body, independent of all others, and only to be bound by its own voluntary act." —*Madison Papers*, No. 39.

The States ratified the Constitution, and the citizens of each State owed obedience to it by reason of the ratification by that State. Their allegiance to it was through their State, given by its command, transferred by its act.

. . .

The discussions during this period had caused a searching investigation of the nature of the Federal Government. Its character as a national Government had been asserted. The powers and rights of the States had been questioned. The ratifying conventions demanded that all uncertainty on this point should be dispelled. The First Congress proposed and within six months nine States adopted the amendment to the Constitution, that

"All powers not delegated to the United States by the Constitution, nor prohibited by it to the States, are reserved to the States respectively, or to the people."

The pure character, the spotless patriotism, the unfaltering firmness of Washington sufficed to delay the struggle between confederation and consolidation in the early administration of the new Government. It came in the days of John Adams. The alien and sedition laws were the occasion. The States of Virginia and Kentucky declared their fixed opinion and purpose. Other States responded; the struggle was severe, but its termination gave possession of the administration for twenty-four years to Jefferson and Madison and Monroe, and that party which adhered to the declaration of principles contained in the Resolutions of 1798 and 1799. They declare that the powers of the Federal Government result "from the compact to which the States are parties;" that they are "limited by the plain sense and intention of the instrument constituting that compact;" that they "are no further valid than they are authorized by the grants enumerated in that compact;" and that "in case of a deliberate, palpable, and dangerous exercise of other powers not granted by the said compact, the States who are parties thereto have the right and are in duty bound to interpose for arresting the progress of the evil, and for maintaining within their respective limits the authorities, rights, and liberties appertaining to them."

Mr. Speaker, I have entered into this historical examination not for the purpose of insisting upon the use of mere names, or of discussing any questions which are just now rather speculative than practical. They all find their solution in the logical deductions from these premises. I desired rather to assert the true theory and nature of the Government in order to solve this pending question. I have desired to maintain that the States are sovereign; that their powers are inherent; that they comprise the undelegated mass; that the Federal Government is their agent, derives all its powers from them, exercises its powers in their name; that its duties are few and defined, and its powers are few and simple, sometimes exclusive and far-reaching, but always limited to the grants declared in the Constitution. I have done this in order that I might bring vividly to the mind of each gentleman here that this Government was designed to be a confederation of States, not a consolidated empire, and to beg them, amidst the temptations of these evil days, to adhere to the wise design of its original formation.

The experience of seventy-five years has confirmed the wisdom of the fathers. The States administering their own internal affairs, the Federal Government regulating their international and inter-State relations, have each fulfilled their respective duties and exercised in harmony their respective powers. We have had peace and prosperity; we have had liberty and social order; we have had variety of institutions in the parts, and unity and vigor in the whole; we have solved the problem of large confederations; we have reconciled the liberty of the citizen with the expansion of empire; individuals have been free; communities have been self-governing; minorities have been protected. The theory of State sovereignty, the theory of State rights, has done this. I beg gentlemen not to depart from it.

. . .

The question being on the amendment submitted by Mr. WHEELER,

Mr. GANSON called for the yeas and nays.

The yeas and nays were not ordered.

The amendment was disagreed to.

The substitute proposed by Mr. PENDLETON was disagreed to.

The joint resolution was then ordered to a third reading, and was accordingly read the third time.

Mr HOLMAN demanded the yeas and nays upon the passage of the joint resolution.

The yeas and nays were ordered.

The question was taken; and it was decided in the negative—yeas 93, nays 65, not voting 23; as follows:

YEAS—Messrs. Alley, Allison, Ames, Anderson, Arnold, Baily, John D. Baldwin, Baxter, Beaman, Blaine, Blair, Blow, Boutwell, Boyd, Brandegee, Broomall, Ambrose W. Clark, Freeman Clarke, Cobb, Cole, Creswell, Dawes, Deming, Dixon, Donnelly, Driggs, Eckley, Eliot, Farnsworth, Fenton, Frank, Garfield, Gooch, Griswold, Hale, Higby, Hooper, Hotchkiss, Asahel W. Hubbard, John H. Hubbard, Hulburd, Ingersoll, Jenckes, Julian, Kasson, Kelley, Francis W. Kellogg, Orlando Kellogg, Littlejohn, Loan, Longyear, Marvin, McClurg, McIndoe, Samuel F. Miller, Moorhead, Morrill, Daniel Morris, Amos Myers, Leonard Myers, Norton, Odell, Charles O'Neill, Orth, Patterson, Perham, Pike, Price, Alexander H. Rice, John H. Rice, Schenck, Scofield, Shannon, Sloan, Smith, Smithers, Spalding, Starr, Stevens, Thayer, Thomas, Tracy, Upson, Van Valkenburgh,

Elihu B. Washburne, Webster, Whaley, Wheeler, Williams, Wilder, Wilson, Windom, and Woodbridge—93.

NAYS—Messrs. James C. Allen, William J. Allen, Ancona, Ashley, Augustus C. Baldwin, Bliss, Brooks, James S. Brown, Chanler, Coffroth, Cox, Cravens, Dawson, Denison, Eden, Edgerton, Eldridge, English, Finck, Ganson, Grider, Harding, Harrington, Herrick, Holman, Hutchins, Philip Johnson, William Johnson, Kalbfleisch, Kernan, King, Law, Lazear, Le Blond, Long, Mallory, Marcy, McAllister, McDowell, McKinney, William H. Miller, James R. Morris, Morrison, Noble, John O'Neill, Pendleton, Pruyn, Radford, Samuel J. Randall, Robinson, Rogers, James S. Rollins, Ross, Scott, John B. Steele, William G. Steele, Stiles, Strouse, Stuart, Sweat, Wadsworth, Ward, Chilton A. White, Joseph W. White, and Fernando Wood—65.

NOT VOTING—Messrs. William G. Brown, Clay, Henry Winter Davis, Thomas T. Davis, Dumont, Grinnell, Hall, Benjamin G. Harris, Charles M. Harris, Knapp, McBride, Middleton, Nelson, Perry, Pomeroy, William H. Randall, Edward H. Rollins, Stebbins, Voorhees, William B. Washburn, Winfield, Benjamin Wood, and Yeaman—23.

So the joint resolution was not passed, two thirds not having voted in favor thereof.

During the call of the roll,

Mr. WEBSTER stated that his colleague, Mr. DAVIS, of Maryland, was detained from the House by illness, and was paired with Mr. KNAPP, also detained by illness. Mr. DAVIS would have voted in the affirmative and Mr. KNAPP in the negative.

Mr. STEELE, of New York, stated that his colleague, Mr. DAVIS, had paired with Mr. WINFIELD.

Mr. COX stated that Mr. VOORHEES had paired with Mr. ROLLINS, of New Hampshire.

Mr. McBRIDE stated that he had paired with Mr. HALL, otherwise he would have voted in the affirmative.

Mr. ASHLEY changed his vote from the affirmative to the negative, for the purpose of submitting at the proper time the motion to reconsider.

Mr. HARRIS, of Illinois. I, when very busy, was requested by Mr. GRINNELL, of Iowa, to pair with him on this question. Without reflection or thinking that it required a vote of two thirds to carry the resolution, I agreed to it, which I now regret, and but for which I should vote in the negative.

The vote was announced as above recorded.

22

"Rejection of the Anti-Slavery Constitutional Amendment,"

New York Times

June 17, 1864, p. 4

The Anti-Administration portion of the House, arraying itself against the proposition to submit this amendment to the States, has deprived it of the requisite two-thirds, and an end is thus made of it for the present Congress. The vote stood *ninety-four* Yeas to *sixty-five* Nays, only four Democrats—BAILEY, GRISWOLD, ODELL and WHEELER—voting in its favor. We deeply regret this. It imposes a needless delay upon the consummation of a great measure, without which the struggle between the South and the North can reach no end. Reconstruction is impossible so long as Slavery exists in the land. The institution, in instigating the rebellion, has committed an inexpiable crime, and the people are fixed in their determination that it shall die the death. Its Northern friends are doing it but a poor service in seeking to prolong its agony. They are doing the country a worse service yet. The public mind, so long harrassed by questions touching Slavery, needs repose. It is high time that a definite and final policy were settled upon—that the only solid foundation for a reconstruction should be recognized and accepted.

But the opponents of the Administration choose to have it otherwise. They are not willing to submit the matter to the decision of the States, in accordance with the method prescribed by the Constitution. Some of them say that the matter cannot expediently be touched now, as it would irreconcilably incense the rebel Slaveholding States. Others say that it never can be touched—that Slavery is a domestic State institution, inviolable under the reserved State rights, and alike beyond the reach of the Federal Constitution whether amended or not. Whatever the argument or the pretext, it is plain that the party means to adhere to the old line of action, and to sustain the institution all the same, whether loyal or rebellious.

The Union Party will of course cheerfully enough accept the issue thus forced upon them. They set forth their approval of the amendment in the Baltimore resolutions in the most distinct terms.

. . .

The Union party, then, has two momentous objects before it: the reelection of President LINCOLN, so as to insure that the war shall be prosecuted until the last rebel soldier lays down his arms, and the election of two-thirds of the members of the next Congress, so as to give the States authority to entertain the amendment abolishing all Slavery in the land forever.

23

"The Great Victory: Lincoln Triumphantly Re-elected!,"

Washington Reporter (PA)

November 9, 1864, p. 3

We barely have room to announce to our readers the soul cheering intelligence that Abraham Lincoln has been re-elected to the Presidency for the next four years. The cause of Freedom and the right has been nobly sustained at the ballot box, and the heart of every loyal man in the land must leap for joy at the result.

Below we give such returns as have come to hand up to the time of going to press:

. . .

LINCOLN'S ELECTION ADMITTED
New York, Nov. 9.—The Tribune claims New England, Pennsylvania, Delaware, New York, Maryland, Ohio, Indiana, Michigan, Illinois, Wisconsin, Minnesota, Iowa and Kansas for Lincoln. Total 190 electoral votes independent of the Pacific States, which it says have probably chosen 11 Lincoln electors. It claims over 10,000 majority in the State, and that members of Congress have enough gained to the Union to secure the requisite two-thirds in the House for the prohibition of slavery by constitutional amendment. It makes the New York delegation stand 22 Union to 9 Democratic.

The *World* concedes Lincoln's election, claiming only New York, Kentucky, New Jersey, and Missouri for McClellan, with Pennsylvania, Delaware, Oregon, California, and Nevada in doubt, but most likely for Lincoln.*

24

Frederick Douglass, "The Final Test of Self-Government"

November 13, 1864†

We have just passed through another Presidential election, the most momentous and solemn that ever occurred in our country or in any other. All elections are important in this country, especially are all Presidential elections so, but this election was one to determine the question of life or death to the nation. Other elections have arisen, and have been settled as to the proper management of the ship of State. The question in this contest was whether we should, with our own hands, scuttle the ship and send her to the bottom.

. . .

I take this election to mean:

. . .

Fourth—It means that the Constitution of the United States shall be so changed that slavery can never again exist in any part of the United States.

So much, I think, has been decided by the election of last Tuesday. That I am not mistaken in this, you have only to refer to the nature of the canvass.

You will bear me witness that on the part of the opponents of the Administration, next to the cry that the war is a failure, there was none so freely and so generally used as the cry against the negroes. Relying upon all that is mean, base, selfish, narrow, proud, bigoted, vulgar to the public mind, they hoped to excite popular opposition by fastening upon the Union party the charge of being an abolition party. The people heard it all, and saw it all, and have accepted it all. They *are* the abolition party. The wily pro-slavery orators and un-

scrupulous pro-slavery editors have charged the Union party with being a negro party, and the people have answered, "we are not ashamed of the negro."

25

Abraham Lincoln, Annual Message to Congress

December 6, 1864‡

At the last session of Congress a proposed amendment of the Constitution abolishing slavery throughout the United States, passed the Senate, but failed for lack of the requisite two-thirds vote in the House of Representatives. Although the present is the same Congress, and nearly the same members, and without questioning the wisdom or patriotism of those who stood in opposition, I venture to recommend the reconsideration and passage of the measure at the present session. Of course the abstract question is not changed; but an intervening election shows, almost certainly, that the next Congress will pass the measure if this does not. Hence there is only a question of *time* as to when the proposed amendment will go to the States for their action. And as it is to so go, at all events, may we not agree that the sooner the better? It is not claimed that the election has imposed a duty on members to change their views or their votes, any further than, as an additional element to be considered, their judgment may be affected by it. It is the voice of the people now, for the first time, heard upon the question. In a great national crisis, like ours, unanimity of action among those seeking a common end is very desirable—almost indispensable. And yet no approach to such unanimity is attainable, unless some deference shall be paid to the will of the majority, simply because it is the will of the majority. In this case the common end is the maintenance of the Union; and, among the means to secure that end, such will, through the election, is most clearly declared in favor of such constitutional amendment.

---

* [In the end, Lincoln lost in only three states: Kentucky, Delaware, and New Jersey. —Ed.]

† "The Final Test of Self-Government: An Address Delivered in Rochester, New York, on 13 November 1864," in *The Frederick Douglass Papers, Series One*, ed. John W. Blassingame et al. (New Haven, CT: Yale University Press, 1991), 4:33–37.

‡ Lincoln, *Speeches and Writings*, 2:657–58.

26

US House of Representatives, Debates on Abolition Amendment

January 6–12, 1865[*]

JANUARY 6, 1865

Mr. ASHLEY. I desire to call up this morning, pursuant to notice previously given, the motion to reconsider the vote by which the joint resolution proposing an amendment to the Constitution in reference to slavery was rejected.

. . .

Mr. ASHLEY. Mr. Speaker, *"If slavery is not wrong, nothing is wrong."* Thus simply and truthfully has spoken our worthy Chief Magistrate.[†]

The proposition before us is, whether this universally acknowledged wrong shall be continued or abolished. Shall it receive the sanction of the American Congress by the rejection of this proposition, or shall it be condemned as an intolerable wrong by its adoption?

If slavery had never been known in the United States, and the proposition should be made in Congress to-day to authorize the people of the several States to enslave any portion of our own people or the people of any other country, it would be universally denounced as an infamous and criminal proposition, and its author would be execrated, and justly, by all right-thinking men, and held to be an enemy of the human race.

I do not believe such a proposition could secure a single vote in this House; and yet we all know that a number of gentlemen who could not be induced to enslave a single free man will nevertheless vote to keep millions of men in slavery, who are by nature and the laws of God as much entitled to their freedom as we are. I will not attempt to explain this strange inconsistency or make an argument to show its fallacy. I content myself with simply stating the fact.

It would seem as if no man favorable to peace, concord, and a restored Union could hesitate for a moment as to how he should vote on this proposition.

As for myself, I do not believe any constitution can legalize the enslavement of men. I do not believe any Government, democratic or despotic, can rightfully make a single slave, and that which a Government cannot rightfully do it cannot rightfully or legally authorize or even permit its subject to do. I do not believe that there can be legally such a thing as property in man. A majority in a republic cannot rightfully enslave the minority, nor can the accumulated decrees of courts or the musty precedents of Governments make oppression just. I do not, however, wish to go into a discussion of the question of slavery as an abstract question. It is a system so at war with human nature, so revolting and brutal, and is withal so at variance with the precepts of Christianity and every idea of justice, so absolutely indefensible in itself, that I will not uncover its hideous blackness and thus harrow up my own and the feelings of others by a description of its disgusting horrors, or an attempted recital of its terrible barbarism and indescribable villainy.

It is enough for me to know that slavery has forced this terrible civil war upon us; a war which we could not have avoided, if we would, without an unconditional surrender to its degrading demands. It has thus attempted to strike a death-blow at the national life. It has shrouded the land in mourning and filled it with widows and orphans. It has publicly proclaimed itself the enemy of the Union and our unity as a free people. Its barbarities have no parallel in the world's history. The enormities committed by it upon our Union prisoners of war were never equaled in atrocity since the creation of man.

For more than thirty years past there is no crime known among men which it has not committed under the sanction of law. It has bound men and women in chains, and even the children of the slave-master, and sold them in the public shambles like beasts. Under the plea of Christianizing them it has enslaved, beaten, maimed, and robbed millions of men for whose salvation the Man of sorrows died. It so constituted its courts that the complaints and appeals of these people could not be heard by reason of the decision "that black men had no rights which white men were bound to respect." It has for many years defied the Government and trampled upon the national Constitution, by kidnapping, imprisoning, mobbing, and murdering white citizens of the United States guilty of no offense except protesting against its terrible crimes. It has silenced every

---

[*] *Cong. Globe*, 38th Cong., 2nd Sess., 138–42, 149–55, 168–79, 189–96, 221–24, 234–39 (Jan. 6–12, 1865).

[†] [Here, Ashley quotes Abraham Lincoln's letter to Albert G. Hodges. See this volume, 1D, doc. 16. —Ed.]

free pulpit within its control, and debauched thousands which ought to have been independent. It has denied the masses of poor white children within its power the privilege of free schools, and made free speech and a free press impossible within its domain; while ignorance, poverty, and vice are almost universal wherever it dominates. Such is slavery, our mortal enemy, and these are but a tithe of its crimes. No nation could adopt a code of laws which would sanction such enormities, and live. No man deserves the name of statesman who would consent that such a monster should live in the Republic for a single hour.

Mr. Speaker, if slavery is wrong and criminal, as the great body of enlightened and Christian men admit, it is certainly our duty to abolish it, if we have the power. Have we the power? The fifth article of the Constitution of the United States reads as follows:

...*

The question which first presents itself in examining this provision of the Constitution is, what constitutes two thirds of both Houses? or, what, in the eye of the Constitution, is two thirds of the entire number of members to which all the States, including the States in rebellion, would be entitled, if they were all now represented, or is it two thirds of the members who have been elected and qualified?

This question would have entered largely into the discussion of the subject now under consideration had not your predecessor, Mr. Speaker, decided, and this House sustained him in declaring, that a *majority* of the members *elected* and *recognized* by the House made a constitutional quorum.

...

If I read the Constitution aright and understand the force of language, the section which I have just quoted is today free from all limitations and conditions save two, one of which provides that the suffrage of the several States in the Senate shall be equal, and that no State shall lose this equality by any amendment of the Constitution without its consent; the other relates to taxation. These are the only conditions and limitations.

In my judgment, Congress may propose, and three fourths of the States may adopt, any amendment, republican in its character and consistent with the continued existence of the nation, save in the two particulars just named.

If they cannot, then is the clause of the Constitution

just quoted a dead letter; the States sovereign, the Government a confederation, and the United States not a nation.

The extent to which this question of State rights and State sovereignty has aided this terrible rebellion and manacled and weakened the arm of the national Government can hardly be estimated. Certainly doctrines so at war with the fundamental principles of the Constitution could not be accepted and acted upon by any considerable number of our citizens without eventually culminating in rebellion and civil war.

...

To thinking men nothing seems more absurd than the political heresy called States rights in the sense which makes each State sovereign and the national Government the mere agent and creature of the States. Why, sir, the unity of the people of the United States antedates the Revolution. The original thirteen colonies were never in fact *disunited.* The man who had the right of citizenship in Virginia had the same right in New York. As one people they declared their independence, and as one people, after a seven years' war, conquered it. But the unity and citizenship of the people existed before the Revolution, and before the national Constitution. In fact this unity gave birth to the Constitution. Without this unity and preexisting nationality—if I may so express myself—the Constitution would never have been formed. The men who carried us through the revolutionary struggle never intended, when establishing this Government, to destroy that unity or lose their national citizenship. Least of all did they intend that we should become aliens to each other, and citizens of petty, independent, sovereign States. In order to make fruitful the blessings which they had promised themselves from independence, and to secure the unity and national citizenship for which they periled life, fortune, and honor, they made the national Constitution. They had tried a confederation. It did not secure them such a Union as they had fought for, and they determined to "form a more perfect Union." For this purpose they met in national convention, and formed a national Constitution. They then submitted it to the electors of the States for their adoption or rejection. They did not submit it to the States as States, nor to the governments of the several States, but to the citizens of the United States residing in all the States. This was the only way in which they could have submitted it and been consistent with the declaration made in the preamble, which says, that "we, the people of the United States, in order

* [Ashley quotes the entire text of Article V. —Ed.]

to form a more perfect Union, &c., do ordain and establish this Constitution." The whole people were represented in this convention. Through their representatives they pledged each other that whenever the people of nine States should ratify and approve the Constitution submitted to them, it should be the Constitution of the nation.

In the light of these facts, to claim that our Government is a confederation and the States sovereign seems an absurdity too transparent for serious argument. Not only is the letter of the Constitution against such a doctrine, but history also. Since the adoption of the national Constitution *twenty-two* States have been admitted into the Union and clothed with part of the national sovereignty. The territory out of which twenty-one of these States were formed was the common territory of the nation. It had been acquired by cession, conquest, or purchase. The sovereignty of the national Government over it was undisputed. The people who settled upon it were citizens of the United States. These twenty-one States were organized by the concurrent action of the citizens of the United States and the national Government. Without the consent of Congress they would have remained Territories. What an absurdity, to claim that the citizens of the New England States, or of all the States, or of any section of the Union may settle upon the territory of the United States, form State governments, with barely inhabitants enough to secure one Representative in this House under the apportionment, secure admission as a State, and then assume to be sovereign and master of the national Government, with power to secede and unite with another and hostile Government at pleasure, and to treat all citizens of the United States as alien enemies who do not think it their duty to unite with them. This is the doctrine which deluded many men into this rebellion, and which seems to delude some men here with the idea that the national Constitution cannot be amended so as to abolish slavery, even if all the States in the Union demanded it save Delaware.

. . .

Had the framers of the Constitution desired the protection and continuance of slavery they could easily have provided against an amendment of the character of the one now before us by guarding this interest as they did the right of the States to an equal representation in the Senate. They did not do it, because, as the history of the convention abundantly proves, the great majority of the framers of the Constitution desired the speedy abolition of slavery, and I contend that, so far

from the Constitution prohibiting such an amendment, it has expressly provided for it.

. . .

It is past comprehension how any man with the Constitution before him, and the history of the convention which formed that Constitution within his reach, together with the repeated decisions of the Supreme Court against the assumption of the State rights pretensions, can be found at this late day defending the State sovereignty dogmas, and claiming that the national constitution cannot be so amended as to prohibit slavery, even though all the States of the Union save one give it their approval.

. . .

In this connection we ought not to overlook that provision of the Constitution which secures nationality of citizenship. The Constitution guaranties that the citizens of each State shall enjoy all the rights and privileges of citizens of the several States. It is a universal franchise which cannot be confined to States, but belongs to the citizens of the Republic. We are fighting to maintain this national franchise and prevent its passing under the control of a foreign Power, where this great privilege would be denied us or so changed as to destroy its value.

. . .

I hold that whenever three fourths of the States *now* represented in Congress give their consent to this proposition it will legally become a part of the national Constitution, unless other States, now without civil governments known to the Constitution, establish governments such as Congress shall recognize, and such States, together with any new States which may be admitted, shall be represented in Congress *before* three fourths of the States *now* represented adopt the proposed amendment; in which event the States thus reorganized or admitted must be added to the number of States *now* represented in Congress, and the ratification of three fourths of the States thus recognized, and none others, is all that will be required to adopt this amendment.

. . .

In this House we have authoritatively declared that a majority of the members elected and qualified are a quorum competent to transact business. The Senate at this session have adopted this rule also. Two thirds of this quorum, then, if this decision be correct, as I believe it is, may constitutionally pass the proposition before us. If we may constitutionally pass this amendment by a vote of two thirds of a quorum of this House and Senate as now constituted, three fourths of the States now represented in Congress may constitutionally adopt it, *provided* they do so before any new States are admitted, or before a rebel State government is organized and recognized by the joint action of Congress and the Executive. I believe this is the true theory of the Constitution. Certainly it is the only theory consistent with national existence.... Certainly no thoughtful man who has carefully examined this subject will defend the absurdity of the constitutional existence of political communities which we call States after their constitutional State governments have been destroyed by the action of their own citizens.

Speeches were made at the last session, and indeed at every session of Congress since the rebellion, to prove that the several acts of secession of the rebel States being illegal, were therefore void, and that the State constitutions in those States not only remained, but that the government of such States could at any time be put in motion without the consent of Congress, whenever ten or more loyal men could be found to assume the Governorship and a few of the subordinate offices therein. Loyal citizens of the rebel States are fast being cured of this fallacy. They have learned by experience that the Government of the United States is supreme, and that local governments in rebel States cannot be put in motion without the consent of Congress. The mass of men did not at first seem to recognize the fact that while acts of secession were illegal and void as affecting the rights of the national Government, its jurisdiction and sovereignty, nevertheless it was such a crime that those committing it forfeited all rights guarantied them by the national Constitution under their State organization.

...

In a constitutional point of view, if there is no loyal State government, such as I have described, but in its stead a government unknown to the Constitution established by the action of its citizens, then, in fact, there is no constitutional State government, and, of course, no State known to the Constitution. The States then in rebellion have no constitutional governments. They have civil organizations, however, hostile to the United States; organizations which are recognized as *de facto* rebel governments. When the rebellion is suppressed there will be no constitutional State governments, in fact, in one of the rebel States, and certainly the rebel *de facto* government cannot remain or be recognized by us after the rebellion is put down. The people residing

within the limits of these so-called States will be under the exclusive jurisdiction of Congress, because in point of fact they cannot be subject to the laws of a State which has no State government known to the national Constitution.

...

Certainly, during the time it remains in rebellion and is unable to maintain a State government it is not a State. If so, then, for *practical* purposes, whether of national administration or for the adoption of this amendment, States in rebellion and without civil governments which Congress can recognize, are not States within the meaning of the Constitution, and cannot act upon this amendment to the Constitution, or do any other act which a loyal State of the Union may lawfully do.

In pursuing this argument we must keep steadily in view the fact that the United States are not a confederation, but a nation; that the national Constitution is the supreme law of the land, and that the Government organized under it is clothed with the sovereignty of the whole people. The first and highest allegiance is due from the citizen to the national Government; he is also subject to the laws *constitutionally* enacted by his own local State government. If there be no local State government in existence the citizen is legally subject only to the laws of Congress. In the absence of a constitutional State government in any portion of the territory of the United States, where a State government formerly existed, Congress has all the authority of a State government within such territory.

...

There is another consideration which ought not to be overlooked when weighing the practicability and expediency of this measure, and that is its financial aspect. Doubtless many gentlemen think this question has less connection with our finances and the credit of the country than any other before us. Not so. In my opinion, and I know I but utter the opinion of many practical business men, the passage of this amendment will give the Government a credit, both at home and abroad, which no victory of our arms, important and invaluable as many of them have been, has yet given us. Its passage will be a guarantee for peace, unity, stability, prosperity, power. It will be a pledge that the labor of the country shall hereafter be unfettered and free, and I need not say that under the inspiration of free labor the productions of the country will be tripled and quadrupled. It will be a pledge to the industrious German, and to all the free laboring men of Europe who are seeking homes among us, that they shall no longer be excluded, as they have been practically, from a country whose climate is softer and fertility greater than any on the continent.

...

Pass this amendment and the brightest page in the history of the Thirty-Eighth Congress, now so soon to close, will be the one on which is recorded the names of the requisite number of members voting in its favor. Refuse to pass it, and the *saddest* page in the history of the Thirty-Eighth Congress will be the one on which is recorded its defeat. Sir, I feel as if no member of this House will ever live to witness an hour more memorable in our history than the one in which each for himself shall make a record on the question now before us. I implore gentlemen to forget party and remember that we are making a record, not only for ourselves individually, but for the nation and the cause of free government throughout the world. While members of the Thirty-Eighth Congress we cannot change the record which each must now make, and those who do not return to the next Congress can never reverse their votes of today, but must forever stand recorded, if voting against this amendment, among those voting to justify the rebellion and perpetuate its cause.

...

Mr. ORTH.

...

The bill now under consideration proposes to submit the following amendment of the Constitution to the several States for adoption or rejection, according to the terms prescribed by that instrument, and if ratified by the votes of three fourths of the States will then become part of our fundamental law.

...*

The effect of such amendment will be to prohibit slavery in these United States, and be a practical application of that self-evident truth, "that all men are created equal; that they are endowed by their Creator with certain unalienable rights; that among these, are life, liberty, and the pursuit of happiness."

This bill originated in the Senate during the last session of Congress, in obedience to what was believed to be the general sentiment of the American people, and passed by the necessary vote of two thirds of the members of that body. It was then sent to this House for concurrence, and after considerable discussion was defeated by a vote of 95 in the affirmative and 66 in

---

the negative, (twenty-one members not voting,) being twelve votes less than necessary to make the two-thirds vote required by the Constitution. The question now before us arises upon a motion to reconsider such vote, action upon which was continued from the last to the present session of Congress.

Probably it was right that the question of reconsideration should thus have been postponed. During the last session of Congress we were just entering upon an exciting political canvass; this very question of slavery, its further continuance or its utter destruction, entered largely into the issues and discussions of that canvass; and in a Government like ours, resting upon the will of the people, and deriving its "just powers from the consent of the governed," it was well to have another and more definite expression of the public will. We passed through that canvass; nearly every one of us on this floor went directly before our own people with our respective records of the last session accompanying us, and the result of that canvass is now a part of our nation's history. No man can question or gainsay the popular verdict; it has been expressed in unmistakable language, and he who is willing to bow to the voice of those whom for the time being he represents in this Hall, cannot doubt the action which the people now expect at his hands.

...

JANUARY 7, 1865

The SPEAKER. The next business in order is the consideration of the business in which the House was engaged at the adjournment yesterday, being the motion to reconsider the vote by which the House on the 15th of last June rejected a joint resolution (S. No. 16) submitting to the Legislatures of the several States a proposition to amend the Constitution of the United States, on which the gentleman from Ohio [Mr. BLISS] is entitled to the floor.

Mr. BLISS.

...

Upon what reasoning and recognition of facts does any member of this Congress claim the possible power, under [Article V], to take the initiatory steps to the change proposed? Are the States whose people, in part, are in rebellion against the General Government out of the Union in theory and in fact? Are they foreign Powers, and their inhabitants foreign people, not subject to the Constitution and laws of the United States? If so, why do we raise and send mighty hosts to enforce, by the sword, the bayonet, and the cannon, obedience

---

* [Orth quotes the text of the proposed amendment. —Ed.]

and subjugation to that Constitution and to those laws? If the people of the so-called seceded States are not citizens in the Union, why are our courts engaged, under an act of Congress, in confiscating their estates for acts of treason against their Government? Treason implies citizenship; it cannot be committed by an alien or an enemy. If those States are not out of the Union in theory of law, and if their people owe the allegiance to the Government of the United States which is claimed of them, then clearly those States are among the number of States three fourths of whom must unite their voices upon any proposition to amend their Constitution.

That they are not so legally in the Union, and so to be regarded as States with a controlling portion of their people in rebellion, is a new and recently assumed proposition, and at war with every executive manifesto, proclamation, and declaration from the first act of secession till now.

. . .

The success of this proposition would dash the cup of hope from the lips of a majority of the people of all the adhering States. It is the desire of a great majority of our people to reconstruct the Union upon its old basis. Upon that basis compromise can be made and the war honorably closed; but upon no other or more restricted plan can it be done. Subjugation of the South, and sway over it, can be accomplished only by standing armies. We cannot dictate in any other way the abandonment of their constitutional and reserved rights. Can we afford the blood, the expense, the general suffering, the lack of all substantial success, which must attend upon such policy?

. . .

Mr. ROGERS. Mr. Speaker, it is the first time in the history of this country, until the present party came into power, when any body of men claimed that in the Constitution of the United States, and by virtue of the laws of the several States before they formed it, each State had no right to legislate and control its own domestic institutions according to its own judgment exclusively. In this question there is not only involved at this time the propriety of interfering with the Constitution of the country, but behind that a grave and serious question, in my judgment, arises, whether there is any power in the confederated Government of this country by any act of legislation and confirmation of the Legislatures of three quarters of the States to interfere with the domain of any State whatever, or its right to control the institution of slavery or any other domestic institution, which

was not delegated to the General Government but reserved to the States exclusively.

I say, sir, that all the parties of the country, not only the Democratic party, but the old Whig party, and the Republican party, until lately, always claimed and held that this institution of slavery was peculiarly under the province of the individual States, and that when the States entered into this confederated Government the powers that they did not delegate to that Government were expressly reserved to the States; that no power not delegated to the General Government could by the force of any amendment to the Constitution be taken away from the States, because they had only confederated themselves together for the purpose laid down in the organic act, and because it would be an act of the creature not given by its creator.

. . .

If it be true that the States where slavery existed never delegated the right to interfere with that institution, what right has the Congress of the United States or the people of other States, through their Legislatures, to interfere with slavery in another State, which institution is peculiarly and solely the creature of the State—a right which was never delegated to the General Government, and to interfere with which has always been held by all parties we had no right? Solely and alone it has been always held that the institution belonged exclusively to the jurisdiction of the States.

. . .

If the position in reference to the amendment of the Constitution taken by gentlemen on the other side of the House be true, then the other relations of the States, the marital rights, the rights of husband and wife, of parent and child, of master and servants; the right of licensing hotels, the right of making private contracts, the rights of courts, the manner in which they shall obtain evidence, the allowance of parties to be witnesses, the jurisdiction and powers of State courts, the rights of suffrage for State officers, constitutions of States and all the rights which now belong to the States, upon the same principle may be interfered with, abolished, and annulled. Those rights, like those connected with the institution of slavery, belong solely and exclusively to the jurisdiction of the States, and were never delegated to the General Government. Does any man here believe that Congress, by a constitutional amendment, can so far alter the organic law of the land as to interfere with marital relations in the States; interfere with the manner in which evidence shall be given; take away the constitutional provision that a man shall enjoy property by descent in certain ways defined by the organic law of a State and blot all States laws out of existence? I ask, do gentlemen here believe that by constitutional amendment the General Government would have a right to do away with all those express and reserved rights of the States, and which were never delegated to that General Government, and never constituted a part of the jurisdiction of the Congress of the United States or of the people, except that the people of each State could act and legislate upon those individual concerns according to their own judgment exclusively, and the dictates of their own consciences?

. . .

But it is proclaimed that because the Declaration of Independence declares that all men are born equal, having certain inalienable rights, among which are life, liberty, and the pursuit of happiness, it never was intended that slavery should exist lawfully. I presume that no right-minded man will pretend that the framers of the Declaration of Independence, when they said that all men were born equal and had certain inalienable rights, intended to include slaves, because slaves at that time never had held any political rights. Slaves had been held here long before the formation of the Constitution; the institution had been transmitted by England and other European nations to the colonies here; slaves were treated here as property liable to be bought and sold, and not as citizens within the meaning of the Declaration of Independence or of the original laws of the country. I will now read from the Dred Scott decision, 19 Howard, page 410:

> "It then proceeds to say, 'We hold these truths to be self evident, that all men are created equal; that they are endowed by their Creator with certain unalienable rights; that among them is life, liberty, and the pursuit of happiness.'
>
> . . .
>
> But it is too clear for dispute, that the enslaved African race were not intended to be included, and formed no part of the people who framed and adopted this Declaration."

. . .

But, says the gentleman from Ohio, slavery is the cause of the war. Sir, slavery is not the cause of the war any more than were seamen the cause of the war of 1812.

. . .

The history of our country will, in pages red with blood, record that this war was caused by the acts of the abolitionists of the North; of those men who interfered with the institutions of the South. Those men are responsible for all this bloodshed which is now wetting American soil, and causing the earth to groan beneath the deadly weight of the commingled bones of our brethren. I charge here to-day that this interference with slavery has alone severed our glorious Union; blighted our national prosperity; wrecked our civil and political liberty; studded our country with the graves of noble soldiers; caused a hundred fields to weep with brothers' blood; and the screams of wives and mothers to emanate from domestic circles at the ghastly appearance of a tyrant's assassin dragging from the death-bed of a wife or the grave of a child the husband and father, to be incarcerated in a dungeon or cell. I implore you, in the name of truth, do not charge upon slavery the cause of this war. By the history of this country I charge that such men as Wendell Phillips, Horace Greeley, Lloyd Garrison, and those in power, have been the promoters of this war, and the blood of this nation rests upon them. Thank God, I am free from it.

. . .

I see before me patriotic men from the State of Kentucky; the State which has stood between the ire of the North and the ire of the South; a State that has been true to the Constitution; whose sons here represent the principles ever held by that great statesman Henry Clay; a State that stands by the landmarks of the organic law of the land as the only palladium of our civil liberty. In the name of God, is it justice, is it magnanimity, is it in accordance with that injunction of Scripture, "Do unto others as ye would have others do unto you," to strip from those men the valuable rights of property which were considered sacred until this civil war raised its hydra head? Is it just and right to take away from those men now, after they have for three years and a half interposed their State for the protection of our firesides and our families, to take away their property without any compensation? By what right do we propose to take away this property without paying for it? The Constitution says that private property shall not be taken for public use without just compensation. Now, if we regard at all the rights guaranteed by the Constitution, by what right do we propose to take away the property of the loyal men of Delaware, Kentucky, and other States, without just compensation?

. . .

Mr. DAVIS, of New York.

. . .

472

But we are told, while asserting this principle of legal or civil equality, that we are violating the fundamental principle of the Constitution under which we live, by the measure now under consideration. I can see no such violation, and even if there were a technical violence done to the letter of the Constitution I should hold it defensible for the purpose of preserving the life and the power of the Republic which our fathers framed for the perpetuation of civil liberty.

…

And I submit to my friends on the other side of the House that the day is come when they should act fearlessly and honestly upon this subject. Is there a gentleman there who does not believe that the American people in their majesty and in their power have decreed the absolute and perpetual annihilation of slavery? Has not the popular verdict, which went forth in November last, proclaimed that that is the unalterable decision of the American people? Is there one who will deny that the next Congress, which according to law will convene here one year from December, 1864, will possess the requisite power to pass the amendment now proposed and submit it to the people? Is there any one who does not know that it will be in the power of the President of the United States, whenever this proposition may be rejected by a vote of this House, to call within sixty days an extra session of that Congress? And although at large expense and at great annoyance to our people, the President can present this one question to their consideration and decision, and then by their act they can announce that this proposition shall be submitted to the vote of the American people.

…

Mr. HIGBY. Mr. Speaker, the debate upon this question has taken a very wide range. Much of the ground that was occupied at the last session of Congress seems to have been swept over again at this session, as if to remind us of facts and arguments which we as Representatives may have forgotten, or which the people themselves may have lost sight of. Many gentlemen have over-looked in their remarks, and probably have forgotten, what has transpired between the last session of Congress and the present; that the policy pursued by the Administration has been indorsed by the vote of the people; that four hundred thousand majority of the votes of the people was given to sustain that policy; that the proclamation issued by the President of the United States on the 1st day of January, 1863, was indorsed as a part of that policy; that the action of Congress in ref-

erence to this question of slavery, since the beginning of the rebellion, was also indorsed; that the action of Congress at the last session in reference to this very subject was indorsed by the people in the reelection of, I believe, every member of the present House upon the Union side who was put in nomination. It will be borne in mind, sir, that at the last session the Senate by an overwhelming majority, far more than two thirds of that body, passed the same joint resolution that is now under discussion; that though this resolution when it came to this body failed to receive a constitutional majority, yet there were nearly or quite thirty more voting in favor of its passage than those who voted against it. These facts were well understood by the people of the nation when they voted at the last election.

…

JANUARY 9, 1865
Mr. YEAMAN. Mr. Speaker, our Government being based upon the idea of the right and the capacity of the people to govern themselves, and the whole scheme being but a mean to ascertain and execute the will of the people, it follows as a necessary sequence that this will, when legally expressed, must be submitted to.

…

After much hesitation and earnest reflection, I have concluded to vote for the resolution submitting to the people of the States the proposed amendment to the Constitution, which, if successful, will forever settle the vexed and distressing question of slavery. In doing this I beg to assure gentlemen that I have come to this conclusion, viewing the subject from a national, and even from a Kentucky stand-point, and have derived little or no assistance from those views common to the members of what is termed the radical party of the North. Being among those who were defeated at the last presidential election I would not now render "a reason under compulsion, if reasons were as plenty as blackberries." And as they are nearly as plenty, and as they are found in great numbers on my own side of the river, I will offer a few. Without any extended argument the vote could be justified on any one of these grounds:

First, the passage of this joint resolution does not determine the matter, but only refers it to the people, the source of all power.

Second, that a man with an earnest respect for the people, and a profound regard for our system of government, might very consistently vote for its submission, and then in his State vote against its ratification.

Third, seeing the people have determined to do it, it becomes the part of wisdom to let it be done as quickly as convenient and with no unnecessary opposition. Let the agony be over and the rubbish cleared away.

. . .

It has been urged that as slavery was in existence when the Constitution was framed, and was by that instrument recognized and guarantied, it thus became a vested interest, and that it is incompetent by subsequent amendment to divest that interest, especially in States refusing to adopt the amendment; and that it is incompetent for the General Government in any form to regulate domestic and State institutions. To my mind this is a singular misapplication of legal reasoning. The argument is based on the extremest point of State rights, State sovereignty, compact, league, &c. It is well known I do not belong to that school. It is applying to the constitutional, fundamental legislation of the people, acting in their sovereign capacity, the same rules and limitations which do apply to statutory enactments and to the legislative powers of Congress as delegated and limited by the people. This is in the nature of an original compact of government, springing from the source of all power, the people. It is competent for them to construct a Government as they please. Surely, in the original instrument or contract, they could have declared all slavery abolished. The contracting power is inherent in them, and they have pointed out the mode by which the instrument may be amended. It is equally competent to do by amendment what might have been done by original compact. If it was competent to declare that three fifths of the slaves should be represented in this House, it was equally competent to declare that none of them should be or that they all should be. It is not a question of construction or of legislative power. The argument I am combating would limit the power of the people in framing a Government. It would deny to the people of a State the power to alter a fundamental law once made and interest acquired under it. I have not a particle of doubt as to the competency and binding effect of the amendment when ratified by the requisite number of States. The Constitution is but a law, the law of original institution by the people, as distinguished from an enactment of Congress. They made it, and they can change it. If they can change the tenure of office or enlarge or restrict the elective franchise, they may prescribe what shall be property and what shall not. Is it not better to satisfy this demand for this one amendment than by the aggravation of a refusal provoke the calling of a convention that may overhaul and remodel and possibly disfigure our entire constitutional fabric?

. . .

Mr. ODELL.

. . .

Mr. Speaker, the effect of this action by this body is only in its operation to submit to the people, to your constituents and to mine, sir, the proposition of amendment of the Constitution. It remains for them to decide it by their suffrage. We shall then all have with them an opportunity of expressing our opinions upon the question at the *ballot-box*. I know of no good reason why I, as a Democrat, believing in the right of the people to rule, should arrogate to myself, in my position as a Representative, the exclusive right of a voice upon this subject. They have, under our Constitution, an equal right with myself; and I will not deprive them by my action of the privilege of exercising it.

Mr. Speaker, I am fully aware of the fact that my position and intended action upon this all-important question will not be in accord with my friends upon this side of the Chamber. I yield to none of them in my attachment to the party with which I have ever acted. I cherish as fondly as any the memories of the great and good men that have been its standard-bearers, and many of whom have passed away; and I have as much confidence in its future, as a power for good in the government of this great nation, as any man in the country. Yet I believe this thing of slavery has lifted its hydra head above the Government of my country. It has been for years a dead weight upon our party. And the time, in my humble judgment, has now come when as a party we ought to unloose ourselves from this dead body. We ought no longer to consent to be dragged down by its influence. We ought to accept the facts of history as they are transpiring around us, and march on with the world in its progress of human events.

The times now favor, and the way is open for the great Democratic party to turn its back upon the dark past and its eyes upon the bright future.

. . .

Mr. WARD.

. . .

Without pursuing this point, I would say that slavery has always been, and is, regarded as a domestic question. The right to abolish it does, and ought to, rest with the States in which it exists. Since the organization of the Government the law of climate and soil has controlled the subject, and has caused the abolition of slavery in six of the original States, and either abolished or prohibited it in all but nine of the new States since admitted. This Government is one of delegated powers, and those not conferred are reserved to the States respectively or to the people. In regard to slavery the Constitution is silent, and therefore no power exists to amend it in the respect indicated; and in addition, in my judgment, that instrument contemplated that all the States should participate in any amendment thereof. Sir, I do not stand here as the apologist of slavery, but merely to insist that we have no right to incorporate the proposed amendment, and that even if the right exists it is a most injudicious time for the exercise of the power when we should desire to bring back the seceded States to loyalty and obedience. Our action in this respect cannot fail to add fuel to the flame, widen the breach already existing, further embitter the South, and prolong the sanguinary contest. I do not regard this question as having been decided by the late election. The issue there involved was the vigorous prosecution of the war for the restoration of the Union. Entertaining these ideas, I cannot vote for the proposed amendment.

...

Mr. MALLORY. Mr. Speaker, it is not my purpose to detain the House by an extended argument on this question now. At the last session of Congress I had the honor to express my views upon it elaborately, and I do not desire to repeat those views now, because I do the House the justice to suppose that it remembers what I said on that occasion. Mr. Speaker, gentlemen may say what they please about the proposed amendment of the Constitution of the United States, but no man can successfully deny the assertion I now make, that it is a radical change of the Government of the United States.... It is an effort to take from the States of this Union, by constitutional amendment, the great power of regulating their domestic and social affairs in their own way, and I deny the power to do that by Congress, even through an amendment of the Constitution adopted in accordance with the mode pointed out for amending the instrument.

...

The President of the United States pays us a very high compliment indeed in his last annual message. He calls upon this Congress, before its expiring hour, to reconsider its action upon this question, and to do now what we refused to do at the last session. What reason does he propose to us for that change? What arguments does he produce in favor of it now that he and others did not adduce at the time this action was before urged upon us? None at all. He simply says: "Gentlemen, it will be done by the next Congress, and as the result is inevitable, as three fourths of the next House of Representatives will be in favor of it, why postpone the result? why defer it longer? why not accept your fate and bow to it submissively?" He asks us to abandon our principles, to give up our convictions, and yet in almost the same sentence he says, "If you want a man as President who will do otherwise than I have done on the slavery question you must find him and put him here, for I shall not change my opinions." Are we not as honestly convinced that we are right, and were right then, as the President of the United States is convinced that he is right? Have we not the same right, and is it not equally our duty to act on our convictions, as it is his right and his duty to act on his convictions? I know of no obligation resting upon a member of this House to change his views at the bidding of the President of the United States, or "any other in authority," not resting on the President himself to change his mind at the dictation of Congress; yet he says he cannot change, but the gentlemen of the House of Representatives can, and he hopes they will. Well, I fear some of them will. The wish or order of the President is very potent. He can punish and reward.

...

JANUARY 10, 1865
Mr. KASSON.

...

We are told here the change is radical; that we have no power or authority to make it; in other words, that we are proposing to introduce into the Constitution an element and doctrine so much outside of the scope of the Constitution, as originally established, as to deserve the appellation now of a "radical" and unjustifiable change. And one of the gentleman upon the other side of the House, I think the gentleman from Kentucky, [Mr. MALLORY,] demanded at the close of his argument yesterday, "If you do this thing what obligation will exist upon the States or the people to adhere to a government thus radically changed?" To that I wish now to call the attention of the House.

And first, I ask permission to read what occurred in the Convention that framed the Constitution, and the reasons given for that action, showing that the position taken by gentlemen upon that side of the House yesterday was in direct contravention of the spirit of the fathers who made the Constitution itself. For example, quoting from the third volume of the Madison Papers, when the very question of the action of the Convention upon this subject was referred to and was under consideration, Mr. Madison declared that he "thought it wrong to admit in the Constitution that there could be property in man;" and Mr. Randolph moved that the word "servitude" be stricken out and the word "service" inserted; and then follows the reason, as given in the Madison Papers, for the change:

> "The former [*servitude*] being thought to express the condition of slaves, and the latter [*service*] the obligation of free persons."

It was so done.

Not only that, but this subject was wrought into the very texture of the Constitution itself; for that Convention prohibited the importation of slaves into this country after the year named in the Constitution; that is to say, it authorizes the prohibition of that importation after the year 1808, and that prohibition was made effectual by subsequent law.

I refer to this to show that we are only treating upon one of the same class of questions which were treated by the men who made the Constitution itself; and therefore it is now within the legitimate scope of any constitutional amendment affecting this subject.

. . .

And now I call the attention of gentlemen upon that side and upon all sides of this House to another fact: that there are but two limitations in the Constitution of the United States upon the power to amend it. In every other respect that Constitution may be amended as fully as the constitution of any State in this Union may be amended. I refer to the fifth article, which gives the power to amend, and prescribes the mode in which the amendments shall be accomplished. It says, after prescribing that mode:

> "Provided that no amendment which may be made prior to the year 1808 shall in any manner affect the first and fourth clauses in the ninth section of the first article" —

That relates to the importation of foreign persons, meaning negroes.

> "and that no State, without its consent, shall be deprived of its equal suffrage in the Senate."

Upon these two points, or rather the one now remaining point, you are not permitted by the Constitution to amend it. Upon every other point within the range of conventional action, as recognized by civilized countries, you have full power to amend the Constitution.

. . .

Mr. MALLORY. I desire to ask the gentleman a question in relation to another matter. Will the gentleman tell me whether he believes that, by an amendment to the Constitution we could so change our Government as to convert it into a monarchy, or an aristocracy, or a despotism?

Mr. KASSON. If the gentleman will ask me a practical question relating to this subject, I will answer him.

Mr. MALLORY. This is a practical question. This amendment proposes radically to change the Government.

Mr. KASSON. I do not propose to discuss here the courses of the planets or the phases of the moon. I keep to the question as closely as I can, and I seek to rescue it from that abyss of party politics into which my friend from Kentucky sought, yesterday, to prostrate it.

. . .

Mr. MALLORY. I wish to ask the gentlemen one more question: Will he hereafter, when this question shall have been submitted to the various States for ratification, admit that the States now in rebellion shall be counted in ascertaining the proportionate number of States ratifying the amendment?

Mr. KASSON. I am not aware, sir, that there is any proposition upon that subject before the House.

Mr. MALLORY. The question must come up in the future, and I ask the gentleman in relation to that future.

Mr. KASSON. "Sufficient unto the day is the evil thereof."

. . .

Mr. KING.

. . .

This House and the Senate, as at present organized, constitute Congress, and we have a right to propose amendments to the Constitution. I do not suppose that the framers of the Constitution ever contemplated that eleven States, or any other number of States, should, upon any proposition which did not suit them, absent themselves. But it is a plain proposition that Congress, whenever two thirds of both Houses shall deem it necessary, may propose amendments to the Constitution. If we have not the power to do so because the Representatives of eleven States are absent, then all our acts are void. They are not what they purport to be on their face, acts passed by the Congress of the United States. That is one argument. Then, sir, the adoption of the Constitution required the consent of all the States, or, in other words, the States that did not agree to it were not to be bound by it, because in article seven of the Constitution it is expressly declared that all the States agreeing to it should be bound by it. But that is not the rule when these amendments are proposed. Three fourths of the Legislatures of the States, on the recommendation of two thirds of Congress, can propose and ratify amendments. Now, if the constitutional provision was that an amendment should receive the assent of all the States, just as that was required in the original adoption of the Constitution, I admit that the question might be raised whether or not we could proceed in this matter without the assent of those States that are now absent; many gentlemen here believing them yet in the Union, although they have thrown themselves outside of its pale for the time being. But that is not the constitutional provision.

...

JANUARY 11, 1865
Mr. PENDLETON.

...

I have been endeavoring to show that the limitations in the letter of the Constitution were not the only limitations upon the power of amendment. And I have done it for the purpose of leading gentlemen of this House to a conclusion I am prepared to take. I have shown that you cannot, under the power of amendment, contravene the letter and spirit of the Constitution; that you cannot subvert republicanism; that you cannot destroy the liberties of the States; that you cannot decide the status of the citizens of the States. I would lead them to the conclusion that there is no power on the part of the Federal Government—on the part of three quarters of the States I intended to say—to adopt the amendment that is now proposed; and that if you do it, if you attempt to impose that amendment upon the dissenting States by force, it will be their right to resist you by force, and to call to their aid all the powers which God and nature have given them to make that force effective.

...

Nobody pretends that the States are clothed with the powers of sovereignty by the Federal Constitution. Nor does that instrument necessarily strip them of the sovereign rights which they had before the Constitution was made. The States have sovereign powers to-day except so far as that Constitution, by their voluntary act of adoption, has taken those powers from them. They do not derive power from the Federal Government. It inheres in them, and I would like to inquire of my colleague from the Toledo district, [Mr. ASHLEY,] if he denies the sovereignty in the States because they have agreed to suspend, or, if you please, to delegate certain powers of sovereignty which would otherwise belong to them, upon what basis can he pretend there is sovereignty in the Federal Government, which has not now and never had any authority except that which is expressly delegated to it by these States themselves.

But, Mr. Speaker, the gentleman from Ohio [Mr. ASHLEY] is led by his anxiety to pass this amendment into the declaration of another doctrine, which although not entirely novel, is somewhat new upon this floor. He holds to the doctrine that ordinances of secession destroy State governments, but do not affect the relations of the States, that is, of the territory and the people to the Federal Government. He holds that an act of secession is an abdication by the people of their rights but not a release from their duties; that it destroys, not the tie which binds them to the Union, but their form of Government, leaving them subject to the jurisdiction of the Federal Government and its absolute sovereignty with all the rights of local government, and he deduces from this the conclusion that the seceding States have no voice on this amendment, but are absolutely bound by it. That doctrine was promulgated by a Senator from Massachusetts [Mr. SUMNER] nearly three years ago in a series of resolutions presented to the Senate, and my colleague will remember that they met with no more indignant response than from the honorable, able, learned, and patriotic gentleman from Massachusetts [Mr. THOMAS] who then had a seat upon the floor of this House.

...

Mr. YEAMAN. What number of States can amend the Constitution?

Mr. PENDLETON. In some particulars, where the power is granted, three fourths of the States can. In other particulars it cannot be done except by the consent of all of the States bound by it.

Mr. YEAMAN. That brings me to the question I wish to ask the gentleman, and that is this: what is there in this particular amendment which makes it an exception to the general rule, and takes it out of the operation of the amending power?

Mr. PENDLETON. That question I have fully answered on another occasion in this House. It does not lie within the scope of my argument now. The doctrine of the gentleman from Ohio, [Mr. ASHLEY,] to which I have just referred, is as large in its operation, though I think hardly as logical or conclusive, as the position taken by the gentleman from Pennsylvania, [Mr. STEVENS.] That gentleman is famous more for a sledge-hammer power of logic than for its scholastic accuracy.

…

JANUARY 12, 1865
Mr. SMITH.

…

While I admit, sir, the just rights of each individual State; while I would accord to each State in this Union all the rights to which it is entitled, and would maintain them to the utmost; while I would adhere to the letter and spirit of the Constitution in respect to all the rights guarantied to each State, I conceive that there is nothing so obnoxious, so abominable, so ruinous to a republican form of government as that doctrine of *ultra* State rights which has been asserted recently upon the floor of Congress. It subverts all the principles of this Government; it is in conflict with the true principles of republicanism, and it brings us into a position into which we would not be brought otherwise—perfect desolation and ruin.

…

Sir, the doctrine enunciated by a great statesman in 1832, that this is a Government of the people, is true to-day. This Congress emanated from the people; the Constitution emanated from the people; the States emanated from the people; and the people, not of Ohio, not of North Carolina, not of Kentucky, not of any other individual State, but the people of the whole country, have a right to control it as their best judgment may dictate; and when the people of this country see proper to alter or amend their fundamental law, whatever that amendment may be, if it is in harmony with that instrument itself and in accordance with the feelings and best interests of the people, he who dares proclaim the sentiment that it is not only the right but the sacred duty of a single individual State of this country to resist such an amendment when adopted, announces himself as a revolutionist now and forever, and deserves the desecration of men who favor law and order in the land. When this Government was formed, it was formed not by the individual independent sovereignties; it was formed by a united people who had assembled in their representative capacity for the purpose of making a stronger and more perfect Union; and they declared that that instrument which was to be the fundamental law of the Government might be amended in the way their interests might dictate.

…

Mr. Speaker, in the adoption of this amendment we do not throw upon the Government and upon the community a people, as has been represented by the gentleman from New York, [Mr. FERNANDO WOOD,] powerless, illiterate, inhuman, and unkind in their disposition. They are a good people; they are an affectionate people; they are an industrious people when properly treated. But there is one idea in this whole system which has kept back the people of the whole South, and that is that one man, and one man alone, has held a whole county, almost—three, four, and five thousand acres of land—and worked it for his individual benefit with five hundred men; whereas if those five hundred men were free there would be five hundred tenements on the same property, and prosperity and advancement would be in proportion to the interest felt and realized in the community. All the northern or free States fully exemplify this truth. The States of the North have outstripped us in States South in manufactures, in machinery, in inventions, in schools, churches, and all that tends to make a nation great and good and powerful. Her people to-day are well fed, well clad, and prosperous; her churches attended, her schools filled, and all happy and progressive; while the South, filled with slaves, is naked, starved, and begging intervention on the grounds of humanity and benevolence. Sir, it is slavery, slavery, which keeps the South down, unprosperous, and undeveloped.

…

Mr. COX. Mr. Speaker, when we left these Halls last year there was a prospect that the administration of the Government would have been changed by the election. The political conventions of the two parties met. The party of the Administration made this amendment a part of their creed. They went before the people claiming the power to abolish slavery by constitutional amendment. Nowhere did the opposite party take ground against the power; everywhere they took ground against its exercise. The convention which met at Chicago adopted their creed. It called for a cessation of hostilities, with but one view, a national convention, in order to reestablish union. Not giving up the principles laid down in the Kentucky and Virginia resolutions of 1798 and 1799, when moved by my colleague [Mr. LONG] in the convention, which, rightly considered, constituted a main foundation of its political creed, it laid them on the table on my own motion, as abstractions unsuited to the demands of the agonized country. Regarding peace as the great practical need of the hour, the convention waived all other questions to reach that. How? By the Constitution, in its fifth article, which provides that a *national convention* shall be called for proposing amendments to the Constitution. This proposition of the convention was at once our weakness and our strength: our weakness when misunderstood by the people, our strength when rightly interpreted. My colleague [Mr. PENDLETON] accepted that platform. In casting my vote for him [for Vice President], I knew that he indorsed it. He indorses it yet. If he had been elected to that office, which he would have graced so well, we might to-day have been appealing to Legislatures, North and South, and not in vain to two thirds of them, to call the convention at the will of the people. The North would have yielded and the South would not have held back. That my colleague and myself well know. In that august assembly the distinguished men from both sections would have been present. What would have been the scope of their action? What the subject of their debates? Need I ask? It would have been the settlement of all grievances, North and South; questions of debt, doubtless; questions of guarantee to State and municipal rights, doubtless; but beyond doubt, this *vexata questio* of slavery, this *teterrima causa belli*, and the agitations and legislation growing therefrom.

Mr. Speaker, I read this morning, with what truth I know not, that a commissioner is now in Richmond with the confidence and assent of the Administration, meeting, perhaps, a commissioner on the part of the confederate authorities; and the rumor is that they have agreed to call a national convention. [Sensation.] I know not whether there is anything in it. My friend from New York who sits behind me [Mr. FERNANDO WOOD] says that there is not, and he is presumed to know more on that subject than I do. [Laughter.]

If, in the providence of God, such a convention were called or were now in session, and this question came up in a full representation of all the States, who would think of disputing its power to modify, change, alter, and abolish, either at once or gradually, by constitutional amendment, the institution of slavery? Not a man. While, therefore, in a state of war, and with nearly half the States in default and absent, I may deny the

wisdom of acting either by the one mode or the other, pointed out for the amendment of the Constitution in this particular—I will not deny a power so essential to peace, safety, and sovereignty. No ingenious refinement or dazzling eloquence shall lead me to deny a power which may yet prove our salvation, when wisely used.

. . .

My colleague [Mr. C. A. WHITE] holds that the States are unlimited and absolute in their sovereignty, and therefore the Federal Government is not sovereign. I ask him to beware where this doctrine leads. But may not the States in their unlimited and sovereign convention, deriving their powers from the original consent of all, give up portions of their sovereignty, modify it, as Mr. Calhoun holds, by the amendatory clause? May they not thus speak the most potential voice of the people of the States in all affairs? It is the people of all the States who consent to amending the Constitution, and by a mode which allows two thirds of both Houses to propose the amendment, which is to be sent to the Legislatures for the ratification of three fourths. First and last and all the time, the States are the constituents of the Federal Government, and as such, and by their State action, they can create and they can destroy. I am of the State-rights school so far as this question is concerned, and of the strictest sect.

Mr. FERNANDO WOOD. I desire to call the attention of the gentleman from Ohio to the language of James Madison in the Federalist:

"That *useful alterations* will be suggested by experience, could not be but foreseen. It was requisite, therefore, that a mode for introducing them should be provided. The mode preferred by the Convention seems to be stamped with every mark of propriety. It guards equally against that extreme facility which would render the Constitution too mutable, and that extreme difficulty which might perpetuate its discovered faults. It moreover equally enables the General and the State governments to originate the amendment of *errors* as they may be pointed out by experience on one side or on the other."

Again, sir, Hamilton says:

"For my own part, I acknowledge a thorough conviction that any amendments which may, upon mature consideration, be thought *useful, will be applicable to the organization of the Government, not to the mass of its powers*; and on this account alone I think there is no weight in the observation just stated."

Mr. COX. The only comment I make upon the quotations of the gentleman from New York is this: Madison in the Convention opposed and voted against the proposition of Roger Sherman to except all internal police of the States from the amendments of the Constitution. The quotation is in harmony with his vote.

. . .

I am sustained in my view, by the history of the Convention which framed the Constitution. Was this question considered by the Convention? It was. In Elliot's Debates, volume five, page 357, it appears that General Pinckney "reminded the Convention that if the committee should fail to insert some security to the southern States *against an emancipation of slaves* and taxes on imports he should be bound by his duty to his State to vote against their report." Again, when the report was made, this clause of amendment came in on the 15th of September. It was discussed by Sherman, Morris, Gerry, Mason and Madison. Mr. Sherman did not like the mode proposed, for fear it would, by three fourths of the States, do things fatal to particular States, as abolishing them altogether, or depriving them of their equality. Colonel Mason thought it dangerous and exceptionable. Mr. Madison defended the present clause. Mr. Sherman moved to annex to the end of the article a further proviso, "that no State shall, without its consent, be affected in its internal police, or deprived of its internal police, or deprived of its equal suffrage in the Senate." Mr. Madison opposed it. It was lost—three to eight. Then Mr. Sherman moved to strike out the fifth article altogether. That too failed. The article was then further amended by the existing clause, that "no State shall be deprived of its equal suffrage in the Senate." (Elliot, volume 5, page 352.) Thus it passed.

The argument from contemporary history is therefore conclusive. The intention of the creator is the best criterion as to the character of the creature. Here we have it, not only implied by the absence of an exception, but by the positive disallowance of it by the Convention. That intention was to limit the amending clause only in two particulars. This one before the House is neither of the two.

27

"Fernando Wood and the Peace Rumors," Reaction to Speech of Samuel Cox (D-OH), *New York Herald*

January 13, 1865, p. 5

During his speech in the House to-day, Mr. Cox, of Ohio, alluded to the various rumors in regard to peace, and to the rumors in circulation of persons going to Richmond in behalf of peace, but remarked that the gentleman behind him, Mr. Fernando Wood, of New York, had just said there was no truth to them.

. . .

THE DEBATE ON THE CONSTITUTIONAL AMENDMENT

The entire session of the House was taken up to-day in discussing the constitutional amendment. The speech of the day was that of Mr. Cox, of Ohio. His speech caused considerable commotion among the democratic members. He opposed the amendment, but held that Congress had power to amend the constitution, taking an opposite stand from that of Mr. Pendleton yesterday. He presented points in a clear and forcible manner, and refuted the fallacy of his democratic colleagues. His speech benefited the measure, and increased the chances of its passage, by completely vindicating the right of Congress to so amend the constitution. The friends of the measure are very much encouraged, and are now more hopeful of its passage than at any time since it has been under consideration. In fact it is now believed that a sufficient number of democrats will change their votes to secure the necessary two-thirds vote. It is doubtful, however, if the final vote is taken for ten days or two weeks yet.

28

Missouri, "Emancipation Ordinance Adopted Almost Unanimously,"

New York Daily Tribune

January 12, 1865, p. 1

BY THE ASSOCIATED PRESS
St. Louis, Wednesday, Jan. 11, 1865
The State Convention just passed the following ordinance of emancipation by a vote of 60 to 4:

"Be it ordained by the people of the State of Missouri in convention assembled that hereafter in this State, there shall be neither Slavery, nor involuntary Servitude, except in punishment of crime whereof the party must have been duly convicted, and all persons held to service, or labor as slaves are hereby declared free."

29

US House of Representatives, Debates on Abolition Amendment

January 13, 1865*

The SPEAKER. The regular order of business is the consideration of the business in which the House was engaged at adjournment yesterday, being the motion to reconsider the vote by which the House on the 15th of last June rejected a joint resolution (S. No. 16) submitting to the Legislatures of the several States a proposition to amend the Constitution of the United States, on which the gentleman from Missouri [Mr. ROLLINS] is entitled to the floor.

Mr. ROLLINS, of Missouri. Mr. Speaker, I desire to submit a few observations to the House upon the important proposition now pending before the final vote is taken upon it. The remarks which I shall make will be rather in the nature of a personal explanation than any elaborate argumentation of this question. At the last session of Congress when the vote was taken upon this

proposition I voted against it. On this occasion when the vote is taken I propose to vote for it. I have changed my views in reference to the expediency of this measure; and while I do not suppose that anything I may say will have any influence whatever in changing the vote of any gentleman upon this floor, I am satisfied with the reasons which have induced me to change my opinion and my action; and it is perhaps due to myself, humble as I am, due to those I represent and who take any interest in the opinions which I may entertain or express here, to present to the House and the country some of the considerations which have induced me to change my action and my vote.

. . .

Sir, if I could save this Constitution and this Union by preserving the institution of slavery in its present status in the various States I would do it most cheerfully. Perhaps I would go further than many of my friends on the other side of the House: if I could save the Constitution of my country and the union of these States even by extending the institution of slavery, I would do it. And why? Not because I am the especial friend of the institution of slavery, but because I regard as the paramount and most important question of the times the preservation of our own liberties, of our own Constitution and free Government. And, sir, I accept also the other view of the proposition: if I could save the Constitution and the Union by the partial destruction of slavery I would partially destroy it; and if I could save the Constitution and Union of my country by the total destruction of slavery—cutting it up by the roots, cutting out the cancer at once—I most unquestionably would do it; for I regard the preservation of these as paramount to and far higher than any question affecting the freedom or slavery of the African race upon this continent. In other words, I adopt precisely the sentiment so felicitously expressed by the President of the United States in a letter which he addressed to Mr. Greeley more than two years ago;[†]

. . .

When I cast the vote which I did before upon this proposition, I had no doubt in regard to the power of Congress to submit this amendment to the States; and the vote I gave at that time was given on the ground of expediency alone. For at that time, as I have stated, I was in favor of pursuing a more conciliatory policy. I be-

---

* *Cong. Globe*, 38th Cong., 2nd Sess., 257–91 (Jan. 13, 1865).

† [See Abraham Lincoln to Horace Greeley, Aug. 22, 1862, this volume, 1D, doc. 12. —Ed.]

lieved at that time that by pursuing such a course and assuring the people of the South that our object was to preserve their rights under the Constitution they might be induced to return. And I was willing that they should return with the institution of slavery preserved as it then existed in different States of this Union. And I believe now that if political events had taken a different direction from what they have taken in all probability those States would be invited to return with all their rights, and along with the rest their right to the institution of slavery.

And I will make this further remark, that it was this general leading consideration that induced me to support the distinguished and patriotic man who was nominated for the Presidency in opposition to the present President. It was because I believed the one would offer and be satisfied with more liberal terms than the other, and that there would therefore be in all probability a better chance of preserving the Constitution and the Government under the administration of that man than by a continuance of the administration of Mr. Lincoln. But I confess here to-day that when I look at all the changes which would have necessarily resulted from a change of Administration, in its men and its policies, I am inclined to doubt whether, *under all the circumstances*, the people have not at last acted more wisely than I did. I do not claim to be infallible.

While I do not take the voice of the majority, however large, as the sole rule of my action, I am always willing to defer to it, and to treat with respect the opinions of a majority of the people of my country.

...

I do not believe, sir, with my friend from Ohio [Mr. cox] that we have a right to make any amendment whatever to this Constitution, that there is no limitation except the express limitation contained in the clause which I have just read.... Now, I do not believe that any amendment can be made to this instrument which has for its object, or whose direct tendency would be, to destroy the very object and purposes for which the Constitution was established. Therefore, sir, any amendment to this Constitution which would destroy "a more perfect union," which would fail to "establish justice," which would fail to "insure domestic tranquillity," which would fail to "provide for the common defense," or to "promote the general welfare, and secure the blessings of liberty to ourselves and our posterity," is not an amendment which may be proposed by Con-

gress, or may be adopted and ratified by the States; and every Representative who votes must be a "law unto himself" whether any amendment proposed is in accordance with the Constitution.

Mr. COX. I desire to ask the gentleman a question. Who is to be the judge whether a proposed amendment comes within the scope of the preamble?

Mr. ROLLINS, of Missouri. I will be the judge myself, so far as I may be called upon to vote for or against it.

Mr. COX. I would prefer, according to my peculiar logic, to allow the States themselves to be the judges. Therefore I infinitely prefer the gentleman's first proposition—that the power of amendment is not limited except by the terms of the clause of the Constitution on that subject.

...

Mr. ROLLINS, of Missouri.

...

I believe, then, sir, that this amendment is in accordance with the express letter of the Constitution. I believe that it is in accordance with the preamble of the Constitution. I believe that it is in accordance with the true spirit, meaning, and intent of that instrument, and the objects and purposes for which it was framed by our forefathers, and that if all the States could be induced to adopt it it would go far to strengthen the Government, by preventing future dissension and cementing the bonds of the Union, on the preservation of which depends our strength, our security, our safety, our happiness, and the continued existence of free institutions on the American continent.

...

I am a believer in the Declaration of Independence wherein it is asserted that "all men are created equal." I believe that when it says *all men* it means every man who was created in the "image of his Maker" and walks on God's footstool, without regard to race, color, or any other accidental circumstances by which he may be surrounded. I know that astute politicians, crafty and ambitious men, in various periods of the Republic have tried to draw a distinction between this man and that man because he happens to have a different colored skin; that the Declaration was applicable alone to white men, and not to the black man, the red man, or any other than the white man. That the word "all" meant a part, not "all!" But, sir, I believe that that general clause in the Declaration of Independence was meant, by the immortal man who penned it, and by the immortal men who signed it, and by a large majority of the great men of that day North and South, to assert the great principle, founded in the rights of man, founded in reason, and in strict accordance to the law of morality and of the Divine will, that "all men are created equal," without distinction of race or of color. And although our ancestors failed to apply the principle, although they were derelict in duty in living up to the great enunciation of principles which they made to the world and mankind, it is no proof to my mind that they did not mean exactly what I say they meant in the expression to which I have referred.

Mr. Speaker, all these considerations are influencing me in the very vote which I shall give upon this amendment; but I desire to say that my experience upon the subject of slavery has been quite singular and diversified. An anti-slavery man in sentiment, and yet, heretofore a large owner of slaves myself—not now, however—not exactly with my consent, but with or without my consent. The convention which recently assembled in my State, I learned from a telegram a morning or two ago, had adopted an amendment to our present State constitution for the immediate emancipation of all the slaves in the State. I am no longer the owner of a slave, and I thank God for it. Although I think this subject might have been disposed of in a better way, causing less inconvenience to our people, and doing in fact the slave no harm, I make no complaint of the convention for that act; and although there is no clause of compensation, I very gracefully yield to the public sentiment, and to the action of this distinguished body of men called in my State to consider its welfare.

...

Mr. STEVENS.

...

From my earliest youth I was taught to read the Declaration of Independence and to revere its sublime principles. As I advanced in life and became somewhat enabled to consult the writings of the great men of antiquity, I found in all their works which have survived the ravages of time and come down to the present generation, one unanimous denunciation of tyranny and of slavery, and eulogy of liberty. Homer, Aeschylus the great Greek tragedian, Cicero, Hesiod, Virgil, Tacitus, and Sallust, in immortal language, all denounced slavery as a thing which took away half the man and degraded human beings, and sang peans in the noblest strains to the goddess of liberty. And my hatred of this infernal institution and my love of liberty were further inflamed as I saw the inspired teachings of Socrates and the divine inspirations of Jesus.

Being fixed in these principles, immovably and immutably, I took my stand among my fellow citizens, and on all occasions, whether in public or in private, in season and, if there could be such a time, out of season, I never hesitated to express those ideas and sentiments, and when I first went into public assemblies, forty years ago, I uttered this language. I have done it amid the pelting and hooting of mobs, but I never quailed before the infernal spirit, and I hope I never shrank from the responsibility of my language.

...

When, fifteen years ago, I was honored with a seat in this body, it was dangerous to talk against this institution, a danger which gentlemen now here will never be able to appreciate. Some of us, however, have experienced it; my friend from Illinois on my right [Mr. WASHBURNE] has. And yet, sir, I did not hesitate, in the midst of bowie-knives and revolvers and howling demons upon the other side of the House, to stand here and denounce this infamous institution in language which possibly now, on looking at it, I might deem intemperate, but which I then deemed necessary to rouse the public attention, and cast odium upon the worst institution upon earth, one which is a disgrace to man and would be an annoyance to the infernal spirits.

Mr. Speaker, while I thus denounced it and uttered my sentiments in favor of universal freedom everywhere, I found in the Constitution of my country what I construed, whatever others may think, as a prohibition from touching slavery where it existed; and through all my course I recognized and bowed to a provision in that Constitution which I always regarded as its only blot; and I challenge the scrutiny of my respective colleague on the Committee of Ways and Means, or any other gentleman, through all the records of utterances in this House, to find one single motion or one single word which claimed on our part to touch slavery in the States where it existed. We admitted that it was there, protected by that instrument. We claimed that in the Territories we had full power over it, and in the District of Columbia, and I, with those who acted with me, could not hesitate as to what our duty required in excluding it from the free soil of the country and confining it to the spots it already polluted. I claimed the right to abolish it in the District of Columbia, as Congress was the only

Legislature on earth that could touch it here. I heard the great man of the West once say that it was a sin and a shame to believe that there was no power on earth that could abolish it over every inch of ground in the world. But, sir, I did not claim early to act upon it here, but I rather proposed to let it rest until a more propitious moment should arrive before we acted upon it.

Such, sir, was my position, and the position of the party with which I acted in this Hall—not disturbing slavery where the Constitution protected it, but abolishing it wherever we had the constitutional power, and prohibiting its further extension. I claimed the right then, as I claim the right now, to denounce it everywhere, even in foreign lands, so that if such language could anywhere affect public sentiment it might do so. I claimed the right then, as I claim it now, to hedge it into the smallest space; but no man with whom I acted ever proposed to violate the Constitution for the purpose of touching slavery.

So much on that point. One other word, not directly on that. The gentleman from Ohio [Mr. PENDLETON] says that I go on the maxim that "what is broken in one thing is broken in all," and that hence, if there was one infraction of the Constitution it was dissolved. That is the coinage of the gentleman's own fertile brain. I never uttered such a sentiment nor held it. The Constitution may be violated in many parts, and remain intact in all others. The gentleman had, perhaps naturally enough, confounded what I had said with what he finds in a sacred book, where it is said that a violation of the least of the commandments is a violation of all. It was not I that said it, but another much greater.

Ingenious gentleman argue, in many honest men will delude their consciences in voting, in favor of still sustaining the institution on the ground that the Constitution does not allow an amendment on this point. They go on the ground that the subject of slavery has not been intrusted to us by the States, and that therefore it is reserved. Now, as the Constitution now stands, that is true. But we are not now inquiring whether we have jurisdiction over slavery. We are inquiring whether the States have granted to us the power of amendment. That is the subject—not the subject of slavery, not the subject of religion, not the subject of anything else—but, have the States yielded to Congress the right to amend? If they have, then the whole question is answered. Not only have they granted that power, but wherever they intended to except anything from the power of amendment, they have said so. My learned friend knows that

when a statute excepts certain things, everything else is meant by it.

...

No lawyer who wishes to understand it can deny that, with the exceptions contained in [Article V's] proviso, the power to amend the Constitution is unlimited. There is no subject on earth relating to Government that you cannot touch. Nowhere in that original instrument did the States grant the right of legislating on the subject of religion; and yet the very first amendment that was made under this power refers to the subject of religion and the freedom of speech, showing the fallacy of the arguments of those who say that you can amend only the subjects granted to Congress.

Perhaps I ought not to occupy so much time, and I will only say one word further. So far as the appeals of the learned gentleman [Mr. PENDLETON] are concerned, in his pathetic winding up, I will be willing to take my chance, when we all molder in the dust. He may have his epitaph written, if it be truly written, "Here rests the ablest and most pertinacious defender of slavery and opponent of liberty;" and I will be satisfied if my epitaph shall be written thus: "Here lies one who never rose to any eminence, and who only courted the low ambition to have it said that he had striven to ameliorate the condition of the poor, the lowly, the downtrodden of every race and language and color." [Applause.]

I shall be content, with such a eulogy on his lofty tomb and such an inscription on my humble grave, to trust our memories to the judgment of after ages.

Mr. BALDWIN, of Massachusetts.

...

Our national Union was established by the Declaration of Independence. Previous to that Declaration there were no States; there were only colonies and dependencies of Great Britain. The Union and the States came into existence together as a nation. By the Federal Constitution this national Union was organized, consolidated, and made more perfect. This doctrine of independent State sovereignty was not tolerated in the constitutional Convention, for the men who controlled that Convention and represented the spirit of the country meant that this Republic should be a great and inseparable nation. After the national Government was fully organized, and during the administration of John Adams, while the country was agitated by a storm of political excitement, the factious vehemence of the Opposition gave birth to this doctrine, that the national Union is merely a compact, league, or agency of independent

State sovereignties. I refer, of course, to the notorious Kentucky and Virginia resolutions of 1798–99. I do not think the men of that time who were concerned in this business understood very well what they did. Certainly they did not mean all that has since been meant by the nullifiers and secessionists.

…

Mr. Madison, as I have said was never afterward quite at ease in regard to these resolutions. When Mr. Calhoun and his followers brought them forth again to justify their attempt to overthrow the Government by means of nullification, Mr. Madison protested, and denied with great earnestness that the Virginia resolutions had any such meaning as the Calhounists found in them. His private correspondence of that date is full of references to this subject.

…

In calling attention to these passages in the private correspondence of Mr. Madison, my aim is to show how completely he, the writer of the Virginia resolutions, repudiated the doctrines of the Calhounists, modern secessionists, and other advocates of independent State sovereignty, who have appealed to those resolutions, the old utterances of partisan monomania, as if they contained a very sacred political gospel. The founders of our Government intended that the great American Republic should be a nation, a sovereign Power, with right to defend its own existence by whatever means may be necessary, and to stand forth among the nations of the earth mighty and glorious in the power of free principles and free men, able to crush with irresistible force all enemies domestic or foreign. Nothing was further from their intention or their favor than this doctrine of State sovereignty which transforms the national Union into a loose league, with no central authority to enforce allegiance and assert national sovereignty, a mere sham, a structure that may fall to pieces at a word from any of the parties to it.

30

Tennessee, "Slavery Declared Forever Abolished," *New York Times*

January 15, 1865, p. 1

CINCINNATI, SATURDAY, JAN. 14.
The *Commercial* has a special dispatch from Nashville, which says:

"The Tennessee State Convention have unanimously passed a resolution declaring slavery forever abolished, and prohibiting it throughout the State.

The convention also passed a resolution prohibiting the Legislature from recognizing property in man, and forbidding it from requiring compensation to be made to the owners of slaves.

A resolution was also adopted abrogating the declaration of State independence, and the military league made with the Confederate States in 1861; also abrogating all the laws and ordinances passed in pursuance hereof.

All the officers appointed by the acting Governor since his accession to office were confirmed.

The propositions of the convention are to be submitted to the people for ratification on the 22d of February, and on the 4th of March an election is to be held for Governor and members of the Legislature.

Nearly three hundred delegates participated in the proceedings of the convention, and the greatest harmony and good feeling prevailed."

31

US House of Representatives, Debates and Passage of Abolition Amendment

January 28–31, 1865[*]

JANUARY 28, 1865
The House then proceeded to the consideration of the motion to reconsider the vote by which the House, at its

[*] *Cong. Globe*, 38th Cong., 2nd Sess., 478-84, 523-31 (Jan. 28-31, 1865).

last session, rejected the joint resolution (S. No. 16) submitting to the Legislatures of the several States a proposition to amend the Constitution of the United States so as to prohibit slavery in the several States;

…

Mr. HIGBY. Mr. Speaker, amid the long debate that has occurred upon this question, not only at the last session but also at this session, three classes of objections principally have been raised upon the other side of the House. One of them is that the Constitution of the United States contains no provision by which we can make an amendment of the character proposed in the resolution now before the House; another, joined with the objection I have just named, is that it is inexpedient at this time to make this amendment; and the third objection is, that slavery is the true condition of the African race.

…

The first of these statements savors of the argument which has been used for scores of years, that the States were complete sovereignties when they organized the General Government. The proposition is very simple, very direct. It is a matter of fact in history that the States were never separate and independent. As dependent colonies, they united together for the purpose of gaining their independence and securing a separation from the mother country. They were dependent colonies at that time, but through their union and their united action independence was obtained. And, having obtained their independence, the very first action on their part was to establish a constitution for a General Government over all.

…

It is said, sir, in this House that the Constitution cannot be amended in the manner proposed in this resolution and in regard to the subject-matter embraced, notwithstanding the Constitution provides the mode and method by which it may be amended. There is but one method provided for amendment. It is the mode attempted by this joint resolution.

…

But, sir, the objection is raised that certain articles of the Constitution prescribe the powers that are granted to the General Government and the rights reserved to the States, and which are not granted to the General Government. I ask the gentlemen who raise this objection where in the Constitution they find it. They do not find it anywhere in the first seven articles of the Constitution adopted by the Convention and ratified by the States. They do not find it there, but they say that we will find it among the amendments. I turn to them and find certain rights are reserved—articles nine and ten are the ones they refer to.

Article nine provides that "the enumeration in the Constitution of certain rights shall not be construed to deny or disparage others retained by the people;" and article ten provides that "the powers not delegated to the United States by the Constitution, nor prohibited by it to the States, are reserved to the States respectively, or to the people." Here is where they find ground for their argument. Mr. Speaker, until these amendments were added to the Constitution there were no rights reserved to the States. I do not think that will be disputed.

Now, sir, where did these amendments originate? If they have not come to the Constitution by virtue of this power of amendment they do not belong to it. If any rights have been reserved to the States they have been reserved by these express words of the Constitution, and these express words are given to the Constitution by a two-third vote of the House and Senate, and by the ratification of the Legislatures of three fourths of the States, and these are simple amendments of the Constitution by the method which the Constitution proposes, and by pursuing precisely the same process we are trying to pursue in order to make this amendment.

Again, sir, is it pretended that anywhere in the Constitution it has been expressed that it requires the assent of every State to an amendment, or that we are required to pursue any other course than the one that is prescribed and expressed? These amendments have been made by this same process; and in those amendments it is not declared that to take away any one of these rights will require the assent of every State of the Union. These amendments have not attempted to amend that portion of the Constitution which instructs us how amendments shall be made, but simply express and declare the reservation of those rights to the States or peoples of the States not enumerated in the powers granted; and, sir, whatever a two-third vote in Congress has proposed, and the ratification of the Legislatures of three fourths of the States have added to the Constitution, a two-third vote of Congress and a ratification of three fourths of the States can take away. And will it be pretended that there is not the same power, and by precisely the same process, to remove from the Constitution articles nine and ten?

…

Mr. PATTERSON. Mr. Speaker, while I yield my convictions to the more experienced judgment of other gentlemen upon this floor with great deference upon most questions, I must be permitted still to entertain the opinion that debate upon the resolution before the House was, in the outset, injudicious. For it necessarily kindled party prejudices and feelings by fanning the embers of old issues destined soon to be buried beneath the ashes of civil war. But while I think it would have been better to have "given our thoughts no tongue," but simply a vote, yet, "being in," we must so conduct the discussion that our acts may not shame our words. If our Government were purely national, a majority of the people could amend the Constitution; if purely federal, it would require a concurrence of each State of the Union; but being a combination of both, a majority of the votes of the Legislatures or conventions of three fourths of the States was fixed upon by the framers of the Government as a compromise method of amendment. Here, I apprehend, is the cause of our divergence upon this overshadowing question. We take the one side or the other according as our reading and habits of thought have led us to give prominence to the federal or national element.

. . .

Sir, there is but one conclusion which can be logically reached on this question. If our Government were purely confederate, the consent of each party to the contract would be necessary to an amendment of the Constitution. If it were purely national, a major vote of the whole people would make it binding upon all, though the unanimous vote of entire sections were against it, for the organic law is their legislation. But being a mixture of both, the people have made it the law that the major votes of three fourths of the States, however given to any amendment, shall be binding upon all. That is the Constitution, and New Hampshire, and Kentucky, and every other State must be bound by an amendment so ratified, though the unanimous votes of the State should be cast against it. And the right of Congress to recommend amendments by prescribed methods is as broad as the right of amendment itself. I do not deny that a State, under these circumstances, may repudiate the plighted faith of the fathers, and elect a revolution rather than submission. But, sir, when any one of the old sister-hood of thirteen, or any daughter since born into the family of States and reared into a vigorous and prosperous maturity by the fostering care of the Government, shall thus prove recreant to the original bond, let her not complain if she is forced to drink the cup of blood and desolation to its very dregs, and let the unhallowed footsteps of no man desecrate these Halls consecrated to liberty who would justify or palliate "the deep damnation of her taking off."

And now, sir, are there any limitations except those specified in the Constitution to the right of amendment? One gentleman asserts that limitations are "to be found in its intent, and its spirit and its foundation idea." Another tells us we are to look for limitations in the preamble to the Constitution. But as the preamble is only a general expression of the intent, and spirit, and underlying idea of the instrument itself, the difference between the honorable gentlemen is one of definitions, and not of ideas. Justice, tranquillity, defense, the general welfare, and liberty are the ends of government; but the English definition of justice and liberty in the twelfth century is not the definition of the nineteenth. Our interpretation of these terms in the future of our history will vary with education and local prejudices. The means which we should feel authorized to employ for the public defense and general welfare might have been deemed extravagant, and possibly revolutionary in the piping days of peace.

To say that this power is limited by the *idea* of the Constitution, however or wherever expressed or implied, is as indefinite as to say that extension is limited by space. Who, sir, is to determine the intent of the organic law, and the proper means by which its objects are to be secured, but the people themselves? And will not their ideas advance and change with the progress of civilization? That there are moral limitations to legislation and to popular sovereignty, I should be the last to deny. This constitutes the higher law, which when violated either by legislative assemblies or by popular majorities, justifies, nay sanctifies the exercise of the right of revolution. But our fathers were not guilty of the extreme folly of attempting the impossible task of enumerating all possible applications of the divine law of limitations.

. . .

The right to change the limitation of State powers must reside in the constitutional majority to whom, by a vote of the people of all the States, the paramount interests of the nation were confided at the first. There probably never was a more delicate and difficult task confided to the judgment of statesmen than the division and proper adjustment of powers between the General and State Governments by the Constitutional Convention. All the past of our colonial and revolutionary life centered there. All the great interests of our moral, social, and political future hung upon it. The proper balancing of these governmental forces could only be hoped for through the teachings of experience. The Convention understood perfectly well the difficult nature of the work devolved upon it. Would it not, therefore, be a reflection either upon the wisdom of the fathers or our own sanity to suppose they did not make provision in the Constitution for such a readjustment of powers or elimination of adverse elements as the future should prove to be necessary to harmonize the action or perpetuate the existence of free institutions?

"I trust the friends of the proposed Constitution," says Hamilton, "will never concur with its enemies in questioning that fundamental principle of republican government which admits the right or the people to alter or abolish the established Constitution whenever they find it inconsistent with their happiness."

I go still further, sir, and claim that the right of gradual and peaceful revolution was purposely framed into the groundwork and superstructure of our institutions so as to obviate forever the necessity for violent and bloody revolutions.

. . .

Nor need we be frightened with the horrors of miscegenation which have been drawn with such artistic skill by my learned friend from Ohio. This deadly Upas is only the product of a night, which has grown without roots and lost its promise of political fruits in the rhetoric of flowers. The African, sir, has been driven North by the force of slavery. Let him be free, and he gravitates to the tropics as naturally and as certainly as the winged people of the air migrate at the approach of winter. The laws of nature will not accommodate themselves to the policy of party politics.

Some gentlemen, too, seem to fear a fair competition between free white and black labor. Now, if the black man belongs to a more intellectual and vigorous race than we, then he ought to triumph in the conflict, and will. But if the white man has a larger brain, stronger and more enduring muscles, and a more active temperament than the black, then he will conquer in this legitimate conflict, and will gradually push the weaker race from the continent, leaving this heritage of liberties to our children after us to the latest generation. Can any man doubt the result?

JANUARY 31, 1865

The SPEAKER stated the question in order to be the consideration of the motion to reconsider the vote by which the House, on the 14th of last June, rejected Senate joint resolution No. 16, submitting to the Legislatures of the several States a proposition to amend the Constitution of the United States; and that the gentleman form Ohio [Mr. ASHLEY] was entitled to the floor.

Mr. ASHLEY. I yield to the gentleman from Pennsylvania [Mr. MCALLISTER] to have read a brief statement.

Mr. McALLISTER sent to the Clerk's desk and had read the following:

When this subject was before the House on a former occasion I voted against the measure. I have been in favor of exhausting all means of conciliation to restore the Union as our fathers made it. I am for the whole Union, and utterly opposed to secession or dissolution in any shape. The result of all the peace missions, and especially that of Mr. Blair, has satisfied me that nothing short of the recognition of their independence will satisfy the southern confederacy. It must therefore be destroyed; and in voting for the present measure I cast my vote against the corner-stone of the southern confederacy, and declare eternal war against the enemies of my country.

[Applause from the Republican side of the House.]

Mr. ASHLEY. I now yield to the gentleman from Pennsylvania, [Mr. COFFROTH,]

Mr. COFFROTH. Mr. Speaker, I speak not to-day for or against slavery. I am content that this much-agitated question shall be adjudicated at the proper time by the people. It is my purpose to state in all candor the reasons which prompt me to give the vote I shall soon record.

. . .

The first inquiry is, has Congress this power? I turn to the Constitution, and find article fifth provides—
. . .*

It is not claimed that Congress itself can engraft this amendment into the Constitution without being ratified by three fourths of the States. Then, sir, under the Constitution, Congress has no power beyond discriminating what shall or ought to be submitted to the people. The members of this House assume no responsibility, they enact no amendment, but as faithful Representatives they submit to the people, the source from whence their power comes, the proposed amendment.

* [Coffroth quotes Article V in full. —Ed.]

"Governments are instituted among men, deriving their just power from the consent of the governed." All political power is invested in the people. At their will constitutions can be remodeled and laws repealed.

...

Again, it is argued that this amendment is unconstitutional; that the Congress of the United States has no legal authority to propose this amendment, nor have the States in ratifying it the constitutional power to destroy or interfere with the right of property. Learned gentlemen of this House differ on this subject. The Constitution itself provides the remedy by which all these differences of opinion can be legally adjudicated. Section two of article three provides:

"The judicial power shall extend to all cases in law and equity arising under this Constitution."

In my opinion, if any person is injured by this amendment, he has a judicial remedy before the highest court of the country.

If the States of the South desire to retain slavery, they can do so by refusing to ratify this amendment. There are thirty-five States. In order to adopt this amendment twenty-seven States must ratify it. Eleven States have seceded from the Union. This is more than is required to defeat the amendment. Certainly no one will pretend to argue that this amendment can be adopted without being submitted to the eleven seceded States. If it was, these States would not be considered a part of the Union. In fact it would be, to all intent and purpose, recognizing them as independent States, and not being under the control of the Federal Constitution.

If this view is taken, then this amendment can do no harm to the people of the States in the, Union. In June last my objection to this amendment was that it was taking away the property of the people of the States that remained true to the Union; that the Constitution was made the means to oppress rather than protect the people. Since that time Missouri and Maryland have abolished slavery by their own action, and the Governor of Kentucky in his message recommends to the Legislature of that State gradual emancipation. The same objection which was then urged against this amendment cannot now be urged.

It is argued that new State governments will be formed in the seceding States under the control of military governors, and this amendment ratified by them. Whether this amendment would be binding upon the people of the seceded States thus ratified will depend entirely upon the result of this war. If after a long struggle, and each of the contending armies or Powers will conclude to adopt the wise and humane policy of a peaceful solution of the difficulties now existing, all of the acts of the State governments formed by military power will be invalid, and the old organization of these States recognized. In this event the ratifications by the new-made State governments will not be worth the paper upon which they are written. If the South achieve her independence, then this amendment will only apply to that which does not exist. If the people of the South are subjugated and their State lines obliterated, and they are ever admitted into this Union under new constitutions, each and every one of the constitutions will have to come free from slavery before the State will be admitted.

The South would not remain in the Union under the Constitution as it now is; they demanded stronger guarantees for the institution of slavery. Can any intelligent person believe that after fighting as they have for nearly four years they will except that which they rejected before the war? If they will not come back under the Constitution, why not abolish slavery; strike from our statute-books every enactment which protects it; make our Constitution and our laws free from the subject of slavery? And then, when this unfortunate, inhuman, barbarous, and bloody war has been prolonged until every heart shall turn sick with its carnage and the reports of its wrongs and outrages, and the people demand a cessation of hostilities until it be ascertained if glorious peace cannot be accomplished by compromise and concession, there will be no obstacles in the Constitution to defeat the accomplishing of a much desired result. We will be free to give new guarantees or new amendments to protect the rights and property of every person who shelters himself under the American Constitution.

...

Many of the honorable gentlemen of this House with whom I am politically associated may condemn me for my action to-day. I assure them I do that only which my conscience sanctions and my sense of duty to my country demands. I have been a Democrat all the days of my life. I learned my Democracy from that being who gave me birth; it was pure; it came from one who never told me an untruth. All my political life has been spent in defending and supporting the measures which I thought were for the good of the party and the country.... If by my action to-day I dig my political grave, I will descend into it without a murmur, knowing that I am justified in my action by conscientious belief I am doing that will ultimately prove to be of service to my country, and knowing there is one dear, devoted, and loved being in this wide world who will not bring tears of bitterness to that grave, but will strew it with beautiful flowers, for it returns me to that domestic circle from whence I have been taken for the greater part of the last two years.

. . .

Mr. ASHLEY. I now yield the remainder of my time to the gentleman from New York, [Mr. HERRICK.]

. . .

Mr. HERRICK. Mr. Speaker, the joint resolution now before the House submitting to the Legislatures of the several States an amendment to the Constitution of the United States, comes before us under circumstances widely different from those existing when at the last session of Congress the same resolution failed to receive the requisite two-thirds vote of this body.

The eventful year which has elapsed has wrought great changes in the situation of the country affecting this important question, and I approach its discussion at this time with quite altered views, as to its expediency, from those which governed me when I last addressed the House upon the same subject. The brilliant successes that have rewarded the gallant efforts of the military and naval forces of the nation, and the result of the presidential election, which has since transpired, have necessarily exercised an important influence over the public mind in both the loyal and insurgent States; and this question has assumed a very different aspect from that which it bore at the last session of Congress. The rejection of the people at the polls of the proclaimed policy of the Democratic party has closed many avenues to reconciliation which then remained open, and the waning strength of the rebellion has brought its leaders to the verge of desperation. Perils which then seemed imminent have faded away, and others of quite different tenor menace us in the future.

. . .

It is weak, Mr. Speaker, it is criminal for him, from a false pride in preserving an imaginary consistency, to remain stationary when all the rest of the world is moving forward, and to regulate his words and actions by what he has said or done in the past.

. . .

Mr. Speaker, at the last session of Congress I voted against this resolution from a solemn conviction of duty. And as I shall now vote for it from a similar conviction,

it becomes me to explain to the House and the country what considerations prompt me to assume a new attitude upon the question before us. Events which will now govern my action have superseded the arguments which influenced the vote I recorded last year. The considerations which then rendered the amendment proposed impolitic, in my view, have ceased to operate, and reasons of great force, which were not then in existence, have arisen to make it now expedient, and to warrant me in reversing my former action.

In my humble judgment the rejection of this measure at that time was demanded by the best interests of the country, which now, on the contrary, seem to call for its adoption. Mr. Speaker, circumstances have changed, and I shall now vote for the resolution, as I formerly voted against it, because I think such action on my part is best calculated to assist in the maintenance of the Government, the preservation of the Union, and the perpetuation of the free institutions which we inherited from our fathers. These are the great objects for which the loyal people of this country have struggled during the last four years with a courage and self-devotion to which history affords no parallel, and poured forth their blood and treasure with an unhesitating patriotism that has astonished the world. So long as a Representative seeks these objects, regardless of partisan or political prejudices, he cannot be rightfully charged with inconsistency, no matter how widely the means he may find it necessary to employ at one time or another, to adapt himself to ever-varying circumstances, may differ. I believe this is the only consistency that is truly desirable. It is certainly the only one to which I make any pretensions.

. . .

It is altogether immaterial, for the purposes of this discussion, whether the power of three fourths of the States to alter the organic law is altogether unlimited, except by the reservation in the amending clause of the Constitution. It may well be doubted whether the people do not possess certain inalienable rights, of which a minority, however small, cannot be divested by a majority, however large. But the States formed the Federal Government by a grant to it of their sovereignty over certain specified subjects, and it must seem to follow that they can also confer upon it any other rights or powers which they themselves possess, in the manner prescribed by the Constitution itself. By the adoption of that Constitution the States transferred to three fourths of their number their entire sovereignty, which can be at any time exerted to augment or diminish the functions of the General Government, save in the two particulars excepted by special limitation. Three fourths of the States can, by an amendment of the Constitution, exercise throughout the United States any power that a State individually can exercise within its own limits.

The institution of slavery is purely a creation of law, and completely under the control of the State in which it may exist, at whose pleasure it may be modified or abolished. What the State may do, the higher power to which by the adoption of the Constitution the State voluntarily ceded its whole sovereignty, except in two particulars, is certainly competent to do, whenever it chooses to assert its authority. In amending the Constitution, three fourths of the States actually represent the whole; and the agent is invested with all the powers that belong to his principle.

...

The Democratic party, while sustaining the Government, believed that the interests of the country, of humanity, and of the cause of liberty would be best consulted in a peace, in which both parties must give up something for the sake of agreement. They believed that there was no impassable gulf between the North and the South which should prevent them from coming together again under the same Government, and that the issue of slavery might be of the greatest importance in any negotiation which might be undertaken to restore peace and reestablish a perfect Union. They thought that both of the combatants, weary of the carnage and devastation that were desolating the land, and taught by dearly-bought experience to respect the bravery and determination of each other, would gladly consent to a peace upon the basis of mutual concession—the South surrendering its project of a separate nationality and the North its hostility to the institution of negro slavery.

These were the views which prevailed in the Democratic party a year ago, and made it then practically a unit in opposition to the measure now before the House proposing the abolition of slavery by an amendment of the Constitution, in accordance with its own provisions. As a life-long member of that time-honored political organization, whose history is the history of the Government in its proudest days, and whose policy, carried out by a long line of wise and patriotic statesmen, made this country what it was four years ago, I raised my voice and recorded my vote as a member of this House against the joint resolution now under consideration.

The tone of the public mind at that time seemed to me, as it no doubt seemed to all who agreed in opinion with me, to foreshadow a change of Administration and the accession to power of the Democratic party, which we believed would be able to check the red tide of war and induce the South to return to the Union, by showing a conciliatory spirit and giving it the fullest assurance that all its rights and privileges under the Constitution, as it exists, should be preserved, and their continued enjoyment of them for the future guarantied by such constitutional changes as might be requisite to effect that object. The two parties into which the people were divided prepared for the presidential election with a distinctly-understood issue. The party of the Administration incorporated this amendment in the platform of principles upon which they entered the canvass. The Opposition boldly declared for a cessation of hostilities and a national convention to redress all grievances, settle all difficulties, and make an honorable and lasting peace by a satisfactory compromise. It was well understood that the principal business of this contemplated national convention, should it ever assemble, would be to put at rest, at once and forever, by the agency of amendments to the Constitution, the vexed question of slavery, which has disturbed the harmony of the country ever since its agitation was commenced, when Missouri applied for admission into the Union. There was therefore no conflict of opinion between the two parties as to the power to amend the Constitution in regard to the institution of slavery. Stripped of all side issues the main question presented to the people for their decision was whether slavery should be abolished and the seceded States coerced into allegiance to the Constitution, as it is now proposed, to amend it, or whether the war should be speedily terminated and the aegis of the Constitution thrown around the social system of the South. The people by a large majority sustained, the first proposition and fully indorsed the policy of the Administration on the slavery issue, and I am now disposed to bow in submission to that popular decree.

...

Now, Mr. Speaker, let me ask my Democratic colleagues upon this floor, of what possible advantage will the defeat of this measure be to our party at this time, in full view of the fact that our political opponents have the power to pass it immediately upon our adjournment in spite of us, and boldly proclaim their intention to do so at an extra session of the Thirty-Ninth Congress, to be convened immediately after the 4th of March?

Looking at the subject as a party man, from a party

point of view, as one who hopes soon to see the Democratic party again in power, this proposition seems to present a desirable opportunity for the Democracy to rid itself at once and forever of the incubus of slavery, and to banish its perplexing issues beyond the pale of party politics, no longer to distract our counsels and disturb the harmony of our movements. It has been our seeming adherence to slavery, in maintaining the principle of State rights, that has, year by year, depleted our party ranks until our once powerful organization has trailed its standard in the dust and sunk into a hopeless minority in nearly every State of the Union; and every year and every day we are growing weaker and weaker in popular favor, while our opponents are strengthening, because we will not venture to cut loose from the dead carcass of negro slavery.

. . .

Mr. KALBFLEISCH.

. . .

I contend Mr. Speaker, even admitting, which I do not, that the Constitution needs amendment in reference to the question of slavery, that this is not the proper time to agitate, much less to act upon, so grave and important a question. Let us wait until the nation shall calmly repose in peace, and all feelings of enmity towards our erring brethren of the South shall have subsided, and good-will and harmony again prevail over all sections of the country.

. . .

There is, Mr. Speaker, another reason which should induce us to approach the consideration of this question with great caution. Adopt this amendment to the Constitution, force it upon the States now in rebellion, and let the result be then restoration to the Union, and who can predict what stumbling-blocks may be thrown in the way of the execution of the Federal laws on the subject? The abolition of slavery forced upon them without their consent and against their will, it is but natural to suppose that the people of those States will not feel particularly anxious to aid in carrying the measure into practical effect. Every one remembers the trouble experienced in the execution of the Federal law known as the fugitive slave law in some of the States which now claim to be filled to overflowing with what in modern parlance is called "loyalty to the Federal Government," but which, in my humble opinion, oftener partakes of the nature of party fealty than of that of true patriotism. In opposition to that law, some of the States adopted enactments going to the extent of disfranchis-

ing officials or citizens attempting or aiding to enforce it. Is there not, at least, danger to be apprehended that other States, following this example, may in like manner attempt to thwart and interfere with the execution of laws carrying into effect the abolition of slavery? Would it not be better to wait until the people of these States themselves, by their own action, provide for the practical abolition of slavery, or rather for the removal of the corpse from which, we are told, the life has long since departed.

. . .

It is claimed by some that the result of the recent presidential election affords conclusive evidence of the fact that the people are in favor of amending the Constitution of the United States so that it shall abolish and prohibit slavery. This I deny. Whatever may have been the hopes and wishes of ultra abolitionists, I insist that this was not the issue made up and presented to the people. In my own State, at least, I know that this was not the case. What is the record in connection with this question? At the last session of Congress this same resolution was submitted and it failed to pass. The people had every reason to suppose that would be the end of it.

. . .

Mr. ASHLEY. I call the previous question upon the pending motion to reconsider the vote by which the House on the 15th of last June rejected a joint resolution (S. No. 16) submitting to the Legislatures of the several States a proposition to amend the Constitution of the United States.

Mr. STILES. I move to lay the motion to reconsider on the table; and upon that I demand the yeas and nays.

The yeas and nays were ordered.

The question was put; and it was decided in the negative—yeas 57, nays 111, not voting 14; as follows:

YEAS—Messrs. James C. Allen, William J. Allen, Ancona, Bliss, Brooks, James S. Brown, Chanler, Clay, Cox, Cravens, Dawson, Denison, Eden, Edgerton, Eldridge, Finck, Ganson, Grider, Hall, Harding, Harrington, Benjamin G. Harris, Charles M. Harris, Holman, Philip Johnson, William Johnson, Kalbfleisch, Kernan, Knapp, Law, Long, Mallory, William H. Miller, James R. Morris, Morrison, Noble, John O'Neill, Pendleton, Perry, Pruyn, Samuel J. Randall, Robinson, Ross, Scott, William G. Steele, Stiles, Strouse, Stuart, Sweat, Townsend, Wadsworth, Ward, Chilton A. White, Joseph W. White, Winfield, Benjamin Wood, and Fernando Wood—57.

NAYS—Messrs. Alley, Allison, Ames, Anderson, Arnold, Ashley, Baily, Augustus C. Baldwin, John D. Baldwin, Baxter, Beaman, Blaine, Blair, Blow, Boutwell, Boyd, Brandegee, Broomall, William G. Brown, Ambrose W. Clark, Freeman Clarke, Cobb, Coffroth, Cole, Creswell, Henry Winter Davis, Thomas T. Davis, Dawes, Deming, Dixon, Donnelly, Driggs, Dumont, Eckley, Eliot, Farnsworth, Frank, Garfield, Gooch, Grinnell, Griswold, Hale, Herrick, Higby, Hooper, Hotchkiss, Asahel W. Hubbard, John B. Hubbard, Hulburd, Ingersoll, Jenckes, Julian, Kasson, Kelley, Francis W. Kellogg, Orlando Kellogg, King, Knox, Littlejohn, Loan, Longyear, Marvin, McAllister, McBride, McClurg, McIndoe, Samuel F. Miller, Moorhead, Morrill, Daniel Morris, Amos Myers, Leonard Myers, Norton, Odell, Charles O'Neil, Orth, Patterson, Perham, Pike, Pomeroy, Price, William H. Randall, Alexander H. Rice, John H. Rice, Edward H. Rollins, James S. Rollins, Schenck, Scofield, Shannon, Sloan, Smith, Smithers, Spalding, Starr, Stevens, Thayer, Thomas, Tracy, Upson, Van Valkenburgh, Elihu B. Washburne, William B. Washburn, Webster, Wheeler, Williams, Wilder, Wilson, Windom, Woodbridge, Worthington, and Yeaman—111.

NOT VOTING—Messrs. English, Hutchins, Lazear, Le Blond, Marcy, McDowell, McKinney, Middleton, Nelson, Radford, Rogers, John B. Steele, Voorhees, and Whaley—14.

So the motion to reconsider was not laid on the table.

During the call of the roll,

Mr. ROLLINS, of Missouri, stated that Mr. ROGERS, of New Jersey, had been confined to his room several days by indisposition.

Mr. CRAVENS stated that Mr. VOORHEES was still detained at his home in Indiana in consequence of severe sickness in his family.

The previous question was then seconded, and the main question ordered.

The question being on the motion of Mr. ASHLEY, to reconsider,

Mr. ANCONA called for the yeas and nays.

The yeas and nays were ordered.

The question was put; and it was decided in the affirmative—yeas 112, nays 57, not voting 13; as follows:

YEAS—Messrs. Alley, Allison, Ames, Anderson, Arnold, Ashley, Baily, John D. Baldwin, Baxter, Beaman, Blaine, Blair, Blow, Boutwell, Boyd, Brandegee, Broomall, William G. Brown, Ambrose W. Clark, Freeman Clarke, Cobb, Coffroth, Cole, Creswell, Henry Winter Davis, Thomas T. Davis, Dawes, Deming, Dixon, Donnelly, Driggs, Dumont, Eckley, Eliot, English, Farnsworth, Frank, Garfield, Gooch, Grinnell, Griswold, Hale, Herrick, Higby, Hooper, Hotchkiss, Asahel W. Hubbard, John H. Hubbard, Hulburd, Ingersoll, Jenckes, Julian, Kasson, Kelley, Francis W. Kellogg, Orlando Kellogg, King, Knox, Littlejohn, Loan, Longyear, Marvin, McAllister, McBride, McClurg, McIndoe, Samuel F. Miller, Moorhead, Morrill, Daniel Morris, Amos Myers, Leonard Myers, Norton, Odell, Charles O'Neill, Orth, Patterson, Perham, Pike, Pomeroy, Price, William H. Randall, Alexander H. Rice, John H. Rice, Edward H. Rollins, James S. Rollins, Schenck, Scofield, Shannon, Sloan, Smith, Smithers, Spalding, Starr, Stevens, Thayer, Thomas, Tracy, Upson, Van Valkenburgh, Elihu B. Washburne, William B. Washburn, Webster, Whaley, Wheeler, Williams, Wilder, Wilson, Windom, Woodbridge, Worthington, and Yeaman—112.

NAYS—Messrs. James C. Allen, William J. Allen, Ancona, Bliss, Brooks, James S. Brown, Chanler, Clay, Cox, Cravens, Dawson, Denison, Eden, Edgerton, Eldridge, Finck, Ganson, Grider, Hall, Harding, Harrington, Benjamin G. Harris, Charles M. Harris, Holman, Philip Johnson, William Johnson, Kalbfleisch, Kernan, Knapp, Law, Long, Mallory, William H. Miller, James R. Morris, Morrison, Noble, John O'Neill, Pendleton, Perry, Pruyn, Samuel J. Randall, Robinson, Ross, Scott, William G. Steele, Stiles, Strouse, Stuart, Sweat, Townsend, Wadsworth, Ward, Chilton A. White, Joseph W. White, Winfield, Benjamin Wood and Fernando Wood—57.

NOT VOTING—Messrs. Augustus C. Baldwin, Hutchins, Lazear, Le Blond, Marcy, McDowell, McKinney, Middleton, Nelson, Radford, Rogers, John B. Steele, and Voorhees—13.

So the motion to reconsider was agreed to.

The question recurred on the passage of the joint resolution.

Mr. ASHLEY. I demand the previous question.

Mr. MALLORY. I rise to a question of order. My point of order is that a vote to reconsider the vote by which the subject now before the House was disposed of in June last requires two thirds of this body. That two-thirds vote has not been obtained.

The SPEAKER. The Chair overrules the point of order. The rules of the House authorize every bill and joint resolution to pass by a majority vote. The Constitution of the United States, however, declares that no constitutional amendment shall pass except by a two-thirds vote. On the question of the passage of the joint resolution the constitutional provision will operate, and not till that time. All other questions are governed by the rules of the House.

The Chair will state that this has been the uniform usage of the House in regard to bills vetoed by the President. In such cases all votes up to the time of taking the question on the passage of the bill over the President's veto are decided by a majority vote; but on the final vote a two-thirds vote is necessary.

Mr. MALLORY. My action upon this question of order will depend a good deal on the response to a proposition which I am about to make to the gentleman from Ohio, [Mr. ASHLEY.] There are gentlemen belonging to this side of the House who can be here to-morrow, but who are not here to-day, who are anxious to vote upon this question. If the gentleman from Ohio will agree that the vote shall be taken at a fixed hour to-morrow, all action upon this side of the House for delay will cease.

Mr. ASHLEY. It has been the universal understanding that we were to have a vote to-day. Gentlemen upon the other side of the House will bear me witness that I have prolonged this debate against the protest of gentlemen upon this side of the House and of leading friends of the measure in the country; and I think it does not come with a very good grace from the gentleman from Kentucky, in view of the time which has been extended to his friends on that side of the House, that he should demand now, when notice was given again and again that a vote would be taken to-day, that it shall be postponed until to-morrow. It seems to me that if gentlemen choose to absent themselves from the House their action ought not to operate either to keep us in session here or justify members in resorting to the usual parliamentary rules to procrastinate and put off the vote.

Mr. MALLORY. I was not aware that any understanding had been arrived at as to a vote on this question to-day. It was postponed till to-day, but at that time there was certainly no understanding that there should be a vote to-day.

Mr. ASHLEY. In reply to a question by the gentleman from Pennsylvania, [Mr. STILES,] I gave notice last week that the vote would be taken to-day; and at the beginning of the discussion this morning I fixed three o'clock as the time the vote would be taken, instead of which we have procrastinated it almost an hour to accommodate gentlemen upon the other side of the House.

Mr. MALLORY. Did that understanding exist upon this side of the House? If it did and if gentlemen will say so, I shall take no action in this matter.

SEVERAL MEMBERS. It was so understood.

Mr. ASHLEY. I cannot yield any further. I desired this morning to be heard on this question, and came into the House intending to close the debate, as under the rules I had a right to do. The time, the subject, and the occasion, all united to make it desirable; but I yielded the time to gentlemen on the other side, until it is now nearly four o'clock, and members on all sides of the House demand a vote. I therefore decline to take up the time of the House, and demand that the main question shall now be put.

Mr. BROWN, of Wisconsin. I ask the gentleman from Ohio to yield to me to offer a substitute for the joint resolution.

Mr. ASHLEY. I cannot yield for that purpose. I have a substitute myself, which I should much prefer to the original joint resolution, but I do not offer it.

The SPEAKER. No motion to amend would be in order at this stage. The joint resolution has passed its third reading, and is now on its passage.

Mr. ELDRIDGE. Mr. Speaker, the gentleman from Ohio says that he has a substitute which he himself prefers to this joint resolution. If so, why does he not offer it to the House? There certainly will be no objection on this side.

Mr. ASHLEY. I do not offer it, because I would not procrastinate this discussion or hazard the passage of the measure.

Mr. ELDRIDGE. It seems to me that if the gentleman has a better substitute, he should propose it. [Calls to order.]

The previous question was seconded, and the main question ordered; which was on the passage of the joint resolution.

Mr. DAWSON called for the yeas and nays. The yeas and nays were ordered.

The question was taken, and it was decided in the affirmative—yeas 119, nays 56, not voting 8; as follows:

YEAS—Messrs. Alley, Allison, Ames, Anderson, Arnold, Ashley, Baily, Augustus C. Baldwin, John D. Baldwin, Baxter, Beaman, Blaine, Blair, Blow, Boutwell, Boyd, Brandegee, Broomall, William G. Brown, Ambrose W. Clark, Freeman Clarke, Cobb, Coffroth, Cole, Colfax, Creswell, Henry Winter Davis, Thomas T. Davis, Dawes, Deming, Dixon, Donnelly, Driggs, Dumont, Eckley, Eliot, English, Farnsworth, Frank, Ganson, Garfield, Gooch, Grinnell, Griswold, Hale, Herrick, Higby, Hooper, Hotchkiss, Asahel W. Hubbard, John H. Hubbard, Hulburd, Hutchins, Ingersoll, Jenckes, Julian, Kasson, Kelley, Francis W. Kellogg, Orlando Kellogg, King, Knox, Littlejohn, Loan, Longyear, Marvin, McAllister, McBride,

McClurg, McIndoe, Samuel F. Miller, Moorhead, Morrill, Daniel Morris, Amos Myers, Leonard Myers, Nelson, Norton, Odell, Charles O'Neill, Orth, Patterson, Perham, Pike, Pomeroy, Price, Radford, William H. Randall, Alexander H. Rice, John H. Rice, Edward H. Rollins, James S. Rollins, Schenck, Scofield, Shannon, Sloan, Smith, Smithers, Spalding, Starr, John B. Steele, Stevens, Thayer, Thomas, Tracy, Upson, Van Valkenburgh, Elihu B. Washburne, William B. Washburn, Webster, Whaley, Wheeler, Williams, Wilder, Wilson, Windom, Woodbridge, Worthington, and Yeaman—119.

NAYS—Messrs. James C. Allen, William J. Allen, Ancona, Bliss, Brooks, James S. Brown, Chanler, Clay, Cox, Cravens, Dawson, Denison, Eden, Edgerton, Eldridge, Finck, Grider, Hall, Harding, Harrington, Benjamin G. Harris, Charles M. Harris, Holman, Philip Johnson, William Johnson, Kalbfleisch, Kernan, Knapp, Law, Long, Mallory, William H. Miller, James R. Morris, Morrison, Noble, John O'Neill, Pendleton, Perry, Pruyn, Samuel J. Randall, Robinson, Ross, Scott, William G. Steele, Stiles, Strouse, Stuart, Sweat, Townsend, Wadsworth, Ward, Chilton A. White, Joseph W. White, Winfield, Benjamin Wood and Fernando Wood—56.

NOT VOTING—Messrs. Lazear, Le Blond, Marcy, McDowell, McKinney, Middleton, Rogers, and Voorhees—8.

So, the two thirds required by the Constitution of the United States having voted in favor thereof, the joint resolution was passed.

During the roll-call,

On Mr. ENGLISH and Mr. GANSON voting "ay," there was considerable applause by members on the Republican side of the House.

The SPEAKER called repeatedly to order, and asked that members should set a better example to spectators in the gallery.

Mr. KALBFLEISCH and other Democratic members remarked that the applause came, not from the spectators in the gallery, but from members on the floor.

The SPEAKER. Members will take their seats and observe order.

The SPEAKER directed the Clerk to call his name as a member of the House.

The Clerk called the name of SCHUYLER COLFAX, of Indiana, and Mr. COLFAX voted "ay."

[This incident was greeted with renewed applause.]

The SPEAKER. The constitutional majority of two thirds having voted in the affirmative, the joint resolution is passed.

[The announcement was received by the House and by the spectators with an outburst of enthusiasm. The members on the Republican side of the House instantly sprung to their feet, and, regardless of parliamentary rules, applauded with cheers and clapping of hands. The example was followed by the male spectators in the galleries, which were crowded to excess, who waved their hats and cheered loud and long, while the ladies, hundreds of whom were present, rose in their seats and waved their handkerchiefs, participating in and adding to the general excitement and intense interest of the scene. This lasted for several minutes.]

Mr. INGERSOLL. Mr. Speaker, in honor of this immortal and sublime event I move that the House do now adjourn.

The SPEAKER declared the motion carried, and again the cheering and demonstrations of applause were renewed.

Mr. HARRIS, of Maryland. I demand the yeas and nays on the motion to adjourn.

The yeas and nays were ordered.

The question was taken; and it was decided in the affirmative—yeas 121, nays 24, not voting 37; as follows:

YEAS—Messrs. Alley, Allison, Ames, Ancona, Anderson, Arnold, Ashley, Baily, Augustus C. Baldwin, John D. Baldwin, Baxter, Beaman, Blaine, Blair, Blow, Boutwell, Boyd, Brandegee, Broomall, William G. Brown, Chanler, Ambrose W. Clark, Freeman Clarke, Cobb, Cole, Cox, Creswell, Henry Winter Davis, Thomas T. Davis, Dawes, Dawson, Deming, Dixon, Donnelly, Driggs, Eckley, Eliot, English, Farnsworth, Frank, Garfield, Gooch, Grinnell, Griswold, Hale, Herrick, Higby, Hotchkiss, Asahel W. Hubbard, John H. Hubbard, Hulburd, Hutchins, Ingersoll, Jenckes, Julian, Kasson, Kelley, Francis W. Kellogg, Orlando Kellogg, Kernan, King, Knox, Littlejohn, Loan, Longyear, Mallory, Marvin, McAllister, McBride, McClurg, McIndoe, Samuel F. Miller, Moorhead, Morrill, Daniel Morris, Amos Myers, Leonard Myers, Nelson, Norton, Odell, Charles O'Neill, Patterson, Pendleton, Perham, Pike, Pomeroy, Price, William H. Randall, Alexander H. Rice, John H. Rice, Edward H. Rollins, James S. Rollins, Schenck, Scofield, Scott, Shannon, Sloan, Smithers, Spalding, Starr, Stevens, Strouse, Stuart, Thayer, Thomas, Tracy, Upson, Van Valkenburgh, Wadsworth, Ward, Elihu B. Washburne, William B. Washburn, Whaley, Wheeler, Williams, Wilder, Wilson, Windom, Winfield, Benjamin Wood, and Woodbridge—121.

NAYS—Messrs. James C. Allen, William J. Allen, Coffroth, Denison, Eden, Edgerton, Eldridge, Grider,

Harrington, Benjamin G. Harris, Charles M. Harris, Holman, Kalbfleisch, Knapp, Law, Long, Morrison, Noble, Radford, Samuel J. Randall, Ross, Stiles, Townsend, and Joseph W. White—24.

NOT VOTING—Messrs. Bliss, Brooks, James S. Brown, Clay, Cravens, Dumont, Finck, Ganson, Hall, Harding, Hooper, Philip Johnson, William Johnson, Lazear, Le Blond, Marcy, McDowell, McKinney, Middleton, William H. Miller, James R. Morris, John O'Neill, Orth, Perry, Pruyn, Robinson, Rogers, Smith, John B. Steele, William G. Steele, Sweat, Voorhees, Webster, Chilton A. White, Fernando Wood, Worthington, and Yeaman—37.

The House thereupon (at twenty minutes past four o'clock, p. m.,) adjourned.

32

"Exciting Scene in the House of Representatives, Jan. 31, 1865,"

Frank Leslie's Illustrated Newspaper

February 8, 1865, p. 345

33

US Senate, Notice of House Vote and Presidential Signature

February 1, 1865*

A message from the House of Representatives, by Mr. MCPHERSON, its Clerk, announced that the House had passed without amendment the joint resolution (S.R. No. 16) submitting to the Legislatures of the several States a proposition to amend the Constitution of the United States. A subsequent message announced that the resolution had been enrolled, and that the enrolled resolution had received the signature of the Speaker of the House. It was then signed by the Vice President, and transmitted to the President of the United States, who, by his Secretary, Mr. NICOLAY, soon announced that it had been approved and signed by him.

* Cong. Globe, 38th Cong., 2nd Sess., 532 (Feb. 1, 1865).

Artist unknown. The Huntington Library, San Marino, California; 499751 (Uncatalogued).

B. RATIFICATION

Introduction to Part 2B

1. "The Constitutional Abolition of Slavery—The Great Measure of the Age," *New York Herald* (Feb. 2, 1865)
2. "Speech of Mr. Lincoln on the Constitutional Amendment," *New York Herald* (Feb. 3, 1865)
3. New York, Governor Fenton's Message, Speeches and Vote on the Abolition Amendment, *Albany Evening Journal* (Feb. 1–4, 1865)
4. "The Great Amendment; Progress of Ratification," *New York Tribune* (Feb. 4, 1865)
5. "Dr. Lieber's Letter to Senator E. D. Morgan on the Amendment of the Constitution Extinguishing Slavery," *New York Tribune* (Feb. 4, 1865)
6. Massachusetts, Unanimous Ratification of Abolition Amendment, *Salem Register* (Feb. 6, 1865)
7. Charles Sumner, Resolutions Regarding the Number of States Necessary for Ratification, *New York Tribune* (Feb. 6, 1865)
8. "Is the Union Destroyed?" (On Sumner's Resolutions), *New York Times* (Feb. 6, 1865)
9. Virginia, News of Ratification, *Press* (Feb. 9, 1865)
10. Delaware, Governor William Cannon's Message, Legislature Rejects Amendment (Feb. 7–8, 1865)
11. Indiana, Debates and Ratification (Feb. 8–13, 1865)
12. Speech of Frederick Douglass, *Liberator* (Feb. 10, 1865)
13. Kentucky, Governor Thomas Bramlette's Address to the Legislature (Calling for Conditional Ratification), *Cincinnati Daily Enquirer* (Feb. 11, 1865)
14. Vice President Elect Andrew Johnson, Speech at the Tennessee State Constitutional Convention, *Washington Reporter* (Feb. 15, 1865)
15. "The Abolition Amendment," *Crisis* (Feb. 15, 1865)
16. Kentucky, "The Constitutional Amendment Rejected," *New York Daily Tribune* (Feb. 24, 1865)
17. Louisiana, Ratification of Amendment, Call for Black Suffrage, *Salem Register* (Feb. 27, 1865)
18. New Jersey, Debates and Failure to Ratify (Feb. 9–Mar. 1, 1865)
19. "The Constitutional Amendment," *Daily Age* (Mar. 7, 1865)
20. Abraham Lincoln, Speech on the Status of Louisiana (Lincoln's Last Public Address) (Apr. 11, 1865)
21. Assassination of President Lincoln, *New York Times* (Apr. 15, 1865)
22. "This Hour Belongs Exclusively to the Negro," Speeches at the Thirty-Second Anniversary of the American Anti-Slavery Society, *New York Times* (May 10, 1865)
23. Andrew Johnson, Proclamation Creating a Provisional Government for the State of North Carolina (May 29, 1865)
24. Andrew Johnson to Provisional Mississippi Governor William L. Sharkey (Aug. 15, 1865)
25. *Equal Suffrage, Address from the Colored Citizens of Norfolk, Va., to the People of the United States* (June 26, 1865)
26. Provisional South Carolina Governor Benjamin F. Perry to Secretary of State William Seward (Nov. 1, 1865)
27. Secretary of State William Seward to Provisional South Carolina Governor Benjamin F. Perry (Nov. 6, 1865)
28. South Carolina, Ratification and Accompanying Resolution (Nov. 13, 1865)
29. "South Carolina," *New York Times* (Nov. 16, 1865)
30. Andrew Johnson to Provisional Mississippi Governor William L. Sharkey (Nov. 17, 1865)
31. "The Amendment to the Federal Constitution," *Daily Eastern Argus* (Nov. 17, 1865)
32. "The Meaning and Scope of the Great Amendment," *New York Tribune* (Nov. 17, 1865)
33. "Manhood, the Basis of Suffrage," Speech of Hon. Michael Hahn of Louisiana at the National Equal Suffrage Association of Washington, DC (Nov. 17, 1865)
34. "What the Amendment Amounts to in South Carolina," *New York Daily Tribune* (Nov. 18, 1865)
35. "Power Given to Congress by the Constitutional Amendment," *New York Times* (Nov. 20, 1865)
36. General Benjamin Butler to Henry Wilson (Nov. 20, 1865)
37. Mississippi, Joint Committee Report and Rejection of Proposed Amendment (Nov. 27–Dec. 2, 1865)
38. Alabama, Ratification and Statement of Understanding (Dec. 2, 1865)
39. Georgia, Message of Provisional Governor James Johnson on the Proposed Amendment, *Press* (Dec. 11, 1865)

Introduction to Part 2B

When Lincoln signed the Thirteenth Amendment and directed his secretary of state William Seward to submit the proposal for ratification, the immediate question became *which* states would be allowed to ratify. The country was still engulfed in a civil war and would remain so for months. Would rebel states be allowed to vote on ratification, and if so, when? If allowed to vote, would these states be allowed to reject and thereby *defeat* the proposed amendment? In the beginning, the issue was more theoretical than real; if every Northern state and those states now under the control of the Union army voted in favor of the amendment, no rebel votes would be necessary to meet the three-quarters majority required by Article V.

In the early months of 1865, supportive Northern newspapers were optimistic about ratification (doc. 1). President Lincoln looked forward to the amendment's resolving any questions that remained about the legal status of slaves freed under his Emancipation Proclamation. The Thirteenth Amendment, Lincoln declared to an applauding crowd on February 2, 1865, would be "a king's cure for all the evils" (doc. 2).

A number of Northern states, including New York, Massachusetts, and Pennsylvania, as well as the border states of West Virginia and Maryland, quickly ratified the amendment (see doc. 4). In Massachusetts, the vote was unanimous (doc. 6). In the more politically divided state of New York, however, the proposed amendment triggered substantial debate (doc. 3). Democrats echoed their congressional counterparts and insisted that constitutional abolition was an "encroachment upon the rights of the States," warning that immediate emancipation was "dangerous both to the interests of the country and of the blacks themselves" (doc. 3). In response, Republicans argued that Article V had already been used for the adoption of amendments binding the states. According to Senator Bailey, this included the adoption of provisions in the original Bill of Rights, including amendments two, four, five and six.[1] Other advocates

argued that history itself had proven that slavery was "incompatible with a free government [and] should be abolished" (doc. 3). "What is there sacred about Slavery?" demanded Mr. Van Buren, and "[w]hy cannot the people rid themselves of an evil so foul and fatal as chattel bondage?" In the end, the New York House voted seventy to forty in favor of the amendment, with the Senate concurring seventeen to eight—both votes indicating a significant, if minority, opposition (doc. 3). About a week later, a similar debate and outcome occurred in Indiana (doc. 11), with Republicans blaming slavery for the Civil War and Democrats claiming the amendment violated the reserved rights of the states. The final vote was twenty-six to twenty-two in the Indiana Senate and fifty-six to twenty-nine in the House, once again indicating substantial opposition (doc. 11).

Northern states that had voted against Lincoln in the presidential election of 1864 also rejected the Thirteenth Amendment: Delaware and Kentucky in February (docs. 10 and 16), and New Jersey in early March (doc. 18). In Kentucky, Governor Thomas Bramlette encouraged the legislature to ratify the amendment on the condition that the state receive compensation for its emancipated slaves (doc. 13). The legislature instead voted to reject the amendment outright on a vote of twenty-one to twelve (doc. 16). In New Jersey, a congressional committee suggested submitting the amendment to the people in a state referendum (doc. 18). The proposal was rejected, and the amendment failed to pass in a tied vote of thirty to thirty. Newspapers aligned with congressional Democrats cheered the states' rejections (doc. 15) and criticized ratifications by "bogus" governments such as those of West Virginia and Virginia (doc. 19). Virginia posed an especially interesting case, as its

---

1. As did many other Reconstruction-era Republicans, Bailey apparently believed that a number of provisions in the Bill of Rights bound the states as well as the federal government. This, despite the Supreme Court's ruling to the contrary in *Barron v. Baltimore* (1833). The documents in this collection contain a number of examples of similarly "nationalist" readings of the Bill of Rights, even before the ratification of the Fourteenth Amendment.

ratification of the amendment came in a vote by the state's government-in-exile, which assembled in Alexandria, Virginia, and was led by Governor Francis Harrison Pierpont. Having set themselves up as the "true" government of Virginia, the Union-supporting Pierpont administration authorized the creation of the state of West Virginia and voted to ratify the Thirteenth Amendment on February 3, 1865. As a result, one "Virginia" ratified the Thirteenth Amendment, while another "Virginia" continued to wage war against the Union.[2]

Only slightly less controversial was Louisiana's ratification vote. President Lincoln recognized Louisiana's government as having restored its relations with the Union despite the state's relatively low number of Union supporters. In a speech delivered on April 11, 1865, only a few days after Lee's surrender at Appomattox and three days before the president's assassination, Lincoln dismissed the argument about whether rebel states were in or out of the Union as a "pernicious abstraction" (doc. 20). Instead, Lincoln urged, supporters of the Thirteenth Amendment should simply join him in recognizing Louisiana as a member of the Union, stating, "If we reject Louisiana, we also reject one vote in favor of the proposed amendment to the national Constitution. To meet this proposition, it has been argued that no more than three fourths of those States which have not attempted secession are necessary to validly ratify the amendment. I do not commit myself against this, further than to say that such a ratification would be questionable, and sure to be persistently questioned; while a ratification by three-fourths of all the States would be unquestioned and unquestionable" (doc. 20).

As Lincoln's comments concede, counting the ratification votes of only those states that had remained in the Union would raise questions of legality under Article V of the Constitution, which seemed to require a three-quarters majority by *all* the states in order to pass, civil war or not. Radical Republicans like Massachusetts senator Charles Sumner insisted that Article V required nothing more than a three-quarters favorable vote by those states still in the Union (doc. 7). Newspapers like the *New York Times* immediately attacked Sumner for his reading of Article V and accused Sumner of presuming the Union had "ceased to exist" (doc. 8). Lincoln hoped to avoid the dispute altogether by finding some way to secure the proper number of ratification votes from all the states.

But as of March 1865, it was not at all clear that this could be achieved. With several Northern states having already rejected the amendment, it appeared Congress would either *have* to only count loyal states as the constitutional denominator or somehow convince the former slaveholding rebel states to embrace permanent abolition (doc. 19). Thus Lincoln defended Louisiana's thinly supported loyal government if only to gain an additional vote in favor of ratification. Three days later, Lincoln was assassinated (doc. 21). The fate of the Thirteenth Amendment now fell to his Democratic vice president, Andrew Johnson.

A former senator from Tennessee, Andrew Johnson had refused to join the Confederacy when his state seceded at the beginning of the war. After Union armies drove out the rebels, Lincoln appointed Johnson as Tennessee's military governor. Johnson was so successful in the role that Lincoln chose him as his presidential running mate.[3] In a speech delivered just prior to leaving Tennessee to join Lincoln in Washington, DC, Johnson congratulated the state's recent constitutional convention for having drafted an abolitionist constitution. In his remarks, Johnson boasted that he had "sent a message to Abraham that the death-knell of slavery had been sounded in Tennessee." As for additional protections for freedmen, Johnson demurred:

> I shall say nothing of the future condition of the negro, nor of the elective franchise. First, reorganize; time and experience will regulate the rest. Let us first get rid of slavery; let there be no bickering or conflict till we get that out of the way. This being done, we will take up other questions, and dispose of them as they arise. Who could have anticipated, three years ago, that we would have progressed thus far? Let us, like wise men, hold ourselves in readiness to manage new questions which may arise in the future. There is no need of giving ourselves trouble prematurely. (doc. 14)

It would be several months before Andrew Johnson revealed his answers to the "other questions" regarding black civil rights. When Johnson took the oath of office on April 15, 1865, the most immediate issues for the new president involved reestablishing law and order in the

2. See Eric L. McKitrick, *Andrew Johnson and Reconstruction* (Chicago: University of Chicago Press, 1960), 126.

3. See McKitrick, *Andrew Johnson*, 90.

former Confederate states and securing ratification of the Thirteenth Amendment.

Two of Johnson's first moves were organizing state governments and appointing provisional governors in a number of the former rebel states. Johnson directed his appointed governors to hold conventions for "altering or amending" the states' constitutions and for each state to establish "a republican form of government" (doc. 23). This meant drafting state constitutions abolishing slavery and ratifying the proposed Thirteenth Amendment (doc. 24). If the former rebel states saw fit to go the extra mile and enfranchise educated blacks, Johnson believed this would "completely disarm" radicals who were "wild upon negro franchise" and who wished to "keep the southern states from renewing their relations to the Union" (doc. 24). Johnson hoped to facilitate the rapid readmission of the former rebel states, and he encouraged the provisional governments to pass laws protecting the civil rights of freedmen as a show of good faith. As Johnson wrote to Provisional Governor William L. Sharkey of Mississippi in November 1865, "It is earnestly hoped that your Legislature will without delay place the State in an attitude which will enable her to resume all Constitutional relations between her and the Federal Government. Let the Amendment to the Constitution of the United States, abolishing Slavery be adopted. Let such laws be passed for the protection of freedmen, in person and property, as Justice and equity demand" (doc. 30).

If the Southern states followed Johnson's advice, the Thirteenth Amendment would avoid "questionable" ratification by only Northern states. This would also pave the way for the Southern states' early readmission to the Union—Johnson's preference and one that marked a major political divide between the new president and congressional radical Republicans. The legislatures of the provisional state governments were dominated by white Southerners who knew chattel slavery was dead and who desired to have their states rejoin the Union as quickly as possible. If ratifying the proposed amendment facilitated their representatives' return to Congress, then there was little lost in doing so and little to be gained by refusing. Nevertheless, the Southern legislatures hesitated—not due to a desire to maintain slavery but because of concerns about the expansion of federal power under Section Two of the proposed amendment.

On November 1, 1865, South Carolina's provisional governor B. F. Perry wrote to Secretary of State William Seward regarding the state's progress toward ratifying the Thirteenth Amendment. According to Perry, members of the legislature had "no objection to adopting the first section of the amendment proposed" but feared "that the second section may be construed to give congress power of local legislation over the Negroes and white men, too, after the abolishment of slavery" (doc. 26). In late November 1865, the Mississippi legislature rejected the proposed amendment due to similar concerns about Section Two. According to a Mississippi legislative committee report:

> The committee cannot anticipate what construction future Congresses may put on this [second] section. It may be claimed that it would be "appropriate" for Congress to legislate in respect to freedmen in the State. This committee can hardly conceive of a more dangerous grant of power than one which, by construction, might admit federal legislation in respect to persons, denizens and inhabitants of the State.... The committee are apprehensive that if this second section be incorporated in the Constitution, radicals and extremists will further vex and harass the country on the pretension that the freedom of the colored race is not perfect and complete until it is elevated to a social and political equality with the white. (doc. 37)

A frustrated Andrew Johnson instructed Secretary Seward to respond to Southern states' concerns about Section Two. In a widely published letter to Provisional Governor Perry, Seward dismissed concerns about the potential breadth of congressional authority granted by Section Two of the Thirteenth Amendment. According to Seward, "The objection which you mention to the last clause of the constitutional amendment is regarded as querulous and unreasonable, because that clause is really restraining in its effect, instead of enlarging the powers of Congress" (doc. 27). Newspapers around the country reprinted and commented—both positively and critically—on Seward's dismissal of "querulous and unreasonable" constructions of Section Two (docs. 31, 32, 34, and 35).

On November 13, 1865, having been assured of a narrow construction of federal power, South Carolina ratified the Thirteenth Amendment. In doing so, however, the legislature added a statement of understanding to their official notice of ratification:

> *Resolved*, That any attempt by Congress towards legislating upon the political status of former slaves,

or their civil relations, would be contrary to the Constitution of the United States, as it now is, or as it would be altered by the proposed amendment, in conflict with the policy of the President declared in his Amnesty Proclamation, and with the restoration of that harmony upon which depends the vital interests of the American Union. (doc. 28)

On December 2, 1865, Alabama followed the same course as South Carolina, ratifying the amendment and declaring:

1st That the foregoing amendment to the Constitution of the United States, be and the same is hereby ratified to all intents and purposes as part of the Constitution of the United States,

2d *Be it further Resolved,* That this amendment to the constitution of the United States, is adopted by the Legislature of Alabama with the understanding that it does not confer upon Congress the power to Legislate upon the political status of Freedmen in this State. (doc. 38)

In Georgia, Provisional Governor James Johnson encouraged the state legislature to ratify the amendment and characterized concerns about the potential breadth of Section Two as "erroneous and unfounded and unwarranted, either by the language employed or the objects to be obtained" (doc. 39). According to Governor Johnson, "The Congress passing it, the different departments of the Government, and most of the Legislatures of the several States ratifying it, construe the amendment to be nothing more or less than a declaration against involuntary servitude, conferring therewith on Congress the restricted power to carry such declaration into execution by necessary and proper laws. Such is the natural import of the language employed, and such doubtless will be the construction given it by the different departments of the Government in all controversies that may hereafter arise" (doc. 39).

The Georgia legislature briefly considered adding an explanatory clause similar to those added by South Carolina and Alabama but ultimately rejected the idea and simply ratified the amendment on December 6, 1865 (doc. 40).

When Georgia ratified the Thirteenth Amendment, it became the twenty-seventh state to do so. As of December 1865, if one counted every state in the United States (including West Virginia and the states of the former Confederacy), the United States consisted of thirty-six

states. If all the state ratifications were deemed valid, then Georgia's vote meant that the Thirteenth Amendment had met the three-quarter majority required by Article V for national ratification. On December 18, 1865, a few days after the opening session of the Thirty-Ninth Congress, Secretary of State Seward announced Congress's ratification of the Thirteenth Amendment (doc. 42). In doing so, he rejected radical Republican theories of rebel "state suicide" and counted the votes of every ratifying state in both North and South.

The focus of constitutional and political debate now turned to the legal rights of the Southern freedmen. Although the Thirteenth Amendment had abolished slavery, a number of Southern states continued to enforce older (or newly enacted) "black codes," which constrained the personal and economic liberties of freedmen. In a November speech delivered to the National Equal Suffrage Association in Washington, DC, newly elected Louisiana senator Michael Hahn warned that these codes were meant to keep freedmen in a state of quasi-slavery:

If we permit a town council to ordain that colored persons shall not remain within the corporate limits, except during certain hours of the day, and then only with a written pass from their former owners as employers, and to prescribe a punishment for persons who may transact business with or lease rooms or houses to colored persons without such written permit, we permit the institution of slavery still to exist shorn of its name. I have read, even since my arrival in this city and in your own papers, ordinances passed at Franklin and elsewhere in Louisiana, which contain such provisions. This discrimination against the colored man cannot be allowed to continue, if we are earnest in desiring freedom to all men.

The freedom of speech and of discussion on subjects so sacred as those connected with the rights of man; the right of the people to keep and bear arms, and peaceably to assemble and petition the Government for a redress of grievances, should be secured to all citizens alike. (doc. 33)

Although Section Two of the Thirteenth Amendment authorized Congress to enforce the abolition amendment, not even civil rights advocates were sure that the amendment authorized congressional protection of black civil rights. In their *Equal Suffrage Address,* Virginia freedmen warned that ratifying the Thirteenth

Amendment would have no effect on the Southern black codes, writing, "[E]ven the late constitutional amendment, if duly ratified, can go no further; neither touch, nor can touch, the slave codes of the various southern States, and the laws respecting free people of color consequent therefrom, which, having been passed before the act of secession, are presumed to have lost none of their vitality, but exist, as a convenient engine for our oppression, until repealed by special acts of the State legislatures."

To the signatories of the address, the only effective solution to such discriminatory state legislation was black suffrage. Giving freedmen the ballot was not only necessary—it was also their constitutional right as citizens of the United States:

We have now shown you, to the best of our ability, the necessity of the recognition of the right of suffrage for our own protection, and have suggested a few of the reasons why it is expedient you should grant us that right; but while we stand before you, pleading with you, for our fellows, on the grounds of humanity and political expediency, we would not have you forget that our case also stands on the basis of constitutional right. No sane person will for a moment contend that color or birth are recognized by the Constitution of the United States as any bar to the acquisition or enjoyment of citizenship. (doc. 25)

In this, the freedmen echoed Frederick Douglass, who had been making the same point ever since the Thirteenth Amendment had first been sent to the states for ratification. In a February 1865 speech published in the *Liberator*, Douglass insisted that the North seize the moment and grant freedmen the right to vote:

I am for the "immediate, unconditional and universal" enfranchisement of the black man in every State in the Union. (Loud applause.) Without this, his liberty is a mockery; without this, you might as well almost retain the old name of slavery for his condition. ... I fear that if we fail to do it now, if Abolitionists fail to press it now, we may not see, for centuries to come, the same disposition that exists at this moment. (Applause.) Hence, I say, now is the time to press this right. (doc. 12)

Abolitionists such as Wendell Phillips agreed with Douglass. Although Phillips supported suffrage for both blacks and women, he believed that "we must take up

but one question at a time, and this hour belongs exclusively to the negro" (doc. 22). The focus on black suffrage became an increasingly pronounced bone of contention between civil rights advocates and women's rights advocates such as Susan B. Anthony and Elizabeth Cady Stanton (see, e.g., vol. 2, 1A, doc. 11).

Despite these early calls for black suffrage, most Republicans avoided the topic and focused instead on the potential need for federal legislation protecting freedmen's civil rights. Since there appeared to be little, if any, authorization for such legislation in the text of the original Constitution, the scope of Section Two quickly became a topic of public debate. In his intentionally published letters to the Southern provisional governors, President Johnson signaled his administration's narrow interpretation of Section Two. Radical Republicans, in turn, rejected Johnson's reading of the amendment and plotted how they might establish a broader reading when members of the Thirty-Ninth Congress took their seats in December. In a November letter to Massachusetts senator Henry Wilson, General Benjamin Butler advised that the incoming Thirty-Ninth Congress publicly declare their broad interpretation of Section Two and rely on the same in passing civil rights legislation (doc. 36).

Aware that the issue would dominate the next session of Congress, newspapers published battling editorials regarding the meaning and scope of the pending Thirteenth Amendment. According to Portland, Maine's *Daily Eastern Argus*, "The construction put upon the amendment by President Johnson is the only fair one. That claimed by the radicals is absurd" (doc. 31). The *New York Tribune*, on the other hand, editorialized that "hereafter, Congress is charged with the duty of protecting in the full enjoyment of his liberties each inhabitant of our country, and clothed with the power requisite to its fulfillment of this high obligation. Congress now has power to 'legislate for the negroes'" (doc. 32). Similarly, the *New York Daily Tribune* lamented that "[w]e are at a loss to imagine what the President intends by his construction of the second clause of the article above quoted. As matter of history appearing from the debates in Congress it is certain that section was intended by its movers and by the two Houses which adopted it to confer upon Congress full power to secure real as well as nominal freedom to slaves" (doc. 34). The *New York Times* took a position somewhere in the middle, suggesting that "[i]t will be the duty of Congress, under this Amendment, to see that this freedom of labor is preserved; but further than that, Congress will have no cognizance" (doc. 35).

As pressing as was the issue of black civil rights, equally pressing was the ratified amendment's potential impact on Republican political power. Under the original Constitution, slaves counted as three-fifths of a person for the purpose of determining membership in the House of Representatives and the electoral college (part 1, section C, docs. 6 and 7). Once freed, the former slaves would count as a full, five-fifths person, thus *increasing* the political power of the former rebel states upon their readmission to Congress. As long as blacks remained disenfranchised, ratifying the Thirteenth Amendment could have the ironic effect of derailing the Republican effort to secure freedom for blacks in the South.

Early in the ratification process, Republican strategists recognized the potential problem and began to grapple with the political windfall Democrats would enjoy upon the ratification of the Thirteenth Amendment. On February 4, 1865, the *New York Tribune* published a letter from Francis Lieber[4] to Senator E. D. Morgan in which Lieber explained the problematic relationship between the three-fifths clause and the Thirteenth Amendment:

If, then, "all other persons," that is slaves, are declared free, and the foregoing provision of the Constitution is not amended, we simply add two-fifths to the basis of apportionment of Representatives in the Southern States; in other words, the number of Representatives in Congress from the States in which slavery has existed will be increased by the present amendment. As, however, these States, and especially those in which the colored citizens exceed in number the whites, will not give the common suffrage to the citizens of African extraction, (as, indeed, many of the Northern States, for instance, Pennsylvania, do not give it, and as other States give the right of voting to colored people on the condition of possessing freeholds only,) the result of the amendment as now proposed, without an additional amendment, would be an increased number of Southern Representatives in Congress of the same number of white citi-

zens. In this case the rebellion, though ultimately subdued at the cost of torrents of our blood and streams of our wealth, would be rewarded with an enlarged representation. No loyal citizen can wish for such a consummation. How is the difficulty to be avoided? (doc. 5)

Lieber's proposed solution was the addition of a fourteenth amendment along the following lines:

"Representatives shall be apportioned among the several States which may be included within this Union, according to the respective numbers of citizens having the qualifications requisite for electing members of the most numerous branch of the respective State Legislatures. The actual enumeration of said citizens shall be regularly made by the census of the United States, but a special census shall take place before the next new apportionment of representatives shall be made by the Congress of the United States." ... Believing, as I do, that this subject deserves the attention of the American people, I have not hesitated to make use of your permission to address to you this public letter.

During the Thirteenth Amendment ratification debates, Democrats cited Lieber's letter as evidence that the Republicans would not be satisfied with merely one constitutional amendment. As state representative Leon Abbett warned his colleagues during the New Jersey ratification debates, "Gentlemen imagine that this amendment will end this negro discussion. On the contrary, its adoption will only serve to open the door to the most disturbing questions. This initiative legislation is only the beginning of the end" (doc. 18). Freedmen's associations also were aware of the Thirteenth Amendment's potential increase of Southern Democrats' voting power, and they used the issue in support of their demands for suffrage. In their June 1865 *Equal Suffrage Address*, the "Colored Citizens of Norfolk, Virginia" explained to their brothers in the North:

You have not unreasonably complained of the operation of that clause of the Constitution which has hitherto permit the slavocracy of the South to wield the political influence which would be represented by a white population equal to three fifths of the whole negro population; but slavery is now abolished, and henceforth the representation will be in proportion to the enumeration of the whole population of the South, *including people of color,*

---

4. According to Michael Les Benedict, Francis Lieber was, at that time, "the most influential political theoretician in America." See Michael Les Benedict, *A Compromise of Principle* (New York: Norton, 1974), 74.

and it is worth your consideration if it is desirable or politic that the fomenters of this rebellion against the Union, which has been crushed at the expense of so much blood and treasure, should find themselves, after defeat, more powerful than ever, their political influence enhanced by the additional voting power of the other two fifths of the colored population, by which means four Southern votes will balance in the Congressional and Presidential elections at least seven Northern ones. (doc. 25)

Although the looming problem of Democrats' increased representational power was clear, politically acceptable solutions were not. One option was to refuse Southern states' readmission until adequate protections for freedmen were securely in place. But how could Republicans justify excluding any state from Congress whose vote had been counted for the purpose of ratifying the Thirteenth Amendment? And how could Southern states be treated as "outside" the Union when for four years Republicans had claimed that *no state* could ever legitimately claim to be "out" of the Union? Republicans thus faced a difficult choice: either they could accept the ratification votes of the Southern states and readmit their representatives to Congress, or they could refuse them readmission and deny the need for their ratification votes on the questionable grounds that they had successfully exited the Union. On December 20, 1865, the *New York Times* commented on the ratified amendment and the conundrum facing Republicans, reporting, "The Executive Department, which certifies to the ratification of the amendment by eight of the late insurrectionary States, is but consistent in remitting to them, as fast as possible, the full exercise of all powers. Congress, however urged by extreme men, will not dare to dispute the ratification, and undo the legal effect of the certificate. And yet it must either go that desperate length, or soon, by an inexorable logical necessity, admit the rights of all the States to be constitutionally represented in its seats" (doc. 42).

In the end, Republicans of the Thirty-Ninth Congress would attempt to cut the Gordian knot by both counting the ratification votes of the Southern states *and* excluding their representatives from Congress. Doing so would set the stage for a dramatic standoff between the Democrat president and the Republican Congress — a standoff that would trigger national debate regarding the constitutional status of the Republican Congress and the need for a fourteenth amendment.

1

"The Constitutional Abolition of Slavery—The Great Measure of the Age," *New York Herald*

February 2, 1865, p. 4

The proposition which has been adopted by both houses of Congress for the incorporation into the federal constitution of an amendment ordaining that "neither slavery nor involuntary servitude, except as punishment for crime, whereof the party shall have been duly convicted, shall exist within the United States or any place subject to their jurisdiction," may justly be placed at the head of all the legislative measures of the government from the beginning as the great distinguishing measure of the age. It marks a new era in our political history and a new departure in the great work of restoring the Union and of widening its political and moral influence among the nations of the earth.

We are especially gratified at the success of this great measure, considering the earnest support which it has received through our editorial columns from the beginning. After a careful examination of the slavery question at the last session of Congress, embracing the irreparable damages inflicted upon the institution by this terrible war, and the "confusion worse confounded" resulting from the tinkering, illegal and incongruous emancipation experiments of President Lincoln and Congress, we reached these conclusions: first, that this institution of slavery must die; secondly, that the time had come for a national settlement of the question; and thirdly, that the settlement provided in the constitution of the United States, and nothing else, would be a valid, complete and conclusive settlement. In the outset the chances of success to this important movement in the present Congress were exceedingly doubtful. It was, upon its first trial, defeated in the House; but since that day, the voice of the people in the Presidential election, the great and impressive achievements of our army and navy, and the abolition projects that have been agitated by Jeff. Davis and his rebel confederates, have reversed the House vote of the last session, and passed this constitutional measure over to the ratification of the States.

All that is wanted now to incorporate this amendment into the constitution, as a part of the "supreme law of the land," is the ratification by a majority in each house of the Legislatures of three-fourths of the thirty-six States belonging to the Union. Can this be done? It can. We have no doubt of it. The loyal States, including the late slave States of Maryland, Missouri, West Virginia, Arkansas, Louisiana, and Tennessee, and the slave States of Delaware and Kentucky, number twenty-eight, or three-fourths of the whole number. Every one of these States, we believe, as soon as prepared for authoritative action, will endorse the measure, assuming that in some of them the vote cannot fairly be taken until something more shall be done than has been done in the work of their reclamation from the rebellion. But before the end of the year we expect the decisive fact to be recorded that three-fourths of the States have ratified this constitutional amendment, and that slavery is thus extinguished throughout the country, and that all our political troubles resulting from it are at an end.

In this view we hope to record the State of New York—first in population, wealth and political power in the Union—as first in this ratification. Governor Fenton has already called the attention of the two houses of the Legislature to the subject, and they will probably act upon it to-day or to-morrow. If not, we may expect to be beaten by a half dozen other States. Kentucky, set down in the negative, with New Jersey and Delaware, by the *Tribune*, is zealously taking the slavery bull by the horns, and will unquestionably bring him to the ground. The Presidential election and the late abolition ordinances of the Tennessee State Convention have brought about a complete revolution in Kentucky. Her Legislature, we predict, will be among the first in the field for the ratification. Nor have we the slightest misgiving in reference to New Jersey or Delaware; for the prevailing current of public opinion will carry everything before it. This pressure of public opinion, which has carried over the balance of power from the democratic party in Congress to the support of this constitutional amendment, will carry it over all the broken elements of opposition in the several States, including the rebellious States as they are reclaimed.

We are informed that Mr. Seward attached great importance to the passage of this proposition through Congress, as the initial point for negotiations for peace with Jeff. Davis on the basis of a reconstruction of the Union; that Davis, thus being headed off on the slavery question, at home and abroad, has intimated his readiness to give up his confederacy as a hopeless cause. What-

ever may be the truth upon this point, it will suffice for the present that this constitutional abolition of slavery is secured; that it will kill off Southern fire-eaters and Northern abolitionists, in removing from the country this fearful bone of contention, this combustible institution of slavery, this firebrand of sectional agitations, election riots, border ruffianism and civil war. We may look forward now to a reconstruction of the Union, of our political parties, and of Northern and Southern society upon a harmonious footing; and we may as confidently expect, whether all these volunteer and informal peace missions are moonshine or green cheese, that the armed resistance of the rebellion, root and branch, will now very speedily be utterly demoralized, broken up, dispersed and dissolved.

2

"Speech of Mr. Lincoln on the Constitutional Amendment," *New York Herald*

February 3, 1865, p. 8

WASHINGTON, FEB. 2, 1865.
The serenading party last night having played several airs before the White House, the President appeared at the centre upper window under the portico, and was greeted with loud cheers.

The President said he supposed the passage through Congress of the constitutional amendment for the abolishment of slavery throughout the United States was the occasion to which he was indebted for the honor of this call. (Applause.) The occasion was one of congratulation to the country and to the whole world. But there is a task yet before us—to go forward and consummate by the vote of the States that which Congress so nobly began yesterday. (Applause, and cries "They will do it," &c.) He had the honor to inform those present that Illinois had already to day done the work. (Applause.) Maryland was about half through; but he felt proud that Illinois was a little ahead. He thought this measure was a very fitting, if not an indispensable adjunct to the winding up of the great difficulty. (Applause.) He wished the reunion of all the States perfected, and so effective as to remove all causes of disturbance in the future; and to attain this and it was necessary that the original disturbing cause should, if possible, be rooted out. He thought all would bear him witness that he had never shrunk from doing all that he could to eradicate slavery by issuing an emancipation proclamation. (Applause.) But that proclamation falls far short of what the amendment will be when fully consummated. A question might be raised whether the proclamation was legally valid. It might be added that it only aided those who came into our lines, and that it was inoperative as to those who did not give themselves up, or that it would have no effect upon the children of the slaves born hereafter. In fact, it would be urged that it did not meet the evil. But this amendment is a king's cure for all the evils. (Applause.) It winds the whole thing up. He would repeat that it was the fitting, if not indispensable adjunct, to the consummation of the great game we are playing. He could not but congratulate all present, himself, the country and the whole world, upon this great moral victory.

3

New York, Governor Fenton's Message, Speeches and Vote on the Abolition Amendment, *Albany Evening Journal*

February 1–4, 1865

FEBRUARY 1, 1865, P. 3[*]
"The Constitutional Amendment Congratulatory Message of the Governor to the Legislature"
    State of New York
    Executive Department
    Albany, Feb. 1, 1865
    To the Legislature:
A proposition to amend the Federal Constitution forever abolishing Slavery throughout the United States has been adopted by both Houses of Congress. I lose no time in calling your attention to this great event, for the purpose of recommending that immediate measures be taken for a ratification of the proposed amendment by this State. The importance of this action of Congress,

[*] [See also *Journal of the Assembly of the State of New York* (Albany, 1865), 201–2. —Ed.]

in opening the way for the extinguishment of Slavery, cannot be overestimated. Our National history presents nothing of greater consequence. The institution of Slavery—always an element of discord—has more than once threatened the country with civil war.

At length the menaced evil came, but the strength of the Rebellious power is slowly waning, and under Providence the violent and wicked outbreak which has so severely tried the endurance and patriotism of the people is giving way. At this opportune period Congress provides a measure which will forever remove this source of strife and national disaster. If the States exhibit the wisdom of the National Legislature, it may be done. To this end let us hope and let us act. Then the day is not distant when the Constitution of the United States will harmonize with the Declaration of Independence—the Nation will be free!

I am confident that the ratification of the amendment by the States will form a sure guarantee of the future prosperity, security and peace of our common country; and I see no reason why the Legislature may not act in this matter at once. Such a course would comport with the dignity and power of New York as well as with her conceded influence in the sisterhood of States. Let her Legislature be the first to act. Let Slavery be abolished so far as New York can do it; and I could wish that it might be done without a dissenting voice. Is it not an occasion for us to act together? Why, then, can we not unite now that the opportunity is presented to remove an institution which has not only been productive of evil, but which has done so much to demoralize our social condition and embitter our political action.

    R. E. FENTON.

FEBRUARY 3, 1865, P. 2
Speech of Senator Bailey
In Senate—February 2.
Mr. President—When I offered this resolution yesterday, I hoped it would pass without a dissenting voice. I supposed that all men of all parties, here at the North, were prepared to take this step so necessary for the settlement of our national difficulties. I thought our legislature would hail this amendment with joy, and hasten to impress the State's broad seal of approval upon it.

But Slavery dies hard. It has long been in its death throe, apparently, but its friends, by assiduous nursing, have so far been able to preserve some signs of vitality. This devotion is not very wonderful, after all. As hideous as this monster is, there are vast interests personal and political dependent upon its life. Although it is sustained by the sweat and groans of four millions of human beings, yet it gives fortunes to its attendants, and political importance to its worshippers.

But perhaps I should say that this once was so. It is hardly true at present. Its power to reward is gone. Its followers at the South are Rebels liable to swift destruction, and the faithful at the North are fugitives and wanderers vainly seeking the power and offices which their souls love. But notwithstanding their deplorable case, a few of their number still cling doggedly to Slavery and defend its right to rule pertinaciously as when it governed the Nation. To them, it is a divine institution more sacred than the honor, the integrity—nay, than the existence of the country. All these must be sacrificed, if need be, that Slavery may live. It may rebel against the Government, mangle and kill hundreds of thousands of our citizens, fill hundreds of thousands of hearts with anguish, load our people with taxation and cover the land with carnage; and yet no man must raise his head against it.

Again, there are those who say that they are willing that Slavery should perish, but insist that it should die by its own volition. There are others who concede that our armies may strike it down when they find it in their way. These last forget and ignore the fact that Slavery is the creature of law, and that it can only be effectively destroyed by law. It may be weakened and rendered unprofitable by contact with our armies, but it can only be eradicated by legal or constitutional enactment.

It is insisted here that there is no power to amend the Constitution so as to prohibit Slavery in the States without the consent of each State to be affected thereby. In other words, that an amendment proposed by Congress and adopted by two-thirds of the States, would be void as to any Slave State not assenting thereto. This is equivalent to saying that the people of the United States have not the power to prohibit Slavery by an amendment of the Constitution, adopted in the manner prescribed by article five of that instrument. This argument is based upon that pernicious and fallacious doctrine of "State Rights," so industriously taught of late—a doctrine invented by John C. Calhoun, adopted by Slavery as its rule of faith and conduct; and which has resulted in this horrible rebellion at the South, and threats of rebellion here at the North.

It holds that the States are so completely sovereign and independent, in all matters not conferred upon the general government by the Constitution, the nation has no power to take from it any one of its present rights or privileges. This is saying in effect, that after the formation of the present constitution, it was impossible to confer upon the national government any new, further or additional powers, because, in so doing, just so much power would be taken away from the several States.

This argument also is forced to the logical conclusion that the Union is a confederation and the Constitution a covenant or compact between sovereign States.

As has been proved a thousand times, the Constitution of the United States was formed by the people, and not by the States. It created a nation—not a confederation. This Constitution was to be the "supreme law of the land, anything in the constitutions or laws of any of the States to the contrary notwithstanding." The nation is thus sovereign—the States are subordinate. This Constitution provides for its own amendment. It authorizes it to be done in a certain prescribed manner, but it does not define the nature or character of the amendments which may be made. The power to amend is general and unlimited; there is no restriction whatever. These amendments are to be added in the same manner as the original instrument was framed. They are to be adopted by the people; for what they do through their authorized agents, they do themselves. But it is scarcely possible to add an amendment to the Constitution without interfering with the rights, or restraining the powers theretofore exercised by the States, or by taking directly from the States some of their privileges and powers and transferring them to the general government. This may be illustrated by examining the amendment proposed and adopted in 1789.

Article two of these amendments declares that the right to keep and bear arms shall not be infringed. Prior to this, the States had the entire control of this matter, and here that control is taken away. And it may be well to inquire why, if the people may amend the Constitution so as to secure to all the right to use the arms furnished by the gunsmith, they may not so amend it as to secure to all the right to use the arms given to them by the Almighty?

Again, articles four, five and six prescribe the limits within which search warrants may issue—require the presentment of a Grand Jury in order to hold a person to answer a capital or otherwise infamous crime—protect criminals from being witnesses against themselves, prevent private property from being taken for public use, without just compensation—require that criminals shall have the assistance of counsel—make a trial by jury necessary in all cases at common law, and preventing any fact tried by jury from being re-examined in any Court than according to the rules of the common law.

These are broad sweeping provisions retaining the powers of the States in many important particulars, and over all of which, they had entire jurisdiction and control prior to the adoption of these amendments. Here then are many important instances in which an amendment of the Constitution has taken away from the States powers they previously possessed, and otherwise interfere with what are here called their "reserved rights." And if it be true that there is no power to take away or interfere with their "rights"—then the amendments of 1789 are void.

It is manifest that the people in framing the Constitution, took just so much from the powers of the States as was necessary for the purpose, and conferred them upon the General Government, and at the same time reserved to themselves by this Fifth Article, right to take just so much more in the future, as might become necessary. In fact they reserved for themselves the same right to amend this Constitution, which the people of the States have to amend theirs. And inasmuch as they had the right when they made and adopted the Constitution to confer upon the government thereby created any powers they deemed necessary, and to restrict and limit the powers of the States—whether in regard to coining money, levying war, enslaving negroes, or anything else; so when they amend that instrument, they may determine these and similar subjects at pleasure. In other words, the people have the same power over any and all subjects when amending the Constitution, that they had when framing it. In both cases they act in their independent sovereign capacity, and no power on earth can control them.

...

Speech of Senator Hastings

Mr. HASTINGS said he perceived that some Senators had prepared to debate this question, and he disliked to make any remarks off hand upon so important a matter, but there were one or two points he desired to present.

First. The Constitution may be amended in any manner which tends to carry out or accomplish more effectually the aims of its framers and adopters, and the objects for which it was established.

Second. That this amendment is eminently calculated to further those aims and objects.

When the Convention framed and the people adopted the Constitution, they formed a government differing in many respects from any which had ever existed. It was an almost untried experiment. The Convention foresaw that by the light of experience amendments, changes might be found to be necessary or desirable. The practical workings of the new Government might develop defects in the organic law, or changes of circumstances which might be produced by time, might call for corresponding changes in that law, therefore the Constitution itself wisely provides for its own amendment, and fixes the manner in which the amendment shall be made.

But these changes must relate to matters which are legitimately within the scope and efforts of governments.

Now let us see what was designed to be effectual and accomplished by the Constitution. (Mr. H. read from the preamble), *"We the People of the United States in order to form a more perfect Union, establish justice, ensure domestic tranquility, provide for the common defense, promote the general welfare, and secure the blessings of liberty to ourselves and our posterity do ordain and establish this Constitution."*

Now will the tendency of this contemplated amendment, if adopted, be to further these avowed objects—to carry them out to accomplish them, or will it not?

The Senator from the 3d. (Mr. Murphy) takes the ground that this amendment can be adopted only as the Constitution itself was adopted, and that it can be binding only on those States which assent to it. But this clearly is not so. Of course the Constitution was not binding upon any State until assented to. It was a new compact or agreement, but when assented, all its provisions are binding, and one of those provisions is that three quarters of the States may adopt amendments which shall be binding upon the other fourth, with or without their assent. By that bargain they are now bound. Without this provision for amendment it would have been necessary that each amendment should be ratified by every state. Now it is not necessary. It is by virtue of their bargain we bind them. And it was a good bargain. The power is safely reposed in three quarters of the states. There is no danger that it will be abused.

Mr. MURPHY—"Will the Senator from the 12ᵗʰ (Mr. H.) permit me one question?"

Mr. HASTINGS—"Certainly, sir."

Mr. M.—"Can the people of the United States establish Slavery in the State of New York without her consent?"

Mr. H.—"As a mere question of political power, I have no doubt they may so amend the Constitution as to do that thing."

Mr. M.—"Without her consent?"

Mr. H. Without her consent. But there is no danger of their doing so.

. . .

FEBRUARY 4, 1865, P. 2
*Debate in the Assembly on the Joint Resolution
to Ratify the Constitutional Amendment*
Remarks of Hon. Mr. Gleason

Mr. SPEAKER—The action of Congress upon the amendment to the Constitution of the United States prohibiting Slavery has been awaited with the deepest interest, not by our country alone, but by all civilized nations. Our decision was to determine whether we were to be, as we claimed, the leaders of human progress, or whether we were to prove false to our own teachings, and to retrograde from our high standard. Amid anxiety and doubt and fear, the moment came! Taught by our past history, taught by our own consciousness, taught, above all, by the bitter experience of four years of civil war, we have at last learned the lesson that Slavery, being incompatible with a free government, should be abolished. In 1865 Congress completes the work of 1776, and proclaims to the world that we are *now* a nation of freemen.

. . .

Remarks of Mr. Keegan

Mr. KEEGAN protested against the passage of this resolution as an encroachment upon the rights of the States. It was not within our province to interfere with the domestic affairs of Georgia or South Carolina. In behalf of his constituents, he protested against this attempted innovation upon the rights of the States.

Remarks of Mr. Van Buren

Mr. SPEAKER—I do not intend to make any extended remarks at the present time, but beg the indulgence of the house to say a few words upon this grave and important subject.

Sir, the important fact gathered from history, that all great wars have resulted in good to the human race, is strikingly exemplified in the progress of this contest. Since the days of the Jews, the hand of Providence, it appears to me, has never been more evident than in the affairs of this country during the past few years.

The heart of Pharaoh was never more hardened, the eyes of the Egyptians were never more blinded, than have been those of the enemies of this Republic in their strange devotion to the hideous institution of Slavery. And now the waters of the Red Sea are sweeping their hosts to destruction.

. . .

Men talk to us of the unconstitutionality of amending the Constitution upon the subject of Slavery.

Sir, what is a Constitution? It is neither more nor less than a compact made by the people of the United States, for their better government, and the preservation of their rights, and it contains, within itself, a provision for its own amendment.

I find no limit, sir, to that power. Can it be possible that any man in his senses can gravely argue, that the sovereign People, who created the Constitution, have no power to amend it?

If so, that instrument instead of being the expressed voice of a free people, is the veriest despotism the world ever saw. The right to amend has never been disputed until it is proposed to touch the institution of Slavery. What is there sacred about Slavery? Why cannot the people rid themselves of an evil so foul and fatal as chattel bondage?

I am surprised, I am disappointed the grand old Democratic Party, of which I was once proud to be a member, when Freedom is the watchword and not Slavery, is putting itself upon record against this great measure of progress.

. . .

Remarks of Mr. Creamer

. . .

I shall at once proceed to briefly answer the gentleman from Suffolk, and to inform him why it is that the Democratic members of this House cannot make the vote on these resolutions unanimous by voting for their adoption. To my mind there are two most formidable and convincing reasons why the action of Congress should not be ratified by this Legislature. The first objection, sir, that occurs to me is that the immediate abolition of slavery throughout the States is both unwise and impolitic. The ablest statesmen of our country in the past have always scouted such an idea as being neither safe nor judicious. The best friends of the negro in former days, when fanaticism and prejudice did not cloud their reason, always pronounced immediate emancipation as being dangerous both to the interest of the country and of the blacks themselves. President

Lincoln himself, no longer ago than the Fall of 1862, in his annual message to Congress, discussed and defended the impropriety of giving immediate freedom to the negro. He, on that occasion, you will remember Mr. Speaker, proposed and submitted a plan of colonization to Congress, and in the case of the failure of his scheme, he thought that gradual emancipation, to be consummated about the year 1900, was the only remedy that remained for the disposition of this vexed question.

. . .

The condition of the negroes of the South in the past days of Southern life I am afraid was a paradise to the fate that awaits the laboring white man of the North. The inevitable weight and hardship that taxation will impose on the poor this time forward, will, sir, be enough to bear, without piling on besides the millions of money that it will take to pay for the sustenance of three millions of helpless negroes.

But, sir, I am influenced by more cogent and forcible reasons than these, in the course that I pursue in opposing these resolutions, and in my determination to vote against them. The unconstitutionality of Congress in the adoption of the proposed amendment, is to my mind the most insurmountable objection of all that can be offered against them. . . . That the General Government is one made up of powers delegated by the several States, cannot but be admitted by every intelligent and fair-minded citizen. Their harmonious working of our State and National Governments has in days past been the admiration of leading statesmen at home and abroad. The National Government, with its powers enumerated and prescribed, seldom conflicting with the reserve rights of the States, presented a masterpiece of statesmanship that the world never witnessed before.

. . .

In connection with this, I will refer you to Article 10, "Amendments to the Constitution of the United States," which expressly declares that powers not delegated to the United States are reserved to the States respectively. Now, in the adoption of the Federal Constitution, the several States either delegated to the United States or reserved to themselves the power to abolish Slavery; which course did they pursue? . . . Here the question occurs, how do we know that they did not? Why, sir, by the subsequent action of every State in the North in exercising the power they had never delegated, in abolishing Slavery themselves. Either the States had power to abolish Slavery or the United States had the power; the States themselves, therefore, in exercising the power,

prove conclusively that it was never given to the National Government—it never had the power, it has not the power to-day.

. . .

Remarks of Mr. G. Parker

Mr. G. PARKER was astonished to see any man rise on this floor, and oppose a measure which was to give freedom to four million slaves. He had given his time, his money, and his blood in this glorious cause; yet to-day was the proudest day of his life. The gentleman from New York (Mr. CREAMER) had referred to the Constitutional question. He asked him to show him anything in the Constitution, or anything in the Debates of the Fathers of the Constitution which says we cannot amend the instrument in this particular. We are called upon to amend the Constitution in a manner in strict accordance with its provisions. He was astonished that any man should deny this power.

. . .

Remarks of Mr. L. J. Burditt

. . .

I am in favor of as speedy a termination of this civil war as is consistent with a restoration of the Union under the Constitution, as it is.

I am also in favor of the abolition of Slavery in the States wherein it now exists, in the same manner as it has heretofore been abolished in the free States where it formerly existed, giving to other States, over a strictly local matter, the same right we have heretofore exercised and enjoyed.

I am not in favor at this time of amending the Constitution of the United States. I prefer that Slavery should be abolished by proclamation as a war measure, or as a military necessity, than by an amendment to the Constitution, believing that the amendment would tend to prolong the war and prevent the restoration of the Union.

That it would deprive the States, as such, of a right heretofore held to be sacred and inalienable—the right to permit or prohibit Slavery. I shall therefore vote against the resolution.

Remarks of Mr. Shephard

Mr. SHEPHARD favored the resolutions because they stood out as a great headland in human history. The first of those epochs was the giving of the Ten Commandments, then the advent of Christ, then the reformation of Martin Luther, then the Declaration of Independence, and now the enunciation of the idea of Universal Freedom.*

4

"The Great Amendment; Progress of Ratification," *New York Tribune*

February 4, 1865, p. 1

NEW YORK

Albany, Friday, Feb. 3, 1865.

The following is the vote of the Assembly of New York on the resolutions ratifying the action of Congress on the Slavery Prohibition Amendment:

Yeas ... 72

Nays ... 40

Mr. Penfield was the only Democrat voting in the affirmative.

The following is the vote of the Senate on the same proposition:

Yeas [17]†

Nays [8]

When the Amendment to abolish Slavery passed the Assembly this afternoon, a salute of one hundred guns was fired by order of Adjt. Gen. Irvin.

...

MASSACHUSETTS

Boston, Friday, Feb. 3, 1865.

Both branches of the Massachusetts Legislature this afternoon unanimously passed the bill ratifying the Constitutional Amendment abolishing Slavery.

MARYLAND

Baltimore, Friday, Feb. 3, 1865.

The Senate of Maryland today passed the Constitutional Amendment abolishing Slavery in concurrence with the action of the House previously reported.

PENNSYLVANIA

Harrisburg, Pa., Friday, Feb. 3, 1865.

Both Branches of the Legislature to-day adopted a bill ratifying the Constitutional Amendment abolishing Slavery.

WEST VIRGINIA

Wheeling, W. Va., Friday, Feb. 3, 1865.

The Congressional amendment abolishing Slavery in the United States was unanimously ratified by both branches of the West Virginia Legislature to-day.

5

"Dr. Lieber's Letter to Senator E. D. Morgan on the Amendment of the Constitution Extinguishing Slavery," *New York Tribune*

February 4, 1865, p. 1†

SIR:—As the election, on the 8th of November last, has added one of the highest national acts to the history of our time, so the amendment of the Constitution which yesterday passed the House of Representatives, will be the greatest effect of the present revolt, if, as we all hope, three-fourths of the State Legislatures give their assent.

The same year, 1788, saw the framing of our Constitution and the first cultivation of the cotton-plant in Georgia; and in course of time this textile plant gave renewed vitality and expansion to slavery, festering in our great polity, until the gangrene broke out in the deep woe of a wide and bitter civil war. The year 1865 will cure our system of this poisonous malady. Seventy-seven years is a long period; the reckless rebellion has brought grief to all and anguish to many hearts, but if the effect of the fevered period be the throwing off of the malignant virus, the Nation will stand purified, and the dire inconsistency which has existed so long between our Bill of Rights of the Fourth of July, and our fostering protection of extending bondage will at last pass away. The sacrifices which we have made will not have been too great.

---

* [The New York Senate voted to ratify the amendment on February 2. The Assembly ratified the amendment the next day on a vote of 72 to 40. See *Journal of the Assembly of the State of New York* (1865), 226. See also "New York Has Spoken!," *Albany Evening Journal*, Feb. 3, 1865, 3. —Ed.]

† [Here the paper lists the names of the senators. —Ed.]

† [The same letter was published in the *New York Times*, Feb. 6, 1865, 5. —Ed.]

The amendment which is now offered to the American people runs thus:

"NEITHER SLAVERY NOR INVOLUNTARY SERVITUDE, EXCEPT AS A PUNISHMENT FOR CRIME, WHEREOF THE PARTY SHALL HAVE BEEN DULY CONVICTED, SHALL EXIST WITHIN THE UNITED STATES, OR ANY PLACE SUBJECT TO THEIR JURISDICTION."

These are simple and straightforward words, allowing of no equivocation, yet, considered in connection with some passages in the Constitution, they require some remarks, which I address to you, Sir, as one of the United States Senators from New York, and as my neighbor in this city.

The amendment extinguishes slavery in the whole dominion of the United States. The Constitution as it now stands, (Article 1, section 2, paragraph 3,) however, directs that Representatives "shall be apportioned among the several States, which may be included within the Union, according to their respective numbers, which shall be determined by adding to the whole number of free persons, including those bound to service for a term of years, and, excluding Indians not taxed, three-fifths of all other persons."

If, then, "all other persons," that is slaves, are declared free, and the foregoing provision of the Constitution is not amended, we simply add two-fifths to the basis of apportionment of Representatives in the Southern States; in other words, the number of Representatives in Congress from the States in which slavery has existed will be increased by the present amendment. As, however, these States, and especially those in which the colored citizens exceed in number the whites, will not give the common suffrage to the citizens of African extraction, (as, indeed, many of the Northern States, for instance, Pennsylvania, do not give it, and as other States give the right of voting to colored people on the condition of possessing freeholds only,) the result of the amendment as now proposed, without an additional amendment, would be an increased number of Southern Representatives in Congress of the same number of white citizens. In this case the rebellion, though ultimately subdued at the cost of torrents of our blood and streams of our wealth, would be rewarded with an enlarged representation. No loyal citizen can wish for such a consummation. How is the difficulty to be avoided?

Let us first remember the following three points:

1. In the practice of every State of the Union those citizens vote for electors of the President of the United States who have a right to vote for Representatives in Congress. Immediately after the adoption of the Constitution of the United States, the Legislatures of several States elected the electors; but a more national spirit soon prevailed, and in all the different States of the Union the people elected the electors, except in South Carolina. There the Legislature retained the election of electors down to the breaking out of the rebellion, on the avowed ground that thus the State obtained a greater influence, this election of electors in South Carolina always taking place after the election by the people had been consummated in all the other States.

2. In every State those citizens who have a right to vote for the most numerous branch of the State Legislature, have also the right to vote for members of Congress.

3. In every State of the Union it is the State itself which determines by its own Constitution, who shall have the right to vote for members of the State Legislature.

These considerations, then, would lead to the suggestion, that the apportionment of members of Congress ought to be made according to the numbers of citizens who in each State have the right to vote for the State Legislature, or for its most numerous branch.

This suggestion may be embodied in an amendment additional to the one just passed, in such words as these:

Representatives shall be apportioned among the several States which may be included within this Union, according to the respective numbers of citizens having the qualifications requisite for electing members of the most numerous branch of the respective State Legislatures. The actual enumeration of said citizens shall be regularly made by the census of the United States, but a special census shall take place before the next new apportionment of representatives shall be made by the Congress of the United States.

You will observe that the words used in this proposition of an amendment have been taken, as far as it was possible, from the Constitution itself. Article I, section 2, paragraphs 1 and 3.

Believing, as I do, that this subject deserves the attention of the American people, I have not hesitated to make use of your permission to address to you this public letter, and have the honor to be,

Sir, your very obedient,
FRANCIS LIEBER.
Hon. E.D. Morgan, Senator of the United States, Washington.
New-York, Feb. 1, 1865.

6

Massachusetts, Unanimous Ratification of Abolition Amendment, *Salem Register*

February 6, 1865, p. 2

The most prominent subject of interest before the Legislature last week was the proposed amendment to the Constitution of the United States, abolishing Slavery. On Thursday, Mr. Scudder of Dorchester, Chairman of the House Committee on the Judiciary, introduced, on leave, a bill to ratify and confirm the proposed amendment, and moved that it be passed through the several stages under a suspension of the rules. Several members objected, on the ground that no formal or official communication had been received announcing the adoption of such a proposed amendment, and that there was no need of this extraordinary haste, as the position of Massachusetts on the subject could not possibly be misunderstood. On the other hand it was urged that the information was sufficiently positive to base action upon—that promptness on this great and all important proposition was peculiarly proper—that the Governor had received official notice by telegraph, from the President's private Secretary, of the adoption of the proposition by Congress—that other States had already acted—and that Senator Sumner urged Massachusetts to adopt the amendment at once without waiting for more formal notice. After much discussion the motion to suspend the rules was lost, by a vote of 89 to 84, two thirds not having voted therefore, and the subject was referred to the Committee on Federal Relations.

On Friday, when the matter came up in the Senate, that body refused to concur in the action of the House, and forthwith passed the bill through its several readings, under a suspension of the rules, every Senator voting in the affirmative.

In the House on the same day, when the bill came back from the Senate, with its action endorsed thereon, a motion to recede from the previous reference was made, and discussed for some time with great animation. The result was that the House receded by a vote of 120 to 70, suspended the rules by a vote of 123 to 55, and passed the bill through its several stages at once,

every member present recording his vote in its favor. Thus, both branches of the Legislature of Massachusetts have UNANIMOUSLY ratified this great and glorious amendment, the adoption of which will entirely and forever abolish Slavery throughout the United States.

7

Charles Sumner, Resolutions Regarding the Number of States Necessary for Ratification, *New York Tribune*

February 6, 1865, p. 5[*]

Mr. SUMNER offered the following, which were ordered to be printed:

Concurrent resolutions declaring the rule in ascertaining the three-quarters of the several States required in the ratification of a Constitutional Amendment:

Whereas, Congress, by a vote of two-thirds of both Houses, has proposed an amendment to the Constitution prohibiting slavery throughout the United States, which, according to the existing requirement of the Constitution, will be valid to all intents and purposes as part of the Constitution when ratified by the Legislatures of three-fourths of the several States; and

Whereas, in the present condition of the country, with certain States in arms against the National Government, it becomes necessary to determine what number of States constitutes the three-quarters required by the Constitution, therefore,

Resolved by the Senate, the House of Representatives Concurring, That the rule followed in ascertaining the two-thirds of both Houses, in proposing the amendment to the Constitution, should be followed in ascertaining the three-quarters of the several States ratifying the amendment; that, as in the first case, the two-thirds are founded on the simple fact of representation in the two Houses, so, in the second case, the three-quarters must be founded on the simple fact of representation of the Government of the country, and the support thereof, and that any other rule establishes one basis for the proposition for the amendment, and another for its

[*] [See also *Cong. Globe,* 38th Cong., 2nd Sess., 588 (Feb. 4, 1865). —Ed.]

ratification, placing one on a simple fact, and the other on a claim of right, while it also recognizes the power of Rebels in arms to interpose a veto upon the National Government in one of its highest functions.

Resolved, That all acts, executive and legislative, in pursuance of the Constitution, and all treaties made under the authority of the United States, are valid, to all intents and purposes, throughout the United States, although certain Rebel States fail to participate therein, and that the same role is equally applicable to an amendment of the Constitution.

Resolved, That the amendment of the Constitution prohibiting slavery throughout the United States will be valid, to all intents and purposes, as part of the Constitution, whenever ratified by three-fourths of the States *de facto* exercising their powers and prerogatives of the United States under the Constitution thereof.

Resolved, That any other rule requiring the participation of the Rebel States, while illogical and unreasonable, is dangerous in its consequences, inasmuch as all recent presidential proclamations, including that of emancipation; also, all recent acts of Congress, including those creating the national debt, and establishing a national currency, and also all recent treaties, including the treaty with Great Britain for the extinction of the slave trade, have been made, enacted or ratified, respectively, without any participation of the Rebel States.

Resolved, That any other rule must tend to postpone the great day when the prohibition of Slavery will be valid, to all intents and purposes, as part of the Constitution of the United States—but the rule herewith declared will assume the immediate ratification of the prohibition and the consummation of the national desires.

8

"Is the Union Destroyed?" (On Sumner's Resolutions),

New York Times

February 6, 1865, p. 4

Senator Sumner has introduced resolutions into the Senate which, if adopted, will recognize as complete the dissolution of the American Union. They relate to the ratification by the States of the amendment to the Constitution just passed by Congress. They declare that this amendment will be valid, and will become part of the Constitution, whenever it shall be ratified by three fourths of the States actually exercising the functions of States under the Constitution; in other words, by three fourths of the *loyal* States of the Union.

. . .

It is true that the action of each House of Congress, in making laws and proposing amendments to the Constitution, is perfectly valid, although taken in the absence of representatives from the rebel States. But this is because the Constitution itself expressly provides for the absence of members, in defining what shall constitute a quorum in each House. "Each House," says the Constitution, (Art. 1, p 5,) "shall be the judge of the elections, returns and qualifications of its own members; and *a majority of each shall constitute a quorum to do business.*" Whenever a majority, therefore, is present in each House, Congress may "do business;" and whatever it does will be just as valid, in all respects, as if every member was present. The Constitution takes no notice of the absence of any member of Congress, provided a majority of all the members are present. Now the absence of members from the rebel States has not destroyed the *quorum* necessary in each House to do business.

But no such rule applies to the ratification by the States of amendments to the Constitution. Upon that subject the Constitution holds the following language:

"The Congress, whenever two-thirds of both Houses shall deem necessary, shall propose amendments to this Constitution,—which shall be valid to all intents and purposes, as part of this Constitution, when ratified *by the Legislatures of three-fourths of the several States, or by conventions in three-fourths thereof,* as one or the other mode of ratification may be proposed by the Congress."

The action of Congress in proposing the amendment requires only a quorum, which the Constitution defines to be a majority in each house. The *ratification* of the amendment requires three fourths *of all the States*; there is nothing in the Constitution to authorize any other conclusion. The fact that one rule obtains in the one case is no reason for assuming that it must obtain in the other. In the one case it is distinctly laid down; in the other it is not,—and that makes all the difference in the world.

The decision of this matter turns wholly on the question, *How many States constitute the Union?* And this depends on the question whether the States, some of whose people are in rebellion, are in the Union or not. If they are not, then Mr. SUMNER'S resolutions are just and sound. If they are, they are unsound, and announce an unconstitutional doctrine. Mr. SUMNER assumes that the rebel States are out of the Union. In other words, he assumes that the Union is actually divided; that the United States, as a nation, has ceased to exist, and has given place to two nations, with two Governments, each exercising authority over a distinct and separate territory. This is the principal actually involved and asserted in his resolution. It has been indirectly assumed in various propositions already submitted to Congress, and in some which have been adopted by that body. But in these resolutions it is distinctly and clearly set forth—so distinctly and so clearly that it will be very difficult, and, we trust, impossible to conceal from the country the real nature of the proposition submitted to the action of Congress.

9

Virginia, News of Ratification, *Press* (Philadelphia, PA)

February 9, 1865

A dispatch from Alexandria, Va., says a certified copy of the proposed anti-slavery amendment to the Constitution of the United States was received by the Governor of Virginia from Secretary Seward to-day, and was promptly laid before both houses of the General Assembly, and was unanimously ratified by the Senate. The House will take action tomorrow, where there will be only two dissenting votes.

By thus sending a certified copy of the Congressional joint resolution to the Governor of Virginia, which is intermediate between Wheeling and Richmond, it would appear that the executive branch of the Government recognizes the State of Virginia, notwithstanding the House of Representatives has refused to receive members from that Commonwealth.

10

Delaware, Governor William Cannon's Message, Legislature Rejects Amendment

February 7–8, 1865

NEW YORK TRIBUNE, FEBRUARY 9, 1865, P. 4
State of Delaware, Executive Department
Dover, Feb. 7, 1865
To the Senate and House of Representatives of the State of Delaware, in General Assembly met:

The Congress of the United States, by the requisite majority of both Houses, has submitted the following Constitutional Amendment to the Legislatures of the several States for ratification:

. . .*

Having received official information of the vote cast in Congress, I take the earliest opportunity to lay the amendment before the General Assembly. In doing so, I must express my hearty concurrence in its object, and recommend most earnestly its immediate ratification.

A due regard to the claims of impartial justice; to the unity, welfare and security of our Government; to the necessity of removing the cause of our present unhappy civil strife; to a reunion of our country upon a sure basis; to a speedy return of permanent and honorable peace; and to the cause of enlightened progress, commends this step to our warmest sympathies. An opportunity is offered to men of all parties to unite, with devoted loyalty, upon measures the promise the most salutary results; and each one can now share in the honor of declaring that henceforth and forever the REPUBLIC SHALL BE FREE.

Let us start upon a new career of liberty, happiness and prosperity; let us build up for posterity a pure and free Government; let us dignify the labor to which, in the Providence of God, each one of us is called; let us make the immortal Declaration a glorious and beneficent fact; and let us render thanks and praise to God, whose service is perfect freedom, for the progress that we are making, under His guidance and in obedience to

---

*[Cannon quotes the text of the Thirteenth Amendment. —Ed.]

His will, in consummating the highest and noblest purpose of human government—universal religious, civil and personal liberty.

WILLIAM CANNON

—Of course, the Legislature will disregard and defy this appeal; for the majority is 'Democratic,' and Slavery—in Delaware as elsewhere—is the 'being's end and aim' of the base counterfeit which profanes the name of Democracy. Almost any sober, reputable Democrat will now tell you: "I am opposed to Slavery; *but* I believe in letting every State decide for itself." Well: here is Delaware with a Legislature that might abolish Slavery if it would, or might ratify the Constitutional Amendment; but it will do neither, because its Democratic majority knows that it owes its ascendancy to Slavery and to nothing else.

PHILADELPHIA INQUIRER, FEBRUARY 9, 1865, P. 1
Delaware Rejects the Constitutional Amendment
Dover, Del., Feb. 8.—The Delaware Legislature has rejected the proposed amendment to the Constitution of the United States, by a three-fourths vote in the Senate, and a two-thirds vote in the House.

11

Indiana, Debates and Ratification

February 8–13, 1865*

SENATE: WED. FEB. 8
The joint resolution [S. 16] accepting and ratifying certain amendments to the Constitution of the United States proposed by Congress to the Legislatures of the several States, was read the second time.

...

Mr. COBB suggested that as this act was the result of such a rapid change in the minds of members of the present Congress, it were better not to follow hastily. The Constitution of this country is no ordinary matter. It is a beacon light to the people of this country; they should obey it and not make changes in it unless there is an important and imperative demand that it should be made.

Brevier Legislative Reports of the General Assembly of the State of Indiana (South Bend, 1865), 7:173-238.

It would require the Legislatures of about twenty-seven States to endorse this amendment, before it will be an amendment to the Constitution, and there are not that many in session—there are but twenty-three that will meet any time soon. Hence it could not be adopted as a part of the Constitution at a very early day, and we only show a want of deliberation, by hastily acting upon it.

...

Mr. OYLER ... [H]e was induced to say that he was not one of those who thought all wisdom lies buried in the grave. He recognized and realized the circumstances that surrounded our fathers when they adopted the Constitution. An institution foreign to the spirit and purpose of the government was accepted as an incubus and a blot; but it was there, and it was for the fathers to do the best they could with it as they found it. They could not have maintained their position before the world had they then blotted out this hated institution of slavery. This is the only and the real reason why the institution was allowed to have an existence at the time it became a part and parcel of the compromises of the Constitution. In my political life it has been my fortune to recognize this principle and to contend that it not be interfered with directly or indirectly. I was willing to leave it as it was—to leave it to the progress of public opinion—to the march of truth and right, of rectitude and justice, and hope for that day when the hearts of the American people should rise above the sordid consideration of dollars and cents.

By stealthy and insidious steps friends of the institution asked to extend this foul blot over the territories, and at last undertook to spread it beyond its limits. Then I, with thousands of others, demurred. Then I thought it right to answer to the convictions of my early education, and say, "thus far shalt thou go, and no farther." And I have no hesitation in saying, if I know the motives and influences that actuated me, that, had the advocates of this institution let it stay where it was, no voice or vote of mine would have been raised against it. To slavery, and slavery alone, can be attributed the loss of so many valuable lives, and so much treasure, and to it may be charged this foul, wicked, and unjust rebellion. Had there been no slavery in the United States, there would have been no rebellion in 1861. Believing that slavery is justly and truly chargeable with all these wrongs, and that as long as it has a place on our statute book—as long as it is not openly condemned—this country can have no permanent or certain peace. I am one of those that will be proud to give my vote to ratify the amendment which has been passed by the Congress of the United States.

...

SENATE: THURS. FEB. 9

Mr. DOWNEY ... With reference to the justice of the matter, I have no doubt. I hold that there are certain rights which all men possess, and of which they cannot rightfully be deprived, so long as they do not, by their own acts, forfeit the same. I recognize the right of each person to personal security, personal liberty, and to possess and enjoy property. These are spoken of as the absolute rights of individuals. In our Declaration of Independence they are denominated "inalienable rights," and are said to consist in "life, liberty and the pursuit of happiness." They belong to all men in a state of nature, without reference to society. For the origin of them we do not look to any Charter or Constitution. They are the gifts of God. Government may and should protect these rights, but it does not confer them.

Yet, important as these rights are, they may be forfeited by the crimes of those who possess them. Amercements, imprisonments, and even deprivation of life may be necessary to promote the ends of good government; and for this purpose slavery and involuntary servitude may, according to the amendment proposed, still continue to exist. But unless these rights are thus forfeited by the individual, human government cannot deprive him of them, without, to that extent, being chargeable with injustice and oppression.

I distinguish between these rights of which I have been speaking and those which are merely relative, and which have their origin in the regulations of human society. As these originated in society, so they must be controlled by it. A failure to distinguish between these rights and those of which I have already spoken, gives rise to much confusion of ideas, and a great amount of fanaticism. Some cannot, or will not, distinguish between the right to live, to be free and to enjoy the fruits of one's labor, and the right to vote, to sit on a jury or to hold an office. Yet it will be seen by any one that the former are the natural rights of the individual, while the latter are wholly dependent upon the regulations of society. It does not follow that if you recognize and secure to the colored man his natural rights, that you must confer upon him all those relative rights which you have conferred upon the white man, and make him his equal.

...

Mr. BENNETT ... discussed the question of negro equality, and said he had no fears on that subject. He believed the Anglo-Saxon race superior to all others; was willing to see all have a fair chance in the race of life, and if the foremost negro overtook and passed the hindmost white man, so be it; he was willing to run the race fairly, and if the nigger beat him he would give him his hat.... He also discussed the question of what should be done with the freed negro. Said he would, if he had time, suggest many plans that he deemed expedient, but would answer the question by asking what would the negro do with his rebel master? He was willing to leave that question to the wisdom of a beneficent Creator, and the future legislation of this great country.

...

Mr. CULLEN ... The system of slavery has been the disturbing element in our society, the Pandora box from which all our troubles have flown since the wheels of government were set in motion. Aye, sir, it had well nigh prevented its formation; and nothing but humiliation and compromise on the part of our fathers with this iniquity would suffice to give birth to our nationality; and since that time, all the convulsions of our country are clearly traceable to it as their chief source and fountain. In 1820–21, upon the admission of Missouri, this question shook the continent as with a terrible earthquake, from centre to circumference, and nothing but a bowing to the behests of slaveholders in the further spread of this blighting curse, saved the nation from internal strife and civil war. In 1832, under the pretext of the tariff question, but in reality to protect the labor of slaves, South Carolina, under the leadership of Calhoun, threatened secession and intestine war. In 1850, upon the admission of California, our Government rocked to and fro like a cradle, and the wisest of our statesmen could see nothing but dissolution and the grim visage of war, in all directions; when, from his retirement, the Sage of Ashland [Henry Clay] stepped forward, and with his mighty voice spoke peace to the troubled waters. From 1854 to 1856, the virgin soil of Kansas was watered freely with the blood of its own citizens in a contest between slavery and freedom. In 1860, and from that time to this, war—bloody, desolating, destructive war, with all its sacrifices of life, health and treasure, slavery has ushered and kept upon us.... Sir, while we behold these pictures of sadness, shall we as Indiana Senators, proud of our heroic deeds and soldiery, refuse to concur in removing the blighting, withering curse?

...

HOUSE OF REPRESENTATIVES: THURS. FEB. 9

Mr. BUSHKIRK ... I feel constrained by a sense of duty to resist the ratification of the joint resolutions of the Congress of the United States for the prohibition of slavery in the several State of the Union; and it is due to myself and people I represent, that I should briefly give the reasons that control my action. I do not expect, sir, nor do any on our side of the House expect, or think for a moment, that by anything we can say here the result will be changed. So far as the action of the House is concerned, we regard that as fixed and certain. The joint resolution of the gentleman from Wabash will be passed in the House, and it is equally certain that it will pass in the Senate, and this action of Congress will be ratified by the authority of the legislature now assembled. But this is no reason why those of us who are opposed to it should not give our voices upon the matter.

...

I desire to say that I do not to-day speak in the interest of slavery. I have neither interest in, nor sympathy with slavery. That is not the ground of objection to the resolution. If the people where slavery exist think proper to abolish slavery, it will meet with my hearty approval, and I shall be thankful for it. Nor do I intend to be drawn into a line of argument that can be construed into a defense of justification of the institution of slavery. I am opposed to the ratification of the amendment proposed in the joint resolution, on three grounds:

First. The exercise of the powers claimed will result in a virtual change of our form of government.

Secondly, It will be an impediment, an obstruction in the way of the restoration of the Union under the Federal Constitution; and—

Thirdly, If I vote for the amendment I shall feel constrained to follow out the principle to its natural, logical and legitimate results, and give to the African race the rights they will be entitled to after the condition of slavery shall have been abolished, and they shall be elevated to the character of citizens of the commonwealth.

...

SENATE: THURS. FEB. 9

...

Mr. BRADLEY ... I hold, Mr. President, that there is a great principle involved in the joint resolution before us. And that principle is, whether the constitution of our country can be amended so as to destroy the private rights of citizens accruing under State laws, and in violation of State enactments. I hold that this cannot be done against the consent of any one of the States belonging to the compact. It is written in the constitution, that all powers not delegated to it are expressly reserved to the people of the respective States. Is this a delegated power? Has a similar proceeding ever been attempted before in the history of our country? Has Congress ever attempted to control or intermeddle with the local institutions of the States?

If there are any powers belonging to the people of the States, which have heretofore been well defined, and acknowledged upon the part of all, has it not been the power to regulate their domestic institutions in their own way? Has not the right of property, as obtained by the citizen from the State organizations, been held as amongst the most sacred of all rights? And then the question arises, if this right can be invaded in the manner proposed? Cannot every other right that the citizen supposes he is in the enjoyment of be invaded and wiped out by a similar process? Legislators, then, should look well to it before they strike down a great principle that lies at the very foundation of our governmental organization.

...

Mr. HORD ... Mr. H. urged, as an additional objection to the proposed amendment, that it tends to centralize power in the hands of the General Government. State sovereignty is the only security to personal liberty. He argued that we had not the power to make the amendment in the manner proposed, and that if the latter day doctrine of the Republican party is correct that the right of amendment is unlimited, then government does provide for its own destruction. The States made the Constitution, the Constitution did not make the States. The Supreme Court of the United States, in numerous cases, has decided that the United States are sovereign, and that their powers are only limited by the Constitution.

...

Mr. DUNNING desired to know if he understood the Senator to say that the Constitution of the United States was framed by the States in their sovereign capacity, and that the Constitution was an agreement between the States as sovereignties?

Mr. HORD. Yes, sir.

Mr. DUNNING then called attention of the Senator to Story's Commentaries sections 152–53: "The Constitution of the United States is not a compact or treaty between different sovereignties, &c."

Mr. HORD. The Supreme Court of the United States,

in a number of cases, have held that the States are sovereign.

Mr. DUNNING. That is not an answer to Chief Justice Story.

...

Mr. BENNETT demanded a call of the Senate.

It was ordered, and the Secretary reported 15 absentees.

The joint resolution then passed the Senate by yeas 26, nays 9.

...

Mr. WILLIAMS moved to amend by allowing any Senator who may desire to record his vote.

The latter motion was agreed to, and Messrs. Barker, Brown of Wells, Carson, Cobb, Corbin, Douglas, English, Fuller, Gaff, Hanna, Mason, Newlin and Staggs, recorded their votes in the negative.

...

YEAS ... 26.

NAYS ... 22.

And so the joint resolution passed.

HOUSE OF REPRESENTATIVES: FRI. FEB. 10

The CHAIRMAN reported the bill—Mr. Whiteside's joint resolution, No. 13—to the House without amendment.

...

Mr. Harrison's argument, condensed, was as follows:

1st. It is a proposition to change the organic law of the land; by the exercise of a power not delegated by the Constitution to Congress.

2d. The Constitution declares that all power not delegated by the Constitution to Congress, nor prohibited by it to the States, is reserved to the States respectively or to the people.

3d. Slavery is a local and domestic institution, and is the creature of local and State laws. At the adoption of the present Constitution slavery existed in twelve of the thirteen original States, and the right to hold slaves was then considered, as it has been ever since, a reserved right in the States, and not a delegated right.

4th. All power is inherent in the people, and our government is founded on the theory that it derives all its just powers from the consent of the governed. The slaveholding States are to be governed by this amendment, without being even consulted, and deprived of their property without compensation.

5th. This amendment, if adopted and ratified by three-fourths of the States, is an abandonment of our former position in regard to the conduct of the war, and relates back to that abolition heresy that was uttered and put forth in 1858, that there was an irrepressible conflict going on between freedom and slavery; that this government cannot exist part slave and part free. Our past history for more than three-quarters of a century, is a sufficient answer and refutation to this heresy.

6th. Suppose this amendment is ratified by three-fourths of the States, slavery will then have been abolished by law; but will not the rugged issue remain to be resolved by force of arms and at the point of the bayonet? The war will then go on for this purpose, and slavery will have to be abolished amidst the war of artillery, the rattle of musketry, and the crash of armed hosts.

The present Constitution is adequate for all purposes, of war as well as of peace, amidst the earthquake those of civil strife and the conflicts of a foreign war, in every struggle which our country has hitherto been engaged, it has borne us triumphantly through. Under it the rebellion can be suppressed and the Union of our fathers restored.

Does this kind of legislation tend to better the condition of the slave? I, for one, have been disposed to doubt the philanthropy of those who profess to be the exclusive friends of the negro. Freedom to the slave under the policy of the Administration leads but to degeneration and the grave.

This amendment can only be justified on the ground of revolution; that it is right to adopt it simply because we have the power to do it. For these and other reasons that I might urge, I shall vote against the proposed amendment.

Mr. BOYD said the opposition to this joint resolution proceeded as though there was no war. He did not discuss the constitutional question. But the lawyers claimed a right higher than the Constitution—the right of the people. The power of the people to make the Constitution certainly could change it.... He showed how the liberation of the slaves of the South was weakening the armies of the South and add them to our own armies, to the relief of our own brave boys, both in the ditches and on the battle-field, and it was but common justice that such should not be returned to slavery. It did not follow that because the blacks were free, they should be invested with all our legal and social rights.

...

Mr. LASSELLE . . . He should vote against this amendment, for a very few reasons. In the first place, involved questions of right, of power and expediency.

It would seem at first blush that we have the power, because there is no prohibition. But he showed that no amendment could be adopted to the Articles of Confederation before the Constitution, without the consent of every State. It was the declaration of the fathers, and a tradition of the people, that no right of a State, nor any right of property, shall be interfered with or disturbed. Prohibitions of change and amendment of the Constitution were in the Constitution itself, with regard to the right of States, &c., as, that the equal right of all States to equal representation in the Senate of the United States, shall not be impaired without the consent of such State. From this, he argued at least the doubtfulness of the power to pass this amendment, because it affected the rights of States and property. And he computed the number and value of slaves, asking if gentlemen could regard it as an equitable thing to strike down the right of property? ["Yes;" "yes"]

He could not, though admitting, as he did, the intrinsic evil of slavery. And he referred to the fact, that the State of Delaware had but day before yesterday declared by an overwhelming majority, in both branches of the Legislature, that she would not ratify this amendment. There was reason to think also that Kentucky would make the same remonstrance. We had every assurance that Kentucky would reject it. Was it right to force a law on these States, depriving their citizens of their property? Even rebels, although they had committed the highest of crimes, had some rights under the law.

. . .

Mr. DUNHAM regretted exceedingly that his physical health would not permit him to do this great subject justice. In his judgement this was the most important question which had ever devolved upon the American people. To solve it, it required all the intellect of our minds and all the patriotism of our hearts. He had lamented to see, listening to this discussion, personal and malignant strife urged by gentlemen on the other side. They had even charged those who differed with them on this question with rebel sympathizing—with disloyalty. They were charged with this simply because they exercised the God-given liberty of thought, and proposed to act conscientiously as their reason and judgment dictated.

. . .

But gentlemen say that our words here encourage traitors. We oppose this proposition and the present war policy, not that we love the rebellion, but because we want to put it down, and want a policy that will put it down. Did gentlemen think Democrats could not appreciate the destiny of this country?—could not take into their minds the great idea, a comment over whose glad plains the two oceans clap their hands in an ecstasy of praise to the Supreme. Talking about loyalty, did gentlemen know what loyalty is? Loyalty is fidelity to the governing power. The officials of this country were with the governing power, and the public officer that grasps at and exercises powers not empowered by the people is a usurper—a traitor—a disloyal man. A clause in the Declaration of Independence which says "all men are created free and equal," was an expression of the determination of our fathers to be rid of all aristocratic domination. Our fathers counted the nigger out.

They did not agree with Ben Butler, when he said the other day that "they are of us." With reference to State Sovereignty, it was a sufficient reply to the sneer of the gentleman from Jefferson (Mr. Wright) against State sovereignty, to say that those attributes of sovereignty which he enumerated as delegates to the General Government, were delegated by sovereign States. The power of amendment of the Constitution was confined in its exercise to the charge of principles not delegated, not radical fundamental. The majority now sought to change the Constitution of that Union as our fathers made it—you sought to furl and trail the glorious flag under which, from the Atlantic to the Pacific, and from the St. Lawrence to the Darien's isthmus, we had achieved all our glories. God Almighty had formed this country for one people. Look at its mountains and its rivers; its prairies and its forests! What God had joined together no one could put asunder. Loyalty! That sentiment did not come from our noble Governor. It did not come from Presidents, Congresses, or any magnates. Great God! The Governor was not our master. From the President of the United States down to the lackey that blacked boots, all were servants of the people.

He challenged the learned gentleman that had followed him, to show one syllable of the delegation that power to Congress. The power of amendment contained in the Constitution extended only to the powers and principles already incorporated in that instrument. He did not care whether you had one tyrant or thirty or a hundred thousand. Liberty was where the whole people promiscuously, through each other, made their own laws and institutions. Tyranny was where one set of men, not chosen by the other set, made laws for the whole. Therefore, if three-fourths of the States undertook to control the other fourth, it is tyranny. If three-fourths of the States, in regard to this amendment, trampled upon the rights of the other fourth, they not simply violated the Constitution, but they were guilty of absolute tyranny.

He had been of those who had been sanguine of the long existence (quoting from Jefferson) of our federal Union. Now he doubted it much, and saw the event not far distant, this question (of slavery) like a fire bell in the night, had awakened him and filled him with alarm. New England puritanism had struck this bell, and filled the country with terror, solely for the purpose of obtaining sectional and political power.

He read from Mr. Jefferson's letters, by way of special enlightenment of the gentleman from Lawrence (Mr. Boyd), Jefferson would be rid of slavery "by expatriation." Was this the Jeffersonianism of Republicans in this Hall? The President—Father Abraham—it was boasted by a Republican newspaper, took a negro into his carriage, whilst his white servant was riding outside, and Charles Sumner took a negro into the Supreme Court of the United States, and caused him to be admitted as a practicing lawyer, in the place where once stood Daniel Webster! He further illustrated this Republican Jeffersonianism. He read copiously from a late speech by Major General Butler, closing with a recommendation to make the negro, who is among us and of us, equal with us before the law.

Mr. D. pursued his theme, and demonstrated that it was the purpose of the party advocating this amendment, to elevate the negro to the proud position of an American citizen. How are the mighty fallen, when Sambo gets up and exclaims, "I, too, am an American citizen." Jefferson had said that he was willing to abolish slavery provided he could have expatriation of the African—a separation of the races and the preservation of the proud Caucasian from contamination. Where two races live together, one must be held in subjection, or the inferior must be absorbed by the superior.

. . .

Mr. Speaker PETTIT . . . The loose objection that this proposed action is not Constitutional meant, he supposed, [that it] was not competent to put into the Constitution by way of amendment what is contrary to the spirit of the Constitution. In opposition to this objection, he showed at length, that where there is a general grant of power, with no limitation upon it, it includes everything under it. Had he stated the objection correctly?

Mr. BROWN. He put it on the ground that sover-

eignty begins with the States. Amendments must be subordinate to the delegated powers. Jefferson and Madison held that the Federal Government had no right to interfere with slavery. He had therefore submitted, that this amendment could not be applied.

Mr. PETTIT. The Constitution unamended does not confer the power.

Mr. BROWN. We can only amend in so far as the Constitution invites amendments. Can we amend the Constitution so as to fasten slavery on the State of Indiana? If not, how can you exclude it from Kentucky by amendment?

Mr. PETTIT. Ratifying this amendment, then, we simply part with a reserved power—We treat with what belongs to us so far, let it be conceded for argument, we add to the powers of the General Government. But he read again from the constitutional provisions for amendment in the 5th and 1st articles. Except upon those two subjects this clause confers upon Congress plenary power to propose amendments. The very contrary of the gentleman's restriction was in the Constitution; if he would undertake it. He glanced at the significant fact that the word "slave" is not in the Constitution, and quoted the language of Madison thereupon. He went into the convention that framed the Constitution.

. . .

HOUSE OF REPRESENTATIVES: SAT. FEB. 11

. . .

Mr. GREGG took the floor and proceeded to deliver some of the reasons why he could not vote to ratify the proposed amendment. . . . How long before it will be proposed to make white and black equal before the law? He regarded the Constitution as ample in its provisions to create the Union and bind it together in perpetual Union. This was demonstrated in the successful administration of the Constitution for sixty years. Besides, this was no time to change the Constitution; it was rather a special time when we ought to come together for the defense of the Constitution, and lock our shields over it. When peace returns, then, and not till then, would come the appropriate time to amend the Constitution.

. . .

Mr. FOULKE. He had no fear of the bug bear of negro equality. It might be that legal restrictions against intermarriages with the inferior race might be necessary. He saw the cause of the commencement of the war in the encroachments of slavery. Was slavery so sacred a thing that we should not touch it? It had impoverished our territory; it was the enemy of schools; it was the most dangerous foe of Democracy, and in this treasonous rebellion it had committed the greatest of all crimes, for which it must die.

...

HOUSE OF REPRESENTATIVES: MON. FEB. 13
Mr. WHITESIDE ... Nice deductions had been made, subtle arguments adduced, upon the subject of delegated and reserved powers—a mass of refinements about Federal and State power had been evolved; yet, beyond and below all this learning lies the fundamental truth, that the *people* made the government, both State and national, marked out the spheres of their operations, and lodged powers, in one or the other, consistent with the purposes for which they were created. The gentleman from Monroe had talked of States rights, as if the rights of States were inalienable, as if they had been fixed by the decrees of Providence—something established by the laws of nature. The only inalienable rights of which he had any knowledge was the right of every man, black or white, on God's green earth, to eat the bread won by the sweat of his own brow, and while he was upon that branch of the subject, he would pause to remind the gentleman from Monroe that, nevertheless, Providence, through a mysterious partiality, had gifted him with a fair skin, his right to life, liberty and the pursuit of happiness, was no more sacred than that of the blackest negro goaded to the toil of a slave upon the plantations of the South.

...

The yeas and nays were then ordered and taken, resulting—yeas 56, nays 29.

...

So the question passed the House of Representatives, and the title was reported by the Clerk, and authenticated amid shouts of irrepressible applause from the floor and the lobbies. And immediately there was the response of a concerted national salute booming southward from the front of the Capitol.

12

Speech of Frederick Douglass, *Liberator* (Boston, MA)

February 10, 1865, vol. 35, no. 6, p. 22

I have had but one idea for the last three years to present to the American people, and the phraseology in which I clothe it is the old abolition Phraseology. I am for the "immediate, unconditional and universal" enfranchisement of the black man in every State in the Union. (Loud applause.) Without this, his liberty is a mockery; without this, you might as well almost retain the old name of slavery for his condition; for, in fact, if he is not the slave of the individual master, he is the slave of society, and holds his liberty as a privilege, not as a right. He is at the mercy of the mob, and has no means of protecting himself.

It may be objected, however, that this pressing of the Negro's right to suffrage is premature. Let us have slavery abolished, it may be said, let us have labor organized, and then, in the natural course of events, the right of suffrage will be extended to the Negro. I do not agree with this. The constitution of the human mind is such, that if it once disregards the conviction forced upon it by the revelation of truth, it requires the exercise of a higher power to produce the same conviction afterwards. The American people are now in tears. The Shenandoah has run blood—the best blood of the North. All around Richmond the blood of New England and of the North has been shed—of your sons, your brothers, and your fathers. We all feel, in the existence of this Rebellion, that judgments terrible, widespread, far-reaching, overwhelming, are abroad in the land; and we feel, in view of these judgments, just now, a disposition to learn righteousness. This is the hour. Our streets are in mourning, tears are falling at every fireside, and under the chastisement of this Rebellion, we have almost come up to the point of conceding this great, this all-important right of suffrage. I fear that if we fail to do it now, if Abolitionists fail to press it now, we may not see, for centuries to come, the same disposition that exists at this moment. (Applause.) Hence, I say, now is the time to press this right.

13

Kentucky, Governor Thomas Bramlette's Address to the Legislature (Calling for Conditional Ratification),

Cincinnati Daily Enquirer

February 11, 1865, p. 1

Gentlemen of the Senate and House of Representatives:

I herewith lay before you, for your consideration and action, a joint resolution of Congress, approved on the 1st instant, proposing to the Legislatures of the several States a Thirteenth Article to the Constitution of the United States, which article is in the following words, viz:

"ARTICLE XIII.

"Section 1. Neither slavery nor involuntary servitude, except as a punishment for crime, whereof the party shall have been duly convicted, shall exist within the United States, or any place subject to their jurisdiction.

"Section 2. Congress shall have power to enforce this article by appropriate legislation.

"Approved February 1, 1865."

I might content myself with submitting this question to you for action, without incurring the responsibility of any suggestions; but upon a matter of such vital importance to the people of Kentucky, involving, as I believe, their well-being and security, such course would not comport with my views of constitutional obligation, and the duties and responsibilities of the office of Chief Executive of the Commonwealth.

The views of the present Executive upon the subject of the proposed amendment, as a national question, are known and of record. We have no new lights upon this subject which could in the least modify or change those views. We still believe it was not wise, as a national policy, pending the rebellion, to propose amendments to the Constitution, which fix, irrevocably, an ultimatum of adjustment that had better have been held under the control of the Government. But our views of national policy have been overruled by those having authority to determine; and the question now presented, though national in its operation, is local for our consideration. We are not now called upon to consider the policy or impolicy of national action, but the bearing which this measure is to have upon us as a State and people. We should therefore approach it divested of all partisan asperities and sectional passions and prejudices, and meet it with the dispassionate consideration and prudent judgment of statesmen charged with the highest interests and most important securities and trusts of a brave, manly and patriotic people.

No intelligent man, whatever may be his desires upon the subject, can hope for the perpetuation of slavery in Kentucky.

Every State which surrounds us has abolished slavery. The laws for the rendition of fugitives are repealed, and no possible hope of their re-enactment. The most valuable slaves have enlisted in the army or fled to other States; those that remain are hopelessly demoralized, and rendered not only valueless, but burdensome. These facts are of general notoriety and indisputable.

Although much of this state of affairs has been brought about by what we have deemed uncalled for and unnecessary interference with the subject of slavery, yet it has been part of the bitter fruits of rebellion; and the facts exist and cannot be changed by denying them or closing our eyes to their existence. Whether the proposed amendment be ratified by you or not, slavery has been foredoomed by rebellion, and cannot be maintained.

It is not, therefore, a question for us to determine—Shall slavery continue or not? but how shall it end? Though we may believe that the several States should have been left to adjust this question, yet will *mere mode* compensate for the dangers, hazards, and expenditures which we are likely to incur by refusing the mode proposed, and standing out for our own, which we deem better? In a word, if you agree that slavery cannot be continued, is it not better to accept a practical and legitimate mode of ridding our people of all the dangers and harassments of its further continuance, than risk the dangerous ordeal through which we must pass in order to reach our own mode of accomplishing the same end? Will the difference in abolishing it, by amendment to the Federal Constitution, or by amendment to the State Constitution, justify the hazards of the experiment?

The people of Kentucky have never permitted the negro to intercept their loyalty to our Government.

They have ever thrust aside and refused to accept the negro as an issue. We have steadily adhered to our Government, regardless of the effect on the status of the negro. We have opposed incorporating the negro as a National element of strife. Shall we now permit the negro to stand between us and our Government? If of any value, the negro is certainly of less value now than when we refused to accept him as an issue. Will we not, by refusing, upon some reasonable terms, to accept the proposed amendment permit the negro to interpose between us and our Government? We are not to blame for such an issue, for we ever opposed it. But will we not have cause to reproach ourselves if, at this late period of our struggle, we accept such an issue? These questions are suggestive, and I will elaborate them.

But what have we a right, under all the circumstances, to demand, as just and reasonable, if we accept the proposed amendment?

Our slave property was assessed for taxation in 1860, before the war began, at $107,494,527. In 1863 the effect of rebellion and unfriendly legislation reduced the valuation to $57,511,770; and in 1864 to $34,179,246.

In view of the sufferings of our people, the loyal stand ever maintained by our State, our losses by the direct and indirect action of our Government pending our struggle to maintain our national life, may we not, with confidence, demand as a condition of our acceptance of the proposed amendment, that Congress shall appropriate the last assessed value of slaves—$31,179,246—to the use of the State, to be used in compensating the owners for the slaves so emancipated? England, in the act of 1833 abolishing slavery, appropriated £20,000,000 to compensate the owners. It cannot be that our Government will be less just, if we accept the amendment upon condition that the assessed value of 1864 be paid to the State, to compensate owners who are to be affected by the proposed amendment; the acceptance to be declared when notice of the appropriation is officially given to the Chief Executive of the Commonwealth. Those who believe that the adoption of this amendment will have the effect to shorten our struggle with rebellion cannot refuse to vote the appropriation, as it will, upon their own theory, be economical. Those who hold to our views cannot refuse it, because it is just and right.

The past is beyond our control; the present only is ours; but, by wise and prudent councils, the future may be shaped by us. Deprived of all control over the past, shall we cheat ourselves of the future by inconsiderately or rashly throwing away the present opportunity to shape our destiny?

The good of our own people—security to them of life, liberty, and the pursuit of happiness, should be our chief and great concern, in acting upon this momentous question. To forfeit present benefit and imperil future security, because of disapprobation of the past, is not the wisdom of the safe and prudent statesman. If we could defeat the final adoption of the proposed amendment by our refusal to ratify it, the policy or impolicy of doing so would then be a legitimate question of debate. But whether we ratify or not, the end must come; it is a fixed fact; slavery must end. Shall we accept the fact, although we had no hand in bringing it about; or shall we close our eyes to its existence? Though we may close our eyes to the fact, yet it will still remain, and will affect us as materially as if we looked upon and accepted it.

By refusing the conditional acceptance suggested, will you not greatly endanger the quiet and security of our people, and subject them to untold harassments by protracting the issue, without the possibility of gaining any thing thereby? Will you not risk the loss of all against nothing to be gained? Better accept it unconditionally, than to reject it altogether.

The prudent farmer, after the storm has swept over his orchard and torn a branch from a favorite tree, leaving it attached by only a few shattered fibers, will cut off the branch and cast it away, that it may not draw the sap which would go to heal the wound, to feed for a season the sickly life of the torn branch, then carry back its decay to the parent trunk. Shall we be less wise? Would he be deemed wise or prudent who, having an arm shattered by a bushwhacker, and pronounced by the surgeon to be incurable save by amputation, yet would obstinately refuse amputation, solely upon the ground that he was not shot in open battle or fair fight? Would such refusal change the character of the wound, or lessen the danger of mortification and death? Shall we refuse to have the shattered limb of slavery amputated, when none can think of saving it, merely because it has been destroyed by rebels and Abolitionists combined?

As you love our country, and would save our suffering from people from evils which no pen can adequately trace, I beseech you to lay aside all passion, prejudice, and partisan asperities, and meet this gravest and most vital question to the present and future of our State, which you may ever be called upon to solve, like states-men and patriots who comprehend the crisis, and dare to meet the responsibilities of the occasion. If not will-ing to act without first consulting your constituents, better take time to consult them, and then act, than postpone this question to the future. Such are the con-victions which, deeply impressed upon my mind, are freely and frankly stated for your consideration.

  THOS. E. BRAMLETTE
  Governor of Kentucky.

14

Vice President Elect Andrew Johnson, Speech at the Tennessee State Constitutional Convention, *Washington Reporter* (PA)

February 15, 1865, p. 1

The Nashville Times has the following report of a speech delivered by Governor Johnson on the 14ᵗʰ instant, on the adjournment of the State Convention which abol-ished slavery in Tennessee.

  Gentlemen: I come here to-night to be a listener, with the rest of you, to your nominee for Governor; but, as there seems to be a disappointment, I shall try to enter-tain you for a brief time. Gentlemen, I congratulate you in the sincerity of my heart on the successful conclusion of your labors. It is the greatest work of the age. In the great revolution which is going forward, you have per-formed your part nobly. This I say without flattery; your work has been well-done. In this momentous struggle, in the development of the great principles of human lib-erty, you have discharged your duty manfully.

  Who would have thought, three or four years ago, that Tennesseans would have been permitted to as-semble in this Capitol, for such a purpose, without being molested, or driven from its halls? The mighty principles of human rights and liberty have been pitted against monopoly and slavery. Yesterday you broke the tyrant's rod and set the captives free. [Loud applause.] Yes, gentlemen, you sounded the death knell of negro aristocracy, and performed the funeral obsequies of that thing called slavery. You have opened the grave and

let the carcass down, and all that remains is for you to seal the pit on the 22 of February, the anniversary of the day which gave birth to the father of his Country. Con-secrate your work on that day.

EMANCIPATION OF BLACKS AND WHITES

I feel a heartfelt gratitude that I have lived to see it done, and that I have been permitted to perform my little part in the great drama. The blow has been struck, and slav-ery lies prostrate. An insolent, insincere, ignorant, un-feeling, hypocritical, nefarious, diabolical slave aristoc-racy has been tumbled to the ground.

  They who never learned that "Worth makes the man, and want of it the fellow," who lived on the real or imagi-nary honors of a buried ancestry, must go down. Your sessions have been, on the whole, harmonious, not-withstanding some little bickering, which I think will pass away with your adjournment.

  While you think that you have emancipated black men, I tell you that you have emancipated more white men than black men from the insolent domination of the slaveholder. Yes, the time was not long ago when you dared not speak your sentiments. Even in East Tennes-see, where there were only a few slaves, and we always spoke more freely, do you remember the power which the slaveholder exercised? How many of our people were compelled to live on barren ridges and cultivate the stony spots, while a few slaveholders owned thou-sands of broad acres in the fertile valleys, which they tilled with their bondsmen? Even you felt their power, and knew the contempt they felt for you.

  Because many years ago, I dared to speak of these things, I was denounced as an agrarian and demagogue, who appealed to the prejudices of the people. Thank God, I have lived to see the day when the people of my State have declared themselves free. I must now urge you to redouble your efforts and carry out your work when you go hence. If you consummate it with the same resolution, the foul blot of human slavery will be re-moved from the escutcheon of the State.

  I shall say nothing of the future condition of the negro, nor of the elective franchise. First, reorganize; time and experience will regulate the rest. Let us first get rid of slavery; let there be no bickering or conflict till we get that out of the way. This being done, we will take up other questions, and dispose of them as they arise. Who could have anticipated, three years ago, that we would have progressed thus far? Let us, like wise men, hold ourselves in readiness to manage new questions which may arise in the future. There is no need of giving ourselves trouble prematurely.

THE NEW STATE

Gentlemen of the Convention, or primary meeting, or assembly of the people, whichever you may choose to call it—you have already lived to see a great work done. The news has gone forth over the land on the wings of lightning. As I stated the other day I had got a dispatch from Governor Fletcher, announcing Missouri was free, so I sent back yesterday a message to him that in my own State over five hundred delegates had unanimously abolished slavery. I also sent a message to Abraham that the death-knell of slavery had been sounded in Tennessee. If we elect a legislature, redistrict the State, and elect Senators and Congressmen, they will certainly be received at Washington, and the whole trouble of reconstruction will be at an end. Our State will be as much a State as ever, having only lost its distracting element of slavery, and therefore stronger for the loss.

. . .

Nor let any man suppose that I think that any portion of the populace should be turned forth as loafers without work. The sooner we get out of this transition state—which is always the worst—the better for us, the better for the negroes. In five years from now the labor of the black man will be more productive than ever, for freedom simply means liberty to work and enjoy the products of one's labor. Let us try to comprehend the times in which we live, and the great principles which are at work. There is a breaking up of old combinations, and men are coming together by their natural affinities. Old parties are disintegrating, and new ideas, thrown out among men of mind, form the basis of new parties. Here is the great contest of philanthropy, of sound reason, of humanity, whose foundation is the Christian religion; a bow of promise, whose base rests upon the horizon, and whose span arches the universe.

15

"The Abolition Amendment," *Crisis* (Columbus, OH)

February 15, 1865, p. 20*

The gallant little State of Delaware has been the first to repudiate the spurious and fraudulent abolition amendment to the Federal Constitution, its Legislature having refused, by a decisive vote, to ratify the amendment submitted to it. Delaware—small as she is, and insignificant in extent and population compared with many of her sister States—has too much dignity, self-respect and chivalry, and knows too well the value of her own sovereign rights to wantonly strike down those of other States by adding her support to the enforcement of a measure which had its origin in the hotbed of Abolition Federalism. The traditional integrity of that little State—her independence and unswerving loyalty to the Constitution and its compacts—will shine from out the cloud of fanaticism and revolution with a lustre and brilliancy of which her children in all lands may be proud. She selected not the path of abolition fanaticism of her own accord—neither could she be bribed or bullied into it by the overshadowing oligarchy at Washington. By this course her people have proven consistent with the history and traditions left them by the first Revolution.

Gov. Bramlette, of Kentucky—in harmony with the vacillating and dubious course which has characterized his administration from the beginning—has recommended the adoption of the amendment; but it is doubtful whether the Legislature of the State will sanction by their votes this last and most outrageous usurpation of the Federal Government. Let Kentucky look at the men in Congress by whose votes this amendment was adopted—let her investigate the filthy means by which they were induced to vote for it—let her reflect upon the history of the elections in that State—and then ratify this outrage upon the Constitution if she can.

In Indiana the Democracy in the Legislature are

* [Originally established by Democrat Samuel Medary, the newspaper *The Crisis* supported the policies of Northern "peace democrats," or "copperheads," as they were derisively called by Republicans. —Ed.]

making a gallant fight against the humbug amendment. We wish their prospect of success was better. The patriotic people of that State are naturally opposed to it, but the same agencies which forced the fraud through Congress may effect its passage in the Legislature.

The same may be said of New Jersey.—There the amendment is being discussed and has not yet been adopted, but the parties are so evenly balanced that there is scarcely a hope that the attempted alteration of the Constitution will be successfully resisted.

16
Kentucky, "The Constitutional Amendment Rejected,"
New York Daily Tribune
February 24, 1865, p. 1

FRANKFORT, WEDNESDAY, FEB. 22, 1864
In the Senate to-day the reports of the Judiciary Committee on the Constitutional Amendment were taken up. Mr. Robinson's minority report, favoring ratification on condition of compensation, was rejected by a decisive vote—Yeas, 9, Nays, 21. A substitute for the report of the majority was offered by Mr. Flake, that the Legislature ratify unconditionally, was also rejected by a vote of Yeas, 11; Nays, 22. The final vote rejecting the Amendment was Yeas, 21, to Nays 12.

17
Louisiana, Ratification of Amendment, Call for Black Suffrage, *Salem Register* (MA)
February 27, 1865, p. 2

The constitutional amendment abolishing Slavery was ratified by the State of Louisiana on the 17th, by both branches of the Legislature.

Mr. Hills has introduced in the Louisiana Legislature a memorial signed by about 5000 colored men, asking

for the right of suffrage. Read, and referred to a select committee.

18
New Jersey, Debates and Failure to Ratify
February 9–March 1, 1865*

On Thursday, February 9th, MR. CLEAVER, of Essex, introduced the following bill:

An Act to ratify an amendment to the Constitution of the United States.

1. *Be it enacted by the Senate and General Assembly of the State of New Jersey*: That the amendment to the Constitution of the United States proposed at the second session of the Thirty-Eighth Congress, by a Resolution of the Senate and House of Representatives of the United States of America, in Congress assembled, to the several State Legislatures, be, and the same is hereby, upon the part of this Legislature, Ratified, and made a part of the Constitution of the United States of America—said Amendment having been approved on the first day of February, A. D., eighteen hundred and sixty-five; and is in the following words, to wit:

Article XIII
Sec. 1. Neither Slavery nor involuntary servitude, except as a punishment for crime whereof the party shall have been duly convicted, shall exist within the United States, or any place subject to their jurisdiction.
Sec. 2. Congress shall have power to enforce this Article by appropriate legislation.

The bill was read a first time, by its title, and referred to the Committee of the Judiciary.

Thursday, February 23d.—MR. L. ABBETT, of Hudson, Chairman of the Judiciary Committee reported the bill to the Assembly, with the following amendment:

* *Debates in the Eighty-Ninth General Assembly of the State of New Jersey on the Bill to Ratify an Amendment to the Constitution of the United States* (Trenton, NJ: J. R. Freese, State Gazette Office, 1865).

2. *And be it enacted*, That this act shall be submitted to the People at the next general election to be held in this State. The clerk of each city and township in the different election districts of this State shall provide at each Poll on said election day, a box in the usual form for the reception of the ballots herein provided: and each and every elector of this State may present a ballot, which shall be a paper ticket, on which shall be printed or written, or partly written and partly printed, one of the following forms, "For the Amendment to the Constitution of the United States," or "Against the Amendment of the Constitution of the United States." The said ballots shall be so folded as to conceal the contents of the ballot, and shall be endorsed "Act to ratify an Amendment of the Constitution of the United States."

3. *And be it enacted*, That after finally closing the polls of such election, the Board of Election shall immediately and without adjournment proceed to count and canvass the ballots in relation to the proposed act, in the same manner as they are by law required to canvass the ballots given for Governor, and thereupon shall set down in writing and in words at full length, the whole number of votes given, "For the Amendment of the Constitution of the United States" and the whole number of votes "Against the Amendment of the Constitution of the United States," and certify and subscribe the same, and cause the copies thereof to be made, certified and delivered, as prescribed by law in respect to the canvass of votes given at an election for Governor. And all the provisions of "An Act to regulate elections," approved April 16, 1846, and the supplements thereto, shall as far as applicable, apply to the submission of the People herein provided for.

4. *And be it enacted*, That this Act shall not become a law until it is ratified by the People, in pursuance of the Constitution and the provisions thereof.

5. *And be it enacted*, That this act shall take effect and become a law immediately after the People have ratified the same in the mode pointed out in this Act.

L. ABBETT, Chairman,
WM. M. ILIFF,
JAS. C. GOBLE.

MR. CLEAVER, of Essex, from the minority of the Judiciary Committee, presented the following report:

That, whereas, great legal uncertainty attends the proposition made by the majority of said Committee, to submit to a popular vote the Act ratifying the Amendment to the Constitution of the United States, as the same was proposed at the second session of the Thirty-Eighth Congress "to the several State Legislatures;"

And whereas, Congress has the clear and undoubted right to elect whether such ratification shall be by "the Legislatures of three-fourths of the several States, or by Conventions in three-fourths thereof." (See Art. 5, of the Constitution of the United States),

And whereas Congress has *not* proposed that said ratification should be by "Convention," nor by a vote of the people, but *has* proposed and elected that said ratification shall be by "the several State Legislatures:"

Therefore, and in order to remove all doubts touching the absolute and unconditional ratification of the said amendment to the Constitution of the United States, on the part of the State of New Jersey, and in order that the proposition of ratification, as made by Congress, may be acted upon by the body to whom it was remitted by Congress for that purpose—the minority of your Judiciary Committee recommend the passage of Assembly Bill No. 115, without amendment.

JAMES D. CLEAVER,
C. C. LATHROP.

FEBRUARY 23, 1865.
The bill and reports were ordered printed, and made the special order for Tuesday, February 28.

TUESDAY, FEBRUARY 28.—The House of Assembly, after the expiration of the morning hour, proceeded to the consideration of the special order, being the reports of the Judiciary Committee, on the bill to ratify the Amendment to the Constitution of the United States, the question being on the agreement by the House, to the amendments proposed by the majority of the Committee.

After debate on the amendments, the question was taken on agreeing to said amendments, and it was decided in the negative as follows:

Yeas . . . 19

Nays . . . 38

The bill was then read and agreed to, and ordered to be engrossed for a third reading.

DEBATE

The House met at half-past two o'clock on the same day, and proceeded to the consideration of the Bill to Ratify the Constitutional Amendment.

The Bill was read the third time, and the question stated by the Speaker: "Shall this bill pass?"

Speech of Hon. P. C. Brinck.

Mr. SPEAKER:—I read from the 5th section of the Constitution of the United States, as follows:

...*

By which it appears a plan has been provided for an alteration of that Constitution. The subject has been officially brought to our attention by the Executive of the State.

The only mode by which the Amendment under consideration can be ratified, so far as the State of New Jersey is concerned, is through this legislative body, conjointly. We cannot throw the responsibility (if we would) upon the people of the State.

...

Speech of Hon. James C. Goble.

...

What amendments are proposed to be made that we are called upon by our vote to ratify and confirm? It is to amend the Constitution so far and in all respects as it relates to involuntary servitude or the abolition of slavery in the United States. Its advocates tell us this is all; it is very small; very short; easily attended to; very soon passed; very innocent; it cannot possibly injure any one; while it will prove a lasting blessing to the whole country. They say it is the voice of humanity, of reason, of pure religion. For my part, I cannot see these points; but I confess I see the very reverse all the way through. To me it seems much larger, and to embrace much more than would seem to be conveyed in the few lines in which the proposed amendment is couched.

...

But what is the nature of the amendments now proposed? Simply one idea permeates the whole, and that is, negro emancipation, negro freedom, and negro equality. This they ask for, this they intend, and this they tell us they will have, cost what it will. They will violate

the Constitution, break all oaths, kill every white person by a perpetual war, bankrupt the nation, and wreck the American Republic to accomplish their fiend-like object. When Abraham Lincoln came into power, he called the colored people niggers, then negroes, declaring that they were a different race, that they could not live with us, that they must colonize and go by themselves. In less than a year from that time, and ever since, they have by him and his party been styled "American citizens of African descent," while it appears to me that the negro tendency is still upward with the party in power. Marked distinctions and preferences have been given to the negro on many occasions by them. They soon will be, not only equal, but superior to the white race, if this abolition mania prevails much longer and spreads much farther.

...

I admit, Mr. Speaker, the fact that there is a provision in the Constitution to amend the same.... Let us examine this provision of the constitution a little for our benefit, and see if we are prepared to ratify the amendments with the legislative vote of New Jersey. Observe, 1st. These amendments were intended to be entrusted with the friends and not the declared bitter enemies of the constitution. Compare that elevated assemblage of men who made the constitution, and who made it on the white basis, with the body of members of both Houses of Congress, who, with a few honorable exceptions, are determined to amend (or kill) the constitution, so that the negro shall be the equal, if not superior, to the white man. 2d. The Congress and two-thirds of both Houses of which shall propose, &c. Was there any such a Congress present? Did two-thirds of all the members of both Houses vote amendments? These questions can only be answered in the negative. 3d. When two-thirds of both Houses shall deem it necessary. Have two-thirds of both Houses deemed it necessary? Have they set forth the great importance of the amendments—the great benefits resulting therefrom to the general government—to the different States of the Union, east, west, north and south? Or do these amendments spring from the political dogmas of the party in power, whose intellectual faculties are greatly impaired from a prevalent disease, called "the negro on the brain?" These amendments owe their origin decidedly to the latter. 4th. Two-thirds of both Houses shall propose amendments to this constitution. Now if there were honestly two-thirds of both Houses who voted for the amendments, it can only be for the proposal of them. They may offer them, and that

---

* [Brinck quotes the full text of Article V. —Ed.]

ends all their power. Why should these amendments be proposed, but to give the people an opportunity to examine their merits, have them put into county and district canvass of all the counties and districts of the several States, that the Legislatures of all the States shall be composed of members who were elected upon the great issue of constitutional amendments. This Legislature was not so elected. We are not ready for the question. We cannot vote upon it. We were sent here to support, not to amend the Constitution of the United States. We have all, and severally, sworn to do so. Everything honorable, sacred and just requires us to keep our oaths. I hope these amendments will be put at issue by their advocates and friends next fall, at our annual election throughout the State, and thus elect a legislature prepared to vote for or against these amendments.

. . .

Speech of Hon. Charles C. Lathrop.

. . .

It has been said by the gentleman from Hudson (Mr. Abbett), and others, that this question was not before the people at the last election, and that therefore it ought not to be acted on now. But this subject was virtually before the people in that late canvass. The question as to whether the power of slavery, which had plunged our land into a sea of blood, should continue to rule this country, or be overthrown, was the question which influenced the action of the people in my part of the State at least. As early as April 8th, 1864, the Senate of the United States passed this amendment of the Constitution, and it was well known to be pending before the House of Representatives, and the matter would be considered by the people. In fact it was the most momentous of all questions in the canvass, as to whether slavery should die in order that the Republic might live, and from my section, not a member was elected to the legislature that did not favor this measure.

. . .

When the proclamation of emancipation was issued by President Lincoln, it was denounced by the Democratic party as unconstitutional. I had, myself, considered it of no avail except as a war measure. It was issued more for foreign effect than for anything practical it might accomplish at home. The Democracy then universally insisted that the only way slavery could legally be reached was by an amendment of the constitution, and proposed that such action should be had. We now stand on Democratic ground, and I now call upon the

Democrats of this House to redeem these pledges. I appeal to them to take rank with the immortal sixteen Democrats in the House of Representatives, who stood so fearlessly and so boldly in Congress, voting for this measure, and against an institution that had broken up and destroyed their party, as it had before done to the party with which it was my pleasure, formerly to be associated, the old Whig party.

. . .

Speech of Hon. D. E. Culver.

. . .

In passing this amendment presented to us, without a provision for compensation to loyal slave-owners in the loyal States of Delaware and Kentucky, we should break our solemn faith pledged to them in the constitution that all their property should be held sacred, which under it is not to be taken away without payment of its full and fair value. I admit, sir, that for the good of the whole, the property of the citizen can be taken, but not without consideration. The States of Delaware and Kentucky have never seceded, and then to what a depth have we fallen, when for their loyalty, we propose to reward the citizens of those States by such unjust and ungenerous treatment. I trust that the State of New Jersey will never do so mean an act; leave it to patriots of Massachusetts and other northern States, after they have shipped off and sold the most valuable of their slave property to the people of the southern States, even while men are living who witnessed the transactions, to rush with indecent haste through the legislatures of those States, bills to free those slaves and their descendants by violence and without even so much as an apology.

. . .

Speech of Hon. Robert Moore.

. . .

I contend that it is not only competent and expedient to thus amend the constitution, but that this is the time for the adoption of such an amendment. Would that the same *patriotism* that animated the breast of the illustrious author of the Declaration of Independence, animated the breast of every member of this assembly. The question on the constitutional amendment would then be settled in this House. Let us endeavor to follow in the footsteps of the illustrious Jefferson, who was a strong advocate of emancipation in his day. His patriotic fears for the future made him extremely anxious to rid the country of this dangerous element. I recollect reading one of Mr. Jefferson's letters to Mr. Holmes, of Maine, that in speaking of slavery he says: "This wolf that we have by the ears we can neither hold fast nor safely let go." But the time has now come when we can safely let him go.

...

Can New Jersey hesitate to join in this good work? Missouri, Maryland and West Virginia have already enrolled themselves in the number of free States, and though Delaware and Kentucky still hesitate, the party of freedom is growing in those States, and will soon be able to control their policy. Tennessee, Arkansas and Louisiana are ready for this great reform, and will give it their sanction. Will New Jersey be alone among the Free States, and stop the progress of Freedom, when slave States set her an example?

...

Speech of Hon. Leon Abbett.

Mr. SPEAKER: I have no love for slavery. It neither enlists my sympathies nor commends itself to my judgment. I trust the hour may speedily come, when throughout the whole land it shall be abolished by State legislation. I stand here not to defend slavery but to maintain the sovereignty of the States as guaranteed by the Constitution. The liberties of this people can never be preserved except by a recognition of all the rights of the States. Every blow struck at these rights is an assault upon the liberties of the citizen. Since the formation of the General Government there has been a contest as to the extent of the powers delegated to the Federal Union and those reserved by the States. The National Government is aggressive. It seeks to extend its powers by a too liberal construction of the charter creating it. The States have ever been jealous of the tendency towards centralization. They have felt that their very existence as independent sovereignties rested upon the limitation of these powers by a strict construction of the provisions of the Constitution. So profoundly were they impressed with the necessity of erecting a strong barrier against the encroachments of Federal power, that they amended the Constitution by inserting the following article:

> "The powers not delegated to the United States by the Constitution, nor prohibited by it to the States, are reserved to the States respectively, or to the people."

The rights of the States remained secure under this provision until the party in power, unable to encroach upon State rights by construction of the Constitution, have sought to accomplish this purpose by its amendment. The object is still the same. The proposed amendment seeks to remove from the States the control of their own local matters and subject them to Federal legislation.

...

The Democratic party cannot abandon a great principle of government for the problematical good that may possibly result from immediate emancipation by national legislation. It is better to secure emancipation by State legislation.

...

The first section [of the amendment] abolishes slavery.

The second gives Congress the power to enforce this provision by legislation. It gives Congress the power to *compel* the loyal States of Kentucky and Delaware to free their slaves. The Federal Government may enter these sovereign States, and by force compel its citizens to give up, without compensation, their slaves, which have been recognized as their private property since the formation of the government. If this be not an infringement of the rights of States, I can imagine no assumption of power that might not be equally justified, provided it came in the shape of a Constitutional Amendment.

...

This proposed amendment is but the entering wedge. If this be driven home, other attempts will follow until the constitution be rent asunder. Were this amendment to be enforced as the law of the United States, it would free four million slaves. The constitution provides that representation in Congress shall be apportioned among the several States according to their respective numbers, which shall be determined by adding the whole number of free persons, including those bound to serve for a term of years, and excluding Indians not taxed, *three-fifths of all other persons.* If these slaves were free the Southern States, instead of having only three-fifths of four millions in the next apportionment, would have the entire number represented. These freedmen would not have a vote, but the white men of the South would have an additional number of representatives in Congress, and their political power would be largely increased. Is it probable that the party in power desire this? Would it not ask for a further amendment? No gentleman upon the other side has dared to suggest this; but we have seen the response already from one of their prominent men (Prof. Lieber*). He states distinctly that such a state of facts could not be tolerated. That this amendment would require another giving representation based upon the number in each State entitled to vote. The object of this further action is either to decrease the number of representatives from the Southern States or compel them to allow the negroes to vote. First, we are to take their property away without compensation, and then force them to allow negro suffrage or submit to a decrease of national representation. Gentlemen imagine that this amendment will end this negro discussion. On the contrary, its adoption will only serve to open the door to the most disturbing questions. This initiative legislation is only the beginning of the end.

I have been surprised that every gentleman on the other side who has spoken on this subject, has stated that the decision of this question depended on the vote of New Jersey, and that all now needed to complete the ratification of the amendment was her vote in its favor. Surely gentlemen must have forgotten the express provisions of the constitution. An amendment is only "valid as part of this constitution when ratified by the legislatures of three-fourths of the several States, or by conventions in three-fourths thereof." There are now thirty-six States in the Union. It therefore requires twenty-seven to make this amendment "a part of the constitution." Eleven States are now in actual rebellion, namely, Virginia, North Carolina, South Carolina, Georgia, Alabama, Mississippi, Florida, Tennessee, Louisiana, Arkansas and Texas. Take these from the thirty-six, and you have only twenty-five. You then require, to adopt the amendment, not only all of the loyal States, but two of the States now in actual rebellion. Moreover, the loyal States of Delaware and Kentucky have decided against the amendment. It therefore requires two more of the seceded States. Four States in actual rebellion must assent to this amendment before it can become part of the constitution. If we count four of these States in favor of this measure, then, and only then, it is true that the vote of New Jersey is also needed to settle the question. Does the Republican party intend to count four of these eleven States? Can it be possible that it contemplates the perpetuation of such an outrage on the American people and the rights of the

* [See "Dr. Lieber's Letter to Senator E. D. Morgan," this section, doc. 5. —Ed.]

States? The Senate of the United States, preponderatingly Republican, has refused to count the votes of these eleven States in the electoral college. While the question was under discussion, Senator Hale said that if the election depended on the votes of Tennessee, Louisiana and Alabama, and they were counted, the party against whom they were counted would not have submitted. That such an act would have produced a second revolution and deluged the North with blood. Senator Wade said, "that the President's proposition that one-tenth of the rebellious States could bring back those States into the Union without any ceremony, was a dangerous one. Louisiana had nothing but the shadow of a civil government. Nothing but the sham semblance of a government could be had in a State till the majority of its people are loyal. The whole State was under military control. There could be no free action where the military authority was supreme. The elections in these Southern States were all shams. Military power had controlled them, and the people had no voice in the matter. The same communities that repealed these ordinances of secession would have done any thing else they were told to do just as well." I know that several organs of the Republican party have counted the States of Tennessee, Virginia, Louisiana and Arkansas to make up the requisite number of twenty-seven. I did not expect that such a policy would be approved by any member of this House. I see, however, by their statement, that the vote of New Jersey alone is needed, that the Republican members of this House deliberately sanction such a course. Shall I, then, by my vote, make myself party to such a fraud? And here it may be relevant to inquire, in whom does the law vest the discretion to receive or reject the votes of these "sham" State governments? In the Secretary of the United States, William H. Seward! The official notice of ratification is transmitted to him, and when the number of such ratifications amounts to three-fourths of the several States, he is required "forthwith to cause the said amendment to be published in the newspapers authorized to promulgate the laws, with his certificate, specifying the States by which the same may have been adopted, and that the same has become valid to all intents and purposes, as part of the Constitution of the United States." I am unwilling to trust William H. Seward with such discretionary power. He is too much of a partisan, to leave any doubt in my mind what his action would be. He would count four "sham" State governments, and declare the amendment adopted and the entire military power of the country would be used to enforce his decree.

…

Speech of Hon. James H. Nixon.

…

The gentleman from Hudson founded his argument upon the doctrine of State sovereignty. That formed the basis of all he said. If his premises had been correct, his argument might have had some force; but he built upon a sandy foundation and the whole structure must fall. I am not a little surprised that the gentleman should contend so earnestly at this late day in favor of the theories of John C Calhoun. State sovereignty has been a dangerous doctrine in this country, a veritable Pandora's Box, full to overflowing with direful plagues. The States of this Federal Union are not sovereign in the sense in which the gentleman uses the term. The chief attributes of sovereignty were surrendered by them when this government was formed. The Constitution of the United States which our fathers agreed should be the supreme law of the land, says—no State shall coin money, nor emit bills of credit, nor pass ex post facto laws, nor laws impairing the obligation of contracts, nor maintain armies and navies, nor grant letters of marque, nor make compacts with other States, nor hold intercourse with foreign powers, nor grant titles of nobility. Wherein does the sovereignty of the States exist after such a surrender? To call them sovereign is a perversion of language. The States were once sovereign. They were so under the articles of confederation, and if the gentleman's speech had been made then, it might have had some weight. But it was to do away with State sovereignty and form a more perfect union, that the present government of the United States was organized.… The people, and not the States, established this government. A contract requires two parties, here there is but one—we the people.

…

The Congress of the United States, having passed by a two-thirds vote the amendment which has been read several times in your hearing, have submitted it to the legislatures of the various States for ratification, according to the first method prescribed for ratifying amendments in the fifth article of the Constitution. The gentleman from Hudson labored hard to prove that there is something dangerous in the second section of the proposed amendment. He sees, or thinks he sees, some new and extraordinary power conferred upon Congress that will pave the way to future invasions of the rights of the States. He seems to look upon it as an indirect usurpation of the part of Congress. Let us look at both sections, for there are only two.

…[*]

Now, Mr. Speaker, I can discover no ground for the gentleman's fears. They are but the creatures of his imagination. The section proposes to give no unusual power to Congress. I would be willing to strike it out, for it would not in the least change the effect of the amendment. It gives to Congress no power which it does not already possess, for what article is there in the Constitution that Congress cannot enforce by appropriate legislation? It is the duty of Congress to prevent and punish any infringement of the Constitution, which is the supreme law of the land, and this second section in no way adds to or limits Congressional power.

The object of the amendment cannot be stated more clearly than in the language of the amendment itself. It proposes to do away with slavery, forever, in the United States and in all places subject to their jurisdiction.

…

There seems to be in the minds of some a sanctity about slavery which makes it almost sacrilege to touch it even in a way which they admit is constitutional. They tell us that our fathers never meant that we should interfere with it, but I never heard anything that I thought deserved the name of an argument adduced in support of the doctrine. If the framers of the Constitution meant any such thing, why did they not include it among the subjects already alluded to, upon which Congress has no right to amend the Constitution? That would have settled the matter. They did not do it, and the reason is plain to all who have read the history of the times and know the character of the great men of that day.

…

The vote was taken and the bill was lost, as follows:

Ayes … 30.

Nays … 30.[†]

---

[*] [Nixon quotes the full text of both sections of the amendment. —Ed.]

[†] [According to the *Daily Age* (Philadelphia, PA), the vote, taken on March 1, was "30 yays to 34 nays." See *Daily Age*, Mar. 2, 1865, 2. The paper also reported, "The result was received with cheers and hisses in the lobbies. It was a strict party vote." —Ed.]

19

"The Constitutional Amendment,"
Daily Age (Philadelphia, PA)

March 7, 1865, p. 2

The action of the New Jersey Legislature rejecting the constitutional amendment abolishing slavery throughout the United States, defeats that measure. So far, eighteen States, including West Virginia, and that other bogus organization which met at Alexandria, and claimed to act for the real State of Virginia, have ratified the amendment, and three have rejected it—Delaware, Kentucky and New Jersey. As it requires twenty seven States to engraft the proposed amendment upon the Constitution, nine are yet to vote in the affirmative before the design of the Abolitionists can be consummated. The States that it is claimed have a right *now* to vote upon the amendment are—

Name of State	Meeting of Legislature
Arkansas	Now in session
Connecticut	May 3, 1865
California	Dec. 4, 1865
Iowa	Jan. 7, 1866
New Hampshire	June 7, 1865
Oregon	Sept. 10, 1866
Tennessee	April 3, 1865
Vermont	Oct. 12, 1865

Of these, Arkansas, as at present organized, is no more entitled to vote through her Legislature now in session than was the faction that met at Alexandria, in Virginia, entitled to represent that old Commonwealth. The whole affair, so far as its legality and constitutionality are concerned, is an insult to the people of the United States. Tennessee was excluded by the Abolitionists themselves from participation in the election of a President in 1864; and with what show of right or justice can it now be claimed that her Legislature has a right to vote upon a proposition to amend the Constitution of the United States? The claim is preposterous; and amendments engrafted upon the organic law of the land by such means will be no more a part of the Constitution, in truth and righteousness, than if they had been placed there by the will of the Emperor of China.

20

Abraham Lincoln, Speech on the Status of Louisiana (Lincoln's Last Public Address)

April 11, 1865[*]

We meet this evening, not in sorrow, but in gladness of heart. The evacuation of Petersburg and Richmond, and the surrender of the principal insurgent army, give hope of a righteous and speedy peace whose joyous expression can not be restrained. In the midst of this, however, He from whom all blessings flow, must not be forgotten. A call for a national thanksgiving is being prepared, and will be duly promulgated. Nor must those whose harder part gives us the cause of rejoicing, be overlooked. Their honors must not be parceled out with others. I myself was near the front, and had the high pleasure of transmitting much of the good news to you; but no part of the honor, for plan or execution, is mine. To Gen. Grant, his skillful officers, and brave men, all belongs. The gallant Navy stood ready, but was not in reach to take active part.

By these recent successes the re-inauguration of the national authority—reconstruction—which has had a large share of thought from the first, is pressed much more closely upon our attention. It is fraught with great difficulty. Unlike a case of a war between independent nations, there is no authorized organ for us to treat with. No one man has authority to give up the rebellion for any other man. We simply must begin with, and mold from, disorganized and discordant elements. Nor is it a small additional embarrassment that we, the loyal people, differ among ourselves as to the mode, manner, and means of reconstruction.

As a general rule, I abstain from reading the reports of attacks upon myself, wishing not to be provoked by that to which I can not properly offer an answer. In spite of this precaution, however, it comes to my knowledge that I am much censured for some supposed agency in setting up, and seeking to sustain, the new State government of Louisiana. In this I have done just so much as, and no more than, the public knows. In the Annual Mes-

[*]Lincoln, *Speeches and Writings*, 2:697–701.

sage of Dec. 1863 and accompanying Proclamation, I presented a plan of re-construction (as the phrase goes) which, I promised, if adopted by any State, should be acceptable to, and sustained by, the Executive government of the nation. I distinctly stated that this was not the only plan which might possibly be acceptable; and I also distinctly protested that the Executive claimed no right to say when, or whether members should be admitted to seats in Congress from such States. This plan was, in advance, submitted to the then Cabinet, and distinctly approved by every member of it. One of them suggested that I should then, and in that connection, apply the Emancipation Proclamation to the theretofore excepted parts of Virginia and Louisiana; that I should drop the suggestion about apprenticeship for freed-people, and that I should omit the protest against my own power, in regard to the admission of members to Congress; but even he approved every part and parcel of the plan which has since been employed or touched by the action of Louisiana. The new constitution of Louisiana, declaring emancipation for the whole State, practically applies the Proclamation to the part previously excepted. It does not adopt apprenticeship for freed-people; and it is silent, as it could not well be otherwise, about the admission of members to Congress. So that, as it applies to Louisiana, every member of the Cabinet fully approved the plan. The message went to Congress, and I received many commendations of the plan, written and verbal; and not a single objection to it, from any professed emancipationist, came to my knowledge, until after the news reached Washington that the people of Louisiana had begun to move in accordance with it. From about July 1862, I had corresponded with different persons, supposed to be interested, seeking a reconstruction of a State government for Louisiana. When the message of 1863, with the plan before mentioned, reached New-Orleans, Gen. Banks wrote me that he was confident the people, with his military co-operation, would reconstruct, substantially on that plan. I wrote him, and some of them to try it; they tried it, and the result is known. Such only has been my agency in getting up the Louisiana government. As to sustaining it, my promise is out, as before stated. But, as bad promises are better broken than kept, I shall treat this as a bad promise, and break it, whenever I shall be convinced that keeping it is adverse to the public interest. But I have not yet been so convinced.

I have been shown a letter on this subject, supposed to be an able one, in which the writer expresses regret that my mind has not seemed to be definitely fixed on the question whether the seceding States, so called, are in the Union or out of it. It would perhaps, add astonishment to his regret, were he to learn that since I have found professed Union men endeavoring to make that question, I have purposely forborne any public expression upon it. As appears to me that question has not been, nor yet is, a practically material one, and that any discussion of it, while it thus remains practically immaterial, could have no effect other than the mischievous one of dividing our friends. As yet, whatever it may hereafter become, that question is bad, as the basis of a controversy, and good for nothing at all—a merely pernicious abstraction.

We all agree that the seceded States, so called, are out of their proper relation with the Union; and that the sole object of the government, civil and military, in regard to those States is to again get them into that proper practical relation. I believe it is not only possible, but in fact, easier to do this, without deciding, or even considering, whether these States have ever been out of the Union, than with it. Finding themselves safely at home, it would be utterly immaterial whether they had ever been abroad. Let us all join in doing the acts necessary to restoring the proper practical relations between these States and the Union; and each forever after, innocently indulge his own opinion whether, in doing the acts, he brought the States from without, into the Union, or only gave them proper assistance, they never having been out of it.

The amount of constituency, so to speak, on which the new Louisiana government rests, would be more satisfactory to all, if it contained fifty, thirty, or even twenty thousand, instead of only about twelve thousand, as it does. It is also unsatisfactory to some that the elective franchise is not given to the colored man. I would myself prefer that it were now conferred on the very intelligent, and on those who serve our cause as soldiers. Still the question is not whether the Louisiana government, as it stands, is quite all that is desirable. The question is, "Will it be wiser to take it as it is, and help to improve it; or to reject, and disperse it?" "Can Louisiana be brought into proper practical relation with the Union sooner by sustaining, or by discarding her new State government?"

Some twelve thousand voters in the heretofore slave-state of Louisiana have sworn allegiance to the Union, assumed to be the rightful political power of the State, held elections, organized a State government, adopted a free-state constitution, giving the benefit of public schools equally to black and white, and empowering the Legislature to confer the elective franchise upon the colored man. Their Legislature has already voted to ratify the constitutional amendment recently passed by Congress, abolishing slavery throughout the nation. These twelve thousand persons are thus fully committed to the Union, and to perpetual freedom in the state—committed to the very things, and nearly all the things the nation wants—and they ask the nations recognition and its assistance to make good their committal. Now, if we reject, and spurn them, we do our utmost to disorganize and disperse them. We in effect say to the white men "You are worthless, or worse—we will neither help you, nor be helped by you." To the blacks we say "This cup of liberty which these, your old masters, hold to your lips, we will dash from you, and leave you to the chances of gathering the spilled and scattered contents in some vague and undefined when, where, and how." If this course, discouraging and paralyzing both white and black, has any tendency to bring Louisiana into proper practical relations with the Union, I have, so far, been unable to perceive it. If, on the contrary, we recognize, and sustain the new government of Louisiana the converse of all this is made true. We encourage the hearts, and nerve the arms of the twelve thousand to adhere to their work, and argue for it, and proselyte for it, and fight for it, and feed it, and grow it, and ripen it to a complete success. The colored man too, in seeing all united for him, is inspired with vigilance, and energy, and daring, to the same end. Grant that he desires the elective franchise, will he not attain it sooner by saving the already advanced steps toward it, than by running backward over them? Concede that the new government of Louisiana is only to what it should be as the egg is to the fowl, we shall sooner have the fowl by hatching the egg than by smashing it? Again, if we reject Louisiana, we also reject one vote in favor of the proposed amendment to the national Constitution. To meet this proposition, it has been argued that no more than three fourths of those States which have not attempted secession are necessary to validly ratify the amendment. I do not commit myself against this, further than to say that such a ratification would be questionable, and sure to be persistently questioned; while a ratification by three-fourths of all the States would be unquestioned and unquestionable.

I repeat the question, "Can Louisiana be brought into proper practical relation with the Union sooner by sustaining or by discarding her new State Government?"

What has been said of Louisiana will apply generally to other States. And yet so great peculiarities pertain to each state, and such important and sudden changes occur in the same state; and withal, so new and unprecedented is the whole case, that no exclusive, and inflexible plan can be safely prescribed as to details and collaterals. Such exclusive, and inflexible plan, would surely become a new entanglement. Important principles may, and must, be inflexible.

In the present "situation" as the phrase goes, it may be my duty to make some new announcement to the people of the South. I am considering, and shall not fail to act, when satisfied that action will be proper.

21

Assassination of President Lincoln, *New York Times*

April 15, 1865, p. 1

PRESIDENT LINCOLN SHOT BY AN ASSASSIN.

———

The Deed Done at Ford's Theatre Last Night.

———

The Act of a Desperate Rebel

———

The President Still Alive at Last Accounts.

———

No Hopes Entertained of His Recovery.

———

Attempted Assassination of Secretary Seward.

———

DETAILS OF THE DREADFUL TRAGEDY.

———

[OFFICIAL.]

War Department
Washington, April 15—1:30 A.M.
Maj.-Gen. Dix:
This evening at about 9:30 P.M., at Ford's Theatre, the President, while sitting in his private box with Mrs. LINCOLN, Mrs. HARRIS, and Major RATHBURN,* was shot by an assassin, who suddenly entered the box and approached behind the President.

* [The correct spelling was "Rathbone." —Ed.]

The assassin then leaped upon the stage, brandishing a large dagger or knife, and made his escape in the rear of the theatre.

The pistol ball entered the back of the President's head and penetrated nearly through the head. The wound is mortal. The President has been insensible ever since it was inflicted, and is now dying.

About the same hour an assassin, whether the same or not, entered Mr. SEWARD's apartments, and under the pretense of having a prescription, was shown to the Secretary's sick chamber. The assassin immediately rushed to the bed, and inflicted two or three stabs on the throat and two on the face. It is hoped the wounds may not be mortal. My apprehension is that they will prove fatal.

The nurse alarmed Mr. FREDERICK SEWARD, who was in an adjoining room, and hastened to the door of his father's room, when he met the assassin, who inflicted upon him one or more dangerous wounds. The recovery of FREDERICK SEWARD is doubtful.

It is not probable that the President will live throughout the night.

Gen. GRANT and wife were advertised to be at the theatre this evening, but he started to Burlington at 6 o'clock this evening.

At a Cabinet meeting at which Gen. GRANT was present, the subject of the state of the country and the prospect of a speedy peace was discussed. The President was very cheerful and hopeful, and spoke very kindly of Gen. LEE and others of the Confederacy, and of the establishment of government in Virginia.

All the members of the Cabinet except Mr. SEWARD, are now in attendance upon the President.

I have seen Mr. SEWARD, but he and FREDERICK were both unconscious.

EDWIN M. STANTON,
Secretary of War.

22

"This Hour Belongs Exclusively to the Negro," Speeches at the Thirty-Second Anniversary of the American Anti-Slavery Society, *New York Times*

May 10, 1865, p. 1

The first session of the thirty-second anniversary of the American Anti-Slavery Society was held yesterday morning, at 10:30 o'clock, in the Church of the Puritans, (Rev. Dr. Cheever's.) The heavy fall of rain in no way interfered with the entire numerical success of the occasion, as at 9:30 the spacious edifice was crowded to its fullest capacity. Upon the platform sat the venerable Wm. Lloyd Garrison, the perpetual President of the Society, Wendell Phillips, George Thompson, of England, Mrs. Francis Watkins Harper, Thomas Garrett, of Delaware, Robert Purvis, of Philadelphia, Samuel May, Jr., Rev. J.T. Sargent, Hon. George B. Lincoln, of Brooklyn, and Edmund Quincy, Esq., of Boston, and one or two others of note. The entrance of Messrs. GARRISON and PHILLIPS was the signal for enthusiastic applause and most friendly greeting on the part of the audience.

After a voluntary upon the organ, the meeting was called to order by Mr. GARRISON, who read the following song of Mrs. JULIA HOWE, which was sung by the choir, the vast audience joining in the "glory" chorus with fine effect:

HYMN OF THE REPUBLIC.
The John Brown Air.

Mine eyes have seen the glory of the coming of the
  Lord;
He has trampled out the vintage where the grapes of
  wrath were stored;
He hath loosed the fateful lightning of his terrible
  swift sword;
His truth is marching on.
Chorus—Glory, glory, hallelujah, etc.

I have seen him in the watch-fires of a hundred
  circling camps;
They have builded him an altar in the evening dews
  and damps;

I have read his righteous sentence by the dim and
   flaring lamps
His day is marching on.
Chorus—Glory, glory, hallelujah, etc.

I have read the fiery gospel writ in burnished rows
   of steel;
"As ye deal with my contemners, so with you My
   grace shall deal;
Let the hero, born of woman, crush the serpent with
   his heel,
Since God is marching on."
Chorus—Glory, glory, hallelujah, etc.

He has sounded forth the trumpet that shall never
   call retreat;
He is sifting out the hearts of men before his
   judgment-seat;
Oh, be swift, my soul, to answer him! be jubilant,
   my feet!
Our God is marching on.
Chorus—Glory, glory, hallelujah, etc.

In the beauty of the lilies Christ was born across the
   sea,
With a glory in his bosom that transfigures you and
   me;
As he died to make men holy, let us die to make
   men free,
While God is marching on.
Chorus—Glory, glory, hallelujah, etc.

Mr. GARRISON then read an appropriate selection from the Scriptures, which was followed by a prayer from Rev. SAMUEL MAY, JR.—a prayer of thanksgiving to the Lord for the abundant harvest which has resulted from the labors, trials and humiliations of the society; of thanks, that in the hour of the nation's peril so great and good a man as the late President of the United States was permitted to preside over our councils so long, and of fervent petition that the Lord would yet direct the nation with wisdom from above in the times yet to come, so that the bondmen might be made, in spite of the demon compromise, free and equal with all men, giving them the fullest recognition as an equal man and son of God.

. . .

SPEECH OF WENDELL PHILLIPS
Mr. PHILLIPS was then introduced and said:

MR. PRESIDENT, AND LADIES AND GENTLEMEN: I am very sorry to say, as you perceive, that I am laboring under a heavy cold, and am not at all able to make a speech. I come upon the platform simply to redeem the pledge made by the committee in their advertisement that I should be one of the speakers, and I know you will be considerate of my feeble voice, and allow me to make not a speech, but a few suggestions, which seem to me pertinent to the occasion. Everything on this platform is looked at in the light of the interest of the colored race. It is as Abolitionists that we meet here, and, therefore, all general considerations of citizenship are to be subordinated to Abolitionism. What I shall say on this occasion is in regard to the next national step to secure to the colored man his new-found rights. If the anti-slavery amendment to the constitution shall be indorsed, the parchment will guarantee to the slave his liberty. Our duty as Americans and clear-sighted Abolitionists is in the re-formation of the elements of State, so that the great forces of society shall guarantee the right recognized by the parchment. No freedom is real or emancipation effectual unless we arrange the forces of society that underlie law, so that they may secure to the freedmen their rights now and for all time.

. . .

The New President
The new President, in taking charge of the ship of state, announces the purposes which will guide his course, when he says that treason is a crime to be punished, not a mere difference of opinion, and the question now is, with the light of four years' experience, and with the announcement from the Presidential chair, what shall be the destination of our people? What shall be done to assassins? If the hand of DAVIS, red with the blood of our Chief Magistrate, be brought under the fetter, we must leave him in the charge of the government, but when we speak of the greatness of the people, aliens, not rebels, on the other side of the picket, we ask what shall be the policy of the government, which will be the quickest and surest guarantee for the liberty of the negro? One thousand men banded together by determined principle, intellectual, fierce, cunning and brave are the rebellion. It is not safe that these thousand men should continue to dwell in North America. Living or dead here is no place for them. . . . I would

have an act of Congress select one thousand men, the leading men of the South, and announce to the world that these are alien enemies, and thereby forever forbid, under pain of death, any one of them being found again in our territories. [Applause.] An act of Congress, under the war powers with no relation to treason, can declare them public enemies, aliens, who shall not be naturalized, nor permitted to come here. Of course, when they are banished their property falls into the hands of the government, to which I would add that of ten thousand more, the subordinates in the conspiracy, who are not strong enough to banish them, but enough to be crippled, and having the land, would then give it to the loyal white and black people of the South. Land I consider one of the two important elements in a politic reconstruction. Now for the other. Political power is in the ballot. In revolutionary times, except in South Carolina, every man, black and white, born free, voted, with the exception of a property qualification in some States. Our fathers were too wise to require book learning as a primary qualification for the use of the ballot. I am surprised that so masterly a mind as that of JOHN S. MILL should make such a mistake as to say that men should read before they can vote. Does he suppose that education is the exclusive prerogative of colleges? It is by work, not reading, that good voters are made. Whoever works develops his intellectual capacities, and taking men by the masses, they who work and don't read are half a century ahead of those who read and don't work, and this is the reason that the slaves will make better voters than the poor whites of the South. The negro inherited a brain which work had cultivated for four generations, and whether the soldier goes to him for advice, or the merchant for counsel, the negro is the only one who, at the South, can give either what he needs. Fairly considered, the only class ready for suffrage in the South is the negro. I would not exclude the white man on account of his ignorance, [Laughter] but the only class which, as a class, has had the education of work, is the black man. I scout as irrelevant the whole question of suffrage in connection with simple information. I read a circular the other day of a benevolent association, and it solicited subscriptions "to elevate the degraded black." I stopped there and thought that if we would remember that black lips and black hearts were the ones which alone gave comfort and sympathy to our armies, and that when SEWARD said that the war would change the status of no one; that the negro saw

the hand of God behind the bullet, and if then we could speak of the degraded black, we were like the Borubon, who never forgets and never learns anything. History will say that the Christianity and intellect of America culminated under a black skin. I would give to white and black the right of suffrage, and then have in our hands the two elements of success, *land* and the *ballot*. Slavery did not create the rebellion. It was the determination of a thousand men, to model a government based on classes and castes like that of England. They dared not confess it, as it would not fire the Southern heart. So this aristocracy used slavery as the instrument to rouse the South. The Anti-Slavery Amendment has torn that weapon from their hands, but the purpose remains the same. You can't kill or appall them, but you can flank them, as GRANT flanked LEE. He flanked him at every step, and finally at Burkesville, which has not, however, and will not come to us this fifteen years yet. Now, the hatred of the poor black and white, which still characterizes the people of the South, is as strong as ever. What shall be done with it? We must check it by new parchment securities. We must reconstruct South Carolina. She can put on her statute books to-day that no black man shall vote. Now, I like State rights, for, if properly bounded, it is good; but carried to the CALHOUN extreme, it is damnable, and that we may check State Rights at the proper time and place, I want to have another amendment passed which shall read thus: no State shall at any time make a distinction of civil privileges between the children of parents living on or born on her soil, either of race, condition or color. [Applause.] I hope some day to be bold enough to add "sex." However, my friends, we must take up but one question at a time, and this hour belongs exclusively to the negro. Let us see to this, that no State shall make a distinction among its citizens either of race, color, or condition, and when, as Abolitionists, we have achieved that, we will have checkmated States Rights, and put the negro in the full enjoyment of his liberty. Until then we leave him in the power of those who have always oppressed him, who have had him for years beneath their feet, and who yet hate him with a perfect hatred. When we have secured this we will remember the freedmen. We know that their little houses are destroyed, that their beasts of burden were either taken by SHERMAN or stolen by WHEELER; their tools are worn out or lost or stolen, and not much can be expected from them for some time to come. Friends, the beauty of this hour we find in the race with which we have to deal. The white men of the South sit sullen, morose, defiant; the black man sits loving, Christian and grateful. One of them said to a friend of mine in SHERMAN's army: "The soldiers have taken away my two horses, and I have nothing with which to work; but, thank the Lord, they have given me my freedom, and I am happy." I thank the Lord that there sits holding the helm of the State to-day a man who knows by experience, by the burning of his own roof, by the exile of his family, and by the terrible sufferings of himself, the bitterness of this pro-slavery caste, and who has given official utterance to the sentiments that "treason is a crime to be punished, and not a mere difference of opinion," and to-day, unless the telegraph tells untrue, he announces that the land and the ballot are the guarantee of the Union in the hand of the black man.

At the conclusion of his address, Mr. PHILLIPS was heartily applauded.

SPEECH OF MRS. F. W. HARPER

Mrs. F. W. Harper, colored, was then introduced and said:

This is one of the happiest mornings of my life. The last year has brought us great satisfaction and grand victories, and at last we see the dawn of peace and the promise of perpetual liberty. God has turned out to us the silver lining of the war-cloud and we behold two growing beauties—victory and peace. The grandest successes of the war are not the victories gained, but the advance in the cause of freedom. If the war has been closed without crushing slavery, our victories would have been defeats and our struggles would have been worse than useless. Place yourself in the condition of a freedman; yesterday a slave, today your chains are snapped asunder; yesterday you had a wife, but you saw the stinging lash and the knotted whip applied, with no power to help; today she is yours to defend with your love, and to guard with your care; yesterday your children were sold, one by one, to the highest bidder; today they are yours, gather them in your arms, and lull them to their slumbers; yesterday your home was at the will and caprice of another; today your home is humble, but freedom is at last the guest of your home. The signing of the Declaration of Independence was the shining epoch in your history, but this amendment forms the commencement of a grander era. And yet there is something fearfully sublime in the judgments of God. We are now of a rising race; we have become the pivot on which the nation has trembled in tears and blood. There is no use

in cursing those whom God himself has blessed. What turned the tide of secession in your battles? Three times you started for Richmond and were turned back. The first time you stopped to send back the slave, and you were defeated; again you started, and again did wrong, and again were defeated; your General burrowed in the mud, and buried in silence the thunders of your cannons before the wooden guns of your enemy. It was not only Little Napoleon, who sat like a nightmare on the Army of the Potomac, but big Slavery as well. You had something stolen in the tent of America, souls written over with the hand of Divinity, and the chains you left unbroken coiled about the feet of the soldiers, and you were not permitted to go up to victory. But when at last you voted in the Fall, Congress caught the infection, giving slavery the only right it ought to have—the right to die. In less than a month Charleston was yours, and in three months Richmond was yours, and LEE and JOHNSTON had surrendered. You had power and skill before, but you had not hold of the hand of the freedman, nor the hand of God. Jesus told you two thousand years ago what to do with the negro: "Whatsoever ye would that men should do unto you, do ye even so unto them." You called the slave a chattel, and you must not think your duty done when you write enfranchisement upon his brow. I don't believe in leaving the question to the loyal white men of the South. Who are they? Where were they during the four years of the war? Where when your brothers died, when your sons were murdered in prisons? Did they bathe the flag in secret tears? If so, while white men were loving it in the dark, black men were defending it in the light, and I say it would be unpardonable meanness if now you should say, "You are good enough for a soldier, but not for a citizen." It's not a decent form of government which permits the rebel to whitewash himself by an oath of allegiance, and leaves the loyal negro beneath his feet. Let the whole North rise up as one man, and say, these men who defended us in the hour of peril, shall be protected in the hour of peace.

. . .

SPEECH OF WILLIAM LLOYD GARRISON

Although I am announced, my friends, as one of the speakers at this meeting, I must confess that there is no need of my saying anything. My vocation as an Abolitionist, thank God, is ended. [Sensation.] There is no one to be converted—that is, no one who is loyal in spirit, who loves his country and means to stand by it.

...

Where is slavery? If the rebellion is put down, slavery is put down; they are one and inseparable. The proclamation of ABRAHAM LINCOLN broke the fetters of three millions of slaves, and for that act alone he will be held in lasting remembrance through all time. [Applause.] For his willingness to serve the poor and the humble, he laid down his life; and was ever man so mourned as he has been? Not simply because he was honest, and came up from the people; not because he was upright and able alone, but because of the consciousness that he incarnated the great cause of universal freedom, and was willing to lay down his life in defence of his principles. What has become of slavery in Louisiana? voted down; in Maryland, voted down; in Arkansas and Kentucky it rests on a rope of sand without form; in Delaware there are a baker's dozen slaves, but Delaware is a very small State, and her slavery is nothing.

The National Decree

It is the nation's decree that slavery shall die the death, so that twenty-one States have voted for the anti-slavery amendment to the constitution, and only three against. Shall we wait for reconstructed States to come in, and then, perchance, be defeated? No. To twenty-five loyal States and none other was this question submitted; and we might as well wait for the felon's time to expire in the State's Prison before we should decide a question of city or town interest, as to wait the action of rebels before we vote and decide on this amendment to the constitution. [Applause.] It is amended beyond all controversy, and if it should be decided in the negative, we know that no more Slave States can come in. The three States which have voted against it are Kentucky, Delaware and New-Jersey. They will yet make haste to come in, and to amend their conduct by falling into line. They stagger now under the weight of their infamy, and cannot long remain. But if they should be perverse, thank God we can do without them, and they are to us of no consequence whatever.

His New Position

I rejoice to stand no longer isolated, and to be looked at as if I were a monster with seven heads and ten horns, with blasphemy written upon my forehead. But now, lost in the great ocean of public opinion, I am but a drop in the sea. Abolitionism is no longer distinctive, but common; and now that abolitionism is triumphant we wont have any more anti-slavery agitation, and our work being ended we must mingle with the millions of our fellow countrymen putting into the grave of slavery whatever sprang from it. We still find a prejudice against the colored people — but man, man must be recognized where ever he appears. Aliens and foreigners come over here and we take them into our arms of protection and say this shall be your home and you shall be citizens like us, and shall we say less to those who are native born here, who have made the field gory with their blood, and who in our hour of despair and trouble gave up all, forgave all and came to our rescue? We have not saved ourselves alone. Two hundred thousand stalwart slaves threw themselves into the scale, and rebellion and slavery have kicked the beam and been crushed.

Andrew Johnson

Thank God we have a man at the helm ready for any emergency. ANDREW JOHNSON, of Tennessee. [Applause.] Was ever a more splendid testimony shown than has been evoked in his case? What a hold ABRAHAM LINCOLN had upon the hearts of us all we thought we could not spare him, and we prayed and hoped, and trusted that his life would be spared during his term of office, and that he might reconduct to peace and prosperity; but the spirit of slavery assassinated the noble man, and the nation was paralyzed for the hour. The assassin could take the life of our honored and trusted head, but could not shake the nation in its safety, security or power. ABRAHAM LINCOLN passed away, and nothing was missed, so far as the government was concerned. From ABRAHAM LINCOLN we have ANDREW JOHNSON, and he is, perhaps, in some respects better fitted for the emergency, and to see that justice is done to the traitors. I like to see people act independently, and then I always judge them by their own measure. For my part, I don't believe in capital punishment at all, but it seems to me if this nation captures JEFF. DAVIS, and does not hang him, it will be recreant to itself and false to humanity. If we are to punish any one, let us take this colossal criminal whose garments are dyed with the blood of thousands, rather than the less conspicuous and perchance misled. Thank God, my friends, that we have lived to see this day, that slavery is destroyed and that blissful days are in store for us, our children and for all mankind.

At the conclusion of Mr. GARRISON's speech the meeting adjourned to 3 1/2 P.M.

23

Andrew Johnson, Proclamation Creating a Provisional Government for the State of North Carolina

13 Stat. 760, May 29, 1865[*]

Whereas the fourth section of the fourth article of the Constitution of the United States declares that the United States shall guarantee to every State in the Union a republican form of government and shall protect each of them against invasion and domestic violence; and whereas the President of the United States is by the Constitution made Commander in Chief of the Army and Navy, as well as chief civil executive officer of the United States, and is bound by solemn oath faithfully to execute the office of President of the United States and to take care that the laws be faithfully executed; and whereas the rebellion which has been waged by a portion of the people of the United States against the properly constituted authorities of the Government thereof in the most violent and revolting form, but whose organized and armed forces have now been almost entirely overcome, has in its revolutionary progress deprived the people of the State of North Carolina of all civil government; and whereas it becomes necessary and proper to carry out and enforce the obligations of the United States to the people of North Carolina in securing them in the enjoyment of a republican form of government:

Now, therefore, in obedience to the high and solemn duties imposed upon me by the Constitution of the United States and for the purpose of enabling the loyal people of said State to organize a State government whereby justice may be established, domestic tranquillity insured, and loyal citizens protected in all their rights of life, liberty, and property, I, Andrew Johnson, President of the United States and Commander in Chief of the Army and Navy of the United States, do hereby appoint William W. Holden provisional governor of the State of North Carolina, whose duty it shall be, at the earliest practicable period, to prescribe such rules and regulations as may be necessary and proper for convening a convention composed of delegates to be chosen by that portion of the people of said State who are loyal to the United States, and no others, for the purpose of altering or amending the constitution thereof, and with authority to exercise within the limits of said State all the powers necessary and proper to enable such loyal people of the State of North Carolina to restore said State to its constitutional relations to the Federal Government and to present such a republican form of State government as will entitle the State to the guaranty of the United States therefor and its people to protection by the United States against invasion, insurrection, and domestic violence: Provided, That in any election that may be hereafter held for choosing delegates to any State convention as aforesaid no person shall be qualified as an elector or shall be eligible as a member of such convention unless he shall have previously taken and subscribed the oath of amnesty as set forth in the President's proclamation of May 29, A. D. 1865, and is a voter qualified as prescribed by the constitution and laws of the State of North Carolina in force immediately before the 20th day of May, A. D. 1861, the date of the so-called ordinance of secession: and the said convention, when convened, or the legislature that may be thereafter assembled, will prescribe the qualification of electors and the eligibility of persons to hold office under the constitution and laws of the State—a power the people of the several States composing the Federal Union have rightfully exercised from the origin of the Government to the present time.

And I do hereby direct—

First. That the military commander of the department and all officers and persons in the military and naval service aid and assist the said provisional governor in carrying into effect this proclamation; and they are enjoined to abstain from in any way hindering, impeding, or discouraging the loyal people from the organization of a State government as herein authorized.

---

[*] George P. Sanger, ed., *United States Statutes at Large* (Boston: Little, Brown, 1866), 13:760.

24
Andrew Johnson to Provisional Mississippi Governor William L. Sharkey
August 15, 1865[*]

Executive Office, Washington, D.C.,
Aug. 15, 1865

Governor William L. Sharkey,
Jackson, Miss.

I am gratified to see that you have organized your convention without difficulty. I hope that without delay your convention will amend your State constitution, abolishing slavery and denying to all future Legislatures the power to legislate that there is property in man; also that they will adopt the amendment to the Constitution of the United States abolishing slavery.

If you could extend the elective franchise to all persons of color who can read the Constitution of the United States in English and write their names, and to all persons of color who own real estate valued at not less than two hundred and fifty dollars and pay taxes thereon, you would completely disarm the adversary and set an example the other States will follow.

This you can do with perfect safety, and you would thus place Southern States in reference to free persons of color upon the same basis with the free States. I hope and trust your convention will do this, and as a consequence the radicals, who are wild upon negro franchise, will be completely foiled in their attempts to keep the Southern States from renewing their relations to the Union by not accepting their Senators and Representatives.

Andrew Johnson,
President United States.

[*] *The Papers of Andrew Johnson, May–August 1865*, ed. Paul H. Bergeron (Knoxville: University of Tennessee Press, 1989), 8:599–600.

25
Equal Suffrage: Address from the Colored Citizens of Norfolk, Va., to the People of the United States
June 26, 1865[†]

Fellow Citizens:

The undersigned have been appointed a committee, by a public meeting of the colored citizens of Norfolk, held June 5th, 1865, in the Catharine Street Baptist Church, Norfolk, Va., to lay before you a few considerations touching the present position of the colored population of the southern States generally, and with reference to their claim for equal suffrage in particular.

We do not come before the people of the United States asking an impossibility; we simply ask that a Christian and enlightened people shall, at once, concede to us the full enjoyment of those privileges of full citizenship, which, not only, are our undoubted right, but are indispensable to that elevation and prosperity of our people, which must be the desire of every patriot.

The legal recognition of these rights of the free colored population, in the past, by State legislation, or even by the Judiciary and Congress of the United States, was, as a matter of course, wholly inconsistent with the existence of slavery; but now that slavery has been crushed, with the rebellion sprung from it, on what pretext can disabilities be perpetuated that were imposed only to protect an institution which has now, thank God, passed away forever? It is a common assertion, by our enemies, that "this is a white man's country, settled by white men, its government established by white men, and shall therefore be ruled by white men only." How far are these statements true and the conclusion reasonable? Every school-boy knows that within twelve years of the foundation of the first settlement at Jamestown, our fathers as well as yours were toiling in the plantations on James

[†] *Equal Suffrage: Address from the Colored Citizens of Norfolk, Va., to the People of the United States; also an Account of the Agitation among the Colored People of Virginia for Equal Rights. With an Appendix Concerning the Rights of Colored Witnesses before the State Courts* (New Bedford, MA, 1865).

River, for the sustenance and prosperity of the infant colony. Since then in New England, New York and the middle Atlantic States, our race has borne its part in the development of even the free North, while throughout the sunny South, the millions upon millions of acres, in its countless plantations, laden with precious crops, bear witness to the unrequited industry of our people. Even our enemies and old oppressors, themselves, used to admit, nay, contend for, the urgent necessity of our presence and labor to the national prosperity, for whenever slavery was to be defended, they were always ready to prove that the negro must be the laborer in the South, because a white man's constitution could not withstand the climate.

Again, is it true that this government owes its existence entirely to white men? Why, the first blood shed in the Revolutionary war was that of a colored man, Crispus Attucks, while in every engraving of Washington's famous passage of the Delaware, is to be seen, as a prominent feature, the wooly head and dusky face of a colored soldier, Prince Whipple; and let the history of those days tell of the numerous but abortive efforts made by a vindictive enemy to incite insurrection among the colored people of the country, and how faithfully they adhered to that country's cause. Who has forgotten Andrew Jackson's famous appeal to the colored "citizens" of Louisiana, and their enthusiastic response, in defence of the liberty, for others, which was denied themselves? Then did the peaceful stability of the government of the United States, during the (to all but the colored race) happy years, that preceded the late rebellion, owe nothing for its continuance to the colored people? Fellow citizens, was not the maintenance of that peace and order, and thereby of your prosperity, wholly owing to the submissive patience with which our race endured the galling slavery of which they were the victims, in the faith and assurance that God would yet work out their deliverance? Then what has been the behavior of our people during the past struggle? Have we in any way embarrassed the government by unnecessary outbreaks on the one hand, or thwarted it by remissness or slackness in response to its calls for volunteers on the other? Let the fact that, in the short space of nine months, from what was called the contraband camp, at Hampton, near Fortress Monroe, and from other parts of this State alone, over *twenty-five thousand* colored men have become soldiers in the army of the United States, attest our devotion to our country. Over

200,000 colored men have taken up arms on behalf of the Union, and at Port Hudson, Olustee, Milliken's Bend, Fort Wagner, and in the death-haunted craters of the Petersburg mine, and on a hundred well fought fields, have fully proved their patriotism and possession of all the manly qualities that adorn the soldier.

Such, as every one knows, have been the relations and attitude of the colored people to the nation in the past, but we believe our present position is by no means so well understood among the loyal masses of the country, otherwise there would be no delay in granting us the express relief which the nature of the case demands. It must not be forgotten that it is the general assumption, in the South, that the effects of the immortal Emancipation Proclamation of President Lincoln go no further than the emancipation of the negroes then in slavery, and that it is only constructively even, that the Proclamation can be said, in any legal sense, to have abolished slavery, and even the late constitutional amendment, if duly ratified, can go no further; neither touch, nor can touch, the slave codes of the various southern States, and the laws respecting free people of color consequent therefrom, which, having been passed before the act of secession, are presumed to have lost none of their vitality, but exist, as a convenient engine for our oppression, until repealed by special acts of the State legislatures. By these laws, in many of the southern States, it is still a crime for colored men to learn or be taught to read, and their children are doomed to ignorance; there is no provision for insuring the legality of our marriages; we have no right to hold real estate; the public streets and the exercise of our ordinary occupations are forbidden us unless we can produce passes from our employers, or licenses from certain officials; in some States the whole free negro population is legally liable to exile from the place of its birth, for no crime but that of color; we have no means of legally making or enforcing contracts of any description; we have no right to testify before the courts in any case in which a white man is one of the parties to the suit; we are taxed without representation, and, in short, so far as legal safeguards of our rights are concerned, we are defenseless before our enemies.

. . .

You have not unreasonably complained of the operation of that clause of the Constitution which has hitherto permitted the slavocracy of the South to wield the political influence which would be represented by a white population equal to three fifths of the whole negro population; but slavery is now abolished, and henceforth the representation will be in proportion to the enumeration of the whole population of the South, *including people of color*, and it is worth your consideration if it is desirable or politic that the fomenters of this rebellion against the Union, which has been crushed at the expense of so much blood and treasure, should find themselves, after defeat, more powerful than ever, their political influence enhanced by the additional voting power of the other two fifths of the colored population, by which means four Southern votes will balance in the Congressional and Presidential elections at least seven Northern ones. The honor of your country should be dear to you, as it is, but is that honor advanced, in the eyes of the Christian world, when America alone, of all Christian nations, sustains an unjust distinction against four millions and a half of her most loyal people, on the senseless ground of a difference in color? You are anxious that the attention of every man, of every State legislature, and of Congress, should be exclusively directed to redressing the injuries sustained by the country in the late contest; are these objects more likely to be effected amid the political distractions of an embarrassing negro agitation? You are, above all, desirous that no future intestine wars should mar the property and destroy the happiness of the country; will your perfect security from such evils be promoted by the existence of a colored population of four millions and a half, placed, by your enactments, outside the pale of the Constitution, discontented by oppression, with an army of 200,000 colored soldiers, whom you have drilled, disciplined, and armed, but whose attachment to the State you have failed to secure by refusing them citizenship? You are further anxious that your government should be an example to the world of true Republican institutions; but how can you avoid the charge of inconsistency if you leave one eighth of the population of the whole country without any political rights, while bestowing these rights on every immigrant who comes to these shores, perhaps from a despotism, under which he could never exercise the least political right, and had no means of forming any conception of their proper use?

We have now shown you, to the best of our ability, the necessity of the recognition of the right of suffrage for our own protection, and have suggested a few of the reasons why it is expedient you should grant us that right; but while we stand before you, pleading with you, for our fellows, on the grounds of humanity and political expediency, we would not have you forget that our case also stands on the basis of constitutional right. No sane person will for a moment contend that color or birth are recognized by the Constitution of the United States as any bar to the acquisition or enjoyment of citizenship.

...

Signed, on behalf of the colored people of Norfolk and vicinity, June 26th, 1865.

Dr. Thomas Bayne, Norfolk, Chairman of the Committee.

Jno. M. Brown, Pastor of the African Methodist Episcopal Church, Bute Street, Norfolk, Va.

Thomas Henson, Pastor of the Catharine Street Baptist Church, Norfolk, Va.

Wm. Keeling, 96 Church street, Norfolk, Va.

Geo. W. Cooke, 21 Fox Lane, Norfolk, Va.

Joseph T. Wilson, 26 Hawk street, Norfolk, Va.

Thos. F. Paige, Jr., 27 Hawk street, Norfolk, Va.

H. Highland Garnet, Pastor 15th St. Presbyterian Church, Washington, D.C., Honorary Member.

26

Provisional South Carolina Governor Benjamin F. Perry to Secretary of State William Seward

November 1, 1865[*]

Columbia S.C., Nov. 1, 1865

I will send you today the whole proceedings of the state convention properly certified as you requested. The debt contracted by South Carolina during the Rebellion is very inconsiderable. Her Expenditures for War purposes were paid by the confederate Government. She has assumed no debt or any part of any debt of that Government. Her whole state debt at this time is only about six millions 6,000,000 and that is mostly for railroads and building new state House prior to the War.

The members of the legislature say they have received no official information of the amendment of the Federal Constitution, abolishing Slavery. They have no

[*] Johnson, *Papers*, 9:324–25.

objection to adopting the first section of the amendment proposed but they fear that the second section may be construed to give congress power of local legislation over the Negroes and white men, too, after the abolishment of slavery. In good faith South Carolina has abolished slavery and never will wish to restore it again.

The legislature is passing a code of laws providing ample & complete protection for the Negro. There is a sincere desire to do everything necessary to a restoration of the Union and tie up and heal every bleeding wound which has been caused by this fratricidal war. I was elected U.S. Senator by a very flattering vote. The other senator will be elected today.

B. F. Perry

27

Secretary of State William Seward to Provisional South Carolina Governor Benjamin F. Perry

November 6, 1865*

His Excellency B.F. Perry,
Provisional Governor of South Carolina:
Washington, November 6, 1865.

Your dispatch to the President of November 4 has been received. He is not entirely satisfied with the explanations it contains. He deems necessary the passage of adequate ordinances declaring that all insurrectionary proceedings in the State were unlawful and void *ab initio*. Neither the Constitution nor laws direct official information to the State of amendments to the Constitution submitted by Congress. Notices of the amendment by Congress abolishing slavery were nevertheless given by the Secretary of State at the time to the States which were then in communication with this government. Formal notice will immediately be given to those States which were then in insurrection.

The objection which you mention to the last clause of the constitutional amendment is regarded as querulous and unreasonable, because that clause is really restraining in its effect, instead of enlarging the powers of Congress. The President considers the acceptance of the amendment by South Carolina as indispensable to a restoration of her relations with the other States of the Union.

WILLIAM H. SEWARD.

28

South Carolina, Ratification and Accompanying Resolution

November 13, 1865

*Johnson, *Papers*, 9:325. [See also "South Carolina Legislature," *New York Times*, Nov. 16, 1865, 2 (reproducing Seward's letter). —Ed.]

SOUTH CAROLINA SENATE JOURNAL (SPECIAL SESSION, 1865), NOV. 13, 1865, P. 74

1. *Resolved, therefore, by the Senate and House of Representatives, of the General Assembly of the State of South Carolina, in General Assembly met, and by the authority of the same*, That the aforesaid proposed amendment of the Constitution of the United States be, and the same is hereby accepted, adopted and ratified by this State.

2. *Resolved*, That a certified copy of the foregoing preamble and resolution be forwarded by his Excellency the Provisional Governor to the President of the United States, and also to the Secretary of State of the United States.

Mr. TRACY offered the following as an amendment thereto:

Resolved, That any attempt by Congress towards legislating upon the political status of former slaves, or their civil relations, would be contrary to the Constitution of the United States, as it now is, or as it would be altered by the proposed amendment, in conflict with the policy of the President declared in his Amnesty Proclamation, and with the restoration of that harmony upon which depends the vital interests of the American Union.

The amendment was agreed to, and the resolutions, as amended, were agreed to, and were ordered to be sent to the House of Representatives for concurrence.

SOUTH CAROLINA HOUSE JOURNAL (SPECIAL SESSION, 1865), NOV. 13, 1865, P. 96

On motion, a message was ordered to be sent to the Senate, asking leave to amend the resolutions by striking out the third in the series.

The following message was received from the Senate:

In the Senate, November 13, 1865
Mr. Speaker and Gentlemen of the House of Representatives:
Senate does not grant leave to your House to amend the resolution of the Senate, ratifying the proposed amendment of the Constitution of the United States, by striking out the third resolution.
By order of the Senate.
F. J. Moses, President, *pro tem.*

The resolutions from the Senate were then concurred in, and were ordered to be returned to the Senate.

29

"South Carolina," *New York Times*

November 16, 1865, p. 4*

We have already announced the gratifying intelligence that South Carolina had ratified the constitutional amendment abolishing slavery, by a strong vote, in both branches of her Legislature. This leaves only *two* votes necessary to its validity. One of them is certain to be given by New-Jersey, and we have every reason to believe that several more will come from the Southern States.

We publish this morning an important message from Gov. PERRY to the South Carolina Legislature, in advance of its action upon this subject. It will be noticed that this body hesitated in its action, not from any desire or purpose to retain or restore slavery, but because it feared Congress might, under the second clause of the amendment, claim the power to legislate for the negroes *after* their freedom had been established. Gov. PERRY presented this matter to the President, who replied, through the Secretary of State, that he regarded it as "querulous and unreasonable." The President holds, that Congress under this clause has no power to make laws concerning the negroes except for the purpose of carrying their *emancipation* into effect. After they are free Congress can do nothing except to maintain their freedom. With this explanation the Legislature took prompt action on the subject and ratified the amendment.

We hail this action of South Carolina as of good omen. It encourages the hope and belief that other Southern States will promptly follow her example, and that we shall very speedily have this amendment ratified by the Legislature of every State in the Union. This would give it a moral weight which otherwise it could never have, and would do more than anything else to keep the whole subject from ever again becoming a disturbing element in the politics of any section of the country.

The sentiment of South Carolina on the adoption of the amendment was natural and proper. It is not strange that she should hesitate about giving her sanction to a provision of the constitution which *might* authorize Congress to take the negroes under its exclusive legislative control. But the explanations made at Washington removed all difficulty on this score, and her action was then prompt and satisfactory.

* [Secretary of State Seward's letter describing the concerns about Section Two of the Thirteenth Amendment as "querulous and unreasonable" was widely, and sometimes critically, reported. See, e.g., "The Resurrection of South Carolina and the Constitutional Amendment," *New York Herald*, Nov. 15, 1865, 4; "Querulous and Unreasonable," *Daily Ohio Statesman* (Columbus), Nov. 17, 1865, 2. —Ed.]

30

Andrew Johnson to Provisional Mississippi Governor William L. Sharkey

November 17, 1865*

To William L. Sharkey

Washington D.C., 17 Nov. 1865

Gov Sharkey has heretofore been notified, will continue to exercise any and all the functions of Provisional Governor of Mississippi. He will please report from time to time, what progress is being made in the restoration of the functions of the State, and make such suggestions, as he may deem proper, and calculated to accomplish the great work in which he is engaged.

It is earnestly hoped that your Legislature will without delay place the State in an attitude which will enable her to resume all Constitutional relations between her and the Federal Government.

Let the Amendment to the Constitution of the United States, abolishing Slavery be adopted. Let such laws be passed for the protection of freedmen, in person and property, as Justice and equity demand. The admission of negro testimony, they all being free, will be as much for the protection of the white man, as the Colored.

I do hope that the Southern people will see the position that they now occupy, and avail themselves of the favorable opportunity of once more resuming all their former relations to the Government of the United States, and in doing so restore peace, prosperity, happiness, and fraternal love.

Governor Sharkey will please show this dispatch to B. G. Humphreys, Governor elect.

Andrew Johnson
President U.S.

* Johnson, *Papers*, 9:400.

31

"The Amendment to the Federal Constitution," *Daily Eastern Argus* (Portland, ME)

November 17, 1865, p. 2

When we wrote a word of congratulation that South Carolina had adopted the amendment to the federal constitution forever prohibiting slavery in the United States we knew not how the scruples of the convention had been overcome in regard to the claim set up by the radicals that the amendment would give them the right to legislate for the negro after slavery should be abolished. The message of Gov. Perry on this subject has now come to hand and it affords a full explanation. It seems that there was not the slightest objection on the part of the convention to the complete prohibition of slavery; but there was an apprehension on the point we suggested, which made the convention hesitate. Gov. Perry states that he telegraphed to Washington on the subject as follows:

"I stated that South Carolina had abolished slavery in good faith, and never intended or wished to renew. That the Legislature was then considering a wise, just, and humane system of laws for the government and protection of the freedmen in all their rights of person and property, and that there was no objection to the adoption of the proposed amendment to the Federal Constitution, except an apprehension that Congress might, under the second section of that amendment, claim the right to legislate for the negro after slavery was abolished. I likewise stated that no official notice had ever been received by the Legislature of the proposed amendment to the Constitution of the United States."

The reply was that neither the Constitution nor laws direct official information to the States of amendments to the Constitution submitted by Congress, but that the notice would be forwarded. To the objection suggested the reply was:

"The objection which you mention to the last clause of the constitutional amendment is regarded as querulous and unreasonable, because that clause is really restraining in its effects, instead of enlarging the power of Congress"

The assurance by the administration, including the Attorney General and also Secretary Seward who signed the dispatch, allayed all fears on this point, and the opposition to the passage of the amendment at once ceased. It was accordingly adopted. The Amendment is in these words:

"Neither slavery nor involuntary servitude except as a punishment for crime whereof the party shall have been duly convicted, shall exist within the United States, or any place subject to their jurisdiction.

Sec. 2. Congress shall have power to enforce this article by appropriate legislation." (Approved February 1, 1865)

The construction put upon the amendment by President Johnson is the only fair one. That claimed by the radicals is absurd. The language cannot be tortured into such a meaning. The second section confines the action of Congress simply to the enforcement of the prohibition contained in the 1st section and gives no color to interference with negroes after they are free.

With this official construction of the amendment it is probable that all the Southern States will adopt it; and the New York Express is of the opinion that under these circumstances even the Kentucky legislature, a majority of which was elected in opposition to the amendment, will adopt it. If so, Delaware will also fall in, and the sanction of the abolition of slavery, forever, will become unanimous. We hope to see that result, and think we shall see it within a year. The slavery question has cost the country dearly enough. It is not effectually settled. Let the seal of extinction be forever put upon it, by the adoption of this amendment by every State and all excuse or pretext for further clamor on the subject will thus be forever ended. This done, the negro suffrage question will soon get its quietus. Every State and Territory, in which the issue has been made thus far, has decided against it—Connecticut, Wisconsin, Minnesota, Nevada and Colorado—and others will give a similar decision when the question, pure and simple is presented. The whole matter will be left to the individual States, where it properly belongs; and in due time, no doubt, negroes who are properly qualified will be permitted to vote, unless that course would be likely to engender and aggravate the antagonisms of race, as many now believe and fear it would. South Carolina has done nobly; let her sister States follow the praiseworthy example.

32

"The Meaning and Scope of the Great Amendment," *New York Tribune*

November 17, 1865, p. 4

Congress, by a two-thirds vote in either House, has initiated, and already twenty-five States have ratified, by a majority vote in either branch of their respective Legislatures, the following important Amendment to the Federal Constitution:

"ARTICLE XIII.

"Sec. 1. Neither slavery nor involuntary servitude, except as a punishment for crime, whereof the party shall have been duly convicted, shall exist within the United States, or any place subject to their jurisdiction.

"Sec. 2. Congress shall have power to enforce this article by appropriate legislation."

The States which have thus far ratified this amendment are as follows:

State.	Time.	State.	Time.
Illinois	Feb. 1, 1865.	Virginia	Feb. 9.
Rhode Island	Feb. 2.	Indiana	Feb. 13.
New York	Feb. 3.	Nevada	Feb. 16.
Maryland	Feb. 3.	Louisiana	Feb. 17.
Massachusetts	Feb. 3.	Missouri	Feb. 24.
Pennsylvania	Feb. 3.	Wisconsin	Feb. 22.
West Virginia	Feb. 3.	Vermont	Mar. 9.
Michigan	Feb. 3.	Tennessee	Apr. 5.
Maine	Feb. 7.	Arkansas	Apr.—.
Ohio	Feb. 8.	Connecticut	May 4.
Kansas	Feb. 8.	Iowa	June 30.
Minnesota	Feb. 8.	New Hampshire	June 30.
		South Carolina	Nov. 13.

South Carolina having thus given the bill a fresh impetus, we may confidently expect to see it further impelled by several of the States which reluctantly followed her into the Rebellion which dug the grave of the "peculiar institution." New Jersey—whose late Legislature was induced to reject the Amendment—has in consequence chosen one which will surely and speedily accept it. So, we trust, will Oregon and California. Dela-

549

ware would probably do likewise, now that her soldiers are at home once more, if a new Legislature were now to be chosen; she will do it, if needful, next year.

But it will *not* be needful. Even if we count Colorado a thirty-seventh State, and thus render twenty-four States requisite to perfect the ratification, the number will soon be made up. We should gladly celebrate this consummation on our approaching National Thanksgiving; but, if the privilege be then denied us, we can wait a little, not doubting that the end is secure.

South Carolina, it will be noted, hesitated to ratify, until spurred thereto by a sharp message from the President through the State Department—not because she had any lingering hope of being enabled to retain or restore Slavery in name, but from dislike to sec. 2 of the Amendment, and apprehension that it would be held to bar her enactment or retention of any such "Black Code" as her late Rebels still hanker after. The grounds of her reluctance to ratify are fairly set forth in a recent *Richmond Enquirer* as follows:

"But the Constitutional Amendment has not been adopted, because *the people of Virginia will not consent to give to Congress the right to legislate for and control any part of her people.* This may be State rights, and, as such, may be very obnoxious to the Radicals. But, suppose the State persists in her refusal, what then? Gov. Pierpont is not a Provisional Governor; he is a Governor by election. Virginia has her Legislature, not by the grace of President Johnson, but by the provisions of the Federal Constitution. Her people are in the Union, though her Representatives may not get into Congress, and her people can live outside of Congress. It is a matter of opinion and choice whether or not a State shall ratify the Amendment; if it is compulsory, it is not binding, or it is binding only so long as force compels a pretended acquiescence in it. If the force is to be always exerted, then the Constitution is destroyed and the Republican Government a failure."

—*The Enquirer* seems ignorant of the fact that the [loyal] Legislature of Virginia *did* ratify the Amendment last Winter, so that no further action is required of that State. It is now desired only that a few more of the same sort shall follow her excellent example.

—But, presuming the success of the Amendment assured, how much shall it be held to mean?

The N.Y. Times—which is currently believed to be

occasionally inspired from the State Department—says of the recent action of South Carolina:

"It will be noticed that the Legislature hesitated in its action, not from any desire or purpose to retain or restore Slavery, but because it feared Congress might, under the second clause of the Amendment, claim the power to legislate for the negroes *after* their freedom had been established. Gov. Perry presented this matter to the President, who replied, through the Secretary of State, that he regarded it as 'querulous and unreasonable,' The President holds that Congress, under this clause, has no power to make laws concerning the negroes, except for the purpose of carrying their *emancipation* into effect. After they are free, Congress can do nothing except to maintain their freedom. With this explanation, the Legislature took prompt action on the subject, and ratified the Amendment."

The Press (Philadelphia) has an "Occasional" Washington letter from its Editor (Col. Forney) on this subject, which says:

"The reluctance of the original seceders to sanction this drastic and searching Amendment, illustrated in the South Carolina Legislature, a few days ago, was produced by the *fair construction* given to the second section of the new Article. The South Carolina leaders saw that their slaves were not only set free by the Constitutional Amendment, but that Congress was empowered to legislate to 'enforce' the universal decree. They were not misled by the absurd theory born of some weak or scheming brain, that under the second section they could apply to Congress for remuneration or compensation for their 'property!' The legislation of Congress is to 'enforce' abolition—to perfect emancipation—not to pay the old slave-masters. And, when Mr. Seward telegraphed to Gov. Perry that his objections to this section were 'querulous and unfounded,' *he meant that the duty of Congress was too plain to require an interpreter.*"

—We hold *The Press* entirely right in the premises, and trust it faithfully reflects the views of the President of the United States. The Constitutional Amendment aims at the absolute, unconditional Abolition of Slavery throughout the United States; but it does not stop here. Hitherto, the personal liberty and civil rights of each citizen were held and enjoyed under the protection of the States respectively; hereafter, they are to be upheld and guarded by the Nation. Hitherto, a State might cruelly oppress any portion of her own people; hereafter, Congress is charged with the duty of protecting in the full enjoyment of his liberties each inhabitant of our country, and clothed with the power requisite to its fulfillment of this high obligation. Ours must henceforth and forever be a Union of Free States and a Nation of Freemen, or Congress will be grossly delinquent and culpable. Gov. Perry's objection to the second section of the Constitutional Amendment may, indeed, have been "querulous and unreasonable," since it is unwise to resist the inevitable or to object to the strongest possible guaranties of individual and general liberty; but we cannot regard his construction of the great Amendment as strained or illogical. If Congress shall forbear to "legislate for the negroes," or for others, it will so forbear simply because the States act so wisely and justly that no further legislation is needed.

33

"Manhood, the Basis of Suffrage," Speech of Hon. Michael Hahn of Louisiana at the National Equal Suffrage Association of Washington, DC
November 17, 1865*

Fellow-citizens, while we strive to secure the object we have in view—the right of suffrage to all American citizens, regardless of color—we must overcome obstacles and difficulties of a serious character which still beset us, and the continued existence of which may threaten to prevent our immediate success. It is necessary, in beginning our work, to see that slavery throughout the land is effectually abolished and that the freedmen are

*Manhood the Basis of Suffrage: Speech of Hon. Michael Hahn of Louisiana, Delivered before the National Equal Suffrage Association of Washington, on Friday evening, November 17, 1865 (Washington, DC: The Association, 1865). [Hahn was shot and severely wounded during the New Orleans Riot on July 30, 1866. See Joseph G. Dawson III, ed., The Louisiana Governors: From Iberville to Edwards (Baton Rouge: Louisiana State University Press, 1990), 148–52. See vol. 2, 1B, docs. 10 and 11. —Ed.]

protected in their freedom, and in all the advantages and privileges inseparable from the condition of freedom. It is a mistaken idea to suppose that slavery is already abolished. The national authority has declared emancipation. The national arms, in a bloody contest against slavery, have triumphed. The legislation and literature of the country treats slavery as abolished. But I, who come from the South and have seen the working of the institution for over a quarter of a century, tell you—and I do it regrettingly—that slavery in practice and substance still exists. Let us not mince matters; let us call things by their right names. Even pro-slavery leaders are now, with feigned alacrity, ratifying the Constitutional Amendment. Aware of the fact that this nation will no longer tolerate slavery in any State, they have come to the conclusion to adopt the first article of the amendment.

But when the second article of the amendment is reached considerable murmuring is heard. They are willing to declare that slavery is dead; but they do not seem willing that the nation should throw its protecting arms around liberty and secure the substance as well as the name of freedom. Hence they are quite slow, hesitating, and reluctant in ratifying the second section. Many good lawyers deem the second section unnecessary, and hold that the language of the first section is amply sufficient to empower Congress to do all that might be embraced in the other section. The apparent unwillingness, however, of the pro-slavery leaders to vest in Congress authority to secure by "appropriate legislation" the abolition of slavery is of deep significance, and does not show a real sincere desire to wipe out every vestige of the degrading institution. The nation should insist on an unqualified ratification of the whole amendment, and then Congress should apply itself to the passage of laws carrying out and enforcing the principles which it embodies.

The important question arises what laws, appropriate in their character, should be passed to secure these objects? A moment's reflection must satisfy us that more work on this subject will be required than we at first may imagine. Congress should see to it that no slave codes are enacted in any States or districts which, in substance and reality, revive all the features of the institution, except the name. It is very easy to say, "we recognize the death of slavery," and still to enact laws applicable to colored persons which, in all but the name, are a revival of slavery. If we permit a town council to ordain that colored persons shall not remain within the corpo-

551

rate limits, except during certain hours of the day, and then only with a written pass from their former owners as employers, and to prescribe a punishment for persons who may transact business with or lease rooms or houses to colored persons without such written permit, we permit the institution of slavery still to exist shorn of its name. I have read, even since my arrival in this city and in your own papers, ordinances passed at Franklin and elsewhere in Louisiana, which contain such provisions. This discrimination against the colored man cannot be allowed to continue, if we are earnest in desiring freedom to all men.

The freedom of speech and of discussion on subjects so sacred as those connected with the rights of man; the right of the people to keep and bear arms, and peaceably to assemble and petition the Government for a redress of grievances, should be secured to all citizens alike. The infamous enactments, prescribing the severest penalties for such persons as should dare to discuss the rights of colored persons or endeavor to teach them to read and write, should be entirely abrogated and trampled under foot. If men can be indicted and imprisoned for agitating the question of colored suffrage, there is no freedom of speech.

…

Laws concerning apprenticeship and vagrancy should make no distinction between men on account of color, or between freedmen and those born free. Under the color of such laws, the most insidious approaches to slavery may be instituted, and the institution itself practically re-established. And when I say that there should be no distinction on account of color or caste in the drafting of such laws, it must not be omitted that there should be no difference or partiality in their execution, for by partiality and prejudice the most execrable tyranny may be practiced to one race, while the other would be held practically exempt.

Public charities for the benefit of asylums and public institutions, and pensions for the wounded, the widow or the orphan, should be hereafter so organized as not to ignore the soldiers in the cause of the Union, no matter what their color.

The nation should insist upon it that the benefits of public education should no longer be denied the colored children of the South. The taxes gathered from all persons, white and black, have been too long applied to the purposes of the white population exclusively, and there should now be no unwillingness to allow the colored man the benefits of government, especially in the education of his children. The nation is vitally interested in the education of the masses, and should show firmness in making this demand. On all these subjects you may safely anticipate much difficulty and evasion, and they should therefore be well considered by the patriotic and philanthropic citizen.

I have thus hurriedly mentioned some of the obstacles which are still in the way, and must not be kept out of view while pursuing the consummation you so devoutly wish. Although they have been set forth very imperfectly, and in an irregular and incoherent manner, they must have convinced you that much still remains to be done. But let us not be discouraged. The cause is worthy of our constant labors and noblest efforts.

While liberty shall be thus secured to all men throughout the land, it is a necessary and concomitant step to extend the right of suffrage to every good American citizen, regardless of color. Many difficulties will be encountered, many obstacles thrown in the way, and many bitter prejudices must be overcome before we can expect to reach the point we aim at. The arguments against colored suffrage which will meet us at every step will be varied and numerous, and presented with much feeling and warmth. Our task is to examine and refute them thoroughly, temperately, and boldly.

Many persons are ready and willing to bury partially their prejudices against the colored men, and give such of them the right to vote as can read and write. This basis of intelligence on the suffrage question is rapidly making converts and gaining the support of some of our most enlightened statesmen. But they forget that the poor African—I mean by descent, not by birth—has never had spread before him the means of acquiring that kind of intelligence which they insist on as a requisite for suffrage. Book knowledge has been denied him by the power of severe penal enactments. Indeed, he has been legislated upon and treated more as if he were a beast of the field than as a human being. And yet the very legislation which thus considered him as a beast without mind and incapable of mental culture, carried with it and on its own face the falsity of this position, by prescribing punishment to men who would seek to cultivate the negro's mind! Here is consistency for you.

…

When Napoleon the Great unlike his nephew—saw the inconvenience, nay, impossibility of maintaining French colonies in North America, and ceded his possessions along the Mississippi valley to the United States, it was agreed by solemn treaty that—

"The inhabitants of the ceded territory shall be incorporated into the Union of the United States, and admitted as soon as possible, according to the principles of the Federal Constitution, to the enjoyment of all the rights, advantages and immunities of citizens of the United States; and in the meantime they shall be maintained and protected in the free enjoyment of their liberty, property, and the religion which they profess."

It is time that this treaty provision, so long ignored and violated, should be enforced. It is time that the claims of large numbers of worthy citizens, unfortunate in their color, should be recognized and allowed. It is time that the principles laid down in our Declaration of Independence, and the sentiments of justice and liberality which should characterize our system of government, be allowed their due sway in this, the second birth of our nation. The spirit of the white man, which would ostracise from a participation in the Government of the country his fellow citizen of a darker hue, is the most miserable and selfish spirit which can spring from the human heart. The unyielding desire to confine suffrage to our own race and deny it to others on no other pretext than that of color, is unworthy of Republicans. In restoring the various departments of the Government over the whole country let us endeavor to be just, impartial, and generous in our measures. Let the leaders of the rebellion, who went forth with all their might to destroy the Government under which we live, be just to those who were faithful to that Government and suffered in its cause. Let the returned Confederate, forgiven by the Government and received and treated as was the prodigal son, not seek to deny the rights of man to those who triumphed in the late war.

The only question which now seriously divides the country is that of suffrage. Let us, in healing up old sores and putting our house to order, be generous, just, and patriotic; and now, for all time to come, dispose of this question in accordance with the principles of humanity and true republican government. The glorious character of the results to be accomplished, the future harmony of all sections of the country and classes of the people, should induce us to enter the contest for this principle cheerfully, energetically, and boldly. As long as this right is denied, there is no peace in the land.

Rest assured the rights of our colored citizens will not long be withheld. Every day of reflection and observation adds hundreds to its advocates. The spirit of progress is aroused throughout the land, and the people cry—"There is no step backwards." You may try to resist the course of events; you may try to destroy sympathetic feelings of the heart and the reasoning faculties of the mind; you may attempt to throw obstacles across the path of the onward march of civilization and humanity, but you will fail. A cause which is sustained by the heart and mind of man, and blessed with the grace of God, must triumph.

34

"What the Amendment Amounts to in South Carolina," *New York Daily Tribune*

November 18, 1865, p. 6

The message of Provisional Governor Perry of South Carolina throws not a little light on the reported ratification of the Constitutional Amendment by the Legislature of that State. The collocation of the correspondence between the President and his Governor presents the business in a somewhat dramatic way. The President writes repeatedly to Perry that he wants South Carolina to adopt the amendment because it will place her in a most favorable attitude before the nation—as a candidate, that is, for admission to Congress. Gov. Perry replied that he is very anxious to get his representatives in, and would pass the amendment for that purpose but for an apprehension that Congress might, under its second section, claim the right to legislate for the negro after Slavery had been abolished. The President hastens to reassure him by the statement that the clause referred to ("Congress shall have power to enforce this article by appropriate legislation") is really restraining in its effects, instead of enlarging the power of Congress. Upon that assurance, and upon the reiterated hint of the President that time is precious (Congress meeting in December), and that the present opportunity, if neglected, is not likely to occur again, Gov. Perry sends his message to the Legislature, and the Legislature adopts the amendment.

It is very plain that Gov. Perry understands, and has caused his Legislature to understand, two things: *First*, that if his State Government, as at present organized, be competent to ratify an amendment to the Constitution, its claim to the admission of its representatives to Congress will be hard to dispute. *Second,* that the adoption of the amendment will not prove a bar to the reestablishment of Slavery, provided the State is left free to enact its own code for the government of the nominally emancipated blacks. On these grounds a grave question is raised on the validity of the approval of the amendment by the South Carolina Legislature as at present constituted, and on the practical effect of a constitutional provision which State legislation is competent to nullify.

We are at a loss to imagine what the President intends by his construction of the second clause of the article above quoted. As matter of history appearing from the debates in Congress it is certain that section was intended by its movers and by the two Houses which adopted it to confer upon Congress full power to secure real as well as nominal freedom to slaves.

It was intended that the law itself should declare what otherwise would be left to be inferred by judicial interpretation. It adopted and expressed a familiar principle of the Constitution, that where a power is granted, all powers incidental and essential to the complete execution of the grant, are implied if not expressed. There is a rule of interpretation that where a statute undertakes to make a specific grant in general terms, the general words are limited by the specific, and by the context referring to the same subject matter. But in the present instance, we fail to see what limitation of the general power can be drawn from words which are at least as broad as any judicial decision could adopt upon the construction of any statute designed to give force to the provision of universal freedom.

The other question is not less important. When Gov. Perry says he wants to reserve to the State the power to make its own laws about the freedmen, and when he adds to that the statement that the Legislature was even then considering "a wise, just, and humane system of laws for the government and protection of the freedmen," we perfectly understand his position. He says, in fact, to the Legislature of South Carolina: "Pass the amendment, it will amount to nothing." For the code which he pronounces wise, just, and humane, is that infamous slave code, the leading provisions of which we explain in our article on Tuesday—a code that does in fact annul the amendment, defy the Federal Government, and remit the negro to a Slavery scarcely less cruel, rigorous, and durable than that which we foolishly believed to have been destroyed. If South Carolina can pass those laws and enforce them, she may

laugh at constitutional abolition, and if her ratification of the amendment is accepted as legal, she will be invading Congress on the pretense of being a Free State at the same moment when the lash is echoing from every plantation, and when involuntary servitude will exist for the punishment of no crime except the old crime of having a black skin.

35
"Power Given to Congress by the Constitutional Amendment,"
New York Times
November 20, 1865, p. 4

The long avowed objection of the late slaveholding states to the Constitutional Amendment is directly against the second section, which reads thus: "Congress shall have power to enforce this article by appropriate legislation." It is said there is danger that under this, Congress will assume the full guardianship of the freedmen, and that perpetual discord must come of it.

If there be any such danger, that second section is not its cause. Congress would have just as much power if that second section did not exist. There is no article in the constitution, whether mandatory or prohibitory, which Congress has not the power to legislate upon, so that it shall be maintained inviolate. The constitution forbids the States to enter into any treaty; to grant letters of marque; to coin money; to pass any law impairing the obligation of contracts; to do divers other things specified. Nobody ever doubted that Congress has power to enforce these prohibitions "by appropriate legislation," whenever needful, though there is no express provision to that effect. The same power must *inherently* exist to enforce this new inhibition of slavery and involuntary servitude. This second section was appended to the body of the Amendment in an excessive anxiety to shield it from sophistry and quibble.

The prohibition of slavery and involuntary servitude in the Constitution of the United States necessarily imposes upon the Government of the United States an obligation to take care that no such system exists, and upon the legislative branch of that government to enact laws, with appropriate penalties, against it. The State that opposes that Congressional power really opposes the prohibition itself; for it would have that prohibition nothing but a dead letter. The fact that this power may be abused is no argument against it. There never yet was a civil power, of any character whatever, that was not liable to be perverted. Men are not always faithful in the discharge of public duty. But for all that, public duty must be imposed upon men. That public duty which relates to slavery and involuntary servitude can be no exception. Congress must be trusted for "appropriate legislation" on this subject, as well as all others within its constitutional sphere. It may come hard to the South to see such work done over the remains of their old idol, but there is no possible help for it. Whatever else happens, *in no form* shall this abomination be set up again.

Few in the South, we suppose, are so demented as to believe in the possibility of restoring slavery as it was. Even without any national law upon the subject, there would be as little likelihood of a return of the South to barbarism outright, as to a social condition wherein one-third of its population answered to the definition given in the Black Code of Louisiana: "A slave is one who is in the power of a master to whom he belongs. The master may sell him, dispose of his person, his industry and his labor; he can do nothing, possess nothing, nor acquire anything, but what must belong to his master." The great object is to prevent the establishment of some milder type of servitude. The colored man was made an absolute chattel by the old slave law; from that, there is every gradation of involuntary servitude, up to the very lightest system of apprenticeship. Were the Southern States left entirely to their own control, it would be not only possible, but probable, that the weaker race would be subjected by law to some of the less severe kinds of bondage. The temptation to such a resort would be very strong, in the face of the difficulties which must attend the getting into successful operation a self-regulating system of absolutely free labor. The firmest friends of this system admit that time and effort are necessary to make it effectual. It is intended that this end shall not be thwarted by any weakness of faith, or any undue greed, in the South. This Constitutional Amendment will hold the South, as probably nothing else could, not only to the renunciation of chattel slavery, but to the maintenance of the full and perfect right of the colored man to bargain, as he best can, for his labor. He must be no more subject to any legal disabilities in this respect than is the colored man in the North; in other words, he must be subject to no such disabilities whatever.

It will be the duty of Congress, under this Amendment, to see that this freedom of labor is preserved; but further than that, Congress will have no cognizance. The question of giving suffrage to the freedmen will remain as much beyond its sphere as before. So will the question of admitting their testimony into the State courts. The Amendment relates to no form of legal oppression, but that pertaining to labor. The fear expressed in some of the Southern Legislatures that the Amendment will be made the pretext for an assumption of the entire control of the colored race of the South by Congress is altogether groundless. It is true that prior to the re-admission of the Southern States to the enjoyment of their full constitutional rights, the President and Congress will ask to be satisfied that there is an honest purpose to secure the freedmen every natural right; but when the readmission has been actually consummated, the treatment of the freedmen outside of the range of this Amendment, must be left entirely to the good faith and justice and enlightened interests of the States in which they live.

We consider that the great safeguard is secured, in making freedom of labor constitutionally inviolable. For years to come, the want of labor will be the greatest of all Southern wants. The restoration of the South from its desolation, and the further development of its immeasurable resources, can come only from hard work. The demand for this will, at best, far exceed the supply. The guarantee to the freedmen of perfect liberty to make their own bargains for their work, of itself gives them an immense power. It makes it the direct interest of the stronger race to deal fairly by the weaker. It renders necessary a policy of conciliation, of inspiring confidence, of supplying moral as well as material motives that shall encourage and stimulate. Preserve this independence of labor inviolate, and, as the South is situated, it will, we believe, insure the freedmen the gradual gain of all other rights. Were labor a drug in the South as in the Old World, no such result would follow. But being the foremost of all needs, the race upon whose volition it mainly depends has a complete power of self-protection and a key that, rightly used, will open the way to any future advancement.

36
General Benjamin Butler to Henry Wilson
November 20, 1865[*]

My Dear Sir: Enclosed please find my idea of the way in which to commence the fight with southern injustice to the negro.

I deem the Preamble necessary because Congress ought to declare in some form that legislation and legislative satisfaction of legislation are both valid when done by the required majorities of those states only who were loyal. We have so treated legislation in other matters, why not in regard to the Negro? If you cannot reckon loyal majorities only, then our National debt is without legislative sanction, our appropriation bills void, and our treaties unratified. The amendment has received the sanction of three-fourths of all the legislatures of all the states that had any legislatures at the time it was submitted.

Now, suppose two-sevenths more States than now are framed out of territories such as Colorado, Utah, New Mexico, or by the division of the old States, is the amendment to be void if not adopted by these legislatures? Nobody could doubt on that question. Well then, why are the other States which have no legislatures to be counted, at least till they have them more than these which may hereafter be made out of new territory. Again, the Preamble is necessary as a declaration that the freedmen have become citizens of the United States by the operation of the Amendment, and thus to overturn the lingering remains of the authority of the Dred Scott decision. Again, the Preamble is necessary in view of the construction Seward has given of the Second Section of the Amendment.

South Carolina, by the message and according to the recommendation of her Provisional Governor, has put on record this construction as a contemporaneous explanation of the meaning; at this time she adopts the amendment with intent to claim a breach of faith in any other opposing legislation of Congress. Let Congress, therefore, put on record a declaration accompanying legislation on the subject of matters defining the true intent, meaning, and interpretation of that Second Section, so that hereafter no sophistry can claim that the word "appropriate" is a restraining word.

The whole Preamble seems to be necessary in order to hold the weak-kneed brethren of the Republican party, who, troubled upon the question whether the states are in or out of the Union, will be carried by the claim that they ought to vote to admit some states so as to have the ratified constitutional amendment by the requisite majority. Indeed, the whole Preamble and bill has been drawn so that whoever shall vote for it will vote to give life and effect to the Constitutional amendment and in favor of liberty and equal rights, not raising, however, any question of the rights of suffrage, and whoever votes against the bill votes against the Constitutional amendment, against equality of rights, and for the black code of the South with its whipping of women and hunting of men with guns and hounds.

The second section of the bill seems to be necessary for the reason, upon examination of the proposed amended black codes preparatory to reconstruction at the South. It will be seen that they all provide that vagrancy or indisposition of a negro to work is a crime for which the negro shall be sold in servitude as a punishment by the decision of a petty magistrate or justice of the peace. To give a jury trial to the negro in such cases will throw an impediment in the way of those codes, which, in my judgment, in practice will be insurmountable. My object has been not to make a code of laws which shall be applicable to the freedmen, but to put on record by this bill the most solemn legislative declaration, and an act which should at once sweep away all distinctive laws *against* him.

If you shall get from this note or draft of the bill sent with it any suggestions which will be of use to you, and therefore aid to the common cause, I shall have attained all I hope from the thought I have given to the subject.

I am very truly yours, B.F.B.

---

[*] *Private and Official Correspondence of Gen. Benjamin F. Butler* (Norwood, MA: Plimpton Press, 1917), 5:679–80. [The document includes the note, "another copy directed to Hon. Thaddeus Stevens." —Ed.]

37

Mississippi, Joint Committee Report and Rejection of Proposed Amendment

November 27–December 2, 1865[*]

The joint committee on state and Federal relations to which was referred the message of the Governor and accompanying documents . . . having reference to the adoption of an amendment to the constitution of the United States, as article XIII proposed by congress on the 1st day of February, 1865, to the several state legislatures, which is in the following words:

> Article 13—Section 1. Neither slavery nor involuntary servitude, except as punishment for crime, whereof the party shall have been duly convicted, shall exist within the United States, or any place subject to their jurisdiction.
>
> Sec. 2. Congress shall have power to enforce this article by appropriate legislation.

They report that, after a careful consideration of the subject, they have come to the following views:

The first and main section of the article has already been adopted by Mississippi, in so far as her territory and people are concerned.

It was substantially and almost in terms incorporated into the State constitution by the late convention. Now is it possible for the State by any act, or in any mode, conventional or otherwise, to change the status fixed by the convention? The freedmen could not by subsequent constitutional amendment be enslaved. The provision of the federal Constitution having reference to the foreign slave trade, and the laws of Congress passed upon the subject, prohibit the importation of negroes from Africa, or elsewhere, so that, as the matter now stands, it is impossible to reestablish or re-introduce slavery here, or elsewhere in the south.

The late State constitutional amendment was adopted in perfect good faith. The people have accepted it, and will adhere to it in the like spirit. Under no circumstances can the persons who were lately slaves be again enslaved. The adoption of the proposed amend-

[*] Dunbar Rowland, ed., *Publications of the Mississippi Historical Society*, Centenary Series (Jackson, 1916), 1:32–34.

ment as Article XIII can have no practical operation in the State of Mississippi. The absolute freedom of the African race is already assured here. It is an accomplished fact. The second section is subject to more grave objections. It confers on Congress the power to enforce the article by "appropriate legislation." Slavery having been already abolished, there is really no necessity for this section, nor can the committee anticipate any possible good that can result from its adoption. On the contrary, it seems to be fraught with evils which this legislature and the people of the State of Mississippi are most anxious to guard against. Slavery may be regarded as extinct everywhere in the United States. At this moment it legally exists nowhere, except in Kentucky and Delaware. It is there tottering to its fall. Its continuance must very soon cease.

Whatever may be the sentiments and preferences of those States, it is quite certain that slavery cannot be perpetuated there, liberation having obtained everywhere else. The proposed amendment is not needed, then, to coerce Kentucky and Delaware into emancipation.

It is the anxious desire of the people of Mississippi to withdraw the negro race from national and State politics; to quiet forever all subjects and questions connected with it, and, so far as forecast and precaution can do so, to forestall and prevent the outbreak of agitation hereafter.

The committee cannot anticipate what construction future Congresses may put on this section. It may be claimed that it would be "appropriate" for Congress to legislate in respect to freedmen in the State. This committee can hardly conceive of a more dangerous grant of power than one which, by construction, might admit federal legislation in respect to persons, denizens and inhabitants of the State.

If there be no danger now, the committee fear the time may come that the public mind might be influenced on this subject to the degree of endangering the reserved rights of the States.

The committee are also of the opinion that the present is not a propitious time to enlarge the powers of the federal government. The tendency is already too strong in the direction of consolidation. The liberties of the people, and the preservation of the complex federative system, would be better insured by confining the federal and State governments in the respective spheres already defined for them.

It would be unwise and inexpedient to open a subject

which your committee had believed extinct, as themes for radicals and demagogues to use to the detriment of the best interests of the country. Mississippi cannot give her deliberate consent to leave open any question from which agitation can arise, calculated to disturb the harmony so happily being restored among the States and the people. This section may be interpreted to refer to Congress to judge what legislation may be appropriate. It is so uncertain and indefinite that it cannot be conjectured what congressional action may be deemed "appropriate" in the extremes to which parties have gone and may henceforth go. It is the common interest of the people in all quarters of the Union, now that vexed questions connected with the negro race are all merged and settled in liberation, that the public mind should be withdrawn from anything unpleasant and irritating in the past, and the door be as effectively closed as human wisdom can devise against future agitation and disturbance from this cause. The committee are apprehensive that if this second section be incorporated in the Constitution, radicals and extremists will further vex and harass the country on the pretension that the freedom of the colored race is not perfect and complete until it is elevated to a social and political equality with the white. The tendency of the section is to absorb in the federal government the reserved rights of the State and people, to unsettle the equilibrium of the States in the Union, and to break down the efficient authority and sovereignty of the State over its internal and domestic affairs. In any aspect of the subject, this section is unproductive of good, and may be fruitful of most serious evils.

Connected as the first section of the proposed article is with the second, and both being included in the same article as an amendment to the Constitution, and a ratification of the first, and a rejection of the second, being, as your committee think, inoperative and of non effect—

Resolved, therefore, by the legislature of the State of Mississippi, That it refuses to ratify the proposed amendment of the Constitution of the United States.

Adopted by the house of representatives November 27, 1865.

Concurred in by the senate December 2, 1865.

38
Alabama, Ratification and Statement of Understanding
December 2, 1865*

JOINT RESOLUTIONS of the General Assembly of the State of Alabama ratifying an amendment to the Constitution of the United States:

Whereas the Congress of the United States on the 1st day of February 1865 adopted a Joint Resolution submitting to the several States a proposition to amend the Constitution of the United States as follows:

Resolved by the Senate and House of Representatives of the United States of America, in Congress assembled, (two thirds of each House concurring,) that the following Article be proposed to the Legislatures of the several States, as an amendment to the constitution of the United States, which, when ratified by three fourths of said Legislatures shall be valid to all intents and purposes:

Article XIII.

Sec 1st Neither slavery nor involuntary servitude, except as a punishment for crime, whereof the party shall have been duly convicted, shall exist within the United States, or in any place subject to their jurisdiction.

Sec 2. Congress shall have power to enforce this article by appropriate legislation;

and the said foregoing proposed amendment, having been laid before this General Assembly, by the Provisional Governor of this State, for consideration and action:

Now, therefore resolved by the Senate and House of Representatives of the State of Alabama in General Assembly Convened:

Documentary History of the Constitution of the United States of America, 1786–1870, House of Representatives, Document No. 529; 56th Cong., 2nd Sess. (Washington, DC: Department of State, 1894), 2:609–10. [See also "The Alabama Legislature Passes the Constitutional Amendment; Joint Resolutions Adopted," *New Orleans Times* (LA), Dec. 6, 1865, 2. —Ed.]

1st That the foregoing amendment to the Constitution of the United States, be and the same is hereby ratified to all intents and purposes as part of the Constitution of the United States,

2d *Be it further Resolved,* That this amendment to the constitution of the United States, is adopted by the Legislature of Alabama with the understanding that it does not confer upon Congress the power to Legislate upon the political status of Freedmen in this State.

3d *Resolved by the authority aforesaid*, that the Governor of the State be, and he is hereby requested to forward to the President of the United States, an authenticated copy of the foregoing preamble and Resolutions

...

Approved Dec 2d 1865.

39

Georgia, Message of Provisional Governor James Johnson on the Proposed Amendment, *Press* (Philadelphia, PA)

December 11, 1865, p. 1[*]

Governor Johnson, in his message to the Legislature on the 4th instant, uses the following language, in urging upon that body the adoption of the constitutional amendment:

On the first of February last the Congress of the United States, by joint resolution, proposed to the Legislatures of the several States of the Union an amendment to the Constitution of the United States, declaring that hereafter neither slavery nor involuntary servitude, except for crime, should exist in the United States, or in any place subject to their jurisdiction; and that Congress should have the power to enforce the proposed article by appropriate legislation. A copy of the proposed amendment is attached, and it is submitted to the consideration of the Legislature, with the hope and desire that it may be adopted and ratified. A very common objection is made to it on the ground that it may confer, by implication, on Congress the power of regulating, generally, the internal policy of the State. Such a construction is believed to be erroneous and unfounded and unwarranted, either by the language employed or the objects to be obtained.

The Constitution of the United States confers, among other things, upon Congress the power to regulate commerce with foreign nations and among the States, to declare war, to raise and support armies, and to provide for calling forth the militia. It is further provided, that Congress shall have power to make all laws which shall be necessary and proper to carry into execution these enumerated powers; but it has never been contended that, because of such authority, Congress was therefore invested with the right to abolish State courts, to prescribe the qualification of jurors, or to declare who should exercise the right of suffrage. Moreover, this amendment is strictly cumulative, and it is not intended by it, either to repeal or modify any of the existing provisions of the Constitution; and, therefore, it will still be for the several States to prescribe, each for itself, who shall be electors for the most numerous branch of their assemblies; and, as a consequence, who shall be qualified electors for members of Congress.

The Congress passing it, the different departments of the Government, and most of the Legislatures of the several States ratifying it, construe the amendment to be nothing more or less than a declaration against involuntary servitude, conferring therewith on Congress the restricted power to carry such declaration into execution by necessary and proper laws. Such is the natural import of the language employed, and such doubtless will be the construction given it by the different departments of the Government in all controversies that may hereafter arise. Under other circumstances, a proposition to ratify such an amendment, would not be entertained by you. Although the "cannon's roar and the trumpet's clangor are no longer heard," society still moves on in its restless way, and it is necessary that we should accommodate our action to the inexorable demands of inevitable results, that the permanent welfare of our people may be secured, and our State restored to her former political rights and relations.

Georgia has, in good faith, abolished slavery. She could not revive it if she would; and the ratification of this amendment will make the people of the United States homogenous—will remove from among us that cause of bitterness and sectional strife which has wasted our property and deluged our land in blood. Furthermore, by yielding to this requirement readily, we shall

[*] [See also *Daily Ohio Statesman* (Columbus), Dec. 21, 1865, 1. —Ed.]

submit a most effectual argument, tending to open the halls of the National Legislature, and the strongest plea that could be addressed to the clemency and magnanimity of the Government.

In turn, let me entreat you to bring forward your prejudices and animosities and offer them a sacrifice on the altar of our common country, that we may once again present to mankind the spectacle—the pleasant happy spectacle, of "brethren dwelling together in unity."

J. Johnson
Provisional Governor of Georgia

40

Georgia, "Ratification of the Constitutional Amendment" (and Statement of Understanding),
New York Times
December 17, 1865, p. 1

THE CONSTITUTIONAL AMENDMENT
The Proceedings of the Georgia Senate
In the Georgia State Senate, Dec. 6, the President announced that the unfinished business of yesterday was the first in order, that was the resolution ratifying the amendment to the constitution of the United States abolishing slavery.

On motion the house resolution on the same subject was received in lieu of the original.

On motion of Mr. SIMMONS, the resolution was amended so as to require copies of the same to be sent to the President and Secretary of State.

Mr. THORNTON, of the Twenty-fourth District, moved to refer the resolution to the Committee on the State of the Republic. His object in this motion was to have the matter further considered before final action. He wished also to see what the President of the United States would have to say in his annual message on the subject. That message, or a synopsis of it, was expected in the newspapers that would soon reach the capital. If the President made the ratifying of the amendment to the constitution a condition precedent to our admission into the Union, he should vote for the resolution; other-

wise, he should most unquestionably vote against it. He should vote against it with the lights before him.

Mr. JAMES F. JOHNSON, of the Thirty-fifth District, was opposed to the reference. The Senate had to meet the question, and the sooner the better.

Mr. O. L. SMITH, of the Sixth District, would vote for the reference if he expected any additional light to be thrown upon the question by the message of the President. He had no such expectations. The Provisional Governor, who is on intimate terms with the President of the United States, has given us no reason to conclude differently. There was no reason to suppose the President would require less of Georgia than he has of Florida or Carolina. It was well understood that the President has made the ratifying of the Amendment to the Constitution of the United States a *sine qua non* to the admission of our members of Congress and a complete restoration of the State to civil government. It was physic that all disliked very much to take, but it was physic that must be taken, and no additional light would settle their stomachs or coat the pill; and he would recommend that they take it straight and without delay.

Mr. STROZIER, of the Tenth District, could not see why the Senate should be refused the information it desired in reference to the views of the President in his message. It seemed that there was a general disposition to seek to get back into the Union, regardless of the violation of principle. He had always endeavored to act on principle, and desired to do so in this instance if he were permitted. If the refusal of their admission into the Union in case they did not adopt the Constitutional Amendment was held *in terrorum* over the Legislature, then, as an automaton, he would walk up and vote for the amendment; but if he were free to vote, he would not. He saw no reason why the ratification of the amendment should be imposed on them as a prerequisite for admission into the Union; and he could see no reason why if this were required other and more onerous requirements should not be made by the President. It was first required that they should abolish slavery; that had been done by a body of higher power than was there. The abolition of slavery in the State had been done by the convention, and could not have been done by the Legislature; but now they hear it said that the Legislature must do a thing that is contrary to all principle.

. . .

The ratification of the proposed amendment would seem to place it in the power of Congress to legislate for the black race within our midst. Hence, if the resolution be adopted, the necessity for some explanatory clause which the House resolution does not contain.... If the Legislature could do nothing except at the bidding of the President, it had better adjourn and go home.

...

Mr. CASEY, of the Twenty-ninth District, moved the previous question, which was sustained.

The House resolution, as amended, was passed by yeas 26, nays 13.

...

RATIFICATION OF THE
CONSTITUTIONAL AMENDMENT

The Georgia Legislature ratified the Constitutional Amendment, unconditionally, as follows:

Therefore be it Resolved, by the Senate and House of Representatives in General Assembly met, That the said amendment to the Constitution be, and the same is hereby ratified and adopted.

The following amendment was rejected, that the ratification might be transmitted without qualification:

"Be it therefore resolved, that in ratifying the amendment to the Constitution of the United States, we do so believing that the Congress of the United States has the power only to make permanent the emancipation of slaves, and that all rights of citizenship can be conferred only by the States respectively, and such, we understand and believe, to have been the object contemplated in the second section of said amendment, and that nothing therein contained, authorized Congress to interfere with the internal affairs of the States."

41

Secretary of State William Seward, Proclamation of Ratification

13 Stat. 774, December 18, 1865*

To all to whom these presents may come, greeting:

Know ye, that whereas the congress of the United States on the 1st of February last passed a resolution which is in the words following, namely:

* Sanger, *Statutes at Large*, 13:774–75.

"A resolution submitting to the legislatures of the several states a proposition to amend the Constitution of the United States.

"Resolved by the Senate and House of Representatives of the United States of America in Congress assembled, (two thirds of both houses concurring,) That the following article be proposed to the legislatures of the several states as an amendment to the Constitution of the United States, which, when ratified by three fourths of said legislatures, shall be valid, to all intents and purposes, as a part of the said constitution, namely:

"Article XIII
"Section 1. Neither slavery nor involuntary servitude, except as punishment for crime whereof the party shall have been duly convicted, shall exist in the United States, or any place subject to their jurisdiction.

"Sec. 2. Congress shall have power to enforce this article by appropriate legislation."

And whereas it appears from official documents on file in this department that the amendment to the Constitution of the United States proposed, as aforesaid, has been ratified by the legislatures of the States of Illinois, Rhode Island, Michigan, Maryland, New York, West Virginia, Maine, Kansas, Massachusetts, Pennsylvania, Virginia, Ohio, Missouri, Nevada, Indiana, Louisiana, Minnesota, Wisconsin, Vermont, Tennessee, Arkansas, Connecticut, New Hampshire, South Carolina, Alabama, North Carolina, and Georgia; in all twenty-seven states;

And whereas the whole number of states of the United States is thirty-six; and whereas the before specially-named states, whose legislatures have ratified the said proposed amendment, constitute three-fourths of the whole number of states in the United States:

Now, therefore, be it known, that I, William H. Seward, Secretary of State of the United States, by virtue and in pursuance of the second section of the act of congress, approved the twentieth of April, eighteen hundred and eighteen, entitled "An act to provide for the publication of the laws of the United States and for other purposes," do hereby certify that the amendment aforesaid has become valid, to all intents and purposes, as a part of the Constitution of the United States.

In testimony whereof, I have hereunto set my hand, and caused the seal of the Department of State be affixed.

Done at the city of Washington, the eighteenth day of December, in the [L.S.] year of our Lord one thousand eight hundred and sixty-five, and of the Independence of the United States of America the ninetieth.

William H. Seward.

Secretary of State.

42

"The Consummated Amendment,"

New York Times

December 20, 1865, p. 4

In the last hours of the Thirty-sixth Congress, which expired with JAMES BUCHANAN's administration, the following amendment to the constitution was proposed to the states by each branch of Congress, the vote in the Senate being *twenty four* to *twelve*, in the House *one hundred and thirty-five* to *sixty-five*.

"ARTICLE 12.—No amendment shall be made to the constitution which shall authorize or give to Congress the power to abolish or interfere, within any State, with the domestic institutions thereof, including that of persons held to labor or service by the laws of said State."

That was the last overture of conciliation made to the slave power, which was already in flagrant treason, and had withdrawn most of its representatives from the national capitol. It was reported, with other propositions, by the majority of the great Pacification Committee, of which Thomas Corwin was chairman. Four years and ten months from that time, the following article is announced by the Secretary of State to have been duly ratified by twenty-seven States, and to be now a part of the Constitution:

"'ARTICLE XIII.—Section 1. Neither slavery nor involuntary servitude, except as a punishment for crime whereof the party shall have been duly convicted, shall exist within the United States or any place subject to their jurisdiction.

"'Sec. 2. Congress shall have power to enforce this article by appropriate legislation.'"

The 18th of December, 1865, will be forever memorable in the annals of the Republic as the point in time at which all slavery, within its limits, was extinguished forever. Never, in all civil history, has there been so signal a retribution of treason as this annihilation of slavery by the very constitution against which treason, for the behoof of slavery, aimed its parricidal blow. It is extremely fit, too, that the very constitution which, as a last offering to peace, it was proposed to turn into a shield for the perpetual immunity and protection of slavery, should, when that peace was repelled, have been converted into the sword of its destruction. What adds to the poetic justice of this marvelous ordering, is that the coup de grace has been given by the very votaries of slavery who turned traitors for its sake.

Of the twenty-seven ratifying States, no less than ten were slaveholding at the beginning of the rebellion, namely: Maryland, Missouri, Virginia, North Carolina, South Carolina, Georgia, Alabama, Louisiana, Arkansas and Tennessee. All of these, save the two first, were part of the "Confederacy" which made traitorous war upon the nation. The old Roman triumphal procession began with the lictors and closed with the captives, chained to the chariots. In our triumphal procession, the conquered march with the lictors, and share with them the *fasces* and the axes. The moral sublimity is immensely upon the side of the American Republic.

Yet there are Americans who find nothing to admire in this; and who are crying out for the worst possible humiliations and indictions upon these subdued and repentant States. They call themselves anti-slavery men, and yet laugh to scorn the participation of these States in the immolation of slavery. They cannot tolerate the grandest spectacle in history, and no doubt do their utmost to transform it into a carnival of vengeance. We are amazed that such men have the audacity to confront the Christian manhood of this American nation with their devilish, unforgiving temper. There never was a poorer blunder than the calculation that the majority of the Northern people will share this spirit. The almost universal approbation which the President's message elicited, is a confirmation strong as holy writ that the great American heart is still generous. No public man, whatever his personal strength or position, can set himself against this sentiment without being inevitably crushed by it, sooner or later.

This certificate of the ratification of the Constitutional Amendment by the necessary number of States, is the first official recognition by the government of the constitutional equality of the late insurrectionary States with the other States. It, therefore, is doubly momentous. It makes an end forever of slavery, and, at the same time, vitalizes the essential principle of restoration. It is impossible for the government which has recognized the voice of South Carolina to be equally potent with that of Massachusetts, and that of Georgia to have the same effect as that of New York, in the amendment of the organic law of the Union, to deny them equal functions in the Union. The very highest power of a State is to say *yea* or *nay* to a proposed amendment to the constitution. The active exercise of that function necessarily involves all other powers. The Executive Department, which certifies to the ratification of the amendment by eight of the late insurrectionary States, is but consistent in remitting to them, as fast as possible, the full exercise of all powers. Congress, however urged by extreme men, will not dare to dispute the ratification, and undo the legal effect of the certificate. And yet it must either go that desperate length, or soon, by an inexorable logical necessity, admit the rights of all the States to be constitutionally represented in its seats.

TABLE OF CASES